ISBN 978-0-265-92494-5
PIBN 10910674

PUBLIC RECORD OFFICE, LONDON

LISTS AND INDEXES
No. LV.

List of
EARLY CHANCERY
PROCEEDINGS

Preserved in the

PUBLIC RECORD OFFICE

VOL. X.

BY ARRANGEMENT WITH
HER MAJESTY'S STATIONERY OFFICE, LONDON

NEW YORK:
KRAUS REPRINT CORPORATION
1963

Volume VIII.

File 973, No. 6, *for* Hemstridge *read* Henstridge.
   ,,   No. 48, *add* [SUFFOLK?].

Volume V.

File 384, No. 25, *for* Fyneley *read* Fyveley (*i.e.* Filey).
File 449, No. 34, *for* Tadboll *read* Tudboll.

Volume IV.

File 302, No. 50, *for* Deovanter *read* Deonanter.

Volume I.

Chronological table, Bundle 26, *for* 6 Henry IV *read* 1 Henry V.
Bundle 31, No. 36, *add note*, Directed to George, bishop of Exeter (1460-1464).

℈ (382)14578(11017) Wt 1117—24

EARLY CHANCERY PROCEEDINGS.

VOL. X.

FILE 1325.

1   Thomas ADAM and Margaret his wife *v.* Thomas son of Edward TOMLYNSON.
Messuage and land in Well late of Thomas Spirling, former husband of the said Margaret.
Faded.   CAMBRIDGE.

2   Robert BOSSALL, brewer, *v* Christopher LEPTON, gentleman.
Messuages and lands in Richmond and Stockton-on-Tees.   YORK, DURHAM.

3–4   Gilbert Smythe and others for themselves and all inhabitants of BOURTON *v.* Richard
YNGOLDESBYE, gentleman.
Common of pasture in Lenborough appendant to the manors of the Castle in Buckingham and
of Bourton.   BUCKS.

5   Richard BRENT *v.* John BYNHAM.
Manors and lands late of William Brent of Cossington, esquire, deceased, father of complainant.
            SOMERSET.

6–9   John BROWNE, son and heir of Walter Browne *alias* Clement of Semley, *v.* Walter
OBORNE (Obourne).
Messuage and land in East Knoyle bought of Edward Browne *alias* Clement.   WILTS.

10   Ralph BYRD, parson of Checkendon, *v.* John RAYMOND.
Lease of complainant's parsonage by ———— Justice, his predecessor.   OXFORD.

11   Richard Colebache and others, inhabitants of COLEBATCH (in Bishop's Castle and Clun)
v. Robert Shepard and others, inhabitants of BROCKTON (in North Lydbury).
Share of a fifteenth payable by the hundred of Purslow.   SALOP.

12   William EDWAYE, vicar of Mynton (*i.e.* Mindtown?) *v.* William WYE of Lyniell (*i.e.*
Linley in More?).
Dilapidations under a lease by William Davys, late incumbent. *Mutilated.*   [SALOP?]

13   John FEREFORD *v.* William COOKE of Thorncombe.
Action on a bond for a debt paid partly in goods.   DEVON.

14   Thomas GRANTHAM, clerk, *v.* Katherine HASYLWOOD and others.
Parsonage of Kirkby-Underwood.   LINCOLN.

15   John HALL of Wellingborough, husbandman, *v.* Hugh PRATT and Robert LOLLE.
Messuage and land in Ashby St. Mary entailed on Thomas Hall, great grandfather of complainant.
            NORTHAMPTON.

16–19   Henry JOHNS, parson of Llanrwst, *v.* Elice PRYCE and David OWEN.
Occupation of complainant's parsonage under a lease from Robert Salusbury, his predecessor,
whose incumbency was annulled for marriage.   DENBIGH.

20   Christopher, son of John JOHNSON, and William WARDELL *v.* James, son of Christopher
THACKER.
Joint lease of mills in Derby from the bailiffs and burgesses of Derby to the said John Johnson
and Christopher Thacker.   DERBY

21–25   Robert KYRKEHAM, knight, *v.* John, son and heir of Simon NORWYCHE, esquire.
Manor and parsonage of Cotterstock and lands in Cotterstock and Glapthorne, late of the chantry
of Cotterstock, granted by Henry VIII in exchange for a messuage and land in Armston and the
keepership of More Hay Laund and Horeshawes in the forest of Rockingham.   NORTHAMPTON.

26   John LLOYD, servant daily attendant on Lord Montagu, *v.* ELIZABETH verch David
ap Res and others.
Messuage and land in Worthenbury and Mulsford (in Threapwood) of the demise of Edward ap
Edward Phelipp.   FLINT.

27–28   William MERKE *v.* Stephen BECKYNGHAM, esquire, lord of the manor of Tolleshunt
Major.
Felling trees on land in Tolleshunt Major inherited by complainant with land in Tolleshunt Darcy
from William his father, and detention of deeds.   ESSEX.

29–30   William, son and heir of John MOPTIDE of Bramston (*i.e.* Brandeston?) *v.* Thomas
SKYNNER.
Messuage and land in East Bergholt of the entail of John, son of William Bramston of East Bergholt,
clothman, sold on complainant's supposed death by Humphrey his brother.   SUFFOLK.

31   William NORRES of Speke, co. Lancaster, knight, and Thomas MASSY of Chester, esquire,
v. William PYCKERYNG, knight, and Edward ELRYNGTON, esquire.
Rent of the monastery of Valle Crucis due to the said Pyckeryng and paid to the said Elryngton.
            DENBIGH.

32–33   Thomas PATRICKE, clerk, v. James BAYLLIE, Robert PINCHWARE and Isabel GARDINER.
Tithes of complainant's parsonage of Wadingham.   LINCOLN.

34   Robert PECOKE, parson of Casterton (Brygcasterton), v. William BROWNE, gentleman.
Profits of complainant's benefice during vacancy after the deprivation of John Abraham.
        RUTLAND.

35   Christopher PETYLL, vicar of Bovey Tracy, v. John SOUTHCOTT, esquire, and Thomas his son.
Occupation of complainant's vicarage and glebe under a lease from George Mannynge, his deprived predecessor.   DEVON.

36–38   Marmaduke POPHAM of Durley, gentleman, v. Roger WALROND (Walderne) of Wells, gentleman.
Lease of the manor of Durley late of Elizabeth, executrix, and late the wife of William Prowes.
        SOMERSET.

39–40   Robert PYPER v. Giles DAVY.
Messuages and land in Udimore pledged to defendant.   SUSSEX.

41–42   James son and heir of Alan RAWLYN v. Allen son and heir of John RAWLYN and others
Messuage and land in Newton.   NORTHAMPTON.

43   George RITHE and Elizabeth his wife, late the wife of Thomas, son and heir of Anthony Rigge, v. John FULLER.
Messuages and lands in Cumberworth, Anderby, Thorpe, Ulceby, Croft, Friskney, and Welton.
Damaged.   LINCOLN.

44   John SCROPE and Elizabeth his wife, late the wife of Robert Roche, v. William ROCHE her son, and William ROCHE, brother of the said Robert.
Theft of deeds relating to the manor of Autby in North Thoresby (Awdeby) with appurtenances in North Thoresby (Thuresby), Beesby (Beysby) and Calthrop of the gift of Thomas Newce, deceased, father of the said Elizabeth.   LINCOLN.

45   Henry SMYTH, Thomasyn his wife, and Alice and Elizabeth BRETTON v. . . . ARGOLLE.
gentleman.
Detention of deeds relating to messuages and land in Stock (Hartforde Stocke), Chelmsford, Ramsden Bellhouse, and Ramsden Crays, late of John Bretton and Ann his wife, parents of the female complainants.   ESSEX.

46–49   William SOUTHALL v. Robert NOKE and Robert SADDOCKE.
Manor of Ives (in Bray) with appurtenances in Bray and Maidenhead claimed under leases respectively from Anne of Neves and the prior and convent of Bisham.   BERKS.

50–53   George STAPILTON, gentleman, and Agnes his wife, executrix,, and late the wife of Mark Averye of Barstable, v. Rose, executrix, and late the wife of Robert Langadon *alias*, COLENDER.
Price of spices and other goods bought of the said Mark by John Godisland, deceased, of whose widow the said Robert was executor.   [DEVON.]

54   William STAPILTONE, gentleman.
Commission to inquire as to lands and goods of Nicholas Buckmayster, deceased, complainant having a lease of the lands (*not specified*) from William Buckmayster his son.   ———

55   Nicholas STRELLEY, knight, v. Isabel late the wife of Bryan SANDFORTHE.
Crown lease of a grange and land in Thorpe [Rig]nell (in Cantley; *see* Monasticon VI, 124), late of the prior and convent of Worksop. *Faded.*   YORK.

56   Thomas THORPE and Edith his wife v. Thomas COLTE.
Annuity charged on lands in Northill (Norrell?) by Maude Langham, deceased, mother of defendants.
Faded.   BEDFORD.

57–58   Griffith TREGARNE *alias* Richard, LL.D., v. Henry HAW, gentleman, and Thomas EGERTON, yeoman.
Rectory of Hilgay, to which complainant was presented by the abbot and convent of Ramsey.
Mutilated.   NORTHAMPTON.

59–61   John WEST of London and Elizabeth his wife, daughter and heir of Alice, wife of William Vaughan, and formerly wife of Thomas Rowleie, v. Richard PANTON *alias* Bullyngbroke, son of William Panton.
Detention of deeds relating to lands in Stony Stratford stated by defendant to have been pledged by the said Alice.   BUCKINGHAM.

62   Walter WHALLEY, gentleman, v. John BABYNGTON, esquire.
Manor of Rampton of the demise of defendant.   NOTTS.

63–68   Thomas WOOD v. Peter VAVASOUR, knight, J.P.
Grange of [Hu]ggate of the demise of the late master of the order of Sempringham and convent of Ellerton. *Faded.*   YORK.

69   ——— v. John MOUNTE STEPHEN, servant to the bishop of Peterborough.
Manor of Wethington (*i.e.* Werrington?) of the demise of the said bishop. *Faded.* NORTHAMPTON.

FILE 1326.

1–3   John ALDHOUS of Westleton *v.* Robert ALDOSE.
Land in Stradbrook, Wilby, or (*sic*) Wootten (in Stradbrook and Wilby), late of John Aldhous, deceased, father of both parties. D. X, 66 (which gives complainant the *alias* of Goddard). SUFFOLK. ·

4–5   Robert [ALDRIDGE], bishop of Carlisle, *v.* Edward MICHELL, clerk, Christopher OKELAND and Christopher HUNSDEN.
Tenths and clerical subsidies collected by defendants. (The said Michell pleads that he has already obtained judgment in this court.)   CUMBERLAND.

9–14   William, son and heir of Thomas ALEN, *v.* John and Robert ALEN.
Detention of deeds relating to lands in Aldwich, Betlow, and Tiscot in Tring, and in Cheddington.   HERTS, BUCKS.

15–16   Robert ALEYN *v.* Thomas VAUGHAN, gentleman.
Double lease of a messuage and land in St. Albans. (Defendant pleads that the matter is already in suit in this court.)   HERTS.

17   John ANDERSON and Alice his wife *v.* John BARTON and others.
Messuages and land in Wilberfoss (Wylberforde), Newton(-upon-Derwent) and Stamfordbridge, late of Robert Tyndall and Maude his wife, deceased, grandfather of the said Alice.   YORK.

18–24   William ANDERSON, gentleman, *v.* John MORLEY, esquire.
Profits of the manor of Holme chargeable with the maintenance during their minority of Edmund, grandson of defendant, and Elizabeth, daughter of complainant, under a contract for a .marriage which did not take place. *Answer on paper.*   YORK.

25   John ANDREWE *v.* Alice ANDREWE, his stepmother (' mother in lawe ').
Land in Aylesbury, late of William Jeffes, deceased, grandfather of complainant.   BUCKINGHAM.

26–28   The same *v.* the same.
Goods of John Andrewe, deceased, younger brother (*sic*) of complainant. (Defendant states that her husband sold her land in Quainton.)   BUCKINGHAM.

29–30   Richard ANDREWES, esquire, *v.* Thomas NEWENHAM, knight.
Closes of pasture at Newbold in Catesby of the demise of William Newenham, knight, deceased, father of complainant.   NORTHAMPTON.

31–33   ANNES verch William ap Howell *v.* John NICHOLAS, vicar of Llanasa.
Seizure of horses of the bequest of William ap Howell, father of complainant, which were alone saved from a flood at Morfa Gwespyr in Llanasa.   FLINT.

34–35   Robert APRYCE of Washington, co. Huntingdon, esquire, *v.* Agnes, late the wife of John DURRANT, and formerly of Humphrey Ardes.
Action on a forged bond to charge a rent on lands in Wiggenhall St. Mary, Wiggenhall St. German, and Wiggenhall St. Mary Magdalen in favour of Elizabeth daughter of the said Humphrey and Agnes on her marriage with Edward, younger son of complainant. (Complainant gives his own account of the settlement.)   NORTHAMPTON.

36–37   Humphrey ARDEN and Elizabeth his wife *v.* William BUCKNAM (Buckingame).
Stables and land near Exeter late of Martin Coffyn, former husband of the said Elizabeth. DEVON.

38   Joyce ASBYE *v.* Ralph WORSLEY, esquire, her divorced husband.
Refusal to complete an assurance ordered by this court (*decree recited*) of lands in Cannock, Norton (Canes?), Leacroft (in Cannock), Wyrley (Worley), Haddysforde, Whitgreave, Durston, Stretton (by Brewood), Sandon, Aldridge, Smallrise (in Sandon), Burston, Weston(-on-Trent), Exson, Stafford and Twyford, and waste of timber and ironstone. *Damaged.*   STAFFORD, LEICESTER.

39   The same (Askebye) *v.* William COLMAN.
Rents of a mill and lands in Cannock, part of the premises. (The list of complainant's lands is repeated, omitting Twyford, and adding Saul and Fernehall. Whitgreave is spelt Whygh Eve.)
,   STAFFORD.

40   The same *v.* George MARTYN of Walsall, yeoman.
Price of ironstone and contract for mining in Cannock. (Complainant states that the divorce being only *a mensa et thoro*, she cannot sue in her own name at common law.)   ˜STAFFORD.

41–43   The same *v.* John SALTE, husbandman.
Cutting and carrying oaks in Cannock, claimed by defendant under a contract with the said Worsley during his marriage.   STAFFORD.

44–45   The same *v.* John JUSTES, husbandman.
Rent of lands in Cannock. (List of lands as in No. 39. adding Swarkeston and Knight Washbourne.)
.   STAFFORD, LEICESTER, DERBY, WORCESTER.

46–47   John ASKE *v.* Henry PORTINGTON of Sawcliffe in Risby (Savelyff), co. Lincoln, late his guardian.
Legacy of John Aske of Houghton, father of complainant, of whom both parties were executors, and account of his possessions, being tithes of corn and hay and lands in Londesborough, some of which produced lead ore. *Mutilated.*   YORK.

48   Thomas ATKYNSON *v.* Reynold GODFFRAY.
. Messuage and land held of the King's manor of Bottesford.   LINCOLN.

49–51   John AVERELL and Joan his wife *v.* John MYLWARD.
Legacy of Henry Cattell, whose widow Felice was afterwards married to John Mylward, father of defendant.   WORCESTER.

52–58 George AWDELEY *alias* Tuchet, knight, *v.* Richard CUMBERBACHE, Ralph TOMSON, and others.
Digging millstones on land held of the manor of Tunstall and stated by the said Tomson to be in Rode.   STAFFORD, CHESTER.

59–61 John AYLMER, husbandman, *v.* Richard AYLMER, his brother.
Moiety of a messuage and land in Burton (*rectius* Girton?) bought of Thomas Hutton of Dry Drayton, esquire, at the cost of both parties.   CAMBRIDGE.

62–63 Thomas AYLWARDE *v.* John RAYNBOWE of Hanwell, co. Oxford, and Alice his wife.
Refusal to complete a sale of a messuage in Napton-on-the-Hill.   WARWICK.

FILE 1327.

1–2 John ABROKE and Joan his wife *v.* Edward FYLDE.
Woodland in Bexhill, late of Richard Holyar of Hoo, deceased, father of the said Joan and of Joan (*sic*), wife of the said Edward.   SUSSEX.

3 Nicholas ADAMS of Townstall *v.* William ALLERTON *alias* Sele and others.
Detention of deeds relating to a messuage and land in Dartington, and poaching. DEVON.

4 Nicholas ADAMS of Dartington, gentleman, *v.* . . . AYLEWORTH.
Crown lease of Dartington park(?). *Faded.*   DEVON.

5 John ADDYNGTON *v.* Robert ADDYNGTON.
Messuage and land in Potterspury. *Faded.*   NORTHAMPTON.

6 Richard AGNES of Great Bowdon, baker, *v.* William AGNES and others.
Detention and destruction of deeds relating to a messuage, cottage and land in Great Bowdon, late of Richard Agnes, deceased, grandfather of complainant.   LEICESTER.

7 Thomas ALCHORNE *v.* John MYCHELBOURNE, yeoman.
Action of debt in contempt of an injunction by Lord Audley in this court, and claim to lands in Ditchling. *Damaged.*   SUSSEX.

8 John ALDERSEY, yeoman of the Guard, *v.* Thomas JOHNSON and Ralph ALDERSEY, clerk.
Land in Barton-on-the-Hill, late of Robert Aldersey, yeoman, deceased father of complainant.   CHESTER.

9–10 John ALDERSON, yeoman of the Guard, *v.* Geoffrey GARTH and others.
Detention of deeds relating to a messuage and land in Swaledale.   YORK.

11 Nicholas ALDYE of Folkestone, gentleman, *v.* the mayor and sheriffs of CANTERBURY.
Action by Thomas Rolfe, gentleman, for price of sheep sold after disposing otherwise of the best of those shown to complainant. *Certiorari.*   KENT.

12–14 The same *v.* the said ROLFE.
Action for repayment of a loan offered in composition for the above bargain, and slanderous affidavit on the Exchequer.   KENT.

15–17 John ALEN, yeoman, *v.* William STERE, tenant to Roger Knollys, gentleman.
House and land in Dunchurch of the demise of the abbot and convent of Pipewell. WARWICK.

18 Ralph ALESBY *v.* Thomas MALTBY the elder, and Thomas MALTBY the younger.
Debt for oxen, etc., the bond for which is lost.   ———.

19 John, nephew and heir of Robert ALEY, *v.* John HEYSEMAN.
Wrongful occupation of a messuage and land in the manor of Kingston by Lewes, by conspiracy with John Crane, lord of the manor, and Joan Aley, late the wife of the said Robert. SUSSEX.

20–22 The same (Alee) *v.* the said John CRANE and Simon MACHYN.
House, barn, and land in Rottingdean held of the said manor.   SUSSEX.

23–24 John ALLEN and Isabel [his wife], a daughter and heir of Thomas Belcher, *v.* Roger KNOLLES of Cold Ashby, co. Northampton, gentleman.
Detention of deeds relating to a messuage called the *Swan* in Dunchurch and lands there and in Toft, Thurlaston and Birdingbury (Berdeberye).   WARWICK.

25–28 James ALTHAM, citizen and clothworker of London, *v.* William WETHERIIOLL (Wytherall, Wetherherd).
Messuage and land in complainant's manor of Malham claimed under a lease from the abbot and convent of Fountain.   YORK.

29–34 The same *v.* John LAMBERD of Calton, gentleman, Richard HODSON, Thomas AUNDERSON, William SMYTH, William A(I)RTON and George BARROW.
Lands in Calton and elsewhere in the same manor. *Answers wanting.*   YORK.

35 The same *v.* Robert DEANE, husbandman.
Messuage and land called Tren House (Tranehowse) in Malham.   YORK.

36–39 John ALYN *v.* Richard youngest son and heir of Richard ABERGE, and Robert ABERGE.
Messuage and land in Worthing held by Richard Aberge (Berge), deceased, nephew of the defendant Richard, of Lord Dacre's manor of Old Court.   SUSSEX.

40 Richard A MAN of St. Bride's, London, hilt-maker, *v.* John JUDDE of Great Packington, and Alice his wife.
Detention of deeds relating to land in Little Packington, formerly of ——— Cokyn. WARWICK.

41 Margaret ANDREWES *alias* Paynter *v.* John WAYMAN.
Messuage, garden and quay in Harwich, late of John Barbar, deceased father of complainant.   ESSEX.

42–44   Thomas ANDROWE of Bereden *v.* Philip Weders (Wethyar), mayor of ARUNDEL.
Arrest of complainant and his goods at Arundel on a charge of smuggling counterfeit coin.
Mutilated.   SUSSEX.

45   John ANNE, esquire, *v.* Thomas POPE, knight.
Detention of deeds relating to closes of pasture in North Aston pledged to defendant.   OXFORD.

46–48   William ANNE of Aylesbury, son and heir of the said John, *v.* John DENTON of Blackthorne,
esquire, his brother-in-law.
Manor of North Aston.   OXFORD.

49   George ANNESLEY *v.* William OGAM, esquire.
Detention of a lease made by John Seyntleger, esquire, of the manors of Great Linford and Piperdes
(*i.e.* Peppetts in Chesham ?)   BUCKINGHAM.

50–52   Hopkin APPOELL, citizen and merchant tailor of London, *v.* Nicholas ALDEY, gentleman.
Lodge and park of Folkestone (Folston), with lands (*described*) bought of defendant partly by payment
of his fine for his share in Wyatt's rebellion. *Mutilated.*   KENT.

53   Robert APPRYCE, captain of 100 men in the Tower, attendant on Thomas Abrudges,
esquire, *v.* Thomas APPRYCE.
Messuage and land held of the late prior of Great Malvern's manor of Baldenhall (in Hanley
Castle).   WORCESTER.

54   Nicholas ARNOLD, knight, *v.* Richard LEIGH, knight, and others.
Site of the manor of Newent, with lands (*described*), the office of bailiwick, and an annuity, and the
parsonages of Newent, Dymock and Pauntley, which the said Sir Richard was engaged to obtain
of the King for complainant.   GLOUCESTER.

55   . Joan ARNOLDE *v.* William MAWESON.
Messuage and land in Kessingland and goods, late of Thomas Arnolde, deceased, brother of com_
plainant.   SUFFOLK.

56–59   William ARNOLDE of Okehampton *v.* Henry VAWDON and Richard his son.
Messuages and land at Croft (in Okehampton) and Blagdon (in Ashbury), late of William Arnolde,
deceased, grandfather of the said William and Richard.   DEVON.

60–62   John, brother and heir of Humphrey ARUNDELL, *v.* Robert HYLL, esquire, J.P., steward
of the manor of Colquite (in Lanteglos by Fowey).
Mill, cottage and close in the said manor of the demise of Lord Thomas Howard and Thomas
Pwnynges, knight.   CORNWALL.

63   Richard ASKUGH *v.* Henry ROO.
Refused to complete a sale of tenements in Harlaxton (Harleston).   LINCOLN.

64–65   Thomas ASPLEN of Enfield, husbandman, *v.* John BRETT of High Cross, maltman.
Action on bills for a debt already paid.   MIDDLESEX.

66–67   Christopher ASSHETON *v.* Thomas HALL, esquire.
Obligation wherewith complainant is charged so as to hinder a payment ordered by this court. _____

68–69   Walter AUSTROPP, grandson and heir of William Shene, *v.* John OVEREY of Toynton,
merchant, son and heir of William Overey.
Messuages in Conisby.   LINCOLN.

70   Agnes AVYE *v.* John AVYE the younger.
Land in Carlton, late of John Avye, deceased, husband of complainant.   NORTHAMPTON.

71–75   Hopkyn Morgan AWBREY, dwelling in London, *v.* Rice ap Gryffyth ap Jevan (MELYN).
Lands in Glentowyth (*i.e.* Glyn-tawy ?), late of complainant's father. *Mutilated.*   BRECON.

76   John AWSOPE of Bradbourne, husbandman, *v.* John AWSOPE of Hognaston, husbandman.
Price of cattle and corn.   DERBY.

77   William AWTOR, nephew and heir of John Nyes, *v.* William BULGAR and Agnes his wife.
Detention of deeds relating to a burgage, garden and orchard in Axbridge conveyed by defendants
to the inhabitants of the borough.   SOMERSET.

78–84   Christopher, grandson and heir of Thomas AYLMER, *v.* Thomas ADYNGTON, John
CRAMPHORN, Anne his wife, and John FAWSSETT (Forssett) and Magdalen his wife.
Cottage and land in the said Adyngton's manor of Harlow.   ESSEX.

85–87   Henry AYNESWORTHE of Winkbourne, co. Notts, gentleman, *v.* William MURR of
Fossdyke, yeoman.
Detention of deeds relating to messuages and land in Kirton-in-Holland late of Robert Daukes,
husbandman, deceased.   LINCOLN.

FILE 1328.

1–2   Thomas ABBOT and Katharine his wife, executrix and late the wife of Philip Hauckes_
worth, *v.* Andrew and John BARKER, executors of Philip Barker.
Goods of the said Haukesworth in the hands of Thomas Barker, clerk, deceased, whereof the said
Philip Barker was administrator.   DERBY.

3   Nicholas ABBOT and Richard BARNES, feoffees to uses, *v.* William SMYTHE, gentleman,
surveyor of Crown revenues in the county, and Edmund PUNTER, yeoman.
Messuage and land in Husborne Crawley given 80 years ago by John Rosse for payments of
fifteenths, amending of highways, relief of the poor, and other common necessary uses, whence a
payment was made for the obit of the said Rosse.   BEDFORD.

4–5   Roger ABERE (Bere) of St. Lawrence, Thanet, *v.* Thomas ROLFE and John his brothers.
Bond given to the said Thomas for a debt of the said John since paid.   KENT.

6   Henry ABNEY *v.* Richard BULLOCK.
Refusal to complete a conveyance of land held ot Sir Richard Freyston's manor of Mendham.
SUFFOLK.

7   William, grandson and heir of Robert ADAM of Wisbech *v.* Richard WHELPDALE and Katherine his wife.
Detention of deeds relating to a messuage and land in Newton.   CAMBRIDGE.

8   Ralph AGARDE *v.* George VERNON, knight, and Robert FORSTER.
Refusal to complete a lease of a close of pasture in the lordship of Tong.   SALOP.

9–10   John ALEN of Kegworth, chaplain, *v.* Robert COTTON, alderman of Leicester, and Anthony GRAUNGE, his son-in-law.
Action by the said Graunge in the said Cotton's court.   LEICESTER.

11–13   Robert ALGOOD, yeoman, *v.* Joan, late the wife of John NAYLER and Robert their son.
Former Crown lands in Wratting and West Wickham. *Answer wanting.*   CAMBRIDGE.

14   William ALLEN(?) of Calne, gentleman, *v.* John BARWYKE.
Barn and land in Hillmarton of the demise of the prior and convent of Bradenstoke. *Damaged.*
WILTS.

15–16   Robert, son and heir of William ALLEYN *v.* Philip ALLEYN.
House and ground in Whaplode.   LINCOLN.

17–18   Thomas ALRYCHE (Arlege) *v.* Henry GODSON and Thomas KEWETT, gentleman.
Messuage and land in Ashow, formerly of Thomas Alryche, deceased, grandfather of complainant.
WARWICK.

19   Elizabeth, late the wife of John AMADAS, and administratrix of his goods, *v.* Richard BULLER, esquire.
Bond given for defendant's preferment in marriage. *Mutilated.*   CORNWALL.

20   John ANDERDON of Launcells *v.* Nicholas MANNYNG.
Tenements called Middle and West Stanbury in Moorwinstow and demised to William Mannyng, since deceased, by John, father of complainant. *Faded.*   CORNWALL.

21   Walter APDAVID of London, baker, *v.* John APDAVID and William APDAVID of Hook.
Land at Penliworth in the lordship of Chirkland, late of David Apdavid, deceased, father of the said Walter and John.   DENBIGH.

22–24   Edward APPEN (Ap pen, Penne), gentleman, *v.* Henry, son and heir of Roger SPARR, and Richard COXE.
Meadow called Hacley (*i.e.* Hagley?) meadow, late of Edmund Appen, father of complainant.
See File 942, No. 29.   WORCESTER.

25   Stephan APPERE (Appare), Jane his wife, sister and heir of Thomas Yorke, and Roger BODENHAM, esquire, her son, *v.* James YATE of Aldbourn, co. Wilts.
Detention of deeds relating to land in Crewkerne claimed in this court by James Lacye.
SOMERSET.

26   Hugh, John, and William APPOWELL *v.* Philip ROGER.
Detention of deeds relating to a gavelkind messuage and land in Mamhilad, late of Walter Appowell, deceased, father of the said Hugh and grandfather of the other complainants. D. XIV, 42.
MONMOUTH.

27   William, son and heir of Hamond ARDERNE of Timperley, gentleman, *v.* Thomas VAWDREY, yeoman, and Thomas STRETTYLL, priest.
Land in Bowdon (Bawden). *See File 1189, No. 51.*   CHESTER.

28   William ARMYN *v.* Thomas HORSEMAN.
Land in Willoughby, late of John Bellow and John Broxolme. *Mutilated.*   [LINCOLN.]

29–30   William ARNEDEN, gentleman, *v.* Nicholas BUXE and William W(H)ALLE, canons and treasurers of the college of Chester.
Annuity payable out of the said college.   CHESTER.

31   Nicholas ASSHETON, vicar of Kendal, *v.* Anthony NEVELL, knight, and others, executors of Thomas Magnus, late vicar.
Dilapidations.   WESTMORELAND.

32–35   Christopher ASTELEY *v.* Richard LEY, guardian of Thomas Myrfen, and Elizabeth, late the wife of Thomas ASTELEY.
Messuage and land in the manor of Laughton (-en-le-Morthen), late of John Asteley, deceased, grandfather of complainant and father of the said Thomas.   YORK.

36   John ATKYNSON *v.* Thomas BARON and Katharine his wife.
Refusal to complete a sale of a messuage and land in Spalding.   LINCOLN.

37–40   Bartholomew AVERELL *v.* Bryan STEPVAN (Strevan), citizen and fishmonger of London.
Detention of a lease made by John [Stokesley], formerly bishop of London of the manor of South-minster. (Interpleader by Ralph Bassett and William Averell, executors of John Averell.)
ESSEX.

41–44   John AYLWORTHY, esquire, *v.* Robert DAVISON, citizen and merchant tailor of London.
Plate pledged to defendant.   LONDON.

FILE 1329.

1–3   William ABBOT, esquire, *v.* Henry CORNYSSHE, gentleman.
Keepership of the capital house of Glastonbury and the other buildings of the abbey. SOMERSET.

4–6   Richard ABYE, husbandman, *v.* Robert BROWNE, John CLEMENT, Richard MYDDEL-TON, bailiff of Wintringham, and others.
Depasturing of common appendant to messuages and land in Wintringham, denial of justice, amercement for slander in court, and oppressive distress.   LINCOLN.

7–8   Humphrey ADAMS, husbandman, v. Thomas KETILBY, late of Hollin (in Pensax), co. Worcester, gentleman.
Messuage called Nethercote and land in Neen Savage of the demise of defendants. *Answer wanting.*
    SALOP.

9   Stephen ADAMS, esquire, and Elizabeth his wife, executrix, and late the wife of John Jenyns, knight, v. Ralph JENYNS, executor of Bernard Jenyns, former guardian of the said Sir John.
Statute staple given by the said Sir John and annulled by a release since lost.   ———

10–11   Fouke, son and heir of Thomas ADENBROKE, v. John ADENBROKE and Thomas his son.
Detention of deeds relating to a messuage and land in Rowley.   STAFFORD.

12–13.   John ALDERSEY v. Giles SPENCER, LL.D.
Presentation to the church of Blofield. *Mutilated.*   NORFOLK.

14   Thomas ALDERSEY and others v. Anne ALDERSEY.
Goods of Ralph Aldersey, citizen and merchant of Chester, late defendant's husband, whose executors complainants are.   CHESTER.

15–16   John ALLSOPP of Hognaston, husbandman, v. John ALLSOPP of Hognaston, called 'Lyttell John,' and Lawrence FERNE.
Price of wool.   DERBY.

17   Martin ALYN of London, joiner, and Anne his wife, executrix and late the wife of Chad Scotte, v. Thomas BLURTON of Rugeley, cutler.
Horse, money, and other property of the said Scotte left in complainant's house at his death.
    LONDON, STAFFORD.

18–20   Robert AMERYKE and Jane his wife v. Emma BENTLEY, executrix of Thomas Bentley of Dunstable.
Goods of Martin Hardwyke, the former husband of the said Jane. *See File* 1331, *No.* 33. [BEDFORD.]

21–22   Emma BENTLEY v. Robert AMERYKE.
Sale of land of the said Thomas in Wellingborough, etc. *Bill and answer wanting. See File* 1331,
Nos. 33-34.   NORTHAMPTON.

23–25   Richard AMILL of Folkington (Foington) v. John AMILL.
Land (*described*) in Worthing, late of Robert Amill, deceased father of both parties.   SUSSEX.

26   John ARMERER, parson of Penshurst, v. John GAWIN.
Rectory of Penshurst, demised to defendants by John Mowne, late parson, deprived for marriage. (Endowment to the effect that Mowne had two wives living.)   KENT.

27   . . . ASPSHAWE v. William BRAT of Tregamon.
Money entrusted to defendants by William Aspshawe, since deceased, father(?) of complainant.
Faded.   MONTGOMERY.

28   Edward ASSER of Great Warley, and Joan and Margery ASSER, v. Joan ASSER, administratrix of the goods of Richard Asser, deceased.
Annuity charged on lands in Roxwell in the parish of Writtle (*sic*) by John Asser, yeoman, deceased, father of complainants and of the said Richard.   ESSEX.

29   Peter ATKYNGSON of Crosby, yeoman, son and heir of William Atkyngson, v. Guy BABTHROP.
Detention of deeds relating to a messuage and land in Winterton, late of Robert Stewenson of Crowle, husbandman.   LINCOLN.

30   . . . ATKYNSON, clerk, v. William HOUGHTON, clerk.
Debt the bond for which is destroyed. *Mutilated.*   ———

31–32   Richard ATKYNSON and Anne his wife, daughter and heir of Edward Brymyngham, esquire, v. James BULSTRED (Bolstred), gentleman.
Detention of deeds relating to the manors of Shutford, Nether Worton, and Great and Little Tew.
    OXFORD.

33   The same and the said Anne, great-granddaughter of William Birmingham, v. . . .
Cottages and land in Shutford. *Mutilated.*   OXFORD.

34–35   John ATMAYRE (Atmer) v. Nicholas EVERARD.
Price of lease of a messuage and land in Brandon.   SUFFOLK.

36–38   Thomas AUDELEY, kinsman and heir of Henry Audeley v. Hugh LOSSE, esquire, and Thomas BOCHER, his servant.
Messuages in Philliplane (*i.e.* Philpot Lane?) and St. Michael Bassishaw and a curtilage in All Hallows the Great ('in the Hey') to have been demised to the said Henry, who advanced the money for purchase from the Crown.   LONDON.

39   John AUNCELL v. Edmund THAXSTER.
Messuage and land in East Ruston, late of William Auncell, deceased, grandfather of complainant.
    NORFOLK.

40–41   Richard AUNGER, husbandman, v. Godfrey SWAYNE.
Lease by defendant of a tenement called the *Hand* and land and rights of pasture in Chesterton, terminated by his forfeiture.   CAMBRIDGE.

42   William AWBREY, LL.D., principal of New Inn, Oxford, v. THOMAS ap Thomas.
Fees for teaching and maintaining defendant's son in New Inn.   OXFORD.

43   The same v. Christopher VAUGHAN, gentleman.
Do.   OXFORD.

44–46   John AYLEWORTHE, esquire, v. Thomas BERDDE and others.
Felling trees in Dartington.   DEVON.

FILE 1330.

1–2   Edward BALLARD and Henry TRENT *v.* William THREVES *alias* Long *or* Thorp, grandson and heir of Thomas Longe.
Land in Radcliffe-on-Trent. D. XI, 28.   NOTTS.

3–8   Thomas BALLE and Joan his wife, great-granddaughter of John Harrye, *v.* Richard BRODIE (Bradye).

F/   Land in the Lordship of Tingrith in the parish of Blackmore.   ESSEX.

9–10   Reynold BARGELEY, Katharine his wife, Thomas TAILOW, Agnes his wife, and Joan HALE *v.* Edmund SMYTH of Kirby Lonsdale, co. Westmoreland.
Messuage and land in Bunny, late of Robert Johnson, deceased, uncle of the female complainants.
NOTTS.

11–12   William BARKER of Foots Cray, co. Kent, and Thomasyn his wife *v.* Richard JOYNOUR of Fletching.
Detention of deeds relating to land in Wivelsfield (Willesfield).   SUSSEX.

13–15   Richarde (*sic*) late the wife of Nicholas BARNEHOUSE *v.* Humphrey, son of John BARNEHOUSE, deceased.
Detention of deeds relating to the manor of Prescott (in Culmstock), and messuages, lands, rents, and services there and in ¦˙·nborough (in Culmstock), Colompstocke, Culmestocke (*sic*), Uffcolompp, Uffeculumpp (*sic*), Kentisbeare and Wellington.   DEVON.
SOMERSET.

16–19   The same *v.* Hugh STUKLEY, gentleman.
Failure to convey the premises as awarded by arbitration. D. XIII, 82.   DEVON.
SOMERSET.

20   The same, executrix of the said Nicholas, *v.* John HARWOOD, gentleman, his brother-in-law, overseer of his will.
Goods of the said Nicholas, and tally of a legacy to complainant. *Mutilated. See D. IX. 60.*
DEVON, SOMERSET.

21–23   Thomas BASSETT of Langley, gentleman, and others, executors of William Bassett of Blore, knight, *v.* John, Richard and William FYTZHERBERT, executors of Anthony Fytzherbert of Hamstall Ridware, King's serjeant-at-law.
Action for a penalty for non-conveyance of the manor of Meynell Langley, already provided for by an assignment of the manors of Blore and Grendon. Answer wanting.   DERBY, STAFFORD.

24–25   John BAWDEN *alias* Wullcomb and Pascaw his son *v.* Walter SHERE.
Share of a messuage and land in Egg Buckland, late of Alice Bawden *alias* Wullcomb, deceased, whose daughters were married to the said John and Walter.   DEVON.

26–28   Robert BEALE of Exeter *v.* John JERE and others.
Messuage and land at Kennford in Kenn, late of Joan Frenche.   DEVON.

29   Edmund BEAWPRE, esquire, supervisor of the will of Harry Lambert, *v.* Agnes, late the wife of Reynold HYLBRANDE, and Thomas his son.
Legacy of the said Lambert, whose executor the said Reynold Hylbrande was, for the foundation of a chantry in Outwell or alternatively for charitable purposes (*described*).   NORFOLK.

30   Ralph BELFELDE and Thomas COWPER, gentleman, executors of Simon Aynsworth, *v.* William BRETON.
Messuages and lands in Helthwayte, purchased jointly by deft and the said Aynesworth, from Lord Robert Dudley and William Glaseour.   YORK.

31   · John BELLOWE of Newstead, esquire, *v.* Thomas CONSTABLE, gentleman, and Barbara, his wife.
Shop in the South Sanctuary, Grimsby, of the demise of Leonard, son and heir of John Collaye of Grimsby, butcher.   LINCOLN.

32–35   Thomas BELTON, clerk, and others, supervisors of the will of Edmund Belton, *v.* John TORSEY and Robert MARKHAM.
Messuage and land (also described as two cottages) in Amcotts, claimed by the said Markham under a lease from Richard Bellyngham of Manton, esquire.   LINCOLN.

36–38   Myles BERNYS of Manton, in Rutland, deprived vicar of Buckminster, *v.* Matthew BAYLYE, now vicar.
Seizure of complainant's goods in the vicarage.   LEICESTER.

39   The inhabitants of the precinct of BLACKFRIARS *v.* Thomas CAWARDEN, Knight, and others. Destruction of the parish church of St. Anne within the said precinct, and occupation of the churchyard.   LONDON.

40–43   John grandson and heir of William BLAKETT *v.* David VYNCENT, gentleman.
Messuage, land, rent and common of pasture in deft's manor of West Sheen. D. IX. 46. SURREY.

44   Jerome BLYTHE, gentleman, *v.* Philip, Charles, William, and Edward TOWNSENDE.
Messuage and land in Norton, late of Richard Blythe, deceased, father of complainant. *See* File 1291, No. 41.   DERBY.

45–47   The King's and Queen's tenants of BOLINGBROKE *v.* Richard, brother and executor of John GOODRICHE (Goodryke) of Bolingbroke, merchant.
Legacy to found a school in Bolingbroke in lieu of one formerly kept by a chantry priest diverted by deft. to a school in Louth.   LINCOLN.

48-51   John BONER of Chard and Isabel his wife, daughter of John Estmond, deceased, v. John
         BOROWE and Alice his wife.
Land in East Chinnock with a cottage containing three acres in West Chinnock of the demise of the
late prior and convent of Montacute (Mountayne).   SOMERSET.

52-57   Leonard BOSGRAVE and Joan his wife, daughter of Thomas Arundell, knight, attainted
         of felony, and late the wife of Robert Fytz James, v. James FYTZ JAMES, knight, and
         Richard FYTZ JAMES, gentleman.
Keepership of the park of Evercreech demised by the bishop of Bath and Wells to Nicholas
Fytz James, esquire, father of the said Robert.   SOMERSET.

58-60   Henry BOWER (Bowyer) alias Turner, a base son of William Bowyer, knight and alderman
         of London, deceased, by Thomas Fyshe, his next friend v. Francis CHALONER, gentleman.
Manor of Wick and lands and a messuage in (Hackney) Wick, Hackney, Stepney, Stratford and
Hoxton.   MIDDLESEX.

61-64   Joan BOYSE v. John REDFORD and Susan, his wife, executrix and late the wife of
         Thomas Purchyn, and daughter of complainant.
Account of a brewhouse, a woad-house, lands and goods in the parish of the Sub-Deanery of
Chichester, whereof the said Purchyn was complainant's bailiff.   SUSSEX.

65   John BRABAND, parson of St. Michael's, Crooked Lane, and Robert INGRAME and
         Nicholas LEVERET his churchwardens, v. Joan BROOKE, George ASHE, and Alice, his wife.
House obtained for a parsonage. Mutilated.   LONDON.

66-67   William BRACEBRIDGE, gentleman, v. Thomas BRACEBRIDGE, esquire.
Manor of Kynnesburye. Writ and interrogatories only. See Files 1291, No. 51; 1331, No. 51.
                                                                              [WARWICK.]

68   William BRADSTOCK v. William BUTTON, esquire, lord of the manor of Crowe.
Tenement in Ringwood of the demise of William Fawkenour. Mutilated.   HANTS.

69-74   The dean and chapter of BRISTOL v. Joan MARWOODE.
Rent of the parsonage of Halberton (Holberton), of the demise of the late monastery of
St. Augustine's, Bristol.   DEVON.

75-76   William BROMBYE v. Thomas MONSON, gentleman.
Sale of land in Clixby on a bad title.   LINCOLN.

77-78   William BROMFYLDE, merchant tailor of London, and Florence his wife, late the wife of
         Edmund Pease, merchant of London, v. William SAKVYLE of Dorking, gentleman.
Transactions following on the robbery of the said Pease and Sakvyle by Christopher Nokkes.
Mutilated.   LONDON, SURREY.

79-80   Ralph BROODHEDD of Lichfield, yeoman, son of John Rowley alias Broadhede, v. William
         CARTER of Beamhurst (in Checkley), husbandman.
Messuage and land in Stramshall (Strongeshelf).   STAFFORD.

81   John BURCHAR, parson of Llangower, v. HOELL, ap Morgan, LOWRYE verch Res, his
         wife, and others.   MERIONETH.
Close at Dwygraig in Llangower belonging to complainant's glebe.

82-85   Elizabeth BURGEYN v. Nicholas HEDDON, James STONER, and John Passmore.
Messuage and land in Barnstaple of the demise of Laurence Prowse, esquire, grandfather of
complainant. Mutilated.   DEVON.

FILE 1331.

Ralph BAGENALL, knight, v. Thomas TYTSOR.
Trespass on meadow in Penkhull and detention of deeds. See File 1335, No. 2.   STAFFORD.

2-5   John BALARDE v. Robert ACTON.
Messuage and gardens in Lewes late of Peter Balarde, deceased, father of complainant. SUSSEX.

6-7   Thomas BALLE v. Lewis WALKER and others.
Sowing land in Newton of the demise of James Fulgam, knight, with ' cockell, darnell and drake,'*
and cutting and carrying an oak therefrom.   STAFFORD.

8-11   Richard son and heir of Alice BANGES v. William ARNOLD, gentleman, and Thomas
         BANGES.
Messuages and land in Smallburgh and Barton late held of the said Arnold's manor of Smallburgh
by the said Alice and William Banges her husband, father of the said Richard and Thomas
                                                                                    NORF.

12-13   Philip BARKER v. Henry GRENE and Joan his daughter.
Purse or bladder found by defts. and cried in Huddersfield church.   YORK.

14   William, nephew and heir of Henry BARKER of London, haberdasher, v. John SOMER.
Detention of deeds relating to tenements in St. Margaret Pattens.   LONDON.

15-18   Robert, son and heir of Andrew BARTON of Smithhills (in Dean), co. Lancaster, esquire,
         v. John HOPKYNSON, gentleman, son and executor of Henry Hopkynson.
Messuages and land in Hulme, North Muskham, Carleton (i.e. Little Carleton in South Muskham),
Coddington and Newark.   NOTTS.

19   The same v. the same.
Destruction of fences, digging ' bastyng stones,' and other damage pending the above suit.
                                                                                    NOTTS.

20-22   John BATE v. Francis LEEKE, knight.
Mansion-place and land in Bottesford and Plungar of the bequest of John Leeke, esquire, and formerly
of the prior and convent of Belvoir. Damaged.   LEICESTER.

* See Wright's Dialect Dictionary s.v. " drawk."

23–24   Thomas BATEMAN, carpenter, *v.* John COLLYNS, Alice his wife, Thomas HEWES, and Dorothy his wife.
Land in Meopham awarded to complainant in this court against John Power and Joan his wife.
                                                                                                    KENT.

25   Christopher BAXENDALE of Misterton, co. Notts, yeoman, *v.* Ralph WALMESLEY.
Messuage in Acreton (*i.e.* Accrington?).   LANCASTER.

26   John BAYNES, vicar of Wistow, with its chapels of [Kil]by and Newton (Harcourt), *v.* Edmund WITHE.
Tithes, whereof those of the ' procyncte ' of Fleckney, Kilby, and Newton alone belong to deft. as rectorial. *Mutilated.*   LEICESTER.

27–28   Stephen BECHE, executor of Humphrey Beche, *v.* Thomas IDLY, administrator of the goods of Edward Artwyke, clerk, deceased.
Verdict falsely obtained for rent of the parsonage of Little Ilford to which the said Artwyke was presented and deprived 21 months later.   ESSEX.

29   Christopher, descendant and heir of Thomas BEE of Ninebanks, co. Northumberland, *v.* Joan, executrix and late the wife of Richard PLUMBER.
Detention of deeds relating to lands in Chingford, late of the said Richard, and Alice, formerly his wife.   ESSEX.

30–31   Stephen BENET *v.* Robert BERRYE.
Price of hides sold to William Dawe on deft's pledge for payment.   CORNW.

32   William, son of John BENET, deceased, *v.* James DEANE his uncle.
Messuages and land in Overton of the demise of Corpus Christi College, Oxford.   HANTS.

33–34   Emma, executrix and late the wife of Thomas BENTLEY, *v.* Robert AMERYKE (Meryck).
Money promised to deft. on his marriage with Jane Marten, daughter of the said Thomas and Emma, but satisfied by a grant of land in Dunstable. *See File 1329, Nos.* 18–20.   BEDFORD.

35–36   Frances BITHELD (Bethelde), daughter of Bernard Duffeld, *v.* Roger TREDARTHE.
Seizures of goods from a messuage in Exeter formerly called the Black Friars and now Russell's Place.   DEVON.

37   John BLYTHE *v.* William STANFOURTHE and others.
Detention of deeds relating to a messuage and garden in the parish of Appthorpe.   N'HAMP.

38   William BODELEY, of London, farrier, *v.* Thomas MOMFORD the elder and Thomas MOMFORD the younger.
Meadow in Norton granted on a nine years' lease by Hugh Balle.   STAFFORD.

39–40   John BODY of Wiveliscombe (Wylsecombe), husbandman, kinsman and heir of Luce Comberhedd *alias* Bodyn, *v.* John YONG and John TAYLOR.
Messuages and land in Wellington of the bequest of John Comberhedd of Cannington, clerk, brother of the said Luce.   SOMERS.

41   Roger BONDE *v.* George LLOYD, steward of the Queen's manor of Estonton (*i.e.* Easting-ton?).
Obtaining a bond from complainant under pretence of its being a receipt for his copy.   GLOUCS.

42   Roger BONFESSOR *v.* John VENYS *alias* Poller(d).
Refusal to quit a tenement in Salcombe at the end of his lease.   DEVON.

43–45   James BONGAYE of Beccles *v.* Francis and John REDE.
Refusal to complete a sale of land in Ellough and Weston. *Mutilated.*   SUFF.

46   Robert BONHAM, esquire.
Commission to examine witnesses in a suit in this court against John Raymond, esquire, and others for a lease of the manor of Pigotts in Saling.   ESSEX.

47   Henry BOROWE *v.* William FOXE.
Detention of deeds relating to a messuage and land in Stradbroke and Ho[rham?] of the bequest of William Borowe of Yarmouth, father of complainant. *Mutilated.*   [SUFF.]

48–50   Richard BRANSON, Amy his wife, John POLLARD and Margaret his wife *v.* Thomas MARLER and Joan his wife, *alias* Androwes *alias* Paynter.
Messuage and land in Erwarton late of Thomas Spearman, deceased, father of the female complainants and some time husband of the said Joan.   SUFF.

51–52   Thomas BRASEBRYDGE, esquire, *v.* John, son of Henry MERYMAN and Edward and John HEWETT.
Messuage and land in Kingsbury. *Damaged. See Files* 1291, *No.* 51; 1330, *No.* 66.   WARW.

53   William BRAYE of Abingdon, miller, *v.* Warham SAYNTLEGER, gentleman.
Mill called Henward Mill in Sutton [Courtney] or Drayton, of the demise of the late abbot and convent of [Abingdon]. *Faded.*   BERKS.

54–55   Francis BRINETON *v.* Edward CHOLMELEY.
Wrongful release of a debt of Henry Stafford, Lord Stafford, to William Cholmeley, esquire, deceased, whose executors both parties are. (The name of a second complainant appears to have been erased.)   ————

56–57   Alice BROKEBANKE *v.* John SPALDYNG and William FOXE.
Shop and pasture in St. John's, Wigford, late of Edward Vessie, deceased, father of complainant.
                                                                                                    LINCOLN.

58   Edmund BROME v. Roger, John, and Thomas MORRIS.
Refusal to complete a lease of a messuage and land in Bromyard.   HEREF.

59   Thomas BROME v. John HERYNGE.
Detention of deeds relating to a messuage and land in Heveningham and Ubbeston.   SUFFOLK.

60–62   William BROWNE of Swineshead gentleman, v. Harry HERDSON of London, skinner, [and the sheriffs of LONDON].
Frivolous suits concerning lead sold by deft. to William Easterdale of Grimsby (Grenysby), merchant, of whom complainant bought it. *Certiorari and Subpoena.*   LINCOLN, LONDON.

63–65   The same v. the same.
Do.   LINCOLN, LONDON.

66   Richard BRASSHE v. John DYER and others.
Messuage in St. Germans.   CORNW.

67   William BRYGGYNNESHAWE and Agnes his wife, late the wife of William Aldwyche, v. John RUSSELL.
Execution of will of the said Aldwyche, who died possessed of a messuage and land with stock in Lee leaving the said Agnes and John as his executors.   BUCKINGHAM.

68–71   Christopher BRYSTO v. Nicholas BRYSTO.
Detention of deeds relating to land in Lee (in Fittleworth) bought of John Lee, yeoman, father of both parties. D. IX. 22.   SUSSEX.

72·   Richard BULLE v. Robert BROWNE.
Damages sustained in defending deft.'s title to a messuage and land in Great Munden demised to complainant.   HERTS.

73–74   Robert BURLEY of Ufford, in Northants, labourer, v. Elizabeth BURLEY and John WESTWOOD.
Messuage and land in Hoddesdon, late of William Burley, labourer, deceased, father of complainant and husband of the said Elizabeth.   HERTS.

75–78   Anthony BURROWE, gentleman, v. George COTTON and Thomas REVE.
Arrears of rent of the parsonage of Blackwell and chantry lands in Walkeringham, Mattersey, Welham, Hayton, Nottingham and Bingham included in a purchase by complainant.   DERBY, NOTTS.

79   John BUSCHE, esquire, and others, v. Francis STRADLING.
Land in ' Carleton Medowe called Radclyff Medowe ' (*parish omitted*).   SOMERS.

80–85   Edmund, son and heir of Thomas BYLES, esquire v. William HYCHYN, gentleman, William HOBB(YS), and others.
Messuage and land in St. Stephen's by Saltash declared by defts. to belong to the dean and chapter of Windsor.   CORNW.

FILE 1332.

1   John BARTON v. William AMERY and others.
Detention of deeds relating to pasture in Barlaston. *Mutilated*   STAFFORD.

2   Randall BAXTER(?) of Acton, co. Middlesex, Amy his wife, Francis . . . of Bocking, co. Essex, Margery his wife, William COX(?), Joan his wife, . . YK . . and Joan (*sic*) his wife v. William HOWELL *alias* Carver, and Agnes his wife, aunt of the female complainants.
Detention of deeds relating to land in Magor, late of Thomas Byrde, deceased. *Damaged.*   MONM.

3–4   Avery BAYLYE, nephew and heir of Alice Wallys, v. John TOWYLL, John RYDGWAY, John MOLTON, Robert HART, and others.
Detention of deeds relating to a messuage and land in West Teignmouth whereof the said Towyll and Rydgway were enfeoffed by John Wallys, husband of the said Alice, against her will.   DEVON.

5   John BEAUMONT (*name cancelled*) v. William TYPSELL, ' a man of warre.'
Action on a bond valid only on defendant's obtaining the restoration of complainant's confiscated goods. *Corpus cum causa.*   [SURREY ?]

6–8   Richard BEARE v. William, son and heir of William PARKER *alias* Hooper, and Joan PARKER *alias* Hooper.
Land at Middle Braddon in the parish of Marstowe, late of John Beare, deceased, father of complainant.   [HEREF.]

9   Richard BELAMYE v. John BEAMONT and James DEYN.
Detention of deeds relating to a messuage and land in Wirksworth bought of Nicholas Hudson and Dorothy his wife.   DERBY.

10–11   John, grandson of William BENNET and of Margaret his wife v. Edward WYSSON and Joan ARTOR.
Messuage and land formerly held of the manor of Newnham by William Chambers, clerk.   HERTS.

12–14   Agnes BENNETT, Thomas CURTEYS and Elizabeth his wife, daughter of the said Agnes, v. Thomas PAYNE, esquire, and Joan PARKER.
Messuage and land in Hutton adjudged to complainants in the Queen's Bench (the said Payne pleads that the case has already been referred to the common law from this court).   SOMERSET.

15–16   Denise BEREFORDE of Linacre Hall v. Alice, late the wife of Stephen BEREFORDE, and administratrix of his goods.
Arrears of rent of a water-mill and tithes in Chesterfield, and loan.   DERBY.

17   John BLAKE *v.* Thomas ROWSE.
Tenement at Knighton in the manor of Wembury formerly demised to William Buell by the prior of Plympton.   DEVON.

18-19· Thomas BOCHER *v.* William WENBORN.
Iron in sows to be delivered at the New Furnace in Heathfield as price of wood in Burwash bought of William Fowle.   SUSSEX.

20   Edmund [BONNER], bishop of London *v.* John BARLEY.
Rent of malt payable for the parsonage of Ashwell.   HERTS.

21   Edmund [BONNER], bishop of London *v.* John GUYTHIAM, gentleman.
Manor of Faunhope belonging to the bishopric.   [HEREF.]

22-23   George BRAYE of London, gentleman, *v.* John COURTNEY, gentleman. ·
Messuages, barn and land in Lanivet' late of Reynold Braye, deceased, father of complainant.   CORNWALL.

24   . . . · BREERTON, esquire, *v.* Christopher HOLFORD.
Forgery of a conveyance of salt-houses in Nether Droitwich and Fulwyche in the name of Ralph BREERTON of Iscoed, co. Flint, esquire, deceased. *Damaged.*   [WORCESTER.]

25-26   Joan BROKE of London *v.* William DUNCOMBE, gentleman.
Rent charged on land in Eddlesborough, formerly wages of a priest in the church of Ivinghoe.   BUCKINGHAM.

27-30   Robert, son and heir of Isabel (Elizabeth) wife of Robert BROKKYLSEBEE, deceased, *v.* Thomas INKERSFYLD.
Detention of deeds relating to a messuage and land in Austin.   YORK.

31-34   George BROKWAYE *v.* Anne, late the wife of David BROKEWEY.
Manor of Ferne in Donhead St. Andrew (Veerne) and messuage and land in Donhead St. Andrew, Shaftesbury, and Gillingham, late of John BROKWAYE, deceased, grandfather of complainant and father of the said David.   WILTS, DORSET.

35-37   Elizabeth, late the wife of Thomas BRUDENELL, knight, and administratrix of his goods *v.* Robert HOPKYNS.
Account as under-sheriff to the said Sir Thomas.   WARWICK, LEICS.

38-42   The same *v.* Thomas BRUDNELL.
Lands in Glapthorne, Cotterstock, Oundle and Benefield. *See File* 1194, *No.* 70.   N'HAMP.

43-46   Robert BRUSHEFELD *v.* Richard and Robert COTTES and Thomas GOODWYN.
Messuage and land in Monyash claimed by Richard Staley and entrusted to defendants pending investigation of title. *See File* 1290, *No.* 63.   DERBY.

47-49   David BRYAN (Briane) of Lincoln *v.* John HENNAGE of Kirkby by Kingerby, gentleman, and Oliver ASKERBY of Asgarby, his servant.
Bargain of corn, and price of glass, belfries and gates [belonging to the priory of Elsham?]. *Mutilated.*   LINCOLN.

50-51   The same *v.* Thomas EMONSON, mayor of Lincoln, Richard BURRELL and Christopher JOHNSON, sheriffs, and William COWPER, a servant of the city.
Refusal of process against the said Asgarby and Hennage and imprisonment for entering the council chamber without leave.   LINCOLN.

52   Thomas BUNGAY, Alice his wife, Leonard PYNCHEBEK, George FORSTER and Mildred his wife *v.* Richard COTTON, knight, Henry LACY, gentleman, his steward, and William THORNELL *alias* Scoller.
Messuages and land late held of the said Sir Richard's manor of Bourne by Adam Forster, deceased, grandfather of the said Leonard and father of the female complainants. *See File* 1333, *No.* 46.   LINCOLN.

53-54   William BURNELL of London, gentleman, *v.* Robert SAVELL, esquire.
Cell or rectory of Woodkirk claimed under leases respectively from King Henry VIII and the prior of Nostell.   YORK.

55-56   Roger BURYE *v.* Richard VAVASOUR, gentleman, and Dorothy his wife.
Messuages, cottages, land, and turbary in York, Walden, Terrington, Thirtleby, Kirby-Knowle, Rounton, Rudby, Ayton, Helmsley, Barton-in-Ryedale, Nunnington, Hornby, Hawxwell, Pickhill (Pycall), Patrick-Brompton, Northallerton . . . Myre (*i.e.* Ainderby-Myers?), Little Crakehall and Richmond bought of the late King by Matthew White and Edward Burye, deceased, brother of complainant. (Many tenements are described in the answer.)   YORK.

57   Thomas Garlande and others, in the name of the inhabitants of BUXTON, *v.* Roger COTTRELL and Robert, Roger, and Thomas his sons.
Chapel of St. Anne in Buxton already awarded to complainants in this court. (Defendants are accused of permitting young persons coming to drink of St. Anne's well to drink and dance in the chapel.)   DERBY.

58   Margaret BYLLINGTON of Tottenham, co. Middlesex *v.* John and Thomas MUTTON, Randolph BYLLINGTON and Rose his wife.
Annuity charged on lands in Grovenant in favour of complainant and Thomas her husband by Peter Mutton, father of defendants John, Thomas, and Rose, his executors.   FLINT.

59   Ralph BYRDE, parson of Checkendon, *v.* Bridget, late the wife of John RAYMONDE, esquire.   ·   OXFORD.
Parsonage of Checkendon claimed under a lease from a former parson.

FILE 1333.

1-2   John, son and heir of Hugh BALDWYN, and administrator of his goods, *v.* Edward BUCKMASTER and John AXSTON (Axstell).
Land at Prestwood (in Great Missenden) held in fee, and messuage, and land in Great Missenden held for the life of William Felowe.   BUCKINGHAM.

3-4   Wilfred BANASTER *v.* Thomas HODGESON, executor of Matthew Thomson, gentleman.
Detention of deeds relating to lands (*undescribed*), late of William Banaster, deceased, father of complainant.   YORK.

5   Edward BANDE, parson of Tockenham (Tockenham Woke) *v.* William ALLEYN.
' Cotes or tofts ' and other lands belonging to complainant's glebe, but claimed by deft. as lord of the manor.   WILTS.

6-7   Edmund BARKER, yeoman, grandson and heir of Edmund Barker, *v.* Robert GARDYNER and Thomasyne his wife.
Detention of deeds relating to the messuage and land in Sibton.   SUFFOLK.

8-10   · Jerome BARNABE, prebendary of Netheravon, *v.* William, brother and executor of Simon SYMONS, his predecessor.
Dilapidations of the parsonage and church.   WILTS.

11-13   Thomas BARRINGTON *v.* John HODGETTES.
Crown rent of a mill in Walsall, sublet by deft.   STAFFORD.

14   John BARTRAM *v.* Thomas BADDELEY.
Messuage and land in Barlaston. *See Files 945, No.* 10; *946, No.* 14; *954, No.* 14.   STAFFORD.

15-16   The same *v.* Thomas BUSBYE, gentleman.
Messuages and lands in Barlaston, Cocknage (in Trentham) and Blackwood.   STAFFORD.

17-18   Ellen, late the wife of William BASSETT, knight, *v.* William BASSETT, esquire.
Detention of deeds relating to the manor of Woodcote, late of John Cootes, esquire, former husband of complainant.   SALOP.

19-20   John BASSETT of St. Magnus, London, fletcher, *v.* the bailiffs and officers of DUNWICH.
Action by Thomas Halydaie in the name of Richard Bodon, for price of herrings and candles. Certiorari.   SUFFOLK.

21-24   William BEERDSLEY and Anne his wife *v.* Hugh BOWDE and Edmund BERDELL.
Goods of Roger Marshall of Lichfield, deceased, father of the said Anne, stated by defts. to have been administered by Isabel, his wife. D. X, 25.   STAFFORD.

25   Edward BELLINGHAM of Aldrington *v.* Edward BELLINGHAM of Haughton, his brother (*sic*).
Land and sheep-pasture in Aldrington claimed by deft. on the ground that his mother has not released her right of dower in Haughton. *Damaged.*   SUFFOLK.

26   John BELLOW *v.* William CRAYKE, gentleman.
Money advanced for purchase of the interest of Christopher Estofte, gentleman, in a messuage and pasture in Beverley.   YORK.

27-29   Richard BENTON of London, yeoman, *v.* Thomas GYTTYNS of Aston in Worthen, yeoman, and John and Edmund his sons.
Loan to the said Edmund.   LONDON, SALOP.

30   John, brother and executor of Ralph BERE of Henley-on-Thames, *v.* Robert ST. . . . . , executor of Joan, executrix and late the wife of John Hoggys of the same.
Legacy of the said Hoggys. *Faded.*   OXFORD.

31   William BETTES of Haddenham *v.* Richard KYRCKBY, gentleman.
Manor and lands in Landbeach, promised to complainant on his marriage with Margery, daughter of deft.   CAMBRIDGE.

32-35   Richard BLACKEWELL, gentleman, *v.* George VERNON, knight.
Lands in Topcliff and Blackwell and tithes in King's Sterndale, Cowdale, Stadon (all in Buxton), and Ashford, demised by the late prior and convent of Lenton with the collectorship of all their rents and tithes in the Peak.   DERBY.

36-37   Richard BLACKWALL the younger *v.* Humphrey STAFFORD.
Breach of conditions (*described*) of an under-lease of a messuage land and stock in Blackwell. DERBY.

38-39   William BLAKE and Elizabeth his wife, daughter and heir of George Astewell, and Joan his wife *v.* Thomas, son and heir of John LEEKE.
Land in Astrop, formerly of Stephen Somerton. *See File* 1307, *Nos.* 16-22, *the last being the replication in this suit.*   NORTHAMPTON.

40   Thomas BLANCK the elder, citizen and haberdasher of London, *v.* John BOWYER, gentleman, and others.
Manor of Warborough.   OXFORD.

41   Elizabeth late the wife of James BLUNT *v.* Elizabeth BYRYTON and Thomas FOOTE of Bridge Sollers.
Lands in Grendon Bishops, late of John Blunt, esquire, deceased, father of the said James and Elizabeth Byryton, and goods.   HEREFORD.

42   John BOCHER of Oxburgh, co. Norfolk, Joan his wife, John DAYE of Thorndon, Katherine his wife, John LAWND of Tybenham, co. Norfolk, Margery his wife, Henry TYLER and Margaret his wife, v. Thomas COLMAN and Eleanor his wife.
Land in Burgate and Wortham, late of Elizabeth Browne, deceased, whose heirs are the female complainants. *Pedigree given.*   SUFFOLK.

43-45   William BOLLES, esquire, and Lucy his wife, late the wife of John Parnell, v. Erasmus HENNYNGHAM and Elizabeth his wife.
Messuages and land in Sampford (?) . . . . . . *Faded.*   [DEVON.]

46-48   John BOSSE v. William THORNELL, *alias* Scoler, late the husband of Katherine Sutt.
Land in Bourne, late of John Bosse, deceased, father of complainants. *See File 1332, No. 52.*   LINCOLN.

49   Thomas BRADSHAWE of the Lee (*i.e.* Leigh?), co. Stafford, gentleman, v. Robert FARRYER, yeoman.
Detention of deeds relating to a messuage and land in Wyndfeld (*i.e.* Wingfield?)   DERBY.

50   Thomas BRADY v. Matthew BRADBERY, gentleman, and Margaret his wife, executrix and late the wife of Thomas Farour.
Debt for malt.   NORFOLK.

51   Robert BROKBANK and Dorothy his wife v. Henry HYLLS.
Tenement in a street called the *Chekker* in King's Lynn.   NORFOLK.

52   Robert BROKEBANK, esquire, v. the same.
Messuage in King's Lynn.   NORFOLK.

53   George BROUGHTON, *alias* Smythe, v. Richard HEYDOCKE and William BEE.
Messuage and garden in Rugeley, late in the tenure of Maude Heydocke.   STAFFORD.

54-56   Matthew BROWNE, knight, v. Roger COMBER, Thomas, grandson and heir of Richard MASCALL, Thomas MYDDLETON (Mylton, Amylton), and Stephen BORDE.
Meadow in complainant's manor of Little Walsted. *See File 1288, No. 89.*   SUSSEX.

57-63   John BUDDE v. Joan BUDDE and Anthony ACKLAND, gentleman.
Land held of the manor of Chittlehampton by John Budde, deceased, father of complainant and late the husband of the said Joan. (Customs of the manor discussed.)   DEVON.

64-65   James BULSTRED, gentleman, v. William RAYNYSFORD, knight.
Actions on a bond for an exchange of lands (*not here specified*) which has been carried out.   [OXFORD?]

66-67   Thomas BULSTRODE v. Robert RAWSON and Anne his wife.
Loans, price of goods (*described*) and horse-hire paid on behalf of Andrew Bulstrode, deceased, brother of complainant and former husband of the said Anne. *Answer wanting.*   [OXFORD?]

68-70   Robert BURS[TON?] of Norbury, weaver, for himself and other inhabitants of Norbury v. Thomas STAYNSON and Thomas CROSSE.
Chalice and other goods of the parish church of Norbury, whereof the said Burston and Staynson are churchwardens. *Damaged.*   STAFFORD.

71-73   Margaret BUSSHOPE v. John, Alice and Thomas BUSSHOPE.
Tithe of corn in Brailes, late of John Busshope, deceased, husband of complainant.   WARWICK.

74-79   Robert BYDDELL of the Inner Temple v. Margery and John WHETELEY and Thomas STONE.
Crown lease of a grange and pasture in Dale.   DERBY.

80   John BYRGEE of Bordeaux v. the Mayor and Sheriff's officers of LINCOLN.
Action of trespass by the wife of John Dove, in the collection of whose debts complainant has been concerned. *Corpus cum causa. Mutilated.*   LINCOLN.

81   Michael BYSSHOP v. . . . . FORTUNE, John AVERY, and Joan, his wife.
Messuage, etc., late of Thomas Bysshop, deceased, grandfather of complainant. *Mutilated.* SUSSEX.

FILE 1334.

1-2   Richard BALLARDE v Robert BALLARDE.
Messuage and land in the parish of Chyld [erditch], late of William Ballarde, deceased, father of both parties. *Mutilated.*   ESSEX.

3   Thomas BARKELEY, scholar at Westminster, son and heir of William Barkeley, v. Edward WELCHE and Jane his wife, mother of conplainant.
Refusal to join in a suit against Richard, son and heir of Michael Lyster, knight, for a lease of the site of the manor of Dinedor with a mill and lands.   HEREFORD.

4   John BARKER, yeoman, and Joan his wife, late the wife of John Fletcher, v. John GOLTYS of Thaxted, farmer.
Obtaining a judgment of a messuage and orchard in Thaxted by a false assurance that certain rooms and half the fruit of the orchard were reserved to the said Joan for life.   ESSEX.

5   Alice BARNEHAM, kinswoman and heir of Joan late the wife of William Leman, v. Bryan BARKER, subsequent husband of the said Joan.
Messuage and dye-house in East Street, Chichester, of the demise of William Hanowse.   SUSSEX.

6-12   John BASSETT of Seaton, co. Rutland, v. Robert KYRKHAM of Vyncent (*i.e.* St. Vincent's in Cosgrove?), co. Northampton, knight.
Refusal to permit an assignment of tenancy of the manor of Haddon. *Damaged.* HUNTINGDON.

13 John BASTARD *v.* John, son and executor of Geoffrey GYLBERD of Bovey Tracy.
Money promised to complainant on his marriage with Tamsyn, daughter of the said Geoffrey.
DEVON.

14 William BAWTRE *v.* Thomas BROWNE.
Land in Bicker and Swineshead late of Edward Bawtrye of Boston, deceased, father of complainant.
LINCOLN.

15 Humphrey BAYLYE of Williton, labourer, *v.* Robert BAYLYE.
Joint lease from the late abbot of Ford of a tenement called Ley-in-Lynton.
DEVON.

16 William BAYLYE *v.* Thomas HALLE, esquire.
Seizure of household goods and tools for a plough from complainant's house at Freshford.
SOMERSET.

17-18 George BECKETT and Elizabeth his wife *v.* John CLARKE.
Messuages and gardens in Stevenage, late of William Howe, deceased, grandfather of the said Elizabeth.
HERTS.

19 John BEGETT *v.* . . . . .
Forgery of deeds relating to a barn and land in Sturton and Fenton of the demise of Richard Holgate and Margaret his wife. *Mutilated.*
[NOTTS.]

20 Richard BEKENSAWE, esquire, *v.* Anthony BROWNE of South Weald, co. Essex, and Joan his wife.
Manor of Becconsall (Bekensawe) pledged to defendants on lease.
LANCASTER.

21 Robert BEKET of Cortuther (in Menheniot) *v.* John CONNOKE of Liskeard, tanner.
Land in the borough of Liskeard, late of Gilbert Beket, deceased, father of complainant.
CORNWALL.

22 Alice BELL *v.* Robert SMITHE *alias* Pewterer of Derby.
Messuages and lands in Atherton and elsewhere. *Mutilated.*
DERBY.

23 John BELLOWE of Newstead, co. Lincoln esquire, *v.* John and Richard MIDDLETON, executors of Robert Middleton.
Price of the Guildhouse in Welwick.
YORK.

24 Hugh BENET, Katherine his wife, Walter DEWE and Joan his wife, *v.* Simon BRODMEDE and Katherine his wife.
Detention of deeds relating to a messuage and land in Crediton (Kyrton) late of Robert Hampton, deceased, father of the female complainants.
DEVON.

25 William BENNETT *v.* James his son and Thomas SHELLEY of Berehyll.
Fraud in the settlement of a cottage in Serley on the said James at his marriage with Margaret, daughter of the said Thomas. *Mutilated.*

26-29 William BERDMORE *v.* James WOODRUFF and Ellen his wife.
Building lease of land in Marchington Woodland.
STAFFORD.

30-31 William BICKYNS of Warwick, shoemaker, *v.* Lawrence ELSTON, parson of Abyngton (Adyngton).
Money promised to complainant on his marriage with defendant's daughter. *Faded.* WARWICK.
CAMBRIDGE?

32-35 John BLACKMAN, citizen and grocer of London, *v.* Joan, daughter and executrix of Peter WAKEFELD of Pontefract, chapman.
Part of price of spices and other goods (*described*).
LONDON, YORK.

36-37 Nicholas BLAKEDON *v.* John HYLPP, mayor of Thornbury, Edward HOLBROKE and others.
Seizure of goods from complainant's house in Thornbury after it was burnt, imprisonment, and conspiracy for assault and non-payment of debts.
GLOUC.

38-44 George, son of Ralph BLAKWALL and of Dorothy his wife *v.* Robert MARSHALL and others.
Moiety of tithes of Bradwell, divided between the late monastery of Lenton and the dean and chapter of Lichfield.
DERBY.

45-46 Laurence BLAKWE(Y), clerk, *v.* Thomas GRENE.
Chamber and close belonging to Moseley chapel in King's Norton.
WORC.

47-49 John BORRETT of Laxfield *v.* John PYERS and Katherine his wife, late the wife of Robert Branche and executrix of Robert Aylmer.
Action on a bond for a debt which complainant could not pay when due, being on service at Boulogne.
SUFFOLK.

50-53 Ralph BOSVILE, gentleman, *v.* Humphrey NASHE and Elizabeth his wife, late the wife of Richard Everingeham.
Messuages (*tenants named*) in Penistone, Thurlestone, Carlecotes, Swindon (both in Penistone), Waldershelf, Bradfield, Wortley and Tankersley. (Defendant also mentions Whitwell and Northope and recites the said Richard's marriage settlement.)
[YORK.]

54 Thomas BOWES, citizen and grocer of London, *v.* the Lord Mayor and Sheriffs of LONDON, and John MESHERVYE, citizen and haberdasher of London.
Action on a bond for performance of an arbitral award never rendered by all the arbitrators. *Certiorari and subpœna.*
LONDON.

55 John BOURRINGE, Margaret his wife and others, *v.* John PORT, gentleman.
Messuage and land in Ilam, Castern and Stanshope (both in Ilam). *Damaged.*
STAFFORD.

56   Richard BRANDE of Elmdon v. Nicholas BARKER of the same.
Arbitral award for payment of a loan made to Thomas Bell.   ESSEX.

57-59   Thomas BRENT ' in the parishe of Sake ' v. John HYLL.
Messuages and land in St. Teath bought of John Vowler (Fowler) and Joan his wife whereof defendant
claims a lease.   CORNWALL.

60-63   William BROCKHURSTE and Anne his wife v. Joan GERVIS and Thomas SWANCOTE.
Cattle, deeds, etc., late of Robert Badger, deceased, father of the said Anne.   [STAFFORD ?]

64   Richard BRODE v. William CARTER and others.
Detention of deeds relating to messuages and land in Almeston (in Woolfardisworthy) and Bideford.
                                                                                            DEVON.

65   Robert, grandson and heir of Robert BROKLYNG v. John MERKANT and Robert RAFF.
Detention of deeds relating to land in Wilby and Brundish.   SUFFOLK.

66   Rowland BROMLOWE v. Simon KEMSEY of Hull, co. York, esquire.
Crown lease of a tenement in the manor of Wilderley (in Church Pulverbatch).   SALOP.

67-69   Thomas BROWNE v. William ASSHEWELL.
Sale of a messuage in King's Lynn in breach of a trust.   NORFOLK.

70-71   Thomas BROYTE and Margaret his wife v. Humphrey, son and heir of Thomas CORYE.
Messuage in Cake Street, Mildenhall, late of Thomas Maye, deceased, grandfather of complainant.
                                                                                           SUFFOLK.

72-73   William BRYAN, a minor, by Richard Byng (?) and Margaret his wife v. John, son of Robert
            JOHNSON, deceased.
Messuage and land in Saddington late of John Bryan, deceased, a cousin of complainant.
                                                                                          LEICESTER.

74   William, great grandson and heir of Lawrence BRYTTLE and of Isabel his wife, v. William
            CHAUNT.
Detention of deeds relating to land in Odcombe of the gift of John Estebroke, deceased.
                                                                                          SOMERSET.

75   The same v. the same and Richard NYGHELLYN.
Wrongful occupation of the same.   SOMERSET.

76-77   John BUCKNYLL and Margaret his wife, executrix and late the wife of Richard Taylour
            of Ledbury, v. John POPLEY of Bristol, cooper.
Action for a debt disproved by an account suppressed by defendant.   HEREFORD, GLOUCESTER.

78   John BUDDE v. Anthony ACKELAND, gentleman and John CHAPELL.
Land held of the manor of Chittlehampton by John Budde, father of complainant. Damaged.
                                                                                            DEVON.

79-81   John BUKKYNGHAME v. Thomas MA(K)POWDER.
Detention of a lease of a messuage and land in Howlosworth (v.e. Holsworthy?) made by John
Clarke.   DEVON.

82-85   William BUKNAM v. Robert BARKER.
Action on a bond for price of goods (schedule annexed) partly paid.   SUFFOLK.

86   Henry BULLYANT, John GARDENER and Agnes his wife v. Robert HARRY.
Messuage and land in Frostenden sold to defendant by Robert, his father, deceased, also father of
the said Agnes and of Margaret late the wife of the said Henry.   SUFFOLK.

87-89   William BURGH v. Henry son and heir of William BRIGGS and George WATSON.
Nuisance caused by converting a pond (' pounde ') in Crediton (Kyrton) used for watering cattle into
a hemp-pit, in breach of the statute 12 Richard II, c. 13.   [DEVON.]

90-91   Thomas BURNAM of Aldingbourn, husbandman, v. Edmund SWYNDELL of Washington,
            yeoman, executor of John Swyndell, priest.
Balance of money given to the said John as complainant's guardian and to his use by John
Swyndell his father.   SUSSEX, HANTS.

92-96   Nicholas BURWAYE, gentleman, son and heir of John Burwaye and grandson and heir of
            Robert Jakes and of Elizabeth his wife, v. John NOWELL and Anne, his wife, daughter and
            heir of John Fowler.
Messuages and land in Wellsborough (in Sibson). Damaged.   LEICESTER.

97-99   Paul BUSSHE, late bishop of Bristol, v. George HERDERT, knight, executor of John
            Cradocke, and Mary, late the wife of Matthew HERBERT, his son.
Arrears of rent of the parsonages of Portbury, Tickenham and Clevedon.   SOMERSET.

100-102   Thomas BUTLER v. Richard CRAWLEGH (Crowley).
Joint purchase of a messuage and land in Swalcliffe from William Hanshawe.   OXFORD.

FILE 1335.

1   Thomas BADGER of Bidford, co. Warwick, v. Francis, son and heir of Simon MOUNTFORD, .
            esquire.
Refusal to complete a lease of pasture in Wednesbury.   STAFFORD.

2-3   Anne, sister of Ralph BAGENALL, knight, v. Thomas TYTTENSOR (Tyndestar).
Messuage and land in Penkhull claimed by defendant as part of the manor of Newcastle-under-
Lyme. See File 1331, No. 1.   STAFFORD.

4-7   Thomas BAKER, executor of William Baker of West Walton v. John WALTER of Griston,
            Agnes his wife, Hugh his son, and John WALTER of Fersfield.
Bond given by the said John Walter of Fersfield to the said William and entrusted by him to the
said John Walter of Griston.   NORFOLK.

8–9   William BAKER of Langford Budville, husbandman, v. Nicholas COURTNEY and Philippa
his wife.
Land in Chipley (in Langford Budville) said by complainant to be held of the manor of Garnival's
Week (in Milverton) and by defts. of that of Chipley.   SOMERS.

10   Henry BALAM of Newport v. John GLASEOUR, rector of Whippingham, and the sheriffs
of LONDON.
Action on a bond for performance of an arbitral award concerning tithes. *Subpœna and certiorari.*
LONDON, HANTS. (I.W.)

11–13   Robert BANESTER and Agnes his wife, executrix of John Whytyng, v. Richard WALKER.
Debt of John Walker, deceased, brother of deft.

14   Robert BARKER of London, merchant tailor, v. William WOODALL and Mary his wife,
executrix and late the wife of John Souche of London, leather-seller.
Bond for a debt already paid in angels at 7s. 6d. each.   LONDON.

15   William BARKER, master of King Edward's free school at Berkhamsted, Roger NORWOOD,
usher there, and John WOODHOUSE, yeoman, their tenant, v. William FORSTER, Elizabeth
his wife, William FONGE, and John DYSSHE.
Claim to lands of the school as heirs of John Incent the founder. *Mutilated.*   HERTS.

16   James BARLOW and Margaret his wife v. John and Peter DAMPORTE.
Tenement (*place not given*) of the demise of Thomas Damporte of Henbury, deceased, father of
both defts., from which complainants have been ejected by a subsequent purchaser.   CHESTER.

17–20   Joan BARTLET, late the wife of Nicholas Hurtland, and Thomas HURTLAND v. Richard
MOMPESSON, esquire and Thomas HOGGES, his servant.
Lands in Andersfield (in Goathurst) and Lexworthy (in Enmore) of the demise of Edmund
Mompesson, esquire, deceased, nephew of the said Richard. D. XI, 25.   SOMERS.

21   William BAYLY, executor of Agnes late the wife of John Bayly, v. Thomas, son and heir
of William HALLE, esquire.
Messuage and land in Freshford of the demise of deft. and his father.   SOMERS.

22   Edward BAYNTON, esquire, and Agnes his wife, formerly Agnes Ryse, v. Charles STOURTON,
Lord Stourton.
Part of the manors of Kilmington, Norton, Stourton, Brook, Wanstrow and Yarnfield, messuages and
lands there (except in Stourton) and in Gasper in Stourton (Geyspore), Penselwood (Penne),
Wincanton, Marston Bigott, Charlton Musgrave, and Beckington and the hundred of Norton Ferris
(Norton Stourton), settled on the said Agnes for life by William Stourton, late lord Stourton.
SOMERS.

23–26   John BEARE of Moorwinstow, husbandman, v. John SAUNDER of Ashwater, gentleman.
Money promised to complainant on his marriage with Joan Twyston, a kinswoman of deft.
CORNW., DEVON.

27   Lawrence BENFELD of Alverstoke, co. Hants, v. John PYTTE.
Messuage near Weymouth quay late of Maude Benfeld, deceased, mother of complainant.
DORSET.

28–29   Peter BERE v. Thomas BERE.
Lands in Menheniot, Liskeard and Doneckys Wyll late of William Bere, deceased, father of both
parties.   CORNW.

30–33   John BEVER v. John HULSON of London, scrivener, and Edmund, son of Richard HYLL.
Messuages and land in Lambeth bought of the said Hulson.   SURREY.

34   Richard BLAKWALL of Blackwell, gentleman v. William NEWTON the younger, of
Moyslowe Castle, gentleman.
Price of work.   DERBY.

35   Simon BLANK of Newark, ironmonger, and Reginald COLLETT of Langthorp, co. Lincoln,
husbandman.
Petition against an injunction to evacuate the parsonage of Winthorpe, of the demise of John
Goonston, parson, deprived for marriage.   NOTTS

36–42   The same v. William HALLYDAY, now parson.
Lease of the parsonage.   NOTTS.

43   John BODENHAM and Alice his wife v. JEVAN àp David of Llanstephan, tailor, and
William PHELIPS of the same, gentleman.
Cattle delivered by the said Jevan in part payment of a debt to complainant who entrusted them
to the said Phelips.   RADNOR.

44–47   Alexander BORNE v. Cuthbert EMERSON.
Land in Cosgrave held of the manor of Easton Mauditt (Est Maldett). *Mutilated.*
N'HAMP.

48   Thomas BOROWE and Ellen his wife, late the wife of Henry Langwade, v. Thomas
SHERBOURNE, esquire.
Refusal to grant a copy for a tenement in deft's manor of Sharnborne (Sherbourne) in Snettisham.
NORFOLK.

49 50   The same (BOROUGH) v. Richard and Peter JOHNSON and John HAYE.
Disturbance in occupation of the same.   NORFOLK.

51   Richard son of Richard BOSTOK v. Ralph DUTTON of Hatton, son of Peter Dutton, knight.
Mills in the manor of Tattenhall, of which manor deft. has a Crown lease.   CHESTER.

52–53   Eustace BOTHE v. Eleanor SKYPWORTH of Habrough.
Bedding (*described*) awarded to complainant by arbitration.   LINCOLN.

54   Henry BOWNE v. Christopher MADDER of Bonsall, husbandman, and William his elder brother.
Refusal to complete an entail of land in Matlock on complainant and Elizabeth daughter of the said Christopher.   DERBY.

55   William BRAKE v. Thomas THORNETON of York, apothecary, and others.
Bond given on defts' behalf to John Thorneton and others.   YORK.

56   William BRAKENBURY, esquire, son of Anthony Brakenbury, deceased, v. Lancelot NEVELL, gentleman.
Messuages and lands in Denton and Houghton and the lordship of Shipley.   DURHAM.

57   Richard BRERETON of Tatton, knight, v. Peter LEYCESTER of Tabley, esquire.
Marriage to deft's daughter of Geoffrey Brereton, aged 11 years, son and heir of complainant and of Jane his wife, daughter and heir of Geoffrey Massye of Tatton, knight.   CHESTER.

58   William grandson of Humphrey BRETT v. George BRETT.
Manor of Doxey of the demise of John Burchyer, late Lord Berners.   STAFFORD.

59   Owen BREWERTON, gentleman, servant to Sir Robert Rochester, knight, controller of the Household, v. JEVAN ap Hoell ap Gruffydd.
Messuages and land in Wepre late of Richard ap Jevan, deceased, grandfather of complainant.
                                                                                FLINT.

60   Mark BROUGHTON of Seaton, co. Rutland, v. John FREMAN.
Manor of Sandys and messuages and lands in Great Stewkley.   HUNTINGDON.

61   Thomas BROWNE of Westminster v. Walter BROWNE, rector of Chelwood (Chelworthe).
Lease of deft.'s rectory promised in return for loans and board at complainant's house at Kendal.
                                                           SOMERSET, WESTMORELAND.

62–64   Andrew BRYNGTON, citizen and fishmonger of London, v. Elizabeth, late the wife of Nicholas BULLE, citizen and goldsmith of London.
Silver delivered to deft. to be changed for gold for a journey to Scarborough. LONDON.

65–67   Morice BUCKETT of Caldecote, weaver v. Robert PECKE of the same, clerk of the peace for the county.
Threats to ruin complainant.   CAMBRIDGE.

68   Richard BUKLER v. Katherine, late the wife of Walter BUKLER, knight.
Annuity out of the manor of Fairford promised on complainant's marriage with Katharine Racland.   GLOUC.

69   John BULLER of Woode, co. Somerset v. William POUNDE, esquire, and others.
Manor of Chale late of Alexander Buller, deceased, grandfather of complainant. HANTS.

70   William BUSSHE v. Thomas CULPEPER the elder.
Manor of Yanworth, obtained of the Crown by Thomas Culpeper the younger, executed for treason
Damaged. See Cal. S.P. Dom. 1547-1580, p. 8.   GLOUC.

71   Robert BUSSHELL of London, yeoman, v. Thomas HYNE, husband of Katherine late the wife of Robert Wilson, and William HYNE.
Bond to secure a gift by the said Wilson of a leasehold messuage in Ince with goods therein.
                                                                                CHESTER.

72–73   George BYNGHAM and George TOFTES v. Anne late the wife of Richard NEVILL.
Detention of deeds relating to the priory of St. Gregory's without Canterbury, etc. (*as in File 1291, No. 69*).   KENT.

74–75   The said George TOFTES v. the said Anne NEVILL.
Detention of a lease to complainant of land in Chartham, Petham, and Nackington, and of other deeds.   KENT.

76–79   George BYNGHAM of Shepherdswell, gentleman, and Anne his wife v. William and John WEVELL and others.
Messuage and land in Newchurch formerly of Benignus Adams of Dattle, co. [Sussex], deceased, former husband of the said Anne and kinsman of the said John and other defendants. *Damaged.*
                                                                                KENT.

FILE 1336.

1   Henry BAKSTER and Anne his wife v. —— GLEGGE, widow.
Interception of a gift of money. *Faded.*

2–3   William BAMBOROWE v. John MAYE and William MARDOCKE.
Tithes of Ashfield and Thorpe of the demise of Thomas Mannynge, late prior of Butley, and his convent.   SUFF.

4–6   Robert BARKER of Ipswich, merchant, v. Ralph MARSHAM of Norwich.
Perjury in an action on a bond for delivery of salt.   SUFF., NORF:

7   . . . BARNARD v. Joan BARNARD.
Tenement late held of Thomas Mylle's manor of Alensmore by John Barnard, deceased, father of complainant and husband of defendant. *Mutilated.*   [HEREFE.]

8–9   William BARNES v. Edward GREVELL, knight, and Basil FEILDING and William SHELDON, esquires.
Detention of deeds relating to the manor and lordship of Ditchford Friary, of the entail of William Willyngton of Barcheston, esquire, uncle of complainants, whose executors defendants are. See D. XIV, 36.   WARW.

10   Edmund BEAWPRE, esquire, for himself and all the inhabitants of Outwell, v. John REPPES and William HUNSTONE, esquires, and others.
Conspiracy to appropriate dykes (described) between Outwell and Emneth.   NORF.

11   John BELLOE of Newstead, co. Lincoln, esquire, v. John WILSON and Jane his wife, late the wife of Hugh Clydere, gentleman.
Lands and rents in Swanland, Kirk Ella and West Ella bought of . . . Sissotson of Willerby. Faded.   YORK.

12–14   The same (Bellowe) v. John WRYGHT.
Pasture land in Cadney and Housham. (Annexed is an answer from Thomas, son of John Mounson, concerning an exchange of lands in Cadney and Housham for others in Oxton and Housham).   LINCOLN, [NOTTS].

15–17   Humphrey BENTLEY v. Alice BELL and others.
Messuage in Derby, with household goods (described). (Annexed is an answer by John, son and heir of Thomas Ofelde, claiming the remainder after the death of the said Alice).   DERBY.

18   Richard BENTON, yeoman, v. William TYPSELL of the borough of Southwark and Robert WELLES, goldsmith, and George SMITHE, 'merchant man,' both of London.
Action on a counterbond for price of plate and jewels bought of the said Welles and Smithe and partially recovered by them.   SURREY, LONDON.

19–20   George BESTE v. John son and heir of John TREVANTRES.
Messuages and lands in Tregantrys and Boysvaghe Tregantrys late of John Beste, deceased, father of complainant.   CORNWALL.

21–22   Thomas BETENSON, Cicely his wife and Elizabeth late the wife of Roger DODECOTE v. Joan LEE.
Burgage in Newport late of William Lee, deceased, husband of defendant and cousin of the female complainants.   SALOP.

23–24   John BETTES v. John CASTRE and Barbara his wife.
Loan made at Field-Dalling.   NORF.

25–28   John BLACKWELL, parson of Belbroughton, v. William CONYERS.
Lease of the said parsonage made with a false date by Edmund Cooper, late parson, deprived for marriage.   WORC.

29   John BLAKEHALL v. Roger FORDE of Broadhempstone.
Bond given on defendant's behalf for performance of an arbitral award.   DEVON.

30–32   William BLOUNT, great-grandson and heir of Nicholas Sutton, v. Thomas SHEPEY of Stapelton, yeoman, son and heir of Robert Shepey.
Land called the Windmill Hill in complainant's manor of Osbaston.   LEICESTER.

33–35   Thomas BLYTHE of Hemsworth (in Norton) v. Thomas DENHAM, esquire, and Thomas PARKER.
Moiety of a messuage and lands in Little Norton. Mutilated. D.X, 30.   DERBY.

36   William BOLLES of Felley, esquire, v. Richard WHALLEYE, farmer of the rectory of Ratcliffe-on-Trent, and Richard BRADSHAWE, bailiff of the late priory of Thurgarton.
Payment in respect of the said rectory ordered by the Chancellor and others as commissioners.
     DERBY.

37–39   Thomas BONVILE of Ilminster, gentleman, son and heir of John Bonvile, v. Stephen PAYNE and Agnes his wife, late the wife of Guy Bonvile, John BAYLLE the elder and John BAYLLE the younger.
Manors of East and West Dillington (in Ilminster) and Clapton (in Crewkerne), and a messuage dovecote and lands in South Petherton, East Lambrook, Kingsbury and Whitwell. SOMERSET.

40–42   Alice BRAKENBERYE, executrix and late the wife of William Middleton, v. Edward HARRYS, gentleman.
Tenements in Plymouth and Cornworthy late of Thomas Vowell, deceased, father of complainant and father-in-law of defendant.   DEVON.

43   Katherine BRAYE, administratrix of the goods of Ralph Eton of London, deceased, v. Margaret, late the wife of Owen GRYFFYTH of the same, gentleman, and Owen MORYCE.
Debt of the said Gryffyth, whose executors defendants are.   LONDON.

44–45   Owen BRAYE, esquire, and Anne his wife, daughter and heir of John Danaster, esquire, v Francis DAWTREY, knight, husband of Anne late the wife of the said John.
Waste of woods in the manors of Twitchin in Horsell and Hill Place in Bisley (now in Horsell) and lands there and in Chertsey and Chobham.   SURREY.

46–47   John BRENNENOKE alias Whyte of North Molton v. Thomas GRENE, late of Timberscombe, skinner, administrator of the goods of Richard Lawhyll (Lowhyll), vicar of Timberscombe, deceased.
Bequest of money and a bed by the said vicar, whose servant complainant was. DEVON, SOMERS.

48–50   William BRERETON of Brereton, co. Chester, knight, v. John, son and heir of Richard FULSTOWE.
Rents and services due from lands in Dalby.   LINCOLN.

51–54   Thomas BRILL, administrator of the goods of Elizabeth Watlington, *v.* Richard WATLING-
TON.
Money payable in consideration of a bequest by the said Elizabeth of wools in her shop at Reading
and other goods.   BERKS.

55–56   Robert BROKE, husbandman, Agnes his wife, Ralph HEMMYNG, Katharine his wife
and Elizabeth FELD *v.* Thomas TAYLOR, clerk.
Detention of deeds relating to a messuage and land in Haselor late of Ralph Feld, deceased, father
of the female complainants.   WARW.

57   . . . BROUHAM *v.* Thomas ELLES.
Goods of complainant's father. *Damaged.*   WESTM.

58   George BROUGHTON of London, gentleman, *v.* Arthur CHAMBORNE, knight, and Thomas
GOSSE.
Debt of the said Gosse.   LONDON.

59–65   Philip BROWNE, Agnes his wife and Roger their son *v.* Richard ROBERTES (Robyns),
Richard BAKER and Rose his wife.
Half a messuage and land in Spreyton bought of John Speke, esquire, since deceased.   DEVON.

66–67   Alice BUCKE of Dedham *v.* Robert STOWE of the same.
Grain and other goods entrusted to defendant.   ESSEX.

68–69   Humphrey BUCSTONE *v.* Thomas (John) SQUYER and Joan his wife.
Messuage and garden in Derby of the feoffment of Anthony Trappes, gentleman.   DERBY.

70–71   William, grandson and heir of Margaret, wife of William BULKELEY *v.* Arthur BULKELEY.
Detention of deeds relating to a mansion called Gorley and land in Fordingbridge.   HANTS.

72   Thomas BULLER *v.* John HEATHER of Derby.
Loan to defendant when acting as the King's victualler. *Damaged.*   DERBY.

73   Edward BURNE of Alvington and Elizabeth his wife, daughter and executrix of Thomas
Williams *v.* Richard IBLE of Lydney, tailor.
Land in Lydney of the demise of John Eddy.   GLOUC.

74   William BURTON *v.* Robert, brother of John MARSHALL, deceased.
Close of pasture in Pinner of the demise of defendant and of Henry Marshall his nephew.   MIDDX.

75   Nicholas BYER *v.* John CHAMPNEYS, knight, and John KYNGTON and Edward LANE
his servants.
Distress in Dartford for a bond given on behalf of Richard Jones for a loan of 12 pieces of gold called
sovereigns. D.X, 24.   KENT.

FILE 1337.

1–4   Henry CALDWALL, clerk, son and heir of Thomas Caldwall, *v.* John MORETON, gentleman.
Messuage and land in Gnosall, obtained by defendants by collusion of Robert Osburne,
churchwarden.   STAFFORD.

5   The same *v.* the same.
Messuage and land in Gnosall, charged with an obit for the soul of John Browning, esquire.
                                                                                                    STAFFORD.

6   Richard CAPLE of London, son of William Caple, and of Margaret his wife *v.* Thomas CAPLE
his elder brother.
Money and goods of the gift of the said Margaret seized in the mansion-house of Caple.
                                                                     HERTS. (*rectius* HEREFORD.).

7–8   William CAVENDISSHE, knight, and Elizabeth his wife *v.* Francis LEEKE, knight.
Messuages and land in Langford (Lanford) of the grant of Thomas Leeke. *See Files* 846, *No.21,
and* 1027, *No.* 21.   NOTTS.

9–12   John CHAPLEYN and Alice his wife *v.* William BROWNE (Brome), of Aisholt, father of the
latter.
Money promised to complainants on their marriage, including half the cost of the wedding dinner and
compensation for an unsuitable tenement.
                                                                                                   SOMERSET.

13   John CHEKYN *v.* Richard LOVE.
Messuage and land in Donington in Holland, late of Thomas Chekyn of Parndon, co. Essex, deceased,
grandfather of complainant.   LINCOLN.

14–15   The same *v.* Robert WRYGHTE.
Price of a tenement in Donington, held of the manor of Monkshall. *Damaged.*   LINCOLN.

16   John CHETWYN of Ingestre, co. Stafford, esquire, *v.* William GRENE of Atherstone.
Under-lease of land belonging to the parsonage of Grendon. *Faded.*   WARWICK.

17   John CHUBBE of Ugborough, husbandman *v.* Thomas HACCHE and John WHYTHYLL
of the same.
Bond given to complainant for a debt of John Ryder and others.   DEVON.

18–19   John CLEMENT, doctor of physic, *v.* Alban HYLLE, doctor of physic.
Wrongful occupation of a messuage in the Barge in Bucklersbury, late of Sir Thomas More, with
furniture (*described*) including 'a table of Sir Thomas More's face', and waste. *Answer wanting.*
                                                                                                   LONDON.

20 The same v. Elizabeth, late the wife of Anthony WINGFELDE, knight, and Robert WINGFELDE, knight.
Wrongful occupation of messuages and lands in Hornchurch, partly of the demise of Winchester College, waste, and seizure of household goods (described, including arms) and deeds. *See File 1342, No. 16.* ESSEX.

21–24 William CLYBERYE v. Richard LEVESON (Lewson), knight.
Extorting a bond for sale for 80*l.* of a messuage and land in Lilleshall worth 14*l.* yearly besides timber. SALOP.

25–26 Robert CLYTHERO v. John WARNER *alias* Pytman.
Lease made by Gilbert Latham, late master of St. Katharine's by the Tower, and the brethren and sisters thereof, of the manor of Quarley, with half the profits of court, fines and heriots. HANTS.

27–29 Isabel COKE and Anne PYKERYNG v. Robert WRYGHT and Elizabeth his wife, late the wife of William son of Richard Thymylby and daughter of Hamond Whytchcote.
Manor of Thorpe, in Thorpe by Aylesby and Laceby, late of John Woer, deceased, father of complainants. LINCOLN.

30 John COKE, ' beinge but a pore servinge mane,' v. THOMAS ap Lewis, and David DAVIE and William VAUGHAM, who promised to be his sureties.
Lease of sheep.

31–32 William COMONS v. John son of Richard BATEMAN.
Meadow in Windermere parish whereof Thomas Comons, uncle of complainant, was disseised by Reynold Bateman. WESTMORLAND.

33–36 Sylvester COMPTON v. John ASSHELOCKE, parson of Beckington.
Lands in Beckington claimed by defendants as forfeited to his manor for non-residence and waste. SOMERSET.

37–39 Humphrey CONYNGESBY and Francis BEDULF v. Thomas SALWEY.
Manor of Stanford and land there, late of Humphrey Salwey, deceased, grandfather of defendant and great-grandfather of complainant. WORCESTER.

40–41 Richard CORNEWELL, canon of Hereford, v. John HARFORD of Bosbury, co. Hereford, gentleman, and William PRYOR and others, his assigns.
Contempt of an injunction as to the prebend of Inkberrow. (The answer belongs to another suit.) WORCESTER.

42–44 Alice COWPER of Lewes, in Sussex, v. Marion, executrix and late the wife of Matthew AUSTEN of Tenterden.
Detention of goods of Stephen Cowper of Andover, in Hants, late husband of complainants by colour of a forged will. *See File 1294, No. 63.* KENT.

45 Stephen COWPER of Tenterden v. Marion, executrix and late the wife of Matthew AUSTEN.
Money paid at current rates to the said Austen as executor of Stephen Cowper of Andover after it had been debased by proclamation from the rate existing when delivered by the said Stephen Cowper of Andover. KENT, HANTS.

46–47 Thomas son and heir of William COWPER v. William GREY, husbandman.
Parsonage of Cudham of the demise of the late prioress and convent of Kilburn. KENT.

48–53 Thomas COWPLEDICKE of Colchester, gentleman, v. John PLAYNE and Ellen TYSON (Tynson) *alias* Sylham.
Lands in Dover, St. Margaret's, Buckland, and elsewhere late of John Cowpledicke, esquire, lieutenant of Dover, deceased, uncle of complainant. (The said Playne states that he has transferred his rights to the Queen.) D. XII, 31. KENT.

54 Ralph CRANE of Middleton, yeoman, v. Roger FOXE, Robert his son and Dennis BASSE-FORD of Brampton, gentleman.
Messuage called Hopton Hall and land in Youlgreave late belonging to a chantry there. DERBY.

55–58 Oswyn CRESWELL, esquire, v. Thomas GRAYE, William SMYTHE, and others, tenants of Ellington.
Rent of ' bygge ' payable for wayleaves (*described*) to bring ' wayre ' through the manor of Cresswell for manure. NORTHAMPTON.

59 James CRYCHLEY of Lichfield, draper, v. Richard HYLL, servant to the bailiffs of Lichfield.
Refusal to serve a capias on John Huddleston surety for a judgment debt of William Robynson of Drayton Bassett, esquire. STAFFORD.

60–61 John, son of Robert CUTT of Harpenden, husbandman v. Elizabeth, late the wife of Edmund BARDOLF, esquire, and Edmund their son.
Land in defendant's manor of Rothamsted (in Wheathampstead) formerly of Richard Feld. HERTS

FILE 1338.

1–6 John CARDEN of London, by Thomas Lawrence his father-in-law, v. Owen CARDEN Lowcross Hale and other lands (*described*) in Tilstone late of John Carden of Lewes, in Sussex, deceased, father of complainant. *Damaged.* D. X. 38. CHESTER.

7 Thomas CARPENTER, dwelling in London, v. Thomas MORGAN, gentleman, and others.
Meadow in Coleford. GLOUCESTER.

8–9 Thomas CATESBY v. Edmund (Edward) HORSFELD of Hetherfeld, co. York.
Bond given for 'a judgment debt awarded against Edmund Waterhouse, partner of defendant, for price of ' yonge brasell,' ' olde brasell,' alum and other wares. LONDON.

10-11   Richard CAVELEY, gentleman, v. Richard WHALLEY, esquire.
Manors of Whatton and Aslocton of the demise of William Gascoyn of Gawthorpe, co. York, knight.
                                                                                        NOTTS.

12-14   Richard CHAMOND, esquire, executor of Jane, late the wife of John Chamond, knight, and
Margaret his wife v. John ARUNDELL of Trerice, co. Cornwall, knight.
Manor of Upcott in Welcombe and messuages, a corn-mill and land in Welcombe and Hartland of the
demise of the said Sir John and Lady Chamond and goods of the latter.   DEVON.

15-17   Richard CHYCHESTER, administrator of the goods of Anne Raymond alias Woode,
deceased, v. MARGARET, executrix and late the wife of John Furse.
Legacy of John Raymond, father of the said Anne, whose executrix was Agnes (Annes) his wife,
first wife of the said Furse.   _____

18-21   Thomas CLOTWORTHY and Ermot his wife, daughter of John Radlye of North Molton,
co. Devon, deceased, v. Sylvester VYCARIE.
Debt secured by a lease of defendant's house in Exton, which he has purloined.   SOMERSET.

22-28   John COGHEN of Atlow, husbandman, v. Ralph GELL of Hopton, gentleman, and
Rowland FERNE his nephew.
Lands in Hognaston claimed in right of Ashbourne rectory and the late monastery of Rocester
respectively. D. X, 56. 2 bills, one asking for a commission, and the other for a subpœna.   DERBY.

29-31   Robert COKES, John GOODMAN, and Thomas PAWLYN, v. Ingram WOD, husband of
Alice, executrix and late the wife of Thomas Fuller.
Detention of deeds relating to a messuage and land in Alkham late of Robert Napleton, deceased,
great-grandfather of the said Cokes and grandfather of the other complainants.   KENT.

32-36   Robert COLE v. Richard COLE, grantee to uses.
Land held of Lord Oxford's manor of Oldhall in East Bergholt by Robert Cole of Stratford, deceased,
father of complainant. (Nos. 34 and 35 appear to belong to another suit.)   SUFFOLK.

37-39   Harry COLSEY and Elizabeth his wife, granddaughter and heir of Thomas Philippes, v.
Elizabeth late the wife of Richard COCKES, and William his grandson.
Detention of deeds relating to a messuage in Stanverton.   GLOUCESTER.

40   Richard COMBES of Cheltenham, yeoman, v. Edward SMYTH, constable of Walton in
Deerhurst (Durest Walton).
Resistance to service of a writ on William Smyth, husbandman, in an action in the Court of Requests
(XXIII, 116?).   GLOUCESTER.

41-43   John COOKE, Elizabeth his wife, Thomas BAWCOM, Ellen his wife, Richard YONGE and
Maude his wife v. Richard MAYE, Francis WARDE, and Roger BERYE (Byrre).
Messuages and lands in Worcester entailed by Emolyn Nasshe on Humphrey Fylde and Agnes his
wife, parents of the female complainants. Answer wanting.   WORCESTER.

44-48   Thomas and William CORYTON v. Richard CORYTON and Walter CODE and others,
feoffees to uses.
Legacy of Peter Coryton, father of the said Thomas, William and Richard payable out of the
manors of Yolande, Trencreek (in Blisland, or Tencreek in Liskeard), Penfrane (in St. Pinnock),
St. Pinnock, Bodwen (in Helland), Helland and Lamellyn (in Liskeard). D. XI, 1.   CORNWALL.

49-50   John COWPER v. Christopher PLANKNEY and others.
Crown lease of land in the manor of Upton. D. XI. 29.   BERKS.

51-55   John COWPER and Elizabeth his wife, daughter of John Hay, deceased, v. Katherine late
the wife of Thomas ROLFF, and William their son.
Sheep entrusted to the said Thomas, whose executors defendants are, to bring up the said
Elizabeth with the profits during her infancy, and to restore them on her marriage.   ?

56-58   Thomas COWPER v. William WALL, John RUSSELL and others.
Lands in Rowley late of Margaret Bryan, deceased, mother of complainant.

59-60   Henry CROFTON and Alice his wife v. William PHYLPOTTES.
Land held of the manor of Garway by John Harvy, deceased, great-uncle of the said Alice and
father-in-law of the said William.   HEREFORD.

61-70   John CRYMES v. William TAYLOUR, William SMYTHE, clerk, Richard BYRCHE,
William HALLE, Edward BAGSHAWE, William TOROLDE (Torroldoo) and others.
Wrongful occupation of portions (described) of the manor of Wetton. Damaged.   STAFFORD.

71-73   The same v. the said HALLE and others.
Felling timber in the same in contempt of an injunction from this court.   STAFFORD.

74-75   Thomas CULPEPER of Beddysburie (i.e. Bidborough?) v. Lewis WEST, esquire.
Refusal to complete a sale of messuages and lands in Canterbury, Hackington, Colver (i.e. Reculver?),
Hyrron (i.e. Herne), and Rainham.   KENT.

FILE 1339.

1-3   John CAKHO of Whitstable, in Kent, mariner, v. Grace BASTARD.
Tenement in St. Leonard's, Colchester Hethe (i.e. Hythe), late of John Cakho, deceased father of
complainant.   ESSEX.

4-7   William, son of John CARLINGTON, deceased, v. Lancelot ALFORDE, esquire, and others.
Messuage called 'Fyshehouse' and land in Wawn of the demise of the late abbot and convent
of Meaux. 2 replications.   YORK.

8–11   The same and Ellen CARLINGTON, late the wife of the said John *v.* the same.
Meadow in Wawn of the like demise. *2 replications.*   YORK.

12–15   Thomas CARY of Cockington, esquire, *v.* John CARY of Okehampton his elder brother,
Robert son of the latter, and Humphrey LOVEYS.
Double sale of the manor of Northlew by the said John and Robert.   DEVON.

16–20   Leonard CHAMBERLAYN of Woodstock, co. Oxford, knight, *v.* John GUYNETH, vicar
of Lenton(?), executor of Stephen Vaughan, esquire.
Money advanced by the Chamber of London to Dame Margery, late the wife of the said Vaughan
and now wife of complainant, on account of her children by the former. (The replication and
rejoinder appear to belong to another suit.) D. X, 26.   LONDON.

21–22   George CHATTE and Joan his wife *v.* Robert HANSON and Thomas CAWTHORNE.
Detention of deeds relating to a messuage, land and rent in Sturton.   NOTTS.

23   Robert CHENEY *v.* Joan HILL and Oliver her son.
Closes of pasture in Wyndenbury (*i.e.*, Wybunbury?) late of John Cheney, father of complaniant.   CHESTER.

24–26   Mereill, late the wife of John CHRISTMAS of Colchester, esquire, *v.* George CHRISTMAS
her son.
Bequest of leasehold pasture near Colchester castle, goods, and money payable out of lands in
Bradwell, Tillingham, and St. Lawrence. *Damaged.*   ESSEX.

27–30   John CLARKE *v.* Thomas SHUGGEBOROUGH, William TOWNE, and Thomas CLERKE.
Detention of deeds relating to a messuage and plough-land in Willoughby, of the demise of the
dissolved college of Asteley, co. Leicester (*rectius* Warwick).   WARWICK.

31–32   Thomas CLERK of Terling, tanner, *v.* James KNOTTESFORD of Fairstead(?), gentleman.
Tenement in Terling demised by Lord Audley in exchange for another.   ESSEX.

33   Harry CLERKE of Newport, tailor, *v.* Thomas GRAUNT and Katherine his wife.
Messuage and land in Broughton late of Harry Clerke of Broughton, deceased, father of complainant.   HANTS.

34   William CLYFF, husbandman, *v.* Roger BASTARD.
Messuage and land in the Manor of Charleton of the gift of Arthur Plantagenet, knight, and his wife.   DEVON.

35–38   John CLOWNAM, late of Handford, co. Stafford, *v.* Thomas HAND, Joan his wife, a
daughter and heir of John Clownam, and others.
Messuage and land in Doveridge. *See File* 1295, *No.* 21.   DERBY.

39–40   Elizabeth COKEYN (Cocken) of Orton-on-the-Hill (Overton under Arderne), late the wife
of John Bradshawe, *v.* John and William, sons of John BYDILL, deceased.
Manor of Shackerstone and pastures, woods, and commons there. *Damaged.*   LEICESTER.

41   Thomas COLLEWALL of Hitchin (Hinchym), bellows-maker.
Petition for a commission in a suit in this court against John Gardyner and others.   HERTS.

42   Robert, son of Peter COLSTINSOCKE, deceased, *v.* Peter COLSTINSOCKE of Wood-
Newton, co. Northants, yeoman, and Robert VENABLES.
Messuage and land in Appleton and reversion of messuages and land in Stockton, Hughterton (*i.e.*,
Hunsterston?), Barterton, Helsby, and Lostock Gralam, after the death of Ellen Colstinsocke.
See File 1295, *Nos.* 32–35.   CHESTER.

43   Ellen late the wife of Peter COLSTINSOCKE *v.* the same.
Do.   CHESTER.

44–50   John COLYNS of Houghton Regis, husbandman, *v.* Joan COLYNS.
Messuage and land held of the manor of Eaton [Bray?] by Henry Colyns, husbandman, deceased
father of complainant and husband of deft. (No. 49 is an interpleader of John Collyns son of deft.,
by Henry Francklyn, his guardian.)   BEDFORD.

51   John CONNOCK of the borough of Liskeard, yeoman, *v.* William TREMORKYN, gentleman.
Refusal to complete a sale of land at Treverbyn in St. Neots.   CORNWALL.

52   Richard COWPER of Warnham, co. Sussex, drover, *v.* George SNELLYNGE, bailiff of
Kingston-on-Thames.
Seizure of a cow and calf from a 'yeates' into which complainant had driven them at Kingston.   SURREY.

53–55   John COXE of Axbridge, linen-draper, *v.* John LYNENG the elder and John LYNYNGE
the younger, both of Tarnock (in Badgworth).
Action on a bond for price of stallions already paid.   SOMERSET.

56–58   George CRESWELL *v.* Mary late the wife of John HORNER.
Share of North Layton Grange in North Stainley (Kyrkestanley) of the demise of George Horner,
father of the said John.   YORK.

59–61   The same *v.* the said John and Katherine his mother.
Do. D. XIV, 2.   YORK.

62–63   Mary, late the wife of John CULPEPER, esquire, *v.* John PENVEN, parson of Bishops-
bourne and Barham, John CLERKE and others.
Parsonages of the said parishes of the demise of Nicholas [Ridley,] bishop of Rochester, late parson.   KENT.

64–69   Philip CURSON and Bridget his wife and Elizabeth and Robert KARVYLE.
Messuage and land in Watlington late of Thomas Karvyle of Rowton Holme, gentleman, former
husband of the said Bridget. *Mutilated:* D. XIV, 64.   NORFOLK.

B 4

FILE 1340.

1–5   Robert CALTON and Anne his wife *v.* Thomas BABYNGTON, esquire, Adam EARE
(Eyere) and others.
Detention of deeds relating to lands in Ashover.   DERBY.

6   Robert CALTON *v.* William BASSETT, esquire, and others.
Next presentation to the parsonage of Cheadle of the gift of Thomas Stackhouse, master of Michael-
House, Cambridge, and the fellows thereof.   STAFFORD.

7–9   John CARTER *v.* William DENHAM *alias* Howsden, executor of Joan, executrix and late
the wife of William Pynner, and Thomas BARRE.
Legacy of John Carter of Langley, father of complainant, whose executors were the said Pynner
and Barre.   ESSEX.

10   Simon CATESBY of Marston Waver (*i.e.* Lea Marston) *v.* Thomas SHUKYSBOROUGHE.
Manor of Upper and Lower Shuckburgh late of Thomas Catesby, deceased, father of complainant.
See File 1208, *No.* 12.   WARW.

11   Thomas CHAPMAN, clerk, *v.* Richard WADE of Chichester, draper.
Lease of the Chancery living of Marston made by John Hungerford, late parson, after his deprivation
for marriage.   SUSSEX.

12–13   Robert son and heir of Richard CHATFYLD of Chailey, husbandman, *v.* Robert CHATFYLD,
brother and executor of the said Richard.
Land in Westmeston of the demise of Richard Chatfyld of Sidlesham, yeoman, and Agnes his wife.
                                                                                    SUSSEX.

14   William, son of Edmund CHATTERTON, deceased, *v.* Christopher DYSMER, clerk of the
peace.
Entail of messuages and lands in Lydeard Millicent, Manton, Purton, Braydon and Shaw entrusted
to defendant to show to Lord Chancellor Audley.   WILTS.

15   Christopher CHEVERALL, esquire, *v.* . . . HUNT.
Bond concerning a farm called Pymperyn to be obtained of Henry Portman. *Mutilated.*
                                                                                    [DORSET?]

16   Robert CHIPPER *v.* Thomas MA(I)STER, clerk.
Detention of a copy of court roll of a tenement in the manor of Stoke-under-Hamdon granted to
both parties and to Elizabeth, now deceased, kinswoman of defendant and wife of complainant.
                                                                 SPALDING   SOMERSET.

17–19   Henry CHITTING, gentleman, and Robert ~~SPARLING~~, parishioners of Wortham, and George
JERVYS, one of the ' parsones' of the same, *v.* Thomas BUCKENHAM, husbandman.
Destruction of seats and a rood-loft in the church of Wortham. (Defendant pleads an injunction
of the late reign for the destruction of images.)   SUFF.

20–23   Miles CHYLDE, John WHYCHYNTON and others *v.* Francis CHAMBERLAYNE and Anne
his wife.
Land in the manor of Hease charged with an obit in the church of Norwood. (Plea overruled that
the matter is determinable in the manorial court.) *File fragmentary.*   [MIDDX.]

24–25   Simon CLARE *v.* Thomas GRAVE.
Lands in the lordship of Ware sold by defendant to Simon Ryse of Blakesware, deceased, uncle of
complainant.   HERTS.

26   Andrew CLARKE *v.* Thomas MYLLES.
Detention of deeds relating to a messuage and land in Wokingham.   BERKS.

27–28   John CLERKE *alias* Pers *v.* Robert son of Richard BLAKE, deceased.
Messuage and land in the manor of East Lavington *alias* Lavington For' or Lavington Bayton.
                                                                                    WILTS.

29   William CLIF, yeoman, *v.* Richard BOODE, gentleman.
Detention of a lease of a tenement in Whitby made by the abbot and convent of St. Werburgh's
(Walburges), Chester.   CHESTER.

30–31   Anne, late the wife of Edward COCKKETT (Cookett), esquire, and Thomas COCKKETT,
gentleman, her son *v.* George WALLE, gentleman.
Detention of deeds relating to bullaries of salt water and lands in Droitwich, Hadzor and Newland
(in Salwarpe). *Demurrer for insufficiency only. See Files* 1206, *No.* 38; 1276, *No.* 5. WORCESTER.

32–33   Nicholas COGGESWELL with wife, daughter and heir of Katherine Robynson,
v. Robert CRANEWELL and Margaret his wife (stated by the said Robert to be deceased).
Detention of deeds relating to messuages and land in Bishop's Hatfield.   [HERTS.]

34–35   John COKE of Edburton, co. Sussex, son and heir of Eve (Ive) Coke of Ringmer, co. Sussex, *v.*
Alen BRAYNE.
Detention of deeds relating to land in Whixall.   SALOP.

36   William COKE *v.* Henry CHAMBERS.
Tithes of Attenborough (Adynbroughe), complainant having the Crown lease of the parsonage. NOTTS.

37–38   Humphrey COLLES, esquire, *v.* Nicholas VANS, gentleman.
Detention of a release made by James Tuchett, Lord Audley, to the late Duke of Somerset of the
manor of Nether Stowey. *Subpoena duces tecum.*   SOMERSET.

39   John son and heir of John COLLYN and of Argentyne his wife *v.* John ASSYTTYLL and
others.
Detention of deeds relating to a messuage and land in Plymouth.   DEVON.

40   Robert COLMAN of Mickfield and Elizabeth his wife, late the wife of John Bury of Offorth
          (*i.e.* Offton?) *v.* Robert PHYLLYPPE and Margaret his wife.
Reviver of a suit for a messuage and land (*place not given*) late of John Hall, grandfather of the said
Elizabeth.   SUFF.

41–42   Margaret COMBURBAGE *v.* Roger MASSY.
Messuage and land in Woodhouse (in Altrincham or Frodsham?) late of Edmund Comberbage and
Joan his wife. *2 Bills. Damaged.*   CHESTER.

43   Robert COOKE, yeoman, *v.* Robert VEESEY and Anne late the wife of Randall HEYGATE.
Manor of Chambers in Feering (Fedrynge) of the demise of John Warren, gentleman.   ESSEX.

44–45   Thomas COOKE, labourer, *v.* John WARD, yeoman.
Refusal to complete a sale of cottages and land in Maulden.   BEDFORD.

46   Robert COOTYS and Elizabeth his wife, a daughter of John Broke of Bramford, *v.* Joan
          BROKE, executrix and late the wife of the said John.
Legacy of the said John.   ?

47–50   James and Robert COPPYNG *v.* John COPPYNG.
Bond for arbitration concerning lands in Boughton Monchelsey.   [KENT.]

51   William COURTMYLL, clerk, *v.* Nicholas HOLLOWALL.
Loan.   ———

52–55   Ralph COUCHE (Coche) *v.* John KYLLYGREWE the elder, esquire, and John KYLLY-
          GREWE the younger.
Pasture within the walls of the West Wood in Penryn, ' kellage and busshellage ' of the haven of
Falmouth (Falffouthe), and messuages and land in Budock and the borough of Penryn. *Titles
given.*   CORNW.

56   Thomas COWPER of East Dereham, mercer, and others, for themselves and all the
          inhabitants of East Dereham ' except those which be hereafter specially named ' *v.* . . .
Plate, bells, books and other ornaments of the church of East Dereham. *Mutilated.*   NORF.

57–59   Robert CROKLYNG *v.* John MARKANT and Robert RA(L)FF.
Detention of deeds relating to land in Wilby and Brundish. *See File* 1293, *No.* 63.   SUFF.

60–63   Alan son and heir of John CROSLANDE *v.* John son and heir of Thomas CROSLANDE.
Messuages and land in Penystone. *Faded.*   [YORK.]

64   Henry, son of John CRYMES *v.* Mary and Edward CRYMES.
Messuages in St. Lawrence Lane, Old Jewry, of the demise of the dean and chapter of St. Paul's.
                                                                                                       LONDON.

FILE 1341.

1   William CARDYNALL of Great Bromley *v.* Thomas DARCY, Lord Darcy of Chich.
Hindering carriage of timber bought of deft. in Bentley park and cutting and carrying timber from
complainant's manor of Bobells (*i.e.* Bovills in Little Clacton?). *Mutilated.*   ESSEX.

2–3   Thomas CAREWE, esquire *v.* Thomas KYNGDOME (Kyngdone) gentleman.
Tithe corn and land in Quethiock belonging to the rectory of Haccombe.   CORNW., DEVON.

4   Nicholas CARSEWELL of Tavistock *v.* Margery, executrix and late the wife of Edward
          COMBE.
Old gold coins entrusted to deft. *See File* 1293, *No.* 12.   DEVON.

5   Christopher CASTELL, labourer, *v.* Anthony BUSTARD, esquire.
Cottage and garden in Dunston of the demise of Francis Bustard of London, grocer, deceased,
brother of complainant. *Commission (commissioners named).*   OXFORD.

6–7   Joan CATER *v.* Clement COLE and John SMYTH.
Inn, cottages and land late of John Cater, deceased, brother of complainant. *Mutilated.*
                                                                                                       OXFORD.

8   Nicholas CAVELL *v.* John DOWDYNGE (Duddynge) and others.
Plunder of lands in Milverton in contempt of a decree of this court. . *Mutilated.*   SOMERS.

9–10   George CAWERTE (Calvarte) *v.* Leonard BROWNE, yeoman.
Pasture in Coningsby whereof deft. claims a Crown lease.   LINCOLN.

11   George CHALDECOTE *v.* Anne and John CHETTELL.
Composition for a judgment obtained by defts. as executors of Henry Chettell. *Mutilated.*
                                                                                                       DORSET.

12   Francis CHALONER, gentleman, and Agnes his wife *v.* Cecily, late the wife of William
          EYNS of London, draper.
Manor of Wyke (*i.e.,* Hackney Wick?) and land in Hoxton of the entail of William Bowyer, knight,
late mayor of London.   MIDDX.

13   William CHANER, yeoman *v.* John KNIGHT, James WYTHOWE (Whytha), steward of
          the court of Cheadle, and Hugh WHITACRE.
Conspiracy to evade payment of a debt.   STAFFORD.

14   George CHAPMAN, parson of Bushey, *v.* John MASON.
Parsonage of Bushey, claimed under a lease by John Synger, late parson, deprived for marriage.
                                                                                                       HERTS.

15–17   John CHAPMAN *v.* George CHAMBERLAYN, gentleman.
Latitats sued out for trespass at Barnham Broom.   NORF.

18-21   Anne CHETELL *v* Joan late the wife of Robert REVE (Ryves).
Burgage in Blandford Forum late of Henry Chetell, deceased husband of complainant. *Replication wanting.*   DORSET.

22   Richard CHURCHEHOWSE and Joan his wife, granddaughter and heir of Humphrey Blonte, *v.* Thomas BUTLER.
Manors of Lulworth St. Andrews and Gatemerston (in Lulworth) and lands in Lulworth, Winfrith Newburgh, Knighton, West Burton, Dorchester, Wareham and Stoborough.   DORSET.

23   William CHYLDE of St. Clement Danes, co. Middlesex, *v.* Henry WYNTON.
Detention of a Crown grant of the manor of Wolferlowe with right to felons' goods.   HEREFORD.

24   Anthony son of Thomas CLATWORTHY and Alice his wife *v.* Oliver DOWNEMAN, father of the said Alice.
Money, goods, and a farm called 'Hacke' promised to complainants on their marriage.
[SOMERSET?]

25   Ralph CLAYTON, yeoman of the Guard, *v.* Thomas ALTAM of Grindleton and William COTTAM of Thornley.
Goods of Henry Clayton, deceased, brother of complainants.   LANCASTER.

26-27   Thomas CLERK of Terling, yeoman, *v.* Lancelot MADYSON of Sandon, yeoman.
Money entrusted to defendant.   ESSEX.

28-31   Edward CLARKE administrator of the goods of John Sturdy, deceased *v.* Harry CORBETT and John SEBORNE, executors of William Seborne.
Cattle and piece of land in Dryther . . . of the bequest of Elizabeth Newton. *Damaged.*
[HUNTINGDON?]

32   Robert CLERKE of Hingham, tailor, *v.* John ISAKKE and Agnes his wife.
Refusal to complete a sale of a croft in Hingham.   NORFOLK.

33   John CLEVYS *v.* Thomas SEMAN.
Action on a bond for assignment of a Crown lease of the parsonage of Bindon.   DORSET.

34   Anthony CLEYMOND of Skirbeck *v.* Thomas PAYNELL, esquire.
Bond for induction of William Erith into the parsonage of Fishtoft.   LINCOLN.

35-39   William CLYFF, husbandman, *v.* Richard LUKE.
Messuage and land in the manor of Charleton late of Arthur Plantagenet, knight, and his wife.
DEVON.

40   William CLYFFORDE, grandson and heir of Roger Clyfforde, knight, and of Lady Jane Courteney his wife *v.* John ROGERS, knight.
Detention of deeds relating to the manor of Ibberton (Iverton).   DORSET.

41-42   Thomas, son of Edward COCKETT, deceased, *v.* Thomas HOLLYS, knight, Henry REYNOLDES and others.
Legacy payable out of the manors of Knettishall, Hopton and Borowe Hall (*i.e.*, Bury's?) in Hillington, etc.   SUFFOLK, NORFOLK.

33-44   John COCKHILLES, Joan his wife, and John their son, *v.* John VOYSYE.
Miswriting the name of the said John the son in a lease of a messuage and land in East Heland (*i.e.* East Healing?) and common of pasture in a place called the Island, all in Fremington, defendant having promised to insert it when the said John should be born.   DEVON.

45   Robert COKE of Ashburton, co. Devon, *v.* John COKE.
Messuage and land at Backwyll in the parish of Chelve (*sic*) late of William Coke, deceased, great-uncle of complainant.   SOMERSET.

46-47   Ralph COLIER, clerk, *v.* Thomas TWYDALL.
Parsonage of Ludborough.   LINCOLN.

48   The same, minor canon of [Lincoln], *v.* Peter LEGHE.
Do. (Mention is also made of a cure of souls in Tychemere (*i.e.* Titchmarsh). *Mutilated.*
LINCOLN, NORTHAMPTON.

49-50   William CONLEY, husbandman, *v.* Oliver SAYNT JOHN, esquire.
Land in Abbot's Ripton *alias* Ripton St. John of the demise of John Seynct Jhone, knight, father of defendant.   HUNTINGDON.

51-53   John COOKE and Alice his wife, late the wife of Walter Bonham, knight *v.* Henry SCHERINGTON, esquire, executor of William Scherington, knight, Thomas WATTES, and Jane ALLAN.
Bequest by the said Sir Walter, whose executors are the said Sir William and Thomas, to the said Jane his concubine of money obtained by compelling the said Alice to sell her lands.
HANTS, LONDON.

54   Robert COOKE and William POWLER *v.* Humphrey TURNER, yeoman.
Price of cattle.   ————

55   John CORNYSHE of Tavistock, yeoman, *v.* William GOODYNG of the same.
Detention of a bond for a debt already paid.   DEVON.

56-57   Richard COUPER of Warnham *v.* Thomas, son of John CARYLL, esquire.
Crofts formerly of Richard Agate and Margery his wife, formerly held of defendant's manor of Horsham.
SUSSEX.

58   The same *v.* the same.
Do., the manor being called Nottham.   SUSSEX.

59–65   Ralph COWCHE *v.* John KYLLYGREW of Arwennack, esquire, Nicholas ROWMOW and John LOVE.
Four mills in the manor of Penryn of the demise of John [Voysey], bishop of Exeter. D. XI, 13.
Mutilated. (The court awarded one of the mills to complainant pending a full hearing.) CORNWALL.

66   Thomas COWPE *v.* William WALLE and John BODNALL.
Land in Rowley late of Margaret Bryan, deceased, mother of complainant.   [?]

67–69   Ralph CRECHE *v.* Robert FYTCHE.
Action on a bond for a debt paid by defendant's order to the executrix of his creditor.   DERBY,

70   John CROSSE *v.* George STERE.
Land in Langford Budville of the demise of Roland Lee, late archdeacon of [Taunton].   *Faded.*
SOMERSET.

71   William CROSSE *v.* the sheriffs of LONDON and William FOWLE of Benenden (Bennyngton), co. Kent, clothier.
Action on a bond for price of cloth compounded for. *Certiorari and subpœna. Mutilated.*
LONDON.

72–76   John CURREY, labourer, *v.* William STAUNTON, Margery his wife, Robert ESCOT (Hiscoke), Sibly his wife, and James GAMON.
Tenement in Bridgerule demised by Humphrey Leigh, gentleman, to John Currey, deceased, father of complainant and of the female defendants.   DEVON.

77–79   John CURTES, parson of Northlew, *v.* the stewards of the court of LYDFORD.
Action by Philip Denys on a bond extorted by a charge of complicity in the disturbances of the year 3 Edward VI. *Certiorari.* (An answer by the said Denys is included.)   DEVON.

FILE 1342.

1–2   Richard CAGER and Agnes his wife *v.* Nicholas DERING, esquire.
Messuage and land in Hawkley, held of defendant's manor of Newton Valence. *See File* 1293, No. 1.
HANTS.

3–5   Nicholas CARTER of Youlgreave *v.* Ralph CRANE.
Farm of Hopton Hall of the demise of George Varnon, knight, and others. *Damaged.*   DERBY.

6   Richard CASTELL *v.* Lawrence ROBYNSON, *alias* Baker.
Part price of wool.   ——————

7–9   Edmund CATERALL, parson of Wick Rissington, *v.* Alexander COTON.
Lease of complainant's parsonage made by John Poole his married predecessor to defendant.
GLOUCESTER.

10–11   John CATTON *v.* Stephen, son of Thomas ANGOLD, and Robert GYLLE, his stepfather.
Land in Hopton of the feoffment of Francis Bolde.   SUFFOLK.

12–15   John CHECHESTER *v.* Anthony BERYE.
Messuages and lands in Chipping Torrington, Rowley (in Parracombe), St. Giles [in-the-Wood], Aylescott (in West Down) and Ilfracombe late of Margaret Burye, deceased, grandmother of complainant and mother of defendant. *Mutilated.*   DEVON.

16–22   John CLEAMENT, doctor of physic, *v.* Elizabeth, late the wife of Anthony WYNGFELDE, knight, and Robert WYNGFELDE, knight, their son.
(Continuation of File 1337, No. 20. The said Sir Robert pleads that the premises were forfeited by complainant's departure beyond seas without licence). *Mutilated.*   ESSEX.

23–25   William CLEMENTT *v.* Henry WYLLYAMS and others.
Occupation of messuages and land in the manor of Beckington during complainant's absence in the King's wars beyond seas.   SOMERSET.

26–27   Maurice CLENOKE, parson of Gatcombe, *v.* George HUSYE, gentleman, and others, his assigns.
Lease of the parsonage of Gatcombe made by Lambert Peche, parson of Gatcombe, when married.
HANTS. (I.W.)

28   The same *v.* the same.
(Draft of No. 26?)   HANTS. (I.W.)

29   Thomas COLEPEPER, gentleman, *v.* Robert CAMOCK.
Manor of Kelvedon Hall, late of Thomas Blenerhasset, knight, grandfather of Mary, wife of complainant. *Damaged.*   ESSEX.

30   John COOPER, knight, *v.* Thomas WYLKES, merchant of the Staple of Calais, and the mayor and sheriffs of LONDON.
Actions concerning a sale of the manors of Hodnell, Old Hodnell and Ascott. *Subpœna and certiorari. Damaged.*   LONDON, WARWICK.

31–33   Humphrey COTON of the Boulde, gentleman, and Anne, his wife, *v.* Agnes HOGESON and John, her son.
Messuage and pasture in Great and Little Loxley. *Answer wanting.*   STAFFORD.

34   [Joan] late the wife of John COVENTRE of Westminster, shoemaker, *v.* William HYLL.
Boots and shoes supplied for the siege of Boulogne to Thomas Palmer, knight, of whose band defendant was captain. *Mutilated.*   MIDDLESEX.

35   The same *v.* the same.
Divers goods supplied in like manner.   MIDDLESEX.

36–40   Martin COWPER *v* John THYNNE, knight.
Farm called Hill Deverell, demised by William [Fitzalan], late earl of Arundel, to John, brother of complainant.   WILTS.

41–42   Henry CRAMPE, yeoman *v* William BOXER.
Detention of deeds relating to land in Southweald and Shenley late of Henry Crampe, deceased, father of complainant and of Joan wife of defendant.   ESSEX.

43–46   George CREDE *v* William LONG and Henry TOPP.
Land held of the manor of Gillingham by Edward Clement *alias* Browne.   DORSET.

47–49   The same and William his son *v* John WYLLYAMS and the said Edward.
Action on a statute merchant given by Nicholas Udale, deceased, for a debt since paid. *See File* 1110, No. 21.   [WILTS *or* DORSET?]

FILE 1343.

1–2   William COURTE (?) *alias* Perye *v*. Robert HAWKYNS of Crewkerne, barber.
Exaction of tithes of Estham (*i.e.* High Ham) by defendant when not in orders, by the procurement of [William] Barlowe, late bishop of Bath and Wells. *Mutilated.*   -   SOMERS.

3–6   John CARRE of Nottingham *v*. Robert BASPOLE.
Messuages and lands in South Elmham, late of Richard Carre, deceased, great-uncle of both parties.
                                                             SUFFOLK.

7–8   Robert CHESTER *v*. John RECHE of Leiston.
Detention of deeds relating to a messuage and land in Debenham.   SUFFOLK.

9–14   Thomas grandson of John CHYRY *v*. John CHER(R)YE.
Detention of deeds relating to a messuage and land in Great Munden. *2 suits.*   HERTS.

15–17   Edward, son of Walter CLARKE, deceased, *v*. George HORSMAN and Frances his wife, daughter and heir of ——— Tymperleye, gentleman.
Messuage and land in Hynklesham and Hadley.   [SUFFOLK.]

18–19   Peter CLAYS (Elyshe) and Elizabeth, his wife, *v*. Thomas, son of Stephen PONCHON (Punshon).
Tenements in St. Martin's and St. Bride's, Fleet Street, late of William Seyton and Clemens his wife, formerly Clemens Sawle, great-grandparents of complainant. *See File* 875, *No.* 59. LONDON.

20–21   Robert COOKE of Whytstone (*i.e.* Wheston near Tideswell?) *v*. Philip BERKER.
Land in Tideswell of the demise of Ingram Clyfforde, knight.   DERBY.

22–26   John COCKSON *v*. Alice KIRKE, William her son, Robert STURDYVANT *alias* Tyler, Agnes his wife, Thomas ARCHER and Joan his wife.
Messuages and land in Donington-upon-Bain, late of Robert Brewer, deceased, uncle of complainant.
                                                             LINCOLN.

27–30   The same *v*. the same, except the said Agnes and Joan.
Messuage and land in Donington, late of Agnes Cockson deceased, mother of complainant.
                                                             LINCOLN.

31–33   Robert COKER of Princes Risborough, husbandman *v*. John HAMPDEN of Kimble, esquire, son of William Hampden.
Messuage and land in Hampden of the demise of John Hampden, knight.   BUCKINGHAM.

34–36   Alice COLBYE *v*. Jane BREWIS.
Manor of Hawkers and Lynbourne Mill of the bequest of Thomas Brewse, knight, deceased, grandfather of complainant, and of Thomas, late husband of defendant.   ?

37–40   Thomas CONYERS, esquire, *v*. John TENAUNT of Bedale, yeoman, and John LEING of Hackforth in Appleton (?), husbandman.
Land in Askyue (*i.e.* Aiskew in Ainderby Myers?) late of John (Henry) Conyers, deceased father of complainant.   YORK.

41   Richard CORNEWALL, canon of Hereford, *v*. John HERFFORD.
Prebend of Inkberrow of the demise of Rowland Tayllour, LL.D., since deprived and deceased.
                                                             WORCESTER.

42   Stephen COWPER of Chichester, yeoman, and Stephen COWPER of Tenterden, tanner, *v*. Bryan JOHNSON, and others.
Messuages and lands in St. Giles, Cripplegate, Leigh, Eastwood, Plumstead, Wateryng (*i.e.* Wakering?) and Prittlewell, late of John Cowper deceased, uncle of complainants. LONDON, ESSEX, KENT.

43   Anne, late the wife of Christopher CRAKENTHROPP, of Newbiggin, Esquire?
Money payable by Thomas Dalston on the marriage of his daughter with Henry, son of complainant. *Mutilated.*   WESTMORLAND.

44–47   John CRUSE of Liskeard, executor of John Bealbury, *v*. William LOWER of St. Winnow, gentleman.
Plate entrusted to defendant by deceased. *See File* 1103, *No.* 32.   CORNWALL.

48–51   Richard CURRY *v*. Thomas MARRYS of Exeter.
Rent of defendant's land at Bowden in Week St. Mary of the grant of John Marres.   CORNWALL.

FILE 1344.

1-2   CADWALADER ap Robert of London, servingman, *v.* Richard VYCHAN and others his tenants-at-will.
Detention and forgery of deeds relating to messuages and lands in Llanvllyn or Llanyollyn (*i.e.* Llanuwchllyn?) and Dolgelly.   MERIONETH.

3   William CALOWE *v.* Alice, late the wife of Anthony BARBYE, esquire.
Land in Holbeach and Whaplode. *Mutilated.*   LINCOLN.

4   Leonard CALVERD of Owlecootes in Craven (*cf.* Owlshaw in Gisburn) *v.* Richard DANCER, clerk, and William his brother.
Goods of Thomas Calverd, clerk, brother of complainant, who died in the said William's house in Gisburn.   YORK.

5-6   John CAPPER of London *v.* Ralph BROKE.   ·
'Wichehouse or saltehouse' in Nantwich of the demise of Roger Partryche.   CHESTER.

7   The dean and chapter of CARLISLE *v.* John, Edward and Roger WARCOPPE.
Lands in the parish (*sic*) of Rutter belonging to the hospital of St. Nicholas by Carlisle.   WESTM.

8   Nicholas CARTER *v.* Margaret BRYNE and John FREKE.
Messuage and land in Henstridge bought of ——— Freke.   SOMERS.

9   Tristram CARTER of St. Katherine's by the Tower and Barbara his wife *v.* Godfrey NICOLS, cobbler, and John JOHNSON, shoemaker, both of London.
Claims on goods of John Jacobs, deceased, former husband of the said Barbara, whereof complainants are administrators. *Mutilated.*   LONDON.

10   · John CARY, parson of Linkenholt *v.* John CHEYNEY of Woodhay, co. Berks, 'who shamefully moordered your Lordeshipps servante gentle Maister Parrys.'
Claim to a lease of complainant's parsonage.   HANTS.

11   Thomas CASELON and Elizabeth his wife, late the wife of Simon Dygby, gentleman, and formerly of Thomas Gaynesforde, esquire, *v.* William CAWSTEN.
Land in Oxted, part of the farm of Sunt, of the gift of the said Gaynesford,   SURREY.

12   John CASSE *v.* John PIRRY and Joyce his wife, late the wife of William Casse.
Messuage and land at Woodrow in Hatfield Broadoak, late of Thomas Casse, deceased, father of the said John and William Casse.   ESSEX.

13   William CATIRBANKE (?), clerk, *v.* Thomas BAWMFORD of Uttoxeter, tanner.
Tenement in Uttoxeter.   STAFFORD.

14-15   Thomas CHAFFYN of Mere, gentleman, *v.* Elizabeth (Margaret) executrix [and late the wife] of George PERCYE.
Reviver of a suit for the parsonage of Mere, wherefrom complainant was ejected by Thomas Arundell, knight, since attainted. *Damaged.*   WILTS.

16   John CHAPMAN, gentleman, son and heir of Allen Chapman, *v.* Henry CALTON and Elizabeth his wife.
Detention of deeds relating to messuages and land in Babraham.   CAMBRIDGE.

17   The same *v.* Nicholas SMYTHE.
Plate entrusted to defendant by the said Allen.   [CAMBRIDGE.]

18   Richard CHYDY[OK ?], administrator of the goods of Anne, late the wife of Walter At Wood, deceased, *v.* Margaret, executrix and late the wife of John Furse.
Legacy to the said Anne from John Reymond, her father, whose widow and executrix took to husband the said Furse. *Mutilated.*   ———

19-21   Thomas son and heir of James CHYNOWETH *v.* Thomas RETYN, gentleman, and George WATTERTON.
Messuage and land in Penbuthyneowe, exchanged with Richard Chapell, since deceased, for entailed lands in Trelidgwith (Treglyswith), both in Constantine, the latter being supposed to be held in fee simple.   CORNWALL.

22   Henry CHYVERTON, gentleman, *v.* Elizabeth TOLCARN.
Plate (*described*) entrusted to defendant by John Tolcarn of North Petherwin, gentleman, and bought by complainant.   CORNWALL, DEVON.

23   Adlard, Henry and Joan CLARE, *v.* Walter CLARE, their father, and Roger WELLES.
Legacy of Roger Dowce of Hainton, whose executors defendants are.   LINCOLN.

24   Richard CLERKE of Shrewsbury (?), burgess, *v.* Thomas DAVYS of Coyne.
Testoons and groats delivered to complainant and accounted for by him in bargains of cattle, the value of the coins having been twice diminished by proclamation meanwhile.   [SALOP?]

25-26   Thomas CLERKE *v.* Laurence STEPHEN and Agnes his wife, late the wife of Robert Clerke.
Goods of William Clerke, deceased, father of complainant and brother of the said Robert.   ———

27   William, son and heir of William CLOPTON, esquire, *v.* Richard SYMONDES.
Detention of deeds relating to lands in Clopton Ryen Clyfforde (in Stratford-on-Avon), Hatton (in Hampton Lucy), Teretford (?) and Bridgetown (opposite Stratford). *Damaged.*   WARW.

28   George COCKET *v.* Thomas SMYTHE, yeoman.
Hindering William Cocket, brother of complainant, from letting a messuage at Langton as his attorney.   LINCOLN.

29   William COLLARD of Potterspury, yeoman *v.* James SKOTT.   ·
Detention of deeds relating to a messuage and land in Denshanger obtained in exchange from Henry Skott.   N'HAMP.

30   Robert, son and heir of Edmund COLLES of Shrewsbury and of Anne Churcheyard his wife.
Petition for a commission to inquire as to a declaration obtained from the said Edmund on his
deathbed by Alice Foster, his second wife, that complainant was not born in wedlock. *Mutilated.*
                                                                                                SALOP.

31   William COLLYN and Agnes his wife *v.* Nicholas COLLYN.
Detention of deeds relating to a messuage and land in Okley. *Mutilated.*   WARW.

32–25   Thomas COLWELL of Hitchin *v.* John GARDYNER and others.
Messuages and land in Saffron Walden (Walden Audley) and Littlebury, late of John Colwell, deceased,
brother of complainant.   ESSEX.

36–37   John, son and heir of Humphrey CONYNGESBY, esquire, and Robert CONYNGESBY, his
guardian by royal grant, *v.* Oliver BRYGGER, Richard LEWCE, clerk, claiming to be feoffee
to uses, and others.
Seizure of deeds from the manor-house of Neen Sollars.   SALOP.

38   Mary COOKE *v.* Thomas CLARKE.
Breach of a contract of marriage, and refusal to share the profits of a bargain of the manor of Powers
Hall (in Witham) obtained by complainant's help.   ESSEX.

39   Rose CORNEWALL *v.* John LYNSEY, executor of Elizabeth, late the wife of Christopher
Moryez, knight.
Lease by the prior of St. Mary Spital of a house and garden in St. Botolph's [Bishopsgate]. LONDON.

40–43   Thomas COTIS (C_{ottes}), gentleman, *v.* William BASSETT, esquire.
Annuities charged on the manor of Blore by defendants and William Bassett, knight, his father.
                                                                                               STAFFORD.

44–48   John COTTON *v.* Thomas COTTON.
Messuage, barn and land at Cotton Bridge in Kingsbury, late of Ralph Cotton ancestor executor of
both parties. *Pedigrees given.*   WARW.

49   John COURTENAY, Elizabeth his wife, Giles GRAYNFYLDE, Margaret his wife, Ralph
COOCHE, and Jane his wife *v.* John GODOLPHYN, esquire, uncle of the female complainants,
and James, his son.
Messuages and land in Trengove (in Constantine), Pellawyn, Prospidneck (in Sithney), Anhell (in
Truro?), Tretharrape, Car[l]igham (*i.e.* Carleen in Sithney), Bosseghan (in St. Anthony-in-Meneage),
Bosworles, Trembleath, Chyrose (in Breage), Gwenna (in Breage), Trenowth (in Mabe), Redruth,
Trevithick (in St. Columb Major), and the borough of Helston late of Richard Trengoffe of Nans,
deceased, father of the female complainants.   CORNW.

50   William COURTMYLL, curate of the parish of Fawnwyche (*rectius* Swanwyche, *i.e.* Swanage?)
v. John POOLE, farmer of the parsonage of Fanwich.
Fees for performing divine service.   DORSET.

51–52   John COWPER, citizen and fishmonger, of London *v.* Thomas FULLWOOD and John
BEANE.
Money and goods of complainant obtained from Andrew Prynce, his servant, at Lowestoft, when
frantic after a blow on the head.   SUFFOLK.

53–54   John CRESCEYE *v.* Margery, late the wife of Thomas LEVESEY.
Messuage and land in East Markham demised by complainant in return for board. *See File* 1295,
No. 67.   NOTTS.

55   John CROOKE *v.* William SMYTH.
Part price of cattle.   ————

56   John CUDWORTH of Thurgoland, yeoman, *v.* John REYNEY and Thomas CUDWORTH
of Thurgoland.
Tenement called Smithley in Wombwell, of the entail of John Hawle, grandfather of complainant.
                                                                                                YORK.

57   Thomas CUMBERFORD, esquire, *v.* William BABYNGTON, esquire, and Anthony, his son
and heir apparent.
Land in Tynmour (*i.e.* Tamhorn?) of the demise of Thomas Cumberford, grandfather of complainant.
                                                                                               STAFFORD.

58   John CURWEN, esquire, *v.* JEVAN ap Jevan and Howell DAKYN, yeomen, both of Carne,
co. Montgomery.
Detention of mares entrusted to defendant, who was to take one-third of their colts, and of deeds
relating to a messuage and land in Kidlington.   OXFORD.

FILE 1345.

1   Robert DADE of Great Thornham, in Suffolk, executor of Robert Warren of Sturton, co.
Suffolk, *v.* John SHELTON, knight, and others.
Detention of deeds relating to a messuage and land in Shelton and Fritton.   NORFOLK.

2   Annes, late the wife of Thomas DAGGAR *v.* Thomas WEBBE.
Messuage and land held of the manor of Langridge.   SOMERSET.

3   Robert DAKEN *v.* Oliver and Alice BUXTONS, executors of Richard Buxtons.
Money promised on complainant's marriage with Elizabeth Buxtons, natural daughter of the said
Richard.

4   Valentine DALE, advocate in the court of Arches, son and heir of John Dale, *v.* Robert
SMYTH.
Detention of deeds relating to the manor of Sarson in Amport (Savageston) and lands in Monkston
and Abbot's Ann. *Answer in File* 1347, *No.* 9.   HANTS.

5–8   John DAMPORTE (Davenport), esquire, attendant on William [Herbert], earl of Pembroke, Katherine his wife, Peter SCAKERLEY (Shakerley), and Elizabeth, his wife, v. Randolph MAYNWARYNG of Peover, knight, father of the female complainants, and Ralph LEYCESTRE, knight.
Alienation contrary to promise of lands called Badeley, Fadeley, Swanneley, Wartington, and Old Whittington.   CHESTER.

9   Arthur DARCY, knight, v. Thomas SHYERS and Richard HANCOCKE.
Land in complainant's manor of Sawley. See File 1213. No. 3.   YORK.

10   Hugh DAVID, clerk, v. (Rice) Llewelyn APRICE and others.
Price of corn, rent, and other debts.   CARDIGAN.

11–13   John DAVIES v. Ralph HANNAM, yeoman.
Cottage and land held of deft's manor of Evercreech.   SOMERSET.

14   Thomas DAVIS v. the sheriffs of LONDON.
Action by John Whitterige, citizen and merchant of London, on a bond for arbitration. *Corpus cum causa*.   LONDON.

15   Hugh DAVYES v. MORYS and DAVID ap Owen ap Meredith.
Refusal to complete a sale of a messuage, barn and land at Ryll (*i.e.*, Reilth?) in Mainstone.
                                                                                              SALOP.

16–17   John DAVYS v. JOHN ap Griffith ap Hoell ap Dicus.
Messuage and land in Mold (Mollesdale). *Mutilated.*   FLINT.

18   Giles DAWBENEY and William MARYETT, executors of Thomas Bonyfaunt, v. Robert DAVYSON.
Action concerning messuages and gardens in Southwark demised to the said Bonyfaunt by Agnes Wryght. *Injunction. Mutilated.*   SURREY.

19–21   Henry DAWBENEY, gentleman, v. Thomas HUNTE, parson of Sharrington.
Removal of books and ornaments (*described*) from the church of Sharrington, whereof complainant is patron.   NORFOLK.

22   John DAWES of London, grocer, v. John, son and executor of John BATENAR of Lewes, co. Sussex, mercer, and Thomas FOSTER, under-sheriff of Warwick.
Action on a bond for a debt partly satisfied in money, goods, and assignment of other debts.
                                                                                              WARWICK.

23–24   John DAWSON v. the bailiffs of LUDLOW, and John ALSAP and Walter TAYLOUR, late bailiffs.
Action arising out of a seizure of square tin salts, which defts. claim to have been exposed for sale without being duly marked. *Certiorari and subpœna.*   [SALOP.]

25   Thomas DAYE, receiver to George [Day], bishop of Chichester, v. John SKORY, late ' usurped ' bishop.
Action on a bond for the income of the bishopric, whereof payment was suspended by the Queen's letters patent.   BISHOPRIC OF CHICHESTER.

26   John DEAN, parson of Binfield, v. John MALTUS.
Dilapidations of the parsonage, whereof deft. claims a lease at an unduly low rent.   BERKS.

27   George DEANE of Great Dunmow, tailor, v. John SAFFULL, yeoman.
Refusal to complete a lease of a messuage called the *Swan*, and land in Great Dunmow.
                                                                                              ESSEX.

28   Richard DEANE v. William SYMON of Fordham, husbandman, ... his wife, and Geoffrey MASCALL, husbandman.
Messuages and land in Bergholt, late of Isabel Deane, deceased, grandmother of complainant.
                                                                                              ESSEX.

29–32   Nevill son and heir of Henry DELAHAYE, gentleman v. Thomas ROYDON, esquire [and William his son?]
Manors of Wateringbury, Chart, and Fowlkes, and lands in Wateringbury, Mereworth, East and West Malling, East and West Peckham, Yalding, Nettlestead, Brenchley, Capel, Tudeley, Pembury and Teston, of the demise of Henry, late abbot of St. Mary Graces, and his convent. *Mutilated.*
                                                                                              KENT.

33–36   William DENE v. Sylvester (*sic*), late the wife of John BUTTLER, knight, and administratrix of his goods.
Messuage and land in Stoke held of the manor of Hawkesbury.   WORCESTER.

37   William DENYS and Alice his wife v. Philip DENYS.
Manor of Otterton and half the manors of Spreton, Sourton and Bowerseley (*i.e.* Bowsleigh in Bratton Clovelly?).   DEVON.

38   Edward, grandson of Thomas DERBY, deceased, v. Thomas BARNES, gentleman.
Lands (*described*) held of deft's manor of Soham.   CAMBRIDGE.

39–40   James DEY v. James BRIGG.
Refusal to complete a lease of the manor of Sale, on which complainant has spent money at deft's request.   NORFOLK.

41–42   Robert DEY of Gransden, labourer, v. William RYCHARDSON of Caldecote, husbandman.
Legacy (*described*) of John Dey of Caldecote, husbandman, father of complainant, whose executor deft. is.   CAMBRIDGE.

43–44   Richard DICKYNSON and Anne his wife v. Thomas, son and heir of John DOCKW(E)RAY.
Tenement in Fulbourn, late of John Ware, deceased, father of the said Anne.   CAMBRIDGE.

45   Edward DOCKRELL and Ursula, his wife, administratrix of the goods of [Margaret] . . .
v. Thomas and John, sons and executors of William MYLLYS of Sou[th]am[pton].
Moiety of a ship and wine [formerly of]? Anthony Guydott, knight. *Mutililated.*   [HANTS].

46-48   Maude DREWE *v.* Robert FULFORD, esquire, James MORTYMER his servant, and
John MYLL.
Loan of plough gear from complainant's house at Newton St. Cyres.   DEVON.

49   . . . DUDERIGE *v.* John FELD
Lands in Mynsterwor[th]. *Damaged.*   [GLOUCESTER].

50-53   Gregory, son and heir of Newell DURGES *v.* Thomas COKH.
Detention of deeds relating to tenements in St. Peter of Mancrofte and St. John, [Norwich].
Mutilated.   NORFOLK.

54   Robert DYKENSON of Misterton, husbandman, *v.* Thomas CALTON (Colton) of Clayworth
Price of goods sold by John Dykenson, deceased, father of complainant.   NOTTINGHAM.

55   Nicholas DYLLON *v.* Thomas INCLEDON.
Suppression of a copy whereby John Seintleger, knight, demised half a pasture in Ilfracombe to
both parties jointly with Urith, wife of complainant.   DEVON.

56   John DYMOCKE *v.* Thomas GREENE, late under-sheriff of Suffolk.
Money obtained of John Brend of Westleton in execution for a debt due to complainant.
        SUFFOLK.

57-58   William DYREHAM of Truro, yeoman, *v.* Richard VICTOR.
Messuages and land held of the Queen's manor of Tybesta in Creed. (Deft. states that tenures
require to be renewed every seven years).   CORNWALL.

FILE 1346.

1-2   John DANNELL (Danyell) of Messing, esquire, *v.* Adam RAYNOR, Robert CLOOBER
Richard, servant to George FOSTER, and others.
Cutting and carrying timber in Great Birch and Easthorpe (No. 2 is an answer by George Forster).
        ESSEX.

3-4   John DANYELL *v.* John STONE, parson of Sutton Bingham, and Richard SOPER.
Messuage and land in Sutton Bingham.   SOMERSET.

5   Arthur DARCYE, knight, and Mary his wife *v.* Hugh PARTRYGE.
Detention of deeds relating to chantry lands in Thornbury, Oldbury, Moreton, Wilford, Kington
(Kyngeston) and Tockington, late of Miles Partryge, knight, brother of defendant, attainted of
felony. *See Calendar of Patent Rolls, Edward VI, Vol.* v. *p.* 191.   GLOUCESTER.

6   Edward DAVIES *v.* Robert LEWES and Hugh BOCHER of Gresford, co Denbigh.
Tenements and gardens in Shrewsbury.   .SALOP.

7   John DAVY *v.* William HOLBEK and Mary his wife.
Refused to complete a lease of a messuage and garden in Kingston-upon-Hull.   YORK.

8   John DAWNSEY, esquire, *v.* Bartholomew DAWNSEY.
Crown lease of the manor of Marlow mortgaged to defendants. *Mutilated.*   [BUCKINGHAM.]

9-15   John DAWSON of East Leake, husbandman, *v.* Thomas CARTEWRIGHT, William
SKYNNER and others.
Messuage and land at Basingfield in West Bridgeford, late of William Dawson, deceased. (No. 14
is a certificate signed by J. Chaworth and others that a seizure of goods at Gamston has been
compromised before them.)   NOTTS.

16-18   Nicholas DAYE *v.* the mayor and bailiffs of OXFORD, and John WATE and others, all
of Oxford.
Actions for assault and obstruction of a watercourse at the King's weir in Oxford, wherein complainant is prejudiced as tenant to George Owen, esquire, who claims a meadow called ' Portemede '
alias ' Portmanhethe ' against the city in right of his manor of Wolvercote.   OXFORD.

19-22   Nicholas DAYLOND (Darland) *alias* Lane, of Honiton, husbandman, *v.* Thomas MENYFE,
of Awliscombe, butcher.
Money promised by defendant in marriage with Alice, his daughter.   DEVON.

23-24   William DEAKEN, guardian of Susan ap Hoell, *v.* HUMPHREY ap John ap Jevan.
Lands in Mathrafal, late of John ap Hoell, deceased, father of the said Humphrey.   MONTG.

25-26   William DENES *v.* William SALYSBURY and James OLYVER.
Detention of deeds relating to a messuage and garden in Barnstaple, and of a rent of wax, honey,
raisins, and pepper reserved on chantry lands there.   DEVON.

27   Maurice DENYS, knight, *v.* Richard WHALLY, esquire.
Detention of deeds relating to the manors of Tanton (*i.e.* Staunton?), Whatton and Hawksworth.
        NOTTS.

28-32   John, son and heir of Joan DOCKER *v.* John HERCYE (Hersey), knight, and William
WHYTE, husbandman.
Detention of deeds relating to messuages and lands in East and West Retford (Stretforde) and
Babworth.   NOTTS.

33   John DODYNGTON of London, gentleman, and ———— his wife, executrix and late the
wife of Edward Stretburye of London, gentleman, *v.* Richard FEELDE, gentleman.
Advowson of the church of Lutton with Washingley, for which the said Stretburye found the
purchase-money.   NORTHAMPTON.

34 John DOTSON v. Harvey FAIRCHYLD.
Slander at Bodmin sessions concerning complainant's conduct as constable. CORNWALL.

35–37 William DRURY of Aisthorpe, son and heir of William Drury, v. William, son and heir of Henry DRURY.
Messuage and land in Fillingham, late of Henry Drury, deceased, brother of the said William the elder and Henry. LINCOLN.

38–41 John DUDRUDGE v. John SPERKE.
Promise of a year's maintenance for complainant and Isabel his wife, daughter of defendant, in defendant's house at Dittisham. DEVON.

42–45 Richard DUNNE, clerk, and others, freeholders of Willen, v. William, son of John [MORDAUNT], Lord Mordaunt.
Enclosure of the driftway to complainants' common in the said Lord Mordaunt's manor of Willen. *Demurrer for insufficiency overruled.* BUCKINGHAM.

46–48 Thomas DUTTON, gentleman, and Mary his wife, v. Joan, late the wife of Robert TAYLOUR.
Goods of the said Robert, whose executors complainants are. GLOUCESTER.

49–51 William DYRDOO and others v. John MATHEWE, William KNAPLOCKE and John STONE.
Cottages and lands in the Queen's manor of Gillingham. *See File 975, No. 94.* DORSET.

52–55 Christopher DYSMARS v. William CHATTERTON.
Composition of a debt to Edmund Chatterton, esquire, father-in-law of complainant, and father of defendant. D. IX, 12. [WILTS.]

56–60 Christopher DYSMARS, clerk of the peace, v. Robert HUNGERFORD, esquire, sheriff.
Fees due for prisoners (*named*) delivered from Fisherton gaol. 2 *suits* D. XIV, 10. WILTS.

61–62 The same v. James STUMPE, knight, son and executor of William Stumpe, esquire, sheriff.
Do. WILTS.

63 Christopher DYSMARS v. [Thomas WHYTE].
Bond for arbitration concerning a messuage in Winterbourne Monkton. *Mutilated. See Files* 1117. *No.* 45; 1213, *No.* 88. WILTS.

64–65 John DYSON, clerk, servant to William Benson, late dean of Westminster, v. Hugh LATYMER, Rowland TAILOUR, and others, executors of the said Benson.
Expenses of the said Benson's household at the parsonage of Hendon. *Detailed account annexed.*
MIDDLESEX.

FILE 1347.

1–4 Thomas DALE v. John, great-grandson and heir of John WYBUNBURYE.
Reviver, on deft's coming of age, of a suit for the manor of Brynshalle and messuages, land, and rent in Wybunbury, Nantwich, Checkley, Swettenham, Bridgemere (Brygemor) and Adderley. D. XIV, 6. CHESTER, SALOP.

5–7 Valentine DALE, an advocate of the Court of Arches, v. Thomas BRUYN, David ap Llewelyn LLOYD, and GRIFFITH ap Hoell.
Leases of the parsonage of Llandissell made by Stephen Grene, late parson, since deprived for marriage. [CARDIGAN.]

8 The same v. John PRYNE.
Profits of lands in Yatton claimed by deft. in payment for a debt of John Dale, father of complainant. *Rejoinder only.* SOMERSET.

9 The same v. Robert SMITHE.
(*Answer to File* 1345, *No.* 4.) [HANTS.]

10–11 John and William DAMARY, Thomas DAMARY of Latton, Nicholas DAMARY, and Egewyn and Eleanor DAMARY of Bevington, v. Richard BRANT.
Legacies of William Damary, husbandman, father of complainants, and of Margery his wife and executrix, afterwards wife of deft. WILTS, WARW.

12 Alice DAMSELL v. John CURTES of Horsley, co. Gloucester, husbandman.
Deeds entrusted to deft. concerning tenements in the manor (*sic*) of Hankerton, Chedglow, and Crudwell. WILTS.

13–15 Leonard DANETT v. William NEALE of Stivichall (Stycholl).
Detention of deeds relating to a messuage in Little Park Street, Coventry. WARW.

16–18 Nicholas DANYELL of Crediton (Kyrton), co. Devon, clerk, v. John CHAPELL, yeoman.
Seizure of household goods (*described*) from complainant's house at St. Teath. (Deft. states that complainant was parson of St. Teath, but deprived for marriage.) CORNW.

19–21 Arthur DARCY, knight, v. Thomas TALBOTT, knight, son and heir of Edmund Talbott, esquire, and others.
Ground called Robinson's Close *alias* Angrom, in complainant's manor of Gisburn. *See File* 1213, *No.* 6. YORK.

22–23 Arthur DARCYE, knight, v. George and Francis GAY(O)LE (Gaill).
Manor and grange of Achum (*i.e.*, Acomb?) in Rufforth. YORK.

24 Thomas DARELL and John COBNOTTE (?) v. Thomas COWSTOCKE, servant of Thomas Michell.
Administration of the will of Edward Markwyke of Hamsey, whose executors were complainants and the said Michell. SUSSEX.

25-26   Bartholomew, Thomas, William and Jarmyne DAUNCE *v.* John DAUNCE, their elder brother.
Non-payment of legacies of William Daunce, esquire, father of all parties, out of the issue of the manor of Cassiobury, and forfeiture of a lease of warrens in Letcombe Regis whereof complainants have the reversion.   HERTS., BERKS.

27   John DAVERS, gentleman, *v.* Robert BARFOTE, gentleman.
Manor of Shackerstone (Shaxton), late of John Davers, gentleman, deceased, father of complainant.
                                                                                         LEICS.

28   DAVID ap Howell *v.* Howell ap David DICUS and others.
Tenements in Llangwnadle and Aberdaron of the entail of David ap Jevan ap Dicus, grandfather of complainant.   CARNARVON.

29   DAVID ap Rees *v.* JOHN ap Robert.
Messuages and land in Trevyn (*i.e.* Tre-Evan) late of Rees ap Jevan, deceased, father of complainant.   DENBIGH.

30   DAVID ap [Hoell] ap David *v.* Henry MATHEWE and Katherine his wife.
Detention of deeds relating to lands in . . sen. *Mutilated.*   GLAMORGAN.

31   Jevan DAVID ap Rice *v.* RITHERCH ap David and others.
Messuages and land in Llanbadarn Vawr late of Engharad verch Jevan, deceased, mother of complainant.   CARDIGAN.

32   DAVID ap Howell of London, waterman, *v.* Gwillim THOMAS and HOWELL ap Gwillim.
Land in Llanbeder acquired of Howell ap Gwillim Lewys.   RADNOR.

33   Edward DAVY *v.* Robert GARRET.
Price of a yoke of oxen bought on deft's behalf.   ————

34-35   Isabel DAVYE *v.* John LEWGEY (Lowgey) and Elizabeth (Joan) his wife.
Land in Mapledurham, late of John Sparhawke of Purley, co. Berks, husbandman, deceased, father of complainant.   OXFORD.

36-38   The same *v.* the same and William HOWSE, son of the said Elizabeth by William Howse, her former husband.   OXFORD.

39   Simon, George and William DAWSON *v.* Richard ALMOND *alias* Almo their stepfather.
Detention of deeds relating to gavelkind lands in Marden, late of John Dawsonne, deceased, father of complainants.   KENT.

40   George [DAY], bishop of Chichester, the Queen's almoner, *v.* John BYKER of Nackington, husbandman.
Debt due to James Hale, knight, who drowned himself in the common river in the liberties of Canterbury. *Mutilated.*   KENT.

41   The same *v.* Robert CHILDERHOWSE.
Horses of the said Sir James.   KENT.

42-44   Nicholas DENBAWDE of Cornwood *v.* John CHUBBE of Ugborough.
Action on a bond given on behalf of William Rede of Hanger, deceased.   DEVON.

45-48   Thomas DENNYS, clerk, *v.* John RICHMAN.
Seizure of tithe corn belonging to complainant's parsonage of Fetcham (Fletcham). *2 answers.*
See D. XII, 14.   SURREY.

49-50   Walter DENYS (Dynys), knight, *v.* Robert TAYLLOUR *alias* ap Rycé.
Crown lease of the manor of Weston.   SOMERS.

51   William DERRY and Joan his wife, late the wife of William Harry and administratrix of his goods, *v.* Elizabeth, executrix and late the wife of Thomas HARRY, father of the said William.
Moiety of leasehold land in Loddiswell promised to the said Joan on her marriage with the said William Harry.   DEVON

52-53   James DEY *v.* Richard BULWER.
Cattle entrusted to deft.   NORFOLK.

54   Thomas DOBBYS of Canterbury, yeoman *v.* Anthony AUCHER, knight, resident at Calais, and James AUCHER and others, his tenants.
Occupation of the rectory of Eastry in contempt of an order of the King's and Queen's Bench.
                                                                                         KENT.

55-56   Simon DOBLE, husbandman *v.* William BROWNE, gentleman.
Tenement in the King's manor of Lydeard. (Deft. pleads that the demise to complainant was by an unauthorized official.)   SOMERS.

57   Owen DODDE *v.* Ralph HASSOWE.
Messuage and land in Hankelow of the demise of Robert Huxley.   CHESTER.

58   Francis Hynde, esquire, and others, for themselves, and all freeholders of the manor of DODDINGTON, and William Walbott and others for themselves and all copyholders of the same, *v.* William STEWARD and others of Ely, Gilbert and Edward KYNNEWORTH of Downham, and Robert DYNNESDALE and Thomas HAMMOND of Manea.
Right of pasture, and cutting pasture and wood in Stony Fen and Block Fen (the latter now in Manea).   CAMBRIDGE.

59-60   John DONNE of Southwark, innholder, *v.* Thomas TURNER and Matthew DOD, husbandmen.
Messuage and garden in Newtown (' the newtowne of Cadeuin ') late of Mores ap Edward, deceased, grandfather of complainant.   MONT.

61–63   Matthew DORYNGTON of Stafford, mercer, *v.* Richard, son of Ralph AUDYENCE.
Messuage and land at Cowley in Gnosall, late of Robert Doryngton, deceased, father of complainant.
STAFFORD.

64–65   John son of Robert DOUGHTIE, deceased *v.* Thomas and John HARWELL.
Land in Duddlewick (in Stottesden) of the demise of Thomas, late abbot of Shrewsbury.   SALOP.

66   Baldwin DOWCE and Elizabeth his wife, late the wife of Anthony Hall, *v.* John COCKES.
Parsonage of Heckforde (*i.e.*, Heckfield?) of the demise of the warden and scholars of New College
(' St. Marye Colledge of Winchester '), Oxford.   HANTS.

67   Thomas DRAX, esquire, *v.* John HAGLEYE.
Meadow in Darfield, late of Thomas Drax, deceased, father of complainant.   YORK.

68–70   William DRAYCOTES of Market Rasen, shoemaker, *v.* William MOLLINSON
(Monston), esquire.
Messuage and land in Camthorpe (Canthorpe), Thornton [le-Moor], and Owersby, demised to
Thomas Draycottes, grandfather of complainant, by the prior and convent of Royston. D. XII, 16.
LINCOLN.

71   Maude DREWE *v.* Robert FULFORDE, James MORTYMER, his servant, and John MILL.
Loan of plough-gear from her house at Newton St. Cyres.   *See File* 1345, *No.* 46.   DEVON.

72–73   Leonard DRURY and ⸺ his mother *v.* William DRURY.
Lands late held in borough English of the manor of Fillingham by John .Drury, deceased grandfather of both parties.   LINCOLN.

74   Peter DUKKET of Broughton Astley *v.* Geoffrey (George) WYLFYTH.
Money promised to complainant on his marriage with Alice, daughter of deft.   LEIC.

75   Humphrey DYCKYNS *v.* Ralph SANDES and others.
Messuage and land in Wolverley (Woverley) late held of the chapter of Worcester by Hugh Ward
and Ellen his wife.   WORC.

76   Thomas DYE *v.* Maude LLOYD of Daywall (in Whittington), and Thomas LLOYD, son
and heir of Roger ap Hugh of the same, gentleman.
Refusal to complete a lease of land in Ifton and Wigginton (both in St. Martin's).   SALOP.

77–78   William DYGHTON of Grantham, co. Lincoln, *v.* Peter DYGHTON.
Detention of deeds relating to a messuage and croft in Wakefield, late of William Dyghton, deceased,
father of both parties.   YORK.

78–81   John DYSON, clerk, *v.* John CANTERELL and Alice, his wife.
Money and household goods (*described*) entrusted by complainant to Cicely, his mother, who died
in defts' house at Glascote in Tamworth.   WARW.

FILE 1348.

1–5   John EDBROKE, *v.* Giles HYLLYNG, vicar of Winsford, and John TYBBE, clerk.
Annuity granted by the said Hyllyng to the said Tybbe, and by him assigned to complainant.
[SOMERS.]

6–7   John EDBROKE of Winsford, administrator of the goods of Ellen Atkyns of the same,
deceased, *v.* John WYNDHAM, knight, and George VERNEY, vicar of Whytherage (*i.e.*,
Withypool?).
Detention by the said Sir John of a bond for 100 ' owlde angelles ' entrusted to the said vicar
by the said Ellen.   SOMERS.

8–9   John EDERIGE and Joan his wife, late the wife of William Symondes, gentleman, *v.*
Griffon AMERADETHE.
Erection of a mill in Thorverton in prejudice of the dean and chapter of Exeter's mills, to which
the tenants owe suit.   DEVON.

10   Anthony EDMONDE, Thomas LOVENDEN, Eleanor his wife, John AUSTEN, and Agnes
his wife, *v.* Adlard WELBY, gentleman.
Lands in the Queen's manor of Gedney, late of William Chater, deceased, father of the female
complainants, and of Margaret mother of the said Anthony.   LINCOLN.

11   William EDMUNDES of Wimborne Minster, co. Dorset, cordwainer, *v.* Hugh HUGMAN.
Lands in the manor of Christchurch Twynham, late of Richard Edmundes, deceased, uncle of
complainant.   HANTS.

12   EDWARD ap Rise of Norwich, yeoman, *v.* THOMAS ap Jevan ap Rise, Alice his wife, and
Richard ap Griffith.
One-third of a messuage and land in St. Asaph (Llanelwyn) late of Rise ap Griffith, deceased,
father of complainant.   FLINT.

13   Henry EDWARD of Lelant, yeoman of the Guard, *v.* Alice, late the wife of John TREVISSA
of the Guard, deceased, and administratrix of his goods.
Complainant's pay received by the said Trevissa from the paymaster of the Guard and the clerk
of the check.   MIDDX., CORNW.

14–16   John EDWARD and others, for themselves and all other copyhold tenants of the manor
of Woodhurst, *v.* John BEDFORD, Sir Thomas POPE, and others.
Fen in Warboys (Warburshe) wherein complainants claim pasture for cattle without number, and
the right to cut sedge.   HUNTINGDON.

17   Peter EDWARDE, husbandman, *v.* Katherine DAVYE and John and Humphrey OLIVER.
Forcible ouster from half a tenement in the manor of Cardinham, promised to complainant on his
marriage with Wylmote, daughter of the said Katharine, and seizure of looms and other goods.
CORNW.

18–19   William EDWARDES, [yeoman] of the Guard, *v.* JEVAN ap Renolde of Mold.
Land in Leeswood pledged to deft.   FLINT.

20–26   Hugh EDWARDES *alias* Hugh ap Edwardes (sic) ap Hoell *v.* JEVAN ap David ap John, RES ap Jenkyn, and JEVAN ap Hoell.
Messuages and lands in Berriew. *2 sets of answers. Rival pedigrees given.*   MONTG.

27–29 ' John EDWARDES *v.* Henry WILCOKES.
Copyhold land called 'a berie lotte' in the Princess Elizabeth's manor of Shitlington. ·(Deft. states that 'berie lottes' are not copyhold, and carry no rights of common.)   BEDFORD.

30–31   Richard EDWARDES and Jane, his wife *v.* EDWARD ap Daye.
Goods of Hugh Daye, deceased, brother of deft. and former husband of the said Jane.
DIOCESE OF LONDON.

32   William EDWARDES of London, innholder, *v.* Thomas EGERTON.
Land in Hampton.   CHESTER.

33   Katherine, late the wife of John EGERLEY *v.* Simon S[EIN]TCLERE of Thame.
Detention of deeds relating to a messuage in Milton, and lands elsewhere. *Damaged.*   OXFORD.

34   Elizabeth, late the wife of Henry EGLYNGTON *v.* Francis LEE and Francis TEMPLE.
Manor of . . . and lands in Ellesborough and Great and Little Kimble, of the demise of John Verney, esquire, and Dorothy his wife. *Mutilated.*   BUCKINGHAM.

35–37   John ELCOCK *v.* EDWARD ap Thomas.
Messuage and land in Llangibby, late of Edward ap Thomas *alias* Sadler·of Bristol, saddler.   MONM.

38–42   Robert ELDRED *v.* Nicholas BOWETT, gentleman, and Joan his wife.
Manor, messuages, cottages, and land in Ingoldsby, late of Henry Willoughby, deceased, great. grandfather of complainant.   LINCOLN.

43   Henry ELIOTT *v.* John GAYNSFORD, executor of Nicholas Gaynsford, and the mayor, aldermen and sheriffs of LONDON.
Action on a bond for price of a messuage and land in the Boulonnnais, lost at its cession to France. *Subpœna and certiorari.*   FRANCE. LONDON.

44   William ELKEZ, parson of More, *v.* William JONEZ and others.   SALOP.
Parsonage and glebe of More.

45   Edmund, son and heir of John ELLMES, esquire, *v.* Elizabeth, executrix and late the wife of Thomas BRUDENELL, knight.
Surplus income of the manor of Wolffehowse and lands in Stamford, late of the said John, whose executor the said Sir Thomas was. (The said John also held lands in Henley, Rotherfield Greys, Watlington Hill, Fawley, Hambleden, Skirmett in Fingest, Turville and Wallingford)
RUTLAND, LINCOLN, OXFORD, BUCKINGHAM, BERKS.

46   The same, grandson and heir of William Elmes and of Elizabeth, his wife *v.* Thomas PYGOTT of Doversell, esquire.
Lands in the manors of Littlecote and Missenden. *Mutilated.* *See File 1217, No. 11.*
BUCKINGHAM.

47–40   John ELLYS, husbandman, son of John Ellys, deceased, *v.* John, son of Charles COPLE-STONE, Thomas STUKELEY, his guardian, and others.
Messuage, land and mills in Chawley, formerly in dispute between the said Charles and John Davy and Avis his wife. D. IX. 18.   DEVON.

51–53   The churchwardens and parishoners of ELMLEY LOVETT *v.* Robert ACTON, knight, and Charles his son.
Lands in the said Sir Robert's manor of Elmley Lovett demised to complainants' predecessors by King Edward IV.   WORC.

54–56   Charles ELTON, gentleman, *v.* Richard ELTON, merchant tailor, his .younger brother, and William DAWKES, mercer, both of London.
Fraudulent conveyance of one-third of the manor of Frankes. *Mutilated.*   ESSEX.

57–61   Richard Cattlyn and others, being the most part of the inhabitants of ELTON (Aylton, Allyngton) *v.* Robert SAPCOTE, esquire.

62–64   George, second son of George ELYOT of Stretford, esquire, deceased, *v.* Henry ELYOT his cousin.
Rent of land in Alderbury, held by the said George, the father, together with the manor of Upwick and other lands.   HERTS.

65–69   Joan, executrix and late the wife of John ELYOTT, *v.* Robert BANKES and Elizabeth his wife, late the wife of Thomas Elyott of Shalford and [Richard AMBROSE and] Henry POLSTEDE.
Action on a bond for a debt already paid to the said Thomas, whosè executors are the defendants other than Robert Bankes.   SURREY.

70–72   John ELYOTT of Plymouth, esquire, *v.* John GYLBERT.
Orchard or garden in the borough of Ashburton, late of Edward Elyott, esquire, deceased, father of complainant.   DEVON.

73–76   William ELYS *v.* William SOUTHWOODE and William and Robert SOUTHWOODE his nephews (?).
Tithes, barn and land in the manor and borough of Chulmleigh (Chymley) of the demise of William Luxton, late parson of Broadwoodkelly, and Robert Bisshop of Bondleigh (Baundley).   DEVON.

77   John ELYSTON and Agas his wife, a granddaughter and heir of Henry Palmer, or Matthew LANE and Alice his wife.
Detention of deeds relating to a messuage in Tolberstrete and a shop in the High Street of Banbury.
OXFORD.

78–80 · Richard ELYTHOURNE v. Ellen ELYTHORNF, alias Mores, his divorced wife.
Embezzlement of goods and of deeds relating to messuages in Long Ditch and Tothill Street,
Westminster. *Answer wanting.* MIDDX.

81 John ERNE of Liss and Joan, his wife, executrix and late the wife of John Ede, v. Thomas
EDE.
Leasehold, late of Richard Talbot of Binstead, deceased, whose executor was the said John Ede.
HANTS.

82. Gabriel EMERSON of London, yeoman, v. Thomas SOUTHERNE and others.
Parsonage of Paglesham demised by rival parsons. ESSEX.

83–84 Christopher son and heir of Vincent ENGEHAM v. Daniel and William EVERINGE.
Occupation of leaseholds called Boxlye Lease near Sandwich and Shelvinge in Woodnesborough by
conspiracy with Elizabeth, stepmother of complainant. KENT.

85 Francis ENGLEFYLDE, knight v. Richard BENSON, clerk.
Messuages and land in Kinnersley, Letton and Almeley, late of Anne Dalabere, deceased, aunt of
complainant. HEREFORD.

86–88. Henry ERLE and others, feoffees of lands granted for repairs of the church of Callington
and its ornaments, v. Anthony WYLL, bailiff of Landrake.
Rent charge on lands in Callington for the above purpose by John Cole, sometime parish priest of
Southill. D. XIV, 51. CORNW.

89–96 James ERLE and George WALTON v. George VERNON, Elizabeth, late the wife of Philip
AYER (Eyre) and Richard OFFERTON, yeoman.
Messuage in Eccleshall and tenements in Sheffield and elsewhere, of the entail of Paul Botton,
ancestor of complainants. *Pedigree given.* YORK.

97–100 William ERMYSTED (Ernestede), clerk, master in Chancery, v. Robert GRENE, yeoman.
Next presentation to the church of Severn-Stoke, of the gift of Henry [Clifford], earl of Cumberland.
WORC.

101–102 Hugh ERSWIKE of Sandon, esquire, v. Elizabeth KEMSEY and others:
Pasture land in Gayton, late of the chantry called Our Lady's service in the church of Leigh.
STAFFORD.

103 George ESCROPE v. John HALL (Nall) and John VEALL.
Lands in Aldbrough in Holderness. YORK.

104–107 Thomas ESSEX, knight, and Margaret his wife, daughter of William Sandes, knight, and
late the wife of William Rogers, esquire, v. John ROGERS, knight, father of the said William,
and Richard ROGERS, esquire.
Manors of Stoford, Barwick, and Sparkford, one-fourth of the manor of Wanstrow, and lands there,
part of the marriage settlement of the said Margaret. *Mutilated.* SOMERS.

108 John ESTON, executor of William Wymond of Rye, v. John STYLL of Stone, executor of
Dame Juliana Brownyng.
Bond for conveyance of lands. *Mutilated.* KENT.

109–111 Richard ESTON v. William, son and heir of William BUTTON, esquire.
Mill and land in Winterbourn Earls, of which complainant assured his title by compromising a suit
by Alice Hyll in this court (*File* 1131, *No.* 33). WILTS.

112–115 Richard ESTON v. Thomas CAPELEYN (Chaplyn).
Tenement next the *Cornish Chough* in Salisbury, late of William Eston, deceased, grandfather of
complainant. WILTS.

116 Thomas EVERARD and Joan, his wife v. Andrew STANE and Agnes, his wife.
Tenement in the manor of Bethersden and Powers, late of Andrew Maryan, grandfather of the said
Joan. *Damaged.* [KENT]

117–119. Thomas, son of John EYLES (Giles) v. Thomas WASSHER, late husband of Anne formerly
the wife of the said John.
Site of the manor of Eastergate (Gate) and tithes in Yapton and Shapwick of the demise of the late
abbess and convent of Sion. D. XIV, 30. SUSSEX.

120 George EYRE of Abney v. Robert BARBER of Tideswell.
Price of wool and cattle. DERBY.

FILE 1349.

1 Thomas FAWKENOR and Rose his wife, late the wife of Thomas Hall, citizen and painter
of London, v. Nicholas BROMFELD, Christopher GALLAUNT, and Richard HALL of
London, brother of the said Thomas.
Land in the manor of Edmonton surrendered by the said Thomas Hall to the said Bromfeld and
Gallaunt to the uses of his will. MIDDLESEX.

2–3 · Andrew FEELDE v, Thomas SPARKE.
Lease of Greenfields Grange in Flotton, promised in exchange for a lease of the manor of Pulloxhill by
Thomas Palmer, knight, since attainted. BEDFORD.

4 Robert FERON, parson of St. Ethelburga's (' Seint Albroughe within Busshopsgate ') v. John
DAY, late parson, deprived for marriage.
Tenths and subsidies due by defendant. LONDON.

5–7 John FERRERS of Tamworth, esquire, v. Walter HARECOURTE.
Bond given by complainant on behalf of Humphrey Ferrers, knight, his father, to Thomas Ensour,
whose widow defendant has married. WARWICK.

8   John FISSHER, parson of Stisted, v. Elizabeth, claiming to be the wife of William WAKFELD, late parson, Stephen, his son, and Robert PANNELL.
Waste in complainant's parsonage, whereof defendants claim a lease from the said William. *Faded*.
ESSEX.

9-10   George FLECHER, citizen and goldsmith of London v. Robert HARDINGE, citizen and salter of London, and Thomas DYCKEFELDE, salter.
Bond given to the said Dyckefelde for a loan by the said Hardinge, made in ' ozenbrigges ' and plate which were not of the value represented.
LONDON.

11   Alice FLETCHER v. John CROSSELAR.
Tenements without the west gate of Chichester of the bequest of Walter Maringe. *Mutilated*.
SUSSEX.

12-14   Thomas FLYNT, Margaret his wife, and Katherine POLE v. John DARBY.
Detention of deeds relating to the manor of Hodnet, of part whereof defendant claims a Crown lease.
SALOP.

15-16   Philip FORMAN, yeoman, grandson and heir of John Forman, v. Edward FORMAN.
Detention of deeds relating to the *Bull* inn at Abingdon.
BERKS.

17   Myles FORREST of Morborne, esquire, v. William PALMER.
Tenement called the *George*, and land in Stutton.
HUNTINGDON.

18   Robert FOWELYN of Theberton, clerk, v. John COTTYNGHAM of Middleton.
Meadow in Fordley, late of William Ulffe of Theberton. *See Files* 452, *No.* 2 ; 586, *No.* 3. SUFFOLK.

19-20   Thomas FOWLER, husbandman, v. William LUMBERD and Alice, his wife, executrix and late the wife of John Everye of Donyatt; co. Somerset, husbandman.
Money payable in consideration of complainants marriage with Joan, daughter of the said John, on his obtaining possession of a tenement in Combrawleigh on the death of Agnes, his mother. DEVON.

21-23   William FRANCKELONDE, citizen and clothworker of London, v. Richard BROWNE, Beatrice his wife, and William LLOYD.
Under-lease by the said Lloyd of portions (*described*) of a messuage of the said Beatrice in All Hallows the Great.
LONDON.

24-26   John FRANKE the younger v. Margaret FRANKE, his stepmother (' mother yn lawe ').
Messuage and land in Terling, with goods, late of Robert Franke, deceased, father of complainant.
ESSEX.

27   John FRELANDE v. Thomas TOPPE, yeoman.
Conditions of a lease of a farm in Stockton.
WILTS.

28-30   Thomas FRETWELL v. Stephen TUPMAN and John SHEPPARD.
Messuage in Wickersley. *Pedigree in answer*.
YORK.

31-33   Christopher (John) FRY v. Arthur FYFARDE (Fefford), clerk, executor of Alexander Marten.
Lands in Hawkesbury (Hakesbury) of the gift of John Marten, father of the said Alexander.
GLOUCESTER.

34   Robert FRY and Alice, his wife, late the wife of John Ros[ogan?] v. John TREMBEARE.
Detention of deeds relating to tenements and a mill-pool head in Loscowelyck and St. Austell, and of rents.
CORNWALL.

35-36   Nicholas FRYE, late of Buckland-Brewer, v. Richard WANELL.
Detention of deeds relating to messuages and lands in Hatherleigh, Okehampton, South Brent, Buckfastleigh and Plymouth.
DEVON.

37-38   Jerome FRYGER v. Alexander RAME.
Detention of a bond for a debt already paid.
[LONDON].

39   The same, a Venetian resident in London, v. the mayor, alderman, and sheriffs of LONDON, and James PYSTYLECHE (Pelsaleche), Venetian.
Action of debt in the sheriffs court, pending a suit in this court. *Certiorari and subpœna*. LONDON.

40-43   The same (Frysard) v. the same (Petzaloche).
Rings entrusted to defendant, and claimed by him as won at cards.
[LONDON.

44   John FRYNCKE of Plympton St. Mary, son of Richard Fryncke, v. John BYCKFORD of Brixton, smith.
Messuage and land in Brixton, pledged to defendant.
DEVON.

45-46   John FULLER v. Robert, son and heir of William ABBOTT.
Messuage and land in Carlton, late of William Fuller of Chelyngton, deceased, father of complainant. *Mutilated*.
[BEDFORD].

47-49   Nicholas FURNESSE v. George and William DOUGHTIE and Thomas and Nicholas MYSTERCHAMBERS.
Messuage and land in Saltfleetby, of the demise of the said Nicholas Mysterchambers. LINCOLN.

50-52   John FURSE of Torrington v. John NEWCOURT of Georgeham, gentleman.
Double lease of a cottage, and of the weighing of wool and yarn in the manor of Holsworthy. DEVON.

53   Anthony FURTHO of Furtho, co. Northants, esquire, and Elizabeth his wife v. Edward WATSON, gentleman.
Water[-mill] and land in Harrowby and Manthorpe, late of Robert Stonesby of Knypton, co. [Leicester], deceased, grandfather of the said Elizabeth. *Mutilated*.
LINCOLN.

54-56   Nicholas FYDENS, citizen and surgeon of London v. Anthony SALMON.
Manor of Heldes Hall in Selston formerly of John Helde. *Pedigree given. Faded*.
[NOTTS].

57–59   The same *v.* William WHYTE of Louth.
Parsonage of Fotherby, claimed by deft. under a lease from the prior of Nun-Ormesby (Normormesby).   LINCOLN.

60–64   Basil FYLDING, esquire, and John LYNWODE and Andrew FOSTER of Sutton, his tenants, *v.* Thomas WREN.
Lands in Wentworth (Wyntforde) with fold-course and right of common.   (Annexed is an answer and rejoinder by Robert Steward, dean of Ely, and his chapter).   CAMBRIDGE.

65   John, brother and heir of Thomas FYNCHE *v.* Robert HAMONDE and Elizabeth his wife.
Detention of deeds relating to messuages in Swaffham Market, one held of the manor of Haspaldes, and the other of the Duchess of Richmond.   NORFOLK.

66–69   John FYPERS *v.* John, son of William JOURDE(Y)N.
Lands in Willingham, late of Marion Fypers, deceased, mother of complainant.   CAMBRIDGE.

FILE 1350.

1   Philip FARMAN, yeoman, *v.* Thomas TONKES.
Detention of deeds relating to a tenement called ' le Moyses ' in the market-place of Abingdon.
                                                                                           BERKS.

2–4   The same (Forman), grandson of John Farman, *v.* John LANGLEY.
Detention of deeds relating to a tenement in St. Helen's Street, Abingdon, entailed on John Brereton and others.   *See File* 1349, *No.* 15.   BERKS.

5   Wilham FELTON of Ewdenes, yeoman, *v.* Robert FELTON his brother.
Detention of deeds relating to a messuage and land in Worfield, late of Richard Felton, their father, deceased.   SALOP.

6   Walter and Baldwin, sons of John FENWIKE of the Hurst, deceased, and administrators of his goods, *v.* Constance FENWIKE.
Occupation of a messuage, land, and a fishery in the Tyne called Walker, of the demise of John a Fenwike of Wallington, in contempt of orders of divers Wardens of the Marches.   N'HUMB.

7   John FERRERS, esquire, *v.* Thomas LYSLE.
Lands in Lea-Marston charged with a rent to defendant as successor of the prioress of Markyate.
                                                                                           WARW.

8   . . . FITCHE, alderman of the craft of bakers of Chester, *v.* Robert HANCOCKE and others.
Breach of regulations for sale of bread in the city.   *Damaged.*   CHESTER.

9–13   Thomas FITZHERBERT, knight, and Anne, his wife, *v.* Ellis STAYLEY, Thomas SAVAGE, Hugh AYRE, clerk, and others, tenants of the manor of Castleton.
Rights of common in Castleton moor.   (The said Savage answers twice.)   DERBY.

14–17   John FITZ RICHARD *v.* Richard MARKAM, esquire.
Crown lease of a messuage and land in Sedgebrook, whereof defendant has bought the reversion.
                                                                                           LINCOLN.

18–19   Thomas FLAVELL and Anne, his wife, *v.* Richard CHAMBER.
Land in Purson and Astrop, late of Hugh Parsons and Eleanor, his wife, deceased, grandparents of the said Anne.   N'HAMP.

20   Edmund FORDE *v.* LAURENCE Nowell, clerk.
Rent charged on the parsonage of Harting, of which parsonage and of other lands defendant obtained possession by the aid of Andrew Dudley, knight, since attainted.   SUSSEX.

21–23   Thomas FOSCROFTE, one of the Queen's messengers attendant on the Chancellor, *v.* Peter SMYTHYMAN.
' Messuage or inne lying in Scott rent in the quenez strete of Westminster,' with a stable and gardens.   MIDDX.

24   Robert FOSTER, Isabel his wife, John JERVYS, Elizabeth, his wife, and Joan NORTHE *v.* John CLARKE.
Legacies of William Northe of Essendon, father of the female complainants, defendant being supervisor of his will.   HERTS.

25–26   John FOWLER *v.* Humphrey HAYWARD.
Refusal to complete a conveyance of a tenement in the Queen's manor of Cirencester.   *Mutilated.*
                                                                                           GLOUC.

27–28   Robert FOXE, vicar of Boreham, *v.* Thomas WALES.
Rent of land (*described*) in Boreham belonging to the vicarage.   ESSEX.

29–30   Richard FRANCES of Screilby and Joan his wife, daughter of John Smyth of Storton, *v.* William BALDYNG.
Goods of the said John, whose executors were the said Joan, and Joan his wife, afterwards the wife of John Baldyng, father of the said William.   LINCOLN, NOTTS.

31   Anthony FRANKESSHE, gentleman, *v.* John WATSON of Allerton, merchant, and others.
Detention of deeds relating to messuages and land in Ripon.   *See File* 1220, *No.* 39.   YORK.

32–33   Anthony FRERE *v.* Thomas DAYE of Snaith, and Isabel, his wife, daughter and heir of John Frere.
Lands late held of the manor of Drax in borough-English by William Frere, deceased, father of the said Anthony and John (defendant denies that the lands are customary).   YORK.

34   Richard FRESTON, knight, cofferer to the Queen, *v.* John CLERK of Finningham.
Failure to deliver copies of court rolls of the manor of Wickham-Skeith as ordered by this court.
                                                                                           SUFF.

35   Robert FRY and Anne, his wife, late the wife of John Rosog(an?) v. John DELAMAYN.
Tenements in St. Austell. *Faded. See File 1260, No. 23.*   CORNW.

36-37   Roger FULLER and another v. Uryan BRERETON, knight, Jane, his wife, late the wife of
Edmund Bray, knight and William, son of William COKE.
Tenement in the said Lady Jane's manor of Eyton (*i.e.* Eaton near Congleton?). *Mutilated. See*
D. IX. 79.   [CHESTER.]

38   Robert FYNDELER v. Robert LOSEBY.
Crown lease of lands. *Faded.*   LEIC.

39   Richard FYSSHER v. Matthew STAUNCEALL and Agnes, his wife.
Price of oxen sold to John Fyssher, deceased, son of complainant and former husband of the said
Agnes.   SOMERS.

40-42   John FYTZJAMES, archdeacon of Taunton, v. John HOWELL, doctor of physic.
Contempt of an injunction of this court concerning the archdeaconry of Taunton.   SOMERS.

43   The same v. Baldwin HILL, clerk.
Entry on the parsonage of Nettlecombe without induction by complainant.   SOMERS.

FILE 1351.

1-2   Robert FAIREMAN of London, goldsmith, v. Owen CLAYTON and William TRACYE,
executors of Laurence Smyth, merchant tailor and citizen of London, John CATER, of
London, vintner, and the sheriffs of LONDON.
Action on a counterbond for a loan made by the said Cater in anticipation of the debasement of
the coinage. *Subpœna and corpus cum causa.*   LONDON.

3-4   Edward FARMER v. Richard LARGE and another.
Two water mills in Abingdon. *Faded.*   .BERKS.

5   Thomas FARNABY of Truro, joiner, v. Piers ROSEMENEWAS.
Silver cup, late of William Farnaby, deceased, father of complainant.   CORNW.

6-8   Nicholas FAYREWETHER of Kenton v. John, son and executor of Edmund FREMAN
of Hadley.
Loan to the said Edmund.   SUFF.

9   Richard FEELD v. Edward NORTH, lord North.
Delivery to Richard Whalley, esquire, of a book of accounts between him and complainant.
                                                                            [NOTTS. ?]

10   William and John FELDE v. Thomas GERVEIS.
Action for a debt discharged by pasturage of a close in Nyland.   SOMER.

11   Thomas FELDYNG v. John ORMESON and Margery, his wife, administrators of the goods
of Nicholas Hasond, deceased.
Legacy of Thomas Feldyng of Leicester, deceased. *Mutilated.*   LEICS.

12-13   Richard FERON v. Peter, son and executor of Richard WYNDER.
Land in Blindcrake of the demise of the said Richard.   CUMBERLAND.

14   John FERRERS, *alias* Baker, and Alice, his wife, v. Sir John SYDNHAME of Brympton.
Land at Sandell in the manor of Old Cleeve of the demise of William Duffill, late abbot of Cleeve,
and his convent. *Mutilated.*   SOMERS.

15-20   John FERROUR, *alias* Frauncis, chaplain, John FYSSHER, *alias* Shereman, Christopher
COURTE, esquire, and others v. Robert MOLEHOUSE (Mollowes) and John SPARKE.
Land in Wattisfield and Walsham. *Mutilated.*   SUFF.

21   John FITZHERBERT v. George BLACKWELL, gentleman, and Robert (Roger) BARKER,
yeoman.
Part price of wool sold to the said Barker. *Mutilated.*   ————

22   Margaret and Mary FITZRYCHARDES v. Richard [IVOTT].
Stalls in the market-place, barn, and lands (*described*) in Rayleigh of the entail of Thomas Alleyne.
Faded. D. XIV, 44; *see also* D. XIV, 19.   ESSEX.

23-24   Thomas Abraham and others (*named*) and all the tenants of the manor of FLAMSTEAD, v.
George FERRERS, gentleman, lord of the manor, and others.
Exaction of fines on entry in excess of the customary 1d. per acre, threat to deprive them of lands
called ' newe landes,' and destruction of enclosures made by agreement with a former lord. HERTS.

25-29   Henry FLEMYNG and Thomas NORTHALL, yeomen, administrators of the goods of Henry
Flemyng, vicar of Brewood, deceased, v. Thomas SAWYER.
Money and jewels (*described*) of the said vicar, partly stolen by Thomas Wolfe, his servant.
                                                                            STAFFORD.

30   Hugh FLUDE, son of John Flude and of Anne Apperedethe, v. Dave FLUDE ap John ap
Madoc, his stepfather, and John ap Robert TRAFFORTHE.
Bill of divorcement of the said Dave and Anne, borrowed to make possible the former's second
marriage.   ————

31-32   William FODEN of Stafford, yeoman, v. Ellen MARKHAM of Oxton (Oxon), co. Notts.
Messuage and land in Church Broughton of the demise of deft.   DERBY.

33-34   [James] FOLJAMBE, knight, v. Richard WHALLEY of Welbeck, esquire.
Corn-rent reserved on the parsonage of Gringley by the late abbot of Worksop. D. XIV, 21.
                                                                            NOTTS.

35   Edmund FORDE, esquire, v. Thomas RYTHE.
Action on a bond, fraudulently obtained, concerning lands in Hastings. *Damaged.*   SUSSEX.

36–37   Matthew, son of John FORDEMAN v. Agnes, late the wife of the said John, and administratrix of his goods, and Stephen FORDEMAN.
Messuage and land in Bransley (*i.e.* Brenchley?) of the gift of the said John.   KENT.

38–42   William FOREST of London, butcher, and Beatrice, his wife, v. John LEIGH of the Booth, knight, Richard OLDEFELDE, and Margaret MOSCROPPE.
Burgage in Over Knutsford late of Robert Moscroppe, deceased, father of the said Beatrice and brother-in-law of the said Margaret.   CHESTER.

43   Robert FORSTER v. [John TASELER].
Farm in Layer-de-la-Haye. *Damaged.*   ESSEX.

44   John FOX of Norwich, yeoman, v. Francis CLOVYLE, esquire, and Elizabeth, his wife.
Debt of Lawrence Hey, whose executrix is the said Elizabeth.   NORF.

45–49   Alice FRANCKELIN v. Edith, late the wife of Nicholas WILLIAMZ and mother of complainant, and William WYLCOCKES.
Manor of Sherston, demised by the late Duke of Somerset to the said Nicholas, Edith and Alice.   WILTS.

50–53   William FRAUNCES of Ketton, co. Rutland, labourer, v. Richard COLLYNSON, husbandman.
Land in North Thoresby, formerly of John Norcot, deceased, great-grandfather of complainant and of Elizabeth, wife of deft. *See* D. XIV, 20.   LINCOLN.

54–56   John FULLERE, son of Margaret, wife of Philip Meredith, citizen of London, v. Nicholas AVENAND of London, tailor, and Frances, his wife, daughter of the said Margaret.
Action on a bond for a payment already made for deft's marriage. *Damaged.*   LONDON.

57   James FULYAMBE, knight, v. Roger GRENHALGH, esquire.
Marriage settlement of complainant's daughter with deft.'s son, including lands in Sutton-in-Ashfield, Newbold, Clayworth and Beckingham.   NOTTS.

58–60   Richard FYNCHAM, gentleman, v. William BLACKWOODE and others.
Land in Brancaster and Deepdale late of John Fyncham, gentleman, [grandfather?] of complainant. *Mutilated.*   NORF.

61   Mark FYNCHE v. John, son of John GRENEHILL.
Croft in Sudbury late of Richard Fynche of Harrow, yeoman, deceased, father of complainant.   MIDDX.

62–66   Thomas FYNNY v. Humphrey THYCKEBROME.
Water-course, mill, land and pasture in Thickbroom (in Weeford) already in dispute in this court (*File* 1221, *No.* 73.) *Damaged.* D. XII, 19.   STAFFORD.

67–68   John FYSSHER and Elizabeth his wife v. John HODGEKYNS and Elizabeth his wife, late the wife of Thomas Bedforde of Coventry.
Expenses and labour of the said Elizabeth Fyssher in treating a disease of the said Bedforde.   WARW.

FILE 1352.

1   John GASCOIGN, knight, and Margaret, his wife, v. William FAWCONER, gentleman.
Debt due to Francis Bryan, knight, a debtor of complainants, on the death of Margaret Staples.
[YORK?]

2–3   John GASON, gentleman, v. Thomas ROLFE.
Action on a bond for price of corn and rent of lands in Ickham and Wingham, belonging to the 'spitall of pore prestes' in Canterbury, which lands deft. refused to warrant.   KENT.

4   Richard GAYE v. Thomas FLOURE.
Messuage and garden in Poole, late of Matthew Tyler, deceased, uncle of complainant.   DORSET.

5   William GEFFEREY, Robert ROLFFE, John BACHELER, and Alice, his wife, v. John HAVELL.
Land in Westham and Pevensey, late of Robert Havell, deceased, uncle of the said Gefferey and Rolffe. *Mutilated.*   SUSSEX.

6–12   Ralph GELL v. Thomas HELLOTT and Anthony LOWE.
Detention of deeds relating to a messuage and land in Wirksworth.   DERBY.

13–14   Henry GESTE v. David PENRY(TH).
Crown lease of St. Margaret's chapel or hermitage of Mork in St. Briavels (Brevelly), with an orchard and grove.   GLOUC.

15   Oliver GIBBES, parson of Moclestone, v. Edward ASHETON, knight, and Robert ASHETON, late parson.
Parsonage of Moclestone, whereof the said Robert was deprived for marriage. *Mutilated.*
[SALOP *or* STAFFORD]

16   Richard GILBEY and Elizabeth, his wife, v. Thomas WHITBROKE.
Money and rings delivered by the said Elizabeth, before her marriage, in respect of a house in All Hallows, London Wall. *Mutilated.*   LONDON.

17–19   William GLASEOUR of Chester, and James his son, of London, v. Peter JACKSON, priest.
'Lordshipp, towne, or towneshipp' of Eastham with 'oxions' of land, 'fysshe yordes,' etc., of the demise of the dean and chapter of Chester.   CHESTER.

20–23   Robert GLENNFELD, gentleman, v. John NORMAN, and others.
Lands in Saxmundham, Kelshall, and Carlton, late of William Worseley of Norwich, co. Norfolk. *Commission.*   SUFFOLK.

24   Nicholas GODFREY of Stony Stratford, and Emma, his wife, v. Cuthbert EMERSON.
Messuages and land in Henslope, late of Thomas Lenell, clerk, deceased, uncle of complainant.
                                                                                                          BUCKINGHAM.

25–28   Philip GODFREY, of Salisbury, tailor, v. John HAWLES (Hollys) and Henry DYMOCKE.
Messuages in the parishes of St. Martin and St. Thomas, Salisbury, late of Henry Godfrey, deceased, father of complainant.   WILTS.

29–30   The same v. Henry CLYFFORD, esquire.
Falsification of evidence as a commissioner in the last suit.   WILTS.

31–33   The same v. Joan, late the wife of Henry DYMOCKE, and daughter of the said Hawles.
The said messuages in the parish of St. Thomas.   WILTS.

34–36   The same v. Michael DYMOCKE, kinsman and heir of the said Joan.
Reviver of a suit by Henry Godfrey, deceased, father of complainant, for [the last-named] messuages *Mutilated.*   WILTS.

37–38   William GODOLHAN, knight, v. William ISAM, gentleman.
Controllership of the coinage of tin, and custody of ' guolle ' (*i.e.* the gaol ?) of Lostwithiel.
                                                                                                          DEVON, CORNWALL.

39   Simon GODSALVE of Cheselborne (Cheselborowe), husbandman, v. Thomas BYRTE, yeoman.
Forgery of a bond for a payment to be made at the end of a tenancy in Osmington.   DORSET.

40–41   John GOLDER v. Leonard ALNOTT, both of Oakley, husbandmen.
Sale of a lease of a messuage and land in Wotton, after forfeiture for non-payment of rent.
                                                                                                          BUCKINGHAM.

42–45   Laurence GOLDYNG and Joan his wife, late the wife of Robert Kent, v. Stephen son and executor of John GYBON, and John HODGES and Elizabeth his wife, executrix and late the wife of Thomas Keynsham.
Gold and silver entrusted to the said John Gybon aud Thomas Keynsham.   —————————

46–48   Harry GOLLOFER, of Maudlyn Syffeld (*i.e.*, Fifehead Magdalen) v. Alice, executrix ᴀ＿‥ late the wife of Thomas HICKES of Stalbridge, butcher.
Sale of a lease from the late abbot of Sherborne, of meadow in Stalbridge.   DORSET.

49   John GOODMAN and Joan his wife v. Edmund PAKE.
Messuages and land in Tewin, late of Roger Strete, deceased, great-grandfather of the said Joan.
                                                                                                          HERTS.

50–52   Margery late the wife of William GOODWYN, and Joan COLTER, v. John, son and heir of Robert COWLES.
Messuages and land in Framlingham (Framyngham) late of John Say, deceased, father of the said Margaret and grandfather of the said Joan.   SUFFOLK.

53–54   Valentine GOODWYNE and Margaret his wife, a daughter of John Myller of Thornham, v. Thomas PAYNE of Castleacre, supervisor of the will of the said Myller.
Messuage and closes in Titchwell, with money, sheep, and pasture therefor in Brancaster of the bequest of the said Myller, and repairs of houses.   NORFOLK.

65–58   Thomas GOUGHE of Whitchurch v. George PAYNE, gentleman.
Refusal to complete a conveyance of the farm of Innes Court in Bedminster.   *Mutilated.* SOMERSET.

59–60   Humphrey GRAUNDORGE and George HILTON v. Roman CHETTELLES.
Bond given on deft's behalf to Alexander Popham, esquire, for rent of the vicarage of Donington-in-Holland.   LINCOLN.

61–63   Roger GRAYE, gentleman, v. William WYRSDAYLE and Cuthbert BOTHE.
Compounded tithes late of the monastery of Revesby.   LINCOLN.

54   John GREBBY and Richard SHERMAN, executors of Stephen Sherman, v. Richard NICHOLLES, gentleman.
Detention of a lease of land in Walpole made by the late prioress and convent of Elstow. NORFOLK.

65–66   William GRESCROFT v. John, son and heir of Leonard BAWDRY.
Messuage and land in Leake bought of the said Leonard.   LINCOLN.

67   Robert GROVE of Donhead, gentleman, receiver of Sir Thomas Arundell's lands, v. Nicholas ENGELBERT, bailiff of Ryme.
Balance of deft's account paid for him by complainant.   WILTS, DORSET.

68–70   Richard GRUFF, son and executor of Thomas ap John ap Gethyn, v. John AYLESBURY and David BAKER.
Lands called ' Pylcoghe ' of the demise of Gruffydd ap David Lloid or of John, his son.   MONTG.

71–74   Thomas GRYFFYN, knight, and Jane, his wife, v. Henry CAPELL, knight.
Manors of Wyke (*i.e.*, Wick St. Lawrence?), Ubley (Obleyge), Stone Easton, Midsomer Norton, Angersleigh, Walton, Thornfalcon, Alston, Marres (in Weare), Aldwick (in Batcombe and Blagdon), Child Oakford, Aust, Downhatherley, Twygbarwe (*i.e.*, Twigworth?) and Cootes, and lands there, late of Richard Newton, deceased, father of the said Jane, and grandfather of deft.
                                                                                             SOMERSET, DORSET, GLOUC.

75–76   The same, described as of Braybrooke, co. Northants, v. the same and William DALE of Yatton, yeoman.
Goods of Elizabeth, late the wife of the said Richard Newton, in her house at Wyke.   SOMERSET.

77–82 John GUYNETH, parson or provost of Clenokvaure and vicar of Luton, co. Bedford, v. Robert VAGHAN, *alias* Robert ap Richard ap Robert, RETHERCH (Retheraugh) ap David, and others.
Tithes of Llanvaxlan (*i.e.*, Llanfaglan?), Llangenwyn, Llangaffo, and elsewhere. *Damaged.*
CARNARVON, ANGLESEY.

83–85 Thomas GWENTE v. James STEVYNS and others.
Land in the manor of Buckland, of the demise of the abbot and convent of St. Peter's, Gloucester, wherein defts. claim common of pasture as copyholders. D.XIV, 48. *See File* 1275, *No.* 24.
GLOUCESTER.

86–87 Richard GYBSON of Erith, gentlemen, v. Christopher LASSELLES of Breckenbrough, esquire.
Seizure of tools and deeds in a vexatious action of debt. HUNTINGDON, YORK.

88–90 Jerome GYLBERD, gentleman, v. Roger GRACE and Margaret, his wife.
Detention of deeds relating to a messuage in the parish of Holy Trinity, Colchester, which were entrusted to defts. during the late rebellion. ESSEX.

91–92 Richard, grandson and heir of John GYLMYN, v. Robert, Amy, and William GYLMYN.
Messuage and land at Bradstone in Slimbridge. *See File* 1227, *No.* 78. GLOUCESTER.

FILE 1353.

1 Edward GADRIGE v. William MARCHAUNT.
Messauges and lands at Walcombe and Penn, in Wells, held of the manor of Emborrow (Emboroughe).
SOMERSET.

2 John GARLAND of Exeter v. John FOSTER and others.
Detention of deeds relating to land (*described*) in Loders. DORSET.

3–6 George GATCHETT (Catchett) of London, yeoman, grandson and heir of Robert Gygges, v. John DAVYSON (Dawson) and William EGER.
Detention of deeds relating to closes in the county of the city of York. 2 *replications.* YORK.

7 Alexander GATE, parson of Tolleshunt Knights (Tolson Militis) v. Thomas BAKER.
Lease of the parsonage made to Jerome Songer by Edward Popley, late parson, deprived for marriage.
ESSEX.

8–9 Elizabeth GATE v. Richard CANONE.
Forgery of a will in the name of William Watkyns of Salisbury, draper, deceased, nephew of complainant. WILTS.

10–11 Osmund GAY and Margaret his wife, late the wife of John Fynche of Milton by Sittingbourne, v. Christopher ROPER, esquire, guardian of Harry Fynche, deceased, eldest son of the said John.
Rent due for quitting the said John's house called ' Groveherst.' KENT.

12–13 William GAYER of Marazion v. Thomas HENRY of Rescrowe.
Action on a bond for a debt of John Arundell of Lanham, knight, partly paid in tin. CORNWALL.

14 Thomas GEORGE, husbandman, son of Thomas George, deceased, and of Anne Tuersley, his wife, v. John SMITHE of Godalming, clothier, his guardian to whom he was formerly apprenticed.
Farm called Tuesley (Tuersley) with land, rent of a mill, etc., in Godalming and elsewhere, whereof defendant has extorted a lease, and obtained a conveyance by colour of a marriage settlement on his daughter. SURREY.

15–17 John GILBERT of Ashford, yeoman, and Avice, his wife, v. Thomas and William GYBBON.
Land in Bethersden, late of James Gybbon, deceased, uncle of the said Avice, defendants being administrators of his will. KENT.

18–20 John GLANFELDE (Glawyn), husbandman, v. William STRECHELEYE.
Tenements in the manor of Jacobstowe of the demise of Francis Stretcheleye, esquire, deceased, father of defendant. D. XIII, 16. DEVON.

21 Nicholas GLYN, gentleman, v. Elizabeth TALCARNE.
Plate (*described*) acquired under a statute merchant executed by John Talcarne, esquire, to warrant the manor of Treire in St. Eval (Treyer). CORNWALL.

22–25 John, great-grandson and heir of Robert GOCHE of Bacton (Bawton), v. William GOODRICKE and Elizabeth, his wife, daughter of William Dobbs, deceased.
Detention of deeds relating to a messuage and land in Wetherden and Wyverstone. 2 *suits.*
SUFFOLK.

26–28 John GODOLGHAN (Godolphyn) of Gwennap, v. John PENPOLL.
Removal of 200 ' semes of sender otherwise called pyllyan ' from complainant's blowing-house at Pensingnans. CORNWALL.

29–32 Valentine GODWYNE and Margaret, his wife, v. Robert WYND and Richard ROBYNS, executors of John Wynd.
Under-lease by John Myller, deceased, father of the said Margaret, of the manor of Brancaster with fold-courses, on condition that she should have a certain number of sheep feeding thereon. *Damaged.*
NORFOLK.

33–39   George GOLSTON of Mamhead, co. Devon, grandson of Piers Golston of Coton, gentleman, deceased, *v.* Edward, son and heir of Thomas SPROTT (Spratt), Edward FRYTHE, William FREMAN, and others.
Lands in Lichfield, Shenstone and elsewhere. (2 answers by Freman are included). *Faded.*
STAFFORD.

40–43   Richard, son of Thomas GOODHANDE, deceased, *v.* Robert APRICE and Miles FOREST, esquires.
Lease from defendants of the manor of Aswick in Whaplode.   LINCOLN.

44   Ralph GOODWYN, executor of Christopher Haward, *v.* Richard FULMERSTON.
Messuage called New Place and land in Ipswich and Stoke of the demise of Andrew Sy[l]yarde, Mary his wife, and others. *Mutilated.·*   SUFFOLK.

45   William GOODWYN *v.* Clement CLERKE.
Rent of land in Bocking, formerly of John Thurkell.   ESSEX.

46–47   Davye. GOUGHE of London, gentleman, *v.* Joan SPENCER and others.
Lease from the dean and chapter of Christ Church, Oxford, of the rectories of **Myfod**, [Welsh]pool, and Guilsfield, in reversion, after a former Crown lease.   MONTG.

48   John GRANEWE of Hoxne, grandson and heir of Robert Thruston, *v.* Edmund PYGOTT.
Detention of deeds relating to a messuage and land in Osmondiston.   NORFOLK.

49   Richard GRAY *v.* Richard JONSONE of Gringley (Grinlie), husbandman.
Failure to repay two ' old rialls ' of gold and to deliver a purchase of barley.   NOTTS.

50   ————, son and heir of Thomas GRAYE and of Alice, his wife, *v.* Thomas BRADLEY, and William FITZWILLIAMS, knight.
Tenement in Theydon Garnon (Garneys) late of William Fowche of Epping, deceased, father of the said Agnes. *Faded.*   ESSEX.

51   Thomas de GRAYE, clerk, *v.* Christopher COOTE, esquire.
Debt of defendant and of Lady Anne Knyvett, his wife. *Mutilated.*

52   John GREATRAKES *v.* Thomas DAKYN of Ible and Christopher·HOULSTON of Ivonbrook (Inbroke) Mill.
Seizure from complainant's house of Grange Mill, in Ible, of goods and deeds entrusted to him.
DERBY.

53–55   John GRENE of Tunstall, husbandman, *v.* John SAYER of Knighton.
Loan.   STAFFORD.

56   Robert GRENE of London, haberdasher, and Luce, his wife, executrix and late the wife of Roger Lloyd, citizen and merchant tailor of London, *v.* DAVID ap Howell of Llanddewi-brefi.
Debt the bond for which is lost.   LONDON, CARMARTHEN.

57–58   John GRENEHYLL (Gyrnehyll) *v.* Cuthbert, nephew and heir of William PATENSON.
Messuage, cottage, and land in Watford, late of Agnes Patenson, late the wife of the said William.
D.. XI, 8.   HERTS.

59–62   Robert GRENLYNGE of Fressingfield *v.* Richard·GRENLYNGE.
Manor of Shelton Hall in Stradbroke, demised by Anthony Wyngfeld, knight, to defendant and Robert, his brother, since deceased, father of complainant.   SUFFOLK.

63–64   Agnes GREY of Kenilworth, late the wife of Lawrence Grey, *v.* Richard KNYVETT, esquire.
Forcible ouster from the parsonage of Radford, in contempt of a judgment of the King's Bench
WARWICK.

65   James GREYNE of Lincoln's Inn, gentleman, *v.* Richard BULLMER of Northallerton, merchant.
Money paid on defendant's behalf to Christopher Andderton of Thavies Inn, gentleman.
MIDDLESEX, YORK.

66–69   Jan (*sic*) GROVE (Agrove) *v.* John TEMPULLMAN.
Close in Woolsthorpe, late of William Grove, deceased, father of complainant.   LINCOLN.

70–73   William GUYE (Quye) of Canewden, co. Essex, labourer, *v.* John THURGER of the same, husbandman.
Messuage and land in Abynton Magna, late of Agnes Quye, grandmother of complainant who claims to be her heir in borough-English   ESSEX (*rectius* CAMBRIDGE).

74–75   Robert GYGNERE of Isleham, co. Cambridge, *v.* Thomas STUTEVILE (Stutfylde), esquire.
Land in Worlington (Wudlyngton), late of James Gygnere, deceased, father of complainant.
SUFFOLK.

76–78   Walter GYLL *v.* Adam BONVILE and Joan, his wife, daughter and heir of John Scose.
Messuage and land in Loddiswell of the demise of the said Scose.   DEVON.

79–81   Robert GYRLYNGTON *v.* Denise PLOMPTON and William WOODROFF, executors of Isabel Plumpton, of Plumpton, co. York.
Rent charged by the said Isabel on the manor of Sacombe.   HERTS.

FILE 1354.

1   John GALLANT and Joan his wife, executrix of Nicholas Walpole, clerk, *v.* Nicholas LOWTHE.
Failure to repay a loan and detention of deeds.   [NORFOLK?]

2   Richard GALLEY *v.* William BUCKLEY, both of Beaumaris, merchants.
Frivolous suit and slander arising out of the adultery of Margaret, wife of complainant and step-daughter of deft. *Damaged.*   ANGLESEY.

3–5   John GANTENNY *v.* John and Grace WARRE and John MORE.
Meadow in Pixton (in Dulverton)   SOMERSET.

6   William GASCOY[GNE] of Cusworth, knight, *v.* William WYNTRYNGHAM of Whytley.
House belonging to the chantry of Daryngton, late of William Keen.   [YORK].

7–9   Peter GATE *v.* Germyn SHREYFFE (Sheryffe) and John GODFREY, administrators
of the goods of William Campbell, deceased.
Loan of horses and of 'tenne poundes in golde, that is to saye tenne angel nobles and tenne half
suffrens.'   NORFOLK.

10   John GAYNSFORDE, gentleman,
Commission to examine witnesses (including Lord Grey of Wilton) as to the genuineness of a
surrender by Nicholas, his brother, of a lease of the manor of Great Brickhill and lands there.
BUCKINGHAM.

11   Richard GAYWODE of London, salter, *v.* . . . . . ., yeoman.
Land called ' Kenlamore' late of Richard Hardyng and John . . . *Damaged.*   MIDDLESEX.

12–15   John GEFFEREYS and others, inhabitants of the manor of Bloxham, *v.* Richard FYNES,
esquire, lord thereof.
Extortion of 'excessive fines, and other restrictions of tenancy contrary to custom. *Damaged.*
D. XIV, 8.   OXFORD.

16–17   Thomas GEMNAN of Mardon and Richard SYMONS (Symond) of Fittleworth, yeomen,
and Thomas BROWN, *v.* George FOWLER of Harting, yeoman.
Money payable by deft. on marriage with Alice, executrix and late the wife of Edward Brown of
Littleworth, tanner, deceased, father of the said Thomas   SUSSEX.

18–19   The same and Richard BROWN, another son of the said Edward, *v.* the same.
Do. the two first-named complainants being supervisors of the will of the
said Edward.   SUSSEX.

20–21   Gilbert GERRARDE and others, executors of Nicholas Hussey, *v.* Richard BONES (Bonnes,
Boones).
Debt.   LINCOLN.

22–26   William GERVYS *v.* [John] FYTZJAMES, archdeacon of Taunton, and Richard FYTZ-
JAMES.
Lease of a mill and pasture in Wells of the bequest of Thomas Clerke, esquire. *Will recited.*
SOMERSET.

27   Thomas GETHYN, parson of Northop, *v.* John SALISBURY, knight.
Parsonage of Northop, demised to deft. by William Parfoy, late parson, deprived for marriage.
Damaged.   [FLINT].

28–30   George GILLE *v.* John CHAPMAN.
Fold-courses in Babraham belonging to a tenement called the *Lamb* and to lands late of the monastery
of Sawtrey.   CAMBRIDGE.

31–33   Robert GLASYER of Petersfield *v.* John ROCHE of East Meon.
Refusal of acquittance for instalment of a debt.   HANTS.

34–35   John GLOVER of Wheatley *v.* William GLOVER and John STORRES.
Messuages, cottages and land in Langford (*i.e.* Glanford ?) Brygg.   LINCOLN.

36–37   Robert GODARDE *v.* William SHIPTON.
Action for price of corn growing in Brampton, partly paid for and less in quantity than represented.
HUNTINGDON.

38–39   William GODBERE and Alice, his wife, late the wife of Thomas Whyte and administratrix
of his goods, *v.* Richard CHANON and others.
Detention of deeds relating to tithe corn in ' Fluxton Mowe' in Ottery St. Mary of the demise
of the college of Ottery St. Mary.   DEVON.

40–42   Richard GODDYNG and Katherine his wife *v.* John DODDE, husbandman, and John, his
son.
Windmill and land in Burnham and Puriton late of John London, deceased, father of the said
Katherine and of Cristyan, wife of the said John Dodde the elder.   SOMERSET.

43   Richard GODFREY of Colchester, beer-brewer, *v.* Benjamin CLERE, surviving executor
of John Steven of Colchester, beer-brewer.
Price of malt and hops, and joint purchase of wood in Boxted.   ESSEX.

44   James GODOLPHYN, esquire, and Mary, his wife, late the wife of John Luttrele, knight, *v.*
Robert OPY.
Detention of household goods and of deeds relating to the manor, borough, and castle of Dunster,
and of messuages and land there.   SOMERSET.

45   Thomas GODYNG *v.* the bailiffs of IPSWICH.
Action by Robert Barker on a bond given on behalf of William Buckname of Ipswich, merchant.
Certiorari.   SUFFOLK.

46–47   Edmund GOLAND *v.* Henry, son and heir of Thomas JOHNSON, knight.
Wrongful distress on two-thirds of the manor of Stainbrough Lowe, and messuages and land in Stainbrough (Deft., being tenant of the other third, states that the said Sir Thomas was also seized of lands
in Linton, Grimston, and Worsborough). *Damaged.* D. XIII, 63.   YORK.

48–49   Thomas GOLDESTONE and Anne, his wife, late the wife of John Caynho, *v.* Richard
BEDELL.
Messuage and land in Leighton Bromswold of the entail of John Dykons, father to the said Anne.
HUNTINGDON.

50–52   Robert GOLDYNGE v. John BARLEY, his father-in-law.
Tenement in Luton, pledged to deft., by whom it was purchased for complainant and partly paid for.   DEVON.

53–54   Anthony GONBYE, gentleman, v. Robert HILL, executor of John Hyll, clerk.
Silver-gilt cup entrusted to the said John.   ——

55   John GOODALE v. John GODDERD, gentleman, and William GENT.
Messuage and land in Shipton Sollers, Shipton Oliffe, Brockhampton, Compton, and Sevenhampton, held of the manor of Shipton Sollers.   GLOUCESTER.

56–57   William GOODDYNGE (Gowdyng) v. William SPRYE and Thomas (Robert) FORDE.
Rent of a messuage and land in Whitchurch, late of Thomas Dennys, knight.   DEVON.

58–63   John GOODLADE v. Nicholas RECHERDSON (Richardson), Edward KYRBY and John COPLEDIKE.
House and land in the manor of Ross in Holderness.   YORK.

64–65   George GOODMAN, husbandman, for himself and all the inhabitants of West Laughton, v. William COWPER and John GOTCHE.
Seizure of a chalice and of deeds relating to a house and lands in East and West Laughton and Bowden Magna, whereof a proportion of the issues should be used for repair of the highway, in West Laughton.   LEICESTER.

66–68   Mary GOODRIKE v. Richard GOODRICK of London, her divorced husband.
Intermarriage with Dorothy, late the wife of George Blage, knight, and detention of complainant's lands and goods. 2 answers, both pleading that the matter is determinable in the ecclesiastical court.
                                                                                 LONDON.

69–70   William GOODWYNE and Elizabeth his wife, late the wife of John Peirce, v. John PEIRSE, son of the said John.
Annuity of the bequest of the said John the father.   SUFFOLK.

71   William GOSEMAN v. George KENNEY (Kynney).
Refusal to complete a lease of a tenement in the parish of Kennyngham (i.e. Kenninghall?).
Mutilated.   NORFOLK.

72–73   Richard GRATWYCK of Cowfold, yeoman, v. Joan, executrix and late the wife of William LEDBETTER, kinsman and executor of William Ledbetter.
Lease of lands in West Grinstead promised in exchange for the farm of Washington.   SUSSEX.

74–75   John GRAVELL (Greavell) v. William BUTTON of Alton, co. Wilts, esquire, son and heir of William Button.
Messuage and land at English Batch in Englishcombe of the grant of John Husey, knight.
                                                                                 SOMERSET.

76–77   Thomas GREGGE and others, for themselves and all the inhabitants of Gonerby, v. Thomas KNOTTE, alias Roper.
Land in Gonerby, now the site of a common hall etc., granted by Agnes Pykard for payments to the curate in Lent, and for repair of the church. See File 1355, No. 45.   LINCOLN.

78–79   John GRENE v. John (sic) his younger brother.
Land, in Great Maplestead, late of Thomas Grene, deceased, father of both parties.   ESSEX.

80   John GRENE and others of Allensmore and Thruxton, yeomen, v. Gwilliam John PHELIPE of Llanigon, husbandman.
Cattle entrusted to deft. to pasture.   HEREFORD, BRECON.

81–83   John GRENE and Margaret, his wife, a daughter of John Pooyd, deceased, v. Agnes, executrix and late the wife of John PO(O)DE.
Land in North Somercotes of the demise of the gild of Our Lady there.   LINCOLN.

84   Edward GREVILL, knight, son and heir of John Grevill, knight, v. Thomas PARTYNGTON, knight.
Detention of deeds relating to the manor of Crendon, late of Edward Grevill, knight, deceased.
                                                                                 BUCKINGHAM.

85   The same, son and heir of Thomas Grevill, v. Stephen HALES.
Detention of deeds relating to a messuage and land called Cranwelles.   BUCKINGHAM.

86   John GRIFF of Newport, co. Gloucester, son and heir of John Griff, v. Charles HARBERT, knight.
Detention of deeds relating to messuages and lands in Monmouth.   MONMOUTH.

87   John GRIFF, parson of Burton, v. John PEROTT.
Lease of the parsonage by John Battie (?), late parson, deprived for marriage. Fdded.
                                                                                 PEMBROKE.

88–89   Robert GRONE (Grono), clerk, v. Thomas JOHNS, clerk.
Parsonage of Eglowsell (now Llangadwaladr).   ANGLESEY.

90–91   The same v. the same and Reynold and Richard MERycKE.   ANGLESEY.

92–93   William and Mary, children of Robert GROVE, deceased, v. Richard DADE.
Joint purchase by the said Robert and Richard of lands in the manor of Donhead.   WILTS.

94   Foulke GRYFFITH of London, yeoman, v. Richard PYGGOTTE.
Gelding of the bequest of Evan ap David ap Price of Llanufydd, gentleman.   DENBIGH.

95–96   James GRYFFITH ap Powell v. David MORTIMER (Mormare), son-in-law of Richard Gryffyth ap Res, and HENRY ap Powell.
Messuage and land at Cilfwyr in Manordeifi (Kilvoyer) late of Thomas ap Price ap Weskyn (the said Mortimer describes complainant as ruler of the country).   PEMBROKE.

97-102 Thomas GRYGGES of Rye and Alice his wife, granddaughter and heir of Richard Allen,
      v. Thomas (William) son of Thomas CHEYNE, and Constance, late the wife of the latter.
Detention of deeds relating to a messuage and land in Warbleton.   SUSSEX.

103 James GUNTER of Mounckton, co. Monmouth, esquire, *v.* James BOYLE, gentleman.
Part price of the grange of Aberdehoneth, late of the abbey of Dore, and bought of the Crown to
deft's use.   HEREFORD.

104 Anthony GURNEY, esquire, *v.* Thomas GRANGER, clerk.
Refusal to complete a sale of the reversion of the manor of Bury Hall in Great Ellingham after the
death of Elizabeth, late the wife of complainant.   NORFOLK.

105 William GYBBES *v.* Richard TRYPPER.
Loan by Katherine Robertes of North Nibley, whose executor complainant is.
      GLOUCESTER.

106-108 John and William, sons of John GYBBYNS, deceased, *v.* Andrew WEKES, gentleman
Tenements in the manor of Easter Nynehead promised to complainants by William Wykes, brother
of deft.   SOMERSET.

109-110 Richard GYLL and Agnes, his wife, late the wife of Matthew Hynde, gentleman, and formerly
      of Edmund Lee, *v.* Francis, son and heir of John HYNDE, knight, J.C.P.
Messuage, lands, rents, and services in Swaffham Prior held by the said Lee, together with lands
in Swaffham, Bulbeck, Reach and Bottisham. *Mutilated.*   CAMBRIDGE.

FILE 1355.

1-4 James GARDEN, yeoman, *v.* the mayor of CHICHESTER, and Bryan BANCKES.
Action on a bond for a debt already paid. *Corpus cum causa and subpœna.*   SUSSEX.

5 Thomas, son of Henry GARDENER, deceased, *v.* William HOWE.
Messuage and land in Tiffield of the demise of the hospital of St. John the Baptist, Northampton.
      N'HAMP.

6 Richard GARDYNER, husbandman, *v.* William WALGRAVE, gentleman.
Forcible ouster from lands in Brent Pelham, because complainant's wife had testified in the spiritual
court to the misconduct of defendant's wife. *See File* 1283, *No.* 2.   HERTS.

7-10 Stephen GARRET and Mary, his wife, executrix of Christopher Wryght, *v.* Thomas OFFLEY
      and William HEWETT, late sheriffs of London.
False return to a *fieri facias* for a debt of Robert Wryght, whose executor the said Christopher was.
Faded. (Annexed is an answer of defendants and Guy Wade to a bill of the same complainants.)
      LONDON.

11 Thomas GATWARD *v.* Richard RAMSEY.
Reversion of marsh in . . .che, late of Spinney priory. *Faded.*   CAMBRIDGE, SUFFOLK.

12-14 John GAWSYM (Gawson) of Westminster, nephew and heir of John Gawsym, *v.* Richard
      WATKYNS and Thomas GOLUP (Gallope).
Manor of East Axnoller (in Beaminster) and lands there and in Beaminster, Pickett (in South
Perrott), Langford (in Stratton ?), Demelpole, Wykwyldlond (*i.e.* Wyke in Halstock), and West
Corscombe. *See* D. IX. 70.   DORSET.

15-19 Richard GAYE *v.* Thomas FLOREY (Flowre).
Messuage, curtilage and garden in Poole, late of Matthew Tyler, deceased, grandfather of complainant.   DORSET.

20 William GEFFREY, chancellor of Salisbury, *v.* John HAMME.
Messuage and land under the castle of Old Sarum, generally given by the bishop to the Chancellor
' for his paynes and dylygence in the correction in the bookes within the said churche.' *Mutilated.*
      WILTS.

21 John GEST *v.* Christopher SKOT and John THWAYT.
Messuage and land in Bydell (*i.e.* Bedale ?).   YORK.

22-24 Bryan GODFREY and William LOVELACKE *v.* the sheriffs of London, and Thomas GORE.
Action of debt in contempt of an order in bankruptcy. *Certiorari and subpœna.*   LONDON.

25 Thomas GODYER of Topsham, merchant, *v.* William PETHERYCK.
Part price of a butt of sack.   DEVON.

26 Thomas GOODKNAPP *v.* James CARTER of Aylesby, yeoman, and Edward MADESON,
      knight.
Messuage, cottages, and land in Ulceby by Thornton-Curtis, entailed by William Goodknapp of
Kingston-upon-Hull, merchant, uncle of complainant.   LINCOLN.

27-28 The same *v.* Andrew CARTER.
Surplus issues of the premises assigned in payment of a debt to the said Sir Edward.   LINCOLN.

29-30 Richard, son of Edward GOODWYN, deceased, *v.* John TURNER and others.
Goods of the said Edward, whereof complainant is administrator. (Defendants plead that complainant's father is John Goodwyn, still living.)   STAFFORD.

31-34 William, son and heir of Richard GOUGHE *v.* Richard THOMAS.
Lands in the parish of Berkeley and manor of Hampton. (Defendant pleads that complainant is a
minor in his ward.)   GLOUC.

35-37 John GOUGHE and Joan, his wife, *v.* Robert HYCH, gentleman, and others.
Price of a lease of the *Crown* inn and land at Glastonbury sold to Robert Wardford.   SOMERS.

38   William GRAUNT and Mary, his wife, v. William, son and heir of William BAYLIEF (Bayllye) of Keevil, gentleman.
Tenement in the manor of Winkfield promised to complainants on their marriage.   WILTS.

39   John GRAVESEND v. Francis SHERLEY and Richard ELRYNGTON, esquires.
Land in Wiston, late of Peter Bulloker, gentleman.   SUSSEX.

40–42   Roger GREAVES v. Stephen and William PYE.
Refusal of charges of Carlton ferry across the Trent.   NOTTS.

43–44   Hugh GREFFITH, prebendary of Westminster, v. Richard SHELLEY, esquire.
Messuage in Westminster belonging to complainant's prebend.   MIDDX.

45   Thomas GREG and others, for themselves and all the inhabitants of Gonerby, v. Thomas KNOTT alias Roper.
Land in Gonerby bequeathed to the inhabitants before the memory of man by Thomas Dymock, knight. See Files 1503, Nos. 9–10, 1354, No. 76.   LINCOLN.

46   Thomas GRESWOLD and Richard his son v. Richard SERJAUNT.
Detention and threatened destruction of deeds relating to lands in King's Norton and elsewhere, late of Marion Fitter, deceased, aunt of Alice, mother of the said Richard Greswold. WORC., WARW.

47–49   Henry GRETE v. William, younger son of John CROTON and of Joan Grete, his wife.
Detention of deeds relating to a messuage and land in Midhurst. See File 1372, No. 37. SUSSEX.

50   GRIFFITH ap Thomas v. Henry ADAME and others.
Loan.   PEMBROKE.

51   GRIFFITH ap Rise v. RISE ap Griffith ap Judithe and others.
Messuage and land in Gwyddelwern, late of Griffith ap David, deceased, grandfather of complainant.
        MERIONETH.

52   GRIFFITH ap James v. WILLIAM ap Rice and others.
Messuage and land in St. Dogmells.   PEMBROKE.

53–54   James GRIFFITHE ap Hoell, esquire, v. GRIFFITH ap Hoell and Jenckyn SWELLIN alias Griffeth.
Reviver of a suit against Swellin ap Griffeth for goods which complainant could not formerly, specify.   ———

55–57   Margaret GRIGBYE of Mersham, grand-daughter and heir of John Brode, gentleman, v. John IPPYNGBURY.
Messuage, garden and orchard in Maidstone to which defendant lays a claim through Henry Wyatt, knight.   KENT.

58–60   Thomas GROVE, Joan, his wife, William WYCHE, Agnes, his wife, and Katherine HARRYSON v. William MAWDESBY (Mawdesley).
Messuage and land in Langley Marish formerly of Giles Squier, deceased, grandfather of defendant and of the femals complainants. D. X. 67.   BUCKS.

61   GRUFFYDD ap Jevan ap Gyttyn v. ANNE verch Llewellyn.
Messuages and land in Teremynyth (i.e. Tir-y-mynach in Llanbrynmair) of the grant of David ap Owen, sometime abbot of Ystrad Marchell.   MONTG.

62–64   Lewis GRYFFETH of Bury St. Edmunds, in Suffolk, v. Anthony WEKES.
Procuring complainant's arrest at Salisbury, extortion of a bond by a promise of obtaining his trial, and plunder of his house at Salisbury.   WILTS.

65   James GRYFFYTH ap Hoell of London, esquire, v. Jenkyn DAVID ap David.
Tithes and oblations of the parsonage (sic) of Ystrad collected for complainant during his absence abroad.   CARDIGAN.

66–69   Thomas Wylliams GRYFFYTH ap Gwylym v. Res GRYFFYTH, knight, and JOHN ap Gwylym.
Land in Tremadoc in the commot of Isgorfai claimed under rival leases from the said Sir Res, and from Edward his brother.   CAERNARVON.

70–75   William GRYMSTON, John WEBBE, and Anne, his wife, v. Sibell GRYMSTON, William MOGERIGE and William AYRE of Salisbury, merchant.
Rent in Kensham (i.e. Kingsholme?) late of William Grymston of Salisbury, deceased, father of the complainants William and Anne, and husband of the said Sibell.   GLOUC.

76   David ap Evan GWYNNE v. HOWELL ap David Appowell and MORRIS ap Evan ap David.
Lands in the parishes of Treyservante and Trescobe, late of Katherine Gryffyth, alias Heyre, deceased, mother of complainant.   MONTG.

77–80   William GYE (Guy), parson of Woodchurch, v. Humphrey CLARKE, gentleman.
Tithes of corn and a chamber in the parsonage of the demise of Thomas Courthop, late parson, deceased, who was married.   KENT.

81   Jerome GYLBERT of Colchester v. George ROBERTES of the same, shereman.
Debt, complainant being unable to compel his witnesses to give evidence.   ESSEX.

82   William, son and heir of Paul GYLLOUR (Gylliour) v. William GYLMYN.
Detention of deeds relating to a messuage in Coney Street, York.   YORK.

83   John GYON v. Thomas and John POLGLASE.
Cattle. Fragment.   [CORNW.

FILE 1356.

1   Richard HADDON v. Anne ARMORER and Roger YONGE her son.
Closes of pasture in Hoxton of the demise of William Clyff, prebendary of Hoxton in St. Paul's Cathedral.   MIDDLESEX.

2–4   Robert HAKYN (Hacon) and Agnes his wife, late the wife of John Hummes, v. Harry LEGAT and John BAXTER.
Joint tenancy of the manor of Cransford.   SUFFOLK.

5   The same v. the same, John GARNICHE and Nicholas GODBOLD.
Do.   SUFFOLK.

6–12   Elizabeth, late the wife of William HALL of Bradford, esquire and George, Nicholas, Paul, and William HALL his sons v. Thomas HALL gentleman, his eldest son.
Execution of the will of the deceased including annuities payable out of messuages and land in West Lavington and Trowle (in Trowbridge or Bradford-on-Avon). *3 answers, one in duplicate.*   WILTS.

13–16   Randall HALL v. John BLITHE, doctor of physic.
Detention of a lease of the parsonage of Horningsay drawn by William Blyth, late master of St. John's College, Cambridge, but not confirmed by the fellows.   [CAMBRIDGE.]

17–19   The same v. Richard KYRKELYE, gentleman.
Entail of one-third of the manor of Landbeach promised on complainant's marriage with Margaret daughter of defendant. *2 answers, one not headed.*   CAMBRIDGE.

20   Thomas HAMLEN and Joan his wife, late the wife of John Smythe, v. Hugh EVANS and others.
One-fourth of ' Frith called the Mayne ' in the town and parish of Sowre (*i.e.* Sourton?) of the demise of William Courteney, knight, since deceased.   DEVON.

21   The same v. Richard FAYERWETHER and others.
Do.   DEVON.

22–23   Robert HARECOURT of Ronton, esquire v. Thomas BOLTE, executor of John ap Harry, clerk, LL.D.
Detention of a bond for a debt already paid, and of a gelding and a ring given to the said John.   STAFFORD.

24   Christopher HARRYS v. Agnes and John HARRYS.
Half a ' tack ' of land (*place not given*).   NORTHUMBERLAND.

25   John HARRYS, gentleman, on behalf of all the inhabitants of Liskeard, v. John CONNOK and others.
Messuages and lands called feoffees' lands belonging to the church of Liskeard.   CORNWALL.

26–27   George HARRYSON v. Thomas WYLSON.
Land and marsh in Dunwich bought of the executors of John Nulsforde.   SUFFOLK.

28–30   Adam HARTE v. Thomas ADAMS and Margaret his wife, executrix and late the wife of Thomas Sporlyng.
Land in Walpole.   NORFOLK.

31   Roger HATCHMAN, gentleman, v. George PENNY.
Action at the common law for a messuage and land in Bensington and Warborough (Pensyngton and Woborugh) awarded to complainant by this court (*see File* 1179, *No.* 1).   OXFORD.

32–33   Edmund HOWELL of Willand, weaver, v. John RO(O)DE and others.
Messuages and land in Sampford Peverell late of Thomas Howell, deceased, grandfather of complainant.   DEVON.

34–38   William HAWELES (Hawlles) of Smallbrook (in Newchurch), gentleman, grandson and heir of Robert Haweles, v. Margaret and William HOLLYS.
Land in Brading pledged to William Dameles, deceased, grandfather of the said William Hollys.   HANTS (I.W.).

39–40   James HAYDOCKE, gentleman, and Margaret (Margett) his wife v. Percival SMALPAGE, gentleman, and Agnes his wife.
Money and reversion of a house and garden in Bartholomew Close lands called Rowney lands, the farm of Sacombe Bury and the manors of Higham and Lilychurch, all of the bequest of Thomas Byll, physician to King Edward VI, and father of the said Margaret and husband of the said Agnes. *Damaged.*   LONDON, HERTS, [KENT].

41   James HEBYLTHWAYTE, clerk to Henry Judd, one of the Six Clerks, v. William, CALVERD and others.
Rents of lands in Caldbridge late of the monastery of Coverham.   YORK.

42–43   Nicholas, youngest son and heir of Roger HENNE, v. John ERDISWYKE (Erswyke), gentleman, and Hugh WHELOK.
Messuages, garden, and curtilages in Stafford held in borough-English.   STAFFORD.

44–45   John HERBERT, Jane his wife, late the wife of Lord [Grey of] Powis, and Edward GREY. son of the latter, v. Thomas and Richard VERNON, David LLOYDE ap Edward and others.
Castle and borough of Welshpool and Llanvylling (in Mechain) ; manors of Teirtre (in Butlington and Welshpool), Ystrad Marchell (in Welshpool), Caereinion, Mechain Uwchcoed, Mechain Iscoed and De . . . . , granges of Stirchley (Strytcheley), Crow Meole (Corneyll) Monk Meole (Mounkneyll,) and Bicton, rent in Andover, tithes of Hatton, the site of the monastery of Buildwas, and messuages, cottages, and lands in Garthbowar(?), Llanfair (Caereinion?), Llangyniew, Castell Caereinion, Llanfihangel, Llanullynge (*i.e.* Llanfyllin ?), Llanfechan, Llansaintffraid, Llanwddyn, Pennant, Hirnant,

Llangynog, Llanerchudal, Llanrhaiadr, C[har]leton, Pontesbury, Uppington, Deeping, Gosford, Ra . . ey, Ruyton, Lythe, Albrighton, Upton, Shrewsbury, Addreynton (?), Raydon (in Hope Bowdler), Bridgnorth, Buildwas, Longdon and Tyerne (sic), Brockton, Ulvere, Walton, and elsewhere. *Much damaged.* MONTGOMERY, SALOP, HANTS, YORK, DERBY, STAFFORD.

46–54 Richard HERYNGE, husbandman, v. Richard and Thomas COKKES, John GARDYNER, Robert WREXHAM, and Thomas ARNOLDE.
Land in Wanborough late of William Herynge, deceased, grandfather of complainant. (Defts. plead a joint tenancy.) WILTS.

55–57 Alexander HODGES v. Michael COLLES and John YOUNGE.
Loan to John Hembreye of Pawlete, deceased, of whose goods defts. are administrators. [SOMERSET.]

58–60 Thomas HOLDEN, administrator of the goods of Katherine his mother, v. Henry FYSSHER and others.
Goods of the said Katherine in the parish of St. Dionis Backchurch (' Seynt Dennys in Lymestrete '), which defendants declare they were appointed by the Lord Mayor to divide between complainant and his brother and sisters. *Replication wanting.* LONDON.

61 Richard HORDE of London, gentleman, v. William NORTHE of the same, bricklayer (John Roo).
Refusal to accept a demise of a messuage and land in Osmaston, which complainant is under bonds to make. (LEIC.)

62 Paul HOUGH and Wilmote his wife v. John WHITE, father of the latter.
Land of the demise of Reginald Pole at Knolle in the manor of Braunton Deane. DEVON.

63–66 John HUETT v. Richard POYNES.
Land at Yearnor in Porlock late of John Luttye and Joan his wife, grandparents of both parties, and manor of Marsh and ' bargaynes ' and gardens in Dunster late of Robert Luttie, [son] of the said John. *Damaged.* SOMERSET.

67 Roger HUGH and Joan his wife, daughter and heir of Philip Soper, v. John PARKER of North Molton, Esquire.
Distress of cattle at Broad Clist, which complainants cannot replevy because they do not know where they are. DEVON.

68–69 Richard HUNT v. Thomas MATYN (Matton) and Thomas his son.
Tithe corn of Compton Bremmer in Enford promised to complainant on his marriage with Elizabeth niece of the said Thomas the elder. WILTS.

70 Thomas HUXLEY, clerk, v. Maude late the wife of Richard HUXLEY.
Cattle and household goods entrusted to the said Richard.

71 John, grandson and heir of Walter HYCHEMAN of Kempsford, co. Gloucester, v. Jane STEVYNS and others.
Toft in Upper Inglesham. BERKS.

72 John HYDLEY of Halesowen, yeoman, v. Walter JONES and Agnes his wife.
Messuages in Catshill (in Bromsgrove). *See Files* 1234, *No.* 45 ; 1238, *No.* 47. WORCESTER.

73–75 Richard HYLL, husband of Joan late the wife of Thomas Samwell, v. Thomas FYLDE yeoman.
Refusal to complete a sale of half a burgage in Stratford-on-Avon being part of a tenement called *Chobson's Inne.* WARWICK.

FILE 1357.

1 Thomas HACHEMAN, yeoman, and John WADE, husbandman, v. Owen GWYN.
· Action on a bond for the appearance in London of Richard Lane of Gussage All Saints, to discuss the title to the demesne lands of Burton. D. XII, 35. DORSET.

2–4 William HACKWYLL of Torrington, clothier, v. Richard DAVYE, [one of the town councillors of Torrington ?]
Refusal to concur in a lease of a house in the High Street of Torrington given to the town by Roger Vysicke. DEVON.

5–6 Dorothy, late the wife of John HALES, and daughter of William Carrant, knight, v. George, son of Thomas SPEAKE, knight, deceased, and administrator of his goods, and William CHIPETT *alias* Samson.
Action on a bond detained by the said Chipett, and given by him and complainant on behalf of the said Sir William. [SOMERSET ?]

7–8 Robert HALL v. Henry THOMSON of Gargrave.
Money entrusted to defendant. YORK.

9–10 John HAMOND *alias* Barker of Coddenham v. Edmund GOSNOLD of the same.
Closes in Hemingstone (Hemston) and Barham of the demise of Robert Letten, knight. SUFFOLK.

11–12 Robert HAMOND of Hampton, gentleman, v. Joan, executrix and late the wife of Aldred FYTZJAMES, gentleman.
Price of beer. MIDDLESEX.

13 William HAMOUNDE, clerk v. John HUTCHINS of Wiveliscombe.
Deeds entrusted to defendant, including a bond by Thomas Cappes, esquire, and Richard Fitzjames, gentleman. SOMERSET.

14-15   William HAMPTON v. Robert MYDDELMORE and Marjory his wife, late the wife of James Leveson.

Claim of dower in a messuage called Watling Street Grange and land in . . . ylsull, said to have been satisfied in the said Leveson's will. *Mutilated.*   STAFFORD.

16   Thomas HANCOCKES *alias* Boycote v. Richard HYGON and Thomas WYLCOX.

Messuages and land in Boycote late of Thomas Hancockes *alias* Boycote, deceased, father of complainant.   SALOP.

17-22   Richard HARBERT and Joan his wife, late the wife of Thomas Davys of Hampton, in Gloucester, v. William WYGSTON, knight.

Lands in Shortley, Stoke and Atherstone-on-Stour. D. XII, 28.   WARWICK.

23   John HARPER v. Thomas GEATOUR and William HADDON esquire.

Lease of a barn and land in Cobham for which the said Haddon has been paid. [KENT *or* SURREY.]

24-28   William HARRISON (Henryson) v. Robert CHALONER.

Messuage and land in Wakefield of the entail of Oliver Fowler, grandfather of complainant. *Damaged.*   YORK.

29-31.   Edward HARRYSON v. Ralph HARRYSON.

Messuages and land in Bakewell late of Thomas Harryson, deceased grandfather of both parties.   DERBY.

32   John HARRYSON v. William DALLANS and Alice his wife, executrix of William Harcastell.

Price of oil supplied to John Harcastell of Boston, deceased, father of the said William.   LINCOLN.

33-35   Richard HARVYE *alias* Harford v. William CHAPELYN of Taunton, merchant.

Tenement in Cannon Street, [Taunton?] held of defendant's manor of Taunton Dean (Taunton Prioratus, Taundeyne).   SOMERSET.

36-39   John HASILLE of Coddenham, draper, v. Thomas SKYNNER *alias* Lyncolne of Bergholt (Bargolde), clothmaker, husband of Margaret late the wife of William Halle.

Failure to warrant a house and lands in Coddenham and Gosbeck late of Jeffrey Reynoldes. D. IX, 54.   SUFFOLK.

40   Katherine late the wife of John HAUKYN v. [John HUBBERDE of Walton?].

Exchange of Customary lands in [Kir]keby (*i.e.* Kirby-le-Soken?) and Thorpe for land in Dovercourt. *Damaged.*   ESSEX.

41-42   William HAWKYNS of Plymouth, merchant, v. William WIKES, mayor of Plymouth, Lucas COCK, and John DERRY.

Wreck and stores at Plymouth bought of Lope de Kerryon, a Spaniard resident in London. DEVON.

43-44   Richard HAWLE of Chastleton, gentleman v. George OSBASTON (Osboldaston) and John HAWLE.

Detention of deeds relating to a messuage and lands in Swerford, Stratford, and Alveston (Alston) late of John Hawle, deceased, father of complainant, styled by the said Osbaston Edward Hawle.   OXFORD, WARWICK.

45   Henry HAWTREY, gentleman, and Jane his wife, executrix and late the wife of John Brabazon, gentleman, v. Elizabeth late the wife of Bartholomew BROKESBY.

Land in Melton Mowbray of the demise of the said Bartholomew and Elizabeth and of William Ryppyngton.   LEICESTER.

46   Thomas HAYES of Bykley v. Robert EVERS.

Rent of land called ' Benecrofte ' in . . . lton. *Mutilated.*   ?

47-49   James HEATHE (Hether) and Elizabeth his wife, daughter and heir of Richard Brayfeld and of Anne his wife, v. Anthony ANKETHILL (Anthyll) and Mary his wife, late the wife of William Page, gentleman, both guardians of Matthew son and heir of William Page.

Cottages, and right of pasture for sheep, a dovecote, and a mill in Warminster and Devizes (' the Vyes ') late of John Page, deceased father of the said Anne.   WILTS.

50-51   John HELHAM and Margaret his wife v. John FLEMMYNGE.

Messuage and land in Broxted (Broxhed), late of Thomas Flemmynge, husbandman, father of defendant and of the said Margaret.

                                                        ESSEX.

52-57   John HELIER of Trent, co. Somerset, husbandman v. Robert COWTHE *alias* Spycer and Thomas VELE.

Tenement in Yetminster of the demise of John Yonge, baker, master of the almshouse of St. John the Baptist and the Evangelist in Sherborne and the brethren thereof.   DORSET.

58-59   Thomas HENMAN of Ecclesfield, co. York, v. Edward KYRBY, Ellen his wife, Thomas HAVREFELD, Margery his wife, great-granddaughter and heir of Bennet Henman, Thomas HAVREFELD her son, and others.

Messuages and land at Kinder (Chynder) in Glossop late of Richard Henman, deceased great-grandfather of complainant.   DERBY.

60   Robert HERBERT of Ripple v. Richard HERBERT.

Forcible entry on messuages and land in Castlemorton bought of William Herbert. WORCESTER.

61   John, Robert, Richard and Edward HEWES v. William BUTLER, clerk.

Goods of Margery Butler *alias* Hewes, deceased, mother of complainants and sister of defendant.   DENBIGH.

62–63   Henry HEYDON, esquire, Anne his wife and John DAUNTESEY, gentleman, v. Robert
LAWRENCE.
Land (described) belonging to the manor of Shipton Sollars, late of Edward Twynnho, deceased,
father of the said Anne and of Katherine late the wife of the said John.   GLOUCESTER.

64–67   The same v. the same.
Do.   Replication wanting.   GLOUCESTER.

68–69   The same v. John GODDARDE, gentleman, and William GENT.
Land and common belonging to the same claimed as part of the manor of Nether Hampen
(in Shipton Oliffe).   GLOUCESTER.

70–71   Anne HEYGATE v. Lancelot MADYSON.
Messuage and land in Sandon and Danbury late of Reynold Heygate, deceased, husband of
complainant.   ESSEX.

72   William HILDERSHAM of Stachewourth (i.e. Stetchworth?), co. Cambridge, v. the mayor
and sheriffs of LONDON, and John BODIE, gentleman, 'secutory' to the Earl of
Huntingdon.
Action on a bond for money to be paid for the said Bodie to use his influence with the earl concerning
a water-mill in Duffield moor.   DERBY.

73   Maurice HILL, Margaret his wife, Thomas BROWNE and Eleanor his wife v. John
HOOPER.
Messuage and land called Curham in Halberton and land in Tiverton late of William Jerman,
deceased, great-grandfather of the female complainants.   DEVON.

74–76   Robert HILL v. Thomas MORE.
Action for delivery of deeds relating to the site of Taunton priory. Mutilated.   SOMERSET.

77–79   Thomas HILL v. William BUCKENAM, citizen and merchant of Exeter.
Part price of one-fourth of the manor of Hockworthy, and of lands, rents, reversions, and services
there.   DEVON.

80   William HILL v. Edward MORE.
Parsonage of Shipton, whereof Thomas Palme[r?], knight, has the advowson together with the
manor. Damaged.   SALOP.

81   Thomas HOBBYS v. . . .
Tenement in the late Duke of Somerset's manor of Stockton Lovell. Mutilated.   SOMERSET.

82–83   Thomas HOLCROFTE, knight, v. John WARDE of Capesthorne, gentleman.
Services due from lands held of complainant's manor of Over. 2 bills.   CHESTER.

84   Reynold HOLLYNGWORTH v. [William ABBOTTE?].
Tithes of corn and hay in Barking demised by the abbot and convent of Barking to Ralph Tracey.
Mutilated.   ESSEX.

85   Thomas HOPKYNS, vicar of Stanton Lacy, v. John (Thomas) BROME, late vicar, and
others.
Lease of the vicarage in anticipation of defendant's deprivation for marriage.   HEREFORD.

86–88   John HORSAM v. Edward WATSON, esquire.
Land in Dingley pledged to Edward (John) Watson of Rockingham, father of defendant, since
deceased.   NORTHAMPTON.

89–90   Walter HORTON of Catton, co. Derby, executor of Anne his mother, deceased, late the wife
of Thomas Toye, esquire, and formerly of Thomas Sprotte, gentleman, v. Richard son and heir
of John STONE.
Meadow at Delves in Wednesbury (Wallstode Delves) of the demise of William Sareson of West
Bromwich and Joan his wife, daughter and heir of Robert Nightyngale of Wednesbury.   STAFFORD.

91–94   Joan, executrix and late the wife of William HOSKYNS of Beaminster, v. John SAMWAYES
of Shilvington.
Loan the bond for which is embezzled.   D.X. 57.   DORSET.

95   William HOUSDEN of Great Chesterford, yeoman, v. Richard HAMOND of Debden,
yeoman.
Part of goods of John Egersall of Witham, deceased, promised to complainant by Thomas Egersall his
brother, administrator thereof.   ESSEX.

96–99   William, grandson and heir of Robert HOWE, v. Christopher BURGOYNE, gentleman.
Deeds entrusted to defendant relating to a house and land in Fen-Drayton.   CAMBRIDGE.

100–104 Thomas HUET v. John EWAN.
Embezzlement of deeds relating to a joint lease to both parties of a tenement in the manor of Bishops-
teignton.   DEVON.

105–107 Thomas and John HUMFREY, grandsons and heirs of Dackyn ap Gittyn ap Madwyn, v.
ROGER ap Jevan, son and heir of Jevan ap Llewelyn.
Messuage and land at Edgerley in Kinnerley 'partable betwyxt heyres males as other land guyldable
ys betwyxt coparceners.' (Defendant claims that he has bought the premises after forfeiture for
felony.)   SALOP.

108–110 William HUNSTONE of Wrangle (sic; rectius Walpole?) co. Norfolk, esquire, v. William
KYDDE.
Detention of deeds relating to messuages and land in Boston, Skirbeck and Wrangle.   LINCOLN.

111   William HUNSTONE of Walpole, co. Norfolk, v. the mayor and burgesses of BOSTON, or
so many of them as to the Chancellor shall seem fit.
Messuages and lands in the above places promised to complainant by Nicholas Throgmorton, knight,
and others, but conveyed to defendant.   LINCOLN.

112–113 John HUTTON of Dry Drayton v. John HASENOR (Hasinar) of Cambridge, brewer.
Beer promised in exchange for malt. CAMBRIDGE.

114 Thomas HUYCKE, D.C.L., v. Redderch David GWYN.
Parsonage of Dinas of the demise of John Harry, clerk. PEMBROKE.

115 Robert HYGDON v. John ROBERTES.
Messuage and land in Barrow of the bequest of Robert Hygdon of North Kelsey, father of
complainant. LINCOLN.

116–121 John HYPPYSLEY, gentleman, and Mary, his wife, daughter and heir of Thomas Flowre, v.
Ralph LATHAM esquire.
Tenements held of defendant's manor of Gaines in Upminster and claimed by him as forfeited for
waste. ESSEX.

122 . . . son and heir of William HYPPYSLEY v. Richard SEWARDE, gentleman.
Detention of deeds relating to a messuage called ' Mawndrelles ' and land [in Huntspill?]. *Mutilated.*
SOMERSET.

FILE 1358.

1–4 Reynold HALL v. Edward MOUNTAGU, knight, Ellen his wife late, the wife of William
Dygby, esquire, and formerly of John Moreton, esquire, and Francis SMYTHE, esquire.
Messuage and land in Wyfordby. (The said Ellen also claimed dower of her first marriage in
Brentingham Sproxton, Garthorp, Ashby Folville, and Melton Mowbray.) LEICESTER.

5–9 Henry HALLE, parson of Edith-Weston v. Reynold CONYERES, esquire, servant to the late
Duke of Northumberland.
Entry on complainant's parsonage before the commencement of a lease, assault on his sister, refusal
to do repairs agreed on, etc. *Replication in duplicate.* RUTLAND.

10–12 William HALYDAY, parson of Winthorpe and late canon of Croxton (Crosson), v. John
GORSTON, late parson, deprived for marriage, Simon BLANKES and Reynold COLLETT.
Dilapidations (*described*) and unlawful lease of the parsonage. NOTTS.

13 William HAMELDON of Maulden, gentleman, v. David LLOID ap Robert ap Hoell of
Beddgelert, gentleman.
Refusal to become surety as promised for a debt of Lewis ap Ryse of Llanlleneur, yeoman.
BEDFORD, CARNARVON.

14: Richard HAMON v. Margery late the wife of Roger PERSONS.
Meadow whereof the said Roger fraudulently obtained a lease from Francis [Talbot], earl of Shrewsbury. *Mutilated.* SALOP.

15–17 John grandson and heir of Richard HAMOND v. Richard HAMOND.
Detention of deeds relating to a messuage and land in Debden. ESSEX.

18–20 Thomas HANSLOPE v. Thomas VERNEY, knight, and Richard VERNEY, knight, his
son.
Lease of lands in Kineton (Kyngeston) and Compton [Verney]. *Mutilated.* WARWICK.

21–23 Thomas, son of John HARPER, deceased. v. John LAWES and Richard STRATFORDE.
Detention of deeds relating to a close in Wyngfold late of Agnes Stratford, deceased
[SUFFOLK or DERBY.]

24–28 William, Anthony and John HARRYS v. Griffith MEREDYTH, esquire.
Lands belonging to the Barton of Marwood, of the demise of [John Bourchier], earl of Bath. D. XI, 2.
DEVON.

29–30 Robert HARRYSON v. John ETWALL.
Messuage and land in Cheadle late of John Harryson, deceased father of complainant. STAFFORD.

31 John son and heir of Elizabeth HART v. William PARKER.
Detention of deeds relating to land in Marshwood. DORSET.

32–34 William HARTE of Chippenham v. Giles GORE, gentleman, son and heir of Thomas Gore,
esquire, and Walter CLARK.
Lands in Sopworth and Alderton late of William Harte, deceased, father of complainant. WILTS.

35 Roger Hayward and others, life tenants of the manor of HARTPURY, for themselves and
all other tenants, v. Walter COMPTON, lord thereof.
Destruction of timber whence the tenants obtained their supplies, refusal of common and seizure
of a house built by them in the churchyard of Hartpury. *Faded.* GLOUCESTER.

36 Hugh HATTON, draper v. Thomas ROSE, gentleman, servant to the Duke of Suffolk, and
William PEKE, draper.
Refusal to complete a lease of a tenement in Lutterworth. LEICESTER.

37 William HAYNTON of Nettleton, husbandman, v. Thomas HOLTBY, yeoman.
Refusal to give bond for price of a messuage and kiln-house in Caistor. LINCOLN.

38 Robert son and heir of Robert HENNYNGE v. Nicholas son and heir of Thomas
HENNYNGE.
Messuage, barn and land in Arundel awarded to complainant in a previous suit. *See Files 1179,
No. 22; 1228. No. 41.* SUSSEX.

39–40 William HERBERT, esquire, son of Walter Herbert, knight, and his wife William son of
Matthew HERBERT, esquire, Katherine his wife Nicholas BAGNALD, knight, and Ellen
his wife v. Richard BULKELEY, knight, and others.
Messuage and land in Penwentles, Rhos-mynach, Llysdulas (both in Llanwenllwyfo), and Clorathe.
ANGLESEY.

41   Richard HOCHYNSON *v.* Peter MEON and others.
Bond given for part of a debt of Oswald Wilstroppe, knight.   [YORK?]

42   .   .   .   HOELL, executor of William Vaughan, clerk, *v.* Robert COOKE.
Rent of the rectory of Carew. *Mutilated.*   PEMBROKE.

43   Robert HOLLAND and Agnes his wife *v.* George KYRTON and Elizabeth his wife, executrix
and late the wife of Thomas Wylson, executor of Margaret, executrix and late the wife of
John Ingram.
Legacy of Janet Holland, mother of the said Agnes, entrusted by her to the said Ingram. LINCOLN.

44-46   Thomas HOMFRAY of Sherborne, husbandman, *v.* Thomas DUTTON, gentleman, and
Francis SANDBACH (Stanbache) his attorney.
Obtaining judgment against complainant in the King's Bench without his knowledge. *Damaged.*
                                                                              GLOUCESTER.

47-49   William HORSSEY *v.* Robert HYLL.
Cloth and woad payable as price of messuages and implements in the hundred (*sic*) of Staplegrove and
manor of Taundeane. *Mutilated.*   SOMERSET.

50   Thomas HOWE *v.* Andrew CUTLER, citizen and merchant tailor of London.
Lease of the manor of Charleton, forfeited by John Tylneye, esquire. *Mutilated.*   [GLOUCESTER?]

51-55   Thomas HUNT, clerk, *v.* Henry DAWBENEY of Sharrington, esquire.
Refusal to complete a bond for balance of an account, complainant having surrendered other bonds
proving the debt.   NORFOLK.

56-59   Thomas HUNTYNGFELD *v.* Richard HENRY and Elizabeth his wife. ·
Land held of the manor of Wilby. *Answer faded.*   SUFFOLK.

60-61   William HUYTT, alderman of London, *v.* Geoffrey, son of George WASTNES of Headon,
esquire, and Robert OGLETHORP, late of Wallingwells.
Loan to the said George, whose executors defendants are.   NOTTS.

62   Roger HYCHESS *v.* Matthew MADOCKE.
Money and an ox obtained under pretence of settling complainant's lawsuit with William Lorzingham,
priest, and Richard Robertes.   —

63   William HYDE, esquire, *v.*   .   .   .
Messuage in Bradwell, part of the marriage settlement of Elizabeth, daughter of complainant, with
John, son and heir-apparent of Edmund Odyngselles, esquire. *Mutilated.*   OXFORD.

64   William HYLL *v.* Robert PORTER of Stalington Grange and Ellen his wife, executors
of John Hyll.
Legacy of Joan Hyll of Stoke, mother of the said William and John, whose executors were the said
John and Robert.   STAFFORD.

65-68   Robert HYNGESTON and Joan his wife, executrix and late the wife of John Hale, *v.* John
CROCKER, esquire, son and heir of John Crocker.
Entry on a tenement in the manor of Hemerdon (in Plympton St. Mary) and suit for it without
providing another tenement in exchange as agreed. *2 bills.*   DEVON.

69-71   Thomas HYNTON *v.* Thomas COX.
Land in complainant's manor of Yardescot or Yerelescott (*i.e.* Earlscourt in Wanborough?).
                                                                            WILTS.

FILE   1359.

1   Thomas HACKER, parson of Egmere, *v.* Thomas BULMAN, late parson deprived for
marriage, and Henry CASTELL.
Lease of the parsonage to the said Castell and destruction of the church and the boundaries of the
glebe.   NORFOLK.

2-3   William HALL, clerk, *v.* Mark COXSON.
Hospital of Elishaw in Elsdon (Illeshawe).   NORTHUMBERLAND.

4-6   Nicholas HALSWELL of Halsw[ell], esquire, *v.* John BYLLEYE, grandson of William
Lynge, deceased.
Moiety of messuages and land in Goathurst and Walton bought by complainant of Margery, great-
granddaughter of the said William.   SOMERSET.

7-11   Thomas HALYDAY *v.* John GENTILLMAN.
Messuage in the market-place and tackle-house at the dam of Dunwich late of John Halyday,
deceased, father of complainant, and husband of Margaret afterwards the wife of defendant.
                                                                            SUFFOLK.

12-15   John HAMOND, citizen and linendraper of London, *v.* Elizabeth HYNDE.
Detention of deeds relating to a messuage and land in Stamford late of William Hepall. LINCOLN.

16-19   John, son and heir of William HAMPDEN of Great Kimble, esquire, *v.* George PAULET,
knight.
Manors of Great Hampden and Bledlow late of John Hampden, knight, deceased. *Rival entails
given.*   BUCKINGHAM.

20-23   Alice HARPER and others to the number of thirty, copyhold tenants of the manor of Elmley
Lovett, *v.* John SETON, knight, and Charles his son, lords thereof.
Procuring complainants' forfeiture by neglecting to hold courts. *Schedule of customs annexed.*
D. XIV, 11.   WORCESTER.

24–25 · Richard HARRYNGTON, gentleman, *v.* John LONGE, kinsman and heir of Robert Shefford. Croft in Northampton formerly of John Warren, deceased, great-grandfather of complainant. *Mutilated.* . NORTHAMPTON.

26 William HARRYSON *v.* Robert CHALLENNER, esquire. Land in Wakefield late of Oliver Fowler, deceased, grandfather of complainant. YORK.

27–28 Adam HARTE *v.* Thomas ADAMS and Margaret his wife. Land in Walpole. *Faded.* NORFOLK.

29 John HASARDE of Lyme Regis, merchant, *v.* Alice, executrix and late the wife of William TUDBOLL (Tyboll) of Lyme Regis, merchant. Price of two butts and a hogshead of sack. DORSET.

30 Lewis HAVARD and Jennet his wife, of the parish of Stone [?], co. Oxford, and Watkin WYLLIAM of Salisbury, co. Wilts, *v.* DAVID ap Jevan and John DAVID ap Jevan. Messuage, barn and land in the parish of St. Michael late of William Watkyn, deceased, former husband of the said Jennet and father of the said Watkin. BRECON.

31 Peter HAWKYN *v.* John HEYMAN. Contempt of an award for partition of a house and land in Landrake late of John Hawkyn, deceased, father of complainant and father-in-law of defendant. CORNWALL.

32 William HAYES of Bridgewater *v.* Richard TUKSWELL of Marlyneh. Detention of a stray ' red hesker ' (*i.e.* heifer?) cow. *Mutilated.* [SOMERSET.]

33 Giles HELLINGE, clerk, *v.* Thomas CLARKE. House, lands, etc., belonging to the prebend of St. Decuman's in Wells cathedral to which complainant was appointed on the death of John son of defendant. SOMERSET.

34 John, son of John HELYAR(D), and others, executors of the said John the father, *v.* Christopher ASHTON, gentleman. Detention of a lease of the parsonage of Charlbury made by George Darce, Lord Darcy. OXFORD.

35–36 William HERBERT, Lord Herbert and Earl of Pembroke, *v.* David VAGHAN ap David ap Ithyll, John Hugh GRYFFETH, and others. Detention of deeds relating to Eyton park, cutting and carrying oaks thence, etc., on the plea that it belongs to the Queen's lordship of Holt castle. DENBIGH.

37 Robert HIGGYN, John PADIKE, and others, copyhold tenants of the manor of Chalton, *v.* William LEGG, bailiff to the Earl of Worcester and Robert ROBSON. Procuring false verdict as to the customs of the manor by impanelling the youngest men as jurors, and other oppressions. HANTS.

38–39 Richard HILL *v.* John BURNARD and others. House in Taunton and goods late of Robert Hill, deceased. SOMERSET.

40–41 Rowland HILL, knight, *v.* Ralph TENCH and Thomas LEYCESTER. Slandering complainant's title to lands in Newhall, part of his manor of Nantwich. CHESTER.

42–43 Thomas HOGON, gentleman, *v.* John WHYSHARD. Detention of deeds relating to land in Little Fransham. NORFOLK.

44–48 John HOLBECHE and Elizabeth his wife, great-granddaughter of John Bole and of Elizabeth his wife, *v.* John MEWES, esquire. Detention of deeds relating to half the manor of Compton in Freshwater. HANTS (I.W.)

49–50 Jasper HOLDELL and Agnes his wife, late the wife of Henry Glamfelde *alias* Smythe of Bergholt (Barfolde), both guardians of Stephen Glanfelde his son and heir, a minor, or John PERYMAN. Detention of deeds relating to a messuage and lands (*described*) in Tattingstone. SUFFOLK.

51–54 John HOLMEMAN of Ebony, co. Kent, *v.* Richard HOLMEMAN his uncle. Land in Northiam late of Richard Holmeman, deceased, grandfather of complainant. SUSSEX.

55 Robert HOLOWEY, Joan his wife late the wife of Richard Gybson, and John GYBSON her son, *v.* Henry [CHAPMAN?]. Cottage and land in the manor of Aston Clinton. *Faded.* BUCKINGHAM.

56 William HOPKYNS *v.* Thomas MANERYNG and others. House and land in New Woodhouse. SALOP

57 Henry HOSKYNS of Beaminster (Bewmaster) *v.* Stephen DENYS. Seizure of the court-book of the manor of Beaminster (Bemyster) Secunda of the demise of Richard Clarcke, prebendary of Salisbury. DORSET.

58–63 John son and heir of Christopher HUNT *v.* Christopher WRIGHT. Messuage and land in Shardlow whereof defendant claims a lease. DERBY.

64–67 John HURTE, yeoman, *v.* John FORMAN and others. Imprisonment at Derby by means of an action on a bond for arbitration, which complainant performed, and seizure of deeds relating to a messuage and land in Marchington and others. DERBY, STAFFORD.

68 Roger HYLLARY, parson of Sock-Dennis, *v.* Thomas PHELYPPES, gentleman. Destruction of the chancel of complainant's church and seizure of the glebe. SOMERSET.

69 Augustine HYTCHE *v.* Henry PYKERYNGE. Refusal to complete a sale of a messuage and lands in Kempston Hardwick, Wootton and Wilshamstead. BEDFORD.

FILE 1360.

1–2   Nicholas HADLYNGE of Floore, husbandman, and Emma his wife v. Richard HALL, vicar of Kilsby, and William HALL, bailiff of the town.
Messuage and land late held of the bishop of Lincoln's manor of Kilsby by William Tayllour and Agnes his wife, mother of the said Emma.   NORTHAMPTON.

3   Thomas and Alice HAMWOOD v. John HAMWOOD.
Goods of Elizabeth Hamwood of Kingsbury, deceased, mother of complainants.   SOMERSET.

4–5   Thomas HANDLEY v. William TASKER and others.
Ellerton Grange, demised to Thomas father of complainant by the late prior and convent of Norton. *Answer wanting.*   STAFFORD.

6–10   William HARDWICK v. Richard HUMFREY of Barton, esquire (gentleman), and William CURTEYS, husbandman.
Messuage and land in Holcot late of complainant's grandfather Robert Hardwick, whose widow was the mother of the said Curteys.   NORTHAMPTON.

11   William HARMON, gentleman, v. John HARMAN and others.
Conspiracy to procure the revocation by Joyce Mountforde, mother of complainant, of a bequest of a farm in Hampton, and to falsify her will.   WARWICK.

12   Robert HARRYSON v. John WALSON and William LAMME.
Messuages and land late belonging to a chantry in Beckingham.   NOTTS.

13–17   Thomas HARRYSON v. John CORBETT of Trowell, co. Notts.
Detention of deeds relating to messuages, a cottage and land held of the manor of Ilkeston of the inheritance of William Lacye.   DERBY.

18–19   John HARVIE v. Agnes late the wife of Rowland HINCE (Hintes), Roger PARTRICHE (Perteche), and others.
Share of messuage and land in King's Bromley and Lupin (in King's Bromley) late held of the said Partriche's manor of King's Bromley by James Awby, deceased, cousin of complainant and nephew of the said Agnes.   STAFFORD.

20   John HAWLE, yeoman, and William his son, servant attendant on William Smyth, esquire, a clerk of the Privy Council, v. JOHN ap David.
Refusal to complete a conveyance of a messuage and land in Newtown as security for a loan.
                                              MONTGOMERY.

21   . . . son and executor of Alice HAYWARDE v. Gabriel PAWLYN.
Reviver of a suit for the Crown lease of the manor of Halliford (Holongforde), formerly of the monastery of [Westminster]. *Mutilated.*   MIDDLESEX.

22–23   Thomas HEALDE(?) v. William MARTYNE of Beech and Robert his son.
Detention of deeds late of Thomas Handley. *Mutilated.*   STAFFORD.

24–26   Francis HEWET v. John LEGETT and Richard ROGERS.
Messuage and land in Sturton-in-the-Clay claimed by defendants in right of Richard Holgate and Margaret his wife.   NOTTS.

27–30   Robert HILL, husbandman, v. William BRAMPTON, gentleman.
Land in Letton, Cranworth, and Shipdham late of Richard Hyll, deceased, father of complainant.
                                              NORFOLK.

31   George HINDE(?) and many others, priests and conducts of Our Lady gild and Trinity gild in Boston, v. William HUNSTONE, esquire.
Lands charged with complainants' maintenance and bought of the Crown by defendants. *Faded.*
                                              LINCOLN.

32–35   William HODGYS of Middle Chinnock v. John BELLEW, John BROXOLME, George PAYN, gentleman, and Katharine his wife.
Parsonage of Charlton Adam with the advowson fraudulently obtained by William Hodgys, deceased, son of complainant and former husband of the said Katharine.   SOMERSET.

36–38   Richard HOIGGE (Hodge) v. John and Henry, sons and executors of Robert COMER.
Money and tenement in Comton Busshoppe (*i.e.* Compton Bishop?) promised to complainant on his marriage with Jane daughter of the said Robert.   [SOMERSET?].

39   John HOLLAND v. Nicholas HOLLAND and his servants.
Messuage and land in Glossop late of Guy Holland, father of the said John and Nicholas.   DERBY.

40–45   The same v. the same.
Manor of Lees in Glossopdale.   DERBY.

46   Thomas HOLLIS of Flitcham, knight, and William GRYVE of Stiffkey (Stukeye) v. Edmund SKYPWITH of Fordham, gentleman.
Goods and debts of Thomas Sele, clerk, whose executors complainants are.   NORFOLK.

47–49   John HOLMES v. Lady Anne BERKELEY.
Refusal to complete a lease of the Bridge House in Sileby promised by her surveyors.   LEICESTER.

50–51   John HOPKINSON, gentleman, son and executor of Henry Hopkynson, v. Agnes, late the wife of Andrew BARTON of Smithhills (in Bolton), co. Lancaster, esquire, and Robert BARTON of the same, esquire, and Ralph BARTON of Gray's Inn, gentleman, their sons.
Messuage and lands in Holme and North Muskham of the demise of the said Andrew, who also held messuages and lands in Carlton, Coddington, Newark and Carburton.   NOTTS.

52-56   Nicholas HOPKYNSON and Agnes his wife *v.* Andrew TUSSER, Thomas HOUGHTON, and Matthew WATKYN[SON].
Detention of deeds relating to a messuage and lands (*described*) in Seagrave and Sileby given by the said Thomas to the said Agnes on her marriage with John his son.   LEICESTER.

57   Thomas [HOWARD] duke of Norfolk, *v.* John MICHELL of Stamerham.
The new or little park of Northurst.   SUSSEX.

58   .   .   .   HOWLDESWORTH, great-nephew and heir of Robert Howldesworth, clerk, *v.* John LACY, Richard his son, and others.
Lands in Southowram late of the said Robert, who was robbed and murdered. *Damaged.* YORK.

59-61   Richard HUCHYNSON *v.* Thomas BANKES, esquire, and others.
Extortion of a second fine for building lease of a croft in Bank-Newton with 'towe key gate or pasture for ij kyen.' (The said Bankes states that complainant was banished by the sheriff's turn from the liberties of Craven and Staincliff as a ' petie mycher').   YORK.

62-64   John HYDON, administrator of the goods of John Hydon his brother (*sic*), deceased, *v.* Richard CURRANT of Bodmin and others.
Business debts due to deceased.   CORNWALL.

65-66   Eleanor, executrix and late the wife of John HYNDE of Bishop's Hull, mason *v.* Walter, brother and executor of John TUELL, clerk.
Price of making the stonework of defendant's house in Taunton.   SOMERSET.

FILE 1361.

1-3   Richard HALL of Hinton by Brackley, co. Northants, yeoman *v.* Robert FROGGE.
Messuage and garden in Pilgrim Street, Newcatle-on-Tyne, late of Richard Hall, deceased, grandfather of complainant.   N'HUMB.

4-7   William HALLE and William THOMAS *v.* Robert NOYES of Ramridge (in Weyhill), son and heir of Thomas Noyes.
Messuage and land in Weyhill (Wee) of the demise of John Rogers, knight. *Damaged.* HANTS.

8   Perkyn HAMLYE of Redruth, labourer, great-grandson and heir of Roger Hamlye and of Melyor his wife, *v.* Richard ERESYE, esquire.
Land in Treleghe Warthe (*i.e.* Treloy in St. Columb Minor ?) of the grant of John Penpons, esquire.   CORNWALL.

9   William HANCOKE of Westhorp (in Byfield) *v.* Richard SCHARELL of London, woolpacker, and Agnes his wife.
Messuages and land in Greatworth [and Westhorp ?] late of Richard Hancoke deceased father of complainant and of Richard Hancoke, former husband of the said Agnes. *Mutilated.*
NORTHAMPTON.

10-12   William HARMON, Elizabeth his wife and Anne ROBERTES *v.* Thomas CHARNOCKE and John LONGTREE, esquire.
Corn taken from the parsonage of Standish in excess of that sold by Richard Standyshe, late parson, whose executrices the female complainants are. *Damaged.*   LANCASTER.

13   James HARR and Elizabeth his wife *v.* John COLE.
Messuage and land in Higham by Stoke late of Thomas Cole, deceased kinsman of the said Elizabeth.
SUFFOLK.

14   William HARREYS, gentleman, *v.* John FURLONGE.
Detention of deeds and waste of a mansion and land called ' Radforde.' *Mutilated.*   DEVON.

15   Thomas HASILFOTE and Barbara, his wife, executrix and late the wife of John Fletcher, *v.* Bertram ANDERSON, and others.
Exclusion of the said Barbara's attorneys from the weighing of lead and tallow to be delivered at Newcastle-on-Tyne. *Mutilated.*   N'HUMB.

16   John HATTON of Whiston *v.* Roger SMYTHE and Hugh PRENE, late bailiffs of Bridgnorth.
Permitting the escape of Harry Smythe, against whom they had awarded a *capias*, and evasion of responsibility.   SALOP.

17-19   William HAYNES of Olney, co. Bucks, *v.* Giles BAKER and others.
Messuages and land in Heathfield late of William Haynes, deceased, grandfather of complainant.
SUSSEX.

20   John HEDGE *v.* Andrew TOMSYN.
Tenement in Withycombe of the demise of John Pollard, vicar, since deprived with a proviso binding subsequent vicars according to local custom.   DEVON.

21-22   Robert HELFORD (Holford) and others *v.* William CLOPTON, esquire.
Refusal to complete a lease of pasture in Stratford.   WARWICK.

23-25   The mayor and Burgesses of HELSTON *v.* Nicholas CURRY and others.
Toll of hides· foreign bought and foreign sold in Helston market, from which defendants claim exemption as burgesses of Bodmin.   CORNWALL.

26-27   John HENBOROUGH of North Curry *v.* Thomas SYMMES and Thomas HAWKYNS.
Land in North Petheston late of John Mychell, deceased, great-grandfather of complainant.
SOMERSET.

28   John HENNAGE, esquire, *v.* Thomas PALFRAMAN and Elizabeth late the wife of Robert PALFRAMAN.
Parsonage of Edlington demised to complainant in succession to the said Robert by the abbot of Bardney.   LINCOLN.

29–30   HENRY ap Thomas, a son of Thomas ap Ellys of Facknat, v. WILLIAM ap John JOHN ap
William and THOMAS ap Harry (ap P_{arr}y).
Diversion of a watercourse belonging to a mill in Nannerch. *Damaged.*   [FLINT or DENBIGH.]

31   ' Patrick [HEPBURN], earl of Bothwell v. William CROWDER, citizen of London.
Plate and jewels pledged to defendant for a debt on complainant's journey northwards with the
late Duke of Northumberland.   LONDON.

32–33   James HETH and Elizabeth his wife, granddaughter and heir of John Page, v. Peter
MORGAN of Bitton, co. Gloucester, gentleman, Robert BATHE of Bishopstrow, clothier,
and Matthew PAGE.
Cottage, land, a messuage, a dovecote, and a mill in Warminster, Devizes (' the Vyes '), and
Tilshead.   WILTS.

34–36   Anthony HEVENYNGHAM of Ketteringham, knight, son and heir of Sir John Hevenyngham,
v. William BOSWELL.
Land in Rushall bought of Robert Feasaunt. *Faded.*   NORFOLK.

37   Humphrey HILL of Bewdley, tanner, v. John MONOUX.
Burgage in Bewdley with site of a booth in the market-place.   WORCESTER.

38   Rowland HILL knight, v. John BROWN, of Upton, miller.
Messuages, mills and land in Upton late of the monastery of Haughmond. *Commission.*   SALOP.

39   Isabel, granddaughter of Thomas HOBBES and of Isabel his wife v. John BAMPTON.
Messuage and yardland ' of the olde gastre ' held of the manor of Pucklechurch.   GLOUCESTER.

40   William HOCHYNSON v. William BARNARD and Thomas WARDALE.
Messuages, cottage and land in Louth late of William Browne, deceased, uncle of complainant.
    LINCOLN.

41   Alexander HODGES v. John HODGES.
Joint tenancy of a messuage and land in Stogursey in reversion after the death of John Hodges,
father of complainant.   SOMERSET.

42–44   Stephen HODGYS v. Richard SCALLAND, parson of Melbury Bubb (Melberybupton),
late his master.
Detention of a feather-bed and bolster of the gift of Thomas Whyte, clerk, and an ox whereof he had
the pasture in lieu of wages.   DORSET.

45   Peter HOGGES v. William HARRYES and other.
Land in the lordship of Cardington late of Richard Hogges, deceased father of complainant. SALOP.

46   Thomas HOLBACHE v. William HOLBACHE his uncle.
Refusal to complete a sale of a moiety of lands in the manor of Old Fillongley.   WARWICK.

47   Elias HOLCOMB of Branscombe, gentleman, v. Robert HERT, gentleman.
Refusal to surrender a lease of land in East Teignmouth, defeasible on the reappearance of the
former tenant, who had left the country.   DEVON.

48   John HOPER of Liskeard v. Joan late the wife of John DELAMAYN and administratrix of
his goods.
Price of leather.   CORNWALL.

49   Ralph HOPTON, knight, v. Thomas SMETHWEKE.
Pasture in the manor of Marston Bigott bought of Edward, Duke of Somerset, ' before the cause of
hys attaindour.'   SOMERSET.

50–51   William HOPTON of Oxford v. John BAKER of the same, clerk.
' Old angels called old edwards ' and other coin and plate (*described*). *Answer wanting.* OXFORD.

52–53   William HORNE, yeoman, v. John PERYN alias Glover.
Burgages in Dorchester late of complainant's uncle Michael Horne, deceased, whose wife Edith
was defendant's great-grandmother. *Answer wanting.*   DORSET.

54   Giles HORSYNGTON of Pucklechurch, co. Gloucester, gentleman, v. Richard NORWELL
of Collurne, mercer.
Messuage and words in Collurne. *Mutilated.*   [WILTS.]

55   Edmund HORWELL v. William WESCOTE.
Lands in Broadwoodwidger whereof complainant purchased the reversion in succession to Joan
Gosecote (Griscote).   DEVON.

56   HOWELL ap Cadwalader, servant to the Earl of Arundel, v. CADWALADER ap Hugh.
Land in Darowen (Drowan) late of Hoell ap Hoell ap Philip *alia* Hoell Vaughan, deceased, kinsman
of complainant. *Pedigree given.*   MONTGOMERY.

57   HOWELL ap Cadwalader of Mainstone, servant attendant on the Earl of Arundel, v. . . .
Lands in Kyllwylsey . . . sburie, and Ednop (*i.e.* Edenhope in Clun). *Mutilated.*   SALOP.

58   John HOWLETT v. Thomas BASTON.
Messuage and land in Doncaster late of William Howlett, deceased, father of complainant.   YORK.

59   William HUCCHYNS and Joan his wife, late the wife of Gilbert Beckett, v. Robert
STAWARD and others, feoffees to the use of the said Beckett's will.
Profits of the manor of Cartuther (in Liskeard) and of lands in North and South Treweda (*i.e.*
Treweatha in Liskeard), the borough, manor and sanctuary of Liskeard, Wilton in Duloe, Mylcomb
in Linkinhorn, Coldienick (in St. Germans), Patrieda in Linkinhorn (Paderda) and elsewhere.
Damaged.   CORNWALL.

60–63   Christopher son of John HUDDESFELD v. Thomas COWLEGH.
Close of meadow in Mere of the demise of the warden and priests of the chantry of Our Lady there.
    WILTS.

64   HUGH ap Harry ap Llewellyn of R . . . market *v.* MEREDITH ap David ap Tuder and Gwen verch Jevan his wife.
Messuages and land in the town of Gweryvion.   CARNARVON.

65   HUGH ap Hoell of Lyneham, co. Oxford, husbandman, son and heir of Thomas ap Hoell, *v.* Jenkyn RES.
Detention of deeds relating to messuages, water-mills, and land in Gwenddwr.

66–71   The same *v.* the same, Hyggyn John HOELL, son and heir of Margery verch Hoell, wife of John Hoell, and JOHN ap Rosser.
Do.   BRECON.

72   Richard ap Owen *alias* HUMFRYE of London, *v.* Owen ap John SARE of Weston, yeoman.
Land in Lurkenhope in the lordship of Tempseter late of Rice ap Morris. deceased, uncle of complainant. *Mutilated.*   SALOP.

73   HUMPHREY ap Griffith of London, serving-man, *v.* ROBERT ap Thomas ap Eder and GRIFFITH ap David.
Seizure of cattle and household goods.   CARNARVON.

74–77   Thomas HUNTYNGFELD and Richard son of John VEER *v.* Andrew RYVET and Elizabeth his wife, daughter of the said Huntyngfeld.
Manor of Barley Hall (in Stradbroke) and messuages and lands in Stradbroke, Brundish, Laxfield, Fressingfield, Wingfield, and Wilby.   SUFFOLK.

78–79   Richard HUSSEY of Newbury, co. Berks, administrator of the goods of Philip his father, deceased, *v.* Richard STEVYNS and John HAYNES.
Messuage and land in Pontesbury of the demise of Joan Fletcher, kinswomen and heir of Roger Hynton.   SALOP.

80–83   Maude, late the wife of William HUTCHESON and Alexander and Joan her children *v.* John, son and heir of Walter SALISBURY.
Messuages and land in Pilton of the demise of James Cowman, gentleman, whereof complainant has the reversion.   DEVON.

84   John HUXLEY and Elizabeth his wife *v.* Henry DELVES, knight.
Legacy of Richard Huxley, father of the said John.   [CHESTER.]

85–87   Henry HYGFORD and Joan his wife, late the wife of Thomas Hall *v.* Richard, son and heir of Richard PARSONS.
Messuage and land in Nether Worton (Coton) bought of Thomas Hatteclyf.   OXFORD.

88   Hugh, son of Humphrey HYLL, deceased, *v.* Nicholas HYLL his brother and Joan UNDERHYLL.
Land in Bromsgrove promised to complainant on his marriage with Sible, daughter of the said Joan.   WORCESTER.

89   Agnes HYNCE of King's Bromley, daughter and heir of Thomas Awby of Abbot's Bromley *alias* Bromley Pagettes, *v.* Humphrey WELLYS, esquire.
Detention of deeds relating to messuages, cottages and land in the lordships of Prestwood and Marchington.   STAFFORD.

FILE 1362.

1–5   Richard INCKPEN and Anne his wife *v.* Richard CABELL (Cavell) and Robert ACOURTE.
Lands (*described*) in the manor of Keyford (in Frome) late of George Twynyho, esquire, deceased, former husband of complainant.   SOMERSET.

6–8   Robert INGLOND, yeoman, *v.* Richard WHETELEY, gentleman.
Refusal to complete an assignment of a lease of the parsonage of Islington as ordered by Lord Rich. late chancellor.   MIDDLESEX.

9   John INGRAM *v.* Thomas STAMPE and John WATSON.
Detention of deeds relating to a messuage and land in Bucknall.   LINCOLN.

10–12   Margaret INNE *v.* John WALRON, John WYLKYNS, and Thomas EDWARDS.
Crown lease of lands in Dunster late of the monastery of Cleeve. *Mutilated.*   [SOMERSET.]

13–15   Rose IRBY *v.* James BLACKBORNE of Grimoldby and Henry OVERTON.
Embezzlement of a bond for a payment to be made to the said Overton to complainant's use.   LINCOLN.

16–18   Edward IRELAND, gentleman, *v.* Richard FOWLER, parson of Hambleton.
Legacies of Richard Ireland of Uppingham, gentleman, father of complainant, and of John Ireland his executor, prebendary of the dissolved college of Leicester, whose executor defendant claims to be.   RUTLAND.

19–22   Anthony IRISHE *v.* George de LALYNDE, knight.
Land and wood at Langford in Parley date of Robert Irishe deceased father of complainant.   DORSET.

23–25   The same *v.* Richard RANDALL.
Land in Edmonsham late of the same.   DORSET.

26–28   Fremon (Fromond) IRYSHE *v.* Richard BADGER.
Lands in Downton and Breamore and goods of the bequest of Maud, late the wife of Richard Barrowe and mother of complainant. D. XII, 9.   WILTS, HANTS.

29   Thomas ISSBELL, husbandman, v. Stephen ROTHERAM and others.
Arrest on a bond made without complainant's knowledge for conveyance of a close of pasture in Cottingham.   YORK.

30   Thomas JACKLYNG and Audrey, his wife, sister and heir of Edward Medley, v. John MEDLEY.
Detention of deeds relating to a messuage in Walcot and a cottage in Folkingham.   LINCOLN.

31   Philip JACKSON of Mosborough, co. Derby, v. Howell BEDWORTHE and Thomas Upgriffith GOGH, Marchers and Welshmen.
Close of pasture in St. Martin's, Oswestry, of the demise of the said Howell.   SALOP.

32–33   Michael JACOBE of St Austell v. John NOTTELL, Mewen HENDY, and William COOTHE.
Messuage and closes in Bodmin.   CORNWALL.

34   William JAGGER, William SMYTHE, and Elizabeth .   . v. Andrew MAYSTER.
Debt due to John Vallew, whose executrix is the said Elizabeth. *Fragment.*   ——

35–38   Nicholas JAGGES v. Edward HALL, James GARNET and others of Newcastle-upon-Tyne, Archibald THOMPSON, and Leonard MERES.
Bond delivered by John Hill of Corpusty, complainant's factor, since drowned, to the said Thompson and Meres for goods bought of him by the other defendants.   NORTHUMBERLAND, NORFOLK.

39–42   Thomas JACKSON, Anne, his wife, John OSLEY, Margery, his wife, and Robert ROBSON v. William OSGARBIE, William DANETT, and Agnes his wife, late the wife of —— Ollynsworth.
Price and profits of a corn-mill in Middle Rasen, late of Robert Robson, deceased, father of the said Anne, Margery, and Robert.   LINCOLN.

43–45   Richard JAMES of Ridge and Joan, his wife, executrix of Richard Watson, v. Guy FOSTER, gentleman.
Debt for goods and services.   HERTS.

46   Howell JANKYN of Portsmouth v. Jevan THOMAS and others.
Messuage and land in the cantred of Selif (Cantesely).   BRECON.

47–48   John JAXSON *alias* Tompson of Stamford, brewer, v. William CUNEY (Connye), gentleman.
Bargain for grain for which a licence was required.   LINCOLN.

49–51   Bartholomew JECKELL of Newington, co. Middlesex, esquire, yeoman purveyor of the Stable, and Richard (*sic*) his wife, executrix of Nicholas Barnhouse, *alias* Harwood, of Bristol, gentleman, v. Thomas RIC(H)ARDES of Bristol.
Action for a debt of the said Nicholas, the said Bartholomew being absent in his office.   GLOUCESTER.

52   Thomas JERBRIDGE v. Agnes JERBRIDGE.
Detention of deeds relating to a messuage and land late of Christopher Jerbridge, deceased, uncle of complainant. *Fragment.*   [NORFOLK?]

53   George JERNEGAN, esquire, v. Edward CARWYTHAM, gentleman.
Rights reserved on a grant of the reversion of the disparted part of Okehampton. *Mutilated.*   DEVON.

54   William JESOP, yeoman, v. John DAWSON, both of Mattersey.
Sale of cattle owned jointly by both parties.   NOTTS.

55–56   Robert JOHNES, vicar of Llanvaer (*i.e.* Llan-fairdyffryn-Clwyd) in the lordship of Ruthin, v. Thomas MYDDELTON, gentleman, and Lowrie, his wife.
Inducing the inhabitants of Llanvaer and Ffynogion not to pay tithes. (*See File* 1365, *No.* 58.)   DENBIGH.

57–62   Reynold JOHNS, yeoman of the guard, son and heir of Anne Jenkyn, v. Morice HUGH, gentleman, John THOMAS, Katherine his wife, and others.
Detention of deeds relating to a messuage and land in Llantrissaint.   MONMOUTH.

63   Richard JOHNS, servant to Lord Paget, v. Roger EDOW and John DAVID.
Lands in Iscoed, and elsewhere, of the inheritance of Lord Derby and Edward Pyllyston, knight.   FLINT.

64   Thomas JOHNSON of St. Albans, and Joan his wife, late the wife of William Johanes, and formerly of John Kylby, v. John SAYMORE, gentleman, and Alice, his wife.
Lands in the manor of Tittenhanger adjudged to the said Johanes in this court   (*File* 830, *No.* 39).   HERTS.

65   David JONES v. Jevan .   .   . of Llanver (*i.e.* Llanfair-Waterdine), co. Salop, and Howell ap Matthew BEDO.
Waste of woods in Beguildy. *Mutilated.*   RADNOR.

66–69   Griffith JONES of Wickhambreux, co. Kent, yeoman, v. Jevan DAVID ap Rice and others.
Detention of deeds relating to land in Llanedy, late of Mabeley Howell, deceased, mother of complainant.   CARMARTHEN.

70–72   Robert son and heir of Thomas JOURE v. Richard PEXSALL, knight, and John and George RYGDON.
Messuage and land in the manor of Peper Harow, of the demise of William Brokes. *Damaged.*   SURREY.

73   Thomas JURYE, clerk, v. John SYDNEHAM, esquire.
Parish church of Street and Walton, to which complainant was inducted on the deprivation of John Best for marriage.   SOMERSET.

FILE 1363.

1-6 Thomas and Richard, sons of Philip INCLEDON, deceased, *v.* John COLOMORE, Katherine wife of Thomas PEARD and late the wife of William Incledon, and others.
Tenement in Braunton of the demise of Patrick Bedlowe. *See* D. XII, 2. DEVON.

7 John INGOLDESBY, gentleman, and Ralph INGOLDESBY, citizen and mercer of London, *v.* [Thomas DAWKES.]
Double bond for price of cloth. *Damaged.* LONDON.

8 Leonard IRBY *v.* John NEVILL, lord Latimer.
Manors of North Bovey, Larkbeare, and Downecary (*i.e.* Cary in St. Giles's-in-the-Heath?). *Damaged.*
DEVON.

9-11 William ISGARE and William RICHARDES, churchwardens of Sherston Magna, *v.* Thomas HAYES.
Suppression of a 'grete legger boke' containing the sums due from each householder for the maintenance of the church of Sherston, and refusal of his own share. WILTS.

12 Henry ISSAM *v.* Thomas BROKE.
Sale of geldings entrusted to defendant.

13 Robert IVE of West Kington, co. Wilts, esquire, *v.* Robert BRADSTON.
Refusal to complete a sale of rents and services in the manor of Hampton and Patchway (Pathshawe).
GLOUCESTER.

14-15 Henry JAGGES and Cecily his wife *v.* Robert CAUNCELOUR of West Harling.
Messuage and land in ' Wyckellwood *alias* Wyclewood ' late of Ralph Brew(y)en, deceased, uncle of the said Cecily. NORFOLK.

16-17 Anne JAMES, executrix and late the second wife of Edmund Tebbe, *v.* Robert CHERSEY (Charsey) and James SCAMPION.
Lease of land and wood in Deptford, whereof defendants have the reversion. KENT.

18-19 Constance JAMYS *v.* Robert John (John) JAMES and John JAMES.
Messuages and lands in Madron late of John James Jacke Vartyn and Jane his wife, grandparents of complainant. CORNWALL.

20-22 John ap John *alias* JANSON of London, buckler-maker, grandson and heir of entail of Nicholas ap Thomas, *v.* LLEWELYN ap Jenkin of Howell.
House and land in Nerquys pledged to Jenkin ap Howell, father of defendant, by John Nycholas, father of complainant. [FLINT.]

23 The same *v.* John ap Llewelyn JOHN.
Detention of deeds relating to the same. [FLINT.]

24-27 Christian JAXSON (Jutson) daughter and heir of John Fuller, *v.* Nicholas BOHUN (Boham), esquire.
Land in Chelmondiston (Chempton). SUFFOLK.

28 Joan JEBETT, Hugh TOWNESENDE, and Agnes his wife, mother of the said Joan, *v.* Crystyan JEBETT, Robert SALESBURY, and Reynes his wife.
Messuage and land in Bilston late of John Jebett, deceased, father of the said Joan and Reynes.
LEICESTER.

29-31 John JENKYNS, husbandman, *v.* Richard BUCKEMAYSTER.
Detention of deeds relating to a messuage and land in Eaton (defendant describes the search for his own lost deeds). BEDFORD.

32-34 William JENKYNS of St. Andrew's, Eastcheap, merchant tailor, *v.* JOHN ap Griffith *alias* John a Benylam, RICE ap John his son, and Katherine DAVID ap Bedo ap Jenkyn.
Messuages and land in Churchstoke late of David Jenkyn, deceased, father of complainant.
SALOP, MONTGOMERY.

35 John JENYNGES *v.* William STREME and Henry STOUGHTON, his servant.
Refusal to complete a sale of a messuage in Manea. CAMBRIDGE.

36-37 Richard JETTER, gentleman, *v.* Richard, son and heir of George FEILDE.
Detention of deeds relating to meadow in Wyberton late of Richard Jetter, deceased, father of complainant. LINCOLN.

38 JEVAN ap David *v.* Ba . . . ap Res and another.
Tenements in Llanded (*i.e.* Llanddetty?) and . . . ecombe. *Damaged.* BRECON.

39-42 Henry JEWSE and Isabel his wife, late the wife of Thomas, son and heir of Michael Dormer, knight; *v.* Michael, son of Jerome HAMPDEN, gentleman.
Messuages, lands, wood and cottages held of Sir John Browne's manor of Headington. *Mutilated*
OXFORD.

43-44 William JOANS of London, mercer, *v.* John William VAUGHAN of Lanthrethall, gentleman.
Messuage and land late of Howell ap Jenkyn of Shenfreth, deceased, uncle of complainant.
MONMOUTH.

45 JOHN ap Jevan, ROBERT ap Gruffydd ap Llewellyn, and Katherine his wife, sister of the said John, *v.* GRWFFYDD ap Llewellyn ap Grono.
Lands in . . . anyvythe (*i.e.* Llanufydd) promised to the said Robert and Katherine on their marriage. *Faded.* DENBIGH.

46-47 JOHN ap Howell, son and heir of Howell Hepkinge (ap Hoppking), *v.* John JAMES, husband of Gwenllian late the wife of the said Howell.
Land in Lanarth. MONMOUTH

48   JOHN ap Jevan of Mortlake, co. Surrey, v. ROBERT ap John.
Land in Dymeirchion late of Jevan ap Jevan, deceased, father of complainant.   FLINT.

49–50   Richard JOHNS, servant to Lord Paget, v. Ralph BROUGHTON and David ap POVA.
Lands in Shocklach late of Randolph Hanmer.   CHESTER.

51–52   Thomas JOHNS v. HARRY ap Jevan ap Walter.
Loan. 2 bills.   CARMARTHEN.

53–55   John JOHNSON of New Windsor, fellow of Eton, v. Thomas HALE, citizen and grocer of
London.
Bargain of grocery intended for resale.

56–58   William, son and heir of John JOLYF, v. Robert and Thomas CABORNE.
Messuage and land in Tetney. (The said Thomas denies complainant's parentage.)   LINCOLN.

59   Griffith JONES v. William LATHEBURY.
Suppression of an account for corn, and false action in the King's and Queen's Bench for a loan.
D. XIV, 54.   KENT.

60   John JONES v. Thomas DASSEWYN, deceased.
Loan to Thomas Ley of Hell (sic) in E[n]veld, deceased, of whose widow, Margaret, defendant is
executor. Damaged.   STAFFORD.

61   Thomas JONES, clerk, v. John MEREDITH and THOMAS ap Jankyn, gentleman.
Parsonage of Llanwenarth to which complainant was presented by Philip and David Flower,
gentlemen.   MONMOUTH.

62   Thomas ap Jevan ap David ap Jevan ap Blethyn, alias Thomas [JONES], v. John, son of
Robert SALYSBURY, deceased.
Messuages and land in the 'countye' of Kynmerth (i.e. commot of Cynmeirch). Mutilated. See
File 912, No. 17.   DENBIGH.

63–66   William JONES, yeoman, v. Christopher BYTTENSON and Emma his mother.
Refusal of rent of the manors of Long Ditton and Thames Ditton as reduced by agreement.
          SURREY.

67–68   John and Richard JONSON, by John Gayton, their guardian, and Joan, his wife, their
mother, v. William JOHNSON.
Land in Hunton purchased with a legacy of Thomas Jonson, father of complainants and brother of
defendant.   KENT.

69–71   James JORDEN v. Joan, late the wife of Henry BRADSCHAWE (Bradshoe), esquire.
Detention of wages, clothing, and money.   .   ———

72–74   Hugh (John), grandson and heir of John JUDD, v. John CLYFFORDE, husbandman.
Messuage and land at Preston in King's Walden. (Defendant claims a title from John Bushe,
purchaser of lands in Temple Dinsley, Kitchin, Offley, Letchworth, and King's Walden.)   HERTS.

75–77   John JUDDE, citizen and skinner of London, v. Thomas BOUGHTON.
Messuages and land in Hornchurch, late of Thomas Mirfyn, alderman of London, deceased, grandfather of complainant.   ESSEX.

FILE   1364.

1–2   William KEANE of Este Harty (i.e. Harptree?), freemason, v. Thomas ANDROWES.
Closes of pasture in Frome Selwood, demised by Robert Leversage, esquire, to Thomas Keane,
deceased, father of complainants.   SOMERSET.

3–4   Edward KEBEL, husbandman, v. John POPE and WALTER Thomas.
Close in Caundle Bishop, of the demise of William Brownesop, parson of Holwell, co. Somerset.
          DORSET.

5–6   John KEBLE of Lockerley, co. Hants, gentleman, v. Nicholas VAUX.
Action at common law for the filazership of the Common Pleas, whereof defendant was deprived,
among other things, for 'fawlse accusation and sklaunderouse ympeaching of Sir Humfrey Browne,
knyght, one of the justices of the said courte, and of dyvers other justices of peace and other
worshipfull of the said countie of Sowthampton concerning matters of religion.'   HANTS.

7   William KELAM and Jane his wife v. Thomas FLETCHER, yeoman.
False imprisonment in order to obtain the said Jane's share of lands in Carnarvon, late of Edmund
Foxwyste, her father, deceased.   CARNARVON.

8   Robert KELEWAY, gentleman, v. Thomas HOLEWALE, gentleman.
Refusal to grant an annuity out of lands in Wootton Glanville, as ordered by the Earl of Bedford's
commissioners, to Chrystyan, his wife, daughter of complainant, driven mad by his 'lewde and evyll
behavyour.'   DORSET.

9–10   Thomas KEMBLE of North Whidhill, yeoman, v. Thomas TRYNDER of Latton,
husbandman.
Surrender to John Berklye, esquire, of a bond for conveyance of lands in Great and Little Chelworth
jointly purchased from him by both parties.   WILTS.

11–12   Eleanor, late the wife of William KEMPE, knight, v. Thomas KEMPE, knight, her son.
'Hockewoodes and underwoodes' in the manor of Stouting and Stanforth, held with those of
Asshmerfeld (i.e. Ashenfield in Crondale?), Crondale and Hadlow.   KENT.

13   John KENALL, parson of Hinton (Waldrist), v. Ralph POLLYNTON, clothier.
. Receipt of complainant's tithes and ejection from the parsonage, glebe, and sanctuary lands.
          BERKS.

14–15   Robert KENE of Great Wilbraham, tailor, v. Robert SCOTTE.
Messuage and land in Borough (i.e. Burrough Green?) late of John Kene, deceased, grandfather of complainant. CAMBRIDGE.

16   Edward KENESTON v. Thomas and George VERNON, esquires.
Detention of deeds relating to the manor of Karyryon and another and the lordship and castle of Charlton in dispute in this court as the inheritance of Edward Grey, lord [Grey of] Powys, deceased, Faded. SALOP, MONTGOMERY.

17–20   William KENRYCKE of Spilsby, draper, v. Agnes KENRYCKE.
Goods of John Kenrycke of Torksey, deceased, father of complainant and husband of defendant. LINCOLN.

21   John KENSYTON(?) and Thomasyn his wife v. the mayor and commonalty of PLYMOUTH and Thomas CLOWTE.
Action concerning a distress for an annuity granted to the said Thomasyn by Thomas Bull in lieu of dower in the borough of Plymouth. Certiorari and subpœna. Mutilated. DEVON.

22   Margery, executrix and late the wife of William KENT, v. Elizabeth CRISPYN.
Defendant of Edmund CRISPYN, clerk, deceased, whose executrix defendant is. ———

23   William son and heir of Thomas KENYNGHAM v. Gerard KENYNGHAM.
Detention of deeds relating to a messuage and land in Preston-in-Holderness. YORK.

24   Richard KERISON v. William HUGHSON, parson of Fritton.
Detention of bonds given for a debt since paid. NORFOLK.

25–27   John KERY of London, salter, v. Humphrey KERY of Binweston, executor of Thomas Kery of the same.
Part price of a gelding and of an adder. LONDON, SALOP.

28   Henry KETILL, Alice his wife, Robert BACON, John BOKENHAM, Isabel his wife and Henry OSBORNE, v. Roger STANNOUGHE, steward of the manor of Seething, Robert his brother, and John BROWNE.
Conspiracy to make a false title to land in the said manor late of Richard Broke. NORFOLK.

29–30   John KETTELL, William REDE and Margaret his wife v. Robert WHITNEY, knight, grandson and heir of James Whitney, and Henry TAYLLOUR his tenant.
Messuages and land in Pencombe late of Richard Byterley, great-grandfather of the said John and father of the said Margaret.
HEREFORD.

31–33   Thomas, son of John KINGE, deceased, v. Robert BELLYNGHAM.
Messuage and land in Lacock late of Lacock Abbey, whence Margaret, wife of the said John was expelled by William Sharington, knight, since deceased. WILTS.

34–37   Thomas, grandson and heir of Thomas KINGE, v. William and Thomas KINGE his uncles and William TASSHE.
Detention and falsification of deeds relating to a messuage and land in Moulton. LINCOLN.

38–39   Nicholas KINGSTON v. John KNEVETT, draper, and Robert WOOD, brewer, citizens of London.
Detention of deeds relating to messuages and gardens at Stratford-atte-Bow held of the lordship of Stepney. MIDDLESEX.

40–41   John KIPPYNG v. William GILBERT and Robert GODFREY.
Tenements in Great Yarmouth, one in Well Rowe, late of William Kippyng, deceased uncle of complainant. NORFOLK.

42 .   Richard KNAVESBORROW v. Brian, executor of Jane, late the wife of Brian STAPYLTON, knight.
Exaction of rent of a messuage and land in Walkingham Hill payable to the Crown and formerly to a chantry in Tuerington (i.e. Terington? Not in indexes to Certificates or Particulars of Chantries.)
YORK.

43   Robert KNIGHT v. George DAWBRIDGECOURT, gentleman.
Bond given for price of a lease of the site and demesnes of the manor of Berkley on a promise to warrant complainant's title against John Newebery. SOMERSET.

44–45   Valentine KNIGHT alias Brothers v. Thomas WELLES.
Land in Offley St. Legers and King's Walden, late of Valentine Knight alias Brothers, deceased, grandfather of complainant. HERTS.

46–49   John KNOLLES of Hordwell, grandson and heir of Harry Knolles, v. Stephen WARWYKE of Ashley-in-Milton and Richard STEPHENS of Milton.
Detention of deeds relating to a messuage and land in Christchurch Twynham. HANTS.

50–54   John KNOTTYSFORDE of Muche Mawburn (i.e. Great Malvern?) co. Worcester, esquire, Jane his wife, Thomas PORTER of Overington, co. Warwick, gentleman, Anne his wife, Bartholomew HUSSEY of Burley, co. Hants, Mary his wife, James DUFFELD of Medmenham, co. Bucks, and Frances his wife, v. Dame Isabel (Elizabeth) SPENCER of Wormleighton.
Waste of the parsonage of Maston (i.e. Prior Marston) and lands in Napton after a lease of the reversion to Robert Stafford, knight, and Jane his wife, both since deceased, parents of the female complainants. WARWICK.

55–57   John KNYGHT v. Thomas CREWE, son and heir of John a Crewe.
Burgage half a house, and land in Holt late of Thomas Knyght, deceased, father of complainant.
DENBIGH.

58–62   Thomas KNYGHT and Joan his wife v. Agnes, late the wife of Thomas CHYPSEY of
Northampton, grocer.
Waste of lands in Preston and Piddington bequeathed in reversion by the said Thomas Chypsey
to complainants together with lands in Northampton.   NORTHAMPTON.

63   William KNYGHT v. ROBERT ap Rice and Jane his wife.
Detention of deeds relating to a messuage called the *George* in Farnborough.   KENT.

64–66   William KYCHYN v. Thomas BURTON and William FERYMAN.
Messuage, land, and dovecote in Bleasby, late of John Kychyn, deceased, father of complainant.
     NOTTS.

67   Peter KYDWELLY of Brown Candover, gentleman, v. Anthony MORE, Nicholas VAUS, and
William EAST.
Detention of deeds relating to messuages and lands in Preston Candover, Polehampton, Overton
or (*sic*) Kingsclere acquired of William Sommer.   HANTS.

68   Jane KYGHELEY v. Marmaduke GASCOYGNE, esquire, and others.
Legacy of Thomas Kygheley, esquire, brother of complainants, whose executors defendants are.
     YORK.

69–72   John KYLBECK v. Thomas WATERTON, knight.
Loan for redemption of lands in Lee, Upton and Whitbar, mortgaged by Robert Waterton, knight,
deceased, father of complainant. *Damaged.*   LINCOLN.

73   John KYME, servant to William Petre, knight, and Richard his brother v. William
MARKEWICKE, yeoman.
Detention of deeds relating to a barn and land in Arlington and Wilmington.   SUSSEX.

74–75   Thomas KYME of Friskney, esquire, and William KYME of London, gentleman, sons of
Thomas Kyme of Benningworth, deceased, v. John DYON, gentleman.
Action on a bond for warranty of lands in Friskney.   LINCOLN.

76–77   John KYNGMAN v. John HUDDER (Hodder) and John GOULE.
Refusal to complete a conveyance of land in Whitchurch late of Eleanor Lane and others. *See
File 1239, No. 70.*   DORSET.

78–79   Anne late the wife of John KYNGSTONE and Thomas their son and heir, v. John, son of
George ROLLEZ, deceased.
Messuage and land in Roborough of the entail of the said John. *See File 1305, No. 45.*   DEVON.

80–83   Robert KYNSEY, vicar of Ware, co. Herts, son of Edmund Kynsey of Warmingham,
husbandman, v. Ralph son of Ralph BOSTOCKE of Barrow, and John HIGSONE.
Detention of deeds relating to chantry land in Middlewich.   CHESTER.

84–85   Thomas KYNTON v. Christopher TEMMYS of Churche Eaton (*i.e.* Water Eaton?),
gentleman.
Detention of a lease of Benyger (*i.e.* Beanacre in Melksham?) entrusted to him to obtain a better
one from Francis Pawmes, esquire.   WILTS.

86–87   Richard KYRKE v. Oliver BURTON.
Refusal to complete a sale of peas and corn growing at High Toynton.   LINCOLN.

88   Walter KYRLE of Walford, gentleman, v. John SYBRAUNCE and Elizabeth his mother.
Detention of deeds relating to the manor of Coughton (in Walford).   HEREFORD.

89–90   Walter KYSSOKE of Salisbury and Joan his wife, v. Richard BRYAN her uncle and late her
guardian.
Legacy of William Bryan(t), father of the said Joan.   WILTS.

FILE 1365.

1   Nicholas and Henry LA, husbandman, executors of William La, v. William MARTYN.
Detention of deeds relating to a messuage and land at Porth in St. Austell. *See File 1368, No. 32.*
     CORNWALL.

2–4   Thomas LACYE v. Nicholas HOLMES, clerk.
Farm in Sturton of the demise of George Lascelles of Gay . . .. *Damaged.*   NOTTS.

5–7   Ralph LAKE (Leeke), gentleman, v. James FOLJAMBE of Walton, knight.
Overstocking a common in Hasland whereof the lord is John Seliocke of Hazlebarrow (in Norton),
gentleman, a debtor of defendant.   DERBY.

8   Robert LAMYNGE of Scarrington (Scarryngton), yeoman, v. ——— ROOSE and Thomas
LAMYNGE.
Under-lease of part of the said Roose's lands in Carcolston.   NOTTS.

9–11   William LANCASTER of Milverton and Thomas HILL of Kingston v. John HOLMER and
Alice his wife, late the wife of Thomas Broke, husbandman.
Legacies of the said Broke to his children, whose guardians complainants are.   SOMERSET.

12–15   John LANCYE v. John LOVERYNG of Bittadon.
Detention of plate (*described*) and other goods, and of deeds relating to lands in East Down.
     DEVON.

16–20   John LANE of Kettering, gentleman, v. Richard HUMFREY, esquire, and John HUMFREY,
gentleman.
Lands in Isham late of John Lane, deceased, father of complainant.   NORTHAMPTON.

21–22 John, son of Robert LANGDON, esquire, deceased, and administrator of his goods, v. John BROWNE, Margaret his wife, late the wife of the said Robert, and Jasper LANGDON *alias* Browne, her son.
Messuage called North and South Penhale and lands in St. Martin's (by Looe), and goods, adjudged to complainant by arbitration. CORNWALL.

23–24 Thomas LANGDON of South Cadbury, fisherman, v. Robert BARON of North Cadbury.
Obtaining a white gelding by means of a forged warrant of replain. SOMERSET.

25–27 Alexander LANGFORD of Trowbridge, clothier, v. Egeon WYLSON.
Detention of deeds relating to a moiety of messuages and lands in Trowbridge and Studley formerly of Thomas Bradford and Dorothy his wife, now wife of defendant. WILTS.

28 Nicholas LAVER of Kingston, v. William WILLIAMS of Knowle.
Action on a bond for a debt as well as for the debt itself. DORSET.

29 Thomas LAWE of Graveley, co. Cambridge, husbandman, v. Hugh BARBER and John PURSELL.
Double lease of a messuage and land in Offord Darcy and Offord Cluny. HUNTINGDON.

30 John LAYNE v. Robert LAYNE his brother and Thomasen LAYNE.
Lease of a messuage and land in Seynt Tyve from Thomas Dotson and John Menwyneck, gentlemen.
Mutilated. [CORNWALL.]

31 Thomasyn LAYNE (Leyne) v. John LEYNE, Margaret his wife, and Roger HORNEBROKE.
Forgery of a lease of a tenement called Tchey held of the said Menwyneck and Dotson. [CORNWALL.]

34–35 Richard LECHE v. William LECHE.
Loans to Gregory Leche, deceased, father of both parties. DIOCESE OF EXETER.

36–37 Reynold, son of Geoffrey LEE, esquire, v. John MARKHAM, knight.
Office of steward of the archbishop of York's lordships of Southwell and Benningworth, partly surrendered to defendant by Thomas Hennage, knight, complainant having the reversion.
NOTTS, LINCOLN.

38 Francis LEEK, knight, v. Roger GRENEHALGH of Teversall, esquire.
Exchange of leaseholds in Glapwell and Sutton-in-Ashfield. *Mutilated.* DERBY, NOTTS.

39–40 John LEGETT v. Thomas MYRFYN and Christopher BAXTER.
Lease of lands to Richard Holgate and Margaret his wife for a week with remainder to complainant for fifty years. *Mutilated.* NOTTS.

41–44 John LEGH, knight, v. Henry [NEVILLE], earl of Westmoreland.
Tithe corn of Billingham, Newton, Cowpen and Woolviston (Wolstone in Beauley). D. XIV, 47.
DURHAM.

45 Edward LEIGHTON of Wattlesborough, co. Salop, esquire, son and heir of John Leighton, v. Thomas HUCKES, esquire.
Manor of Clopton in Mickleton (Micheton), and land and rent in Clopton, Mickleton, Honeybourn, Keyndon (*i.e.* Quinton?) and Marston. GLOUCESTER.

46 Richard LEIGHTON v. John TILLEY, Denise his wife, and others.
Obtaining a prohibition from the Council of the Marches against suing for damages for a false indictment of robbery, whereof he was acquitted. *Mutilated.* SALOP.

47 Thomas LEVERETT of London, fishmonger, v. Robert WITTON.
Messuage, land and oil-mill in Wisbech late of John Leverytt, deceased, grandfather of complainant.
CAMBRIDGE.

48 William LEVERETT of Newark-upon-Trent v. Roger CAPESTAKE, gentleman.
Loan. *Commission (named).* NOTTS.

49–50 David LEWES v. Francis BARET.
Precentorship of Llanddewi-brefi and prebend of Llanfair Clydogau formerly of Rowland Mericke, clerk. *Mutilated.* CARDIGAN.

51 John LEWES, parson of St. Mary Magdalen's, Southwark, v. William HARRY and others.
Loan by Morgan Lewes, clerk, whose executor complainant is. SURREY, CARMARTHEN.

52 Robert LEWES v. Thomas SKARGELL of Sheffield, butcher.
Pasture in Sheffield entailed on Thomas and Joan, parents of complainant. YORK.

53 John LEWIS of London, merchant tailor, v. Jevan David GLASE (Glays) of Brecknock.
Gelding entrusted to defendant during complainant's stay in those parts. LONDON, BRECON.

54 Philip LEWYS v. Philip JENKYN and Richard WILLIAMS.
Messuages and land in Llanvaches and elsewhere late of Lewis ap Philip, deceased, father of complainant. *Damaged.* MONMOUTH.

55 William LEWYS v. the mayor and bailiffs of OXFORD, and Thomas COGEYN, one of the latter.
Action for impounding sheep. *Certiorari and subpœna. Mutilated.* OXFORD.

56–57 William LLEWELYN (Fowellen), citizen and salter of London, v. John HARRIS.
Manor of Leighton and messuage, lands, and woods there of the bequest of Thomas Kery, citizen and salter of London, uncle of complainant. MONTGOMERY.

58–59 David LLOID, warden of West Harnham, co. Wilts, and MORRIS ap Johns, v. Thomas MILTON.
Tithes of Llanfair[-dyffryn-Clwyd] in the lordship of Ruthin (defendant pleads a judgment of this court in a suit by Robert Johns, vicar). *Mutilated. See File 1362, No. 55.* DENBIGH.

60 Jevan LLOID ap Elis v. HOWELL ap John ap Tydyr.
Land with common of pasture appendant. *Mutilated.* MERIONETH

z 11017 E

61   John LLOYD of Leaden Roding, co. Essex, clerk, *v.* Robert ap David LLOYD of Corwen
and others.
Glebe and tithe of Llangar, whereof complainant is parson.   MERIONETH.

62   Robert Thomas LLOYD *v.* William CLERKE of Bladford (*i.e.* Blackford?), yeoman.
Price of cattle.   SOMERSET.

63–64   Morgan LLOYDE (Flloyde), *v.* John HAYWARD.
Costs awarded in the bishop of London's court in a suit for tithes at Shepperton.   MIDDLESEX.

65–66   John LODGE of Bower Chalke *v.* William HANNAM, gentleman, and Elizabeth his wife.
Loan to John Baylie, former husband of the said Elizabeth.   WILTS.

67   John LONDON *v.* Agnes, executrix and late the wife of John BAUGH.
Cattle entrusted to the said John at Tibberton.   WORCESTER.

68   John LONGE *v.* John HAULE.
Meadow in Lawford.   ESSEX.

69–72   William LONGSTON and Joan his wife, executrix and late the wife of Thomas Lyne, *v.*
Alice LYNE, mother of the said Thomas.
Money awarded by arbitration in lieu of half a tenement in Henbury promised to the said Thomas on
his marriage.   GLOUCESTER.

73–76   James LONGWORTH of Tysoe, gentleman, *v.* John STAMFORD of the same, yeoman.
Bond given concerning defendant's contract of marriage with a sister of John Cox.   WARWICK.

77   Richard LORKYN of East Bedford, yeoman, *v.* Henry BAKER, blacksmith.
Defendant awarded by arbitration, which complainant could not pay because ' busyed with the
Quenes affayres.'   MIDDLESEX.

78   William LOVE and others, in the name of the inhabitants of Hilgay, *v.* William HULLYER,
parson, of Hilgay.
Actions in divers courts for ' tythe of fieringe called sedge.'   NORFOLK.

79   Thomas LOVELL and Anne his wife *v.* David FYNES (Vynes).
Annuity charged on lands in Letton and Shipdham by John Cusshen of Hingham, gentleman,
deceased, father of the said Anne.   NORFOLK.

80–82   Simon LOW, citizen and merchant [tailor?] of London *v.* Joan late the wife of Walter YATE,
and Richard YATE, gentleman, her son.
Manor of Arlingham released by the said Joan to the said Richard.   GLOUCESTER.

83   The same *v.* the same, Elizabeth wife of the said Richard, and others.
Claim of dower of the said Elizabeth in parts of the said manor, including a fishery in the Severn,
and damages. *Mutilated.*   GLOUCESTER.

84–91   The same *v.* Robert CURTES, John BAWME, John TYE and others.
Trespasses (*described*) on the manor of East Deeping. *A Replication wanting. See* D. XIV, 37.
LINCOLN.

92   The same *v.* Henry LACY, gentleman.
Do.   LINCOLN.

93   The same *v.* George HOLLAND.
Continuance of a suit in this court for the manor of Deeping St. James after recovering a deed
whereby he could sue at common law.   LINCOLN.

94–97   The same *v.* Harry REPPS, gentleman.
Messuage called Middleton in Mendham, and lands and rent there and in Homersfield, Sancroft,
and South Elmham formerly of Elizabeth Holland, deceased.   SUFFOLK.

98–99   Simon LOWE *v.* John SEYMER and John BONDE.
Messuages and land in Burton acquired of Alexander Seymer. *Mutilated. See* File 1270, *No.* 27;
1317, *No.* 25.   OXFORD.

100   Elizabeth, Joan, and James LOWRANCE, executors of William Lowrance, *v.* Roland
DURRANT, gentleman.
Lease of lands in Saptone (*i.e.* Sapperton?) by James Durrant of Chesterfield, deceased, father of
defendant.   DERBY.

101–102 Thomas, son of William LUCYE, esquire, *v.* Roger BROWNE late collector of his rents,
and . . . MASON.
Sale of woods called Beryngton Heye on complainant's behalf. *Damaged.*   WORCESTER.

103 105 Anne LUMLEY and Joan KELYNGE *v.* William NEWMAN.
Goods of Margery Kelynge, deceased, including a ' styllytorye,' whereof complainants are administrators, stated by defendant to have been pledged by her and Anthony Dryland.   ——

106–107 George and William, sons of Joan LUND, deceased, *v.* Francis CALCOT.
Manor, grange and farm of Apley of the demise of Robert Tyrwhyte, knight.   LINCOLN.

108   Thomas LUTELEY, cursitor in Chancery, *v.* Robert BATE, rector of Church Lawford.
Lease of defendant's rectory promised in exchange for obtaining a licence for non-residence.
WARWICK.

109   John and Charles LUTLEY of Crofton, gentlemen, *v.* William HEDE.
Gelding entrusted to defendant.   SALOP.

110   Richard LYDE *v.* Robert COTERELL.
Crown lease of tithes of Upper and Lower Kinsham in Presteign (*sic*) late of the monastery of
Wigmore.   HEREFORD.

111–115 Henry LYE v. William son and heir of William STEVYNS and John WALE (Walle, Waule).
Messuages and land in Christchurch and Milton late of John Lye, deceased, father of complainant.
HANTS.

116–118 John LYMBURY v. Nicholas BOYLE of Long Sutton.
Sale of reversion of a tenement in Compton Dundon (Dondo) on a bad title. SOMERSET.

119 The mayor and burgesses of LYME REGIS v. Alice late the wife of William TUDBOLL of
the same merchant.
Balance of the said Tudboll's account as receiver of the town rents. DORSET.

120 William LYNGE v. Thomas BEDYNGFYLD.
Action at common law, pending a suit in this court (*File* 1306, *No.* 62) for land in [Monk-]Soham
the rent whereof is payable to the use of the inhabitants of Soham.
SUFFOLK.

FILE 1366.

1 Peter LAKE of Exeter, merchant, v. John MALYN of Calais, gentlemen, and the sheriffs of
EXETER.
Action for part price of woad, defendant having failed to appear at the place of payment appointed
by arbitration. *Mutilated. Injunctions. See File* 1306, *No.* 1. DEVON.

2–4 John LANE the younger v. John LANE the elder and George LANE.
Messuages and land in the manor of Wheatley late of Robert Lane, deceased, grandfather of
complainant and father of defendant. NOTTS.

5–6 John LANGMAN, clerk, v. Matthew LAPP.
Vicarage of St. Kew, whereof defendant claims a Crown lease. CORNWALL.

7–8 Richard LAURENS v. Thomas son and heir of Thomas NORRES.
Messuage and land in Snettisham late of Richard Cupper, deceased, grandfather of complainant.
NORFOLK.

9 William LAWSON v. Harry LANE.
Part price of a share in a lease of the manor of Bourton-on-the-Water belonging to complainant in
right of Elizabeth his wife, deceased, sister of complainant. GLOUCESTER.

10–12 Stephen LAYRE and Anne his wife v. William LAMBERT of Paswicke (*i.e.* Pattiswick?)
carpenters.
Detention of deeds relating to lands in Danbury held jointly with John Lambert, yeoman and
Elizabeth his wife both since deceased. ESSEX.

13–14 Anthony LECHE of Standlake, carpenter, and Agnes his wife, daughter of Alice Genyver,
deceased, v. Thomas TUCKWELL (Stuckwell) of Longworth, co. Berks, husbandman.
Crop of corn on the land of the said Alice, promised to the said Agnes and Richard Were her brother
on the marriage of the said Agnes with defendant. OXFORD, BERKS.

15–16 Richard LECHE and Alice his wife v. John, son and heir of Roger CROWCHE, husbandman.
Obtaining a conveyance of a messuage and land in Husborne Crawley from John Sleyn of Twmswik
(*i.e.* Tingewick?), co. Buckingham, husbandmen, father of the said Alice when ' strawfte and
lunatyke.' BEDFORD.

17–18 Hugh SEE v. John OSWYN, clerk, servant to the late Duke of Northumberland.
Manor of Woodford Grange and lands in Wombourne and Trysull late of the priory of Dudley,
which was granted to the said Duke. STAFFORD.

19–24 Reynold SEE, gentleman, v. Walter TRAVERS of Nottingham, goldsmith, and James
THURLAND and Nicholas ENGLISHE, complainant's sureties.
Action for cost of making brooches and a ring, which were of much baser gold than contracted for.
NOTTS.

25 . . . LEE *alias* Cocke v. . . .
Land in defendant's manor of Flamstead. *Mutilated.* HERTS.

26–28 Francis LEEKE, knight, v. Oliver WOODHEED.
Detention of deeds relating to a messuage and land in Clown. DERBY.

29–31 The same v. Richard BOCHER, stepson and executor of Robert Knutton, complainant's
bailiff.
Rents of lands in Scarcliffe, Palterton, Ault-Hucknall, Rowthorn (in Ault-Hucknall), Staynmore, and
Bolsover, and loan. (*Replication wanting.*) DERBY.

32–40 Henry LEIGHE, esquire, Agnes his wife, Robert TRUMPE, and Joan his wife, v. Agnes,
executrix and late the wife of Robert THIMBLETHORPE, and George and Bertram his sons.
Reviver of a suit before Lord Wriothesley for a messuage and land in Worstead late of Robert
Camond, deceased, father of the female complainants. *Both suits included.* NORFOLK.

41–42 Raynold LESSYE v. Roger BURFORD (Bufford) and Elizabeth his wife, late the wife of
William Owner.
Goods of Ralph Owner of Dunwich, deceased, whose executors were the said Richard and William.
SUFFOLK.

43 Nicholas LES[TRAUNGE?], knight, v. James HAWES, citizen and merchant of London.
Arrest on a statute staple for a loan with interest at 25 per cent. after agreeing to arbitration.
Audita querela. LONDON.

44 Christopher LEWENS, gentleman, v. William BARRET of Hampton, co. Surrey, gentleman.
Detention of deeds entrusted to defendants. KENT.

E 2

45–48   Thomas LINCOLN, great-nephew and heir of John Bacon, *v.* Thomas ADAM and William
ORDING.
Messuage and land in West Keale and Keale Coates. *Bill in duplicate.*   LINCOLN.

49–50   Morres LLEWELLYNG and Emma, his wife, late the wife of Leonard Gosney, *v.* Nicholas
CORYNGDON.
Land and a watercourse in Mark.   (Defendant states that in this manor, on a grant of a reversion,
the existing tenant must sue for a renewal of his estate).   SOMERSET.

51   John LLOID *v.* RICE ap Morgan and others.
Land in Aberglyn late of Lewis Lloid, deceased, father of complainant.   CARMARTHEN.

52   Hugh LLOYD, ordinary yeoman of the guard, *v.* RICE ap Howell ap Robert.
Lands in Echeldrey (*i.e.* Ucheldref in Llanflewyn?) late of Katherine wife of complainant.
                                                                                    ANGLESEA.

53   John LONG of Westminster, one of the Queen's bedesmen, *v.* James TOOLY.
Messuage and orchard in Ide late of Richard Long, deceased, father of complainant.   DEVON.

54   Henry LONGE, clothier.
Petition for directions in the trial of an action of defendant against John Geryshe, late of Melksham,
clothier, who has pleaded threats uttered at Southampton, where the action must therefore be
tried.   HERTS.

55–60   Philip LONGE *v.* Joan EYER, concubine and executrix of Giles Eyer, dean of Chichester.
Plate and household goods entrusted to the said Giles, which defendant states to have been recovered
by suit in this court during the said Giles's lifetime.   SUSSEX.

61   William LONGSDEN and Juliana his wife *v.* Richard BARREY and Ellen his wife, executrix
of John Harryngton and mother of the said Juliana.
Goods promised to complainants on their marriage.   ———

62   Thomas LOVETT *v.* John COLE.
Bond for conveyance of lands in Weedon Beck (Wydon in the Street).   N'HUMB.

63–64   John LUCAS, esquire, *v.* Anthony HARVYE, esquire.
Detention of deeds relating to the manor of Huish Champflower and the advowson of the church
there.   SOMERSET.

65   John LUTER *v.* the mayor of OXFORD.
Action by Fabian Humfrey for price of woad alleged to be unmerchantable. *Certiorari.*   OXFORD.

66   Roger LYMMER *v.* Joan, executrix and late the wife of Thomas STRUTT.
Debt for wheat bought of Robert Miller, whose executor complainant is.   ———

67–70   William LYNE (Lynde) of Snape, husbandman, *v.* Robert DUXE of Swefling, husbandman.
Conveyance of a close of land in Bruisyard extorted by a false charge of theft.   SUFFOLK.

71–73   William son of Francis LYNGEN *v.* Hugh FOXE, Robert HUGHES, and others.
Manor of Cotton and messuages and lands in Westbury and Wortham late of William Lyngen of
Huish, gentleman, deceased, uncle of complainant.   SALOP.

74–75   John LYNSEY of London, armourer, *v.* Humphrey MOSELEY, gentleman.
Messuages in St. Peter's Cornhill of the bequest of Elizabeth, late the wife of Christopher Noryce,
knight.   (Complainant states that by the custom of the City, leases of church lands are not vacated
by the death of a parson or churchwarden.)   LONDON.

76   The same *v.* the same and the mayor and sheriffs of LONDON.
Action by the said Moseley concerning the premises. *Certiorari and subpœna. Damaged.*
                                                                                    LONDON.

77–80   Hugh LYPYATE and Susan his wife *v.* Peter TOLPOT (Tolpate) and Anne his wife.
Messuages and gardens in Lambeth Marsh late of Thomas Huntlowe, alderman of London, deceased,
kinsman of both parties. *Rival pedigrees given.*   SURREY.

FILE 1367.

1–2   James LACYE *v.* Robert HUNGERFORD, esquire, nephew and heir of Thomas Yorke of
Helthroppe (*i.e.* Throope in Stratford Tony?), co. Wilts, esquire, and STEPHEN ap Peeres(?)
Manor of Estham in Crewkerne, advowson of the church of Estham, and messuage and land in
Crewkerne at the gift of John Lacye, grandfather of complainant. *Faded.*   SOMERSET.

3–4   Stephen son and heir of Richard LACYE *v.* Anne late the wife of John KNEVET, esquire.
Reviver of a suit concerning the site of the manor of Horham Thorpe Hall, etc. (*File 1242, No.* 3).
Mutilated.   SUFFOLK.

5   John LADYMAN *v.* John ABINGTON.
Messuages and lands in Brent Eleigh and Monks Eleigh, late of John Hunt the elder, deceased,
grandfather of complainant. *Each damaged.*   SUFFOLK.

6   Edward LAKYN of Kenley.
Petition for a commission to John Gateagre, esquire, and others to inquire into his title of Kinnerton
grange and Ritton marsh (both in Wentnor).   SALOP.

7   Richard LAMBERD of London, weaver, *v.* Hugh NEWALL, yeoman.
Price of white sackcloth.   LONDON.

8–9   Henry LANE and Henry OSBORNE, bellows-maker, *v.* William WYLLYNGTON, esquire,
Ambrose CAVE, knight, and others.
Lease from Thomas Fyssher, gentleman, of lands in Aston, Witton, Handsworth, and elsewhere,
claimed by defendants as forfeited for non-payment of rent. *Faded.*   WARWICK, STAFFORD.

10–11 Henry LAWRENCE of the Middle Temple, gentleman, v. Henry PO(Y)SHE and William
LAWLES.
Land in Romney Marsh of the demise of John Cheyney, gentleman, son and heir of John Cheyney
of West Woodhay, co. Berks, esquire. KENT.

12–15 John LAVERAUNCE v. John RE(Y)NOFF and Clere COURTIER.
Refusal to complete an assignment of a lease made by the mayor and burgesses of Totnes of a house
and a garden in Totnes. DEVON.

16–17 Thomas LAYER, clerk, v. Thomas HALL, steward of the late college of Stoke, and Robert
DAVYE, vicar of Ickleton, co. Cambridge.
Presentation to the parsonage of Ashen, conveyed by Matthew Parker, dean of the said college, and
his chapter since the statute for the dissolution of colleges. ESSEX.

18 Thomas LECHE v. Edward [LECHE his brother?]
Meadow and cottage in King's Sutton and Astrop late of John Leche his father. NORTHAMPTON.

19–24 Francis LEDEGATE (Ledgiat) v. Lawrence son and heir of William PALMER.
Messuage and land in Braytoft late of William Ledegate, deceased, grandfather of complainant.
LINCOLN.

25–30 Reynold son and executor of Geoffrey LEE v. Christopher and Ursula MOUNTFORDE and
others.
Farm in Bysshopburton and wardship of Geoffrey brother of complainant. *Mutilated. See File
1306, No.* 24. [YORK.]

31–34 Richard grandson and heir of Alexander LEEKE v. Thomas DADSLAY, and Nicholas
JULYAN his tenant at will.
Messuage and land [in Bottesford and Normanton] claimed by the said Dadslay through Robert
Erswell of Barston. *Bill wanting.* WARWICK.

35 William LENSEY and Anne his wife, sister and heir of John Grace, v. Thomas WYTTON.
Moiety of lands in Standon awarded to the said Anne by a commission from the Court of Requests.
HERTS.

36–37 . . . LETHUM v. Roger CAPSTAKE.
Account of sale of woods in Gringley park and other business of William Nevell, esquire, master
of both parties. *Damaged.* NOTTS.

38–40 Thomas LEWES of the Middle Temple, gentleman, and Alice his wife, v. William WYKES,
gentleman, late clerk of the kitchen to the Earl of Pembroke.
Price of corn bought of George Poole of Shepperton, gentleman, late the husband of the said Alice.
MIDDLESEX.

41 LEWIS ap David of London, yeoman, v. Lewis APPENDRYE and Robert VAUGHAN.
Messuage and land in Painscastle late of David ap Jenkin, yeoman, deceased, father of complainant.
RADNOR.

42 LEWIS ap Mores of Whitechapel, baker, v. John ap Llewellyn *alias* ESTER.
' Table, manger, and boyer ' of Lewis, son of defendant. LONDON.

43 LEWIS ap Owen of London, gentleman, v. JOHN ap Owen and MORICE ap David.
Land in Berriew (Berhuewe) of the grant of Hugh ap Owen, gentleman. MONTGOMERY.

44–51 Harry Jevan LEWYS of South Newton, v. Mansell BYLLINGTON (Abillington, Ablyngton)
the elder and the younger.
Loan. (Answer taken by commission at Hawarden.)
WILTS, [FLINT].

52 Joan late the wife of Thomas LEWYS and William their son v. William PLATEFOTE,
gentleman.
Parsonage of Barkway of the demise of Thomas, late abbot of Colchester. HERTS.

53 John, son and heir of Matthew LEYTYE and of Agnes his wife, v. Richard, son and heir of
James TRESAGHER and of Joan his wife.
Reviver of a suit by the said James and Joan against Matthew Hoskyn, clerk, brother of the said
Agnes, for messuages and lands in Tresuthan (*i.e.* Treswithan in Camborne?) Trevrevowrthe,
Rosewryne, the borough of Penryn, Tregrasek (*i.e.* Pengersick in Breage?), Spernane (in Breage) and
Prestlowe. CORNWALL.

54 Philip LLENWARNE of Shaftesbury, co. Dorset, v. Sebyll LLENWARNE, John her son,
and Thomas WEBBE.
Messuage and land in Much Birch late of Richard Llenwarne, deceased, father of complainant.
HEREFORD.

55 LLEWELYN ap Griffith and Maude his wife, v. Edward GRYFFYTH and others.
Land in Llangayng late of William Edward Llewelyn, deceased, brother of the said Maude.
CARMARTHEN.

56 Jevah LLOID, yeoman of the Chamber, v. THOMAS ap David ap Res and WILLIAM ap
Hoell ap John.
Refusal to complete a sale of a messuage and close of pasture in Newborough. ANGLESEY.

57–60 Thomas LLOID *alias* White of Bristol v. Sebill late the wife of Hugh LEWYS and Joan
LYPPARD *alias* Meredith.
Messuages, and land in Stapleton and Willey late of John Lloyd *alias* Whyte, deceased, father of
complainant. HEREFORD. (HAVERFORD *in Bill.*)

61 Res LLOYD, servant attendant on the Earl of Arundel, v. Res HERGEST.
Under lease of a tenement in Llansaintffraed to Stephen Doone, complainant's enemy, contrary to.
promise. RADNOR.

62–64   The same v. DAVID ap David.
Land in Llanvareth claimed by defendant through Hoell ap David his wife's grandfather.   RADNOR.

65   Roger ap Jevan LLOYD, servant to Lord Rich, v. Jevan Dyo LLOYD and others.
Conspiracy to indict complainant of felony.   RADNOR.

66   The same v. David ap Jevan ap David LLOYD.
Claim under a wrongful award in a frivolous suit.   *Mutilated.*   RADNOR.

67   William LOKAR, bailiff of Simon Lowe, v. Richard YATES, gentleman, John his brother,
and others.
Assaults and forcible entries at Arlingham.   *Supplicavit.   See File* 1365, *Nos.* 80–83.   GLOUCESTER.

68–70   Thomas LONG v. Thomas HALLE.
Pasture in Trowle of the demise of Thomas Halle (de Aula) of Bradford, esquire, grandfather of
complainant.   WILTS.

71–72   Arthur LONGEVYLE and Anne his wife, daughter and heir of Geoffrey Myddelton, v. Richard
NYCOLLES and Richard SAYE.
Messuage and land in Tilney.   *See File* 1244, *No.* 47.   NORFOLK.

73   Luke LONGLEY v. John AMORE and Margaret his wife.
Price of sheep sold at Crimplesham to John Rowland, former husband of the said Margaret.
                                                                                       NORFOLK.

74   John LORYNGE of Arlsey (Alrycheseye), co. Bedford, husbandman, and Margaret his wife,
late the wife of Thomas Dryver, yeoman, v. Edward BROKETT, gentleman.
Messuage and land in Graveley, Stevenage, and Wymondley, claimed on behalf of John Dryver,
son of the said Thomas and Margaret, born after his mother's remarriage.   HERTS.

75–77   Nicholas LOVELAKE and Parnell his wife v. John POLWHEYLL.
Messuage, quay, and orchard in Plymouth late of James Pylkyngton and Radegund his wife,
deceased, great-grandparents of the said Parnell.   DEVON.

78–79   The same v. Ellis WARWYKE.
Detention of the deed of entail of the above.   *Subpœna duces tecum.*   DEVON.

80–81   The same v. the same.
Messuages and land of like descent in Plymouth, Sutton Prior, Sutton Vautort, and Nethercombe.
                                                                                       DEVON.

82   William LOWRE v. John CRUYS, executor of John Bealburye, 'a poste and a notable
rebell.'
Plate of the said Bealburye seized by complainant when serving under Lord Russell in the suppression
of the western rebellion.   CORNWALL.

83–85   Robert LUCE, citizen and leather-seller of London, v. Thomas FULSEHURST of Crewe,
knight, and Robert, his son and heir apparent.
Conveyance, invalidated by statute, of messuages and lands (tenants' names given) in Barthomley
and elsewhere, with rents including a rent called 'tylth and ward,'   *Mutilated.*   CHESTER.

86–89   Roger, son of Richard LUCE, deceased, v. Edmund RYTHE, steward of the manor of
Trematon, and others.
Tenement at Burraton in the said manor.   CORNWALL.

90   John LUMLEY, lord Lumley v. Percival LUMLEY *alias* Vavysour.
Profits of the manor of Bradbury, a coal-mine in Stubclose, messuages and lands in Haughton and
Great Chilton and the agistment of Lumley park.   DURHAM.

91–92   Thomas Locke and George Roman, churchwardens of LYDLINCH, for themselves and all
their parishioners, v. Bartholomew and Richard ROMAN.
Lands in Lydlinch given by Thomas Husey, esquire, for the repair of the parish church.   *Answer
wanting.*   D. XIV, 63.   DORSET.

93–95   Richard LYELL, master in Chancery and precentor of Wells, v. William HAYMAN.
Parsonage of Pilton and Wotton, demised to defendant by George Dogean, late precentor.   D. IX, 52 ?
                                                                                       SOMERSET.

96–98   John LYLYNGSTON of Milbrook, husbandman, v. Thomas HUNNERESTON (Homerston)
of Hitchin and ———— his wife.
Part price of wethers sold to William Wylot of Milbrook, husbandman, deceased, former husband
of the female defendant.   BEDFORD, HERTS.

99–100 Elizabeth LYNTON v. Ralph HOPTON, knight, Thomas GOSMERE (Cosyns), and Oswald
RADDOKE.
Messuage and land in Ditcheat held of the manor of Glastonbury.   *See File* 1138, *No.* 103
                                                                                       SOMERSET.

101–104 John LYON, gentleman, v. Richard INGOLDSBYE of Cowley in Preston, gentleman,
Winifred his wife and Francis their son.
Lease of part of the manor of Lenborough with pasture for sheep.   BUCKS.

105   Richard LYSTER, grandson and heir of Saveacre Dalaber, esquire, v. George DALABER,
esquire, and John, Richard, Thomas, William, James and Nicholas DALABER.
Manors of Clehonger, Kinnersley, Chilson (in Madley) and Meercourt (in Allensmore).   HEREFORD.

106–107 Thomas LYTLE of West Thorpe (*i.e.* Thorpe by Newark?) v. Christopher STORRE of
Newark.
Detention of deeds and of malt.   NOTTS.

108   Joan, Marion, Anne, Elizabeth, and Ellen, sisters and heirs of Robert LYVER(E)D, v. Edith,
late the wife of Edward WILLMOT, their guardian in socage.
Detention of deeds relating to land in Steventon.   *Mutilated.*   BERKS.

FILE 1368.

1   John MACHELL, alderman and sheriff of London, v. Elizabeth, late the wife of Peter WAKEFELDE, and Jenett WAKEFELDE.
Price of worsted and fustian sold to the said Peter.   LONDON.

2   John MAISTERSON v. Ralph BROKE.
Tithes of defendant's lands in Leighton.   CHESTER.

3-6   John MANBY and Elizabeth his wife v. Thomas VYNCENT, Margaret his wife, daughter of Thomas Alen of Mattishall, and others.
Forgery of a will in the name of William Straycocke, deceased, father of the said Elizabeth and former husband of the said Margaret, disposing of messuages and land in Yaxham.   NORFOLK.

7   Randall MANEWARINGE, knight, v. John DAMPORTE, esquire, and others.
Detention of deeds relating to the tithe of Over Peover belonging to the parsonage of Rostherne and that of Chelford belonging to the parsonage of Prestbury.   CHESTER.

8   Harry and William MANNELL v. Edmund ACTON, Alice his wife and Juliana MANNELL.
Money and household goods of George Mannell of Alby, deceased, whose executors complainants are.   NORFOLK.

9   Walter MARCHAUNTE v. John GYBBES and Joan his wife, late the wife of John Pawle.
Money advanced to pay defendant's tenement in Wookey Hole.   SOMERSET.

10-13   Benet MARGITT, alias Hellande, husbandman, v. Alexander WOLCOMBE, esquire.
Refusal to complete a lease of messuages and land at Helland in Probus.   CORNWALL.

14-17   Thomas MARKEHAM, vicar of South Creake, v. James BYGOTT (Bygett), gentleman.
Tithe of wool and lambs demised by Thomas Lemon, late vicar, for less than its value.   NORFOLK.

18   Anthony MARLER of London, mercer, and William WELE, v. William GOODBOROW.
Messuage and land in Wilmington of the demise of Thomas Kyrrey of London, salter, deceased, uncle of the said Wele.   KENT.

19-22   Thomas MARLETT v. John YONG and Thomasyn, his wife.
Messuages and lands in Shipley, late of John Marlett, deceased, elder brother of complainant and former husband of the said Thomasyn.   SUSSEX.

23-24   John MARSHALL, yeoman, v. William HOUSDEN and others.
Messuages, cottages, and land in Bishop's Stortford (Stertford, Startford) and Great and Little Hallingbury, late of John Marshall, deceased, grandfather of complainant. *Answer wanting.*   HERTS, ESSEX.

25-26   John MARSHALL, husbandman, v. Robert PAYNE of Croxton, co. Cambridge, gentleman.
Messuages and land at Wintringham in St. Neots of the demise of Thomas Rauns, late prior of St. Neots, and his convent.   HUNTINGDON.

27-28   Edward MARTEN v. Robert HARDY (Herdy) of London.
Detention of deeds relating to land in Boughton Monchelsea of the bequest of John Orgar.   KENT.

29   Edward MARTEN of Caxton, husbandman, v. John and William MUNES.
Messuage and land in Madingley, late of William Marten, deceased, father of complainant.   CAMBRIDGE.

30-31   Humphrey son of John MARTEN v. William MILL of Launceston.
Refusal to sign a contract not to alienate his lands, promised to complainant on his marriage with Alice his daughter.   CORNWALL.

32   William MARTEN v. Nicholas and Philippa LAA.
Messuages and land on St. Austell and St. Blazey, partly complainant's own, and in part held jointly with defendants by William Hygo his ward. *See File 1363, No. 1.*   CORNWALL.

33-35   John MASTYN v. Nicholas HASARDE.
Action on a bond for delivery of Gascon wines to be laden on complainant's ship *Coxes Barke* of Southampton, which was robbed of her outward cargo by pirates.   HANTS.

36   John MASTER, husbandman, son of William Master and of Alice his wife, both deceased, v. William THOMSON.
Land in Chilthorne Domer, late of William Horley of Nethway (in Brixham), co. Devon, esquire.   SOMERSET.

37-39   Thomas MATHEWE of Buckfastleigh, co. Devon, joiner, v. Ralph COUCHE of Penryn, gentleman, and Harry TREMAYNE.
Tithing corn of Mevagissey.   CORNWALL.

40-41   William, son of Robert MAUNDRELL, deceased, v. Richard his brother and Edward BAYNTON.
Lease of a tenement in Rowde (Rodde), made according to complainant by Queen Katherine [Parr] and according to defendant by Queen Katharine [Howard].   WILTS.

42-43   Thomas MAWLE (Mall) v. Lancelot SPERE.
Refusal to complete a sale of messuages and land in Stoke by Nayland held of the manors of Stoke and Leavenheath (Levenhaye).   SUFFOLK.

44-46   Nicholas MAWNDRELL v. John, son and heir of Richard WAKE of Hartwell, co. Northants, esquire.
Refusal to complete a lease of a messuage and land in Clevedon.   SOMERSET.

E 4

47   Richard MAYE, Joan his wife, Robert MAYE, Dorothy his wife, and Lucy, daughter and heir of Robert PERESON and of Grace his wife *v.* Thomas BOCHER of Wisbech.
Messuage and land at Parson Drove in Leverington, late of John Costym (Costyn) of Wisbech, deceased, father of the said Joan, Dorothy and Grace.   CAMBRIDGE.

48   John MAYNE of Peamore (in Exminster), yeoman, *v.* Thomas WHYTFELDE.
Detention of deeds relating to messuages and land in Braunton.   DEVON.

49   Robert MAYNEWARINGE of Mertyn [?serjeant-attendant-on] the King and Queen, *v.* the homage and suitors of the manor of NEWHALL (in Heswall) and Thomas TAYLOR.
Action for a tenement in the said manor. *Certiorari and subpœna. Mutilated. See File* 1310, *No.* 6.   CHESTER.

50–51   Richard MEARE (Meyre) *v.* Constance MEYRE.
Tenement in Stapleford, late of William Meare, deceased, father of complainant. *Mutilated.* NOTTS.

52   John, son and executor of Thomas MEDE, *v.* Joan, late the wife of John FORDE of Blackawton, yeoman, and Nicholas his son, his executors.
Silver girdle of 28 ounces pledged to the said John Forde.   DEVON,

53–54   John MERSSHALL, prebendary of Haydor with Walton, *v.* Robert DAVY *alias* Baker, grandson and heir of Joan wife of William Meed.
Tenement· in complainant's manor of Walton, late of Robert father of complainant, hanged for felony.   BUCKINGHAM.

55–58   Anne, late the wife of William MERYAT and daughter of Margaret Clapsho, deceased, *v.* John WYNTER.
Messuage and land in West Tisted, held of the manor of Merryfield.   HANTS.

59–61   Joan late the wife of Robert MERYTONE.
Petition for commission to inquire as to a right of way to a meadow in Braughing from the manor of Mutfords in Little Hormead, demised by the chancellor as master of Trinity Hall, Cambridge, and the fellows thereof.   CAMBRIDGE.

62–63   Henry METCALF, Frances his wife, Peter BAYLAND, and Joan his wife, *v.* Alice, executrix and late the wife of Robert PETT.
Legacies of John Yardley, father of the female complainants, whose executor the said Pett was.

64–67   William MODY of London, grocer, *v.* John ASSHENHURST and Joyce his wife, executrix and late the wife of John Moseley of Ashbourne, yeoman.
Price of groceries (*schedule annnexed*).   LONDON, DERBY.

68–69   Thomas ALLSHOP *v.* the same.
Money accruing to complainant as apprentice to the said John Moseley. *Faded.*   DERBY.

70–73   Charles MOGRYDGE of Winterbourne Stoke, gentleman, son and heir of George Mogrydge, *v.* Thomas MYCHELL and Edith his wife, executrix and late the wife of the said George.
Household goods of the said George (*described*), including two cotterels, two bell candlesticks, two querns, a ' mesyng fatte ', a salting-tub (' sylte '), and 6 cart-horses with their ' harmes, houkes and cheynes.'   WILTS.

74   The same *v.* Robert COWSLED and others.
Detention of money and of deeds relating to messuages and land in Henstridge, entrusted to defendants by the said Edith.   SOMERSET.

75   Joan late the wife of John MOGRYDGE, William ERLE, and Maude his wife, *v.* John HICK(H)EY, supervisor of the will of the said Mogrydge and John his son.
Messuage called Bingwell and land held of the manor of Tiverton.   DEVON.

76   Robert MOLEHOWSE *v.* Henry PECKE.
Detention of deeds relating to land in Wattisfield and Walsham, late of the free chapel of Redgrave and Botesdale.   SUFFOLK.

77   Henry, grandson, and heir of Humphry MOLYNS, esquire, *v.* Thomas COLEPEPER, esquire.
Detention of deeds relating to the manors of Mongewell, Mackney (in Brightwell), Sandell (*i.e.* Sandhill in Fordingbridge?), Fountayne, Jaylers Crosse and Galbridge (in Martock), and messuages and lands in Beckley (?), Sotwell, Wittenham, West Corscombe, Masterton (Mostorn), and elsewhere. *See File* 1245, *No.* 60.   OXFORD, BERKS, HANTS, SOMERSET, DORSET.

78   John MONKE of Launceston, yeoman *v.* John LEN of the same, gentleman.
Bond to warrant a tenement called Goodmansley against Gabriel Lennard, stepson of complainant, to whom he has conveyed it. *Mutilated.*   CORNWALL.

79   Philip MORCOMBE and Margery his wife *v.* William BROWNYNGE, clerk.
Share of goods of John Brownyng of Holysworthie, tanner, deceased, father of the said Margery and brother of defendant, whose will was burnt in the episcopal registry by the western rebels.   [DEVON.]

80   John MORE, gentleman, *v.* John TYLLYS and Alice his wife.
Close in Bristow late of Thomas More, gentleman, deceased, father of complainant.   NORFOLK.

81   Mary, late the wife of John MORE and granddaughter of John Monson, knight, deceased, *v.*
Tenements in Keelby. *Mutilated.*   LINCOLN.

82   Richard son and heir of John MORE, by William Warham, knight, his *prochein amy, v.* Anthony MORE, gentleman.
Manor of Horwoods and lands called Horwood's Lands in Preston Candover, formerly of John Horwodde. *Pedigree given.*   HANTS.

83-87   Robert MORE of Shipston-upon-Stour v. Thomas WOODALL, and Richard BROWNE of London, salter.
Cloth belonging to John Ryder *alias* Pitt, indebted to complainant.   WORCS, LONDON.

88-89   Thomas, son and heir of John MORE of Sherfield, gentleman v. Thomas PARMYNGER (Barmyger).
Land in Hartley Westpall held of the manor of Holdshott.   HANTS.

90   Thomas MORE, citizen and merchant tailor of London, and Amy his wife v. John SPENCER of Althorpe, knight, executor of Richard Catisby of Ashby St. Leger, knight.
Money promised by the said Sir Richard on the marriage of the said Amy his daughter.
          LONDON, NORTHAMPTON.

91-92   William MORE, kinsman and heir of William Malyns of Horley, co. Oxford, v. Edmund RYCHARD.
Detention of deeds relating to a messuage and land in Tysoe.   WARWICK.

93   Ralph MORGAN of London, baker, v. OWEN ap Owen, esquire, and JAMES ap Lewys, yeoman.
Detention of deeds relating to messuages, cottages, a mill and land in Eglossawen, Kemmes, Cardigan, Whitechurch, Treygmor, and . . . oythe.   CARDIGAN, PEMBROKE.

94-98   Thomas MORGAN of Hurst, son of Alice late the wife of David Lewys of Salisbury, draper, v. John KEYVELOCKE (Keyloake) of Minsterworth and Margery late the wife of William MICHELL.
Messuages and chantry rent in Westgate Street *alias* Eburgestrete in the parish of St. Nicholas, Gloucester, formerly held by the said Keyvelocke to the use of Andrew Whytmaye, clerk, deceased, his brother-in-law.   GLOUCESTER.

99   William MORGAN v. HENRY ap Richard.
Detention of deeds relating to lands in the lordship of Goldcliff.   MONMOUTH.

100   John MORLEY, husbandman, v. Thomas BAKEWELL.
Detention of money and goods of John Morley, deceased, father of complainant, and of a tenement in Hollington bought therewith and held of the honour of Tutbury.   DERBY.

101   John MORTON, yeoman, grandson and heir of John Morton, v. Joan REYNOLDYS and others.
Detention of deeds relating to messuages and lands in the borough of Week St. Mary, West Style (*cf.* Steelhill in Week St. Mary), Penalam (in Jacobstow?), Stowe and St. James (*i.e.* Jacobstow?)
          CORNWALL.

102   Thomas MOUNTGOMERY of Shrewsbury, draper, v. William TUDDER of the Oak (in Bicton).
Loan to John Tudder of Shrewsbury, deceased, whose executor defendant is.   SALOP.

103   John MOYNE v. James DANYELL and Richard CHEKE.
Cottage and land in the manor of Beaminster Secunda of the demise of the said Danyell and of Henry Hoskyns.   DORSET.

104   John, nephew and executor of John MUDGE, v. John THORNE.
Money entrusted to defendant by Alice late the wife of the testator.   ————

105   William MURSTON the elder v. Edmund BRUDENELL, esquire, and Robert HOPKYNS.
Parsonage of Slawston bought of John Campynet, gentleman.   LEICESTER.

106-108 William MURYELL, [citizen] and grocer of London, v. Thomas and Robert NEWTON and others.
Contempt of a decree in a former suit (*File* 1146, *No.* 60) concerning a messuage and garden in St. Peter's, Derby. *Mutilated.* D. IX, 32.   DERBY.

109-110 Richard MYCHELL and Margaret his wife, daughter and heir of Richard Garton, v. Francis GARTON, gentleman and Ursula GARTON.
Messuages, barn and land in Billingshurst and Pulborough settled on the said Richard Garton by William his father, deceased, husband of the said Ursula. *Damaged. See Files* 806, *No.* 33; 1223, *No.* 5; 1309, *No.* 70.   SUSSEX.

111-112 John MYLDENHALE, yeoman, v. Thomas DRORIE and John W(H)ARLTON.
Detention of deeds relating to a messuage and land in Fincham.   NORFOLK.

113   John MYLL, grandson and heir of William Awalley, v. Arthur BANE.
Detention of deeds relating to tenements in Preston and Kirkham.   LANCASTER.

114   Thomas MYLLINGTON, citizen of London, v. the sheriffs of LONDON, and Richard DEGRO.
Action of debt after promising forbearance so that complainant might obtain the means of payment.
Certiorari and subpœna.   LONDON.

115   John MYLSENT and John ADAMS, executors of Thomas Adams of Cambridge, v. John WOOD and Godfrey SWAYNE, executors of John Fanne of the same.
Bonds for the marriage settlement of Margaret Swayne, step-daughter of the said Thomas Adams, with the said Fanne, satisfied by a conveyance of a brewhouse in Chesterton.   CAMBRIDGE.

116-122 Francis MYNSHULL, esquire, v. Maude late the wife of Thomas WALLEY, John MYNSHULL, esquire, and James HAUGHTON, gentleman, his executors, and others.
Messuage and lands in Wimboldsley formerly of John Whitmore of Thurstaston.   CHESTER.

FILE 1369.

1   Thomas MANLEYE and John SMYTHE v. John MOLTON.
Bail given before the justices of the liberty of Peterborough.   NORTHAMPTON.

2-3   Thomas MAPOWDER, gentleman, v. John BUCKINGHAM.
Refusal to complete a sale of a leasehold messuage (' myce ') and land in Holsworthy paid for in money and cloth.   DEVON.

4   John MARAM and Edmund GYLBERT v. John BOLMAN.
Bond for price of barley bought of Thomas Shepman of East Dereham, husbandman.   NORFOLK.

5-6   Roger MARCHALL, gentleman, v. Ambrose BECKWYTH of Middleton, gentleman, his stepfather, and others.
Messuage and land in Sawdon and Naburn late of William Marchall, deceased, father of complainant.   YORK.

7-10   Edmund MARSHALL of Bishop's Tawton v. Anthony ACLAND of Chittlehampton, gentleman.
Acquisition of reversion of a tenement in Goodleigh, which defendant claims to be void by the custom of the manor for lack of the consent of the tenant for life.   DEVON.

11-20   John MARTEN, parson of Bittadon, v. Edmund BURNET, John STAMPE (Skampe), and James GOSLAND.
Seizure of complainant's goods while in hiding as a Papist. (The said Burnet states that he arrested complainant by the Earl of Bedford's command during the rebellion in the west.)   [DEVON.]

21-26   The same v. Humphrey HOLMAN and others.
Access to water called Frogmeare ford and to the market town of Ilfracombe awarded to complainant by arbitration. Faded. (Annexed is an answer by Walter Ley and others.)   DEVON.

27-29   William MARTEN of Beech v. Thomas BERDMORE, bailiff of the manor and leet of Swinnerton, and others.
Forcible entry and seizure of deeds relating to complainant and Thomas Handley, claimed by defendant as a distress for an amercement imposed in the said leet.   STAFFORD.

30-31   John MARTYN, vicar of Somerton, v. Humphrey WORTHY, gentleman.
Detention of deeds relating to complainant's vicarage claimed under a lease from William Radbard (Roodbart), late vicar.   SOMERSET.

32-35   Roger MASCALL v. Robert FYSKE, Joan his wife, late the wife of John Cottell, John COTTELL his son, John GOODWYNE, steward of the manor of Woodbridge, and Thomas CRAPNELL, bailiff.
Tenement in the manor of Woodbridge acquired of Robert Cottell, brother of the said John the elder. Mutilated.   SUFFOLK.

36   William MASON v. Thomas FLETCHER, one of the craft of common bakers of Chester, William FLETCHER, alderman thereof, and John FARTLEFFE and Nicholas WEDDERBYE, stewards.
Fee and expenses for soliciting confirmation of the ordinances of the said craft.   CHESTER.

37-39   Robert MASSY, gentleman, v. John GRYFFYTH, gentleman.
Crown lease of the manor of Maysemenan to Thomas Saulesbury, since deceased.   DENBIGH.

40   John MASSYE of Etchells v. Roger COMBES.
Refusal to complete a sale of wheat.   CHESTER.

41-42   Robert, younger son of Robert MASSYE, deceased, v. John MAYNWARYNG and others.
Messuages and land in Shocklach, Aldersey and Barton, formerly of Randolph Massye, and in Coddington formerly of William Massye, brothers of complainant. Damaged. (Defendants cite a decree of the Council of the Marches.) See File 1370, No. 36.   CHESTER.

43-45   Harry MASYN the younger, yeoman, v. Richard HOLBETON.
Debt of John Masyn, deceased, brother of complainant, already paid.   DEVON.

46   George MATHEWE and Alice his wife, executrix [and late the wife of Thomas Smythe?] v. Thomas SMYTHE and others.
Farm called Woodecote (in Leek-Wootton?). Mutilated. See File 1245, No. 42.   [WARWICK?]

47-49   Humphrey MAWTHELL, late chantry priest of St. Anne's, Bewdley, v. Thomas HOPKYS, clerk.
Detention of letters patent conferring a pension on complainant.   WORCESTER.

50-53   Thomas MAYNARD and John POLLOXFEN, executors of Thomas Polloxphen, v. Robert STEPHYN and Thomasyne his wife, late the wife of Andrew Pyttes.
Refusal to complete a sale of oaks at West Pitten in Yealmpton.   DEVON.

54-56   William MEDOWES, husbandman, v. Simon WYLDON (Wylder), late villein regardant to the manor of Brailes.
Messuage and land in Over-Brailes surrendered by defendant in consideration of his enfranchisement.
D.X.42   WARWICK.

57-58   Nicholas, son and heir of Thomas MEGGES, v. Thomas ROWSE, esquire.
Reversion of the manor of Sutterton after a bequest for a term of years to the late prior and convent of Ely. Mutilated.   [LINCOLN.]

59-61   James MELLOR and others v. William GRYM and others.
Destruction of enclosures on the waste of Vincent Mundy's manor of Warslow.   STAFFORD.

62   The warden and scholars of MERTON College, Oxford, v. William FARR and Humphrey
        LEYGH.
Detention of deeds relating to lands in [Stratton St. Margaret]. *Mutilated.*   WILTS.

63–64   The same v. Richard (John) INGRAM.
Destruction of a chapel in the rectory of Wolford and other waste.   WARWICK,

65–66   John MOARE of Gloucester, tailor, v. Henry TWENYNG, husbandman.
Refusal to complete a sale of a tenement and watermill in Painswick.   GLOUCESTER.

67–70   John MOGFORTH v. Katherine SHERMAN and John, her son.
Messuage and land (*place not named*).   [DEVON *or* CORNWALL ?]

71–73   John MONNES of London, ironmonger, v. John HASELWOOD and Roger DYNHAM.
Double bond for price of wine, the said Hasylwood having fled into sanctuary and elsewhere to avoid
receiving payment.   LONDON.

74–76   Hugh MORE v. John EVELEGH, attorney in the Common Pleas.
Manor of Holcombe and messuage and land in Ottery St. Mary and Banton pledged for payment
of complainant's debts.   (Defendant states that the matter is pending in the Court of Requests.)
Bill mutilated. D. IX 9.   DEVON.

77–78   John MORE of London, shoemaker, grandson and heir of Joan Boylle, v. William BAKER.
Tenement and bakehouse ' beyond the river of Tye ' in St. Martin's, Hereford, late of Roger Corowe.
deceased, brother of the said Joan.   D.X, 61.   HEREFORD.

79–80   John MORGAN, gentleman, v. John VYDYAN.
Detention of a lease of Brislington, made by Lord De la Warr.   SOMERSET.

81   Rethergh MORGAN v. RETHERGH ap John, Anne his wife and Rethergh JAMES.
Price of cattle and other goods.   ———

82–85   Lawrence MORSE v. James LEONARD and Alice his wife.
Lands (*described*) in Barking and Dagenham late of Thomas Barbour, deceased, uncle of complainant
and former husband of the said Alice. *Mutilated.*   ESSEX.

86–91   Richard MORYS of London, baker, v. Edward LONGFORD of Chirbury, Katherine his
        wife, late the wife of Hugh Davys, and DAVID ap Hoell.
Messuage and land in the parish (*sic*) of Rorrington (now in Chirbury) of the gift of the said Hugh.
D. XI, 34.   SALOP.

92–94   John, grandson and heir of Richard MURDEN, by William Warner of Ratley and Joan his
        wife, complainant's mother and guardian in socage, v. John SMYTHE, Anthony RANDELL,
        and others.
Messuages and lands in Bramstone, Long Buckby, Daventry, Napton, and Whitnash.
                                                                              NORTHAMPTON, WARWICK.

95–96   Thomas MYLLER, husbandman, v. Edward, son of John MERYWETHER, deceased.
Lands in Shepherdswell late of Thomas Myller of Nonington, deceased, grandfather of complainant.
                                                                                                KENT.

97   William MYLLES, gentleman, v. Dorothy late the wife of William WYLDE, Wyatte her
        son, and William GYFFORDE her son-in-law.
Lands (*described*) in the manor of Croydon forfeited by the said William Wylde and Dorothy.
                                                                                               SURREY.

98–100 The same and others, tenants of the manor of Croydon, v. the said Dorothy.
Reviver of a suit against the said William Wylde for copyhold lands in the said manor.   SURREY.

101–103 Thomas son of Edward and Sybil M . . . v. Richard MEDWELL and Alice his wife.
Closes in the manor of Evesham of the demise of the late abbot and convent of Evesham. *Mutilated.*
                                                                                              WORCESTER.

FILE 1370.

1–3   Thomas MACHELL v. Richard MACHELL and John his son.
Manor of Crackenthorpe and messuages, a mill, land, and rent there and in Keisley in Dufton
(Kesclyve), Appleby, Brampton, Lazenby (Lesingby) and Kirkoswald late of John Machell, deceased,
grandfather of the said Thomas and Richard.   WESTMORLAND, CUMBERLAND.

4   The same v. Henry MILNER and others.
Tenements of defendants in the manor of Crackenthorpe.   WESTMORLAND.

5   The president and scholars of MAGDALEN College, Oxford v. Elizabeth late the wife of
        [Edmund] MARVYN, knight, J.Q.B.
Wood called Prior's Rede adjoining Alice Holt, in a farm formerly held with that of Thedden (in
Alton) by the ancestors of defendant.   HANTS.

6–9   The same and Ralph STANNOWE, gentleman, farmer of their manor of Gaton (in
        Brandiston), v. George HORSEMAN, esquire, owner of the manor of Booton.
Rights of common and fold-course in Brandiston and Booton heath.   NORFOLK.

10–11   Thomas MALLET v. John BOYDELL.
Mortgage of the reversion of a messuage and land called [Ranw]orthy and Postrydge in Durley and
Spaxton. *See File* 1247, *No.* 1.   SOMERSET.

12–14   Agnes MAN v. Nicholas MAN.
Messuage and land in Reddisham late of Robert Manne, deceased, husband of complainant and
father of defendant.   SUFFOLK.

15–18   Henry MARABLE v. Thomas BOLLES and Anne his wife.
Messuage and land in Kirton-in-Holland late of Robert Marable, deceased, brother of complainant and husband of the said Anne.   LINCOLN.

19   MARCILA varth David v. GRIFFITH ap Evan ap Richard, clerk, and Maud his wife.
Detention of deeds (*place not named*) and goods.   —— ——

20–22   MARGARET verch Robert and ROSE . . . v. EDWARD and JOHN ap Edward ap Davy.
Cattle and land in Whitton late of Robert ap Johane of Evyn, deceased, father of complainants, whose executors defendants are. *Mutilated.*   SALOP.

23–24   William MARLER v. Richard NYCKLYN, Richard DENTON [and others?], parishioners of the Holy Trinity, Coventry.
Messuages and land in Coventry late of John Paddon, deceased, grandfather of complainant, who also granted closes of pasture in Coventry to the said parish. *Mutilated.*   WARWICK.

25–27   Richard MARSHALL, yeoman, v. John JACKSON of East Rainton, yeoman.
Tenement in West Rainton demised by the dean and chapter of Durham to Thomas Trippe, yeoman, afterwards attainted of felony.   DURHAM.

28   William MARSHALL, parson of Marston Moretaine, v. Richard WESTONE, esquire.
Tithe corn claimed in right of the chapel of Wroxill by defendant, who obtained a Crown lease thereof in spite of a decree of the Court of Augmentations.   BEDFORD.

29–30   George MARTEN of Walsall v. Nicholas MOORE.
Detention of a bond for a debt from which defendant had deducted 2s. for payment before it was due.   STAFFORD.
     The same v. Eleanor, executrix and late the wife of Thomas POMFRETT.
Price of lease of a bloom-smithy payable in charcoal.   STAFFORD.
     The same v. Richard CROSSALL.
Price of work.   STAFFORD.

31   Peter MARTEN of Helston v. John VYVYAN, esquire. ·
Tin works, 'knack mylnes' and blowing and grinding mills for tin in Wendron (Seynt Guendon) pledged to defendant as surety for a debt since paid.   CORNWALL.

32–34   Richard MARTYN, esquire, and others, feoffees to uses, for themselves and all the inhabitants of Long Melford, v. Edward and Thomas ABBOTT.
White rents and woods of the manor of Bower Hall in Pentlow, granted by John Hill of Melford, clothier, for payment of the king's [tax] of Melford or for alms when there was no tax.
                                                                                      SUFFOLK.

35   Elizabeth late the wife of John MASON and Henry her son v. William STARTE.
Detention of a demise made by John Hall of land in Harpford (Herforde).   DEVON.

36–38 . Robert MASSY v. John MASSY (Masey), John MANWARYNGE and others.
Messuages and lands in Clutton Edge, Shocklach, Coddington, Great Aldersey, and Barton late of Randolph Massy, deceased, brother of complainant and of Roger, father of the said John Massy.
See File 1369, *No.* 41.   CHESTER.

39–42   Thomas MATHEWE v. John son of Richard ODYNGZELLES and John LANGBROKE, servant of complainant.
Lease of the manor of Cabornes in Stanford-le-Hope. D. X, 17.   [ESSEX?]

43–44   John MAYE v. Thomas, grandson and heir of William SWYTSER.
Messuage and land in North Cray late of John Maye and Denise his wife, deceased, grandparents of complainant.   KENT.

45   Thomas MERCHE v. John BRAYE, lord Braye.
Messuage, barn and land in Burgham (Burkham) late of William Merche, deceased, grandfather of complainant.   SURREY.

46–49   MEREDITH ap Jevan of Chenies, co. Buckingham, v. JOHN son and heir of Rice ap David.
Land in Llananno late of Jevan ap Cadogan, deceased, father of complainant.   RADNOR.

50–51   Hugh ap David ap Evan MEREDITHE v. LEWIS ap Griffith ap Jevan ap Madocke.
Land in Trawsfynydd late of Evan ap Meredith, deceased, grandfather of complainant.
                                                                                     MERIONETH.

52   David MEREDYTH and . . . his wife, v. Hugh ap David GOZ of Dythur, gentleman.
Lands [in Dythur?]. *Mutilated.*   [MONTGOMERY?]

53   William [?ap Rich]ard MERVYN of Margam, yeoman, v. John FRANKLYN.
Price of oxen. *Mutilated.*   GLAMORGAN.

54–55   Francis MERYNGE, esquire, v. John and Henry STOWE.
Lease of the rectory of Newton late of the monastery of St. Katherine, Lincoln.   LINCOLN.

56–57   Jacomyne, executrix and late the wife of Boniface MEWRES of London, beer-brewer, v. Charles FRANKE.
Refusal to account for partnership in a brewhouse called the *Hartes Horne* in All Hallows, Barking, and obtaining an award in an arbitration which complainant could not attend. LONDON.

58–60   William, son of John MICHELL and of Joan his wife, v. Thomas, William and John SPEDE.
Messuage and land in Old Cleeve of the demise of William Dovell sometime abbot of Cleeve.
                                                                                     SOMERSET.

61–62   Richard MIRFELD, servant to the bishop of Winchester, v. Nicholas TEMPEST, esquire, Thomas and Henry HEPWORTH, and others.
Manors of Tong and Collynghed and messuages and lands there and in Holm and Ryecroft (both in Tong) late of Peter Mirfeld, esquire, father of complainant, and manors of Morley, Fyncheden, Howley (in Ardsley), Mirfield, Hopton, Dighton, Batley, Bolton (?), Newstead, Wakefield, Gildersome, Kirkheaton, and Little Smeaton, and messuages, mills, land and rent in the same places and H[uddersfield?], Stubbs, Womersley, Soothill, Ossett, Saxton, Woodkirk, Little Bowling, Drighlington, South Byram, Chekynley, and Frysby, late of John Mirfeld, his grandfather.
                                                                                                                    YORK.

63–68   The same v. Thomas WATERTON and John TEMPEST, knights, Henry TEMPEST, esquire, and others.
Do.   YORK.

69–71   Henry MOLYNS v. Humphrey MOLYNS.
Manor of Mongewell, late of William Molyns, esquire, deceased, father of complainant.   See Files 1245, No. 60; 1368, No. 106.   OXFORD.

72–75   John MORDAUNTE, lord Mordaunt, v. John OKEDEN, gentleman, and Cecily, his wife, late the wife of Thomas Basskett, gentleman.
Claims of common in complainant's manor of Dawlish.   D. XII, 22.   DORSET.

76–79   The same, and John MORDAUNT, knight, his son and heir apparent, v. John son and heir of Thomas LENTON.
Pasture (described) in Lowick in dispute between the manors of Lowick and Aldwinkle.
                                                                                                               NORTHAMPTON.

80–83   John MORE of Wing, co. Bucks, v. Roland HOLLAND of Bridgnorth.
Manor and parsonage of Ratlingcope, late of the monastery of Wigmore.   SALOP.

84–85   Richard MORE, prisoner in the King's Bench, v. Jasper POUNT.
Debt of Thomas Stukeley, esquire, for which he had pledged the farm of Wotton.   DORSET.

86–87   The same v. Barnard DUFFELD (Dovell), his fellow-prisoner.
Lease of the parsonage of Shapwick lent with money, and debts of complainant fraudulently collected by defendant.   DORSET, LONDON.

88–89   Maurice MORECOK v. Dame Joan HAMCOTES (Amcotes).
Messuages, gardens, and orchards in Faversham and the Isle of Harty, late of Henry Hatche, deceased, cousin of complainant.   KENT.

90   Thomas MORELAND and Alice, his wife, late the wife of Robert Worgan, v. Edward and William WORGAN.
Detention of deeds relating to land in Newland.   Mutilated.   GLOUCESTER.

91   Henry [MORGAN], bishop of St. David's, v. Jeffrey TAYLER.
Parsonage of Carew, claimed under a lease from Robert Ferrar, the deprived bishop.
                                                                                                                PEMBROKE.

92   Cecily, late the wife of William MORLEY, v. Mary, late called Lady DARRELL, alias Mistress Mauncell, and George DARRELL.
Trespass on a messuage and land in Leverton (in Chilton Foliat parish, co. Wilts, but in Kintbury hundred, co. Berks), in contempt of an order of this court.   BERKS.

93–95   Robert MOSLEY and others, inhabitants of Bilston, v. Hugh LEE of Woodford Grange, yeoman.
Lands for the support of a priest in the chapel of Bilston, confiscated as chantry lands. STAFFORD.

96–98   John MUDDELL v. Thomas DEPLAKE (Diplake, Duplacke).
Tenement in the manor of Mayfield, late of Richard Muddell of Godstone, co. Surrey, deceased, father of complainant.   D. X, 32.   SUSSEX.

99–102   Richard MYLLER v. Richard WEST, yeoman, both of Hulcote (in Easton-Neston).
Office of bailiff of the manor of Easton-Neston of the gift of John Willyams, knight.   NORTHAMPTON.

FILE 1371.

1–2   John NALLE of West Bromwich, esquire, v. Francis MOUNFORD, gentleman.
Refusal to complete a lease of messuages, cottages, and lands in Walsall and Wednesbury.
                                                                                                                STAFFORD.

3–6   Nicholas NAPPER v. John MASTER.
Refusal to complete a lease of a messuage and land at Milton in Martock.   SOMERSET.

7   William NAULL of West Bromwich v. executrix and late the wife of John PRATTYE of Yardley.
Loan of oxen.   STAFFORD.

8   Henry NAYLER, citizen and clothworker of London, v. Anthony BLOWE.
Bond for debt of defendant, to Lawrence Sheres of Islington, innholder.   MIDDLESEX.

9–11   Baldwin NEDE v. the mayor and bailiffs of OXFORD, and Augustine WYLMOT (Wylmyn) and others.
Actions for trespasses in the Port Meadow (' Portemede alias Portemanheyte ') of Oxford, in dispute between the said mayor and bailiffs and the manor of Woolvercot. Certiorari and subpœna.
                                                                                                                OXFORD.

12–13   Thomas NEVYLE, knight, v. Thomas SMYTH, gentleman.
Detention of a lease made by Anthony Browne, viscount Montague, of a messuage in St. Mary Overies, Southwark.   SURREY.

14–17   Richard NEWETT v. John ROWELL alias Newett.
Messuage and land in Sutton and Dingley late of Agnes Newett, deceased, claimed by complainant
as his grandmother and by defendant as his great-grandmother. (No. 16 belongs to a cross suit).
NORTHAMPTON.

18–19   John NEWMAN v. William ABBOTTE, yeoman.
Lands in Bishop's Stortford (Startford) late of John Newman, deceased, father of complainant.
HERTS.

20–21   Richard NEWMAN v. Thomas STREPER.
Refusal to complete a sale of sheep agreed on at Newport. See File 1265, No. 71.
HANTS (I.W.)

22–23   Benedict, late the wife of William NEWNHAM, knight, v .Thomas COWPER and Edmund
SUTTON, esquires.
Lease of the parsonage of Kirklington, whereof the said Cowper is tenant in reversion. NOTTS.

24   Symon NEWNO, yeoman, v. William GEOFFREY of Monk-Okehampton, husbandman.
Messuage and land in Iddesleigh.   DEVON.

25–27   Robert NEWTON v. William NEWTON.
Land in Epworth late of Richard Newton, deceased, father of complainant.   LINCOLN.

28   Robert NEWYTT v. Robert BANASTRE .
Plate, napery, and deeds late of Richard Newytt, clerk, deceased, whose executor complainant is.
[NORTHAMPTON ?]

29   Thomas NICHOLES, yeoman, v. John and Walter NICHOLAS (sic)   .
Messuage and land in Dillyng (i.e. Dilwyn ?) late of Walter Nicholes, deceased, father of complainant.
HERTS (rectius HEREFORD ?)

30   John NICOLLES of Brundish, gentleman, v. Elizabeth, executrix and late the wife
of John TASBURGHE of Norwich, esquire.
Action on a bond for price of lands in [South Elmham St. Michael and St. Peter], which defendant
had promised not to put in force until they were discharged of her late husband's debts. Damaged.
SUFFOLK.

31–32   The same v. the same and Francis CLOVELL, esquire, now her husband.
Do.   D. XIV. 45

33–38   Thomas NICOLSON, citizen and merchant tailor of London, and Anne his wife v.
Christopher JONES, grandson of David ap Hoell, Jevan MORGAN, and others.
Tenements in Abergavenny and its suburbs late of David Watkyns, deceased, grandfather of the
said Anne.   MONMOUTH.

39   George NODES, yeoman, nephew and heir of Anthony Clarke, gentleman, v. William
CLARKE.
Detention of deeds relating to a messuage and land in Barking.   ESSEX.

40   John NORBERY of Frodsham and John NORBERY of Gray's Inn v. John DUTTON,
esquire, and others.
Manor and lordship of Frodsham.   CHESTER.

41–42   Nicholas NORBON, Blue Mantle pursuivant-at-arms, v. David VINCENT, groom of the
Privy Chamber to Edward VI.
Action for forcible entry on a messuage and land in Richmond late of John Norton otherwise
Richmond [herald], deceased, father of complainant.   SURREY.

43   Gilbert NORCLIFFE and Agnes and Jennet NORCLIFFE his nieces, and wards v. John
NORCLIFFE and others.
Messuages and lands in Barkisland and Southowram, formerly of John Norcliffe, deceased, grand-
father of the said Gilbert.   YORK.

44–47   Richard NORFOCKE (Norfold) v. William TAYLOR.
Land in Dunston of the demise of George Gryffyth, knight.   STAFFORD.

48–49   William NORRES and Cecily his wife, daughter and heir of William Scull, v. Thomas
BENSON, son-in-law of Thomas Erley.
Messuage in Kingston-on-Thames.   MIDDLESEX (sic ; rectius SURREY).

50–52   The same v. the same.
Other tenements in Kingston.   SURREY.

53   William NORRYS v. [John LAVERS].
Detention of a mare and oats entrusted to defendants and failure to repay a loan. Mutilated. ——

54   William NORTHE, husbandman, v. Emma, late the wife of Gabriel THROGMORTON of
Warboys, esquire.
Forgery by the said Gabriel of a surrender of a messuage and land in his manor of Ellington.
HUNTINGDON.

55–57   William NORTON of London, coppersmith, v. Thomas LAXTON and Robert his son.
Messuage and land late held of the manor of Gretton by John Norton, deceased, father of complainant.
NORTHAMPTON.

58   Ralph, son of Roger NORWOOD, esquire, Joan his wife and William TAUTY the elder
and the younger, his tenants v. John BRYDGES, lord CHANDOS.
Tenements in the said Norwood's manor of Leckhampton.   GLOUCESTER.

59–63   John son and heir of Robert NOTT v. Vincent MOGFORD alias Crucie and Agnes his wife,
mother of complainant.
Messuage and land in Lapford wherein the said Agnes claims dower.   DEVON.

64–68   Richard NOTTYNGHAM of Stoneleigh, [miller,] *v.* Richard DENTON, Stephen and Christopher HALES, Richard STONEFELD, and Ralph UNDERHILL.

' Walke myll ' and land in Stoneleigh, with ' loppes and shreddes ' of trees, and fishery between Finham and Stoneleigh bridge, of the demise of John Hales of Coventry, esquire, brother of the said Stephen and Christopher. *Mutilated.*   [WARWICK.]

69   Thomas NOTTYNGHAM of Aldeburgh, co. Suffolk, merchant, and George FATHER of Harleston, co. Norfolk, mercer, his surety, *v.* Robert NORTON, gentleman.

Action in London for a debt which the said Nottyngham is ready to pay.

70–71   Robert NOYES and John his son, *v.* John SEINT JOHN, esquire, and Nicholas his son.

Seizure of corn from the manor of Littleton in Kimpton. (Defendant pleads a decree of the Court of Requests. *See Proceedings of the Court of Requests*, XIV, 71).   HANTS.

72   William NOYS *v.* John OSBORN, esquire, groom of the Privy Chamber to Edward VI.

Lease by John Poynet, late bishop of Winchester, of the rectory of Shipton, invalidated on the ground that he was not lawfully bishop.   HANTS.

73–77   George NUNNE *v.* Thomas, son and heir of Robert SPRYNGE, gentleman.

Corn-rent of the manor of Pakenham Hall, demised with tithes of Pakenham by the late abbot and convent of St. Edmunds.   SUFFOLK.

78–80   John NURTON (Norton, Nourton) and Gregory ROWSEWELL, for all the inhabitants of North Curry, *v.* William LYTE, esquire.

Land in North Curry given for a ' conducte ' priest, repairs of bridges, and ' any maner of harneys or other common charges.'   SOMERSET.

81–82   William NUTTALL *v.* John PERESON, his uncle.

Procuring a surrender of a tenement in Newnham, in the isle of Ely, late held of the Bishop of Ely's manor of Ely Porta by Katherine Wrenche, sometime the wife of Thomas Denys.   CAMBRIDGE.

83   Thomas NUTTINGE, yeoman, and others, executors of Roger Nuttinge, vicar of Minster Lovell, *v.* Robert LUCAS of Asthall Leigh, husbandman.

Tithes of Minster Lovell claimed by complainants to pay first fruits and other debts of the said Roger.   OXFORD.

84–85   Constance, late the wife of John NYCOLLES, *v.* Thomas, son and heir of William BEDELL, gentleman.

Collusive suit for lands in Willingale Doe, Norton, and Ongar against William Pawne and Ellen, his wife, late the wife of the said William Bedell.   ESSEX.

86   Reynold NYGHTTYNGALE *v.* the bailiffs of LICHFIELD.

Action by John Bagnold for assault. *Certiorari.*   STAFFORD.

87   Thomas NYX *v.* Richard TYRE.

Price of Crown lease of a yardland in Sewsterne, being about 20*a.* land, meadow and pasture.   LEICESTER.

88–91   Robert NYXON of Yalding, co. Kent, carpenter, *v.* John JUDKYN.

Cottages, land, and messuages in Rothwell, Orton and Kettering, late of Edward Nyxson, deceased, uncle of complainant.   NORTHAMPTON.

FILE 1372.

1–2   Alice late the wife of Robert ODELL, and Thomas, his son, administrators of his goods, *v.* John SMYTH of Chichele (Chycherley), co. Buckingham.

Pasture ground and cattle in the manor of Brokeborough (*i.e.* Brogborough in Lidlington ?)   [BEDFORD.]

3   George OGLANDER, gentleman, *v.* Maude, late the wife of Sampson THOMAS.

Detention of an entail of messuages and lands in London, Islington, Hackney, Hoxton, and Southampton made by Thomas Thomas, customer of Southampton, deceased, father of the said Sampson, and grandfather of Elizabeth, wife of complainant.   MIDDLESEX, HANTS.

4–5   Andrew and Dorothy OGLETHORPE, administrators of the goods of William Oglethorpe, late the husband of the latter, *v.* Thomas SCOUTHORPE, son-in-law of Clement Oglethorpe.

Manor of Farnehauby and Esthalworth of the demise of the dean and chapter of Windsor.   YORK.

6–7   Thomas OKYS of Flashbrook, yeoman, *v.* John GRENE of Tunstall in Adbaston.

Forgery of a will in the name of William Okys, father of complainant, and brother-in-law of defendant.   STAFFORD.

8–9   Edmund OLDE *v.* the mayor and commonalty of EXETER, John BRAGGYN, and Thomas PAYNE.

Lease of the moiety of Cowley Marshes in Exeter, whereof complainant has failed to repair the banks for lack of ' stakes, frith, and gower ' which should have been delivered by the said mayor and commonalty.   DEVON.

10–13   The same *v.* the said mayor and commonalty.   DEVON.
Do.

14   William son and heir of Robert OLDMYXON, *v.* John OLDMYXON and others.

Manors of Oldmixon in Hutton, and Knighton in Stogursey. *See File* 1148, *No.* 12. SOMERSET.

15–16   Joan OLYVER *v.* Christopher MATHEWE and Wylmoth his wife.

Messuage and land in Milverton, late of the chantry there, demised to Robert Olyver, deceased, father of complainant and former husband of the said Wylmoth.   SOMERSET.

17-19   Thomas ONLEY of Pulborough, co. Sussex, gentleman, and Gertrude his wife, late the wife
of Richard Lee, v. William KINGSWELL, gentleman.
Waste of woods in the farm-place of Shalden of the demise of the said Richard and John his father.
.HANTS.

20-21   Thomas ORDEWAY, citizen and shoemaker of London, and Katherine his wife, daughter
and heir of John Ingram, v. John TOWNELL and Joan his wife.
Reviver of a suit for a messuage and land in Holbrook abated by the said Katherine's marriage.
Answer wanting.   SUFFOLK.

22-23   William son and heir of William ORME v. William GROVE.
Detention of a grant made by William, abbot of Halesowen, and his convent of tithe corn of Rowley,
which defendants states to have been extorted from a co-grantee by the late Duke of Northumberland.   STAFFORD.

24   John OSBASTON, and Humphrey and Anne YARDLEY, children of Anne Merecot (Morecot),
v. Richard WILLES and Henry MORECOT, executors of William Morecote.
Plate and other goods late of Joan Mylton, deceased, wife of the said William and grandmother
of the said John and of Anne Morecot.   ————

25   George OSBORNE of London, goldsmith, executor of Margaret, executrix and late the wife
of Walter Sawkyns of London, wax-chandler.
Petition to examine witnesses as to an oral lease by Bartholomew Jykett of a barn and lands in
the manors of Brownswood (Bramswode) and Stoke Newington. *See File* 1237, *No.* 47.
MIDDLESEX.

26   . . . [late the wife?] of Thomas OSMERE v. Thomas BOYCOTE and Thomas
ATT WELLE, feoffees to uses.
Refusal to refeoff complainant of messuages and land in East Sutton. *Faded.*   KENT.

27   William OTTYE, deputy and attorney to George [Day], bishop of Chichester, as the Queen's
almoner, v. Thomas MYKELFELD of Sawtry, co. Huntingdon, yeoman.
Debt due to Robert Ewen of Little Walden, suicide.   ESSEX.

28-30.   Edward OVER v. John SMYTHE, Hugh BRYNGHELOWE and Barbara, late the wife of
John OVER and guardian in socage to Jacob his son.
Messuage and land in Beaconsfield late of Nicholas Over, deceased, [grandfather?] of complainant.
Mutilated.   BUCKS.

31-33   William OVER, yeoman, v. John and Robert HAYWOOD, great-grandson of Alice Curtes.
Tenement and garden in Wooburn.   BUCKS.

34   Elizabeth, late the wife of Jasper OWEN, knight, v. Robert CATLYN, esquire.
Detention of the will of Henry [Stafford], lord Stafford and earl of Wiltshire.   ————

35   OWEN ap Jevan v. FLEWELLIN and David GYTTO.
Land in ' Clagevelowe in the countie of Cardithe [in] Southwalles ' (*i.e.* Llangevelach ?)
[GLAMORGAN ?]

36   John, son and heir of Roger OWRES v. John LAMBERT.
Detention of deeds relating to tenements in Wethersfield, Shawford and Gosfield.   ESSEX.

37-39   William OWTON of Midhurst, clothier, v. Alice GRETE.
Money of Joan Greate of Midhurst, sister of the said Alice, whose executor complainant is. *See File*
1355, *No.* 47.   SUSSEX.

40   The dean and chapter of OXFORD v. Humphrey CUMBERFORDE, esquire.
Rent of the manors of Wigginton and Cumberford (in Wigginton).   STAFFORD.

41   The chancellor and scholars of [OXFORD] University v. Thomas DEVIES and others.
Parsonage of Holme Cultram. *Mutilated.*   CUMBERLAND.

FILE 1373.

1-7   Anne, late the wife of John PAKINGTON, knight, v. John LITELTON, esquire, Thomas
PAKINGTON, knight, Humphrey PAKINGTON, and John, his son.
Manor (*sic*) of Extons (Hextones) and Arley, messuages and lands in Bromsgrove and Fulham, lands
called Harvington and Cadball Hey, and the manor and parsonage of Chaddesley Corbet. *Mutilated.*
STAFFORD, MIDDLESEX, WORCESTER.

8-10   The said Humphrey v. the said Anne and William SHELDON and others, executors of George
Roll, her brother-in-law.
Action on a bond for assignment of jointure, which complainant claims to have been done. *See File*
1312, *No.* 8.   WORCESTER.

11-12   Thomas PAKYNGTON, knight, v. John WALWYN, gentleman.
Forgery of a custumal (*provisions given*) of the manor of Aylesbury.   BUCKS.

13   Ralph PALMER, gentleman v. Thomas PYGOTT, esquire.
Refusal to complete a lease of pasture in Doddershall. *Mutilated.*   BUCKS.

14   Thomas PALMER, parson of Stoke Climsland, v. Robert BENYE.
Waste (*detailed*) of complainant's parsonage.   CORNWALL.

15-17   Randolph (Randoll) PARKER and Joan his wife, great-granddaughter and heir of Hugh
Hadfelde, v. Roger son and heir of John COMBERBACHE and Roger HADFELD.
Messuage and land in Congleton (the said Comberbache claims that the case should be tried in the
Court of the Duchy of Lancaster).   CHESTER.

18   Thomas PARKINSON, B.D., parson of Willingham, *v.* Lancelot RYDLEY, D.D., late parson, deprived for marriage, and Henry RYDLEY.
Lease of the parsonage.   CAMBRIDGE.

19   Joan PARKYNS and John her son *v.* Hugh TREVILLYAN, gentleman.
Tenement in the manor of Challacomb of the demise of John Trevillyan, esquire.   DEVON.

20–23   Thomas PATMERE, gentleman, son and heir of Henry Patmere *v.* Jerome GYLBERD, gentleman.
Detention of deeds relating to ' grovettes ' and other lands in Colchester, Lexden, and Esterford, said to be claimed by William and Thomas Ball. *See File* 1312, *No.* 17.
ESSEX.

24–27   Thomas PATTESHALE *v.* John TAMWORTHE, esquire.
Manor of Sawdon and lands there and in Great and Little Baddow, Moulsham, Springfield, Boreham, Purley and Danbury late of Joan Otley, deceased, wife of Thomas Otley and grandmother of both parties.   ESSEX.

28   John PAWLYE *v.* [Thomas CONDOROWE of the borough of Truro, porter and keeper of tin.]
Detention of tin delivered to defendant according to the custom of the county. *Faded.* CORNWALL.

29   Roger PAYNE and Alice his wife, executrix and late the wife of Thomas Sandham the younger, *v.* Isabel ROCKE.
Detention of a lease of Colworth (in Oving) made by William Erneley, esquire.   SUSSEX.

30–33   Thomas and John, sons of John PEARS *alias* Paynter, *v.* William GRAUNTE of Moyles Court, overseer of his will.
Farm called Upper Burgate in Fordingbridge of the demise of William Coke.   HANTS.

34   John PECKE of Trumpington, yeoman, *v.* Robert BALLARD and Anne his wife. ·
Debt of complainant to George Richardson of London, former husband of the said Anne, paid in wool.   LONDON.

35   Alice, late the wife of John PEMBERTON of Kirton, yeoman, and Cuthbert their son, *v.* Romayn CHETYLS (Chyttyls).
Lease of the vicarage of Donington which can only be sued on by the lessor or his executors the said John having died intestate.   LINCOLN.

36–38   The said Cuthbert *v.* the same.
Reviver of the above on the death of the said Alice.   LINCOLN.

39–41   Joan PEMBERTON of North Petherton, co. Somerset, *v.* Percival AYRE (Eyre, Eyer) and Stephen MYCHELL, both of Boston, yeomen.
Money collected by John Pemberton, late husband of complainant, for rents and Crown dues of the parsonages of Kirton and Donington, and obtained by defendants on his death in ' passynge the langewasshys between Hollande and Northfok.'   LINCOLN.

42   The same *v.* Hugh PHELLIPPS and Eleanor his wife.
Goods left by the said John in defendant's house.   LINCOLN.

43–46   Nicholas PENNANT and GRIFFITH ap Harry (Apparry), executors of Robert Evans, gentleman, *v.* GEORGE ap Owen and Richard NICHOLLS.
Lease of the rectory of Condover and other deeds entrusted to defendants by the said Evans.
SALOP.

47   Walter PERMYTER *v.* Thomas, son of Robert HARDYE, deceased.
Refusal to complete a conveyance of tenements in Bushey (Bursue) in Corfe Castle.   DORSET.

48   John PEROTT *v.* Thomas EGEBASTON.
Action on a bond for an annuity payable from messuages, ranch, and water-mills in Cullompton, defendant not having proved his title as agreed.   DEVON.

49   Robert PEROTT, yeoman, *v.* Michael THRALE, gentleman.
Rent reserved on tithes in Luton, complainant being lessee of other tithes there and in . . . Challeye (*cf.* Chaul End in Caddington) called Luton tithes.   BEDFORD.

50–51   William, son and heir of John PEVERELL *v.* Thomas WALTON, his tenant.
Detention of deeds relating to lands in Moorlinch (Morlyng) and High Ham.   SOMERSET.

52   David PHILLIPS of the Inner Temple, gentleman, *v.* William LEWES, yeoman.
Land in Llanginning (Saint Kynnynges) bought of Philip and Maurice ap Gwilliam, yeomen.
CARMARTHEN.

53   The same *v.* Henry NICHOLAS, yeoman.
Land in St. Cleers, late of Owen Phillips, gentleman, deceased, father of complainant. CARMARTHEN.

54–57   William PIGION and Eleanor his wife, daughter and heir of William Hermer, citizen of Norwich, *v.* Henry WARD and Margaret his wife, executrix and late the wife of the said William Hermer.
Messuages and lands in Norwich, Postwick and Plumstead, and legacy of sheep.   NORFOLK.

58   Grace, daughter and heir of Richard PLAYFOTE *v.* Thomas PLAYFOTE of Milton.
Dwelling-house in Kingeston, in the parish (*sic*) of Stamshowe, with a barn, horse-mill and other buildings and land in the liberties of Portsmouth.   HANTS.

59   Richard, grandson of Richard POLE, esquire, *v.* . . .
Messuage and lands at Hallasey in Coates (' Hombacye otherwise Hallissey ') and elsewhere, and goods. *Mutilated.*   WILTS, GLOUCESTER.

60–66   David POOLE (Powle), LL.D., *v.* John WILLYAMS, clerk.
Archdeaconry of Gloucester. *Mutilated.*   GLOUCESTER.

67   John POPE of London, gentleman, *v.* the sheriffs of LONDON.
Action of debt by Jasper Fyssher of London, goldsmith, a commission having issued for complainant's
bankruptcy. *Corpus cum causa. Mutilated.*   LONDON.

68   Anthony PORTER *v.* Edward BUTLER and Thomas TOORNER.
Lease of the manor and parsonage of Mickleton, late of Walter Barton of Reading, co. Berks.
GLOUCESTER.

69–70   Margaret, late the wife of John PORTER *v.* Ralph PORTER.
Detention of deeds relating to a messuage and land in Longsdon in the lordship of Horton.
STAFFORD.

71–76   Robert POTTON of Ipswich, clothworker, *v.* William AMYS of Washbrook, yeoman, and
Thomas COWPER of Ipswich, merchant.
Bond given on behalf of defendants.   SUFFOLK.

77–78   Thomas son and heir of William POWLE *v.* Randall (Reynold), [brother and executor] of
John GOOD.
Refusal to complete a lease of cottages and land in Woollavington. *Damaged.*   SOMERSET.

79   The same *v.* William WILLOWES.
Purchase of the same.   SOMERSET.

80–83   Thomas and Joan, children of John PRATTIE, deceased, and Alice PRATTIE, guardian
of the said Joan, *v.* Edward LYTTELTON, gentleman, and his servants.
Land, in the lordship of Birmingham demised together with a mill by Edward Byrnyngham, esquire,
said by defendant to have been attainted of felony.   WARWICK.

84   John PRESTON and others, for themselves and all the inhabitants of Malham, *v.* John
LAMBERT of Calton, gentleman.
Destruction of the chapel of Malham being more than a mile from the parish church of Kirkby-in-
Malham-Dale (Malady).   YORK.

85–87   Hugh PRUSTE *v.* Thomas BLACKEDON *alias* Gyffard and John his son.
Money entrusted to defendants for payment to Thomas Hatche of South Molton.   DEVON.

88–89   The same *v.* the said Thomas BLACKDON, and John HUSBANDE, clerk.
Rent of tithe corn of Hartland. *See File 1149, No. 78.*   DEVON.

90   Edmund PULKRE *v.* William CURTEZ and others.
Messuages and land in the manor of Sutton Courtney late of Edmund Pulkre, deceased, father of
complainant.   BERKS.

91   The same *v.* John TRELOCKE and Agnes, his wife, sister of complainant.
Lands in Sutton Courtney and Sutton Wick, late of the said Edmund, the father.   BERKS.

92   The same *v.* Osmond PULKRE his uncle, Oliver WELLESBOURNE and the homagers of
SUTTON COURTNEY.
False verdict as to other lands therein.   BERKS.

93   John PYCKTON of Hambledon, co. Bucks, yeoman, Lawrence GYLBERT of South Stoke,
co. Oxford, and Ellen his wife, *v.* Matthew CURSELL.
Messuage and land in Aston Upthorpe, late of Thomas Moryn, husbandman, deceased, great-
grandfather of the said John and grandfather of the said Ellen.   BERKS.

94   Roger PYGOT *v.* Robert PIGOT and Sewell WYLLET.
Messuages and lands in Fenny Stratford, late of Thomas Pygot, esquire, serjeant-at-law, father of
the said Roger and Robert.   BUCKS.

95   Richard PYKERYNG and Agatha his wife, *v.* Robert A MERE of Broyle.
Messuage and land in Chichester late of Nicholas Hulles.   SUSSEX.

96–99   Ralph PYLMER and Margery his wife, daughter and heir of Robert Skryven, *v.* Richard
SHELD.
Detention of deeds relating to land in Deerhurst.   GLOUCESTER.

100–101 Richard PYPE and George BASFORDE, citizens and leather-sellers of London, *v.* Bryan,
son and heir of Randall PYE, esquire, and Alexander SLATER, miller, son of Christopher
Slater, deceased.
Water-mill in Whitwell bought of Sir Thomas (William) Holles.   DERBY.

102   Walter PYTCHER and Joan his wife, executrix and late the wife of Thomas Dewseynge
(Dowseynge), *v.* Thomas, son of John FYFTELYNGE of Hardingham.
Life interest of the said Joan reserved with other things on a sale of messuages and land in Hingham.
NORFOLK.

103   Roger P . . ., administrator of the goods of Gilbert Lawson, tallow-chandler of London,
deceased, *v.* Henry DURHAM, of Beverley, late merchant of Hull.
Account of alum, flax, soap and other goods sold by defendant on the said Lawson's behalf.
Mutilated.   LONDON, YORK.

FILE 1374.

1   Robert PAGEITT *v.* Joan EREWYKER.
Detention of deeds relating to a messuage and land in Bradninch.   DEVON.

2–3   Dorothy, late the wife of John PALMER, esquire, and executrix and formerly the wife of
John Gyfforde, esquire, *v.* Roger GYFFORDE, her son.
Rent of the parsonage of Hillesden, of the demise of the late abbot and convent of Notley. BUCKS.

4–5   Ralph PALMER of Waddesdon, gentleman, v. Richard HOLDEN.
Meadow in the 'lotte meads' of Quainton, formerly of John Lamborne of Waddesdon, gentleman.
BUCKS.

6–9   Richard PARK, husbandman, v. William SEDLIE, esquire.
Messuage and land of the demise of defendant, in the manor of Loughton.   ESSEX.

10–13   Walter PATE v. Richard WARREN.
Messuage and land in Loughton, late of Thomas Pate and of Agnes his wife, deceased, grandparents of complainant.   CAMBRIDGE.

14–16   Thomas PATMER of Hadham, co. Herts, v. Thomas, son of Maude WHYTLEY.
Land in Norcott bought of John Grymesdiche.   CHESTER.

17–20   Thomas, grandson and heir of Thomas PEASE, v. John NEWDIGATE, gentleman.
Refusal of admission to a tenement in defendant's manor of Herfelde of the gift of Nicholas Webbe.
Faded.   ?

21–24   Robert PENNYCOOKE v. Thomas TRICE of Godmanchester.
Messuage, land, and 'odgrowes' of wood in Woodwalton pledged to defendant.   HUNTINGDON.

25–26   John grandson and heir of John PERSON v. Anthony NEYSAM and Joan his wife, daughter and heir of Nicholas Person.
Messuage and land in Tydd St. Mary.   LINCOLN.

27   John PERSONS v. William IDWYN and Anne, his wife.
Lands held in coparcenery of the 'senery' and manor of Holt.   WORCESTER.

28–29   Richard PETTYE v. Thomas ANDREWES, knight, and Edward LIGHTFOOTE, late priest.
Tenement in the said Sir Thomas's manor of Ilmington of the demise of Thomas Sandys, lord Sandys.   WARWICK.

30   William POLE and Thomasine, his wife, late the wife of William Beaumont, v. George HAYDEN.
Action to compel complainants to reside on their tenement in defendant's manor of Bere. Mutilated.
DEVON.

31–32   John, grandson and heir of John POLLYNG, v. William POWLYNG.
Land stated by complainant to be in Bilston, and by defendant to be in Chellesworth.   SUFFOLK.

33–36   John PORTER, gentleman, v. George and Henry WALKER, William BLOWE, and Peter TYDDERTON.
Claim of common in Ilam Moor and Dovedale in right of tenements in Castern (in Wetton).
STAFFORD,

37–38   John PORTER of Barton Hartshorne, gentleman, v. Richard DUKE of Newnton gentleman.
Refusal to complete a settlement of lands (not specified) on the marriage of Roger his son, with Joan daughter of complainant.   BUCKS, OXFORD, WARWICK.

39–40   Duplicates of the above, dated 7 June, 1622, and stating that they were copied after the fire, according to proclamation.   BUCKS, OXFORD, WARWICK.

41–43   Thomas PORTYNGTON and Avery MOSELEY, churchwardens of Althorp, and Christopher YONGE and others, feoffees to uses, v. Gilbert SMYTH, late churchwarden.
Messuage and land in the manor of Keadby, given for the repairs of the church of Althorp, and claimed by defendant under a lease from Katherine, duchess of Suffolk.   LINCOLN.

44–47   William PRATT v. Hugh MORECROFTE.
Messuage in Kelvedon late of William Pratt and Agnes his wife, grandparents of complainant.
ESSEX.

48–51   William PRYDE and Robert CLYVERS, churchwardens of Holwell (Holeway), v. Humphrey WATKYNS, gentleman.
Messuage and land in the defendant's manor of Holwell of the demise of John Portyngton, late abbot of Abbotsbury, and his convent.   SOMERSET.

52–55   Anthony PYKERYNG and John his son v. John PELL.
Messuage and land in Threckingham and Stow, said by complainant to have belonged to Elizabeth Mason, and by defendants to Robert Baxter, clerk.   LINCOLN.

56–59   John PYPER v. Henry TREFRYE.
Messuage and land at Lewarne in St. Neots, of the demise of John Trevrye of Tremver (i.e. Tremoore in Lanivet ?), deceased, father of defendant.   CORNWALL.

60–61   Humphrey PYRRY and Dorothy, his wife, late the wife of Thomas Russell, v. Hugh LIDIAT, father of the said Dorothy.
Detention of deeds relating to messuages and lands in Himley, and of a legacy of John Lidiat, his brother.   STAFFORD.

FILE 1375.

1–2   Thomas PACKER and Edmund BENDBOWE v. Thomas BROCKEBANKE.
Action, against the said Packer concerning a sale of corn in Cheltenham, and against the said Bendbowe for replevin thereof. Mutilated.   GLOUCESTER.

3   Ralph PALMER of Knowle, capper, v. John GYBBYNS, clerk, and Martin DARKER.
Messuage and land in Knowle, promised in fee in exchange for the advowson of the church of Winslow.   WARWICK, [BUCKS].

4   Thomas PALMER v. Richard WENTWORTH and others.
Action in the King's and Queen's Bench for a copyhold in [W]illiton formerly of John Aligh, knight.
Faded. See File 1182, No. 21.   [SOMERSET.]

F 2

5   Alexander PARKE, yeoman, son of John Parke, v. Robert THORNTON.
Detention of deeds relating to a messuage and land in Beltoft.   LINCOLN.

6-8   Thomas PARKER and others v. Robert FUTTER and Richard MIDDILDICHE (Middilche), feoffee to uses.
Land in Bressingham the issues whereof were supposed to be used by the churchwardens to the common profit of the inhabitants. *Mutilated.*   NORFOLK.

9-10   Robert PARTRICHE v. Robert ALLEN (Alyen).
Tenement in Henstead (Hempsted) of the entail of Richard Pounde, deceased, great-grandfather of complainant.   SUFFOLK.

11-12   Harry PATENDEN v. William HUGGYNS, husband of Joan, late the wife of Alexander Patenden.
Claim to rent in East Peckham, based on deeds which defendant has refused to show.   KENT.

13-17   Thomas PATESHALL v. John ALEYN (Allen) and George MEDLEY.
Messuage and land in Chawrie, *alias* Broxted, formerly held of the said Medley's manor of Tiltey by Robert Savell (Sawell). *Rejoinder in duplicate.*   ESSEX.

18-19   William PATTUCKE of Stafford, innholder, v. Anthony HART of the same and John PHELLEPES.
Price of a mare sold to complainant but successfully claimed against him by John Spounner.   STAFFORD.

20-21   George PAYNE of Winscombe, gentleman, v. John ROYNON (Runnyon) of Bickford, esquire.
Refusal to complete a sale of messuages, lands, and rent in Axbridge, Cheddar, Compton Bishop, Upper and Lower Weare, and Allerton (Alryngton).   SOMERSET.

22-23   John PAYNE of Carson, gentleman, collector of first-fruits and tenths, v. John ROGERS, knight, sheriff, of Somerset, and Richard his son and under-sheriff.
Information as to extortion of bonds from complainant's sureties.   SOMERSET.

24   Robert PAYNE and Elizabeth his wife v. John MARSHALL.
Waste of trees and hedges on a messuage and land at [Win]teringham in St. Neots of the demise of the prior and convent of St. Neots. *Mutilated.*   HUNTINGDON.

25   John PEERSE, curate of St. Olave's, Southwark, v. John BAYNYARD and John WEBBE, clerk.
Detention of deeds relating to the next presentation to the vicarages of Luppitt and Pelynt.   DEVON, CORNWALL.

26   Hugh PENRYN of London, tailor, and Thomas his brother v. Morres ap John WYN, Margaret his wife, and others.
Messuage called Ewern Ebrame in Deythur.   MONTGOMERY.

27   Richard PERWYCHE of Dingley, co. Northants, gentleman, v. Anne late the wife of Thomas FLETCHER.
Detention of deeds relating to the manor of Lubbenham and messuages and lands in Salterton, Newcastle, Whitmore, Whetmore (*i.e.* Wetmoor in Stretton?) and Milwich late of Richard Perwyche, grandfather of complainant. *Mutilated.*   LEICESTER, STAFFORD.

28-31   Thomas PEVERELL of Southwark, Agnes his wife, John JEFFRESON, Katherine his wife, and Joan BUSSE, v. John, son and heir of William BYSSHE.
Land in Burstow, late of John Busse, deceased, father of the female complainant.   SURREY.

32   Isabel PETTER of Pollesworth, . . ., and Elizabeth his wife, v. Robert PAWLETT (?)
Messuages and lands late of Ralph Burton (?), ancestor of the female complainants. *Mutilated.*
[WARWICK.]

33-34   Roger PHILLIPP v. Matthew PYNCKENEY and Thomas HUTCHYN, bailiff of Lady Sheffield's soke of Snaith.
Messuage in Cowick with tolls, tallage, and other profits.   YORK.

35-36   William PITCHER, Agnes his wife, JOHN RUTLAND, Joan his wife, John SWANE, Christian his wife, Anne NEWPORTE, Alice GOLDYNG, and Joan JAMYS, v. John WALTER, yeoman.
Land in Griston and Walton late of Harry Palmer, deceased, father of the female complainant.   NORFOLK.

37-41   Randall, Thomas, William, Barnaby, Margaret, Elizabeth and Francis, children of Thomas POLE, esquire, deceased, v. John MYNSHALL and Richard HOUGH, esquire, feoffees to uses.
Manor of Netherpool (*now a separate parish*) and other lands in Eastham, the profits of which were to be employed to complainants' advancement.   CHESTER.

42-43   Jane late the wife of Otis POLGREENE v. Humphrey POLGREENE, his brother.
Lands in Govan and an annuity in Bospolvyn (in St. Columb Major), promised in lieu of dower in Polgreene (in Newlyn East?) and Bospolvyn.   CORNWALL.

44-46   The same v. the same.
Detention of deeds relating to messuages and lands in Lanner (in Gwennap), St. Stithian's, Gwennap, and elsewhere.   CORNWALL.

47   Simon PONDER of London, pewterer, v. the sheriffs of LONDON, and Thomas ALTHAM, citizen and clothworker of London.
Action against complainant alone for a debt of John Heppeworthe, for which he was bound jointly with John Lute, warden of the Clothworkers' Company. *Subpœna and certiorari.*   LONDON.

48–51　Giles POOLEY, gentleman, and Alice his wife, *v.* John PULHAM, yeoman.
Meadow in Framlingham ' at Castell ' late of Giles Tendeslowe, deceased, father of the said Alice.
SUFFOLK.

52　John POPHAM and Amy his wife, posthumous daughter of Howell Adamz, *v.* Roger APWILLIAMZ, son of Robert Apwilliam, deceased.
Land in Seintatham pledged by the said Howell. *Mutilated.*　　[GLAMORGAN.]

53–56　John POWELL of Westminster *v.* Humphrey DAVID.
Tenement in Llanbrynmair, formerly of Jevan Bache, great-grandfather of complainant.
MONTGOMERY.

57　Thomas POWELL of Warwick, draper, *v.* William PHYLYP and JEVAN ap Morgan.
Refusal to complete lease of a messuage and land in Llanstephen (' Seynt Stevyns parysshe.').
RADNOR.

58　Peter POWER of London, shoemaker, *v.* Martin DANYELL.
Debt to Pascowe Power, deceased, of whose goods complainant is administrator.
LONDON, CORNWALL.

59-65　John PRICE, knight, *v.* Edward PLANKNEY, Ralph MORES, John REDMAN, and others.
Registrarship of a commission appointed 26 Henry VIII for visitation of exempt religious. *Mutilated.*

66–67　Elizabeth PROWSE *v.* Marmaduke POPHAM, gentleman.
Manor of Durleigh and lands there of the demise of Robert Welshe, master of the hospital of St. John Bridgwater, and his brethren. *Damaged.*　　SOMERSET.

68　Hugh PRUSTE of Hartland *v.* Edmund SPECKOTT, esquire, and others, executors of Richard Graynfilde, knight, son and executor of Roger Graynfilde, esquire.
Price of wines and other goods, and set out of tithes of Moorwinstow.　　DEVON, CORNWALL.

69-71　Isabel, executrix and late the wife of John PRYGG, *v.* Joan, late the wife of Robert DYER and administratrix of his goods.
Trading account.　　SOMERSET.

72　Edward PYLSTON, knight, and others, parishioners of Gresford.
Commission to inquire for church goods stolen in anticipation of Edward VI's command to sell them.　　DENBIGH.

73–75　John PYTT and Agnes his wife, late the wife of John Buckland *v.* Edmund FORD.
Land in defendant's manor of Harting of the demise of the feoffees of Roger Lewkner, knight, and Constance his wife. *Answer wanting.*　　SUSSEX.

FILE 1376.

1–2　Robert PACHELL (Pechell), husbandman, *v.* Robert YVES.
Messuage and land in Billinghay which defendant claims to belong to a manor now dismembered so that courts cannot be held.　　LINCOLN.

3　Thomas PAINE of Hutton *v.* Richard ROGERS, late under-sheriff, and Francis STRADLINGE.
Action by the said Stradlinge on a bond for a payment extorted by the said Rogers.　SOMERSET.

4–5　William PALLMER, esquire, *v.* William HYNDE.
Lease of lands in Burton-on-the-Hill granted to complainant on condition of respite of a debt.
GLOUCESTER.

6–7　John PALMER, Crystyan his wife, daughter and heir of Eleanor Henberye, and Richard their son, *v.* Philip CROME, surveyor to Thomas Mayle, knight.
Refusal of admission to overland and other lands held of the said Sir Thomas's manor of Puriton, part of which lands defendant claims to be demesne.　　SOMERSET.

8-10　Peter PALMER *v.* John BARWYKE, late customer of Bristol.
Money expended as defendant's deputy.　　GLOUCESTER.

11　William PALMER, gentleman, *v.* Edward GRYFFYN, esquire, attorney-general.
Detention of a grant made by the late abbot and convent of Peterborough of the office of bailiff of the manor (*sic*) of Cottingham and Middleton. *Endorsed* with an abstract of contents and the words ' Speke to the attorney.'　　NORTHAMPTON.

12–13　John PARKER *v.* William HARRYSON.
Cottage and land late held of the manor of Waltham Holy Cross by Richard Parker and Joan his wife, parents of complainant.　　ESSEX.

14–15　Roger, grandson and heir of Roger PARKER *v.* William, grandson of Humphrey DOWNES.
Messuage and land partly ' shutynge upon the Porte Waye ' in the lordship of Haughton and Coton Clanford (in Seighford). *Answer wanting.*　　STAFFORD.

16　John PARROT of Cullompton *v.* William GAGE of Ottery St. Mary, son of John Gage.
Lease of land in Payhembury (by the name of all his messuage, etc. in Payhembury, North Charlton and Kentisbeare) already leased to William Broke and Alice his wife.　　DEVON.

17–18　Thomas PARRYS, citizen and mercer of London, *v.* John FOSTER.
Balance of a debt of John Herbert, esquire, and Lady Jane Powys his wife, which defendant had promised to pay in wool.　　LONDON.

19   Robert PARTON v. the bailiffs and aldermen of WORCESTER, and William LYTTELTON, gentleman, town-clerk.
Action on a verbal promise to convey a meadow in St. Martin's, Worcester, the jury being packed. *Certiorari and subpœna.*   WORCESTER.

20   John PASWATER v. Ralph COCKE.
Lands in Biggleswade late of William Westerdale, clerk, deceased, uncle of complainant. D. XI, 35. *See File* 1312, *No.* 13.   BEDFORD.

21   Joan late the wife of Richard PAULYN v. Richard, Agnes, and Stephen PAWLYN.
Goods given away by deceased when a hundred years old, leaving nothing for complainant and her children.   CORNWALL.

22–23   Lord Chidiock PAWLETT v. Richard BATTYE, yeoman.
Messuage and land in Ripon.   [YORK].

24   The same v. William FAYREFAX, knight.
One-third of the manor of Bilbrough, formerly of Ralph Battye, clerk.   [YORK].

25   The same v. the same.
Do.   and one third of the manor of Sandworth (*cf.* Sandwith Lane in Bilbrough).   YORK.

26   Edward PAWMPLYN and Henry LYNTON, yeomen, v. Martin GARROTT and Christian his wife.
Plate and goods of Alice Cotes, deceased, whose executors complainants are.   [CAMBRIDGE?]

27   John PEARLE v. John EVANS *alias* Taylor and Philip JENKYN.
False title to lands in complainant's lordship of 'Callow; whereof defendant was formerly steward. *Mutilated.*   HEREFORD.

28   Edmund PECKHAM, knight, v. William CAPINDALE and others.
Windmill and land in Nottingham bought of Hugh Broke.   NOTTS.

29   John PEKDEN, husbandman, son of Richard Pekden, deceased, v. [Richard MYCHEL-BOURNE of Ditchling, gentleman, and John CHYLDE his tenant, a sheriff's bailiff].
Occupation of a messuage and land in Stanmer of the demise of John Pears, late dean of Malling, and his college, in contempt of a commission from this court. *Mutilated.*   SUSSEX.

30–33   Bartholomew PEROT (Parrott) v. Agnes JENKYNS, late the wife of John Davy.
Messuages and land in Great Brickhill acquired of the said Davy by a feoffment which defendant declares to be to uses.   BUCKINGHAM.

34   Joan late the wife of Robert PERS v. Henry THYRKYLL, a rebel, son and executor of Ralph Thyrkyll.
Extortion of money and detention of deeds relating to a tenement in Yarmouth bought of the said Ralph. *See File* 1044, *No.* 25.   NORFOLK.

35–37   John PERYAM, clothier, son of John Peryam, v. Edward HYLMAN and Alice his wife.
Detention of deeds relating to lands in East and West Teignmouth.   DEVON.

38–39   Richard PERYN of London v. George VYNCENT of Southampton, merchant.
Promise to return 55*l.* in money or canvas out of 400*l.* awarded to defendant by arbitration.
LONDON, HANTS.

40–41   Nicholas PERYS of Launceston v. Thomas HUMFREY of Lawhitton, merchant, and John BROWNE.
Detention of a bond for a debt already paid.   CORNWALL.

42   James PHILCOKE, an executor of Hugh Philcoke, v. ―――― an executrix and late the wife of John WRIGHT, John WRIGHT, and Ralph FOXLEY.
Non-payment of a debt of Robert Loráuns, whose executor was the said John Wright, deceased, and suppression of a bond for the same. *Mutilated.*   ――――

43–46   William PHILLIPOTT of Newark, merchant, v. Richard GRAVES of Langford.
Refusal to become surety as promised for a debt of John Graves for pins and other pedlar's ware.
NOTTS.

47–48   Morgan PHYLYP, precentor of St. David's, a student at Oxford, v. WILLIAM ap Rice of Haverford.
Prebends of the Spittall and Trefgaron and a cursal prebend annexed to the precentorship. *Faded.*
CARDIGAN, PEMBROKE.

49   John PLAW . . . and others, yeomen, with all the other inhabitants of Langham v. Thomas HILTON.
Rent granted by Margaret Odham for payment of the ' holy mote rente ' of Langham. *Mutilated.*
SUFFOLK.

50–51   Richard, son of Simon PODYCHE v. Thomas HEWAR(DE), gentleman, and others.
Messuage and land in Emneth of the gift of John Swynkar of Wisbech.   CAMBRIDGE.

52–54   Edward POLE, gentleman, v. John FOWLER of Chichester, baker.
Messuage, land, and will in the manor of Kemble of the demise of Richard Onis (*sic*), abbot of Malmesbury.   WILTS.

55   Richard POLLARD, yeoman, v. Francis CHERLEY (Sherley), esquire.
Messuage and land in Ratcliffe, formerly of St. Katherine's chantry in Melbourne, in Derby.
LEICESTER.

56–58   William, son and heir of William POLLARD by Christian his wife, v. John POLLARD.
Detention of deeds relating to a messuage called Mead Place and lands in Bramdean and Cheriton.
HANTS.

59   William PONCELL v. John and Thomas COLE.
Land late of complainant's father at Brinscombe in Weare.   SOMERSET.

60   Thomas POWELL v. John DAVID ap Jevan ap Rice and others.
Lands late of David ap Kadogan. *Mutilated.*

61   William POWELL, parson of Rhoscolyn ' otherwyse called Guynfayn,' v. John Lewys ap Jevan LLOYD, bastard [son of Lewis ap Jevan Lloyd, late parson?].
Lands of the said parsonage. *Mutilated.*   ANGLESEA.

62–65   Thomas POYNTER of Whitchurch, clothman, executor of John Browne, v. William BENET.
Wages of the said Browne as defendant's servant.   HANTS.

66–68   Thomas PRATTE of Rugby, poulterer, v. Richard HALLE, bailiff of Kilsby, William HALL, bailiff, and Richard BURNHAM.
Messuage and 2 ' quartrons ' of land late held of the manor of Kilsby by Roger Alsoppe.
NORTHAMPTON.

69–75   John PREDYAUX of Orcherton v. William and Agnes PREDYAUX.
Detention of deeds relating to the manor of Street and messuages and lands there and in Burleston and Fuge (all in Blackawton) late of John Predyaux of Orcherton, deceased, grandfather of the said John and William. *See File* 1253, *Nos.* 50–52.   DEVON.

76   Nicholas PREDYE v. John BYDGOOD of [Langford] Budwell and John ENGLYSSHE, steward of the court of Milverton.
Action in the said court for a supposed debt to Robert Bydgood, deceased, brother of the said John. *Mutilated.*   SOMERSET.

77   Hugh PRICE v. EDWARD and GRUFFYDD ap Res ap Ithell and others.
Close of pasture in Merton, formerly of Thomas ap Thomas.   FLINT.

78–80   John PROCTOR of Sturton, yeoman, v. William RYMYNGTON of the same, husbandman.
Threshing a ' tuffolde ' of peas bought for winter feed of complainant's cattle, so that he should not know the quantity. (*See* Wright's Dialect Dictionary.)   NOTTS.

81   Robert PROCTOUR and Winifred his wife, daughter of William Blytheman, esquire, deceased, v. George LASSELLES, esquire.
Money given to defendants in consideration of a marriage between his son and the said Winifred, which did not take place. (The marriage settlement included land in Sturton and the town of Brentcliff, *i.e.,* Brentshill in Barton?)   NOTTS.

82–83   Bartholomew PUTHALLE v. Joan EGLISFELD.
Tenement late held of the manor of East Ham by John Cole, ancestor of complainant. *Pedigree given. Mutilated.*   [ESSEX].

84–89   The same v. the same.
Do., the lands being held of the late abbot of Stratford, and defendant appointing the steward of the manor.   ESSEX.

90   Anthony PYKERYNG and Anthony WILLIAMSON v. Francis CAWDRON, Mary his wife, and James DYSNEY, gentleman, brother of the latter.
Manor of Burton Pedwardine and plate and other goods late of Thomas Colston, deceased, former husband of the said Mary, the said Anthony, Anthony and James being his executors. *See File* 1312, *No.* 78.   LINCOLN.

91   Thomas P . . . v. Thomas HUNTE and Joan his wife, executrix and late the wife of Ralph Huggens of Kyrkbye.
Loan. *Faded.*

FILE 1377.

1   Adrian QUINYE of Stratford-on-Avon, mercer, v. John COMBES, gentleman.
Detention of deeds relating to a messuage land, and a barn in Stratford-on-Avon.   WARWICK.

2–4   John QUYCKE v. William HULLAND, esquire.
Tenement in the manor of Honiton Sege of the demise of Nicholas Holland, esquire, deceased, father of complainant.   DEVON.

5–8   Thomas QWYCKE, parson of Cranoe, v. Thomas GOODRYCHE.
Claim to complainant's parsonage under a lease from Nicholas Wyddon late parson deprived for marriage.   LEICESTER.

9   Thomas RANDELL, John his son, and Thomasyn, wife of the latter, v. Henry RANDELL.
Messuage and land called Willestrew in Lamerton of the demise of William Randell, gentleman, father of the said Thomas, whose heir defendant is.   DEVON.

10   John RANDOLF of Peter[sfield], clothier, v. Mawdlyn ROBERTES of Southampton (a man).
Debt to Thomas Vyncent of Win[chester], clothier, deceased, whose executor complainant is. *Mutilated.*   HANTS.

11–15   William RASTELL v. Francis STYLECRAG (Steelecragge).
Messuages, cottages and gardens in the parishes of Our Blessed Lady (*i.e.* St. Mary Aldermanbury?) and St. Michael Bassishaw, claimed under leases respectively from the prior of Elsing Spital and the Crown. *Mutilated. Rejoinder wanting.*   LONDON.

16–23   Richard RATCLIFFE, cousin and heir of Jeffrey Ratcliffe, gentleman, v. Edward MONTAGUE, knight, and Robert FERNHAM, esquire.
Messuages and lands in Mountsorrell, Rothley, Barrow, Quorn, Woodham, Belton and Long Whatton. D.XI, 9.   LEICESTER.

F 4

24   Elizabeth, executrix and late the wife of John RAVESSHE, clerk comptroller of the household of the late Duke of Somerset, v. Richard WHALLEY, esquire, chamberlain to the Duke.
Wages appointed to the said John, after the arrest of the Duke, by the commissioners of the late King's
council.

25-29   William RAWKYNS and Cybell his wife, daughter and heir of Thomas Lovell of Etchil-
hampton, co. Wilts, v. Anthony DENTON, master of the town of Wells, and the burgesses
(brethren) of WELLS.
Messuage called the *Meremede* with land and common of pasture in Wells.   SOMERSET.

30   The same v. the same.
Do. (house and defendant not named).   SOMERSET.

31   Henry RAYE, Denise [his wife, and their child?], v. John BONHAM, knight.
Pasture called ' Leyfeld ' of the demise of Lady Anne Mountjoye, wife of defendant.   *Mutilated*.
          WILTS.

32   William RAYME v. John PORTER, clerk.
Refusal to complete a demise of land in Wheatley (Queteley).   NOTTS.

33   James RAYNBOROWGHE of Ipswich, clothier, v. the bailiffs of IPSWICH and Matthew
GOODWYNE.
Action for a debt of Thomas Raynborowghe, brother of complainant, who has absconded. *Certiorari*
and subpoena.   SUFFOLK.

34   Richard READE, vicar of Highworth, v. John BOLLER.
Claim to the vicarage under a lease from Edward Denton, late vicar, deprived for marriage. WILTS.

35-36   Richard READINGE, yeoman, v. Thomas HODGES of London, soaper.
Detention of deeds relating to land in Basing late of ' Elizabeth Reading, deceased, mother of
complainant. *See File 1378, No. 23.*   HANTS..

37-38   Alice late the wife of John RECHE v. John SYNKLER, esquire, and Edmund CASTEL(S)-
TON his servant.
Tenement in the manor of Ashburton demised by Hugh Woldham (*sic*), late bishop of Exeter, to
Margaret Herle, former wife of the said John Reche. *Mutilated.*   DEVON.

39-40   Thomas REDE and Anne his wife v. Edmund BACON.
Detention of a draft settlement of the parsonage of Tugby on Thomas, son of Richard Nel(l)e of
Keythorp in Tugby (Cathorpe) and Anne daughter of complainant, at their marriage. (Interpleader
by the said Richard.)   LEICESTER.

41   Thomas REDYNG of Underley (in Wolferlow) and Katherine his wife v. Thomas DAVYS of
Bucknell, gentleman.
Board of defendant's son while at grammar school.   HEREFORD, SALOP.

42-48   John REEDE, citizen and haberdasher of London, and Mary his wife v. Geoffrey HAMLYN
and John (Anthony) COOTES.
Lease of the parsonage of Sheriff Hales late of Anthony Cootes, deceased, father of the said Mary
and husband of Christian afterwards wife of the said Geoffrey.   STAFFORD.

49   George RESOGAN of St. Stephen's-in-Brannel v. Thomas TREFRIE, esquire, and Robert
RESOGAN.
Lands in St. Endellion late of John Resogan, deceased, father of complainant.   CORNWALL.

50-52   Gregory REVELL, yeoman of the guard v. the mayor and approved men of GUILDFORD,
and John DABORNE of the same, clothier.
Action on a bond for price of kerseys, which complainant claims to have signed as a witness only.
Certiorari and subpoena. Answer wanting.   SURREY.

53-57   Thomas RICHARDES and Agatha his wife v. William JELLARDE (Gillott), fishmonger.
Plate and money (*schedule given*) late of William Stockeley, deceased, former husband of the said
Agatha and father-in-law of complainant.   LONDON.

58   William ROBERDES of the Inner Temple v. John FRYER.
Detention of deeds relating to land in Kessinglanand and Gisleham formerly of Richard More.
          SUFFOLK.

59   Griffith ROBERTES v. WILLIAM ap Jevan ap Rees and JOHN ap William his son.
Payments for ' battles and comyns ' of the said John at St. Mary Hall, Oxford.
          OXFORD, CARNARVON.

60   William ROBERTS of London, baker, v. WILLIAM ap David, clerk, and HUGH ap
William.
Lands in Llanfairfechan late of Robert ap Howell, deceased, father of complainant. CARNARVON.

61-64   William ROBYS of Wetherby, tailor, v. Christopher PARKYNSON and another.
Messuage and land in Wetherby late of the commandery of Ribston. (The custom of the manor with
regard to successions is disputed.) *Mutilated.*   YORK.

65   Anthony ROLESLEY v. William ROO, Joan his wife, and others.
Messuage and land in Breadsall of the demise of John Dethicke.   DERBY.

66   John ROLFF v. Thomas, son of Richard GLYDE, deceased.
Detention of deeds relating to a messuage and land in Brightling.   SUSSEX.

67   Richard ROLLESLEY v. Anthony ROLLESLEY.
Detention of an entail of the manor of Orleston and of other deeds. *See File 1464, No. 42.* DERBY.

68-70   John ROSEAR and John KYNG v. Richard DODYNGTON and John his son.
Messuages, shop and land in Stogursey late of Richard Lucas, deceased, cousin of complainant.
D. XII, 3.   SOMERSET.

71-73 John ROULLANDSON, servant to Cuthbert [Tunstall], bishop of Durham, *v.* Anthony
LANGHORNE.
Land in Natland demised to Jervauxe Roullandson, father of complainant, by Walter Striklande,
esquire. WESTMORLAND.

74-76 Thomas ROWSELEY *v.* John HEMMYNGTON the elder and John HEMMYNGTON the
younger.
Action on a bond for a debt already paid. CAMBRIDGE.

77-78 William RUMBOLD *v.* John CHAMBERLYN.
Detention of a bond for a debt already paid. NORFOLK.

79 Thomas RUNKHORNE, clerk, executor of Hugh Salisbury, gentleman *v.* Richard RODOM,
gentleman.
Lands in Backford, Tattenhall, and Ferne (*i.e.* Farndon?) bequeathed by the said Hugh to Alice
his daughter for life in marriage with John Lee, gentleman. *Mutilated.* CHESTER.

80-84 Nicholas RUSSELL, citizen and haberdasher of London, *v.* Roger MATHEWE of Taunton
and Isabel his mother.
Price of caps sold to Edward Mathewe, deceased, father of the said Roger. LONDON, SOMERSET.

85-86 William RYCHARDSON, parson of Braunston and chaplain to the Queen, *v.* William
WRYGHT and others.
Detention of deeds relating to complainant's parsonage and withholding of tithes and other profits.
NORTHAMPTON.

87-90 Nicholas RYGBYE *v.* John WYN ap David ap Powell, nephew and heir of John Powell *alias*
Breurton, clerk, D.D.
Messuage in the borough of Wrexham of the demise of Henry Standyshe, late bishop of St. Asaph.
DENBIGH.

91 Roger RYSSHETON *v.* John WHYTEHEDE *alias* Holden, vicar of Ryall.
Lease of defendant's vicarage. RUTLAND.

FILE 1378.

1-5 William RADBORNE *alias* Heyword and Agnes his wife, daughter and heir of Edward
Shorte, *v.* Thomas MORRES, gentleman.
Messuage, land, and a dovecote in Shilton, Redewe next Baunston, and Yelford. *Replication
wanting.* BERKS (*now mostly* OXFORD).

6 John RAINBO *v.* Richard CAMESWELL, esquire, surveyor of the King's and Queen's lands
in the county.
Crown lease of a moiety of messuages and land in Hanwell. OXFORD.

7-9 John RAMESKAR of Baslow, co. Derby, son and heir of Richard Rameskar, *v.* Thomas
grandson and heir of Thomas BOTHE.
Messuage in Gildingwells and land in Letwell (Lekewell). YORK.

10-11 William RATCLYF of Exeter, merchant, *v.* George ARRUNDELL, gentleman.
Loan to complainant, who has since become bankrupt. DEVON.

12 James RATLYFF, citizen of Norwich, *v.* William STEDE.
Messuage in Norwich demised by William Staller for fealty only. NORFOLK.

13 Thomas RAWE, vicar of Wantage, *v.* Robert ALDEWORTH and William ESTMONDE.
Lease of the vicarage and land made by Oliver Stonyng, late vicar, deprived for marriage. BERKS.

14-18 James RAWLYN *v.* Allyn RAWLYN, Thomas COBBE, and Thomas BAXTER, clerk (the
two latter not named in the original bill).
Messuage and land in [West?] Newton late of John Rawlyn, deceased, father of complainant.
NORFOLK.

19-21 Willaim RAWLYNS, vicar of Gulval, *v.* John PLEMYN *alias* Bossolowe, nephew and heir of
Thomas Plemyn.
Garden at Trevarrack (in Gulval) belonging to complainant's glebe. CORNWALL.

22 Thomas RAYNER *v.* Nicholas FANNE and others.
Lease of a farm in Thaxted and other goods late of Richard Rayner, deceased, father of complainant,
whose executors defendants are. ESSEX.

23-24 William READYNG *v.* Richard READYNG.
Messuage and land in Basing late of John Reading of Tadley, weaver, deceased, father of complainant and brother of defendant. *See File* 1377, *No.* 35. HANTS.

25-26 Thomas REDD (Rede) and Alice his wife *v.* William BERYFF.
House in the Holy Trinity, Colchester, late of Richard Vyne, deceased, father of the said
Alice. D. XV, 25. ESSEX.

27 Richard REDE *v.* Robert CLAXSON and Charles COLLYNWOOD.
Land in Wrangle. LINCOLN.

28-29 Richard REDE, knight, *v.* Ellen, executrix and late the wife of William GOODWYN of
Bermondsey, gentleman.
Crown rent of the rectory of . . . ram of the demise of the late abbot and convent of Chertsey.
Faded. SURREY.

30-32 John RICHARDES of Uxbridge, co. Middlesex, labourer, *v.* John HENNAGE, esquire, and
Anne his wife.
Detention of deeds relating to the capital messuage and farm of Helmdon late of Edward Gos[ford?],
deceased, grandfather of Anne late the wife of complainant. *Damaged.* NORTHAMPTON.

33   Roger RISHETON v. Richard, William and Ralph COWBURNE.
Forcible resistance to removal of mills from Little Harwood.   [LANCASTER.]

34–35   John ROBERTES, groom of the ewry, v. JOHN ap Griffith ap Hugh, gentleman, and others.
Rectory of Cilcen of the demise of Geoffrey Jones, parson.   FLINT.

36–37   William ROBYNSON of Drayton, esquire, v. James CRUCHELEY.
General warranty of a messuage and land in Lichfield, late of the hospital of St. John there, obtained
under pretence that it was against John Fitzherbert only, on whose behalf complainant had sold
them.   STAFFORD.

38   Agnes ROGGERS v. John CARSEWELL, gentleman.
Tenement in the manor of Colyton late of Francis Roggers, deceased husband of and complainant.
Mutilated.   DEVON.

39   John ROLLE and others (*named*), for themselves and all the inhabitants of St. Giles's, v.
John MALLET, esquire, and John COKER.
Land in St. Giles's whereof the rent has been used time out of mind for repairs of the church.
DEVON.

40   Edward ROLLESLEY of London, barber, v. Anne ROLLESLEY.
Detention of deeds relating to tenements in St. Peter's, Paul's Wharf, St. Benet's, Paul's Wharf, and
New Brentford late of John Rollesley, gentleman, deceased, brother of complainant and husband of
defendant.   MIDDLESEX.

41–45   William ROMBALDE of Crux Easton, husbandman, v. John GAMBOND, parson of East
Woodhay, and Hugh FITZRICHARDE, gentleman.
Lease of the said Gambond's parsonage with the chapel of Ashmansworth, to commence when he
should be appointed to the hospital of St. Mary Magdalen without Winchester.   HANTS.

46   Peter ROOS and other inhabitants of Chorlton, Shenton (?) Swinshed, Radwod and Stable-
forde, all in Eccleshall, v. Humphrey VYSE, gentleman.
Cottages given time out of mind for repair of the chapel of Chorlton.   STAFFORD.

47–50   John ROWLES (Rolles) of London, hosier, v. James DAYNE (Deane).
Closes of pasture in Wirksworth of the demise of Nicholas Hudson and Dorothy his wife.   DERBY.

51   John ROWSE v. Humphrey DOCWRAY.
Manor of Ditton Hall of the demise of Thomas, lord Vaux of Harrowden, and Elizabeth his wife.
CAMBRIDGE.

52–53   Ralph RUDERD (Ruddeard) v. Reynold SHENE and Alice his wife, late the wife of George
Roger.
Land in Longnor late of William Roger, father of the said George.   STAFFORD.

54   John RUFFORD, husbandman, v. John NEWMAN and others, yeoman.
Forcible ejection from a messuage and land in Ravenstone (Ranston) of the demise of Francis Bryan,
knight, deceased.   BUCKINGHAM.

55   William RUSHTON of Highworth, butcher, and Joan his wife v. Roger WODSHAWE of
Lambourne, husbandman.
Legacy of ——— Jones of Devizes (Thevise), whose widow and executrix afterwards married
defendant.   WILTS, BERKS.

56–60   Richard son and heir of Thomas RUSSELL v. Hugh LIDIATE and Humphrey PIRRY,
stepfather of complainant.

61   William son and heir of William RYSLEY v. Thomas WOODWARD and John ARDEN,
gentlemen.
Double lease of land in Chitwood. *Damaged.*   BUCKINGHAM.

FILE 1379.

1–2   Robert RABBETT v. Alice Nicholas, Richard, William, Edward and Peter RABBETT.
Detention of deeds relating to land in Boughton Monchelsea, which defendants claim to be pledged
for money due at their majorities.   KENT.

3   Nicholas RAND v. George CUTLARD of Fokyngham, [co. Lincoln].
Action on a bond for tenancy of messuages and land in Collingtree and in Gold Street, Nottingham.
Damaged.   NORTHAMPTON.

4–5   Richard RANDALL, husbandman, v. Anthony IRYSHE, gentleman, and others.
Common in Stanbridge Heath appendent to a messuage in Edmondsham.   DORSET.

6–7   William RASTELL v. Thomas WHITE, knight, alderman of London.
Dwelling called ' Scalles Inne ' in Medelane in the parish of St. Michael, called ' Whittington College'
of the demise of Henry [Grey], marquis of Dorset. D. XIV, 27.   LONDON.

8–11   James RATCLIF of London, gentleman, v. George RATCLIFF of Cartington (in Rothbury),
co. Northumberland, knight, and John RATCLYFF alias Moore, gentleman, servant to
Lord Dacre.
Manors of Castlerigg, Tallentire, and Derwentwater, and messuages and lands in Crosthwaite
(Crosswater, Groweswetter, Crostwhayter, Crostherte) late of John Ratcliff, knight, deceased.
Rival pedigrees given. (A demurrer that the matter is in suit before the Council of the North is
overruled.) *See File 878, No. 6.*   CUMBERLAND.

12   James RATCLYFF v. John BARR.
Messuage in Lord Conyers's manor of Kirkby-in-Ashfield.   NOTTS.

13-15　　William RAWLYN and Margery his wife v. William FYTZHUGH.
Messuage and land in Wilden. D. IX, 27., BEDFORD.

16-17　　William RAYDALL, parson of Radwell, v. William PLOMER, churchwarden.
Pulling down the sacrament in the church of Radwell, prohibition of saying mass, refusal to account for 'church goods, wrongful occupation of church lands, neglect of tillage, enclosure of common, etc.
The same v. John SPERLINGE of Baldock.
Seizure of goods while complainant was under arrest for religion. HERTS.

18-19　　Thomas RAYNES and William BOULSIER, husbandmen, v. John WYBARNE, gentleman, fellow of Gray's Inn.
Frivolous suits for trespass in Pembury. KENT.

20　　Thomas READE and others, inhabitants of Chatteris, v. William SABERTON and others, inhabitants of Sutton.
Common in Black Fen (now in Chatteris): *Damaged.* CAMBRIDGE.

21　　Peter REDE v. William PLATFOTE, under sheriff.
Money obtained on a judgment for complainant against John Harvy of Frostenden (Frossyngton). SUFFOLK.

22　　Robert REDE v. John ROE.
Detention of price of sheep, and failure to complete a sale of a messuage and land in Stony Stanton. LEICESTER.

23　　John REIGNOLDES of Great Kimble, co. Bucks, v. John ap David FLOID, Guelliam (Guenthan) his wife and others.
Lands in Rethlyn, late of Matto ap Tedre. DENBIGH.

24　　Harry REPPYS, esquire.
Commission to examine witnesses as to a settlement by Elizabeth Hollond on her marriage with complainant of the manor of Middleton in Mendham and lands in Mendham, Homersfield, Sandcroft, and South Elmhan. SUFFOLK.

25　　RES ap Hoell of Newcurt, yeoman, v. John GRIFFYTH of Brecknock and others.
Debts due to Margaret verch Jevan, mother of complainant. HEREFORD, BRECON.

26-28　　Alice, late the wife of William RESKYMMER, esquire, and a daughter and heir of John Densell, serjeant-at-law, v. William CAVELL and Dorothy his wife, late the wife of Laurence Courtney.
Manors of Polrode (in St. Tudy), Bolland (*i.e.* Bolleit in St. Buryan?) Scawen, Drym in St. Buryan (Tredrym), Ventonvedna (in Sithney), and Selena in Buryan (Sulena), of the grant of John Skewys, esquire; and marriage of Joan Dawnaund, a ward of complainant. *See File* IIII, *No.* 117. CORNWALL.

29　　Peter REYNELL v. William CASTELL.
Cottage in the late Duke of Suffolk's manor of Holbeton. *Mutilated.* DEVON.

30　　Richard REYNER, yeoman, v. John WYLSON, clerk, Katherine his wife, and George GABATUS and John DAMMES, husbandmen.
Messuages, cottages, and land in Darlton late of Thomas Reyner, deceased, father of complainant and former husband of the said Katherine. NOTTS.

31　　REYNOLD ap John ap Madocke, clerk, v. JOHN ap Herry ap Howell.
Detention of deeds relating to lands late of Ryce Wyn, deceased, great-grandfather of complainant.
Commission. FLINT.

32　　Robert REYNOLDE, clothier, v. . . . . HARBOTTEL, merchant.
Loan at rates of from 20 to 60 per cent. ' *Mutilated.* ————

33　　John REYNOLDS, gentleman, an ordinary marshal of the Household, v. JOHN and THOMAS ap Jevan ap Gruffydd ap David.
Messuages and lands in Trawsfynydd and Festiniog. MERIONETH.

34　　RICE ap Owen ap Dackyn of Berwick (*rectius* Berriew?) v. John Gogh DAVID ap Meredith of Tyrynenche (*i.e.* Tyr-y-mynach?).
Action on a bond for a debt already paid. MONTGOMERY.

35　　RICHARD ap Griffin ap Ithell, an infant, by David Edwards his guardian, v. ROBERT ap David ap Griffith ap Robert and WILLIAM his son.
Messuages and lands in Allington; Burton, Gresford, Brymbo, Broughton and Wrexham late of William ap Madocke ap Llewelyn, deceased, great-uncle of complainant. DENBIGH.

36-38　　Anthony RICHARDSON, vicar of North Shoebury, v. Henry HENDY.
Rent of money and corn payable out of the parsonage whereof defendant is farmer. *Answer wanting.* ESSEX.

39-41　　John RICHARDSON, merchant of the staple of Calais, v. Laurence SHARPE of South Kyme, carpenter.
Contract to build a house in Conisby like the guildhall there, which defendant says he could not do because of the rise in the price of victuals. LINCOLN.

42　　Lybeus RICHARDSON v. Thomas RICHARDSON and others.
Reviver of a suit for a pasture in [Toynton All Saints] (*File* 1314, *No.* 39). LINCOLN.

43　　William ROBERSON and another v. Richard BRAYE of Kennington.
Action on a bond for a debt partly paid. *Mutilated.* KENT.

44　　ROBERT ap Hugh, clerk, v. Hugh GOUGH, clerk, and others.
Parsonage of Newborough whereof the said Gough was deprived for marriage ' and for other evyll opynyons.' ANGLESEA.

45   John ROBERTES v. Edward NICHOLSON of Market [Deeping?], yeoman.
Money promised for obtaining a lease of the manor of Langtoft from John Fewter, esquire. *Faded.*
                                                                                    LINCOLN.

46   Stephen ROBERTES v. Percival AUSTYN of Staplehurst.
Messuage and garden in Goudhurst, late of Walter Robertes, deceased, father of complainant.
Mutilated.   KENT.

47   William ROBERTES of London, baker, v. WILLIAM ap David, clerk, and HUGH ap
William.
Messuage and land in Llanfairfechan, late of [Robert] ap Hoell ap Tyder, father of complainant.
Damaged.   CARNARVON.

48–52   Anthony ROBERTSON (Robenson) of Toft, esquire, v. Stephen SALMON and Richard
HODGE, executors of Rose Tavernour, deceased.
Action for a debt already paid, on a bond mislaid by John Tavernour of Boston, gentleman, deceased,
husband of the said Rose.   LINCOLN.

53   ROGER ap Ryce v. Evan MEREDITH *alias* Blanneth and others.
Messuage and land in Dyserth late of William ap Ryce of Hereford, deceased, father of complainant.
                                                                                    RADNOR.

54–63   ROGER ap Owen of Southwark, waterman, v. Rece VAUGHAN ap Morgan, DAVID ap
Jevan, THOMAS ap David ap Jevan and others.
Messuages and land in Mallaen (in Caeo and Cilycwm) late of David ap Res Griffyth, deceased, great-
great-uncle of complainants.   CARMARTHEN.

64   Agnes RÓGERS v. John CARSWELL.
Land in Ottery St. Mary late of Robert Rogers, deceased, brother of complainant.   DEVON.

65–68   Nicholas ROKEWODE v. Richard HEYDON, esquire.
Goods (*schedule annexed*) of Sir Humphrey Style, deceased, whose executors both parties are.
Mutilated.   2 answers.   ———

69–71   John and Thomas ROLL v. William ASCOUGH and Richard his son.
Crown lease of half the manor of Panton to John Roll, deceased, father of complainants. LINCOLN.

72   Thomas ROMNEY v. Harry BYRKEHEVED, prothonotary of the county [of Lancaster].
Office of deputy to defendants promised on complainant's marriage with his daughter. *Mutilated.*
                                                                                    [LANCASTER].

73–75   Nicholas ROOSE (Rose, Rosse) v. Walter ROSE his nephew.
Land in the prebendal manor of Alrewas. *Mutilated.* D. XI, 32.   STAFFORD.

76–77   Walter son and heir of Thomas ROSE v. Humphrey COTTON, farmer of the said manor,
Nicholas BURWEY his steward, and the said Nicholas ROOSE
Burgages and land at Sandford in Alrewas and a messuage and land held of the manor. STAFFORD.

78–79   William ROSE v. John SMYTHE and others, feoffees to uses.
Detention of a deed of feoffment of messuages in Thame and lands elsewhere.   OXFORD.

80–81   Richard ROSEWALL, husbandman, v. Henry PASCOW, Simon MATHEW, and others,
inhabitants of St. Ives.
Appointment of complainant to collect the port-farm of St. Ives without assessing it on the mariners
of the town. (Defendants plead that certain persons undertook to pay.)   CORNWALL.

82   Thomas ROUS of Henham, esquire, v. John BRAYE.
Detention of deeds relating to land in Bradfield belonging to complainant's manor of Hacheston.
                                                                                    SUFFOLK.

83–84   John ROWLAND of Hove, husbandman, v. George his elder brother.
Copyhold land and goods of Alice Hardam, deceased, mother of both parties, which descend to
complainant as the youngest son.   SUSSEX.

85   Henry ROWPER and Elizabeth, his wife, late the wife of Thomas Symes, v. Joyce
SYMES.
Rent of a tenement called the *Whet Sheff* in Daventry and frame of timber of the bequest of the
said Thomas.   NORTHAMPTON.

86–87   Thomas RUMBOLD of Newport [Pagnell], co. Bucks, v. John PYE and Richard ROBYNS,
gentleman, steward of the manor of Cranfield.
Timber in a close in the said manor bought of Edmund Pedder, gentleman   BEDFORD.

88   Stephen RUSSELL, yeoman, v. William MORYN.
Price of a colt and a cow.   ———

89–90   Guy RYCE and others, for themselves and the other parishioners of Pamber, v. the provost
and scholars of QUEEN'S COLLEGE, Oxford.
Failure to maintain service in the priory church of Pamber as required by the Act of Parliament
dissolving the priory (of Monk Sherborne).   HANTS.

91–92   William RYCHARDSON and others, inhabitants of Caldecote, v. Robert PECKE, clerk of the
peace for the county.
Seizure of a chalice and extortion of money for the Duke of Northumberland's rebellion.
                                                                                    CAMBRIDGE.

93–95   Thomas RYCHE of Huntington v. Thomas TUTTESHAM and Isabel (Elizabeth) his wife,
late the wife of Thomas Bereworth of Hadlow, gentleman.
Refusal to complete a sale of land in Linton under the will of the said Bereworth to build on his
lands in Tonbridge. D. XI, 26.   KENT.

96   William RYCHERD of Constantine v. John TRYSPRYSYN and Jane PENKEVELL.
Refusal to complete a lease of a messuage and land at Rosemerryn in Budock.   CORNWALL.

97   John RYGMAYDEN, esquire v. Alice HARTELEY.
Messuage and land in Cabus belonging to complainant's manor of Woodacre in Garstang (Wedacre), and forfeited for receiving ' inmakes ' there (*i.e.* a married couple) without licence.   LANCASTER.

98–99   William RYVE (Reve), Isabel his wife and Francis their son v. Richard HARDEWYCHE.
Land of the manor of Westbury of the demise of Thomas Hornour, knight (defendant pleads that the matter is already in suit in this court, *i.e. File* 1258, *No.* 28, and in the King's and Queen's Bench).
SOMERSET.

FILE   1380.

1–3   John SABYN of East B[rent ?], husbandman v. John EDGYLL.
Gelding entrusted to defendant and afterwards damaged.   SOMERSET.

4–6   William SECOLL v. Robert MARTEN his son-in-law.
Detention of deeds relating to lands in Eynsham.   OXFORD.

7–10   William SEDLEYE v. John, son and heir of John BANDE, esquire.
Messuage and land late held by Thomas Howe of defendant's manor of Corringham.   ESSEX.

11–13   Thomas SEGREY of Woburn, pewterer, v. Richard CRYMES, citizen and haberdasher of London.
Interest of 12 per cent. on a loan secured on leaseholds in Woburn.   BEDFORD.

14   Thomas SEKYNGTON of Coleshill v. John HUNT and Michael PURFREY, esquire, both of the Middle Temple.
Failure to make an award whereto complainant is bound concerning the manor of Seckington and a messuage and land [in Coton ?]. *See Files* 1161, *No.* 11; 1265, *No.* 13.   WARWICK, DERBY.

15–17   Alexander SEMER and Elizabeth his wife, v. William GERARD, Richard COMPTON, and James his son.
Detention of a bond for conveyance of tenements in Corton and Whitcombe (in Corton Denham). *Tenants named.*   SOMERSET.

18–22   John SEYMER v. Francis ROLLESTON.
Lands in Gresley. *Damaged.*   DERBY.

23   Henry SHELLEY and his wife, daughter and heir of Richard Sackvyle, esquire, v. John LEEDES, esquire.
Manor of Chipstead, advowson of the church and messuage and land in Caterham.   SURREY.

24–26   George SHERE v. William CRUCE.
House and land called Tofton (*i.e.* Tatson ?) in Bridgerule.   DEVON.

27–28   Hugh SHERPE of Plumpton husbandman, v. John HOMES and others.
Messuage and land in Binstead late of Henry Sherpe, deceased, grandfather of complainant (Joan, wife of the said John Howes joins in the answer, which is mutilated).   SUSSEX.

29   Thomas SKRYMPSHER v. John SKRYMPSHER, esquire, his eldest brother.
Refusal to make assurance of a rent in the manor of Meer and lands there and in Forton, Aqualate, Sutton and Warton, late of Thomas Skrympshyre, deceased, father of both parties. *See D.* XIII, 26, *and File* 1268, *No.* 26.   STAFFORD.

30–32   John SKULLARDE of Andover, yeoman v. John SKULLARDE the younger.
Alienation of lands in Chute and Vernhams Dean by Thomas Skullarde, deceased, uncle and guardian of complainant and father of defendant.   WILTS, HANTS.

33–35   John SKYNNER v. William COLLYN the elder and William COLLYN the younger.
Land in Hemyock late of Hamond Cropjoy, deceased cousin of complainant. *Pedigree given.*
DEVON.

36   John SLEDDE and Charles HOSKYNS, citizens and merchant tailors of London, v. John BUTTERALL, executor of John Allen of Stamford, merchant.
Debt for goods (described, including six yards of ' fustyan in apes ').   LONDON, LINCOLN.

37–38   Edward SLEGGE, gentleman, v. William ANNE, esquire.
Land formerly of the fraternity of Aylesbury, between Walton bridge and the common ditch there. D. XI, 12. *Dismissed because in suit at common law.*   BUCKINGHAM.

39   Hugh SLOLYGHE v. [John CHICHESTER, esquire].
Land of the demise of the said Chichester in the manor of Sherwill. *Damaged.*   DEVON.

40–43.   Roger SMALE, administrator of the goods of William Peers, clerk, v. William WYNE of Queen-Camel, husbandman, and Alice his wife.
Money, said to be ' a lace (lasce) and two angle nobles bowed about the same,' entrusted to the said Alice.   SOMERSET.

44–45   Gilbert SMYTHE, gentleman, v. Alice late the wife of John AWELD of Leckhampstead and Thomas his son.
Loan to the said John, whose executors defendants are.   BUCKINGHAM.

46   Ambrose SOMER v. Hugh MARE and Nicholas (*sic*) his wife.
Tenements in the manor of Ilfracombe of the demise of Henry [Gray], duke of Suffolk.   DEVON.

47–49   John SOWTER v. Thomas TURNER.
Destruction of seals of a bond for a debt of Thomas Welles (Walles).   [BERKS *or* SUFFOLK.]

50   Joan, executrix and late the wife of John SPEGHT, v Humphrey BENTLEY, surveyor to Lady Tailboyes.
Messuages and lands in East and West Retford, Cotham, Welham [in Clarborough] and Moorgate [in North Retford] of the demise of Thomas, son and heir of Christopher Wymbisshe, esquire.
NOTTS.

51-54   George, son and heir of Thomas SPEKE, knight, v. Anne late the wife of the said Sir Thomas, and Christopher DODYNGTON, esquire.
Exchange between complainant and the said Lady Anne, for the purpose of his marriage settlement, of lands in the manors of White Lackington, Atherstone in White Lackington (Athelardeston), East Dowlish, and East Wonford.   SOMERSET, DORSET, DEVON.

55-56   John SPENCER, esquire, v. Richard LYON and William TAYLOUR.
Trespasses on messuages and lands in complainant's manor of Worstead during Ket's rebellion and afterwards.   NORFOLK.

57-58   Robert, great grandson and heir of Robert STABULL, v. Humphrey QUERNEBY, mayor of Nottingham.
Land in the woman's market at the east end of the flesh-shambles, Nottingham, claimed by defendant in right of the town. See File 1468, No: 50.   NOTTS.

59-60   Robert STANNEWEY and Thomas KNEVETT, churchwardens of St. Sepulchre's ' commonly called the rounde paryshe,' v. James FLETCHER, alderman of Cambridge.
Seizure of plate, vestments and books of the church (described), and overcharge for repairs. Answer and replication wanting.   CAMBRIDGE.

61-63   Henry STAVELEY, husband of Mary, executrix and late the wife of Thomas Cosyn, v. Richard BLACKWALL, husband of Alice, executrix and late the wife of John Prest.
Under-lease by the said Prest of meadow in Clerkenwell, formerly of the Hospitallers. D. XIII, 56.   MIDDLESEX.

64-66   William STODARDE, clerk, v. William WYLLOTT and others, tenants-at-will of Robert Stodarde, a miner.
Messuages and land in Horley late of Thomas Stodarde, deceased, father of complainant. See File 1383, No. 49.   SURREY.

67   Thomas STOURMER v. William HEMYNGTON.
Moiety of lands in Westmourdon. Damaged.

68   Thomas STRADLYNGE of London, knight, v. William AVAN.
Distresses on land in Avan during complainant's imprisonment in the Tower by command of the late Duke of Northumberland.   GLAMORGAN.

69   William STRONGE v. Richard PERSONS and Agnes his wife.
Lease of land in Stogursey secretly obtained by William Stronge, deceased, father of complainant and husband of the said Agnes.   SOMERSET.

70-72   The same v. John POLE and Robert MORE.
Suppression of a demise of the messuage of Faringdon in Stogursey made by the said William the father.   SOMERSET.

FILE   1381.

1-2   William SAKEVYLE of Dorking, esquire, one of the servers of the Queen's . . . board, v. DAVID ap Evan, Jevan DAVID ap Gytto, and others.
' Comorth ' payable in the manor of Llanll . . . Faded. .   CARDIGAN.

3-5   John SAMER of Downham, husbandman, v. John WYNDELL of Cranham, husbandman.
Messuage and land in Ramsden Crays late of William Samer, deceased, father of complainant.
ESSEX.

6-8   John son and heir of Robert SANDER, by Robert Ede and Elizabeth his wife, his mother and guardian, v. John SANDER.
Land in Lopham of the gift of John Sander, deceased, father of the said Robert and of defendant.
NORFOLK.

9-12   Francis SAUNDERS of Wantisden, co. Suffolk, grandson and heir of John Saunders, citizen and draper of London, v. Katherine (Bridget) late the wife of Richard WYGMORE, gentleman.
Messuage and garden in Mark Lane. Replication wanting. See File 1315, No. 7.   LONDON.

13   William SAUNDERS, late of Kibworth, gentleman, v. Henry SACHEVERELL.
Lease of the manor of Saddington pledged to complainant after its expiration.   LEEDS.

14   Anthony SAUNDERSON of Harledon v. William ALLYNSON and others.
Tenement called ' Croslak ' in Fryslyngton (Frylyngton) obtained of William Ligh in exchange for another in dispute in this court.   ?

15-16   Jane SAYNT JOHN, late the wife of Humphrey Tyrrell, esquire, v. Alexander SAYNT JOHN, esquire, her husband, and George TYRRELL her son.
Lands and goods owned by complainant before her marriage.   ———

17   Robert SAYNTQUYNTYNE and Jane his wife, late the wife of Ralph Burton, v. Roger BURTON, son of the said Ralph and others.
Grange and lands in Pickering of the demise of the late abbot and convent of Rievaulx.   YORK.

18   The same *v.* Christopher HORSSER and others.
Do.   YORK.

19   The same *v.* Hugh WYDDE and others.
Do.   YORK.

20–22   William SAYVELL of Halifax, mercer, *v.* Maurice (Morysen) de MARINE, merchant stranger of London.
Action for a debt satisfied by a bond of Henry Falowfeld of London, merchant.   YORK, LONDON.

23–25   Robert, son and heir of Sylvester SEDBORROWE, by William Arrondell his 'prichyn amye,' *v.* Bartholomew STAVELEY, gentleman, his uncle.
Detention of deeds relating to messuages and lands in Minehead (Mynete), Culbone, Porlock and Brushford. *See File 1270, No. 18.*   SOMERSET.

26–27   Ralph SEGERS(T)ON of Liverpool, merchant, *v.* the sheriffs of LONDON, and Dorothy, late the wife of Walter YONGE of London, merchant tailor, and others, his executors.
Action for a debt for cloth partly paid by John Parker; master of the Rolls in Ireland. *Certiorari and subpœna.*   LONDON; LANCASTER.

28–30   Ellis SERLE of Combe Raleigh, husbandman, *v.* John SERLE.
Refusal to complete an under-lease of land in Wulferchurche (*i.e.* Wolford in Dunkeswell?), held of the manor of Bower Hayes, and of common of pasture on Wulferchurche and Dunkeswell downs.
DEVON.

31   William, son and heir of John SEWALL, *v.* Edmund FREND.
Detention of deeds relating to land in Boughton, Holme and Thorpland.   NORFOLK.

32–33   Thomas, son and heir of Thomas SEXTEN, and Robert WALLSHE his tenant, *v.* John WYSEMAN.
Lands (*described*) in defendant's manor of Maplestead, forfeited by the verdict of a jury not all of the homage.   ESSEX.

34   William SHAWE and Philippa, his wife, late the wife of John Pengelly, *v.* John [CARMYNOW, esquire.]
Rent assigned by the Council of the West in lieu of dower to Katherine, late the wife of John Pengelly, and mother of the said John. *Mutilated.*   CORNWALL.

35–37   Robert and William SHEPARDE *v.* John STRELLEY (Sturley, Stirley) *alias* Bowyer.
Tithe barn and tithe corn of Stratforth (*i.e.* Startforth) of the demise of the late abbot and convent of Egglestone. *Mutilated.* D. XIV, 49. *See Files* 1158, *No.* 61; 1267, *No.* 50.   [YORK.]

38–43   John SHERE *v.* Ralph HORTOPPE, clerk, and others.
Seizure of goods (*schedule in duplicate*) at complainant's house at Bridgerule, on the ground of his conviction of felony.   DEVON.

44   John SHORTE of Laneras *v.* Thomas JENKYNS.
Detention of herrings shipped on complainant's behalf from Carlingford (Cardyngford) to St. Ives.
CORNWALL.

45–48   George SKYRROWE, vicar of Harmston (Armeston), *v.* Thomas MYDDYLBROKE, husbandman, and others.
Messuage and land in Harmston belonging to complainant's glebe.   LINCOLN.

49–51   Thomas SMYTH and others (*named*), with all the inhabitants of Waterfall, and Humphry GOLDE, Richard FELTEHOUSE, and others (*named*), with all the inhabitants of Grindon, *v.* Edward ASTON, knight.
Rights of common on Morridge in defendant's lordship of Bradnop (in Leek).   STAFFORD.

52–53   Thomas SMYTHE of Campden, esquire, and Catherine, his wife, executrix and late the wife of Robert Wynter, esquire, *v.* Richard WYLDE.
Forgery of a deed in the name of the said Robert. *Damaged.*   [GLOUC.] WORC.

54–56   William SMYTHE, husbandman, and Ellen (Helen), his wife, *v.* Humphrey (H)ORTON, vicar of Marston, and others.
Rooms in the vicarage of Marston and houses of the demise of William Wayn, late vicar.   DERBY.

57–60   Thomas SNOWE, yeoman, *v.* John, son and heir of Herbert FYNCHE of Sanders (*i.e.* Sandhurst?) co. Kent, gentleman.
Refusal to complete a lease of a barn and land in Hailsham.   SUSSEX.

61   Edmund SOMERSETT and others *v.* William HORSEY, esquire, and Bartholomew HORSEY.
Enclosure, occupation of land 10 'goodes' in length and 6 feet in breadth, and other trespasses at Marbin in the Queen's manor of South Damerham. *Supplicavit*   WILTS.

62   Thomas SONDFORD of London *v.* John and Elizabeth BAUGHE and William HIBINE.
Detention of deeds relating to the manor of Edgton, late of Richard Sondford of the Lee, deceased, grandfather of complainant.   SALOP.

63–65   Nicholas SOUTHCOTT of London, mercer, and Ellen, his wife, daughter and heir of John Copland, *v.* Agnes FLEMYNG, Robert RAWSON, Joan his wife, Richard WENTWORTH, Alice his wife, Thomas ELLES, and Thomasyn his wife.
Messuages and lands in Crofton, Hardwick, Wragby, Folby, Sharleston, Hartshead, Quarnby in Lindley (Wherneby), North Elland, Pontefract, Wakefield, Sandall, Barsland (*i.e.* Barkisland), West Hardwick and Bankrode, bought of John Flemmyng, gentleman, deceased, husband of the said Agnes, and father of the said Joan, Alice and Thomasyn.   YORK.

66–67   John SOWTER of Derby, plumber, and Agnes, his wife, *v.* Elizabeth STAFFORD and Alice, her daughter, wife of John GRENEWAYE.
Close in Hanbury, late of Thomas Fynymore, deceased, father of the said Agnes.   STAFFORD.

68   Thomas SOWTHERNE, treasurer of Exeter cathedral and vicar of Cornwood, v. Walter HELE, gentleman.
Rent of houses in Cornwood.   DEVON.

69   Thomas SPELMAN v. Joan DERLYNG.
Share of a messuage and lands in Little Chart, Sutton Valence, Marden, Staplehurst, Boughton Monchelsea, and Langley, late of John Mascall of Chart, deceased. *Pedigrees given.* D. XIV, 13.
       KENT.

70   Thomas SPROTTE and Laurence, his wife, late the wife of Loye Rolentyne, and _____ daughter and heir of the said Loye, v. John HEFTER, bailiff of the court of Mark and Oye, and John ARDEN.
Frivolous suit to hinder process in an action in this court. *Faded.*   CALAIS.

71-74   John STARKEY of London, mercer, v. Augustine HYNDE, alderman of London, John LOVYS, and Joan his wife, daughter of the said Augustine.
Messuages and lands in All Hallows, Lombard Street, and Stepney, late of Thomas Starkey, deceased, brother of complainant and former husband of the said Joan.   MIDDLESEX.

75-77   Hugh STARKYE, esquire, v. Thomas HOLCROFTE, knight.
Messuage and land in Woodford, bought of John Warde of Capesthorn.   CHESTER.

78   William STEPHENSON, Richard LAPLOVE, and Agnes, his wife, mother and guardian of the said William, v. Christopher HORDERN.
Messuage and land in Fulford, late of John Stephenson, deceased, father of the said William.
       STAFFORD.

79-81   Joan STEVYNS of Burthopp (*i.e.* Burderop?), late the wife of Thomas Stevyns, and Thomas STEVYNS of Baydon, v. John WALDRON of Little Hinton, husbandman.
Action on a bond given on behalf of Richard Edwardes for price of sheep, of which complainants are prepared to pay the balance.   WILTS.

82-84   John STOKDALE of Foston, yeoman, v. Henry VERNON, esquire, son and heir of Henry Vernon, knight.
Money and a tenement in Sudbury, promised on taking service with defendant.   DERBY.

85-87   Thomas STUKELEY and John FORDE, gentlemen, v. John WYLKOCKES, keeper of the bishop's palace at Exeter.
Detention of court-rolls of the manor of Ashburton, demised to complainants with the borough by John, late bishop of Exeter.   DEVON.

88   Robert SUTTELL of London v. John JEFFEREY.
Cattle of the bequest of Anthony Suttell.   LONDON.

89-91   John SWETYNG of London, yeoman, v. Miles, nephew and heir of Robert WARTON, and Thomas BOWMAN.
Detention of deeds relating to a messuage in Micklegate-in Selby, of the grant of Jane, daughter of the said Robert.   YORK.

92   Robert SWYFTE of Rotherham, brother and heir of Alexander Swyfte, v. Edmund HOLMES of Retford.
Money and goods entrusted to defendant by Agnes, late the wife of the said Alexander.
       YORK, NOTTS.

FILE 1382.

1   Agnes SANTAWBYN, executrix and late the wife of Thomas Megges, esquire, v. George AUSTEN.
Chests of cypress and other goods lent to Alice Golson, who died in defendant's house.   _____

2-4   James SAULTORNE (Salthorne) v. William BAGELHOLE (Bagelhale, Bagenhalle).
Exchange of a steer for another which proved to be the property of Henry Bonde (Bande, Bounde).
       [CORNWALL?]

5-6   Andrew and Giles, sons of Margaret SAYNTTABIN, deceased, and administrators of her goods, v. John SAYNTTABIN, their elder brother.
Seizure of the said goods at Parracombe.   DEVON.

7   WILLIAM SA . . . of Ly[don?]hall, gentleman, v. John ALCOK and Henry CHESSHER.
Land in Admaston (in Wrockwardine). *Faded.*   SALOP.

8-9   Thomas SELWOODE of Chard, merchant, v. John MORRYCE.
Action for cloth bought in partnership with complainant by John Morryce, deceased, son of defendant.
       SOMERSET.

10   Henry SERLE of Histon, gentleman, v. William PEPES, Eleanor, his wife, and Thomas PYTCHARD.
Lands (*described*) in Trumpington, late of Alice Askynne, deceased, complainant's aunt. *Continued in File 1473, No. 18.*   CAMBRIDGE.

11   John SEYGER of Wymondham, yeoman, v. Robert KENSEY, yeoman.
Land in Wichlewood, late of John Seyger, deceased, father of complainant.   NORFOLK.

12   The same v. Henry SYMONDES.
Delivery of a bond entrusted to him for a debt of the said Kensey.   NORFOLK.

13–17   Thomas SEYNTON v. James BOX, clerk, and Thomas PALMER.
Messuages and land in Easthorpe (in Southwell) late held of the manor of Southwell by Agnes Barrye (Barra), deceased, cousin of complainant.   NOTTS.

18–21   John SKERNE v. Margaret, William and Thomas HUSSEY.
Houses called Downeland and Ham with other houses and lands in Kingston-upon-Thames and tenements in St. George Street, Southwark, St. Sepulchre's without Newgate, and Skerne late of Swythen Skerne, deceased, husband of the said Margaret and grandfather of complainant.
                                                          SURREY, LONDON, YORK.

22–24   Henry SKOTT, vicar of Swanbourne, v. William CURLE.
Lease of complainant's vicarage made under a false date by Edmund Cowper, late vicar, deprived for marriage.   BUCKINGHAM.

25–28   Edward SLEGGE v. John RUFFE, Robert RAYE, and Thomas WOLFE.
Undue influence in obtaining a purchase of Crown lands in Girton and St. Giles's, Cambridge.
                                                                                     CAMBRIDGE.

29   John son of John SLEPE v. Thomas LYTLETON, gentleman.
Refusal to complete a sale of a tenement in St. Winnow.   CORNWALL.

30   Henry SLYFORDE, esquire, v. James HARRINGTON, esquire, son and heir of John Harrington, knight, and others.
Mansion-house of Pinchbeck of the demise of the said Sir. John and office of bailiff of the manor, of his bequest.   LINCOLN.

31   Hugh SMITH and Margaret his wife v. CADWALADER ap Rece.
Detention of deeds relating to a tenement in Edge.   SALOP.

32   Edward SMYTH, husbandman, executor of William Watson, v. John FENNE.
Messuage and land in Halton bought of defendant.   LINCOLN.

33   John SMYTH of London, parson of Merthyr Tydfil, v. John ap Jevan PHILLIPE.
Rent of complainant's parsonage.   GLAMORGAN.

34   Thomas SMYTHE v. the sheriffs of LONDON.
Action of debt by Richard Hochon to hinder complainant's recovery of houses in Coleman Street and part of a yard in the Ball Alley. Certioriari. Faded.   LONDON.

35   Robert SNELLING of D[orche?]ster v. Owen REYNOLD of Melcomb Regis.
Burgage in [Dorchester?] late of Richard Snelling, uncle of complainants, and Edith his wife both deceased. Mutilated.   DORSET.

36–38   John SPENLOF v. Thomas son and heir of Richard JOHNSON and others.
Land in Trusthorpe late of Thomas Spenlof, deceased, father of complainant.   LINCOLN.

39–40   John SPENSER of East Bergholt, co. Suffolk, clothier, v. William TALBOT and John GOODALL, executors of Thomas Spenser of Louth, draper, his father.
Moiety of chattels and of rents of leasehold (not specified) of the bequest of the said Thomas.
                                                                                       LINCOLN.

41   Richard STANSEFELD of Retford, executor of John Draper, clerk, v. Gasyon ULLYOTT of Walkeringham, yeoman.
Colt entrusted to defendant.   NOTTS.

42–45   Walter STAPLEHILL of Exeter, gentleman, v. Raymond NORLEGH and others.
Action for warranty of a close called Chevelegh Park in the parish of Stalerton (i.e. Talaton?) acquired of John Southcote of Bovey Tracy, esquire. See File 1268, No. 66.

46–52   Robert STEPHYNS alias Weyver of Chulmleigh v. Henry DULON (Dulyn), esquire (gentleman) and Isabel his wife late the wife of Richard Bury, esquire.
Messuages and land in Dolton held of defendants manor of Halsdon.   DEVON.

53   Joan late the wife of Richard STOFORD and others v. Thomas POMEREYE, knight.
Lands in defendant's manor of Parkham of the demise of Giles late lord Daubeney.   DEVON.

54–56   Thomas STONARD of Ash by Sandwich v. Thomas HOLLY of Sandwich.
Action on a bond for delivery of a former bond, which was not done till after the time specified.
                                                                                           KENT.

57–58   George STOWFORD v. John TOSE (Toose, Towse), grantee to uses, and Robert FARRANT.
Messuage and land in the manor of Ottery St. Mary acquired of John Curham.   DEVON.

59–61   John, son of William STYLE and of Elizabeth his wife, both deceased, v. Thomas REDE, gentleman.
Land in the manor of Nether Winchendon late of the abbot and convent of Notley. D. XI, 19.
                                                                                     BUCKINGHAM.

62–63   Harry SWAYNE of Tiverton, clothier, v. Richard FRANKE of Cambridge, draper.
Insufficient bond for balance of a debt assigned to complainant by Harry Averell of London, draper.

64–66   Humphrey SWYNERTON, esquire, v. Richard STYCHE.
Detention of deeds relating to the prebend of Hilton.   STAFFORD.

67   John SYMONDES, master of the hospital of St. John [the Baptist, Bath], and the brethren and sisters thereof, v. Matthew COLTHURST, esquire, and Peter BEAWSHING.
Common of pasture for sheep and cattle in Lansdown (Lemsdowne) and King's Mead, both in Walcote held of defendant's manor of Barton. Faded.   SOMERSET.

FILE 1383.

1 Thomas SALWEY (?), gentleman, v. Francis BEDELL, gentleman, and John LEVESON.
Detention of deeds relating to lands in Cannock, Stafford, Hednesford, Norton Saredon, Salt, Stretton, Whitgreave and elsewhere, the keepership of Cheslyn Hay, and the 'chymarge' of Cannock formerly of Humphrey Salway. *Damaged.* D. X, 63. STAFFORD.

2 John SAUNDRYE, clerk, v. Thomas and Richard BOSSYNS.
Action in the stannary court of Penwith and Kerrier for a debt paid to Roger Kympe to whom the same Thomas was 'given' for complicity in rebellion. CORNWALL.

3 John SAVELL, vicar of Ather (i.e. Haydor?), v. Richard BROKILLESBYE, gentleman.
Tithes. LINCOLN.

4 Thomas SCUDAMORE v. THOMAS ap John ap Hoell.
Land in Llancillo late of John ap Jenkin Scudamore father of complainant. HEREFORD.

5-8 The same v. Richard Thomas Guillim PHILIPP of Langua.
Other land in Llancillo late of the said John. *Much damaged.* HEREFORD.

9 William SHADWELL and Joan his wife v. William REVE.
Farm [called] Burbage Savage held of Edward late earl of Hertford by John Reve, deceased, former husband of the said Joan [and father of defendant.] *Mutilated.* WILTS.

10 Francis SHAKERLEY, gentleman, v. Richard BRUER.
Boundaries of land in Ditton. KENT.

11 Dennis SHELDEN v. Henry and Hugh SHELDEN.
Messuages and lands in Carlton, Chelmorton and Mo[nyas]he entailed on complainant by Hugh Shelden, deceased, father of all parties. NOTTS, DERBY.

12-14 Humphrey SHELLEY, yeoman, v. John SHELLEY, William FURNYFALL, Alice his wife, late the wife of Robert Shelley, Thomas ASBURY and others.
Messuage and land in Aston by Stone bought of Robert Darknall of London, esquire. *See File 1064, No. 18.* STAFFORD.

15-16 John SHELLEY, son of the said Robert, v. the said ASBURY.
Detention of a lease made by the late prior of Stone of a messuage and land in Aston. STAFFORD.

17 William SHEMAN, Ellen his wife, Robert CRISPE and Agnes his wife, v. Humphrey COMBERFORD of Comberford (in Wigginton), esquire.
Meadow in Wigginton late of Thomas Drake, deceased grandfather of the female complainants. STAFFORD.

18-21 Thomas SKEVYNGTON, gentleman v. William SKEVYNGTON.
Messuages, cottages and lands in Gumley, Foxton, Lawton, Lubbenham, Kilby, Great Bowdon, Illstone (Ilverston), and Ratby late of William Skevyngton, knight, deceased, father of complainant and grandfather of defendant. LEICESTER.

22 [Thomas SMITH*, knight,] and Dame Philippa his wife late the wife of John Hampden, knight, v. John HAMPDEN of Kimble, gentleman.
Site of the manor of Great Hampden promised to the said Dame Philippa on her persuading the said Sir John to entail the manor on defendant. *Mutilated.* BUCKINGHAM.

23-25 William SMITHE, Margaret his wife and Elizabeth CLEMETTES (Clementes) v. David ap JOHNES.
Messuages and land in the parish (sic) of Latton late of John Evance, deceased, father of defendant and grandfather of the female complainants. RADNOR.

26 Roger SMYTH, husbandman, v. John, son and heir of John PORTER, knight.
Messuage and land in Rodsley held by . . . . , deceased, together with the manors of Culland (in Osleston), Rodsley, Osleston, and Winster, and messuages and lands there and in Westbroughton, Ostole, Underwood and elsewhere. *Mutilated.* DERBY.

27-29 Joan, executrix and late the wife of Thomas SMYTHE, v. Richard SMYTHE.
Messuage and lands held of the manor of Maplederwell. HANTS.

30-32 William SMYTHE v. John GRYGGE and Cicely his wife, late the wife of John Ledford.
Sheep entrusted to the said Ledford by Rabridge Coper, widow, for delivery to John Smythe, since deceased, brother of complainant, at the end of his apprenticeship. ——

33-38 William SMYTHE alias Fowller, Robert GOODALE alias Smythe, Agnes WALWYNE and others v. Thomas PARRY, serjeant cofferer to the Princess Elizabeth, and Henry WYLCOTE his servant.
Tenement in the Princess's manor of Shitlington. BEDFORD.

39-43 John SNELSON of London v. Richard BOSTOKE, Joes his wife, Thomas STANLEY, esquire, and others.
'Wichehouses' in Middlewich and messuages there and in Burwardsley (Bursley) late of Hugh Snelson, deceased, father of complainant and husband of the said Joes. CHESTER.

44-47 Henry STANDYSHE v. Thomas STANDYSSHE, clerk.
Grant by William Standysshe, gentleman, since deceased, of the reversion of land in his manor of Galdon (i.e. Walton?) in succession to John Zelocke. SOMERSET.

48 John STEPHENS v. Robert ROBOTHAM, gentleman, and Grace his wife, late the wife of Robert Bull, and administratrix of his goods.
Decree obtained in this court, against which complainant proposes to appeal by citing his former co-defendants as witnesses. *See File 1314, No. 47.* LONDON.

---

* *See Lipscomb's Buckinghamshire, II, 233.*

49-51   Robert son of John STODARD v. William STODARD, clerk, and John GYLMAN, gentleman.
Messuages and lands in Horley and the parish of Christ Church (*i.e.* late Grey Friars) of the grant of Joan Watson, mother of the said William. *See File* 1380, *No.* 64.   SURREY, LONDON.

52   The said William v. Richard MORFYN and Thomas ELLYS.
Detention of deeds relating to a messuage and land in Horley of the grant of the said Joan.   SURREY.

53-58   William STOKES v. Anne SOMERSALL and Richard JOHNSON.
Lands, rent and messuages in South Croxton and Walton-on-the-Wold (*tenants named*) late of John Malorie. *Rival pedigrees given.*   LEICESTER.

59   The churchwardens of STONE v. William CROMPTON of London, merchant.
Destruction of the parish church of Stone, whereof defendants had obtained a lease. *Mutilated.*   STAFFORD.

60-63   Roger STRATTON and others (*named*), husbandman, for themselves, and all the inhabitants of Houghton Conquest, v. Joan CONQUEST.
Seizure by Edmund Conquest, esquire, late the husband of defendant, of lands conveyed for the relief of the charges of the town, and embezzlement of church goods, money raised for the 'furniture' of soldiers, etc.   BEDFORD.

64-68   James STREATE v. Thomas HANNYNGE.
Tenement in the manor of Attysborowe demised by Marmaduke Mauncell, esquire, to John Streate, deceased, father of the said James, whose widow married defendant.   SOMERSET.

69-73   John SUMNER v. John MOUNTSTEVYN, servant to John, bishop of Peterborough.
Building a windmill on the manor of Werrington (Wethyngton) of the demise of John, bishop of Peterborough.   NORTHAMPTON.

74-75   William SYMONDES of Datchworth (Thatchforthe) co. Herts, yeoman, administrator of the goods of Christopher Symondes of Ruston, clerk, his brother, deceased, v. Reynold LEE and Robert GOWCHE (Gowge, Googe), esquires.
Goods of the said Christopher, said by the said Lee to have been distrained for Crown rent and tithes in Fiskerton.   NOTTS.

76   Henry SYSSARSON of London, cordwainer, and Elizabeth his wife v. Christopher ASSHTON of Fyfield.
Price of shoes and other goods bought of Richard Bartram of London, cordwainer, former husband of the said Elizabeth.   LONDON, BERKS.

77   Henry S . . . of Bristol, skinner, v. Joan, executrix and late the wife of John WILLIAMS of Portbury (?) mariner.
Debt of the said John for cloth. *Mutilated.*   SOMERSET.

FILE 1384.

1   John SADLER and Margaret his wife v. William SWANYKE, clerk, and John SWANYKE of Whitchurch, co. Salop, yeoman.
Messuages and land at Swanwick in Norbury (Swanyke) late of Ralph Swaynyke, deceased, father of the said Margaret.   CHESTER.

2-4   Thomas, son and heir of Richard SALTE v. Anne (Agnes), late the wife of John WEBBE.
Detention of deeds relating to land in the manor of Yoxall and packing a jury.   STAFFORD.

5   John SALYSBURY v. John SMYTH, mayor of Barnstaple, and the bailiffs and burgesses of BARNSTAPLE.
Action by the said Smyth in his own court on a contract for transport of goods from abroad. *Certiorari.*   DEVON.

6-8   Alexander and William, sons and executors of William SAMER (Seimer, Seymer) v. John SCOTTE of Gravesend, woodmonger.
Lands in East Hanningfield pledged for a debt of deceased.   ESSEX.

9   Francis SAMWELL of Northampton, gentleman, v. John HORPOLE his tenant.
Repairs of a water-mill in the Abbot's Meadow at Duston held by complainant on lease of the Crown.   NORTHAMPTON.

10-12   Henry SANDYFFORDE of Bristol, skinner, v. Thomas CRICKLAND.
Refusal to carry out a composition for complainant's debt, awarded by commissioners in bankruptcy.   SOMERSET.

13   Robert SAUNDERSON, executor of Richard Norres, clerk, v. Robert CAULTON and Thomas BOLT, clerk.
Presentation to the church of Cheadle granted by the master and scholars of Trinity College, Cambridge, to the said Caulton in order to present the said Norres's nominees.   STAFFORD.

14-17   Richard SCOTT and Joan his wife v. Robert, son and heir of Thomas TOWNENDE.
Messuage, garden and orchard in Haxey (Axhaye) late of John Pople, deceased, father of the said Joan.   LINCOLN.

18   John SELLYNG v. Richard SELLYNG, his elder brother.
Messuage and land in Carlton Colville, the deeds whereof were obtained from Gregory Payne by threatening to bring him before Robert Kette, the captain of the rebels.   SUFFOLK.

19-21   John SELYOCKE of Hasylboroughe (*i.e.* Hazlebadge?), gentleman, v. Robert SMYTH of London, gentleman.
Failure to cancel a bond (*sic*) given jointly to Thomas Dignham, gentleman.   DERBY, LONDON.

22   The same *v.* Richard WHETALL, merchant stapler of Calais.
Usurious bond.   DERBY, CALAIS.

23-27   Thomas SHERBROKE *v.* William BERNARD, son and heir of Joan Wentworth.
Reviver of a suit for a messuage in Louth (*File* 1264, *No.* 25). *See also File* 1270, *No.* 30. D. X, 47.
                                                                 LINCOLN.

28-29   William SMETHER, butcher, *v.* Thomas STOFFOLD (Stowal, Stovall).
Messuage and land in Cranley, late of Richard Smether, deceased, grandfather of complainant.
                                                                 SURREY.

30   John SMYTH *v.* John SYBLES.
Detention of deeds relating to lands in Ledbury.   HEREFORD.

31.   Robert SMYTH of Derby, pewterer, *v.* Humphrey BENTLEY, late of Derby, gentleman.
Delivery of deeds and bonds and conveyance of a tenement in Derby by defendant's advice.
Mutilated.   DERBY.

32-34   Henry SMYTHE and Elizabeth his wife *v.* Thomas, son and heir of Thomas FAYTHEFULL.
Messuage and land at Frobury in Kingsclere, late of Philip Beynham, deceased. *Pedigree given.*
                                                                 HANTS.

35-37   William SMYTHE *v.* John SMYTHE of Henley, his brother, executor of Thomas Smythe,
a third brother.
Goods given to complainant by the said Thomas for the finding of Richard and Agnes his children.
(Defendant pleads a verdict at *nisi prius*, delayed by Wyatt's rebellion).   OXFORD.

38-40   Edmund SOME of King's Lynn, merchant, *v.* Katharine, late the wife of Robert REYNER
of Peterborough, merchant, and William their son.
Price of ' amys ' iron and soap sold to the said Robert, whose executors defendants are.
                                                                 NORFOLK, NORTHAMPTON.

41   Thomas SOUTHERNE, treasurer of Exeter cathedral, *v.* Walter STAPILHILL (Stepelhill) of
Exeter, gentleman.
Compensation promised for trespass of —— Darte and —— Geste on land in Ide.   DEVON.

42-45   Edward SOWGATE, husbandman, son of Adam Sowgate, *v.* Robert SA(W)YER and William
FYNCHE, husband of Jane, late the wife of the said Adam.
Detention of deeds entrusted to the said Robert to make a five years' lease of a messuage and land
in Ospringe to the said William and Jane. *See File* 1268, *No.* 44.   KENT.

46-47   John SPADARD *v.* Matthew HENSTON and John HORNBY.
Lands in Honeybrook (in Wimborne Minster), Up-Wimborne, and Wimborne Minster formerly of
Robert Spadard. *Mutilated.* (Defendants plead that the matter is in suit in the Court of Requests.)
                                                                 DORSET.

48   Thomas SPRYGGES *v.* Adam STURGES.
Messuage called the *Olde Swanne* in Market Harborough with a garden abutting on the river
Welland, formerly of Henry Man.   LEICESTER.

49-51   Robert son and heir of Hugh STANFORD, Richard GRAFTON, and Agnes his wife, late the
wife of the said Hugh, *v.* the dean and chapter of SALISBURY and Robert ELYOT their
tenant.
Messuages, barns, mills and land in Stratford-under-the-Castle, late of William Stampford, deceased,
father of the said Hugh. D. XIV, 32. *See File* 1184, *No.* 51.   WILTS.

52   Thomas STANLEY, lord Monteagle *v.* Henry SAVYLL, knight.
Rent due from the manor of Tankersley to that of Brierly. *Answer in File* 1385, *No.* 54.   YORK.

53-55   Joan, late the wife of James STAVELEY, citizen and vintner of London, *v.* Marcelyne
HALES of Romford, gentleman.
Messuage and land in Hornchurch adjudged to Elizabeth Gyfford in a previous suit (*File* 992,
No. 57). *Replication wanting.* D. IX, 25.   ESSEX.

56-60   William STEKE(S) *alias* Ewen, a minor, by John Shepherd, gentleman of the Queen's chapel
and Jane his wife, late the wife of William Steke, his guardians, *v.* John GARDYNER,
gentleman.
The same *v.* the same and John FITZ and Anne his wife, late the wife of Thomas Gardyner
and mother of the said John.
Nineteen tenements called St. Mary's Inn (' Seynt Mary or Syng Mary ') in the parish of St. Clement
Danes.   MIDDLESEX.

61-63   Philip, son and heir of John STEVYN(S) and of Denise his wife, sometime Denise Proutz, *v.*
Thomasyn, late the wife of Robert Stevyn.
Messuages and lands at Rippleside and elsewhere in Barking.   ESSEX.

64   William STOKES, of London, minstrel, *v.* William HIBBS, husbandman.
Cottage and land in [Courteenhall] of the gift of William Stokes, father of complainant. *Mutilated.*
                                                                 NORTHAMPTON.

65   William STRAY *v.* Giles NYCOLLES and Thomas GREMYTT.
Messuage and land in Bishampton.   WORCESTER.

66-67   Ralph, great-grandson and heir of Thomas STUBBES of Butterton, *v.* William MORETON
and Richard his son.
Lands in Astbury of the grant of Hugh Egerton.   CHESTER.

68   Robert STYLE of Ash-Bocking *v.* Humphrey PALMER, clerk to one of the Six Clerks.
Failure to enrol a decree in an action against Lionel Talmache, since deceased (*File* 1067, *No.* 58.)
Mutilated. A decree in the suit in question is enrolled (D. III, 10.).   SUFFOLK.

69–70   John SWASHTON *v.* William DAVYE.
Detention of deeds relating to land in White Roding. (Defendant pleads a decree in the Court of Requests. · *See Court of Requests Proceedings*, XXII, 54.)   ESSEX.

71   David SYMPSON *v.* William LATHAM of Sandon, esquire, son and heir of William Latham of London, goldsmith.
Refusal to complete a sale of the manor of Beachampes in Wyck[ford] and Runwell.   D. IX, 43.
ESSEX.

FILE 1385.

1–2   John SADLER of Newbury, husbandman, *v.* Gilbert POWNSSEYE of Blandford St. Mary, butcher.
Warranty of sheep.   BERKS, DORSÉT.

3   William SADOK *v.* Robert DIGHTON, clerk.
Detention of bills entrusted to complainant by James Seller, parson of Wath.   YORK.

4   Richard SAGE and Katherine his wife, daughter and heir of Thomas Rolffe, *v.* John PAXON.
Detention of deeds relating to a messuage and land in Hatfield Peverel.   ESSEX.

5–7   Thomas SAGE *v.* Polydore WALKYNGES.
Refusal to complete a demise of a tenement in defendant's manor of Farrington.   *Mutilated.*
SOMERSET.

8   William SALTER *v.* Thomasyn late the wife of Robert SALTER.
Moiety of land in the manor of Woodbeare (in Plymtree) late of the said Robert.   *Mutilated.*
DEVON.

9   John SALYSBURYE of Grays Inn, servant to the Earl of Pembroke, *v.* David LLOYD ap Nicholas of Pentrewide, co. Salop and RICHARD ap John ap Elys of Llandegla.
Messuage and land in Creigiog and Creigioguwchllan late of Robert Salysbury, deceased, father of complainant.   DENBIGH.

10   Richard SAMBACHE *v.* Anne, late the wife of ——— COLTON, and formerly of Robert Catysbye.
Action on a bill for a debt already paid to the said Catysbye.   WARWICK.

11–15   Miles SANDES, clerk, *v.* Thomas WHYTYNG of Bratoft, yeoman, and Alice his wife.
Coin and silver articles entrusted to defendants. *Answer in duplicate.*   LINCOLN.

16–17   William SARJEANT *v.* Audrey RICHARD and John HAMPDEN esquire.
' Leies ' of meadow, including a ' hadley ' or ' hadd ' (*i.e.* headland ?) in Kimblewick and arable there and in Rounden (all in Kimble). *Answer wanting. See File 1264, No. 15.* BUCKINGHAM.

18   Henry SAVELL, knight, *v.* Robert and Nicholas SAVELL.
Detention of deeds.   [YORK ?]

19   John SAWNDERS and Henry COLYNS, masters and wardens of the butchers of Coventry, and their fellowship, *v.* John EDWARDS, butcher.
Selling meat in Coventry outside the shambles, and refusal to join the said fellowship.·   WARWICK.

20   Elizabeth late the wife of Thomas SCAMPTON *v.* Robert FINLEY.
Extortions from complainant and others by colour of a Crown lease of lands in Thurmaston.
LEICESTER.

21   Richard SELLERS of Baston, co. Derby, and Elizabeth his wife *v.* Richard and William LEIGHE, gentlemen.
Messuages and land in Rothwell and Carlton.   YORK.

22   Henry SERLE *v.* Thomas FYSHE.
Conversion of the goods·of William Boyer, knight, mayor of London, deceased, whose executors both parties are, and action concerning the manor of Hackney Wick (' Wyke in the parishes of Hackney and Shepneth and in Leyghton ').   MIDDLESEX, ESSEX.

23–24   John SEYMOR, esquire, *v.* Francis ROLLESTON, gentleman.
Tenancy of the priory of Gresley, formerly held by Henry Cruche, gentleman, together with the rectory and lands there and in Castle Gresley, Linton, Swathlingham (*i.e.* Swadlincote ?), Drakelow, Bowthorpe, Oakthorpe, Donase (*i.e.* Donisthorpe ?)·and Thorpe.   DERBY.

25   John SHAKELFORD, husbandman, *v.* Peter PYNK.
Tenements held of Lord Audley's manor of Bradley.   HANTS.

26   Ralph SHAWE, vicar of Brimpton, *v.* William PENBROKE.
Messuage and land belonging to complainant's church in the manor of Brimpton.   BERKS.

27   William SHEPARD of Swinstead, butcher, son of Thomas Shepard of Silkstone, yeoman *v.* Henry, Richard and Elizabeth SHEPARD, executors of the said Thomas.
Legacy of the said Thomas, and money given to him for complainant by Isobel Burton.
LINCOLN,· YORK.

28–29   Richard SHERWYN of Penkridge, miller, son of Edward Sherwyn, *v.* David CAWER-DYNE (Carden), gentleman.
Land, mill and fishery in Mavesyn Ridware of the demise of Robert Cawerdyne, esquire, grandfather of defendant.   STAFFORD.

30   Thomas Burynton and Robert Irland, wardens of the mercers, goldsmiths, and ironmongers 'under one gyld and fraternitye' in SHREWSBURY, v. John MACKWORTH, alderman of Shrewsbury.
Non-payment of rent of the Mercers' Hall in Shrewsbury, distributable to almsmen dwelling in the churchyard of St. Chad, and breaking up the doors of the hall.   SALOP.

31   Dorothy SLYGHT v. John LAWRENCE.
Messuage and garden in . . . ckforde. *Mutilated.*

32   William SMARTE the younger, son and heir of Eleanor Gillet, v. Denise PARSEMORE.
Messuage and land in Bradley of the entail of Thomas Hatche and others.   DEVON.

33   John SMYTH of Marlborough and Elizabeth his wife v. John MONDY of Shalbourn and others.
Land at Stanmore in Beedon of the bequest of William Monday, former husband of the said Elizabeth.   BERKS.

34–36   John SMYTH, husbandman, v. Thomas SMYTH, labourer, and others.
Lands and cottages in Horseheath and Shudy Camps late of John Smyth, deceased, father of complainant.   CAMBRIDGE.

37   Thomas SMYTH, yeoman, and others, all of Caldecote, v. Robert PECK of the same, clerk of the peace for the county.
Money entrusted for the Duke of Northumberland's rebellion.   CAMBRIDGE.

38   Richard SNEYDE of the Inner Temple and Alice his wife, late the wife of George Leche, v. William LECHE, son of the said George.
Refusal to account for goods of the said George, whose executors are the said Alice and William, and wrongful occupation of a shop in Northgate Street, Chester.   CHESTER.

39–42   Thomas SOOLE (Sowle) v. Gregory GOSE.
Messuage and yard in Great Yarmouth late of Robert Soole, deceased father of complainant.
        NORFOLK.

43–44   Richard SPENCER, citizen and fishmonger of London, son and heir of William Spencer, v. Richard WARDE the elder.
Detention of deeds relating to a shop, garden and barn (*described*) in Derby.   DERBY.

45–46   Lancelot SPERE v. William his eldest brother.
Land late held of the manor of Netherhall in Stoke by Thomas Spere, deceased, father of both parties, complainant being heir by the custom of the manor and defendant at common law.
        SUFFOLK.

47–48   John SPERLYNG and Richard FARRANT v. Thomas MISTERCHAMBERS.
Information of an assault committed on Nicholas Furnesse of Saltfleetby, yeoman, at service of a subpoena at Louth.   LINCOLN.

49–52   Edward [STANLEY], earl of Derby, v. John NEWDEGATE, esquire.
Detention of deeds relating to the manor of Colham (in Hillingdon).   MIDDLESEX.

53   The same v. John NORTON, esquire.
Manors of Thirsk, Kirkby, Malzeard, Wrote, and Burton-in-Lonsdale.   YORK.

54   [Thomas STANLEY] lord Monteagle, v. Sir Henry [SAVILE].
(Continuation of File 1384, No. 52). *Faded.*   YORK.

55   William STANLEY of Newark-upon-Trent, draper, v. Peter HUCKYT.
Price of cloth.   NOTTS.

56   Geoffrey STARKY of Haykensall (*i.e.* Hackensall?) co. Lancaster, gentleman, son of John Starky, v. Lawrence SMYTH, knight.
Messuages (*described*), gardens and rent in Chester late of the hospital of St. John the Baptist.
        CHESTER.

57   William STAMFORDE of Packington, gentleman, v. Thomas LANE.
Detention of deeds relating to a messuage and land in Handsworth acquired of Humphrey Wyrleye of Stafford, deceased, and William his son.   STAFFORD.

58–59   Roger STAVELEYE v. William MOUNTFORDE; yeoman.
Houses and land in Hatherton held of the late Duke of Northumberland's manor of Wolverhampton.
        STAFFORD.

60–62   John STEVENS, cousin and heir of Goddard Eglentyne, v. Thomas son of William HAYE.
Detention of deeds relating to land in Battle. *Answer wanting.*   SUSSEX.

63–64   Leonard STEVYNSON v. Thurstan MEADE (Medde).
Action on a bond after agreement to accept a lesser sum than therein specified.   SOMERSET.

65–67   Matthew [STEWART], earl of Lennox and Margaret his wife, v. Christopher DENBY, knight.
Witton Moor, granted to complainant with the manor of East Witton by King Henry VIII.
        YORK.

68   John STOKER of Wyke, esquire, v. William HEBBES.
Messuage and land in Corton late of John Stoker, deceased, father of complainant.   DORSET.

69   Robert STONYSBYE, gentleman, and Bartholomew HYLTON, grandson and heir of Bryan Stabeler, v. William GRYMSTON and others.
Annuity due from the said Grymston's lands in Mouthorpe in Grendall Lyght (*i.e.* Mowthorpe in Kirby Grindalythe).   YORK.

70–71   Humphrey STORER, husbandman, v. Robert BROWNLOW, farmer to George Vernon, knight.
Right of way in Trusley.   DERBY

72   Richard STRADFORD v. the constable of WINDSOR castle.
Imprisonment on a castle warrant sued out by Richard Emerson concerning corn, malt and money delivered to him. · *Certiorari.*   BERKS.

73   Thomas STRADL[YNGE], knight, v. William Hopkyn DAWKYNS.
Land and tithes called the chapel of Henllys in Llanddewi.   GLAMORGAN.

74–75   Anthony STRELLEY, knight, v. THOMAS ap Robert ap Hoell and others.
Rents and services due from Crown lands. *Mutilated.*   SALOP.

76   Edmund STURE v. William STROODE, esquire.
Manor and hundred of Ermington of the demise of Francis Stonore of Stonor, co. Oxford, knight.   DEVON.

77–78   Richard SWALE, yeoman, Agnes his wife, and John CHARDEZ v. Richard VAVISOR, gentleman.
·Manor of Little Askham demised by John late abbot of Bridlington to John Chardez, deceased, former husband of the said Agnes and father of the said John..   YORK.

79   Thomas SYBELY v. Christian SIBELEY his daughter-in-law.
Land at Henton in the manor of Martock of the demise of King Henry VII.   SOMERSET.

80   Gilbert SYMPKYNS v. John LONDON of Woodstock, yeoman.
Information of purchase of wool contrary to the statute 5-6 Edward VI., c. 7, defendant being neither a woollen manufacturer nor a merchant of the Staple.   OXFORD.

FILE 1386.

1   Richard son and heir of Philip TAILER v. William PHILIPES, gentleman, and others.
Detention of deeds relating to a messuage called Sowell Sonke.   PEMBROKE.

2–3   John TAILOUR v. John DANYELL.
Land in Alrewas of the demise of George Gryffith, knight.   STAFFORD.

4   John DANYELL v. John TAYLLOUR.
Cottage and land in Allerwas late of Richard Ellyngton, deceased, grandfather of complainant.   [STAFFORD.]

5–7   William TALPOTT, late of Petersfield, yeoman, son and heir of William Talpott, v. John CHAMPION, late of the same.
Land in the tithing of Nursted said by complainant to belong to the manor of Nursted and by defendant to that of Weston both late of the abbot and convent of Durford, co. Sussex.   HANTS.

8   John TAVERNER, yeoman,˙Jane his wife, William TAVERNER, yeoman, and Thomasen his wife, all of Endellion, v. Nicholas Dyer, husbandman.
Land in St. Teath.   CORNWALL.

9   Thomas TAYLOUR, vicar of Kidderminster, v. Edward BLUNT.
Close of pasture in Kidderminster, part of the endowment (*described*) of the vicarage on the dissolution of the priory of Maiden-Bradley. *Mutilated.*   WORCESTER.

10   Richard THACHAM of Idmiston, husbandman, v. Thomas COOKE of Bishopstoke, co. Hants, gentleman.
Messuages and land in Winterburn and Woodford late of John Thacham, deceased, father of complainant.   WILTS.

11–14   Edward THACKER v. William WHETECROFTE and others.
Messuage and land in Heage of the demise of Thomas Thacker of Repton, deceased, father of complainant.   DERBY.

15–16   Alice late the wife of John THOMAS of Bristol, tailor, and administratrix of his goods, v. John WEBBE of Newnham, yeoman.
Non-deliver of 'fyve skore thousande woode . . . to be cutt and made after the reste of tallwoode or billyttes'   GLOUCESTER.

17   William THOMAS, clerk, v. Anthony AMORYE, gentleman.
Occupation of the rectory of High Bickington, although 'by the dexteritie of the lawes . . . he . . . must of force forsake the same.'   DEVON.

18   Richard THOMSON v. James ASLABY.
Horse and gown late of James Thomson, deceased, father of complainant.   [YORK?]

19–22   The same v. Francis ASLABY; son and executor of the said James.
Reviver of the preceding.   [YORK?]

23–25   Richard THORNE v. Margaret, late the wife of John CANDYSHE, (Cavendysshe), knight, kinsman of complainant, and formerly the wife of Robert Sheffelde, knight.
Annuity granted by the said Sir John for past service out of the manors of Woode (*i.e.* Melwood in Owston?) and Bournham (*i.e.* Burnham in Haxey) and messuages and land in Woodeburnham and Axholme.   LINCOLN.

26   Richard THORNEDEN, D.D., parson of Adisham with the chapel of Staple annexed, v. John WYSEMAN, gentleman.
Lease of the parsonage made by Thomas (John) Brande, late parson deprived for marriage, to Christopher Nevynson, whose widow defendant has married.   KENT.

27   The same v. Thomas WYSEMAN.
Same lease.   KENT.

28 ·   Joan THORNEGATE of Upham [and Richard COWSYN] *v.* Richard TYCHEBOURNE and others.
Obtaining a *latitat* against the said Cowsyn whom they are suspected of having robbed, and threats, *Damaged.*   [HANTS.]

29–30   Robert THURGOOD of Magdalen Laver, yeoman, *v.* Henry SERLE.
Manor of Marshalls and messuages and land, all in North Weald Bassett, bought of William Fitz-willyam, knight.   ESSEX.

31–33   Edward THURLAND of Lound in Haughton (Houghton Lownd), esquire, *v.* Thomas BURTON of Cotes, gentleman.
Price of lead bought of the King and sold to defendant.   NOTTS, LINCOLN.

34   John THYRLBORN of Girton *v.* [William MUNSEY] of Cambridge, burgess and tailor(?)
Bond given by Thomas Thurlborn, husbandman, for delivery of malt. *Mutilated.*   CAMBRIDGE.

35   John TIDERLEY, vicar of Northam, *v.* Christopher BERY and others.
Tithe and glebe of Northam. *Faded.*   DEVON.

36 · Robert TOLEY of Stickney, *v.* John TOLEY his uncle.
Messuage and land in Hatton bequeathed to complainant by William Toley, his father.   LINCOLN.

37–39   Lawrence TORKYNTON, gentleman, *v.* Mark BROUGHTON.
Legacies of Henry Torkynton, deceased, father of complainant and former husband of Katharine wife of defendant.   [HUNTINGDON?]

40   Robert TOURSON *v.* Edmund and Anthony TYSON and others.
Land at 'the water syde' (*i.e.* Waterbeach?)   CAMBRIDGE. (?)

41–45   William TOWLE *v.* John MANSER and William VOWELL (Wowell).
Tenements in North Creake and Burnham Thorpe.   NORFOLK.

46   John TOWYLL of Teignmouth *v.* Thomas SIMON *alias* Mychell, clerk.
Detention of deeds relating to land in Dawlish acquired of Richard and . . .   Hert, gentlemen.   DEVON.

47–48   John TOWYLL, husbandman, *v.* James, brother and heir of Robert WYTTON.
Messuages and land in Saxilby and Hardwick, late of William Towill, deceased, father of complainant.   LINCOLN.

49   Richard TRAFFORD *v.* Robert HOLLYNGWORTHE and Agnes his wife.
Messuage in Melton Mowbray bought of John Beaumont, esquire.   LEICESTER.

50–52   John, son and executor of John TREGEAN, Katherine his wife, and Francis his son, *v.* Hugh POMERYE and Joan, his wife.
Refusal to renew a lease made by Edward Pomerye, knight, of land in Halbote, a wood called Breffa, and a grove of alders near Penwerne (all in Cuby?). *Mutilated.*   CORNWALL.

53   John TREMAYN of Tregonon (*i.e.* Tregony?), gentleman, *v.* William THOMAS, of Creed (Saynt Crede), yeoman, and Thomas TEAGE.
Conspiracy to defeat a conveyance of land in the manor of Tybesta (or Creed).   CORNWALL.

54–60   George TRESHAM, gentleman, [bailiff] of the manor of Moulton, *v.* William HAYNES.
Lease of part of the demesnes of the manor, including rabbits and a dovecote. *Damaged.* *2 replications and rejoinders.*   NORTHAMPTON.

61–62   John TREVELACKE of Gerran *v.* William CRYSTOFER and Harry TREGYDELL (Tregryll).
Messuages and land in Creed.   CORNWALL.

63–64   Thomas TREVELYAN *v.* John TREVELYAN, esquire, his elder brother.
Manor of Knolle and messuages, burgages, lands, wills and a rent of 1*d.* in Owlknoll, Chekeston, Berrynarbor, Wolmershays, Champnehays, etc. (*as in* File 1164, *No.* 30, *reading* Lynch *for* Lynet *and* Tortyslynch *for* Hertyslynch.   SOMERSET, DEVON, DORSET.

65   William TURNER *v.* Roger CAPSTOCKE his stepdaughter's husband.
Dispute as to the manor of Belsize (in Castor), of the demise of the late abbot of Peterborough and assault. *Faded.*   NORTHAMPTON.

66–67   John TURVY, labourer, *v.* Thomas COOKE (Cole), yeoman.
Cottage let by defendant in Horningsea.   CAMBRIDGE.

68   George TYLER *v.* Arthur LAWELEY of Alveley, yeoman.
Loan.   SALOP.

69   Ralph TYLLYNGTON of Norwich, beer-brewer, *v.* Ralph SYMONDES of Cley, gentleman, and John BYRD, husbandman.
Fraud in taking complainant's wheat for the late King's use.   NORFOLK.

70   John TYRART of London, vintner, *v.* the sheriffs of LONDON.
Action by John Awdrey of London, weaver, for sale of wine contrary to the Act 7 Edw. VI, c. 5, complainant having a Crown licence to keep a tavern in the precinct of the Black Friars. *Certiorari.*   LONDON.

FILE 1387.

1–2   David, son and heir of Thomas TAILLOUR, *v.* Thomas COPPENER.
Detention of deeds relating to land in Pembridge (Penrigge).   HEREFORD.

3–4   Edward TAILOUR of Hadley, co. Middlesex, esquire, and James CROSSE *v.* Thomas STILER, Edmund ONIONS (Inyons) and others.
Lands in Morton extended for a debt of Thomas Forster of Enileth, co. Salop. *Damaged.*   STAFFORD.

5–6   The same v. John LAMBOURN (Lambard) and others.
Pasture in Aspley extended for the same debt.   BEDFORD.

7- 9   Anne TAPPE v. John MOWLE.
Debt.   SOMERSET.

10–13   John TAPPLE(Y)S (Topleyes) and Emot his wife, late the wife of William Eyton, v. Nicholas
BERZSFORTH (Barsford) and others.
Land in Vincent Monday's lordship of Warslow, late of John Stone. 2 answers.   STAFFORD.

14   John TAYLLOUR v. Robert BRAYLEGHE, clerk, and others.
Goods including four 'lyrons' (i.e. beams) bought of John Browne, parson of Langton, killed in the
rebellion in co. Devon, whose goods were given to defendants by the Earl of Bedford.   [DORSET.]

15–21   John TAYLOUR of Tetford, yeoman, v. William TUPHOLME, and William SMYTHE and
others, his servants.
Messuages and land in Ashby (Askeby) by Horncastle and Mid-Thorpe in Ashby (Myddell Thorpe)
late of Robert Clarke, grandfather of complainant. See No. 57. D. IX, 44.   LINCOLN.

22–23   John TAYLOUR and Margaret his wife, v. John TYCHEBORNE and Robert and John
SELYARD.
Legacy of Richard Tychborne of Edenbridge, gentleman, father of the said Margaret, whose
executors defendants are.   KENT.

24–25   Walter TAYLOUR v. Thomas TAYLOUR his brother.
Land in Frittenden pledged by complainant and redeemed with money found by him. D. IX, 20.
                                                                                  KENT.

26   Richard TESDALE, Rycharden his wife, Henry THWAYTES, Alice his wife, Thomas
ADAMS, and Mildred his wife, v. Robert GRENESTRETE.
Messuage and land in Teynham, late of John Abram, deceased, uncle of the female complainants.
                                                                                  KENT.

27–28   Hugh THOMAS of Abergavenny, mercer, v. the sheriffs of LONDON, and Alice WATKYNS
of Abergavenny, draper, and Thomas CARTER, fishmonger.
Action by the said Carter for price of linen carried by complainant to the said Alice. Certiorari and
subpœna.   LONDON, MONMOUTH.

29–33   John THORNES and Joan his wife v. Richard JOHNSON and John HALLAM his lessee.
Messuage, barn, kiln-house and land in Stoke Bardolph and Gedling, late of Richard Johnson,
deceased, grandfather of the said Joan and father of the said Richard.   NOTTS.

34–35   Thomas THREDER v. Thomas ALE(E) alias Coke, husbandman, and Joan his wife.
Jury-packing in an action for lopping trees on land of the demise of defendants in Flamstead.
                                                                                  HERTS.

36   Stephen THWAYTES v. Robert SAUNDERSON.
Loan the bond for which is lost.   LONDON.

37–38   Andrew TOOK, vicar of [Wiggenhall] St. German's and petty canon of Norwich, v. William
BUTTES, gentleman.
Vicarage of St. German's claimed under a lease from John Sayer, late vicar, deprived for absence.
                                                                                  NORFOLK.

39   Hugh TREVANION, knight, late feodary of the Duchy of Cornwall, v. William SOMASTER,
gentleman.
Detention of books and records which came to defendant's hands as complainant's deputy. Mutilated.
                                                                                  CORNWALL.

40   Edward TREVOUR, sewer of the Chamber, son of Robert ap Edward alias Trevour, v. David
ap John alias TREVOUR, gentleman, servant to the Earl of Pembroke.
Water-mill and land in Esclusham adjudged to complainant in a former suit. Mutilated. D. X, 3.
See File 1271, No. 59.   DENBIGH.

41   John TREVOUR of London v. Richard WILLIAMS.
Loan.   LONDON, ANGLESEA.

42–43   Thomas TREWE of Stoke Nayland, clothier, v. William CLARKE.
Goods delivered to Giles Pachet on complainant's verbal security.   SUFFOLK, RUTLAND.

44–49   Alexander TROTT and Alice his wife v. William HAWKYNS, gentleman, and Elizabeth
BULL.
Messuage, dovecote and land in Plymouth, late of Thomas Bull, deceased, grandfather of the said
Alice.   DEVON.

50–52   The same v. Michael STEPHYN.
Messuage and land in Cofflete (Cockflete) and Hareson, both in Brixton, late of the said William.
                                                                                  DEVON.

53–54   Richard TRUE of Tonbridge, ironfounder, v. Andrew FORMENGER of the same.
Wages and expenses for blowing 13 'foundayes' and two days at the late Duke of Northumberland's
furnaces at South Frith (in Tonbridge).   KENT.

55   Oliver TRUXTON, common carrier between Ludlow and London, v. Walter NICHOLLES of
Burford, clothier.
Fine paid in Blackwell Hall by complainant for a cloth of defendant which was found deficient in
length and weight.   SALOP, LONDON.

56   Robert TUCKEY and Juliana his wife v. Walter ROME and Isabel his wife.
Land in Kingston Seymour of the demise of John King, esquire.   SOMERSET.

57–59　　William TUPHOLME of Boston, merchant, v. Thomas WEST and John MAY(RE).
Detention of deeds relating to meadow in Ashby by Horncastle, late of Thomas Tupholme, deceased, grandfather of complainant. *See No.* 15.　　　　　　　　　　　　　　　LINCOLN.

60–62　　Tristram TURNER and Alice his wife, daughter of William Benett, deceased, v. John, grandson of Robert BRETT, Robert APLEN and Andrew his son.
Double demise of a tenement in the manor of White Staunton.　　　　　　　SOMERSET.

63–67　　Thomas TURNOUR, citizen and woodmonger of London, v. John SLANNYNG.
Rent of a messuage, wharf and crane in the parish of St. James Garlickhithe late belonging to a chantry in the parish church. D. XIV, 46.　　　　　　　　　　　　　　LONDON.

68　　　　Henry TWYNNYNG, husbandman, son and heir of Thomas Twynnyng, v. Henry BERDE.
Messuage, water-mill, and land in the lordship of Painswick, of the demise of Arthur Plantagenet, knight.　　　　　　　　　　　　　　　　　　　　　　　　　GLOUCESTER.

69–70　　Thomas and Ralph TYLSTON v. Richard BOSTOCKE and John BROMELEY.
Compensation for goods of complainants late in the hands of Roger Tylston their kinsman, confiscated on defendant's statement that the said Roger was ' a rebellion.'　　[CHESTER *or* SALOP ?]

71–72　　John TYNGLE of London, cutler, v. John SYMSON of Pinchbeck, late his master.
Sheep which defendant promised to deliver on demand with their increase.　LONDON, LINCOLN.

FILE 1388.

1–3　　Richard TAILOR and Joan his wife v. Libeus ALCOCKE, yeoman, son of Libeus Alcocke.
Messuages and land in Halton and Spilsby, late of William Pynder, deceased, father of the said Joan. *Answer mutilated.*　　　　　　　　　　　　　　　　　　　　LINCOLN.

4–5　　Richard TAILOUR v. Robert OWXSTON, vicar of Stillington.
Refusal to complete a lease of land in Stillington.　　　　　　　　　　YORK.

6　　　　John TALCARN v. Elizabeth his mother.
Plate, featherbed, and other goods, in complainant's house at Petherwin, entrusted to defendant.　　　　　　　　　　　　　　　　　　　　　　　　　　DEVON.

7–8　　William TANFELDE, esquire, and Elizabeth his wife v. Thomas BURGES.
Manor of Cold Hall (in Great Bromley)late of Thomas Clovyle, esquire, father of the said Elizabeth. D. XIII, 4.　　　　　　　　　　　　　　　　　　　　　　ESSEX.

9　　　　Robert TATTON v. Robert KEMPE.
' Bownes and averages and other services ' due from a tenement in the manor of Etchells.　CHESTER.

10–11　　John, brother of William TAYLOUR of Milbourn, deceased, v. Thomas NELE.
Tenement in the manor of Whitchurch of which the copy is withheld by William Basseley, gentleman, now lord.　　　　　　　　　　　　　　　　　　　　　　　　WILTS.

12　　　　Thomas TAYLOUR of Banham, co. Norfolk, v. John TAYLOUR.
Tenement in Pomfret late of Robert Taylour, deceased, father of complainant.　　YORK.
Footnote that an attachment was directed to the sheriff of York.

13–15　　Jane TEMMES and John LUDLOWE, gentleman, her son, v. Ambrose HAWKYN.
Felling timber on a messuage and land of the demise of complainants in Monk-Sherborne (West-sherborne).　　　　　　　　　　　　　　　　　　　　　　　　HANTS.

16–18　　Robert TEYNTER, vicar of Winscombe v. George PAYNE, gentleman.
Vicarage of Winscombe, which defendant occupied by the sufferance of ——— Cham, late vicar, deprived for marriage.　　　　　　　　　　　　　　　　　　　　SOMERSET.

19　　　　Howell THOMAS ap Hopkyn of Llantrissaint v. Philip LOARGHE, late of Chepstow.
Price of oxen.　　　　　　　　　　　　　　　　　　　　　　　MONMOUTH.

20–21　　Hugh THOMAS v. Alice WATKYNS.
Sale of linen. *Bill wanting.*　　　　　　　　　　　　　　　　　　？

22　　　　Robert THOMAS, servant to John Veigh[an ?] of London, esquire, v. Harry PHELIPE and others.
Detention of deeds. *Mutilated.*　　　　　　　　　　　　　　　　BRECON.

23　　　　THOMAS ap Hoell v. John DAVID ap Jevan ap Res of Newchurch and Lewis David Thomas DEE of Colver.
Messuage and land called ' Tere Cadowgan .'　　　　　　　　　　　　RADNOR.

24　　　　THOMAS ap Morgan v. James GODSLOND.
Seizure of wheat and bean bought at Barnstaple.　　　　　　　　　　DEVON.

25　　　　THOMAS ap Robert ap Roger v. THOMAS ap Roger.
Land in Nantglyn granted by defendant to Roger ap Robert (*sic*), deceased, father of complainant.　　　　　　　　　　　　　　　　　　　　　　DENBIGH.

26　　　　William THOMPSON, of Ripon, miller, v. Richard SEYLL, clerk.
Money promised in marriage with Jennet, sister of defendant, etc.　　　　YORK.

27–30　　Alice THORNETON of Hawkhurst, co. Kent v. Mary BRYERTON *alias* Cambridge, late the wife of William Adcocke.
Messuage and land in Hingham late of Bryan Adcocke, deceased, father of complainant.　NORFOLK.

31–33　　John THORNEY, Alice his wife, Edmund COWPER and Margaret his wife, v. Henry FULLER, husband of Joan granddaughter and heir of Richard Scoles, and others.
Detention of deeds relating to a messuage and land in Osmonston otherwise Scoles, late of Harry Framysham (Fransham) deceased, father of the female complainants.　　[NORFOLK.]

34-36 Michael THRALE of Luton, co. Bedford, v. John HEYWORTH, gentleman and Joan his wife.
Lease, in lieu of wages, of 30a. land at Hatcham barn, invalid because described as in Kent, where only half an acre was situated.   SURREY, KENT.

37-42 William THRELKYLL, vicar of Steeple, v. George STONERD, esquire.
Glebe claimed by defendant as part of his manor of Steeple Grange, and tithe.   D. XIV, 38.
ESSEX.

43-46 John THURDON v. Richarde WHITE, widow (sic) and Richard her son.
Messuage and land at Thurdon in Kilhampton late of Roger Thurdon, deceased, father of complainant.
CORNWALL.

47-48 Nicholas TOMPSON, Alice his wife, and Margaret late the wife of Robert BRYAN v. Thomas and John MORER.
Annuities charged on a malt-mill, messuage and lands in Kingston and Ham under the will of William Morer, father of defendants and of the female complainants.   SURREY.

49 Geoffrey TOTTHYLL and Mary his wife, administrators of the goods of Gilbert Kyrke her father, deceased, v. John SOUTHCOTT of Shillingford, gentleman, her stepfather.
Money, stock of a shop in Exeter, and half the rent of a tenement in Silverton.   DEVON.

50 John TOWNE of Queenhill (Quynell), yeoman, v. Robert GOWER of Witley, gentleman.
Messuage and land of the demise of defendant (place omitted).   WORCESTER.

51-52 Frances, late the wife of Richard TOWNELEY of Townley (in Burnley), knight, v. John TOWNELEY, gentleman.
Administration of the goods of the said Sir Richard under a forged will.   LANCASTER.

53 Henry TOWNERAWE v. William, lord VAUX [of Harrowden].
Lease of a messuage and land in Laxton promised in succession to one from Thomas Vaux, lord Harrowden, and Elizabeth his wife, both deceased.   NOTTS.

54 . . . TOWNROWE v. Richard Ralph and Robert CUTLER.
Lease of lands in Cherbroughe wrongfully obtained from Ambrose Dudley, knight. Mutilated.
[NOTTS.]

55-56 John TOWYLL of Thurlestone, husbandman, v. John TOWYLL of Newton Bushel, baker, and others.
Messuage and land in Kingskerswell late of John Towyll, deceased, grandfather of complainant.
DEVON.

57-58 John TREDGOLDE, guardian in socage to Thomas Westwood, v. John WESTWOOD.
Messuages and lands in Magdalen Laver, High Laver, Sawbridgeworth (Sapsforth), and Harlow late of Thomas Westwood, deceased, father of the said Thomas and brother of defendant.
ESSEX, HERTS.

59-60 William TRESHAM, D.D., v. John BAYARDE, parson of Greens-Norton.
Rent charged on defendant's parsonage by Griffith Jones, late parson, and William (Parr), marquis of Northampton, patron of the living.   D. IX, 2.   NORTHAMPTON.

61-62 Edward TREVOUR, gentleman, son and heir of Jane B(r)ereton, John YERWERTHE and Elizabeth his wife, sister of the said Jane v. Owen BRERETON.
Copyhold, burgage and customary lands in Holt, Gresford and Wrexham of the bequest of Randolph B(r)ereton of Borras, esquire.   DENBIGH.

63 Thomas TROLOPPE v. William SAVELL of Halifax, Richard WENDON of London, draper, and Henry SUTTON.
Imprisonment for a debt due to the said Savell and partly recoverable from the said Wendon.
Mutilated.   LONDON.

64-65 Jane late the wife of John TRYGGES v. Hugh BANCROFT, his apprentice.
Maladministration of the goods of the said John and failure to carry out an arbitral award. Mutilated.

66 John TRYTTE of Brimfield v. John CONOPE (Canope) and Margaret his wife, cousin of complainant.
Waste in a tenement in the town of Drayton, lordship of Stockton, and liberty of Leominster. Paper.
Request for a survey by the Queen's steward of the liberty.   HEREFORD.

67-68 William son of John TULLY v. William FORDON and Joan his wife, executrix and late the wife of Richard Lee (?).
Apparel and household goods (described) and deeds relating to tenements in the lordship of Hints.
SALOP.

69-71 John TURLE of Rowley, nailer, son of William Turle, v. William PERKES alias Pershowse and Elizabeth his wife, executrix and late the wife of the said William Turle.
Bequest of apparel and tools of a nailer's shop.

72 John TYLLNEY, gentleman, v. William MORE and Humphrey SUTTON.
Lands (not specified).   DERBY.

FILE 1389.

1 Hugh UP ROSSER v. ——— (not named).
Messuages and land called Coyid Glasson late of Roger Up Rosser, deceased, grandfather of complainant.   RADNOR.

2-3 John son and heir of John UTTERBY of Middle Rasen v. Thomas WALKER, priest, Richard UTTERBY, and others.
Detention of deeds relating to a messuage and land (place not named). Answer wanting. LINCOLN.

4–5   John UVEDALE (Udale) *v.* Henry DYGBY, gentleman.
Lease of a close of pasture in the manor of Waltham-on-the-Wold made by Henry [Manners], earl of Rutland and stated by defendant to be conditional on forgiving a debt of the earl.   LEICESTER.

6   ·   Henry VAGHAN of London, buckler-maker, and Margaret his wife, late the wife of David Lloyed *v.* JOHN ap Griffith and REYNOLD ap David.
Dower of the said Margaret in a messuage and land in Tremalygouz.   ANGLESEY.

7–9   John VALENTYNE and Margaret his wife, late the wife of John Saunders of Chigwell, *v.* Henry JOHNSON.
Pasture in Woodford of the demise of the late abbot and convent of Stratford Langthorne.   ESSEX.

10–11   Harry VALYANT *v.* Thomas FUTTER.
Conveyance of a tenement in Over Rickinghall so drawn by defendant as to convey all complainant's lands in Over and Nether Rickinghall.   SUFFOLK.

12–15   John VAN HORNE, merchant of the Steel Yard, *v.* James CLYVE (Cliff) of London, salter.
Price of stockfish for which defendant and others were jointly and severally bound. D. IX, 39.
        LONDON.

16–18   Charles VAUGHAN of Shapweke *v.* THOMAS ap Ryce, son of Rice David ap Guyllym, LLEWELYN ap Watkyns and others.
Manor of Llechrydd in Llanelwedd of the entail of Richard Vaughan, knight, deceased, father of complainant.   RADNOR.

19–21   Cuthbert VAUGHAN and Elizabeth his wife *v.* Thomas TWYSDEN.
Messuage called Chilmington and lands in Chart, Kingsnorth, Shadoxhurst, Ivychurch, and Eastbridge late of William Twysden, esquire, former husband of the said Elizabeth and brother of defendant, his executors.   KENT.

22   David Lloid ap Griffith VAUGHAN of Llanrwst *v.* Griffith SALUSBURY, serving-man.
Falsification of a commission in a suit for lands in Istovoboill and Mathebroyd.   DENBIGH.

23   Richard VAUGHAN executor of Morgan Gwynn, *v.* DAVID ap Thomas.
Land in Cilycwm pledged by Gwilliam (ap) David ap Rice to the said Gwynn to be redeemed only after 100 years.   CARMARTHEN.

24–26   Richard VAUGHAN, clerk, student at Oxford, *v.* John ap Morgayn ap Rice LLOYD, gentleman.
Parsonage of Bishopstone, claimed under a lease of John Lipyngton, late parson, deprived for marriage.   GLAMORGAN.

27   Thomas VAUGHAN, gentleman, *v.* Thomas Gitto SAER..
Crown lease of the grange of Tyrnewythe. *Mutilated.*   ?

28   Thomas VAUGHAN of Brislington, co. Somerset, son and heir of John Vaughan, *v.* Morgan THOMAS of Howick, gentleman.
Messuage and land in Nash in the lordship of Goldcliff of the bequest of Thomas Vaughan of Bristol.
        MONMOUTH.

29   Thomas VAUGHAN, overseer of the will of George his brother, for himself and Henry, Edmund, Thomas, John, Jane, Anne and Alice, infant children of the said George, *v.* Gregory WARREYN, husband of Joan late the wife of the said George.
Detention of goods of the said George and vexatious suit in this court for the farm of Kinsbourne Bury in Harpenden.   HERTS.

30   Thomas VAUX, lord [Vaux of] Harrowden, *v.* John GOSSE.
Occupation of the manor of Brant-Broughton under an invalid lease.   LINCOLN.

31–34   Richard VENABLES, of the Queen's guard, *v.* Thomas LANGHAM, gentleman.
Rectory of Orton Underwood of the demise of Robert [King], bishop of Oxford.   LEICESTER.

35–39   Michael VENDOVER (Wendover), citizen and grocer of London *v.* Thomas QUADRING, esquire.
Messuage and land in North Rauceby late of Simon Kirke, deceased, grandfather of complainant.
        LINCOLN.

40   Richard VERNEY, knight, son of Thomas Verney, knight and of Alice his wife, *v.* Vincent GODDARDE his brother-in-law.
Debt for which complainant pledged pasture in Kyngston (*i.e.* Kineton) and Compton (Verney), and which defendant promised to release on obtaining a lease of the manor of Ogbourn.
        WARWICK, WILTS.

41   George VERNON of Sutton, co. Worcester, esquire, executor of Thomas Acton of the same, esquire, *v.* Robert ACTON of Ribbesford co. Worcester, knight, brother of the said Thomas.
Action on a bond for conditions of a Crown lease of the farm of the foreign and park of Walsall, whereof the said Thomas was dismissed by the Duke of Northumberland.   STAFFORD,

42–47   Mary, late the wife of George VERNON, esquire, *v.* Thomas FLYNT, Margaret his wife daughter of Humphrey Vernon, deceased, and Katherine POLE, her sister.
Manors of Westbury, Whitley, and Welbatch (in Stapleton) and lands there and in Hodnet formerly of Richard Ludlow, knight, grandfather of the said Alice. *Mutilated. Parts of two suits? See File 1080, No. 67.*   SALOP.

48–50   John VYAN (Vians) *v.* John WYLDE *alias* Mer(y)ell).
Land at Wornditch in Kimbolton late of Richard Bull and Joan his wife, deceased, grandparents of complainant.   HUNTINGDON.

51   Thomas VYASE *v.* William WYLKYNGSON and others.
Lease of a close at Stoneferry in Cottingham entrusted to defendants.   YORK.

52-56   Margaret late the wife of Nicholas VYCARY *alias* Taylor *v.* Thomas ALSTONE, Agnes his
wife and Robert his son.
Land in the manor of Hodditch (in Thorncombe).   (Defendant denies that widows have right of
succession in the demesne lands of the manor).   DEVON (*now* DORSET).

57-58   Agnes VYLLARDE, by Nicholas Vyllarde her father and guardian in socage, *v.* Alice
DEWPELOCKE.
Messuage and garden in St. Mary's Lane, Lewes, of the bequest of Daniell Maryate.   SUSSEX.

59-63   Thomas VYNCENT, gentleman, and Felice his wife *v.* Thomas SPARKE, master of the
hospital of Greatham and bishop of Berwick, Thomas SALVAYN, clerk, Ralph STOKE-
DALE, and Felice his wife.
Messuage and salt-cote in Greatham held of the late master of the said hospital by William Bayker,
whose executors are the said Felice and Felice.   DURHAM.

64   Peter VYNTE *v.* Richard PLATFOTE and Richard MELTON.
Messuage and land in Congham late of John Marys, deceased, grandfather of complainant.
NORFOLK.

65-67   Humphrey VYSE of Stone (Stawne), gentleman, *v.* Francis ROSSE, esquire.
Detention of deeds relating to a messuage and lands mingled with those of defendant in Chorlton.
STAFFORD.

68-71   Thomas VYVYAN, vicar of St. Just (Yewst) *v.* Thomas GODOLPHIN, gentleman, and
others.
Non-payment of the last quarter's rent of the vicarage under a lease by William Trealeighe, late
vicar, seizure of lease, and other damage, including destruction of ' pekons.'   CORNWALL.

FILE 1390.

1-4   Ralph WALKER *v.* William TAYLOUR, parson of Tatenhill, administrator of the goods of
John Taliour, late parson.
Repair of the parsonage and glebe buildings.   STAFFORD.

5   Henry WALSTED *v.* John EVANS and Thomas LUCKOCKE.
Price of cloth bought from complainant's shop in Walsall.   STAFFORD.

6-10   Thomas son and heir of Henry WARD *v.* William WARD, William PRIORMAN *alias*
Hemsley, and Thomas NEDESON of Newland.
Land in Botheney of the entail of Thomas Warde, deceased, and Matilda his wife.   (The answer is
filed during Heath's chancellorship.)   YORK.

11-16   Edward WARREN, knight, *v.* Elizabeth LEGH.
Debt of Richard Leigh of Baguley, esquire, deceased, husband of defendant.   CHESTER.

17-18   Edmond WATERHOUSE of Huddersfield, co. York, clothier, *v.* the mayor, aldermen and
sheriffs of LONDON, and Thomas BARLOW of London, merchant.
Action for a debt falsely entered in the said Barton's book. *Certiorari and subpœna.*   LONDON.

19-22   John WATERTON (Walterton) *v.* Nicholas MYCHAEL.
Messuage and close of pasture in Wakefield of the entail of Robert Waterton the elder.   ,   YORK.

23-24   Polidour WATKINS *alias* Vaughan of Houndstreet, son and heir of Richard Watkyns, *v.*
George AVANHAM.
Detention of deeds and occupation of land in complainant's manor of Marksbury.   SOMERSET.

25   Anne WEBBE, daughter of William Grymston of Salisbury, deceased, *v.* Sybly GRYMSTON
and William MOGGERIDGE.
Annuity of the grant of Fulk Grevyll of Beauchamp's Court, knight.   WILTS, WARWICK.

26-27   Elizabeth late the wife of William WELLES, freeman of Yarmouth and merchant, *v.* Nicholas
FYRMAGE and Denise his wife, executors of the said William, John HACON, steward of the
borough-court of Yarmouth, and John MORE.
Widow's portion of goods and of messuages, cottages and land in Yarmouth.   NORFOLK.

28-29   The same *v.* the said FYRMAGE.
Goods of the said William, whose daughter is the said Denise.   NORFOLK.

30-31   Thomas WELLS of Twyford, esquire, and Margaret his wife, executrix of Ralph Foster, of the
same, *v.* Francis FLEMMYNG, knight.
Land (*described*) in Romsey late of the abbess of Romsey.   HANTS.

32-35   Edmund WELLYS *v.* John ROOKE of Saxmundham (Sacmondes), tailor.
Refusal to complete a sale of a messuage and lands in Badingham and Dennington.   SUFFOLK.

36   Andrew WESTON *v.* John BROKEMAN and [William?] CARDYNALL.
Price of the manor of Bovills (in Ardleigh) bought of the said Brokeman and resold to the said
Cardynall. *Mutilated.*   ESSEX.

37   Susan WESTON, administratrix of the goods of the said Andrew, *v.* the same.
Reviver of the preceding? *Mutilated.* D. IX, 31.   ESSEX.

38   Robert and Thomas WESTON *v.* Richard WOODROFF and William BUTTON, esquire.
Land in Calne held of the manor of Cheverell Hales of the demise of Robert Balfronte, clerk, master
at the almshouse of Heytesbury.   WILTS.

39   Robert WETHERSBYE, esquire, and Elizabeth his wife, late the wife of John Clopton
of Long Melford, co. Suffolk, esquire, *v.* William CLOPTON, son of the said John.
Life interest of the said Elizabeth in the manor of Down Hall (in Rayleigh).   ESSEX.

40   Gilbert WHELER of Rollright, gentleman, son and executor of John Wheler, *v.* William son and executor of Ralph SHELDON.
Debt already paid to the said Ralph.   OXFORD.

41   Hugh WHITFORD, parson of Whitford, *v.* David OWEN.
Money obtained under pretext of being collector of a clerical tenth and of an annuity due to the bishop of St. Asaph.   FLINT.

42–43   Hugh WHYTE *v.* Margaret BERY, late the wife of John Derrat.
Tenement in Broomfield of the demise of ——— Byckome.
      SOMERSET.

44   Walter WHYTHALL *v.* Randall BRERETON, esquire.
Pasture in the lordship of Cheddleton late of Richard Chedulton, deceased, ancestor of complainant.
Pedigree given.   STAFFORD.

45–48   John WHYTING, B.D., parson of Therfield, *v.* Andrew MEVERELL, gentleman.
Parsonage of Therfield of the demise of William Burham, late parson, deprived for marriage.   HERTS.

49–51   John WILLIAMS, lord Williams of Thame, *v.* George OWEN, esquire.
Crown lease of Cumnor wood, defendant being lord of the manor. *Answer wanting.*   BERKS.

52–53   The same *v.* the same.
Detention of the ledger of Abingdon abbey, and wrongful occupation of lands in Wytham, Hinksey, Cumnor and Sunningwell.   BERKS.

54   The same *v.* Francis ROLLESTON of Lea (' the Lee ') esquire.
Detention of deeds relating to land in Ashover late of the priory of Beauchief.   DERBY.

55–56   The same *v.* JOHN Upe Morrys, son of Morrys ap John Lloid.
Land called Gornogo or Gwernogo(ff) late of the monastery of Cwmhir.   RADNOR.

57   The same *v.* John WALWYN.
Do.   RADNOR.

58   Christopher WILLION of Gargrave *v.* Nicholas WILSON of the same and Adam SQUIRE, bailiff of the Earl of Cumberland's court of Gisburn.
Horse distrained for a debt of complainant since paid.   YORK.

59   Henry WILLIS, B.D., vicar of Bibury, *v.* [Robert WORTHINGTONE].
Vicarage of Bibury and chapel of Winson, with tithes of Arlington, Ablington, and Winson, claimed under a lease from William Sheldon, late vicar, deprived for felony. *Injunction. Damaged.*
      GLOUCESTER.

60   Hugh WILLOUGHBYE and Elizabeth his wife, late the wife of John Laurens, *v.* Henry LAURENS, son of the said John.
Manor of Solton in West Cliffe, and messuages, lands, and rents there and in Rowling (in Goodnestone near Wingham), Buckland Rivers, Bridge, Nackington and Upper Hardres adjudged to complainants in this court for the life of the said Elizabeth with remainder to defendant. *See File* 1482, *No.* 99.   KENT.

61   Maurice WOGAN of Sherrington, co. Bucks, *v.* Ryse THOMAS ap Evan, farmer of the ferry of Llanstephan.
Loss of a horse and pack of complainant owing to a hole in the ferry-boat.   CARMARTHEN.

62   Alexander WOLLACOMBE, gentleman, *v.* Gilbert DRAKE, gentleman.
Lands in Exmouth and Littleham and money promised in exchange for the manor of Whytesley (*i.e.* Whitsleigh in St. Giles-in-the-Heath). D. IX, 1.   DEVON.

63–64   Thomas WOODRIFFE of Hope, co. Derby, and Margaret his wife, *v.* William BRERETON, knight.
Messuages and land in Alsager (Awsinger) late of Thomas Bukeley of Eaton, deceased, cousin of the said Margaret.   CHESTER.

65   Richard WOODWARD, servant to the Queen, *v.* Haminet SOWTHERN *alias* More.
Closes in Boughton of the demise of the dean and chapter of Chester.   CHESTER.

66–67   The dean and chapter of WORCESTER *v.* Thomas GRENDON.
Double conveyance by the Crown of the advowson of the church of Dean. *See Calendar of Patent Rolls, Edward VI,* I, 237-8; III, 293.   BEDFORD.

68–70   John WORDESEY and others, administrators of the goods of Richard Hopkyns, deceased, *v.* John JENNYNS, Maude his wife and others.
Seizure of the said goods, including a ' yowke ' and a pair of ' gobertes,' from the said Richard's house at Walsall.   STAFFORD.

71–72   Richard WOTTON, yeoman, *v.* Richard son and heir of William MYTTON, esquire.
Pasture in Shrewsbury demised to Robert, father of complainant.   SALOP.

73   The same *v.* the same.
Do., defendant being the lessee of the abbot of Buildwas.   SALOP.

74–75   John WRIGHT *v.* Robert and Roger TAVERNER.
Action for price of Crown lands in Ribston and elsewhere acquired through the Earl of Bedford, the grant to whom proved to be void.   YORK.

76   Richard WRIGHT, painter-stainer and citizen of London, *v.* Roger and Randolph TAILIOUR.
Moiety of land in Bostock granted to complainant by Thomas Leftweich, esquire, in reversion after the death of Richard father of defendants.   CHESTER.

77   Robert WRIGHT.
Commission to examine witnesses as to the pledging of land in Lady Norton's manor of Debden to John Peppis, gentleman, since deceased.   ESSEX.

78   John WYDMERPOLE· and Joan his wife, daughter and executrix of William Basford, v.
Robert BENBRIGGE, overseer of the will of the said Basford, and others.
Goods of the said Basford and messuage and land in Hemington of the demise of Walter Devereux,
lord Ferrers.   LEICESTER.

79–80   William WYLL v. John ROWE (Rawe), son-in-law of Bartholomew Bucke.
Detention of deeds relating to a tenement in the borough of Plymouth   DEVON.

81   Lewis WYLLYAMS, yeoman of the wardrobe to the late Duke of Somerset, v. the sheriffs
of LONDON, and Robert HICKES of London, ironmonger.
Action for price of velvet and sarcenet ordered by complainant on the Duke's account. *Certiorari
and subpœna.*   LONDON.

82   John WYLSON of West Mersea, co. Essex, mariner, v. Thomas LORDE.
Messuage and garden in Orford, late of Rowland Wylson, deceased, father of complainant.
                                                                          SUFFOLK.

83   Richard WYLSON of Baldock, co. Herts, beer-brewer, and Juliana his wife, daughter and
heir of Richard Skegge and of Agnes his wife, v. Thomas PYGOTTE, esquire, and THOMAS
his son.
Land in Littlecote (in Stewkley) formerly of Henry Skegge of Dunstable in Bedford, weaver.
                                                                          BUCKS.

84–87   Robert son of John WYNTER v. Thomas grandson of James CAPS, gentleman.
Tenement and cottage in defendant's manor of Whytesfeld.   SOMERSET.

FILE 1391.

1–3   Thomas WAKE, esquire, grandson and heir of Roger Wake, v. John WYRLEY (Wourley).
Detention of deeds relating to the manor of Milton-Clevedon.   SOMERSET.

4–8   John son and heir of Thomas WALDRAM v. Richard MARTYN.
Detention of deeds relating to lands intermingled with those of defendant in Cadby, and refusal to
make a severance.   LEICESTER.

9–10   William WALGRAVE v. Richard and Thomas GARDYNER and Robert SMYTH.
Messuage and land in Brent Pelham. *See Files 1283, No. 2 ; 1321, No. 2.*   ESSEX.

11   Edmund WALLE of Passenham, sawyer, and Ellen his wife, late the wife of Roger Palmer
(Pasnam), v. Thomas PALMER, half-brother of the said Ellen.
Forgery of a conveyance of a messuage and land in Passenham. *Mutilated.*   NORTHAMPTON.

12–13   Edward WALLYS v. William VAUS.
Close of pasture late held of the manor of Cranfield by Edmund Pedder, gentleman.   BEDFORD.

14–15   Ralph WALROND of Tiverton, clothier, v. William BUCKNAM (Buckenham), executor of
Philip May, both of Exeter, merchants.
Payment made on behalf of the said May in London.   DEVON.

16   Ralph WAREN, ·son and heir of entail of Robert Waren, v. Christopher ASKUE, esquire. ·
Detention of deeds relating to messuages and lands in North and South Ockenden, Upminster, and
the hundred of Hoo. *See No. 20.*   ESSEX, KENT.

17   Henry WARNER of Great Waltham, esquire, v. Edward CRANE, citizen and grocer of
London, Robert KEMpE, an executor of John brother of complainant, Henry BERNARD,
servant to Lord Rich, and others.
Tampering with a jury in an action concerning sale of woods in Great Stambridge.   ESSEX.

18–19   Christopher WARREN v. Edward BYBBYE of Manchester, draper.
Debt of James Williamson of Manchester, draper, paid by defendant in cloth of less value than
represented. *Faded.*   LANCASTER.

20   Jane, late the wife of Robert WARREN, citizen and merchant tailor of London, v. Thomas
POYNES, gentleman.
Detention of·goods (including a kirtle of caffa and four ' boungraces ' of satin) and of deeds relating
to messuages and lands in Upminster, North Ockenden, All Hallows St. Mary's, and Stoke in the
hundred of Hoo, and Long Melford. *See No. 16.*   ESSEX, KENT, SUSSEX.

21–23·   The same v. Thomas KNOTT, now her husband, and Christopher SA(L)MON, gentleman,
late barber to King Henry VIII.
Waste of lands in Upminster and North Ockenden late of the said Robert.   ESSEX.

24   William WATERS of Lavenham (Lanam), co. Suffolk, draper, v. Elizabeth WATERS.
Messuage and land in Hitchin of the demise of William Conyngesbye, esquire.   HERTS.

25   Thomas WATKYS of Aston, serving-man, v. John HYGGYNSON.
Refusal to complete a bond concerning a joint lease of pasture in·the lordship of Preen (?). *Faded.*
                                                                          SALOP.

26–27   Richard WEDGEWOOD, gentleman, v. Richard MICHELL and others.
Messuages and land in Horton late of Richard Wedgewood, grandfather of complainant. STAFFORD.

28–31   Henry WELLYS of Overton, co. Hants, gentleman, and Mary his wife, daughter and heir of
Richard Pole, v. William·STANNEY and Gertrude his wife.
Manor of Godlingstone and messuages and land in Swanage (Sandewiche), Corfe and Kingston.
                                                                          DORSET.

32-35   William WENHAM v. John FAWKENOUR, gentleman, Thomas GRATEWICK and
         William his brother.
Lease of the prebend of Bishopstone obtained by the said Fawkenour to complainant's use.
                                                                             SUSSEX.

36-39   Thomas WETTON of London, haberdasher, v. Helen, executrix and late the wife of William
         BASSET, knight, grantee of the monastery of Tutbury.
Meadow in Tutbury of the grant of John Porte, knight. D. X, 55.   STAFFORD.

40-42   Richard WHALLEY, esquire, v. William BOLLES.
Manor of To[ton?], formerly demised to Simon Callyes. *Mutilated.*   NOTTS.

43-44   Richard WHALLEY, esquire, v. Richard FEELD and John HANBYE.
Purchase of Crown lands in Limber Magna to the said Hanbye's use. *Mutilated.*   LINCOLN.

45   Christopher WHICHECOTE of London, merchant and Lucy his wife, a daughter of Thomas
         Boswell of the New Hall in Darfield, v. Anthony AYRE, gentleman, executor of the said
         Boswell.

46-51 The same v. the same, Martin ANNE, husband of Elizabeth, executrix and late the wife of
         the said Boswell, and Hugh WORALL, esquire.
Legacy payable out of lands in Gateforth, Burton, Selby, Barugh (in Darton), Greasborough and
Wath.   YORK.

52-54   Walter WHYTTOCK v. Polydore WATTEKYNS *alias* Vaughan.
Refusal to complete a sale of land in Cameley, and non-payment of price of a gelding and money
lent. *Mutilated.*   SOMERSET.

55   Richard WILKYNSON of Isell v. William son of Laurence FYSSHER, and Thomas PORTER
         of Alanby, esquire, steward of the honour of Cockermouth.
Land in Setmurthey (Setmorthowe) demised by John father of complainant for a term lately
expired.   CUMBERLAND.

56-59   Jane WINTER v. Richard LITTLEY and Emma his wife, executrix and late the wife of
         Humphrey Reynoldes of Coventry, gentleman.
Milborne Grange, messuages and land in Stoneleigh, and the parsonage of Cubbington, of the bequest
of the said Reynolds.   WARWICK.

60-62·   The same v. the said Emma REYNOLDES.
Do.   WARWICK.

63-64   John WODCOKE and John PRINGE v. John WESTOVER.
Messuage and land in Churchstoke (i.e. Stoke Abbott?) late of Agnes, wife of William Bakelford,
grandmother of complainants and great-grandmother of defendant.   DORSET.

65-69   Edmund grandson and heir of Robert WOODROVE (Woodrowe) v. Henry BAYNEBRIGGE
         (Benbricke), Elizabeth and Agnes BAGSHAWE, granddaughters of Gervase Woodrowe,
         and others.
Messuages and land at Wormhill in Tideswell (Tydsworth, Tyddesdale) of the entail of Christopher
Bagshawe (Bachyshawe) and others. D. X, 39.

70-72   Timothy WOTTON, Andrew MEVERELL and Anne his wife v. Charles WOTTON *alias*
         Richardson and Thomas WOTTON.
Manor of Saxelby and messuage in St. Gregory's, London, late of Matthew Wootton, gentleman,
deceased.   LINCOLN.

73-75   John WRIGHT, labourer, v. John (Thomas) WRIGHT *alias* Carver, Libeus RICHARDSON,
         and others.
Messuage and land at Hanney in Spilsby late of Thomas Wright, deceased, father of complainant.
                                                                             LINCOLN.

76   The same v. the same except the said Richardson.
Do. *Damaged.*   LINCOLN.

77-78   Richard WRIGHT v. Geoffrey TEYNBYE.
Lands in Barton-on-Humber.   LINCLON.

79   Walter WYLLIAMS of Chedzoy, co. Somerset, and Jennet his wife, daughter of Laurence
         Phelipes and of Agnes his wife, both deceased, v. David William RYCE and others.
Park, marsh, and other lands in Penvay of the demise of Arnold Butler of Pembrey, esquire.
                                                                             CARMARTHEN

80-83   John WYLMOTT, esquire, v. Henry LAKE, Agnes his wife, and Thomas SOUTHDON.
Messuage and land in Whitstone of the demise of John Carewe, esquire.   DEVON.

84-86   Egion WYLSON and Dorothy his wife v. Thomas WALRON.
One-half of one-third of the manor of Langridge with appurtenances in Langridge, Tadwick in
Swainswick (Totwycke), Lansdown and Westcomb.   SOMERSET.

87   Ryce WYNE, yeoman of the Chamber, son of Ryce ap Jevan ap Llewellyn, v. John
         GREFFYTH ap Nycolas.
Common of pasture for a horse, pigs and geese appurtenant to a house and land called Leeswood
(' the Lyswod ').   FLINT.

88-89   Thomas Maria WYNGFELDE v. Ambrose COLE his stepson.
Slander and robbery of goods and deeds at Ipswich. *Mutilated.*   SUFFOLK.

90   William WYNTER of London, esquire, v. Roger GREGORY, husbandman.
Manor of Brodewyke late of John Wynter, father of complainant.   GLOUCESTER.

91   William WYTHYE of Grays Inn Lane, tailor, v. EDWARD ap Powell.
Loan.   LONDON, SALOP.

FILE 1392.

1-3   Roger WALROND v. Marmaduke POPHAM, gentleman.
Manor of Durleigh and land there of the demise of Robert Welshe, master of the late hospital of St.
John, Bridgewater, and the brethren thereof.   SOMERSET.

4-5   John WARNER v. Thomas BUTTIS, esquire.
Repairs of a mill and mill-house in Great Ryburgh due under complainant's lease.   NORFOLK.

6   John WARREN v. Anthony BUSTARDE, esquire and others.
Repudiation of a lease of lands in the said Bustarde's manor of Brampford Speke.   DEVON.

7-10   John WARREYN of Fyfield and Thomas HEYTHE and Jane his wife, his tenants, v.
Leonard WOODLAND of Chippenham.
Action for trespass on a messuage and land in Pewsey, the title-deeds being in this court.
       WILTS.

11-15   Andrew son of Walter WARWYKE and Walter SPEALTE v. Bartholomew FORTESCUE,
esquire.
Refusal to complete a sale of land in Holbeton.   DEVON.

16   William WATSON v. Richard BULLOCKE and James MOYSIER.
Partition of the manor of South Holme acquired of the Crown (field-names given).   YORK.

17-18   Henry WAYNMAN, clerk, v. Robert JOHNSON, clerk and Thomas JOHNSON.
Debt.   ———

19-20   Margaret WESTHAWE, executrix of Richard Westhawe, v. Thomas LAURENS of Norwich,
merchant, and Alice his wife.
Debt of Nicholas Calver of Little Walsingham, mercer, copyhold tenant in Little Walsingham and
father of the said Alice.   NORFOLK.

21-24   · Geoffrey and John, grandsons and heirs of John WESTON, v. Herbert and Thomas FYNCHE.
Messuages and lands in Linstead, Bapchild and Tonge wrongfully sold by John Chilton, late steward.
of Wye. *Will recited.*   KENT.

25-26   William WESTON v. Thomas BRUER.
Toft and croft held of the late Earl of Southampton's manor of Swanwick in Titchfield.   HANTS..

27-31   Thomas WHARTON, lord Wharton, v. Thomas MAULEVERER, knight.
Money payable as part of a contract of marriage between Henry son of complainant and Joan
daughter of defendant.   ———

32-33   . . . WILLIAMSON v. Richard HARRISON.
Common of pasture in Everton, defendant being farmer of the vicarage. *Faded.*   NOTTS.

34-35   William WILLOUGHBY, lord Willoughby of Parham, v. Robert PAWLYN, late constable of
Orford, and other inhabitants there.
Arrest of goods claimed by a servant of complainant and dispute as to rights of common. (Interro-
gatories and deposition, concerning the powers and duties of the burgesses).   SUFFOLK.

36-38   Thomas WOODHOUSE of London pewterer, v. John SKARVELL.
Messuage and land formerly held of the manor of Lavant by Thomas Luke. *Replication wanting.*
       SUSSEX.

39-41   Richard WOODWARD v. Thurstan LANT (Lont).
Land in Snelston sublet by defendant.   DERBY.

42   Richard WORTLEY of Thame, fletcher, v. Thomas HENDIE.
Refusal to give bond for conditions of a lease of a messuage and land at Moreton in Thame.
       OXFORD.

43   . . . WYKES, yeoman, v. Thomas his brother.
Loans of cattle and money. *Mutilated.*   SALOP.

44   Mary WYMBISSHE v. [Ambrose DUDLEY and Lady Elizabeth TAILBOYSE his wife, late
the wife of Thomas Wymbisshe, esquire.]
Refusal to complete a sale of a close of pasture in Tooting Bec. *Mutilated.*   SURREY.

45-46   Edward WYNGATE v. Thomas HUMERSTON (Hamerston) and Margaret his wife, executrix
and late the wife of William Smyth of Huchyn.
Debt for goods supplied. *Mutilated. Answer wanting.*   [HERTS?]

FILE 1393.

1-2   Richard WADESLEY and William RODDESBYE v. John RODDESBYE.
Goods of Agnes Roddesbye, deceased, sister-in-law of defendant, whose executors complainants
are. *Mutilated.*   ———

3   Edward WARCOPP v. William PRESTCOSYN.
Loan.   WESTMORELAND.

4-6   William WARDEN and Elizabeth his wife, granddaughter and heir of John Coles, v. William
FYSSHER.
Land in Great Billing claimed by defendant under a lease from the parson.   NORTHAMPTON.

7   Edward WATSON, esquire, v. James ALTHAM, citizen and clothworker of London, Giles
           ALLYNGTON, knight, sheriff of Huntingdon and Thomas LOVETT, esquire, sheriff of
           Northampton.
           Refusal by the said Altham to avow a suit against the other defendants for moneys levied on a
           statute staple whereof he had promised to renounce execution.   HUNTINGDON, NORTHAMPTON.

8–9   William WEALE of London, gentleman, v. Humphrey KERY of Binweston (in Worthen),
           gentleman.
           Compounding debts due jointly to complainant and to Thomas Kery, deceased.
                                                                                 LONDON, SALOP.

10–12   William WEAVER of Whitechapel, co. Middlesex, collar-maker, and Marion his wife v.
           William PHELPPOTT and Thomas DONNE.
           Messuages and land in Llangarran late of Richard Phillip of Treduchan in Llangarran (Tradraham.
           waylarde), deceased, cousin of the said Marion. See File 1321, No. 12.
                                                                                 HEREFORD.

13   Robert WEBB v. John GOSSON, gentleman.
           Refusal to complete a lease of a tenement in Berkshire in the parish of St. Aldate's (Sainte Toles) in
           the city of Oxford (sic) and of land in Long Wittenham.   BERKS.

14–16   Nicholas WEBSTER and Agnes his wife v. Agnes GEE.
           Messuages in [Ro]thley late of Robert Vincent, deceased. Damaged.   LEICESTER.

17–20   Leonard WELBECKE of Garsington v. John HOWELL of Iffley.
           Joint debt of complainant and John Alexaunder which it was agreed that the latter should pay.
                                                                                 OXFORD.

21–24   Thomas WELDISHE v. James BLACKE and Richard PEMERTON.
           Messuages and land in Linton of the bequest of William Weldishe, father of complainant.   KENT.

25   The dean and chapter of WELLS v. John TOGOOD, parson of Wraxall.
           Reviver of two suits for an annuity charged on the said church.   SOMERSET.

26–27   John WIGAN of London v. William FOX.
           Messuage and land in Ewloe of the demise of Ryse ap Edward of Pell, whereof defendant claims to
           have been awarded provisional possession by the Council of the Marches.   FLINTS.

28–29   Thomas WILKES, merchant of the Staple of Calais, v. John SEYNTLOWE and Edward
           GREVYLL, knight.
           Lands in Napton, Old Hodnell, Ascote, Burton-Dasset (Cheppyng Dassett), Birton, North End, and
           Knightcote (both in Burton-Dasset) of the entail of John Spenser. Damaged. See File 1322, Nos.
           43–44.   WARWICK.

30–35   Anthony WILL of Callington v. William WESCOTT, Sampson CRABBE and others.
           Messuages and land at Frogwell (in Callington).   CORNWALL.

36–39   Owen WODD v. Thomas GYLL.
           Messuage and land in Leek of the demise of Ralph Bagenall, knight.   STAFFORD.

40–43   George WODE v. Richard WHYTLAWES and William BENT (Benett).
           Site of a stable in a street called ' Shoplocke ' in Shrewsbury, and pasture at Coton in the liberties
           of Shrewsbury, all of the bequest of Robert Wode, brother of complainant.   SALOP.

44–45   John, son of John WYATT of Fonthill Gifford, tanner, v. Nicholas VINCENT alias Brooke,
           servant to John Mervyn, knight, overseer of the will of the said John Wyatt the father.
           Bequest of leather, ' rindes ' and other necessities for tanning.   WILTS.

46   Thomas WYLL v. Martin COLE of East Allington.
           Detention of deeds relating to a tenement called Odicknoll in the manor of Odicknoll in St. Mary
           Church.   DEVON.

47   The same v. John WYLL his son.
           Detention of deeds relating to the same and other land there and to a tenement in Compton (in
           Marldon?) held of the manor of Paignton.   DEVON.

48–49   Myles WYLSON of Manchester v. Christopher FRAUNCIS.
           Messuage and leasowe in Kingswinford late of William Wylson, brother of complainant, and Jane his
           wife.   STAFFORD.

50   Thomas WYLDSMYTH v. Myles and Edward WYLSON.
           Pasture-ground in Amblecote of the demise of the said William and Jane. [STAFFORD or WORCESTER].

51–53   Agnes, late the wife of John WYNDE and formerly of Nicholas Baskerfeld, v. Thomas
           PAYNE of Castleacre.
           Lease of the manor of Titchwell obtained by defendant only, after receiving money from complainant
           to obtain a joint lease.   NORFOLK.

54   John WYNYETT of North Petherton, husbandman, v. Thomas BAKER, yeoman, late
           servant to John, earl of Bedford, deceased, the King's and Queen's lieutenant of the forest of
           Dartmoor, and others.
           Refusal to make complainant the said Baker's deputy in the four foresterships of Dartmoor.
           Mutilated.   DEVON.

FILE 1394.

1–3   William WAKE, yeoman, Joan his wife and Ralph their son v. Henry TWYNYHOO,
           gentleman.
           Refusal to complete a lease of a capital messuage, cottage and land at Bagbury in Evercreech in
           reversion after the death of Thomas Wake, father of the said William.   SOMERSET.

4–6   John WALKELEY of King's Stanley, husbandman, v. William RYCARDES.
. Refusal to complete the marriage settlement of complainant's son and defendant's daughter.
                                                                        GLOUCESTER.

7   . . . WALKER, clerk, v. Robert ROBOTHAM and Grace his wife, administratrix of the
        goods of Robert Bulle, deceased.
Expenses of complainant relating to the prebend of Berkswich and Whittington in [Lichfield]
cathedral. *Mutilated*.   STAFFORD.

8   William WALLER of Ottery St. Mary, gentleman v. Walter YEA.
Price of lease in reversion of a ' justement grounde ' in Bishop's Nympton (Nymet). *See File* 1396,
No. 16.   DEVON.

9   Humphrey WALROND of Bradfield (in Uffculme), son and heir of Henry Walrond, v.
        William HODY.
Boundaries of Hoo D$_o$w$_n$ in Brixham, defendant having embezzled the deed of enclosure. DEVON.

10–12   William WALSAM v. Thomas WARDE of Clayworth, William SWAYNSON and John
        SMYTHE, labourers.
Price of cattle sold to the said Warde, for which the other defendants had become sureties.
                                                                        NOTTS.

⌠13   John WATKYNS v. Richard WATKYNS.
⎮   Messuage and land in Pencoyd of the gift of defendant.   HEREFORD.
⎨
⎮   The same v. Thomas FOSTER.
⌡   Meadow in King's Caple of the demise of defendant.   HEREFORD.

14   William WATSON, citizen and draper of London, v. Cuthbert ELLISON, mayor of
        Newcastle-upon-Tyne.
Part price of flax. *Mutilated*.   N'HUMB.

15–16   William WAYTE of Hartwith, husbandman, v. Marmaduke BECKWITH, gentleman.
Obtaining an inquest for damages without informing complainant, in contempt of an injunction
from this court. *See File* 1166, *No.* 29.   [YORK.]

17   John WEBBE, yeoman, and Katherine his wife v. John STANEFORDE.
. Messuage and land in Nether Tysoe held of the late abbot of Kenilworth's manor of Kineton.
                                                                        WARWICK.

18   The dean and chapter of WELLS v. William TURNOUR, late dean, John CAERDEMAKER,
        chancellor of the cathedral, and John BESTE and James BOND ' syngle ' canons.
Money payable by defendants in their admission ' in the name of a caucyon ' (The first three
defendants' names are marked ' marryed men.')   SOMERSET.

19–21   Richard WHALLEY of Welbeck, esquire, v. William GASCOIGNE, knight.
Lordship of Whatton.   [NOTTS.]

22–23   The same v. Maurice DENNYS, knight.
Action for conveyance of the manors of Taunton (*i.e.* Staunton?), Whatton and Hawkesworth,
which complainant could not do because imprisoned by the late Duke of Northumberland in the
Tower.   NOTTS.

24–27   Richard WHALLEY, esquire, appointed to administer the money of the late Duke of
        Somerset at his first arrest v. John (Richard) RAVESSHE, comptroller of the household of
        the said Duke, and Thomas WETHERALL his clerk of the works.
Falsification of a statement of defendant's wages.   ————

28–29   Elizabeth WHARTON v. Evan CARTER and Miles ANDR . . .
Goods of Robert Wharton, husband of complainants, killed at Kendal. *Faded.*
                                                [WESTMORELAND], WORCESTER.

30   John WHITE of Bristol, gentleman, v. George HARBART, knight, executor of John
        Craddock of Bedminster.
Debt of the said Craddock. *See File* 1395, *No.* 46.   SOMERSET.

31–35   John WHATELEY (Wheatley, Whatley), vicar of Crowle, v. John COMBES, gentleman.
. Tithe hay and corn and profits of the Easter book of complainant's vicarage, defendant being patron
and entitled to a pension therefrom.   WORCESTER.

36   Hugh WHITE and Mary his wife v. John LONGLEY, father of the said Mary.
Money and apparel worth 20 nobles promised to the said Mary on her marriage. ————

37   Martin WHYTFORD, husbandman, and Henry JAGOWE, yeoman, both of Tregony, v.
        Nicholas HERLE, esquire.
Damages awarded against defendants for taking from Paul Wyllyams at Roche a horse which
defendants claimed as his.   CORNWALL.

38–39   Francis WILKES of Broom (in Bilston), gentleman, v. Thomas THROCKMERTON,
        esquire, and William RYCE, gentleman of the Privy Chamber.
Messuage and land in Willenhall held of the manor of Stow Heath, and pledged to William Horwood,
late Attorney-General, deceased. *Mutilated.*   STAFFORD.

40   John WILSON v. Roger CHURCHMAN of Windsor, yeoman.
Refusal to complete a lease of land in Staines.   MIDDLESEX.

41–42   Robert, son of Robert WILSON, v. Nicholas GARLYCK of Thossell (*i.e.* Tidesdell?) and
        Robert his brother.
Unlawful distresses on a messuage and land at Hargatewall in Wormhill (Hardykwall) of the
demise of Francis Hopkyns. *See File* 1186, *No.* 61.   DERBY.

43-44   The same *v.* the said Nicholas.
Refusal to complete a lease of the same (?). *Damaged.*   DERBY.

45-46   William WINDESOR, lord Windsor, *v.* James [BLUNT], lord Mountjoy.
Reviver of a suit against William late lord Mountjoy for the manors of Barton, Sutton, Sapperton, Alkmonton, Bentley, Hatton, Little Longstone (Langewisdon), Brushfield (Brightrichfelde), Totley in Dronfield (Tottyngsley), Hazlewood, Alvaston, and Allerton, the mansion-house of Fole in Checkley (Fald Madley Allfeithe, Alsighe), lands and a water-mill in Fole, Totton (*i.e.* Toot Hill in Checkley), Alvaston, Ambaston,Thulston in Elvaston (Thurleston) Alvestone (*i.e.* Elvaston) and Thurvaston, the mansion of Hampton Lovett Tikynhapletre, messuages, land and 12 'dulmers' (*i.e.* bullaries?) of salt water in Hampton Lovett and Droitwich (Bartwiche), and the mansion of Telton, Cottesmore, and Greatham. (The pedigree differs from that in the Complete Peerage.)   DERBY, LEICESTER, STAFFORD, WORCESTER, RUTLAND.

47   William WITHERS, vicar of Butleigh, *v.* William GOUPPEY.
Lease of the said vicarage by John Whyte, late vicar, deprived for marriage.   SOMERSET.

48   Robert WOOD and Katherine his wife *v.* Richard AWNYON of Chester, shoemaker.
Tenement late of Margery Howe, deceased, mother of the said Katherine. *Damaged.*   CHESTER.

49   Ralph WRIGHT, parson of Pluckley, *v.* John MORE and Richard DERING, gentlemen.
Wrongful occupation of complainant's parsonage.   KENT.

50-52   James WRYGHT *v.* John son and heir of Nicholas SAUNDERSON.
Meadow in Carlton late of John Wryght, deceased, father of complainant.   NOTTS.

53   Edward WRYGHTE (?), husbandman, *v.* George IVELEY and others.
Chapel and glebe of [Chapel-en-le] Frith. *Damaged.*   DERBY.

54   Godfréy WUDDUS and William SHAWE *v.* Nicholas GEPSON and others.
Goods of Roger Newbold, deceased, whose executors complainants are.   ———

55-56   Roger WURTHINGTON, Alice his wife, and John their son *v.* Elizabeth late the wife of Henry WYGLEY, and George WYGLEY.
Occupation of a messuage and land in defendant's manor of Scraptoft in contempt of a verdict given at Leicester. *Answer wanting.*   LEICESTER.

57   Thomas WYDALL of Glentham *v.* Peter MAYNERS and others.
Loan the bond for which is lost.   LINCOLN.

58-60   Edward son and executor of Henry WYGLEY *v.* George SYMKYN.
Waste of lands in the manor of Scraptoft by colour of a forged copy of court roll.   LEICESTER.

61   Richard WYCKBROK of Bishop's Waltham, draper, *v.* Emery LYKES, servant to ——— Capplyn of Southampton.
Purchase in exchange for cloth (*described*), of canvas on complainant's account in St. Malo which proved to be of less value than represented.   HANTS.

62-63   Thomas WYLCOKE and Patrick HOWARD, [churchwardens] of South Lynn, *v.* Harry BLASBYE and James BAKER, late churchwardens.
Price of church ornaments (*described*), partly lent to the said Baker and the rest paid to the commissioners for the sale of church goods.   NORFOLK.

64   John, son of Robert WYLLIAM *alias* Cornysshe and of Joan his wife, *v.* Richard BULLER, esquire, and Joan WYLLIAM *alias* Cornysshe, stepmother of complainant.
Tenement at Kingsmill in the manor of Landulph. (It is stated for custom that a grantee cannot surrender his estate without the consent of his successor named in the same grant).   CORNWALL.

65-66   William WYLSON, labourer, son and heir of Henry Wylson, *v.* George ZOUCHE, esquire, and Thomas LUDLAM of Ripley, tailor.
Messuages and land in Ripley of the demise of the late abbot and convent of Darley.   DERBY.

67-69   Eleanor WYSEMAN, guardian of Edmund son and heir of John Wyseman, *v.* Charles WYSEMAN.
Composition concerning lands in Thornham Magna and Parva, Stoke [Ash] and Wetheringfelde (*i.e.* Wetheringsett?) late of Thomas Wyseman, deceased, father of the said John and Charles. *Mutilated.*   SUFFOLK.

70   [The said?] John *v.* the said Charles.
Lands in Thornham, Brockford (in Wetheringsett) and Stoke [Ash]. *Mutilated.*   SUFFOLK.

FILE 1395.

1-2   Reynold WADDYNGTON, parson of Haceby, *v.* William TOWNROWE, late parson, deprived for marriage, Robert FORCET of Walcot, gentleman, and William BOTHE, yeoman.
Forgery of a lease of the said parsonage in the name of the said Townerowe.   LINCOLN.

3-5   Joan WALFORDE of Bocking *v.* Thomas SYLESDON, gentleman.
Land in Finchingfield late of John Walforde, deceased, husband of complainant.   ESSEX.

6-13   George WALLE and others *v.* William WESTE, knight, Edmund his son, and George NEWPORTE, esquire.
'Seales or leades or bullaryes of salt water callyd fates otherwyse callyd salte fates otherwyse boylinge fates otherwyse salte howses [otherwyse] boylinge leades otherwyse salte leades or wychebowses' and woods in Droitwich. *See File 1276, Nos. 5 and 30.*   WORCESTER.

14 ·William WALPOLE. Joan his wife, late the wife of William Shadworth, and Robert SHAD-
WORTH her.son, v. Henry and Thomas SHADWORTH.
Legacy of the said William Shadworth, whose executors defendants are.   ———

15 Thomas WALSINGHAM, servant to George Owen, esquire, the Queen's physician, v. the
mayor and bailiffs of OXFORD and Richard BROKES, burgess of Oxford.
Action for calling the said Brokes a rebel and a liar, arising out of a dispute between the said Owen
and the city of Oxford concerning common in St. Giles's Field. *Certiorari and subpœna. See File*
1397, *No.* 25. ·   OXFORD.

16 Arthur WARCOPPE, gentleman, v. Hugh BYRD and Thomas HYLL, husbandman.
Pasture in Colby late of Bernard Warcoppe, father of complainant.   WESTMORLAND.

17–20 Thomas WARDE and Elizabeth his wife, niece and heir of William Chase, v. Thomas
WETHERALL.
Farm in Isleworth of the demise of the said Chase.   · MIDDLESEX.

21 Nicholas son and heir of John WATKYNSON v. Thomas FYSSHER and others.
Detention of deeds relating to a messuage and land in Knottingley.   YORK.

22 Roger WATKYS and Rose his wife v. William MENLOVE.
Burgages and land in the lordship of Wem, late of John Bollar·of Brewood, co. Stafford.   SALOP.

23 Ralph WATSON, parson of Nuthurst, v. Richard WASTLYN *alias* Saunders.
Parsonage of Nuthurst claimed under a lease from Gregory Doddes, late parson deprived for
marriage.   HANTS.

24–27 William WATTES of Canterbury v. Thomas HARLAKENDEN.
Messuage and land in Ivychurch, late of William Watt(es), deceased grandfather of complainant
D. XII, 4.   KENT.

28 William WEALE, student at the law, and others, sons of William Weale of Shrewsbury, dyer,
deceased v. Robert GYTTYNS.
Messuage, barn, and land in Shrewsbury and Coleham of the demise of ——— Hoord of Bridgnorth.
                                                                                      SALOP.

29 Edmund WEKES v. Hugh WEKES and Anthony HONYCHURCHE.
Suppression of a new lease of land in Broadwoodkelly, late of Henry Wekes, father of the said Edmund
and Hugh.

30 William WELSTODE and John his brother and next friend v. Thomas GOBY of Wimborn
Minster, beer-brewer.
Legacy of William Welstode of Wimborn Minster, father of complainants, and cost of maintenance
of the said William the son, for which defendant had received 200 sheep.   DORSET.

31 William WENHAM v. John FAWKENER, gentleman.
Lease of the parsonage of Busshoppreston (*i.e.* Preston by Hove?) which defendant promised to
obtain in exchange for a former lease.   SUSSEX.

32 Richard WEST v. William STRYNGER and Joan his wife.
Messuages in Billingshurst and [Wisborough] Green late of Richard West, deceased, father of complainant.   SUSSEX.

33–34 William Feltham and Nicholas Lece (Lease), churchwardens of WESTHALL, for themselves and all the inhabitants, v. Richard son and heir of Thomas DAVYE.
Land in Westhall called the ' gylde lande of Seyncte Trenyte.'   SUFFOLK.

35 The same churchwardens, with the rest of the inhabitants, in the name of the town v. Richard
MYHELLES.
Rent charged by Thomas Gooche, late vicar, on a tenement occupied by defendant in Westhall.
                                                                                      SUFFOLK.

36–37 Richard WESTON, husbandman, and William his son, v. Christopher BRADWELL.
Site of the manor of Marston and lands of the demise of Thomas Arthur. (Defendant pleads the said
Richard's dilatory proceedings at common law).   STAFFORD.

38 Richard WESTON v. William RAYNSHAWE·and others.
Tenement in the borough of Stafford bought of John Russell (?). *Damaged.*   STAFFORD.

39 Edward Bagshawe and William· Halle, for themselves and the inhabitants of WETTON, v.
John GRYMES of London, clothworker.
Seizure of the church of Wetton by colour of a purchase of the manor.   STAFFORD.

40–41 John WEVINGE· of Ashton Keynes v. Benett JAYE of Purton.
Detention of deeds relating to messuages and land in Chelworth. (Defendant pleads a decree of the
Court of Requests).   WILTS.

42–44 Robert WHELER of Cowley, co. Gloucester, labourer v. Thomas HAWKES, yeoman, great
grandson and heir of Richard Reynalde of Walsall and of Annes his wife.
Lands late of John Bavyn of Pershore [co. Worcester], grandfather of complainant. *Damaged.*
                                                                                      STAFFORD.

45 Christopher WHYTE v. Leonard WYLKYNS.
Close of pasture in the manor of Chilcot (in Wells) of the demise of John Uvèdale, prebendary of
Wells.   SOMERSET.

46 John WHYTE of Bristol, esquire, v. George HERBERT, knight, executor of John Cradocke,
gentleman.
Loan to the said Cradocke· repayable out of the issues of the parsonage of Bedminster. *See File*
1394, *No.* 30.   SOMERSET.

47   Robert WIGMORE, esquire, v. William GRESSHAM, esquire, and John GRYFFYN.
Action concerning land in complainant's manor of Roughton, which should have been suspended during arbitration.   NORFOLK.

48   WILLIAM ap William and John CLEMENT v. Lewis APPRYCE.
Cottage and land in Kerry late of William Brekenock, deceased, grandfather of complainants.   MONTGOMERY.

49   WILLIAM ap David of Oswestry, yeoman, v. Meredith ap John TAYLOUR.
Price of flax and 'wosters.'   SALOP.

50-51   George WODE of St. John Zachary, London, goldsmith, and Katherine his wife, v. William PALMER.
Legacy of Thomas Palmer of Carlton, father of the said Katherine and William   LONDON, NORTHAMPTON.

52   John WOLDNALLES, labourer, v. David POLE, official of the bishop of Coventry and Lichfield, and the sheriff of STAFFORD.
Imprisonment on an excommunication at the suit of the late Duke of Northumberland for withholding of tithes in Walsall. *Subpœna and corpus cum causa.*   STAFFORD.

53   George WOLFITTE, clerk, and Geoffrey WOLFITTE v. Alice late the wife of Richard DRAYCOTE and John DRAYCOTE.
Lease of the parsonage of Wysall (Wysho) made by the late monastery of Worksop and lost at the dissolution.   NOTTS.

54-55   Richard WOLMER of Bloxham, esquire, v. Christopher TOMPSON.
Parsonage of Wellingore with lands and deeds promised to defendant's son on his marriage with complainant's daughter. *Commission.*   LINCOLN.

56-59   Robert WOODFORD of London v. Francis SMYTH.
Manor of Ashby Folvill formerly of John Folvyll, ancestor of complainant and of Mary, wife of defendant. *Damaged.* D. XIII, 52.   LEICESTER.

60-64   Edmund WOODROVE v. Henry BAYNBRYGGE and others.
(Continuation of *File 1391, Nos. 65-69*). *Damaged.*   DERBY.

65-67   Robert WOOLBY of Wainfleet, yeoman, c. John BAWDEWYN.
Messuage in Ashby by Horncastle late of Richard Neve, deceased, grandfather of complainant.   LINCOLN.

68   Francis WORSELEY of Helpes[tone], grandson and heir of Myles Worseley, v. Nicholas FETHERSTONE.
Detention of deeds relating to a messuage and land at Deeping gate in Maxey. *Mutilated.*   NORTHAMPTON.

69-70   William WORTLEY (Worley) of Whissendine, labourer, Joan his wife, and Agnes MANNE v. John (A) MANNE.
Legacies of Thomas Man, father of the female complainants and brother of defendant.   RUTLAND.

71-72   Elizabeth WRIGHT, an infant, by John Gedge of Earith her guardian, v. Henry CORBETT of the same.
Legacy of Stephen Wright of Somersham, father of complainant, whose executor defendant is.   HUNTINGDON.

73   Robert WRIGHT.
Subpœna to obtain the evidence of John Corbett, gentleman, steward of the manor of Debden, and others, as to land there pledged to John Peppis, deceased, by commandment of Lord Rich, then chancellor. *See File 1321, No. 47.*   ESSEX.

74   William WYKE, vicar of Deverell Langebrege, v. William HAYNES.
Non-performance of conditions of presentation to the said vicarage for which complainant gave bond in 100l. *Mutilated.*   [WILTS.]

75-76   Walter WYLDE of Cromer, mariner, v. William MANGLES, Elizabeth his wife and others.
Messuage in [Cromer] of the demise of John Fevers. *Mutilated.*   NORFOLK.

77-79   Simon WYLDON, husbandman, grandson of William Wyldon, v. William PALMER, gentlemen, and Thomas BROOKES, his servant.
Seizure of copy of court roll and crops of a tenement in the said Palmer's manor of Brailes.   WARWICK.

80-82   William WYLLCOKES v. John COWYCK and Margaret his wife, executrix and late the wife of Richard Seller.
Detention of deeds relating to tenements in Southwark, Wooburn, Little Marlow, Wycombe, Great Missenden, and Wendover late of Walter Wyllcokes, deceased, father of complainant, whose executor the said Seller was.   SURREY, BUCKINGHAM.

83-85   Robert WYLLYAMSON v. Robert ASSHETON his father-in-law.
Goods and a tenement in Edlaston promised to complainant if he should lose a tenement he then possessed.   [DERBY].

86-87   Edmund WYLSON v. Henry FOXALL and Seth WALTHEWE, executors of Agnes Walthewe.
Detention of deeds relating to a messuage in Birmingham and of a legacy of the said Agnes to Sence Walthewe, wife of complainant.   WARWICK.

88-90   Anthony WYNTER and Edmund NYCOLLES, administrators of the goods of William Marshall, parson of Wetherley, deceased, v. William DEWSNOPE, clerk.
Arrears of rent of the said parsonage. D. XII, 20.   LEICESTER.

FILE 1396.

1   Roger YALDEWYN and Elizabeth his wife, administratrix of the goods of Thomas Jutton late her husband and of John Jutton, v. John BROKEHURST.
Lease of a messuage and land in Kirdford obtained by defendant to the use of the said John Jutton.
SUSSEX.

2-8   Thomas YARBROUGHE of Keddington (Kenyngton), labourer, v. George SERJEANTE, Robert, son and heir of Richard YERBURGHE, and Alison late the wife of George RAYNOLD.
Messuage and land in Cockerington formerly of Roger Yerburghe, deceased, great-grandfather of complainant.
LINCOLN.

9-14   Elizabeth, late the wife of Charles YARBURGHE, esquire, v. John AUNGEWYNE, esquire, an executor of John Ely her tenant by knight's service, and Christopher SCOPHOLME of Saltfleethaven.
Wardship of John son of the said John Ely and of a messuage and land in the manor of Theddlethorpe.
LINCOLN.

15   John YATE v. Walter FAWCETT and Joan his wife, aunt of complainant.
Procuring a conveyance of land in Tettenhall Regis, late of Roger Yate, deceased, brother of complainant.
STAFFORD.

16-17   John son of Walter YEA and of Alice his wife v. William WALLER, gentleman, and John SNOWE of Bickwell (in Rose Ash).
Suppression of a lease of half a messuage and land in Bishop's Nympton (Nymet). *See File 1394, No. 8.*
DEVON.

18-19   Thurston YEARDLEY of Egham v. Michael GRENE.
Manor of Milton with mill and land of the demise of the president and scholars of Corpus Christi College, Oxford.
SURREY.

20-22   Christopher YERBURGH, gentleman, and Margaret his wife, v. Richard SKEPPER, gentleman.
Refusal of arbitration before John Coppuldyk, knight, the Queen's steward of the honour of Bolingbroke, concerning lands therein.
LINCOLN.

23   John YERWORTH and Elizabeth his wife, late the wife of Robert Pole, v. Thomas WYLKES, and others.
Messuage called ' wychhowses,' ' leades to wall salt in belonging to the same, and messuages and lands in Nantwich and Saltersich of the demise of Thomas Smyth, knight.
CHESTER.

24-26   Robert Courme and others, customary tenants of YETMINSTER UPBURY, v. Anthony DALABER, yeoman, lessee of the manor.
Neglect to keep courts and wrongful entry on the lands of some of the tenants whose rights are described at length.
DORSET.

27   William YONG, esquire v. William EYTON.
Manors of Cainton (in Bolas) and Stoke-upon-Tern late of Francis Yong, esquire, deceased, father of complainant.
SALOP.

28   William YONG v. Matthew . . . , John HOUSBAND and Edward LLYLLO.
Land in Carnarvon late of John Yong, deceased father of complainant.
CARNARVON.

29-30   Humphrey YORKE of Hannington v. Robert ALEN.
Land in Lamport (Lamparde) late of Margaret, wife of John York, deceased, uncle of complainant.
NORTHAMPTON.

31   John YORKE v. Richard MORTON.
Crown lease of messuages, cottage and land in Morton (in Great Ness).
SALOP.

32-35   George YOUNGE v. John HOLBEME, executor of John Holbeme.
Messuages and lands in Ugborough of the demise of the said John the elder and of Margaret his wife.
DEVON.

FILE 1397.

1   Edmund [BONNER], bishop of London, v. George SHEPESHEDE (Shepeside) and others.
Waste of Rydmarley park by colour of complainant's deprivation.
[WORCESTER.]

2   . . . , Alice his wife, John HAYLEY, Elizabeth his wife, and John son and heir of Agnes MASSYE v. Henry MORETON and Margery his wife.
Messuage cottage and land at Bentley in Stoke late of Thomas Walkelate, deceased, father of the said Alice, Elizabeth, Agnes, and Margery. *Faded.*
STAFFORD.

3   . . . , Jane his wife, William, son and heir apparent of Matthew HERBERT, esquire, Katherine his wife, . . . and Ellen his wife v. Res GRUFFYDD, knight.
Manor of Penryn and several hundred messuages and lands in Clynnog, Llanvayr (*i.e.* Llanfaer-isgaer ?) Carnarvon, Dinorwic, Ucheldref, Penhesgyn, and Crynlyn (all in Llansadwrn), Castell Mathafarn Wyon, Pentraeth, [Mathafarn Ucha and Mathafarn Isa ?], Castell (in Penmynydd) Llandisnan (*i.e.*, Llandyfnan?), Llodart Escop (in Llandyfrydog?), and Llansadwrn, Tregarnedd (in Llangefni), Llanidan, Porthamel (in Llanedwen), Llanfair-yn-y-Cwmwd, Llangeinwen, Rhoscolyn, Bryngwallen (in Llanerchymedd) and Newborough; Llechylched, and Llegh gar var wy (*i.e.*, Llechcynfarwydd?); Llandebrodoch (*i.e.*, Llandyfrydog?), Rhosmynach (in Llanelian), Amlwch, and Llanelian; and many other places (*named*); late of Edward Gruffydd, esquire, deceased, father of the female complainants. *Mutilated. Commots given.*
CARNARVON, ANGLESEA.

4   Thomas son and heir of Margery . . . AS v. Henry HALL and Thomas LEGHE.
Gardens, etc., in Towcester. *Mutilated.*
[NORTHAMPTON.]

H 4

5-8   Ralph [WY]CH . . . and Margery his wife *v.* Maurice STERE and Alice his wife.
Land in the manor of Chelverton (Chelsam Euwitere, Chelston) of the bequest of John Lambe,
brother of the said Alice. *Faded.*   NORTHAMPTON.

9   Thomas . . . *v.* William BANDE, gentleman.
Parsonage of Buckland Abbots (*i.e.* Buckland Newton?). *Damaged.*   DORSET.

10   . . . , husband of Joan executrix and late the wife of John Fensham *v.* John and Henry
BEVELL.
Detention of deeds relating to lands in Dunstable of the demise of the fraternity of St. John the
Baptist, [Dunstable], and the churchwardens there. *Damaged.*   BEDFORD.

11   Hugh . . . [of C]aynham, yeoman, *v.* William CAMEL and John his son.
Yearly payments due for use of a sow, tithe, and money. *Mutilated.*   SALOP.

12   . . . and . . . , executors of William Cashe, *v.* Andrew COLLINGEHAM, gentleman.
Price of debt for which defendant. proposes to wage his law. *Mutilated.*   LINCOLN.

13   . . . of the Inner Temple, gentleman, *v.* DAVY a Penry.
Payment of two instead of three dishes for grinding every two bushels of corn at complainant's mill
of Llanwynno. *Mutilated.*   CARMARTHEN.

14   . . William . . . . , one of the guard of Guines, *v.* EDMUND ap Rece ap Morys and Hugh
. . . . LLOYDE.
Land in the parish of Kerye. *Mutilated.*   MO[NTGOMERY.]

15   . . . , prisoner in Ludgate *v.* Thomas GODWYN.
Action of debt, pending an action in this court concerning the purchase of the vicarage of Dunton
Bassett. *Damaged.*   LEICESTER.

16   . . . *v.* Richard HENRYE and Elizabeth his wife.
Lands in the manor of Wilby. *Mutilated.*   SUFFOLK.

17   . . . *v.* JOHN ap Richard, ANNE verch Richard his wife, and RICHARD ap David ap
Ethell.
Messuage in Caerfallwch. *Mutilated.*   FLINT.

18   . . . of Hurstbourne, esquire, *v.* John KYRKBY, gentleman.
Detention of deeds relating to a farm called Paynes Hole. *Mutilated.*   HANTS.

19   . . . and Parnell his wife *v.* Philip LAMPRYER.
Share of lands of Clement Lampryer, deceased father of the said Parnell, valued at 406 quarters of
wheat yearly. *Damaged.*   JERSEY.

20   Lewis . . yeoman of the wardrobe to Edward late Duke of Somerset, *v.* the sheriffs of
LONDON and Robert HICKES, ironmonger.
Action for a debt of the Duke for velvet and sarcenet, to particulars of which complainant had sub-
scribed the date of payment promised by the Duke. *Certiorari and subpœna. Mutilated.* LONDON.

21   . . . *v.* John LONGE and John ROCHE.
Trespasses in Acton Beacham. *Mutilated.*   [WORCESTER.]

22   . . . , executor of . . . Bealbury, *v.* William LOWER, gentleman.
Plate pledged to defendants. *Mutilated.*   CORNWALL.

23   . . . *v.* the sheriff of MIDDLESEX.
Arrest for a debt satisfied by a lease of a manison house and land at Crandon in Bawdrip (Grandon)
to Robert Graunte, of Bradford, co. Wilts, whose debts were assigned by King Edward VI to John
Osborne, gentleman. *Habeas corpus. Mutilated.*   MIDDLESEX, SOMERSET.

24   . . . , yeoman of the Guard, *v.* Emma . . . and OWEN ap Guillim.
Land in Beguildy. *Mutilated.*   RADNOR.

25   . . . *v.* [the mayor and bailiffs of OXFORD and] Thomas COGEYN,
Action for trespass on the Port Meadow of Oxford. [*Certiorari and*] *subpœna. Mutilated. See File
1395, No.* 15.   OXFORD.

26   FOWKE ap Thomas of London, yeoman, *v.* Foulke PIGGOTT, priest.
Seizure of Margaret verch Jenet, wife of complainant, under pretence of marriage, and of farm
stock and deeds. *Mutilated.*   DENBIGH.

27   . . . ap Morrys of Ruthenland, gentleman, *v.* ROBERT ap David, Margaret his wife and
John their son.
Detention of deeds entrusted to defendants concerning lands in Llangum Dymmayle. *Mutilated.*
                                                                            DENBIGH.

28   . . . , citizen and merchant of London *v.* Richard SAKEVILE, knight, and Henry
SHERINGETON, gentleman, next of kin to William Sheringeton, knight, deceased, and
administrator of his goods.
Bond given jointly by complainant and the said Sir Richard and Sir William for performance of
covenants by the late Duke of Northumberland. *Mutilated.*   ————

29   . . . *v.* Edward SLEGGE, alderman of Cambridge.
Closes in St. Giles's, Cambridge. *Mutilated. See Star Chamber Proceedings, Philip & Mary, II,* 55.
                                                                            CAMBRIDGE.

30   B . . . of Bristol, merchant, *v.* Francis STRADLING.
Meadow in Bedminster (other tenants' names given). *Faded.*   SOMERSET.

31   . . . *v.* William WYNGFELD, deprived parson of Burnham Thorpe, and Henry CAN-
TRELL.
Forgery of a lease of the said parsonage in the name of the said Wyngfeld. *Mutilated.*   [NORFOLK.]
                (The remaining documents in this bundle are illegible.)

FILE 1398.

1   Robert ABBOTT, executor of Richard Abbott, v. Robert SMYTHE.
Loans of money and goods to Robert Smythe *alias* Rothwell of Great Limber, deceased, father of complainant.   LINCOLN.

2   William ABBOTT v. Thomas CLEMENT.
Lease of land in Heston (in Hartland), acquired by defendant from ˙John Arundell of Lanherne, knight, on a promise to convey it to complainant.   DEVON.

3-6   Richard ABYE, husbandman, v. Robert BROWN, Richard LINLEY, and others, jurors of the court of Wintringham, and Richard MIDDELTON, bailiff.
Failure to make presentments for wrongful depasturing of Wintringham common, and unlawful distresses. *Mutilated.*   LINCOLN.

7-9   Bartholomew ACHE v. Anthony COKESHED.
Refusal to complete a sale of land (*described*) and a barn in Chulmleigh seven years from purchase as promised. *Mutilated.*   DEVON.

10-12   John ADAMES of Waltham St. Lawrence, co. Berks, labourer, and Elizabeth his wife, v. Thomas GRYME.
Land in Hartwell, late of Edward Gryme, deceased, grandfather of the said Elizabeth.
                                                                            NORTHAMPTON.

13-14   Ralph ADDERLEY of Dovebridge Holt v. Robert PORTER, yeoman, and Thomas his son.
Lands in Fulford and Sayerley (both in Stone). *2 bills.*   STAFFORD.

15-19   Henry ALAMBIE, parson of South Kelsey, v. Thomas MOUNSON, esquire, and Nicholas BROUGHTON.
Portion of complainant's glebe demised to the said Thomas by George his brother, late parson.
                                                                            LINCOLN.

20-22   Nicholas ALDRIGE, husbandman, v. John PERSE of Awbridge (in Michelmersh), husbandman.
Land in Wellow, late of Thomas Aldrige, deceased, father of complainant.   HANTS.

23   William ALDRYCHE v. Ursula GRAY.
Messuage, garden and cottage in Norwich, late of Thomas Aldryche, grandfather of complainant.
                                                                            NORFOLK.

24-27   Ralph ALEN of Bentley, husbandman, v. William MARTYN.
Lease of half a messuage in Beech and lands in Swinnerton occupied therewith obtained from Robert Martyn, son of the said William and Elizabeth his wife.   STAFFORD.

28   William ALEY, late of Langford, yeoman, v. Robert COGGAN of Chard, chapman.
Gelding lent for a journey home from London.   DEVON, SOMERSET.

29-30   Alexander ALLAN of London, barber-surgeon, v. George JACKSON.
Messuages, cottages and land in Thirn, Thornton-Watlass, Lower Ellington and Kirkby Fleetham.
                                                                            YORK.

31   Thomas ALSOPE of Ashbourne, mercer, v. John BUKLOW and others.
Seizure of sheep of complainant at Parwich together with those of Agnes Bukloo, deceased, mother of the said Thomas and John.   DERBY.

32-37   James ALTHAM, alderman of London, v. John LAMBERT of Calton, esquire.
Manor of Malham.   YORK.

38   Thomas ALYN of Rugeley, innholder, v. Richard . . .
Price of pasture in Rugeley bought of John Weston, gentleman. *Mutilated.*   STAFFORD.

39   Walter ALYNSON of Blandford Forum, tailor, v. Thomas PERHAM, parson of Long Cheselborne.
Refusal to complete a sale of wheat and barley.   DORSET.

40   Matthew AMCOTTES and Mary his wife, late the wife of Henry Rokeby of Kirk-Sandall, v. Robert ATHERTON of Clement's Inn, gentleman.
Messuages, cottages and lands in Brampton and Lenton.   YORK.

41   Griffith AMERYDET of Exeter, gentleman, v. John PETER *alias* Anthony.
Jointure of the wife of another John Anthony, which should have been reserved on a sale of lands in Northlew, bought of him and sold to defendant.   DEVON.

42-43   Humphrey ANDREWES v. Robert and Richard TAYLOUR of Shutford, co. Oxford.
Bond given for defendant's appearance at Worcester sessions to prosecute certain persons for felony.   WORCESTER.

44   Thomas APPRYSE, tailor, son and heir of Ryse ap David, v. OLIVER ap Morris and others.
Detention of deeds relating to a messuage in a street called 'Pentrerewill' in Newtown and another in Kilcowen.   MONTGOMERY.

45-47   Robert APULBY of Bingham, gentleman, v. Richard STAPULTON, knight, formerly his master.
Non-payment of a loan for which defendant has obtained the documents for purposes of account.
                                                                            NOTTS.

48-50   Christopher ARGENTYNE, Elizabeth his wife, and Lewis, their son v. John MORE, knight.
Capital messuage, barton, and other lands, with a free fishery, belonging to the manor of Combe Rawleigh, demised by defendant without a warranty against a rent payable to James Nott, esquire.   DEVON.

51   Francis ARMIGER *v.* John KYNGE.
Detention of deeds relating to lands in Stratford and Glemham of the grant ot John, son ot Thomas
Truston.   SUFFOLK.

52   Walter ASHETON of Cotts, yeoman, *v.* Edith BROWNE of Wotton-under-Edge.
Part price of wool the bond for which is lost.   ✎   GLOUCESTER.

53   John ASKEW, yeoman, *v.* Hugh OSBORNE.
Crown lease of lands in Great Ponton (Pawnton) belonging to the manor of Grantham. LINCOLN.

54–57   . John ASCUE, Hugh OSBORNE, and others, *v.* John and Richard ASCUE.
Crown loan of lands in the manor of Great Ponton (Pawneton) in the soke of Grantham, stated by
defendants not to be copyhold.   LINCOLN.

58–62   Thomas ASSHETON and Elizabeth his wife, late the wife of Thomas Bradburie *v.* Mary
        [PERCY], countess of Northumberland, and others.
Parsonage and vicarage of Ecclesfield with rent in Hall Hartley, the chapel of Bradfield and ' the
porcion within the lymytes and boundes of the parishe churche of Sheffilde.'   [YORK.]

63–64   Thomas ATKINS of London, grocer, *v.* the mayor and sheriffs of LONDON, and Emanuel
        LUCAR and Richard PEGREM of London, haberdasher, his son-in-law.
Action of debt following on proceedings in bankruptcy, the said Pegrem having promised to respite
a debt from Stourbridge fair to Ely fair. *Certiorari and subpœna.*   LONDON, CAMBRIDGE.

65   Edward ATKYNSON of Brampton, yeoman, *v.* James FOLJAMBE, knight, son of Godfrey
        Foljambe, knight.
Land in Ingmanthorpe (Dingmanthorpe,) late held of the manor of [Temple] Normanton by
Roger [Atkynson], deceased, grandfather of complainant. *Mutilated. See Files* 792, *No.* 35; 1121,.
No. 23.   DERBY..

66   Richard AWNGER of Chesterton, husbandman, *v.* Godfrey SWAYNE of the Middle Temple,.
        student.
Vexatious suits and contrivance of complainant's non-appearance. *Mutilated.*
                                                                            CAMBRIDGE, LONDON..

67–69   William AYAR *v.* Thomas TOOPE of Poole, draper.
Debt of Nicholas Hynton paid to defendant.   DORSET..

70   Anthony AYLEWORTHE of Aylworth (in Naunton), co. Gloucester, *v.* Stephen WEBB.
        and William RYDER, executors of Thomas Beele.
Action in the court of Salmonsbury *alias* Slaughter for price of the manor of Pole Howse (*i.e.* Pull
Court in Bushley?) and land in Bushley and Longdon, already paid for in money, goods (*described*)
and permission of occupation.   WORCESTER.

71–72   Robert AYNESWORTH of Ainsworth, co. Lancaster, yeoman, *v.* Roger BANASTER and.
        James BULLEN.
Messuage and land in Acton, late of Simon Aynesworth of London, yeoman, deceased; brother of
complainant.   CHESTER.

73–81   The same *v.* the same Richard MAYNWARING, knight, Richard ORMESHAWE, clerk,
        Ralph STURROPP, Hugh WENTWORTH and Margaret HAMMETT.
Do.   CHESTER..

FILE 1399.

1   . . . ABEDOWEGOGHE of London, labourer, *v.* Richard APRECE, gentleman, and.
        others.
Lands in Llanbadarn, late of Gooddogan Abbed[owegoghe?], deceased, father of complainant.
Damaged.   /   RADNOR..

2   . . . ABURFORTH *v.* John CHAPMAN.
Goods of John Aburforth, deceased, father of complainant, which defendant had contracted to·
carry from Thaxted to Bosbury. *Mutilated.*   ESSEX, HEREFORD.

3–5   Robert ACTON of Ribbesford, co. Worcester, knight, *v.* Thomas WALSYNGHAM, esquire,.
        son and executor of Edmund Walsyngham, knight, lieutenant of the Tower.
Action on a bond to warrant lands in Ham and Croydon free from encumbrances, in spite of an
exception made by the said Sir Edmund of the lessor's rent.   SURREY..

6–7   The same *v.* John, son of William JACKSON.
Occupation of a messuage called Ham and lands in Croydon after notice to terminate the lease.
                                                                                          SURREY..

8–9   Richard AGARD and Elizabeth his wife, executrix, and late the wife of John Bristowe *v.*
        Randal SCARYOTT.
Tenement in Nantwich. *Much damaged.*   CHESTER.

10–13   William AGARD, yeoman, *v.* Agnes late the wife of John SOWTER and John their son.
Action for a debt due to the said John, the father, partly paid by an under-lease to the said Agnes
of land in Markeaton (Marton).   DERBY..

14–15   Richard, youngest son and heir of William ALEN, husbandman, *v.* Richard ELVYNGTON,.
        son-in-law of William Shurley, esquire, deceased.
Land in the manor of Wiston (Wystneston) of the demise of Ralph Shurley, esquire. *Mutilated.*
                                                                                           SUSSEX

16–18   Thomas ALEN, parson of Stevenage, co. Herts, *v.* Thomasyn NEWLANDE.
Land in Wittersham (Wrytlesham) wherein defendant claims an annuity by gift of William Clark,
sometime her husband.   KENT..

19-21   Edward ALGER v. Richard LEES of Ashmorebrook (in Lichfield), shereman.
Damages awarded in an arbitration concerning a messuage and land in Cannock (Channocke).
STAFFORD.

22-24   John ALLEYNE v. George MEDDLEY, George HADLEY and Thomas PATESHALL.
Tenement in the manor of Tyltey. *Mutilated.*   [ESSEX.]

25-28   William ALSOPPE *alias* Parker and Anne his wife v. William SALYSBURY, gentleman.
Detention of a lease of a tenement in ' Crockstreate,' Barnstaple, pasture in Bishops Tawton, and
meadow in Barnstaple conveyed by John de Borowe of Dover to the said Anne and to Lettice,
wife of defendant.   DEVON.

29-31   Thomas AMERYE of Pinner v. Thomas EDEN, gentleman, and John, grandson and heir of
John WALESTON (Wallexton).
Land and house (*described*) in Ruislip, formerly of John Amerye and Joan his wife, grandparents
of complainant.   MIDDLESEX.

32   Roger AMYCE, Elizabeth his wife, and Mary their daughter v. Sir John THYNNE.
Crown lease of land in the manor of Deverell Langbridge, afterwards acquired by defendant.
Mutilated.   [WILTS.]

33-36   John son of John ANDERDON v. Nicholas, son of John MANNING.
Driving sheep from complainant's land in Moorwinstow(?) and other trespasses. *Faded. Deposition
included.*   CORNWALL.

37   Roger ANDREWE of Great Torrington, co. Devon, v. Christopher COCKE of Camelford and
Emma his wife.
Detention of deeds relating to a messuage in Fore Street, Bodmin.   CORNWALL.

38   Richard ANNYS v. George BULL.
Messuage in Womadon (*i.e.* Wymondham?) whereof both parties were enfeoffed jointly by Robert
Annys, and of which complainant pledged his share to defendant.   LEICESTER.

39-40   Richard APEVAN and Thomas and Myles WOORRYE, sons of Woorrye ap Evans, deceased,
v. Harry FRANKLYN.
Messuage and land in Llangewg in the lordship of Gower, late of William Hopkyn, deceased, grandfather of the said Richard and Woorrye.   [GLAMORGAN.]

41-42   The same v. RICHARD ap John.
Messuage and land in Llangiwg, late of Jenkyn (ap) William ap Hopkyn, deceased, uncle of the
said Richard and Woorrye.   GLAMORGAN.

43-45   Edmund APPLEYARD v. Hugh GARNER, fishmonger, and of John MILNER, tailor.
Household goods and lease of meadow in Loughborough. *Faded.*   LEICESTER.

46-47   Hugh APPOWELL and William son and heir of Morgan APPOWELL v. Margaret
MERYKE (Apmeryk) and others.
Messuages, watermill and land in Llangonoyd, late of Thomas Davy, deceased, great-grandfather
of the said Hugh and Morgan, and grandfather of the said Margaret.   GLAMORGAN.

48-50   The same and John APPOWELL, brother of the said William, v. Morgan WILLIAM and
Gwirvill his wife, late the wife of Roger Watkyn.
Messuages in Mamhilad, late of Walter Appowell, deceased, father of the said Hugh and Morgan.
MONMOUTH.

51-53   Nicholas APPULBY, parson of Colton, v. Francis STYWARD, gentleman.
Land in Colton claimed by complainant as glebe and by defendant as belonging to the late monastery
of Wymondham.   NORTHAMPTON.

54   Roger APSHAWE, merchant and citizen of Chester, v. George COLIER of Stone.
Debt for goods supplied, the bond for which is lost.   CHESTER, STAFFORD.

55   The same v. Robert COLIER.
Debt for ' spruce skynnes,' the bond for which is lost.   CHESTER, STAFFORD.

56   Richard ARGENTYNE, clerk, v. the bailiffs of IPSWICH.
Action by Robert Wingfelde of Brantham, gentleman, for a payment, the conditions of which (*not
specified*) have not been fulfilled.   SUFFOLK.

57-58   Thomas ASTELEY v. William, son and heir of Richard BYLLYNGTON.
Messuage and land in Bescote, late of Michael Selman, deceased, grandfather of Joyce wife of
complainant.   STAFFORD.

59   Mary, late the wife of Anthony ASTLEY of Orslow (in Church Eaton), gentleman, and
administratrix of his goods, v. Elizabeth LONDON *alias* Lun.
Detention of a bond given by John Mounslow of Caughley, gentleman.   STAFFORD, SALOP.

60   William ASTMORE v. George MYDDYLMORE.
Rectory of King's Norton. *Mutilated. See File* 1287, *No.* 50.   [WORCESTER.]

61-63   John ATMER v. Roger WODEHOUSE, knight, and John WALTER.
Detention of a deed relating to turbary in Great Breccles, claimed by complainant, together with
a fold-course and common of pasture.   NORFOLK.

64   William ATWEEKES of Heston, co. Middlesex, v. Richard TYLL of Croydon.
Messuage and land in Thorpe.   SURREY.

65   John AUDELEY, gentleman, v. Nicholas BAGGNALL, knight.
Manor of Buglawton of the grant of John, late Lord Audley. *Mutilated.*   CHESTER.

66-67   William AVEREY of Benefield, embroiderer, v. William PALMER of Coweleton (*i.e.*
Colly-Weston?), esquire, and Robert DEXTER.
Land held of the said Palmer's manor of Myddelton.   NORTHAMPTON.

68–69   Alice AWNSELL and Edmund her son v. Robert, son of William BONDE.
Messuage at Nasty in Great Munden of the demise of defendants and of Thomas Bonde.   HERTS.

70–72   Henry AYLMER of Battisford Tye v. Henry HUBBERT, esquire.
Lands and messuages (*described*) in defendant's manor of Lynges in Battisford, forfeited for sub-
letting a part, complainant having failed to obtain the lord's leave through insanity.   2 bills.
SUFFOLK.

73–74   Edmund AYSSHELEY and Katharine his wife v. Alban (Albert) HYLL and Alice his wife,.
late the wife of John Masye.
Land and fulling-mill and a bakehouse held of the manor of Newton St. Cyres.   *Damaged.*   DEVON.

FILE 1400.

1–4   John ABURFORTH of Bosbury, co. Hereford, son and heir of Agnes Aburforth, v. Richard
ABURFORTH of London, gentleman, his brother, and Alice ALMON.
Farm called Woodhams and land in Thaxted, late of Thomas Cobbe, deceased, father of the said
Agnes and Alice.   D, XV, 40.   DEVON.

5–6   Richard ADAMS, husbandman, and Elizabeth his wife, executrix and late the wife of
Roger Wilcockes, or Richard WROTTESLEY of Wrottesley, co. Stafford, gentleman.
Messuage and land in Broseley, demised by Thomas Sutberey, formerly prior of Wenlock, and his
convent to John Bayly and Joes his wife, sometime the wife of the said Wilcockes.   SALOP.

7–9   William ALCOCKE v. John HART, bailiff of the liberty of Romney Marsh.
Procuring judgment in a suit against William Gylbert for a messuage and land in Newchurch
pending a *certiorari* from this court.   KENT.

10–11   Richard ALEN of Lichfield, husband of Margaret late the wife of John Lee, v. Hugh LEE,.
gentleman, and Edward LEVESON.
Lease of a moiety of the tithe corn of the parsonage (*sic*) of Wombourne, Trysull and Seisdon, made·
by Fulk Lee, gentleman, and entrusted to defendant.   STAFFORD.

12–14   Richard ALEYN, citizen and haberdasher of London, v. John BADLOND of Kingsland.
Messuage and land in Eardisland (Eresland), Burton, Leominster, and Middleton, adjudged to·
complainant in a suit in this court by Humphrey Bell, since deceased.   *See Files 717, No. 32;*
947, No. 18.   HEREFORD.

15–18   Thomas AMERYE v. William PADDON, Edmund FLINGE and Joan his wife, late the·
wife of Davy Paddon.
Messuage and land in Teignmouth.   DEVON.

19   Anthony AMORYE v. Ralph BARNEFELD.
Refusal to complete a lease of land in Woolfardisworthy.   *See File 1402, No. 18.*   DEVON.

20–21   John ANDREWE and others v. Walter and John YONGE.
Mill held of Humphrey Arundell's moiety of the manor of Batteshorne (in Honiton).   *Mutilated.*
DEVON.

22–25   Thomas ANNOTT of Lowestoft v. Agnes, wife of Richard WATSON, and formerly of John
Rowte of the same.
Price of herrings sold to the said Rowte, of whose goods defendant is administratrix.   SUFFOLK.

26–29.   The same v. the same.
Do.   SUFFOLK.

30–32   The same v. the said Richard and Agnes.
Do.   SUFFOLK.

33   Roger APIE v. Katherine MEREDYTH and Roger her son.
Messuage in Orcop, formerly of Robert Apie.   *Mutilated.*   HEREFORD.

34–37   Robert APRICE v. William APRICE, his uncle, and Roger TYTLOWE of Crowley, co.
Huntingdon.
Annuity charged on messuages and lands in Wiggenhall St. Peter and St. Mary Magdalen by Robert
Aprice of Washingley, co. Huntingdon, grandfather of complainant.   NORFOLK.

38   Christopher son of Robert ARDEN v. Edward BASSETT, servant to Nicholas Poyntz,
knight.
Tenement on Cleve Hill in the parish of Mangotsfield (Mangerfeld), held of the manor and hundred
of Barton Regis, of the gift of Matthew Bamfeld.   GLOUCESTER.

39–42   Edward ARNOLD, executor of Anne, daughter of John Volensbye, v. Thomas CORNE,
chaplain, executor of Thomasyn Volensbye.
Legacy of the said Thomasyn.   ———

43   John, younger son of John ASKE, deceased, v. [Henry PORTYNGTON, overseer of the
will of the said John the father].
Detention of goods of the said John the father and of a lease of the tithes of Houghton and of land
there and in Londesborough.   *Mutilated.*   YORK.

44   Francis ASLEYBYE, esquire, v. John THORNETON.
Next presentation to the parsonage of Settrington of the gift of Francis Standley, esquire.   YORK.

45–47   Edward ASTON, knight, v. John, son and heir of John LAUNTE (Lont).
Messuage and land in Brystowe (*i.e.* Burstall?) late of John Aston, knight, deceased, father of
complainant.   LEICESTER.

48–49   William AUBURY (Awbrey), D.C.L., principal of New Inn, Oxford, and EDWARD ap
Edward of Oxford, glover, executors of John Thomas, parson of Selattyn, co. Salop, v.·
John EDWARDES, of Chirk, esquire, assignee to uses.
Next presentation to the church of Llanrhaiadr-in-Mochnant.   DENBIGH.·

50   Richard AUTON v. Edmund BROUGHTON of Stewkley, co. Huntingdon.
Refusal to complete a lease of the parsonage of Tydd St. Giles.   CAMBRIDGE.

51   Thomas AWDER of London, haberdasher, v. John FAYE and John JAYM.
Debt, the bond for which is lost. *Footnote that an attachment has been granted.*   LONDON.

52   John AYMESWORTHE, executor of Edward Gregson, parson of Fladbury, v. Christopher
HALES, gentleman, parson of Fladbury (*sic*), and Stephen HALES.
Goods of the said Gregson and profits of his parsonage to the end of the year in which he died.   WORCESTER.

53–57   Anthony, Thomas and Robert, sons of Edward AYRE, esquire, deceased, v. Francis LEKE,
knight.
Lease of the manors of Holme and Danston, and of lands in Birley in Brampton, Branpton (Brampston), Whittington and Whitwell, whereof defendant has the reversion.   DERBY.

FILE 1401.

1   Richard ACTON of London, yeoman, v. John ALCROFT.
Messuage and land in Timperley, formerly of Hamlet Ardern. *See Files 715, No. 19; 941, No. 31;
and 1189, No. 51.*   CHESTER.

2–3   Anne, late the wife of Ralph ALDERSEY, v. Thomas ALDERSEY and others, executors
of the said Ralph.
Goods of Robert Byrkenheade, deceased, former husband of complainant.   CHESTER.

4   John ALDERSON, yeoman of the Queen's chamber, v. Jeffrey GARTH.
Debt of John Dente, deceased, whose executor defendant is.   [YORK?]

5–6   John, son of Adam ALDERSON, v. Leonard LOFTHOUSE, guardian of William and
Agnes, children of James Dent.
Detention of deeds relating to land in Reeth and Harkerside (in Grinton).   YORK.

7–8   Richard ALDRYCHE v. Robert, grandson of Robert SPATCHET.
Detention of deeds relating to a close in Rumburgh of the grant of William Wethers.   SUFFOLK.

9   John ALEYN of Greenhill (in Norton) v. Alice, late the wife of Richard ALEYN of
Waleswood and others.
Forgery of a will in the name of the said Richard omitting a legacy to complainant.   DERBY, YORK.

10–12   John ALFREY v. Richard, son and heir of Thomas INFYLD, feoffee to uses.
Refusal to enter on messuages and land in East Grinstead and Worth granted to complainant by
Peter Alfrey, his great-uncle, and now in the possession of complainant's brother.   SUSSEX.

13–14   Richard ALLEYN v. John HOPTON of Rockhill in Greet (Rochell), grandson and heir of
John Hopton, gentleman.
Lands in Greet, late of William Alleyn, deceased, grandfather of complainant.   SALOP.

15   Thomas AMORE v. Nicholas GUNHAM.
Principal and profits of a legacy from complainant's parents entrusted to defendant. *Mutilated.*
     SOMERSET.

16   Thomas ANDERDON (*rectius* Anderson?) and John and Richard, brothers of Katharine
ANDERSON, deceased, v. Matthew, son and heir of Richard CLATON.
Legacy to the said Katharine, of whose goods complainants are administrators, payable out of
lands in Appleby. *Mutilated.*   LINCOLN.

17–21   Robert APPLEBYE of Bingham, gentleman, and Elizabeth his wife v. Henry SACHA-
VERELL, gentleman.
Messuage and lands in Barton, bought of Elizabeth Bowgham of Hingham, mother of defendant
and a 'tabler' at his house. (Annexed is a replication to an answer of George Metcalfe.)   NOTTS.

22–26   John ARCHER v. John APRICE and Elizabeth his wife, late the wife of Richard Collyns.
Messuage in Henley-on-Thames, late of Richard Archer, deceased, grandfather of complainant.
Replication wanting.   OXFORD.

27–28   The same v. the said John APRICE and William COLLYNS, son of the said Richard.
Do, the said Elizabeth being dead.   OXFORD.

29–30   Robert ARDALL v. John DAVY of Dunstable, husbandman.
Ring promised to complainant on his marriage with defendant's daughter.   BEDFORD.

31   William ARMERE, gentleman of the Queen's henchmen, and Elizabeth his wife v.
[Thomas WENTWORTH], Lord Wentworth, and Richard, a son and heir of Ambrose
EDGOR *alias* Cary.
Attempt to invalidate a sale by the said Richard Edgor of a cottage and land in Poplar held of the
said Lord Wentworth's manor of Bishop's Hall, on the ground that no partition was made at the
said Ambrose's death.   MIDDLESEX.

32–33   Christian ARNOLD of Okehampton, late the wife of William Arnold, v. William LANG-
FORD of Week St. Germans.
Messuage and land in the manor of Norton Bawson (*i.e.* Norton in Broadwoodwidger?) claimed
under leases from successive chantry priests of Marldon.   DEVON.

34   Thomas ARUNDELL, esquire, v. William SHELDON of Bewdley, co. Worcester, esquire.
Instruction to the under-sheriff not to receive the post fine on a conveyance of the manor of
Hartshill and lands there and in Ansley (Ancely), so as to impair complainant's title thereto.
     WORCESTER.

35–37   Hugn ASCUE, knight, *v.* Francis SCLYNGESBY, esquire.
Detention of deeds relating to the house of the late Crossed Friars of St. Robert of Knaresborough and lands (*described*) there.   YORK.

38–40   William ASLOCKE of Wymondham, gentleman, and Elizabeth his wife *v.* John CLERE, knight.
Refusal to acknowledge a conveyance by John Sygar of land in defendant's manor of Gonviles (in Wymondham).   NORFOLK.

41   John ASSHEWELL *v.* Richard COLLYER.
Messuage and land in Burrington.   HEREFORD.

42–43   Robert and Roger, sons of Richard ASTERLEY, *v.* John CORBETT.
Detention of deeds relating to a messuage and land at Farley (in Pontesbury).   SALOP.

44–46   John AVEREY of Congresbury *v.* John MUTTELBURY, Richard COOKE (Cock), and Thomas CURTYS and Roger ORTON, bailiffs of John Sydenham, knight.
Seizure of cattle and removal to the Bishop of Wells's orchard.   SOMERSET.

47   John AWBREY of London, clothworker, *v.* Thomas Morgan AWBREY.
Price of goods supplied.   LONDON, BRECON.

FILE 1402.

1   John, Robert, Humphrey, Thomas, Edward, Margaret, Alice and Grace, children of Humphrey BAGSHAWE and of Agnes his wife *v.* John PASCALL.
Legacies of Robert Arthure, brother of the said Agnes, whose executor defendant is. *See File* 1291, *No.* 2.

2–3   William and Roger, sons of Roger BARBER of Eversholl, deceased, and John BIRTE, their uncle, *v.* Joan ALBON and William BARBER of Willeshampsted.
Debt of Thomas Everett to the said Roger the father, of whose goods defendants and the said Birte all claim to be administrators.   [BEDFORD.]

4–7   The same *v.* the same.
Cattle of the said Roger the father.   [BEDFORD.]

8–11   William BARBER of Faringdon and Richard WRYGHT of Wantage, butcher, *v.* Toby PLEDALL, gentleman.
Refusal to acknowledge a conveyance of land held of defendants' manor of Faringdon.   BERKS.

12–13   John BARKER *v.* William FREBARNE.
Messuage and land in St. Osyth's (St. Toses), late of John Sager, deceased, uncle of complainant.
                                                             ESSEX.

14–17   Thomas BARNABY of London, gentleman, *v.* James MORELEY, citizen and ironmonger of London.
Action on a bond for a debt of Thomas Woodman, satisfied by a composition before William Lord Howard, Lord Admiral, and by seizure of a ship at Dover.   LONDON, DOVER.

18–20   Ralph BARNEFELD *v.* Anthony AMEREY, gentleman.
Refusal to complete a sale of land in Woolfardisworthy (Wolsworthi). *See File* 1400, *No.* 19.
                                                             DEVON.

21–26   John BARWYKE and Elizabeth his wife *v.* John TOWTE and Edith his wife, late the wife of John Berell.
Share of a messuage and land in Fremington, late of John Munsys, deceased, father of the said Elizabeth and Edith.   DEVON.

27–28   Thomas BAWNE (Browne) and Bridget his wife *v,* Richard EYRE and others.
Messuages and land in Normanton and Goton (*i.e.* Gotham?), late of George Eyre, deceased, father of the said Bridget and Richard.   NOTTS.

29–30   John BAYLY . . . *v.* Ellen FORD.
Bond given to William Forde of Bedford in satisfaction of a debt of John West of the same, tanner, in lieu of rent of pasture in the manor of Putnoe, adjoining Clapham park. *Mutilated.*
                                                             BEDFORD.

31   Edmund BEAWPRE, esquire, for himself and the other inhabitants of Outwell, *v.* John REPPES and William HUNSTON, esquires, and others, inhabitants of Marshland.
Dykes, etc. (*described*), separating the half-hundred of Clackclose from the hundred of Marshland.
                                                             NORFOLK.

32–35   Richard BENNET of Hampreston, co. Dorset, son and heir of William Bennet, *v.* John ORCHARDE, Richard URRY, John GODFREY, Richard KINGE and John ERELES-MAN.
Forgery of deeds and wrongful occupation of land in Shalfleet, claimed by defendant or right of Thomas Deve, deceased, father-in-law of the said Orcharde, Urry and Kinge.   HANTS (I.W.).

36–38   Thomas BENSON *v.* Hugh AUCAR (Awgar, Awgarde) and Margaret his wife, executrix, and late the wife of Richard Graye.
Prices of messuages and gardens in Deptford Strand sold by the said Graye, but afterwards bequeathed by him to the said Margaret to sell for the benefit of his children.   KENT.

39   Hugh BENTELEY and Margaret his wife, late the wife of Robert Porter, *v.* William MASSE and Katharine his wife, mother of the said Margaret.
Messuage and land in Longdon (Longisdon) and Leek of the gift of Agnes Stepulton   STAFFORD.

40   Dennis BERISFORD of Brampton *v.* Alice BERISFORD.
Loan to Stephen Berisford, deceased, husband of complainant, and mother of defendant.   DERBY.

41   Laurence BERNARD v. William LYTE, gentleman.
Detention of deeds relating to a barn and fishery in Northover of the demise of Thomas Spencer, late prior of the hospital of St. John the Baptist, Bridgwater.   SOMERSET.

42   William BODELY v. Thomas MERE and Anne his wife, executrix and late the wife of John Stevenson.
Bond given to Alexander Wagge·on behalf of the said Stevenson.   ———

43–46   John, son of John BOND, v. John BENGER, both yeomen.
Messuage in Longcot of the demise of Thomas Braybroke, gentleman.   BERKS.

47–50   John BONDE and Ralph AGAR[DE] v. Henry SUTTON, knight.
Manor of Kelham.   NOTTS.

51   The same v. the same.
Do. *Replication only.*   NOTTS.

52–55   Robert BOSSALL, citizen and brewer of London, and Isabel his wife v. Thomas, son and heir of John TROUGHTON.
Messuages in Richmond and Stockton-upon-Tees, late of Thomas Huntrott, deceased, grandfather of the said Isabel.   YORK, DURHAM.

56   Mary BOURN of Bletchington, co. Oxford, v. Thomas YEARD and others.
Manor of Long Sutton and other lands entailed by John Bourne, late the husband of complainant.   SOMERSET.

57–58   John BOWER v. Thomas COLLARD, yeoman, and Alice his wife.
Detention of deeds relating to a messuage and land in Swingfield, Folkestone, and Elham, late of Robert Bower, yeoman, deceased, father of the said John and Alice.   KENT.

59   John, son and heir of Robert BOWKER, v. Thomas OKES, yeoman.
Messuage, cottage and land in complainant's manor of Flashbrook granted to another Thomas Okes, deceased. *Damaged.*   STAFFORD.

60–61   [John] HAWRDEN, principal of Brasenose College Oxford, and the scholars thereof, v. Stephen and William NYCHOLLES and others, inhabitants of Hinksey.
Meadow called Bassett's Fee in Boetley (*i.e.* Botley in Cumnor?). *Mutilated.* OXFORD (*now* BERKS.)

62–64   Robert BRAYNE of St. James's by Bristol, servant to the Queen,. and Thomas CHESTER of Bristol, merchant, v. Charles MORGAN, gentleman.
Messuages and land in Bristol acquired of Leonard Maleverye of Hanbrook, gentleman, and Elizabeth his wife.   GLOUCESTER.

65–66   Thomas BREDGE and Joan his wife v. Thomas ROMNEY, gentleman.
Detention of a lease made by the dissolved college of Stoke, of lands in Stoke, Ashdon, Birdbrook and Ridgwell (Rodeswell).   ESSEX.

67–69   The same v. Thomas CROPLEY.
Do. *Mutilated.*   ESSEX.

70   Richard BRISHE of Tewkesbury, fisherman, v. Danie PARTE, gentleman.
Frivolous suit. *Injunction.*   GLOUCESTER.

71   Robert BROCAS, esquire, v. Edmund ASSHEPOLE.
Waste in the manor of Little Brickhills, formerly of Henry·Carye, esquire.   BUCKS.

72–73   John BROKE of Kidderminster v. Richard FOXALL of Coventry, merchant.
Action for balance paid to defendant's servant of a debt for goods supplied. WORCESTER, WARWICK.

74   William BROKESBY, gentleman, v. Thomas WYMBERSLEY.
Forgery of a bond for enjoyment of a Crown lease of messuages, mills and land in Breedon, Tongue and Kirby Bellars. *Faded.*   LEICESTER

75–76   Henry BROMELL (Brannell) and Joyce his wife, sister and heir of Richard Morys, v. Howell ap Res BAUGHE.
Messuages and land in the manor of Treport pledged to defendant by the said Morys.   SALOP.

77–79   John BROMLEY v. Robert BROWNE, Joan HOLLYER, late the wife of John Bromley, deceased, son of complainant, and others.
Messuage, cottage and land in Shareshill, late of John Hyll, father-in-law of complainant. STAFFORD.

80–83   Thomas BROOKE v. Christian HUL(S)BUSSHE, merchant of the Hanse, and Dericke (VAN) HASSALL, his factor.
Refusal to execute a defeasance of a bond given on behalf of Henry Couche of Gresley, esquire, which had been corrected after being wrongly drawn.   DERBY.

84   The same v. the same.
Action at common law pending the above suit.   MIDDLESEX.

85   John BROWE, Joan his wife, Nicholas DYKESBECKE, Edith his wife, and Elizabeth COCKE v. Agnes CANON of Southwark.
Inn in Myllane, Ware, late of Thomas Cocke, deceased, father of the female complainants. HERTS.

86–89   John BUCKNALL, husbandman, v. Thomas, son of William BUCKNALL.
Erection of a water-mill in Bucknall so as to drown a coalmine of the demise of the said William and Thomas.   STAFFORD.

90–93   Thomas BUCKWORTH, esquire, King's and Queen's serjeant-at-arms, v. Humphrey LYNGHOKE.
Land in Terrington.   NORFOLK.

94   John BUTLER v. John MARSHALL of Great Tew, co. Oxford, yeoman.
Detention of a lease made by Richard Ingram, esquire, of a messuage and lands in Long Compton, delivered to prevent·the lessor from taking it away.   WARWICK.

95–96   John BUTLER v. John SAMWAYS.
Messuages and lands called Chedington pledged to defendant for money since repaid.   DORSET.

97   William Baker and others, churchwardens of St. James's, BURY ST. EDMUNDS, on behalf of the parishioners, v. Thomas BYRDALL and John GRENEGRESSE, executors of Isabel, executrix, and late the wife of Henry Dauney.
Money bequeathed for the rebuilding of the church.   SUFFOLK.

98–99   Anthony BUSTARD of Adderbury (Alderburie), gentleman, v. Henry COLE, D.D., provost of Eton, and Maurice OWGAN (Hoogan, Augan, Ogan).
Corn-rent of the parsonage of Bloxham, late of the abbess and convent of Godstow. *Answer wanting.*   OXFORD.

100   The same v. the said provost and Roger COKE and Elizabeth his wife, executrix, and late the wife of the said Maurice.
Receiver of the preceding. *Mutilated.*   OXFORD.

FILE 1403.

1   The master and scholars of BALLIOL College, Oxford, v. Robert RICHES, the younger.
Detention of deeds relating to a messuage and land in Wootton, formerly of Robert Riches, the elder.   OXFORD.

2   Robert BARTLE of Strelley (Sturley), co. Notts, v. Robert GYRLING of Harleston, co. Norfolk, and Ellen his wife, executrix, and late the wife of Robert Parmentar.
Judgment debt received by the said Parmenter on complainant's behalf in the court of Eye.
                                                                                   SUFFOLK.

3–4   Anthony BATE and Ellen his wife, late the wife of Robert Lovet, and formerly of Ralph Orcharde of Derby, weaver, v. James ORCHARD, son of the said Ralph.
Messuages, etc., in Derby of the bequest of the said Ralph adjudged to complainant in this court (*suit missing*).   DERBY.

5   William BAWLE v. Henry BAWLE.
Messuage and lands (*described*) in Wellingborough, late of James Bawle, deceased, grandfather of complainant.   NORTHAMPTON.

6–7   William, son and executor of John BAYLEY of Christchurch, v. John LESTER of the same.
Price of cattle.   HANTS.

8   Robert BEALE of Exeter v. Thomas ERLE and others.
Messuage and land at Kennford in Kenn of the grant of Joan Frenche.   DEVON.

9–12   William BELDON, household servant to the Chancellor, v. Edmund DOBSON and Peter HUDLESSE.
'Carres or pittes' of the demise of the Chancellor in 'Yoorke feldes otherwise called Nonne Feldes,' in the county of the city of York.   YORK.

13–17   William BELL, vicar of Kirkburn, v. Robert SMALWOOD, parson of Foxholes, Gilber. WARTER (Walter), and William SYGSTON.
Detention of deeds relating to a messuage and lands in Battleburn and Tibthorpe.   YORK.

18   Thomas BERRIE v. William BENNETT.
Detention of deeds relating to land in South Somercotes of the grant of William Langton, gentleman.   LINCOLN.

19–20   John BLACKGREVE and William SMYTHE v. Thomas OSBORNE.
Spoons and other household goods of Thomas Smythe, deceased, brother of the said William and of Alice, wife of the said John.   NOTTS.

21   John BLAKEMAN of Barton v. Edmund BAWDON.
Messuage and land in Bradley, late of Roger Blakeman, deceased, father of complainant. STAFFORD.

22–23   Jerome BLITHE of Norton and Anne his wife, daughter of Isabel Eare, deceased, v. Godfrey BOSEVILL and others.
Manor of Oxspring (Oxbringe) and messuages, lands and mills there and in Thurlestone by Birchworth, Cudworth, Orthwate, Darton and Brierly. *See File 1194, No. 39.*   YORK.

24–25   Gilbert Smyth and others, in the name of all the inhabitants of BOWTON v. Francis INGOLSBYE.
Common in the lordship of Lenborough claimed by complainants as tenants of the manor of Bourton and of the Castle manor in Buckingham.   BUCKINGHAM.

26–29   Peter BOWDEN and Joan his wife, daughter of Margery Palmer, v. John BOROUGH.
Lands in Northam of the grant of William Hyllyngs.   DEVON.

30–32   Elizabeth, daughter of John BOWMAN, v. Christopher FLETCHER of Cambridge.
Messuage and land in West Wratting.   CAMBRIDGE.

33–34   Edmund BRADOCK, gentleman, v. Henry, son and heir of Henry MALKYN.
Messuage and land at Over Longsdon in Leek late of Francis Bradock, esquire, deceased, grandfather of complainant.   STAFFORD.

35–38   Henry, son and heir of William BRECKNALL, v. William WYLLS.
Wrongful occupation of a messuage and land in Harberton, enticing away complainant's apprentice and frivolous suit.   DEVON, CORNWALL.

39   Richard BREDENAY (?) v. John CHECHESTER, esquire.
Refusal to complete a lease of land in Great Torrington. *Damaged.*   DEVON.

40–46   Isabel BRERETON, late the wife of Humphrey Vernon of Hodnet, esquire, deceased, v. Mary, late the wife of George VERNON, esquire, son and heir of the said Humphrey, and William COTTON of Cotton, esquire.
Manor of Rowton *alias* Rowlton and messuages, lands, a water-mill, a horse-mill and rent there and in Elwardyne (*i.e.* Ellerdine in High Ercall) and Longford. *See File* 1080, *No.* 67.   SALOP.

47–48   Thomas BREWER, parson of Lyng, v. George GRANGE and Michael DUNNYNG, executors of Richard Dunnyng, late parson.
Dilapidations.   NORFOLK.

49–52   John BRIDGEWATER, parson of Yelling, v. Christopher TYE, Mus. Doc.
Parsonage of Yelling.   HUNTINGDON.

53–54   The same v. Christopher TYE, gentleman.
Demise of the said parsonage.   HUNTINGDON.

55–60   Robert BROCKE, late dean of the dissolved college of Burton-on-Trent, v. Robert MOWER (Mooer), late one of his prebendaries.
Account as complainant's deputy.   STAFFORD.

61   Margaret, late the wife of William BROWNE, and daughter and heir of William Hastings and of Margaret his wife, v. Nicholas JAGGES.
Messuage and land in Corpusty of the bequest of William Neale, clerk.   NORFOLK.

62   Roger BROWNE v. Edward THORNTON, husbandman.
Rye and money entrusted to defendant.   ————

63   Robert BROWNELOWE, yeoman, v. Humphrey STORER and Arthur EYRE.
Rights of way to a messuage and land in Trusley.   DERBY.

64   Richard BROWNSWORDE, late of London, woolwinder, v. John DALTON.
Detention of deeds relating to an inn called the *Lyon* and land in Farningham.   LONDON.

65–67   Nicholas BRYCKELBANKE of Manningtree, merchant, v. John BOROUGH and Richard COLE.
Execution on a bond for conveyance of lands in Little Bromley and a messuage in Manningtree under an order in bankruptcy, which conveyance was delayed at defendant's own request. D. XII, 45.   ESSEX.

68–69   Eleanor BRYTT v. George MYDDILTON, gentleman.
Settlement of lands and services in Mells, Chilton, Yeovil (Evell), Henford by Yeovil (Hynford), Kingston Montague, Dinnington and East Coker, promised on the marriage of George, son of defendant, with Alice, daughter of complainant. *Mutilated.*   SOMERSET.

70–73   Philip BUDSIDE and Margery his wife v. John son and heir of Robert KYLYOWE.
Detention of deeds relating to the manor of Lansalloes and one-fourth of messuages and lands there.   CORNWALL.

74–76   John BULL v. William COVE, gentleman, steward of the manor of Boulge.
Fabrication of buttals of land in Burgh, complainant being tenant of lands there both within and without the said manors.   SUFFOLK.

77   John BOWMAN, citizen and pewterer of London, v. Richard DAVERS and Frances his wife.
Messuage and land late held of the manor of Barton by Timothy Rowdon of London, gentleman.   GLOUCESTER.

FILE 1404.

1–3   Walter BABYNGTON of Ottery St. Mary, gentleman, v. Harry, son and heir of Thomas STYLE and of Joan his wife, uncle and aunt of complainant.
Refusal to complete a purchase of one-third of a messuage and land at Larkbeare in Talaton.   DEVON.

4–5   Roger BAGULEY and Elizabeth his wife v. Robert PHILPOTTES.
Rectory of Lynton of the demise of the prior of the late 'house of Jesu of Bethleem of Shene.' *Mutilated.*   [HEREFORD.]

6–8   Thomas, son and heir of William BAKER, v. Thomas MILDMAY, esquire.
Lands held of the manors of Howards and Stranges in East Walton, which manor defendant claims under a Crown lease alleged by complainant to be invalid.   NORFOLK.

9–12   William BANKES of Rotherham, ironmonger, v. Nicholas ROBYNSON and John WYLFOURTH, executors of Thomas Robynson of Eckington, scythe-smith.
Debt for 'syxe hundreth spruse iron,' *See No.* 78.   YORK, DERBY.

13–14   John BARBAR and John WYNCHE v. John CAUNFELD.
Refusal to complete a sale of barley. *Mutilated.*   BEDFORD.

15   John BARBER, gentleman, v. Robert BARNEFELD of Newport, co. [Salop].
Detention of deeds relating to the manor of Flashbrook, etc. *Mutilated.*   STAFFORD.

16–17   John BARBOR of Flashbrook, esquire, v. William STAUNFORD, esquire.
Destruction of boundaries between defendant's own lands in Rowley and others let to him by complainant.   STAFFORD.

18–20   William BARKROFTE and Agnes his wife, daughter and heir of John Marshall v. Thomas HOLMES.
Detention of deeds relating to a messuage (described by defendant) in Stow by Quy (Stokequy).   CAMBRIDGE.

21-23   John BARNEY, esquire, v. Edward SPANYE.
Detention of an award between defendant and the inhabitants of Langley in a dispute concerning
common. *Mutilated.*   NORFOLK.

24   William son and heir of John BARTON v. John BARTON.
Detention of deeds relating to a messuage and land in Foxearth.   ESSEX.

25   Robert BAYLYE v. Roland BACKHOUSE of Hathern, clerk.
Frivolous suit in this court for the chantry house of Stretton Parva, wherein complainant has
spent 20s., being half his substance.   LEICESTER.

26   William BEESTON, ale-brewer, v. John BROWNINGE.
Judgment debt concerning houses in Bermondsey (Barmsey, Bramsey) Street, already compounded for.   SURREY.

27-31   Robert, son of Robert BELAMY, deceased, v. Joan BELAMY, late the wife of the said
Robert, and William MOTLEY, administrators of his goods.
Debt due to the said Robert and cancelled by him.   [NOTTS?]

32-34   Christopher BELL and Thomas LAURENCE, his surety, v. the sheriffs of LONDON and
William MOSYER.
Action for price of goods not supplied up to the agreed value. *Certiorari and subpœna.* LONDON.

35   Joan BENNETT v. Richard BUSSHE.
Crown lease of a messuage and land at Penquite in St. Germans. *Damaged.*   CORNWALL.

36-37   Humphrey BENTLEY v. Alice BELL and others.
[Detention of deeds relating to] tenements in Derby and of household goods. *Faded.*   DERBY.

38   John BERNE v. Thomas COWPER.
Detention of deeds relating to messuages, gardens and buildings in Norwich.   NORFOLK.

39-42   Arthur son of William BETELCOMBE v. John SCREVEN and Richard GODARD,
executors of the said William.
Legacy payable at complainant's majority.   ———

43-44   John BLACKALL of Exeter, merchant, v. John COURTNEY, gentleman.
Tin, an action of trover for which is impossible because it is no longer in defendant's hands. DEVON.

45-49   Godfrey BLACKSHAWE and John NEWBOLD v. Bridget, late the wife of Dennis
BERESFORDE.
Promise to indemnify complainants as sureties of Richard Berysford of Chesterfield, gentleman,
brother of the said Dennis.   DERBY.

50-56   Thomas BLENKENSOP of Holbecke, esquire, and Stephen NEVYNZON of Canterbury,
D.C.L., v. Robert DALSTON (Dauston), gentleman, Thomas KENDALL and Leonard
DENT.
Tithe, corn and buildings in King's Meaburn of the demise of William, late abbot of York, and his
convent. (The said Dalston pleads that the lease is void by Act of Parliament and of tenements
not usually leased.)   WESTMORLAND.

57   James BRANDE v. John RYCHEMAN, yeoman.
Pulling down the chapel of Bistern which defendant had contracted to repair if complainant would
obtain a priest for it from William [Herbert], Earl of Pembroke.   HANTS.

58-61   John BRAY and Eleanor his wife, daughter and heir of Nicholas Burges, v. Elizabeth
DOWE.
Detention of death relating to land (*described*) in Burgh.   NORFOLK.

62-63   Walter BRIGHT v. William HAMOND and William FELD, executors of William Harty-
stonge.
Shipment of corn at Blakeney creek. *Mutilated.*   NORFOLK.

64-68   Anne BRIGHTMAN v. Joan, late the wife of Richard ELLYS.
Detention of deeds relating to lands in Stebbing.   ESSEX.

69-70   John BROCKETT, knight, v. William HAMOND, gentleman.
Rent payable out of land in Lenton to complainant's manor of Brockett Hall *alias* Appylton Hall.
                                                                                      YORK.

71   Thomas BUCHER v. William TOMPSON.
Water-mill and land in the manor of Ramsbury claimed under rival leases from the Earl of
Pembroke and the late Duke of Somerset.   WILTS.

72   William BURNE the elder of Brewood, son and heir of John Burne, v. William· BURNE
the younger, and John COKE.
Detention of deeds and heriots relating to a messuage and land in Congreve (in Penkridge).
                                                                                      STAFFORD.

73-77   John BURROWES v. Reynold ROBOTHAM and Alice his wife, executrix, and late the
wife of John Heathcote.
Price of oxen sold to Richard Heathcote of Kirkby-in-Ashfield, father of the said John Heathcote.
                                                                                      NOTTS.

78-81   John BURROWES of Southburn (Brome), scythe-smith, v. Nicholas ROBYNSON and
John WILFOURTH, executors of Thomas Robynson of Eckington.
Debt for 'amyse iron' and steel, and loan. *See No. 9.*   YORK, DERBY.

82–88 . William and Robert BUSTYNG *v.* James BOLEYN, knight, John, a son and executor of Robert HARWARD of Booton (Bowton), and Richard ALLYSON.
Mill in the said Sir James's manor of Cawston pledged for a debt to the said Robert. *See File* 1196, *No. 67.* NORFOLK.

89 Margery BYLLYNGES of Calais, administratrix of the goods of Cornelius Byllynges, deceased, *v.* William HORNER, executor of Owen Horner, bailiff of Shoreham.
Balance of a debt. *Mutilated.* SUSSEX.

FILE 1405.

1–2 Joan, late the wife of William BACON and daughter of Thomas Olyver, *v.* Richard HAYTER, husbandman.
Tenement in the manor of Britford (Burford) of the demise of the late Earl of Huntingdon. WILTS.

3 John BACON *v.* William PAGE, his stepfather and guardian, and others.
Land in Drinkstone, late of John Bacon of Hessett, deceased, father of complainant. SUFFOLK.

4 Bartholomew BAILLE of Peterborough, co. Northants, and Agnes his wife *v.* William BRIDGE and Henry SKELYS of Pickering Lythe.
Cottage and land at Ruston in Wykeham, late of Ralph Hartley, deceased, grandfather of the said Agnes. YORK.

5 John BAKER *v.* [William LYGHT].
Hindrance of a compromise with the dean and chapter of Wells concerning the wardship of Thomas Norton, stepson of complainant, and of his manor of Stathe, with its appurtenances in Stathe, Saltmoor (within Stoke St. Gregory) and Andersley. *Damaged. See D.* IX, 71. [SOMERSET.]

6 Lawrance BAKER of South Stoneham *v.* John SEARLE, steward of the manor of Stone, and Agnes, late the wife of Walter BAKER of Southampton.
Land in Fawley held of the said manor by grant of the said Walter. HANTS.

7–8 Paul BALE and Agnes his wife, late the wife of Jeffrey Hobb, *v.* John GEFFORD, esquire, and Thomas HOBB, son of the said Jeffrey and Agnes.
Messuages and lands called Bremridge Barton (in South Molton) of the demise of John Coblegh, esquire, and others to the said Jeffrey, Agnes and Thomas. DEVON.

9–11 Richard BALLARDE, yeoman, *v.* Thomas FELTON, gentleman, husband of Jean, late the wife of William Shelton.
Right of way to land in Stanford Rivers and High Ongar of the successive demise of the said William and Joan. ESSEX.

12 Robert BALLARDE *v.* Nicholas BALLARDE.
Attempt to cut off an entail made by Clement Ballarde, father of both parties, of the manor of Horton by Chartham and Sappington (in Petham) and lands in Chartham and Petham. KENT.

13 John BANBURY *v.* John PECK and Anne his wife, late the wife of John Smyth of Winchelsea.
Debt of John Crane, gentleman, promised to complainant in lieu of his interest in the will of the said Smyth. SUSSEX.

14 Henry BANKES, vicar of South Petherton, *v.* John COLLYENS (Cullyns) of the same, mercers.
Vicarage of South Petherton, of the demise of Thomas Hooper, late vicar deprived. SOMERSET.

15 Thomas BARKLEY, scholar of Westminster, *v.* Richard LYSTER, esquire, son and heir of Richard Lyster, knight.
Lease of the manor of Dinedor to William Barkley, deceased, father of complainant. HEREFORD.

16 Richard BARNARDE, husbandman, *v.* Richard his father, Henry BODDENHAM of Wilton, esquire, and Thomas FELTHAM of Fovant.
Messuage and land in Kingston Deverell, demised by the said Henry to the said Richard and Richard jointly. *See D.* XV, 49. WILTS.

17 Beatrice, executrix and late the wife of Richard BASEDEN, *v.* Richard COPPINGER, gentleman, executor of Thomasyn, executrix and late the wife of Ralph Symondes, citizen and fishmonger of London.
Action on a bond intended for warranty of a lease by William Lorde, citizen and fishmonger of London, of a tenement, wharf, garden and pond in Stewside in St. Margaret's, Southwark.
SURREY.

18 Robert BATELL *v.* Henry FORTESKEWE, esquire. .
Pasture in Witham and lands held of defendant's manor of Bluntishall. ESSEX.

19–25 Thomas BAYLYE and Margaret his wife, executors of William Trust, late her husband, *v.* Lettice, late the wife of Thomas NEWSOM and formerly of William Trust, and Thomas TRUST.
Loan of the manor of Maidwell. NORTHAMPTON.

26 Cuthbert BAYNEBRIGE *v.* William WILSON and James PEKE.
Tenements in Middelton of the feoffment of Thomas Maynard. DURHAM.

27–28 Christopher BAYRD *v.* William and Elizabeth DENT and others.
Detention of deeds relating to messuages and lands in Tealby (Tuelbye). LINCOLN.

29 . John BEARE, husbandman, *v.* Thomas CLEMENT.
Messuage and land in Harton in Hartland. DEVON.

I 2

30–31   John BEDYLL, citizen and tallow-chandler of London, v. William BREYNWOOD of London, scrivener.
Detention of deeds entrusted to Edward Breynwood (Brentwood) of London, scrivener, deceased, concerning a messuage in Thames Street, in the parish of St. Magnus.   ·   LONDON.

32–33   Christopher BELLINGE v. John HALKE.
Refusal to complete a sale of land in Hastingleghe. *Damaged.*   [KENT.]

34–35   William BENNET of Swineshead v. John PARKER of Lincoln and William SYMSON.
Land in Sutterton, late of John Parker of Boston, deceased, kinsman of complainant and the said John.   LINCOLN.

36   John BENTON v. Thomas GREVE.
Meadow in King's Norton of the demise of Thomas Myddelmore, gentleman.   WORCESTER.

37   Robert, son and heir of Nicholas BERNET and of Denise his wife, v. John SAXPES.
Land formerly held of the manor of Warbleton by William Stokke.   SUSSEX.

38   William BLACKENDEN, Millicent his wife, Edward CRAYFORD, Mary his wife, Arthur CHOWTE and Elizabeth his wife v. Philip CHOWTE, esquire.
Detention of deeds relating to the manor of Thornton *alias* Bartletts (in St. Nicholas at Wade), Northolme, North Ryckett, and Madford (in Hemyock), and a messuage and lands in the manor of Mekynbroke (in Chislett, Herne and Hoath) and Madford, late of Henry Lee, esquire, deceased, father of the female complainant.   ·   KENT, SOMERSET, DEVON.

39–41   The inhabitants of BLACKFRIARS v. Thomas CAWARDEN, knight.
Occupation of the church of St. Anne's, first to show King Henry VIII'S ' pavylyons, maskes and revelles,' and then for defendant's private profit. *Damaged.*   LONDON.

42–45   Agnes BLANNEY of London, late the wife of Hugh Blanney, v. William NEWALL.
Detention of a lease of pasture in Shrewsbury and dilapidations.   (The answer appears to belong to another suit.)   SALOP.

46   The same v. the same.
Do. and lease of a messuage in Fish Street, Shrewsbury.   SALOP.

47   William BOLLES, esquire, Crown receiver, of cos. Notts, Derby and Chester, v. [Richard WHALLEY, esquire?]
Account as receiver of four bailiwicks. *Mutilated.*   NOTTS.

48   Elizabeth, late the wife of John BOLTON of Rochester, deceased, and administratrix of his goods, v. Michael BOLTON of Bolton Hill and William PRICE of Haverfordwest (Hereford West).
Lease in reversion from the master and fellows of Christ's College, Cambridge, of the rectory of Manorbier.   PEMBROKESHIRE.

49–54   William BOOTE of Alfreton v. Robert BROKE, esquire, Lady SHEFYLDE, his wife, William HOLLYS, knight, Thomas ZACHEVERELL, gentleman, and others.
Parsonage of Blackwell and land claimed by the said Zacheverell as the site of a coal-mine whereof he has a Crown lease.   DERBY.

55   Thomas BORNE, Joan his wife, Alice ALEYN, Mary . . . , and Edward B . . . . and Elizabeth his wife v. Robert ABERGE.
Reviver of a suit by John Aleyn, deceased, father of the said Joan, Alice and Elizabeth, and grandfather of the said Mary, for a messuage and land held of Lord Dacre's manor of Old Court. *Damaged.*   SURREY.

56   William BORNE and Joan his wife v. John BRENDON, esquire, and Anne his wife.
Refusal to complete a lease of a messuage and land at Nutley in Tavistock.   DEVON.

57–59   Richard BOSTOCKE, yeoman, son of Richard Bostocke, v. Ralph DUTTON, esquire, and others.
Messuages, cottages, land, mills and fishery in Tattenhall of the demise of John Audley, Lord Audley.   CHESTER.

60–63   Joan, executrix, and late the wife of Hugh BOWDE of Lichfield v. Mark WYRLEY and Nicholas BOYD (Birde).
Lease of Darnford mill and lands in Lichfield to all parties jointly by John Sandland, chantry priest of St. Katherine's chapel in Lichfield Cathedral.   STAFFORD.

64   Anthony BOWES of Boston [co. Lincoln], merchant, v. the mayor and sheriffs of LONDON and Richard YONGE, citizen and grocer of London.
Action of account as deputy to the said Yonge in the common packership of cloths, wool and fells in London, after withdrawing complainant's account book. *Certiorari and subpœna.*   LONDON.

65–68   Ralph BOWRYNGE v. Henry and Agnes B(E)YRDE.
Detention of deeds relating to a messuage cottage and land in Shenstone and ' the ' Wall.   STAFFORD.

69   Roland BRAMTON v. Richard JOHNSON.
Information of export of salt hides from Beaumaris contrary to the statute 27 Henry VIII, c. 14.   ANGLESEA.

70–71   Elizabeth BRANDON of Halstead (in Stixwould), co. Lincoln, late the wife of Charles Brandon, knight, and formerly of James Strangways, of West Hawlsey, knight, v. George GENRAYES, gentleman.
Rent issuing from defendant's manor of Bilton.   YORK.

72–75   George BREDYMAN and Edith his wife v. Thomas TYRINGHAM, esquire.
Close in Hinwick belonging to complainant's manor of Puddington. D. XV, 39.   BEDFORD.

76–77   Thomas BRENT of Stoke [Climsland] v. John HYLL, his tenant-at-will.
Lands, rents and services in St. Teath bought of John Vowler and Jane his wife. *2 bills.*
CORNWALL.

78–81   John BRODE and Joan his wife, daughter and heir of John Trecarell v. Stephen IVE, Joan
his wife, John SYMM, John BROWNE the younger, and Joan his wife.
Messuages and lands called Worthy Penpeth in Tintagel (now in Lanteglos), claimed in right of
Thomas Hendre. *Pedigree in answer.*
CORNWALL.

82   .   John BROKE v. George PRESTON.
Forgery and other fraud relating to a messuage and lands of William, brother of complainant, in
Enfield, Edmu[n]dsey (in Gosfield) and Cheston. *Mutilated.*   MIDDLESEX, ESSEX, HERTS.

83   Robert BROKEBANKE, gentleman, v. William CODYNGTON.
Messuage and land in Coleby.
LINCOLN.

84   Richard BROMYCHE of Castle Bromwich, co. Warwick, administrators of the goods of
John his brother, deceased, v. Margaret DERBY and Nicholas BROMYCHE (Bromesdych).
Legacy of John Bromyche, father of complainant and husband of the said Margaret, land in
Bromsgrove and goods of the said John.
WORCESTER.

85–89   Humphrey BROWN, knight, J.C.P., executor of William Compton, knight, v. Edward
GREVILL, knight, and Abraham his grandson.
Manor of Goldicote and lands, rents and services there and in Aldermarston (*i.e.* Alderminster,
co. Worcester?), bought by the said Sir Edward and alienated before payment.
WARWICK [WORCESTER?]

90   The same v. the same.
Power of the manor of Goldicote. *Mutilated.*
WARWICK.

91–92   Richard BROWNE v. William and Edward, sons of James STEPER, deceased.
Windmill, water-mill and profits of fairs and markets in Kirton-in-Lindsey of the demise of the
widow of Thomas, Lord Burgh.
LINCOLN.

93   Robert BROWNE of Rampton, co. Notts, yeoman, v. George WHYTE.
Messuages in Micklegate and Skeldergate, York, formerly of Christopher Tomlynson, deceased,
ancestor of complainant. *Pedigree given.*
YORK.

94–95   Thomas BRYNTON v. Richard LEGGE, bailiff of Wenlock.
Failure to make return to a writ of error, complainant having deposited the sum in dispute with
him.
SALOP.

96   .John BUCKLAND, gentleman, v. Nicholas, James, and Thomas FRANCES, and Robert
GOODWYN, husbandman.
Tithe, corn and a tenement in Martock with goods and deeds late of Richard Buckland, gentleman,
deceased, uncle of complainant, and stepfather of the said Nicholas, James and Thomas.
SOMERSET.

97   Thomas BUCKNOLL of Ubberley in Hanley (Ubleye), gentleman, v. Francis CRADOCKE
of Bucknall, yeoman.
Watercourse passing through land in Stoke late of William Bucknoll, father of complainant.
STAFFORD.

98   Robert BUNELL and Robert HOLBECK, citizens of London, v. James DAVERES.
Tenements in St. Dunstan's-in-the-West of the grant of Elizabeth Daveres, some time the wife of
Thomas Holbecke, deceased, father of the said Robert. *Mutilated.*   LONDON.

99   William BURMAN, yeoman, v. Alexander WYLSON, yeoman.
Rent of a messuage (*described*) in Royston of the demise of Thomas Lee, gentleman, defendants
having purchased the reversion.   CAMBRIDGE or HERTS.

100–102   Joan BURRYTTE v. Thomas WOTHERWYKE, yeoman.
Goods of complainant acquired by defendants during her illness.   ———

103   Alice BURTON of Loftmarish (in Pickering), late the wife of Roger Burton, v. Stephen
HOLFORD, gentleman.
Abduction of complainant's daughter. *Mutilated.*   YORK, CHESTER

104   Henry BUXTON, Thomas SHERIFF and Joan his wife v. John son and heir of John
THOMPSON of Boothby, and Leonard BROWNE, executor of John Browne of Skinnand.
Legacy of Henry Buxton, grandfather of the said Henry and Joan, whose executors were the said
John and John.
LINCOLN.

105–108   Henry BYRCHE, gentleman, v. Roger BARBOUR of Luton and John BARTON of Egginton, yeomen.
Action on a bond for a debt, the original amount and the amount paid being in dispute. . BEDFORD.

FILE 1406.

1   Richard BABACOMBE, by John Babacombe his guardian, v. Richard BABACOMBE his
uncle.
Messuage and land in Buckland Brewer, late of John Babacombe, deceased, grandfather of complainant.   [DEVON.]

2   Stephen BABBE of Chadleigh v. John THORNE and Thomasyn his wife.
Goods, including a ' spete basyn,' of the bequest of Richard Babbe, father of complainant, whose
executors are the said Stephen and Thomasyn.   DEVON.

3   Guy BABTHORPE, esquire, v. Robert CUNNYNWORTHE, Joan his wife and others.
Detention of deeds relating to the manor of Drakes (in Middle Rasen). *See File 1410, No. 1.*
LINCOLN.

4   Robert BACKEHOWSE of Andover, co. Hants, v. John [NEVILL], Lord Latimer.
Messuage and land. *Mutilated.*   WESTMORLAND.

5   James BADELEY v. William BRODEHERST.
Price of two geldings, the bond for which was stolen from complainant.   STAFFORD.

6   Beatrice, executrix and late the wife of Thomas BAKER, gentleman, v. John SKYLLE.
Lease of the parsonage of Great Dunmow.   ESSEX.

7-9   Edward BAKER and Rose [his wife?] v. Margery, late the wife of John FOSTER.
Debt of George Pekham paid to the said John. *Mutilated.*   ————

10   Alice BALL v. George COSTERDYNE and Thomas LEE.
Messuage and land in Dorrington in the lordship of Whitchurch, late of Richard Ball, deceased,
father of complainant.   SALOP.

11   John BALLARD, husbandman, v. George SAMON.
Messuage and land in the manor of Salford Abbots of the demise of the late abbot and convent
of Evesham.   WARWICK.

12-13 Thomas BARBOUR v. Ralph BARBOUR and William and James HALL.
Messuage called Grindsbrook (Grymesbroke) in Edale, with lands (*described*) and rights of common
held on a joint loan by complainant and the said William and James.   DERBY.

14-16 Robert BARKER v. Jerome SONGER, gentleman.
Messuages, lands and cattle belonging to Janett Chyld's chantry in Witham.   [ESSEX.]

17   John son of Peter BARNARD v. William CARTER.
Detention of deeds relating to a messuage and land in Wickham St. Paul and Gestingthorpe.
                                                                  ESSEX.

18   John BARNARDISTON v. Robert WYNDE, executor of John Wynde.
Frauds with regard to a bond given by complainant for a debt of the said John Wynde to Christopher
Miller, already in dispute in this court   (*File* 1408, *No.* 9.) *Injunction and dissolution of injunction.*

19-21 Hugh BARNESBY v. Christian, late the wife of Thomas PLEYER, and Griffin CURTEIS,
steward of Sherston Magna.
Messuage and land in the said manor of the demise of Anne, duchess of Somerset.   WILTS.

22-24 William, younger son and heir of William BASELEY, v. Robert BROWNE.
Messuage and land in the manor of East Knoyle, claimed by defendant as forfeited by complainant's
mother through remarriage without licence.   WILTS.

25   William BASSET, esquire, grandson and heir of entail of William Basset, v. Helen BASSET,
his father's wife.
Manor of Mey[nell Langley?], held of the manor of Ekyngton. *Mutilated.*   [DERBY.]

26-27 George BATEMAN v. Thomas and Margaret BATEMAN.
Contempt of an arbitral award concerning an unexecuted draft will of Thomas Bateman of Flinton
South Elmham (*sic*), esquire, deceased, father of all parties.   SUFFOLK.

28   Robert BATTELL and Richard MAPLE, gentlemen, v. Edmund ATKINSON *alias*
Somersett.
Manor of the Barbican and houses in St. Botolph's without Aldersgate of the demise of Charles
[Brandon], late Duke of Suffolk, and Katharine his wife. *Mutilated.*   LONDON.

29   Geoffrey BAYLYE, clerk, v. John POPE, claiming to be vicar-general of the Archbishop
of Canterbury in the diocese of Lincoln, and Peter LEE.
Refusal to institute complainant on a Crown presentation to the church of Welton by Louth.
                                                                  LINCOLN.

30   Richard BELL v. Matthew BOOLE.
14a. land in Aslackby, late of Richard Bell, deceased, father of complainant.   LINCOLN.

31-32 The same v. the same.
16a. like land. (Defendant pleads a decree in the former suit.)   LINCOLN.

33   [The same?] v. . . .
Lands in Greyby and Asklaby, late of John Barrett of Theralby and others. *Mutilated Bill wanting.*
                                                               [LINCOLN.]

34   John BENGEMYN, citizen of Norwich, v. Agnes SOTHERTON of the same.
Action for a loan which had been compromised on account of the fall of money.   NORFOLK.

35   Stephen BENNET and Mark OLYVER, burgesses and late bailiffs of Launceston, v. John
ANDREWES.
Action for debt for the escape of Richard Carlyan from the custody of complainants' successors
after having been brought to hear mass. *Commission and injunction.*   CORNWALL.

36-41 Richard BENNYS of Larling, co. Norfolk, husbandman, grandson and heir of John Bennys,
v. John STARKE (Storke).
Detention of deeds relating to land (*described*) in Dallinghoo. *2 suits.*   SUFFOLK.

42-44 The same v. William, son and heir of William GARDENER.
Do.   SUFFOLK.

45   Francis BERTYE of Hackney v. John LYTTELTON.
Instalment of debt for leases and goods which defendant had been ordered by the Chancellor to
pay. *Mutilated.*   MIDDLESEX, WORCESTER.

46-47 Edward BEVERLEY, gentleman, v. Richard and William PHILLIPSON.
Messuages and land in Worlaby, late of John Beverley of Elsham, gentleman, deceased, father of
complainant.   LINCOLN.

48 Roger BLAKEWAY v. William CHURCHE and others.
Messuage and land in Huntington of the demise of the late prior and convent of Wenlock. SALOP.

49 William BLAKEY of Rye v. the Lord Warden and Admiral of [the CINQUE PORTS].
Imprisonment by William Crispe, esquire, lieutenant of Dover castle and vice-admiral of the said ports, at the suit of John Lambertson and others, Dutchmen. *Corpus cum causa. Damaged.*
KENT.

50 John BLAKGRAVE, Alice his wife, and William and John SMYTHE v. William HAKE and others.
Leasehold, messuages and lands in Barrow-on-Trent and Milton of the bequest of Edmund Smyth, yeoman. DERBY.

51 Thomas BLOUNTE v. John WILSON, parson of Colton.
Price of a gelding. STAFFORD.

52-53 Henry BODELEY of Westminster v. John FORD.
Land in Norton Woodhouse, late of Thomas Bodeley, deceased, father of complainant. STAFFORD.

54-58 William BOLLES v. George PETYTE and Bonaventure BOLLES.
Parsonage of Attenborough (Adenburgh), late of the priory of Felley. *Mutilated.* D. XV, 2. *Two answers, one appearing to belong to another suit.* NOTTS.

59-62 Humphrey BONEVILLE, gentleman, v. William, son of Hugh FOUNTAYN of Ugborough, gentleman.
Right of way from a messuage, mill and land of complainant in Ivybridge to Ermington church.
DEVON,

63 Nicholas BONYFANT, clerk, v. William, James and Robert BROCKE, executors of Thomas Canydyne, parson of Blaby.
Wages for serving the chapel of Countesthorpe. LEICESTER.

64 William BOWDEN *alias* Yeo v. John BROCKEDON.
Money and goods hidden in a bucket and entrusted to defendant during the rebellion in the west.

———

65 Richard BOYCE of Boxley, co. Kent, and Margaret [his wife], sister and heir of Ralph Bellingham, esquire, v. Richard ELDRYNGTON, Thomas BELLINGHAM, gentleman, born in Flanders, and others.
Manors of Thakeham, Charflete, Clothall (in West Grinstead), Lyminster and Covertes, and lands in Thakeham, Sullington, West Grinstead, Clayton (in Sullington?), Heckingfelde, Lyminster, Wyke, Littlehampton, Preston and Arundel. *Mutilated.* *See File* 1407, *No.* 27. SUSSEX.

66 John BRACE and others v. George NEWPORT, bailiff of Droitwich.
Contempt of a decree concerning bullaries of salt water and a wood called Owood. WORCESTER.

67 Thomas BRACEBRYDGE, esquire, v. the sheriffs of LONDON and Mary, late the wife of John CRYMES of Wetton, and Thomas MOUNTGOMERY of London, clothworker.
Action for plate pledged and redeemed on behalf of defendant by George Griffyth of Wichnor, knight. *Certiorari and subpoena.* LONDON, STAFFORD.

68 The same v. John NETHERMYLL, executor of Julyne Nethermyll.
Waste of lands in Kingsbury occupied by defendant on a writ of *elegit* for a debt now satisfied.
See File 1291, *No.* 51. WARWICK.

69-72 George BRADSHAWE v. Anthony ABELL and Elizabeth his wife, mother of complainant.
Half the manor of Orton-on-the-Hill, with other lands and goods, settled on complainant on his marriage with Francis, daughter of Roger Fowke. LEICESTER, WARWICK.

73-75 Thomas BRADSHAWE v. James FERYBY.
Sale of a horse at Barton [-on-Humber?] belonging to Dr. Ramridge, dean of Lichfield. *Mutilated.*
[LINCOLN?]

76 Robert BRAYTHEWAIT v. John GODWEN and John DAYE.
Crown lease of tithes of ' the barre ' of Luston. HEREFORD (' HARTFORD ').

77-78 John BREWER of Springfield, shereman, v. George COKKERELL, parson of Springfield.
Land in Springfield, late of John Brewer, deceased, father of complainant. ESSEX.

79 Charles BROCAS(?) v. John GUNNELL and others.
Seizure of money and goods at Waresley (Waseley). *Faded.* HUNTINGDON.

80-81 Robert, son of Robert BROKKYLSBEE of Glentworth (Glentford), and of Isabel his wife, v. John BATTEE.
Messuage and land in Blyton. LINCOLN.

82-85 Valentine BROWNE of London, esquire, v. Roger NABBE and others.
Wetley Moor and Milne Herne, portions of complainant's manor of (Leek) Frith. STAFFORD.

86 John BUDE of Winchester and Elizabeth his wife v. Thomas PERY.
Rent of a house in Whitchurch bequeathed to the said Elizabeth with lands there by Robert Botrell, her father. HANTS.

87 John BULL of Sproughton, co. Suffolk, yeoman, v. Henry DAYENS and John WOODE.
Dispute about a horse in the *Lion* inn at Esterforde (*i.e.* Easterfield). *Faded.* ESSEX.

88 John BULL v. William LAWRENCE.
Messuage and land in Sprowton. *Mutilated.* [SUFFOLK.]

89 John BULLEN of Colnbrook v. William and Ellen, children and executors of Alice WYDNAM of the same.
Action on a bond for payment of an annuity to the said Alice and of debts of other persons (*described*). BUCKINGHAM.

90-92   Thomas BURRYNG (Burren) of Huycke (*i.e.* Highweek?) *v.* John, nephew and heir of
John KNYGHT, and John, son and heir of Robert SCOBLE.
Messuage and land in Dartington.   DEVON.

93   John BURTON, labourer, *v.* Robert BURTON, 'naymed to be the sonne of your sayd
orator.'
Cottage in Laceby conveyed to defendant on a promise to provide for him during his life. LINCOLN.

94   John BURTON, gentleman, executor of Nicholas Fetherstonehaugh of Deeping Gate, co.
Northants, gentleman, *v.* Michael FETHERSTONHAUGH, gentleman.
Price of a leasehold and hay at Newland in Stanhope.   DURHAM.

95   Ralph BURTON *v.* Edward ALTHAM and Fortune his wife, executrix, and late the wife of
Thomas Fowle.
Messuages (*described*) in St. Margaret's, Lothbury, of the demise of the master and fellows of Jesus
College, Cambridge.   LONDON.

96   Nicholas BUTLER *v.* Thomas and Joan BUTLER.
Manor of Alrewas, late complainant's grandparents, William Butler and Joan his wife, daughter
and heir of Thomas Youxall.   STAFFORD.

97   Richard BUTTES and Maude his wife, late the wife of John Hoberde, *v.* Thomas TOWER.
Action on a bond given by the said Maude on a promise of marriage by defendant. *Mutilated.*

98   Robert BYDDELL *v.* Ralph WHETELEY and Richard his son.
Detention of an assignment of a Crown lease of Southouse Grange in Dale.   DERBY.

99-103   Thomas BYLDON, citizen of Chester, *v.* Robert RASTELL (Rostyll) of Birmingham and
Dorothy his wife.
Part price of herrings sold at Lichfield on Palm Sunday.   STAFFORD.

104-105 John BYLLYNGHURST, Joan his wife and Margaret BOXFOLDE *v.* William BETFELD.
Messuages, land and marsh in Witley and Thursley, late of John Boxfold (Boxold), deceased, late
the husband of Joan now wife of defendant, and uncle of the female complainant.   SURREY.

FILE 1407.

1-3   Thomas BABYNGTON and Margaret his wife *v.* Hugh WESTON, D.D., late dean of
Westminster and rector of Lincoln College, Oxford.
Promise to obtain for complainant an assignment from William Cottesforde, yeoman, of a lease of
the parsonage of Long Combe.   OXFORD.

4-5   Maude, daughter of Thomas BAGOT, esquire, and of Jane his wife, and an heir of the latter,
v. Francis, son and executor of Richard BYDULPH, esquire.
Money promised to complainant by the said Richard on his marriage with the said Jane.
                                                                           STAFFORD.

6-7   Henry BAKER *v.* Thomas HAMLYN of Penny-Cross, husbandman.
Refusal to complete a lease of a messuage and land in Burrington.   DEVON.

8-10   John BALL of Eckington, scythe-smith, *v.* Roger BLOUNT, bailiff of the manor of
Eckington, William GREVES and John EUSE.
Grant of licence to mine on complainant's lands in the manor of Eckington, the custom being that
every tenant may mine on his own lands.   DERBY.

11-14   Henry, son of Thomas BARLEY, deceased, citizen and grocer of London, *v.* Robert
SMITH, gentleman.
Legacy of the said Thomas entrusted to defendant by the custom of the city.   LONDON.

15   George BASSETT, Alice his wife, Thomas HEWETT and Elizabeth his wife *v.* George
DRURY.
Share of a messuage and land in Thetford required by defendant and Roger Gent of Brettenham,
deceased, as security for a debt of John Aleyn, gentleman.   NORFOLK.

16-20   Alice, late the wife of Richard BAYLY(FF)E, *v.* William LAMBERT of Winchester, gentleman, Giles DYSER, and John, son of William BAYLYE.
Promise of a lease of closes of pasture in Maiden Bradley on the death of the said Richard. WILTS.

21-22   William BEKKETT of Colchester, yeoman, *v.* Robert SHOYLE of Mayland, yeoman.
Detention of a bond for price of wool and of balance overpaid therefore. *Mutilated.*   ESSEX.

23-26   Thomas BELLYNGHAM, gentleman, *v.* Richard ELRYNGTON (Aldryngton) and Thomas
GULDFORD, esquires.
Manors of Charflete, Yapton, Barnes and Clothall (in West Grinstead), and lands, rents and
services in Lyminster, Yapton, Claybury, (West) Grinstead, Thakeham, Arundel, Poling, Little-
hampton and elsewhere of the entail of Ralph Bellyngham, deceased, brother of complainant.
Damaged.   SUSSEX

27   The same *v.* the same.
Manors of Thakeham, Charflete, Lyminster and Covertes, and messuages, lands and rent in Thakeham, Cullington, Westgrenestrete (*i.e.* West Grinstead?), Clayton, Hethingfild, Lyminster, Wick
in Littlehampton (Weke), Littlehampton, Preston, Arundel, Horsham, Yapton and West Firle,
late of the said Ralph. *See File* 1406, *No.* 65   SUSSEX

28-31   John BENETT, gentleman, *v.* Robert KYNGE, citizen and grocer of London.
Messuage called the *Windmill* and others in St. Sepulchre's, Newgate, of the demise of Robert
[King], bishop of Oxford.   LONDON.

32–33   Edward BENNETT, clerk, *v.* John TOPLES (Topley).
Price of lead.   [DERBY.]

34–35   The same *v.* the same.
Do.   DERBY.

36–41   John BENTLEY, husbandman, *v.* Francis CLOVYLE, esquire, and John BRASYER, his tenant.
Refusal to complete a lease of land held of the said Clovyle's manor of Thriplow.   CAMBRIDGE.

42–44   William BIRDE of London, merchant tailor, *v.* John BIRDE.
Messuages and land in Wolverley (Overley) and Churchill of the entail of Richard Birde, father of both parties.   WORCESTER.

45–46   Robert son and heir of Richard BLYANTE *v.* John POOLEY, esquire
Detention of deeds relating to a messuage and lands (*described*) in Great Bricett and Ringshall.   SUFFOLK.

47–51   Thomas BOLTE, clerk, executor of William Bolte, *v.* Jane, executrix, and late the wife of Thomas CHATWYN, esquire.
Price of sheep.   ———

52–54   John BONAM and others, feoffees to uses, *v.* John MICHELL, yeoman.
Detention of the will of William Totham and other writings relating to lands in Canewdon, bequeathed for an obit and the relief of the poor.   ESSEX.

55–61   Thomas BOWES and Cecily his wife, executrix of William Eynuz (Eynes) *v.* George BURGEN and George CREDE, gentlemen, and Henry SERLE.
Bond given for account of the goods of William Bowyer, knight, alderman of London, whose executors were the said Eynuz and Serle.   LONDON.

62–65   Ralph BOWNER (Bowlmer), knight, and others, executors of Anthony Gyrlyng, esquire, *v.* Elizabeth GYRLYNG, late his wife, and John SAXFORD, gentleman, her brother.
Goods of the said Anthony, who had required by his will that the said Elizabeth should leave them or their value to his children.   SUFFOLK.

66   John BREARTON and Robert FYLTON *v.* James HUTT.
Closes of pasture in Carden of the demise of Hugh Page, yeoman, since deceased.   CHESTER.

67–69   Henry BRETON of Monkton, administrator of the goods of John [Salcote *alias* Capon], bishop of Salisbury, deceased, *v.* John BARNEBYE, the bishop's servant.
House in Foster Lane and goods of the bishop, including plate and an ' uttermost vesture called a thymmere,' which complainant had to deliver by the course and usage of the Exchequer.   LONDON, WILTS.

70   James [BROOKE], bishop of Gloucester, *v.* the dean and chapter of GLOUCESTER.
Refusal of payment of tenths net incomes of impropriate parsonages.   GLOUCESTER.

71–73   Thomas BROWNE *v.* John LANGE (Longe).
Rights of pasture and tillage on Halsdon moor in Cookbury (Kokabery).   DEVON.

74–75   William BROWNE *v.* Alyn NYCOLS of Foxearth.
Debts due for the parsonage of East Mersey, whereof complainant has bargained for a lease in reversion by Gregory Fox of Peldon, whose widow defendant has married.   ESSEX.

76   John BULBECKE, gentleman, *v.* Robert SEWALL and William GAYMARDE.
Close of pasture in Clevedon of the demise of John Wake of Hartwell, co. Northants, and other lands.   SOMERSET.

77–79   Gilbert BULL *v.* Katharine, late the wife of Robert RAYNER and William their son.
Contract with the said Robert, whose executors defendants are, to buy all complainant's corn at the price current in Peterborough market.   NORTHAMPTON.

80–84   John BURYE *v.* Henry IPSYCHE.
Land in Little Maplestead and Pebmarsh pledged to . . . Carter by William Burye, father of complainant. *Mutilated.*   ESSEX.

85–88   Nicholas BUSSHELL *v.* Henry, son and heir of Thomas GEFFREYES.
Messuage and land in Sherstone acquired of John Bate and Sybil his wife.   WILTS.

89–90   John BYE, servant to the Lord Treasurer, *v.* John DAYNE, his stepfather.
Messuages and lands in Basingstoke and Bramley, late of John Bye, deceased, grandfather of complainant.   HANTS.

91–95   Thomas, Peter and Joseph, sons and heirs of Thomas BYRCHETT, *v.* Humphrey BLECHYNDEN, husband of Elizabeth, late the wife of the said Thomas the father.
Detention of deeds relating to gardens and a barn in Pley[den] and messuages in Rye. *Demurrer for insufficiency overruled. Mutilated. See File* 1408, *No.* 39.   [SUSSEX.]

FILE 1408.

1   James BADELEY *v.* Thomas BERRYN.
Price of iron sold at Stafford.   STAFFORD.

2–5   Robert BAGSHAWE *v.* Christopher BAGSHAWE of Lytton.
Messuages and land in Tideswell and Chapel-en-le-Frith, formerly of Christopher Bagshawe, deceased, ancestor of both parties.   DERBY.

6–8   Roger BALLE of Hadleigh, clothmaker, *v.* John BALLE.
Seizure of deeds relating to a messuage and lands in Hersey, late of Joan Wryght.   NORFOLK.

9–10   John BARNARDISTON of Northill (Northevile), gentleman, v. Christopher MILLER of Lynn, his brother-in-law, George HARRYSON, attorney of the latter, Edward MOLYNOX, gentleman, and John BAKER, under-sheriff of Bedford.
Conspiracy for a collusive suit on a bond for securing an investment made on the said Miller's behalf of money partly obtained by the sale of land in Necton. *Answer wanting.*
BEDFORD, NORFOLK.

11–12   William BARSHAM v. Cicely BARSHAM.
Messuage and land in Wood-Norton, Hindolvestone (Hilderstone) and Guestwick (Geystweyt), late of Thomas Barsham, deceased, brother of complainant and husband of defendant.   NORFOLK.

13–16   John BATTYN v. the mayor and bailiffs of TREGONY, Nicholas FLAMANK, and Henry JAGO and others, jurors.
Embracing in an action for trespass by the overflow of water from complainant's mill called Nansa mill. *Certiorari and subpœna. Mutilated.*   CORNWALL.

17   Robert BAYLES v. Ralph BOUGHE.
Action on a bond for arbitration concerning furs (*described*). *Mutilated.*

18–20   Henry BEDELL (Byddell) v. William and Henry WALL and Richard BENBOWE.
Felling timber on a close of pasture in the lordship of Tipton acquired of the Charterhouse of Warwick.   [STAFFORD.]

21   Thomas BELL, vicar of Kingerby, v. Thomas ELWAND.
Tithe hay of Kingerby. *Mutilated.*   LINCOLN.

22   John BEMISH, yeoman, v. Nicholas POWLTER and John POOCK.
Tenement in New Street, Great Dunmow, late of John Bemish, deceased, grandfather of complainant.   ESSEX.

23–25   Richard BENNET of Hampreston, co. Dorset, v. John ORCHARD, John ELLERMAN and others.
Wrongful occupation of land in Shalfleet, late of William Benett, deceased, father of complainant, and detention and forgery of deeds.   HANTS (I.W.).

26–28   John BENTLEY v. John STUARD and John HAS(W)ELL.
Tenement in Bottisham, late of Richard Bentley, deceased, father of complainant.   CAMBRIDGE.

29   John BERYMAN v. Joan, late the wife of Simon ARTHUR, his tenant.
Tenement and burgage (*described*) in Bideford acquired of Lawrence Prouz.   DEVON.

30   Richard BLACKEWALL v. Ralph BRADSHAWE of Osmaston.
Price of lands.   DERBY.

31–38   Robert, son of Richard BLAKE, deceased, servant to Edward Baynton, knight, esquire of the body to the late King, v. Dame Isabel BAYNTON and John HYCHECOCKE.
Manor of East Lavington (Stepull Lavington, Lavington Forum, Lavington Beynton) of the demise of the said Sir Edward.   WILTS.

39   Humphrey BLECHYNDON and Elizabeth his wife, late the wife of Thomas Byrchet of Rye, yeoman, v. Thomas BYRCHET, son of the said Thomas, and Thomas NEVE.
Forcible entry and seizure of money and goods (*described*) at Rye, etc. *Mutilated. See File 1407, No. 91.*   SUSSEX.

40–41   George BLOMEVYLE (Blomefeld) v. William MORE of Edwardstone, co. Suffolk.
Sale of lands (*described*) in Little Dunham, partly on a bad title. *Mutilated.*   [NORFOLK.]

42   John BRABANDE, parson of St. Michael's, Crooked Lane, v. the churchwardens of ALL HALLOWS.
Rent out of what is now the site of part of the chancel of the church of All Hallows awarded in this court to the church of St. Michael's. *Mutilated.*   LONDON.

43–44   Robert BRACKELEY of Newport v. William KINDGE, son-in-law of Ellen Pocoke.
Lease of lands in Whippingham made by the priest and patrons of the chantry of Newport to John Pocoke, deceased, husband of the said Ellen. *Mutilated.*   HANTS (I.W.).

45   Francis BRADSHAWE of London v. Susan, late the wife of John BLUNT of Burton, gentleman, and Edward his son and executor.
Tenements called the 'Connyngry' house and pasture and 'Siddalowe Codd' of the demise of the late abbot and convent of Burton. *Mutilated.*   [STAFFORD.]

46–47   Christopher BRADYE and Agnes his wife, daughter of William Long *alias* Pymmer, deceased, v. William HOWSDON, uncle and former guardian of the said Agnes.
Profits of a messuage and close in Newport. (Defendant pleads that corn was taken away by John Long *alias* Pymmer of more value than the profits.)   ESSEX.

48–50   Christopher BRAMPSTON of Lincoln, baker, v. Robert HUCHINSON.
Goods (*schedule given*) for which defendant proposes to wage his law.   LINCOLN.

51–53   William BRASEBRIDGE v. Thomas BRASEBRIDGE, esquire, [his father], George GRYFFYTH, knight, and John LUCAS *alias* Gryne and Anthony ROWLEY, servants of the said Thomas.
Conveyance of lands (not specified) to the said Lucas and Rowley contrary to a promise made on complainant's marriage with Anne, daughter of Julyan Nethermill. *Mutilated. See File 1410, No. 45.*   [WARWICK ?].

54   John BRAY and Eleanor his wife, daughter and heir of Nicholas Burges, v. Elizabeth DOWE.
Detention of deeds relating to land in Burgh, adjoining the manors of Chysselden and Vasse.   SUFFOLK.

55–62 Robert son and heir of William BRAYTHEWAIT *v.* Gilbert DAWSON, Thomas MEADE and others.
Cottage in Kirkby Malzeard, granted to the parish church, with reversion in case it should be taken away from the maintenance of divine service. YORK.

63 Richard BRENT of Cossington, esquire, *v.* George SYDENHAM.
Obtaining complainant's signature to Latin documents which he did not understand concerning a messuage in Rooks Bridge (in East Brent) and a wood in Langford. SOMERSET.

64–67 Christopher BRISTOWE of Lee, co. Surrey, *v.* John, son and heir of Robert FRESTON.
Price of tenements in Altofts, Stanley and York, partly bought by the said Robert and partly sold by him on behalf of complainant and Ursula his wife. *Damaged.* D. XV, 20. YORK.

68–69 Anne BROWNE *v.* Charles BROWNE, her husband.
Ill-treatment and desertion, defendant stating that he sent her away for fear she should poison him. *Faded.* ———

70 Christopher BRYTYFE *v.* Christopher KETTELL.
Price of a tenement in the manor of Forncett. NORFOLK.

71–73 Robert BULLOCK of Cokethop (in Ducklington and Yelford), husbandman, *v.* Francis FETYPLACE, esquire.
Pasture in Standlake of the demise of Anne of Cleves, defendant being a former lessee. OXFORD.

74–75 Joan BUNNE *v.* Richard HELDER *alias* Spycer, grandson and heir of Walter Spicer.
Messuages and land in Lynly *alias* Lylly, late of John Bunne, deceased, great-grandfather of complainant. *Mutilated.* HERTS.

76–78 John BURKEHAM of Ticehurst, blacksmith, *v.* Richard BRABONDE and Thomas HUMFREY.
Land in Salehurst, late of John Burkeham, deceased, father of complainant. SUSSEX.

79–80 John, son of Nicholas BURNESTON, deceased, *v.* Nicholas ROBYNSON.
Tenement in the manor of Spalding. *Mutilated. Bill wanting.* [LINCOLN.]

81–82 Thomas BURYTON of Wargrave, gentleman, son and heir of William Buryton, *v.* Griffith BARTON, gentleman.
Detention of deeds relating to lands in Streatley, Moulsford and Basildon, late held together with a messuage (*described*) in Reading by John Kente and others. BERKS.

FILE 1409.

1–4 Michael BAKER, executor of Joan, executrix, and late the wife of Thomas Robyns, *v.* Thomas HOBSON, gentleman.
Tenement called North Hamstead in Shalfleet, with rights of warren of the demise of John, late prior of Christchurch and his convent. HANTS (I.W.).

5–6 Peter BAKER *v.* John SHERWYN, pewterer, and Elizabeth his wife, late the wife of George Isatson citizen and butcher of London.
Messuage and buildings in Pentecost Lane, formerly in the parish of St. Nicholas Shambles, and now in that of Christ Church within Newgate. LONDON.

7 Edward BALDEWYNE of Nayland, executor of Robert Cooper, *v.* John WAGE and John FLEGG.
Forgery of a will in the name of John Thorpe, priest of Stowmarket, a creditor of the said Cooper. SUFFOLK.

8–9 Henry BANKES, vicar of South Petherton, *v.* John CULLEN (Culleynes) of the same, mercer.
Vicarage of South Petherton, demised to defendant by Thomas Hooper, late vicar, deprived for marriage. SOMERSET.

10 William BASELEY of Stockland, co. Dorset, yeoman, son and heir of Thomas Baseley, *v.* John EVELEY, gentleman, attorney-at-law, Thomas MYCHELL, Richard CALMADY and others.
Contempt of a verdict in the Common Pleas concerning a messuage and land in Talaton. DEVON.

11–12 John BETTY *v.* Henry his brother.
Dye-house, etc., in St. Mary Stepps, Exeter, pledged to defendant on his becoming surety for complainant's debts. DEVON.

13–16 Anthony son of John BIDDEGOODDE *v.* Simon son and heir of Anthony WOURTH.
Tenement in the manor of Worth (in) Washfield, claimed by defendant as demesne. DEVON.

17 Edward BODLEY *v.* John PYDDESLEY.
Rent of lands in the manor of Newton St. Cyres for which defendant became responsible on acquiring the lease from complainant. DEVON.

18 Thomas BOLER *v.* Robert GYBBE.
Land in Chappell Fryth. *Mutilated.* [DERBY.]

19–20 Edmund [BONNER], bishop of London, *v.* JOHN ap Guyllyam, gentleman, steward and bailiff of his manor of Fownhope.
Keeping courts in the absence of complainant's ' councell and offycers.' HEREFORD.

21 John BOSTON of Wynslowe *v.* Elizabeth, late the wife of John MACHEN, and administration of his goods.
Price of wool and sheep. [BUCKS *or* HEREFORD.]

22-23   Nicholas BOTHE *v.* William BASSETT, esquire.
Rent charged on the manor of Meynell Langley by William Bassett, knight, deceased, father of defendant.   DERBY.

24   Nicholas BOTHE of Hardwell, serving-man, *v.* Anthony HUNGERFORD, knight, and Dorothy his wife.
Manor of Framptons in East Hendred, late of the priory of Bradenstoke.   BERKS.

25-28   John BOURNE, knight, *v.* Arthur DEDYCOTE of London, Philip DEDYCOTE of Worcester, and John BARLOWE, priest.
Wrongful occupation of the hospital of St. Oswald by Worcester and plunder of its church.
                                                                                 WORCESTER.

29   William BOWLES *v.* Richard WHALLEY.
Parsonage of Attenborough, manor of Toton (Tawton), and tenement in Cropwell Bishop.
Mutilated. See File 1391, *No.* 40.   NOTTS.

30   Thomas BRADWALL *v.* Ralph RYDDEARD, gentleman, and others.
Land at Rudyard in Leek of the demise of Thomas Goodfellowe.   STAFFORD.

31-32   William BRATT (Brett) of Routon *v.* Thomas TORNER (Turner) of Newtown, co. Montgomery.
Lease from Edward Wolridge, gentleman, of a tenement in Cotton and Cowley.   STAFFORD.

33   Thomas BRAYNWOOD and Margaret his wife, daughter and heir of William More, *v.* Robert BROWNE, esquire.
Forcible entry on a messuage and lands in Stow Maries and seizure of deeds and goods for a debt due to William, father of defendant.   ESSEX.

34-35   Richard BRENT *v.* Robert COOKER, esquire.
Plate (*schedule annexed*) entrusted to defendant under the will of William Brent, esquire, father of complainant.   ——

36-38   William BRISLEY of Bromley, collier, *v.* William SKOTT and Juliana his wife.
Action on a bond for conveyance of a messuage and land in Bromley to John Havyatt, citizen and clothworker of London, deceased, uncle of the said Juliana. *Replication wanting.*   KENT.

39   The dean and chapter of BRISTOL *v.* John WARRE.
Rent of the parsonage of Kingston, for which complainants cannot distrain because there is no glebe.   SOMERSET.

40   Anne, late the wife of Robert BROKELSBY, esquire, *v.* William and Francis LEES.
Leasehold in Saxby, acquired of —— Lees, whose executors defendants are.   LINCOLN.

41   The same *v.* Katharine, late the wife of —— LEE of Saxby.
Messuage and land (*not specified*) bought of the said Lee.   LINCOLN.

42-43   John BROXOLME *v.* Richard PELTER.
Action on a bond for delivery of malt partly taken for the King's and Queen's service. *Answer wanting.*   LONDON.

44-47   John BUCKLOWE *v.* John WIGGELEY of Wyrkesworth.
Price of sheep, the bond for which is lost.   [DERBY.]

48-49   Richard BURDEN *v.* John CHECHESTER, esquire.
Refusal to complete a lease of land in Great Torrington, alleged by defendant to be terminable when he should come to live at his house at Wyke (*i.e.* Allensweek?) in Great Torrington. DEVON.

50   Richard BURNBYE *v.* Richard CHYDLEY (Chudley), knight, and others.
Messuages and land in Bratton and Stoke-in-Teignhead.   DEVON.

51-52   Juliana BUTLER *v.* Edward WILLIAMS of Monmouth.
Messuage and land in the lordship of Major and Undy, late of William (V)ychan, whose heir complainant is.   MONMOUTH.

53-54   Nicholas BUTSTON *alias* Broke and Joan his wife *v.* Robert, son and heir of Thomas, WAREN.
Double conveyance of a tenement called Saint Hill in Kentisbeare by John Purse of Plymtrey, deceased.   DEVON.

FILE 1410.

1   Guy BABTHROP of Drax, co. York (*sic*), gentleman, *v.* William BURNELL of London, gentleman.
Assignment of a lease of the manor of Winkbourne (Wyngborne), for which defendant has evaded payments. *See File* 1406, *No.* 3.   NOTTS.

2   Nicholas BACKHOUSE, citizen and mercer of London, *v.* William MATON of Salisbury draper, and Anne his wife.
Goods supplied to Thomas Peterson of Andover, late the husband of the said Anne.   ——

3   William BAGELEY *v.* Robert PHYLPOT, vicar of Linton.
Rectory of Linton, demised with the advowson of the vicarage by the prior and convent of St. John of Bethlehem in Sheen, co. Surrey.   HEREFORD.

4-7   Peter BAKER *v.* Hugh DAVIE and Joan his wife.
Detention of deeds relating to a messuage and gardens in St. Stephen's, Coleman Street, whereof complainant has purchased the reversion after defendant.   LONDON.

8   Nicholas BARHAM *v.* the mayor and sheriffs of London and William CLERKE.
Action for delivery of 8 tons of iron bars. *Certiorari and subpœna.*   LONDON.

9 William BARRETT and Joan his wife v. William ASSHEN, Alice his wife, and John their son.
Messuage and land in West Purie and Paulerspury acquired. of William, son of ·the said William
Ashen. NORTHAMPTON.

10–11 Avery BARWICK, Joan his wife, George THROGMORTON, and Bridget his wife v.
George CLARCKE, gentleman.
Detention of deeds relating to messuages, land and a course tor 80 sheep in Halstow (Hoo?) St. Mary s
and Frindsbury of the entail of John Clarke, grandfather of the female complainant. KENT.

12–13 William BASELEY and Joan his wife, daughter of Robert Woodrouff, v. John WOODE-
ROUFF. ·
Lands in the manor of Hackpen of the demise of John Whytemore, late abbot of Dunkesweu, and
his convent. DEVON.

14–16 The· same v. the same.
Goods (described) of the bequest of John Knolles. DEVON.

17 Robert BASSETT v. Edward BASSETT.
Detention of deeds relating to lands in Loxton of the entail of Giles Bassett. SOMERSET.

18–20 Isabel BAVEN and Alice HEYWOOD v. William OVER.
Land in Wooburn, late of Robert Baven, father of complainant, and Elizabeth his wife, both
deceased. Replication wanting. BUCKINGHAM.

21–22 Robert. BAXSTER, parson of Great Bealings, v. George CAMPE and Thomas HAY-
WARDE.
Rent reserved on a lease of complainant's tithes. SUFFOLK.

23–24 John BEAUMONT and Margaret his wife, daughter of John Barter, v. John COMPTON
(Combton) and Robert SOMERSIDE, executors of the latter.
Land in the parish of St. James in the liberty of Alcester, granted to the said Margaret on her
marriage. DORSET.

25–26 Thomas BEAMOUNT v. George SOMERSETT, knight, Robert (Richard) CUTIS and others.
Messuage and land in the said Sir George's manor of Foxley, and claimed by him as forfeit for
felling trees. [NORFOLK.]

27 Thomas BEKENSALL, citizen and salter of London, v. Thomas TRYNNE, citizen and
brewer of London.
Debt of defendant to John Dames, for which complainant gave security without a counterbond.
LONDON.

28–30 William BEREY, B.D., parson of Kirkby-in-Cleveland, v. Laurence SUTTON.
Lease of the said parsonage of Kirkby made by William Latimer, late parson, deprived for
marriage. YORK.

31 Nicholas BLABIE v. Elizabeth SAMON.
Messuage and land in Southam. WARWICK.

32 Thomas BLOUNT of London, mercer, v. Thomas LAWRENCE and others.
Messuage and land in Chelmarsh, formerly of Thomas Teddestill of Yoden (i.e. Eudon Burnel in
Chetton?). See File 1076, No. 10. SALOP.

33–35 Austin BONNER of Great Glen, husbandman, v. Thomas, grandson and heir of Henry
REYNER.
Messuage and land in Great Peatling of the entail of John Bonner, deceased, uncle of complainant.
D. XII, 17. Replication wanting. LEICESTER.

·36 Edmund BONYTHON, late of Penryn, yeoman, v. Henry JOHN, clerk.
Debt to Udan Vertue, since married to complainant. CORNWALL.

37–38 Richard BORROUGHS, husbandman, v. Humphrey WOODE alias Butler.
Land in the manor of Kentisbeare granted to complainant by the late Duke of Suffolk in view of
his marriage with Wilmet Heathfilde, from which defendant has dissuaded her. DEVON.

39–41 William BOWERMAN, vicar of Doulting, v. John HORNER of Mells, esquire, and John
KYNMAN alias Clarke his servant.
Trespass on a quarry in complainant's glebe, and hindrance to his customers, the said Horner having
a quarry adjoining. SOMERSET.

42–43 John BOURNE, knight, v. Martin CROFTE, gentleman, grandson of John Crotte.
Refusal to seal a contract with divers conditions (described), including conveyance of defendant's
share of the manor of Holt and of the advowson of the church there. WORCESTER.

44 Lawrence BOWREMAN v. Hugh COGAN and John HACKER.
Part price of iron. ———

45 William BRASEBRYGE v. Thomas BRASEBRYGE, esquire, his father, Anthony
[ROWLEY and John LUCAS], servants of the latter, and George GRYFFYTH, knight.
Alienation of the. manor of Kingsbury and other lands contrary to a promise made on com-
plainant's marriage. Mutilated. See File 1408, No. 51. WARWICK.

46 William BRATT v. Thomas TURNER.
Leasehold messuage and land in Ronton,·pledged to defendant. STAFFORD.

47–49 John BRAYE alias Syblye of St. Cleer v. Edward JENKYNG, Thomas BEER, steward
of the court of Trenouth (in St. Cleer), and John STEDE, bailiff.
Action of trespass in the said court, refusal of wages of law, and distress. CORNWALL.

50–52 John BROCKE and Dame Anne SHEFFYLDE his wife v. Ellen, late the wife of Robert
GOUCHE, gentleman. ·
Right to dwell in the manor house of Chilwell, reserved to the said Dame Anne on a demise to the
said John before their marriage, together with lands in Beston and . . desworthe, which demise he
assigned to the said Robert. [NOTTS.]

53   William BROGDON, parson of St. Lawrence Jewry, London, and also of Birkin, v. Ralph DUFFYLDE and others, executors of John Golding, late parson of Birkin.
Dilapidations of the church and parsonage of Birkin.   YORK.

54 `   William BROMLEY, examiner in Chancery, and others, executors of Richard Rea, yeoman of the Guard, v. John REA and Richard OXLEY.
Bequest (described) of deceased's goods which defendants were employed to remove from Thame to Billingsley and Harpford (in Morville).   OXFORD, SALOP.

55–56   John BROWN v. Robert PAYNE.
Action on a bond for a debt already paid.   ————

57   William BROWNE, collector of Crown rents of parsonages of the diocese of Winchester, v. Eleanor, late the wife of William SACKFELD of Dorking, late collector, and administratrix of his goods.
Rent of the parsonage of St. Saviours, Southwark, etc.   SURREY.

58   Richard BROXHOLME, yeoman, v. Robert ELSHAM.
Refusal to complete a sale of a messuage and land in North Kelsey, Lincoln.

59   Elizabeth, late the wife of Thomas BRUDENELL, knight, and administratrix of his goods and Robert BRUDENELL v. Thomas and Richard MAN.
Messuage and lands in Packington bought of John Cockyn, esquire.   WARWICK.

60–62   John and Anne BUCKELOWE v. Thomas ALSOPPE of Ashburne, mercer, and others.
Goods and deeds of the bequest of Ralph Buchelowe of Powwick, father of complainants. DERBY.

63   John BULPAN and Agnes his wife v. Maude ROWDE, late the wife of John Pyllocke, father of the said Agnes.
Land in North Petherton of the grant of John Sompter, great-uncle of the said Agnes. SOMERSET.

64–70   William BURDHEAD v. Amer and Thomas BURDHEAD.
Manor of Denby, late of Richard Burdhead, deceased, grandfather of complainant and father of defendants. (Defendants state that the said Richard also held lands in Clayton, Bircheworth, i.e. Ingbirchworth or Roughbirchworth, Skelmanthorpe, and [P]enyston.)   YORK.

71–72   William BURGES, clerk, v. Nicholas KERISON and others, executors of John Gurnay.
Part price of lands held of the manor of Tasborough.   NORFOLK.

73–75   Matthew BUTLER and Thomas NOTTYNGHAM v. John BULL.
Actions on bonds given for assurance of lands in Bowge, etc.   [SUFFOLK.]

76–78   Simon BUTTRY, gentleman, and Margaret his wife, late the wife of Simon Norwyche, v. Simon MALLORY, gentleman.
Manor of Brampton and messuages and lands there and in Dingley, Oxendon and Chepstow, wherein defendant claims annuities for several persons. Mutilated.   NORTHAMPTON.

79–81   Thomas BUXSEY alias Boxley v. Walter CRETYNGE and others, canons of Wells.
Lease of the rectory of Buckland Abbas. (The answer is by the dean and chapter of Wells).
          DORSET.

82   William BUYS and Alice his wife v. Robert PETHEK.
Lease of a messuage and land at Churleton in Tamerton made by John Treffrye of Tremere jointly to the said Alice and Robert.   CORNWALL.

83–83   Edmund BYSTON of Kelvedon v. George BYSTON.
Tenements in Earl's Colne, late of Robert Byston, deceased, grandfather of complainant. ESSEX.

FILE 1411.

1–3   John CARNESDALE and Joan his wife, administratrix of the goods of Robert Cowper, deceased, v. John ABBES and Edward BALDEN.
Land in Nayland of the demise of Christopher Danby.   SUFFOLK.

4–6   Thomas CAWOOD, gentleman, v. Thomas CHAMPION.
Land in Arborfield, late of Stephen Ca(l)wood, deceased, father of complainant.   BERKS.

7–9   Elizabeth CHACE of Wenden, a minor, v. Simon SAWYER, Thomas MEDE and others.
Tenements in Fulbourn and Walden descended partly from Thomas Chace, her father, and partly from Thomas Maunde   Mutilated.   CAMBRIDGE, ESSEX.

10–11   Andrew and John, sons of William CHAMBER of Leeds, deceased, v. Stephen CHAMBER, his executor.
Legacies. Mutilated.   [KENT or YORK].

12   Simon CHAMBERLEYN, yeoman, v. John DOBBE.
Refusal to complete an assignment of defendant's share of a lease of the parsonage of Blakeney.
          NORFOLK.

13–14   The same v. the same.
Detention of a lease of the same parsonage made by another parson.   NORFOLK.

15–18   William CHAPELAYN, vicar of Fawsley, v. Thomas ANDREWES, knight, John CLERKE, husbandman, and others.
Corn dues called church-shot due from lands in Charwelton and Bramston (Brendeston) to the church of Fawsley as the mother-church of the hundred of Fawsley and deanery of Daventry.
          NORTHAMPTON.

19   Gregory CHARDERER of Askham Richard v. Richard SWALLE and Thomas NELSON of the same.
Detention of deeds relating to land late held by John Charderer, deceased, father of complainant, according to the custom of the manor of Bridlington Abbey.   YORK.

20–23. Francis CHAUNCEY and Alice his wife v. Benjamin GONSON.
Crown grant to Humphrey. Tyrrell of the manor of Shenley and woods in Great Warley. *Mutilated.*
ESSEX.

24–26 Robert CHEPINGHURSTE of Brokenton, husbandman, v. Paul STRETELEY.
Land in Chippinghurst (in Cuddesdon) and Garsington of the entail of Thomas Chepinghurst, deceased, grandfather of complainant. *Demurrer, overruled, that the matter is determinable at common law. Damaged.* OXFORD.

27–28 Oliver CHIDLEY, Dame Dorothy his wife, John FRYE of Wyckecraufte and Joan his wife, v. Edmund WEKES and Jane his wife, executrix, and late the wife of Richard Mallet of Idsley (*i.e.* Iddesleigh, co. Devon).
Debt of Michael Mallet, deceased, whose executrices were the female complainants, satisfied by assignment of a lease of the parsonage of Kingston (in Taunton Dean). SOMERSET.

29–30 Stephen CLEMENT, yeoman, v. John TURNOUR.
Defence of a suit for tithes of a close, late of the priory of Frithelstock, whereof both parties have a joint lease. DEVON.

31–32 Thomas CLEMENT of Hartland, yeoman, v. John BEERE.
Price of a horse. *Damaged.* DEVON.

33–34 William CLYFTON of Barrington, esquire, v. Clement NUSE (Newse) of London, mercer.
Release of a bond given by both parties and others on behalf of Henry Knevet, knight, deceased. *Mutilated. See File 1293, No. 45.* SOMERSET, LONDON.

35–36 John COBBE of South Walsham v. Thomas, his elder brother.
Goods and deeds given by Alice, his mother, in her lifetime and also bequeathed. NORFOLK.

37–39 Charles COCKES of Holborn, co. Middlesex, gentleman, v. John VAYNE and Meryke GREFYTH.
Land in Grosmont of the feoffment of James ap Howell of Garway, co. Hereford, gentleman.
MONMOUTH.

40–43 Nicholas COGESWELL and Katharine, his wife, v. Nicholas PARGAT.
Messuage and land in Bishops Hatfield, late of Nicholas Lanham, deceased, grandfather of the said Katharine. HERTS.

44–46 The same v. Henry RUSSELEY.
Smaller tenement in Bishops Hatfield of like descent. HERTS.

47–52 Richard COLBORN, clerk, v. Robert PARKER and Thomas WRIGHT.
Parsonage of Berford of the demise of John Fawkenour, late parson, denied by complainant to be a clerk. *Mutilated.* [WARWICK?]

53 John COLBYN *alias* Tynker v. DAVID ap Griffith.
Loan. ———

54–55 Matthew COLTEHURSTE, esquire, v. the mayor and sheriffs of LONDON, and Philip GUNTER of London, merchant.
Action on a bond for a debt of Richard Holden, deceased, already overpaid. *Certiorari and subpœna.* LONDON.

56 Richard CONWEY, vicar of Chrishall, co. Essex, administrator of the goods of Humphrey Conwey, deceased, v. Peter CONWEY and others.
Messuages, burgages and land in Rhuddlan (Rutlande) of the demise of Richard Bode, knight, and others. *Mutilated.* FLINT.

57 The same v. Thomas GRYSSET, gentleman.
Detention of deeds relating to the same. FLINT.

58–61 Humphrey CONYNGISBIE, servant attendant on the Chancellor, v. William DEVEROUX, esquire, and John CARTEWRYGHT.
Prebend and manor of Nuneyngton (*i.e.* Nonington in Withington) of the demise of Henry Welche, prebendary. *Mutilated.* HERTS (*rectius* HEREFORD)

62 The same v. the said CARTEWRIGHT.
Contempt of a decree in the preceding suit. [HEREFORD.]

63–64 Edward COPE of Hardwick, esquire, v. Thomas DALE, merchant and citizen of London.
Double payment of part of a debt of Anthony Cope, knight, deceased, father of complainant.
OXFORD, LONDON.

65–69 Richard CORBETT, knight, v. John SOWTHWELL, esquire, and Francis BACON, gentleman.
Action on a bond for a debt which the said Sowthwell had agreed to pay. [SUFFOLK?]

70 John CORNYSSHE of East Allington v. Nicholas, son of John LEYGHE of Ugborough.
Refusal to complete a lease of land in Aveton Gifford. DEVON.

71–74 William COSEBYE, Joan his wife and William their son v. Walter COSEBYE, brother of the first-named complainant.
Messuage, curtilage, ' erbe gardyne and appell gardyne ' (*described*) in Great Totnes, formerly belonging to the chantry house near the bridge. *See File 1209, No. 49.* DEVON.

75–76 The said Walter v. the said William.
Three messuages in Sir Piers Edgecome's manor of Totnes. DEVON.

77 Richard COSOUR v. Thomas PHILYPP.
Messuage and land in Loddiswell. *Damaged.* SOMERSET.

78 Thomas COTES v. Robert his brother.
Messuage and land in Sir Ingram Clyfford's manor of Steeton of the grant of defendant and Richard his father. YORK.

79–80   Richard COUPER, labourer, v. John HARCOURT, knight, and William BYSSHOPP.
Tenement in the said Sir John's manor (sic) of East Grinstead and West Dean.   WILTS.

81–82   Stephen COWPER, husbandman, v. Edward FFORDE.
Land in Ninfield, late of Stephen Cowper, deceased, grandfather of complainant. *Mutilated.*
                                                                                   SUSSEX.

83–86   Stephen COWPER of Bexhill, husbandman, v. John FIRLEY of Penhurst.
Land in Ninfield, late of John Cowper, deceased, father of complainant, and grandfather of Elizabeth
Cowper, an infant stepdaughter of defendant. *Mutilated.*   SUSSEX.

87–92   William COWPER v. Geoffrey PRATTE, Elizabeth his wife, and Henry TAYLOUR.
Detention of goods and of deeds relating to a messuage and lands in Hingham, late of John Cowper,
deceased, great-grandfather of complainant and husband of the said Elizabeth.   NORFOLK.

93–94   Philip COXE of Green Street, serving-man, v. Morgan LAURENCE and others of Skenfreth.
Debt, the bond for which is lost.   ESSEX, MONMOUTH.

95   Ralph CUDWORTHE v. Richard KENTE and others.
Tenement in a street called the ' Kyrgayte ' in Wakefield. *Mutilated.*   YORK.

96   William CULVERWYLL of West Qua[ntoxhead], husbandman, v. John WYNDHAM,
esquire, and others.
Parsonage of Brompton Ralph of the demise of Robert Walshe, parson. *Mutilated.*   See File
1419, No. 83.   SOMERSET.

97   John CURR, husbandman, v. William his brother and William his father.
Messuages, land and rent in Charlton, Charney Street (in Hungerford), Homedewe (*i.e.* Helme
in Hungerford ?) and Hungerford. *See File 1295, No. 76.*   WILTS (*now* BERKS).

FILE 1412.

1–2   Richard CABELL, gentleman, v. Richard CORSELEY of Frome, clothmaker.
Refusal to complete a conveyance of a close of pasture in Frome.   SOMERSET.

3   Silvester CAMPION, [parson of Great Henney], v. Thomas RONDE.
Parsonage of Great Henney, demised by a former parson. *Mutilated.*   ESSEX.

4–6   Roger CAPSTOKE of Caistor, co. Northants, gentleman, v. John MARKEHAM of Ketton,
co. Rutland, gentleman.
Failure to obtain a lease for complainant of the parsonage of Uffington as promised. LINCOLN.

7–8   The same, late collector of rents to William Nevell, esquire, v. Martin AYLESBURY.
Arrears of rent of messuages and land in Torksey and tithes of Torksey and Brampton. LINCOLN.

9–11   Thomas CATESBIE of Whiston, co. Northants, esquire, v. Robert DOLBYN.
Messuage and lands in a park called Segored, in the lordship of Denbigh, late of Thomas Pigot,
esquire.   DENBIGH.

12–13   The same v. John GRYFFYTH.
Mansion house in Denbigh bought of Thomas Pigot.   DENBIGH.

14   The same v. GEOFFREY ap Henry.
Messuage and land in Lewenny bought of the same.   DENBIGH.

15   The same v. Fulke FRANCIS.
Lane in Lewenny bought of Mary, Lady Parr of Horton.   DENBIGH.

16–18   The same v. John ap Evan ap David LLOID, grandson of David Lloid ap Grono ap Teder.
Messuage and land in Kilkeddy and elsewhere. *Mutilated.*   [DENBIGH?]

19–20   Francis CHAMBRELAIN, esquire, son and heir apparent of Leonard Chambrelain, knight,
v. William ISHAM, gentleman.
Arrest in London for an instalment of an annuity granted on the surrender of the keepership of the
park of Ill Brewers. *Mutilated.*   LONDON, [SOMERSET].

21   Robert CHAPMAN of St. Andrew's, Wardrobe, London, son and heir of John Chapman of
All Saints, Derby, v. William A MARE of Derby, draper.
Detention of deeds relating to a messuage in Derby. *Will described.*   DERBY.

22–23   Thomas CLAYFFEALD v. Giles FYLDES, gentleman.
Injunction obtained, ' but suspended owing to the late King's death,' to stop an action of slander
by defendant, who was accused of embezzling the chalice and ornaments of the chapel of Paganhill
(Pakynghill) in Stroud.   GLOUCESTER.

24   The same v. the same.
Contempt of an injunction of this court in an action for slander.   [GLOUCESTER.]

25–28   Margaret CLERKE of Bramford (Braynsforthe) v. Thomas PEDGRAVE.
Forgery of a will in the name of Margery Pytman, sister of complainant, whose executors both
parties were.   SUFFOLK.

29–31   William CLOTTON of Walden, co. Essex, tailor, v. John HORTON, his half-brother.
Salt-house in Northwich, late of Robert Clotton, deceased, father of complainant.   CHESTER.

32–36   Owen CLUNNE, citizen and draper of London, executor of Benedic (Bennet) Jackson,
citizen and butcher of London, v. William JACKSON, executor of Alice, late the wife of
the said Benedic.
Detention of deeds relating to lands in Poplar and Stepney marshes.   MIDDLESEX.

37   The same v. the mayor, aldermen and sheriffs of LONDON and the same.
Action *de rationabili parte bonorum* in contempt of a decree in the above suit. *Certiorari and*
subpœna. Mutilated.   LONDON, MIDDLESEX.

38–39　Edward CLYFTON, vicar of Ugley, v. Edward ELRYNGTON, esquire, and Robert and John FAWCONER, his farmers.
Vicarage of Ugley, claimed under a lease from the late monastery of St. Osyth's. ESSEX.

40–42　William COCKSON of Wisbech, draper, v. Robert LACEY of Huntingdon, gentleman.
Refusal to complete a lease of a messuage called the *Bell* in Wisbech. CAMBRIDGE.

43–44　Edward COKE and others, executors of Alice, executrix, and late the wife of William Coke, yeoman, v. Anthony LUDGATER.
Lease of part of the farm of Felpham, claimed as forfeit by the fall of the top of a chimney built of earth and chalk. *Mutilated. Answer wanting.* SUSSEX.

45–46　John, son of Robert COLE, v. Oliver COLE and Elizabeth his wife.
Half the capital messuage of Aveton Gifford and land there of the demise of John Copleston, esquire, deceased. DEVON.

47–51　Thomas COLES, parson of Manston, v. Grace, late the wife of Christopher LEYETT (Lyatt), esquire.
House and land of the chantry of Our Lady in the church of Manston, united to the parsonage.
DORSET.

52–53　Robert COLTON v. James BYLTON (Belton).
Tenement in Thetford, late of Robert Colton, deceased, father of complainant. NORFOLK.

54–58　Nicholas CONYERS, gentleman, son and heir apparent of George Conyers, gentleman, v. James and Arthur PHILIPPE (Phillipps).
Abduction of Joan, granddaughter of William Conyers of Marske, esquire, affianced to complainant. *Damaged.* (Defendants state that her father threatened that ' yf she would not be maried he would so beat her that he would not leave one hole bone of her.') YORK.

59–65　Andrew CORBETT of Linslade, knight, and Edward MANERING, gentlemen, executors of Robert Nedeham, knight, v. Edward ASTON, knight.
Detention of deeds relating to the marriage settlement of Robert grandson of the said Sir Robert and Frances daughter of defendant, including an undertaking to pay 600 marks to Sir Robert that he might not disinherit his said grandson. BUCKINGHAM.

66–67　Robert COTES v. John, son and heir of Robert FRESTON of London, gentleman, and administrator of his goods.
Action for price of woods of Christopher Danby, knight, in Nayland, sold without his warrant.
SUFFOLK.

68　Thomas Taylour and Simon Cotton, masters of the craft of butchers in COVENTRY, and the fellowship of the same, v. Edmund BAKESTER.
Sale of bad meat at excessive prices outside the shambles, and refusal to join the said fellowship.
WARWICK.

69　Thomas CO . . . v. William STILE.
Shooting fallow deer in complainant's park called Powles Park. *Damaged.* WARWICK.

70–73　Henry CRUCHEFYLDE of South Stoke, co. Oxford, nephew and heir of John Cruchefyld, John LEKE, esquire, and others.
Detention of deeds relating to messuages and lands in Bray. BERKS.

74–78　Richard CURRANT, Maude his wife and Ellen and Allice GROVE, all of Kingston-upon-Thames, co. Surrey, v. Thomas AYLMER and others, executors of William Grove, father of the female complainants.
Annuity rising from lands not specified, leases of ' Frogges Eighte,' ' Groves Eighte,' and other lands and household goods (*described*). OXFORD.

79–82　George CURSON of Croxall, co. Derby, esquire, v. John STRETEHEY, gentleman, son and heir of Thomas Strethey.
Messuages and land in Streethey, late of Thomas Curson, deceased, father of complainant.
STAFFORD.

83　Anthony, Jane and Audrey CUTT, Thomas WULFE and Elizabeth his wife v. Anthony BROWNE, C.J.C.P., Francis KNYGHTON, esquire, and Katherine his wife.
Share of profits of the manors of Rickling Hall, Woodhall, Matching Hall and Barstable Hall, etc., late of Peter Cutt of Bergholt (Barfelde), deceased, father of the complainants other than Thomas Wulfe, and husband of the said Katherine. ESSEX, HERTS, CAMBRIDGE.

FILE 1413.

1–2　Thomas CARY of Haccombe, esquire, v. John SE(Y)WARDE.
Quit-rent reserved by John Cary, grandfather of complainant, on land in Budleigh. DEVON.

3　Barbara, late the wife of Richard CATELYN, serjeant-at-law, v. Rooke GREENE, esquire.
Part of plate and other goods of the said Richard (*described*) recovered by defendant from thieves who stole them on Newmarket Heath. CAMBRIDGE.

4　William CHAMBERS *alias* Irelande v. Thomas HURSTE and Humphrey his son.
Refusal to make a lease, as awarded by arbitration, of lands in Longley, Wellaxall, and Warley, held of the manor of Halesowen. SALOP, WORCESTER.

5　William CHAUNCE of Bromesgrove v. John LYTTLETON.
Site of the manor of Dyars (in Bromesgrove) and other lands of the demise of Sir John Pakington. *Mutilated.* [WORCESTER]

6-8   John CHENEY of Chesham Bois, esquire, v. Richard GOODRYCHE, esquire, and Richard STANES.
Messuage and lands in Newport and Widdington held to the use of George Halle and of Mary his wife.   ESSEX.

9-11   Margaret, late the wife of John CLEBURY, *alias* Margaret Hays, v. James BEDYLL and Joan his wife.
Messuage, mill and land, late of Thomas Hays of Suckley, deceased, father of complainant and of the said Joan. *Damaged.*   WORCESTER.

12 .   John CLEYTON v. William SUTTON and Robert JENYN. ·
Detention of deeds relating to atonement in Appleton demised to the said Sutton and to be settled on his son at his marriage with the said Jenyn's daughter.   CHESTER.

13-14   Richard and Anthony CLYNKARD, executors of Anthony Burtanke, clerk, v. Humphrey MOLLYNS.
Payment for a presentation to the rectory of Mongewell. *Mutilated.*   OXFORD.

15   Thomas CO, chaplain and executor of William Say, knight, v. William SHANBROKE.
Manor of Bengeo (Beniewe), bequeathed by the said Sir William for maintenance of complainant and another priest in a chantry in the church of Broxbourne and for the poor of Broxbourne.
                                                                                        HERTS.

16-18   Margaret, late the wife of Simon COCKE, v. John and Robert COCKE.
Lands in Strood, Frindsbury and Higham of the demise of William Friswell, late prior of Rochester, and his convent.   KENT.

19   Matthew COLCLOUGHE, late alderman of Calais, v. the mayor and aldermen of LONDON, and Charles BROWNE of Calais, gentleman, and man-at-arms.
Action on a bond given on behalf of Oliver Turnour, a commoner of Calais. *Certiorari and subpœna.*   LONDON, CALAIS.

20-23   Robert COLLYOUR v. Robert NOWELL, esquire, executor of John Nowell, clerk.
Rent awarded by arbitration for pasture in Darlaston.   STAFFORD.

24-25   The same v. the same.
Action on a bond for a debt partly satisfied by arbitration.   STAFFORD.

26-27   Anne, late the wife of Robert COLSON, *n.* William EMERSON of Southwark, tanner, and William WYLSON.
Repairs of an inn called the *Spur* and other tenements in Southwark of the demise of St. Thomas's Hospital.   SURREY.

28-29   John COMDEN and Joan his wife v. John BEREWORTH (Berewooth).
Messuages and land in Goudhurst, late of Stephen Bereworth, deceased, grandfather of complainant and of the said Joan.   KENT.

30-31   Richard COMPTON v. Richard MYCHILL.
Right to maintain hedges on defendant's lands in Cannington, adjoining those of complainants.
                                                                                      SOMERSET.

32   Andrew COOKE of Kirton v. William MATTYNS, clerk.
Money entrusted to defendant.   LINCOLN.

33-39   Thomas COTHAM, an infant, by Nicholas Watkynson his guardian, v. John EDNELL and John PENNYNGTON, clerk.
Messuage and land late held of the manor of North Collingham by Alice Cotham, mother of complainant.   NOTTS.

40-41   Humphrey COTTELL, late of North Tamerton, son and heir of Robert Cottell, v. Henry CARLYON, Harry PHYSYK and others.
Land in Ventendavyes (*i.e.* Davies in North Tamerton?). *Former suit described.* CORNWALL.

42-44   William COUPER v. Thomas COUPER.
Copyhold in Upton in the lordship of Southwell and other lands and goods of the bequest of William Couper, father of both parties (*will described*), and jewels and other goods (*described*) of the bequest of Cicely his wife. ·   NOTTS, MONTGOMERY, DERBY.

45-46   Thomas CRAG of Eccleshall, serving-man, v. Richard WOLDRYCHE, Hugh BANKER and William TYLLE.
Chief rents and tithe hay in Whitgreave belonging to the late college of Stafford. STAFFORD.

47-52   William CREKE of Hackleston, husbandman, v. Thomas CREKE, Robert BENDEE and Joan his wife.
Messuage and land in Hardmead, late of William Creke, grandfather of complainant and father of the said Thomas.   NORTHAMPTON.

53-54   Richard son of Laurence CROFTE v. William GRENESTRETE, husband of Benedict, late the wife of the said Laurence.
Detention of a deed of entail of the manor of Stalisfield (Stalkysfeld).   KENT.

55-58   John CRUYS of Paignton v. John TOWLYE of Woodleigh, husbandman.
Refused to complete a conveyance of land in Breyxham promised on condition of complainant's marriage with Alice, daughter of defendant. *Bill mutilated.*   DEVON.

59   Thomazen, late the wife of Edward CRUYS, v. John HOLLWYLL, parson of Georgeham.
Expulsion from defendant's parsonage in breach of a lease, and seizure of the said Edward's will and other deeds from his house in Exeter.   DEVON.

60   Morgan CYCELL v. Nicholas CORR, John YTTON *alias* Fletcher, and Walter GRENE.
Messuages in the Shambles and elsewhere in Bristol of the gift of John Cycell, father of complainant.   GLOUCESTER.

FILE 1414.

1-2   Thomas CARIEW of Haccombe, esquire, grandson and heir of John Cary (Carewe), v. John HALS, esquire.
Marsh, now a pool, in the manor of Leigham in Egg-Buckland.   DEVON.

3   Agnes CASSELAKE, John ZELAKE, Alice his wife, and John RICHARD v. Richard MARTEN.
Messuage and land in Farringdon, late of Elizabeth Tudboll, deceased, kinswoman of the said Agnes, Alice and John Richard.   *Pedigree given.*   DEVON.

4-8   Richard CAVE v. William BAKER, Thomas COMBER (Cumbre), Alice his wife and Job (Joppe) HARBERTE.
Messuages and lands in Steventon and Chipping Faringdon, late of William Johnson, deceased, kinsman of complainant.   BERKS.

9-10   John CAWOOD and William BULL of St. Faith's, administrator of the goods of [John Long], proctor of the Arches, v. Alexander CARLYLE of Whittington College.
Messuage in Paternoster Row of the demise of William Compton, knight.   LONDON.

11-13   Edward CHAMBERLAYNE and William GIFFORD v. Ralph GIFFORD of Steeple Claydon, gentleman.
Refusal to verify a compromise of a statute merchant made to Roger Knolles (Knowelles) of Cold Ashby, gentleman, for which complainants are sureties.   BUCKINGHAM, NORTHAMPTON.

14-16   Thomas CHEKE v. Jane SARGER (Serger).
Detention of a lease made by the dean and chapter of Salisbury of the manor of Folke.   DORSET.

17-18   John CHELTHAM, clerk, master of St. David's Hospital, [Kingsthorpe], v. Francis MORGAN, serjeant-at-law.
Mansion-house and rents of the said hospital claimed by defendant under a lease from the late prior and convent of St. Andrew's, Northampton.   NORTHAMPTON.

19   The same v. Francis SAMUELL, gentleman.
Detention of deeds relating to the same.   NORTHAMPTON.

20-23   John CHUBBE of Ugborough v. John ROUSE and Simon SPERKEWELL *alias* Chapell, executors of William Rede of Hanger (in Cornwood).
Debt of the said Rede, who died seized of messuages and lands in Cornwood and Modbury, 3½ doles in Screchebysallers and shares in divers tinworks.   DEVON.

24-25   Reynold, son and heir of William CHYNALS, gentleman, v. Martin TREWYNARD and Agnes his wife, late the wife of the said William.
Detention of deeds relating to lands in Chynals (in St. Keverne), Lauethna (*i.e.* Lavethan in Blisland?), Tredrizzick and Tredower (both in St. Minver), Tripcony and Trebedanan (*i.e.* Bodannan in St. Endellion or Trebudannon in St. Columb Major?), and delay in execution of the said William's will.   CORNWALL.

26-28   Robert CLAMPARDE (Clamper) v. Richard Edward, James and Elizabeth BURRAGE (Bowrage).
Messuage and land in Brenchley, late of Andrew Burrage, deceased, father of the said Richard Edward and James.   KENT.

29-30   Gilbert CLAYDON of Dullingham, gentleman, v. Leonard BARRET, attorney in the Common Pleas, and others.
Action on a recognizance for conveyance of lands, payment for which has not been completed.   CAMBRIDGE.

31   Margaret late the wife of John COLBEARE v. George KYRKEHAM, esquire, and William SMYTHE.
Messuage, cottages, and land in the manor of Feniton ' Malerby ' of the demise of Lady Joan Kyrham.   *Manorial customs described.*   DEVON.

32-33   Thomas COLLARDE v. Alexander SYDENHAM, gentleman, and Edith SLOWCOMBE.
Messuage and land held of the manor of Huish Champflower.   .   SOMERSET.

34-40   Reynold CONYERS of Wakerley, esquire, v. Thomas GRENEHAM, Joyce his wife, John MARSHE, and Eleanor late the wife of George GRENEHAM.
Manor of Ketton acquired of the said George, son of Thomas Greneham.   RUTLAND.

41   Giles COOK, parson of Woodford, v. Thomas HODGESON.
Deduction from first-fruits of the said parsonage for an annuity granted to defendant.   *Mutilated.*   NORTHAMPTON.

42-45   Isabel COOKE *alias* Watson and John PULVERTOFT, son and heir of Anne Pyckeringe v. Robert WRIGHT and Elizabeth his wife, daughter of Hamond Whitchecot.
Manor of Thorpe and land in Laceby, formerly of John Woogher and Anne his wife, parents of the said Isabel and Anne Pyckeringe.   LINCOLN.

46   John COOKE, Mary his wife, late the wife of William Jenyn of Rayleigh, mercer, and Edward, John and Thomas JENYN, sons of the said William and Mary, v. Margaret, executrix and late the wife of Edward STRANG(E)MAN of Hadleigh, gentleman.
Money delivered to the said Edward upon trusts (*described*), partly for the said sons.   ESSEX.

47-50   Thomas CORNYSHE, prisoner in the Counter, son of Thomas Cornyshe, deceased, v. John MALYN and Giles HILL.
Decree in a former suit concerning lands in Calais.   CALAIS.

51-53   Isabel COTTRELL, executrix of John Cottrell, dyer, v. William WHAT(E)LEY.
Debt of Clement Whateley, deceased, brother of defendant.   WORCESTER.

54   Philip COXE of Green Street, co. Essex, v. Anthony HENDRY, bailiff of Monmouth.
Permitting the escape of Richard Cartener, imprisoned for debt, and detention of his bond.
                                                                         MONMOUTH.

55-57   Alexander CRANE, Agnes his wife and Alice COLMAN v. John CORBOLD.
Messuage and land in Thorndon of the entail of Thomas Colman, grandfather of the female complainants.   SUFFOLK.

58-59   Geoffrey CRAWLEY v. Stephen TEMPLER, clerk, son and heir of Henry Templer.
Lands in Over Wallop, late of William Crawley, grandfather of complainant.   HANTS.

60-61   James CRYCHELEY of Lichfield, draper, v. John HARMAN and Nicholas ROBYNSON of
Morehall, gentleman.
Action for delivery of a bond for which complainant has given a release. STAFFORD, WARWICK.

62-64   John CULHAM v. William, grandson and heir of Edward SHORTE.
Land in Thorndon, late of Thomas Culham, deceased, father of complainant.   SUFFOLK.

FILE 1415.

1-8   John CATTE v. John KEMPE, Thomas REDHOD (Redwoodde), and Richard JODE(?).
Messuage and land in Stourmouth (part stated by the said Redhod to be in Preston), late of John
Catte, deceased, grandfather of complainant.   KENT.

9-14   Richard CHITWOOD of London, gentleman, v. Richard GROSVENOUR and others.
Pasture near Pinford Bridge in the lordship of Bromfield, formerly belonging to the Crown.
                                                                         DENBIGH.

15   Robert CLARE, husbandman, v. Nicholas BIRDE of Lichfield, baker, feoffee to uses.
Cottage and land in Streethay.   STAFFORD.

16-17   Alan CLERKE v. George PORTER of Lincoln.
Goods bought of Robert Huchynson.   LINCOLN.

18-19   William COCKES of Hackney, hackneyman, v. Henry PERRYN and Katherine his wife.
Expenses and recompense for recovering geldings stolen from Christopher Freman of Debden,
deceased, late husband of the said Katherine.   MIDDLESEX, ESSEX.

20   Richard COKE v. John HILLS.
Land in the dean and chapter of Worcester's manor of Boraston. *Damaged.*   SALOP.

21-22   Thomas COLE v. William WATTES.
Rectorial tithes of Stokenham, leased to both parties jointly by William Burgoyne, esquire.
Mutilated.   DEVON.

23-24   John COLPAS, an infant, by Ellen his mother, v. Isabel KNIGHT and Richard her son.
Land and cottage held of the manor (*sic*) of Ramfeld (*cf.* Ramsdean in East Meon) and Langrish
(in East Meon).   HANTS.

25   Philip COPLEY, esquire, and William COPLEY of Cambridge, his son, v. Margaret COPLEY
and others.
Manors of Sprotbrough and Plumtree and other lands.   YORKS, NOTTS.

26-28   John COURTNEY v. Nicholas CLAPPE.
Plate (*described*) entrusted to defendant at Chard and claimed by him as a pledge for a debt.
                                                                         SOMERSET.

29-30   John COVE v. Joan KELLEY.
Manor of East Stoodleigh and capital messuage and barton of Redcliffe (in Northlew), already in
dispute in the Court of Wards.   DEVON.

31   Thomas COWPER of Thurgarton, co. Notts, esquire, v. OWEN ap Meredith and others.
Crown lease of the parsonage of Llanver (*i.e.* Llanfair-Caereinion?).   MONTGOMERY.

32-33   Thomas COXE v. Thomas WRIGHT and Elizabeth his wife.
Detention of deeds relating to messuages, cottages, lands, chief rents and services in Maer (Meyre),
Sidway (in Maer) and Chaldon (*i.e.* Charlton in Maer?).   STAFFORD.

34-36   William son and heir of William CRISPE (Cripse) and others v. Anthony WYNGEFELD,
knight.
Tenements in defendant's manor of Easton. *Mutilated.*   SUFFOLK.

37-38   Thomas CROKE v. Henry TAMPON, and Henry LACYE, gentleman, steward of the court
of Stamford.
Debt to the said Tampon's wife, respited on pledge of a girdle. *Mutilated.*
                                                           [LINCOLN, NORTHAMPTON.]

39-41   Nicholas CROSTWAYT, citizen and pewterer of London, and Frances his wife v. Robert
MYLBORNE.
Messuage in the parish of Holy Trinity, Cambridge, late of Nicholas Warley and Elizabeth his
wife, deceased, parents of the said Frances.   CAMBRIDGE.

42-44   William CRUGE (Crudge) v. Richard POMEROYE, John, son and heir of John SCOBBELL,
and John, nephew and heir of John KNYGHT.
Messuage and land in Dartington, late of John Cruge, deceased, father of complainant.   DEVON.

45   Mary, late the wife of John CRYMES, v. the sheriffs of LONDON and Thomas SUDLOWE.
Action on a counterbond concerning the administration of the goods of the said John. *Certiorari
and subpœna. Damaged.*   LONDON, STAFFORD.

46–47 CRYSLY verch Thomas and many, others *v.* William Chester, knight, master of the DRAPERS' company, and the wardens of the same.
Legacy of Thomas Hoell, merchant of London, dwelling in Seville. *Answer wanting.* LONDON.

48–51 Adam CRYSPYN, husbandman, *v.* Henry DYLLON, esquire.
Leases of the capital mansion and barton of Colleton and of mills, marshes and other lands in Chulmleigh. DEVON.

52–53 Robert CUFLEY, husbandman, *v.* John CUFLEY, his elder brother.
Land in Charlton of the gift of Robert Cufley, husbandman, father of both parties. HANTS.

54–58 John CURTES of Seend *v.* Joan, executrix and late the wife of Nicholas HARRYS his father-in-law.
Lands (*described*) in the lordship of Bulkington of the demise of Henry Longe, knight. WILTS.

FILE 1416.

1–2 Robert, son of Richard CABBELL, *v.* Richard SAMWELL, lessee of the prebend of Wanstrow.
Messuage and land in Wanstrow of the demise of James Rogers, prebendary. *Mutilated.*
SOMERSET.

3–6 Thomas CARLETON, citizen and merchant tailor of London, and Elizabeth his wife *v.* Richard COLLING.
Legacy of Thomas Catesby of Lea-Marston (Wevermarston), esquire, father of the said Elizabeth, whose widow married defendant, formerly his servant. LONDON, WARWICK.

7 George CATESBYE, esquire, and Joan his wife *v.* John GLIN.
Joint tenancy of a messuage, grange and land in Fawley, late of John Glin, deceased, father of defendant, and former husband of the said Joan. HEREFORD.

8–10 Thomas CHAFFYN, esquire, supervisor of the will of Thomas his son, and guardian of Thomas his grandson, *v.* John DACKOMBE.
Lease of the manor of Uffington, delivered by the said Thomas the son in view of his marriage with Joan, daughter of defendant. D. XII, 29. BERKS.

11 Thomas CHAFFYN *v.* Margaret, executrix and late the wife of George PERCYE.
Reviver of a suit for the parsonage of Mere and lands there and in Kingston Deverell. *Mutilated.*
See D. XII, 30.; *File* 1424, *No.* 1. WILTS.

12 Robert CHAMBER and William WALL *v.* [John STELE].
Moiety of a messuage and land in Newton and Heatley (in Abbot's Bromley), formerly of John Bostoke, father-in-law of the said Stele. *Second membrane wanting.* STAFFORD.

13–14 Thomas CHAMBER *v.* Richard CHAMBER, both yeomen.
Detention of deeds relating to a messuage, water-mill and land in Harrietsham and Charing, late of William Chamber, deceased, father of both parties. KENT.

15 Leonard CHAMBERLAINE of Shor[thampton?), co. Oxford, knight, *v.* Alban HILL of London, physician, and Alice his wife.
Detention of deeds relating to a house in Buge . . . (*i.e.* Budge Row?) of the demise of William Holland, clerk, master of the Savoy. *Damaged.* LONDON.

16 Thomas CHARDE and George HYGGYNS *v.* Margaret, executrix and late the wife of John SHEWARDE.
Under-lease of a tenement in Lord Howard's manor of Bradpole. DORSET.

17 Thomas CHARDE *v.* Leonard STOURTON, esquire.
Messuages, mills and land in Bradpole and Bridport. DORSET.

18–21 The masters, fellows and scholars of Trinity, St. John's and Bennet Colleges and Clare and Gonville Halls in Cambridge, and of Merton College, Oxford, and all other the inhabitants of CHESTERTON *v.* Richard, son and heir of Thomas BRAKINGE, esquire, and John WOOD.
Plantation of osiers so as to hinder common of pasture in Chesterton. (The three first membranes appear to be parts of different copies of a bill.) CAMBRIDGE.

22 Richard CLARKE *v.* Anne MARKYE.
Detention of deeds relating to a messuage and land in Ross and Walford of the entail of Alice Clarke, grandmother of complainant. HEREFORD.

23–24 William, son and heir of Charles CLIFFORD, *v.* Thomas DENTON, esquire.
Manor of Hillesden, late of Hugh Conwey, knight, and Elizabeth his wife. BUCKS.

25–29 William COLLYN *v.* Margaret COLLYN.
Manor of Church Hall (in Broxted) and lands in Chaureth and Broxted (Brokeshed), late of Nicholas Collyn, deceased, father of complainant and husband of defendant. ESSEX.

30–34 Robert COLMAN *v.* Thomas ANDREWES of Charlton, co. Northants, knight.
Tenement in defendant's manor of Ilmington of the demise of Thomas Lord Sandys, late lord thereof. *Replication wanting.* WARWICK.

35–36 Robert COMPTON *v.* John BAKER and Dorothy his wife.
Messuage and land in Twinsted of the gift of John Compton, deceased, brother of complainant, and former husband of the said Dorothy. ESSEX.

37 Humphrey, son and executor of Richard CONNYSBYE, *v.* Humphrey KERREY of Kidderminster, clothier.
Debt of defendant paid to John Bearsly. WORCESTER.

38   Andrew CORBETT of Linslade, co. Bucks, knight, v. William BULLOCK.
Messuage and land in complainant's manors of Williamston and Westfeild.   PEMBROKE.

39–41   John CORDALL, gentleman, v. William HAMOND, son and executor of Elizabeth, executrix
        and late the wife of Giles Hamond, carpenter.
Rent and repairs of a messuage in St. John's Street, late of the Hospitallers.   MIDDLESEX.

42–43   William CORYNGTON of Croydon, co. Surrey, and Jane his wife v. John SPENCER of
        Castle Ashby, co. Northants, esquire, and Audrey his wife.
Share of a messuage and land in Limehouse, late of Dame Katherine Jones, deceased, aunt of the
said Jane and Audrey.   MIDDLESEX.

44   Jane, late the wife of Sir Richard COTTON of Warblington, co. Hants, and Ralph his brother
        v. Edward ALMEYRE of Pencyokyn near Holt (i.e. Pant-yr-Ochain in Gresford?), esquire.
Balance of account as steward of the said Sir Richard's lordships of Bromfield, Yale and Chirk.
        DENBIGH.

45   The same, executors of the said Sir Richard, v. Richard BOSTOCKE.
Compromise of price of wood.   CHESTER.

46   Jane, late the wife of Richard COTTON of Bedhampton, co. Hants, knight, v. Robert
FLETCHER, gentleman.
Manors of Great and Little Sutton and Ince and rectory of Bromborough of the grant of the dean
and chapter of Chester.   CHESTER.

47–48   The same v. Anthony COOPE, gentleman.
Houses and lands in the manor of Bedhampton.   HANTS.

49   Peter COURTENEY of North Worton, co. Oxford, grandson and heir of Edward Courteney
        v. Oswald and Christopher CHAMBERS.
Lease by the prioress and convent of Nun-Monkton of the rectory of Walton, whereof William
Gascoyne, knight, had obtained a conveyance by imprisoning Ralph, father of complainant. YORK.

50   Henry CULLIFORD v. Simon DAVY of Kingston in Purbeck.
Parsonage of Corfe Castle of the demise of Thomas Benett, D.D.   DORSET.

FILE 1417.

1   Arthur CAMME v. William KYNGESCOTT, gentleman.
Loan to defendant while a prisoner in the Fleet for contempt of this court.   LONDON.

2   John CAPRON, husbandman, v. William WELSHE, husbandman, his uncle.
Land in Loxton of the demise of Giles Bassett of Uley, co. Gloucester, esquire.   SOMERSET.

3   John CARDEN of London, aged 8 years, by Thomas Lannyns, his stepfather (' father-in-
        lawe '), v. Randolph BRUERTON and Owen CARDEN.
Lands (described) in Coddington and Tilston, entailed on Randolph Carden, deceased, grandfather
of complainant.   CHESTER.

4–5   William CATCHELOWE (Catyslowe) and Joan his wife, daughter of Thomas Fowle, v.
        Thomas RANDOLPH.
Detention of deeds relating to a messuage and land in Ticehurst.   SUSSEX.

6   Thomas CHAFFYN, esquire, v. Thomas ABRAYE and John HEYTON.
Money due from Charles, late lord Stourton, who demised to defendants the site and demesnes
of the manor of Mere.

7   Allen CHAPMAN of Fenstanton, co. Huntingdon, yeoman, and Joan his wife v. John
        CHAPMAN of Thriplow, yeoman, his father.
Land held of the bishop of Ely's manor of Shelford and promised to complainants.   CAMBRIDGE.

8   William CHARLES of Gillingham v. Joan wife of John WHITE.
Exchange of lands in Hoo and Maidstone. Mutilated.   KENT.

9   William CHAUNDELER of South Ockendon, co. Essex, v. Thomas STILGO.
Messuage in Castle Street, Deddington, formerly of John Chaundeler, deceased, father of complainant.   OXFORD.

10   Robert CHETWYN, gentleman, and Katherine his wife, executrix and late the wife of
        Thomas Ponchyon, gentleman, v. Thomas BROWNE, esquire.
Reviver of a suit concerning marsh lands in Plumstead, partly bought by the said Ponchyon.
        KENT.

11–14   Thomas CLARKE, yeoman, v. Edmund HARMAN, esquire.
Manor of Fifield beside Bruern of the demise of Thomas Cade, late master of the hospital of
St. John the Evangelist [Burford]. Mutilated.   OXFORD.

15   John CLARKESON of Kirkton, co. Notts, gentleman, and Elizabeth his wife, a daughter
        of John Rodney (Radney), esquire, v. John [MORDAUNT], lord Mordaunt.
Rents of lands in Sandford. Mutilated.   SOMERSET.

16–18   Nicholas CLERKE of Chesterfield, mercer, v. Elizabeth PARKYNSON.
Loan to William Parkynson of Newbold, butcher, deceased, husband of complainant.   DERBY.

19–21   William, son and heir of William CLERKE, v. John BOSEGRAVE, his stepfather.
Parsonage of Renhold (Renhale) of the demise of John Gostwike, knight.   BEDFORD.

22–24   John CLYFTON and Agas his wife v. Matthew LAYNE and Alice his wife, executrix and
        late the wife of Richard Crowke alias Blaunte, grandson of John Pawlmer.
Messuage in Colber Street and shop in the High Street, Banbury, formerly of Henry Palmer.
        OXFORD.

25–28 John COCKYN of St. Ives, yeoman, v. Henry JAMYS and James NYCOLL.
Messuage in Lelant, late of Thomas Cockyn, deceased, grandfather of complainant. CORNWALL.

29 John COLBORNE, parson of Kelsall, v. Margaret, executrix and late the wife of Tristram
FEREBYE.
Reviver of a suit for rents due to complainant's parsonage. SUFFOLK.

30 John COLE v. John HOLCOMB.
Action for price of a lease of a parsonage which complainant should have bought of Roger Garland
but believed to be void. *Mutilated.* DEVON.

31–32 Robert COMBER of Wartling, yeoman, executor of William his brother, v. Thomas
PLAYNSTE (Playnsted) and Ellen his wife.
Deceased's share of profits of lands in Pevensey marsh under the will (*described*) of John Comber,
father of complainant and former husband of the said Ellen. SUSSEX.

33 Humphrey CONYSBIE, servant to the Chancellor, v. John JAMES.
Tithe hay of Hanbury and repairs of the parsonage, let to complainant in succession to defendant.
WORCESTER.

34 Andrew CORBETT, knight, v. Humphrey COLLES.
Detention of deeds relating to the manor of Red Castle. *Mutilated.* SALOP.

35–36 John COTERELL v. Roger, son and heir of Robert COTTERELL.
Messuage and land at Kinder, in Glossop, late of Ambrose Cotrell, father of complainant. [DERBY.]

37–38 Hugh, son and heir of the said John COTTERELL, v. the same.
Reviver of the above. [DERBY.]

39 Alexander COTON of Clement's Inn v. Anselm GYES of Brockworth; esquire, and Richard
ABYNTON of Dowdeswell, gentleman.
Annuity. *Mutilated.* GLOUCESTER.

40–42 Agnes, late the wife of Richard COUGHEN, yeoman, and administratrix of his goods, v.
William COUGHEN his brother and Henry their father.
Joint tenancy of land in Little Chester of the grant of Dennis Beresford and Thomas Newton.
DERBY.

43–45 John CROKER v. Anne, late the wife of Humphry TALBOTT.
Lease and keepership of Blockley park, and warren in Blockley, and tithes of corn and hay in
Northwyke. WORCESTER.

46–47 John CROSSE, son and heir of Agnes Mose, v. Thomas WATSON and Joan his wife.
Messuage and land in Hockwold and Wilton, partly held of the manors of Scales and Peverynges
(*i.e.* Poynings?). NORFOLK.

48 William CROWSYER v. Rogert TREGONYN.
Detention of loans, wages and share of goods of Thomas Crowsyer, deceased, father of complainant and of defendant's wife. CORNWALL.

49–51 William CURDE, husbandman, v. Simon CLARKE.
Tenement in Cottenham of the demise of John Rogers, chantry priest in the parish church of
Cottenham, confirmed by many others. CAMBRIDGE.

52 Ralph CURSON v. Richard DUNE, both husbandmen.
Exclusion from a parlour and lands reserved on an under-lease of a tenement in Sir George
Gryffithe's manor of Alrewas and waste of trees. *See File 1421, No. 71.* STAFFORD.

FILE 1418.

1–2 Roger CAIPSTOKE of Castor (Kyster), gentleman, v. William LEVERATT of Newark.
Loans, price of goods (*described*) and of timber from Halton woods, and fee for pasturing cattle.
NORTHAMPTON, NOTTS.

Henry CANTRELL, gentleman, v. Peter STANKLYFF, parson of Burnham Thorpe.
Ejection from the parsonage on succession thereto, whereas complainant's lease is valid for a year
longer. NORFOLK.

4–6 Alexander CARVANELL and Mary his wife, executrix and late the wife of Martin Pendrie,
v. John KYLLIGREW and others.
Book of accounts of the said Pendrie which the said Kylligrew claims in two answers as proving
his title to a tin-work. CORNWALL.

7–9 John CAYBORNE v. John SKYPWITH of Burgh-in-the-Marsh, gentleman.
Land in Saltfleetly pledged to defendant for a debt. LINCOLN.

10–13 Francis CHALONER, esquire, and Agnes his wife v. Charles JACKSON, esquire (gentleman).
Manor of Snydale with appurtenances (including a windmill) there and in Loscoe, Normanton,
Aiton, Featherstone, Preston, Sharleston, Warmfield and elsewhere of the entail of Thomas
Chaloner, knight. YORK.

14–17 John CHICHESTER, esquire, v. John ANDROWE and others, feoffees to the use of the
town of Torrington.
Burgage with a 'standing or shoppe' adjoining in Great Torrington. DEVON.

18–19 Roger CHOLMELEY of London, knight, v. Nicholas ALYN.
Detention of deeds relating to the manor of Holme Hall in Quy-cum-Stow. CAMBRIDGE.

20 William CHORLETON, priest, v. Elizabeth HURLETON.
Part price of a gelding sold to Thomas Hurleton, deceased, husband of defendant.

21   Jane CLEBURNE *v.* Richard CLEBURNE of Cliburn, esquire.
Ejection from a tenement in Sleagill contrary· to complainant's tenant-right.   WESTMORLAND.

22   Margaret, late the wife of John CLEBURY, *v.* Peter RUMNEY of Gloucester.
Occupation of complainant's lands and goods by colour of a plea of matrimony in the court of the bishop of Hereford.   DIOCESE OF HEREFORD.

23-26   John CLEMENT, doctor of physic, *v.* John YORKE, knight, late sheriff of London.
Greek and Latin books in print and manuscript and other goods (*list given*) seized in the house of complainant in Bucklersbury on his departure beyond seas in the late reign for.conscience' sake.
LONDON.

27-28   Thomas CLEMENT [? student at the] University of Padua, *v.* John GWYN, clerk.
Prebend of Llanwenog in the church of Llanddewi-Brefi. *Mutilated.*   [CARDIGAN.]

29-30.   Stephen CLEYBROKE *v.* Edmund [BONNER], bishop of London.
Forfeiture of a tenement in defendant's manor of Fulham for breach of an order to pull down a house from which he was excused by defendant in person.   MIDDLESEX.

31-33   William CLOPTON, esquire, *v.* Leonard, grandson of Gerard DAMMETT, esquire, and of Mary his wife.
Bonds for the marriage settlement of complainant's daughter, who died without issue. (The settlement included messuages, lands and rents in Burton Dasset, North End, Knightcote, Radway, St. Mary Cray, Orpington, Chislehurst and Paul's Cray.)   WARWICK, KENT.

34-35   Thomas CODRYNGTON, esquire, *v.* George LUDLOWE, esquire.
Lease in reversion of defendant's manor of Fyfeld, with appurtenances in Wylton, Gerrestone, Bradner, and Trowe, which is parcel of the manor of Norton Bavent, made by Elizabeth Cresner, formerly prioress of Dartford, and her convent.   WILTS, DORSET.

36-38   Thomas COKE, yeoman, *v.* Henry CLERK and Emma his wife, late the wife of John Stowe.
Messuages and land in Aldham acquired of Richard Stowe, grandson of the said John.   ESSEX.

39-41   Elizabeth, executrix and late the wife of Henry COLLYER, *v.* John STOCKER, overseer of his will, and Joan his wife.
Money of the said John.   DORSET.

42-43   John COLLYNS and Agnes his wife *v.* John RICHEMAN.
Loan by John Hudd, deceased, whose executrix the said Agnes is.   SOMERSET.

44-45   Margaret CONYE *v.* Richard WATERTON and Henry YONGE.
Goods of Augustine Waterton of Messingham, gentleman, sometime husband of complainant.
LINCOLN.

46-47   John son and heir of John COOMES of Old Stretford, co. Warwick, *v.* William BLAND, an executor of Richard Comes, uncle of complainant.
Detention of a lease made by Robert Pennell of Worcester, smith, of a messuage in Worcester.
WORCESTER.

48-49   Thomas, Lawrence and Margery CORBOWLD *v.* John WITHE of Stratford and William BOSSET of Little Glemham.
Legacy of William Corbowld of Fornham, whose executors defendants are. *See File* 973, *No.* 48. .   SUFFOLK.

50-51   Anne CORDE(E) of Polstead *v.* Thomas BENDISHE, gentleman, son and heir of John Bendishe.
Messuages and land in Hadleigh, late of Nicholas Bendisshe, gentleman, deceased, former husband of complainant.   SUFFOLK.

52   William COTTESFORDE *v.* Hugh WESTON, late master of Lincoln College, Oxford.
Invalid lease of the parsonage of Twyford. *Ne exeas regnum.*   BUCKINGHAM.

53   Richard COVERT *v.* Hugh ALEE and Humphrey DICKENS.
Monastery of Prees and lands there pledged to defendants.   SALOP.

54-59   Jane, executrix and late the wife of William CRANO, citizen and merchant tailor of London, *v.* John GRESSHAM, knight.
Arrears of annuity released by complainant in ignorance.   LONDON.

60-61   John CRESWELLER and Maude his wife *v.* Joan NEVY *alias* Shynner, executrix of Thomas Nevey of Chichester, barber.
Close of pasture in St. Bartholomew's without the west gate of Chichester.   SUSSEX.

62   John CRUSE (Cruyse) of Liskeard, grandson of John Bealbury of the same, *v.* James BRENDON.
Release to —— Lower of a suit for a debt due to the said Bealbury, whose executors both parties are. *See Files* 951, *No.* 14; 1196, *No.* 14.   CORNWALL.

FILE 1419.

1-2   John CALDEWALL and others *v.* Fulke GREVYLL, knight, and Edward CHOLMELEY and Edward MORE, his servants.
Parcel or 'hagge' of wood sold by the said·Sir Fulke at Littywood in Bradley (Cuttlestone hundred).
STAFFORD.

3   Margaret, late the wife of Thomas CALTON, *v.* John CROFTE and others.
Manor of·Dulwich of the entail of Thomas Pope, knight.   SURREY.

4   William CARANT, knight, son and heir of William Carant, knight, *v.*·Martin ROCHE.
Detention of deeds relating to the manor of Wilkinthroop in Harrington. ·*Mutilated. See File* 1176, *No.* 5.   SOMERSET.

5   John CARLOWE, yeoman, v. Francis NOONE, esquire.
Detention of deeds relating to messuages and lands in Gosbeck, Ash-Bocking and Helmingham.
SUFFOLK.

6   James CASTELL, gentleman, Elizabeth his wife, Andrew REDE and John his son and
heir apparent v. Roger PYERS (Pyres, Peyos).
Detention of deeds relating to messuages and land in Froyle and Farnham, late of Henry Quynby,
deceased, father of the said Elizabeth and of Alice mother of the said John.   HANTS, SURREY.

7   Arthur CHAMBER of the Middle Temple v. William and Meredith GRYFFITH.
Tenement in Lloyntidnon.   SALOP.

8-13   Robert CHATERTON of the Middle Temple, gentleman, and William his brother, studer.\
of Christ Church, Oxford, v. Richard KELSO, Geoffrey COO, Reynold HIGENSON,
Hamlet REDD (Reade), Alice ASHELEY and Henry MORYS (More).
Rents of messuages and lands in Altrincham and Ashley, late of Edmund Chaterton of Nuthurst,
co. Lancaster, deceased, which defendants claim to hold of Hamlet Stockeley.   CHESTER.

14   Rowland CHEEF, master and keeper of the hospital of St. John the Baptist without
Bridgnorth, v. Sir John PARROT.
Tenements in Bridgnorth wrongfully seized as chantrey lands. *Damaged.*   SALOP.

15   The dean and chapter of [CHRIST CHURCH, Oxford] v. Alice, executrix and late the wife
of Gilbert NORRŸCE.
Parsonage of Tetburye, formerly of the abbot and convent of Ensham, and charged with a rent
to the bishop of Worcester. *Mutilated.*   [GLOUCESTER.]

16   John [CHRISTOPHERSON], bishop of Chichester, v. Robert COWPER.
Reviver of a suit by George [Day], late bishop, for lands in Slinfold, held of the manor of
Drungewick.   SUSSEX.

17-20   Isabel, late the wife of William CHYLDE, v. Norman CHYLDE her son.
Messuage, cottage and land in Grimley, formerly of John Chylde, father of the said William.
D. XIII, 1.   WORCESTER.

21   Thomas, son and heir of James CHYNOWETH, v. Thomas RETYN, gentleman, and George
WATERTON.
Messuage and land in Constantine obtained by defendant from Richard Chapell, since deceased,
in exchange for lands now said to be entailed.   CORNWALL.

22   Robert CLAREINGBOLL of Nether Hardres, co. Kent, Joan his wife and Thomas MOTTE
v. Humphrey WELLYS of Horecross, esquire.
Messuage and garden in the borough and tenement of Tutbury, late of Stephen Barry, deceased,
father of the said Joan, and of Marion, mother of the said Thomas.   STAFFORD.

23   The same v. Thomas BETTE.
Do.   STAFFORD.

24-27   The same v. the said WELLYS and BETTE.
Do.]   STAFFORD.

28-35   Matthew CLATON, gentleman, v. Thomas, Edmund (Edward) and Richard, sons and
executors of William ANDERSON of Flexborough, gentleman, his guardian.
Account of goods and leaseholds of Richard Claton, deceased, father or complainant, including the
farm of Thorhelme (*i.e.* Thornholme in Appleby?) and Raynthorpe and the parsonage of Appleby.
Schedule of lands and rents.   LINCOLN.

36   Jane CLEBOURNE of Sleagill v. Thomas HUTTON.
Seduction under promise of marriage.   WESTMORLAND.

37   The same v. George and John BURD.
Slander that the said John had had his pleasure of complainant.   WESTMORLAND.

38-41   Agnes CLYFFE and Christopher WOTTON v. Thomas SWANCOTE (Sawncote).
Moiety of lands in Ecclesall, formerly of Elizabeth daughter of Stephen Brodhurst, ancestress of
complainants. *Pedigree given.*   STAFFORD.

42-44   Henry COBBE v. John MILLETT and others.
Messuage on the east side of Northbrook Street, Newbury, pledged for a debt since recovered
therefrom.   BERKS.

45-48   Elizabeth COCKAYN and Florence his daughter v. Vincent LOWE.
Goods of Thomas Cockayn, deceased, late husband of the said Elizabeth, whose executors all parties
are.   DERBY.

49   Robert COKER of Mappowder, esquire, v. [Richard PERHAM and others, feoffees to uses].
Legacies of Thomas Coker, father of complainant, payable out of the manor of Frome Whitfield.
Mutilated.   DORSET.

50-52   Thomas COLLYN of Linkinhorne, husbandman, and others, tenants of the King's and
Queen's manor of Rillaton, v. Richard HARRY and others.
Destruction of boundaries and 'landstovez' in the said manor whereof defendants were accused
by inquisition in a former suit.   CORNWALL.

53-54   Thomas COMBERFORD, esquire, grandson and heir of Thomas Comberford, v. William
BABYNGTON, esquire, and Anthony his son and heir apparent.
Land demised in exchange for other land in Tymmore.   STAFFORD.

55-57   Anthony, son and executor of Thomas CONYE, v. Hamond SUTTON of Washingborough, esquire.
Action on a bond for conveyance of lands in Kirton or elsewhere on the marriage of the said Thomas with Margaret Waterton, daughter of defendant, the execution of which was delayed by defendant till after the said Thomas's death.   LINCOLN.

58   Henry COOKE v. Geoffrey, son of Richard BURGA(Y)N.
Detention of a lease made by John Ratclyff, knight, of a tenement in Abbotsham.   DEVON.

59-63   Silvester COOPER, gentleman, v. Thomas BULLOCK, esquire, and Richard BULLOCK.
Woods in the manor of Wokefield of which complainant has a Crown lease and defendants an earlier lease of the site and demesne.   BERKS.

64   Thomas COOPER v. John DODGE and others.
Messuage and land in Charing (Charnynge), late of Robert Cooper, deceased, grandfather of complainant. *Damaged.*   KENT.

65-67   John CORSE of London, poulterer, v. Walter PAYNE.
Messuages and land in Litlington, late of Edward Corse, deceased, grandfather of complainant.
                                                                                                                                        CAMBRIDGE.

68-71   Walter COSBY of Great Totnes, executor of William Cosby, v. Wilmot, executrix, and late the wife of Thomas HORWELL.
Debt wrongly released by Margaret, late the wife of the said William and co-executrix with complainant.   DEVON.

72   John COLPAS, an infant, v. Isabel KNYGHT and Richard her son.
(Duplicate of *File* 1415, *No.* 23.)   HANTS.

73   Margaret, late the wife of Richard COTTON, v. John, son and heir of Edward SNELSTON, yeoman, and Elizabeth FALLOWE, his mother.
Messuages and lands in Astle (in Withington) and Turnock and Siddington (both in Prestbury) pledged to the said Edward.   CHESTER.

74   William COX v. Richard PATRICK.
Keepership of the castle and honour of Huntingdon called Baynard's or Bayllol's honour and Crown rents in Huntingdon, Brampton, Great Stewkley, Abbotsley and Great and Little Paxton.
                                                                                                                                        HUNTINGDON.

75-76   Thomas COXE v. Robert BREMNER and Agnes his wife.
Messuage, cottages and land in Over Walton (in Eccleshall) and Chipnall and Sowdley (both in Cheswardine).   STAFFORD, SALOP.

77-79   Richard CRISTOFER and Joan his wife, executrix, and late the wife of John Ackelande of Exeter, v. Thomas TURBOT of Barnstaple, innholder.
Money entrusted to defendant for payment to a daughter of the said John at her majority, which she failed to reach.   DEVON.

80-82   Ralph CRYCHE, executor of Henry CRYCHE, v. Anthony GRENE and Henry NEWTON.
Crown lease of a barn and tithes of corn in Lullington and Coton.   DERBY.

83   William CULVERWELL of Stogumber v. John WYNDHAM of Orchard.
Lease of the rectory of Brompton (Brympton) Ralph. *Mutilated. See File* 1411, *No.* 96.
                                                                                                                                        SOMERSET.

FILE 1420.

1   Nicholas Wootton, J.U.D., dean of CANTERBURY, and his chapter, v. John UGDEN, alderman of Canterbury.
Account of complainant's rents in Canterbury.   KENT.

2   John [CAPON *alias* Salowe], bishop of Salisbury, v. John LEWSON.
Lease of the manor of Sherborne. *Rejoinder only.*   [DORSET.]

3-5   George CARTER of Crundale v. Robert EDOLF of Brenzett.
Fresh marsh in Ivychurch, late of Andrew Shave of Crundale.   KENT.

6   Edward CHAMBER of Royston, gentleman, son of William Chamber, v. John HOPPER, master of the hospital of St. John and St. James in Royston, and Thomas WEBSTER.
Tenements in Bassingbourne, Melbourn and Therfield of the demise of John Collynson, clerk, late master of the said Hospital, and his brethren.   CAMBRIDGE, HERTS.

7-9   Giles CHAUNDELER and Alice his wife v. Joan GARDENER.
Messuage and land in Hartest, late of William Freman, deceased, grandfather of the said Alice.
                                                                                                                                        SUFFOLK.

10-13   Agnes CHEKE v. William PEPULL (Popull) and Agnes, late the wife of John GARD.
Goods (*described*) of the bequest of Joan Gard, former wife of the said John.   ———

14   Thomas CHEKE v. George and John SERLE, executors of Nicholas Serle.
Action on a bond for a debt partly respited.   [DORSET?]

15-18   Rowland Swynborne, master of CLARE HALL, Cambridge, and the fellows of the same, v.   Henry MALLETT, clerk.
Debts of defendant for 'determants' of his commons, as receiver to the said hall, etc., divers of the records of the hall being destroyed. *Mutilated.*   CAMBRIDGE.

19-20   Thomas CLERKE v. Agnes late the wife of Laurence STEPHYN.
Household goods of William Clarke, deceased, brother of complainant. *Bill wanting.*   ———

21-23　　Peter CLEYTON *v.* Elizabeth, late the wife of William CLEYTON, and Anne Heywood.
Under-lease of pasture in Ecclesall of the demise of Thomas Roope.　　STAFFORD.

24　　Henry CLYFFORDE, esquire, *v.* William OSBORNE of Wotton.
Detention of deeds relating to the rectory of Wheatenhurst (Whytmystre).　　GLOUCESTER.

25　　Christopher COCKES and Katherine his wife *v.* Thomas HILL.
Seizure of goods on a false indictment of forcible entry on tenements in Erpingham and Ingworth surrendered to complainants.　　NORFOLK.

26-27　　Lewis CODOGAN of Glastonbury, co. Somerset, *v.* Richard AP JOHN *alias* Cosor, shoe-maker, William AP JOHN his son, and William ADAM.
Burgages and land in Caerleon, late of Morgan ap William Barbar and Katharine his wife, grand-parents of complainant.　　MONMOUTH.

28-30　　Henry, son and heir of John COKK, esquire, *v.* Henry BODENHAM, esquire.
Delay till after the death of the said John of conveyance of a share of lands and houses in Anstey, Ebbesborne Wake, Gerardeston, Steventon, Sutton Courtney, Hergrave (in Sutton Courtney), Shipton, Milton and elsewhere (*tenants named*). *Mutilated.*　　ESSEX, HERTS, WILTS, BERKS.

31-33　　Francis COLBARNE of Clement's Inn *v.* Richard SCOLOWE.
Vicarage of Norton by Evesham, of which defendant was deprived for marriage, of the demise of Thomas Court, now vicar.　　WORCESTER.

34-37　　John COMBES *v.* Adam WYNTROPP.
Detention of bonds for debts (*described in answer*) already paid.　　————

38　　John CONNOCKE of Liskeard *v.* Otes TRELOWDRO.
Price of calf-skins.　　CORNWALL.

39-41　　Robert COOKE, husbandman, *v.* Roger WARREN, gentleman.
Meadow in Feering, leased to complainant by word of mouth.　　ESSEX.

42-43　　Richard COPWOOD of Totteridge, gentleman, *v.* William COPWOOD of the same, esquire, his brother.
Bond given on defendant's behalf to Nicholas Chune, citizen and haberdasher of London.　　HERTS.

44-48　　William COURTHOPE of Cranbrook, clothier, *v.* Thomas URMESTON.
Bond given on behalf of Thomas Wigg, citizen and clothworker of London, who has removed the seal. *See* D. XIII, 3.　　KENT, LONDON.

49-51　　Richard COVERTE *v.* Humphrey DICKINS and Hugh (A(LEE.
Site and lands of the monastery of Preen, pledged for a loan.　　SALOP.

52　　John COWLINGE *v.* Richard LANYEN and Robert TRENCREKE.
Money and 13,000 pounds of white tin delivered to the said Trencreke in satisfaction of a mortgage to the said Lanyen of the manor of Treveglus and other lands, rents and services in St. Merryn.　　CORNWALL.

53-56　　Thomas COWPER of Thurgarton, co. Notts, esquire, *v.* OWEN ap Dan and HOWELL and JOHN ap Evan.
Crown lease of the parsonage of Llanvor.　　MONTGOMERY (*vectius* MERIONETH?)

57-58　　William CREDE *v.* Nicholas NOWELL.
Frivolous suit for lands in Gillingham in the court of the manor, where it is not the custom to allow costs on judgment for defendants.　　DORSET.

59　　[Thomas] CURTEYS, alderman of London, *v.* [Thomas] EYNUS . . . STOKER and others.
Lands of the hospital [of St. John the Baptist, Huntingdon] in Sto[wkey], Folksworth, Stilton and Yaxley. *Damaged. See* D. IX, 36.　　HUNTINGDON [NORTHAMPTON].

FILE 1421.

1　　Thomas DABRICHECOURT, gentleman, Alice his wife, Richard MYDDLELMORE, gentleman, and Anne his wife, *v.* Thomas and Humphrey GRESWOLD, gentleman.
Detention of deeds relating to messuages and lands in Solihull.　　WARWICK.

2-3　　Thomas DANWOOD *alias* Bene of Brentwood, smith, *v.* William his brother.
Land and messuages in Shenfield and Brentwood of the bequest of William Danwood *alias* Bene, father of both parties.　　ESSEX.

4　　Arthur DARCYE, knight, *v.* Richard SKIPWYTHE and others.
Distress of complainant's tenants in Brimley (in Hartwith) for taxes of Sawley, they being con-tributable with the seignary of Bishopside.　　YORK.

5　　John DAVEIS, gentleman, *v.* Thomas GREY, esquire.
Trees growing on lands held of defendant's manor of Barwell which the tenants claim to belong to them by custom.　　LEICESTER.

6-7　　William and Joan DAVELLES *v.* Robert BOURDEN.
Detention of a lease of lands in Highampton made jointly to complainants and Lewis Davelles, esquire, by William Bowden of Black Torrington.　　DEVON.

8-9　　John DAVY of Stockland, merchant, *v.* William WILLES of Taunton, husbandman.
Debts paid on behalf of William Westron of Dulverton, merchant, deceased, whose widow and executrix defendant married.　　DORSET, SOMERSET.

10　　Thomas DAVYE *v.* Thomas COTES.
Messuages and land in Clayworth, late of Robert Davye, deceased, uncle of complainant.　　BERKS

11-14   Edward DAVYS, vicar of Faringdon, v. John DREWYT.
Vicarage of Faringdon, claimed under a lease from John Stele, late vicar, deprived for marriage.
BERKS.

15 ,   John DAVYS v. . . . and WILLIAM ap Res ap William.
Land in Llangwyfan, late of Rice ap David, brother of complainant.   *Mutilated.*   DENBIGH.

16   Richard DAVYS, yeoman of [the Guard?], v. Thomas BEDDOWE and Owen DAVID.
Unthreshed corn at Powsicke.   *Mutilated.*   ———

17-19   Roger DAWSON of London, dyer, v. William BODIE of London, merchant tailor, and Allen BARKER his tenant.
Tenement called the *Rainbow* behind the church of St. Mary Aldermary, pledged to defendant for price of Spanish skins which turned out not to be genuine.   *Injunction.*   LONDON.

20   The same v. [the mayor of LONDON and] the said BODIE.
Action in the mayor's court pending the preceding.   [*Certiorari and*] *subpœna. Mutilated.*
LONDON.

21-24   John DEAN, clerk, v. Gilbert GRENE, clerk, late monk of Combermere.
Refusal to complete a sale of the pension awarded to defendant on the dissolution of his monastery.
CHESTER.

25-26   John DETHYKE, esquire, v. John WYNGFELD and Elizabeth his wife, late the wife of Christopher Dethyke.
Land and right of way in Mydle[ton] promised by the said Christopher in return for building a windmill.   *Mutilated.* (The said Christopher also disposed by will of lands in North Runcton, Setchy, East and West Winch, Hardwick in North Runcton, and South Lynn.)   NORFOLK.

27   James DEYE v. Richard HAWTYNG.
Price of land in Holt and Catherington (*rectius* Sharrington?) sold to defendant for a debt, and deeds lent to be copied.   NORFOLK.

28-32   Ellen and Agnes, daughters and heirs of Richard DICKONS, gentleman, v. Richard HUNT, gentleman.
Messuages and lands in Stamford, Peterborough, and Yarwell.   *Pedigrees given.*
LINCOLN, NORTHAMPTON.

33-36   John DIOT v. ' Dame Ladye ' Katherine GEREYSLEY.
Loan of 60 old angels in pledge for 30l. of white money.   ———

37-39   Christopher DISMERS of Fifield, co. Wilts, gentleman, v. John PLATER, great-nephew and heir of John Plater.
Detention of a deed of feoffment of land in Penn made by William Plater of Newington, co. Surrey, grandson of the said John the elder.   BUCKINGHAM.

40-46   William, son and heir of John DOLBEAR, v. Thomas and Margery MATHEWE.
Right of way to a messuage and land at Summerhill in Ashburton.   DEVON.

47   Jane DORMER of Wing, late the wife of Robert DORMER, knight, v. Katherine, late the wife of Richard DORMER, knight, and John his son.
Chains delivered to the said Sir Richard, whose executors defendants are, to raise money for complainant's husband in the Queen's service.   BUCKINGHAM.

48   The same v. Robert PEARSON, clerk, and Edward SLOWE.
Debt of John Stodard, deceased, whose executors defendants are.   [BUCKINGHAM.]

49-52   George DOWNES v. Edward MOUNTAGU, esquire, son and heir of Edward Mountagu, knight.
Parsonage of Winwick, of the demise of the late prior and canons of Huntingdon.   *Mutilated.*
D. XII, 32.   HUNTINGDON.

53   Ralph DOWNES v. Richard SAUNDERSON and Thomas HOWE.
Ship purchased of the said Saunderson.   *Mutilated.*   GLOUCESTER.

54-57   William DRAKE v. John PENTENEY and others.
Marsh in complainant's manor of Hardley.   *Mutilated.* D. XII, 41.   NORFOLK.

58-60   Anne, late the wife of Mark DRAYCOTT, and Richard their son v. Henry [DRAYCOTT, eldest son of the said Mark], and Edward BOWNE.
Lands in Loscoe and elsewhere held of the manors of Horestone and Duffield.   *Faded.*   DERBY.

61   The same v. the said Henry.,
Frivolous suits for customary lands in Horsley held of the manor of Horestone, after disclosure of title in this court.   *See File* 1115, *No.* 73; *Star Chamber Proceedings, Philip and Mary*, IV, 44.
DERBY.

62   Henry son and heir of Mark DRAYCOTT of Loscoe v. Edward TOFTE.
Lands in Horston and Horsley, partly acquired of George Leversege.   *Mutilated.*   DERBY.

63-67   Richard DREWRY of Lullingstone, co. Kent, clerk, v. John DEYKEN, William COWPER and others.
Land in Wenn, late of Margaret Couper, deceased, daughter of the said William, whose executor complainant is.   *Mutilated.*   SALOP.

68   Robert DUCKETT of London, grocer, v. William INGRAM, constable of Market Bosworth, and others.
Goods of John Elmer, parson of Market Bosworth, seized for dilapidations, complainant having the next presentation to the parsonage.   LEICESTER.

69   Henry DUDLEY, esquire, and Margaret his wife, daughter and heir of Lord Audley of Walden, v. Thomas CASTELL of London, esquire.
Land near the bridge of Ware, late of the priory of Christ Church, London.   HERTS.

70   John DUN, yeoman, v. Owen ap Llewelyn ap Owen and others.
Detention of deeds relating to tenèments in the lordship of Averushtely.   MONTGOMERY.

71–72   Richard DUN, husbandman, v. Ralph CURSON, yeoman.
Common appendant to land of the demise of defendant in the lordship of Alrewas.   *See File* 1417,
No. 52.   STAFFORD.

73–74   Richard DUTTON of Clement's Inn v. John HAWARDEN, esquire, and Richard HALL
(Howell) and Edward MILLENTON, husbandmen.
Messuage and land in Pentrobin acquired of John Hawarden of Wolston, co. Lancaster, esquire,
father to the said John.   FLINT.

75   Thomas DYCKSON of Hemley and Joan his wife v. Robert BULL of Hadley, clothier.
Messuage and lands in Hollesley, late of John Ward, deceased, grandfather of the said Joan.
D. XV, 21.   SUFFOLK.

FILE 1422.

1–4   William DAGGES of London, son of Oswald Dagges and of Margaret his wife, v. Ambrose
NORTON, Wolfram SLE *alias* Sleford and others.
Lands in Grantham and Heuerby or Hayerby (*i.e.* Harrowby?), formerly of Hugh Massingberde.
Faded.   LINCOLN.

5–6   Valentine DALE, LL.D., son and executor of John Dale, gentleman, v. George SYDDEN-
HAM, esquire, husband of Eleanor, executrix and late the wife of Edward Wynter,
gentleman.
Site of the monastery of Cleeve and pasture there demised by King Henry VIII to Anthony
Bustard.   SOMERSET.

7   Richard DANBYE v. Christopher BYCKERS.
Crown lease of lands in the manor of Carthorpe in Burneston, acquired of James Cancellers,
gentleman.   YORK.

8   Leonard DANNET, gentleman, and Cristian his wife v. Robert HOBBY, citizen and
grocer of London, and Grace his wife.
Annuity of the bequest of Edward Dean, former husband of the said Cristian and brother of the
said Grace.   LONDON.

9   John DANYELL of Messing, esquire, v. George FOSTER, esquire.
Cutting and carrying timber from land in Great Birch.   ESSEX.

10   Peter DANYELL of Furnival's Inn v. Peter LEYCESTRE, esquire, and William YANNES.
Land in Over Tabley, late of Thomas Danyell, esquire, deceased, father of complainant.   CHESTER.

11–12   Thomas DAVIS of Batheaston, tailor, v. Harry TAYLOUR.
Rival leases of a tenement in Batheaston by the prior of Bath and John Harrington, esquire,
successively lords of the manor (*sic*) of Batheaston and St. Katharine.   SOMERSET.

13–14   Henry DAVY v. John MANING of Maulden and Robert BETTE.
Messuage (*described*) in Ampthill of the entail of John Davy.   BEDFORD.

15–16   Thomas DAWKENS and Katharine his wife, late the wife of Richard Large, v. Hugh
JO(Y)NES *alias* Sare.
Burgages in Monmouth, late of David ap Hoell *alias* Sare, uncle to the said Katharine.
MONMOUTH.

17   John, son and heir and executor of Ambrose DAWNEY, esquire, v. Jane DAWNEY, late
the wife of the said Ambrose, and Richard her son.
Money in bags and bladders and elsewhere and a gold chain and crucifix, late of the said Andrew.
WILTS.

18–21   James, son and heir of James DEANE, of Wirksworth, v. Thomas JONES and others.
Lead mined in a ' meyre ' of land 29 yards square in Matlock.   DERBY.

22–24   Ellen, late the wife of John DENHAM, citizen and mercer of London, v. John BRIDGES,
gentleman.
Messuage and land in Beguildy, late of John Blaney, deceased, brother of complainant.   RADNOR.

25–28   John DENHAM and Grace his wife v. Richard BRENT, John, son of John HAM and of
Thomasen his wife, and Thomas HAM.
Manor of Maidstone or Mainstone, *alias* Paunesfoteshill, in Romsey, formerly of William Brent
of Cossington, co. Somerset, deceased, father of the said Grace and Richard.   HANTS.

29–32   The same v. Richard BRENT and John LEWYS, clerk.
Do. *Mutilated.*   HANTS.

33   Maurice DENNYS, knight, v. Edward TYBBOTT of Upton Cheney (in Bitton).
Farmhouse and lands (*described*) in Siston (Scieston).   GLOUCESTER.

34–38   John DENTON v. Nicholas, son and heir and an executor of James LEYBURNE, knight.
Annuity payable out of tithes of corn in Scales Moor (near Kentmere) of the demise of the abbot
and convent of St. Mary's, York.   WESTMORLAND.

39   William DETHYKE of Newall, esquire, v. John HOPKYNS and others.
Tithes of the appropriated rectory of Repton.   D. IX, 34.   DERBY.

40   William DEYE v. William HOWARD and Margery his wife.
Land in Monks Toft and Haddiscoe, late of William Welles, *alias* Sever, grandfather of complainant. *Damaged.*   NORFOLK.

41–44   John DONKIN and Constance his wife, executrix and late the wife of John Tom, v. John
PAWLE, yeoman.
Seizure of deeds relating to messuages and land in St. Ives (St. Tyes).   CORNWALL.

45-47   Henry, son and heir of Mark DRAYCOTT, *v.* John ROW.
Lease of lands in Normanton-on-Soar, claimed by complainant to have expired.   NOTTS.

48-49   Jasper DUNRIGE of London, an infant, by William Boddie and Katherine his wife, mother of complainant, *v.* Edmund DUNRIGE of Buckland, grandson and heir of Richard Dunrige of Hatch, and Richard DUNRIGE.
Messuages and lands in Tavistock, Milton and Plymouth, late of John Dunrige of Hatch, deceased, grandfather of complainant. *See Files 497, No. 20; 700, No. 8; 977, No. 72.*   DEVON.

50   William DUSSYNG *v.* Robert WEBSTER and Simon NOCKALL.
Messuages and lands in Calthorpe (Cawthropp) and Wickmere, late of John Dussyng, deceased, father of complainant.   NORFOLK.

51-52   Richard DUTTON of Clement's Inn *v.* Randolph BAMBELL of Chester, alderman, and John HOPER.
Messuage and shops in Chester of the demise of William Clyff, dean of Chester, and his convent, claimed under a lease of the late abbot.   CHESTER.

53   John DYER *v.* Edward COLMAN of Little Waldingfield, clothier.
Action for a debt of William Cookes of London, salter, and others, partly paid, for which complainant had refused to be bound.   ESSEX, LONDON.

54-55   Thomas DYGNAM and Cecily his wife *v.* Richard WARTON of London, fishmonger.
Messuages and land in Agmondesham and Beaconsfield, pledged to defendant by John Jerard, who thereby forfeited them to complainants under the will of John his father.   HERTS, BUCKS.

56-58   The same *v.* the same .
Do., the said Cecily being daughter of the said John the father, and tenant in remainder after the issue of his son.   HERTS, BUCKS.

FILE 1423.

1-2   George DALBIE of Walkeringham, co. Notts, *v.* John LYNNE and William (H)ELSON.
Messuages and lands in Muston, Stenwith (now in Woolsthorpe, co. Lincoln) and Bottesford, late of Stephen Dalbie, deceased, grandfather of complaiant.   LEICESTER, [LINCOLN].

3   Thomas DANYELL *v.* Alice DANYELL.
Manor of Daresbury, late of John Danyell, deceased, father of complainant.   CHESTER.

4   Thomas DANYELL of St. John's Street, co. Middlesex, and others *v.* Richard SMYTH of Southfleet.
Messuage, barn and garden in Chart Street, Seal, late of William Wylkyn, deceased, grandfather of complainants.   KENT.

5   DAVID ap Hoell of London, yeoman, *v.* JOHN ap Morys and others.
Messuages and land in [Llauvair] Waterdine, formerly of Matthew ap Jevan Gethyn, deceased, grandfather of complainant.   SALOP.

6   DAVID ap Morice, household servant to Lord Williams of Thame, *v.* DAVID (Res) and THOMAS ap David.
Messuage and land in Gwenthrew, late of David ap Hoell ap Jevan, deceased, grandfather of complainant.   MONTGOMERY.

7   DAVID ap Pres ap Cona *v.* John WADE of Coventry, mercer, and Jane his wife.
Money entrusted to the said Jane to pay a debt to Richard Dutton of Chester.   WARWICK, CHESTER.

8   DAVID app Pryce of Hendon, gentleman, *v.* WILLIAM app Pryce ap Howell and others.
Bond given on defendant's behalf to William Parker of London, draper.   MIDDLESEX.

9   DAVID ap Richard *v.* JEVAN ap Hoell of Llangirrig and others.
Bond given to Jenkyn ap Gutto Gwallter of Cemmaes for price of goods supplied to defendants.   MONTGOMERY.

10-11   DAVID ap Thomas *v.* RICHARD ap John (Jones), son and heir of John ap Jevan ap David.
Detention of deeds relating to land in Michaelchurch.   RADNOR.

12   Owen DAVID ap William, executor of David ap William, *v.* Roland ap David ap William, yeoman of the Chamber.
Messuages, mills and lands in Porthhyrne, Penheskyn, Castellour, Porthaythwy and Treglias of the demise of William Gryffyth and William his son, knight, and the late bishop, dean and chapter of Bangor.   ANGLESEY.

13-14   John DAVY *v.* William FRANKE, William MAN and others.
Detention of deeds relating to a messuage and land in Kingston-upon-Hull.   YORK.

15   George and Edward DAVYS *v.* Edward MADDOK.
Messuage and land in Bromfield for which complainants cannot sue in the county, being bound apprentices in London.   DENBIGH.

16   Robert DAWBENEY, citizen and merchant tailor of London, *v.* Margaret, late the wife of John MANERS, knight.
Debt of William Coffyn of Haddon, knight, former husband of the said Margaret.
                                                                LONDON, DERBY.

17-20   Thomas DAWSON and Helen his wife *v.* Thomas (Richard) TORSEYE.
Detention of deeds relating to land in Owston (Oxston) in the Isle of Axholme.   LINCOLN.

21-24   Francis DAWTREY of Portsmouth, co. Hants, knight, *v.* Robert WYNGFELDE, knight.
Manors of Letheringham (Leveryngham), Easton, Goddinges (*i.e.* Goodwin's Place in Hoo?) and Charsfield, and lands in Letheringham and Framlingham (Franyngham), extended for an annuity due to Philip Dennys, esquire.   SUFFOLK.

25   Richard DEAN, clerk, v. John HESLERTON of Old Malton.
Goods of William Dean of Old Malton, gentleman, deceased, whose executor complainant is.
YORK.

26–27   William DEANE v. Alen PYLETON.
Messuage and land in Ashprington and Totnes, late of Richard (corrected from John) Baker, grandfather of complainant   DEVON

28   Elizabeth, a daughter of Thomas DELARYVER, deceased, v. Edward DYCHER and Alice his wife.
Detention of an entail of the manor of Brafferton.   YORK.

29–30   Maurice DENYS, knight, and Elizabeth his wife v. Roger HUNT and William WHEATLEY.
Land in Darenth (Durrant), claimed to be included in a sale of a messuage and land in Stone (by Faversham).   KENT.

31   Thomas DENYS, parson of Fetcham (Feteham), v. Alice late the wife of John RICKMAN and John WOODINGE.
Parsonage of Fetcham awarded to complainant in a suit in this court against the said John Rickman.   SURREY.

32   John DENYSON v. William HOLLYNGWOOD and Joan his wife.
Detention of deeds relating to a messuage and land in Terrington.   NORFOLK

33   Clement DERRILL v. Owen BENYON and Nicholas PAYE.
Distress on land held of the Earl of Worcester's manor of Chilton, under pretext of forfeiture.
HANTS.

34   Thomas DEVENYSHE of West Hampnett, esquire, and Anne his wife v. Anthony PELHAM of Buxted, esquire.
Manor of Bucksteep (in Warbleton) pledged to defendant.   SUSSEX.

35   Robert DICKINSON v. Joan, late the wife of James STAVELEY, citizen and vintner of London.
Detention of deeds relating to two messuages called the *Sun* in Lombard Street, etc., of the bequest of the said James in remainder after defendant's death.   LONDON.

36   Roland DORANT, gentleman, son and heir of James Dorant, v. James FOLJAMBE, knight.
Messuages, cottage and land in Chesterfield, Dunston, Newbold and Dronfield.   DERBY.

37   Katherine, late the wife of Michael DORMER, knight, v. John GODDERD and Thomas MATHEWE.
Manors of Wendlebury and March Haddon (i.e. Haddon in Bampton?) and messuages in Brize Norton.   OXFORD.

38   James DRAPER of London, bowyer, v. John BARWYCKE.
Tenements in the parish of St. Albans (Alberous) with a rent reserved to the churchwardens [of that church]. *Mutilated.*   LONDON.

39   John DRAYTON, parson of St. Michael's, Wareham, v. Roger BRAYNE.
Profits of the said parsonage, claimed under a lease from Simon Berwike, late parson and formerly a monk, deprived for marriage.   DORSET.

40–42   Valentine DUCKMANTON of Saynton, co. Lincoln, v. Thomas FRANKYSSHE and Ellen LE(I)STON.
Messuages, cottages and lands in Tickhill, Stancill, Wadworth, Bawtry and Rotherham, late of John Leston, deceased, husband of the said Ellen and cousin of complainant.
YORK, NOTTS, DERBY.

43–45   Richard Rusburgh and Henry Clerke, churchwardens of ST. DUNSTAN'S IN THE WEST, and William Peyhen and others, the parishioners of the same, v. Richard LYSTE, vicar of the same, and Peter NEWCE.
Messuages and gardens in Shoe Lane, in the parish of St. Bride's, conveyed for the said church. (Defendants plead sale and purchase as chantry lands.)   LONDON.

46–48   Christopher DYGHTON and Thomas HAMMERTON, feoffees to uses, v. Thomas HUBLETHORN, cousin and heir of Agnes Bywaters, and John WA[R]DE, his tenant.
Messuages, cottages and land in Sutton-in-the-Marsh, Trusthorpe, Huttoft and Thornton by Horncastle, granted by William Bywaters, late the husband of the said Agnes, for the maintenance of a chaplain in the church of Horncastle and for other religious uses.   LINCOLN.

49–53   John DYNGE v. John GADDYSBURYE (Gadbery), gentleman.
Crown lease of lands in Southwell, obtained by defendant for himself after a promise to obtain it for complainant.   NOTTS.

54   John, grandson and heir of Alice (Allsyn) DYNGLE v. William DYNGLE and Chrystyan his wife.
Detention of deeds relating to messuages and lands in Trengale, Gonemand and Pennant (in St. Endelliom).   ,   CORNWALL.

55   Richard DYSNEY v. Dame Bridget MORYSON and Thomas HUSSEY, esquire.
Trees in the High Park (of Beauvale) bought of William Hussey, knight, deceased.   NOTTS.

FILE 1424.

1–2   William DACKCOMBE, gentleman, and Elizabeth his wife, late the wife of George Percye, gentleman, v. [Thomas CHAFYN?].
Parsonage of Mere of the demise of Peter Vannes, dean of Salisbury. *Damaged.* *See File* 1416, *No.* 11.   WILTS.

3   Christopher DANBY, knight, v. Elizabeth late the wife of Robert FRESTON and John his son.
Arrears of the said Robert as steward of the manors of Newland (in Halstead) and Paul's Cray and deeds.   SUFFOLK, KENT.

4   Roland DANDE of Mansfield, ironmonger, v. John CAPRON of the same.
Loan by Oliver Dande, deceased, father of complainant.   NOTTS.

5   Nicholas DANIELL, clerk, v. John DREWE and John his son.
Seizure of goods and deeds from complainant's house at Holsworthy.   DEVON.

6   Thomas DANYELL of Crediton(?), clerk, v. John CHAPELL.
Seizure of household goods, including ' an iron wyndowe with his frame,' a ' bawe of ewe ' (i.e. a bow of yew), and locks from the door. Mutilated.   DEVON.

7-10   Thomas DANYELL v. Thomas MELLES and Joan his wife, daughter of Thomas Wormsley and of Elizabeth his wife.
Messuages, cottage and land in Quadring, late of Agnes Danyell, deceased, grandmother of complainant.   LINCOLN.

11   Joan, late the wife of Ambrose DAUNTESEY, esquire, and formerly of ——— Lamborne, gentleman, v. Roger MAWDELEY, esquire.
Refusal to complete a marriage settlement of John his son with Elizabeth Lamborne, daughter of complainant.   ———

12   . . . DAVYE v. Thomas COTES and others.
Messuages in Clewer (Cleworthe), late of Robert Davye, deceased, brother of complainant. Mutilated.   BERKS.

13   Davy DAVYS of London, merchant tailor, v. William BRAYN.
Messuage, garden and orchard in Shrewsbury, late of Margaret Pope, deceased, grandmother of complainant.   SALOP.

14-17   John DAWES, citizen and grocer of London, v. Edmund TWYNYHO, gentleman, and William, son of Gerard POWER.
Tenement in Kenilworth for which money was paid to the said Twynyho and George Tresham, gentleman, to obtain a purchase from the Crown.   WARWICK.

18-22   William DAWES and Alice his wife, both of Putney, co. Surrey. v. William and Hugh HYDE and others.
Land in Presteign, held of the manor of Wigmore by Hugh Hyde of Presteign, weaver, deceased, father of the said Alice and Hugh.   RADNOR.

23-25   John DEANE of London v. Thomas VENABLES and others.
Lease for life of a messuage and land in Newhall, stated by the said Venables to be a tenancy at will.   CHESTER.

26-29   Robert DEY and Alice his wife, late the wife of Edmund Harte, v. John HARBOTTELL of Crowfield, merchant.
Land in Caddenham, late of John Norman, deceased, father of the said Alice, and claimed by defendant as part of his manor of Crowfield.   SUFFOLK.

30-31   The same v. John LEADER.
Detention of deeds relating to the same.   SUFFOLK.

32-38   Jane lady DORMER v. Isabel, late the wife of Thomas SAYRE, William her son and Richard FOSTER.
Manor of Wing with lands in Crofton belonging thereto, claimed by defendants under a lease from the priory of St. Mary de la Pré.   BUCKINGHAM.

39   Henry DOTSON v. John his brother.
Lands in Trevylyan, Cardewe (i.e. Cordew in Trevalga), Boscastle, Trevrenga (i.e. Trefrank in St. Clether?), Hendraburnick (in Davidstow) and Taven, late of John Dottson and Joan his wife, both deceased, parents of both parties. Damaged. See File 1296, No. 55.   CORNWALL.

40   Humphrey DOVE of Rowzton (i.e. Rowton, co. Chester?) v. Roger HANCOX of Pattingham.
Debt of William Pyrre(?). Mutilated.   [CHESTER?], STAFFORD.

41   Joan, late the wife of Thomas DOWRANT, of Redbourn, co. Herts, and administratrix of his goods, v. Thomas SAUNDERSON.
Tenement in Great Peatling of the demise of Anthony Wystowe.   LEICESTER.

42   Baldwin DOWSE and Elizabeth his wife, formerly Elizabeth Whyte, v. John COXE.
Lease of a parsonage by the warden and scholars of New College. Replication only.   ?

43   John DRENECK and Thomasen his wife, granddaughter and heir of Richard Laffryan (Lanfrean), v. John LAFFREAN, son and executor of the said Richard.
Messuages and land in St. Austell and Lavrean (Laffrean) in St. Austell.   CORNWALL.

44-45   Richard DREWE of London, waterman v. Richard PERSENSON and others.
Detention of deeds relating to a messuage and land in Scaftworth.   NOTTS.

46-47   Robert DREWE and Thomasyn his wife v. Richard SHEPPERDE, her father.
Concealment of a lease made by James Courteney, esquire, of a messuage and land in Cullompton.   DEVON.

48-49   William DREWRY, knight, and others v. Robert HOLDICHE, esquire.
Compromise of a debt of Richard Corbett, knight.   NORFOLK.

50-53   Peter DUNNE v. Richard BLYKE, esquire.
Lands in Radnor, late of Katherine Dunne, deceased, cousin of complainant and mother-in-law of defendant. Damaged.   RADNOR.

54   Roland DURANT, executor of Thomas Metcalf, v. Robert HOLLYNGWORTH and Francis
GROCE, executors of Agnes, late the wife of John DURANT of Barrowden, gentleman.
Debt of the said John.   RUTLAND.

55–56   John DURRANT and Joan his wife, granddaughter and heir of Thomas Parker, v. Richard,
brother of John PARKER, deceased.
Detention of deeds relating to a messuage and land in Hove (Hoo) of the entail of Robert Swynam.
    SUSSEX.

57   . . . late the wife of John DYALL v. Thomas EDGEWORTHE, gentleman.
Dower in a burgage in Holt. *Damaged.*   DENBIGH.

58   John DYON, gentleman, v. Henry WILLIAMS, parson of Louth.
Claims on a repairing lease of defendant's parsonage which was never confirmed by the bishop and
chapter of Lincoln.   LINCOLN.

FILE 1425.

1–4   John ECCLESTON v. Thomas RABY.
Goods of John Wylde, deceased, whose daughter was married to complainant and his widow to
defendant.   ———

5–9   John, Thomas, Christopher, Robert, and William, sons of John EDEN, deceased, v. Anne,
executrix and late the wife of John HYNDE.
Goods of the said John Eden, whose widow Margaret, co-executrix with complainants, married
the said John Hynde.   DURHAM.

10–12   William EDON, Katherine his wife, Richard BYFOLD, Agnes his wife, Roger GUNE and
Alice his wife, v. John BLEKE.
Detention of deeds relating to a messuage and land in Norton Lindsey late of Richard Ball and
Alice his wife, great-grandparents of the female complainants.   WARWICK.

13–17   Giles EDWARDES of London v. William EVYETT.
Pasture for sheep on lands in Quatford of the demise of the late abbot and convent of Lilleshall.
    SALOP.

18   Humphrey EDWARDES, B.D., archdeacon of St. Asaph, v. John SALESBURY, knight,
and others.
Mansion house, lands, feedings, rents, services, tithes, etc., belonging to the said archdeaconry.
    DENBIGH.

19   William EDWARDES the elder, son and heir of John Edwardes, v. William EDWARDES
the younger.
Detention of deeds relating to lands in Horton in the parish of S . . . (now in Beeding) and
Beeding. *Faded.*   SUSSEX.

20–23   Roger EDWORTH, vicar of St. Cuthbert's, Wells, v. Simon SEWARDE, prebendary of
Dinder in Wells Cathedral.
Corn-rent payable on the compromise of a suit between the parties' predecessors. (Defendant pleads
that on his appointment the prebend was discharged of all burdens by the bishop).   SOMERSET.

24   Philip EGERTON, knight, v. Henry OSBASTON and Peter WYNSHAM.
Messuage and lands in Laughton.   STAFFORD.

25   Thomas ELRYNGTON of Willesden, esquire, v. John CONSTABLE, knight, and Christopher
HYLLIARD, esquire.
Bond precluding complainant from publishing evidence about the death of Roger Barne his farmer
in Holderness.   MIDDLESEX, YORK.

26–31   Roger ELSDON v. Christyan late the wife of Richard COWLE, and John BORYNGTON
her son.
Land in West Sampford of the demise of William Ingelarde, late prebendary of West Sampford, and
claimed by defendants under a lease from Thomas [Darcy], lord Darcy.   DEVON.

32   Emmote, late the wife of Richard ELYETT, v. George HAYDON, lessee of the manor of Beer.
Lands (*described*) in the said manor of the demise of the late abbot of Sherborne. D.XII.1.   DEVON.

33   Gregory ELYNGER of Clopton, husbandman, and Ann his wife, late the wife of William son
of Thomas Elynger, v. Anthony STEBBYNG of Kettleburgh, husbandman.
Detention of deeds relating to lands in Clopton belonging to Thomas Elynger, infant son of the said
William and Anne.   SUFFOLK.

34   John ELYOTT of Marshfield, co. Gloucester, v. John HANHAM.
Messuage and land in Yatton, late of John Elyott, deceased, father of complainant.   SOMERSET.

35–37   George ELYS v. John DENYNGE.
Messuage and garden in Winchester, late of William Colvyle, deceased, kinsman of complainant.
Mutilated.   HANTS.

38–40   Maude late the wife of Richard ENDBROKE v. John FURSMAN.
Burgages and land in the manor of Paignton and in Rowneham of the grant of Joan Fursman,
deceased, aunt of defendant.   DEVON.

41   George ENGLISHE of Belvoir v. Thomas LODGE, alderman, and John PLAT, mercer, both
of London.
Loan to defendant the bond for which has come to their hands.   NOTTS, LONDON.

42–44   Wilfrid son and heir of Thomas ENTWYSELL v. Roger TRYMNELL (Trymley), gentleman,
and others.
Detention of deeds relating to a moiety of messuages and land in Handford and Newcastle-under-
Lyme.   STAFFORD.

45-46　Stephen ERBERI. *v.* Thomas ERBERY, draper, and Thomas GENT, mercer, both of. Bruton (Bureton, Brewton).
Price of a tenement in Bruton, which the said Thomas Erbery declares that he has paid to complainant's creditors.　SOMERSET.

47　James ERMYSTED of Stainforth, husbandman, *v.* John NUTTALL of Tasborough, gentleman.
Price of woollen twills, the bond for which is lost.　YORK, NORFOLK.

48　William ESTABROKE *v.* John BROCKE and others.
Freehold lands. *Mutilated.*　DEVON.

49　John and Edward, sons of John ESTON, gentleman, deceased, *v.* John CARPENTER.
Messuage, wheat-mills and land in Rye held in gavelkind according to the custom of the town. *Mutilated.*　SUSSEX.

50　The same *v.* the same and Robert and Thomas, all sons of John CARPENTER.
Delay in delivering deeds in the above suit.　SUSSEX.

51-52　John ESTON *v.* John ILLARY.
Money payable for a child which complainant had been ordered to bring up. *Mutilated.*　———

53　Richard ESTON of Winterbourn Earls *v.* William BUTTON.
Distress for rent of a tenement and mill in [Win]terb[ourn] Earls which complainant has paid to Alice, wife of John Hyll of London and afterwards of Kyngeston, co. Radnor, gentleman, lessee thereof. *Faded. See File* 1131, *No.* 33.　WILTS.

54-58　John ETHEREDGE of Kerswell, esquire, *v.* Edward FORD, gentleman.
Action on a counterbond for a bond already satisfied.　DEVON.

59　John ETWALL *v.* George, son of Richard REDFORD.
Moiety of lands in Stanton promised to complainant on his marriage with Elizabeth, sister of defendant.　STAFFORD.

60　Robert EUSTAGE (Eustace) of Dedham *v.* John HEYWARDE of Ramsey.
Lands in the manor of Moze awarded to complainant in this court, but demised to defendant by the court of the manor. *Mutilated.*　ESSEX.

61　Richard EVAUNCE, citizen and cordwainer of London, *v.* Reynold ap John WYN and others.
Messuages and lands in Llanfechain and Eastane Colwyn of the bequest of Edward Mathewe of Whitlyngton, co. Salop.　MONTGOMERY.

62　The same *v.* JOHN ap David.
Messuages and land in Llanfechain and elsewhere of the like bequest. *Mutilated.*　MONTGOMERY.

63-66　John EVERINGHAM, citizen and woodmonger of London, *v.* the mayor and sheriffs of LONDON, and Thomas VENOUR of Henley-on-Thames, gentleman.
Action on a bond for arbitration concerning an account for purchase of wood. *Certiorari and subpoena.*　LONDON.

67　Giles EVERTON of Rawton, co. Salop, gentleman, *v.* William and Menry UNDERHYLL.
Encroachment with their ' heyment or fensure ' on a close of pasture in Essington, etc.　STAFFORD.

68-71　Roger EWRYNG and Joan his wife, late the wife of John Broydon, *v.* Thomas BRAMSTON of Bergholt (Barfold), executor of John Deveroll.
Administration of the goods of William Smyth of St. Osyth's, mariner, deceased, father of the said Joan.　SUFFOLK, ESSEX.

72-75　The dean and chapter of EXETER *v.* Thomas JOHNSON and Margery his wife, executrix and late the wife of William Reynoldes.
Writings and money in the hands of the said Reynoldes as receiver to complainants.　DIOCESE OF EXETER.

76-77　Thomas EYON and Alice his wife *v.* William GILBANK.
Detention of deeds relating to a messuage called Gobions and land in Laindon and Colchester, late of Margaret Gillbank, deceased, wife of defendant and mother of the said Alice.　ESSEX.

78　Edmund EYRE, citizen and vintner of London, *v.* Christopher EYRE of Highlow, co. Derby, esquire, and Thomas his son.
Bond given for the guardianship of the goods of Miles Eyre, citizen and vintner of London, dissolved by the death of Mary his widow, daughter of the said Christopher. ' *See File* 1426, *No.* 65.　LONDON.

FILE 1426.

1　Richard EDGE of Horton, yeoman, *v.* Thomas BRODWALL of Crowborough, yeoman.
Debt of William Barlow of Norton, whose executor complainant is.　STAFFORD.

2　Baldwin, grandson and heir of William EDMUND, *v.* Thomas BOWTHEWATER.
Detention of deeds relating to a messuage and land at Longdon in Solihull.　WARWICK.

3　Giles EDMUNDES(?) and Alice his wife, *v.* Joan GARDYNER.
Messuage and land in Hartest(?) late of William Freman, deceased grandfather of the said Alice. *Faded.*　SUFFOLK.

4　Richard EDWARDES *v.* Thomas PYERSON and Richard COKE.
Messuages and land in the manor of Kingswinford of the demise of Thomas Edwards.　STAFFORD.

5　Robert EDWARDES and Edith his wife *v.* John GODD and others.
Share of goods of Joan Godd, deceased mother of complainant, who is her executor, defendants being overseers of her will.　———

6-7 Thomas EDWARDES, husbandman, v. William MARTYN of Long Ashton.
Maintenance of a bastard of John Edwardes of Mangotsfield (Magnesfyld), deceased, brother of complainant, moneys due to whom have been received by defendant. GLOUCESTER, SOMERSET.

8 Thomas EDWARDES of Yelford (Elverd) v. Cuthbert TEMPLE of Standlake, clothier, and Francis FETEPLACE.
Lease of pasture called ' Shirwood ' on a bad title. OXFORD.

9 William EGERTON of Little Swinbourn v. Thomas PHYLPOTTE of Compton Wasshelynge (in Compton), esquire, his brother-in-law, and John MARYNER his tenant.
Lease of the demesnes of the manor of Swaythling in succession to the said Maryner. D. XII, 38. HANTS.

10-13 The same v. John COOKE of Tidworth, esquire.
Lease of the rectory of Houghton. HANTS.

14-15 Edward, great-grandson of John ELAND, deceased, v. Richard HALL and Thomas WELDON.
Detention of deeds relating to a close of land in Carlton, dower of complainant's mother, now the wife of James Browne. See File 1427, No. 48. NOTTS.

16-17 Robert ELDRED of Bourn, yeoman, v. Thomas ELDRED (Aldred).
Messuage, buildings and land in Thurlby, late of Thomas Eldred, deceased, grandfather of both parties. LINCOLN.

18 Ralph ELIOTT (Hellott) v. William and John ELYOTT.
Messuage, cottages and land, part freehold or ' chre ' (i.e. chirograph?) ' holde ' and part copyhold in Breedon and Melbourne, late of John Elyott, deceased, father of complainant.
LEICESTER, DERBY.

19-20 Henry ELLYS, gentleman, v. Edward WYATT, Mary his wife, and Dorothy WALGRAVE.
Gold chain of the gift of Dame Juliana Walgrave, deceased, of whose goods defendants are administrators. ——

21 William ELLYSTON and Helen his wife, granddaughter and heir of Nicholas Heyere, v. Ellis STALEY and Nicholas GARLYCK.
Messuage called ' Redseats,' another messuage in Hardwick, and cottages in Castleton, Bakewell and Bradwell. DERBY.

22-23 Richard ELSEY and Joan his wife v. Thomas JACKESON.
Messuage in Stickney, late of William To(y)lye, deceased, father of the said Joan and of Margaret, late the wife of defendant. LINCOLN.

24-25 William ELTAM of Newchurch v. Michael DENNYS, esquire, brother and heir of Thomas Dennys, knight.
Messuage and land in the manor of Rew (in Ventnor) demised to complainant, William his father, and Thomas his younger brother HANTS. (I.W.)

26-27 Richard ELYATT alias Okeleye of Ashby-de-la-Zouch, co. Leicester, v. William FRAUNCES.
Messuage and land in Alrewas. STAFFORD.

28 John ELYOTT, citizen and mercer of London, v. Thomas HEBBES, esquire.
Action for a payment promised for a debt of Giles Keyllway, esquire, on condition that the chapel of Radour with lands there and in Blackford and Modbury proved to be of equal value.
MONMOUTH, SOMERSET, DEVON.

29 George ELYS of Poole, co. Dorset, v. John DENNYNGE.
Messuage, curtilage and garden in Winchester, late of John Elys and Alice his wife, parents of complainant. HANTS.

30 Joan, Amy, Edith and Alice ELYS, infants, by Richard Waller, their guardian, v. Roger ELYS, husbandman.
Tenements in Speenhamland, late of Thomas Elys, deceased, grandfather of complainant and father of defendant. BERKS.

31 [The same] v. John WYLKYNS of Bad . . . BERKS.

32-33 William EMERSON of Paglesham and Thomas EMERSON of London, yeomen, v. John SALMON alias Myller and John SAVERY of Paglesham, mariner.
Rival leases of the parsonage of Paglesham. ESSEX.

34 Thomas EMOTT of Alphington v. Walter STONE.
Detention of a lease made by Thomas Drewe, gentleman, of a messuage and garden in Ashburton.
DEVON.

35-38 Henry ENGLYSCHE v. John TREVYLYAN, esquire.
Closes in the manor of Nettlecombe of the demise of John Trevylyan, esquire, deceased, father of defendant. See File 1298, No. 30. SOMERSET.

39 Mark Anthony ERRYZO, merchant, of Venice, v. Nicholas NORBORNE, pursuivant, Peter BABYCHE, late complainant's servant, and —— RYVERS.
Frivolous action in the marshal's court for an assault in Southwark. SURREY.

40-41 Thomas ESSEX, knight, and Margaret his wife, late the wife of William Rogers, esquire, v. John ROGERS, knight, and Richard his son.
Manors of Stoford (rectius Cloford ?) and Ba . . . one-fourth of the manor of Wanstrow, etc., of the settlement of John Rogers, esquire. Mutilated. SOMERSET.

42-44 John ESTMOND of Hilton, husbandman, v. William CHYLDE of the same, gentleman.
Action on a bond for a debt already paid. DORSET.

45–46   William ESTON, husbandman, v. Nicholas NAPPER.
Tenement in Yeovilton (Evelton) late of Thomas Eston, deceased, father of complainant.
                                                                    SOMERSET.

47   John ETHEREDGE, esquire, v. Oliver MANWARYNGE, gentleman, and Richard HENSON, clerk.
Claim to tithe of the manor of Kerswell, exempted by composition between the abbot and convent of Montacute and the canons of Exeter.   DEVON.

48   William ETTERICKE of Barford in Wimborne (Minster), yeoman, v. Peter COOPER alias MOUNSELL.
Refusal to complete an assignment of a lease of a messuage and land in Ibberton (Ebrington alias Abberton).   DORSET.

49   Margaret, executrix, late the wife of William ETTYS, citizen and girdler of London, v. William ETTYS, her son.
Seizure of deeds relating to messuages in Bristol and West Ham. Mutilated. GLOUCESTER, ESSEX.

50   The same v. Thomas ARGALL, registrar of wills in the prerogative court of Canterbury.
Will of the said William, disposing of the premises and of messuages in Friday Street, London.
                                                    GLOUCESTER, ESSEX, LONDON.

51–52   William [EURE] lord Eure (Ewrie), v. Robert CREPLYNE of York.
Compromise of a debt.   YORK.

53   William EVANS, parson of Wolves Newton (Nova Villa Lupi), v. David PHILIPPE ap Hoel.
Dilapidations of the chancel of the church, whereof defendant had a lease from David Watkyns, late parson. Mutilated.   MONMOUTH.

54–55   William EVE of Beauchamp Roding, husbandman, brother and heir of Henry Eve of the same, v. Thomas PEACE (Pease) of Stamford Rivers.
Detention of deeds relating to lands in Aythorpe Roding (Ellen, late the wife of the said Henry and afterwards of defendant, is mentioned as also defendant in the latter's answer, but not in the bill).
                                                                     ESSEX.

56–59   John EVELEGH v. Thomas BRADDON and others.
Manor of Holcom, stated by defendants to be in the parishes of Ottery St. Mary and Bampton.
                                                                     DEVON.

60–63   Ralph EVOTTES v. Richard COOK and John HEYLESDEN of North Walsham.
Debts due to William Lytle, a debtor of complainant.   NORFOLK.

64   John EYLAND, citizen and cutler of London, v. Francis BACON, gentleman.
Action on a bond to warrant the title of a messuage and garden in the precinct of the White Friars by Fleet Street.   LONDON.

65–66   Anne [late the wife of] Stephen EYRE, and Roland his son v. Henry EYRE and others.
Tenements in Horsley Gate and elsewhere acquired by Miles Eyre, since deceased. Mutilated.
See File 1425, No. 78.   DERBY.

FILE 1427.

1–4   Richard FACYE v. George MAIOR.
Messuage and land at Winscott in Pyworthy conveyed to complainant's use by Agnes his mother on his marriage with Edith, daughter of Nicholas Trote, gentleman. Replication in duplicate.
                                                                     DEVON.

5–10   Nicholas, son of John FANNE of Thaxted, yeoman, and grandson of William Gace, v. Agnes GACE, late the wife of the said William, and Richard and John his sons.
Verbal bequest of money by the said William, whose executors defendants are.   ESSEX.

11   The same v. the same.
Money entrusted to the said William by the said John Fanne.   ESSEX.

12–13   Philip FARMAN of Adderbury v. Elizabeth, late the wife of Edward FARMAN his brother.
Detention of deeds relating to lands called ' Golyn Landes ' and ' Farmans Landes.'
                                                            OXFORD, BERKS.

14–16   John FARNIFOLDE of Rumboldswyke v. Richard FARNEFOLD of Steyning, son and heir of Richard Farnefolde, and James FARNEFOLDE.
Detention of deeds relating to lands in West Grinstead, Ashurst, Shermanbury, and Stoney Style.
                                                                    SUSSEX.

17   Thomas, son and heir of Thomas FASHYN of Southampton, merchant, v. John de la LOEE.
Corn-rent chargeable on land called ' La Courte de la Loufew ' in the parish of Câtel (' Our Lady Castell '), which defendant has attempted to charge on complainant's manors of Annevill and Lescewe. See File 1120, No. 3.   GUERNSEY.

18–21   Francis, late the wife of Richard FAWKENER, v. Thomas YATE, Elizabeth his wife, and others.
Lands at Milton in Portsea, Kingston, Cliddesden, Ashmansworth, Stoke, Binley (in St. Mary Bourne), [St. Mary] Bourne, and Hurstbourn (Husburne).   HANTS.

22–27   Robert FAYREBOLTE and Margaret his wife, late the wife of Hugh Forrest, v. Joan, late the wife of Richard FORREST, husbandman, parents of the said Hugh.
Moiety of lands in Came and of goods given to the said Hugh and Margaret on their marriage.
                                                                    HEREFORD.

28–29   Richard FELDE v. Richard WHALLEY, esquire, late his master.
Action for an account rendered before Lord North by complainant's instructions.   ———

30   Richard FERNE v. Thomas BROOKE.
Manor of Earl's Court *alias* Kensington of the demise of Anne, countess of Oxford.   D. XIV, 14.
MIDDLESEX.

31–32   The same v. the same.
Do.   *Answer wanting.*   MIDDLESEX.

33–36   John FERRALL of Eastbourne, husbandman, grandson and heir of Agnes Ferrall, v. Nicholas PRYOR.
Wrongful occupation of a messuage and land in Cuckfield by means of deeds obtained by Stephen Borde and others.

37   Robert FILLE v. John RAYNSFOURTH, knight.
Occupation of a house and goods in defendant's manor of Manningtree in contempt of writs of error and *de non molestando*, complainant having denied him a lodging there in his return from beyond seas.   *Mutilated.*   ESSEX.

38–39   John FISSHER v. Richard CHALCROFT.
Detention of leases of lands in Wedmore, formerly of Alice Chalcroft, grandmother of defendant.
SOMERSET.

40–42   Robert FITZHERBERT, gentleman, v. John WARDE and others, executors of William Topleys.
Rent of pasture in Tissington demised to the said Topleys.   *Mutilated.*   DERBY.

43   Richard Smithe and others, inhabitants of FLAWBOROUGH, v. Anthony STAUNTON of Staunton, esquire.
Annuity payable from the church of Staunton to that of Flawborough.   *Mutilated.*   NOTTS.

44–47   Mary FLETCHER of Cambridge, executrix and late the wife of James Fletcher, v. Miles PRAUNCE of the same, brewer.
Detention of documents awarded to the said James by arbitration.   CAMBRIDGE.

48–50   Robert FLETCHER and Agnes his wife v. Richard HALL and John SHEPERD.
Close of pasture in Carlton acquired of Edward Eland, since deceased.   *See File* 1426, *No.* 14.
D. XV, 11.   NOTTS.

51–52   Elizabeth FLOWER of Bristol v. John WEBBE of Newnham, yeoman.
Meadow and three 'stages of fysshynges,' etc., in the late abbot of Gloucester's manor of Ruddle (in Newnham).   GLOUCESTER.

53–56   The same v. Walter FLOWER.
Do.   (Both defendants plead that complainant has a husband living.)   2 *mils.*   GLOUCESTER.

57–59   Richard FLOWER of London, haberdasher, v. Agnes, late the wife of Thomas TAYLE-YOUR and others.
Messuages and lands in Drax, Rawcliffe, and Carleton, acquired of Laurence Nesse, yeoman.   YORK.

60   The same, styled 'citizen,' v. Ralph NESSE and Agnes TAYLOR.
Do.   YORK.

61   Thomas, son of David FLOYD, deceased, v. JEVAN ap Thomas ap Jevan and MEVANWY verch David.
Cattle entrusted to Thomas ap Jevan ap Maddoc, deceased, father of the said Jevan and husband of the said Mevanwy.   ———

62–63   Robert FLYNTE of Lakenham, esquire, v. William, grandson of Amy HELME and John MYUN his guardian.
Encumbrances of the manors of Caster and Markyshall of the demise of the said Amy.   NORFOLK.

64   Thomas FLYNTE and Margaret [his wife] v. Margaret BAYLEY.
Tenement in Westonney of the gift of Humphrey Vernon, esquire, father of the said Margaret.
Mutilated.   MONTGOMERY.

65–66   Roger FOBERY and Margaret his wife v. John WARCOP, gentleman, Henry his son and Ralph TYRELL.
Refusal to complete a sale of portions of a messuage in Foster Lane in the parish of St. John Zachary.   LONDON.

67   John FOGGE, knight, Mary his wife and Edmund EYRE, citizen and vintner of London, v. Christopher EYRE of Highlow, esquire.
Legacy of Miles Eyre, whose executors are the said Mary and Edmund for the marriage of fifty poor maidens in Tideswell, Hope and Hathersage, and other purposes.   *See File* 1425, *No.* 78.

68   Anthony FONSO of Bristol, merchant of Portugal, v. Richard BARETT of Lyme and Edmund MANSEY of Taunton.
Forgery of a receipt for wood in the name of Thomas More of Taunton.   ———

69   John FORDE of Weston-upon-Trent v. William LOVETT of Callowhill in Kingston, yeoman·
Refusal to complete a lease of a close of pasture in Colton.   *Mutilated.*   STAFFORD·

70–71   John FORDE of Horkesley v. Anthony RUSSHE of Thornham (Therneham), co. Suffolk.
Refusal to complete a sale of half the manor of Dengewell in Wix and Great Oakley.   ESSEX.

72–74   Miles FOREST of Morborn (Marborne), esquire, v. William APRICE, son and heir and executor of Robert Aprice of Washingley, esquire.
Debt of the said Robert, of a bill for which complainant was robbed on the highway.   HUNTINGDON.

75   John FORSEY of Sherborne, co. Somerset (*rectius* Dorset), parchment(?)-maker, v. Thomas HALLETT and Alice his wife.
Refusal to pledge a leasehold in the borough of Milborne Port for a loan of 40s.   *Damaged.*
SOMERSET.

76–78   Anthony FORSTER of Newark, esquire, and John SOMMER, clerk, executors of John
        Longland, bishop of Lincoln, v. Agnes and Richard BASSET and Richard WHALLEY,
        esquire.
Wardship of the manors of Fledborough and Normanton, and of messuages, lands, and rents of
assize there and in Wodcotes, Stokeham, Staythorpe, East Drayton, North Clifton and elsewhere
held of the bishop by John Basset, esquire, deceased, husband of the said Agnes and father of the
said Richard Basset. *Damaged.*   NOTTS.

79   The same v. Edmund BONER, bishop of London.
Arrears of rent awarded against defendant in this court as archdeacon of Leicester. *Mutilated.*
See File 1023, Nos. 56–61.   LEICESTER.

80–81   George FOSTER, esquire, v. John TEY, esquire.
Half the price of the marriage of Thomas, son and heir of Nicholas Coveld, in ward of complainant
for lands in Great Birch and Copford held of his manor of Easthorpe, and of defendant for other
lands.   ESSEX.

82   The same v. John DANYELL.
Messuage and land in Easthorpe.   ESSEX.

83–86   Joan, late the wife of William FORTE, v. John NORREYS and William JOHNSON,
        gentleman, deputy-stewards of the manor of South Petherton, John KINGMAN, bailiff,
        John TUCKER, and others.
Lands in Padman Street in the said manor of the demise of Henry [Daubeney], late Earl of
Bridgwater.   SOMERSET.

87   Henry FOSBROKE, gentleman, v. John BRONELEY.
Refusal to complete an assignment of a lease of tithe corn in Nottingham and tithe hay in Beeston.
                                                                                      NOTTS.

88–91   Edmund FOWLER of East Budleigh v. John WEBBER and Thomasyne his wife.
Loan of a chest of napery, brewing vessels, and money.   DEVON.

92   William FRANCKLIN v. Robert LEYS and Alice his wife, late the wife of John, brother of
        complainant.
Action for the manor of [Molton], late of William Greer of Molton, gentleman, the manor of Norton,
late of the abbot of Malmesbury, and lands in Marlborough. *Mutilated.*   SOMERSET, WILTS.

93   Anthony FRANKISHE, gentleman, v William and Lionel CAMONSON and William
        ROUNDELL.
Detention of deeds relating to messuages and land in Ripon. See File 1220, No. 39   YORK.

94–97   John FRAUNCES of Cottenham, yeoman, v. Thomas WEDD.
Messuage and land in Swaffham Bulbeck, late of Joan Danes (Deyns), deceased, grandmother of
complainant.   CAMBRIDGE.

98–101 John FRENCHE and Alice his wife v. Thomasyn CROKEHORNE, daughter of John Brode.
Messuages and lands in Allisdon and Way (both in North Tamerton), late of John Crokehorne of
Tamerton, deceased, father-in-law of defendant and grandfather of the said Alice. CORNWALL.

102–103 William FRENCHE of Okeford Fitzpaine, labourer, v. John STYLL of Fontmell, son and
        heir of John STYLL.
Sale by defendant of land including two ' keyne lease ' in the marsh of Bere, whereof the inheritance
was in Sir George Delaleyne.   DORSET.

104–106 Richard FRESTON, knight, v. Cicely, late the wife of Thomas WE(T)CHE and Thomas
        her son.
Detention of deeds relating to a marsh or alder-carr in Mendham ' on the parte of Norfolke.'
                                                                                    NORFOLK.

107–109 William FRYE, husbandman, and Margaret his wife v. Walter HUNGERFORD, knight.
Lease of a messuage in Warmes   .   .   .   (i.e. Warminster) paid for in the Court of Augmentation
before its dissolution. *Mutilated.* See D. XIV, 12.   WILTS.

110   Robert FULJAMBE of Howell v. Nicholas TAYLOUR.
Goods of John Fuljambe of Heckington, whose executor complainant is.   LINCOLN.

111   John FYNYMORE v. Agnes and Walter DRAKE.
Gold and old money entrusted to Richard Drake, deceased, whose executors defendants are. ——

112–114 William FYSSHAR, Margaret his wife, Nicholas BROWNE and Alice his wife v. Thomas
        HERYNGMAN and Elizabeth his wife.
Messuages and lands in Croydon, formerly of Randolph Barker, for which defendants plead a
former judgment of the Star Chamber. D. XIV, 5.   SURREY.

115   Thomas FYSSHE v. William TERRY and others.
Messuage and land in the manor of Marston 'of the demise of the last prior of Tutbury. DERBY.

116–118 William FYSSHER v. William CROUCHER.
Messuages and land in defendant's manor of Bathampton (Hampton), let by the bishop of Bath
and Wells in villeinage as ' olde aster.'   SOMERSET.

119   John, son of Richard FYSSHER, v. the same.
Tenement in the same manor. *Mutilated.*   SOMERSET.

120–121 John FYTZJAMES, archdeacon of Taunton, v. John PYRREY and Elizabeth his wife.
Parsonage and prebend of Milverton Prima, Langford and Thorne, demised by George Hennage,
predecessor of complainant, to Thomas Sowthwood, yeoman, with various exceptions and charges
(*described*).   SOMERSET.

122   Mary and Margaret FITZRICHARD v. Richard EVOTT.
Assault in lands in Rayleigh awarded to complainants in this court together with stalls in the
markets. *See* D. XIV, 19; 44.   ESSEX.

123-125 John FITZWILLIAM of Kingsley, co. Hants, esquire, v. Joan, executrix and late the wife
of Richard THWAYTES and Thomas AUSTWYCKE.
Tithe, corn and hay of Pontefract, Tanshelf, and Carleton, late of the monastery of Pontefract.
YORK.

FILE 1428.

1-2   John FABYAN, citizen and draper of London, Jane his wife and John GARDENER, v.
the Mayor and Aldermen of LONDON and William PLEASANCE, yeoman, surviving
executor of George Pleasance.
Action on a bond given by Robert Gardener, draper and citizen of London, whose executors are
the said Jane and John Gardener, for a payment to Charles Pleasance, bestowed son of the said
George. *Certiorari and subpœna.*   LONDON.

3-4   Katherine FARNELEY *alias* Ludlowe v. Thomas LUDLOWE, her divorced husband.
Lands belonging to complainant before her marriage.   WORCESTER, SALOP.

5   John FARRE v. John RYDER and others.
Contract to build a mill for which complainant surrendered land in Epworth (' Exworth in the
Isle of Exholme.')   LINCOLN.

6   William FAYERBROTHER of Norrington v. William HANDFORD of London, merchant
tailor.
Recognizance given in complainant's name but without his knowledge.   SURREY, LONDON.

7-9   Richard FAYREFYLDE and Walter SCORYE, v. John BARWIK, esquire, late ranger of
the forest of Savernake.
Money due to complainants as keepers of the said forest in lieu of an allowance of wood.   WILTS.

10   Nicholas [FELDE ?] and Joan his wife v. Harry SCALES and others.
Legacy of Robert Lapham of London, yeoman, son of the said Joan whose executors defendants
are. *Mutilated.*   LONDON.

11   John FENTON v. Joan DORYNGTON and Mathew her son, executors of Robert Doryngton
of Stafford.
Detention of deeds relating to a meeting, and land in Fenton, and of money delivered to the said
Robert for payment of complainant's subsidy. *Mutilated.*   STAFFORD.

12-13   Richard FENYS, esquire, v. Anthony BUSTARDE, gentleman.
Detention of deeds relating to the manor of Bloxham Beauchamp and lands there.   OXFORD.

14   John FERMOR of Yodon (*i.e.* Eudon in Glaseley ?) and William PALMER of Chelmarsh,
v. the steward and bailiffs of BRIDGNORTH and John CORBET of Glaseley, esquire.
Action for an allegation of bribery in a suit before the Council of the Marches for lands in Fernolles.
[*Supersedeas*] *and subpœna.*   SALOP.

15-16   George FERREYS, executor of Elizabeth Bowser, v. John, son and heir of Thomas
SCRYMPSHER of Norbury.
Annuity charged on the manors of High Offley, Tunstall and Lee by Humphrey Bowser, deceased,
whose executrix the said Elizabeth was, and who afterwards sold the manors to the said John.
STAFFORD.

17-18   Richard FERROUR, husbandman, v. Thomas COLE and Thomas WHYT.
Messuage and land at Fenton in Kettlethorpe, late held of the manor of Stowe by Oliver Ferrour,
deceased, brother of complainant.   LINCOLN.

19   William FILLOLL v. John TOGOOD, Thomas AMYLL *alias* Ward and others.
Obstruction of a road leading from Shaftesbury to complainant's tenement in Marnhull.
[DORSET]

20   Thomas FISSHER of Westminster, v. Roger PATRICKSON of Ennerdale.
Town grant of of the bailiwick of Egremont, claimed under a grant from Lord Wharton.
CUMBERLAND.

21   William FISSHER of Carlton, gentleman, v. Anthony ELLYS, under-sheriff of Nottingham,
and William, brother, and attorney of Richard MARSHALL.
Extent on a judgment debt already partly satisfied in cash.   NOTTS.

22   John FITZHERBERT, esquire, of the body to [the King], v. John, son and heir of John
ISACKE.
Refusal to complete a sale to Humphrey Fitzherbert, esquire, father of complainant, of a messuage
and lands (described) in the manor of Gatesbury and the parishes (*sic.*) of Gatesbury and Braughing.
HERTS.

23-25   The same v. the same.
Refusal to complete a sale of part of the same lands to Anthony and Michael Fitzherbert, deceased,
brothers of complainants.   HERTS.

26-27   John FLEMINGE, gentleman, v. Leonard TEDSELL, Agnes his wife, and John, son of
Roger JUKES, deceased.
Messuage and land in Tettenhall and Wolverhampton, late of William Flemminge, deceased,
grandfather of complainant.   STAFFORD.

28-29   Simon FLETE of King's Lynn, co. Norfolk, shipwright, and Agnes his wife, v. Thomas
WULFFE of Cambridge, butcher.
Messuage in Cambridge, late of William Smythson of Cambridge, carpenter, deceased, father of
the said Agnes.   CAMBRIDGE.

30–31   William FLYNTE, parson of Brisley, v. Christopher ATHOWE.
Tithes.   NORFOLK.

32   Stephen FOOLD v. Richard COPLESTON of Copleston, esquire, and others.
Meadow in the said Copleston's manor of Sharnewyke (i.e., Langtree Week?) in Langtree.   DEVON.

33   John FORD, yeoman, v. Thomas BARE.
Refusal to complete a sale of a tenement in Cockfield, held of the Earl of Oxford's manor of
Earl's Hall.   SUFFOLK.

34   William FORDAME v. Harry WALTER and Thomas MORE.
Tenements in Hoddesdon, late of John Bramstone, deceased, grandfather of complainant.   HERTS.

35   Edmund FORDE v. Thomas RITHE and Constance his wife, administrators of the goods of
Henry Wyndesore, deceased, and George RITHE of Lincoln's Inn.
Bargain concerning the manor of Harting.   SUSSEX.

36–38   Thomas FORDE v. Walter SHERE.
Land in Brixton.   DEVON.

39–40   George FORMAN, citizen and skinner of London, v. Paul FORTUNE.
Attachment for a debt of George Vanderhove to whom complainant was wrongly supposed to be
indebted.   LONDON.

41   Philip son and heir of Robert FORMAN v. John PYRRYN.
Messuages and lands in Oxford, Abingdon, Shillingford, Hanney, Kennington, Adderbury,
Rollright, Epwell, Walton, Cowley and Watlington.   OXFORD, BERKS.

42–43   . . . . daughter and executrix of Joan FORSTER, v. Ema (Emote), executrix and
late the wife of Thomas FORSTER, and Joan their daughter.
Arrears of annuity charged on a tenement in Scarborough by William Forster, deceased, husband
of Joan the elder and father of Thomas. *Mutilated.*   YORK.

44   Thomas FORSTER v. Christopher ARON and Richard BAYLY.
Tenement, croft, orchard and garden in Shiffnall.   SALOP.

45–48   William FORSTER v. Elizabeth late the wife of Martin MISTERCHAMBERS.
Money entrusted to defendant on complainant's behalf by Thomas Forster of Louth, deceased, his
father and brother of defendant.   LINCOLN.

49–50   Bartholomew FORTYUNE, citizen, and founder of London, v. Margaret, executrix and late the
wife of Thomas MORAR of Croydon.
Detention of a bond for a debt already satisfied. *Answer wanting.*   LONDON.
                                                                                          SURREY.

51   Elizabeth, the divorced wife of Thomas FOSTER, and formerly the wife of Thomas Pedder,
esquire, and Thomas, and Edmund PEDDER, her sons, v. Henry PEDDER, eldest son of
the said Thomas the father, and Henry Allen.
Messuages and lands in Husborne Crawley, Salford, Milton Keynes, Moulsoe, Meriden and Great
Linford, adjudged to complainants in this court. *Damaged. See File 788, No. 14.*
                                                                                   BEDFORD, BUCKS.

52   John FOSTER and William PLOTE, churchwardens of Aldenham, and others, for all the
inhabitants of Aldenham, v. Philip BOLD and Joan his wife.
Property in defendant's manor of Aldenham, bequeathed by Thomas Stebbyng to the churchwardens
of Aldenham to use the profits at their discretion for divine service.   HERTS.

53   Robert FOSTER of London, dyer, and Elizabeth his wife, v. Nicholas MACKYN and
William MYSTERTON.
Messuage and land in Woodseats, late of Robert Wylkynson, deceased, grandfather of the said
Elizabeth.   YORK.

54–55   John FOWLER of Combrawleigh, v. William . . . MBERD and [Alice his wife?]
Money and land promised to complainant on his marriage with Joan, daughter of John Every of
Donyatt, husbandman, former husband of the said Alice. *Damaged.*   SOMERSET, DEVON.

56–58   William FOWLER v. Leonard WENSLEY.
Refusal to complete a demise of a tenement in Burton-upon-Stather. *Damaged.*   LINCOLN.

59–60   Charles FOXE v. Francis CRESSETT, gentleman of New Inn.
Affray ' thys present Saterdaye mornyng ' in the fields beside Holborn.   MIDDLESEX.

61   John FOXE v. John PROCTOUR and George KERKBYE.
Vexatious suits for a close in Sturton.   NOTTS.

62–63   Thomas FRANCKLYN v. Margaret FRANKLYN.
Detention of deeds relating to messuage, and lands in East Challow and Letcombe Regis, late of
Thomas Francklyn, deceased, father of complainant and husband of defendant.   BERKS.

64–66   The same v. the same.
Joint tenancy of lands in Challow, in consideration of which complainant had let his other lands
there.   BERKS.

67   Richard FRAUNCEIS v. John LYTE of Lytes Cary, esquire, and Joan his wife, late the wife
of William Yonge.
Refusal to complete a sale of a mill and land in Trent.   SOMERSET.

68   John, son and heir of William FRAUNCES of Combe Flory, v. Somerset Knight, v. Robert
GOUGE, Eleanor his wife and William GRAVENER.
Messuages and lands (*described*) in Paddington, late of William son of John Fraunces, deceased, cousin
of complainant.   MIDDLESEX.

69-71 William FRAUNCES of Ketton, co. Rutland, yeoman, v. Thomas (Richard), husband of Elizabeth COLLYNSON.
Messuage and land in North Thoresby, late of Thomas Fraunces, deceased, grandfather of the said William and Elizabeth. *See* D. XIV, 20. LINCOLN.

72 Robert FREMAN v. Henry DETH.
Lands in Gosberton, Pinchbeck, Surfleet, Whaplode, Holbeach and Moulton of the entail of Robert Reynoldson. LINCOLN.

73-75 William FREMAN, husbandman, v. Richard FREMAN.
Messuage and land in Witcham, late of John Freman, deceased, grandfather of complainant. CAMBRIDGE.

76-78 George FREVYLE, esquire, v. Dorothy, executrix and late the wife of John FREVELL, esquire.
Lands in Little Shelford given to complainant with the rest of the manor and its appurtenances in Hauxton, Newton, Harston and Shepreth, by Robert, son and heir of the said John. CAMBRIDGE.

79 Edmund FROGMERE v. John LYNSSEY.
Seizure of a bond from complainant's attorney. *Mutilated.* LONDON.

80 John FRY v. Mary, executrix and late the wife of Nicholas COVE.
Lease of the mansion and demesnes of the manor of West Quantoxhead, entrusted to the said Nicholas by Michael, son of Baldwin Mallett, esquire. SOMERSET.

81 Christopher FRYE and ' Sysley his wyfe of the cytie of Brystowe Marchant,' v. Walter FESARTE.
Land in Buckelsebury of the bequest of John Marten. GLOUCESTER.

82-83 John FRYE the elder and John FRYE the younger, both of Alderbury, v Hugh PILGRIME, executor of Joan Frye.
Messuage and land in West Grinstead, and goods (*schedule annexed*), late of John Frye, deceased, grandfather of complainants and husband of the said Joan. WILTS.

84-85 Andrew FULFORDE, esquire, v. Agnes late the wife of Peter HOWE and John their son.
Messuage and land in Upton Helion granted by the said Peter to all parties jointly. *Subpœna duces tecum.* DEVON

86-89 Andrew, son and executor of Thomas FULLER, v. Margery, wife of William ABBOTT, esquire, John KEYLE, gentleman, her son-in-law and Clement CYSLEY.
Manor of Westbury in Barking of the demise of Dorothy Barley, late abbess of Barking. *Damaged.* ESSEX.

90-91 Dennis FULLER v. William KYNGE.
Messuage and land in Hampstead bought of John, son and heir of Walter Coxson, for which defendant pleads a judgment in the Common Pleas. *See File 788, No. 31.*

92 Joan late the wife of John FUNTEYN v. Dennis BRETT.
Tenement in Sall of the feoffment of James Boleyn, knight. NORFOLK.

93 Roger FYNEMORE of Quemerford v. William ASSHMAN of Whetham.
Detention of deeds relating to lands in [Whetham], Corsham, West Kington, Calstone, Calne and Compton Bassett, late of Walter Fynemore, deceased, father of complainant. *Mutilated. See Files 409, No. 49; 509, No. 20; 787, No. 17; 987, No. 47.* WILTS.

94 Edward FYTZGARRETT, esquire, and Dame Agnes PASTON, his wife, v. Alice late the wife of Thomas CALTHROPPE and Bertram his brother, administrators of his goods.
Account of the said Thomas as receiver of rents of the manors of Thorp, Boughton, . . . Ude, Barney, Sudbury, Middleton Hall and Brandon Hall, the rectory of St. Gregory's, tenements in Birchin Lane, etc. NORFOLK, SUFFOLK, ESSEX, LONDON.

FILE 1429.

1-2 Richard son and heir of Alice GAMELONDE v. Richard son and heir of Leonard COOKE and William NEWMAN.
Messuage and land in Waltham Holy Cross stated by the said Newman to be in the Queen's park there. ESSEX.

3-4 Richard GARDNER v. John and William, sons of William WEBBE, and Thomas BYNGLEY.
Tenement in Odstock, promised by the said William the elder, whose executors defendants are. WILTS.

5 The same v. Katherine WEBBE and William CHUBBE.
Demise of a tenement in Odstock while in dispute in this court. WILTS.

6-7 John GARLYNG v. Geoffrey SCOTT and Joan his wife.
Price of geldings left in defendant's house in Chelmsford during complainant's journey to London. ESSEX.

8-9 Thomas GARRETT v. George EDWARDES, parson of Eversholt, and Thomas POTTES *alias* Johnson.
Lease of the parsonage of Eversholt promised for complainant's trouble in educating the said Edwardes and obtaining him the presentation thereto. BEDFORD.

10-11 Thomas GARRETT v. George TYRRELL.
Messuage and land in Croydon of the bequest of William Garrett. SURREY.

12 John GASCOIGNE of Sutton v. Fulk GREVILL, knight, his brother-in-law.
Loan the bond for which is lost. YORK.

13–16   Henry GASKEN, vicar of Wysall (Wysaw), v. William PYNE, executor of Richard Wilde, clerk.
Lease of complainant's vicarage.   NOTTS.

17–18   John GATEFORD of Penshurst, husbandman, v. John JESOPE (Gisuppe).
Lands in East Malling belonging to Robert Streitfild an infant, stepson of complainant.   KENT.

19–22   Richard GAYEWOOD v. William and George BLACKWALL.
Land in Mansfield bought of the said William, who declares that it was only pledged for reimburse-
ment of a debt. D.XII, 21.   NOTTS.

23–24   Peter GERINGE of Winterton v. Henry ANDERSON and Margaret his wife.
· Old gold and silver late of Richard Gering, deceased, grandfather of complainant.   LINCOLN.

25–28   The same v. Peter ANDERSON of Roxby, yeoman
Damage by cattle in the glebe of Winterton parsonage.   LINCOLN.

29–30   Michael GERMYN v. the mayor, bailiffs and sheriffs of EXETER, and Thomas BORD-
FELDE (Brodfelde).
Action on a bond to be void when defendant had the registrarship of the diocese of Exeter, whereof
he was deprived by the Archbishop of Canterbury. *Certiorari and subpoena. Faded.*   DEVON.

31   William GERY of Bushmead, esquire, v. William PLATFOTE (Platforde), yeoman.
Execution on a statute staple already redeemed.   BEDFORD.

32–33   Matthew GOODDINGE of Ipswich, clothier, v. the mayor of BOSTON, [and Robert BRIAN
(Bryant) of Boston, merchant].
Action on a bond annulled on balance found by arbitration. *Certiorari.*   LINCOLN.

34–35   John GOODMAN, dean of Wells, v. Robert ELIOTT, clerk.
Spiritual jurisdiction of the archdeaconry of Wells. *Mutilated.*   SOMERSET.

36–39   John GOODMAN v. John GROWT.
Parsonage of Stockinge Pelham of the patronage of Jerome Songer. *Mutilated.*   [HERTS.]

40   Jane GOODMAN, late the wife of the said John.
Do.   *Mutilated.*   [HERTS.]

41–42   Valentine GOODWYN and Margaret his wife, daughter of John Myller, deceased, v. Thomas
BUTTES, esquire.
Joint lease of the manor and rectory of Thornham made by Richard Nykkz, late bishop of Norwich.
.   [NORFOLK.]

43–44   John GOONE and Nicholas SMYTHE, churchwardens of Westhall, v. Thomas DAVYE.
Rent of Trinity lands of the gild of Westhall.   SUFFOLK.

45–49   John GOSTWICKE, executor of Elizabeth Gostwicke, v. Thomas VARNEY (Farney),
knight, and Anne his wife, executrix and late the wife of William Gostwicke.
Loan to William Gostwicke, deceased, nephew of the said William. *See File* 1123, *No.* 42. [BEDFORD.]

50–52   Thomas GOUGHE of Whitchurch v. Christopher, son and heir of John KENNE, esquire.
Mansion house and lands of Inyns Court at Bishopsworth (Busshfort) in Bedminster, acquired of
George Payne.   SOMERSET.

53–56   John GRANGER of Godmanchester v. William LARKETON of Islyppe.
Bond given on defendant's behalf for the maintenance of Christopher Collen his stepson.
HUNTINGDON, [N'HAMP.]

57   Hugh son and heir of John GREMES v. Henry JAMES *alias* Trehaverse of Sethen (*i.e.*
Sithney?), co. Cornwall.
Detention of deeds relating to messuages and lands in Tavistock.   .   DEVON.

58–59   Roke GRENE, esquire, son and heir of Edward Grene, knight, v. Margaret GRENE, late the
wife of the said Sir Edward, and formerly of Robert lord Curzon.
Actions for dower of the manors of Great and Little Sampford and Exning barred by a grant of
dower which is in defendant's hands.   ESSEX, SUFFOLK.

60   The said Margaret v. William FYTCHE.
Abetting the said Roke in seizure of goods at [Little Sampford]   *Bill wanting.*   [ESSEX.?]

61–63   John GRENFELD v. Alexander TRYGGES, merchant of Exeter.
Manor of Rowthorne pledged to defendant to obtain money for complainant's journey by command
of the Privy Council to the isles of Scilly (Suleye). (Philip and Mary are spoken of as the late
sovereigns).   DEVON.

64–68   Isabel, late the wife of Richard GRESSHAM, knight, v. John HARBATTELL, administrator of the goods of John Hall, clerk, deceased.
Detention of deeds and issues of the manor of Aldburgh (in Barton-upon-Ure) and messuages
and lands there and in Pott Grange (in Ilton), Swinton (by Masham) and Bromley (in Grewelthorpe).
YORK.

69–72   Thomas GRESSHAM, esquire, son and heir of the said Sir Richard, v. the same.
Profits of messuages and lands of the said Sir Richard in York   .   YORK

73   William GREVE and Isabel his wife v. .   .   .   . and Humphrey JORDANE.
Messuage and land in the said Jordane's manor [of Coxford in Grimstone?]. *Mutilated.*   NORFOLK.

74–76   Fulk GREVILL, knight, and Elizabeth his wife, v. William BOSTOCK.
Manors of Downhatherley, Boddington and Beauchamp Court (co. Warwick), late of Richard, lord
Beauchamp, deceased, great-grandfather of the said Elizabeth. *Damaged.*
GLOUCESTER [WARWICK.]

77–88   Thomas GRYFFYN, knight, and Jane his wife, a daughter and heir of Richard Newton' esquire, *v.* John HORNER and John RUNYON, esquire, and Richard MORGAN, gentleman' complainant's auditor.
Diversion of water from a tucking-mill in Babington, and embezzlement·of the issues of the manor of Court-de-Wick in Yatton, Walton-in-Gordano, Ston Easton, Midsomer Norton, Babington, Clewer, Taunton, Alston Marreys (in Weare), Winsford Bosun, South Charlton and Downhatherley, and lands there and in Claverham, Kingston Seymour, Clevedon, Yatton, Upton, Chilcompton, Compton Dando, Bakyngton (*i.e.* Luckington in Kilmersdon?) Vobster (in Mells), Kilmersdon, Mells, Clewer (*sic*) Alryngton, Weare (Overweere), Biddisham, . . , Huntspill, North Charlton, Acton Burnell, co. Devon (*sic*), and Teniton (lands in many other places named, descended to Giles Capell, knight, and Jane his wife).   SOMERSET, GLOUCESTER, DEVON.

89–90   William GRYFFYN of London *v.* Richard MYNSHALL, William GOLBOURNE and Edmund CRUC of Nantwich.
Pastures in Barterton demised to complainant by his father.   CHESTER.

91   John GRYFFYTH *v.* EDWARD ap Hugh.
Lands at Llanforda in Oswestry, late of the chantry of St. Michael there.   SALOP.

92   Philip GUNTER, citizen and skinner of London, *v.* John HOLMES of North Mimms, co. Herts, gentleman servant to the late Duke of Northumberland.
Forgery of an acquittance of a loan, dated at Euston (*i.e.* Eaveston) so that the issue may be tried where defendant has influence.   YORK.

93–95   William GUNVILE of Gorleston, gentleman, son and heir of Richard Gunvile, *v.* Edward BOWES of London, haberdasher.
Refusal to complete a sale of a messuage and land in Bradwell.   SUFFOLK.

96   Richard GWYN of Lincoln's Inn *v.* FLUELLEN ap Roser.
Houses in Llansannor acquired with lands there for Margaret Fluellen   GLAMORGAN.

97   John GYLE *v.* Thomas GRENE.
Detention of deeds relating to lands in Needham Market, Barking, Darnsden, Battisford (Basforde), Bricett and Kingshall and forgery of a will in the name of Robert, brother of complainant. SUFFOLK.

FILE 1430

1–3   Thomas GABITUS, [parson of Cumberworth,] *v.* John JACKESON *alias* Cowper.
Rent of tithes of Cumberworth of the demise of William Fletcher, late parson. *Mutilated.*
                                                         LINCOLN.

4–5   The same *v.* Richard RAUSON, Elizabeth his wife, late the wife of the said John Jackson, and John JACKSON his son.
Revival of the above.   .   LINCOLN.

6   Christian, late the wife of John GALLEY, and John and James her sons, *v.* John STEDEMAN.
Tenement in Ashwick of the demise of the member and ' confreers ' of the hospital of St. John the Baptist, Bath.

7   Richard GALLYNGTON of Dulcote, yeoman, *v.* John SWAYN of Greyndon, husbandman.
Sixteenth share of a lead-pit and works on Mendip. *Faded.*   SOMERSET.

8   Roger and John GARLANDE *v.* Robert MORE of the Inner Temple and Richard CALMATHIE.
Bail given on behalf of Robert Inne of Lyme, merchant, in an Admiralty suit for conversion of goods shipped thence to Andalusia. *Damaged.*   DORSET.

9   William GARNANS of London, gentleman, *v.* Thomas SMYTHE, attendant on the Council of the Marches.
Tenement in the manor of Foxley in Yazor, of which manor defendant is Crown lessee·in reversion.   HEREFORD.

10–13   The same *v.* the same.
Do.   HEREFORD.

14   John GAYER *v.* Richard CARCLEWE and others.
Messuages in St. Keverne of the gift of Thomas Baghowe.   CORNWALL.

15–17   Thomas GELL *v.* Richard ELSYE and Ralph NEWTON.
Lands in Bakewell, late of Arthur Shakerley and Margaret his wife.   DERBY.

18   Henry GERNYNGHAM, knight, vice-chamberlain to the Queen, and Richard FRESTON, knight, cofferer of the Household, *v.* Richard WENAM.
Refusal of rent payable from the manor of Brent Pelham to Anne, wife of John Knight, and late the wife of John Lucas, esquire, and waste.   HERTS.

19–20   Anne, late the wife of Anthony GILBERT, esquire, *v.* John WADHAM and Nicholas GILBERT, esquire, his executors.
Goods of the said Anthony, including money promised to complainant by her father, Richard Cooke, esquire, on her marriage.   HANTS.

21–23   Nicholas GIRLINGTON, esquire, *v.* John NEWCOM(EN) of Saltfleetby, esquire, and Robert CLARKE.
Collusion in.an action on a bond included in a release by the said Newcomen.   LINCOLN.

24   Richard GLYNNE *v.* John CLOWYS his father-in-law and Margaret, late the wife of Richard MANORES, knight.
Messuage and land in the manor of Gyldmorton of the demise of the said Sir Richard, surveyor.   [LEICESTER.]

25   Thomas GODDESPEAS v. William WARDEN and others.
Messuage and land in Great Brendon, late of William Goddespeas, deceased, father of complainant.
Mutilated.   NORTHAMPTON.

26–27   Dorothy GODFRY v. John GOLDEWELL of Chart, gentleman.
Detention of a bond. *Mutilated.*   · KENT.

28   John GODWYN of Croscombe, clothier, and Alice his wife, executrix of William Yarbery
of Bruton, clothier, v. John MOUNTENEY and Mary his wife, administratrix of the goods
of John Tucker of Bruton, deceased, late her husband.
Debt to John Yarbery, deceased, father of the said William.   SOMERSET.

29   William GOD . . ., husband of [. . . . late the wife of Edmund Denny of Palgrave],
v. George DENNY of the same, brother of the said Edmund.
Goods of the said Edmund, and debts due to him. *Mutilated.*   SUFFOLK.

30–31   William GOLD of Northover, mercer, v. William LYGHT, gentleman.
Messuage and land in defendant's manor of Northover, of the demise of the master and brethren of
the hospital of St. John the Baptist, Bridgwater.   SOMERSET.

32–34   William GOLDBURNE of Clifford's Inn, student of the law, v. William CARISON and
Richard GOOD, his servant.
Land in Wigland of the demise of Edward Goldburne of Overton, father of complainant.
                                                                            CHESTER.

35   Richard GOODE of Tewkesbury v. Joan GOODE.
Bond given by William Goode, deceased, father of complainant and husband of defendant.
                                                                            GLOUCESTER.

36–38   John GOODLADDE of Tooting, co. Surrey, son of John Goodladde and of Joan, his wife,
v. Nicholas RICHARDSON and others.
Messuages and lands, late held by the said Joan of the manor of Ross in Holderness.   YORK.

39   William GOODMAN *alias* Skynner v. Lawrence RASTORNE (Rastall).
Refusal to complete a conveyance of an island called ' Tynseigh ' in the ' Temses ' in the parish of
Westbury.   BUCKINGHAM.

40–42   William GOODRIGGE v. Thomas and Harry GOODRIGGE and Robert SMYTHE.
Land in Tugby, late of John Goodrigge, deceased, father of the said William, Thomas, and Harry.
                                                                            LEICESTER.

43–44   William GOODWYN of Adderley Green (in Caverswall)· v. Thomas, son and heir of Edmund
WHYTMORE.
Impounding cattle at Weston Coyney, pending a suit in this court. *Mutilated. See File 992,
No. 26.*   STAFFORD.

45–47   Philip (William) GOOSEY of Chippenham, administrator of the goods of Richard, his brother,
deceased, v. John COOPER of Lacock, executor of Joan, executrix and late the wife of the
said Richard, Lawrence BAYNERD and John SMITHE.
Purloining a bond for performance of an arbitration by the said Smithe and others, and collecting
debts due to the said Richard.   WILTS.

48   Edward GOSTWYK v. William HAMELDEN.
Grange of Stanford Bury, late of the abbot and convent of Wardon. *See File 1125, No. 27.*
                                                                            BEDFORD.

49–50   Edmund GOWER and Eleanor (Elizabeth), his wife, late the wife of Stephen Cottrell, and
Katharine, Eleanor, Elizabeth, and Martha COTTRELL, daughters and heirs of the said
Stephen, v. John BEREMAN, husband of Agnes, late the wife of Richard Cottrell.
Detention of deeds relating to messuages and lands in Hill Crome, Crome Symondes, Erles Croma
(*sic*), and Boughton.   WORCESTER.

51   William and Robert, sons of John GOWPIE, v. Mary GOWPIE.
Lease of a messuage and land in Budleigh by William Strode of Egham, co. Surrey, to Philip
Gowpie, deceased, his wife (*not named*), and complainants in succession.   SOMERSET.

52–54   John GRENE, Elizabeth, his wife, Richard ALFFELD and Jane, his wife, v. William
VEYSSEY, Sibill his wife, Richard MANSFELD, Jane, his wife, Christopher WOODE and
others.
Messuages, shops and land in St. Sepu.chre's and St. Martin-in-the-Fields, late of William Stede,
deceased, grandfather of the female complainant, but claimed in right of Nicholas Asshlve,
deceased, uncle of the said Sibill and Jane Mansfeld.   MIDDLESEX.

55   Robert GRENE and Alice GRENE, his guardian in socage, v. Robert ARDERNE.
Land at Wilmcote in Aston Cantlow.   WARWICK.

56–57   Thomas GRENE v. John LUNSFORTHE.
Messuage. and lands in Burghersche (*i.e.* Burwash). *Mutilated.*   [SUSSEX.]

58   · Walter GRENE of Bristol v. William BAGER.
Burgage called ' Truggins Yerde ' in Barlondon in the lordship of the castle of New Radnor, late of
Nicholas Grene *alias* Bocher and Ellen his wife, parents of complainant.   RADNOR.

59   Thomas GRENELANE v. Richard SEWARD, gentleman.
Refusal to complete a conveyance of land in defendant's manor of Chilcompton, for which a fine
was to be paid in lead.   SOMERSET.

60   William GREVE of Stiffkey (Stukey), yeoman, executor of Thomas Seele (Scele, Stele),
parson of Roydon (Rydon), v. Katherine, executrix and late the wife of Edmund SKYPP-
WYTH of Fordham, gentleman.
Horses and cattle taken to pasture, and loan of money.   NORFOLK.

61-64   John GREY, knight, v. William DERBY and others, executors of Thomas Browne of Fishtoft, bailiff, of the manor of Frampton.
Profits of the said manor and of the ' brovage ' and agistment of Holland Fen, waifs and strays of the honour of Richmond, etc., of the demise of the heir of Charles [Brandon], late Duke of Suffolk.
LINCOLN.

65   William GREY of the Inner Temple, gentleman, v. Thomas his brother.
Tenement in the manor of Morfe (in Enville). *Mutilated. See File* 1300, *No.* 80,   STAFFORD.

66   Robert, son and heir of Lawrence GREYE, gentleman.
Petition to call Richard and Roger Taverner, gentlemen, to testify to a conveyance of messuages and lands in Kenilworth.   WARWICK.

67   William GREYSHOT v. John and Alice (?) MILLE.
Cottages and land in the manor of Bishop's Sutton. *Damaged.*   HANTS.

68   Lawrence GRYFFITH v. John LLOYD Aprothoughe.
Messuage and land in Llangadock, late of David ap Griffith ap Owen, father of complainant.
CARMARTHEN.

69   Edmond GRYFFYN, servant attendant on the Marquis of Winchester, v. Lawrence MAYNEWARINGE, his brother-in-law, and others.
Seizure of deeds relating to the manors of Barterton and Woolstanwood, late of John Gryffyn, father of complainant.   CHESTER.

70   John GUYNETT, parson of Luton, co. Bedford, v. GRIFFITH ap John ap Evan, clerk, and HUGH ap John ap Howell, gentleman, both of Llangelynin, co. Merioneth.
Rent of the rectory of Clynnog Vawr.   CARMARTHEN.

71-74   Martin GYBSON of Calverley, yeoman, v. John DAWNEY, gentleman.
Action on a bond for payment of defendant's debts, of whom he is ' under the retynue ' in service.
YORK.

75-78   Robert GYE of Dodderidge (in Sandford) v. Peter VAN, dean of Salisbury, and his chapter.
Lease of the rectory of West Allington to complainant and to John his father, since deceased.
DEVON.

79   Ancelme GYES v. Thomas BYRTE and Cicely his wife.
Manor of Holt.   WORCESTER.

80   Ancelme GYES, son of John Gyes of Elmore, esquire, v. [William and John GYES] his brothers.
Annuities charged on the manor of Brockworth. *Damaged.*   GLOUCESTER.

81-82   Robert GYLBERT v. Edmund HUNT, constable of Hindolveston, and late servant to John Robsart, knight.
Seizure of deeds, money and goods and extortion of a bond and a general release by means of a false charge of felony.   NORFOLK.

83-84   William, son of John GYNNYE (Genny), and servant of Nicholas Ligh of Addington, co. Surrey, v. Robert GENNY, William GYNNY of Great Birch, and others.
Messuages and lands in Dewsall, Kilpeck and elsewhere, in which defendants are maintained by John Skudamour, esquire. *Damaged.*   HEREFORD.

FILE 1431.

1-5   Richard GABYTUS v. William (Thomas) THOMLYNSON.
Sale of stolen oxen at Blyton under toll-marks procured at Kirton.   LINCOLN.

6-7   Robert GAMAGE, esquire, v. Miles MATHEWE of Llandaff.
Manor of St. Nicholas and advowson of the church there, offered for sale in order to pay a Crown debt.
GLAMORGAN.

8-9   John GARRANT, yeoman, v. Joan SHARPE, *alias* Garrett and others.
Messuages and lands (*described*) at Porthpygan (in East Looe) of the grant of Robert, brother and heir of John Garrant.   CORNWALL.

10   Robert GAYWOODE of Bishop's Offley, gentleman, v. Ellen and Philip BOUGHEY.
Messuage called the Hall of Sugnall Parva, and lands there, late of Humphrey Gaywood, deceased, father of complainant.   STAFFORD.

11   Peter GERINGE of Wyn[terton], gentleman, v. Robert CLAYTON.
Messuage and land in Colby, bought of Leonard Wenysley. *Mutilated. See File* 1429, *No.* 23.
LINCOLN.

12-14   George GERRADE (Jarrard), v. William WRYGHTE, parson of High (' Greate ') Wycombe.
Money, messuage and land (*place not named*) given to defendant to resign his living.   BUCKS.

15-17   Robert GIRLYNGTON of the Inner Temple, gentleman, v. William RYGISBY.
Rent of Brentford ferry and a messuage and land there held of the Bishop of London's manor of Ealing.   MIDDLESEX.

18   John GLASYER, parson of Newington Bagpath with the chapel of Owlpen, v. John MASON and others.
Claim to the parsonage under a lease from Thomas Mason *alias* Hancoke, brother of the said John Mason and deprived of the parsonage for marriage.   GLOUCESTER.

19-22   Thomas GODFFREY *alias* Porter v. William LUDON.
Messuage and land in the manor of Potterne.   WILTS.

23–25   Frederick GODFREY and Garrard HANSPOLE, executors of Jacomyn, late the wife of
Garrard Copleman, and formerly the wife of John Lovyn, v. John ABBOTT and Joan, his
wife, daughter of the said Copleman.
Lease of a house in the Savoy and goods of the said Jacomyn claimed as goods of the said Garrard
Copleman. *Answer wanting.*   MIDDLESEX.

26   Thomas [GOLDWELL], bishop of St. Asaph, v. John SALISBURY, knight, Robert
SALISBURY, esquire, Dorothy his wife, PEERS ap William and others.
Lands and profits of the archdeaconry of St. Asaph, the archdeacon's house being used as an
alehouse. *Mutilated.*   DIOCESE OF ST. ASAPH.

27   The same v. John CONWEY of Partrevan, esquire.
Occupation of glebe of the archdeaconry and tithes of Dyserth in contempt of an injunction in th
above suit. *Mutilated.*   FLINT.

28   The same v. the same PEERS ap William.
Occupation of lands belonging to the archdeaconry in contempt of a like injunction.   FLINT.

29–31   Joan, executrix, and late the wife of William GOOD, v. Richard GOODE his son.
Site of the manor of Fawley of the demise of John Frelande.   HANTS.

32–37   John GOSSE of Brant Broughton, gentleman, v. Thomas VAUX, Lord [Vaux of] Harrowden,
Elizabeth his wife, James HUNTYNGTON, John GOSSE, and others.
Lease of the manor of Brant-Broughton and other lands of the said Lord Vaux there.   LINCOLN.

38 . . Clement GOTELEY v. John BROWNE his son-in-law.
Detention of a grant of an annuity redeemed by a grant of land in Ashford.   KENT.

39–40   John GOUGH, gentleman, v. John MAN(D)LEY.
Contract to build a new house or parlour.   STAFFORD.

41   Robert GRANTHAM v. Edward BROWNE of Newark.
Messuage in Lincoln, late of Hugh Grantham, deceased, father of complainant.   LINCOLN.

42   Thomas GRAVE and Elizabeth his wife, v. John GEFFREY and Mary his wife.
Detention of a lease of land in Marshwood made by —— Salisbury.   DORSET.

43–44   Richard GRENE, gentleman, v. Francis BERNARD, esquire.
Money and warrants of complainant's will, promised as price of the reversion of a messuage called
'Gobyons' and other messuages and lands in Great and Little Bardfield, Great and Little
Sampford and Sible Hedingham.   ESSEX.

45   Maurice [GRIFFITH], bishop of Rochester, v. Ralph HOPTON, knight, and Christopher
BYTYNSON.
Messuage, orchard and garden in St. Saviour's, Southwark, late of the prior and convent of
Winchester Cathedral.   SURREY.

46–47   The same v. John KNOTTYNG.
Arrears of rent of woods in the manor of Cuxton, the lease whereof to John Lascoy was suppressed
by the last bishop. (Lease of other portions of the manor are mentioned.)   KENT.

48   The same v. Ralph HOPTON, knight, and Christopher BYTTYNSONE.
Messuage, garden and orchard (*described*) now in the parish of St. Saviour's, Southwark, and formerly
in that of St. Margaret.   SURREY.

49–51   Francis GUEVERRA v. Edmund son and heir and executor of Paul WYTHEPOOLE.
Attempt to extend the manors of East Keale, Stenigot Sibsey, Leake and Leverington, for a debt
of John Reade, esquire, father-in-law of complainants, since satisfied.   LINCOLN.

52   Richard GULLOCKE (Gollocke) v. John CHAUNDLER and Walter WHYTLOCKE of
Wotton in Somerset.
Land at Harteley Gate in Wotton of the demise of the said Chaundelar.   SOMERSET.

53–55   The same v. the same and William COCKES.   DORSET (*sic*).
Do.

56   John GUYES, esquire, and Auncelme his son and heir apparent, v. Thomas DUTTON of
Sherborne, esquire.
Manor of Barrington, pledged to defendant.   GLOUCESTER.

57–62   John GWYN, parson of Llanrhaiadr and student at Queen's College, Cambridge, v. David
BIRCHINSHA, and DAVID, ap (Ser) John.
Arrears of rent of the parsonage of Llanrhaiadr, of the demise of Thomas Rouncorne, late parson.
DENBIGH.

63   William GYMBER of London, grandson and heir of William Thomas, v. Henry CROWTE.
Detention of deeds relating to a messuage in Bedford.   BEDFORD.

64   John . . . and Michael GYSOPPE, husbandman, v. Richard and John ASKUE.
Lands in Great Ponton claimed as concealed from the King's and Queen's manor of Grantham.
Mutilated.   LINCOLN.

FILE 1432.

1–3   Peter, Agnes, and Katherine GAMAGE, Owen SMITH, Margaret his wife, Nicholas COVE
(Gove), and Anne his wife, v. John GAMAGE and Richard NORCOCK.
Messuage and land in Walden, bequeathed by William Gamage, father of the said Peter and the
female complainants, to be sold for their benefit on his wife's death. D. XII. 5.   ESSEX.

4   Richard GARLANDE and Joan his wife, v. Nicholas TOPPE, harper, and Joan his wife.
Detention of deeds relating to tenements in Marwood called Church Marwood and Kingsheanton.
See File 993, *No.* 9. ·   DEVON.

5–7   John and Thomas GARRWELL v. Bartholomew GARRWELL.
Messuages and lands in Great and Little Hale and Hedington. *Mutilated.*   LINCOLN.

8–10   Richard GATESKELL, parson of Purley, v. Thomas WYNDMAN, parson of Farnborough
(Ferneborowe).
Wages for serving defendant's cure.   BERKS.

11–13   John GAYER v. John ARUNDELL of Lanhern, knight.
Money advanced by Richard Gayer of Marazion, deceased, father of complainant to defendant while
imprisoned in the Tower.   CORNWALL.

14.   William GLASEOUR of the Inner Temple v. Randall MANWERINGE, esquire.
Malversation as deputy-steward under complainant of the manor of Barnshaw.   CHESTER.

15–17   John GODBOLD v. William MARCHANT, *alias* Tyler.
Action on a bond for a debt ·partly paid.   [SUFFOLK.]

18   The same v. the same, both of Southwold.
Price of hay and butter.   SUFFOLK.

19–20   John GODFREY of Norwich, mason, v. Simon CRABBE of the same, worsted-weaver.
Messuage in St. James's, Norwich, and land in Pockthorpe, late of Ralph Godfrey, deceased, father
of complainant.   NORFOLK.

21–23   Thomas GOODINGE of Ipswich, merchant, v. Christopher LATYMER, esquire.
Conveyance of the manor of Freston. *Mutilated.*   SUFFOLK.

24–28   Eleanor and Ralph GOODRICHE v. Rowland ATKYNS *alias* Goodriche.
Messuage and land in the manor of West End Naunton in Cheltenham and Charlton Kings of the
settlement of Richard Goodriche, deceased, husband of the said Eleanor and father of the said
Ralph.   GLOUCESTER.

29   David GOUGH v. DAVID ap Jevan,·clerk, and OWEN ap Meredith.
[Marriage] and land in Knewill, late of Llewelyn ap Tyddyr, deceased, grandfather of complainant.
Mutilated.
                                                                                 MONTG.

30   John GRAUNGER of Ashleworth, co. Gloucester, husbandman, v. Thomas GRAUNGER.
Cottages and land in Wellam (*i.e.* Welland?) late of John Graunger, deceased, grandfather of
both parties.   WORC.

31–34   Robert, son and heir of Robert GRENE, v. John GUDDYE (Goodye).
Lands in Oldbury claimed under a lease from the monastery of Polesworth. *Damaged.* WARWICK.

35–37   George GRENEHAMME, gentleman, v. William CALDECOTT (Calcott), esquire.
Rents and services of messuages and lands held of complainant's manor of Ketton. RUTLAND.

38   John GRENESLADE, husbandman, v. John WYNDHAM, knight.
Refusal to complete a lease of land in Luxborough.   SOMERSET.

39   ·Ralph GRENEWAYE, alderman of London, v. Bryan BALES and Elizabeth his wife,
late the wife of Richard Pymonde.
Messuage, tenement and burgage in Westgate, Wakefield, and croft in the High Street, all bought ·of
Ralph Bayvett of Wakefield, merchant.   YORK.

40 ·   Thomas GRENEWAYE, brother and heir of the said Ralph, v. the same.
Reviver of the above.   YORK.

41   Edmund G[R]EYE v. William BLAKE. and others.
Rents in Andover. *Mutilated.*   Hants.

42–43   John GREYNFELD, esquire, v. Edmund SPECOTT, John KYLLEGREWE and John
BEVELL.
Crown debt of Richard Greynfeld, knight, deceased, brother of complainant, whose executors
defendants are, concerning lands of the late monastery of Buckland.   DEVON.

44–47   The same v. the same.
Do. *Damaged.*   DEVON.

48–49   Thomas GREYSWOLDE v. Thomas DABRIDGCOURTE, Alice his wife, Richard
MYDLEMORE, and Anne his wife.
Messuages and land in [Solihull?] late of Richard Greyswolde, deceased, grandfather of the female
complainants. *Mutilated. See Files* 992, *No.* 45; 1124, *No.* 50.   WARWICK.

50–51   Alice GRIFFETH, late the wife of Griffeth Lloit, and ELLEN verch Griffeth his daughter,
v. Humphrey ap. Hugh *alias* LLOIT his brother.
Messuages and lands in Gylsall (?).   ·   MONTG.

52–53   George GRUFFITHE, knight, v. Robert COOKE of St. Clement Danes.
Cofferer's debenture for oxen taken from complainant, and money given by him for a fee in Chancery,
in the hands of Anthony Rowley at his death in defendant's house.   LONDON.

54   John GRYFFYTH, LL.B., dean of St. Asaph's, v. Richard PUSKYN, late dean, John
SALESBURYE, knight, and others.
Possessions of the deanery, to which the said Puskyn was presented by the said Sir John and
afterwards deprived. *Damaged.*   DIOCESE OF ST. ASAPH.

55–56   Henry GRYME, administrator of the goods of John Gryme, late parson of Kilve (Culve), v.
Richard ROGERS.
Price of sheep.   SOMERSET.

57-59   John GUYE of Stoke by Guildford, husbandman, v. Peter DAVY.
Messuages and lands in Godalming and Witley, late of Thomas Guye of Shalford, yeoman, deceased,
father of complainant.   SURREY.

60   Agnes, late the wife of Thomas GYBBES, and granddaughter of Edmund Penny, v. Thomas
HARFLITTE.
Contempt of a decree of a Chancery commission concerning land in Ash and costs.   KENT.

61-64   William, son of the said Agnes, v. the same.
Detention of deeds relating to the premises.   KENT.

65   John GYFFORD, esquire, v. Humphrey DOSSET (Dorsett).
Messuage and land at Hatton in the parish of Crewood (vectius Brewood) of the demise of John
Gyfford, knight.   STAFFORD.

66   John, son of William GYLES, v. Richard POMERYE, Anne, late the wife of Tristram
HENSCOTT, John HENSCOTTE, William STROWBRIDGE, and Anne his wife.
Messuage and land in Great Totnes and Ashprington acquired of the said Richard and extended on a
statute staple given by him to the said Tristram, whose executors are said Anne and John Henscott
and William. Mutilated.   DEVON.

FILE 1433.

1-6   William, son and heir of John GARDENER, v. William COLE and Richard GARDENER.
Detention of deeds relating to a tenement in Bramford.   SUFFOLK.

7-8 ·   Thomas GARLAND, husbandman, v. John THORNTON 'of Beltoft.
Messuage and land in Scotton, Haxey and Owston, late of Thomas Garland, citizen and cooper
of London, deceased, nephew of complainant. See File 1300, No. 9.   LINCOLN.

9   William GARNETT of Broxbourne, yeoman, v. Christopher MARSTON of Hertford,
tanner.
Price of oak-bark.   HERTS.

10-14   William GARRYNGTON of East Mersea, husbandman, v. Margaret OFFYNE.
Messuage and land in Tollesbury of the bequest of John Garryngton of Heybridge.   ESSEX.

15-17   Elizabeth, late the wife of Nicholas GAVELL, v. Henry SYDNEY, knight, kinsman and heir
of Nicholas Sydney, and William ROBERDES of Beccles, gentleman.
Lands (described) in Bramfield, held of the late college of Mottingham.   SUFFOLK.

18   John GAYER, great-grandson of John Trembrace, gentleman, v. John BOSSOWOLOWE
and others.
Detention of deeds relating to lands in Ludgvan and Buryan of the bequest of Alice Treffuses.
                                                                                          CORNWALL.

19   John GAYNESFORD, executor of Nicholas Gaynesford, v. Ralph WYDENBURY, executor.
of Katharine, late the wife of the said Nicholas, and Joan his wife.
Jewels, plate, and other goods.   ————

20-21   Walter GEMYNGHAM of Worstead v. William BARNES of Great Yarmouth, yeoman.
Land in Filby, late of Robert Gemyngham, deceased, uncle of complainant.   NORFOLK.

22   Thomas GENT, late bailiff of the manor of Leek, v. Hugh JANNY and others, homagers of
the great court there.
Amercement for levying another amercement wrongly imposed on William Traforde by the said
homagers.   STAFFORD.

23-24   Gilbert GERRARDE of Grays Inn, Alice, daughter of George TRAFFORDE, deceased,
·   and others, v. Edmund TRAFFORDE, knight, and others.
Manor of Quick (Wyke, Whyke), and messuages and lands there in Saddleworth Frith, of the gift
of Ralph Trafforde, esquire. Pedigree in answer. See File 584, No. 7.   YORK.

25   Thomas GILES of London, haberdasher, son and heir of Margery Giles, Thomas WORRALL,
Margaret his wife, and Alice, late the wife of Edward RICE, v. Humphrey BETTERTON.
Messuage, barn and land in Kidderminster, late of Elizabeth Highway, deceased, mother of the
said Margery, Margaret and Alice and of Anne late the wife of defendant.   WORCESTER.

26-27   George GODDARD, gentleman, son and heir of William Goddard, v. William BYLLYNG.
Waste of a messuage called the Crown and others adjoining in Bishopsgate Street in the parish of
St. Leonard, Shoreditch, late of the hospital of Our Lady without Bishopsgate.   MIDDLESEX.

28   Thomas GOLSTON of Mamhead, co. Devon, v. Edward SPRATT, gentleman, and others.
Messuages and lands in Lichfield and Shenstone of the entail of Piers Golston of Coton, gentleman,
deceased, grandfather of complainant.   STAFFORD.

29   John GOODMAN, dean of Wells, v. Philip LAWES and Eleanor his wife, executrix and
late the wife of William Foxe, deputy-provost of the cathedral.
Money advanced by Richard Swanne, formerly provost, an office since abolished, for payments to
the prebendaries of Combe and their vicars, and left in the hands of the said Foxe.   SOMERSET.

30-33   George GOUGHE of Lincoln's Inn, gentleman, v. John GOUGHE of Lydney, son of William
Goughe.
One-half and one-third of the grange and demesne of Wollaston, half a barn and garner and rent
of a house and lands and liberty to fish and make ' puttes and engens ' in the Severn.   GLOUCESTER.

34-35   John, son of William GRAUNGER, v. Richard BRAYE.
Lands and a messuage in Ewell of the bequest of Richard Playstow. (Defendant pleads a previous
trial in the Court of Requests.)   SURREY.

36	John GRENE *v.* James JOHNSON.
Rent of the office of deputy to defendant as usher to the Court of Augmentations, since abolished.

37	Richard GRENEAKERS and others, governors of the grammar school of Clitheroe, *v.*
William FENNAYE and others.
Messuages and lands belonging to the rectory of Almondbury.	YORK, LANCASTER.

38	Christopher GRENYNG, parson of Colne Engaine and vicar of Little Waldingfield, *v.*
Hugh APRYCE and Margaret his wife [late the wife of William Pewson of Westminster, yeoman].
Action on a bond for payments to be made out of complainant's cures, defendants having made no provision for the service thereof. *Mutilated.*	ESSEX.

39–42	Fulke GREVILLE, knight, and Elizabeth his wife *v.* Thomas STAPELDON (Stapelton).
Manor of Lightwood, late of Robert, Lord Willoughby de Broke, deceased, grandfather of the said Elizabeth.	STAFFORD.

43–44	Walter GREY, esquire, *v.* William TREVITT and Edith his wife.
Corn-rent of the capital messuage and demesnes of the manor of Long Bredy.	DORSET.

45–46	Robert GRIFFETH, servant to Nicholas Hare, knight, Master of the Rolls, *v.* JEVAN ap Rice ap David.
Crown lease of a messuage and land in Wickwer.	DENBIGH.

47	GRIFFITH ap Thomas, vicar of Cilcen, *v.* Thomas SALUSBERYE, esquire, J.P.
Imprisonment for lack of sureties on a false report by John ap Griffith ap Hugh, esquire, farmer of the rectory of Cilcen, and other vexatious, whereby he is compelled to leave his vicarage. FLINT.

48	GRIFFITH ap Jevan ap David *v.* RES ap Thomas ap Res and others.
Land in Llan . . . late of David Lloyd ap Jevan ap David, deceased, brother of complainant.

49–50	Richard ap Thomas ap John GRUFFYN *v.* John ap David GETHYN.
Gavelkind messuage and land in the lordship of Wolston, in the parish of Wortham. *Pedigree given.*	MONTGOMERY.

51	James GRYFFYTH ap Powell, esquire, and Sible his wife *v.* MORYS ap Howell and Morrice TAYLOUR.
Bond given together with defendants on behalf of Yevor Bedo(?). *Mutilated.*	HEREFORD.

52–54	Richard GRYFFYTH (ap Griffith) of London *v.* Rowland BOLDE, yeoman.
Seizure of goods from complainant's house in Llangollen by colour for distress of a heriot. DENBIGH.

55	James GRYFFYTHE ap Hoell and Cicely his wife *v.* DAVID ap Watkyn and others.
Loan made by the said Cicely before her marriage.	————

56	Thomas GRYMSE *v.* Walter BEETES and the steward and bailiff of THETFORD.
Action for a debt of Thomas Grymse, father of complainant, satisfied by pledging a house in Brandon Ferry. *Subpœna and certiorari.*	SUFFOLK.

57–59	Richard, son of Richard GUNTER, gentleman, and of Joan his wife *v.* Thomas REVE, an officer of the Exchequer.
Money and plate of complainant's parents said to have been placed into the Exchequer. *Mutilated.*	OXFORD.

60–61	GWENLLIAN verch Meredith of St. Sepulchre's, London, sister (*sic*) and heir of Jevan ap John, *v.* Edward LLOYD, gentleman.
Messuage, barn and land in Sylyng (*i.e.* Silvington?). (Defendant pleads a judgment of the Council of the Marches.)	SALOP.

FILE 1434.

1	Thomas HALYS, gentleman, *v.* John TYRRELL, knight, John his eldest son and Thomas TYRRELL.
Ejection from the manor of Columbers *alias* Columbyn Hall in Stowmarket in contempt of a *certiorari* from this court.	SUFFOLK.

2–5	John, grandson and heir of John HAME, *v.* John BROMEHYL (Bromwell) and AGNES PEDLER.
Detention of deeds relating to messuages in the borough of Newport in St. Stephen's by Launceston.	CORNWALL.

6–7	Richard HANBURY *v.* Michael HEWMAN.
Tenement in Feckenham, late of Richard Hanbury, grandfather of complainant. *Faded.*	WORCESTER.

8–11	Elizabeth HARDYNG, administratrix of the goods of William Hardyng, *v.* John GOSTE.
Mill, cottages and land in Broughton of the demise of the late abbot and convent of Missenden. *Faded.*	BUCKINGHAM.

12–13	Robert, son and heir of John HARECOURT, esquire, *v.* John PEYNNE and Thomas GRETRICKE, executors of Thomas Alton, prior of Ronton.
Arbitral award in respect of the manor of Bouton and a mill and a watercourse there.	STAFFORD.

14–15	William HARMON (Herman), gentleman, Elizabeth his wife, and Anne ROBERTES, *v.*
John LONGTREE and Thomas CHARNOCKE, esquire.
Price of 'seyffes and mettes' of corn sold from the parsonage of Standish on behalf of Richard Standyshe, D.C.L., whose executors are the said Elizabeth and Anne.	LANCASTER.

16–18	The same *v.* Peter ANDERTON, esquire.
Do. *Mutilated.*	LANCASTER.

19   Thomas HARRYSON, nephew and heir of Ralph Clownam of Doveridge, yeoman, v. Thomas
          and John SPONNE.
Messuage and land in Kilbourn formerly of Henry Parkehall of Hilton.   DERBY.

20   Richard HASTINGES, a waiter in the port of London, v. John DETHYK of Warnegay, co.
          Norfolk, merchant stranger.
Conspiracy to avoid forfeiture of wines landed without payment of butlerage.   LONDON.

21   John HAWKES v. Humphrey PERSALL, brother-in-law of Roger Symondes.
Pasture in Hallen (i.e., Hadnall?) the lease whereof was entrusted to defendant.   SALOP.

22 ·   Richard HAYTLEY v. John ORME.
Debt and wager of law.   ⸺

23-25   Randall HAYWARD, esquire, and Anne, lady [Grey of] POWIS, his wife, v. Adrian
          STOKES, esquire, and Frances his wife.
Sites of the monasteries of Stoneleigh and Arbury, manor of Monks Kirby, etc., of the demise of
Charles [Brandon], Duke of Suffolk, deceased, father of the said Anne and Frances.   WARWICK.

26-28   The same (Haworthe) v. John HERBERT, esquire, Jane his wife, William CHARLETON
          and others.
Forgery of a Chancery commission in a suit for dower, and detention of household goods.
          SALOP, MONTGOMERY.

33-35   The same (Hauworthe), v. the said John and Jane.
Continuance of the above suit in contempt of an injunction from the late Chancellor. Answer
wanting.   SALOP, MONTGOMERY.

29-32   The said Randall (Hauworth, Haward) v. the said Adrian and Frances.
Arrears of annuity due to the said Anne now deceased, as part of the estate of the said duke.
Mutilated.   ⸺

36-37   Barbara, executrix and late the wife of Henry HERDSON of London, v. Richard
          BRYDGES, knight, late sheriff of Berks.
Goods of John Hidden extended on statute.   BERKS.

38-39   Roland HEYNES of Bridgnorth v. William ARNEWEY and Alice his daughter.
Gold ' angelles ' or ' angellettes ' received by the said Alice together with a proposal of marriage
from Edward Taylor, which she afterwards rejected.   SALOP.

40-41   Thomas HEYWARD v. WALTER ap Guillam of Ross, esquire.
Household goods of the gift of Edward Hayward of Ross, deceased, brother of complainant.
          HEREFORD.

42-44   Reynold HIGATE of Great Chart, co. Kent, gentleman, and Constance his wife, late the
          wife of William Sympson, v. John, son of Peter JOHNSON alias Dyckland.
Messuage and land in the ' scunage ' of Calais, previously in dispute in this court. Faded. CALAIS.

45-50   Thomas, son and heir of John HILLES, v. Anne RICARDES and Jervis RAMSDEN,
          executors of Stephen Ricardes.
Detention of deeds relating to a messuage and land in the ' den ' of Omenden in Middenden, late of
the said John, one of whose executors was the said Stephen.   KENT.

51 .   Joan HITCHINS v. William HITCHINS and John HAND.
Debt of the said Hand to Humphrey Hitchins, deceased husband of the said Joan, whose executors
were herself and the said William.   ⸺

52-55   William HODGEKYN v. Leonard MOUNT.
Refusal to complete an assignment of a lease from John Seyntleger, knight. Mutilated.
          BUCKINGHAM.

56   Richard HOLFORDE, sewer of the Chamber, and George WARREN, citizen and [goldsmith?]
          of London, v. William RAWLYNSON.
Demand of payment for a lease of a tenement in St. Mary-le-Strand where complainant had a
licence to ' occupie the game of bowlyng and whyte otherwyse called hand owte,' all such licences
having since been revoked by Act of Parliament. Mutilated.   MIDDLESEX.

57   The same (?) v. Robert CHAPMAN and John ELLYS his tenant.
Like suit concerning another house and garden. Mutilated.   MIDDLESEX.

58-59   William HOLFORTHE, citizen and skinner of London, v. the mayor, aldermen and sheriffs
          of LONDON, and Sibill NORRYS and Robert OKEY alias Norrys, her son.
Slander and frivolous action of debt following a matrimonial suit by the said Sibill. Certiorari and
subpoena.   LONDON.

60   Reynold HOLLINGWORTH v. Robert REYNOLDES of London, haberdasher.
Action for a judgment debt of John Crowche. Injunction.   LONDON.

61   Thomas HOOKE v. James SAWNDERSON of Spalding, co. Lincoln, and Thomas PREEST
          his servant.
Hempseed paid for in malt at Downham Market.   NORFOLK.

62-64   Robert HORNESBY and Elizabeth his wife, daughter of Myles Ryder of Crowle (Croyle),
          deceased, v. Lawrence SPONGE.
Household goods of the said Ryder, of whose will the said Elizabeth is executrix and defendant is
supervisor.   LINCOLN.

65   Giles HORSYNGTON of Pucklechurch, co. Gloucester, v. Thomas PAYNE.
Action for price of cheese and butter, in revenge for an action in the Star Chamber (Star Chamber
Proceedings, Henry VIII, File XXV, Nos. 103, 140 and 194; File XXI, No. 80).   LONDON.

66-69   Michael HUDSON v. William LEVERETT of Newark and Dorothy his wife.
Money and goods entrusted to the said Dorothy.   NOTTS.

70–76   ·William HYCHCOCKE and Agnes his wife, late the wife of Roger Germyn and formerly of
John Alport, v. John LANE and Elizabeth his wife, daughter of the said Agnes.
Detention of deeds relating to the manor of Pendeford, of the demise of the late prior and convent
of St. Thomas by Stratford.   STAFFORD.

77–80   Robert HYDE of Lincoln, yeoman, v. Godfrey and Agnes HYDE.
Messuage and land at Little Hayfield in Glossop, late of Nicholas Hyde, parson of Standon, co.
Stafford, and Thomas Skrymsher.   DERBY.

81   Baldwin HYLL, rector of Tallaton, v. John HYLL of Wear.
Money and other considerations due on a lease of complainant's corn-tithes. *Mutilated.* DEVON.

82   William HYLL v. Richard WIGHTMAN.
Advowson of the church of Sibson acquired of Thomas Palmer, knight.   LEICESTER.

FILE 1435.

1–2   John HALE v. Nicholas HAYLE, Joyce his wife, and Edward DASHWEN (Dasshefen).
Goods and lands in Alveley and elsewhere, late of Humphrey Hale, deceased, husband of the said
Joyce, whose executor complainant is. *Answer mutilated.*   SALOP, STAFFORD.

3   Anne, late the wife of Thomas HALL of Worcester, esquire, and Francis their son by William
Tyler of London, his uncle and next heir, v.   .   .   .   .
Manor of Hilles Aston *alias* Whiteladies Aston, advowson of the rectory and vicarage, tithes of corn,
and messuages and lands there and in Nether Aston. *Mutilated.*   WORCESTER.

4–6   John HALL of South Newton, grandson and heir of entail of Richard Hall, v. Thomas
OKELEY.
Messuage and land in Chipping Norton formerly of Thomas Water, clerk.   OXFORD,

7   John HALLS, esquire, v. Richard MEYO.
Barton of Ford with a marsh late of Richard Halls, deceased, father of complainant.   DEVON.

8   William HAMELDEN, late of Stanwich, gentleman, v. William LEVERYCHE of the same.
yeoman.
Action on a bond for a debt partly paid.   NORTHAMPTON.

9   William HAMET, husbandman, v. Richard GENNOWE and John DUNGIELL.
Tenement in the manor of Cottingbek in St. Germans, bought of defendants and of Joan, wife of the
said Gennowe and mother of the said Dungiell. *Mutilated.*   CORNWALL.

10–13   John HANNAM v. Ambrose HANNAM.
Lands in North Cheriton and Lotterford, late of Ambrose Hannam, deceased, father of both parties.
                                                                                SOMERSET.

14–15   Nicholas HARPESFYLD, LL.D., archdeacon of Canterbury and parson of St. Stephen's
without Canterbury, v. Thomas CULPEPER of Bidborough (Bidebury), esquire.
Parsonage and glebe of St. Stephen's.   KENT.

16   John HARRISON and Joan his wife v. Isobel REDHED.
Rent in Westham of the bequest of John Funnell, brother of the said Joan and Isabel.   SUSSEX

17   Lancelot HARRYSON, yeoman of the Chamber, v. John WARCOPE, esquire.
Messuage and land called Ingmire in Sedbergh, held of defendant by the tenant-right of the county
which is no bar to an action at common law.   YORK.

18   Thomas HASTYNGES, knight, v. Anthony OVINGTON.
Detention of deeds relating to land in Ovington.   YORK.

19   George HAWKYNS v. Thomas MEYRE, late of London, and Fortune his wife.
Messuages, barns and land at Upton in West Ham, late of Owen Hawkyns, deceased, father of
complainant and husband of the said Fortune.   ESSEX.

20–22   Henry, son and heir of Thomas HAYE of Litchurch, v. Robert and John, sons of Richard
SHAWE of Carlton, co. Notts, deceased, and William WYLKINSON.
Refusal to complete a lease of land in Quarndon.   DERBY.

23   Nicholas HECKER and John HARISON v. Francis TIRRET and Joan his wife.
Execution for a debt on houses in Rye, where the King's writ of common process does not run.
                                                                                SUSSEX.

24   John HELME, rector of Stocking Pelham, and John GOODEMAN, his farmer, v. John
GROWTE, farmer of Jerome Songer's manor of Stocking Pelham.
Leases of the parsonage made by John Freman, late rector, deprived for marriage, and of the glebe
made by the said Songer, being patron. · *See File 1429, No. 36.*   HERTS.

25–29   William HENDER (Hynder) v. Thomas HAMLEY, Joan his wife, late the wife of John
Lawes (Lowes), and John JENSON.
Tenement in Whitstone acquired of William Dawe and Joan his wife.   CORNWALL.

30   Henry HENTHORNE of Laceby v. Robert SMYTHE of Great Limber.
Obtaining and paying away money entrusted by complainant to Thomas Ward. 3½ *lines erased.*
                                                                                LINCOLN.

31–32   William HERBERT v. John GOLDWYER.
Lands (*described*) in Kenwick of the feoffment of William Beell. D.XI, 42.   BERKS.

33–35   John HEWES *alias* Lloied of Burford, co. Oxford, v. RICHARD ap Jevan ap Owen, son of
Jevan ap Owen Baugh, and others.
Land in Trustow   .   .   .   .   late of Howell ap Jevan Lloid, deceased, father of complainant.
Damaged.   MONTGOMERY.

M 2

36   William HEWET, alderman of London v. John PANTON and others, tenants of the manor of
Beesby (Beysbye, Basby) dwelling in Gunnerby, Wold Newton and Beesby (now in Hawerby).
Frivolous suits and refusal of rents.   LINCOLN.

37   George HEYDON, esquire, v. Thomas CHYLD and others.
Balance of debt the agreement for which is in defendant's hands.   ·

38   Thomas HEYWARD of Ashton v. John SPYSER of Monmouth.
Plate of Eleanor, late the wife of complainant, formerly Eleanor Mutton, whose executor
defendant is.   SOMERSET, MONMOUTH.

39   John and   .   .   . , sons of Richard HIGGINS, deceased, v. Thomas BERDSLEY, overseer
of the will of the said Richard; and Richard BELLINGHAM (Bullingham).
Money, goods, plate, etc. *Mutilated.*   _____

40–43   Rowland HILL, knight, v. Edward WALFORD, William ELCOCK and Richard DARWYN. .
Rights of common in Emlode (*i.e.* Evenlode, co. Worcester ?) belonging to the manor of Lambrough
(*i.e.* Longborough ?).   [WORCESTER ?] GLOUCESTER.

44–45   John HIPPISLEY, gentleman, and Mary his wife v. Lawrance RASTALL, gentleman.
Lease of a ' pasture close or ilond called Tynseigh ' on the ' Temses ' adjoining the parish of Egham
entrusted to defendant by Thomas Flower, gentleman, father of the said Mary. D.XI, 3.   SURREY.

46   The same v. John PAYNE. gentleman.
Lease of the rectory of Banwell of the bequest of the said Flower.   SOMERSET.

47   The same v. Thomas NORRES, yeoman.
Pasture and an island in Egham and Staines of the like bequest.   SURREY, MIDDLESEX.

48   Thomas HOBSON and Alice his wife, late the wife of Andrew Bedman and administratrix
of his goods, v. Richard COOK and Henry TYLER, yeomen.
Detention of a lease of a messuage and land in Sutton made by Francis Wyat, gentleman. *Mutilated.*
                                                                       ESSEX.

49–51   John HODDER the younger, son of William Hodder, deceased, v. John HODDER the elder,
Joan his wife and Walter SAMPSON.
Joint lease to the said John and John of the site of the manor of Barn and half the rest by the
surveyors of Cicely [Grey], ' marques Dorcet,' and Thomas her son.   DORSET.

52–54   William HODGES and Parnell his wife, late the wife of John Gaylerde, v. Thomas BONVILE,
gentleman.
Close of pasture in West Dillington of the demise of John Bonvyle, gentleman, father of complainant.
                                                                       SOMERSET.

55–62   James HOLAND of Colnbrook, co. Middlesex, and Isabel his wife, v. Thomas WYBER,
esquire, Thomas his son, and Roger LANCASTER.
Messuage and land held of the first defendant's manor of Clifton.   WESTMORLAND.

63–64   John HOLLAND v. Nicholas HOLLAND and others.
Manor of Lees in Glossopdale of the gift of Guy Holland, deceased, father of both parties.   DERBY.

65   Leonard HOLLANDE, esquire, and Joan his wife, v. Thomas GUILFORDE and Richard
ELVINGTON, esquires.
Manors of Westferley, Covertes, and Yapton and lands there, late of Ralph Bellingham, esquire,
deceased, grandfather of the said Joan.   SUSSEX.

66   Thomas HOLLE of Heigham v. Richard BULWARD and Margaret his wife.
Land in Earlham between Heigham Heath and the lands of the late abbot of Langley.   NORFOLK.

67–68   Richard, son and executor of Robert HOLTER of Lewes, v. John APTOFTE, executor of
Henry Fitzherbert of Ringbere (*i.e.* Ringmer ?).
Debt.   SUSSEX.

69   Peter HONYBOURNE, citizen and draper of London, v. Humphrey ONESLOWE, executor
of Richard Whitaker of Shrewsbury, clothier.
Action on a bond for a debt already paid.   LONDON, SALOP.

70   John HOPKYNS and James MORLEY of London, merchants, owners of the ship *Elizabeth,*
v. the sheriffs of LONDON and John HASSARD of Lyme, merchant, owner of the ship
Fawkon.
Action on a bond concerning two French prizes taken at sea by the said ships. *Certiorari and
subpoena. Mutilated.*   LONDON, DORSET.

71–73   John HOPWOOD and Anne, his wife, v. Robert, grandson and heir of Robert CLIDEROWE.
Manor of Bailey, messuages and lands there and in Goosnargh, Cumeralgh in Whittington (Comberall)
Broughton, Finningley and Misson, and moiety of the manor of Aukley and of messuages and lands
there.   LANCASTER, NOTTS.

74–79   Thomas HORNE, guardian to William Robyns, an infant, v. John PEYS (Payse) and Joan
his wife.
Messuage and land in Kensworth, late of Thomas Robyns(on), deceased, father of the said William
and husband of the said Joan.   HERTS.

80–83   Paul HOUGH and Willemote his wife, daughter of John White and of Clase his wife, both
deceased, v. Joan WHITE, second wife of the said John.
Messuage and land held of the dean of Exeter's manor of Braunton.   DEVON.

84 Emmott late the wife of William HOUGHTON *v.* John BRISTOWE.
Action in the Common Bench for lands in Staythorpe (Starethorpe) pending a suit in this court.
NOTTS.

85-87 Richard HOUNSELL of Eype, mariner, and Alice his wife, *v.* Nicholas LONGE and Agnes his wife, formerly Agnes Crocker.
Seizure of goods of Matthew Martin of Whitchurch, deceased, father of the said Alice, and abduction of Sara her mother. DORSET.

88-90 William HOWSDEN of Great Chesterford *v.* Richard HAMOND of Debden.
Contempt of an arbitral award concerning a debt of Robert Wright of Debden, yeoman. D. XII, 10.
ESSEX.

91 The same *v.* the steward and bailiffs of the court of WALDEN, and [the same].
Action of debt pending the above suit. *Certiorari and subpœna. Faded.* ESSEX.

92 Walter HUGGARDE of Lincoln, tanner, brother and executor of John Huggarde, *v.* William HUGGARDE of Collingham, also his brother.
Action on a bond intended to be to the use of defendant's children. LINCOLN, NOTTS.

93 Robert HUMFRYE *v.* William LYNGE and Alice, his wife.
One-fifth of lands in Stowlangtoft, late of John Rose, deceased. SUFFOLK.

94 William, brother and heir of Thomas HUNTE of Chawston in Roxton (Cholverston) *v.* Alice HUNTE.
Detention of deeds relating to a messuage, cottages and land in Maulden. BEDFORD.

95-99 Richard HURLESTON *v.* Elizabeth, late the wife of William SNEYD, alderman of Chester, and other executors of the said William.
Money promised to complainant on his marriage with Elizabeth Shalcrosse. CHESTER.

100 James HUXLEY of Bow Brickhill, co. Bucks, son and heir of Richard Huxley, *v.* Ralph DUTTON of Hatton, esquire.
Messuage and land in Sydenhall, formerly of Ralph Huxley and Joan his wife, deceased. CHESTER.

101 Laurence HYDE of Templecombe, co. Somerset, gentleman, *v.* Anthony VENABLES, gentleman, and Dowse VENABLES.
Messuage and land at Aston by Pickmere, in Great Budworth, late of George Woode of Balterley, co. Stafford, gentleman. CHESTER.

102 The same *v.* the same.
Messuage and land in the same place, late of a chantry in the chapel of Stretford, co. Lancaster.
CHESTER.

FILE 1436.

1 Myles HADLEY, LL.B., parson, of Little Gaddesden, *v.* Thomas HEFFE and Edward NEWMAN.
Parsonage of Little Gaddesden. HERTS.

2 Richard HALL, gentleman, uncle and heir of Ellen Hall of London, *v.* John WOODROF, Elizabeth his wife, and others.
Occupation of messuages and land in Edmonton, in contempt of a writ of *habere facias seisinam.*
MIDDLESEX.

3-4 William HALL of Ellastone (?) yeoman, *v.* John DEANE and John LEE.
Messuage and lands (*described*) in Mavesyn Ridware of the demise of Thomas Cawarden, gentleman, and Elizabeth, his wife. STAFFORD.

5-6 John HALYBRED *v.* Robert QUYNCE and Joan, his wife, executrix of John Holt of Taverham.
Detention of deeds relating to messuages in Norwich, and of a bond formerly delivered to the said Joan under a promise of marriage with complainant. *Damaged.* NORFOLK.

7-11 Perkyn HAMLEY of Redruth, labourer, grandson and heir of Roger Hamley and of Nelyor his wife, *v.* Richard ERISY, esquire, son and heir of James Eryssy.
Land in Treleghwartha (*i.e.* Treleigh in Redruth) of the gift of John Penpons, esquire.
CORNWALL.

12 John HARDINGE of Cowley, yeoman, *v.* Richard HARDINGE, his elder brother, and George and Thomas, sons of the latter.
Fraud in drafting a fine for purchase of a moiety of messuages, mills, and land in Cam, Dursley, and elsewhere, formerly of John Draycote. *Faded.* GLOUCESTER.

13-18 William HARRIS of Malden, gentleman, *v.* Vincent HARRYS.
Messuages and land in Cold Norton, late of William Harris of Southminster, deceased, father of both parties. ESSEX.

19-23 The same *v.* the same, Arthur his brother, and Christopher and Edward HARRIS.
Manors of Westwick and Eastwick (in Burnham-on-Crouch) and Baynards in C . . . , late of the said William, the father. ESSEX.

24-26 The same *v.* the said Arthur, John BODE, and others.
Manors of Westwick and Shopland and lands in Burnham, Little Wakering, Foulness, Maldon, Canewdon, Southchurch, Mundon, Shopland, Prittlewell, Great Oakley, Rochford, Crixea, Althorn, Mayland, Lachingdon, Woodham Mortimer, Southminster, etc. *Mutilated.* ESSEX.

27-35 Alice HARVEY of Thetford, co. Norfolk, *v.* William and Richard CORBYN, William HYBBERT, Alice, his wife, and others.
Messuages and lands in Shotton and Ewloe, late of William Harvey, deceased, father of complainant.
FLINT.

36-39   John HATTON of Whiston v. Thomas BOLT, clerk.
Payments made on defendant's behalf.   SALOP.

40   George HAWARD, knight, v. David BARHAM, miller, the churchwardens of MAIDSTONE
         and CLIFF by Lewes, and others.
Information as to messuages and lands in Maidstone given for St. Christopher's and St. George's
lights in the church there, and cottages, gardens and a ' wyshe ' in Cliff of the late fraterhity of St.
Thomas there, all concealed from the Crown.   KENT, SUSSEX.

41   John HAWARDEN, principal of ' the king's halle and the college of Brasenhouse,' and the
         scholars of the same college v. John WILLIAMS, lord Williams of Thame.
Land called Bassett's Fee in Boteley meadow.   OXFORD.

42-44   Thomas HELE v. William KYMPE.
Detention of deeds relating to lands held of complainant's manor of Cassacowen in Blisland.
                                                                              CORNWALL.

45   Thomas HERLEAWYN, yeoman, and Mary his wife, v. Anthony HAWES.
Messuage and land at Bosue in St. Ewe demised by John Arundell of Lanhern, knight, to John
Hawes, since deceased.   CORNWALL.

46   William, son of Roger HILL and of Mary his wife, both deceased, v. John GOODMAN,
         dean of Wells, and John COTTERELL and others, clerks, ' residensies ' of the cathedral.
Tenement in the ' overland ' of the said dean and chapter's manor of Allerton (Alverton).
                                                                              SOMERSET.

47-49   Wilham HILL the elder v. William HILL, complainant in the above suit.
Land and mill in Allerton of the grant of Edmund Somerset, gentleman, and John Basse of Pensford.
                                                                              SOMERSET.

50-52   John HOLBECKE v. Humphrey GYLBYE and others.
Messuage and land held of the manor of Laneham by John Kellome, deceased, grandfather of complainant.   NOTTS.

53-54   William and Henry, sons of John HOLLOWAIE, deceased v. William GLOSSE their
         brother-in-law.
Tenement in the manor of Apps of the demise of the late prior of Christchurch.   HANTS (I.W.).

55-57   Agnes HOLMES of Swaffham v. Joan, executrix and late the wife of John ROLFE of the
         same.
Loan.   CAMBRIDGE.

58-61   Richard HOMMERSLEY of Stafford v. Francis, son and heir of Richard WARDE.
Exchange of pastures in the lordship of Tillington.   STAFFORD.

62-68   Beatrix HOORE v. Robert HOORE, Richard BOWERMAN (Burman), Richard COLLEN-
         SON, Francis AYNESWORTH, John BUSHE, and others.
Burgages and land in Leicester, late of Thomas Hoore, deceased, husband of complainant and father
of the said Robert.   LEICESTER.

69-73   Christopher HOSKINS, an executor of John Norman, clerk, v. Edmund BOWRE and
         others.
Money, plate (described) and goods of the said Norman, whereof he bequeathed 100l. to a priest to
teach school at Kingsclere.   HANTS.

74-76   William HULLOND, esquire, v. Thomas ARSCOTT, gentleman.
Detention of deeds relating to messuages and land in Holsworthy.   DEVON.

77-80   Stephen HUNTER, clerk and others, administrators of the goods of Anthony Style, deceased,
         v. Lawrence HALL.
Lease made by the prior and convent of Durford of lands in Petersfield.   HANTS.

81-83   John HYCHEMAN, a minor, v. Joan STEVENS.
Lands in Over and Nether Inglessham, late of Walter Hycheman of Kempsford, co. Gloucester,
deceased, grandfather of complainant.   [WILTS.]

FILE 1437.

1   Thomas HABGOOD of Chute, co. Wilts, v. John CURY, parson of Linkenholt.
Lease of arable common of pasture, and tithe of milk, calves and corn belonging to defendant's
parsonage.   HANTS.

2-5   John HALL of South Newton v. Richard HOLMARKE (Halmarke) parson of Salford.
Lease of defendant's parsonage to Edmund Annesley, contrary to his promise on the surrender of
complainant's lease.   OXFORD.

6   Thomas HALL.
Petition to examine witnesses in an information for usury laid in the Common Bench against John
Blyth, gentleman.

7   Richard HANDFORDE, citizen and painter-stainer of London, v. the officers of the
         ADMIRAL'S COURT, the mayor and sheriffs of LONDON, and John WARREN of London,
         barber surgeon, Lybeus FOXE of the same, merchant, and Peter van STENCELL.
Double attachment of hides and gloves bought of the said Foxe, at the several suits of the other
defendants. Certiorari and subpoena. LONDON.

8-11   John HARCOURT and Francis STONER, knights, v. Anthony HUDDELSTON, Mary his
         wife, and others.
Reviver of a suit on a counterbond for a debt of Francis Barentyne, deceased, whose goods have come
to complainant's hands. Damaged.   LONDON.

12-14　John son and heir of William HARE v. John WATTON, yeoman.
Detention of deeds relating to a close in Romford. *Mutilated.*　　ESSEX.

15　Thomas HARPER of Southwark v. the bailiffs of KINGSTON and Ellen MYLES.
Action on a composition for a debt. *Certiorari and subpœna.*　　SURREY.

16-18　Thomas HARRYSON, husbandman, v. Thomas LITTILBURIE, esquire, Robert BAN-
BURGH and Andrew CATBYE (Cadby).
Lease of a messuage and land in Hemingby promised by the said Littilburie.　　LINCOLN.

19-22　Henry HART, Margaret his wife, and John CARNESDALE, administrators of the goods of
Robert Cowper of Stoke Nayland, deceased, v. John ABBES.
Land in Nayland of the demise of Christopher Danby, knight.　　SUFFOLK.

23　John HARTE of London, carpenter, and Alice his wife, v. William BROMBY and others.
Messuage and land in Calverton (?). *Faded.*　　NOTTS.

24　John HARTE v. Katherine GRENALL.
Goods of William Harte, deceased father of complainant and husband of defendant, who are both,
his executors.　　LINCOLN.

25-28　George HASELL v. John WATERS.
Refusal to complete a lease of a tenement in Haddenham as formerly made to Thomas Gunstone of
Soham. *Mutilated.*　　CAMBRIDGE.

29-32　Thomas HEDGES (Hodges) v. Edward son of Thomas HART.
Land in Sherston Pinkney, bought of William Morgan and Jerome Halley.　　WILTS.

33-36　Edmund HENLEY and Margery his wife v. John RODDON and William GYFFORDE.
Half a bed of down and bolster and other goods (*described*) given to the use of the said Margery by
John Stone of Offwell, clerk, deceased (Defendants give a different list.)　.　DEVON.

37-40　Roger HENSHAWE, servant to Nicholas West, gentleman, one of the Six Clerks, v. John
FALLOGHES (Fallowes).
Messuage and land in Alderley formerly of Oliver Fallowes.　　CHESTER.

41-42　John and Edward HERENDEN of Boughton Monchelsea v. Thomas FYSHER.
Land in Loose formerly of Aleyn Andrewes, great-grandfather of complainants. *Mutilated.*　KENT.

43-49　Richard HOLFORDE, one of the King's Chamber, v. Thomas LEFTWICHE, Margaret
WOODROFFE, Humphrey TAILOUR her tenant at will and others.
Closes of pasture in Wincham near Great Budworth (Wymncheham) demised by Thomas Leftwiche
of Leftwich to Humphrey Holford, brother of complainant. *Replication wanting.*　　CHESTER.

50　Michael HOMEWOOD v. Richard DUNTON and Eleanor his wife.
Cottage held of the manor of Cuckfield.　　SUSSEX.

51　John HOORDE, gentleman, v. Ralph BENETT.
Corn-mills in the manor of Langacre (in Broad Clist) of the demise of Frances duchess of Suffolk
and others.　　DEVON.

52-55　Richard HOPKYN, master of the hospital of Stoke by Newark, v. John MOLYNEUX
esquire.
Dilapidation of the chapel of St. Leonard belonging to the said hospital, and wrongful occupation
of its lands in Stoke, Elston and Cotham. *Mutilated.*　　NOTTS.

56-58　Thomas HORSEMAN of Old Sleaford, esquire, v. William BROWNE, gentleman.
Action for a debt already paid in oxen. *Mutilated.*　　LINCOLN.

59-60　The same v. Simon HALL of Donington, gentleman, and Reynold HALL.
Money repaid by the Crown on cancelling a sale of chantry lands in Great Hale and of the rectory and
tithe of Meer.　　LINCOLN.

61-63　John HOTHUM, esquire, son and heir of Francis Hotham, knight, and Thomas FUGALL,
parson of Lowthorpe, v. Thomas EYNUS, esquire.
Rectory of Lowthorpe, occupied by colour of possession of chantry lands.　　YORK.

64-66　William HUDSON of St. Alban's, innholder, v. Richard SHARPE.
Instalments of purchase-money of the *Lion* inn in St. Alban's, paid beyond what was due.　HERTS.

67　John HUGH v. Richard SMYTH and others.
Messuages and land in the lordship of Bromfield late of Hugh Gryffith deceased, father of complainant. *Mutilated.*　　DENBIGH.

68　John HUMFREY of Hitchin, tile-maker, v. Robert DRAPER of Ippolitts, yeoman.
Entry on a tenement on Tilehouse Street, Hitchin, on purchasing others adjoining.　　HERTS.

69　Richard HUNT v. Thomas HANBERY, vicar of Coterege (*i.e.* Cotheridge?).
Lease of defendant's tithes. *Mutilated.*　　MARCHES OF WALES [*i.e.* WORCESTER ?]

70-71　Thomas son and heir of Christopher HUNT v. Richard PLA(Y)STON.
Detention of deeds relating to the manor of Shardlow and messuages and lands in Ashton and Wilne
(Wyllen).　.　　DERBY.

72-73　William HUSON, parson of Fritton, v. Robert JOHNSON of Hethel.
Detention of deeds relating to complainant's parsonage, and breach of conditions of the lease thereof.
Mutilated.　　NORFOLK.

74-75　Oliver HYDE, gentleman, administrator of the goods of Robert A(t)wood, deceased, v.
Richard and John BUTLER.
Messuage and land in Radley of the demise of the abbot and convent of Abingdon.　　BERKS.

76　John, Thomas and William HYLL v. Randolph and Henry GRAVENOUR.
Lands late of Robert Hyll. *Mutilated.*　　?

77   Robert HYLLARY of Denver, gentleman, *v.* Richard BELLAMY of Well, yeoman.
Execution on a judgment debt after compromise.   NORFOLK.

78–79   John and Joan HYWOOD *v.* Philip STOCKWELL of New Windsor.
Seizure of jewels, plate, money and goods.   BERKS.

FILE 1438.

1–2   William HACKER *v.* Stephen BORDE of Lindfield.
Refusal of redemption money for the manor of Grant and other lands in Lancing.   SUSSEX.

3–6   John HALE *v.* [the mayor and sheriffs of] LONDON, and Richard HAMDEN, leather-seller,
and others.
False verdict in an action of trover and waste of goods. *Certiorari and subpœna. Mutilated.* LONDON.

7   John HALL *v.* John TREGYAN and others.
Land in Penponce held of the said Tregyan's manor of Rosmodres.   CORNWALL.

8   John HARFORDE and Richard his son, both of Bosbury, co. Hereford, *v.* Walter MAY,
clerk.
Partnership of the bishop of Hereford's part of Prestbury.   GLOUCESTER.

9–10   Joan, executrix and late the wife of Nicholas HARRIS, and William and John their sons,
v. John CARTER, son-in-law of the said Nicholas.
Messuages and land in Seend (Sean) and Bulkington. *Mutilated.*   WILTS.

11–13   William HAWKES of Timsbury, co. Somerset, son and heir of Richard Hawkes, gentleman,
v. Roger SMYTHE, husbandman.
Manor of Egleton and messuages and lands in Upper and Lower Egleton and Bishop's Frome, late
of William Gower, esquire.   HEREFORD.

14–16   William HAWKES of Gloucester and Joan, his wife, late the wife of John Synton, and John
CAMPYON of Mathon, co. Worcester, *v.* Edward STAMPFORD, late of Rowley, co.
Stafford, esquire.
Messuage and land in Ersett (*i.e.* Hergest?) adjudged to the said Joan by several decrees of the
Council of the Marches.   HEREFORD.

17–21   Robert HEATH *v.* William ANNE of Middleton, gentleman.
Judgment obtained at *nisi prius*, pending a suit in this court, on a bond to supply millstones to a
mill at North Aston. *See File* 1312, *No.* 46.   OXFORD.

22–25   Henry HERON of London and Christian his wife *v.* Reynold ALEE, Alice his wife, late the
wife of Thomas Stapleton, and Thomas STAPLETON her son.
Lands in Bollington and Sutton, late held according to the custom of the manor and forest of
Macclesfield by Thomas Champion, deceased, father of the said Alice and of Katherine, mother of
the said Christian.   CHESTER.

26   Thomas HERVEST of Salisbury *v.* Robert RENEGER of Southampton, merchant.
Balance of a debt for lead, the bond for which was delivered on part payment.   WILTS, HANTS.

27–29   Anthony HICKMOT of London, brewer, *v.* William POUGHNYLL of Ludlow, co. Salop,
gentleman.
Crown lease of lands in Welshpool and Machynlleth, late belonging to chantries in the churches of
those parishes.   MONTGOMERY.

30   Walter HIDE *v.* Joan HIDE.
Messuage and land in Stevenage, late of Thomas Hide, deceased, father of complainant.
HEREFORD (*rectius* HERTS).

31–34   Richard HOGETES (Hodgetts), yeoman, *v.* Adam and John (A)PARKE *alias* Pershouse.
Tenement in the lordship of Dudley acquired of John Hogetes of Sedgley, co. Stafford, yeoman.
D. XIV, 56.   WORCESTER.

35   Roger HOLLANDE *v.* Anne VYNSENT.
Passing off a silver-gilt ring for gold.   ———

36–39   William son of Thomas HOOPER *v.* John DRAKE, esquire.
Land and pasture in defendant's manor of Musbury of the demise of the late Marquis of Exeter.
Mutilated.   DEVON

40–41   Robert, grandson of William HORSELEY, *v.* Thomas STANDYSSHE.
Messuages and land in Dorrington.   ·   LINCOLN.

42   John HOWLOTT *v.* Thomas BAYSTON.
Land in Selby. *See File* 1361, *No.* 58.   YORK.

43–44   John HOWSEMAN, clerk, vicar of Canewdon and Henry BAKER, yeoman, *v.* John
MYCHELL, John BONAM and Robert CASSELYN.
Collusive suit in this court for lands in Canewdon bequeathed by William Totham, esquire, for an
obit and the poor. *Mutilated.*   ESSEX.

45   Thomas and William HUNWYCK *v.* William WORLYNGTON, esquire, and Elizabeth
his wife.
Detention of deeds relating to a messuage and land in Great Lees.   ESSEX.

46–48   George HUXLEY *v.* Simon LEYE.
Lease of a tenement called the *Lyon* in Brirckhill on a bad title.   BUCKINGHAM.

49–51   John HYDE of East Hanningfield, son of John Hyde, and nephew and heir of William
Hyde, deceased, *v.* William SANDLE, yeoman.
Imprisonment on a recognizance enrolled in Chancery in the name of John Hyde of Ramsden, to
prevent him from suing for lands of the said William in defendant's hands.   ESSEX.

52–54   The same *v.* the same.
Messuages and lands in Ramsden Belhouse, Downham, Runwell, Wickford and Horndon, late of the said William Hyde.   ESSEX.

55–57   John HYDE, grandson of the said William, *v.* William AYLYFF, esquire, Margaret his wife, and Robert BRETTEN.
Do., except one messuage.   ESSEX.

FILE 1439.

1–5   Ralph HALEY (Halley) *v.* Richard HALLEY, Thomas GOODE, feoffee to uses, and Thomas COTESMORE.
Messuages and land in Brightwell Baldwin, Brightwell Prior, Britwell Salome, and Syrefeld (*cf.* Shirburn) in Watlington, late of Richard Haley, deceased, father of the said Ralph and Richard.   OXFORD.

6–8   John HALL *v.* John FAWKNER, alderman of Lincoln.
Malt promised as a rebate of rent of a house called the *Sargyantes Heade* in Lincoln.   LINCOLN.

9–11   Walter HANCOCKES, labourer, *v.* Richard and John WIGHTWICKE and others.
Meadow late held of the manor of Tettenhall Regis by Thomas Hancockes of Compton and Margery his wife, deceased, parents of complainant.   STAFFORD.

12   Thomas HANLEY *v.* John BARBOUR, esquire.
Ellerton Grange in Adbaston, late of the prior and convent of . . . . . *Mutilated.*   STAFFORD.

13   Charles HANMER, citizen and goldsmith of London, *v.* Richard ATKYS and others.
Messuage and land in Merton of the gift of Roger, elder brother of complainant.   SALOP.

14–16   Thomas HANSHERTE, gentleman, and Amy his wife, late the wife of Nicholas Ruste, *v.* Thomas SOWTHEN.
Debts due to the said Nicholas, which defendant was asked to administer owing to the said Amy's ignorance of law.   [LINCOLN?]

17–18   Humphrey HARTE, citizen and girdler of London, *v.* Richard STAVERTON (Staffarton).
Refusal of admission to a tenement in Warfield acquired of Thomas Bowyar and held of defendant's manor of Heathly.   BERKS.

19–20   Christopher, son and heir of Robert HATCHE, *v.* Edward NORTON.
Detention of deeds relating to a great messuage called the *White Horse* and land in Newmarket.   SUFFOLK.

21–22   George HAWSTED of Bury St. Edmund's, Agnes his wife, and George, Henry, and Margaret HAWSTED *v.* George ROUX (Rokes) and William HAWSTED.
Legacies of Roger Hawsted of Hawstead, deceased, father of the said Agnes, George the younger, Henry, Margaret and William.   SUFFOLK.

23–24   John HAYDON, gentleman, *v.* John EVELEGH, gentleman, and others.
Lands at Straitgate and elsewhere in Ottery St. Mary, with feedings, of the demise of John Fyssher, late warden of the college of Ottery St. Mary, and his canons.   DEVON.

25–26   John, son of Thomas HAYNES, deceased, *v.* Richard HARDYNGE.
Detention of deeds relating to Frombridge mills and lands in Frampton-on-Severn late of John Arrondell, knight, and Elizabeth his wife.   GLOUCESTER.

27   Robert HERBERT *v* William NORTON and Anne his wife, daughter and heir of William Bedford.
Reviver of a suit brought by defendants against William Herbert, deceased, father of complainant, for lands in Thatcham.   BERKS.

28   Thomas HERBERT *v.* Lewis WALTER.
Lands late of Richard Herbert, deceased, father of complainant.   *Mutilated.*   BRECON.

29–30   Richard HERYNGTON and Agnes his wife, late the wife of John Brodock, *v.* William HYDE, esquire, and Richard Holmes.
Lands in Wantage, Letcombe, and Steventon.   BERKS.

31   Ralph HEYDON and Agnes his wife *v.* George FERRES.
Reviver of a suit by Thomas Abraham, deceased, father of the said Agnes, for lands in Flamstead.   HERTS.

32   William HILDERSHAM *v.* the sheriffs of LONDON.
Arrest at the suit of John Holdernes, innholder in St. Dunstan's, for two years' rent already paid.
Certiorari.   LONDON.

33   John HILLARYE and Alice, his wife, daughter of William Toker and of Margery, his wife, *v.* William CATCOTT of Lamyatt, son of John Catcott of Batcombe, and Edward WADHAM, gentleman.
Double sale of a leasehold in Barton by William Adamps of East Pennard, gentleman.   SOMERSET.

34–35   Giles, Peter and John, sons of Robert HILLE *v.* George RODGERS, esquire.
Refusal to confirm a conveyance of lands in the manor of Trebarwith by Eleanor Wynter, mother-in-law of complainant.   CORNWALL.

36   James, son of John HILLER, *v.* Mary, late the wife of Thomas LOCK.
Parsonage of Marten (*i.e.* Merton,) of the demise of the prior of [Merton?]. *Mutilated.*
See File 1476, No. 89.   [SURREY?]

37–39   James HOBBES, husbandman, son of Geoffrey Hobbes, *v.* Paul BALE, Agnes his wife, mother of complainant, and others.
Chamber and pasture in a tenement called Bremridge in South Molton.   DEVON.

40–42   William HODGEKYNSON of Atherstone, co. Warwick, husbandman, *v.* Henry JAMES.
Messuage and land in Hope and Longstone, late of John Hodgekynson, deceased, father of complainant.   DERBY.

43   John, son and heir of Richard HOLDEN *v.* Nicholas LONGE and Anne his wife.
Messuage and land in Fittleworth, Bury, and Slaugham (Slapham).   SUSSEX.

44–46   Henry HOPKYNSON *v.* Richard BLACKWALL, esquire and others.
Detention of deeds relating to a tenement called the *Swanne* and land in Wirksworth, late of the chantry of the Holy Rood in the parish church there.   DERBY.

47   Peter HUBBERT, parson of Dennington, and Robert LYNDE, *v.* Abrae, late the wife of John HOLDYCHE.
Bonds for repayment of advances for seed corn made to poor persons of Dennington out of a town stock of 20*l.* in the custody of complainants and of the said Holdyche.   SUFFOLK.

48–51   Richard HUMBLE and Anne his wife, *v.* William MALBONE of London, draper.
Administration of the goods of Thomas Birkhedde, priest, including the advowson of West Horsley, and a lease of the vicarage of St. Bride's, Fleet Street, defendant being overseer of his will, and his executors the said Anne and Robert Birkhedde, defendant's apprentice.   SURREY, LONDON.

52   . Thomas HYCHE, husband of Joan, late the wife of John Hedge (Hiage), *v.* John BERRAM, knight, and others.
Manor of Bilsthorpe of the demise of Thomas Vaux, lord [Vaux of] Harrowden, and others.
NOTTS.

FILE 1440.

1   Edmund HALES of Corsley, co. Wilts, yeoman, *v.* John PYLTON of the same, miller.
Extortion of a bond to marry defendant's sister by seizure of deeds relating to tenements in Friggle Street (in Frome).   SOMERSET.

2–3   Robert HALL of Gretford *v.* Henry GRYCE of Wakefield, gentleman, son and heir of Thomas Gryce.
Detention of deeds relating to the manor of Firbeck. (Defendant also claims land in Odysthorp held of the manor of Laughton).   YORK.

4–5   Mary, Katherine, Anne, Margery and Elizabeth, daughters of the said Robert, and of Anne his wife, *v.* the same.
Detention of deeds relating to the manors of Styrrap, Orchotes (*i.e.* Oldcoates in Blyth?) and Norney in Styrrap (Orney), and lands in Southwell and West Burton (Burton upon Trante), late of Robert Cressye, grandfather of the said Anne the mother.   NOTTS.

6–7   Thomas HALL *v.* Thomas DYSON, Alice his wife, and John DYSON, claiming to be feoffees to uses.
Messuage and land in Rawmarsh, late of John Hall, deceased, brother of complainant.   YORK.

8–9   John HANKINSON *v.* Hugh HANKINSON.
Burgage, garden and orchard in Congleton, late of John Hankinson, deceased, grandfather of complainant.   CHESTER.

10–12   Edward HARRYS of Cornworthy, gentleman, *v.* William GILES.
Share of a ship bought by both parties of Thomas Stewckley, gentleman.   DEVON.

13–14   John HARRYS, servant to John Merry of Chilswell, gentleman, *v.* William ROWSE of Lillingstone, gentleman.
Acquittance of the said Merry, delivered to defendant in anticipation of a payment for sheep.
BERKS, OXFORD.

15   Thomas HARRYSON *v.* John CORBET.
Forgery of deeds relating to a tenement held of the lordship of Ilkeston and already awarded to complainant in this court. *Mutilated.*   DERBY.

16–18   Robert HARVY of Hartforde *v.* Richard HEDGER of Warblington, butcher.
Loan to George Collyns of Warblington, brother-in-law of complainants, whose executor defendant is. *Mutilated.*   HANTS.

19–21   William HARVYE, executor of Agnes, executrix and late the wife of James Ramshawe, *v.* Edward NYCOLSON.
One-third of the tithe-corn of Langtoft of the demise of defendant.   LINCOLN.

22   John HATHE of Romsley (Ramesley), co. Salop, *v.* Ralph son of George WARLEY.
Rent charged on a messuage and land in Smethwick after assignment of a lease thereof made by another Ralph Warley, gentleman.   STAFFORD.

23–24   John HELYER of Potterspury (Estpurye), yeoman, *v.* Thomas INGE, yeoman.
Detention of deeds relating to a messuage and land in Hansloppe bought of Lewis Dyve, esquire.
N'HAMP.*

25–29   Robert HIGHSTED (Hysted) *v.* John READER and Thomas his son.
Lands in Bredgate (*i.e.* Bredgar) pledged to the said John. *2 replications.*   KENT.

---

* Part of Hanslope, co. Bucks, was locally in Hartwell, co. N'hamp., to which it has since been transferred.

30   Robert HOBBYE, citizen and grocer of London, and Grace his wife, executors of Edward Deane, gentleman, v. Leonard DANNETT.
Seizure of goods and of deeds relating to a messuage and lands called Beaumont Leys by Leicester.
LEICESTER

31–35   Thomas HOLT of Royston, co. Herts, 'mawlstiner,' v. Dr. Thomas Whyte, warden of NEW COLLEGE, Oxford, and the fellows thereof.
Land in Widdington held of defendants and warranted by complainant to Margaret Collens.
2 *replications.*   ESSEX.

36–39   Edmund HOPTON of Calais, merchant, v. Edmund PETYTE.
Price of fabrics (*described*) sold to William Toppe, clerk of the check of the King's and Queen's works at Guines, whose executor defendant is.   CALAIS.

40   Gregory HOPTON and Saige his wife, daughter of James Leche v. Richard UPRISE, clerk.
Houses, lands, rents and services in Newtown, Eskargilliog and Llandinam of the gift of defendants, and in Aberhafesp (Haverhavis) of the gift of the said James and of Anne his daughter.
MONTGOMERY.

41   Roger HOULTE, citizen and goldsmith of London, husband of Cicely, late the wife of William Morfen, v. Thomas GWIN, plasterer.
Messuage and land, late of —— Merewether. *Mutilated.*   MIDDLESEX.

42   Thomas [HOWARD], Duke of Norfolk, v. William WESTE, lord de la Warr.
Felling of trees in Knappstock park in contempt of an injunction from this court.   ——

43   The same v. Avery MYCHELL and John MOORE.
Ironworks connected with walks in the forest of Worth forfeited on the attainder of the late Duke.
Mutilated.   SUSSEX.

44   The same v. William SYMBARB.
Manor of South Brent, awarded to complainant by arbitration on the reversal of his grandfather's attainder.   SOMERSET.

45–48   Nicholas HUDSON, Dorothy his wife, and Richard BELLYME and John ROLLES their tenants, v. Cicely BARTON, and James DEANE (Adene) of Wirksworth, lead-burner.
Messuages and land in Wirksworth awarded to the said Dorothy in a previous suit (*File* 1004, *No.* 68 ; D. I, 26). See also File 1235, *No.* 51.   DERBY.

49–50   Thomas HURBOTT, Elizabeth his wife, Humphrey DEVIAS, Agnes his wife, and Rose YATE, v. Joan, late the wife of Walter FAWCETT.
Pasture in Tettenhall Regis demised to the said Walter by John Yate, brother of the female complainant, while insane. *Damaged.*   STAFFORD.

51   John HYGFORDE, esquire v. Peter TEMPLE, gentleman, and John WESTELEY.
Corn-rent of the site of the manor of Marton and land there, late of the priory of Nuneaton.
WARWICK.

FILE 1441

1   John HAGHE of the Hurste, yeoman, v. Thomas GLEDALL, Alice his wife, and others.
Messuages and land in the Slacke in the parish (*sic*) of Whernby.   YORK.

2–3   Stephen HALES v. Robert MARRYS (Maurice), gentleman.
Refusal·to complete a sale of a lease of the site and demesnes of the manor of Fladbury.
WORCESTER.

4–5   Thomas HALKNYGHT of Salisbury, servant to Thomas Norman, deceased, late canon of [Salisbury], v. Robert PENRUDDOCK, esquire, and Edmund BOWER of Fifehead St. Andrew, yeoman, executor of the said Norman.
Goods of the said Norman, who was indebted to complainant for household bills (*described*).
Mutilated.   WILTS.

6–8   Giles HALL v. Nicholas BONSALL.
Heathcote Grange in Hartington of the demise of the late abbot and convent of Garendon.
DERBY.

9–13   John HALL 'in Holborne,' tailor, v. Simon ADEE (Adye), Alice his wife and others.
Suppression of court rolls of the manor of Cirencester, wherein complainant has inherited a messuage and garden from John Hall his cousin.   WILTS.

14   George HALSTED, Agnes his wife, and Henry, George and Margaret, their children, v. George ROKE and William HALSTED.
Legacies of Roger Halstedd, father of the said Agnes (*sic*), whose executors defendants are.
——

15–16   Robert HALSTED and others, grandsons of Robert Clytherowe, v. Robert and Joan CLYTHEROWE and Richard SHERBORNE.
Moiety of the manor of Auckley, of messuages and lands there and in Finningley and Misson, of the ' free piscarye ' in the water of Torn, and of the advowson of the church of Finningley, late of Ralph Clytherowe, deceased, also grandson of the said Robert.   NOTTS.

17–18   John HANDLEY of London, apprentice, son and heir of Thomas Handley, v. Edward NEWPORTE, gentleman.
Manor of Downton, and messuages, lands, rents and services there and in Hanley William, Ovinsape (*i.e.* Over Sapey), and Eastham.   WORCESTER, HEREFORD.

19-21   John son and heir of Thomas HARDYNG *v.* Richard STRETFOLD.
Lands in Walton by Aylesbury, Weston Turville, and Calcote, belonging to John Bosse's manor of
Stoners and held of the Queen's manor of Bierton.   BUCKINGHAM.

22   John HARFORDE, *v.* Frances, late the wife of Oliver LEDER, knight.
Reviver of a suit for a messuage in St. Thomas's (*File* 1230, *No.* 16).   LONDON.

23   Edward HARPESFEILDE *alias* Mitton of Weston-under-Lizard, gentleman, *v.* Margery
and Richard OFFELYE.
Messuages and land in Brinton and Blymhill.   ,   STAFFORD.

24-25   William HARVY, yeoman, *v.* Thomas son and heir of John HARVY.
Land held of the manor of East Donyland (Estdolylond) by another John Harvy, deceased, father
of complainant.   ESSEX.

26   John HARWARD of Purbeck *v.* John HORSEY, knight and James WORSLEY, esquire.
Counterbond for a bond given by defendants in the Court of Augmentations on behalf of Richard
Hewe of Poole and Edmund Deane of Winson, merchants.   DORSET, SOMERSET.

27   Thomas HASSELLER *v.* Francis BADEROWE.
Lands in Northam and Burgate.   SUFFOLK.

28   John HAYDON of London, merchant, *v.* Thomas HAYDON of Woodbury, his elder brother.
Annuity of the bequest of Richard Haydon of Woodbury, esquire, father of both parties.   DEVON.

29   The said Thomas *v.* the said John.
Land in Withycombe Rawleigh awarded to complainant by arbitration of John Prydyaux, serjeant-
at-law.   DEVON.

30-32   John HAYNES of Ireton Wood, husbandman, *v.* Thomas DAKYN and Margaret his wife,
formerly Margaret Wardell.
Money promised to complainant on his marriage with Elizabeth Wardell, daughter of the said
Margaret.   DERBY.

33   Thomas HAYS of Aston, co. Chester, *v.* Robert EVERS, esquire.
Rents in Belton in Axholme.   LINCOLN.

34   John HAYWARD of Terwick, labourer, grandson of Joan Hayward, deceased, and
administrator of her goods, *v.* Elizabeth DUDMAN and Richard her son.
Messuage and land in Farnhurst of the demise of Robert [Sherborne], late bishop of Chichester.
          SUSSEX.

35-37   Thomas HENDLE (Hendeley) of Otham, esquire, *v.* Thomas ROBERTES, esquire, and
Margery his wife, late the wife of Walter Hendle, knight, brother of complainant.
Detention of deeds relating to the manors of Courshoarne and Angley (both in Cranbrook) and
messuages and lands in Biddenden, Sharlysmoor, Tenterden, Woodchurch, and Appledore, the said
Margery having a life-interest in the parsonage of Cranbrook and the chapel of Milkhouse (in
Cranbrook).   KENT.

38-41   Christopher HENNAGE, gentleman, *v.* William UPTON and Jane his wife.
Manor of Middleton and lands in Arlington and Alfriston entailed on William Hennage, deceased
father of complainant and former husband of the said Jane.   SUSSEX.

42-43   Henry HERDES *v.* Richard (William) DYNSON.
Gold chain entrusted to defendant by Robert Herdes, who then bequeathed it to complainant.

44-47   John HERYNGE *v.* Edward CO(U)CHE and Agnes his wife.
Messuage and land in St. Erney formerly of William Bake and Joan his wife, parents of Elizabeth
wife of complainant and grandparents of the said Agnes.   CORNWALL.

48-49   William HEWE *v.* John PARKER, esquire.
Land late held of the manor of Pixton in Nynehead Flory by Thomas Stephyns, whose widow
complainant took to wife.   SOMERSET.

50-52   John HEWET of Bodmin, an executor of John Typpett, *v.* Stephen LAWRYE his kinsman.
Messuage and land in Tresodderne (in St. Columb Major ?) of the demise of John Tregose, esquire,
and John Rouse.   CORNWALL.

53   John HEYWARD *v.* Ralph INSLEY of Witherby, husbandman.
Bond given on defendant's behalf to William Dewsnopp, parson of Drayton. *Mutilated.*
          LEICESTER.

54-57   Stephen HILLARIE *v.* Stephen WORTHEVALE.
Messuages and land called Copplestone (Copston) in Lesnewth.   CORNWALL.

58   William HODGE *v.* [John WARDE].
Money payable to William Northe for the farm of Mettley Hamens in Braughing (*i.e.* Hamels by
Mentley ?) obtained by defendant in exchange for the manor of Shortgrove Hall in Newport.
          HERTS, ESSEX.

59   Richard HODSHON of Newcastle-on-Tyne, merchant, *v.* Robert STRINGER, yeoman,
and others.
Land at Newbiggin in Lanchester bought of Simon Welberey and Christopher Morland. DURHAM.

60   Hugh HODSON, parson of Skelton *v.* William SUTHACK, gentleman.
Seizure of hay and corn belonging to complainant's parsonage.   CUMBERLAND.

61   William HOLGAT of Acomb (Akham), co. York, and Anne his wife, *v.* John BELLOWE,
esquire.
Messuages and land in Barnoldby late of Christopher Atkyrke of Grimstone, deceased, uncle of
the said Anne.   .   LINCOLN.

62–63   William HOLLANDE, esquire, v. Richard RYSEDEN.
Messuage in complainant's manor of Newcourt in Sheepwash.   DEVON.

64–65   Thomas HOLWAY v. John and Jeffrey DICK.
Tenement in North Langton (i.e. Market Lavington?) of the demise of John Montague, esquire, deceased. Damaged.   WILTS.

66   Richard grandson and heir of Richard HOPKYNS v. Margery HOPKYNS.
Ten half burgages in the borough of Walsall and land in the foreign or lordship of Walsall. STAFFORD.

67   Robert HOTTOFF and Elizabeth his wife v. William GERYE.
Land in Stoneley (in Kimbolton), Hoo (in Pertenhall) and Pertenhall of the settlement of Robert Marleborough of Brigstock, co. Northants, late the husband of the said Elizabeth.
HUNTINGDON, BEDFORD.

68–70   Emmote late the wife of William HOUGHTON v. John BRYSTOWE.
Messuage and land in the manor of Staythorpe of the demise of the prior and convent of Newstead.
NOTTS.

71–72   William HOWPER v. Oliver SEINT JOHN of Southampton.
Sale of the ship Maye Flower, whereof each party owned one-half and failure to account for trading profits.   HANTS.

73–75   William HUDSDON (Hudson) and Anne his wife, administratrix of the goods of Richard Woodwall, deceased, v. Arthur DUDLEY and John BLYTHE, prebendaries of Lichfield.
Promise to obtain a new lease of the parsonage of Arley and Seckley (Sykelehyll) wood, paid for in wine and salt.   STAFFORD.

76–83   William HUMFREY and others v. Geoffrey DANYELL, Nicholas SNELL, Walter SKYLLINGE and Robert MAY.
Messuage and land in Elston of the demise of John Berkley.   WILTS.

84–85   Roger HUNT of London, gentleman, v. John BEERE, esquire.
Messuage, land, rent and common of pasture in Dartford demised by defendant for a ' Mary grote ' and a yearly rent of 19l.   KENT.

86–87   William HURST, parson of Hawridge, v. Francis CORNEWALYS, gentleman.
Tithes claimed under a lease from Edmund Hodson (Huddeson), late parson.   BUCKS.

88   Richard HUTTON, servant to the Queen, v. the sheriffs of LONDON, and Christian JOHNS, alias Crislye ver John, executrix and late the wife of Le[onard?] Johns of St. Michael, Tonygroes.
Action for wages of workmen employed in felling timber at Lantarnam ' in Wales in the countye of Monmothe ' for King Edward's works in the isle of Scilly. Certiorari and subpœna.
LONDON, MONMOUTH.

89   Richard HUXLEY of Portland, co. Dorset, grandson of Robert Huxley, v. Ralph DUTTON.
Lands formerly of Ralph Huxley and Joan [his wife]. Mutilated.   CHESTER.

90   Richard HYCKYNS v. William PASCOWE, clerk.
Annuity promised on obtaining the vicarage of St. Stephen's.   CORNWALL.

91   Thomas son and heir of Richard HYGGYNS, v. William COLLYNS and Elizabeth his wife.
Messuage and lands in Hasbury, Halesowen, and Hagley.   SALOP (now WORC.), WORCESTER.

92   Giles HYLLYNG, clerk, v. Henry CLERKE and Margaret VERNEY.
Prebend of St. Decuman's in Wells cathedral.   SOMERSET.

FILE 1442.

1   John HALL of London and Alice [his wife] v. William BRAMBYE and others.
Messuage and land in Cotgrave. Damaged.   NOTTS.

2–3   John HANCOCK v. John HASYLL.
Messuage and land in Bottisham, late of Isabel Caverley, deceased, wife of John Cawverlay, and aunt of complainant. Answer wanting.   CAMBRIDGE.

4–8   Martin son of Thomas HARLAKENDEN v. John STORYE, D.C.L., master in Chancery.
Messuage and land in St. Pancras held of the manor of Cantelyns, whereof defendant has a lease from the dean and chapter of St. Paul's.   MIDDLESEX.

9   Robert HARRYSON v. George HERBERT, knight, executor of John Cradocke, gentleman.
Failure to save complainant harmless from a bond given by him for sale of Welsh mats on the said Cradocke's behalf while in service with him.   LONDON.

10–11   William HARTE, yeoman, v. John HARTE.
Messuage and garden in Spalding, late of Katherine Harte, deceased, grandmother of complainant and mother of defendant.   LINCOLN.

12   Bartholomew HARVY, gentleman, v. Thomas FYSHER.
Messuage and land in Evedon, late of William Harvy, deceased, father of complainant.   LINCOLN.

13   Francis [HASTINGS], earl of Huntingdon, v. Elizabeth THORPE, and Anthony THORPE, esquire.
Slingsby moor in complainant's manor of Slingsby.   YORK.

14   Alice [late the wife of John] HAYDON and administratrix of his goods v. John SENT.
ALYN.
Tenement in Camborne (?) of the demise of Michael Rosewaren and goods. Mutilated.
CORNWALL.

15-16   John son and heir of Richard HAYWARD v. Gabriel PAWLYN.
Double lease of the manor of Halliford (Haloughford) by the abbot of [Westminster]. *Faded*.
                                                                                    MIDDLESEX.

17   Thomas HELYAR v. William   .   .   .
Messuage and land in Evercriche. *Faded*.   SOMERSET.

18-19   Francis HEWETT of Wales, co. York, gentleman, v. Bryan SANDEFORTH, clerk, and
Alen HEY, yeoman.
Detention of releases made by Richard Whalley of Welbeck, esquire, who is now suing complainant.
                                                                                    YORK, NOTTS.

20   William HEYTHE v. Richard WARTE(S), vicar of Nafferton, and Gilbert WARTERS.
Lease of tithes of Nafferton acquired of Humphrey Conysbye.   YORK.

21   Thomas HEYWARD of Ashton v. Edward CAPLE, executor of William Caple of Caple,
esquire.
Action for a debt paid without obtaining a receipt.   HEREFORD.

22   Richard HIGDEN of Bedminster, co. Somerset, v. William OLDICHE and John and William
his sons.
Land in North Wootton, late of Joan Higden, deceased, mother of complainant.   DORSET.

23   John HILL v. Henry HILL and John his son.
Refusal to surrender a messuage and land in Pencombe at a date ordered by a commission from this
court. *Damaged*.   HEREFORD.

24-27   Richard HOLDFORD, gentleman sewer of the Chamber, executor of Christopher
Wynnyngton, clerk, v. Thomas WYNNYNGTON and others, gentleman.
Seizure of goods of the said Christopher at Audlem.   CHESTER.

28   Hugh HOLT v. Geoffrey (H)ELMES and others.
Messuage in Leicester, late of Robert Holt, deceased, uncle of complainant.   LEICESTER.

29   Richard HOLT, household servant [to Cardinal Pole], v. Matthew and Richard, sons of
George MARDING, yeoman.
Falsification of the term of a lease of the manor and parsonage of Sledmere made to the said George,
whose executor the said Matthew is. *Mutilated*.   [YORK].

30-32   Henry HORNE of Bury St. Edmunds, yeoman, v. Thomas BROWNE of Norwich, butcher.
Messuage in St. Martin's-at-Palace, Norwich, late of Robert Horne, deceased, father of complainant.
                                                                                    NORFOLK.

33   George HORSEY, esquire, executrix of Joan, executrix and late the wife of Jaspar his father,
v. Richard PATE.
Staverton mills, of the demise of the dean and chapter of Exeter.   DEVON.

34   Simon HOWELL, Margery his wife, and Anthony ERESBY v James RANSHEWE and
Alexander BARLEY.
Messuage, and lands in Sale and Manchester, late of Edward Holt, deceased, father of the said
Margery and [grandfather] of the said Anthony. *Faded*.   CHESTER, LANCASTER.

35-38   Gregory HOWS and others, inhabitants of Raveningham, v. John, son and heir of Richard
ULSTOFTE.
Messuage called the ' Gyldehall ' and land in Raveningham, whereof the said Richard was the last
surviving feoffee to the use of the parish.   NORFOLK.

39   Agnes HOWSON, John EXCETER, and Ellen his wife v. James ANDERKYN.
Tenement in Canewdon, late of John Cooke, husbandman, deceased, uncle of the female complainants.
                                                                                    ESSEX.

40-42   Thomas HUBBETHORNE (Hoblethorne) v. Thomas HAMMERTON.
Messuages and lands in Sutton, Huttoft, Trusthorpe and Thornton by Horncastle, late of Agnes
Bywater, deceased, kinswoman of complainant.   LINCOLN.

43-44   John HUCHYN *alias* Glandefyld v. Robert NORTHAM.
Refusal to give bond as promised for warranty of a leasehold in Beaworthy, and claim thereto in
continuance of a former lease.   DEVON.

45   HUGH ap Hoell of Lineham, co. Oxford, husbandman, grandson and heir of Hoell ap Thomas
ap Gwyllym Vaughan, v. JOHN ap Rosse and Jenkyn RYSE.
Detention of deeds relating to messuages, watermills and land in Gwenddwr and within the parish of
Landaffaugthey (i.e., Llandevalley ?),   BRECON.

46   HUGH ap Gruffydd v. LEWIS ap Richard and others.
Lands in Llanufydd (Llanyveth) late of Gruffydd ap David ap Robert, deceased, father of complainant.   DENBIGH.

47   HUGH app Griffith of Almington, co. Stafford, husbandman, v. RICHARD app William,
yeoman, and others.
Messuages and land in Wheldrenewed and Vaynor, late of Greffeth app Davyd app (*sic*) Vaghan,
deceased father of complainant.   MONTGOMERY.

48   HUGH ap Robert ap Grono ap Tona v. ROBERT ap John ap Madocke, Eleanor his wife,
and others.
Land in Sagrate.   DENBIGH.

49   Rowland HUMBLE and Anne his wife v. the mayor and aldermen of LONDON, and William
MALBONE.
Action for a debt of Thomas Brikett, clerk, deceased, of whose will the said Malbone is overseer and
the said Anne an executor. *Certiorari and subpœna*.   LONDON.

50   John and Eleanor, children of Richard HYGGYNS, v. Thomas BARDSLEY [overseer] of his mill, and Richard BULLINGHAM.
Money and goods of the bequest of the said Richard. *Mutilated.*   ———

51-52   Thomas HYLL and Elizabeth his wife v. Edward CHAMBERLAYNE, esquire.
Messuage and land in defendant's manor of (H)astly, late of the Marquis of Dorset. *Mutilated.*   ?

53   William H . . . v. Thomas HAMLEY and Joan his wife.
Detention of deeds relating to a messuage and land in Whitstone bought of William Dawe and Joan his wife.   CORNWALL.

FILE 1443.

1-4   Robert INGE and Margaret his wife v. Robert, grandson and heir of John HILLER.
Messuages and land in Beddington, late of John Waker, deceased, grandfather of the said Margaret.   SURREY.

5-6   John INGRAM v. Robert HENNEAGE, executor of George Henneage, dean of Lincoln. and warden of the college of Tattershall.
Action for sheep payable as rent for a messuage called 'Souche Manour' with lands and stock of sheep in Withcall and Cuckerington.   LINCOLN.

7   William INNYCENT and others, husbandmen, v. William BOOTE.
Action of waste for coal-mining at Newton in Blackwell. *Faded.*   DERBY.

8   Robert IVE v. William WALGRAVE, gentleman.
Tenement in defendant's manor of Brent Pelham. *See Files 1283, No. 2; 1321, No. 2.*   HERTS.

9-10   Edmond JACKESON, clerk, v. Lewis LYES, executor of Anne Jarves.
Loan and power of malt, said by defendant to have been satisfied by a lease of land at Broughton in Eccleshall.   STAFFORD.

11   Simon, son and heir of Robert JACKESON, v. Peter PEERSON *alias* Burneyate, John ROBYNSON, gentleman, and David FLEMMYNGE.
Messuage and land held of the said Robynson's manor of Loweswater in the honour of Cockermouth.   CUMBERLAND.

12-13   Roger JACKSON v. Richard, cousin and heir of Agnes WYERSDALE, and Richard WYERSDALE of Braceby, co. Lincoln, husbandman.
Maintenance and purchase of title of messuages and land in Croxton (Crawson) and B[ranston?] in dispute in this court. *Mutilated.*   LEICESTER.

14   John JACOBBE of Walberswick, innkeeper, v. Thomas WASE of Barford.
Refusal to complete a sale of malt.   SUFFOLK, NORFOLK.

15   Thomas JAMES v. William GYRLYNG.
Land in Newport and goods, late of Richard, brother of complainant. *Damaged.*
                                               HANTS (I.W.).

16   Constance JAMYS, granddaughter, and heir of John Jamys Jacke Vartyn and of Jane his wife, v. Robert John JAMYS.
Detention of deeds relating to tenements in Madron. *Damaged.*   CORNWALL.

17   The same v. John TREVERE and others.
Other messuages and lands in Madron.   CORNWALL.

18-19   Robert JANYNS v. Thomas JANYNS his brother and Thomas DALE of Aylesbury, tailor.
Contempt of an arbitral award as to lands in Hartwell and embracery by the said Dale.
                                               BUCKINGHAM.

20   John JAXSON of Stamford, baker and weaver, v. William CONY of London, gentleman.
Dispute as to a bargain of corn suspended during a proclamation against sale of corn, etc.
                                               LINCOLN, LONDON.

21-22   Thomas JECKELERE, husbandman, v. Anthony BEDYFELD (Benyfeld), esquire, and Edmund his son.
Messuages, land and liberty of a fold in Great Massingham bought of John Warcoppe of Aylesford, co. Kent, gentleman.   NORFOLK.

23   Richard JEFFERY, parson of Pattenham, v. Thomas SAUNDERS and John DUNCOME, executors of Richard Duncome, gentleman.
Parsonage of Puttenham, claimed under a lease from Oliver Chippe, late parson, deprived for marriage.   HERTS.

24-25   Richard JEKYS, gentleman, v. Walter HARECOURTE and Mary his wife.
Mortgage of a manor called the Motte in Tamworth and lands in Tamworth, Wigginton and Coton (in Wigginton). D. XII, 12.   STAFFORD.

26   Humphrey, son and heir of the said Richard, v. the same.

27-29   Do. *Damaged.*   STAFFORD.

30   John JENNYE of Cressingham, co. Norfolk, esquire, v. Thomas MALYVERAY, knight, and Ralph DYCONSON.
Manors of Tockwith and Bilton and messuages, cottages, windmills, lands, and rent there. YORK.

31   The same v. the same and Robert, son and heir of Bryan SNAWSELL of Easingwold, gentleman, and formerly a ward of the other defendants.   YORK.
                                               Ditto

32-33   Thomas JENNYNGE v. Thomas RAYNOLDE.
Messuage and land in Little Chesterford, late of Robert Jennynge of Great Chesterford, deceased, father of complainant.   ESSEX.

34–38   Nicholas JEPSON of Killamarsh, yeoman, v. Peter FRECHEVYLE, knight, and Elizabeth his wife.
Iron-smithies in Stayley of the demise of the said Elizabeth.   DERBY.

39   John JERMYE, knight, v. Robert BROKE, esquire.
Refusal to complete a settlement of the manor of Nacton and other lands on the marriage of Richard his son with Mary, daughter of complainant.   SUFFOLK.

40–41   The same v. Robert CRANE, esquire.
Manor of Mynyottes in Creeting St. Mary, Creeting St. Olave, Creeting All Saints, Coddenham, Earl Stanton, Aspall Stonham, Little Stonham, and Crowfield.   SUFFOLK.

42–45   John JERMYE of Brightwell, knight, v. Bartholomew HALL, gentleman, grandson and heir of Thomas Hall.
Manors of Easton Gosbeck, Myneottes, Stoneham, Creeting, Coddenham, Easnelles in Foxhall, and Stratton. See File 1134, No. 53.   SUFFOLK.

46–49   The same v. the same and Lionel TALMACHE and Robert WINGFELD, esquire.
Do. (The said Talmache claims manors in Helmingham, Gosbeck, and Bentley.)   SUFFOLK.

50–52   The same v. Thomas [HOWARD], duke of Norfolk.
Crown lease of the manor of Foxhole (i.e. Foxhall) acquired of Thomas Pope, knight.   SUFFOLK.

53–54   Robert JERVYS v. James JERMEN and Bridget his wife, late the wife of William Jervys.
Messuages and lands late of Richard Jervys of Whepstead, deceased, grandfather of complainant.
                                    SUFFOLK.

55   Edmund JESOPPE v. Thomas LONDON.
Messuages and land in Occold acquired of Robert London. Mutilated.   SUFFOLK.

56–59   JEVAN ap David ap Hoell v. [Jevan GWILLIM, gentleman?] and others.
Messuages and lands called Tir Eskayr Ithell in Llansawel, Maystrothen, and Maes y Gwiell. Much damaged.   CARMARTHEN.

60   Richard JEVYNE, husbandman, v. Oliver APARKE alias Persehowse.
Messuage and land held of the Crown manor of Sedgley by Thomas Jevyne, deceased, father of complainant.   STAFFORD.

61   Henry JOANES of Dowlish Wake, co. Somerset v. Thomas LUDD of Llangwyfan.
Land in the town of Baghkern and commot of Dogfeilyn, the court of which is held at Ruthin, acquired of John Griffith of Llangwyfan and Richard ap Gwilliam of Llangynhafal.   DENBIGH.

62–64   Walter JOBSON v. John FAWKENER, alderman of Lincoln, and William CLARKE.
Messuages and land in Lincoln, late of William Fawkener.   LINCOLN.

65–67   Edward JONES v. MATTHEW, HENRY, and ROBERT, sons of John ap Madock ap Gruffydd ap Jevan.
Land in Leeswood of the bequest of David Jones, father of complainant.   FLINT.

68–70   Richard, grandson and heir of John JONES, v. Thurstan, son and heir of Roger HOGGETTES.
Messuage and land held of the manor of Sedgley. (Defendant pleads a verdict in the manor-court.)
                                    STAFFORD.

71–72   Thomas JONES, son and heir of John Thomas John Phelipe, v. Thomas WATKYN.
Action in the Duchy Chamber at Westminster for a tenement in Skenfrith. Decayed.
                                    [MONMOUTH.]

73   William JONES v. DAVID ap David.
Goods entrusted to defendants by John Appowell, deceased, father of complainant.   [WALES.]

74–77   John JOYE of Climping, husbandman, son and executor of Richard Joye, v. Edward his brother.
Arrears of corn-rent of a messuage and land in Elsam, demised by the said Richard for his life to defendant.   SUSSEX.

78–81   John JURDEN and Joan his wife, granddaughter and heir of Nicholas Hamond, yeoman, v. Thomas WYNCHECOMBE, esquire, Cristyan his wife, Henry WHITE, esquire, and Bridget his wife.
Messuage, cottage and land in Dagnall, claimed as the inheritance of Henry Bradshawe, grandfather of the female defendants.   BUCKINGHAM.

FILE 1444.

1–4   Thomas, son and heir of William INGLESBYE alias Baker of Brentwood, yeoman, v. John HANKYN and John son and heir of William WHYTE.
Meadow in Shenfield, claimed as the inheritance of Richard Alen, deceased, uncle of the said John Hankyn and William Whyte.   ESSEX.

5–6   The same v. Christopher PLANKNEY, guardian in socage to Thomas Legate.
Messuage in Brentwood and land in Shenfield.   ESSEX.

7   Henry INGLYSSHE v. John, son of John TREVYLYON, esquire, and others.
Lands at West Harwood in Timberscombe, held of the said Trevylyon's manor of Old Knowle. See File 1164, No. 30.   SOMERSET.

8–11   Anthony INGRAM v. John CORBETT, gentleman.
Action on a bond for an arbitral award concerning a messuage and land in Kennett.   CAMBRIDGE.

12–13   INON ap Rice of London, tailor, v. GRIFFITH ap Jevan of Warthye.
Messuage and lands in Llanfihangel (St. Michael's), late of Griffith ap Llewelyn, deceased, grandfather of complainant.   CARMARTHEN.

14-15   John ISAKE *v.* John HAYDON, gentleman, late steward of the manor of Ottery St. Mary, William COR(H)AM his clerk, and Richard ISACKE.
Messuages and land in the said manor late of Thomas Isake, deceased, grandfather of complainant.
DEVON.

16-18   Richard ISATT *v.* William WALDON.
Destruction of a bond for a debt paid only in part.   ———

19   Richard IVE of West Kington *v.* John OLIVER of Bushton.
Messuage and land in Sherston Pinkney, late of Richard Ive, .deceased, great-grandfather of complainant.   WILTS.

20   Alice ap (*sic*) Thomas JAMES *v.* Roger ap Richard FYLPOTT.
Tenement in the parish of Doughton Halley, late of David ap Richard Philpot, deceased, husband of complainant.   MONMOUTH.

21   Edward JANKYN, parson of Garsdon, co. Wilts, *v.* William THOMAS, parson of Crickhowell.
Tithe corn of Crickhowell sold to complainant before defendant's ordination.   BRECON.

22   Bartholomew JEKETT and Rychard (*sic*) his wife, late the wife of Nicholas Barnehouse, *v.* Henry BRAYNE, esquire.
Tenements bought of defendant in Bristol.   GLOUCESTER.

23   The same *v.* Mary SOUTHCOTTE and others.
Manor of Prescott, late of Thomas Marwood and Joan his wife, parents of defendants.   *Mutilated.*
DEVON.

24-26   The same, the said Barnehouse being also called Marwood, *v.* John HOLBROKE, executor of Richard Gage, an executor of Nicholas Derell.
Indenture of lease of the ' sheffe or rectorye ' of Holbeton, entrusted to the said Derell.   DEVON.

27   John JERMAN, yeoman, and Joan his wife, *v.* . . . NER of Uxbridge, co. Middlesex, widow.
Tenement in Amersham, late of John Pletour, deceased, father of the said Joan.   *Mutilated.*
BUCKINGHAM.

28-32   John JERMYN, yeoman, son and heir of Thomas Jermyn, *v.* William BUSSE.
Lands in Cobham of the bequest of John Bradforth, yeoman, whose widow was married to defendant.   KENT.

33   John JERNEGAN, esquire, and others *v.* George BOWES, gentleman.
Account of lands in Gorleston and of goods, late of Richard Gunvyle, esquire, whose executors all parties are.   NORFOLK.

34-39   Henry JERNINGHAM (Jernegan), knight, and Frances his wife, granddaughter and heir of William Kingston, knight, *v.* Thomas DYER of Weston, co. Somerset, knight.
Manor of Haresfield pledged to defendant.   2 *suits*.   GLOUCESTER.

40-41   John Fuller, master of JESUS College, Cambridge, and the fellows of the same, *v.* Thomas CAWARDEN, knight.
Woods in complainants' manor of Horne Court.   SURREY.

42   JEVAN ap David ap Hoell of London *v.* Lewis ICHAN and others.
Lands in Llansawel, late of Jevan ap David Hoell and Isabel ap (*sic*) David his sister.   *Pedigree given.*   CARMARTHEN.

43   JEVAN ap David ap Hoell of London *v.* Griffith ap Jevan LLOID, gentleman, and others.
Messuages and lands in Pencarreg, Kellan, and Llanvayre Igladoge (*i.e.* Llanfair-Clydogau?), late of John ap Hoell Ichan, deceased, great-grandfather of complainant.   CARMARTHEN, CARDIGAN.

44-46   William ap Jevan ap Griffydd ap John *alias* William JEVANS *v.* John his brother.
Messuage and land in Ffestiniog.   MERIONETH.

47   John JEWE, clerk, and Richard and William JEWE *v.* John HAWE.
Goods of William Gybbes and of Thomas Gybbes, his executor, both deceased, whereof complainants are administrators.   ———

48-50   David JEYN of Bristol, tucker, and Elizabeth his wife *v.* Walter FLOWER.
Meadow and fisheries in Ruddle (in Newnham), late of the abbot and convent of Gloucester.
GLOUCESTER.

51-52   Thomas JOBOUR of Offlow, co. Stafford, husbandman, *v.* Robert FOSTER of Tong, co. Stafford, gentleman.
Messuages and lands late of the Crown in Ashton.   *Mutilated.*   SALOP.

53   JOHN ap Jevan of London, clothworker, *v.* Robert JONES (ap Johnes) of Southwark, tailor.
Messuage, etc., in Rythyn, demised by defendant to Robert Edney.   [DENBIGH.]

54   JOHN ap Powell, servant to the Lord Warden of the Cinque Ports, *v.* MORYS ap Richard.
Messuage and land in Llanarmon-Mynydd-Mawr, late of Howell ap Howell, deceased, father of complainant.   DENBIGH.

55   JOHN ap Robert, clerk, son and heir of Robert ap Llewelyn ap . . . , and of Agnes his wife, *v.* John SALYSBURY, knight, and others.
Messuage, cottage and lands in Aberwheeler, late of John ap Edm' ap Griffydd ap Jorwerth.
Mutilated.   DENBIGH.

56   JOHN ap Rees and Llyke his wife *v.* THOMAS ap Richard and THOMAS ap John.
Messuage and land in Llanfrechfa.   BRECON.

57   JOHN ap Howell of Lacock, co. Wilts, clerk, *v.* Christopher VAGHAN and others.
Messuages and lands in Crickhowell and Llangattock.   BRECON.

58-61   Henry JOHNES *v.* John LEGH (Lee) of the Ridge (in Sutton), esquire.
Messuage called the Nunhouse and land at Old Wharton in Davenham.   CHESTER.

62   George Bullock, master of St. JOHN'S College, Cambridge, and the fellows of the same *v.*
Thomas SNAG the elder and Thomas SNAG the younger.
Manor of Blunham and another, late of George Brooke, lord Cobham. *Damaged.*   BEDS., HERTS.

63   Thomas JOHNS and Joan his wife, late the wife of David ap John Robartes, *v.* Robert
GOODYNOUGHE.
Account of a joint purchase of cattle.   ———

64-66   Henry JOHNSON, esquire, *v.* John, Ambrose, and Thomas DUNNE and John HEDLEY.
Manor of Arras, late of Thomas Johnson, knight, deceased, father of complainant.   YORK.

67   John JOHNSON of Bishop's Stortford *v.* John MEADE of Elsdon and Edward MEADE
of Berden, both in Essex.
Refusal to give bond for balance of price of a messuage called Pishobury.   HERTS.

68   Ralph JOHNSON, esquire, *v.* John MAYNE, esquire.
Refusal to surrender a grant of an annuity in exchange for a conveyance of land in Lewisham.
                                                                          KENT.

69-74   Richard JOHNSON and Joan his wife *v.* Robert HAMOND.
Messuages and land in Penge and Beckenham, late of Robert Hamond and Ralph his son, father
of complainant and grandfather of the said Joan. D. XV. 27.   SURREY, KENT.

75   Thomas JOHNSON and Margery his wife, late the wife of William Reynoldes, *v.* Rose, late
the wife of John DRAKE and executrix and formerly the wife of John Cotton, and John
ANTHONY.
Messuage in St. Mary Arches, Exeter, demised by the said brother to the said Reynoldes, and by
him to the said Anthony.   DEVON.

76-78   Thomas JOHNSON ' of the parishe of Berydstowe in the countye of Execetour ' *v.* John
WRAYE, gentleman, John PRYGGES, John YOUNES, and others.
Arrest as a Frenchman and seizure of goods.   DEVON.

79   Anthony JONES of Bishop's Castle, co. Salop, mercer, *v.* DAVID ap Llewelyn.
Shop in Newtown of the demise of defendant.   MONTGOMERY.

80   John JONES of Kyvele *v.* John PRYOR of the same . . . his wife, and Marion his
daughter.
Action on a bond for an arbitral award concerning land. *Mutilated.*   [WILTS.]

81   Thomas JONES *v.* Thomas MARTEN and Joyce his wife.
Double sale of a messuage and land in Frodesley.   SALOP.

82-84   William, son of Thomas JOYCE (Joce), deceased, *v.* Nicholas JOYCE.
Lands in Sturminster Newton Buckland (*sic*) of the demise of Thomas Stukeley, knight. 3 *bills,*
similar, except that two give Dorset as the county and the other Somerset.   DORSET, SOMERSET.

85-86   Margaret JUDDE *v.* Henry LACEY, gentleman.
Share of messuages and gardens, late of John, son of Thomas Lyttill, deceased.   LINCOLN.

87   Robert, son of William JURDEN, *v.* John SACKFEILD, esquire, and Christopher
TERRELL.
Land in the said Sackfeild's manor of Mount-Bures.   ESSEX.

88   Miles JYNNYNGES of Ipswich *v.* Martin FLOWERDEW.
Bond given on behalf of Anthony Russhe, a minor in the King's and Queen's ward, for price of
rings bought of defendant. *Damaged.*   SUFFOLK.

FILE 1445.

1   Michael KASSY *v.* John BYRDLEY.
Detention of deeds relating to a messuage and land in Hanbury, and of wages for pulling cloth.
                                                                          WORCESTER.

2-3   Robert KEANE of Great Wilbraham, tailor, *v.* Thomas SHEPERYCK, husband of Alice,
late the wife of James Loveday.
Land in Burrough Green, late of John Keane, deceased, grandfather of complainant.   CAMBRIDGE.

4   Richard KELSAYE of Boston *v.* Robert KELSAYE.
Debt, the bonds for which have been embezzled.   LINCOLN.

5-7   John KELYNG, citizen and fishmonger of London, *v.* Thomas CHECHELEY and Marion
his wife.
Reviver of a suit by Margaret Harryngton, mother of complainant, for land in the Forde and rent
of lands there and in ' the flowe diche.'   ESSEX.

8-11   John KELYNGTON *v.* Amys CHECHESTER.
Refusal to complete a lease in reversion of land in Twitchen.   DEVON.

12   Peter KEMBRYGE of the Isle of Wight, baker, *v.* the sheriff of HANTS, and William
GUYRLYNG, constable of the Isle of Wight and captain of Carisbrooke castle.
Imprisonment in the said castle without process of law. *Corpus cum causa and subpœna.*
                                                                          HANTS (I.W.).

13-15   Martin KEMPTE (Kemp) *v.* Michael BOROGH.
Promise to pay for a ring bought by Robert Borogh.   CORNWALL.

16-18   Nicholas KENDALL *v.* John, son of John SNELL.
Messuages and land in Micklebring (Mikelborowe) and Braithwell (Baythwell). *See File* 1239,
No. 22.   YORK.

19-21   Christopher KENE of Kenn v. George SPEKE of White Lackington, esquire, and Elizabeth his wife.
Loan to Richard Mallet of Currypool (in Charlinch), esquire, former husband of the said Elizabeth.   SOMERSET.

22-28   Giles, son of Richard KENT of Newchurch, v. John HATTON and Elizabeth his wife, late the wife of Hugh Newe.
Legacy of John Rawlyn of Briddlesford (in Arreton), one of whose executors was the said Newe.   HANTS (I.W.).

29   Richard KENT of Wychemalbank, husbandman, v. Ralph BAGNALL of Nantwich, yeoman.
Money entrusted by Ellen, late the wife of complainant, to Elizabeth, wife of defendant.   CHESTER.

30   Richard KENT and Margaret his wife v. John DAYE alias Brent.
Land in Newton Tony, late of Thomas Taylour, deceased, ancestor of the said Margaret. Mutilated.   WILTS.

31-32   Richard KENT v. Robert GREGORY of Southcot.
Reversion pledged to defendant of a messuage in Tilehurst, held in fee simple by John Kent, since deceased, elder brother of complainant.   BERKS.

33-35   Thomas KENT v. Godfrey WOODHOUS of Dronfield.
Loan.   DERBY.

36   Edward, son of Roger KERDE, deceased, v. Ede, late the wife of Michael KERDE.
Claim to a widow's estate in a messuage and land held of the manor of West Hatch.   .   WILTS.

37   John KESER of Great Peckham, grandson and heir of William Keser, v. Thomas ROIDON, esquire.
Mill and land in East Peckham of the demise of the prior and convent of Christ Church, Canterbury. Mutilated.   KENT.

38   Hugh KETE, aged 10 or 11 years, by John Kete his elder brother, v. Richard, son and executor of Edmund BUSBYE, and James ONSLOWE and John BUSBYE, his assistants.
Reviver of a suit for the farm and parsonage of Hagborne. D. XV, 55.   BERKS.

39   Robert KEYLE, administrator of the goods of Thomas Keyle, citizen,and mercer of London, deceased, v. Edward GORGE, knight.
Reviver of a suit for a mill and pasture in Sturminster Marshall (File 1239, No. 54.)   DORSET.

40   Thomas KEYS, esquire, serjeant porter to the King and Queen, v. Francis LAMBARD, citizen and grocer of London.
Action for a debt whereof defendant was not present to receive an instalment when due. LONDON.

41-42   Robert KING of Moreton, yeoman, v. George BROWNE of White Roding, gentleman.
Locking up the barn of the manor of Marks Hall in White Roding, in which he had permitted complainant to store a crop of peas, oats, and hay.   ESSEX.

43-44   Robert KING, gentleman, v. John BURNARD, Roger WAGGETT, and others.
Tenements in the manor of Muchelney. held by complainants on lease from the Crown.
                SOMERSET.

45   Richard KINWELMERSHE of London, mercer, v. John SPARKE of the same, merchant tailor, an overseer of the will of Richard Husband of the same, ' pastler.'
Recognizance given to defendant by Jane, wife of complainant, late the wife of the said Husband, for the performance of the latter's will.   LONDON.

46-47   Robert KIRKHAM, knight, v. Henry PERKER and William WOODHOWSE, knights.
Goods of Henry Perker, knight, deceased, father of the said Sir Henry, whereof complainant is an administrator. Answer wanting.   ⸻

48-52   Richard KITSONNE and Joan his wife, late the wife of Thomas Chester, v. Stephen PORTER and Margery his wife, executrix and late the wife of William Chester.
Money promised to the said Thomas on his marriage by the said William his father.   ⸻

53-59   John KNIGHT of Knight's Hill, son of Henry Knight, deceased, v. Ralph JENYNS, George BROUGHTON, and Thomas NEWNHAM, knight.
Mortgage of tenements called Leigham.   SURREY.

60-62   Simon KNYGHT v. John MICHELL of Truro.
Action on a bond for price of goods bought for William Hewster, complainant's master, who paid for them.   CORNWALL.

63-64   Robert KNYGHTE v. Robert DARDOO (Dyrdoo) of Gillingham, co. Dorset, gentleman.
Manor of Berkeley of the demise of John Newborough, esquire.   SOMERSET.

65   Humphrey KNYVETON, Ellen his wife, and Anne EYRE v. John BLOUNT, gentleman.
Messuage and buildings demised by defendant to Thomas Blakwall, deceased, father of the female complainants. Mutilated.   DERBY.

66-67   Thomas KNYVETON, esquire, v. James, son of John PERSON.
Messuage and croft in Ashbourne, late of John Knyveton, deceased, grandfather of complainant.
                DERBY.

68   John KYDD of London, [draper, and Margaret his wife] v. William WILLIAMSON of Kings Lynn, late the husband of Alice, formerly the wife of John Skales [and earlier the wife of . . . Dunstan].
Money promised by the said Skales to the said Margaret [and other children of the said Alice by her first marriage]. Mutilated.   LONDON, NORFOLK.

69   John KYDMAN v. John FOKES.
Non-delivery of barley at Brinkley as purchased.   CAMBRIDGE

N 2

70   Morres ap John KYRE *v.* THOMAS ap Llewelyn.
Messuage and land in Kerry (Kyre).   MONTGOMERY.

71   Richard KYRK *v.* William ROTHERHAM, alderman of Lincoln, Thomas HUCHYNSON,
        and others.
Action by the said Rotherham before the mayor of Lincoln for price (already paid) of oaks in
Goltho, sold by him to complainant and the other defendants.   LINCOLN.

72   Thomas KYRLE, gentleman, *v.* Richard HARREIS.
Land in Walford.   HEREFORD.

73-74   . . . KYRLE *v.* the same.
Land in Walford. *Mutilated.*   HEREFORD.

75   William KYTTERIDGE of Chelmsford, mercer, *v.* John PASCALL.
Legacy of William Pascall, uncle of defendant, payable out of lands in Thurrock. *Pedigree given.*
                                                                      ESSEX.

FILE 1446.

1   Robert LACYE *v.* William FRANKLAND and Robert and George RUDD.
Tenement in Danby demised by John Nevill, lord Latimer, to Peter Rudd.   YORK.

2-4   The same *v.* William RUDD.
Tenement in Danby, demised to complainant by the said Lord Latimer in succession to the said
Peter.   YORK.

5-7   Stephen, son and heir of Richard LACYE of Hoxne (Hoxton), gentleman, *v.* Agnes, late the
        wife of John KNYVETT.
Contempt of subpœnas in an action for lands in the manor of Horham Thorpe Hall. *Injunction.*
See File 1242, *No.* 3.   SUFFOLK.

8   John LAKYN *v.* Robert LAKYN.
Messuage and land in Kenley. *Mutilated.*   SALOP.

9   Robert LAMBERT, Florence his wife, and Agnes BRAKENBURYE *v.* Pearce VENABLES
        and Emma AYER.
Household goods of Pearce Wynington, gentleman, father of the female complainants, who died in
the said Venables's house at Witton.   CHESTER.

10-13   Lancelot LANCASTER of Sockbridge, esquire, *v.* Anthony DUCKET.
Actions of novel disseisin of lands in Kendal and of debt arising from the marriage settlement of
William, son of complainant, since deceased, with Katherine, daughter of defendant.
                                                                      WESTMORLAND.

14-17   William LANDER *v.* John ROBERT and Walter ANGOVE *alias* Smyth.
Lands in Stithians, Gwennap and St. Germans, late of John Launder, deceased, father of complainant.   CORNWALL.

18-21   Edward LANE *v.* John FERMOUR, knight, and John ADAMS.
Cottages and land in the said Sir John's manor of Halistocke granted to Joan, formerly the wife
of Thomas Cox and afterwards of complainant. *Mutilated.* D. XV, 6.   D[ORSET].

22-24   Martin LANE, vicar of Chesterfield, *v.* James FOLJAMBE, knight, son of Godfrey
        Foljambe, knight, Bridget BEYRYSFORDE (Basforthe), and others.
Lands in Walton, Boythorpe, Newbold, Tapton, Brinington, Calow, and Hasland belonging to
complainant's glebe.   DERBY.

25-29   The same *v.* the same and Margaret HERST.
Do.   DERBY.

30-31   Giles LANGLEY, vicar of Chieveley, *v.* James, son and executor of John PHILPOT.
Counterbond for a debt to John Llewelyn of Caerleon already paid.   BERKS, MONMOUTH.

32   Gregory LANGSTON of Great Totnes, co. Devon, merchant, *v.* Peter BONAMY, gentleman,
        and others.
Messuage and land in St. Martin's, late of Olyve Tardye, deceased, father of complainant (*sic*).
                                                                      GUERNSEY.

33-37   Margaret LANGTON and Peter STANLEY, esquire, executors of Robert Langton, *v.*
        Thomas HOLTE, knight.
Bond given by the said Robert and Thomas for John Lambert, receiver of the Duchy of Lancaster
for King Henry VIII.   LANCASTER.

38-39   William LANGTON *v.* John DYATT.
House called the *Cardinal's Hat* in Lichfield and land in the fee of Curborough and Elmhurst
(Elynhurst).   STAFFORD.

40-43   Anne LATTON of Chilton, executrix and late the wife of John Latton, *v.* John COUPER.
Theft of leases of the farms and manors of Wantage, Bockhampton, and Upton, and other
documents. D. XII, 34.   BERKS.

44-49   Edward LAWE of Colchester, tailor, *v.* John, son and heir of Thomas LAWE of Brook
        Walden (in Saffron Walden), and George, son and heir of William LAWE.
Messuage and land at Newland End in Arkesden, late of Thomas Lawe, labourer, deceased, great-
grandfather of complainant.   ESSEX.

50-52   Edmund LAWRENCE, yeoman, *v.* John HIGHAM, esquire, husband of Martha, late the
        wife of Thomas Fyncham.
Messuage and land in Brantham, formerly of Humphrey Wyngfeld, knight.   SUFFOLK.

53–54   Anthony LECHE of Standlake, carpenter, v. Richard WEDGE (Wegge).
Share of a crop of corn paid by Thomas Stuckwell of Longworth in consideration of his marriage
with Alice, mother of defendant and of Agnes, wife of complainant.   OXFORD, BERKS.

55–56   Edward LEDES, parson of Snailwell, v. William PASTON, esquire, and Thomas GYLBART,
his tenant.
Common of pasture in Snailwell.   CAMBRIDGE.

57–58   Francis LEEKE, knight, v. Roger GRENEHALL, esquire.
Detention of a bond for a debt already paid by complainant's sureties. See File 1365, No. 38.
                                                                                  [DERBY?]

59–62   Francis LEEKE, knight, v. Simon MUCKLOWE, esquire.
Manor of Crowneast (in St. John Bedwardin) and lands there and in Wichenford and St. John.
See Files 540, No. 16; 848, No. 47; 1245, No. 92.   WORCESTER.

63–67   Thomas LEGH v. James LEGH and others.
Ketleigh Park in Week St. Mary, late of Thomas a Legh, deceased, father of both parties. Bill
Mutilated.   CORNWALL.

68–72   The same v. the said James, and Alice late the wife of the said Thomas the father.
Choice of the best of every kind of goods of the said Thomas the father according to Cornish
custom.   CORNWALL.

73–75   The same, administrator of the goods of Alice, late the wife of John Roche of Lezant,
deceased, v. the same and others.
Goods of the said Alice and John Roche.   CORNWALL.

76–77   Thomas LEGH v. William MYDWYNTER and Charles RUGGE.
Tenement in Aylesbeare of the grant of John Farwell.   DEVON.

78   Thomas LEVESON, esquire, and Cicely his wife v. . . .
Land held of the manor of Kynvarr by Margaret Bradeley. Mutilated.   [STAFFORD.]

79   James LEWES of London v. William David LLOYD.
Messuages and lands in Mount and Warwick of the demise of Eleanor ap (sic) James, late the wife
of Res ap John of Eglwyswrw, co. Pembroke.   CARDIGAN.

80–83   Thomas Lee and John Machell, late sheriffs of LONDON, v. Robert THORNELL and
William WEST, knight.
Action by the said Thornell for the escape of Bryan Rye of Whitwell, co. Derby, a freeman of
London, permitted to go abroad to collect his debts under the Queen's proclamation for permitting
debtors in Ludgate to compound. (The said Sir William claims the wardship of Edward Rye.)
Mutilated.   LONDON.

84–85   John LONGE, clerk, v. Simon (James) KEMPSEY.
Information as to wrongful occupation and neglect of the hospital of God's House in Hull.   YORK.

86   John LONGE of Hougham v. . . .
Bond. Faded.   NORFOLK.

87–89   William LONGEMAN of Woodhay, husbandman, son and heir of Walter Longe (sic), v.
John [WHITE], bishop of Winchester, Richard HAMDEN, steward of his manor of
Highclere, and Thomas LONGEMAN.
Lands called ' cosset landes ' and ' jayle land ' held of the said manor.   HANTS.

90–92   John LORD of Wiston, co. Sussex, clerk, v. Michael BABINGTON of Derby, esquire.
Wages as chantry priest of Ballidon.   DERBY.

93   Robert LOUGHTON v. William PADLEY, yeoman, and John ROGER.
Messuages and land in Bole, late of William Loughton, deceased, father of complainant.   NOTTS.

94–95   John [LUMLEY], lord Lumley, v. Lionel SMYTHE and others.
Wrongful occupation of waste and felling of trees in the manor of Great Lumley in Chester-le-Street.
                                                                                  DURHAM.

96   The same(?) v. Richard LUMLEY alias Vavaster.
Manor of Butterby.   DURHAM.

97–99   John LUTER v. Nicholas HERYCKE and Agnes his wife.
Cloth entrusted at Northampton to John Danporte, late the husband of the said Agnes.
                                                                                  NORTHAMPTON.

FILE 1447.

1   Nicholas LABORNE, yeoman, v. John AMAN and Richard PETAR.
Purse with money and deeds given to Peter Atkyngson of Fetcham, co. Surrey, in possible exchange
for a lease of a messuage in Burton.   LINCOLN.

2–4   William LANE of Cottesbrook, esquire, v. John MOL(L)E, gentleman.
Contradictory leases of pasture in Stutchbury.   NORTHAMPTON.

5   John LANGDON, gentleman, v. . . .
Arbitration between complainant and John Mortofte, gentleman, concerning the manor of Nowers
and lands in Itteringham, Wolterton, Mannington, and Irmingland. Mutilated.   NORFOLK.

6–8   John LAUNCE and Christian TAYLOR, executors of Richard Taylor, v. John, son and
executor of John LOVERINGE.
Goods (described) of the said Richard entrusted to the said John Loveringe the father.   ———

9–11   William LAURENCE of Mintey, co. Wilts, and William and Margaret his children v. James
SOMERFIELDE.
Rival leases of the manor of Yanworth from Thomas Culpeper of Bedgebury, co. Kent, esquire.
                                                                                  GLOUCESTER.

12–13   Hugh LAWE of Oundle, gentleman, v. Nicholas BAILIE, gentleman.
Deed of grant of the next presentation to the church of Barnwell St. Andrew entrusted to defendant.   NORTHAMPTON.

14–17   George LEE and others v. MARCAS ap Owen (Markett ap Evan), Res David ap Jevan LLOYD and others.
Messuages and lands in St. David's, Trogan (i.e. Trefgarn?), Spittal and Lanpeter-pont-Stephen of the demise of the precentor of St. David's whose collector is the said Marcas.
PEMBROKE, CARDIGAN.

18–21   William LEE of Camelford v. Humphrey (John) and Joan ESTON.
Goods of John Lee, deceased, father of complainant.   CORNWALL.

22   Robert LEEKE of London, yeoman, son of John Leeke, deceased, v. Roger METCALF of Harom (in Helmsley), gentleman, and others.
Lands in Thirsk of the demise of John Dyneley, late chantry priest of Sigston.   YORK.

23–25   Charles LEISTOCK, gentleman, v. Thomas ELSDON (Elleson) alias Rauff.
Action on a bail-bond released by John Babtyst, in order to extort a grant of lands in Lyme Regis.
DORSET.

26   John LEKE v. Henry MALKYN, a tenant of the manor of Horton.
Grinding his corn at the mills of Leek and Cheddleton instead of those at Hanley and Groton.
STAFFORD.

27   William LENTALLE, esquire, v. John LENTALLE.
Detention of deeds relating to a messuage and garden in Sandwich and to an account with Richard Rawlings and of goods all late of Elizabeth Lentall, deceased, mother of both parties.
KENT.

28   Hugh LEWES v. John BOND the elder and John BOND the younger.
Falsification of a lease made by Myles Hampden of Burcot Farm in Dorchester (sic), whereof complainant is lessee in reversion.   OXFORD.

29   James LEWES of London v. MEREDITH ap Griffith.
Meadow in Penbryn.   CARDIGAN.

30   Ralph LEYCESTER, knight, v. Roger BURGES.
Detention of deeds relating to messuages and land in Toft and Mobberley (Mounberley). See File 1022, No. 43.   CHESTER.

31–33   Thomas LEYGHTEFOOTE of Morchard Bishop, husbandman, v. Edmund ROLAND, steward of the court of Crediton.
Rent of land in Crediton claimed in right of the late college of Crediton.   DEVON.

34–35   Thomas LEYGHTEN and Elizabeth his wife v. William, son of John PERY.
Detention of deeds relating to burgages and lands in Devizes. (Defendant states that they relate to lands and a rent in Warminster, Helmeford, for which cf. Henfords Marsh in Warminster, and Norton Bavant.)   WILTS.

36   Richard LLOYD, parson of Llantrisaint, v. RICHARD ap William and others.
Forcible entry on complainant's parsonage and collection of his tithes.   ANGLESEA.

37   The same v. Robert PYGOT, late parson.
Do., defendant having been deprived for marriage.   ANGLESEA.

38   Philip LOCKTON, of Swineshead, Jane his wife and Anne and —— DYGHTON v. Justinian CROWE.
Detention of deeds relating to bequests of John Dyghton, deceased, father of complainants other than the said Philip.   LINCOLN.

39   The same v. the same.
Detention of deeds relating to lands and rents in Lincoln, late of Robert Dyghton, deceased, son of the said John.   LINCOLN.

40–42   Richard LOVE v. Nicholas HARVIE.
Land in Wissett, late of Robert Love and Margaret his wife, deceased, parents of complainant.
SUFFOLK.

43–47   Robert LOVE and Anne his wife v. Richard MORTYMER, Joan, late the wife of John WILSON, and others.
Inn called the Red Lion in Baldock, late of Joan, late the wife of William Watson, deceased, and grandmother of the said Anne.   HERTS.

48   Robert LOVE, son of the said Robert and Anne, deceased, v. the said MORTYMER and WILSON and John PLUMMER.
Reviver of the preceding.   HERTS.

49–53   William LOVELES of Henley-on-Thames, co. Oxford, gentleman, and Margery his wife v. LEWIS ap Maurice, son of Maurice Gethin ap Jevan ap Rice.
Tenement in the town and parish of Penantt (i.e. Llanfihangel-y-Pennant), claimed by complainant under a lease from the monastery of Chertsey, and by defendant under a lease from that of Beddgelert.   CARMARTHEN.

54   The same v. ROBERT ap Price ap Evan.
Land in the town and parish of Chachyther (Glachyther), claimed by complainant under a like lease.   CARMARTHEN.

55–57   William LUCKCOCKE alias Tyrrye v. Christopher KENNE, esquire, and John and James BERYE.
Messuages and land in the said Kenne's manor of Yatton, demised ' as olde aster in villynage.'
SOMERSET.

58   Katharine LUTTERELL, a ward of the Crown, *v.* [Richard EGCOMB, knight].
23*a.* English and ¼*a.* Cornish, the course of the water of Tamar, with fishery, a pigeon-house and a fulling-mill and grist-mills with the water thereto belonging, late held of the manor of Calstock by Katharine, late the wife of Piers Egcomb, knight. *Mutilated.*   CORNWALL.

59   John L'YNDESEY, the King's and Queen's armourer, *v.* William BARBAR, formerly a captain in the wars.
Bond extorted by imprisonment in Collyns Alley in the Old Bailey on a supposed command of the Earl of Pembroke.   LONDON.

60   Elizabeth, late the wife of Philip LYNNE, esquire [? and formerly the wife] of John Sewster, esquire, *v.* John LYNNE, brother and heir of the said Philip.
Half the manor of Castle in Bassingbourn and other lands there and in Royston. *Mutilated.*   CAMBRIDGE, HERTS.

61–64   Robert LYSTER *v.* William WHYTE and Cristian his wife.
Lands in the manor of St. John's in Mellis, the court rolls of which have been embezzled.   SUFFOLK.

65–66   William LYTE *v.* Laurence BARNARD.
Lease of a tenement in complainant's manor of Northover, assigned in evasion of the statute 21 Henry VIII, c. 13.   SOMERSET.

67–68   The same (Lyght) *v.* William GOLD, merchant.
Land in the said manor claimed under a lease from the hospital of St. John the Baptist, Bridgwater.   SOMERSET.

FILE 1448.

1–4   William LAMBE and Eleanor his wife, servant to the King and Queen at Calais, *v.* Francis AYSCOUGHE (Askewe), knight.
Manors of Kelsey, Walworth, and Blacktoft and other lands, late of John Hansarde of London, skinner, deceased, father of the said Eleanor.   LINCOLN, DURHAM.

5   John LANGLEY, gentleman, *v.* Henry, Henry and Richard CUTT.
Manors of Wood Hall, Wyggepytt, and Cokeshales in Arkesden and Montenys and Daugeworthes in Elmdon, and messuages and lands there and in Clavering, Wenden, Wicken, Wenden-Lofts (Loughtes), [Saffron] Walden, and Wigpett, late of Henry Langley and of Thomas Langley, esquire, his son, grandfather of complainant.   ESSEX.

6–9   Richard LANYEN *v.* John COWLYNG, Margaret his wife, and others.
Detention of deeds relating to the manor of Treveglos (in Zennor).   CORNWALL.

10   William LARCOME and Anne his daughter *v.* John BOURNE.
Lands (described) in George Essex's manor of Pitney Plonkete, partly in the parish of Hewes. *Mutilated.*   SOMERSET.

11   The same *v.* the same and the said ESSEX.
Tenement in a manor formerly of —— Arundell. *Surrejoinder only.*   [SOMERSET ?]

12–16   Thomas LATHAM *v.* the mayor and bailiffs of NORTHAMPTON, and Agnes, executrix and late the wife of William ELYOTT.
Action for price of a gelding which proved 'lame and perished of his wynde.' *Certiorari and subpœna.*   NORTHAMPTON.

17–18   Ralph LEEKE *v.* Thomas WATERTON, knight, and Henry EVERINGHAM, gentleman.
Purchase of the title of Henry Johnson, esquire, to messuages and land at Wadsley in Ecclesfield and Brandfield, contrary to the Act 32 Henry VIII, c. 9.   YORK.

19–21   John LEGH of Isell, esquire, *v.* Christopher DANBY the younger, gentleman, his son-in-law.
Seizure from the parsonage of Surlingham of Deeds relating to the manor of Surlingham and other manors and lands.   NORFOLK, CUMBERLAND.

22–27   John LEVES of Marleburgh and Joan his wife, late the wife of William Smarte *alias* Collyns, *v.* George REYNOLDES, son-in-law of John Abbott.
House in Andover.   HANTS.

28   Thomas, son and heir of Thomas LEWIS, *v.* Trehern GOZ and others.
Land in St. Michael's (*i.e.* Michaelstone *or* Llanmihangle).   GLAMORGAN.

29   John LEYVET and Isabel his wife *v.* Robert ap Morrys and others.
Loan by Roger Byny, former husband of the said Isabel.   ————

30–31   The dean and chapter of LINCOLN and Kellam WATSON, gentleman, their lessee, *v.* William BEVER and others.
Corn and rent of lands in Edith-Weston called the 'olde rightes' of the church of Hambleton.   RUTLAND.

32–35   Jane LINGHAM (Lyngen) of London, 'shempster,' *v.* John LYNGEN of Hurst (in Westbury), gentleman.
Leasehold, messuages and land in Aston Rogers of the bequest of Wilham Lyngham, father of complainant.   SALOP.

36–39   The same *v.* William LINGEN, gentleman.
Fraudulent acquisition of a deed of feoffment of the manor of Cotton and messuages and lands in Westbury and Worthen pending a suit against John Lyngen, brother of complainant.   SALOP.

40–41   Richard LISTER, esquire, *v.* James and John AWDLINGTON and others.
Manors of Clehonger, Kinnersley, Letton, Dinedor, and Burlton (in Burghill), and lands there and in Chilston (in Madley), Meer Court (in Allensmore), Stretford, Dorston (in Birley), and Alton, Chadnor (Chabner) and Falley (all in Dilwyn?). *See File* 1367, *No.* 105.   HEREFORD.

42   Peter LOCKE of Alverstoke, yeoman, and Joan his wife, daughter and heir of Wilham
        Squyer, v. John STONER and Joan his wife.
Detention of deeds relating to lands in Brading, late of John Stoner and John Punche.
                                                                    HANTS (I.W.).

43-44   Christopher, son and heir of Thomas LONDE (Lounde) v. John JACKSON
Detention of deeds relating to messuages and land in Horkstow. (Defendant pleads a former
decree of this court.)   LINCOLN.

45-46   Cicely, late the wife of Robert LONGE, citizen and mercer of London, v. Edward and
        Richard CROMPTON and others, her tenants.
Action for enclosures in the manor of Condover (Codnour) permitted by a decree of the Star Chamber.
                                                                    SALOP.

47-50   Thomas LONGLONDE v. John WYSE, yeoman.
Messuage and land in the manor of Banbury of the demise of John Longlonde, late bishop of
Lincoln. D. XIII, 10.   OXFORD.

51-53   John LOORDE of Caldon, yeoman, v. William GLEDENHURST and Peter RICHARDSON.
Messuage and land in Farley.   STAFFORD.

54-56   Lawrence LOVETT, esquire, son and heir of Richard Lovett, v. Thomas FARNALL alias
        London.
Messuage and land in Soulbury of the grant of John Mylliett of Liscombe.   BUCKS.

57-58   Simon LOWE v. Katherine, late the wife of Richard DORMER, knight.
Detention of deeds relating to the manor of Burton by Bampton, sold by defendant to Alexander
Seymer. See Files 1270, No. 27; 1317, No. 25; 1365, No. 98.   OXFORD.

59-60   The same v. Edward KYNG and Alice his wife, daughter of Simon Seymer.
Do.   OXFORD.

61-63   Simon LOWE of London, merchant tailor, and John KEYME, gentleman, v. Thomas
        PARRAMORE.
Manor of Sayes in the Isle of Harty and land there, formerly of Thomasyn Chevyn of Feversham.
Mutilated.   KENT.

64-66   Robert LUCAS of Asthall Leigh, tailor, v. William HORLEY (Horsley), vicar of Minster
        Lovell.
Seizure of grain, half of which is due to complainant as lessee of the parsonage of Minster Lovell.
D. IX, 26.   OXFORD.

67-68   Thomas LUCAS v. Edmund LUCAS.
Refusal to complete a lease of a messuage in Horsley. Mutilated.   [SURREY?]

69-70   Thomas LYSON v. Thomas GRENE, Robert PEYKE, and Jennet his wife, daughter of the
        said Grene.
Messuage and land in Brinkhill, formerly of William Grene, deceased, great-grandfather of complainant and of the said Thomas Grene.   LINCOLN.

FILE 1449.

1   Elizabeth, executrix and late the wife of John LANE, v. John KIRBIE.
Pasture in Knaptoft of the 'inhabytans' of William Turpyn, ward to King Henry VIII.
                                                                    LEICESTER.

2   Elizabeth, John, and James LAURENCE, executors of William Laurence, v. Rowland
        DURAUNT, gentleman.
Messuage and land in Chapton of the demise of James D(o)uraunt of Chesterfield, deceased, father
of defendant.   DERBY.

3-6   Thomas LAWRENCE v. James ORME, late the husband of Anne, formerly the wife of
        John Secole.
Messuage and land in Kingham, demised by John Bewfoo, gentleman, to complainant and the said
Anne for the benefit of her children by her first marriage.   OXFORD.

7   Richard LECHE of Duloe, husbandman, v. William LECHE.
Detention of deeds relating to land in St. Keyne, late of James Leche, deceased, father of complainant.   CORNWALL.

8   Oliver LEDER and Lawrence TAYLOR, knights, v. Robert FLETCHER, esquire, and
        William TROWTBECKE, executors of Thomas Roncorn, clerk.
Instalment of an annuity forwarded to the said Roncorn after his death.   LINCOLN.

9   John LEE.
Application for a mandate to John Huchynson, mayor of Lincoln, to take order between him and
Robert Hutchynson concerning a tenement in Lincoln and a judgment debt.   LINCOLN.

10-12   Francis LEEKE, knight, v. Thomas BEVERAGE, parson of Sutton-le-Dale.
Account as bailiff of complainant's lands.   DERBY.

13   Brian LEIDES, gentleman, and William FENTYMAN, clerk, grantees to uses, and Brian
        FENTYMAN v. Thomas FENTYMAN and Joan his wife.
Manor of Kirkby Wharfe, late of Robert Fentyman, deceased, father of the said Brian and
Thomas.   YORK.

14   Giles LENGLEY, clerk, v. James, son and heir of John PHILPOTT (Phelpott).
Land in Traston in Newport (Treston), late of Roger Langleye of Christchurch, deceased, whose
executors were the said Giles and John.   MONMOUTH.

15   . . .: son of Nicholas LEVESEY and of Crystyan his wife, *v.* Sir John BYRON, Henry TOWNEROWE and others.
Site of the manor of Laxton of the demise of the feoffees of Thomas Vaux, lord Vaux of Harrowden. *Mutilated.*   NOTTS.

16-17   Thomas LEWES ap Griffith of London *v.* STEPHEN ap Thomas ap Enyon (Evyon), son and heir of Jevan ap Thomas.
Tenements in the lordship of Radnor, formerly of Agnes verch Enyon of Cascob, great-grandmother of complainant.   RADNOR.

18   Gwenllian LEWIS *alias* Gwenllian verch Henry *v.* Thomas John David PHILLIPP and others.
Tenement called Ulisden.   CARMARTHEN.

19   John LEWIS of London, yeoman, *v.* James WILLIAMS, knight.
Messuage in Henllan, late of Lewis ap Jevan of Carmarthen, yeoman, deceased, father of complainant.   CARMARTHEN.

20-22   William LEWKENOUR, citizen and draper of London, *v.* William MATON of Salisbury.
Debt, the bond for which was lost in a cap-case.   LONDON, WILTS.

23   Thomas LEWYS of London, one of the Queen's guard, *v.* William GRAWELL, gentleman.
Refusal to complete a sale of land in Abergwili.   CARMARTHEN.

24   . . . [LI]GHTFOOT, husbandman, *v.* Edmund ROWLAND, steward of the lordship of Crediton.
Land in the said lordship. *Faded.*   DEVON.

25   The mayor and burgesses of LISKEARD *v.* Thomas COWCHE and others.
Mills and land in Liskeard.   CORNWALL.

26   The same *v.* Roger PEERS and others.
Do.   CORNWALL.

27-28   William LOCKER, citizen and plumber of London, *v.* Thomas HICKELEY.
Detention of deeds relating to a messuage and land in Nant y Meichiad (Michiard).
                                                                                                          MONTGOMERY.

29-30   John William and Leonard, sons of John LOCKETT, *v.* John PENBURIE and John HODGEK(YN)ES, executors of Laurence Penburie, husband of Emma, formerly the wife of the said John the father.
Goods of the said John promised to complainants on his death intestate.   ———

31-33   John LOGGYN of Cubley *v.* Thomas MORE, citizen and merchant of London, his master.
Account of receipts and payments on defendant's behalf.   DERBY, LONDON.

34   John LONGE, clerk, *v.* Laurence ALEN.
Mastership of the hospital of the Holy Trinity, Hull, granted to complainant by the Crown and to defendant by the mayor and aldermen of Hull.   YORK.

35-36   James LOVE *v.* Robert CRANE, esquire.
Arbitration as to land in defendant's manor of Butlers in Newton. *Damaged.*   SUFFOLK.

37-39   Nicholas LOVELAKE and Parnell his wife *v.* Ellis, son and heir of Walter WARWICK.
Messuages and lands in Plymouth, Sutton Prior, Sutton Vautard and Nethercourt, late of William Keytyrige, ancestor of complainant. *Mutilated. Pedigree Given. See File* 1367, *No.* 75.
                                                                                                          DEVON.

40-41   John LOWCHE *v.* William PAGETT and Eleanor his wife.
Detention of deeds relating to burgages and land in Marlborough.   WILTS.

42-44   John LYELL of Honiton, executor of Dr. Richard Lyell his brother, *v.* William and John BULL and others.
Goods of the said Richard, whereof defendants have obtained letters of administration. *Replication wanting.*   DEVON.

45-46   John LYON and others, merchants, *v.* Thomas, brother of John HASYLFOTE, merchant.
Action of trespass for arrest of goods under an Admiralty decree.   LONDON.

47   John LYON, gentleman, *v.* Cuthbert MYTFORD, esquire, and John WETHERYNGTON, gentleman.
Trespasses on land in Mitford and threats, ' dysdayning that a man borne in the south parte of this realme shoulde dwell amonge them.'   NORTHUMBERLAND.

48-50   John LYON, knight, alderman of London, *v.* Anne READE.
Farm in Thrupp. *Answer wanting.*   BERKS.

51-52   Thomas LYVESON, gentleman, *v.* Edward MUSGRAVE and others.
Right of way through defendant's land in Wolverhampton. *See Files* 424, *No.* 44 ; 847, *No.* 10; 1242, *No.* 40.   STAFFORD.

FILE 1450.

1-2   Alice MABATT *alias* Maberley *v.* Robert TOWNESENDE.
Messuage and land in Cassington, late of John Townsend, deceased, grandfather of complainant and father of defendant.   OXFORD.

3-4   John MALLYN of Newark-upon-Trent *v.* Richard DUFFELD of South Scarle, husbandman.
Refusal to sell corn according to a standing agreement, prices having risen.   NOTTS.

5–9   John MARMYON, gentleman, servant to Thomas Cheyney, knight, Lord Warden of the·
Cinque Ports, v. Humphrey, son and heir of James HALES, knight, J.C.P.
Messuages and land in Henley-on-Thames and Assendon (in Henley) entailed on William Marmyon,
grandfather of complainant. *2 bills, one asking for a subpœna, the other for a commission.*
D. XII, 46.   OXFORD.

10–11   John MARWOODE and Agnes his wife, daughter of Robert Burell, v. Andrew BURELL.
Tenements in Bygburye of the demise of Margery . . . and Elizabeth Scobbell. *Mutilated.*
                                                                          [DEVON.]

12–15   Robert MAWRE (Mower) v. Elizabeth (Agnes) PALMER.
Manor of Upton of the entail of Philip Dracot, knight.   LEICESTER.

16–19   Walter MAYNEY v. Edward STOUGHTON of Ash by Sandwich (Edmund Stockton of
Staplehurst), gentleman, son-in-law of Richard Exherst, and Francis and Thomas his sons.
Detention of deeds relating to the manor of Exherst in Staplehurst, bought of John Monnynges of
Dover, gentleman, and Margery his wife.   KENT.

20   Philip MAYNWARYNG, gentleman, usher attendant on the King and Queen, v. Randal
MAYNWARYNG of Coryngham, esquire.
Rectorial tithes of Rosthurne· (Rausturne) of the grant of Randal Maynwaryng, knight, deceased,
brother of complainant.   CHESTER.

21   The same v. Dame Jane COTTON of Bedhampton, co. Hants, Hugh CHOLMELEY,
knight, steward of the manor of Newhall, and Thomas MAYNEWARING [bailiff].
Manor of Newhall, etc. *Mutilated.*   CHESTER.

22   Matthew MAYSON of Dartford, co. Kent, yeoman, and Robert his younger brother v.
Robert and William FESHAR.
Tenement and mill in Wythop, late of Nicholas Mason, yeoman, deceased, father of complainants.
                                                                          CUMBERLAND.

23   John MELLEY, executor of Simon Clare, vicar of Chaddesley Corbet, v. William NEWPORT
of Rushock and others, esquires.   WORCESTER.
Tithe of wood in Chaddesley Corbet.

24–25   John MERCER, citizen and wool-packer of London, v. Edward LYTELTON, knight.
Action on a bond not to alienate land in Lapley, which he was compelled to do by decree of this
court (D. X, 21). *Mutilated. See also File 1309, No. 16.*   STAFFORD.

26   John MILWARD v. William STOWE, Elizabeth his wife and others.
Detention of deeds relating to messuages at Wollescote (Woscot) and Wollaston in Old Swinford.
                                                                          WORCESTER.

27   Thomas MILWARD v. George TUCKEY, gentleman, and others.
Messuage and land in Warley, late of Humphrey Stafford and Margery his wife.
                                                        SALOP, WORCESTER, STAFFORD.

28–30   Richard MOGERYGE of Winterbourn Stoke v. John PLOMLEY and Thomas
FRAUNCEYS.
Wool of the bequest of George Mogeryge, father of complainant. *Answer and replication wanting.*
See File 1368, No. 70.   WILTS.

31   John MONE, husbandman.
Petition to examine witnesses as to lands, rents, and services in Mayfield, late of William Wodde.
                                                                          SUSSEX.

32–33 · John MOONE of Loughborough, clothier, v. Richard HALL.
Leasehold in Loughborough and Cotesfield of the assignment of defendant. *Damaged.*
                                                                          LEICESTER.

34–36   William MOORE of London, draper, v. William ALLESTREE (Alystrye).
Bond given on behalf of William Horne.   DERBY.

37–40   Robert MORDAUNTE, esquire, v. Robert HARTE.
Land in Hempstead promised to complainant on a purchase from John Wakeleyn.   ESSEX.

41   Ralph MORGAN of London, baker, v. JAMES ap Lewis, yeoman, base-born.
Messuages, cottages, mill and land in Malyna, Eglossawe, Whitchurch, and Trigmore, late of
Lewis ap David ap Griffith ap Madog, deceased, great-uncle of complainant.   PEMBROKE.

42   Thomas MORGAN of the Middle Temple, gentleman, v. Matthew ap Res (Richard)
VAGHAN, gentleman, and others.
Messuage and land in Gelligaer (Kellygayre), granted by William ap Howell for complainant's
'maynetenaunce at larninge.'   GLAMORGAN.

43–44   The same v. the said VAGHAN and others.
Messuage and land in Gelligaer of the grant of Henry Morgan of Llandaff, gentleman. GLAMORGAN.

45–46   Giles MORRYS of Coxwell, co. Berks, yeoman, and Margaret his wife v. Thomas HENTON.
Detention of deeds relating to land in Wanborough of the entail of Walter Arden of Hampton
Turville, yeoman, grandfather of the said Margaret.   WILTS.

47–48   Thomas MORTON of Milborne v. John COWARD, husbandman.
Cattle and deeds relating to land in Gillingham entrusted to defendant.   DORSET.

49–51   John MOTTE v. Thomas SKOTTE and Elizabeth his wife, late the wife of John Clerk, and
administratrix of his goods.
Refusal to. complete a sale of a messuage and land in Elsenham.   ESSEX.

52   Stephen MOYLE, Joan his wife and Humphrey, son and heir of Margery, late the wife of
Henry OVEREY, v. Elizabeth, late the wife of Richard WOODLAND.
Detention of deeds relating to lands in Barking late of John Woodland, and in Dagenham late of
William and James Woodland, uncles of the said Joan and Margery.   ESSEX.

53–54   The same *v.* John WOODLANDE, son and heir of the said Richard.
The like as to a tenement in Dagenham, late of Thomas Woodland, another uncle.   ESSEX.

55   Simon, grandson and heir of William MUCKELOWE, *v.* Richard MILL.
Messuages, land, rivers, fishing, and 'stakinges' in Shelsley Kings and the lordship of Martley
of the demise of Thomas West, knight.   *See Files* 540, *No.* 18; 656, *No.* 47; 852, *No.* 85.
WORCESTER.

56–58   John MUDGE of Buckfastleigh *v.* John ELISAUNDER.
Detention of deeds relating to land in.Skeryton (*i.e.* Skirradon in Dean Prior ?).   DEVON.

59   Benett MULLEYNES of Maidstone, co. Kent, *v.* Anthony WALDEGRAVE, esquire.
Messuage and garden in Bures bequeathed by Thomas Mulleynes, father of complainant, to
Katharine his wife by an invalid will.   SUFFOLK.

60–61   The same *v.* Barnaby CLEYDON.
Do.   SUFFOLK.

62–66   Richard MYDMORE, yeoman, *v.* John, son and heir of Thomas PELLOND.
Land in Chiddingly, pledged by Elise Mydmore, deceased, father of complainant.   SUSSEX.

67–68   John MYNSHALL of Minshull, esquire, *v.* Richard HOUGHE.
Share of a judgment debt awarded in this court (*see File* 1375, *No.* 37).   CHESTER.

69–70   The same *v.* John HOUGHE.
Rent of tenements (described) in the manor of Netherford.   CHESTER.

71   John M . . . *v.* Robert PYGOT, clerk.
Tithes of Lantrissaunt of the demise of Nicholas Harpesfelde, LL.D.   *Mutilated.*
DIOCESE OF BANGOR (*sic*).

72   Thomas M . . . *v.* William HOLSTOCKE, both citizens and grocers of London.
Messuage in the parish of St. Martin Thorgyns (*i.e.* Orgar ?).   *Damaged.*   LONDON.

FILE 1451.

1–7   Thomas MADELEY of Denston, gentleman, *v.* Walter, son of Wilham WHYTHALL,
Richard SMYTHE, and William HEYTON.
Messuages and land in Butterton, late of John Madeley, deceased, father of complainant.
STAFFORD.

8–9   John MAISTERSON of Rye and Joan his wife *v.* William STUNT.
Lands in Framfield, Ashburnham, Sedlescombe, and [Wartli]ng, adjudged to complainant in this
court (D..IX, 72).   *Mutilated.*   SUSSEX.

10   William MARSHALL, parson of Marston [Moretaine], *v.* Edward BROKET of Grays Inn,
esquire.
Silver bowl pledged to defendant.   BEDFORD, MIDDLESEX.

11   Thomas MARTYN *v.* Richard BALLE and Margery his wife.
Contempt of a judgment at *nisi prius* concerning a tenement in the manor of Ashwater.   DEVON.

12–15   Ede (Edmund) MASON and Katherine his wife, executrix of John Buntyng, *v.* Thomas
MONYMENT.
Messuage and land in Althorpe (in Fakenham), claimed by defendant as a partial exchange for other
lands in Fakenham.   *Mutilated.*   NORFOLK.

16–20   John MASTER and Agnes his wife, daughter of William Busshopp, deceased, *v.* Humphrey
WATKYNS, Thomas CHAFIE, and Christian his wife, formerly Christian Mychell.
Messuage and cottage in the said Watkyn's manor of Holwell of the demise of the late abbot of
Abbotsbury.   D. XV, 36.   SOMERSET.

21–24   John MAUNCELL, servant to the Lady Elizabeth, *v.* Christopher RUSSELL and Cristian
his wife.
Removing complainant's crops from land in the said Lady Elizabeth's manor of Sturminster
Newton Buckland, demised by him to defendant.   DORSET.

25–28   Walter MAXE of Wilton, gentleman, *v.* Robert (William) CREDE of Salisbury.
Detention of a blank signed document given him for delivery to Robert Maxe to write thereon a
letter of attorney.   WILTS.

29   William MAYDGE *v.* Nicholas SOWNTER.
Refusal to complete an assignment of his life interest in land in Peter's Marland.   DEVON.

30   Elizabeth, late the wife of John MAYEYOW, *v.* Reynold WYLLYAM.
Messuage and land in Preston Candover, late of John More, gentleman, deceased, father of complainant.   HANTS.

31–32   John MEASURE *v.* Roger GRENE and William GRASCROFT.
Detention of deeds relating to land in Leake.   LINCOLN.

33–34   Edmund MERVYN, archdeacon of Surrey, *v.* Richard BAGH, executor of Thomas Bagh,
late archdeacon.
Bonds for a life-annuity payable to the said Thomas from his resignation.   SURREY.

35–37   John MERY and Richard MYLLER *v.* LLEWELYN and JOHN ap Griffith ap Howell,
John LLOYD ap Tuder, and others.
Detention of deeds relating to land in the lordship of Yale and the parishes of Llandegla, Llanarmon,
Bryn Eglwys, Llanferras, and Llandysilio.   DENBIGH.

38–39   The.same *v.* the said JOHN ap Griffith, John LLOYD and others.
Lands in the said lordship and parish bought of John Perrott, knight.   DENBIGH.

40　　·　Thomas MILDMAY, esquire, v. Jeffrey DRURYE and Richard MEREDITH, yeomen.
Detention of deeds relating to the manor of Shouldham, Tottenhill, and Foston (in Tottenhill).
NORFOLK

41 ·　　Elizabeth MISTERCHAMBER, executrix of Joan late the wife of William Forster, v.
[Joan daughter of the said Joan], and Emma (Emote), executrix and late the wife of
Thomas FORSTER.
Rent of messuages and lands in Scarborough. *Mutilated.*　　　　　YORK..

42–45　　Richard MOLFORD (Moumford) v. John MULFORD (Monforde) his brother.
·Tenement in Basing bequeathed to defendant by John Mulford, father of both parties, on condition
that it should not be alienated except to complainant. *Mutilated.*　　　[HANTS.]

46　　Thomas MONSLOWE, parson of Cowden, v. George BRYGER.
Half a year's rent of complainant's parsonage on a lease by Edward Sayer his predecessor.
KENT.

47–48　　William MORDAUNTE, esquire, and Agnes his wife v. Robert FLETCHER, esquire.
Carpet for ·a table, of the bequest of John Bothe.　　　　　[FLINT ?]

49–51　　John MORE and Jennett his wife v. George TREWYNARD and Edith HARLYN.
Detention of deeds relating to lands in the Island and elsewhere in St. Ives (Sentyse), late of Walter
Harlyn, deceased, brother of the said Jennett and husband of the said Edith.　　CORNWALL.

52–54　　Robert, grandson and heir of Margaret MORE v. John CLERKE.
Messuage and land in Burgh, formerly of John Herdone (Heydone?).　　　SUFFOLK.

55–59　　Robert MORGANE, esquire, v. Edward ASTON, knight, great-grandson and heir of Robert
Aston, knight, and Edward COCKE *alias* Clarke his servant.
Messuage and lands (*described*) in Leigh, late of William Morgan, deceased, great-grandfather of
complainant. ·　　　　　STAFFORD.

60　　Richard MORRYN the younger and Alice his wife v. Richard MORRYN the elder and
Gilbert MORRYN. ·
Land in the tithing of Dalditch in Budleigh.　　　　　DEVON.

61–63　　Lewis MORTLAKE v. John SMYTH of Denston, co. Suffolk, esquire, and Richard
MORTLAKE.
Messuages and land in Haverhill, pledged to the said John by John Mortlake, deceased, father of
the said Lewis and Richard.　　　　　ESSEX.

64–65　　William MOWSEHERST, gentleman, v. Richard HASTLYNGE.
Detention of deeds relating to a messuage and land in East Peckham, late of Hugh Mowseherst,
deceased, father of complainant.　　　　　KENT.

66　　·　Roger MUROWE and Thomas SOWTER, churchwardens of Sutton, v. the Lady ANNE
OF CLEVES. ·
Vestments (*described*), books and straw formerly supplied to the church of Sutton by the prior of
Castleacre as impropriator of the rectory.　　　· LINCOLN.

67–69　　George MUTTON of London, gentleman, v. John MUTTON.
Annuity granted by Peter Mutton of Rhuddlan, gentleman, out of lands in Meliden (Melerdyne)
and elsewhere now in the possession of defendant. *See File 851, No. 48.*　　FLINT.

70　　Peter MUTTON, administrator of the goods of the said George, deceased, v. the same.
Reviver of the above.　　　　　FLINT.

71　　Richard MYCHELL and Thomas BREWER of Chard, co. Somerset, merchants, v. William
JACOBE.
Corn-rent of the manor of Tolpuddle and of lands there, late of the abbot of Abbotsbury. DORSET.

72　　John MYLLYNG, late of Barton, co. Oxford, yeoman, uncle and heir of Richard Fryer,
yeoman, v. William WYLDBLOD and Richard PADLAND (Palland).
Detention of deeds relating to lands in Tenbury.　　　　　SALOP (*sic*).

FILE 1452.

1–5　　Sylvester MAKERAS of Royston, co. Herts, labourer, v. William, son and heir of Ralph
SMYTHSON, and others.
Messuage and land in the lordship of Barningham, late of Alexander Makeras, yeoman, deceased,
father of complainant.　　　　　YORK.

6　　Jane MAKERAS, late the wife of the said Alexander, v. William and Thomas SMYTHESON,
executors of Ralph Smytheson of Newsham.
Price of the premises.　　　　　YORK.

7–8　　Elizabeth, late the wife of Richard MAN, and administratrix of his goods, v. John JUDDE
and Alice his wife.
Reviver of a suit for a tenement in Little Packington. D. XI, 39. *2 suits.*　　WARWICK.

9–10　　The same v. Robert BRUDENELL, esquire, and Elizabeth his mother.
Acquisition of the premises from the said John, against whom an injunction had been granted as
above.　　　　　WARWICK.

11–13　　Isabel MANLEY, sister and heir of William Caller, v. Thomas BENET and others.
Detention of deeds relating to a messuage and land in St. John's, Thanet.　　KENT.

14　　Thomas MANNOUXE and Richard GOUGHE for themselves and all the inhabitants of
WOLLASTONE v. William [SOMERSET], earl of Worcester.
Corn rent distributable among the inhabitants of Wollastone from a farm there, late of the abbot
and convent of Tintern. *See File 1310, No. 3.*　　　　　GLOUCESTER.

15–17   Robert, grandson and heir of Margaret late the wife of John MARTEN, v. Thomas HOLTON and Margery PECOKE, wife of the said John at the time of his death.
Messuage and land in Kirton, late of John Brende, deceased, father of the said Margaret. SUFFOLK.

18   John MASCALL v. Thomas NEELLE, Amy his wife, and Dennis OFFYNGTON.
Land in the manor of Plompton, formerly demised to Robert Offyngton. *Damaged.*
[NORTHAMPTON *or* SUSSEX.]

19–20   Thomas MATHEWE, citizen and merchant tailor of London, v. William CHAMBER-LAYNE of Northampton.
Under-lease of water-mills called Clifford Mills by Little Houghton, with a fishery and a barn and land adjoining. NORTHAMPTON.

21   John MATLEY v. Robert BEXWICK.
Messuages and land in Stockport, late of Bartholomew Matley, deceased, father of complainant.
CHESTER.

22–25   Thomas MATSON, gentleman, v. John LEEDES, esquire, and Agnes his wife.
Manor of Chepstede and lands there and in Catteram, Cowlesdon and Walton, late of Richard Sackevile, father-in-law of complainant. *Mutilated.*
[SURREY.]

26–28   Roger MAWDLEY and Robert EVERARDE v. Nicholas GILBERT, gentleman, and John WADHAM, esquire, executor of Anthony Gilbert, gentleman.
Price of goods of Elizabeth Fitzjames, deceased, whose executors were complainants, and the said Anthony. *Damaged. Answer wanting.*
WILTS.

29–30   William MAYCOT, executor of Anne, late the wife of Osmond Gaye, v. William MOWSHERST and others.
Parsonage of Chart and manor of Lambethwick (in Lambeth), late of John Mascall, deceased, father of the said Anne.
KENT, SURREY.

31–34   John MELLERS of Coningsby, co. Lincoln, v. Richard PEYCHE, gentleman.
Messuages, cottages, and land in Conway, Creuddyn, 'le commote' of Isaf, Beaumaris, Carnarvon, and Bangor, late of Nicholas Mellers, father of complainant. DENBIGH, CARNARVON, ANGLESEA.

35–37   Bartholomew, Jacobs, Jeronimo, and Francis MICHAELI, heirs of Bonaventure Michaeli, and Jeronimo ARNELFYNE, merchants of Lucca, and their company, by Augustine de Asexto of Lucca, their factor, v. John and William HAWKINS and others, all of Plymouth, and Peter LAKE of Exeter.
Capture at sea of a ship of Rouen freighted by complainants, concerning which no process from the Admiralty can be served in Plymouth because of the liberty of the town. *Mutilated.*
DEVON.

38–39   Matthew MONKE and Mildred and Joan, daughters of Thomas MAPLYSDEN, v. Thomas BYFLYTTE and Joan his wife, executrix, and late the wife of John Bisshopenden of Catsfield.
Debt of the said Monke remitted by the will of the said Bisshopenden on condition of his paying it to the other complainants at their majority. SUSSEX.

40–42   William MORDAUNT, esquire, second son of John lord Mordaunt, and Agnes his wife v. John BINGLEY.
Tenement in Chester, late of the said Agnes's father. CHESTER.

43–45   The same v. Peter CONWAY.
Stables in Chester of the like inheritance. CHESTER.

46   William MORETOFTE v. John MORETOFTE and others.
Messuage and land in Itteringham, Mannington, Irmingland, and Calthorpe, late of John Moretofte, deceased, father of the said William and John. *Mutilated.* NORFOLK.

47–48   William MORGAN, younger son of William Morgan ap Hoell, gentleman, deceased, v. James GUNTER, William HERBERT of Colbrooke, esquire, John BARRY, feoffee to uses, and others.
Conspiracy to maintain the title of Lewis Morgan Philip, nephew of complainant, to the manor of Gwenegochen. MONMOUTH.

49–53   William MOUNSON, esquire, executor of Thomas Dymocke, esquire, v. George SEYNT-POLL, esquire.
Manor-place of North Carlton and lands there of the demise of the abbot of Barlings and formerly in the occupation of defendant. LINCOLN.

54   Simon MUCKELOWE v. John JONES.
Land in Kempsey, late of Richard Muckelowe, deceased, father of complainant. *See File* 540, *No.* 18.

55–58   Edward MYCHELL of Calstone (Causton), clothiers, and John MYCHELL v. John CHAPERLEYN of Swindon.
Loan. *Damaged.* WILTS.

59–60   John MYDDELMORE, woodward and bailiff of the manor of Bredon, v. Thomas COOKES and John COLE.
Herbage of the said woods. WORCESTER.

61   Richard EYLLES and Thomas COLE v. Thomas ELDRINGTON, Thomas LUTMAN, and John CARYE.
Partnership between the said Lutman and Carye and Richard Holmeden and John Cole, complainant's employers, in a water-mill used for iron-working at Grinstead. *Mutilated.* SUSSEX.

62–63   John MYLSENT, one of the Six Clerks of Chancery, v. Edward BUTLER.
Goods of Frances, late the wife of Oliver Leder, knight, deceased, in Great Stoughton, whereof
both parties are administrators. *Mutilated.*   HUNTINGDON.
64–69   The same v. Thomas BAWDWYN, uncle of the said Frances, and administrator of her
goods (*sic*).
Expenditure on behalf of the said Sir Oliver and Frances.   HUNTINGDON.

FILE 1453.

1–3   William MAN v. David MAN.
Messuage, etc., in Lakenheath of the bequest of Amys Man, mother of both parties. *See File* 852,
No. 7.   SUFFOLK.
4–5   Thomas MANERWING and Margaret his wife, late the wife of ——— Cotten, gentleman,
v. Thomas MONYNGES and others.
Annuity bequeathed by William Monynges, gentleman, out of defendant's lands in Sandwich and
Woodnesborough (Winnesborough).   KENT.
6–7   William MANNE, groom in ordinary of the Queen's Chamber, v. John MASSY, yeoman.
Crown lease of a tenement in Coppenhall, part of the messuages, lands, rents and services, late of
Roger Woodhouse.   CHESTER.
8   The same v. Robert CARRE of Sleaford, gentleman, Michael THOMSON, his servant, and
others.
Messuage and lánds in Asgarby and elsewhere demised by Edward VI to George Layton.
                                                                                        LINCOLN.
9   Peter de MARDARIAGA, Spaniard, v. the sheriffs of LONDON.
Action by Thomas Curteis, knight, now sheriff of London, for a debt for which he had compromised.
Certiorari.   LONDON.
10–13   Anthony MARLER v. Thomas MELLERS and Margaret his wife, late the wife of William
Gressent of London, haberdasher.
Messuage and lands (*described*) in Islington and Harringay, part of Robert Trappes's manor of
Newington Barrow, and a house called the *Falcon* in Gracechurch Street. D. XI, 18.
                                                                                        MIDDLESEX.
14–15   Richard MARSHALL of Doncaster, tanner, and Elizabeth LIGHTFOTE, an infant, v.
William FISSHER of Carlton-in-Lindrick, co. Notts, gentleman, and Leonard ELWODE
his servant.
Goods of Thomas Farrar, parson of Rawmarsh, deceased, whose executors complainants are.
                                                                                        YORK.
16–17   Richard MARSHALL and Maude his wife, late the wife of John Lawrence, v. George
HERBERT, knight.
Annuity bequeathed to the said Maude by John Cradocke her son, whose executor defendant is.

18–21   Humphrey son and heir of John MARTYN *alias* Honychurche v. Joan MARTYN *alias*
Honychurche, executrix [and late the wife?] of the said John, and Edmund ROWLANDE,
overseer of his will.
Messuages and lands in Milton Damerell, North Tawton, and Norton.   DEVON, SOMERSET.
22   John, son of Baldwin MARWODE, gentleman, v. Edward DREWE.
Messuage and lands in Halberton, formerly of John Crosse.   DEVON.
23–25   Thomas grandson and heir of William MASSON v. Christopher, grandson and heir of John
ROTHERHAM.
Messuage by the common well and land in Ekyngton.   [DERBY *or* WORCESTER.]
26–27   John MATHEWMAN *alias* Mathewes v. William BEVER.
Messuage and land at Scoles in the bailiwick of Holme and the lordship of Wakefield, of the devise
of Thomas Mathewe(s), father of complainant.   YORK.
28   John MAWDE v. Elizabeth HADDOK and Thomas her son.
Refusal to give bond for a sale of oats to be delivered at Halifax.   YORK.
29   John MAWDE v. Elizabeth, executrix and late the wife of Thomas HAYDOCK and
Francis his son.
Refusal to complete a sale at Bothome Inn of oats (' shyllynges, commenly called shyllyng grotes ')
to be bought in Blackburn market.   LANCASTER.
30–32   Henry, son and heir of Richard MAYNE, by John Spalt his guardian, v. William MAYNE
his great-uncle.
Detention of deeds relating to lands in Ermington and Ugborough.   DEVON.
33–36   The same v. Richard FRENDE.
Do.   DEVON.
37   Thomas MERSHALL v. Henry ELACOTT, both of Exeter, merchants.
Messuage on St. Petrock's [Exeter] of the demise of John Woddeham, esquire. *Damaged.* DEVON.
38   Richard MICHELL, esquire, v. James BOY(E)SSE.
Messuage and garden in Bridgwater acquired of James Bysse, esquire.   SOMERSET.
39–42   Thomas MODYE, parson of Moulton, v. Richard his brother.
Exclusion from complainant's parsonage, which defendant has been permitted to inhabit at will.
                                                                                        SUFFOLK.

43–44   William MONE, parson of Okeford Fitzpaine, v. John PISTER, esquire (gentleman).
Parsonage of Okeford, claimed under a lease from Thomas Rand, late parson, deprived for marriage.
DORSET.

45–47   John MONSONE, gentleman, v. William SUTTON.
Land in South Kelsey.   Demurrer for insufficiency overruled.   LINCOLN.

48–51   Joan MORE of Bockmer (in Medmenham), late the wife of Thomas More, v. Robert MORE
his second son.
Moiety of lands, late of the monastery of Medmenham, promised in return for goods of the said
Thomas and·a messuage and land in Barby (Barraby), the said Thomas having already received
the purchase-money of complainant's land in Braintree.   ·   BUCKS, NORTHAMPTON, ESSEX.

52   Edmund MORGAN, gentleman, v. Edward LEWYS, esquire, and Jevan WYLLIAM.
Lands in Bedwellty, formerly of Jevan David Powell ap William.   MONMOUTH.

53   James MORLEY of London, merchant, v. the sheriffs of BRISTOL and William PRATT.
Action for ' newland fyshe ' captured from the French by a ship of war partly owned by complainant.   Certiorari and subpœna.   GLOUCESTER.

54–57   John MOUNTEAGUE of Epsom, husbandman, v. John SKETE of London, merchant,
husband of Margaret, late the wife of Oliver Man.
Messuage and garden in Leatherhead, late of Thomas Mounteague and Elizabeth his wife,
deceased, parents of complainant.   SURREY.

58–59   John MOYNYNGES v. Crystyan SMYTHE.
Bale of ' whoode ' (i.e. woad) worth 6l. 13s. 4d. entrusted to defendant.   SUFFOLK.

60   Vincent MUNDY of Marketon, co. [Derby?], esquire, v. James, son of Robert WHITALL.
Suppression of court rolls of the manor of Warslow, inherited with those of Allstonefield and Longnor
from John Mundy, knight, father of complainant.   Mutilated.   [STAFFORD.]

61–62   Richard MUSKETT and George, son and executor of John GROME, v. John WARD and
Walter WARREYN.
Detention of deeds relating to a messuage in Rattlesden and an account of church goods and an
action for the latter.   SUFFOLK.

63–64   Hugh MYCHELL, one of the ' allmowse knyghtes ' of the King and Queen at Windsor, v.
John CLAWSE(Y) alias Chaworthe, yeoman.
Price of land in Northchurch and woods in Somerfylde, sold on complainant's behalf.   HERTS.

65–68   Thomas MYLLE the elder, Critian his wife, and others, v. Thomas MORTIMER. .
Refusal to deliver a lease of closes in Chudleigh (described) made by defendant and Thomas
Pomerye; knight.   DEVON.

69–70   Thomas MYLLER, deceased, v. John EWEYN and Agnes his wife.
Messuage and land in Takeley of the entail of Thomas Myller, deceased, ancestor of the said
Thomas and Agnes.   ESSEX.

FILE 1454.

1–2   Ralph MACCLESFIELD and Thomas BRYNDLEY v. Thomas COXE and Margaret
his wife.
Messuages, cottages, land and rent in Mere in Forton (Meyre), High Olton (in Norbury), Chawton,
Aston and Tunstall (in Adbaston) of the grant of John Darte and Joan his wife, sister of the said
Margaret.   STAFFORD.

3   William MAISTER, gentleman, v. William MIDDELTON, yeoman.
Detention of deeds relating to messuages and land in Uttoxeter.   STAFFORD.

4–7   Francis MALLETT, D.D., dean of Lincoln, v. Martin LANE, vicar of Chesterfield.
Rent of Little Chester payable in lieu of a pension from defendant's church.   D. XIV, 50.   DERBY.

8–9   John MALYN v. Elizabeth, executrix and late the wife of John STOWELL.
Double recovery against Peter Lake of Exeter of money receivable on behalf of complainant.
D. XI, 5.   See also D. XIII, 33.   DEVON.

10   William MAN, groom of the Chamber, v. Rice WYNE.
Expenses of obtaining a Crown lease of a mill and messuages formerly held of Margery Roose.   ?

11   Robert MANBIE of Marlesford and Anne his wife v. Thomas and Margery MARRET.
Tenement in the manor of Woodbridge of the bequest of Thomas Marret, deceased, father of the
said Anne and Thomas and husband of the said Margery.   SUFFOLK.

12–13   William MANLEY, late of Manley, gentleman, prisoner in the Fleet, v. George IRELAND
of Crowton, esquire, and Elizabeth his wife, heir of John Birkhevid of Crowton, esquire.
Annuity of the bequest of the said Birkhevid.   See File 1309, No. 11.   CHESTER.

14–17   .The same v. the said George.
Debt of William Garnerde (Gardener).   Faded.   CHESTER.

18   The same v. Ralph DUTTON of Hatton, esquire, son and executor of Piers Dutton, knight.
Delivery to the said George of a statute staple compounded for by arbitration.   Mutilated.   See
File 975, No. 76.   CHESTER.

19–20   John MARCER v. Matthew ANDREWES of Huntingdon and John WHITE.
Messuage and land in Holbeach, late of John Marcer, deceased, father of complainant.   Answer
wanting.   See D. XI, 40.   LINCOLN.

21   Ellis MARCUS, denizen goldsmith, v. William DENHAM of London, goldsmith.
Action of account for plate entrusted to complainant to be remade.   LONDON.

22-25   John MARYS v. Thomas MARYS and Robert (Thomas) PETHICKE.
Lease of a tenement in Week St. Mary. *Mutilated.*   CORNWALL..

26   William MARSHALL, gentleman, and Alice his wife, late the wife of Richard Gibson, v.
John and Thomas HOWLE.
Detention of deeds relating to marsh in [Hope] All Saints and Blackmanstone. *Mutilated.* KENT.

27   John, David and Robert MARSHE, and Robert, son of Stephen MARSHE, deceased, v.
David FORSTALL and William BLYMSTON.
Messuages and land at Martin (Merton) in East Langdon and West Cliffe of the bequest of John
Marshe, father of the said John, David, Robert the elder, and Stephen.   KENT.

28-30   William MARTIN of Garsington, co. Oxford, yeoman, v. John BRADDESTON, Dorothy
his wife, and William WOLLSHOTTE.
Price of a messuage and land in Comberbury (*i.e.* Congresbury?) repayable on the death of Wilham
Wollshotte, late the husband of the said Dorothy, and father of the defendant William.
SOMERSET.

31-32   John MARTYN, clerk, v. Peter SEYNTLE, esquire, and Thomas GRYFFITH, clerk.
Detention of a deed whereby the dean and chapter of St. George's in Windsor Castle appointed
complainant to be curate of Bradninch.   DEVON.

33 .   Thomas MARVYNDE, a sewer of the Queen's hall, and Henry YONG, his deputy, v. Thomas
BARNES and Robert BUTTON, servants to Christopher Metcalf, knight.
Wapentake-of Buckrose granted to the said Marvynde by King Edward VI together with those of
Harthill and Dickering and that between Ouse and Derwent.   YORK.

34-35   William MARYETE of London, brewer, grandson and heir of Robert Maryet, yeoman,
· v. Richard FRAUNCYS, yeoman.
Messuage and land in Willington (*i.e.* Willingham?) claimed under a demise of Henry Sydney,
knight, and others.   LINCOLN.

36-40   John MASON and·Dorothy his wife v. Richard WYATT and Anne his wife.
Detention of deeds relating to a messuage and land in Bennington and Leverton, late of Peter
Emery, deceased, ancestor of the said Dorothy and Anne.   LINCOLN.

41-43   Leonard (Bernard) MASON, late chaplain to Dr. Daye, bishop of Chichester, v. John
WOOD of Nuthurst, carpenter, and Wilham COLMAN of Henfield, serving-man.
Parsonage of Nuthurst to which complainant was collated on the deprivation of Gregory Dodes
for marriage.   SUSSEX.

44   The same v. the same, John POLLINGTON, yeoman, and Thomas BAKER.
Collusive distress on the same parsonage, whereof the said Pollington is complainant's tenant.
SUSSEX.

45   James MASSEY, gentleman, v. William BRETLAND.
Half a close of pasture in Hollingworth of the gift of James Massey, esquire, father of complainant.
.CHESTER.

46   William MATHEWE, citizen and merchant tailor of London, servant to Walter Davis,
citizen and clothworker of London, v. the mayor, aldermen and sheriffs of LONDON and
Christian HOLLESBUSHE (a foreigner).
Action for price of cloth called ' brissells ' bought by complainant on behalf of his said master.
Certiorari and subpœna.   LONDON.

47   Thomas MAUNSFOLD, clerk, and William WODWARD, executors of James Roolston,
gentleman, v. Roger TYTHERTON of Caldon and George TYTHERTON of Uttoxeter,
executors of Thomas Tytherton, servant of the said Roolston.
Live-stock of the said Roolston (*described*).   STAFFORD.

48   Richard MAYE, ' plymer ' (*i.e.* plumber?), v. Thomas ROWSE.
Detention of deeds relating to land in Gaywood.   NORFOLK.

49 Christopher MAYN, gentleman, descendant and heir of Robert Morton, v. Robert MORTON,
gentleman.
Manors of Limpool and Hesley (both now in Bawtry, co. Notts). Pedigree given. YORK, NOTTS.

50-52   Wilham MAYNARD of London, mercer, v. Alice WOODE.
Goods of complainant in the hands of Paul Stafford, deceased, his apprentice and factor. *Mutilated.*
LONDON, DEVON.

53-56   Philip MAYNEWARYNGE, esquire, v. Jane, late the wife of Richard COTTON, knight,
Hugh CHOLMONDELEY, knight, her steward, and Thomas MAYNEWARYNGE.
Land in the manor of Newhall, late of Randolph Maynewaryng, knight. *Mutilated.* [CHESTER.]

57   James MEDELTON of Salisbury and Joan his wife v. Thomas MORGAN of Cantreff.
Loan of money and cloth of the said Joan before her marriage.   WILTS, BRECON.

58   William MELLER v. Maude late the wife of James MELLER and Ralph their son.
Mill in Wetton of the demise of the late prior of Tutbury.   STAFFORD.

59   Anthony MERYE of Stoke Bruerne, gentleman, v. Thomas BACON, citizen and salter of
London.
Detention of a bond made to complainant by John his brother.   NORTHAMPTON, LONDON.

60   George MEVERELL v. Edward CRYMES and others.
Jewels of Mary Crymes, who had promised to marry complainant.   ————

61   George MIDDELMORE v. William ASTEMER.
Misdescription of a document in a former suit for the glebe and tithes of King's Norton.
WORCESTER.

62   John MIDDELTON *v.* Humphry BENTLY, William CALDEWALL, and others.
Messuages and land in Burton-on-Trent and Horninglow (Hornyngton), late of Thomas Middelton, deceased, father of complainant.   STAFFORD.

63-67 The same *v.* William CALDWALL, Henry BERDMORE, Christopher USHERWOODE, Thomas WETTON, and John SMYTH.
Part of the premises whence complainant was ousted by Humphrey Bentley, gentleman.
    STAFFORD.

68   William MOGERYDGE *v.* John WYLTON.
Refusal to complete an assignment made by Thomas Mompesson of Corton. *Mutilated.* WILTS.

69   John MOLYNEUX *v.* Thomas NELSON and Cicely his wife.
Debt of William Walker of Chilwell, deceased, former husband of the said Cicely.   NOTTS.

70·   John MONESLEY *v.* Thomas LEE and others, grantees to his use.
Promise to grant a presentation to the church of Eardley in consideration that complainant had brought up Anne Lee, a kinswoman of the said Thomas.   SALOP.

71   John MOORE 'of Salisbury, merchant, *v.* Robert TREVOUR, Edward his son, the latter's wife, and the under-sheriff of DENBIGH.
Wrongful occupation of a tenement and imprisonment of complainant's servants. *Faded.*
Injunction and subpœna.   DENBIGH.

72   Hugh MORE, gentleman, *v.* [John EVELEGH].
Manor of Holcombe and messuage and land in Ottery St. Mary and Banton. *Mutilated. See File* 1369, *No.* 74.   DEVON.

73-75 John MORE of Ickleton, labourer, *v.* John and Lettice WALBANKE.
Money entrusted to John More, vicar of East Winch, whose executors defendants are.   NORFOLK.

76   Thomas MORE, esquire, *v.* William CHAPLYN.
Detention of deeds relating to the site and demesnes of Taunton priory.   SOMERSET.

77-79 Francis MORGAN, serjeant-at-law, *v.* Thomas FORSTER, gentleman, and Elizabeth his wife.
Detention in contempt of an arbitral award of deeds relating to the manors of Upbury·(Ubburie), and Bylkemore (both in Pulloxhill), and Blundells (in Silsoe), and lands in Aspley Guise, Birchmore (now in Woburn), Upbury, Pulloxhill, Silsoe, Flitt, Barton-in-the-Clay, Higham Gobion, Maldon, Gravenhurst and Woburn.   BEDFORD.

80   Humphrey MORGAN, citizen and mercer of London, *v.* the mayor, sheriffs and aldermen of LONDON, and Thomas PARYS.
Action for a debt paid on behalf of Richard Capyll for which the said Morgan and Parys were both sureties. *Certiorari and subpœna.*   LONDON.

81-83 John MORTON *v.* Thomas, son and heir of Robert CHAPMAN, John, son and heir of William BELL, and John STEPHYNSON.
Messuage, loft, and garden in Boston, late of Thomas Morton, deceased, father of complainant.
    LINCOLN.

84-87 Thomas MOUNGOMERY *v.* Edward CRYMES.
Detention of a lease of messuages adjoining Blossoms Inn in St. Lawrence Lane. *See File* 1340, *No.* 64.   LONDON.

88   John MOUSON, gentleman, *v.* Humphry LEGERD.
Cottage and common in South Kelsey.   LINCOLN.

89-91 The same (Mounson) *v.* Thomas MOUNSON.
Messuages, cottages and land in North and South Kelsey, late of Thomas Mounson, deceased, father of both parties.   LINCOLN.

92-93 Richard MOWER of Oker (*i.e.* Oakover?) Woodhouses, co. Stafford, yeoman, executor of Thomas Mower, clerk, *v.* Richard HARRYSON.
Wrongful occupation of land of the demise of defendant in the lordship of Weston and detention of a bond.   WARWICK.

94   Roger MOYLE, gentleman, grandson and heir of John Moyle of Bake (in St. Germans), esquire, *v.* John MOYLE, esquire, and Roger SPRYE.
Messuages and lands in Landrake and St. Germans and burgage in Bodmin High Street.
    CORNWALL.

95   Edmund MOYSES of London, haberdasher, *v.* Matthew HYNE of Milnthorpe, yeoman.
Manor of Heversham (Eversham).   WESTMORLAND..

96-99 John MUNES (Monnes) *v.* William COLFORDE.
Distress for sums awarded to defendant (D. IX, 58) and already paid into this court in a suit for tenements within Aldgate and in Romford, St. Botolph's without Aldgate, Whitechapel, Brent-wood and Warley.   LONDON, ESSEX.

100-101 George MUTTON of London, gentleman, *v.* Griffith ap Jevan LLOYD, David LLOYD ap Morgan and others.
Money and 'teles' of oats due as described to complainant as 'raglar' and constable of the county.
    CARDIGAN.

102   Philip MYCHE *v.* Thomas YVE and Thomas SAMWELL.
Lands late held of the manor of Rayleigh by John Myche, deceased, father of complainant.
    ESSEX.

103   Thomas MYDDELTON, gentleman, *v.* John BELL and others.
Crown land in Ripon.   YORK.

104–106 George MYLBORNE v. John ASHECOME, late the husband of Agnes, formerly the wife of John Hartgill, and John ABAROUGHE.
Messuage and land in Ditcheat, late of John Moone of Letsomes Grene, deceased, grandfather of complainant.   SOMERSET.

107–109 Richard MYLLAR and Richard TAYLOR v. William BURDON of Hundleby and John his son.
Action for debts due to the said William and paid to the said John.   LINCOLN.

110–111 Edmund MYSITT, yeoman, purveyor to the Household, v. Gregory LOWELL, Joan his wife, and Edmund TWYNO his tenant.
Manor of Wiggenhall and lands thereto belonging in Watford, of the demise of James Josken of London, gentleman, former husband of the said Joan.   HERTS.

FILE 1455.

1   MADOC ap Harry ap Thomas ap David of London v. JEVAN ap Res ap Jevan.
Lands in Dinlley, mortgaged to defendant's father by David ap Hoell, [? great-] grandfather of complainant.   CARNARVON.

2   [Elizabeth, late the wife] of Richard MADOCKE of Church Ireton, v. Alice, late the wife of [Robert ?] TOPLEYS, Richard her son and William FLETCHER of Wirksworth.
Debts. *Mutilated. See File* 1309, *No.* 7.   DERBY.

3–4   Simon MALORYE, gentleman, v. John STYLE, clerk.
Detention of deeds relating to the manor of Clendon, late of Robert Malorye, deceased, father of complainant.   NORTHAMPTON.

5   Henry MANSER, administrator of the goods of Thomas Arthur, deceased, v. Katherine WYNDE and John CROSSE, executors of Edward Arthur, father of the said Thomas.
Land in Wisbech of the demise of the late Trinity gild there and goods (*described*), late of the said Edward.   CAMBRIDGE.

6   MARGARET, late the wife of ——— ap Thomas v. David ap Evor PHELPOTT and RICHARD ap Jones.
Messuage and land in Michaelchurch settled on complainant at her marriage.   RADNOR.

7–10   Andrew MARYSHE v. William EDWARDES.
Forgery of a bond concerning a joint tenancy of a tenement in Bishop's Nympton (Nymet, Ninyett). D. XI, 23.   DEVON.

11   Thomas MASCALL v. . . . SCOTTE and others.
Lease by complainant of a messuage, mill and land in Lindfield. *Mutilated.*   SUSSEX.

12   Henry MATHEWE of London, gentleman, v. John Gruffithe GOUGHE of Llandaff, gentleman.
Money promised by defendant on marriage with his daughter, since deceased.
                                                                                       LONDON, GLAMORGAN.

13–14   Henry MAYNWARYNG, servant to Stephen [Gardiner], bishop of Winchester, deceased, v. William MELTON (Myltone) of Southampton, gentleman.
Rights of pasture belonging to the parkership of Kingsclere, together with other profits (*described*), defendant being lessee of the herbage of the park.   HANTS.

15   MEREDITH ap Lewis, dwelling in Westminster, v. Walter APPOWELL his guardian.
Goods and jewels of Lewis ap Jenkin of Brecknock, deceased, father of complainant.
                                                                                       MIDDLESEX, BRECON.

16   Richard MERICOCKE, parson of Flourdon, v. James BIGOTT, gentleman.
Parsonage of Flourdon, demised by a former parson, deprived for marriage. *Damaged.*
                                                                                       N[ORFOLK].

17   Thomas MERYMAN, husbandman, son of John Meryman, deceased, v. John SHELTON.
Refusal to complete a lease of a messuage and land in Taddington, late of the chapel there.
                                                                                       DERBY.

18–19   William MICHELL v. Robert HICKES of Wilton, clerk, Robert MARLAND of Taunton, 'harderman,' and others.
Embezzlement at Billerbroke (*i.e.* Bilbrooke in Old Cleeve?) of a bond given by the said Hickes to the said Marland who had assigned it to complainant.   SOMERSET.

20   John MOLYNAX of Drayton, yeoman, v. John PARRET, steward of the manor of Dorchester, and Simon PARRET, his deputy.
Land late held of the said manor by John Molynax, grandfather of complainant.   OXFORD.

21–26   John MOLYNEUX, esquire, v. John MARKAM, knight, William ABBOT, George UPTON and others.
Land in complainant's manor of Thorpe claimed as belonging to the manors of Overhall and. Netherhall in [East] Stoke.   NOTTS.

27–28   The same v. George NORTHE.
Land in Stoke marsh.   NOTTS.

29   John MONKE of Honiton, yeoman, v. Thomas ISAAK of Colaton Rawleigh.
Detention of a bond for a debt already paid.   DEVON.

30   Jo . . . MOORES v. Alice MOORES, mother-in-law (stepmother?) of complainant,
and others.
Trespass and seizure of goods of complainant's father.   ————

31–34   John MORE v. Robert BRIGHT and John BARKER.
Manor of Ratlingcope, and tenements and a mill there whereof the said Bright claims a Crown
lease.   SALOP.

35–37   Robert MOTE of Lambeth v. Henry, son and executor of Robert CHARE.
Collusive suit against William Gardener for land in St. Mary Magdalen nigh the Bridge, [Bermond-
sey], late of the abbot and convent of Bermondsey.   SURREY.

38–41   Vincent MUNDY of Markeaton, co. Derby, esquire, v. Roger TONGE and Thomas FYNNEY.
Land in Allstonefield, where complainant owns two-thirds of the manor. *Boundaries in answer.*
See File 1453, *No.* 60.   STAFFORD.

42–43   George MYDDELTON v. Richard, son of Hugh LOWTHER, deceased.
Embracery, threats of violence, falsification of a writ, and unlawful arrest to prevent the taking
of an extent on a statute staple.   CUMBERLAND, YORK.

44–46   Francis MYNSHULL v. John ANYON, clerk, and William BENNETT, executors of John
Whitemore, and William HOCKNELL and Roger HURLESTON, gentleman.
Messuage, land and common in Wimboldsley. *See File* 1368, *No.* 116.   CHESTER.

47–48   Ralph MYNSHULL of Lincoln's Inn, gentleman, v. Hugh GYBBONS and others.
Lands in Minshull Vernon of the demise of Dowce, late the wife of John Starkye of Wrenbury.
                                                                          CHESTER.

49–53   Richard, grandson and heir of John MYRFELD, esquire, v. Thomas, son of John WENT-
WORTH, esquire.
Detention of deeds relating to the manors of Morley, Fynchedon, Howley (in Ardsley), Mirfield,
Hopton, Dighton, Batley, Bolton, Newstead, Wakefield, Gildersome, Little Smeaton. and Laughton,
and messuages, lands, mills and rent there (except in Hopton and Laughton) and in Kirkheaton,
Hunderfield (*i.e.* Huddersfield?), Stubbs, Womersley, Soothill, Ossett, Saxton, Woodkirk, Little
Bowling, Drighlington, South Owram, Chekinley and Frisby. *See File* 1370, *No.* 61.   YORK.

54–55   The same v. Henry GRYCE, esquire.
Detention of deeds relating to manors of Tong and Collynghed and messuages, mills and land there
and in Holme and Ryecroft (both in Tong), late of Peter Myrfeld, father of complainant, and
messuages, mills, lands and rent late of the said John (as above).   YORK.

FILE 1456.

1   William NANFAN of Pendock, gentleman, v. Sybell, late the wife of Rowland NORTON,
esquire, and Margaret his daughter.
Goods of Richard Monyngton of Masyngton (in Ledbury), esquire, deceased father-in-law of
complainant. *See File* 1147, *No.* 5.   HEREFORD.

2–7   William NANFAN of Marton, gentleman, v. Richard SMYTHE and Elizabeth his wife.
Fees of the keepership of Blackmore Park chargeable on defendant's manor of Hanley Castle.
(Annexed is an answer from John Hornyold, purchaser of the park, with replication and rejoinder.)
                                                                          WORCESTER.

8   Nicholas NAPPER v. Thomas PHYLYPPES.
Partition of a Crown lease of the site and demesnes of Montacute priory.   SOMERSET.

9–12   Ralph NEDEHAM and Elizabeth his wife v. Margaret NEWTON and William and Thurstan
her sons.
Share of a messuage and land in Glossop, late of William Ragg, deceased, father of the said
Elizabeth. *See File* 1311, *No.* 16.   DERBY

13–15   Robert, son and heir of Robert NELE, v. John DYON, esquire, and Rowland BYRKITT.
Land held of the manor of Belchford. *Mutilated. Demurrer for insufficiency.*   LINCOLN.

16   John NETHERMYLL of Coventry, draper, v. John [WATERS], Thomas BRACEBRYDGE,
and others. ·
Agreement concerning woods in Kingsbury. *Mutilated. See Files* 1291, *No.* 51; 1330, *No.* 66.
                                                                          WARWICK.

17–20   Henry [NEVILLE], earl of Westmoreland, v. Humphrey HATTON.
Manor of Talworth of the demise of Robert Smythe, solicitor and tenant at will to Ralph, late earl.
                                                                          SURREY.

21–25   Alexander NEVYLL, esquire, v. Anne NEVYLL.
Detention of a gold chain and of deeds relating to messuages, cottages and land in South Leverton,
· late of Anthony Nevyll, knight, deceased, father of complainant and husband of defendant.
                                                                          NOTTS.

26–30   The said Anne v. the said Alexander.
Corn and hay, late of the said Sir Anthony, lying ' untashed ' in the barns and ' tuffolds ' of
South Leverton and Matterson.   NOTTS.

31–33   John NEWCOM, gentleman, v. Nicholas GYRLYNGTON, gentleman.
Refusal to complete a sale of defendant's moiety of the manor of Barnbow and messuages and
lands there and in Barwick, late of John Grenefeld, deceased, grandfather of both parties.   YORK.

34   Richard NEWDICKE and John APULBY v. John RANDES, Agnes his wife, and others.
Land and a messuage in Leverington, late of Bartholomew Edmundes, deceased, great-grandfather
of the said Newdicke and father of the said Apulby.   CAMBRIDGE.

35–38   Benedict, late the wife of William NEWNEHAM (Newenham), knight, v. William MARK-HAM.
Loveley Grange and other lands in Oxton claimed under a lease from the late abbot and convent of Welbeck.   NOTTS.

39–41   John NEWSOME, vicar of Hotonbusshell, v. William [EURE], lord Eure (Ewry), and others.
Tithe hay of Ayton belonging to complainant's vicarage.   [YORK.]

42   John NEWTON v. Thomas ARUNDELL, knight, and William JOLYFFE.
Manor of Milton awarded against complainant in this court (see D. X, 52; File 1311, No. 35). Mutilated.   DORSET.

43–45   William NEYFF v. William NEYFF his first cousin.
Messuage and land in Lesby (i.e. Legsby or Laceby), late of William Neyff, deceased, grandfather of both parties. D. X, 43.   LINCOLN.

46–48   Lambert NOLLOTH and Alice his wife v. John SHORTYNG and Robert NEWMAN.
Messuages and land in Marston, late of Emma, wife of another Robert Newman, and mother of the said Alice.   NORFOLK.

49   William NORRES of Speke, co. Lancaster, and Anne his wife v. JOHN ap Howell and Elizabeth his wife.
Messuage and land in Wrexham.   DENBIGH.

50   Henry NORREYS, esquire, v. William LENTALL.
Lands in Cookham, formerly of William Norreys, great-grandfather of complainant.   BERKS.

51   Edward NORTH, lord North, v. John WYNCHCOMBE of Newbury and Henry WYNCHE-COMBE.
Bond given on behalf of Robert Renacre. Mutilated.   BERKS.

52–53   Walter NORTHCOT of Crediton v. John WELSHE of the same.
Wardship of Walter, infant son and executor of Joan Harris.   DEVON.

54–55   Robert NORTHLEY (Norley) v. Thomas SOUTHCOT, esquire, executor of Thomas Staplehill.
Park of Chuley (Cheveley) in Staverton adjudged to complainant in the Common Pleas. DEVON.

56   Edward NORTON v. James HYATT, esquire.
Detention of a bond for re-conveyance of a barn and land in Newland pledged to William Halle.
                                                                                               GLOUCESTER.

57–60   Thomas NOTTYNGHAM v. Francis, son and executor of John SOONE, gentleman.
Action on a bond for a debt already paid to the executors of Peter Spere, deceased.   ———

61–63   Robert and John NOYES of Littleton, in Kimpton, husbandman, v. George DABRIDG-COURTE (Dabiscourte), escheator.
Distress at Cholderton (Chelerington) in pursuance of an outlawry subsequent to a pardon.
                                                                                               HANTS, WILTS.

64.   George NUNNE v. John HOLT, gentleman, and others.
Corn-rent of the manor of Pakenham Hall and tithe-corn of Pakenham, formerly of the abbot and convent of St. Edmund's. Descent traced.   SUFFOLK.

65   William NUTTALL v. John PEARSON.
Detention of deeds relating to land and pasture in Ely and Downham.   CAMBRIDGE.

66–69   John NUTTELL of Tasburgh v. William HUGHSON, clerk.
Messuage and land in Long Stratton pledged to defendant.   NORFOLK.

70–73   John NYCHOLAS, Jane his wife, Nicholas POLGLAS and Alson his wife v. Jane TRELY-VER and others.
Messuages and land in Mawgan in Pyder, late of John Bertla, deceased, grandfather of the said Jane, Alsom and Jane.   CORNWALL.

74–77   Agnes, late the wife of William NYE, and Thomas NYE his youngest son and heir, v. John PALMER, esquire.
Messuage and land (described) in defendant's manor of Eccleston (in Angmering). Answer and replication wanting.   SUSSEX.

FILE 1457.

1   Thomas NANFAN, esquire, v. John and William NANFAN.
Lands in Birtsmorton, Castlemorton, Barrow, and elsewhere, late of John Nanfan, esquire, deceased, father of all parties.   WORCESTER.

2–5   Ralph NAYLYNGHURST of Great Baddow, gentleman, v. James DRYLANDE.
Hedgebote, ploughbote, gatebote, cartbote and firebote reserved on a lease of lands called 'Mascalles, Kingstons, and Mascalles Gardeyne,' and omitted from a subsequent modification thereof.   [ESSEX.]

6–9   William NEDEHAM, yeoman, v. George COWPER.
Messuage and land in Fairfield of the devise of William Nedeham, grandfather of complainant.
                                                                                               DERBY.

10–12   Robert NELE v. Robert and Laurence, sons of Robert TRUSSE, deceased, and Matthew NAYLER.
Refusal to complete a purchase of a messuage and land in Horncastle by the said Robert the father, whose executors defendants are. Faded.   LINCOLN.

13 Thomas NEVYNZON, an infant, by Stephen Nevynzon, his guardian, *v.* the president and scholars of MAGDALEN College, Oxford, Thomas WARREN, late mayor of Dover, and others.
Rents and lands in Old Romney, Snargate, lvychurch and elsewhere let by the said president and scholars to the said Warren and to Christopher Nevynzon of Adisham, gentleman. KENT.

14 William NEWBOLTE, butcher, *v.* Nicholas NEWBOLTE, shoemaker, and Thomas KENTE, blacksmith, all of Dronfield.
Depasturing land in Dronfield in excess of agreement. DERBY.

15–16 Edmund NEWENHAM, gentleman, *v.* Benett, late the wife of William NEWENHAM, knight.
Detention of a grant of an annuity in Caldecote (Calcott) made by the said Sir William.
WARWICK.

17 Robert NEWMAN of London, gentleman, *v.* William DAVELL of Coxwold, gentleman.
Messuage and land in Carlton [Miniott?], late of Richard Newman, deceased, father of complainant.
YORK.

18 Wilham NEWMAN of Harlow, co. Essex, on behalf of Giles, William, Elizabeth, Susan, and Maude, children of Rowland Edwardes, late citizen and clothworker of London, and of Cuthbert and Nicholas, sons of Nicholas Fuller, late citizen and mercer of London, *v.* Thomas MORE, citizen and mercer of London, and James STANDISHE of Duxbury, co. Lancaster, esquire.
Fraudulent release of a bond given for payments to the said children on account of the marriage to the said More of Elizabeth their mother, sister to the said Standishe. LONDON.

19 Edward NEWPORT, esquire, *v.* Edward PYE, esquire, his uncle.
Composition for an annuity granted to defendant to qualify him as a justice of the peace. ———

20–21 John NEWPORTE of Bridgwater *v.* John WHITE of Cardiff, executor of John White, controller of customs at Bridgwater.
Bond given to the said controller to indemnify him for a disputed seizure of butlerage-wine at Bridgwater. SOMERSET.

22 Richard NEWTON, husbandman, *v.* William HARRYSON *alias* Turnour, yeoman.
Refusal to complete a sale of messuages and land in Newborough. STAFFORD.

23–25 Robert NEWTON *v.* Robert BROMLEY and others.
Detention of deeds relating to a messuage and land in Horsley. DERBY.

26–27 NICHOLAS ap Rees *v.* John WYN ap Meredith and others.
Village or hamlet called . . . yn Wydd in the 'hundred or comote of Dogvellyn,' of the demise of the bishop, dean and chapter of Bangor. DENBIGH.

28 Walter NICHOLL of Chollacombe, husbandman, *v.* John ROOKE and Maude his wife, executrix and late the wife of John Dunscumbe of the same.
Legacy of the said Dunscumbe. DEVON.

29 Francis NOONE of Martlesham, co. Suffolk, executor of Dame Eleanor Lee of London, 'avowes,' *v.* [Richard LEE of Maidstone].
Manor of Great Delce and tenements in Chatham and Maidstone. *Mutilated.* KENT.

30 Francis NOONE of Gray's Inn, esquire, *v.* Richard LEE of Maidstone, esquire.
Destruction of a subpœna. KENT.

31·33 · Robert NORCLIFFE of London, son and heir of John Norcliff of Rochdale, co. Lancaster, *v.* Henry PRESTLEY.
Detention of deeds relating to messuages and lands in Barkisland and Southowram. YORK.

34–35 The same *v.* Thomas GLEYDALE, William PRESLEY, and John BAYLISDEN.
Messuages and lands in the same places. YORK.

36 The same *v.* William WHITLEY and others.
Detention of deeds relating to a messuage and land in Southowram. YORK.

37 John and Thomas, sons of Thomas NORTHE of Bradway (in Norton).
Commission to examine witnesses as to a lease made by the abbot and convent of Beauchief.
DERBY.

38 John NORTON of London, joiner, *v.* the mayor and jurats of DOVER, and Agnes, late the wife of John BENNET, and Henry HARWOOD her stepfather (' father-in-lawe '), deputy-bailiff of Dover.
Action by complainant for money stolen by the said Agnes, the court being packed by the lieutenant of Dover castle with his soldiers. *Corpus cum causa.* KENT.

39 Richard NORTON *v.* Thomas HAMERTON of Stockwith.
Loan. NOTTS.

40–42 William NORTON and Anne his wife *v.* William HERBART.
Lands (*described*) in Thatcham, late of William Bedford, deceased, father of the said Anne.
Second answer wanting. BERKS.

43 William NORTON of London, saddler or coppersmith, *v.* Thomas LAXTON and John his son.
Messuage and land held of the manor of Gretton by John Norton, deceased, father of complainant.
See File 1371, *No.* 55. NORTHAMPTON.

44 Nicholas NOSEWORTHIE of Totnes, merchant, son and heir of William Noseworthie, *v.* the mayor and commonalty of TOTNES.
Action by John Hackwill for trespass on burgages (*described*) in Totnes. *Certiorari.* DEVON.

45   The same *v.* the same and the said HACWYLL and others.
Do.   *Certiorari and subpœna.*   DEVON.

46   Elizabeth NOTTYNGHAM *v.* Thomas WRIGHT.
Messuage and land in Heptonstall.   YORK.

47–49   James NOWELL *v.* Roger TAYLOUR of Northefelde, co. Warwick.
Detention of deeds relating to a messuage and land in Lytle Barre (*i.e.* Perry Barr ?).
                                                                                 [STAFFORD ?]

50   Robert NOYS, late of Littleton, yeoman, *v.* Anthony BOSWELL.
Money entrusted to Robert Boswell of Combe, deceased kinsman of defendant.   HANTS.

51   Robert NUNNE and Alice his wife, late the wife of John Swanton of Bury St. Edmunds,
v. John WOODWARD, shereman, and Edward CRANE, clothier, both of Stratford.
Bond, one seal of which is broken.   SUFFOLK.

52–53   Ellen NUTTELL, [granddaughter ?] and heir of Thomas Howell, *v.* Robert WOLLWARD.
Detention of deeds relating to a tenement in Balsham. *Mutilated.*   CAMBRIDGE.

54   William NYCHOLAS of Swaffham Bulbeck *v.* Francis SKYFF *alias* Skrogges of Albury,
gentleman.
Cost of bringing up Elizabeth, a lame sister of defendant.   CAMBRIDGE, HERTS.

55   John NYCHOLLES of Alveley, son and executor of Richard Nycolles, *v.* [Joan, executrix
and late the wife of John HALL]:
Detention of money and deeds. *Mutilated*   SALOP.

56–57   George, son and heir of William NYCHOLSON, *v.* Elizabeth BOWSHER, executrix, and
late the wife of the said William.
Detention of deeds relating to messuages and lands in Twickenham, Whitton (in Hounslow),
Heston, Worton (in Isleworth), Isleworth, and East Greenwich.   MIDDLESEX, KENT.

58   John NYCOLS *alias* Marshe and Katherine his wife *v.* William ELSONE.
Cottage and land in Birmingham.   WARWICK.

59–60   Roger NYCOLSON of Barking, smith, and Agnes his wife *v.* George, son of John SHYNGLE-
TON *alias* Lee of Stanford Rivers, deceased.
Detention of deeds relating to land in Little Warley.   ESSEX.

FILE 1458.

1–2   Thomas OCKES of High Offley, yeoman, *v.* John CALDWALL of Alston.
Price of oxen sold by William Ockes of Flashbrook (in Adbaston), deceased, father of complainant.
                                                                                STAFFORD.

3–4   The same *v.* the same.
Detention of bonds and of an inventory of the said William's goods.   [STAFFORD.]

5–7   Thomas ODDYNGSELLES *v.* Richard SNAPE and Edward GRYFFITH.
Messuage and land in Long Itchington, late of Edmund Odyngselles, deceased, father of complainant.   WARWICK.

8–10   Philip OKEDEN *v.* Edward ELDRIDGE and ———, late the wife of John OKEDEN.
Lands in Fordingbridge bought of Philip Baskervyle of Bide, co. Wilts.   HANTS.

11–12   The same *v.* Cicell, late the wife of John Okeden his father.
Land in Linwood bought of the same Philip. *Mutilated.*   HANTS.

13   The same *v.* the same.
Alderwood Park in Cranborne demised to the said John by Queen Anne Boleyn.   DORSET.

14–15   Nicholas OLDEMAN of Henley-on-Thames, son and heir of Thomas Oldeman and of Elizabeth
his wife, *v.* Ralph, grandson and heir of Robert CHOWNE.
House called Goddards (in Hambledon), with lands in Hambledon, Skirmett (in Hambledon) and
Turville.   BUCKS.

16–17   Thomas OLDFELD *v.* Thomas BLACKWALL, vicar of Twyford.
Refusal to complete a lease of vicarial tithes of Twyford.   HANTS.

18   Thomas ONSLOWE *v.* John WARDE and Joan his wife.
Dispute as to the extent of a grant of burgages in Baschurch already considered in this court and
in the Star Chamber *Much damaged* D XI, 14   SALOP

19   The same *v.* Francis WARDE, son and heir of the said John and Joan and Katharine his
wife.
Forcible entry on tenements awarded to defendant in the preceding suit.   SALOP.

20   The same *v.* the same.
Ousted from lands in Baschurch in contempt of former decrees. *Attachment.*   SALOP.

21–22   Thomas COKE, husbandman, *v.* Richard BULWER.
Messuage and lands in Dalling of the grant of Thomas Crane.   NORFOLK.

23   John ORGAR *v.* Robert CAMPYON and Thomas THURNALL.
Lands in Babraham, late of John Orgar, deceased, father of complainant.   CAMBRIDGE.

24   Richard ORMISHAE, clerk, *v.* Thomas TYTTELEY of Pool, gentleman.
Loans of money and corn.   CHESTER.

25   William, son and heir of William OSBORNE, citizen and leather-seller of London, *v.*
Richard BAGOTT, esquire.
Reviver of a suit by the said William the father for land in Heatley and Bagot's Bromley (both
in Abbot's Bromley), formerly of William Osborne his kinsman, deceased.   STAFFORD.

26–28   Anselm OSGERBEE of Beelsby, yeoman, v. John FRYER (Frere) and Alison OSGARBIE
Messuage and land in Middle Rasen, late of John Osgerbee, yeoman, deceased, brother of complainant.   LINCOLN.

29–31   Henry OSMUND v. Joan OSMUND.
Detention of a lease of a messuage and land called Blackborough in Kentisbeare made to John
Osmund, deceased, father of complainant and husband of defendant.   DEVON.

32   William OSSANT v. Thomas HOO.
Action on a bond concerning a lease of the manor of Vewters and of lands in Burnham Overy,
Burnham Norton, and elsewhere surrendered to defendant.   NORFOLK.

33   John OVERTON, husbandman, and Margaret his wife, late the wife of Thomas Phips, v.
John PHIPS.
Detention of deeds relating to a messuage and land in Tysoe bought by the said Thomas of the
said John.   WARWICK.

34   OWEN ap David (ap John) of London, clothworker, son and heir of David ap John ap
Dynyved and of Morvyth his wife, v. LEWIS ap Madoc and DAVID ap John ap William.
Land in Garthewyn.   DENBIGH.

35–36   The same v. JOHN ap William ap Grono of Abergele, gentleman.
Do.   DENBIGH.

37   Richard OWEN, gentleman, v. David LLOYD Llewelyn ap Morys, gentleman.
Price of lands and wool sold by Edward Lloyd, brother and servant of complainant.   ————

38   Robert OWEN, student of Lyon's Inn, London, v. MORRIS, OWEN and HUGH ap John
ap Meyricke.
Life-interest of Gwenhover, late the wife of Robert ap John ap Meyryke, in messuages and lands
in Trevenigan and Trewillmet.   ANGLESEA.

39   William OWEN, gentleman, son of Jane verch David ap William, v. Thomas WYN and
William LEWES ap Morgan.
Messuages and lands in the 'parisshes, towenes, felds, and hamlettes' of Treyvarchoyll, Treyva-
chiad and Treyllwndiaid in the lordship of Maynoll Bangor (i.e. Vaynol in Pentyr?).
CARNARVON.

40   Roger OWTON of London, mercer, v. William OWTON, executor of Joan, mother of complainant.
Multiple actions for the same debt on a bond and otherwise. *Mutilated.*   LONDON.

41–43   Richard Marshall, dean of Christ Church, OXFORD, and his chapter v. Henry BERKELEY,
lord Berkeley, and Robert KNIGHT his chaplain.
Advowson of the church of Wotton-under-Edge and chapel of Nibley, late of the abbot and convent
of Tewkesbury.   GLOUCESTER.

44–48   The Chancellor, masters, and scholars of OXFORD University v. John WAYTE, late mayor
of Oxford.
Dilapidation of St. Mary College, Oxford.   OXFORD.

49   Parnell OXLEY v. Nicholas, son of Edward OXLEY.
Annuity charged on a messuage and land in Tunbridge by Nicholas Oxley, father of complainant.
KENT.

50   Richard OXLEY, clerk, v. John REY, late vicar of Scartleffe (i.e. Scarcliff).
Payment for serving defendant's cure.   [DERBY.]

51–56   Richard OYE v. Robert son and heir of John PYKE, and Robert CLARKE.
Messuage and land in Oadby (Odeby, Odeley), stated by the said Pyke to have been granted by
William Oye for repair of highways.   LEICESTER.

FILE 1459.

1   Agnes, executrix and late the wife of William PALMER, v. John BLOUNT of Burton-on-
Trent, gentleman, and John ALSOPP of Blore Woodhouse.
Messuage in West Broughton and lands in Sudbury and Morton whereof the rent is payable to the
said Alsopp for a debt of the said Blount.   DERBY, STAFFORD.

2–4   George PALMES, clerk, receiver of Crown revenues in the diocese of York, v. Francis
LASCELLES, William HOBSON, John DIGHTON, John NOWELL and others.
Appropriated tithes of Golcar, Beaghall, Gatenby, Sedbergh (Sadburye), Hoggett, Thorpe, Maltby,
Barton, Kippax, and Ripon. *Mutilated.*   YORK.

5   The same v. Robert HALL of York, alderman, and others.
Appropriated tithes of Clifton and parsonage of Wressell.   YORK.

6   The same v. John GRESSAM of London, knight.
Corn-rent of the parsonage of Swine.   YORK.

7   The same v. Jenett SAVELL and others.
Terms of the parsonages of Darton, Bradford, Womersley, Bingley, Acaster Malbis, and Marshe.
YORK.

8   The same v. Richard WHALLEY of Welbeck, co. Notts, esquire.
Farm of the parsonage of Scarborough.   YORK.

9   The same v. Edmund KNEVETT.
Spiritual profits of the parsonage of Kirby-on-the-Hill.   YORK.

10   The same v. Thomas WATERTON of Burn, knight, and John BONY, esquire.
Tithe of West Bretton and farm of the parsonages of Sandall and Warmfield.   YORK.

11   The same *v.* John WRYGHT.
Spiritual profits of the parsonage of Welwick.   YORK.

12   The same *v.* Henry NEVELL of London, knight.
Spiritual profits of the prebend of South Cave.   YORK.

13   The same *v.* William EATON, gentleman.
Pension issuing from the parsonage of Bambroughe (*i.e.* Barnbrough).   NOTTS (*rectius* YORK).

14   The same *v.* Robert GRAVES of Newark, co. Notts, gentleman.
Pension issuing from the parsonage of Walton.   YORK.

15   The same *v.* Robert NOWELL, Robert HALL, Henry GASCOYGN, knights, Marmaduke
CLAREGENETT, and others,
Appropriate tithes of Beaghall, Hollym, Holmpton, Clifton, Burnestone, Gatenby, Sedbergh,
Hipswell, West Stansfield, Checkers, Ryttinges, Wheatley, Balne, Brompton, Norton, Scampton,
. . . orton, Rillington, Holme-on-the-Wolds, Wyllesdale, Rillisdale, Ripon and South Duffield,
pensions of. Howgate, Gilling, Ryther, and West Runckford, and parsonage of Bingley. *Mutilated.*
        YORK.

16   The same *v.* Reginald LEE of Southwell.
Corn-tithes of Fiskerton.   NOTTS.

17-18   The same *v.* Philip LOVELL, Joan SAVELL, Richard WHALLEY, Nicholas FARFEX,
knight, Reynold Lee, and others.
Arrears of rents and tithes in Skelton, Darton, Billington, Scarborough, Golcar, Catterick, Alne,
Tollerton, Wharram Percy, Fiskerton, Ratcliffe, Sutton-on-Trent, Normanton, and the deanery of
Pontefract Castle. *Mutilated.*   YORK, [NOTTS].

19-20   The same *v.* Robert GYER.
Farm of tithes of Thixendale (Thistildall) in Wharram Percy.   YORK.

21-22   John PANSFOTE, gentleman, son of Richard Pansfote of Hasfield (Asfyld), esquire, *v.*
Richard SKULL (Scwll).
Waste of lands (*not described*) intended to be settled on complainant at his marriage. (Defendant
pleads a judgment of this court.)   GLOUCESTER.

23   Thomas PARAMOUR *v.* Thomas, son of William CHEVYN, and John and Robert KERE.
Obtaining the annulment of a fine of the manor of [Says] in the Isle of Harty in complainant's
absence. *Mutilated.* D. XII, 18.   KENT.

24-31   Humphrey PARKER of Stoke by Winchester and Alice his wife, late the wife of John Lee,
gentleman, *v.* Richard RO(Y)DON, grandson and heir of Hamnel Ley, and Katherine
YARDELEY his aunt.
Land in Backford bought of Thomas Gawllowe (Yallowe).   CHESTER.

32-35   Roger PARKER of Cheshunt *v.* Robert HOBSON of London, merchant tailor.
Action on a bond for a debt overpaid by distress.   HERTS, LONDON.

36   Thomas PARKER, vicar of Mildenhall, *v.* Roger WRIGHT, late vicar, deprived for simony,
and Margaret WODOWES.
Ousted from the vicarage by colour of a lease from the said Wright.   SUFFOLK.

37   Anthony PARRY *v.* William . . .
Land in Farnborough held of the royal manor of Hanhams. *Mutilated.*   SOMERSET.

38   Thomas PARRYS, citizen and mercer of London, *v.* William LANE, chaplain of Bristol.
Debt of defendant to William Dormer, citizen and mercer of London, who assigned it to complainant.
        LONDON, GLOUCESTER.

39-42   William PARSONS of Salisbury, freemason, *v.* Margaret, late the wife of George PARSONS.
Burgage in Nether Stowey of the bequest of John Parsons, yeoman, father of complainant.
        SOMERSET.

43-44   John PASCALL of Great Baddow *v.* the mayor, aldermen and sheriffs of LONDON and
Richard BRETT.
Action on a bond for delivery of money and a lease of the manor of Barnhall lost in transit by
complainant's servant. *Certiorari and subpœna.*   ESSEX.

45   The same *v.* the sheriffs of LONDON and George FOYSTER of London, carrier.
Action on a bond for a debt already overpaid. . *Certiorari and subpœna.*   LONDON.

46   Thomas PASCALL of Ipswich *v.* Richard WYLES.
Messuages and land in Pascall, late of Richard Pascall, deceased, cousin of complainant.   SUFFOLK.

47   John PASCHALL *v.* Mary, late the wife of John SPONER, gentleman.
Leases of Dengie Hall and Steeple Grange and goods of Robert Arthur of Great Baddow, deceased,
whose executors were the said Paschall and Sponer, whence legacies are claimed by Humphrey
Bagshawe and others (*File 1291, No. 2.*) *Mutilated.*   ESSEX.

48   Nicholas PAULYN, Eleanor his wife, and others *v.* Richard LE, esquire.
Leasehold in Boxley of the demise of Eleanor Le of London, ' vowes,' defendant having the reversion.
See File 1457, No. 29.   KENT.

49-54   George PAYNE, gentleman, *v.* John CASELEY, late vicar of Winscombe (Wynchecombe)
deprived for marriage.
Bond to assure an annuity to complainant on his resignation, for which complainant has given the
advowson of the vicarage of Wedmore.   SOMERSET.

55   The same *v.* Thomas ARTHUR, gentleman.
Money paid on defendant's behalf.   SOMERSET.

56   Gwenllian PAYNE of London v. David BEDOWE, husbandman.
Lands in Clyro, late of John ap Howell, deceased, father of complainant.   RADNOR.

57-58   John PECKE v. Thomas PADLAYE and others.
Peas sown on land of the demise of William Padlaye. *Mutilated.*   NOTTS.

59   Robert PECOCKE, alderman of York, v. Thomas SOWDEN, mayor of Boston, and William
KYDD, late mayor.
Refusal to award process against William Johnson on a judgment debt.   LINCOLN.

60   John PERNNE of Balsham.
Commission to examine witnesses as to a conditional bequest by John his father of a messuage
and land in East Bilney and North Elmham. (Names endorsed are William Perne, W. Baxter, and
Christopher at Howe.)   NORFOLK.

61   Thomas PEROTT, yeoman, and Thomas his son v. Michael THRALE, gentleman.
Crown rent due for corn-tithes and a barn in Luton and Challey (*i.e.* Chaul End in Caddington?),
late held by Robert Perott, deceased, son of the said Thomas the elder. *Mutilated.* D. IX, 49;
XIV, 58. *See File* 1373, *No.* 49.   : BEDFORD.

62   Hugh PERRYN, esquire, v. Mabel, late the wife of Thomas de LA CLOCHE and Clement
their son.
Land and houses in St. Martin's recovered by the said Thomas against Clement Nordest, husbandman, since deceased, who transferred to complainant his rights therein.   JERSEY.

63   John, youngest son and heir of Richard PERYN, v. Lancelot HARRYSON, citizen and
grocer of London.
Quitclaim of a messuage and land in the manor of Walthamstow obtained by false pretences.
          ESSEX.

64-68   Richard PERYN of Launcells v. Denyse, late the wife of John TREVERTHYN of Newlyn,
butcher, and Christopher his son.
Debt of the said John, whose executors defendants are.   CORNWALL.

69   John PETER *alias* Anthony v. John and Raymond MEDLAND.
Land adjoining a river called ' Hedweyr ' in Hatherleigh.   DEVON.

70   Robert PETITE, an overseer of the will of John Thomas of Hailsham, husbandman, v.
John, son and executor of Richard WYNNAM.
Legacy of the said John Thomas to Mary his daughter, Alice his widow having married the said
Richard.   SUSSEX.

71   Robert PEYCOKE of Over Tabley, husbandman, v. Evan DEANE.
Arrest within the liberties of the Duchy of Lancaster on a suretyship for which defendant had
given an oral release.   CHESTER.

72   Morgan PHILLIPES, B.D., prebendary of Tref Garon (Charon *alias* Trecharon), v. John
WYGLE and others.
Lease of the said prebend by Richard Rawlyns, late prebendary, deprived for heresy and marriage.
See File 1376, *No.* 47.   CARDIGAN.

73   William Thomas PHILLIPPE and John Appowell GETHYN, both of Henley-on-Thames,
yeomen, v. Morice APPRICE, clerk, and others.
Messuage, barn and land in Reatt, late of Rice ap Llewelyn and Evan ap Pretheraghe. RADNOR.

74-75   Roger PHILYPPES v. Thomas PRESTON, William LAYTON, Christopher MAUGHALL,
and others.
Lease of a tenement in Rawcliffe occupied by the said Layton and other goods of William Morlay
alias Adams and ——— Dyconson, felons, claimed by complainant under a grant of royalties and
casualties in the manor of Snaith and Cowick. *See File* 1375, *No.* 33.   YORK.

76   William PICKERINGE of London, knight, son of William Pickeringe, knight, v. Roger ap
John WYN.
Tithes of Bryn-tangor belonging to the church of Bryn-Eglwys, of the demise of King Henry VIII.
          DENBIGH.

77-78   Thomas PIGAS, yeoman, v. Edmund ESTOFTE, gentleman.
Trespass by defendant on land in Reedness bought of him.   YORK.

79-81   Richard PLUMSTEDE of Ely v. John BUCKTON.
Tenement in Churchgate Street, Bury St. Edmunds, acquired of Nicholas Estaw.   SUFFOLK.

82-83   Robert PONYARD of Barkway, gentleman, v. Thomas HOLTE of Royston.
Action on a bond for reconveyance of copyhold in Wedyngton held of New College, Oxford, on
condition of repayment of money.   HERTS.

84   Baldwin PORTER of Coventry, gentleman, v. Thomas OLIVER, yeoman, and Alice his wife,
late the wife of Robert Porter, and formerly of Robert Akars.
Escote Hall and other lands in Berkswell, late of John Porter, esquire, deceased, father of the said
Baldwin and Robert.   WARWICK.

85   John PORTYNGTON of Portington, gentleman, Anne his wife, William YAXLEY of
Boston, gentleman, and Rose his wife v. Thomas LYTLEBURYE of Stainby, esquire, and
Ellen MYDDELTON of Wintringham, administrators of the goods of Rose Eland of
Kingston-upon-Hull, deceased, late the wife of John Eland, knight.
Bequest of a gold chain.   . YORK, LINCOLN.

86   John, son and heir of John POULE, v. John WALTON and others.
Detention of deeds relating to a messuage in Leominster.   HEREFORD.

87   Henry POWCOCKE of Speldhurst *v.* [John, son of William WALLER].
Messuage and land, late of Thomas Saker, deceased, grandfather of complainant. *Mutilated.*
                                                                          KENT.

88   Gregory and Richard PRATT, executors of William Pratt of Ryston, gentleman, *v.* William
ADAMS, gentleman, and Margaret his wife, executrix and late the wife of Thomas Craneham
of Downham, yeoman.
Loan of money and a silver spoon.   NORFOLK.

89–90   Richard PRATTE, administrator of the goods of John Pratte of Ervill's Exton (Ervyldes),
deceased, *v.* John ISEMONGER.
Goods of deceased whose widow defendant has married.   HANTS.

91   Richard PRATTE, student of Cambridge and prebendary of Llandarog (Llandorock) in
the college of Abergwili, *v.* Davy PENRY, gentleman.
Arrears of a pension due to complainant's predecessor for a school in the college of Brecon.
                                                            CARMARTHEN, BRECON.

92   Griffith PRICE of London, yeoman, son and heir of Rice Appowell, yeoman, *v.* David
Thomas BEDDO and others.
Detention of deeds relating to messuages and lands in Llandovery, Pencarreg, and Llanybyther.
                                                                          CARMARTHEN.

93–95   John PROWTE, clerk, *v.* Thomas SOMERLAND of Lytle Byrkyll, innkeeper.
Rings and money belonging to George [Dowdall], deceased, archbishop of Armagh, entrusted to
Henry Long, who died in defendant's house.   [BUCKS.]

96   William PYE, B.D., *v.* the sheriffs of LONDON.
Action by William Harper, alderman of London, on a bond for a debt of Thomas [Radcliffe], Lord
Fitzwater, lord deputy of Ireland, already paid. *Certiorari.*   LONDON.

97–100 Nicholas PYERS of St. Nicholas-at-Wade, Anne his wife, and John MOSEREDE her son
v. George BYNGHAM, gentleman, and George TOFTES, executors of Richard Newell of
Canterbury, gentleman.
Repair of sea-walls in the manor of St. Nicholas Court, of the demise of the president and fellows
of Queen's College, Cambridge.   KENT.

101–102 Peter de Rochia PYMENTILL, merchant stranger, *v.* the mayor, aldermen and sheriffs of
LONDON, and Elizabeth WILFORD and Thomas her son.
Action for balance of an account payable at Viana in Portugal and not in London. *Certiorari and
subpœna.*   LONDON.

103   Piers, son and heir of John PYTTES, *v.* Robert STEPHYN and Thomaysyn his wife.
Detention of deeds relating to a messuage and land at Pitten in Yealmpton.   DEVON.

FILE 1460.

1   William, grandson and heir of John PACHETT, and of Agnes his wife, *v.* William BECKE
and Richard CARPENTER.
Messuage and land in the lordship of Bromsgrove formerly of Thomas Pachett. WORCESTER.

2–3   Anthony, son of William PAGE, deceased, *v.* William BRYDGES.
Detention of deeds relating to a messuage and land held of the manor of Hurst. (Demurrer that it
has not been pleaded that the premises are demisable by copy of court roll, etc.) GLOUCESTER.

4–5   Richard PAGETT, citizen and stationer of London, *v.* the mayor and aldermen of LONDON
and Thomas LENTHORPE, citizen and grocer of London, late servant to Edward Moreton,
deceased.
Action on a bond given in return for a promise to obtain money from Joan, late the wife of the said
Edward, and now the wife of complainant. *Certiorari and subpœna.*   LONDON.

6–7   Ralph PAIGE, gentleman, *v.* John ELWYN (Elvyn), executor of John Elwyn of
Weasenham.
Legacy payable to complainant by direction of Edmund Elwyn, deceased's son. NORFOLK.

8–11   John PALMER of London, draper, *v.* Peter WYTT of Yarmouth.
Money, household goods and herrings promised to complainant on his marriage with Katharine,
daughter-in-law of defendant. *Answer wanting.*   LONDON, NORFOLK.

12   Richard PANNELL (Paynell), esquire, *v.*
Settlement of lands in Boothby [Pagnell] on Francis Pannell and Dorothy Hewes *alias* Newell at
their marriage. *Mutilated.*   LINCOLN.

13–15   John PARKYNS *v.* Gregory LOVELL, esquire, farmer of the manor of Richmond.
Messuage and land in the said manor, late of Henry Parkyns, deceased, father of complainant.
                                                                          SURREY.

16   John PAROTT, knight, *v.* Francis [HASTINGS], earl of Huntingdon.
Wood in Belton, late of the abbey of Grace-Dieu. *Mutilated.*   [LEICESTER.]

17–19   Leonard PATERICKE and Elizabeth his wife, both of Rugeley, co. Stafford, *v.* Robert
WHELER, Thomas RYCROFTE, and others.
Lands at Mewton (in Chisbury) of the demise of John Bad(d)y of Bishop's Castle. *Mutilated.*
                                                                          SALOP.

20–23   John PATRIKE of Ingrave, yeoman, and Joan his wife, formerly Joan Foster, *v.* Geoffrey
VAUGHAN and Walter HYNTON.
Messuage and land in Creshed (*i.e.* Creeksea?), late of Elizabeth, wife of John Patrike, and
mother of complainant.   ESSEX.

24-27   Robert PAWLING and Joan his wife, daughter and heir of Robert Partriche, v. Thomas
PYE and Joan his wife.
Messuages called Cattmers and Caltons in Orford.   SUFFOLK.

28   The said Robert PAWLING and Robert his son v. the same.
Reviver of the preceding on the death of the said Joan Pawling. *Mutilated.*   SUFFOLK.

29   The said Robert the elder and Joan his daughter v. the said Joan PIE.
Reviver of the past suit on the death of the said Thomas.   SUFFOLK.

30-36   William PAWLL of Little Burton v. Richard SMYTH of Sherford, esquire, and William
PYWALL.
Joint lease of a pasture in Stretton Baskerville to complainant and the said Pywall.   WARWICK.

37   Francis PAWNUS and another v. [William LUDLOWE].
Bond given on behalf of Edward Ludlowe, esquire, supposed to be deceased. *Damaged.*   ————

38-39   William PAYNE, yeoman, v. Richard MYDDYLCOTE, clothier.
Rent of a falling-mill with two ' stockes ' in Raydon (*i.e.* Rodden?).   SOMERSET.

40   George PEARSON of London, salter, and Katharine his wife v. RICHARD ap Owen.
Detention of deeds relating to lands late of Bedo ap Gough (*sic*), grandfather of the said Katherine.
Faded.   RADNOR.

41-43   Thomas, son and heir of William PECKE, of St. Neot's [co. Huntingdon], v. Robert
ROGERS and Joan his wife, late the wife of John Chapman.
Messuage and land in Burne demised with clause of re-entry to William Chapman, deceased,
father of the said John.   [LINCOLN?]

44   Nicholas PENNYCOT and Anne his wife v. John ERLEY, gentleman.
Plates, household goods and money late of Jane Dorrell, deceased, whereof the said Anne is
administratrix.   ————

45-49   The same v. George DORRELL (Derrell, Darrell), esquire, and others.
Do. (*described*).   PROVINCE OF CANTERBURY.

50   Roger PENSON v.   .   .   .
Cottage and land in Bloxwich, late held of the manor and lordship of Walsall by William Barker
and Mary his wife. *Mutilated.*   STAFFORD.

51-52   Thomas PERESON and Thomas and Robert LEMINGE his uncles and guardians v. John,
son and executor of Nicholas PERESON.
Dilapidation of messuages and lands on the castle, ditch and elsewhere in Wysby[che], and
detention of plate (*described*) and household goods. *Mutilated.*   [CAMBRIDGE.]

53   Jane PERNELL v. John BERNABEY.
Messuage in Witney late of Thomas Smyth, deceased grandfather of complainant.   OXFORD.

54   John PERSONS of Chatwall, son and heir of Richard Persons, v. John HARLEY and others.
Detention of deeds relating to land in Rodington.   SALOP.

55   Oliver PERYN v. Robert RYCHARD *alias* Bose.
Detention and forgery of deeds relating to messuages and land in Gwinear acquired of Philip John.
    CORNWALL.

56-57   John PETEFYLDE, vicar of Earl's Colnes, v. John LEE, late vicar.
Crown debt of defendant.   ESSEX.

58   Philip PHARYE v. John POND.
Messuages and lands in East Orchard held of the manor of Iwerne Minster.   DORSET.

59-62   Morgan PHILLIPP, B.D., parson of Deddington, co. Oxford, and precentor of St. David's,
v. George A LEE, merchant, WILLIAM ap Ryce, and John BOULTON.
Prebends of Lampeter-Pont-Stephen and Spittall and manors of Trefgaron and Landrodeon.
See File 1376, No. 47.   [CARDIGAN], PEMBROKE.

63   Thomas PHILLIPPS of Montacute, esquire, v. John HORSEY, knight.
Recompense promised for the next presentation to the church of South Perrott.   DORSET.

64   The same v. Thomas WHITE of Poole.
Detention of a bond for a debt already paid by the hands of the said Sir John.   [DORSET.]

65-66   Agnes PHIPTON v. Thomas, Richard and Henry FLEMYNGE.
Lands in Kynges Tetnhall, late of William Phipton, deceased, husband of complainant. *Damaged.*
    [STAFFORD.]

67   Richard, son of William PHYLYPP and Rycherd (*sic*) his wife, v. Anthony GREDYN and
others.
Land in Maker of the gift of John Dymmer.   CORNWALL.

68   Roger PHYLYPPE v. Matthew PENKNEY and Thomas HUTCHYN of Snaith.
Rent, toll and casual taxes belonging to a tenement held of the Duchy of Lancaster. *Mutilated.*
See File 1375, No. 33; 1459, No. 74.   YORK.

69-70   The same v. Richard GLEDOWE, husbandman.
Toll of hay in the manors of Snaith and Cowick, which cannot be collected through ignorance of
the amount.   YORK.

71-72   William PICKERINGE, knight, son of William Pickeringe, knight, v. John EDWARDES.
Parsonages and chapels of Chirk, Halton, Llansaintfraid [Glyn-ceiriog] and Bryn-y-groes.
    DENBIGH.

73-75   Bartholomew PLATE (Plott) v. Thomas WATSON and Agnes his wife, late the wife of
John Edmondes.
Messuage and land at Grafton in Langley, bought of John, son of the said John Edmondes.
    OXFORD.

76   Reynalde POLE, cardinal archbishop of Canterbury, v. John VEYSER and others.
Wreck in the manors of Grain (Grene) and Stoke.   KENT.

77–79   Thomas POOLE v. Matthew COLTHURST, esquire.
Land, water-mill and cottage held of the manor of Combe.   SOMERSET.

80–84   John POPHAM and Amy his wife v. ROGER ap William.
Messuages, cottages and land in the manor of Castleton in St. Athan pledged by Hugh Adams,
father of the said Amy, to Robert ap William, father of defendant.   GLAMORGAN.

85   William POPLE of Sampford v. William LANCASTER, a churchwarden of Milverton.
Contract for rebuilding Milverton church. *Mutilated.*   SOMERSET.

86   Stephen PORTER and Margery his wife, executrix and late the wife of William Chester, v.
John, son and heir and executor of John Baker.
Manor of Langney (*i.e.* Longney?) of the demise of Thomas Cromwell, lord Cromwell, and after-
wards of King Henry VIII.   [GLOUCESTER?]

87   Richard POTTER, esquire, v. Robert CROWE.
Rent of a messuage and land in Westham (*i.e.* Westerham?) bought of William, son of John
Cripps.   KENT.

88   Lewis POWELL of Westminster, yeoman, v. Hoell ap Morgan IGHAN and others.
Lands in Merthyr [Cynog]. *Mutilated.*   BRECON.

89   Thomas POWLE, husbandman, v. Michael and John WATTY, executors of Watty Antron,
        grandfather of complainant.
Bequest of household goods.   CORNWALL.

90   . . . POWLE, one of the Six Clerks of Chancery, and George FILBIE, clerk attendant
        therein, v. Silvester COWPER, gentleman.
Sale of woods (*described*) in the manor of Uckfield. *Mutilated.*   BERKS.

91–92   Miles PRAUNCE v. Margaret, late the wife of John WATTON, and John their son.
Action on a bond for a debt already paid to the said John the father, whose executors defendants
are.   ———

93   The same v. the same.
Part of the above debt which complainant had set off against a debt of the said Margaret. ———

94–98   Thomas PRESTE of Wisbech, co. Cambridge, clerk, v. Thomas KYMME of Stickney and
        Elizabeth his wife.
Messuage and land in Spalding and Pinchbeck, late of Richard Bettes, deceased, great-grandfather
of complainant.   LINCOLN.

99   Thomas, son of Arthur PRESTON, deceased, v. William FARFAX, knight.
Annuity due in exchange for the manor of Bilbrough-on-the-Hill and messuages, cottages, mills,
land and rent there.   YORK.

100   William, John, George and Richard PRETTYE, Christopher LYSTER, Joan his wife,
        ———, Mary his wife, Christopher WITLOCKE and Alice his wife v. [William HODYE],
        Henry CROXSTON, and others.
Money to be raised by sale of copyhold in Little Munden, late of John Prettie, deceased, father of
the first four complainants and of the said Joan, Mary, and Alice. *Mutilated.*   HERTS.

101   John PRIOUR of Bramley v. Sir William WHARAM, husband of Elizabeth, late the wife
        of John More of Sherfield, and Walter BEKENSALL.
Lands in Pamber, Chedwell and elsewhere, late of the said More. *Mutilated.*   HANTS.

102–104 John PROCTOUR v. John WOMOCKE, butcher.
Refusal to complete a sale of a messuage and land in Fenton, formerly of Anthony Thorney,
gentleman.   NOTTS.

105–107 Thomas and John, sons of Thomas PULHAM, v. John CURTEIS and Alice his wife, late the
        wife of the said Thomas the elder.
Land in the manor of North Poorton of the demise of Thomas Arundell, knight, deceased.
                                                                                   DORSET.

108–109 William PYE, D.D., parson of Chedzoy, v. Nicholas MASON, late parson.
Dilapidations by defendant, who was deprived for marriage.   SOMERS.

110–112 Edmund PYKE, Katharine his wife, and Simon and William, their sons, v. John BARWYKE,
        esquire.
Refusal to complete a lease of a messuage and lands (*described*) in Wilcot for which payment had
been made to William Allen of Calne, the former owner.   WILTS.

113   Thomas PYKE of London, skinner, v. Henry CAMPYON and Thomas FYSSHER of
        Itchington.
Licence to export beer granted to Edmund Robertes. *Mutilated.*   LONDON, WARWICK.

114   Ralph PYLMER and Margery his wife v. George, son and heir of Richard SHELD.
Revive of a suit for land in Derherst (*File* 1373, *No.* 96). D. XII, 48.   [GLOUCESTER.]

115–118 Agnes (Annys), executrix and late the wife of Simon PYNDER, v. Christopher EGMANTON,
        gentleman.
Price of geldings which defendant states to have been given for a lease of closes in Adling[fleet].
Faded.   [YORK.]

119   Thomas PYNDER, clerk, v. John KYCHYN.
Debt.   SUFFOLK.

120–121 John PYPER and Joan his wife *v.* John HANFORD.
Messuage and land at Dennington in Swimbridge, formerly of John of Denyngton, ancestor of defendant and of the said Joan. *Pedigrees given.. See Files* 1252, *No.* 89; 1462, *No.* 76. DEVON.

FILE 1461.

1 Alexander, son of Alexander PAGE and of Maude his wife, *v.* Thomas DENYS, knight, and William WARD his steward.
Tenement in the manor (*sic*) of Littleham and Exmouth of the demise of John Mere, late abbot of Sherborne. *Mutilated.* D. XII, 36. · DEVON.

2–4 William PAGE of Cullompton, merchant, *v.* Richard VOWLER (Fowler) of Kingswear, shipmaster, and George PERYMAN, servant of John Petor of Exeter, merchant.
Money paid to defendants in Spain by Henry Foxe, servant of complainant, who had received it for kerseys and linen. D. XV, 41. DEVON.

5–6 William PALLEY of Wigston, yeoman, *v.* Richard CATER.
Detention of deeds relating to a messuage and land in Evington. LEICESTER.

7–8 John PANNELL of Pentlow, yeoman, *v.* Alice and Anthony CARTER.
Excessive distress for a debt due to Geoffrey Carter, deceased, father of the said Anthony, and of [John] the said Alice's former husband. ESSEX.

9 The same *v.* Thomas WALE and the said Alice, now his wife.
Do. ESSEX.

10 Bartholomew PARROTT *v.* William MYLLER.
Detention of deeds relating to an annuity charged on messuages and land in Great Brickhill by John Davy, stepfather of complainant. BUCKINGHAM.

11–12 John PAYNE and Agnes his wife, daughter and heir of John Lopdell, *v.* Thomas BURTON and Agnes his wife, late the wife of Nicholas Lopdell.
Detention of deeds relating to messuages and lands (*described*) in Eastbourne, Willingdon, and Hailsham. SUSSEX.

13–14 Thomas PAYNTER of Tewkesbury, co. Gloucester, husbandman, *v.* George FRANCKELYN.
Price of a messuage and land in Sir Thomas Pope's manor of North Leigh. OXFORD.

15 John PECKE, husbandman, *v.* Isabel, Thomas, and George PADLEY.
Crops of land in Heyton hired of William Padley, deceased. *Mutilated. See File* 1459, *No.* 57. [NOTTS].

16–17 Leonard PECKSON *v.* William CHAUNTRY, executor of John Chauntry.
False valuation of goods of the said John, who owed complainant for grain. ———

18–21 John PEERSON, clerk, *v.* Margaret LEEKE and George ELYNGETHORPE, clerk.
Rectory of Warsop. NOTTS.

22 Margaret PEGLER *v.* William SOMERS and James OSWALDE.
Seizure of a gelding on a false pretence of the Queen's service. ———

23–25 John PENFORD *v.* Matthew PENFORD and others.
Tenement in the manor of Brewood. *Mutilated.* STAFFORD.

26 John PERRYN and Philippa his wife *v.* Philip LAMPRIERE.
Lands late of Clement Lampriere and Janette his wife, parents of defendant, and grandparents of the said Philippa. (Custom of the island described.) *Damaged.* JERSEY.

27–28 William PERWYCHE of Brixworth, gentleman, *v.* Henry BROKE, esquire, and Mary his wife.
Manor of Lubbenham and messuages and lands in Middleton and Collingtree of the entail of Richard Perwyche, esquire, grandfather of complainant. NORTHAMPTON.

29 Francis, son and heir of John PETT, *v.* Philip, son and heir of Robert FORMAN of Abingdon, co. B[erks].
Messuage and land in Adderbury. OXFORD.

30–33 Richard PEYTON, student in Grays Inn, *v.* Frances PEYTON.
Legacy of Robert Peyton of Isleham, knight, father of complainant and husband of defendant. CAMBRIDGE.

34–35 Thomas PHELYPPES of Montacute, esquire, *v.* Thomas CHRISTOPHER.
Account of 'avereynge' money and other profits as complainant's deputy-hayward in the royal manor of Shapwick. SOMERSET.

36 Thomas PINCHESTER, husband of Katharine, late the wife of William Best of the Grocers' Company, *v.* Sir John LION of the same company, alderman of London.
Money lent to King Henry VIII and repaid to defendant for distribution. (Defendant pleads for a remedy quicker than the ordinary Chancery process.) *Commission to the Lord Mayor and others.* LONDON.

37–41 John POLEY, esquire, *v.* Elizabeth, executrix, and late the wife of John HARRYE, esquire.
Marriage settlement of complainant's daughter with William, son of the said John. SUFFOLK.

42–48 Agnes, daughter and heir of Thomas POLLARDE, *v.* Thomas POLLARDE and Richard SMYTHE
Detention of deeds relating to a messuage and lands in Ashington, Washington, Wiston, and Thakeham. *See D.* XV, 3. SUSSEX.

49 · Adrian PONYNGES *v.* Peter KNIGHT.
Land in Burmarsh in Romney Marsh, late of Thomas lord Poynings, deceased, brother of complainant. KENT.

50   . . . POOARE, clerk, v. Nicholas SHEPHERDE of Almondsbury (Amesbury), butcher.
Price of tithe calves. *Mutilated.*   GLOUCESTER.

51–52   William PORCOUR of Mark, husbandman, v. John ESGAR of South Brent.
Waggon, iron ropes, a ' solowghe,' a ' solowghe share,' a ' putteshyde,' and other farm implements
entrusted to John Esger, deceased, father of defendant, and guardian of complainant.
                                                                                        SOMERSET.

53–54   Stephen PORTER and Margery his wife, late the wife of William Chester, v. Richard
KITSON and Joan his wife, late the wife of Clement Poweslye, and formerly of Thomas
Chester.
Debt partly repaid by a lease of land in Langley ended by the death of John Chester, son of the said
Thomas, and ward of the said Clement and Joan.   SUSSEX.

55   John P[ORTMAN ?] v. Nicholas HALSWELL.
Tenement in Badgworth, formerly of Henry Portman. *Faded.*   SOMERSET.

56–57   Hugh POTTER v. Robert WRYGHT.
Messuage and land in Caston belonging to James Bulle, an infant, and claimed by complainant as
his guardian admitted, and by defendant and Katherine his wife, mother of the said James, as
his guardians in socage.   NORFOLK.

58–59   Richard POUNTNAY and John WESTE, churchwardens of Lacock, for themselves and all
the parishioners, v. Grace, late the wife of William SHARINGTON, knight, formerly Grace
Pagett.
Church house of Lacock built on a site of the gift of William Draper.   WILTS.

60–63   Richard PRESTON of Preston, co. Lancaster, gentleman, v. Henry GELLESTROP
(Gollestrop), Edmund JACKESON, and others.
Crown lease of the manor of Fulford to Dame Elizabeth Taylebushe.   YORK.

64–67   William PRETYMAN, grandson and heir of William Pretyman, v. Thomas COLVYLE
(Coveld) and Katherine his wife.
Detention of deeds relating to lands in Cotton, Bacton, Mendlesham and Finingham whereof
defendants claim the reversion.   SUFFOLK.

68   Ries David PRICE of London v. John and Philip HOELL.
Messuage and land in Llangattock, late of David Price, deceased, father of complainant.
                                                                                        MONMOUTH.

69–70   John PROCTOR v. John FOXE of Retford.
Refusal to complete a demise of a messuage and close in Sturton.   NOTTS.

71–73   Hugh PRUST of Gorvin (in Hartland) v. John PRUST.
Tenement called Elmscott and land in Hartland late of John Prust, deceased, great-grandfather of
complainant. *See File* 1149, *No.* 78.   DEVON.

74   Hugh PRYNKLETT v. Thomas and Margaret WYNTER [executors of Joan Evans].
Sale and loan of household goods. *Mutilated.*   ———

75–76   Richard PUTTO of Chelmsford, yeoman, v. John DUN of the same.
Tenement and garden in Moulsham bought of defendant.   ESSEX.

77–78   John PYNKE, husbandman, v. Andrew BROUNSMYTHE, parson of Bradley, and John
MICHELL, vicar of Candover.
Bond given to the said Michell in consideration of a lease of the said Brounsmythe's parsonage,
defeated by his resignation.   HANTS.

79–80   John, great-grandson of Thomas PYWALL, v. Barnaby HOLBACHE.
Lands in the manor of Fyllongley, where defendant's brother is steward. *Mutilated.*
                                                                                        [WARWICK.]

81   Richard P . . . ER of Bow . . . v. [John GYLES, executor of William Gyles].
Payment made on behalf of . . . Cassewell on account of a messuage in Totnes and lands there
and in Bowden (in Totnes), Tybbycombe and Bloden in dispute in this court. *Damaged.* DEVON.

FILE 1462.

1   John PACON, Margery his wife and others v. Richard WINECOTT, clerk.
Land held of the Countess of Bedford's manor of Milton Abbot.   DEVON.

2   Robert PAGE of Carlton, co. Northants, grandson and heir of William Cleypole and of
Margaret his wife, v. Robert KYNG.
Detention of deeds relating to a messuage and land in Billesdon.   LEICESTER.

3–5   John PARKE, parson of Nailstone, v. George MEDLEY, esquire, half-brother of Henry
[Grey], late Duke of Suffolk.
Lease of complainant's parsonage by a lay patron.   LEICESTER.

6   Henry PARKER v. Richard WARNER.
Messuage and land in Little Hormead, late of John Parker, deceased, father of complainant.
                                                                                        HERTS.

7   John PARKER, esquire, v. William HEWE of Nynehead, co. Somerset, yeoman.
Land and common of pasture in Broad Clist.   DEVON.

8–9   John PARROTT, knight, v. . . . NYCOLLES, Robert COOKE, and others.
Crown grant of messuages, cottages and land in Kingsthorpe. *Mutilated.* (Defendants claim a
grant of the manor of Kingsthorpe to the tenants thereof.)   NORTHAMPTON.

10–11 Francis PAWLINES v. Richard, son and heir of John HULPONK.
Messuage and land in Bayhurst. *Mutilated.*   [HANTS.]

12   John, great-grandson and heir of Thomas PAYN, v. John WHELER and Thomas LUTMAN.
Detention of deeds relating to a messuage and land in Ardingly. SUSSEX.

13-15   John PAYNE, husbandman, v. Richard WHYTLEY.
Land in dispute between the manors of Flamstead and Humbershoe. HERTS, [BEDFORD.]

16-17   Thomas PAYNE, gentleman, supervisor of the mill of John Myller, gentleman, v. Agnes
WYND, late the wife of Nicholas Baskervile, gentleman, and formerly of the said Myller.
Wardship of Margaret, daughter of the said John Myller, and of the manor of Peresons and other
lands in Thornham and of the rectory. NORFOLK.

18-21   Richard PAYS (Payce) of Studham, butcher, v. Richard PEYTWYN (Pettwyn) of the
same, painter.
Tenement and garden in Studham, late of Thomas Pays, deceased, father of complainant.
BEDFORD.

22-23   John PEARDE, husbandman, son of Orydge Pearde, widow, v. William FUTTES.
Promise of a lease of lands called Lintoñ in Welcombe. DEVON.

24   John PEDLEY, husbandman, v. John NEWMAN.
Messuage and land in Waresley, late of Thomas Pedley, deceased, father of complainant.
HUNTINGDON.

25-28   Nicholas PEKE v. William ALMON.
Refusal to complete a sale of land in Ash by Sandwich. See D. XIII, 9. , KENT.

29   John and Thomas PELHAM v. William HOLLYNGWOD and Joan his wife.
Messuage and land in Terrington. NORFOLK.

30   John PENFORDE of Horsebrook (in Brewood) v. Matthew PENFORDE and others.
Pasture in Brewood of the demise of William Penforde, father of the said John and Matthew.
STAFFORD.

31   John, son of Alice PETT, v. John WARNER.
Agreement for defeasance of a bond to surrender the reversion of a messuage and land in Braughing.
HERTS.

32-39   John, son of George PETVYN, gentleman, deceased, v. Florence, late the wife of Walter
PETFYN, gentleman, Andrew STOURTON, esquire, and Katharine his wife.
Site of the manor of Rimpton, and lands and a mill there. DEVON.

40-41   William PHILLIPPES of Chichester, merchant, v. James BENNET.
Beer which proved sour when exported to Amsterdam. SUSSEX.

42-43   James PLUMLEY v. Richard WYLKYNSON and Alice, late the wife of Robert MUNNE.
Corn-tithes of Frindsbury and Hoo farmed jointly by the said Plumley and Wylkynson. KENT.

44-47 .   Henry POOLE, husbandman, Dorothy his wife, late the wife of John Smythe, esquire, and
Roger, Francis, Clement, Ambrose, Erasmus, William, Robert, Anthony, George and Margery
SMYTHE, children of the said John, v. Robert, son and heir of Richard SAPCOTES, knight.
Action for rent of lands in Gunthorpe (in Oakham) and Martinsthorpe (Marsthorpe), paid in advance
of the specified time. Mutilated. D. XII, 43. RUTLAND.

48-50   Anthony POPE, esquire, v. Nicholas HARRYSON.
Detention of an entail made by John Pope, father of complainant, of tenements called the
Maydenheade in Petty Wales and Beer Lane. LONDON.

51   William POUNDE, esquire, and Anthony WINSOR, gentleman, v. Joan CHEKE and
Robert ANDROWES.
Lands in Arreton, late of Thomas Troyes, deceased, grandfather of complainants. HANTS (I.W.).

52-54   John, grandson and heir of John PREDYAUX, of Orcherton (in Modbury), esquire, v.
Agnes PREDYAUX of Tavistock, late the wife of John Predyaux, and William their son.
Manor of Strete and messuages and lands there and in Burleston and Fuge (all in Blackawton).
See Files 1253, No. 50; 1376, No. 69. DEVON.

55   Thomas PRESTON of Burwell and Agnes his wife v. William CRYSPE.
Messuage and land in Fordham, late of Robert Sprynge, deceased, father of the said Agnes.
CAMBRIDGE.

56   John PROCTOUR v. Thomas SYGISWYCKE and others.
Joint use of a bull in respect of tenancies in Wynterskell. YORK.

57-58   John PROUSE, esquire, v. John ROWE.
Messuage and land called Waye in Chagford, late of Laurence Prouse of Exeter, deceased grandfather of complainant. DEVON.

59   Tristram PRUDHAM and Joan his wife, late the wife of Thomas Belye, v. Andrew
QUYCKE, clothier, and others.
Tenement in the manor of Newton St. Cyres of the demise of John Howe, late prior of Plympton].
Mutilated. See File 1463, No. 1. DEVON.

60-61   Laurence PRYDE v. Cicely, late the wife of John FLAGGE and others.
Land formerly held of the bishop of Salisbury's manor of Candall Bisshopp by John Hylborn.
[DORSET.]

62-69   Thomas PRYME of Halesworth, Ele his wife, and John FLYCKE v. Elizabeth SUCKLYNG,
stepmother of the said Ele, and William JENTYLMAN her son.
Messuage in Southwold, late of Richard Colford, deceased, grandfather of the said Ele and John.
SUFFOLK.

70-71   Beatrice, late the wife of Thomas PUNCHUN, v. Thomas BROWNE, esquire.
Charges for embanking land bought of defendant. Mutilated. Answer and replication wanting.
KENT.

72–75   Ralph PYNDER of London, grocer, *v.* Jane, wife of Hugh WYLLOUGHBY, knight, said
to be gone beyond seas, and George BERESFORD, gentleman, steward of the lordship of
Arnold.
Cottages and closes in the said lordship bought of the said Sir Hugh when a prisoner in the
Counter in Bread Street, London.   NOTTS.

76   John PYPER and Joan [his wife] *v.* John [HANFORDE].
Detention of deeds relating to a messuage and land in Swimbridge. *Damaged. See File* 1461,
No. 120.   DEVON.

FILE 1463.

1   Alice QWYCKE, executrix of Andrew Qwycke, *v.* Nicholas BROWNSCOMBE and John
ROBERTES.
Heriots in the manor of Newton St. Cyres. *See File* 1462, *No.* 59.   DEVON.

2   John RADBERD, parson of Fontmell, *v.* Henry HASKALL.
Lease of defendant's parsonage by a former parson. *Mutilated.*   DORSET.

3–6   James RAGOZZYN, stranger and merchant, *v.* William WEBBE of Salisbury and Thomas
BINGLEY, merchants.
Action in the King's and Queen's Bench for tin bought of John Melhuys, merchant of Cornwall,
since bankrupt.   CORNWALL.

7–9   Thomas RAMPSTON *v.* John DARNELL.
Messuage and garden in Manningtree awarded to complainant in this court. *See File* 1155, *No.* 1.
                                                                                                    ESSEX.

10–12   Myles RAVEN *v.* William BANKES, both of London, merchant tailors.
Loan repayable for purchase of a messuage in Budge Row in St. John's, Walbrook. (No. 11 is an
answer by Thomas Aynesworth.)   LONDON.

13–16   Alyn RAWLYNS *v.* Richard BALLARD.
Messuages and land in Titton (in Hartlebury) held of the manor of Hartlebury, and acquired in
reversion from John Ballard, deceased, father of defendant.   WORCESTER.

17–18   Elizabeth, late the wife of John RAYMONT of London, *v.* Giles RAYMONT and Robert
VADY.
Messuage in Gold Street, Walden, and land there.   ESSEX.

19–22   John RAYNOUR, parson of Wells, *v.* John BANYARD.
Lease of complainant's parsonage made by James Lomlyn, a layman, and acquired by defendant
in exchange for the presentation to the church of Foulsham.   NORFOLK.

23   Henry REDINGE of Exeter, scrivener, *v.* Thomas MARSHALL of the same, merchant,
and Eleanor his wife.
Bond given on defendant's behalf for part price of a messuage in Exeter High Street purchased of
William Blackall(er).   DEVON.

24   John REDMAN of Great Shelford, co. Cambridge, gentleman, *v.* William HOGGE of
Brandon Ferry, warrener.
Rent of part of a messuage called the *Maides Hedde* in Brandon Ferry acquired of Edmund
Sewarde, yeoman.   SUFFOLK.

25–26   Francis REEDE, gentleman, *v.* Christopher STEDMAN, William SMYTH, and others.
Detention of deeds relating to land in Benacre, Henstead and Wrentham.   SUFFOLK.

27   Henry ROBARTSON of Southwell, merchant, *v.* James INCKERSELL.
Bond given jointly to Reynold Lee on behalf of John Gilbye.   NOTTS.

28–31   Thomas ROBERTSON, D.D., archdeacon of Leicester, *v.* Richard MUNDEY and Peter
CROKER of London, grocers.
Loan to William Bellers of Bristowe, co. Leicester, deceased, whose executors defendants are.
                                                                                                    LEICESTER.

32–36   John ROBYNSONNE *v.* Richard SALKELD, descendant of John Prodishow.
(Continuation of File 1466, No. 41). *Pedigrees given.*
                                                                                                    CUMBERLAND.

37–41   Thomas ROCKLEY of Deptford Strond, co. Kent, *v.* Henry SAVELL, knight, grandson-in-
law of William Fytzwilliam, knight.
Messuage and land in Wentbridge (in Darrington and Thorp Audlin) and Darrington, late of
William Halydaye of East Hardwick, grandfather of complainant.   YORK.

42   Anthony ROSLEY *v.* William CARTER and others.
Detention of deeds relating to messuages and land in Cheadle.   STAFFORD.

43   The same *v.* Richard DETHICKE, parson of Breadsall.
Refusal to complete a lease of tithe-hay in Breadsall to last during complainant's lease of Cottall.
                                                                                                    DERBY.

44   Ralph ROWLET, knight, *v.* Richard RAYNESHAWE.
Action on a bond for arbitration concerning waste done in the manor of Pré (in St. Albans).
Mutilated.   HERTS.

45   Charles RUGGE of Newton Poppleford, baker, and William   . ., clothmaker, *v.*
Thomas LEE and John FAR(E)WELL.
Refusal to complete a lease in reversion of land in Aylesbeare. *Damaged.*   DEVON.

46–48   Robert RYCE and Florence his wife, late the wife of Ellis Wymarcke, *v.* Guy WOOD,
brother of the said Florence.
Debt due to the said Florence by John Grenberye and paid to defendant.   LONDON.

49–50   Eleanor RYCHARDES and others *v.* Richard SPYLLESBURY.
Corn-rent iri the Bishop of Worcester's manor of Hallow of the demise of the late prior and convent of Our Lady of Worcester.   WORCESTER.

51   John RYCHARDSON, merchant of the Staple of Calais, *v.* Lawrence SHARPE of South Kyme, carpenter.
Contract to build a house on complainant's land at Conisby.   LINCOLN.

52–53   Eleanor, late the wife of John WYSEMAN of Great Thornham, co. Suffolk, esquire, *v.* Henry CHYTTYNG.
Joint purchase of the manor of Thornborough in Thornton and other lands from Edward Chambarlayne, esquire. (Bill addressed to Stephen, bishop of Winchester, chancellor.) *Commission.*
                                                                                BUCKS, OXFORD.

54–57   Anthony RUSSHE and the said Eleanor, now his wife.
Petition to make replication in the above suit. *See* D. XIV, 15. *Answer wanting.*
                                                                                BUCKS, OXFORD.

58   The same *v.* the same.
Moiety of repurchase price of the premises. *Mutilated.*   [BUCKS, OXFORD.]

59–60   Robert RYVE, prebendary of Bitton, *v.* John AYLWORTH and John SEYMOUR, esquires.
Lease of the said prebend by George Wolfett, late prebendary, the confirmation whereof by the bishop and chapter of Salisbury is void because they are ' not trewly named accordyng to their corporation.'   GLOUCESTER.

FILE 1464.

1–2   Reynold RABET, gentleman, *v.* William ELMYE of South Elmham, yeoman.
Detention of rents and of deeds relating to lands in Bramfield, Thorrington, Westleton, and Swaffham Bulbeck, late of Reynold, his father, and lands in Halesworth, late of Margaret Hird his grandmother, mother-in-law of defendant.   SUFFOLK, CAMBRIDGE.

3   Thomas RAGLANDE of Wallington, knight, *v.* John BULL, yeoman, and William HOGGE of Brandon.
Action on a bond for sale of barley, which complainant's servants delivered in insufficient quantity.
                                                                                NORFOLK.

4–5   John (Thomas), son and heir of Thomas RANDALL, *v.* Thomas DEARYNGE, gentleman.
Detention of deeds relating to messuages and lands in Stodham (in Liss) and Cokkyslande (*cf.* Crockerislonde in Liss. V.C.H. Hants, IV, 84).   HANTS.

6–8   William RATCLIFF of [Exeter], merchant, *v.* George ARRUNDELL, gentleman.
Action for a loan of which the interest is partly paid.   [DEVON.]

9   Thomas READER, parson of Thornton, *v.* William TATHAM and others, all of Ingleton, husbandmen.
Wrongful occupation of complainant's glebe.   YORK.

10–11   Richard REDINGHURST *v.* Joan, late the wife of Richard JENYNGES, and daughter of Richard Redinghurst.
Messuage and land in Binstead, late of Joan Locke, deceased, wife of the said Richard the elder, and grandmother of complainant.   HANTS.

12–15   Thomas REYNES (Raygnes) *v.* Richard his brother.
Loan.   ——

16–18   Joan REYNOLDES, sometime the wife of Richard Moreton, *v.* William FYSSHER, Margaret his wife, Nicholas BROWNE, Alice his wife, and James and Margery TREWYNE.
Lands and half a burgage in Week St. Mary and Jacobstow, late of Nicholas Moreton (Marten), clerk, deceased, great-uncle of the said Richard, Margaret and Alice. *Pedigrees given.* CORNWALL.

19   William RICE, esquire, Thomas THROCKMERTON, esquire, and Margaret his wife *v.* John LITTLETON, esquire.
Water-mill and land in Tibbington, late of William Whorwood, deceased, father of the said Margaret, and of Anne, wife of Ambrose Dudley, knight, after whose attainder his moiety was granted to the said Rice.   STAFFORD.

20–22   Robert ROBERTES *v.* William FYDLER (Fylder) his son-in-law.
Water-mills in Otford and Alton of the demise of [William] Waram, late ' bushopp ' of Canterbury.
                                                                                KENT, HANTS.

23–24   Thomas ROBERTES *v.* Nicholas WHYTE and Alice his wife, late the wife of Thomas, son of complainant.
Life annuity for which complainant granted messuages and lands in Staplehurst to his said son.
                                                                                KENT.

25–26   John ROBYNS, prebendary of M[o]nmore in the church of Wolverhampton, *v.* John LUSON, esquire (gentleman).
House and land belonging to the said prebend (in Wolverhampton).   STAFFORD.

27–29   John, Richard and George ROBYNSON *v.* Richard HODE, John BURGES his tenant, and others.
Tan-house and land in Robertsbridge, late of Richard Hoode, deceased, grandfather of complainants and of the defendant Richard.   SUSSEX.

30 .   Richard ROBYNSON, gentleman, *v.* John LAYTON of West Layton, co. York, gentleman, and Nicholas YONGE, yeoman, servant to Robert Menell, serjeant-at-law.
Slanders and suits in the courts of the bishopric of Durham for lands in Heighington and Auckland St. Andrew, formerly of John lord Scrope.   DURHAM.

31–33   Thomas ROCHESTER and John WALGRAVE, gentlemen, *v.* William CURSON and
William ANDREWE, esquires.
Detention of deeds relating to the manor of Becke in Billingford and messuages and lands in
Billingford, Bylaugh, Foulsham, Wood Dalling, Wood Norton, Brisley, Bawdeswell, Hoo, Foxley,
Worthing, Swanton, Over and Nether Guist, Sparham and elsewhere.   NORFOLK.

34   Richard ROGERS of Whittington, co. Gloucester, and Emma his wife *v.* Thomas BOYSE.
Moiety of a messuage and land in Elmley Lovett, late of John Carter, deceased, grandfather of the
said Emma.   WORCESTER.

35–38   Thomas ROLF the younger *v.* Thomas ROLF the elder.
Messuage and land in Lyminge, late of Robert Rolf, deceased, great-grandfather of complainant
and grandfather of defendant.   KENT.

39–41   John ROLLE, gentleman, *v.* Thomas CLOTWORTHY and John his son.
Waste of lands in Winkleigh during a lease by George Rolle, esquire, deceased, father of complainant.   DEVON.

42–45   Richard ROLLESLEY, gentleman, *v.* Constance, late the wife of Anthony ROLLESLEY.
Detention of deeds relating to the manor of Osleston. *See File* 1377, *No.* 67.   DERBY.

46–48   John ROSIER of Parham Hacheston *v.* Joan, executrix, and late the wife of Nicholas
SMYTH of Halesworth, and John his son and heir.
Detention of a mortgage of lands called ' Bysshoppes ' and ' Elmhams ' (in Hacheston?) made by
John Seman.   SUFFOLK.

49   Stephen ROTHERAM *alias* . . . am of London, gentleman, *v.* Henry ROWTON, clerk,
and others.
Forcible entry on meadows in Cottingham and seizure of a mare and deeds.   YORK.

50   William and Richard, sons of John ROWESWELL, deceased, *v.* John PARKER, gentleman.
Lands in defendant's manor of Torrel's Preston (in Milverton), of the demise of King Henry VIII.
                SOMERSET.

51   John ROWLEY of Rudgewey *v.* John CROXTON, chaplain, and others.
Burgage, one-third of a salt-house of six leads, barn and rent in Nantwich (Wyche Malbane).
Mutilated.   [CHESTER.]

52   Thomas ROYLE of Newbold *v.* Juliana, executrix, and late the wife of Robert WYLCOCKES.
Bond for price of sheep sold to John Pagett of Ravenstone (Raunson), chapman. (The writ is
addressed to Thomas, archbishop of York, but the date is proved by the mention of the queen's
reign.)   STAFFORD, DERBY.

53–55   Anne RUDSTONE, executrix and late the wife of Thomas Fowler, esquire, *v.* Agnes, late
the wife of Thomas CAREWE of Swaffham Bulbeck, husbandman.
Loan to the said Carewe for the health of the soul of the said Fowler.   ESSEX, CAMBRIDGE.

56–57   Thomas RUNCORNE, parson of Crawley, *v.* William SENTELL.
Common of pasture in the manor of Crawley, whereof defendant is lessee.   HANTS.

58   John, son and heir of Henry RYSHETON, *v.* Ralph RYSHETON.
Detention of deeds relating to the manor of Holt and land in Studley.   WARWICK.

59–65   Thomas RYVETT of London, mercer, *v.* Millicent LEIDES of Milford, Thomas her son, and
George BAWNE, yeoman.
Cottages, lands and messuages in Lowthorpe, Skerne, Kilham and Pockthorpe bought of John
Bransbie, clerk, deceased, brother of the said Millicent.   YORK.

FILE 1465.

1–3   Francis RAIGNOLDE, executor of Robert Raignolde, *v.* Robert COLE.
Action on a bond for arbitration concerning lands in the manors of Spencers and Newhall.
                SUFFOLK.

4–6   John RAMBRIDGE, dean of Lichfield, and Robert ATKINS, his servant, *v.* Peter
BRYSTOWE of London, grocer.
Closes demised to defendant by Henry Williams, late dean, to his own use in view of his impending
deprivation for marriage.   STAFFORD.

7   John RAMSDEN *v.* Robert MEYNELL, serjeant-at-law.
Judgment on a bond given on behalf of William Ramsden for prosecuting a writ of error, which he
could not do because imprisoned by order of the Council.   ————

8–11   Robert RANNEWE, husbandman, *v.* Robert LONGE of Little Thurlow, draper, and Isabel
his wife.
Refusal to complete a sale of tenements in Dullingham.   CAMBRIDGE.

12–14   Humphrey RATCLYFFE, knight, *v.* William CROWDER.
Loan of jewels (*described*) which proved to be false.   LONDON.

15–19   Thomas RAUSLEY and Joan his wife *v.* William MASON and Matthew SMYTHE, sons-in-
law of Richard Beseby, and Christopher GIBSON.
Land in Atterby, late of Thomas Witton, deceased, father of the said Joan.   LINCOLN.

20–21   Christabel RAYNARDE *v.* William HUNTE.
Land in Cotingham, late of John Raynarde, deceased, husband of complainant. *Damaged.*
                [YORK.]

22–23   Margaret, Thomas, William and John RAYNES, executors of Thomas Raynes, *v.* Thomas
BEDWOLFF, cooper.
Loan spent on a bargain of wines.   ————

24   John RAYNHAM v. Roger LANGLEY.
Croft in Stoke by Nayland, late of John Raynham, deceased, father of complainant.   SUFFOLK.

25–27   John, son and heir of John REDE, v. George LOSEMORE and William REDE.
Half a mill, messuage, land and rights of common in the said Losemore to manor of Templeton (Temple).   DEVON.

28–32   William REY, Joan his wife, late the wife of Thomas Lancaster of Denshanger, co. Northants, v. Simon MARKBY alias Swyne.
Messuage and land in Mumby of the demise of the abbot of Bawlings.   LINCOLN.

33   The said Joan v. Elizabeth, late the wife of the said Simon.

34–35   Do., the said William and Simon being dead.   LINCOLN.

36–37   John REYDE (Reade), husbandman, v. William NEWPORTE.
Detention of deeds relating to a messuage and land in Haughley Street, Stowmarket.   SUFFOLK.

38   John REYNOLDES and Cycyle his wife, daughter of Thomas Lowman, deceased, v. Richard CARWYTHEN and Katharine his wife, late the wife of the said Lowman.
Messuages and lands in Honiton (Honnyngton) of the demise of Hugh Pollard, knight.   DEVON.

39–40   Philip RIDEOUT v. Richard SEWARD (Sheward), esquire, and John VAGGE.
Joint demise to complainant and the said Vagge of the reversion of a mill and land in the said Seward's manor of Chilcompton.   SOMERSET.

41   William ROBERDES of the Inner Temple v. Isabel, executrix, and late the wife of Edward BYRD, gentleman.
Messuage and land in Gillingham All Saints. Damaged.   NORFOLK.

42–47   Nicholas ROBERT v. John DALE, clerk of the market of Bodmin.
Wrongful occupation of a messuage in Bodmin, failure to return a gelding lent, and interference with the sale of fish in Bodmin market.   CORNWALL.

48   Giles ROBERTES v. John ROBERTES.
Messuage and land in Charlton, late of William Robertes, deceased, grandfather of complainant.   WILTS.

49–50   Robert, grandson and heir of Robert ROGER, v. Richard ROGER.
Forcible entry on messuages and land in Ewell contrary to a decree of Lord Audley in this court, and action in the Common Bench.   SURREY.

51–55   John ROGERS, knight, and Katherine his wife v. Richard ROGERS, esquire, his son and heir apparent, and John CHETTELL, gentleman.
Annuity promised in return for a mortgage of the manor (sic) of Langton(-Long-Blandford) and Littleton (in Blandford St. Mary) and lands there to raise money for the said Richard's relief.   DORSET.

56   Roger ROLFFE of Hadleigh, co. Suffolk, clothier, v. the mayor and burgesses of BOSTON, and James WEST.
Action for price of wool bought to ' indrape.' Certiorari and subpœna.   LINCOLN.

57–58   The same v. the said mayor and burgesses, and Laurence MERIALL.
Do. Certiorari and subpœna.   LINCOLN.

59   John, son and heir of George ROLLE, esquire, and Margaret his wife v. William SCOURRIER, merchant of Taunton.
Detention of deeds relating to houses, burgages and gardens in Taunton. See File 1314, No. 78.   SOMERSET.

60–63   Francis, brother of John ROLLESTON, deceased, v. Edward ASTON, knight.
Land and tithes in Mayfield of the demise of the prior and convent of Tutbury.   STAFFORD.

64–66   William ROMMESDEN (Ramsden) v. Thomas GRENE and others.
Land at Bramley in Leeds. Mutilated.   YORK.

67–68   John ROUNDE (Bounde) and Alice his wife v. Anne AFFORDE.
Messuages and lands in the manor of Ruscombe Southbury demised to the said Alice and to William and Richard Aforde.   [BERKS.]

69   Richard ROWE v. Simon BRADMEADE.
Refusal to complete a sale of a leasehold in Crediton (Kyrton).   DEVON.

70   John ROWLAND of Hove v. George ROWLAND of Marston.
Goods of Alice Hardham, deceased, mother of both parties.   SUSSEX.

71–74   Michael ROWSE of St. Minver v. John TRENOWTHE.
Messuage and land at Gluvian Wartha in St. Columb (Major), late of John Rowse of St. Breock, yeoman, deceased, father of complainant.   CORNWALL.

75–77   Thomas ROWSELEY v. Edward, brother of John ROWESLEY.
Detention of deeds relating to lands in Royston, etc.   [HERTS.]

78   Laurence ROYDE of Templecombe, co. Somerset, gentleman, v. Anthony VENABLES, gentleman, and Dowse VENABLES.
Messuage and land in Aston by Pickmere of the grant of George Woode of Balterley, co. Stafford, gentleman.   CHESTER.

79   John ROYDON, doctor of physic, v. William PEKYNS.
Falsification of a lease of a messuage and land in Cuddesdon.   OXFORD.

80–81   Grace RUDDE of Croxton, executrix, and late the wife of John Rudde, esquire, v. John HOPKYNSON and —— WYLLIAMSON, clerk.
Closes in Newhouse (Newsome) held of Edward Hanbie by the said John Rudde and by Robert Hopkynson of Kirmington, deceased.   LINCOLN.

82   John RUDIERD v. Alexander WOOLLEY and Charles his son.
Close in Silkstone of the demise of Matthew [Stewart], earl of Lennox.   YORK.

83-85   Lybeus RYCHARDSON v. John EAGER.
Pasture in Toynton by Spilsby formerly in dispute in this court   (Files 1314, No. 39; 1379, No. 42.)
                                                                                LINCOLN.

86-88   Richard RYCHE v. Thomas RYCHE.
Messuage and land in Linton sold to both parties separately by Thomas Tuttesham, gentleman,
and Isabel his wife, and awarded to defendant in this court (see File 1379, No. 93).   KENT.

89   Evan RYES of Frodsham, co. Chester, gentleman, v. Griffith RYCHARD and JOHN ap
        Madock ap Edward.
Repairs of a water-mill in Trimley of the bequest of Ryes ap Evan of Leeswood, gentleman.
                                                                                FLINT.

FILE 1466.

1-2   Thomas RAGLAND, knight, v. John TUCKER and Katherine his wife, niece of David
        Maddock.
Messuage and land in complainant's manor of Molton, claimed under a lease from John Ragland,
knight, his father.   GLAMORGAN.

3-5   John, son of John RANALDES (Reynoldes), v. Thomas TUNBRIGE, gentleman.
Messuage (described) in Buntingford Street in John Fylpote's manor of Aspeden.   HERTS.

6   Crystyne, sister of Richard RAWLE, v. Richard WHYFFYN and others.
Tenement in the manor of Sturminster-Newton Buckland.   DORSET.

7   Michael RAWLYN, husbandman, v. Benett RAWLYN.
Messuages, lands and rents in Trembeth (i.e. Trembleath) in St. Mawgan (in Pyder), late of Isabel
Rawlyn, grandmother of complainant and mother of defendant.   CORNWALL.

8-9   Richard RAWLYNS of Henley-on-Thames, storeman, v. Henry, son of Henry VYNES,
        and others.
Pasture (described) in the lordship of Remenham demised by the said Henry the elder to Robert
and Anne, parents of complainants. Mutilated.   BERKS.

10   The same, alias Rawlynson, v. John BEVINGTON, gentleman, and John VENER, yeoman.
Detention of the lease of the above and forcible ouster.   BERKS.

11   Richard RAWLYNSON v. William MASTEN alias Westall.
Cottages and land in Greasbrough (Gresbroke), Greasbrough Byerlaw, and Rotherham, late of
Robert Masten alias Westall, uncle of complainant.   YORK.

12-14   John READER v. Nicholas ELSTON (Elverston).
Messuages and land in Wormshill bequeathed to both parties jointly by John Pratt of Lenham
to the use of his mill.   KENT.

15   Thomas, grandson and heir of Richard REDE, esquire, v. William, son and heir of Henry
        SQUERRY (Scurry).
Wrongful occupation of messuages and land in Petersfield during the absence of Richard, father of
complainant, in King Henry VIII's service at Térouenne and Tournay. D. X, 37. (See File 1467,
No. 39).   HANTS.

16-18   Joan REIGNOLDES v. William FYSSHER, Margaret his wife, Nicholas BROWNE, Alice
        his wife, and others.
Detention of deeds relating to lands and half a burgage in Week St. Mary and Jacobstow, whereof
the said Margaret and Alice are tenants in reversion, being complainant's daughters.   CORNWALL.

19   Anthony RESTWOLD, esquire, v. Richard VERNEY, knight.
Detention of deeds relating to the manor of Hurst and lands there sold by complainant to Thomas
Warde, esquire.   BERKS.

20-21   REYNOLD ap John of West Horsley, co. Surrey, clerk, v. JOHN ap David ap Richard and
        AGNES verch Griffith.
Meadow in Llanynys in the lordship of Dyffryn Clwyd, late of Madoc ap Llewelyn, deceased,
grandfather of complainant. Bill in duplicate.   DENBIGH.

22-27   The same v. JOHN ap Harry ap Howell and JOHN ap Griffith ap Hugh, grandson and
        heir of Hugh ap Eigyon, clerk.
Messuages and land in Halltin and Ewloe, late of David ap Res, deceased, great-uncle of complainant.   FLINT.

28   RICHARD ap John, yeoman, v. David GOZ ap Griffith ap Edneved and JEVAN ap Moris.
Loan.   LONDON, MERIONETH.

29   RICHARD ap Hoell v. John JEVAN ap Pullo ap David.
Seizure of stock after procuring complainant's imprisonment on a charge of murder.   BRECON.

30   Richard ap Hoell v. JEVAN ap Thomas.
Action on a bill satisfied by a feoffment of land in Llanvigan, the consideration never having been
paid.   BRECON.

31   The same v. THOMAS ap Thomas, husbandman, and THOMAS ap Meredith.
Messuage and land in Llanvigan of the demise of complainant.   BRECON.

32   RICHARD ap John of London, baker, v. MARGARET vergh John and JOHN ap Llewelyn.
Messuage and land in Brogyntyn (Porkynton), formerly of David ap Hoell, grandfather of complainant.   SALOP.

33-34   RICHARD ap Robert, parson of Bryngwyn, v. RICHARD ap Hoell, gentleman.
Lease of complainant's parsonage by Humphrey Lloyd, late parson.   RADNOR.

35   RICHARD ap Llewelyn v. Roger VYCARYS and William CONNOP.
Land in Pembryge, late of Thomas ap Llewelyn (sic), deceased, father of complainant.
HERTS (rectius HEREFORD).

36   RICHARD ap Thomas ap Griffith, serving-man, v. WILLIAM ap Mathewe and others, all
of Chirbury, co. Salop.
Land in Worthin, late of Thomas ap John ap Griffith (sic), deceased, father of complainant.
RADNOR.

37   Nicholas RICHMAN of Great Yarmouth v. Victor MOLLINGE.
Land in Heringham bought of Agnes Bixteley alias Cowper.
NORFOLK.

38   Robert RIGGELEY and Agnes his wife v. William TANNER.
Goods of John Tanner, deceased, brother of defendant, and former husband of the said Agnes. ———

39   ROBERT ap John ap Jevan v. MARGARET verch Jevan ap Tedder.
Land in Dyserth (Thesserte), late of Thomas ap Jevan ap Tedder, deceased, uncle of complainant.
FLINT.

40   John ROBERTES of Clifford's Inn, gentleman, son of Robert ap Howell ap Gruffydd, v.
HUGH ap Meredith ap Ryes.
Land in Penmen Beyno formerly of David Robert, Annes verch Lewis his wife, and others
(named).
CARMARTHEN.

41   John ROBYNSON, great-nephew and heir of Richard ROBYNSON, clerk, v. Richard
SALKED.
Lands in [Brigham] of the late chantry of Mosser founded within the parish church of Brigham.
See File 1463, No. 32; also Calendar of Patent Rolls, Edward VI, vol. II, p. 70.   CUMBERLAND.

42   Thomas ROGER v. John CHECHESTER, gentleman.
Lands in Frythstocke of the demise of the monastery of Frythestocke. Mutilated.   [DEVON.]

43   Owen ROGERS of London, stationer, and Rose his wife v. JOHN ap Griffith ap John.
Messuage and land in Bodfari, late of David Lloid, deceased, father of the said Rose.   DENBIGH.

44   Richard ROKEBYE, gentleman, v. John RASKELL.
Leaseholds in Stoke and Ponton. Mutilated.   LINCOLN.

45-46 Edward, son and heir of John ROLFFE v. Joan ROLFFE.
Detention of deeds relating to a messuage in Bottisham.   CAMBRIDGE.

47   William ROOKES and Margaret his wife v. Nicholas HARVY.
Messuage called the Middle House in Halstead, late of Robert Harvye of Great Maplestead, deceased,
father of the said Margaret.   ESSEX.

48-51 Anthony ROSLEY (Rollesley) v. William CATER and others.
Detention of deeds relating to messuages and land in Cheadle.   STAFFORD.

52-55 Ralph ROSYER of London, esquire, v. Thomas ARRUNDELL, gentleman.
Detention of a bond for a sum already paid in respect of defendant's marriage with Margery West,
step-daughter of complainant. Damaged.   LONDON.

56   Lionel ROULSTON of Pontefract v. Agnes, executrix and late the wife of John LAWE
of Saxby.
Barley which the said John had contracted to deliver.   YORK, LINCOLN.

57   Thomas ROWE of Halesowen, butcher, v. William SOWTHALL of Frankeley, husbandman.
Non-delivery of cattle sold.   [WORCESTER.]

58   Margaret RUDDING of St. Neot's, co. Huntingdon, granddaughter and heir of Thomas
Rudding, v. John PILGRYME of Elmdon, husbandman.
Detention of deeds relating to a messuage and land in Claveton.   ESSEX.

59   William RUDSTONE, gentleman, v. Christopher BURGOINE, esquire.
Money and lease of the manor of Oakington (Okenton, Hoggkenton) promised on complainant's
marriage with Elizabeth, daughter of defendant.   CAMBRIDGE.

60-61 William RUSSKE v. John, son and heir of RUSSKE.
Lands in Castle Thorpe (in Hanslope), late of Thomas Russke, deceased, grandfather of complainant. Mutilated.   BUCKINGHAM.

62-63 Edmund RYDDELSTONE of Manchester, yeoman, v. Francis PENDELTON of the same,
cotton-man.
Seizure of a shop and stock in Manchester demised by defendant to work on shares.   LANCASTER.

64-67 Lancelot RYDLEY, D.D., v. Thomas PARKYNSON [clerk] his brother-in-law.
Parsonage of Willingham whereof complainant expected to be deprived by reason of his marriage.
Damaged.   CAMBRIDGE.

68-70 William, Robert, Thomas and Thomas (sic) RYE v. Salmon WYLKYNS.
Messuage and land in Preston and Luddenham, late of Edward Rye, deceased, father of complainants.   KENT.

71   Christopher RY[SBYE], husbandman, v. Thomas SMYTHE of Carlton, co. Northants,
husbandman.
Messuage and close in the royal manor of Easton, late of Henry Rysbye, deceased, cousin of complainant.   LEICESTER.

72-73 Roger RYSSHETON (Russheton) v. John WHITEHED alias Holden, vicar of Ryall.
Lease of defendant's vicarage. See File 1377, No. 91.   RUTLAND.

74   Thomas RYTHE and Constance his wife, granddaughter and heir of Constance, wife of Roger Lewkenor, knight, v. Edmund FORDE.
Conveyance of the manor of Harting and lands in East and West Harting, Wenham (in Rogate), Rogate and Ashurst (Atchurche) *alias* Fridinghurst (in Chiddingfold) obtained by undue influence from Henry Wyndesore, brother of the complainant Constance. *Damaged.*   SUSSEX, SURREY.

75   John son and heir of Robert RYVETT of Waldringfield v. Andrew RYVETT.
Annuity secured on the site of the manor of Cretingham instead of on the whole manor as promised. *Mutilated.*   SUFFOLK.

76-80   John RYXMAN, vicar of Brixham, v. John PLUMLEY and Edward HARRYS.
Rent (including wine) and tenths of complainant's benefice.   DEVON.

FILE 1467.

1-3   John SACKFORDE v. Anthony RUSSHE, esquire.
Lease of the manor of Mere Hall in P[layford ?], Bealings and Rushmere, and of lands, sheep-courses and fisheries there and in Bucklesham, Martlesham and Newbourne. *Mutilated.*   SUFFOLK.

4   John, son and heir of Richard SANBAGE, v. Richard INGRAM and John his brother.
Lands in Little Wolford of the demise of the said Richard Ingram.   WARWICK.

5-7   Thomas SAVAGE of Stafford, mercer, v. Thomas WATWOOD (Wetwood) and Richard ALYN, bailiffs of Stafford.
False return of no effects to a writ of execution against James Clemence.   STAFFORD.

8-11   Henry SAXY of London, mercer, and William his brother, clerk, v. Edmund [BONNER] bishop of London.
Presentation to the treasurership of St. Paul's, the grant of which by the late bishop has been burnt.   LONDON.

12   Joan, late the wife of Thomas SHADWELL, administrator of the goods of John Dyer, deceased, v. Thomas ASTLEY and John COX of Ludlow, gentleman.
Non-payment of rent of a messuage and land in Leintwardine, and detention of a lease thereof made by the abbot and convent of Wigmore.   HEREFORD.

13   William SHAKESPERE v. Roland DAVID.
Messuage, barn and land in Stockwellgate, Mansfield, late of Robert Shakespere, deceased, father of complainant.   NOTTS.

14-17   William SHAWE of London, skinner, v. John CROWE.
Tenement in Markington, late of Richard Wrightson, husbandman, deceased, great-grandfather of complainant and grandfather of defendant.   YORK.

18-20   Michael SHORTE of Reepham, husbandman, v. William RAWCEBY, Agnes his wife, Thomas STANLEY, and John BOLTON, husbandman.
Lease of a messuage and land in Willingham acquired of the said William and Agnes.   LINCOLN.

21   John SMYTH of Isebroke, co. Glamorgan, husbandman, v. John WATTES, mayor of Bridgwater.
Iron seized as pirate's goods.   SOMERSET.

22   Richard SMYTHE, parson of the church (*sic*) of Brington, Bythorn, and Old Weston, v. Thomas ROWSELEY, gentleman.
Lease of complainant's parsonage.   HUNTINGDON.

23   Thomas SMYTHE of Birmingham v. Joan, late the wife of Hugh ESTWICKE of Bewdley, and Henry Segewyck her brother.
Price of iron sold to the said Hugh, who has taken sanctuary at Westminster and conveyed his goods to the said Henry.   WARWICK, WORCESTER.

24-25   Thomas SMYTHE v. Edward LEWES, son-in-law of William Parramour.
Manor of Over Stanway and messuages and land in Nether Stanway.   SALOP.

26-28   Thomas SMYTHE v. Makelene, late the wife of Thomas STEPHYN and administratrix of his goods.
Action on a bond for a loan already repaid and on another bond for assignment of a lease of mills called ' Crasse Mylles ' in St. Botolph's. *Mutilated.*   MIDDLESEX.

29-31   George SOUTHCOTE v. Richard HARTE.
Clerkship of the peace, to which complainant was appointed by letters patent of King Henry VIII, and defendant by Thomas Denys, knight, *custos rotulorum.*   DEVON.

32-36   George SOUTHEWORTH of ' the Highe Felde,' esquire, v. Herman CURTALL of Derby, surgeon.
Fee to be returned in default of cure. (Defendant pleads that complainant, contrary to his orders, ate eggs at midnight, green apples sodden in milk, and peascods.)   LANCASTER, DERBY.

37   Francis SOUTHWELL, esquire, and Alice his wife, late the wife of John MYNNE, v. Nicholas LUTTRELL, esquire.
Messuages and land in the royal manor of Week Fitzpaine, now farmed by defendant.   SOMERSET.

38   Edward, son and heir of Thomas SPROTT, v. Hugh HYLL.
Seizure from a tenement in Ashmorebrook (in Lichfield) held at will of defendant of goods and deeds relating to messuages and lands there and in Great and Little Abnall and Pipe (in Lichfield), Chorley, Hammerwich, Burtonwood, Longdon, Cannock, Rugeley, Barr, Walsall, and Farewell, and burgages in Lichfield.   STAFFORD.

39–40   William SQUERY, gentleman, nephew and heir of Philip Squery, v. Thomas REDE.
Messuages and land in Petersfield recovered in this court against Robert Acton, knight, and Margaret his wife (D.X, 27.)   *Damaged.   See File 1466, No. 15.*   HANTS.

41   John STANDERWYK, executor of John Pinney, vicar of Stokenham, v. John HALS, esquire, and others, inhabitants of Stokenham.
Arrears of rent of the chapel and tithes of Sherford, part of complainant's benefice.   DEVON.

42–43   John, son and heir of John SWALLOWE, v. Roger WENTWORTH, esquire.
Land in Bocking held of defendant's manor of Bocking Hall and claimed as profit for non-payment of rent.   ESSEX.

44–46   The same v. John WENTWORTH, esquire, son and heir of the said Roger.
Do.   ESSEX.

47–51   Robert SWETE v. Thomas CRAYKE.
Goods of Henry Swete, clerk, deceased, whereof complainant is administrator.   DIOCESE OF LINCOLN.

52–57   Henry SYDDALL, vicar of Walthamstow, v. Edmund WYTHYPOLL, gentleman.
Vicarage and part of glebe of Walthamstow.   ESSEX.

58–64   Robige (Robryge), executrix and late the wife of Robert, son and executor of Thomas SYLLY, v. George HARNYGE, Mary his wife, late the wife of Thomas Compton, gentleman, Peter BRYSTOW, and Henry GAYLORD.
Tenements in Yeovil of the demise of John Burnell and claimed as held of the said Harnyge's manor of Newton Sermonville.   SOMERSET.

65–66   Richard SYMOND of Fittleworth, yeoman, and Thomas BROWNE, a minor, v. Alice BROWNE.
Legacy of Edward Browne of Fittleworth, father of the said Thomas, of whose will the said Symond is supervisor and defendant is executor.   SUSSEX.

67–70 · Hugh SYNCOK, husbandman, v. John WALSHE, Joan his wife, Richard BAGYLHOLE, Thomasyne his wife, and William, son of John CLYVERDON, feoffee to user.
Share of messuages and land at Milford and South Hole in Hartland, late of John Cola, yeoman, deceased, grandfather of the female defendants and of Agnes, mother of complainant.   DEVON.

71   Richard SYSMER v. John SYSMER.
Messuage and land in Liddington and Thorpe, late of Richard Sysmer, deceased, father of both parties.   RUTLAND.

72–75   Brian SYSMER of Over, co. Cambridge, son of the above complainant, v. the same.
Do.   RUTLAND.

FILE 1468.

1–3   The masters, scholars and fellows of ST. JOHN'S COLLEGE, Cambridge, v. John HERON, Edward SLEGGE, and John PYNDER, a fellow of the college.
Lease of Hilton Farm void by alienation and dilapidation.   HUNTINGDON.

4–7   Griffith SALESBURY, gentleman, brother and heir of John Salesbury, v. GRIFFITH ap John ap Meredith, gentleman, son-in-law of Robert Salesbury, deceased.
Lands in Istorabrill and Mathebroyde awarded to complainant in this Court (D. IX, 56).   DENBIGH.

8–9   Alice, late the wife of Christopher SALTER, and Joan and Jane his daughters and heirs, v. Henry SALTER.
Lands in Buckerell, formerly of William Salter, father of the said Christopher and Henry.   DEVON.

10–13   Agnes and Alice, daughters of Richard SAMWELL, deceased, v. William ALBRIGHT, brother and heir of Elizabeth Samwell.
Messuage and land in Offley, late of John Samwell, deceased, brother of the said Richard and husband of the said Elizabeth.   HERTS.

14–15   William SCAILLES, discoverer of concealed lands, v. William GASCOIGNE, knight, Michael WRIGHT of Islington, innholder, and others.
Maintenance in a suit for debts supposed to be due from complainant to the said Wright and paid by the said Sir William.   MIDDLESEX.

16–19   John SCKOSE of Menheniot v. Stephen MABYN of the same, husbandman.
Detention of deeds relating to a messuage and land in Penquite (in St. Ive), late of John Shore, deceased, father of complainant.   CORNWALL.

20   Henry SEMER of Blandford Forum, capper, v. Thomas KEYNELL of Hinton St. Mary, yeoman.
Refusal to complete a sale of a tenement in Blandford and a close in Langton.   DORSET.

21–22   William SEVEGAR *alias* Sugar of Bridgwater, shoemaker, executor of William son of John Baker, v. Simon JENKYN and John BRADLEY.
Half a messuage and land in Bicknoller of the demise of Giles James *alias* Sweting.   SOMERSET.

23–25   Alexander SEYMOR v. Thomas GODDERD.
Messuages and land in Blandford, late of Isabel, mother of complainant (Elizabeth, wife of Alexander Seymor the elder?) and daughter of Tristram Stoke.   DORSET.

26   William SHAFTE and Thomas NELE v. William NELE, father of the latter.
Board and lodging in a messuage called the *Lyon*, in Shaftesbury, promised to the said Thomas on his marriage with the said William Shafte's daughter.   DORSET.

27–28   John SHARPE v. John BOTHOME.
Detention of deeds relating to a messuage called the *Angel* in Derby.   DERBY.

29   William SHELDON, esquire, v. William BARNES.
Land in Chelmscote (in Brailes) and Brailes, late of the gild of St. George in the chapel of St. James, Warwick.   WARWICK.

30   Robert, son and executor of Matthew SHEPARD, yeoman, v. Thomas PERSSEY of Islington, gentleman.
Manor of Farnfields and lands in Harringay of the demise of Hugh Oldham, late bishop of Exeter.   MIDDLESEX.

31–32   William, son and executor of Thomas SHERRARD, v. William MAYOT and Elizabeth his wife.
Money buried by the said Thomas in his house at Cowall for fear of robbers.   STAFFORD.

33–34   Thomas SIMCOKE v. Humphrey HOLFORD his stepfather and Edward GOLBORNE.
Leasehold, messuages and land of the bequest of Thomas Simcoke, father of complainant.
Mutilated.   CHESTER.

35   Edmund SKELTONE of London v. Oswald SKELTONE.
Messuage, tenant-right and land called Lyntwayte, late of Roger Skeltone, deceased, father of complainant.   CUMBERLAND.

36   William SMODINGE, yeoman, v. John MORSE.
Wrongful occupation of land in Aylesford of the demise of John Seath of Milton, gentleman, and Thomas his son, and false charges in the King's and Queen's Bench.   KENT.

37–39   Nicholas SMYTH, gentleman, son and heir of Joan wife of Thomas Smyth, v. George NORTON, knight, and Elizabeth his wife, late the wife of Lord Audley [of Walden].
Land held of the manor of [Saffron] Walden. D. XV, 1.   ESSEX.

40   William SMYTH v. John PANKERS and others.
Cattle and household goods (*described*) of the bequest of Richard Smythe of Farnham, whose executors defendants are.   SUSSEX.

41   Ambrose SMYTHE of Whepstead, co. Suffolk, yeoman, v. Nicholas LEGGE, scrivener.
Bargain of lands in Sturston, Tottington and Stanford. *Damaged.*   NORFOLK.

42   William SNEDE, knight, v. William CLIFF, dean of Chester, and William WALL and Nicholas BUCKSEY, prebendaries.
Lease of a messuage in Northgate Street and two closes in Chester, invalid by reason of a former lease.   CHESTER.

43   Edward, a son and executor of Adam SOWGATE, v. Christopher ROPER, esquire.
Detention of a lease made by the master, fellows and scholars of St. John's College, Cambridge, of a messuage and land called Elverland in Ospringe. *See File* 1384, *No.* 42.   KENT.

44–46   The same v. Robert SAYER.
Do.   KENT.

47–48   William SPARROWE v. John HARVYLL and Margaret his wife.
Loan to the said Margaret as a merchant sole.   ————

49   Ralph SPRATT, citizen and merchant tailor of London, v. Thomas PIERSON of Wrexham, mercer.
Debt due to Thomas Spratt of London, salter, brother and debtor of complainant.
                                                                    LONDON, DENBIGH.

50   Robert, great-grandson and heir of Robert STABULL, v. William ATKYNSON, mayor of Nottingham.
Land (*described*) in the women's market at the end of the flesh-shambles of Nottingham, claimed on behalf of the mayor and commonalty. *See File* 1380, *No.* 57.   NOTTS.

51   Gawyn STANGER of London v. James STANGER, Richard his brother, and others.
Non-performance of an award made by Thomas lord Wharton, lord [warden] of the East and Middle Marches, to compromise an appeal of the murder of Richard Stanger, father of complainant.
                                                            LONDON [NORTHAMPTON].

52–56   Walter STAPLEHILL of Exeter, gentleman, v. Joan STAPLEHILL, Richard CHUDDE-LEGHE, knight, Thomas SOUTHCOTTE, esquire, and Thomas COLLYN.
Manors of Bremyll *alias* Bremlegh (in Trusham) and Chevelegh (in Talaton?), and lands there and in Ashton, Christow, Kennick (in Christow), Tryssame *alias* Trysme (*i.e.* Trusham), Kingsteignton, Ilsington, Highwell, Staplehill (in Highweek), Kylmescroft (*cf.* Kiln Down in Christow), Kyddon (*cf.* Kiddon's Plantation in Higher Ashton), Exminster and Wolcombe. *See Files* 1268, *No.* 66; 1382, *No.* 42.   DEVON.

57   Randolph, son of John STARKEY, deceased, v. John TENCHE, clerk, an executor of the said John, and Ralph TWYSE.
Goods of Mary Starkey, sister of complainant.   [CHESTER?]

58   Robert STARLYNG of Dedham, clothier, v. Mark ANTHONY of London, merchant stranger.
Goods of Geoffrey Rayman, late of London, a debtor of complainant, and debt due to him.
                                                                    ESSEX, LONDON.

59–60   Thomas STEPHYN of Berythropp (*i.e.* Burderop in Chiseldon?), v. Joan his mother.
Action for dower in the manor of Inglesham already compounded for. *Mutilated.*   WILTS.

61–62   Joan STEVENS v. Thomas her son.
Refusal to join in an action against Thomas Key(es), M.A. of Oxford, on a bond for the education of Jerome, also her son.   [WILTS?]

63   John STEVYNS v. Anne, late the wife of Humphrey TALBOT.
Path of Blockley and keepership thereof with a warren, and tithes of corn and hay at Northwick in Blockley (Northewake).   WORCESTER.

64–67   William STOKES v. John BYRON, knight, and Richard HUMFREY, esquire, feoffees to uses, Richard HUDDELSTON, and Margery his wife.
Messuages and lands in Barton-on-the-Wold, Prestwold, Wymeswold, Barrow-on-Soar, Quorndon, Sileby, Woodthorpe, Knight-Thorpe, Thorpe Acre, Sheepshed, Osgathorpe, Belton, Breedon, Castle [Donington?], Nenyborowe (rectius Queniborough?), Slawston, Dodesworth (i.e. Diseworth?) and Cotes, formerly of William Stanton.   LEICESTER.

68–70   Robert STONESBY, gentleman, and Bartholomew HYLTON, grandsons and heirs of Bryan Stabler, v. William GRYMSTON and others.
Rent charged on a messuage and land of the said Grymston at Mowthorpe in [Kirkby] Grindalythe.
                                                                    YORK.

71–72   John SYBSAY, late of King's Lynn, co. Norfolk, gentleman, v. Thomas MASSYNGBERD, esquire.
Messuage and land in Thorpe and Freston, late of William Thorpe of Partney, gentleman, deceased.
Rival pedigrees given.   LINCOLN.

FILE 1469.

1   Eleanor, late the wife of William SACKVILE of Dorking, esquire, and administratrix of his goods, v. Thomas MONYNGES, executor of John Monynges, lieutenant of Dover castle.
Action of debt left undefended on a promise to abide the arbitration of Robert Broke, knight, C.J.C.P., since deceased.   SURREY, KENT.

2–6   Otes SAGAR, vicar of Warmfield, v. Nicholas TEMPEST of Wadland, esquire.
Claim of right of way through a close in Wakefield bought for the foundation of an almshouse.
                                                                    YORK.

7   Robert SAVAGE, parson of St. . . ., Bristol, and William BEDFELDE, churchwarden, v. Thomas PACYE and others.
House built for the parson of the said church by David Leyson of Bristol, merchant, deceased.
Damaged.   GLOUCESTER.

8   John SELYOCK v. Richard CRYMES and John HARRYSON.
Detention of deeds relating to the manors of Dronfield and Redbourne.   DERBY, LEICESTER.

9   John SELYOCKE of Hazlebarrow (in Norton), gentleman, v. Thomas DIGNAM.
Extent of the manor of Dronfield for an annuity whereof the redemption money has been paid.
                                                                    DERBY.

10   Henry SERLE of Histon, co. Cambridge, gentleman, licensed carrier of grain, v. John ALMONSON.
Action on a bond for shipment of grain from Cambridge to Dover, which was stopped at Lynn by the Queen's command.   ———

11   Luke SERRET v. Harry LANGYFFORD.
Land at Sowton in Petertavy.   DEVON.

12   The same v. Stephen and John SOWTON.
Do.   DEVON.

13–18   The same v. William, nephew and heir of Richard LANGIFFORD.
Do.   DEVON.

19   Alen SHARRAT and Anne his wife v. Thomas Cotton of WHITCHURCH.
Contempt of an order of commissioners appointed by this court to permit the redemption of lands pledged by Thomas Mawdley, father of the said Anne.   SALOP.

20–23   William SHAWE, yeoman, v. Giles BRYDGES.
Assessment by the Commissioners of Sewers on pasture in West Ham held of defendant.   ESSEX.

24–26   Thomas SHEREWOOD and Joan his wife v. Richard CHAPMAN alias Tanner of Chideock (Chedwike).
Lands in Whitchurch, late of Mabel . . . dys, mother of complainant. Faded.   DORSET.

27   William SHEREWOOD, student at Oxford, v. John PARSONS, Elizabeth his wife, late the wife of John Horne, and others.
Sheep entrusted by John Gregory to John Horne of Hordley (Herdley), father of the said John, to provide an annuity for complainant.   OXFORD.

28   Ralph SHERMAN, yeoman of the Ewry, and Margery his wife, a daughter of Piers Dutton, knight, v. Ralph DUTTON, her brother.
Money due to the said Margery out of the manors of Halton by Waverton, Brixton, etc., and messuages and lands there and in Waverton, Chowley, Claverton, Pulford, Golbourn-Bellow, Rushall, Tattenhall, Crook-Aldersey (in Carden), Kettlehulme, Marbury, Norbury, Great and Little Barrow, Littleton, Christleton, Wardle (Wordhull), Milton, Allostock, Nether Peover, Hawarden, Mancott, Handbridge and Chester. Damaged.   CHESTER, FLINT.

29–30   Thomas SHITTELWORTH v. Simon HOPSTER.
Price of goods supplied.   ———

31–32   Katharine, late the wife of Thomas SKARDEVYLE, and Robert his youngest son and heir, v. John SKARDEVYLE his eldest son.
Messuage and land held of the manor of Hunston. Answer wanting.   SUSSEX.

33   John SKETE, husbandman, *v.* Thomas GAWDYE of Rockland, esquire.
Building and land in Wortwell, Redenhall, and Denton, late of Nicholas Skete of Norwich, deceased, brother of complainant.   NORFOLK.

34   The same *v.* the same and Francis GAUDYE of London, gentleman.
Do.   NORFOLK.

35   John, youngest son and heir of William SLUTTER, of West Grinstead, husbandman, *v.* Roger GRATWEKE.
Tenement in the manor of H . . . , formerly of the chantry of St. Leonard. *Mutilated.*
SUSSEX.

36   Henry SMYTH of Milton (Medylton), co. Kent, yeoman, *v.* Edward LEWYS.
Messuage in Dudley, late of Thomas Smyth, deceased, father of complainant.   WORCESTER.

37–39   Richard SMYTH *alias* Pergetour *v.* Edmund ANYSLE of Cornwell, executor of Thomas Smyth, and Bartholomew REDHED of Highgate, co. Middlesex.
Messuages and lands in Chipping Norton, Stow and Slaughton, late of Richard Smyth *alias* Pergetour, deceased, grandfather of complainant.   OXFORD, GLOUCESTER.

40–43   The same *v.* Bernard NICOLLSON and John RYDDER, sons-in-law of Thomas Smyth, and Emma Smyth his daughter. •
Messuage and land in Chipping Norton.   OXFORD.

44–48   Robert SMYTH of Derby, pewterer, *v.* Ellen, late the wife of Humphrey BENTLEY.
Messuage called 'Fraunces House' with grounds in Derby.   DERBY.

49   Thomas SMYTH of Petworth, co. Sussex, weaver, and William SMYTH *v.* John STEVYNS of Godalming, weaver.
Messuages, barn and land held of the royal manor of Godalming by Richard Smyth of Godalming, weaver, and Elizabeth his wife, both deceased. *Mutilated.*   SURREY.

50   John SMYTHE of London, grandson and heir of entail of Robert Horne, *v.* Lancelot HARRYSON of London.
Action on a bond for conveyance of messuages and land held of the manor of Walthamstow Tony.
ESSEX.

51   John SMYTHE, clerk, LL.D., collector of tenths, etc., for Cardinal Pole in the diocese of Llandaff, *v.* Thomas MORGAINE, knight.
Parsonage of Caldicott, late of the monastery of Llanthony.   [MONMOUTH.]

52–54   Richard SMYTHE of Boxford, yeoman, and John SMYTHE of Bures St. Mary, mercer, *v.* Robert ROOKE and Katharine his wife.
Bedding and cattle entrusted to defendants by Thomas Smythe, clerk, deceased, whereof complainants are administrators.   SUFFOLK.

55   Robert SMYTHE *v.* Richard EMERYE and John, son and heir of John FANNE.
'Hedde manor,' houses, lands and feedings (*described*) in Thaxted, of which a lease with exceptions was promised by the said John the elder.   ESSEX.

56   Thomas SMYTHE *v.* William REDE, gentleman, administrator of the goods of Ralph Colyn, deceased.
Action on a bond for conveyance of the life-interest of Joan, mother of complainant, since deceased, in a house and garden in the parish of St. Katherine Coleman.   LONDON.

57   Henry SNOWE and Joan his wife, late the wife of William Colynson, *v.* Elizabeth, late the wife of Philip LYN, and John his brother.
Forgery of acquittance of a debt due to the said Collynson, whose executors complainants are.——

58   Edward SOUNDE *v.* Robert SOUNDE and others.
Land in Church Shocklach and Shocklach of the demise of Robert Sounde, father of complainant,
CHESTER.

59   Robert SOUTHWELL, knight, Robert, Michael and William FOSTER, George CRISTMAS, Bridget his wife, —— Cotton, . . . his wife, and Ja[ne FOSTER?] *v.* Alice, executrix and late the wife of George FOSTER.
Issues of the manors of Easthorpe and Great Birch of the bequest of Robert Foster, esquire, father of the said George Foster, Robert, Michael, William and the female complainants. *Mutilated.*
ESSEX.

60–62   Nicholas SPURGEON *v.* John HALE and Robert BRYANT.
Messuage and land in Great Maplestead of the bequest of John Spurgeon, father of complainant.
Terms of will disputed.   ESSEX.

63   Randle SPURSTOE of Wolseley, co. Stafford, esquire, *v.* Robert WADE of Church Minshull.
Leasehold in Tarporley pledged to defendant. *Mutilated.*   CHESTER.

64   William SQUIRE of Hanbury *v.* the bailiffs, aldermen and chamberlains of [WORCESTER].
Action by . . . Wynnes, Dorothy his wife, and George, son of John Newport of Droitwich, gentleman, for a rent of wood payable for the keepership of the park of Feckenham. *Corpus cum causa. Mutilated.*   WORCESTER.

65   Roger STANDYSHE *v.* Thomas FLETWODE (Flytwode), esquire.
Detention of deeds relating to messuages and land in Shevington and Standish.   LANCASTER.

66   Thomas STAPLE and Elizabeth his wife, executrix, and late the wife of John Monoux, *v.* William LYTTELTON.
Part price of timber, stone, and household goods.   WORCESTER.

67		Thomas STAPULLS of Buckby, yeoman, Alice his wife, George CARTER of Bishop's Itchington, Agnes his wife, Thomas BOTT, and John BOTT his guardian in socage v. John KEY, William WYSSETTER, and Margaret his wife.
Detention of deeds relating to messuages and lands in Dunchurch and Toft, late of William Tytley, deceased, father of the female complainants, and of Isabel, mother of the said Thomas Bott. *Mutilated.*									WARWICK.

68		William STAVELEY of London, grocer, v. the mayor and sheriffs of LONDON and Nicholas STAVELEY of London, mercer.
Action on a bond given on behalf of Christopher Staveley of London, grocer, brother of the said William, who was then a minor and his apprentice. *Certiorari, subpœna and commission.*
LONDON, YORK.

69		John STELE of Heteley, co. Stafford, v. Humphrey GRONEDYRDGE, gentleman.
Messuage and land in Donington [in Holland], late of William Stele, deceased, uncle of complainant. *See File* 1352, *No.* 59.							LINCOLN.

70		John STEPHYNS, servant to Mr. Holmes, [master?] in Chancery, v. William STEDMAN of Minsterley.
Rent of sheep-pasture in [Minsterley?] of the demise of Richard Stephyns of Minsterley, deceased, father of complainant. *Mutilated.*							SALOP.

71–72	William STOCKWITH, clerk, v. William SYMCOTTES.
Hospital of St. John the Baptist, Huntingdon, with messuages and lands in Stukeley, Folksworth, Stilton and Yaxley.							HUNTINGDON, NORTHAMPTON.

73		John STODEARD of London, clothworker, v. the sheriffs of LONDON, and Robert [RICHARDES?], Thomas STANNYLANDE, and others.
Action concerning stock in the hands of complainant bequeathed to him and the said Stannylande for six years' use by John Toloes, alderman of London, their master. *Certiorari and subpœna. Mutilated.*									LONDON.

74		Thomas STOKAM v. Robert ROGER and Jane his wife.
Waste and refusal to obtain on complainant's purchase of the reversion of a messuage in Moregate.
NOTTS.

75		Adrian STOKES, esquire, and Frances, duchess of SUFFOLK, his wife, v. Henry [STANLEY] lord Strange.
Sale of wood pending a partition of the manor of Curry Rivell and the forest of Neroche (Roche).
SOMERSET.

76–79	William STOKES, gentleman, v. Robert SHEFFELD.
Land in Great Gidding of the demise of Thomas lord Vaux of Harrowden.			HUNTINGDON.

80		John STORYE, D.C.L., v. John READE of Westminster, gentleman.
Prebend of Kentish Town (Canteloes), claimed under a lease from ——— Layton, late prebendary.
LONDON.

81–83	Jane STOURTON of Up-Cerne, co. Dorset, executrix and late the wife of Roger Stourton, v. Thomas STANTOUR of Horningsham, esquire.
Sheep and cattle pastured by defendant at Longford.					WILTS.

84–87	The same (Sturton) v. Elizabeth, late the wife of the said Thomas STANTOUR and Roger his son.
Do.										WILTS.

88		Giles STRACHY and Joan his wife, executrix and late the wife of William Herne (Heron) of Sudbury, merchant.
Petition for a commission of bankruptcy for the said Herne's debts, the said Joan being his creditor for dower. *Four names endorsed, presumably creditors or debtors.*			SUFFOLK.

89		William STRANGWAIES of Haselbury Brian v. Richard AGAR and Elizabeth his wife, executrix, and late the wife of John B(r)istoo.
Detention of a bond delivered to the said Bristoo to implead John Symcott, a clerk in the King's Bench.									DORSET.

90		John STRETE of London, vintner, v. John AWDREY.
Money obtained under pretext of getting a licence for complainant to sell wines which he had met, though a member of the Innholders Company. *Mutilated.*				LONDON.

91		John STROWDE v. William GYLLET and others.
Detention of deeds relating to messuages, cottages and land at Watercombe in Warmwell.
DORSET.

92–93	Thomas STRUTTE v. Peter HARPER *alias* Clerbecke, both of Southwark, carpenters.
Cost of board and lodging to be set against a loan.					SURREY.

94		Thomas STURMEY of Mourdon v. William DYETTE.
Action on a bond for hire of sheep, whereof payment has been tendered. *Mutilated.*		?

95–97	William, son of Thomas STURTON (Storton, Stourton, Turton) v. Ralph LEAKE of Hasland (Housland), co. Derby, esquire, and Robert, Guy, William and Richard SAMPOLE.
Messuage called the *Crown* and land in Bawtry of the demise of the said Leake. *See File* 1307, *No.* 14.										YORK.

98		Henry, son and heir apparent of Thomas STYLE (Stille) of Talaton, gentleman, v. John EVELEGH, gentleman, Thomas WEKES, and Margaret his wife.
One-third of a messuage and land in Larkbeare settled on complainant at his marriage with Thomazyn Skynner, kinswoman of the said Evelegh. *Faded*				DEVON.

99–101   John, son and heir of John SWETEALL v. Robert CURTEIS of Mendham, co. Norfolk.
Detention of deeds relating to a messuage and land in Somerleyton.   *Replication wanting.*
                                                                           SUFFOLK.

102–103 Humphrey SWYNERTON, esquire, v. Robert NOWELL.
Falsification of a bond given to James Nowell of Hylcotte, deceased, father of complainant.
                                                                           [WILTS ?]

104   John Sym . . ., vicar of . . ., v. Richard MYCHELL.
Lease of tithe corn made by Robert Pytman, late vicar, who ' of his carnall and dyvelyshe mynde
tuke and maryed a wÿff.' *Mutilated.*   SOMERSET.

FILE 1470.

1   The dean and chapter of the cathedral church of ST. AUSTEN, . . ., v. Humphrey
WORTHE, gentleman.
Parsonage of Somerton, of the demise of [Edward Seymour] duke of Somerset. *Mutilated.*
                                                                           SOMERSET.

2   Thomas Trysham, knight, prior of ST. JOHN OF JERUSALEM in England, and his
co-brethren, v. John THROUGHGOOD and Anne COCKE.
Detention of deeds relating to the manors of Clerkenwell, Newington Barrow *alias* Highbury,
Hackney, etc.   MIDDLESEX.

3–5   Henry SALESBURYE of Whitechapel v. Jacomyne, executrix, and late the wife of Boniface
MEURES *alias* Vawse of London, beer-brewer.
Compensation for bad beer supplied for export.   MIDDLESEX.

6   Christopher SAUNDERS, Joan his wife, late the wife of William Cockes, and Nicholas and
John COCKES, her sons, v. Robert MUTTYLBURY.
Life-rents, leases, etc., promised in exchange for the lease of the barton and capital mansion of
Buckerell and of land there.   DEVON.

7–8   Anthony, son and heir of Thomas SAUNDERSON, v. William ALLYSON, John JACSON,
and others.
Messuage and land in Frizington (some of defendants cannot appear in court, being warned by
the Lord Warden of the Marches for service at an hour's notice).   ·   CUMBERLAND.

9–10   Richard SAVERY of Totnes v. Henry FOXE.
Price of sack, which defendant declares to have been taken by the King's butler at Dartmouth, so
that he never received it.   DEVON.

11–13   John SEINT JOHN, gentleman, King's and Queen's serjeant-at-arms, v. George CARR.
Crown lease of Ticknall grange.   DERBY.

14   John SELTFORD and Agnes TWYGG, executors of Richard Twygg, v. William CART-
WRIGHT of Wybunbury, Joan his wife, and Thomas HOLME of Avenbury.
Money and lease of land in Stockton made by Richard [Sampson], late bishop of Coventry and
Lichfield.   CHESTER.

15–16   Isabel, late the wife of Alexander SEYMOUR, v. Thomas MATHEW and John GODERD.
Manors of Wendlebury and Marchehad . . . and messuages and land in the parish of Byrse
 . . . (*i.e.* Bicester ?) claimed by complainant as dower and on behalf of the said Mathew in
reversion. *Mutilated.*   OXFORD.

17   The same v. Peter COWPER *alias* Mownsell and John OLYVER.
Lands entailed by complainant's father. *Mutilated.*   DORSET.

18   George SHARPE, vicar of Wandsworth, v. Myles KNARESBROWE, farmer of the rectory.
Tithes of corn.   SURREY.

19–23   Ralph SHEFFYLDE v. William VAUX, lord Vaux of Harrowden.
Lease of a mill and meadow in Irthlingborough promised on the surrender of a former lease by
Giles, brother of complainant.   NORTHAMPTON.

24   John SHERWOOD v. John ATMERE and John BACON.
Debt of Nicholas Everard for which complainant was bound, and which was assigned to the said
Bacon by the custom of the city of London.   LONDON.

25–27   Edward SHOVELER of Maldon, mercer, guardian *pour cause de norture* of Henry and
Elizabeth Bedwell, v. Thomas EDWARDES, late the husband of Agnes their mother.
Household goods of the bequest of Simon Bedwell of Hullbridge in Hockley, father of the said
wards.   ESSEX.

28   [John] grandson [and heir of Swythen SKERNE] v. Margaret, William and Thomas
HUSSEY.
Houses and lands in Kingston-upon-Thames, Southwark, St. Sepulchre's without Newgate, and
[Skerne]. *See File* 1382, *No.* 18.   SURREY, LONDON, YORK.

29   Simon SMALLEY of Weston, co. Stafford, yeoman, and Maude his wife v. Francis
MOUNTFORDE.
Detention of deeds relating to a messuage called Wynnley (*i.e.* Windley ?) in Sutton Coldfield, late
of Thomas Mountforde, esquire, deceased, grandfather of the said Maude.   WARWICK.

30   Ambrose SMYTH and Agnes his wife v. Roger POTTER and others.
Messuage and land in Whepstead.   SUFFOLK.

31–32   John SMYTH, esquire, son and heir of Sir Clement Smyth, v. Nicholas ANDREWES and
Barbara his wife.
Action for price of a messuage in Knightrider Street already paid.   LONDON.

33-34 Ralph STANDISSHE, fellow of Trinity College, Cambridge, and doctor of physic, *v.* William HARMAN, Elizabeth his wife, and Anne ROBERTES.
Legacy of Richard Standisshe, D.C.L., brother of complainant, whose executors the female defendants are. CAMBRIDGE.

35-36 William STOCKER, clerk, *v.* Thomas BENGER.
Prebend of Milton Manor in Lincoln Cathedral, claimed under a lease from James Courthopp, late prebendary. [OXFORD.]

37 Robert STYLE, executor of John REYNER, *v.* Charles FRAMLINGHAM, administrator of the goods of Dame Elizabeth Tylney, deceased, late the wife of Lionel Tallmage, esquire.
Farm called 'Kyttes of the Felde' and other lands in Ash-Bocking and Hempston. *See File 1067, No. 58.* SUFFOLK.

38-39 John SUTTON *v.* Roger JELYON.
Pasture in Leverton, late of John Sutton, deceased, father of complainant. LINCOLN.

40-41 Godfrey SWAYNE *v.* Edward, son of George LUMBARDE.
Refusal to complete a sale of two messuages near the Round Church in Cambridge, one called the *Horne.* CAMBRIDGE.

42-45 John SWYGO, 'merchant millenor,' an executor of Baptist Boron of London, 'merchant millenor,' *v.* Adrian (VAN) AFFRAN, Dutchman.
Bed-furniture of crimson velvet awarded to complainant in the Admiralty and in this court. *Ne exeas regnum and injunction.* LONDON.

46-49 Richard SYVYAR, Joan his wife, Thomas MORBRED, and Alice his wife, *v.* Robert LAMBE, gentleman, and Mabel his wife, great-granddaughter and heir of Robert Ponte.
Messuages and land in Salehurst, late of Thomas Andrew of Robertsbridge, yeoman, father of the female complainants. SUSSEX.

FILE 1471.

1-2 Andrew SADELER of Aston Tirrold, yeoman, *v.* Anne, executrix, and late the wife of Thomas READE of Abingdon, gentleman.
Refusal to complete lease of a messuage and land in Long Wittenham. BERKS.

3-5 John SAMPSON and Joan his wife, executrix and late the wife of Thomas Jamys, and Isote JAMES *v.* Martin JAMES, clerk, and others.
Goods of the said Thomas, father of the said Isote, of whose will defendants claim to be supervisors. CORNWALL.

6-9 John SAUNDER of Yearde *v.* Thomas TAWKE of Rookley (in Arreton).
Refusal to complete a sale of Westborne (*i.e.* Westbrook in Brading?) in exchange for sheep. HANTS (I.W.).

10-14 Edward SAUNDERS, knight, C.J.K.B., and others, feoffees to uses, and the mayor, bailiffs and commonalty of COVENTRY, *v.* Thomas BONDE.
Land in Old Fillongley granted by Thomas Bonde, grandfather of defendant, to establish a 'beade howse or an almes howse' at the Bablake in Coventry. WARWICK.

15 John, Richard and . . ., gentlemen, sons of Laurence SAVAGE of Wall Grange, esquire, deceased, *v.* Mary, late the wife of Edmund SAVAGE, knight.
Goods entrusted to the said Sir Edmund and to John Savage, knight, for division among complainants. *Mutilated.* STAFFORD.

16 Robert SAY, gentleman, and Agnes his wife *v.* Anthony AGAR of Fleet.
Detention of a copper pan ('lead') and nails and of deeds relating to a messuage (*place omitted*), late of Simon Whyte, former husband of the said Alice. LINCOLN.

17 John SENHOUSE of Seascale, Elizabeth his wife and Anne BARDSEY *v.* Walter STRICKLAND of Sizergh, esquire, and Eleanor EGLESFELDE.
Detention of deeds relating to the manors of Eldenborough (Alenburghe) and Eaglesfield and messuages and lands in Drigg, Carleton, Whinfell, Blindbothel, Gilcrux and Dearham, late of Richard Eglesfelde, esquire, deceased, brother of the female complainants and husband of the said Eleanor. CUMBERLAND.

18-20 George SERLE *v.* Thomas CHEKE and Joan his wife.
Refusal to complete a conveyance of a reversion of pasture in Shalfleet. HANTS (I.W.).

21-25 William SHERLEY of West Grinstead, gentleman, *v.* Francis SHERLEY of the same and others.
Goods (*described in answer*), late of Thomas Sherley, esquire, deceased, father of the said William and Francis. SUSSEX.

26 William SKAILLES and Margery his wife *v.* John JENKYNSON, late of Cusworth, labourer.
Cottage in Womersley of the demise of William Gascoigne of Cusworth, knight, since deceased. YORK.

27 . John SMARTE, parson of Wallington, *v.* Robert NEWPORTE of Sandon.
Occupation of complainant's parsonage under a lease from John Eyreson, late parson, deprived. HERTS.

28 The same *v.* the same and George NEWPORTE his brother.
Contempt of an injunction in the above suit. HERTS.

28 . George SMYTH *v.* Philip OCDEN.
Manor of Linwood, late of Nicholas Smyth, deceased, father of complainant. HANTS.

30 Hugh SMYTH and Richard FENTON *v.* Roger FOLJAMBE, gentleman.
Messuage and land in Sheffield of the bequest of Anne Fenton, mother of the said Richard. YORK.

31   John SMYTH v. John SPENCER, Agnes his wife, Thomas HARRISON, and Thomasyn
his wife.
Tenement in Wirksworth bequeathed with others in Derby, Idridgehay and Higham by Robert
Smyth, uncle of complainant.   DERBY.

32–37   John SMYTHE of Barnstaple, son and heir of Paul Smythe, v. Robert GREEDE (Grade),
Thomas THORNE, and others.
Tenements in the town or burgage (sic) of North-Molton of the bequest of John Hethelurd Atwyll
(sic).   DEVON.

38–39   Richard SMYTHE v. Thomas, son and heir of Robert HUDSON.
Messuage and land in Louth, late of John Smythe, deceased, father of complainant.   LINCOLN.

40   Robert SMYTHE of Derby, pewterer, v. Robert and Thomas, sons of John BROCKHOUSE
(Brookehouse), of the same, tanner.
Money promised by the said John on complainant's marriage with his daughter.   DERBY.

41–43   Anne SPARKE v. Henry MUSKETT.
Land held of defendant's manor of Harleston Hall by Andrew Sparke, late the husband of complainant.   SUFFOLK.

44   John SPARLING of London, ' abiding in service . . . towardes the lawe,' v. Ralph
HARKEY of Harwhaite, yeoman.
Cattle promised in compromise of a slander.   YORK.

45–47   Leonard STAFFORD, parson of Newton Tony, John THISTALTHWATH, gentleman, and
Richard ANDREWES of Dean, yeoman.
Parsonage of Newton Tony, claimed under a lease from John Smithe, late parson.   WILTS.

48–51   Walter STAFFORD, esquire, v. Walter WHITALL, gentleman, Richard WORTHINGE-
TON (Warrington), John STONE, and others.
Claim of common in Bentley Hay, demised to Henry [Stafford], late lord Stafford, with the hays
of Alrewas, Cheslyn, Ogley, Gailey, and Teddesley.   STAFFORD.

52–55   William STANBRIGGE of Frome Selwood v. Richard LECETOUR and Katherine his wife.
Messuage and land in the manor of Wraxall demised jointly to complainant and to John Stokes,
former husband of the said Katherine.   SOMERSET.

56–60   Thomas, grandson and heir of John STANDBRIDGE, v. John STANLEY and Robert
SEBROKE.
Messuage and land in Cheddington, formerly of Hugh Standbridge, grandfather of the said John.
                                                                                                BUCKINGHAM.

61–62   Thomas STANLEY, lord Monteagle, and William PARRE, marquis of Northampton, v.
Christopher and Thomas ROGERSON.
Land in Sedbergh claimed under a lease from the late abbot of Jervaulx.   [YORK.]

63   John STANYFORTH of Gere Lane, smith, v. Thomas HOLME.
Land held of the manor of Eckington by Joan Stanyforth, deceased, mother of complainant.
                                                                                                DERBY.

64–65   Thomas STEBBYNG of Belchamp Walter, butcher, v. Thomas MAN alias Noschall, Crysten
his wife and Henry, son and heir of Edmund IPESWYCHE and of Anne his wife.
Messuage and land in Little Maplestead, late of John Stebbyng, deceased, father of complainant.
                                                                                                ESSEX.

66   Richard STEPHENS of the Middle Temple, gentleman, v. George HUNTLEY, esquire, son
of John Huntley.
Rent of the site and demesnes of the manor of Standish, the lease being destroyed ' by the senester
practisinge and counsell of certen persons whome your Graces oratour dare not name.'
                                                                                                GLOUCESTER.

67   William STEPHENSON, clerk, and John STEPHENSON v. Katherine BELL.
Messuage, barn and land in Leake and Leverton.   LINCOLN.

68   . . . STEPHENSON v. John WESTLAND and Richard CLARKES.
Gavelkind lands in Leake and Leverton. Mutilated. See D. XV, 5.   LINCOLN.

69   Leonard STEPHYNSON, parson of Ilchester, v. Thomas JEFFREY of the same, tailor.
Glebe of Ilchester.   SOMERSET.

70   Henry STORIE and Anne his wife v. Richard GASCON(GE), gentleman.
Land in bold Ingleton awarded to complainant in the late Court of Augmentations.   YORK.

71–73   Leonard STUBBYS v. Thomas SAUNDERSON, yeoman.
Messuage and land in Leake of the demise of complainant.   LINCOLN.

74–77   Richard STUCKEY v. Henry BOCHER.
Messuage and land in Spreyton.   DEVON.

78–79   William SUDBURY alias Gonne of Wickham, yeoman, v. Robert HACON of Rendham,
carpenter.
Price of cattle and rent of land in Rendham to be set against a debt.   SUFFOLK.

80–81   Henry SWAYNE of Tiverton, ' toker,' v. Richard HAGGELEY of the same, ' toker,' and
Edward WEBBER his servant.
Burning of complainant's shop in Tiverton while in defendant's occupation with his receipts as
factor to John Prouse.   DEVON.

82   Alexander SYMSON of Skarthoe, smith, v. Richard, William, and Thomas CURTEYS,
executors of Simon Marchaunt, parson of the same.
Recompense promised by the testator for frivolous suits.   [LINCOLN.]

83   James SYMSON of York v. Richard ABEE.
Refusal to complete a sale of barley.   LINCOLN.

FILE 1472.

1   John [SALCOTE *alias* Capon], bishop of Salisbury, *v.* John LEWSON, esquire.
Manors of Holnest and Burton.   DORSET.

2–6   John SALESBURY, knight, Robert SALESBURY, esquire, and Dorothy his wife, late the
wife of Fulk Salesbury, *v.* Thomas [GOLDWELL], bishop of St. Asaph.
Lease of the archdeaconry of St. Asaph.   FLINT.

7   John SAPCOTE *v.* William ERMYSTED, canon of Westminster, and others.
Rectory and manor of Therfold of the demise of John Whyting, parson. *Damaged.*   [HERTS.]

8–9   Edward SAUNDERS, knight, J.C.P., *v.* William STOKE of Foleshill, esquire.
Claim of rent from messuages (*described*) in Smithford Street, Coventry.   WARWICK.

10   Alice, late the wife of William SAYE, *v.* John CLARK and Anthony DAVERS.
Land held of the manor of Dauntsey.   WILTS.

11   Nicholas SEBORNE *alias* Plomer of Wotton-under-Edge, co. Gloucester, *v.* William
GORWEY.
Tenement in Wootton Bassett of the gift of Robert Seborne, father of complainant.   WILTS.

12–15   Peter SENTHILL *v.* William KEMPE.
Rent of the manor of Akenham. *See File 1270, No. 25.*   SUFFOLK.

16   Brian SEWELL *v.* Oliver WOODHEDD and others.
Messuages and lands in Whitwell and Worsoppe (*i.e.* Worksop ?), late of John Sewell, deceased,
father of complainant.   DERBY, NOTTS.

17   William SHEFFELD, clerk, *v.* John DEAN, rector of . . . and . . . gton.
Half profits of defendant's parishes promised as a recompense for serving them. *Damaged.*
    NOTTS.

18   Arthur SHEPPARD of Shipton Moyne, miller, *v.* John ASIDE *alias* Sadler.
Seizure of brass and pewter from complainant's house during his arrest on a charge whereof he
was acquitted.   GLOUCESTER.

19–21   Richard, grandson of William SHOTE, *v.* William CRUCHE (Crowche), gentleman.
Water-mill and land held of defendant's manor of Hampton by Claverton, late of the bishop of
Bath and Wells. *Mutilated.*   SOMERSET.

22–23   John SKUTTE *v.* John STOCKER.
Annuity payable by defendant to his wife for which complainant has given bond.   ———

24–26   Nicholas SKYRES, administrator of the goods of Humphrey Skyres, deceased, *v.* Richard
DREWE.
Land in Chertsey (Chessey) of the demise of the abbot and convent of Chertsey. *Mutilated.*
    SURREY.

27–28   John SLATER *v.* Beatrice, late the wife of William SLATER.
Closes of pasture in Pinchbeck.   LINCOLN.

29–30   Robert SLATER *v.* the same.
Messuage, stable, horse-mill and land in Pinchbeck, late of Robert Slater and Isabel his wife, parents
of the said Robert and William.   LINCOLN.

31–33   Richard SLY *v.* Robert MORDAUNT (Morden) and John MILLER.
Messuage and land held of the said Mordaunt's manor of Westbury by Robert Bastard, deceased,
uncle of complainant.   BUCKS.

34   Robert SMYTH and Isabel his wife *v.* Thomas STEVYNSON.
Land (*described*) and messuages in Thornton, late of William Nellson, deceased, father of the said
Isabel. *Mutilated.*   LINCOLN.

35–41   John SNEYNTON *v.* Robert NEVELL of Ragnall, son and heir of Robert Nevell, esquire,
and George his son.
Detention of deeds relating to the manor and rectory of Burton.   NOTTS.

42   George SNOWE, yeoman, and Margaret his wife *v.* Thomas JEFFERAY of Chiddingly.
Messuage and land in Hailsham and Pevensey, late of Nicholas Wyllard of Chiddingly, deceased,
brother of the said Margaret.   SUSSEX.

43   Robert SOUTHWELL, knight, late master of the Rolls, and Francis his younger son *v.*
Margaret, executrix, and late the wife of Thomas CALTON of [London?], goldsmith.
Marriage to the said Francis of Mary, daughter of Nicholas [T]r appes of London, goldsmith, and
granddaughter and ward of the said Thomas. *Mutilated.*   LONDON.

44–47   George, grandson and heir of John SPEKE, esquire, *v.* William DENYS, gentleman, and
Alice his wife, late the wife of Henry Denys.
Manor of Spreyton and half the manors of Stourton and Douresley (*i.e.* Dorseley in Harberton ?),
late of John Speke, knight, father of the said John.   DEVON.

48–49   John SPERLYNG *v.* Henry ESEBY and Peter JACKESON.
Messuage and land in Potto of the bequest of Thomas Sperlyng, father of complainant.   YORK.

50   Thomas STAFFORD of Ditchling, co. Suffolk, and Margaret his wife *v.* Stephen HACHE
of Sellinge and Margery his wife, late the wife of Richard Redge.
Land in Newchurch, late of Alice Armynard, deceased. *Pedigree given.* D. XV, 31.   KENT.

51   James STAUNGER *v.* Richard, son of Henry TOLSON.
Obtaining a lease of a messuage and land in Braithwaite in breach of complainant's tenant-right.
    CUMBERLAND.

52   Henry STEPHYN and Jenett his wife v. Richard TRELADEVAS.
Messuages and lands in Leighey, Rescevyn, Rescevyn mill, Bodener Wartha, and Tregelast, late
of William Moryshe, deceased, uncle of the said Jenett and Richard.   CORNWALL.

53 ·   William STEPHAN, fisherman, and Robert PONTEYS, yeoman, churchwardens of All
Saints, Hastings, and John SLYWRYGHT, Stephen DOLVE, Robert ROGERSON, and
others, inhabitants of the same, v. Edward DURRANT, jurat of Hastings, and late churchwarden, and Martin BRABON, feoffees to uses.
Lands in Pett, Farley and Guestling awarded to the said church in this court, and others belonging
to it in Hastings. *Mutilated.*   SUSSEX.

54-55   John STEVYNSON v. John PARKER.
Messuage and land in Gnosall of the gift of Thomas Cecyll and John Bell.   STAFFORD.

56-57   William, son and heir of John STOCKER, v. James CHAPMAN.
Detention of deeds relating to lands, rents and services in Basingstoke, Cliddesden, and Wildmoor
(in Sherfield-upon-Loddon) demised by the said John for his life to defendant and others. HANTS.

58-60   Alexander STOKES of Hatfield v. Henry COLLINWOOD (Callengwood) of Tuxford, co.
Notts.
Wool and lambs of sheep given to complainant by Thomas Stokes, his kinsman, parson of Treeton,
who had lent them to complainant to manure his lands.   YORK.

61   John STORY, LL.D., and Thomas LEVYEN, clerk, v. John COX of London, salter.
Debt to Richard Bowerman, clerk, deceased, whose executors complainants are.   LONDON.

62   Thomas STOUGHTON of Ash and Jane his wife v. JULIANA Pynnor(?) and John her son.
Messuage and land called Little Betshanger, late of Laurence Omer, deceased. *Mutilated.* KENT.

63   Jane, late the wife of Roger STOURTON, esquire, v. Lord Thomas HOWARD.
Messuages and cottage held of defendant's manor of Stockwood.   DORSET.

64-66   Roger STRETON and Joan his wife v. Thomas MADELEY.
Messuages and land in Butterton, formerly of Thomas Madeley, ancestor of the said Joan and
Thomas.   STAFFORD.

67   Ambrose SUTTON of Burton by Lincoln, esquire, v. NICHOLAS Sutton, gentleman, executor
of Nicholas Sutton.
Messuage and land in Willoughton bequeathed to the deceased by John Sutton, esquire, uncle of
complainant, on condition of a payment to Mary Sutton, which has not been made.   LINCOLN.

68   Nicholas SUTTON, executor of Charles Sutton, esquire, v. Robert FLUD.
Action on a bond the acquittance for which was delivered to Robert Arneway of Lincoln's Inn,
gentleman, who was unable to return to England since the loss of Calais.   ————

69   John SYMES, vicar of Woollavington, v. Thomas DAY.
Removal of tithe corn by command of Richard Mychell, lessee of . . .. Pytman, late vicar,
deprived for marriage. *Mutilated.*   SOMERSET.

FILE 1473.

1-5   John SADLER, Joan his wife, Thomas, son and heir of Maryet JOHNSON, Thomas
COCKES, Elizabeth his wife, William AGARD and Margery his wife v. John SOWTER of
Derby, plumber, and Agnes his wife.
Land in Hanbury, late of Thomas Fynymore, grandfather of the said Joan, Maryet, Elizabeth,
Margery, and Agnes. D. XIII, 5.   STAFFORD.

6   John SAKEVILE of Dorking, co. Surrey, esquire, v. David ap Jevan LLOYD and others.
Messuages and land in Lampeter-pont-Stephan (Llanbether), late of William Sakevile, esquire,
deceased, father of complainant.   CARDIGAN.

7-8   Agnes SALYSBURY of London, daughter of Thomas Salysbury of Flint, and late a ward
of the Crown, v. Thomas SALYSBURY, bastard son of the said Thomas, Res THOMAS,
and others.
Messuages and land in Flint, Le Boles (*cf.* Plas-yn-Balls near Flint), Coleshill, and Hawarden.
FLINT.

9-11   Bartholomew SAMFORD v. George, son of John BALCHE, deceased, and of Elizabeth his
wife.
Money promised to complainant on his marriage with Alice, daughter of the said John.
DIOCESE OF BATH AND WELLS.

12   Elizabeth, late the wife of Thomas SAUNDERS, v. Richard MICHELL.
Refusal to complete a sale of a tenement in Cannington.   SOMERSET.

13   Richard SAVAGE v. Mary, executrix, and late the wife of Edmund SAVAGE, knight.
Wages as steward of lands in Lambeth.   SURREY.

14   The same v. the same.
Expenses of repair of buildings and staithes in the same.   SURREY.

15   The master and chaplains perpetual of the hospital of the SAVOY v. the churchwardens of
MAIDSTONE and David BARHAM, miller.
Tenements in Maidstone formerly appropriated for the lights of St. Christopher and St. George in
the church there.   KENT.

16-17   Thomas SECKINTON, husbandman, v. Robert NICCOLLES.
Manor of Seckington and messuages and lands there and in Alvecote (in Shuttington) and Shut-
tingtou. *See File* 1161, *No.* 11. ·   WARWICK.

18-20   Henry SERLE v. William PEPES and others.
(Continuation of *File* 1382, *No.* 10.)   CAMBRIDGE.

21 Isabel SEYMOUR of Bourton, co. Oxford, late the wife of Simon Seymour, esquire, *v.* Thomas GODDARD of Upham, co. Wilts, gentleman.
Detention of deeds relating to the manor of Corston (Coston) and other lands. SOMERSET.

22 John SHARPE, yeoman of the Guard, *v.* Estelen, late the wife of John PAYNE of Carbrooke, and administratrix of his goods.
Books of reckonings and other documents entrusted to the said Payne, and debt. NORFOLK.

23-25 Thomas SHERMAN of London, gentleman, *v.* Peter DODDE and others, executors of Agnes Carrington.
Leasehold in Wettenhall bought of Ralph Sherman, brother of complainant. (Defendants plead a decree of the Council of the Marches.) CHESTER.

26 John SHIPMAN *v.* John BURRE and Alice his wife, executrix, and late the wife of Thomas Leedes.
Action on a bond whereby complainant undertook to make no claim to lands of the said Leedes in West Ham, he having entered thereon to recover trees felled on his own land. ESSEX.

27 Anne SKARNYNG *v.* Edmund her son.
Loan of 100*l.* and of goods and a lease to the like value. ———

28 Edward SLEGGE of Cambridge, gentleman, *v.* John HARRYS and Joan his wife.
Messuage in Aylesbury bought of William Sakevyle and John Dudley. *See File 1380, No. 37.*
BUCKINGHAM.

29-30 John SMITH, yeoman, *v.* Walter SHYLLYNG, esquire, and William MOODYE.
Lease in reversion of a messuage and land in Stockbridge. HANTS.

31-35 Robert SMITHE *v.* Thomas LAVENDER.
Close (*described*) in Caxton, late of William Smythe of Willingham, husbandman, deceased, father of complainant. CAMBRIDGE.

36 John SMYTH of Higham, clerk, grandson and heir of William Smyth, *v.* Anthony COLE.
Detention of deeds relating to a messuage, dye-house, and land in Stratford. [SUFFOLK ?]

37-40 William SPARKE, administrator of the goods of Ralph Sparke, deceased, parson of East Harling, *v.* Thomas WARNER, executor of John Style.
Money and acres received to the said Ralph's use. NORFOLK.

41-42 Thomas SPENSER of Abingdon, yeoman, *v.* Robert MONKE of Henley-on-Thames, butcher.
Part price of oxen and wethers. BERKS, OXFORD.

43 Randall STARKEY of London, merchant, *v.* Thomas HURLESTONE and William BYKERTON.
Close of pasture in Wrenbury of the demise of Thomas Starkey, brother of complainant. CHESTER.

44 Thomas STEPHYNS, parson of Swalchif (*i.e.* Swalecliff), *v.* Robert WEBBE.
Lease of complainant's parsonage by Anker Bright, late parson, deprived for marriage. *Faded.*
KENT.

45-50 John STEVINS of Bourton-on-the-Hill, co. Gloucester, merchant, *v.* Thomas RUSSELL, knight, son and heir of John Russell, knight, and John ABERHALL.
Manors of Holt and Shelsley, extended for a warranty made by John Croftes, deceased, of the manor of Hanley. *Damaged.* WORCESTER.

51-53 Robert, son of John STODARD, *v.* John GYLMAN, gentleman.
Detention of deeds relating to a messuage in Christ Church parish adjoining the church of St. Nicholas Shambles of the demise of the late prior and convent of St. Bartholomew the Great. *Damaged. See File 1383, No. 49.* LONDON.

54 John, son of Richard STONARD, an infant, by Humphry Crosse his guardian or *prochein amye, v.* Thomasyn STONARD and ——, daughter of John STONARD of West Hanningfield.
Messuage called Barn Hall in Stock, late of John Stonard of Buttsbury, deceased, uncle of the said Richard. ESSEX.

55-59 John STORYE, esquire, and Joan his wife *v.* Henry WATTES.
Messuages, barn and land in Wokingham, Hurst and Twyford, late of Richard Wattes, deceased, father of defendant and grandfather of the said Joan. BERKS.

60-62 William STRANGWAIES of Haselbury Bryan, gentleman, *v.* Thomas BAGSHAWE, vicar of Cranborne, co. Dorset.
Detention of a grant of the next presentation to the rectory of Poyntington made by Fulk Grivyll, knight. SOMERSET.

63-64 Edmund STURE (Stere) *v.* William PAYNE.
Damage to fencing during a lease of complainant's park of Okehampton. DEVON.

65 Harry STYCKE *v.* Agnes COLE.
Refusal to attorn or to pay rent for a messuage and land at South Stroxworthy, in Woolfardisworthy, whereof complainant has acquired the reversion after her death. DEVON.

66 Thomas SUTTON *v.* John and Alice WEBSTER and William BONSALL.
Detention of deeds relating to a messuage and land in Over Haddon. DERBY.

67 Nicholas SWALLOWE *v.* John DEY.
Messuage and land late held of defendant's manor of Foxton by John Swallowe, uncle of complainant. CAMBRIDGE.

68-70 John SYMSON, parson of Thurcaston, *v.* Ralph LANGLEY.
Dilapidations of complainant's parsonage and non-payment of rent due on a lease made by Henry Manne, late parson. LEICESTER.

FILE 1474.

1-2   John SADLER v. William, John and Richard SADLER.
Messuages and land in Standlake, late of Thomas Sadler, deceased, father of complainant.
OXFORD.

3-4   John SANDERS v. William HORWOOD.
Detention of deeds relating to messuages and land in Northampton.   NORTHAMPTON.

5-9   Henry SAXCEY of London, mercer, v. Robert TRAPPES, citizen and goldsmith of London.
Contempt of arbitration on an account. *Schedule annexed.*   LONDON.

10-13   Francis SEELE v. Richard HODGESON and Elizabeth his wife, late the wife of William Kaye.
Messuages, cottage and land in S . . ., late of Thomas Newsome, deceased, grandfather of complainant and father of the said Elizabeth. *Damaged.*   YORK.

14-15   Alexander SEYMOUR the elder, gentleman, v. Simon LOWE of London, merchant.
Manor of Burton and messuages, land and rent there late of Simon Seymour, esquire, deceased, father of complainant. *See Files* 1317, *No.* 25; 1270, *No.* 27; 1365, *No.* 98.   OXFORD.

16-17   John SHEPARD v. William HOMBER.
Refusal to complete a sale of land in Shaftesbury.   DORSET.

18-19   Thomas SHIPWRIGHT v. John SHIPWRIGHT.
Messuage and land, late held of the manor of Waghen Rector by John Shipwright, deceased, father of both parties.   YORK.

20-25   John SHOUTHCOTT of London, gentleman, Elizabeth his wife, George SOUTHCOTT, gentleman, and Frances his wife v. Anthony BUTLER of London, gentleman, and William WESTON.
Lands (*described*) in Banbury demised by John Longland, late bishop of Lincoln, to William Robyns, alderman of London, deceased, father of the female complainants. (The said Butler's answer is missing.) D. XII, 50.   OXFORD.

26-27   Richard SHOWARD, esquire, v. Thomas TROPNELL and William his son.
Pollution of a stream running through complainant's manor of Chilcompton by the erection of a dye-house or woad-house in Midsomer Norton.   SOMERSET.

28-30   Bridget, executrix and late the wife of Baldwin SMYTHE, citizen and haberdasher of London, v. Roger CHOLMELEY, knight, Christyane his wife, and Robert STEPNETHE.
Marsh in Woolwich of the demise of the said Sir Roger and Christyane, obtained by complainant on a *fieri facias* from John Merylaw of London, skinner.   KENT.

31   William SOMASTER v. William COURTENEY.
Assault and dispute as to plate, etc. (*described*) of John Paynter, deceased. *Mutilated.* CORNWALL.

32   Roger SPURLINGE v. John MATYWARDE.
Messuage and land in Bury St. Edmunds and goods late of John Spurlinge, deceased, uncle of complainant.   SUFFOLK.

33-40   Edward [STANLEY], earl of Derby, v. Richard LEVESON, knight, son and heir of James Leveson, esquire, and Arthur HODGEKYS (Hotchekyse), gentleman.
Messuage and land at Cockshutt in Ellesmere claimed as belonging to the manor of Petton. SALOP.

41-43   John STANLEY of Westminster, gentleman, v. William FOXE his tenant.
Messuage and land in Ewloe of the demise of Rice ap Edward ap Pell of Wepre, gentleman.
FLINT.

44-46   The same, servant to the Queen, v. John FOXE.
Messuage and land in Mancott obtained of defendant on an extent by Edward Stanley of Ewloe, esquire.   FLINT.

47   Matthew [STEWART], earl of Lennox, and Margaret his wife v. Arthur WOODHED and others, inhabitants of Silkstone.
Rents and ' sutes roial ' belonging to the manor of Silkstone.   YORK.

48   The same v. Robert ROSE.
Manor (*sic*) of Whorlton and Brighton sometime of James Strangwais, knight.   YORK.

49 50   Thomas STODARD, gentleman, v. Dorothy his mother and John MOUNTSTEVYN, gentleman.
Reversion of messuages and land in Gunthorpe, Walton, Warrington, Paston, Eastfield and Thwaites (between Dagsthorpe and Paston). *Mutilated.*   NORTHAMPTON.

51-52   William STOKES, esquire, v. Elizabeth SYSON *alias* Roell.
Detention of deeds relating to messuages and land in Walton.   LEICESTER.

53   John STOOKES v. Thomas LAWTON.
Messuage and land in Clifton Reynes, late of Richard Stookes, deceased, father of complainant.
BUCKINGHAM.

54-55   William STOURTON, yeoman, v. Ralph LEAKE of Hasland, co. Derby, esquire, and Robert, Guy and William SAMPOLE.
Inn called the *Crown* and land in Bawtry demised by the said Leake to Thomas Stourton, father of complainants. *See File* 1307, *No.* 14.   YORK.

56-57   Thomas Waite and William Clement, churchwardens of STRATFIELD MORTIMER, v. Robert TOMPSON, feoffee to uses.
Land in Stratfield Say conveyed by Alice Clerk *alias* Geffrey to the use of the said church. HANTS.

58–60   Frideswide STRELLEY.v. William SAVILL and Robert STRELLEY of Tirlington.
Detention of deeds relating to the parsonages of Great Bowden and Carlton Scroope, the manors of Great Bowden and Harborough, a windmill and lands in Great Bowden, Church Langton, Harborough, Carlton Scroope and Linby, and the parsonage and patronage of the vicarage (sic) of Adbaston, Ratcliff, Basford, and Oxton (Oxen), late of Robert Strelley, deceased, husband of complainant and uncle of the said Savill.   LEICESTER, NOTTS.

61   John STROWDE v. Richard M[OWER?].
Messuage and land in Chiddingfold, formerly held by Lawrence Rawsterne together with the manor of Combes alias Brabis (in Chiddingfold) and messuages, a ' columbary,' land and rent in Godalming, Chiddingfold, Alfold, and Puttenham. Mutilated. Bill wanting.   SURREY.

62–63   William STYRMAN (Sturmyn) v. Thomas IRBY, gentleman.
Lease of pasture in Sutton St. James bought of defendant by John Styrman, father of complainant.   LINCOLN.

64–66   Richard SWANSON of Ware, co. Herts, yeoman, v. Bernard, son of Robert SWANSON.
Messuage and land at Calder Bridge, late held by George Swanson, deceased, father of complainant. (Custom of the county disputed.)   CUMBERLAND.

67–68   John SYGAR of Wymondham, yeoman, v. Henry SYMONDES.
Detention of a bond made by Robert Kensey of Wymondham, yeoman, to William Tassell, gentleman. Decayed. See File 1161, No. 53.   NORFOLK.

69–71   Amy, late the wife, of Robert SYKYS of Markfield, v. John WARNER of the same.
Pasture in the late Marquis of Dorset's manor of Whitwick.   LEICESTER.

72   . . . SYMONT v. the sheriff of LONDON or the keeper of the KING'S BENCH prison
Action by Robert Twyllye, a Frenchman of Rouen, for price of canvas which proved to be decayed and of short measure. Mutilated. Corpus cum causa.   LONDON.

FILE 1475.

1–2   John TAILOUR of Wandsworth, co. Surrey, and Elizabeth his wife, daughter and heir of Thomas Smythe, v. John HUNDEN.
Detention of deeds relating to messuages, a dovehouse, and land in Caxton.   CAMBRIDGE.

3   Thomas TAYLLOR and Elizabeth his wife, daughter of Robert Bovie, deceased, v. James BYDDELL.
Reviver of a suit for a messuage, gardens and barns in Evesham brought by the said Elizabeth before her marriage.   WORCESTER.

4   Henry TAYLLOUR, priest, v. Christopher NELSON, gentleman, and others.
Messuage and land in Rychall (i.e. Riccall?) granted for singing mass at the altar of St. James in the parish church there.   [YORK?]

5–9   John TAYLOUR of Henley-on-Thames, co. Oxford, yeoman, and Margery his wife v. Rowland and George WALKER.
Messuages and land in Harborough and Farndon, late of Richard Borsworth, deceased, grandfather of the said Margery.   LEICESTER, NORTHAMPTON.

10–11   John TAYLOUR v. William WILLOTT and William and John LONGHURSTE.
Damage to land held of the manor of Dorking by ' conye berryes ' made by defendants in lands within the manor.   SURREY.

12–15   Thomas TAYLOUR v. William TAYLOUR.
Messuage in Swallowfield and tenement in Wokingham, late of John Taylour, deceased, father of both parties. D. XI, 6.   BERKS.

16   Robert TW . . . John IDELL.
Messuage and land in Barton held by complainant in right of Alice his wife. Mutilated. LINCOLN.

17   Joan, late the wife of Thomas TEBAT, v. Richard IVE, esquire, and others.
Tenement in the said Ive's manor of Brokenborough in Almondsbury. Mutilated.   GLOUCESTER.

18–20   John TEBOLDE v. Edward ROLFFE.
Messuage in Bottisham bought of Joan, executrix, and late the wife of John Rolffe, deceased, father of defendant.   CAMBRIDGE.

21–22   Francis TEMPLE v. Nicholas EGLETON.
Messuage and land in Ellesborough bought of John Beufoo. D. XII, 39.   BUCKINGHAM.

23–24   The same, gentleman, v. Richard BOLLER and John ELLYS.
Detention of deeds relating to the same.   BUCKINGHAM.

25   Richard THOMSON, labourer, v. James ROBYNSON, yeoman, and Agnes his wife.
Cottages in Nawton Dale and Beadlam (Bodelam), late of William Thomson, clerk, deceased, brother of complainant.   YORK.

26–29   Robert THORNETON, executor of John Thorneton of Kingston-upon-Hull, merchant, v. William CROKKEY, overseer of the said John's mill.
Closes near Kingston-upon-Hull of the demise of the late prior of the Charterhouse by Hull.   YORK.

30   Thomas brother and heir of William THORNETON, and Margaret SMETON, v. [John DOGGETT and Mary his wife, formerly Mary Brereton].
Reviver of a suit for a messuage and land in Hingham (File 1185, No. 13). Mutilated. D. XIII, 6. [NORFOLK.]

31   William THORNHYLL v. Thomas ASSHELOCKE.
Bond. Mutilated.   ↘

32–35   John THROKEMARTON, esquire, v. Richard TRACY, esquire.
Messuage and land called Didcote in Beckford of the demise of the late abbot and convent of
Tewkesbury.   GLOUCESTER.

36   ·   Thomas THURLAND, parson of All Cannings, v. Edward BOYNTON, esquire.
Glebe of All Cannings.   WILTS.

37   Richard THYMŸLBY of Poolham (in Woodhall) v. Edward and Thomas ROSSE, gentlemen.
Judgment obtained in the King's and Queen's Bench in contempt of an injunction from this court.
                                                                               LINCOLN.

38   The same v. the same.
Action on a bond for warranty of the manor of Dunton Hall and lands in Tydd St. Mary, Tydd
St. Giles, and Tydd St. James. *Mutilated.*   [LINCOLN, CAMBRIDGE.]

39–40   William TILCOCKES, late mayor of Oxford, v. Thomas MAYOTT (Mayett) of London,
merchant tailor.
Debt due to Thomas Mallyson, who bequeathed it to complainant to provide work for the poor
of Oxford.   OXFORD.

41–44   John TOMLENSON of Chingford, co. Essex, husbandman, v. Thomas THOMLYNSON.
Closes in Edingly, late of Richard Tomlenson, deceased, father of complainant.   NOTTS.

45–49   The same v. Richard BLACKEBORNE and Margaret his wife, late the wife of the said
Richard Tomlenson.
Messuages, cottages, and land in Edingly of the like descent.   NOTTS.

50   Jervys (?) TOMPSON of Derby v. Lancelot LANCASTER, esquire.
Messuage and land held by tenant right of defendant's manor of Hartsop (Hartstope) by Geoffrey
Tompson, deceased, father of complainant. *Damaged.*   WESTMORLAND.

51   John TOMPSON of London, haberdasher, and Elizabeth SUTTON v. Richard ARGEN-
TYNE, parson of Brantham (Brame otherwise Brentham), and George SUTTON, late
parson.
Lease by the said George of the parsonage of Brantham with the chapel of Bergholt annexed.
                                                                               SUFFOLK.

52–53   Francis TONNERD v. John TONNERD and Goodlacke CHAPMAN.
Half the rent of a brewhouse on the west side of the water of Boston, late of Richard Tonnerd,
deceased, father of the said Francis and John.   LINCOLN.

54–55   Andrew TOOKE, vicar of Wiggenhall St. German, v. William BUTTYS.
Lease of complainant's vicarage by John Sayer, late vicar, deprived for desertion. *Answer
wanting. See File* 1387, *No.* 37.   NORFOLK.

56–58   Robert TOPPE v. Walter BOLANDE.
Farm of Sutton Veny (Fenysutton) of the demise of Walter, lord Hungerford, attainted of treason.
                                                                               WILTS.

59   Thomas TOPPELEYS of Tissington v. Richard HODGEKYNSON and Alice his wife.
Cottage in Parwick. *Damaged.*   DERBY.

60–63   William TOTENHAM, labourer, v. William, son and heir of Hugh MARTEN.
Tenements in Great Wenden, late of Thomas Smyth, deceased, uncle of complainant.   ESSEX.

64–68   Simon TRAPPETT v. Margaret and Robert TRAPPETT.
Messuage and land in Crowfield, late of Simon Trappett, deceased, husband of the said Margaret,
and father of the said Simon and Robert.   SUFFOLK.

69–72   Jane TRELYVER (Trevyner) v. John RESOUGA and Nicholas RESOUGA *alias* Polglase.
Detention of deeds relating to messuages and lands at Moreland, in St. Mawgan in Pyder, and
frivolous suits.   CORNWALL.

73   Thomas TRENCHARD, esquire, v. John HORSEY, knight.
Messuage and land in Sherborne, late of Thomas Trenchard, knight, deceased, father of complainant.   DORSET.

74–76   The same and Eleanor his wife v. the same.
Manor of Pinford (in Sherborne) demised by the late abbot of Sherborne to John Horsey, knight,
deceased, father of the said Eleanor and John.   DORSET.

77–81   John TREVANYON, esquire, and others v. Hugh BUSCOWEN, esquire.
Land in Kea appropriated to the maintenance of the church.   CORNWALL.

82   Thomas TREVILLIAN v. [John his brother].
Manor of Knoll and lands, etc., in Owlknoll, Berrynarbor, Wolmershayes, etc. (*as in File* 1164,
No. 30, *corrected as in File* 1386, *No.* 63). *Mutilated.*   SOMERSET, DEVON, DORSET.

83–86   Alice, late the wife of John TREVILLIAN, and Thomas their son v. John TREVILLIAN
and John STOCCOMB.
Do., *reading* Mene *for* Mere.   SOMERSET, DEVON, DORSET.

87–88   William TUCKER, vicar of Ermington, v. John ROUSSE.
Lease of half the tithes of Ermington made by the prior of Montacute without his convent.
Commission. D. XII, 13.   DEVON.

89   John TULL v. Richard TULL his uncle.
Lease of a tenement in St. Mary Bothaw, bond, and goods (*described*) entrusted to defendant in
complainant's imprisonment by the Duke of Northumberland, etc. *Mutilated.*   LONDON.

90–91   Edmund TWYNYHO and Elizabeth his wife, late the wife of Robert Lytton, knight, v.
Thomas SHOTBOLD.
Will of Katherine Munden, mother of the said Elizabeth, obtained while she was sick and 'wauke.'
Schedule of goods annexed.   [GLOUCESTER?]

92–94   Edmond TWYNYHO of Watton-at-Stone, co: Herts, esquire, *v.* John THYNNE, knight.
Lease of the manor of Kempsford, whereof defendant has the reversion.   GLOUCESTER.

95–96   Anne TYBBENHAM *v.* Thomas TYBBENHAM.
Annuity promised during the occupation of money payable to John Mylls, prependary of Canterbury, an executor of Crystyan Tybbenham of Bungay, mother of both parties.   KENT, SUFFOLK.

97   Matthew TYSE of Ottery St. Mary, surgeon, *v.* William WHETON of Ide, husbandman.
Debt for board, lodging, and medical treatment.   DEVON.

98   Richard TYSON of London, gentleman, *v.* Edmund [BONNER], bishop of London.
Messuages and land at Muswell Hill in the manor of Harringay of the bequest of John Tyson of
London, mercer, father of complainant. *Mutilated.*   MIDDLESEX.

99   Edmund T . . . *v.* William SAXEY and Edward, son of Edward VAUXE.
Under-lease of pasture in Swaffeham by Richard Maunsell and Elizabeth his wife, late the wife
of the said Edward the father. *Mutilated.*   (NORFOLK or CAMBRIDGE.)

FILE 1476.

1   Christopher TAILOUR of Whitechapel, co. Middlesex, *v.* John (J)EVANS.
Household goods in All Hallows, Hereford, entrusted to defendant by Anne his kinswoman, wife
of complainant, on a report of the latter's death on a voyage to Spain in the Queen's ship *Antelope*
to fetch the King.   HEREFORD.

2–4   Frances, late the wife of John TALBOTT, knight, and administratrix of his goods, *v.* John
MORTON, rector of Boningale.
Rectory of Boningale, demised to the said Sir John Talbot in exchange for the next presentation
to the rectory of Longford.   SALOP.

5   Adam TAYLER, clerk, parson of Bar . . . worth (*i.e.* Battisford?) *v.* Margaret, late
the wife of Richard WALLYS of Haddenham and administratrix of his goods.
Bond given on behalf of the said Richard for a debt to the Crown.   SUFFOLK, CAMBRIDGE.

6–9   Richard, son of Roger TAYLER, *v.* Dorothy and John TAYLER.
Detention of deeds relating to burgages in Uttoxeter and lands and a cottage there and in Bramshall,
late of Roger Tayler of Doveridge, deceased, father of the said Roger and John, and husband of
the said Dorothy.   STAFFORD.

10   John TEDDESTILL *alias* Fermer *v.* Thomas TEDDESTILL *alias* Fermer of Kensington,
co. Middlesex, and others.
Messuage and land in Chelmarsh of the entail of John Teddestill *alias* Fermer of Ewdon Burnell
(in Chetton), grandfather of complainant. *See File* 1076, *No.* 10.   SALOP.

11   John and David THOMAS, sons of Thomas ap Edward, deceased, *v.* Angharrett HOWELL,
Ellis ASSHEBULL, and Ewen (*sic*) his wife. ·
Goods of the said Thomas ap Edward in the hands of Howell ap Jenkyn his father-in-law, deceased,
husband of the said Angharrett, and father of the said Ewen.   ⸺

12–14   John, son and heir of John THOMAS of Barnstaple, *v.* Edward THORNE, esquire.
Refusal to complete a sale of the manor of Putford Julian and all other his messuages, lands and
services in West Putford.   DEVON.

15–20   William THOMAS, daily attendant on the Master of the Rolls, *v.* JOHN ap Gwillym and
RICHARD ap Philip.
Land in Treget of the demise of Robert ap Gwillym, father of the said John.   MONMOUTH.

21   Richard THOM . . . *v.* Llewelyn ap Jevan DYO.
Messuage and land in Cilcenin of the demise of Jenkyn Gwyn and Owen Merycke   *Mutilated.*
CARDIGAN.

22   John THORNBAR, husbandman, *v.* Edmund HARRYSON and others.
Destruction of timber of a ' fyer howse ' which complainant was building for his habitation in
Bashalt.   YORK.

23–27   John THORNETON, parson of Settrington, *v.* Francis ASLABY, esquire.
Profits of the rectory taken under a lease from Robert Wysdome, late parson, between his deprivation
and complainant's induction.   YORK.

28–31   William THORNHYLL *v.* William STOURTON, esquire, and Thomasyn his wife.
Detention of deeds relating to lands called Flyntford, Radon, Byffrom, and Selwood.   DORSET.

32   John THORNTON of Little Wakering, co. Essex, *v.* Richard MUDGE.
Salt meadow and other land in Cliff, late of John Lokyn, deceased, great-grandfather of complainant.   KENT.

33   Robert THROWER *v.* Thomas CRESSEY, both of London.
Waste of a building at Collyrow (Colyar Rowe) in Hornchurch, pledged to defendant for expenses
of a journey to Flanders. *Mutilated.*   ESSEX.

34–35   John TILL and others *v.* John WARDE and others.
Tithe hay and corn of Whitgreave, late of the college of Stafford. *Answer wanting.*   STAFFORD.

36   Robert TOPPE of Semley, husbandman.
Petition to examine witnesses as to a lease of the capital site and farm of Birchmore (in Berwick
St. John); with lands, fisheries, etc., by Henry Uvedall of Corfe Castle, co. Dorset, esquire.   WILTS.

37–38   Anthony TORNEY (Turney), gentleman, *v.* Peter LEE and Christopher POTTES.
Under-lease of the manor of Glentham and lands there belonging to the dean and chapter of
Lincoln.   LINCOLN.

39   Geoffrey TOTLE and Mary his wife, administratrix of the goods of Gilbert Kyrke of Exeter, deceased, *v.* Martin SMYTHE of the same.
Part price of coal, iron, etc. *See File* 1388, *No.* 49.   DEVON.

40   John TRAVEYS, executor of John Benet of London, merchant tailor, *v.* the sheriffs of LONDON, and Edward PORTER and Clement (*sic*) his wife, administratrix of the goods of Robert Benett of New Windsor, deceased.
Action on a forged bill obligatory, and debt. *Special certiorari and subpœna.*   LONDON.

41–43   Joan TREHANNEK *v.* William KYLLYOWE, gentleman, constable of St. Teath, and John BRYGHT of St. Tudy, yeoman.
Forcible entry, seizure of jewels, plate and deeds relating to land in St. Teath and false imprisonment at Launceston.   CORNWALL.

44   James TREWYNNARD, gentleman, *v.* Henry JOHN of Helston, clerk.
Plate pledged by William Trewynnard, esquire, deceased, whose executor complainant is.   CORNWALL.

45   Stephen, son of John TRISTRAM, *v.* George ESCOTE and Joan his wife.
Woodland in the parish of Haukeryge belonging to the manor (*sic*) of Exton and Haukeridge.   [SOMERSET.]

46–50   Thomas TRUMBULL and Henry WALLER, citizens and fishmongers of London, *v.* Arthur MALBY of London, fishmonger, and Edmund FLYCKE.
Bond entrusted to the said. Malby concerning a partnership between complainants and the said Flycke for purchase of grain.   LONDON.

51–52   Richard TRUMFLETE, George BULLOCK and Alice his wife, administratrix of the goods of Alice, executrix and late the wife of John Trumflete, deceased, *v.* Richard WATLINGTON.
Payment due under the will of Elizabeth Watlington, whose executor was the said Trumflete, for wool, cloth, etc., bequeathed by her to defendant.

53–55   Austen, son of William TURNELL of Markham, deceased, *v.* William his brother, Nicholas BRAMHALL, clerk, overseer of the deceased's will, and John BOITHE.
Old gold of the bequest of deceased.   NOTTS.

56–63   Ralph TURNOUR of London *v.* William COLLYNG, Eleanor his wife, late the wife of Roger Father, and Roger FATHER, son of the said Roger.
Manor of Colemore (Colmare, Comer) in Astley Abbots, formerly of Thomas Father, deceased, ancestor of the said Ralph and Roger. *See* D. X, 65.   SALOP.

64–66   George TURVYLE of Aston *v.* George SWILLYNGTON of Liddington, esquire, his brother-in-law.
Goods of Jane, mother of complainant, and late the wife of William Turvyle, knight.   LEICESTER, RUTLAND.

67–69   John TWYNE of Canterbury, alderman, *v.* Christopher COURTHOPPE, gentleman.
Tithe-corn of St. Paul's, Canterbury, claimed in right of the hospital of St. Laurence. *Mutilated.*   CANTERBURY.

70   Thomas, son of Edward TWYNEO, esquire, and of Edith his wife, *v.* Richard LANNENG, yeoman.
Land within the homage of Fontmell of the demise of the abbess of Shaftesbury.   DORSET.

71   William TYGHE and Elizabeth his wife *v.* Henry LUNDON and John PECKE.
Tenement in the manor of Ridlington acquired of John Filder.   RUTLAND.

72–73   The same *v.* the same.
Tenement in the same acquired of ——— Johnson.   RUTLAND.

74–80   Thomas TYNGLE, brother of William Tyngle, deceased, vicar of Billingbrough, and John and Edward BUCKBURIE, churchwardens of Billingbrough, *v.* Humphrey QWARNEBY of Nottingham, bell-founder, and William KYME, gentleman, complainants' attorney in the Common Pleas.
Collusion in an action on a bond for maintenance of the church of Billingbrough.   LINCOLN.

81–84   William TYRELL, esquire, and Elizabeth his wife, executrix and late the wife of John Freman, *v.* Valentine DALE and Elizabeth his wife, executrix and late the wife of Richard Forde of London, gentleman.
Bond concerning a separation between the said Freman and Elizabeth, sometime his wife, mother of the said Forde.   LONDON.

85   Thomas TYRINGHAM *v.* [John GRENE].
Refusal to complete a sale of land in Tyringham and Filgrave. *Mutilated.*   BUCKINGHAM.

86   The same (Teringham) *v.* the same.
The like concerning land in Filgrave.   BUCKINGHAM.

87–89   William TYRRELL *v.* Thomas LOCK, esquire.
Parsonage of Merton of the demise of the late prior and convent of Merton.   SURREY.

FILE 1477.

1   Robert son of William TAILLOUR and of Agnes his wife *v.* Henry GRYMES, gentleman.
Refusal of succession to a messuage and lands in defendant's manor of Wetton.   STAFFORD.

2   Frances, late the wife of John TALBOTT, knight, *v.* John BOTHE, gentleman.
Manor and mill-pool of Mobberley, being complainant's dower.   CHESTER.

3   John TARRYE of Cookbury, yeoman, *v.* Joan PEERS and John KNAPMAN.
'Peysed groots' of silver, silver spoons, brass pots and pewter entrusted to defendants.   DEVON.

4   William TAYLOR, yeoman, v. Thomas TEFFE.
Detention of deeds relating to land in Appleby.   WESTMORLAND.

5–6   Thomas TAYLOUR, Myles NYLSON, and John DRAPER v. the bailiff of the manor of
the CLINK and the keeper of the prison there, and Robert BULLEYN of Southwark, smith.
Action on a usurious contract against the Act 5 & 6 Edward VI, c. 20. *Corpus cum causa and
subpœna.*   SURREY.

7–9   Jane TEMMYS v. Ambrose HAUKIN and Owen WHYTE.
Obtaining a general warranty of a messuage and land in Monk-Sherborne (Weste Shereborne),
complainant intending a warranty against herself and John Ludlowe only. *See File* 1388, *No.* 13.
                                                                          HANTS.

10–12   Thomas TENNAUNT and Anne his wife v. Hugh HULME.
Messuages and land in Tilston and Barton, late of William Hulme, deceased, citizen and leather-
seller of London, father of the said Anne.   CHESTER.

13   Robert THOMAS, grandson and heir of Roger Strange, v. EDWARD ap Meredith and John
WYN ap Meredith.
Detention of deeds relating to land in Oswestry (Ocestrye).   SALOP.

14   Ralph THOMSON, yeoman, v. Richard HOLMES, his stepson.
Non-payment of price of closes in Nuneaton and detention of a lease of the same and of other
closes there.   WARWICK.

15–18   John THORNTON v. Walter CHARNELES, keeper of the prison of Burton-on-Trent.
Escape of Francis Bradshawe, against whom judgment for debt had been awarded in the court
of Burton.   STAFFORD.

19   Robert THURLEY v. Michael THURLEY and others.
Land in Guilden, Morden and Ashfield, late of Thomas Thurley, deceased, father of complainant.
                                                                  CAMBRIDGE, HERTS.

20–23   Katharine THYRKEHILL v. Robert LOWDALE.
Messuage and pasture in Diss, late of John Cowper, former husband of complainant.   NORFOLK.

24   Robert TODDY, executor of Thomas Turner, v. William FOWLE.
Debt for work.   ————

25–28   John TOMKYNSON v. Roger TOMKYNSON, John HETH, and others.
Land in Leicester of the bequest of John Tomkynson, father of the said John and Roger.
                                                                        LEICESTER.

29   Nicholas TOPPE and Joan his wife, daughter of Clement Skynner, and of Joan his wife,
deceased, v. Richard GARLAND and Joan his wife.
Detention of deeds relating to a messuage and land in Marwood.   DEVON.

30   Thomas TOPPE of Stockton, yeoman, v. Thomas PAGE of Tisbury, gentleman.
Action on a bond for a debt of John Heldych of Stockton, smith, already paid.   WILTS.

31–33   John TOWILL v. Thomas WEBBE.
Detention of deeds relating to a messuage and land called Aller in Dawlish. *See File* 1386, *No.* 46.
                                                                        DEVON.

34   Richard TOWSEY of London, tailor, v. Edward BARBOUR of Hereford, serjeant, his
lessee.
Rent due to Morgan Man from a messuage in Hereford.   HEREFORD.

35   John TOWSON v. Nicholas EBBESLEY *alias* Hew.
Reversion of a tenement in Lord FitzWarine's manor of Kingston after the death of Philip, father
of complainant.   DEVON.

36   Edmund TRAFFORD of Trafford, co. Lancaster, esquire, v. Ralph CHADWICKE and
others.
Lands in Godley, Newton, Matley, Walton and Sale bought of Hamlet Massye, esquire.   CHESTER.

37   The same, an executor of the said Hamlet, v. Alice BYBBY and Thomas JANNY.
Lands in Salé and Godley.   CHESTER.

38–42   The same and others, executors of Hamnett Massye of Sale, esquire, v. James MASSYE
alias Robynson.
Detention of a bond given by Alice, late the wife of the said Hamnett concerning her dower.
                                                                        CHESTER.

43–45   William TREVETT, executor of William Trevett, and Nicholas VENABLES v. John
STANDON.
Parsonage of Barnham of the demise of the late prior and convent of Boxgrove. *Mutilated.*
                                                                        SUSSEX.

46   John TREVOUR, son and heir of John ap John ap Richard Trevour, and attendant on
Richard Sackevile, knight, v. Owen GOZ ap Lewys, gentleman.
Messuage and land in Strete y Vrnwy of the demise of Richard Trevour.   MONTGOMERY.

47–48   Richard TROTT of Dartmouth, tailor, v. Harry TROTT.
Detention of deeds relating to messuages and land in Newton Bushell, late of Warren Trott,
deceased, father of both parties.   DEVON.

49   Richard TROUGHTON of Southworth, gentleman, and Jane his wife, daughter of William
Porter, deceased, v. John PORTER and Rowland SHERARD.
Messuages and land in Great Markham held according to the custom of the soke of Dunham by
the said William and by Augustine Porter, deceased, father of the said John.   NOTTS.

50–52   The same v. the same and Ellen PORTER, mother of the said John.
Do.   NOTTS.

53–61   The same *v.* Ellen PORTER, late the wife of the said Augustine, and the said SHERARD.
Messuages, rent and land at Lobthorpe in North Witham, late of John Porter of Belton, gentleman,
deceased.   LINCOLN.

62–63   Thomas TUNCKES of Bilston *v.* Thomas BAYLYE and others.
Lease of all the messuages and lands late belonging to the chantry of Willenhall in Willenhall and
Wolverhampton.   STAFFORD.

64   Walter TUNGATE *v.* Robert MARCHE, Robert RUSTE, and others, homagers of Martham.
Refusal to find complainant, heir of John his father, to messuages and [land] in Martham.
Mutilated.   NORFOLK.

65–69   The same *v.* Richard WHYTE and Elizabeth his wife.
Messuages and lands in Potter'Heigham, Horsey, Rollesby, Somerton and Martham, late of John
Tingate, deceased, father of complainant, and husband of the said Elizabeth. *Mutilated.*
                                                                                       NORFOLK.

70   Cuthbert TUNSTALL of London, esquire, *v.* Anthony DACHETT of Greyrigg, esquire.
Lease of half the manor of Docker and of the demesne and the herbage of the park, defendant
having the reversion.   WESTMORLAND.

71–73   Robert TYLER and Joan his wife *v.* John WYKE, father of the said Joan, and John his son.
Land in Lord Oxford's manor of Silverton.   DEVON.

74   Edmund TYLLER and Ellen his wife *v.* Robert BENTLY.
Land in Wethersfield, late of Thomas Bayly, deceased, grandfather of the said Ellen.
                                                                                       SUFFOLK.

75–76   William TYNDALL *v.* William BLASTE (Blaston) of Bristol, merchant.
Removal of wines attached for a debt of Thomas Clerke of Shiffnal.   GLOUCESTER, SALOP:

77–80   Robert TYRWHYTT of Kettleby, knight, *v.* Hamond, nephew and heir of Rise WHICHE-
COTE, esquire.
Manors of Dunston, Anwick, Harpswell, and Melton, messuages and lands in Spital-in-the-Street
(in Hemswell), Upton and Hemswell, and advowson of the chantry in the chapel of St. James,
Melton, of the entail of William Tyrwhytt, knight, ancestor of complainant. *Pedigree given.*
                                                                                       LINCOLN.

FILE   1478.

1   John TAILOR *v.* John HAULFHEDE.
Sale on a bad title of tenements held of Henry Dudley's manor of Braughing.   HERTS.

2   Nicholas TANNER and Alice his wife *v.* John CATTCOT.
Messuage and land at Rudge in Beckington, late of Richard Tre, deceased, father of the said Alice.
Mutilated.   SOMERSET.

3–4   John TATNALL *v.* Ralph KYNGESTON and Margaret his wife.
Barley delivered to the said Margaret at Wendover for malting and loan of money. [BUCKINGHAM.]

5–9   David TAYLOR *v.* John, son and heir of Geoffrey TAILOUR and Thomas COPENER his
lessees.
Land in Pembridge, late of Thomas Taylor, deceased, father of complainant. *See File* 1387,
No. 1.   HEREFORD.

10–12   Edmund TAYLOUR, husbandman, *v.* Matthew [STEWART], earl of Lennox.
Land in defendant's manor of Horton-in-Ribblesdale. *Answer wanting.*   YORK.

13   William THACKER and Thomas THACKER, an infant, *v.* William BEACHER and
Thomas CARIS.
Intimidation of an inquest concerning messuages and lands late of John Thacker, father of the
said Thomas. *Damaged.*   ———

14–17   John THATCHER the younger *v.* John, son of Agnes THATCHER *alias* Argentyne.
Messuages in Kensington, late of John Thatcher of Brompton, deceased, great-grandfather of
complainant.   MIDDLESEX.

18   Robert THEYRE *v.* the mayor and bailiffs of BRIDGWATER, and Richard MYCHELL
of Cannington, esquire.
Action for corn claimed as tithe of Woollavington and entrusted to defendant. *Certiorari and
subpœna.*   SOMERSET.

19   John THOMAS *alias* John Thomas Nicholas *v.* Richard TEAK, clerk, and others.
Seizure of deeds relating to a messuage and land in Sithney.   CORNWALL.

20   Philip THOMAS, clerk of the peace, *v.* Elizabeth, executrix, and late the wife of Richard
SPARKE.
Account of the said Richard as complainant's deputy.   CHESTER.

21   THOMAS ap David, servant to the Lord Warden of the Cinque Ports, *v.* Griffith ap Jevan
LLOID and others.
Messuage and garden in Kyltalgarth.   MERIONETH.

22–23   THOMAS ap William, yeoman attendant on John Throckmerton, esquire, a master of
Requests, *v.* MEREDITH ap Thomas.
Messuage and land in Ruthin.   FLINT.

24   THOMAS and GRIFFEN ap Rys *v.* Morris PENNAUNTE, Douce his wife, late the wife
of Robert ap Jevan ap Rys, and David LLOID ap Rys.
Tenements in Ysceifiog of the bequest of Rys ap David ap Gryffan, father of complainant. ———

25   John THURGOODE v. Robert PERS, labourer, and Emma his wife.
Refusal to complete a sale of a messuage and land in Witcham.   CAMBRIDGE.

26   . . . . brother of Edward THURLAND(?) v. George, Thomas and Elizabeth HYNDE.
Messuages in Gamston.   *Mutilated. See File* 1076, *No.* 25.   NOTTS.

27   John THYNNE, knight, v. John RUSSELL.
Mill and land in Maiden Bradley of the demise of the late prior and convent of Maiden Bradley.
                                                                                       WILTS.

28   Ambrose THYRSTON of London v. THOMAS ap Jevan ap Rice.
Withdrawal of Griffith his son from complainant's service.   LONDON.

29–31   Robert TODDIE v. William FOWLE.
Debt for wool bought of Thomas Turner, deceased. *Mutilated.*   ———

32–35   Anne TORNER v. George, son of William DAUNVERS, and William and John TORNER.
Messuage and land in the said William Daunvers's manor of Adderbury promised to còmplainant
and Thomas, late her husband, father of the said John and William Torner. *Damaged.*
                                                                                  [OXFORD ?]

36–37   Christopher TOWNESEND, citizen and clothworker of London, v. the mayor and aldermen
    of LONDON.
Action by Margaret Ha(y)les on a bond for arbitration between her and William Harbert, gentleman,
now beyond seas under the ' tuyssion ' of William [Somerset] earl of Worcester. *Certiorari.*
(Answer by the said Margaret.)   LONDON.

38   Philip TOWNSEND v. Jerome BLYTHE.
Messuage and land in Norton of the demise of William Blythe, gentleman, father of defendant.
Damaged. See Files 1291, *No.* 41; 1330, *No.* 44.   DERBY.

39   Edmund TRAFFORD, knight, son and heir of Edmund Trafford, knight, v. William
    BALSHAWE, Hugh *alias* Hankyn FAWDON, and others.
Resistance to enclosure of waste in Chorley belonging to the manor of Bollen.   CHESTER.

40–41   John TREDGOLD and Alice his wife v. William ALLENSON (Aleson).
Land in Stoke Nayland, late of Thomas Combirton, deceased, grandfather of the said Alice.
                                                                                       SUFFOLK.

42–46   David TREGENAWEN and John his son v. the steward, bailiffs, etc., of the stannary
    court of BLACKMERE, and Matthew RESCORLA and others.
Forcible entries on a messuage in St. Austell held of the manor of Galowras (in Gorran) on plea
of searching for false coins and action of trespass. *Certiorari and subpœna.*   CORNWALL.

47–48   John TREGUNWELL *alias* Tregyskye of Newlyn, yeoman, v. Thomas COCKE of Mevagissey.
Messuages and land in Tregiskey, Trewinney, Tregassick Wartha (all in Mevagissey) and Tregiskey
Wolas *alias* Crenwyn, formerly of Hockyn Tregunwall *alias* Tregyskye, gentleman, ancestor of
complainant.   CORNWALL.

49   John TREWE of Corfe Castle and Joan his wife v. Agnes SKUTT and John MILLER.
Messuage and land in Wolgarston, late of John Fagon, deceased, grandfather of the said Joan and
father of the said Agnes.   DORSET.

50–51   William, son and heir of Robert TRIGGES, v. George COMYE and Joan his wife, late the
    wife of Don Mychell de Vyves.
House of the prebend of Waltham in the collegiate church of Bosham, and land in Bosham claimed
in this court by Charles Stothern (Suthern).   SUSSEX.

52   Thomas TROWGTON, knight, v. . . . TYPLADY and others.
Messuages in Richmond, late of John Trowghton, deceased, father of complainant. *Much
damaged.*   YORK.

53–56   James, son of John TRUSLOWE, deceased, v. Thomas GODWYN, gentleman.
Grist-mill and land of the demise of defendant's parcel of the manor of Tale in Payhembury.
                                                                                       DEVON.

57   John TRUSTON v. Robert TRUSTON his uncle.
Refusal to complete a sale of his share of a messuage and land in Stratford according to the will
of Thomas Truston his father.   SUFFOLK.

58–59   Joan TUBBE, daughter and heir of John Calway, v. Jasper CALWAY, her bastard brother,
    Pentecost his wife and Oliver PIERS.
Messuages and land in St. Neots, etc.   CORNWALL.

60   James [TURBERVILE], bishop of Exeter, v. John ELYOTT his tenant.
Messuage and demesne lands belonging to the manors of Cuddenbeck (in St. German's parish) and
St. German's.   CORNWALL.

61   James [TURBERVILE], bishop of Exeter, receiver of appropriated tithes assigned by Act
    of Parliament to the Cardinal [Pole].
Petition to examine witnesses as to leases of the parsonage of Broad Clist.   DEVON.

62–74   Laurence TURKYNGTON of Great Stukeley, gentleman, v. Laurence TAYLARD, knight,
    William his son, Giles his brother, and Robert Newell, clerk.
Detention of deeds relating to the manors of Clarivaux and Deanes in Upwood mortgaged to William
Taylard, deceased, by Gerard Stuycley, great-grandfather of complainant. *Damaged.*
                                                                                    HUNTINGDON.

75   William TURLING of Weston, co. Devon, clothier, v. John MAN, mayor of Poole.
Balinger called *Phœnix* sent by complainant to Exmouth but taken to Poole after a voyage to
Ireland.   DORSET.

76–77   Thomas TURNER of Newtown v. William BRETTE.
Share of a messuage called Stred Vallocke and land in Llan . . . ecke, demised jointly to both
parties and others by Llewelyn ap Owen, gentleman.   MONTGOMERY.

78 .   Henry TYLNEY of East Tuddenham, yeoman, v. George CHAMBERLEYNE.
Refusal to admit John Rede, whose title complainant has purchased, as heir to Edmund his father
of land in Bickerstone (Byxton) held of defendant's manor of Barnham-Broom.   NORFOLK.

79–81   Robert TYRRELL, gentleman, v. Elizabeth, late the wife of Thomas HOWE.
Tithes of the manor of Mucking pledged for a debt. *Mutilated.*   ESSEX.

FILE 1479.

1–2   John UMFFREY v. Cristian, late the wife of Robert DRAPER, and Laurence   . . .
Messuage, cottage, and land in Hitchin and Ippollitts. *Damaged.*   HERTS.

3   James UNYON v. Margaret WORLE and Geoffrey WARDE.
Messuages and land at Tiddington in the royal manor of Alveston (Almiston, Alston). *Damaged.*
                                                                                       WARWICK

4–5   Henry UPHILL *alias* Androwe v. Bryan MULES (Myles).
Agreement for sale of a tenement at Wrimston in the parish of Swimbridge and manor of Bishop's
Tawton.   DEVON.

6–7   . Edward UPTON of Nottingham, an infant, by Edward Crewe of the same, tanner, his
guardian, v. Eden UPTON his grandmother.
Messuages and land in Bingham, late of Thomas Upton, deceased, father of complainant. NOTTS.

8–12   William UVEDALL, knight, v. John, son of John GRESSHAM, knight, Katharine, wife of
the said Sir John, and others, his executors.
Marriage settlement of complainant with Ellen, daughter of the said Sir John. *Mutilated.* ——

13   Walter VAHAN, gentleman porter of the castle of Guines, v. John HARRYS of Emok,
yeoman.
Debt the bond for which is lost.   CALAIS, RADNOR.

14   The same v. John APRYCE of Kennarth, yeoman.
Goods borrowed of complainant's wife.   RADNOR.

15–16 Edmund VALEY v. John WESTMYLL.
Lease of land in Whyp . . . ngall (*i.e.* Whippingham?). *Mutilated.*   HANTS (I.W.?).

17   Peter VAN STYNSELL, merchant stranger, v. Lybeas FOXE, citizen and merchant tailor
of London.
Procuring an action of debt by John Waren, citizen and barber surgeon of London, to avoid an
attachment of leather goods for which defendant has not paid.   LONDON.

18   John VANCE of Lambeth, saddler, v. John BEVER of the same, innholder.
Action on an arbitral award, complainant having tendered payment a day late.   SURREY.

19   Elizabeth, late the wife of Thomas VARNON, v. Robert BARKER *alias* Willyamson and
others.
Messuage in Newcastle-under-Lyme, late of another Thomas Varnon.   STAFFORD.

20–22 Charles VAUGHAN and Jane his wife, executrix of Thomas Hussey, v. Thomas LOVELL,
gentleman, Elizabeth his wife, late the wife of Hubert Hussey, Robert PULVERTOFT, and
John FRENCHE.
Manor of Pegges and messuages and land in Ewren Mynster of the entail of Thomas, father of the
said Thomas Hussey and brother of the said Hubert. *Mutilated.*   [DORSET.]

23–24 Elizabeth VAUGHAN of London, late the wife of Thomas Vaughan, gentleman, v. John
(William) BEREMAN of the same, ironmonger.
Lands in Hill Croome and Baughton (in Hill Croome) of the entail of Thomas Trubblevyle
(Turbyll), deceased father of complainant.   WORCESTER.

25–29 John VAUGHAN of Clandon, co. Surrey, esquire, and Anne his wife, late the wife of Henry
Knevett, knight, v. Thomas, grandson and heir of Thomas SHARMAN, and Thomas
SHERMAN the younger.
Manor of Hyde by Lewes, late of Roger Lewkenour, knight, and awarded by Parliament to the
said Sir Henry and Anne (34–35 Henry VIII, c. 46).   SUSSEX.

30–32 The same and William and Cuthbert MUSGRAVE, esquires, v. John [LUMLEY], lord
Lumley, and others.
Forcible entry, seizure of deeds and other damage in the manor of Great Lumley.   DURHAM.

33   Lewis VAUGHAN, servant to Lord Rich, v. Thomas JENKEN, chaplain, and Ryse
VAUGHAN.
Loans at Abburgeyney.   BRECKNOCK (*sic*).

34–35 Walter VAUGHAN of London v. John GRUFITH, son and heir of Grufithe Philipps
Watkyn, and others.
Messuage and land in Llanbeder (St. Peter's) and Partrishowe, formerly of Edward Thomas.
                                                                                       BRECON.

36–40 Walter VAUGHAN, servant in Grays Inn, and Margaret his wife v. Gwen JAMES, late the
wife of James Baker.
Brass pan and sheets pledged by David Lloid, former husband of the said Margaret, of whose goods
she is administratrix.   MIDDLESEX.

41   Anne [de VERE], countess of Oxford, and John ROBERDES, gentleman, her tenant, v. Alverey RANDALL, gentleman.

Manor of Badlesmere and lands thereto belonging.   KENT.

42   John VERE, earl of Oxford, v. Rtchard COLE and Robert his brother.

Subornation of perjury in a suit in this court concerning meadow in Bergholt fen. *See File* 1338, *No.* 32.   SUFFOLK.

43   George VERNON and Richard WRIGHT, executors of James Smythe, v. Sara EDMONDES, his servant.

Gold.   ————.

44-45   Henry VERNON, nephew and heir of Richard Vernon, clerk, v. Richard TYSDALE of London, merchant tailor.

Detention of deeds relating to a messuage in St. Augustine's ' next Paules gate.'   LONDON.

46   Randall VERNON v. George TOUCHET, lord Audley, and William SNEYDE, knight, his steward.

Refusal to admit complainant to land in the manor of Audley.   STAFFORD.

47-49   Henry VEYSYE, gentleman, v. Robert CHAPMAN and Elizabeth his wife.

Messuage in St. Mary's, Cambridge, at the nether end of Market Hill, formerly of Richard Atkynson.   CAMBRIDGE.

50   Nicholas VIZAKERLEY of Stotfold, co. Bedford, yeoman, v. John MANNYNGHAM and others.

Double sale of a tenement called the SWAN in Baldock and land in Welleyn (*i.e.* Willian?).   HERTS.

51-52   John VYCAR and John his son v. Thomas NORMAN.

Tenement called Woolcotts in the manor of Brampton Regis (Kynges Brinton) of the demise of John Norman, late prior of Barlinch, and his convent.   SOMERSET.

53   John VYNCENT v. George STANLEY, gentleman.

Refusal to complete a conveyance of a messuage and land in the manor of Kidlington in pledge for a loan.   OXFORD.

54-57   John VYVYAN of Trenoweth (in St. Columb Major), son and heir of Richard Vyvyan, v. Sampson HICK and Michael ROUS.

Detention of deeds relating to messuages and land at Gluvian in St. Columb Major (Glyvyan Vargh by Tounflore).   CORNWALL.

FILE 1480.

1-2   Katharine WALGRAVE v. Richard SMYTH.

Debt.   ESSEX.

3   William WALROND and Eleanor his wife v. . . . . .

Tenement in the manor of Whitestaunton claimed in the Court of Requests by Nicholas, son of Richard Spragatt (Sprakett). *Damaged.*   SOMERSET.

4   Henry WALSHE, clerk, v. Thomasyn, late the wife of William THOMAS, attainted of treason.

Action for the prebend of Nonington, complainant being absent as lecturer on the Lady Margaret's foundation at Oxford.   HEREFORD.

5-7   William WALTER and Helen his wife, late the wife of John Vyncent, v. Thomas, son and heir of Thomas DEREHAM.

Land (*described*) in defendant's manor of Crymplesham.   [NORFOLK.]

8-11   Robert WALWORTH, parson of Allington, v. Richard MA(W)BORN.

Part of the glebe of Allington claimed under a lease from Richard Thirkell, late parson.   LINCOLN.

12-14   Nicholas WATKYNSON and Elizabeth his wife, late the wife of Thomas ap John, v. Anthony FORSTER, esquire, John MALYN, and many others.

Mansion-house called Elton Hall in North Collingham. *Replication wanting.* D. XII, 8.   NOTTS.

15-16   Thomas WATYS, vicar of Abbotsbury, v. Thomas SYMONS and Giles STRANGWYS, knight, lessee of the rectory.

Dispute as to vicarial tithes.   DORSET.

7 1   John WEBBE of Houghton Regis, husbandman, v. William HOLLAND, bailiff of the liberty of Leighton Buzzard.

Toll in Leighton Market, from which complainant is exempt as a tenant in ancient demesne of the Crown.   BEDFORD.

8 1   John WEBBER v. Robert STRAINGE (Straunge).

Partition of a messuage and land in Black Torrington.   DEVON.

19-21.   Richard WELBY, esquire, v. Richard TOMSON and others, inhabitants of Stixwould.

Claim of right of way and common in complainant's land at Halstead (in Stixwould).   LINCOLN.

22-23   John WELLES, kinsman and heir of Richard Welles, v. William FYNNE (Phynne).

Detention of deeds relating to messuages and land in Clapton (*place omitted in bill ; described in answer*).   SUFFOLK.

24-25.   John, son of John WELLOCKE, deceased, v. Robert FOS[DIKE].

[House and land in] Hadleigh, money and goods, late of the deceased, whose executors both parties are. *Mutilated.*   SUFFOLK.

26–29   Richard WERE of Horsmonden, yeoman, v. William and John ONGLEY and Thomas
AUSTEN.
Detention of deeds relating to a messuage and land in Horsmonden and Goudhurst formerly of
Robert Poille.   •   KENT.

30–31   Margaret, late the wife of Lewis WEST, esquire, v. Thomas CULPEPER, esquire.
Partition of land of Christopher Hales, knight, deceased, Master of the Rolls and father of complainant.   LINCOLN.

32–33   John WESTBYE, esquire, v. William HARDYNGTON.
Messuage and land in Holmes, late of William Westbye, esquire, deceased, father of complainant.
Faded.   LANCASTER.

34   Leonard WESTE, esquire, servant to the Queen, and Barbara his wife v. William GAS-
COIGNE, esquire.
Manor of Thorpe in Balne, entailed by Thomas Gascoigne, esquire, together with the manor of
Burgh-Wallis and lands there and in Skellow, Cam[psall?] and Owston. *Mutilated.*   YORK.

35–37   The same v. Robert EYER, gentleman, and Jane his wife.
Continuation of *File 1482, No.* 48.   [YORK.]

38–41   Hugh WESTWOODE v. Roger REDYNG.
Manor or lordship of Arlingham and land there formerly of Simon Lowe, citizen and merchant tailor
of London. *See File 1365, No.* 80.   GLOUCESTER.

42   George WHITFELD and Anne (Agnes) his wife v. John DICONSON, yeoman.
Land and common of pasture in Partney, late of Walter Wright, deceased, former husband of the
said Anne.   LINCOLN.

43–44   The same v. the same.
Inducing the said Agnes to sell the premises below their value.   LINCOLN.

45–47   Anne, late the wife of Richard, son of William WHYTGROME *alias* Cowper, v. Edward
GRENE, brother-in-law of the said Richard.
Messuages and lands in Broadwater and Sompting.   SUSSEX.

48–49   Richard WILLINGHAM, labourer, v. William CLAY.
Messuage and land in Scawby, late of Robert Chapman, deceased, great-uncle of complainant.
                                                                                       LINCOLN.

50–51   Robert, son and heir of James WODROF and of Phelyse his wife, administratrix of his
goods, v. William GARDENER, second husband of the said Phelyse, and John GROTE-
RAKES his lessee.
Lands in Uttoxeter, Uttoxeter Woodland, Marchington, and Marchington Woodland, and share of
goods under the custom of the county.   STAFFORD.

52   Thomas WODWALL v. John MONHOWSE (Monnox).
Detention of deeds relating to a messuage in Bewdley.   WORCESTER.

53–57   John WOLCOTT, Agnes his wife, and Harry their son v. Gawen CAROWE, knight, steward
of the manor of Exminster.
Meadow held of the said manor.   DEVON.

58–60   Roger WOLHOUSE, citizen and haberdasher of London, v. Richard RAWLYNSON.
Price of haberdashery sold to William Rawlynson of Doncaster, deceased, son of complainant.
                                                                                       LONDON, YORK.

61–66   Richard WOLLET (Wyllett), yeoman, v. John GOODMAN and Robert COCKES, of London.
Arbitration as to a messuage and land in Alkham of which the said Goodman made a secret lease
acquired by complainant without knowledge of old conditions.   KENT.

67   Richard WOOD[LYF] of Baumber, husbandman, v. John WATSON and Alice his wife.
Messuage and land in Ingham, late of Lawrence Woodlyf, deceased, grandfather of complainant.
Mutilated.   LINCOLN.

68–69   Francis, son and heir of John WORSELEY, v. Thomas GRANTHAM, gentleman, executor
of Margaret Brycknell.
Detention of deeds relating to the manor of Grendon and lands in Deeping Gate, Maxey, and
Deeping St. James.   NORTHAMPTON, LINCOLN.

70   Ralph WORSELEY of London, esquire, servant to the Queen, v. John MYNSHULL,
esquire, and others.
Enclosure of complainant's waste in Birkenhead (Birket).   CHESTER.

71–73   Roger, son of John WRIGHT of Kenton, v. Thomas BROME of Ubbeston.
Detention of deeds relating to a messuage and land in [Kenton] formerly of John Ryvet of
Rishangles. *Faded.*   SUFFOLK.

74   Ralph WRYNE of Hesslewood, co. York, son and heir of William Wryne, v. Ralph
DAVENPORTE.
Detention of deeds relating to messuages in Eastgate Street and Watergate Street, Chester. *See
Files 916, No.* 40; *1283, No.* 14; *1323, No.* 37.   CHESTER.

75–78   John WYBUNBURY v. Laurence SAVAGE, Elizabeth his wife, John DAVENPORT, and
others.
Lease of Swottenham Hall and land in Swottenham of the bequest of John Wybunbury, father of
complainant, and former husband of the said Elizabeth.   CHESTER.

79–81   Joan, late the wife of John WYCHEHALSSE, and daughter of John HYEM *alias* Cutwyll
and of Joan his wife, both deceased, v. Hugh and Thomas HELE.
Land in Great Totnes formerly of John Symons.   DEVON.

82   Rowland WYLDMAN of Stonesby *v.* Robert WRYGHT of Castle Bytham.
Money promised on marriage with defendant's daughters.   LEICESTER, LINCOLN.

83-84   William WYLKYNSON *v.* Gilbert ASTELEY of Patshull, co. Stafford, esquire, and
Robert, Alice and Agnes HERDY.
Land at Mykylwhayte in Byngley of the demise of the said Asteley. *Damaged.*   [YORK.]

85-89   Richard WYNNE, vicar of Hore, *v.* Robert MELLER.
Portion of glebe claimed by defendant as sectorial.   LEICESTER.

90-93   The same (Wyne) *v.* Robert and Edmund, sons of Christopher EYERS.
Do. and corn-tithe.   (The said Meller takes part in the rejoinder.)   LEICESTER.

FILE 1481.

1   Randall WADE *v.* Ralph EGERTON of Wrinehill, co. Stafford, knight.
Loan at Northwich.   CHESTER.

2-4   William WADLEY of London, tailor, *v.* [John LYTELTON].
Contempt of a decree of the Court of Augmentations concerning lands (*described*) at Rockley in
Stanton Lacy. *Damaged.*   SALOP.

5   Parnell, late the wife of the said William, *v.* [the same?].
Reviver of the preceding(?). *Mutilated.*   SALOP.

6-8   The same and John GYFFORD and Susan his wife, daughter of the said William *v.* [John
DE VERE, earl of Oxford], John LITLETON, esquire, and William (John) BRAMPTON.
Wrongful occupation of the same. *Mutilated.* D. XII, 42.   SALOP.

9-10   Edmund WAKEHAM and Katherine his wife *v.* Thomas STUKELEY, gentleman, and
Alice his wife.
Legacy of John Burley, deceased, father of the said Katherine, and former husband of the said
Alice, who died seised of a messuage and land in Thurlstone, Bigbury and elsewhere.   DEVON.

11   John WALKER of Sherborne *v.* Humphrey CONYSBY, esquire, and John CALLOWHYLL.
Cottage and land in the said Conysby's manor of   .   .   . *Mutilated.*   WORCESTER.

12-13   John WALSHE, esquire, *v.* Thomas ALYNGTON, gentleman.
Detention of deeds relating to the manor (*sic*) of Cathanger and Staye (Stowye) in Fivehead.
     SOMERSET.

14   Reynold WARCOPE of London, gentleman, *v.* John HARRISON.
Issues of lands in Birkmyre belonging to Henry, son and heir of John Broweham of Brougham,
complainant's ward.   WESTMORLAND.

15-17   Robert WARDE, Joan his wife, late the wife of John Hartknoll the younger, and Thomas
HARTKNOLL, son of the said John and Joan, *v.* John HARTKNOLL the elder, Robert
his brother, and Richard CORNYSHE of Ilfracombe.
Messuages and land at Middle Hagginton in Berrynarbor of the grant of the said John the elder.
     DEVON.

18   Robert WAREN of Harleston, butcher, *v.* Michael LANKESTER of [the same?], butcher.
Rent of land in Kirton due to William Scrutton of Walton, yeoman.   SUFFOLK.

19   William WARREN and Agnes his wife, daughter of William ASTELL, *v.* Joan ASTELL,
executrix, and late the wife of the said William.
Debt assigned to the said Agnes by Richard Fox on a promise of marriage.   ———

20   Arthur WATSON, mercer, *v.* Robert SHERWOOD of Digby, husbandman, and others.
Money promised to obtain a vicar for the parish of Digby.   LINCOLN.

21   Edward WATSON of Rockingham, esquire, *v.* John MARKHAM, gentleman.
' Sore ' falcon promised in exchange for a ' laneret.'   NORTHAMPTON.

22-24   Margaret WATTON of Chesterton *v.* Miles PRAUNCE of Cambridge, brewer.
Detention of deeds relating to a messuage (*described*) in St. Clement's, Cambridge, bought of William
Browne by John Walton, deceased, husband of complainant.   CAMBRIDGE.

25-26   The same and John WATTON, executors of John Watton of Chesterton, *v.* the same and
Katherine his wife, executrix, and late the wife of William Browne.
Action on a bond for a debt already paid.   CAMBRIDGE.

27   William WAULE of Cradley, nailer, *v.* Laurence HYPKYS of Rowley, smith.
Price of iron and hire of tools, including a ' twerne,' a ' cantell ' of iron, and a ' herthstaffe.'
     WORCESTER, STAFFORD.

28-33   John WAYLANDE and Alice his wife *v.* Simon MAWER (Mower) of Freslond (*i.e.*
Freiston?) and Grace his wife.
Share of money entrusted to defendants by Alice Crame of Butterwick, deceased, mother of the
said Alice.   LINCOLN.

34   Humphrey WELLES, esquire, and Jane CHATWYN, executors of Thomas Chatwyn,
esquire, *v.* Joan, executrix, and late the wife of Robert DORRINGTON of Stafford.
Debt of Ralph Bagnoll, knight, paid at the said Robert's request, on promise of the collectorship
of rents in the deanery of Stafford.   STAFFORD.

35   Faith WELTON *v.* John DENE and Robert WOODSHIDE, both of Lowestoft.
Goods of Richard Welton of Lowestoft, deceased, husband of complainant.   SUFFOLK.

36-37   Simon WESTMERLAND of Normanby *v.* Thomas HALTON, administrator of the goods
of Richard Blawe, deceased.
Action on a bond for price of wool already paid.   LINCOLN.

38   Alexander WHEATLEY of Grantham, shoemaker, *v.* Richard ATCOCKE, parson of Wyverbee (*i.e.* Wyfordby?).
Cost of bringing up defendant's illegitimate child.   LINCOLN [LEICESTER?]

39   William WHELER *v.* Stephen CLAYBROKE and Eustace CLYNCHE.
Land in Hendon, late of Katherine Wheler, deceased, mother of complainant.   MIDDLESEX.

40–41   Thomas WHITE, parson of Longworth, *v.* Philip WYBLEN and Edmund STRAUNGE.
Share of a corn-rent payable to maintain a priest in the chapel of Charney.   BERKS.

42–43   Martin WHITFORD, husbandman, and Henry JAGOWE, yeoman, both of Tregony, *v.* Nicholas HERLE, esquire.
Procuring defendants to remove a gelding from Roche, for which they were sued for trespass.   CORNWALL.

44–47   Andrew, son and heir of Andrew WHITYNGE, *v.* Richard WYNTERFLODE.
Land in Little Hedingham held of defendant's manor of Liston Hall.   ESSEX.

48–49   Walter WHYTE of Horningsham, husbandman, *v.* Richard, son of Richard EARLE.
Messuages and land in Melksham.   WILTS.

50–53   John WILKINSON, citizen and merchant tailor of London, *v.* Thomas EASTE and others.
Detention of deeds relating to messuages and lands in Hemyngley, Hundelbie, Braetofte, Erbelouthe, and Hagworthingham, bought of John Parrot, knight.   LINCOLN.

54–57   Thomas WODWARDE *v.* Thomas THORNE.
Refusal to complete a lease of a messuage in Syresham.   NORTHAMPTON.

58–59   Thomas WOLLERYE *v.* John LYSAUNTES.
Messuages and land in Cheltenham. *Mutilated.*   GLOUCESTER.

60   The same *v.* the same, son of William Lysauntes, deceased.
Site of the manor of Lower Lee (Netherlee) in Westbury(-on-Severn), with land, formerly of Simon Rawleyghe.   GLOUCTESTER.

61   Richard WOLLEY of Newark-on-Trent, labourer, *v.* John WOLLEY of Saxondale.
Money received on complainant's behalf from William Ballard of Wymeswold, gentleman. NOTTS.

62–63   George WORSELEY, parson of Nettleton, *v.* Elizabeth, late the wife of William JONES.
Detention of deeds relating to part of complainant's glebe.   WILTS.

64–65   Thomas WORSHEPE of Lowestoft, merchant, *v.* Agnes, late the wife of Thomas BARTON of Harwich, his uncle, and administratrix of his goods.
Ship called the *Houtaylle* of Harwich and money and goods of the bequest of the said Thomas Barton.   SUFFOLK, ESSEX.

66   James WORSLEY of Hamworthy, gentleman, *v.*   .   .   .
Manor of Shapwick, formerly of John Cammell. *Mutilated.*   DORSET.

67   James WRYGHT *v.* Joan, late the wife of John SAUNDERSON, and Nicholas his son.
Reviver of a suit for meadow in Carlton (*File* 1394, *No.* 50).   NOTTS.

68–69   Thomas WRYGHT of Onnely and Elizabeth his wife *v.* Richard OCATE.
Messuage and land in Bignall (Bignehill) and Talke.   STAFFORD.

70–76   Robert WYLKOKE *v.* Richard and Agnes WYLCOCK.
Messuage and land in Shouldham, late of Agnes Wylcoke, deceased, grandfather of complainant.   NORFOLK.

77   Anne WYLKYNSON *v.* Richard STANNYLAND and others.
Messuage and land in Wyrkesopp of the entail of Robert Wylkynson, deceased, grandfather of complainant.   [NOTTS.]

78   William WYLLOUGHBY of Nuneaton, co. Warwick, tanner, *v.* Richard ALLYNSON.
Messuages and gardens in Nottingham, late of Richard Wylloughby, deceased, grandfather of complainant.   NOTTS.

79–81   Henry WYLLYAMS *v.* William MAYNSTON, William HOLLANDE, and Austin WHELER.
Land in Beckington, bought of William Foster and Juliana his wife. *Answer mutilated.*   SOMERSET.

82–85   Thomas and James, sons and executors of Robert WYLSMERE, *v.* Gabriel BUSSHE, an administrator of the goods of Alice, late the wife of the said Robert.
Goods of John Sariche. *Mutilated.*   DIOCESE OF LONDON.

86   Margaret WYLSON of London, late the wife of Robert Wylson of Twoe Peny, *v.* William WYLSON of Twoe Peny.
Seizure of goods.   LONDON, CUMBERLAND.

87–90   Robert WYNDE (Wyend) of St. Ives, tanner, and Richard ROBYNS of Godmanchester, executors of John Wynde of Brancaster, gentleman, *v.* John BARNARDESTON, gentleman.
Collusive suit on a bond given to Christopher Myller.   HUNTINGDON, NORFOLK.

91–93   Edmund WYNDHAM, knight, and Richard NICHOLLES, gentleman, *v.* Humphrey CONYE.
Pasture in Wiggenhall held of defendant's manor of Kenwick in Tilney.   NORFOLK.

94–95   Harry WYNDRYCHE and Joan his wife, executrix of Thomas Smyth of Mutford, *v.* Richard HAMOND and Alice his wife, executrix and late the wife of Thomas Thorneton.
Loan of cattle.   SUFFOLK.

96–97   Peter (Thomas, Walter) WYNSEMORE *alias* Cee of Bristol *v.* Thomas SHOTE (Swite, Sute) and Thomas WILLIAMS.
Cottage held of the manor of Bedminster of the demise of Harry Williams, parson of Bedminster.
         SOMERSET.

98   Richard WYXSTED of Westminster, clothworker, *v.* Thomas DODDE and Anne his wife.
Messuage and land in Vauxhall and Wrenbury, formerly of Thomas Starkie, esquire.   CHESTER.

FILE 1482.

1–3   William WADE of Wilby *v.* Roger WADE.
Legacy of William Wade of Brundish, father of both parties, who died seized of lands in Earl Soham.   SUFFOLK.

4–6   Thomas WATERS, Richard POLLYN, Alice his wife, Thomas HAWKYNS, and Elizabeth his wife, *v.* Thomas, son and heir of Richard BRAY.
Messuages and land in Caddington, late of John Cristian, deceased, grandfather of the said Thomas Waters, Alice and Elizabeth.   BEDFORD, HERTS.

Walter WALKER, yeoman, son and heir of Richard Walker, *v.* James RYLEY.
Detention of deeds relating to a close in Meriden.   WARWICK.

8–9   The same *v.* the same and Thomas WALKER of Warwick, tanner.
Do.   WARWICK.

10–11   William WALSAME, husband of Agnes, late the wife of John Bullocke of Lounde, *v.* Thomas STIRROPE and William GREE.
Bond for payment of legacies to the children of the said Bullocke.   ?

12–17   Robert WALTON, clerk, son and heir of Richard Walton, *v.* Edward PLANKNEY, gentleman, and Thomas GREVE, merchant.
Messuage with appurtenances in Northgate Street, Chester.   CHESTER.

18–19   Reynold WAPPAM of Wiston, yeoman, *v.* John, son of Robert SERLE.
Messuage and land in Chillington, late of Richard Wappam. *Mutilated.*   SUSSEX.

20–21   Edith WARNER *v.* Robert AYSSHE of North Petherton.
Money and apparel promised to complainant at the end of her service.   SOMERSET.

22–28   William WARNER *v.* Thomas LOVELL, knight, son and heir of Francis Lovell, knight, and Thomas RUDDOCKE.
Messuage, land and a fold-course with appurtenances in Bridgeham and Roudham, late of Nicholas Hare, knight, Master of the Rolls.   NORFOLK.

29–30   Henry WATSONE of Ampthill, co. Bedford, labourer, *v.* William JENYNGES.
Cottage and pightle in Baldock.   HERTS.

31   James WATTYE, husbandman, *v.* Thomas ENYS and John TRESPRESON.
Tenement called Rosemeryn (in St. Budock?) of the demise of John Penkevell and William Trespreson.   CORNWALL.

32–33   George WAUTON *v.* Miles WHITSTOKE of St. Olave's (Saint Toylie) in the suburbs of London.
Rings and gown entrusted to defendants.   [SURREY.]

34   Anthony, William, Thomas, Nicholas, Edmund and Jane WEBBE and Edith BRAMSDON, children of Christopher Webbe, deceased, *v.* Agnes and John PLEDALL.
Detention of a lease of the manor of Studley Grange made by the late abbot of Stanley.   WILTS.

35–39   John WEBBER, clothier, *v.* Nicholas OSBORN and Alice his wife, executrix and late the wife of Richard Syth.
Woad seized at Minehead on an unreasonable replevim.   SOMERSET.

40   Alexander WELLYS *v.* Thomas A MERE.
Messuage and garden in Nether Street, Ryde. *Mutilated.*   [HANTS, I.W.]

41–45   Jane WENTWORTH and others, executors of Nicholas Wentworth, knight, porter at Calais, *v.* Paul DAYRELL, esquire.
Lease by defendant of lands in Lillingstone Darvell.   BUCKINGHAM.

46–47   Henry WESCOTT of Stafford Castle *v.* William WESCOTT of Handsacre [his grandfather?].
Sale of lands entailed on complainant at the marriage of Roger, son of defendant, with Eleanor, daughter of John Wolseley of Wolseley. *Mutilated.*   STAFFORD.

48   Leonard WEST, esquire, servant to the Queen, and Barbara his wife, the Queen's woman, *v.* Robert EYRE, gentleman, and Joan his wife.
Detention of deeds relating to a messuage called Rockley Hall *alias* Shirley House and land in Burgh-Wallis.   YORK.

49–52   The same *v.* Richard MOORE.
Wrongful occupation of the same. *Mutilated.*   YORK.

53–54   Richard WEST, parson of South Somercotes, *v.* Nicholas GIRLYNGTON, gentleman.
Forcible ouster from complainant's glebe and seizure of tithe corn and deeds.   LINCOLN.

55   Anthony and Edward WESTON, executors of William Weston, B.D., parson of Godmanchester, *v.* Thomas COLLYNS and Joan his wife.
Money, plate, books, writings, etc.   HUNTINGDON.

56   John WESTON and Parnell his wife, cousin-german of William Sherington, knight,
deceased, v. Henry SHERINGTON, brother of the said Sir William and administrator of
his goods.
Money paid by John Pope to the said Sir William to the use of the said Parnell.   ———

57-58   Richard WHALLEY, esquire, v. Anthony EYRE and Henry HUET.
Detention of deeds relating to the manor of Whitwell.   DERBY.

59   The same v. John ROWELL of London, embroiderer, late his servant, and Paul POPE,
scrivener.
Theft of clothing from chests in Mr. Mering's house called Derby Place.   LONDON.

60   Richard WHALLEY, esquire, late chamberlain to the Duke of Somerset, v. John RAVISHE,
clerk, the Duke's comptroller.
Action for wages disallowed by complainant, after a judgment of this court in the latter's favour.
                                                                               SURREY.

61-63   Thomas WHALLEY, gentleman, v. Ralph WYNDALL of Willoughby, yeoman.
Detention of bonds relating to the discharge of a debt due to Walter Whalley of Willoughby, uncle
of complainant.   NOTTS.

64-65   William WHITEFELD v. George KERY, an executor of Thomas Kyrye.
Annuity of the bequest of the said Thomas, who died seized of lands in Binweston, Leighton
Rogers, Hyssington (Hyston), Wilmington (in Chirbury), Wynsley (i.e. Winsbury in Chirbury?),
Rorrington (in Chirbury), Asterley (in Pontesbury), Wandsworth, Battersea, and Slingesby alias
.   .   . ekerse. Other legacies described. Mutilated.   SALOP, SURREY, KENT.

66-67   The same v. the same and the mayor, bailiffs, etc., of SHREWSBURY.
Actions of debt. Subpœna and [corpus cum causa]. Mutilated.   SALOP.

68   John WHYTE v. Wylmott, late the wife of Nicholas LYDE of Chipping Torrington, and
administratrix of his goods.
Price of leather.   DEVON.

69   Christopher WIGGENS v. John DAVY alias Baker.
Tenement in Walton by Aylesbury, late of Thomas Baker, deceased, great-uncle of complainant.
                                                                                 BUCKS.

70   William WILBON and Robert LUCAS, for themselves [and other inhabitants] of Shefford,
v. John MYLWARD of Gravenhurst.
Land in Shefford acquired for maintenance of the road there.   BEDFORD.

71   Henry WILLAN of Kelshall, co. Herts, v. Hugh JENKYNSON of London, salter.
Bond and fee for apprenticeship of John, brother of complainant, whom defendant failed to teach.
Subpœna duces tecum.   LONDON.

72   Thomas WILLIAMS of London, merchant tailor, v. Richard AUNDERSON of Northaw
(the Northe Halle), gentleman.
Bond for price of cloth (described) bought of William Feildinge of London, merchant tailor.
                                                                          LONDON, HERTS.

73-74   Robert WOOD v. John ap Harry ap John GRUFFITH and Lourie his wife.
Detention of deeds relating to messuages, burgages, lands and rents in Flint and Coleshill, late of
Robert Wood, deceased, father of complainant and husband of the said Lourie.   FLINT.

75   Robert WOODE, Agnes his wife, William HASSAR, and Geoffrey BAYLIE, clerk, v.
Thomas CANTIE of Holton-le-Moor (Howton in the More), labourer, Peter LEE, and
Edward WEBSTER, priest.
Presentation to the church of Welton by Louth, granted by the prior and convent of Ormsby to
Richard Hasser, whose executors are the said Agnes and William.   LINCOLN.

76-79   Hamond WOODHALL v. Nicholas, grandson and heir of Thomas BOOTHE.
Messuage and land in Goxhill (Golsell) of the entail of William Woodhall, grandfather of complainant.   LINCOLN.

80   John WORME v. Nicholas THEWE.
Messuage in the manor of St. Ives, late of Thomas Feld, clerk.   HUNTINGDON.

81   Edward WRYGHT v. Henry KYRKE, chaplain.
Sums payable on an under-lease of the parsonage of Conington. Mutilated.   HUNTINGDON.

82-88   Ellen WRYNE of Hesslewood, co. York, executrix, and late the wife of Ralph Wryne,
gentleman, v. John (Jenkyn), son and heir of John ALDERSEY, gentleman, and William
ALDERSEY.
Messuages, land and rent in Middle Aldersey, Crook Aldersey, Clutton (Clatton), Chowley, and
Coddington. Faded. See Files 922, No. 18; 1086, No. 18.   CHESTER.

89   Roger WURTHYNGTON, Alice his wife, and John their son v. Elizabeth, late the wife of
Henry WYGLEY and George WYGLEY.
Messuage and land in the said Elizabeth's manor of Scraptoft, late of the prior and convent of
Coventry.   LEICESTER.

90   John WYDLAKE of Catcombe, husbandman, great-grandson and heir of Thomas
Sto(w)ye, v. John HUGH.
Detention of deeds relating to a burgage and land in Dunster.   SOMERSET.

91-96   John WYKE v. Nicholas BARBAR, Margery his wife, and Robert FOSTER of Tonge.
Bond of the said Foster bequeathed to complainant by William Wyke of Prior's Lee, yeoman,
father of the said John and Margery.   SALOP.

97   William WYKES and Henry STEPHINS, gentlemen, and John BOWDON, parishioners and governors of the parish of Northlew, in the name of the said parishioners, v. John COVE.
Messuage and land called the Church House in Northlew demised to complainants and others for the repair of the church.   DEVON.

98   William WYLLOWES v. Anne [DE VERE], countess of Oxford.
Land in Camps of the demise of defendant.   CAMBRIDGE.

99–100 Hugh WYLLUGHBY and Elizabeth his wife, late the wife of John Laurens, v. Henry, grandson and heir of Thomas LAWRENCE.
Annuity awarded to complainants in this court out of the manor of Solton (in West Cliffe) and lands in Bridge, Upper Hardres, Rowling (in Goodnestone and Wingham), Nackington, and Parmested (in Kingston). *See File* 1390, *No.* 60.   KENT.

101   William WYLLYAMS of East Parley v. John RYNGWOOD.
Debt of Francis Bucklond, vicar of Sopley, deceased, of whose goods defendant is administrator.   HANTS.

102   John WYLLYAMSON v. the sheriffs of LONDON.
Action by Henry Wood for money entrusted to complainant and repaid. *Certiorari.*   LONDON.

103   Edward WYLMOT of Witney, merchant, v. William BOXE of London and Philip his brother.
Refusal to complete a sale of lands in the tithing of Corbery in Witney.   OXFORD.

104   Thomas Maria WYNGEFELDE of Kimbolton, co. Huntingdon, esquire, v. John BOSGRAVE of Renhold (Rennall), gentleman, servant to the Earl of Bedford.
Rival leases of the parsonage of Dean from the dean and chapter of Worcester and William Chamberlen, parson, deprived.   BEDFORD.

105–106 Mark, son of William WYNTER, deceased, and administrator of his goods, v. John SALTER.
Land in Rogate and Harting of the demise of the abbot of Durford.   SUSSEX.

FILE 1483.

1–7   Edward WALKER of London, yeoman, v. Christopher BYKKERS.
Crown lease of a tenement in Cawthorpe.   YORK.

8   John WALKER of Brokenborough, co. Wilts, husbandman, v. HOELL ap Thomas and others.
Messuages and land in Llanfihangel, late of David ap Rosser, deceased, uncle of complainant.   BRECON.

9   Richard WALLASTON v. the sheriffs of LONDON.
Action by William son and executor of Thomas Poyntell for a debt which should have been set against the profits of a parsonage (*name omitted*).   LONDON.

10   Arthur WALSHE, esquire, and Mary his wife, daughter of Bryan Tuke, knight, v. John NORTON and William HOGBYN.
Detention of deeds relating to the manors of Tatenham (in Sellinge) and Heyton (in Stanford) and a messuage and lands in Sellinge, Stanford, Ostenhanger, Monks' Horton, Lymne, Hurst, and Eastbridge of the settlement of Reynold Scott, knight, former husband of the said Mary.   KENT.

11–14   Matthew WARCOPPE v. Eleanor WILTON.
Price of three ' eskeppes ' of bigg sold to John, son of defendant.   ———

15   Christopher WARREN of Coventry, draper, v. Edward BYBBYE.
Reviver of a suit for part price of cloth, dismissed owing to complainant's absence through illness.   WARWICK.

16   Randall WARREN v. John MATLEY and George RIDGEWAY.
Lease of meadow in Stockport (Stopforthe) promised to the said Warren and Ridgeway jointly by the said Matley.   CHESTER.

17–21   Richard WATTES and Eleanor his wife, a daughter of Joan Hannam, deceased, v. Matthew, son and heir of William GRENE.
Land and common of pasture for a ' heyffecare ' and other beasts in defendant's manor of Wilton (*rectius* Milton) Clevedon.   SOMERSET.

22–26   Katherine, late the wife of William WEBBE, v. John WEBBE his executor.
Detention of deeds relating to tenements in Salisbury.   WILTS.

27–29   Robert WEBBE v. William EVERELL of Oundle, chandler.
Money entrusted to defendant by complainant's uncle, John Webbe, deceased, parson of Benefield.   NORTHAMPTON.

30   The same v. William EVERELL the younger, Edmund ABELL and Eleanor his wife.
Reviver of the above, the said William and Eleanor being executors of William the elder.   NORTHAMPTON.

31   Nicholas WEBSTER and Agnes his wife v. Anne GEE.
Messuages in Rothley, late of Robert Vyncent of Markfield, deceased, grandfather of the said Agnes.   LEICESTER.

32–33   Edmund, son of Henry WEKES, deceased, v. Hugh his brother and Anthony HONYCHURCHE.
Lease of land in Broadwoodkelly, to the said Hugh only, in breach of conditions of surrender of a former lease.   SOMERSET.

34–36   Agnes, late the wife of Thomas WELSTEDE, v. William LOKYER and William BUDDON, husbandman.
Tenement called ' Gauntes Ferme ' of the demise of John Leigh. . . *Mutilated.*   DORSET.

37   Margaret, late the wife of Lewis WEST, esquire, *v.* George TOFTES and others, feoffees to uses.
Writ of error on a fine of lands in Canterbury. *Mutilated.*   KENT.

38–41 `   Margaret WEST, a daughter and heir of Christopher Hales, knight, *v.* William WEST, knight, formerly her guardian, and John ROBYNS of London, draper.
Seizure of bonds given by the said Robyns to Lewis West of Wales, co. York, esquire, deceased, husband of complainant and son of the said Sir William, and action of debt.   YORK, LONDON.

42–43   Lewis WESTE and John DYER *v.* Ralph JOHNSON.
Action on a bond for a debt respited by agreement.   KENT.

44   John WEY of Stoke St. Gregory, weaver, *v.* Agnes, late the wife of Richard BAYNE, deceased, and administratrix of his goods.
Money promised to complainant on his marriage with Joan, daughter of the said Richard   SOMERSET.

45   Richard WHALLEY, esquire, *v.* William BOWLLES, esquire.
Detention of vouchers to an account of the parsonage of Ratcliffe ordered by this court.   NOTTS.

46–47.·   Richard WHALLEY, esquire, *v.* Ralph PYNDER of London, grocer.
Procuring an attachment for a debt satisfied by Hugh Willoughby, knight.   LONDON.

48   Robert WHEATLEY of Netherton, co. York, *v.* James WHEATLEY, parson of Barton-in-the-Beans.
Lease of defendant's parsonage promised in return for goods supplied.   NOTTS.

49   Robert WHETEAKER of Bishopstrow, clothman, *v.* William BROWNE.
Detention of deeds relating to a messuage and land in Cherhill.   WILTS.

50   John WHITEFORD of Edmonton, co. Middlesex, *v.* JOHN ap Gruffydd ap Powell and John LLOID.
Detention of deeds relating to pasture in Llanferras bought of Jevan ap Richard.   DENBIGH.

51–52   John WHRYTTE of Henham *v.* Alice WHRYTTE his ' mother-in-laywe ' (*i.e.* stepmother).
Lands (*described*) in Debden, late of William Whrytte, deceased, father of complainant.   ESSEX.

53   Joan WHYTE *v.* William WHYTE of Newport, co. Bucks.
Promise to assure messuages and lands in Kilburn and Hampstead to William Whyte, deceased, husband of complainant and son of defendant.   MIDDLESEX.

54–56   John WHYTE of Bristol, gentleman, *v.* George HERBERT, knight, executor of John Cradocke of Bedminster.
Debt, defendant claiming to have sold his executorship.   GLOUCESTER, SOMERSET.

57–59   Thomas WHYTE, knight, alderman of London, *v.* John MYDWYNTER and Agnes his wife.
Price of cloth supplied to Edmund Blackburne of Brighton, draper, late the husband of the said Agnes.   LONDON, SUSSEX.

60–61   Robert WILCOCKES *v.* Thomas RAVEN.
Refusal to complete a conveyance of a messuage and land in Knossington (Knoston), formerly of the monastery of Owston (Wooston).   LEICESTER.

62–63   Thomas WILLOUGHBY, esquire, a minor in the king's ward, *v.* George MEDLEY and others, executors of Henry Willoughby his father.
Profits of the manors of Wollaton and Middleton.   NOTTS., WARWICK.

64   William WINDSOR, lord Windsor, *v.* James [BLUNTE], lord Mountjoy.
Reviver of a suit against William [Blunte], lord Mountjoy, for the manors of Brayton, Sutton, Sapperton, Alkmonton, Bentley, Hatton, Langweston (*i.e.* Longstone?), Brightrichfeld (*i.e.* Birchill near Dronfield or Birdfield in Edington?), Totley (in Dronfield), Hazlewood, Fald Madeley (*i.e.* Madeley in Checkley?), Hampton Tovet, Thikenap[le]tre (in Hampton Lovett?), and Alwastre, and water-mill and lands in Fald Madeley, Alseyghe, Cotton, Alvaston, Ambaston, Alleston, and elsewhere, and 12 ' buliveres ' of salt within Hampton Lovet and Bartwich (in Droitwich?). *Mutilated.*   DERBY, STAFFORD, WORCESTER, LEICESTER.

65–66   Robert, son and heir of Robert WITTON, *v.* Thomas PLOMER.
Detention of deeds relating to messuages and lands in Walsoken and Wisbech.   NORFOLK, CAMBRIDGE.

67   Jane WOODHEWS *v.* Humphrey GABATUS of Bonsall, clerk.
Debt, the bond for which is lost.   DERBY.

68–69   Francis WOODHOWSE, gentleman, *v.* John ATTMER.
Manor of Great Breckles and lands there and in Hockham (Heokkham), Shropham, Stow, and Thompson, the deeds of which were seized during Ket's rebellion.   NORFOLK.

70–75   William WOTTON of Salisbury *v.* Edmund BOWER.
Debt of Thomas Norman of Salisbury, clerk, deceased.   WILTS.

76   Anthony WRIGHT *v.* Thomas ESTWOOD and Alice his wife.
Presents given to the said Alice in expectation of marriage.   ———

77–80   Richard WYCHERLEY of Milcott, co. Warwick, son and heir of Richard Wycherley of Wycherley, and Jane his wife *v.* Thomas STURY, esquire.
Messuage and land in Ross Hall (in St. Chad's, Shrewsbury), late of Eleanor Kynaston of Marton.   SALOP.

81   John WYKE *v.* Thomas ALLEN, gentleman, and William ALLESTRE of Derby, glover.
Joint purchase by the said Wyke and Allestre of Cowden Grange and lands in Bakewell in the tenure of George Vernon, knight, and others (*named*).   DERBY.

82–83   Philip WYLLIAMS of Mathern, co. Monmouth, yeoman, v. Thomas BARRELL, vicar of Ashcott, and William WALTON and Richard COMPTON, gentleman.
Lands in a close called Wythies partly of the demise of the said Barrell.   SOMERSET.

84   John WYN of Southwold, merchant, v. the bailiffs of SOUTHWOLD, and James SUCKELYN of the same.
Action for part price of three-fourths of the ship *Mary Grace*, complainant's compurgators being pressed for the king's ships. *Certiorari and subpœna.*   SUFFOLK.

FILE 1484.

1–4   John WALEYS of Low Ham, labourer, v. John HURDE of (Long?) Sutton, husbandman.
Action for part price of cattle retained in part payment of a debt.   SOMERSET.

5   John WALHEYD v. Christopher BRYCKYLBANKES and Thomas HOYLAND.
Messuage and land in Hathersage of the gift of Roger Walheyd, clerk.   DERBY.

6–7   Edward WALKER v. Thomas GYBSON of West Tanfield, glover.
Tenement in the King's and Queen's manor of Carthorp, bought of Richard Danby.   YORK.

8–12   Ralph WALLYS of Aldeby, gentleman, grandson and heir of John WALLYS of Aldeby, v. Robert SKARLET.
Land in Lowestoft.   (Defendant pleads a recovery in the manor-court.)   SUFFOLK.

13   Thomas WALLYS of Andover v. William and Katherine GUNTER.
Debt of Richard Lyster of Hurstbourn Priors paid to William Gunter, deceased, master of complainant, father of the defendant William, and brother of the said Katherine.   HANTS.

14–19   Vincent, son and heir of William WARNER, v. William SAUNDER of Ewell, co. Surrey, esquire.
Manor of Parrock Inhams and messuages, iron-mill and land in Hartfield (Hatfeld).   SUSSEX.

20–22   Roger WARREN, gentleman, v. Margery COBBE, late the wife of John Sewell.
Obtaining a writ of *nisi prius* without notice in an action of dower out of a messuage and land in Alphamstone, Twinstead and Great Henney.   ESSEX.

23–25   William WARREN and Agnes his wife v. Joan, executrix and late the wife of William ASTELL, father of the said Agnes.
Debt assigned to the said William by Richard Fox in consideration of his marriage with the said Agnes, which did not take place.   ———

26–27   Thomas WATERS of King's Lynn v. Ralph WALLER and Mary his wife, executrix and late the wife of Geoffrey Cobbe.
Debt of Thomas Thursby. *Mutilated.*   NORFOLK.

28–31   John WATERTON v. Nicholas MYCHELL.
Messuage and pasture in Wakefield granted to complainant and Robert and John (*sic*) his brother.
See File 1390, *No.* 19.   YORK.

32–37   John WEALE, parson of St. Mildred's, London, and Thomas FERMOUR *alias* Tedstell v. Thomas VERNON, esquire.
Land in Walton whereof complainant owns the chief rent.   SALOP.

38–39   Edmund WEKES, Hugh his brother and Anthony HONYCHURCHE.
(Continuation of *File* 1483, *Nos.* 32–33.)   DEVON.

40–41   Alice WELMAN v. Edmund YONGE, Richard STARTOPP, and others.
Tenement in Aston. *Mutilated.*   OXFORD.

42–43   George WELSSHE v. Henry ANDROWE of Rockbeare.
False presentment at the hundred-court of East Budleigh for bowling and other unlawful games.   DEVON.

44–45   Henry WELSSHE, chaplain to the Lord Chancellor, v. Thomasyne, late the wife of William THOMAS, executed for high treason.
Presentation to the prebend of Nonnington after the death of Polydore Vergil.   HEREFORD.

46   Henry WENTWORTH, gentleman, and Crystyan his wife, late the wife of Edward Gyfford, v. John SEMARE her brother.
Detention of a lease of the impropriate parsonage of Thornborough.   BUCKINGHAM.

47–51   Anthony and Edward WESTON v. Thomas COLYNS and Joan his wife.
Goods of William Weston, B.D., late vicar of Godmanchester, whose executors complainants are.   HUNTINGDON.

52   Robert WHITE v. Christopher EGMONTON.
Messuages, cottages and lands in Garthorp.   LINCOLN.

53–54   William WHITHED of Stamford, innholder, v. William KINDERSELYE, gentleman, under-sheriff.
False return of *non est inventus* to a writ of *scire facias* awarded against Thomas Rose of Lutterworth (Lettelworthe).   LEICESTER.

55–56   John WHYTEPAYN, citizen and scrivener of London, and Elizabeth his wife, executrix, and late the wife of William Lychefeld, citizen and poulterer of London, v. the sheriffs of LONDON, and John WAYLAND, citizen and scrivener of London.
Action on a bond whereon no claim was made in the said Lychefeld's lifetime, for a debt partly cancelled by a bond given on the said Wayland's behalf, and embezzlement of deeds. *Certiorari and subpœna.*   [LONDON.

57   John WILKINSON of London, merchant tailor, *v.* Thomas ROOKE, Stephen WRYT, and·
others.
Detention of deeds relating to a gild-house and land in Hundleby and rent in South Somercotes
and elsewhere(?).   LINCOLN.

58   John WILLE, husbandman, bailiff of the court. of Trematon, *v.* John BOURWOOD and
Henry GRUBB.
Actions of trespass in the Common Pleas for execution of a judgment of the court of Trematon
against defendants as sureties for William Molton of Plympton, co. Devon, merchant. CORNWALL.

59-62   Watkin WILLIAMS of Salisbury, yeoman, son of William Watkyns, *v.* John WALBY,
gentleman.
Land in Llanhambach. (Defendant declared that the suit is brought by Lewis Havorde without
complainant's knowledge.) *See File* 1359, *No.* 30.   BRECON.

63-73   The same *v.* DAVID ap Jevan, JOHN ap David (John David ap Jevan), William DAVID
ap John, and JEVAN ap Hoell.
Messuages and land in Llanfihangel-tal-y-llyn claimed by the second defendant under a gift of
David Eyre.   BRECON.

74-76 ·   Oliver WILSON, citizen and barber surgeon of London, *v.* Thomas, son of Thomas
MALTHOWSE, deceased.
Messuage and land and keepership of woods in Grantley of the demise of William Malory, knight.
                                                                                           YORK.

77-79   Edward WOLFE *v.* Elizabeth WOLFE.
Messuages and lands in Worminghurst, Washington, Shipley, and elsewhere, late of John Wolfe,
deceased, nephew of complainant and husband of defendant. *Mutilated.*   SUSSEX.

80-82   Robert WOODE of Norwich, gentleman, *v.* Alexander MATHER.
Money and plate of Edmund Woode of Norwich, alderman, deceased, father of complainant, whose
executors both parties are. *Answer wanting.*   NORFOLK.

83-84 ·   William, grandson and heir of William WOODE of Waldringfield, *v.* William MARKANT
· of Walton, son and heir of Robert Markant.
Detention of deeds relating to a messuage and land in Hemley.   SUFFOLK.

85-86   William WOODROFFE, gentleman, and William FOSTER, executors of William Foster,
v. Richard FOOTE of Downham Hythe, husbandman.
Cottage and land in Brampton sold to the said Foster.   HUNTINGDON.

87 ·   John WOODWARDE of Chesterfield, yeoman, *v.* John HYLL of Duckmanton, glover.
Debt.   DERBY.

88   Henry WORLANDE of London, cordwainer, *v.* John, son of Clement SMYTHE, knight,
deceased.
Rent of the manor of Mugden Hall and of messuages in St. Mary-at-Hill, wherein complainant has
acquired the life-interest of Alexander Frogenhall, esquire. *See* D. XII, 7.   ESSEX, LONDON.

89   Nicholas WRYGGE of Thame, ' wheler,' *v.* John CHYCHE (Cheche) of the same, husbandman.
Action on a bond after respite of payment.   OXFORD.

90-91   Thomas, son and heir of Richard WULFFE, *v.* William BRADLEY of Cambridge, brewer.
Detention of deeds relating to a tenement in Cambridge.   CAMBRIDGE.

92   Christopher WYGGINS, husbandman, *v.* Edward SLEGGE of London, gentleman.
Refusal to make a general warranty of a tenement in Aylesbury, late of the fraternity of Our Lady
there. *See File* 1380, *No.* 37.   BUCKINGHAM.

93-94   Thomas WYLKYN, husbandman, *v.* Giles ASSHEWELL, husbandman, and Margaret
his wife.
Detention of deeds relating to a messuage and land in Swavesey.   CAMBRIDGE.

95-96   Miles WYLLYAMS of Sutton C[ourt]ney, yeoman, kinsman and heir of Elizabeth, daughter
of Edward ap Howell, *v.* Watkin ap Jevan LLOYD (Beanlloyd).
Messuage and land in Cusop.   HEREFORD.

97-98   Thomas WYLLYS and Isabel his wife, cousin and heir of Joan Frenche, *v.* Thomas JESOP.
Detention of deeds relating to land in Swyre. *Mutilated.*   DORSET.

99   John WYLSON, kinsman and heir of Robert Fyssher, *v.* George GRIFFITH, knight, and
William FYSHE(R).
Messuages and land in the said Sir George's manor of Alrewas. *Pedigree given. See Files* 993,
No. 43; 1006, *No.* 8.   STAFFORD.

FILE 1485.

1-8   Edward WALGRAVE, esquire, and Joan his wife, *v.* Cuthbert [TUNSTALL], bishop of
Durham, and Henry [NEVILLE], earl of Westmoreland.
Occupation of a lead-mine in Eggleston pending a commission from this court.   DURHAM.

9-14   Ralph WALLER and Thomas WISE, gentleman, servant to Thomas Hennage, knight,
deceased, *v.* Katherine HENNAGE, late the wife of the said Sir Thomas, George HENNAGE,
esquire, William USTWATE, and others.
Refusal to complete a lease of the site and demesnes of the late monastery of Wellow, with buildings,
lands, mill, water, tithes and rents there and in Weelsby and Clee. *Mutilated.*   LINCOLN.

15–18   Thomas WALTON, gentleman, and Ann his wife v. Thomas AISHLOCKE and John AISHLOCK, clerk.
Lands in Heytesbury, late of Thomas Aishlock, deceased, husband of the said Ann.   WILTS.

19   William WAREN and others, for themselves and the inhabitants of Castor, Ailsworth, Sutton and Upton, v. [Roger WYNGFYLD, esquire, J.P.].
Rights of common, etc., of the demise of former abbots of Peterborough. *Mutilated.*
NORTHAMPTON.

20   Katherine WAS[TENES and others, children] of George Wastenes of Heydon, esquire, v. Jeffrey WASTENES, executor of the said George.
Legacies of the said George who died seized of a messuage in Wayles in the parish of Treton (*sic*), and of lands there and in Brampton, Laughton, Throxon (*rectius* Thropom, *i.e.* Throapham) and Chapel Anston. *Mutilated.*   YORK.

21   Robert WEBBE, ' one of the most honourable courte of Chauncery,' v. William, son and heir of William EVERELL, and others.
Duplicate of *File* 1483, *No.* 30.   NORTHAMPTON.

22   Richard WERE v. Thomas SOMERFEELDE.
Manor in Yanworth of the demise of Thomas Culpeper of Bedgebury, esquire. *Mutilated.*
GLOUCESTER.

23   Hugh WESTWOOD v. John SELSMAN and James ROLLES of Cam.
Detention of deeds relating to the manor of Arlington and land there. *See File* 1480, *No.* 38.
GLOUCESTER.

24   Richard WHALLEY v.   .   .   .
Manor of Tawton (*i.e.* Toton). *Mutilated. Bill wanting. See File* 1391, *No.* 40.   [NOTTS.]

25–27   William WHYSSHET v. John SAMBORNE, esquire.
Refusal to complete a conveyance of the form of Bathingbourne (in Newchurch).   HANTS (I.W.).

28–30   John WILLIAMS of Ross v. Harry WYLLAN of Enfield, co. Middlesex.
Action on a bond for a lease of the parsonage of Ross as security for a loan spent in suing for the completion of a Crown lease of the manor of Kingstone. *Replication wanting.*   HEREFORD.

31–32   Thomas WILSON of London, beer-brewer, v. Margaret, late the wife of Giles KYRBY, and administratrix of his goods.
Money received by the said Giles as complainant's servant." *Mutilated.*   LONDON.

33–34   John WODDE v. Richard GERMAN and others.
Coal-mine in Lenton of the demise of the said German, and messuage and land there and in Mere and Longton.   STAFFORD.

35   Roger WOLHOWSE of London, haberdasher, v. Richard, father and executor of William RAULYNSON of Doncaster, chapman.
Debt for haberdashery supplied.   LONDON, YORK.

36–37   Robert, son and heir of Robert WOODE, v. (John ap) Harry ap John GRUFFYDD and Lowry his wife, mother of complainant.
Detention of deeds relating to messuages, burgages and land in Flint and Coleshill. (Defendants say that they extend into Bowlles).   FLINT.

38–42   John, son and heir of William WOODYE, v. Henry GYLE, Robert GOODE, and John GREY.
Messuages and lands in Staines, Egham and Thorpe, and barn in Hale.   MIDDLESEX, SURREY.

43–48   The same v. the said GYLE and GOODE and Gertrude GREY.
Do.   MIDDLESEX, SURREY.

49–50   George WORSELEY, [parson] of Nettleton, co. Wilts, v. John KERY, late mayor of Hereford.
Extortion of a bond and rings by imprisonment at Hereford on a charge of incontinence. *Mutilated. Answer wanting.*   HEREFORD.

51–53   James WORSELEY of Hamworthy, gentleman, v. Thomas TRAVERS.
Manor of Shapwick, formerly of John Camell, deceased. *Pedigrees given.*   DORSET.

54   Richard, son and executor of Robert WOTTON, v. William TYDDER and Robert his son.
Messuages in Bicton (near Shrewsbury) of the demise of the late abbot of . . . *Mutilated.*
SALOP.

55–56   Reynold, son of John WYLLYAMS, knight, v. Bridget, late the wife of Walter CHALCOTT of Sulhampstead Banister, gentleman, former husband of Isabel, mother of complainant.
Detention of deeds relating to lands in Burghfield.   BERKS.

57   Thomas and James, sons and executors of Robert WYLSMERE, v. Gabriel BUSHE.
Goods of Alice, executrix, and late the wife of John Saryche, whereof the said Robert and. Gabriel were administrators.   DIOCESE OF LONDON.

58   William WYNDESOR, lord Windsor, and others, executors of Andrew, lord Windsor, v Robert WINGFYLDE, esquire, executor of Humphrey Wingfilde, knight, an executor of John [de Vere], earl of Oxford.
Action on a bond for price of the wardship of Roger Corbett, long since paid.   ————

59   Ralph WYSEWALL and [Elizabeth his wife, granddaughter of Walter Fenymore], v. William ASHEMAN and Anne his wife, executrix, and late the wife of Robert Beynton.
Legacies of the said Fenymore and Beynton, including messuages (*described*) in Calne. *Mutilated.*
[WILTS.]

60   Thomas WYTHYETT v. George SNOWE.
Detention of deeds relating to a messuage and land late of John Criksall, deceased, uncle of complainant. *Mutilated.*   SUSSEX.

61   John W . . . v. John and John (*sic*), sons and executors of William PYKE.
Refusal to discharge complainant in an action by Walter Pyke of Bristol, another son of the said
William, for a debt partly paid to the latter. *Faded.*   GLAMORGAN, BRISTOL.

FILE 1486.

1   John WADE and William BYLKEYE v. John COUNDEY.
Refusal to complete a grant of the reversion of a ' justemente ' or parcel of land in Lesnewth.
                                                                                      CORNWALL.

2–5   William WALDRAM of Kingsey, co. Oxford, v. Thomas, his elder brother.
Parsonage of Aldborne leased to both parties jointly by Joan Styphens of Inglesham, in Berks.
                                                                                      WILTS.

6   John WALLBOTT v. John LYNGHOK, Margaret his wife, William . . .
Goods of William Awstyn, deceased. *Mutilated.*   [NORFOLK?]

7   Thomas WALLYS of Southampton, gentleman, and Margaret his wife, executrix and late
the wife of Ralph Forster, v. [Thomas WHYTE], bishop of Winchester.
Lease of the manor of Twyford, wherein the said Forster built a mill. *Mutilated.*   [HANTS.]

8   Robert WARDE, Joan his wife, late the wife of John Hartknoll, and Thomas
[HARTKNOLL] her son v. John HARTKNOLL of Ilfracombe, father of the said John,
Thomas his brother, and Richard CORNISHE.
Messuages and land in Middle Haggington (in Ilfracombe or Berrynarbor) of the gift of the first-
named defendant.   DEVON.

9   Edith WARNER v. Robert ASHE of North Petherton (Peverton).
Wages in money and goods.   SOMERSET.

10   Thomas WARTER, yeoman, v. John SMALEMAN.
Refusal to complete an assignment of a leasehold in Dudley.   WORCS.

11–17   Thomas WARTER of London, gentleman, v. Thomas SPENCER and Beatrice his wife.
Part price of rings, gems and other goods (*described*) delivered with money (*described*) to William
Parkyn, deceased, son of the said Beatrice, whose executors defendants are.
                                                    LONDON, ARCHDEACONRY OF LEICESTER.

18–19   Nicholas WATKYNSON and Elizabeth his wife, late the wife of Thomas ap John, v. Anthony
FOSTER, bailiff of the liberties of Newark, and others.
Forcible entry at Elton Hall, in North Nottingham, pending a suit in this court.   NOTTS.

20   Nicholas WATKYNSON and Elizabeth his wife, late the wife of Thomas ap John, v. [John
MALEN], Robert PORTE and others, servants of the said Anthony.
Distress on lands in North Collingham pending a suit in this court. *Mutilated. See D. XII, 8.*
                                                                                      NOTTS.

21–23   The same v. John MALLYN, Owen FERMERYE and others.
Do.   NOTTS.

24   Thomas [WATSON], bishop of Lincoln, v. [Jane WRIOTHESLEY], countess of Southampton,
David GRYFFITH, and Thomas ALLEN his bailiff.
Rent claimed out of the manor of Ringden for keeping the Old Temple *alias* Lincoln Place.
                                                                            HUNTINGDON, LONDON.

25   William WATSON and Margaret his wife v. Henry DAY.
Land in Skidbrooke late of William Goodriche, deceased cousin of the said Margaret. *Pedigree
given.*   LINCOLN.

26–28   Henry WAYNMAN, clerk, v. Robert JOHNSON, clerk, and Thomas JOHNSON.
Debt.   ———

29–32   William WAYTE, husbandman, v. Marmaduke BECKWITH, gentleman.
Action for slander concerning an affray at Hartwith, an injunction against it having been dissolved
by the death of the late King. *See Files 1166, No. 29, and 1394, No. 15.*   YORK.

33   John WEBBER of Taunton v. Henry . . .
Debt the bond for which is lost. *Mutilated.*   SOMERSET.

34   Henry WEKES v. Hugh MORRICE and others.
Two-thirds of the demesne of the manor of Dilwyn of the demise of John Seyntlowe, knight, and
Margaret, his wife.   HEREFORD.

35   Gilbert WELLER, Avice his wife, Thomas MORTON, Warborowe his wife, Robert
WILLYAMS and Anne his wife v. Francis BROWNE, esquire, and Anne his wife.
Manors of Winterborn Clenston, Wotton Glanville, Hartley, and Halstock, etc., late of George
Delalynde, knight, deceased, husband of the said Anne and brother of the female complainants.
                                                                   DORSET, WILTS, HANTS.

36–37   The dean and chapter of WELLS v. Philip LAWES and Eleanor his wife, executrix and
late the wife of John Foxe.
Debt of the said Foxe as deputy to Thomas Speke, knight, deceased, provost of Combe in Wells
Cathedral.   SOMERSET.

38   John WELLYS v. Thomas KERLE.
Lands in Walford late held by defendant of Thomas Wellys, deceased father of complainant.
                                                                              HEREFORD.

39   Ralph WESTDENE, late sent into the Fleet prison from Westminster by order of the Chancellor.
Petition in bankruptcy.   ———

40   John [. . .], abbot of WESTMINSTER v. Henry NORTHEY, late constable of St. Martin's-le-Grand.
Action of slander arising out of charges of misconduct in office.   LONDON.

41   Richard son of John WESTON of Rugeley v. John CHATTERTON.
Detention of deeds relating to messuages and land in Horton.   STAFFORD.

42-44   John WAY v. Agnes BAYNE.   SOMERSET.
(Continuation of File 1483, No. 44.)

45   William WEYGHTE, Juliana his wife and Agnes BYSSHOPPE v. Thomas SARGENT, Agnes his wife and Joan, late the wife of Humphrey HADLEY.
Land in Kidderminster late of William Morford, and Margaret his wife, grandparents of the female complainants.   WORCESTER.

46   Richard WHALLEY, esquire, v. William GASCOIGNE.
Manor of Whatton and messuages and lands there.   NOTTS.

47   Walter WHALLEY v. Thomas HUTTON.
Agreement as to the parsonage of Broughton. Commission.   LINCOLN.

48   John WIGHT and Agnes his wife, descendant and heir of Bernard Jenyns, v. John GREY, Lord Grey.
Detention of deeds relating to the manors of Braboeuf in the parish of St. Nicholas, Guildford, and of Polsted in Compton, and messuages and lands in Shalford, Worplesdon, Chiddingfold, Bromley, Albury, Wonersh, Dunsfold and Haslemere. Pedigree given.   SURREY.

49   John WYLKINS, of Burwell, husbandman, v. John GRACE, of Newport, co. Essex, his stepfather.
Detention of deeds relating to a messuage in Haddenham.   CAMBRIDGE.

50.   Griffith WILLIAMS, daily attendant on the Earl of Pembroke, v. . . . TAILLOUR and Robert GREYNDEN.
Lease of a rectory. Mutilated.   ?

51   William John WILLIAM of Llanvair [Kilgiden], yeoman, v. John CONWAYE, gentleman.
Loan at unlawful usury.   MONMOUTH.

52-55   WILLIAM and RETHERGH ap David ap Res and others v. DAVID ap Jevan ap Llewelyn.
Land in the town of Talabolyon and parish of Bettws Co(y)daney.   ANGLESEY.

56   The same v. EVAN ap Lewis ap Evan and HENRY ap Rice.
Messuages and land in Talabolyon.   ANGLESEY.

57   WILLIAM ap Jevan of London v. JOHN ap David and JEVAN ap John.
Messuage and land in Crickadarn, late of Jevan ap David, deceased, father of complainant.   BRECON.

58-59   WILLIAM ap Yevan of London, serving-man, v. John THELLWOLD, feoffee to uses, and others.
Messuages and lands in Llangar late of Yevan ap David, deceased, father of complainant, and others.   MERIONETH.

60   WILLIAM ap Thomas v. WILLIAM ap David ap Evayn ap Grono.
Detention of deeds relating to a messuage and land in Penmon.   ANGLESEY.

61   Richard WILLYAMS v. John THOMAS ap Watkin.
Rent of closes in Devynnock demised while at sea between Ireland and Wales.   BRECON.

62   The warden, scholars and clerks of WINCHESTER College v. Giles PERCY, esquire.
Tithes of Up-Sydling, in the parish of Broad Sydling.   DORSET.

63-65   William WODCOCKE and Elizabeth his wife v. Anne [DE VERE], countess of Oxford.
Wages and expenses in defendant's service. Damaged.   ———

66-67   Humphrey WOOD v. Richard WOLRYCHE.
Action for money due to Ellen, wife of defendant, and paid to the use of Richard his father.   ———

68-69   Ralph WORSELEY, of London, esquire, v. Thomas SHARPE, clerk, and John, grandson and heir of John DEANE.
Messuage and land in Wallasey.   CHESTER.

70-72   Thomas WRAYE, of Kensington, smith, v. Richard AYRE, of Shinfield, husbandman.
Failure to deliver a ton of iron promised in marriage with Alice Fawce, servant of defendant.   MIDDLESEX, BERKS.

73-76   Edward WRIGHT, of Bingham, co. Notts, v. Thomas BURDON, almsman in the Queen's bede-house of Leicester.
Messuage and land in Gadsby, Newbold, Barnsby and South Croxton, late of John Wright and Margaret his wife, grandparents of complainant.   LEICESTER.

77-79   Roger WRYGHT, parson of Church Hopton, v. Thomas CAR(RE)MAN.
Messuages and land in Church Hopton called the 'Maydens Howse.'   SUFFOLK.

80-82   Robert WYGMOR v. William WARDE, John HUGON (Hogon) and William RUGGE.
Detention of deeds relating to a messuage and land in Roughton, late of Ralph Symonde of Cley, esquire.   NORFOLK.

83-84   William, son and heir of William WYLKES, v. William MAUNSELL.
Detention of deeds relating to messuages and lands in Bromsgrove and Clent partly held of the manor (sic) of Bromsgrove and King's Norton.   WORCESTER.

85–88   William WYLKYN of Fulbourn, yeoman, v. Richard RANDE, husband of Alice, late the
wife of Thomas Olyver.
Land in Great Wilbraham, late of John Wylkyn, deceased, grandfather of complainant.
CAMBRIDGE.

89–92   William WYLLOWES v. Anne [de VERE], Countess of Oxford.
Wages earned in defendant's service. *Much damaged.* (Defendant describes benefits received
from her, including a lease of land and rights of pasture in Castell Campes.)   [CAMBRIDGE.]

93–98   Henry WYLLOUGHBYE, esquire, v. George MEDLEY, esquire, and others.
Manor of Smallwood, late of Hugh Wylloughbye, knight, father of complainant.   CHESTER.

99–100   George WYLLUGHBYE v. Richard AGARDE.
Messuage and land in Coton, bought of Edward Ascolle (Astoll, Astele) of Tamworth.   STAFFORD.

101–102   The same, described as esquire, v. Thomas ALDRETT *alias* Grene.
Do.   STAFFORD.

103–104   John WYLLYS, husbandman, v. Richard SMYTH.
Detention of deeds relating to a water mill and land in Dunkerton.   SOMERSET.

105   Robert WYNDE of Gillingham, gentleman, v. Thomas HUYSTOCK.
Land (*place not given*) of the grant of Richard Carrant, esquire.   DORSET.

106–107   John WYNSLAND v. Walter PARKER and Ellen his wife.
Manor of Cranford of the demise of the prior and brethren of St. John of Jerusalem in England.
MIDDLESEX.

108   Thomas WYNTERBOURNE, of London, yeoman, v. Thomas, son of Thomas
WYNTERBOURNE.
Messuage and land in Grove, late of John Wynterbourne of Southcot, deceased, father of
complainant.   BERKS.

109   Edward WYSTOWE, citizen and grocer of London, Elizabeth his wife, John MALYN,
armourer, and Margaret his wife, v. Robert GRYGGES (Gregges), of West Hanningfield,
yeoman, and Thomas and Robert, his sons.
Lease held in Rettendon, late of Edward Grene of London, mercer, deceased, father of the female
complainants. *See File* 1489, *No.* 5.   ESSEX.

110–111   Christopher WYTHERS, of Hungerford, co. Berks, and Joan his wife, v. Thomas
SYMBERBE.
Messuages and land in Harrington formerly of Agnes Longe, deceased, great-grandmother of the
said Joan.   WILTS.

112   Richard WYXSTED of Westminster, clothworker, v. Thomas DODDE and Anne his wife.
Messuage and land of the demise of defendants in Newhall and Wrenbury.   CHESTER.

FILE 1487.

1   Edward YABBE *alias* Hole and Nycholl (*sic*) his wife v. Robert HUGH her father.
Moiety of a messuage and land in the manor of Slapton and goods promised to complainants on
their marriage.   DEVON.

2   William YARRYNGTON the elder and Hugh his son, servant to the Chancellor, v. William
YARRYNGTON the younger, also his son.
Obtaining a conveyance of a messuage and land in Astley contrary to complainant's instructions.
WORCESTER.

3–5   Roger YATES and Margaret his wife, late the wife of Roger Griswold, v. William RAY-
NOLDES, citizen and bowyer of London, Isabel his wife, and John MYLNER.
Refusal to complete a sale of a messuage, cottage and land in Ashow.   WARWICK.

6–8   William YAXLEY v. John OVEREY.
Action on a bond for a debt already paid.   ———

9   Robert YENDALL, vicar of Menheniot, v. John TRELAWNY, esquire.
Right of way to complainant's vicarage.   CORNWALL.

10–13   Leonard YEO v. John YEO, gentleman.
Two-thirds of a messuage and land in Huish.   DEVON.

14–18   William YEO, clerk of Chancery, v. Ralph JACKSON, Ellen EGLEE and Michael her son.
Land and barn in Fulham and Chiswick formerly of Thomas Robynson, deceased.   MIDDLESEX.

19–22   Tristram, son of John YERELYE (Yardeley), v. John HATTON, Michael GRENE, and
Roger COOKE.
Detention of deeds relating to the manor of Milton and Trumpes Mill (both in Egham), of the
demise of the president and scholars of Corpus Christi College, Oxford.   SURREY.

23–25   Richard YOLGRAVE of Dronfield, husbandman, v. Alexander CHAMBERS and William
and John STANYFFORTHE, husbandmen.
Messuage and lands in Eckington and on Lightwood, late of Geoffrey Yolgrave, yeoman, deceased.
father of complainant.   DERBY.

26–30   William son of John YOMAN v. Agnes LOVEDAYE and William SKELTON.
Detention of deeds relating to a tenement in Fyrrebrige (*i.e.* Ferrybridge?).   [YORK].

31   Robert YONG v. John LIGHT.
Detention of deeds relating to the manor of Trent, and surrender of copies of a joint tenancy in
Sherborne.   SOMERSET, DORSET.

32–33 Eleanor YONGE, late the wife of Henry Higgens of Bristol, vintner, *v.* Simon MUCLOO, gentleman, grandson and heir of William Mucloo. *See Files* 540, *No.* 18; 1452, *No.* 54.
Messuage and land in Kempsey of the entail of Edmund Longstone, yeoman, father of complainant. WORCESTER.

34–35 John YORKE of London, knight, *v.* William FAIRFAXE, knight.
Manor of Pallethorpe in Bolton Percy (Pedderthorpe, Paderthorpe). YORK.

36–39 William YORKE of Birmingham and Robert, Stephen, Richard and Hugh YORKE *v.* Thomas CHORLTON and John FOSTER, gentleman, and William CHERCHE.
Pasture in Huntington demised with a messuage and other lands by the late prior and convent of Wenlock to William Yorke, grandfather of complainants. SALOP.

40–42 Roger YOROTH, servant attendant on William [Herbert], earl of Pembroke, *v.* RICHARD ap Jenkyn *alias* ap Jene.
Tenements in the parish (*sic*) of Llangoven and Pen-y-clawdd, late of Jankyn Yoroth, deceased, grandfather of complainant. MONMOUTH.

43–46 Richard, son of William YOUNG, *v.* John RUDGE and Denise his wife, late the wife of John Young.
Messuage and land in Toller Porcorum of the demise of Robert Egarden, gentleman. DORSET.

47–48 George [ZOUCH], lord Zouch, *v.* Richard son of Thomas MARSSHE, and William BACHAM.
Manor of Caddington and lands there. BEDFORD.

49–51 The same *v.* the same.
Do., and lands in Dunstable, Henlow, Edworth, and Kensworth.
BEDFORD. HEREFORD (*rectius* HERTS).

52–53 Susan, late the wife of John [ZOUCH], lord Zouch, and others *v.* John NEWCOURT.
Account of profits of one-fourth of the manor of Hartland, which defendant was to receive to pay a debt of the said Lord Zouch whose executors complainants are. DEVON.

54–58 The same *v.* Raymond NOR(TH)LEIGH and George STOWFORDE (Stofforde), gentleman, bailiffs of the said manor.
Do. DEVON.

FILE 1488.

1–4 John CRESIE and others *v.* William GOODING and others.
Tenements in Wodebridge. *Mutilated.* [SUFFOLK.]

5 . . . his wife, and GOLEY verch David *v.* RICHARD ap John ap Owen and JEVAN ap Ric'.
Messuages and land in Llangadfan, late of Jevan ap David, deceased. *Mutilated.* MONTGOMERY.

6 . . . HOLMES *v.* . . .
Goods of Richard Holmes of Carlton, deceased, brother of complainant. *Mutilated.* NOTTS.

7 William WILBON of Shefford, yeoman, an [executor?] of James Dene, gentleman, . . .
Tenement in Houghton Conquest [of the demise?] of the monastery of Chicksand, late claimed in this court by William Dore. *Mutilated.* BEDFORD.

8 . . . and Elyze WYNDLE of East Ravendale (Randall) *v.* Thomas FOSTER of Binbrooke.
False evidence and detention of deeds relating to lands held of the manor of Melton. *Subpœna duces tecum. Mutilated.* LINCOLN.

9 . . . *v.* Thomas AUSTEN.
Detention of deeds relating to the manor of Duxhurst and land in Staplehurst. *Mutilated.* KENT.

10 . . . dyer, *v.* William (John) BARRET of Bristol.
Compensation promised for woad which proved useless. *Faded.* GLOUCESTER.

11 Thomas . . . STON of Horncastle, yeoman, *v.* John BECKERYNG.
Messuage and land in Sutton, Huttoft, and elsewhere. *Damaged.* LINCOLN.

12 . . . *v.* William BLUNTE.
Tenement held of Christopher Ashedon's manor of Fyfield. *Mutilated.* BERKS.

13 . . . ARD, parson of Driby, *v.* Robert BOWGHAN, gentleman, and Margaret KYME.
Rights of common in the manor of Driby. *Mutilated.* LINCOLN.

14 . . . of Withington, yeoman, *v.* John BRANE.
Refusal to complete a lease of lands in Brane. *Mutilated.* HEREFORD.

15 . . . of Egham, co. Surrey, gentleman, *v.* Roger COK of Chertsey, co. Surrey, and Michael . . .
Manor of Milton *alias* Middelton of the demise of an Oxford college. *Mutilated.* [OXFORD.]

16 . . . *v.* John, son and executor of Michael DORMER, knight, and Ambrose [DORMER?].
Land in Latchford pledged by the said Sir Michael. *Damaged.* OXFORD.

17 . . . *v.* Morice EVANCE.
Debt the bond for which is lost. *Mutilated.* OXFORD.

18 William . . . husbandman, and Mary his wife *v.* Richard FLYNTHAM of Torksey, yeoman.
Messuages and land in Brampton, late of Thomas Pall, deceased, grandfather of the said Mary. *Mutilated.* LINCOLN.

19   . . . *v.* Henry . . . and Margery FREMAN.
Messuage and land in [Ruyton] ' in the hundred of the elevyn townes.' *Mutilated.*   SALOP.

20   John . . . administrator of the goods of Richard Palmer, parson of . . . deceased,
    v. [Peter HOCHYNSON, clerk, William REYNOLDE], gentleman, and William WHYTE.
Part of the said goods awarded to complainant by the bishop's official, for which defendants had
letters *ad colligendum. Mutilated.*   SUFFOLK.

21   . . . husbandman, *v.* William HOOPER of Topsham (Appisham).
Detention of deeds relating to a house and land in Kentisbere and of goods found therein.
Mutilated.   DEVON.

22   . . . *v.* John HORNER, heir of Thomas Horner of Mells.
Lease of land in Westbury on a bad title. *Mutilated.*   SOMERSET.

23   John . . . *v.* John HOTHENY and others.
Leasehold in Holborn and elsewhere. *Damaged.*   MIDDLESEX.

24   Humphrey . . . servant to the Chancellor, *v.* John JAMES of Hill.
Failure to ' walle, wynde, and dawbe ' a sheepcote let by defendant with the parsonage of Hanbury.
Mutilated.   WORCESTER.

25   Thomas COSE(?) *v.* William KYMPE his tenant.
Detention of deeds relating to the manor of Cassacawen in Blisland. *Damaged.*   CORNWALL.

26   . . . labourer, *v.* William LYNACERS and Humphrey HOUEDEN.
Crops in [Rugeley?]. *Mutilated.*   STAFFORD.

27   . . . of Ewhurst, husbandman, *v.* Eleanor MYLLES.
' Stoddes ' of timber and boards entrusted to defendant. *Mutilated.*   SURREY.

28   . . . *v.* William NEWTON, parson of Burythorpe.
Lease of defendant's parsonage promised if mass were again said in England, etc. *Mutilated.*
        YORK.

29   . . . servant to . . . Norman,* canon of Salisbury, deceased, *v.* Robert PENRUD-
    DOCK, esquire, and Edmund BOWER, yeoman [executor of the said Norman?].
Repairs of the said Norman's house and expenses on his account. *Mutilated.*   WILTS.

30   . . . rector of East and West Leake, *v.* John PORT, knight.
Tithes claimed under a lease of complainant's parsonage made by Julian Crosbye, deceased, late
rector. *Mutilated.*   NOTTS.

31   . . . *v.* George RAVEN, priest.
Contract to serve the parish church of Calk. *Mutilated.*   DERBY.

32-34   . . . *v.* Katherine, late the wife of Robert RAYNER of Peterborough, and William
    his son.
Action on a bargain for grain with the said Robert, whose executors defendants are, after sub-
mission to arbitration. *Mutilated.*   NORTHAMPTON.

35   . . . *v.* Robert ROSE, esquire.
Crown lease of the castle and manor of Whorlton, the manor of Breighton, and the reversion of the
manor of Greenhow, formerly in dispute between defendant and William lord Dacre and his sons.
Mutilated.   YORK.

36   Gilbert . . . *v.* William SMYTHE.
Messuage and land in Ware, late of Joan Genynges, deceased, grandmother of complainant.
Mutilated.   HERTS.

37   . . . ERR . . . esquire, *v.* Robert STYLE.
House in the parish of St. Martin's demised to complainant by the churchwardens in payment for
a supply of ordnance. *Damaged.*   JERSEY.

38   Robert . . . King's and Queen's servant at arms, *v.* Thomas TAYLOUR and Thomas
    THROPPE.
Tenement in the manor of Newhall, of which the said Throppe is bailiff. *Mutilated.*   CHESTER.

39   Richard . . . nephew of Jevan ap Hoell *v.* Richard *v.* THOMAS ap Hoell ap Aynyon.
Messuage in Bryngwyn, formerly of Hugh ap David of Michaelchurch. *Mutilated.*   RADNOR.

40-41   . . . *v.* Sir Roger WOODHOWSE and John WALTER.
Turbary and fishery in Breckles. *Mutilated.*   [NORFOLK.]

42   R . . . *v.* William WYTNEY and HUGH ap Howell of Clyro.
Water-mill and land in Bryngwyn. *Mutilated.*   RADNOR.

FILE 1489.

1   Juliana COTRELL *v.* Thomas BAGOTT and John COLERD, yeoman.
Forcible occupation of land in Feckenham and seizure of goods. (To the King.)   WORCESTER.

2   William FAIROK, parson of Frethorn, *v.* James CLIFFORD, patron of his church.
Ouster from the said church by threats in contempt of a former decree of this court. (To the
archbishop of York.)   [GLOUCESTER.]

3   William MIDDELTON *v.* Tristram COUPER, esquire, and others.
Forcible entry and assault at Lostwithiel. (To the bishop of Winchester.)   CORNWALL.

4   [William SEGREVE and . . . his wife] *v.* Thomas CHAWORTHE, knight.
Manor and soke of Mansfield. *Mutilated.*   NOTTS.

* Not in Le Neve.

5   Edward WISTOWE, citizen and grocer of London, Elizabeth his wife, John MALYN, armourer, and Margaret his wife v. Robert GRIGGES, yeoman.
Land called Roughall Park or Wood in East Hanningfield (Handfyld), formerly held by Edward Grene of London, mercer, deceased, father of the female complainants. *See File* 1486, *No.* 109.
ESSEX.

6   Sir Thomas WYGHTFELD v. Sir Hugh THOMAS and Sir Wynter WYNTER, all scholars of Oxford.
Resistance to arrest by the commissary of the university on a charge of intended violence.
OXFORD.

7   Robert WYNTRESHILL v. John, son of William WAYTE, feoffee to uses.
Manors of Wintershull (in Bramley) and Frensshes, etc., late of Robert Wyntreshill, father of complainant. (To Thomas,* bishop of London, keeper.)   SURREY, SUSSEX.

8–9   Nicholas FERYBY, prebendary of Stillington, in York cathedral, v. Thomas, son of John SMYTH of Easingwold and John HEBBULL of Huby.
Threats to complainant and assaults in the said prebend so that the tenants propose to abandon (*guerpere*) their tenancies and the servants their services. *French.* (To the archbishop of York, 1388–1394.)   YORK.

10   Agnes PLOMER v. John WAKERLEY, esquire, and John BILLYNG.
Burgages and lands in Peterborough of the demise of William Barfot, great-grandfather of complainant. *See Bundle* 7, *Nos.* 192 *and* 317. (No heading; *cir.* 1391–1463?).   NORTHAMPTON.

11   John [HEMINGBROUGH?], prior of Durham, v. Thomas MAPPERLEY, Thomas his son, recorder of Nottingham, and the bailiffs of NOTTINGHAM.
Arrest of two cloth-sacks brought to Nottingham by monks of Durham, on a plea for an annuity granted by complainant to the said Thomas. *French. Damaged.* (To Thomas, archbishop of Canterbury, 1399 *or* 1407–9?)   NOTTS.

12   Thomas ASSHEBURNHAM v. Sir Roger FENES, Adam IWODE and others, feoffees to uses.
Refusal to reconvey the manor of Ashburnham and forcible ouster. *French.* (15th century?)   SUSSEX.

13   John BOWERMAN of Deddington v. John HILTON.
Lands in Little Wooton (Orton), Little Tew (Tybba) and Hampton inherited from Geoffrey atte Hall and Galiene his wife. *French.* (To the King, 15th century.)   OXFORD.

14   The men of DENBIGH v. . . .
Violation of liberties [which may extend to?] the boroughs of Conway and Rhuddlan. *French. Faded.* (15th century.)   DENBIGH.

15   Richard EDY of London, brewer, and Joan his wife v. Joan TERRY, Marion, wife of Master ISBURY of Huntingdon, ' baron,' and John CHILD, an officer of the King's Bench.
Abduction of complainant's child on pretext of showing it to the said ' baron ' to cure distraction arising from the loss of his own child and indictment of felony. (To the King; 15th century?)   LONDON, HUNTINGDON.

16   Thomas, son and heir of Edward LANGFORD, esquire, v. Katherine, late the wife of John ARUNDELL, knight.
A mark of gold ' in a pece of silke fast knyte,' delivered to defendant in trust. (To the bishop of Lincoln; 15th century.)   ——

17   John, son and heir of Peter PRESTON, yeoman, v. Richard DAWYS of Nevendon, co. Essex, Katharine his wife, and John BRISTOW.
Land in Enfield. (To the archbishop of Canterbury; 15th century.)   MIDDLESEX.

18   William WEST, priest, v. John HAYNSON, late mayor of Kingston-upon-Hull.
Dismissal from the office of reading and singing divine service in the church of Holy Trinity, Hull. (To the archbishop of Canterbury. Early 15th century.)   YORK.

19   . . . WILFORD of Badburgham v. John WESTRETE, vicar of Badburgham, feoffee to uses.
Messuage and land [in Babraham?] held under the will of John Bevereche. *French. Mutilated.* (15th century?)   [CAMBRIDGE.]

20–23   Joan, late the wife of Robert WOLASHULL, Thomas BOTTISFORD and Agnes his wife v. Bartholomew BROKESBY, esquire.
Messuages, land and rent in Melton Mowbray and Burton Lazars, late of Richard of Waltam and Maude his wife, great-grandparents of the female complainants. (To the King; 15th century?)   LEICESTER.

24   . . . and ·. . . his wife v. Richard HAYNE.
Lands in Salisbury, late of Thomas Bere, mason. *Faded.* (To the archbishop; 15th century.)   WILTS.

25   William . . . v. Agnes late the wife of John PALMER, and John PYNMORE, feoffee to uses.
Messuage in Bristol of the bequest of the said Palmer. *Damaged.* (To the bishop of Lincoln; 15th century.)   GLOUCESTER.

26   Richard KYNGESTON, dean of Windsor, v. John CR(O)UKERNE, clerk.
Vicarage of Saltash to which defendant fraudulently obtained a presentation from Thomas Boteler, complainant's predecessor. *French.* [1402–1417?]   CORNWALL.

27   Richard STOKYS v. Thomas PENDYN, vicar of Almeley, feoffee to uses.
Messuage and land in Almeley, late of Lewis Stokys, deceased, father of complainant. (To Thomas, archbishop of Canterbury; 1412–3 or 1455–6.)   HEREFORD.

---

* Thomas Kempe was bishop of London 1450–1489, and Thomas Savage 1496–1502; but neither appears to have been keeper of the seal.

28   . . . v. John CAUMBRIGGE, late sheriff of Norwich.
Procuring a false return by the coroners on a replevin of goods (described). *Faded. French.*
(*After* 1418.)   NORFOLK.

29   Aleyn CALY and others v. the same and Robert BAKSTER, mercer, also late sheriff.
Do., following a distress on a claim of rent from the fullers of Norwich. *French.* (To the bishop
of Durham; 1418–1424.)   NORFOLK.

30–35 John, abbot of CROYLAND, v. William JOHNSON *alias* Waterson, vicar of Moulton, and
John REDESDALE, yeoman.
Common in a marsh called 'Purcente' in Croyland. (To the King; 1427–1476?)   LINCOLN.

36   John AUMFRE of Avestoke v. Nicholas DURANT.
Assault and subsequent threats. (To the bishop of Bath and Wells; 1432–1443.)   DEVON.

37   Thomas BYTHAM v. Maude, late the wife of Robert SEWKER, and others, his executors.
Annuity promised as composition for a messuage in Wysbech. *French.* (To the bishop of Bath;
1432–1443.)   [CAMBRIDGE.]

38   John CULLOM and Eleanor his wife, daughter and heir of John Guybon, gentleman, v.
Thomas DANYELL and Gregory GUYBON, feoffees to uses.
Tenements in Clenchwarton and West and North Lynn. (To the bishop of Bath and Wells;
1432–1443?)   NORFOLK.

39   John DERKE of London, joiner, v. John ATKYN of St. Albans, glover, formerly his 'doer.'
Detention of deeds relating to lands in St. Albans. (To the Duke of Gloucester; 1432.) HERTS.

40   William ETON of Coventry, merchant, v. Nicholas DADENALL.
Mill and land in Stivichall (Styfford Hale joust Coventre) conveyed to defendant to pay a debt
out of the issues to Thomas Wyldegryse of Coventry, draper. *French.* (To the bishop of Bath;
1432–1443.)   WARWICK.

41–42 Robert FLECHER v. Stephen NELLE and others, late bailiffs of Cambridge.
Action for escape of Piers Basse, prisoner for debt, the present bailiffs refusing to execute the writs.
(To the bishop of Bath. 1432–1443.)   CAMBRIDGE.

43   William HEGON of Gloucester v. John HORSMAN of the same, bladesmith.
Joint purchase of smith's tools (described) from William Olyvere and others. *French.* (To the
bishop of Bath and Wells; 1432–3?)   GLOUCESTER.

44   Alice, granddaughter and heir of John RENAWDE, v. William son of Thomas BLAST, and
John GODERICH.
Forgery of a release of a messuage and land in Crawley in the name of Mabel, wife of the said
John. *French.* (To the bishop of Bath; 1432–1443.)   SUSSEX.

45   John REYNWELL, alderman of London, v. John HAROP and others of Stratford-upon
Avon, husbandmen.
Action in which service of writs was impossible. *Mutilated.* (To the bishop of Bath; 1432–1443.)
                                                                                  WARWICK.

46   Robert SHEPERD v. Walter ASLAK(?), esquire.
Contempt of a *supersedeas* in an action of debt in Forncett court. (To the bishop of Bath; 1432–
1443 or 1467–1472.)   NORFOLK.

47   William TYLNEY and Elizabeth his wife v. John WYND.
Legacy of William Laveryk, father of the said Elizabeth. (To the bishop of Bath and Wells;
1432–1443?)   ————

48   Roger [PRATTE], master of the hospital of ST. GILES, NORWICH, v. Thomas BALLE,
sheriff of Norwich.
Suppression of the record of an assize taken against John Chyrcheman and others for a rent in
Norwich. *French.* (To the bishop of Bath; 1434.)   NORFOLK.

49   John Hygons, prior of ST. OSWALD'S, GLOUCESTER, v. Thomas HERT of Gloucester,
feoffee to uses.
Land in King's Barton by Gloucester, formerly of Edward, predecessor of complainant. *French.*
(To the bishop of Bath and Wells; 1434–1443.)   GLOUCESTER.

50–51 John HALLE v. William EDWYN, feoffee to uses.
Land in Stondon, late of William Halle, father of complainant. *French.* (No heading; 1435.)
                                                                                   ESSEX.

52   Ellen JOCE v. Richard ALCESTRE and William METE.
Assault and robbery in her house at Worcester. (To the archbishop of Canterbury. *Cir.* 1443.)
                                                                                 WORCESTER.

53   Harry Werkeworth, prior of ST. MARY'S, SOUTHWARK, v. Laurence SMYTH(?),
executor of Sir John Brymesgrave.
Bond for arbitration between Robert Weston, late prior, and Nicholas [Mockyng, late] master of
St. Laurence Pountney, concerning a rent claimed from the latter church. *Mutilated.* (To the
archbishop of Canterbury. *Cir.* 1443.)   SURREY, LONDON.

54   Robert CONSTABLE 'of the Receyt' v. John [Kingston], prior of MERTON.
Refusal to complete a lease of the manor of Coombe Neville (in Kingston). (The gift of a livery
gown is appealed to as evidence of the promise.) (To the archbishop of Canterbury; 1443–1485.)
                                                                                   SURREY.

55   John, son of John COTYLLER, deceased, v. Thomas . . .
Detention of deeds relating to a messuage in Stortford. (To John, archbishop of Canterbury;
1443–1452.)   HERTS.

56   John DOREWARD, esquire, v. John Depyng, abbot of ST. OSYTH'S.
Failure to disclose a statement of Thomas Sumpter, mayor of Colchester, deceased, that he had falsified the will of Roger Kyrkele, whose messuage and land in Colchester complainant had bought under his true will. (To the archbishop of Canterbury; 1443–1460.) ESSEX.

57   Richard, son and heir of John FOX, v. Robert GERMAN, feoffee to uses.
Messuage and land in. Plumstead and East Wickham, late of Thomas Chamburleyn, deceased, brother (sic) of the said John. Bill wanting. KENT.

58–61   The same v. John COK and others, feoffees of the said German.
Do. Depositions included. (To the archbishop of Canterbury; 1443–1456.) KENT.

62   John GLOVER, parson of Middelchynnok; v. William SADELER of Bridport, co. Dorset.
Lease of complainant's parsonage to defendant and Richard Pyper, priest, who has failed to serve the church. (To the archbishop of Canterbury; 1443–1450.) [SOMERSET.]

63   Joan, late the wife of Reynold GREY, lord Grey of Ruthin, v. John ENDERBY and others, feoffees to uses.
Manors of Towcester, Burbage, Great Brickhill, Foxley, Winfarthing, Shefford, etc. Damaged. See File 17, No. 81. (To the archbishop of Canterbury; 1443–1448.)
NORTHAMPTON, BUCKINGHAM, NORFOLK, BEDFORD, ETC.

64   Roger LEGH, Clarencieux king-at-arms, v. Thomas CHICHELE of London, tailor.
Forgery of a bill in complainant's name. (To the archbishop of Canterbury; 1443–1460.)
LONDON.

65   John LABOURET, native of the country of Davion and merchant of the isle of Noirmoutiers, v. Nicholas FRYCHOW of Penryn.
[Seizure of] wine of Avion and other goods at sea contrary to the truce with France. Mutilated. (To the archbishop of Canterbury; 1444.)

66   Adam WODESILL v. John WODESILL of Heathfield, his uncle.
Repairs of a tenement in Dallington. (To the archbishop of Canterbury; 1444.) SUSSEX.

67   Robert BERBURY v. John ROGGER, esquire, late sheriff of Oxford.
Committal to gaol under a forged warrant on his account as collector of green wax. (To the archbishop of Canterbury; 1445–1450.) OXFORD.

68   Roger PYE and others, lightermen, v. John TAVERNER.
Wages and 'harnes' for [discharging?] defendant's ship Grace Dieu by command of [Simon] Eyr, mayor of London. Mutilated. (To the archbishop of Canterbury; 1445.) LONDON.

69   Thomas Arundel TRERYS, chaplain, v. Thomas Pomerey, prior of CHRIST CHURCH, London, and alderman of London, Simon HAMMYS, esquire, and Joan CARPENTER.
Extortion of goods (described) by threats and a charge of incontinence. Commission awarded to the dean and chapter of St. Stephen's. (To the archbishop of Canterbury; 1446–1460.) LONDON.

70   Thomas CROXBY, clerk, v. John CARBERTON, mayor of Lincoln, and Robert BUKLEY and Robert SKUPHOLM, 'vycountes.'
Contempt of a writ of error in an action of trespass by John Lutte, barber of Lincoln. (To the archbishop of Canterbury, 1447–8.) LINCOLN.

71   Richard DIRIVALE v. Master Robert APPILBY and others, executors of Thomas Brone, bishop of Norwich.
Recompense promised in the bishop's chamber at Hoxne for complainant's resignation of the benefice of Diss. (To the archbishop of Canterbury; 1447–1450.) NORFOLK.

72   William DONNYNG v. the mayor and sheriffs of LONDON.
Action by Thomas Veyle for a debt mostly paid. Corpus cum causa. (To the archbishop of Canterbury; 1447.) LONDON.

73   John [MOWBRAY], duke of Norfolk, v. John and Robert WYNGEFELD and William GENNEY, feoffees to uses.
Manor of Alconbury Weston, etc., bequeathed by John, duke of Norfolk, father of complainant, to complainant's use after payment of debts and reburial in England by Thomas his grandfather. (To the archbishop of Canterbury, 'my gretely trusted cosyn'; 1447–1460.) HUNTINGDON, ETC.

74–75   John DAVY, merchant of Brittany, v. John MIDDELTON, knight, and Henry HAGERSTON, esquire.
Seizure of goods (described) from complainant's ship at Dunstanburgh. Schedule of names annexed. (To the King; before 1448.) NORTHUMBERLAND.

76   Thomas TUDENHAM, knight, keeper of the Great Wardrobe, v. William CANTELOWE, sheriff of London.
Arrest of a tenant of the said wardrobe in his tenantry without the 'wardroper' or his deputy. (To the Archbishop of Canterbury; 1448–1449.) LONDON.

77   Henry MAY, merchant of Bristol, v. Richard HATTER, mayor of Bristol, and Thomas HOOR and Thomas ASSHE, chamberlains.
Refusal to admit Richard May, complainant's apprentice, to the freedom of the city after the expiration of his indentures. See File 17, No. 213. (To the archbishop of Canterbury; 1449.)
GLOUCESTER.

78   John FRAY, late chief baron of the Exchequer, and others, executors of William FLETE, merchant, v. Alexander MEDE, grantee to uses.
Lands in Whaplode, Holbeach, Fleet and Gedney, formerly of Richard Reed. Decree endorsed. (To the cardinal; 1450–4.) LINCOLN.

79   Richard HERT v. William BROKHERST, both of Islington.
Assault on complainant's ploughman on land held of the prebend of M[ora] in St. Giles's and Shoreditch. [1450–1452?] MIDDLESEX.

80   Richard HERT v. John his brother and others.
Land in Islington, etc. *Copy of proceedings, part in File 7, No. 175; pleadings in French, depositions in English, the rest in Latin.* (To John, archbishop of York; 1450–1452.)   MIDDLESEX.

81-82   John SALTBY, priest, v. John AYLEWARD and others.
False verdicts of assault, and that the complainant's chantry in the church of St. Olave, Jewry, was founded without licence *temp.* Edward II. (To the Cardinal, chancellor; 1450–1454?)
LONDON.

83   John SERLE v. Vincent MORY and others, feoffees to uses.
Lands in Laseythyn whereof complainant was to be refeoffed in the event of his recovery from sickness. (To the Cardinal, *i.e.* Kempe *or* Morton; after 1450.)   ·   [CORNWALL.]

84   Richard WELLES, lord Willoughby, and Joan his wife v. Richard BONYNGTON of Boston, gentleman, and others, executors of Robert, lord Willoughby, father of the said Joan.
Failure to account before the bishop of Lincoln for issues of the manors of Orby, Burgh, Theddlethorpe, Carlton, Saltfleethaven, Fulstow, Fulstow 'Arsyk,' Fulletby, Wispington, Raithby, Partney Thorp, Partney, Fotheringay, Toynton, West Keale, Stickford, Fenton, Welton, Scre[m]by, Mablethorp, etc. (To the archbishop of Canterbury; 1452–1455.)   LINCOLN, NOTTS.

85   Richard TREMANS v. Henry BODRUGAN, esquire.
Arrest at Trelyver, false imprisonment at Bodrugan (in St. Goran), and seizure of bin from Crukbarges moors. (To the archbishop of Canterbury; 1453.)   .   CORNWALL.

86   John HOGON of Bristol v. Clement BAGOT, both merchants.
Voyage to Zeeland already in dispute in this court. (To the Earl of Salisbury; 1454–5.)
GLOUCESTER.

87   George HOUTON v. Anselm RYE.
Refusal to complete a sale of the manors of Coates and Wigwold (in Cirencester). (To the archbishop of Canterbury; 1454).   GLOUCESTER.

88   Homobone GREBE, merchant of Venice under the king's special protection, v. Walter . . .
Bond for delivery of Cotswold wool by Thomas Albert. *Mutilated.* (To the archbishop of Canterbury; 1455.)

89   Robert LAWE v. William LEVESEY, vicar of Walesby, and others.
Detention of deeds relating to a messuage and land in East Markham. (To Thomas, archbishop of Canterbury; 1455–6 or 1460?)   NOTTS.

90   Thomas NEVYLL, knight, Maude lady WILLOUGHBY his wife, Humphrey BOURGHCHIER, esquire, and Joan his wife v. Ralph [CROMWELL], lord Cromwell, and Thomas CHAWORTH, knight.
Settlement of the manors of Houghton, Wyllughby and Grymston (in Wellow) by Ralph, lord Cromwell, deceased, father of the said Ralph and grandfather of the female complainant. (To the archbishop of Canterbury; 1455–6.)   [NOTTS.]

91-92   Philip PATRIK v. Simon BRIGMAN of London, fuller.
Action on a bond for conveyance of a tenement without Bishopsgate to John William Pleyter, sawyer, who refused it. *2 bills.* (To the archbishop of Canterbury; 1455.)   LONDON.

93   Jane and Elizabeth, daughters and heirs of Richard TRELAWNY, esquire, v. Walter LYARD, bishop of Norwich, and others, feoffees to uses.
Manors of Tregrina (*i.e.* Tregrenna in Altarnun?) and Wal . . . *Faded.* (To the Earl of Salisbury; 1455.)   ·   CORNWALL.

94   Thomas POMRAYE(?), knight, and Joan his consort v. John . . .
Forcible ouster from the manors of Clifton, Assheton, S . . . ., Lokesheire, etc., and tenements in Exeter during the said Thomas's absence on service against the rebels in Calais. *French. Damaged.* [1456–1460?]   [DEVON], CORNWALL.

95   Piers THOMAS of Plymouth v. John BARBOUR *alias* John Clyfton, barber, and Radegund his wife, executrix, and late the wife of John Botton of Plymouth.
Cost of boarding Perot Gorey of Bordeaux at the expense of the said Botton. (To the archbishop of Canterbury; 1456.)   DEVON.

96   Oliver TREGESEWE v. Thomas ENYS, feoffee to uses.
Lands (*not described*). (To the archbishop of Canterbury; 1456.)   CORNWALL.

97   William DUNTON, 'awnour' (*i.e.* almoner?), under the King in cos. Suffolk and Essex, v. Robert WODE and others.
Hindrance of complainant from performing his office in Ipswich, and resistance to a writ of *supplicavit.* (No heading. *Temp.* Edw. IV?)   SUFFOLK.

98   Robert WYDITON, citizen and grocer of London, v. [the executors of Henry WYBBE?]
Encumbrance of lands in prejudice of a debt of Richard Honyman. (Mention is made of tenements adjoining the Friars Minors, in Fleet Street and Thames Street, and at Fresh Wharf. *French. Damaged.* (To the Chancellor. Edw. IV or earlier.)   LONDON.

99   John HOO, seaman(?), v. the sheriffs of LONDON.
Action by John Fitzherbert on a bond for assignment of a debt recovered by John [Mowbray], duke of Norfolk, against Robert Strelley, knight. *Corpus cum causa. Faded.* (To Robert, bishop of Bath and Wells; 1467–1472).   LONDON.

100   John SCARBURGH, esquire, Anne his wife, and Nicholas BOLTH[O]RP, citizen, and vintner of London, v. Alice, executrix and late the wife of Geoffrey DALLYNG, citizen and vintner of London. *See File 20, No. 2.*
Joint sale of blankets by the said Dallyng and John Snypston, citizen and vintner of London, whose executors are the said Anne and Nicholas. (To the bishop of Bath; 1467–1472?) LONDON.

101　　[Hen]ry WHETELE of Chislett,, yeoman, v. the bailiffs of CANTERBURY.
Action by John Bolde, clerk, on a bond for delivery of corn. *Corpus cum causa.* (To the bishop of Bath; 1467–1472?)　KENT.

102–105　Nicholas WODEHILL (Woodell) of London, surgeon, v. William CHAPMAN of the same, gentleman.
Action for a loan partly not made and partly to be set off against treatment for wounds (*described*). (To the bishop of Bath and Wells; 1467–1471.)　LONDON.

106　　Thomas YONG v. Guy FAYREFAX, serjeant-at-law, and others, feoffees to uses.
Refusal to join in a suit for the manor of Harefield, settled on John son and heir of William Neudegate at his marriage with Elizabeth daughter of defendant. *See File 33, No. 265.* (To the bishop of Bath and Wells; 1467–1471.)　MIDDLESEX.

107　　John LYLBURN v. the keeper of the MARSHALSEA.
False imprisonment by 'divers mysrewled persons.' *Corpus cum causa. Orders endorsed.* (To the keeper of the Great Seal; 1471.)　SURREY.

108　　Luder BRAMES of Hamburg, of the Hanse, v. John PORTER of Calais and the servants of Lord CLINTON.
Plunder of complainant's ship near Dover and elsewhere. *Commission to persons named. Cargo described.* (To the bishop of Lincoln; 1475–1485.)　KENT.

109　　Richard CLERK of London, brewer, v. the sheriffs of LONDON.
Action by William Bartelot, clerk, for price of goods delivered by him in payment of a debt. *Certiorari. Damaged.* (To the bishop of Lincoln; 1475–1480 or 1483.)　LONDON.

110　　John COWPER v. the mayor and.bailiffs of SOUTHAMPTON.
Action by Thomas Bache in the court of pie-powder, in which counsel and wager of law were both refused. *Certiorari.* (To the bishop of Rochester; 1475.)　HANTS.

111–113　Michael DENYS and Alice his wife v. Robert PARKER, feoffee to uses.
Will of John Loveles (*annexed*), disposing of the manor of Babford, half of the manor of Good-myston, etc. *Mutilated.* (To the bishop of Lincoln; 1475.)　[KENT?]

114　　William [Walwayn], abbot of EYNSHAM, v. William SHEREVE, vicar of Tetbury.
Lease of the parsonage of Tetbury obtained from complainant's predecessor. *Damaged.* (To the bishop of Lincoln; 1475.)　GLOUCESTER.

115　　Thomas POPELOT of Great Horksley, fuller, v. the bailiffs of COLCHESTER.
Action by . . . [C]opynger of Wyleyn (*i.e.* Willingham?), co. Suffolk, on a bond for price of wool already paid. *Certiorari. Mutilated.* (To the bishop of Lincoln; 1475–1480 or 1483–1485.)　ESSEX.

116　　John SAGGEFORD v. Thomas ROGERS.
Land sold to John Rightwys and Thomas Bartylmewe. *Damaged.* (To the bishop of Lincoln; 1475–1485.)　NORFOLK.

117　　Thomas SOMER of London, haberdasher, v. Richard BABKARY of Sherborne, brazier.
Debt the bond for which was stolen from complainant's apprentice by thieves who killed him. (To the bishop of Lincoln; 1475–1485.)　LONDON, DORSET.

118　　Alan WENAGON of Brittany, merchant, v. the sheriffs of LONDON.
Action by Richard . . . for hire of a ship, for which he had failed to obtain a safe conduct. *Corpus cum causa. Mutilated.* (To the bishop of Lincoln; 1475–1480 or 1483.)　LONDON.

119　　. . . and Jane his wife, daughter and heir of William Marton, v. Christopher HOWE(?), feoffee to uses.
Messuages and land in [?Ma]rton and To[llesby?] in Cleveland. *Damaged.* (To the bishop of Lincoln; 1475–1485.)　YORK.

120　　Robert RUSSELL v. Ralph WHITE and others, feoffees to uses.
Messuage in Wokingham, late of John Russell. *Faded. Decrees endorsed.* (To the archbishop of York; 1482–5.)　BERKS.

121　　John, son and heir of William NYCOLL of London, brewer, and of Rose his wife v. John BYRCHEHOLTE and others, feoffees to uses.
Messuage at Charing Cross and land in St. Martin's-in-the-Fields of the gift of Thomas Walpole, master of the chapel of the Blessed Virgin of F . . . beside Charing Cross. *Faded. Decrees endorsed.* (To the archbishop of York; 1483–8.)　MIDDLESEX.

122　　William BAROWE, gentleman, v. John HYCHECOT, clerk, and John BAROWE of Well (in Long Sutton), feoffees to uses.
Messuage and land in Odiham, late of John Barowe, esquire, deceased, father of complainant. *Orders endorsed.* (To the bishop of Lincoln; 1484–5.)　HANTS.

123　　Robert COPPYNG v. [John REYNO]LD and others, feoffees to uses.
Lands, rents and services in [Boughton Monchelsea] and Marden of the bequest of Joan at Woden. *Mutilated.* (To the bishop of Lincoln; 1484.)　KENT.

124　　David MORGAN v. Richard HAKLET of London, skinner.
Action on a bond. (To the King. Henry VII or VIII.)　LONDON.

125　　John DRAPER and Agnes his·wife v. William PRENTES, parson of Lawshall, feoffees to uses.
Price of a messuage and land in Newton sold under the will of John Weston, father of the said Agnes. (To the Cardinal; 1493–1500?)　SUFFOLK.

126　　Alice MERDEN, cousin and heir of John Newe, v. John PRESTE, husbandman, and Alice his wife.
Detention of deeds relating to land in Iwere Minster. (To the archbishop of Canterbury; 1486–1493 or 1504–1515?)　DORSET.

127   Ralph WYLLUGHBY, esquire, son of Hugh Wyllughby, knight, deceased, v. Henry
WYLLUGHBY, knight, administrator of the goods of Margaret, late the wife of the said'
Sir Hugh.
Manors of Carlton-on-Trent, North and South Marnham, Normanton, Skegby, Sutton-on-Trent,
Dummysby (*i.e.* Dunsby?) and Bradmore, ferry in the town of Trent, lands in Sutton-on-Trent,
Broughton Solney, Cropley, and Butler (*i.e.* Cropwell Butlers?), and plate. *Decree endorsed.*
(To the archbishop of Canterbury; 1486-1504.)   NOTTS. LINCOLN.

128   Maude, late the wife of Walter GYLES, and Richard HEYNES his nephew v. John
    . . . TRELL and others, feoffees to uses.
Messuage and land in Salcott and Whitebarewe (*i.e.* Wigborough?). *Faded.* (To the Cardinal,
i.e. Morton *or* Wolsey? After 1493?)   ESSEX.

129   John BARLEY, gentleman, v. Richard WALTER, gentleman.
Detention of deeds relating to lands in Manuden, Henham and Elsenham. *Exemplification of*
proceedings, including depositions. (To the Cardinal; 1498-9.)   ESSEX.

130   Robert JOSSE v. William HOLBORN, feoffees to uses.
Land in Southwold. (To John, archbishop of Canterbury; late 15th century.)   SUFFOLK.

131   Robert WADE v. Adam BREMMAN of Havering and Alice his wife.
Tenements in Orsett, late of Henry (*no surname*) and Margery his wife, grandparents of complainant. *French.* (To the Chancellor; before 1500.)   ESSEX.

132   Nicholas, grandson and heir of John FYNDERN, v. Richard VERNON, knight, John
WARDE of Stenson, and Margery his wife.
Collusive suit for messuages and land in Willington, formerly of Alice Firbrace. (To the King;
cir. 1500?)   DERBY.

133   Robert GRYME, clerk, v. William KARRE.
Action on a bond for wheat partly delivered at Chelmsford. (To the bishop of . . . *cir.* 1500?)
                                                                               ESSEX.

134   John NEWTON, esquire, v. Henry SEWARD, esquire.
Assault on William Doultyn, servant of complainant, between Wells and Glastonbury. [To the
King and Council; temp. Henry VIII?]   SOMERSET.

135-136 Robert LADDE of Great Yarmouth and Margaret his wife, late the wife of Thomas Harrys,
    v. Simon SMYTH.
Detention of deeds relating to the rectory of Gorlestone. (To John *rectius* Thomas, bishop of
Ely; 1551-3.)   SUFFOLK.

FILE 1490.

1   Thomas ABURLEY, yeoman, v. Ann, late the wife of Thomas GRESLEY, knight.
Messuage and land in Admaston, late of Richard Aburley, deceased, brother of complainant and
one of the King's retinue at Calais. *Damaged.* (To the Archbishop of York.)   STAFFORD.

2   Lawrence AILMER, of London, draper, v. John PAY and John STEWARD, his ward.
Manor of Tailefers (in Great Parndon?) and lands called ' Stewardes,' formerly of Richard Steward,
grandfather of the said John. *Damaged.*   ESSEX.

3   Joan, late the wife of John ANDREWE of Honiton, clothier, v. John HUGH and Henry
LAWRENCE, feoffees to uses.
Tenement in Honiton.   DEVON.

4-6   William ANDREWS of Wighton, weaver, v. John DOBBYS, an executor of William Feke,
husbandman.
Land in Wighton bequeathed by the said Feke to Marion his wife, now the wife of complainant,
and wardship of James his son, to whom he bequeathed horses and a messuage and land in Wighton
and Hindringham.   NORFOLK.

7   William ANFLYS of Lynn, v. John . . . and Agnes his wife, formerly Agnes Joyne.
Refusal to complete a conveyance of a messuage called the *Antelope*, in St. Neots. *Damaged.*
                                                                             HUNTINGDON.

8   John ARCHER v. Baldwin HETH and Joan GROVE.
Detention of deeds relating to the manor of Aspley.   WARWICK.

9   Edward ARNOLD, Jane his wife and Michael STRAILE v. Rose, late the wife of Thomas
BOWDON, and William his son, executors of the said Thomas.
Money promised by the said Thomas to Adam Clerke, whose executors are the said Jane and
Michael, on his marriage with the former.   CALAIS.

10   Edward AUSTYN v. Margaret BABYNGTON.
Rent of land in Mildenhall. *Damaged.*   [SUFFOLK or WILTS.]

11   John AYSSHE v. Cristian Faundry, abbess of AMESBURY, and Joan HORNER, her nun.
Detention of deeds relating to messuages and land in Aldbourn and the borough and suburbs of
Marlborough.   WILTS.

12   . . . of London, tailor, v. the Mayor and Sheriffs [of LONDON].
Action by Robert Doly on a bond for a debt overpaid in merchandise. *Certiorari. Damaged.*
(To the Archbishop of Canterbury. 15th century.)   LONDON.

13   Thomas ATKYNSON, executor of John Atkynson, v. Thomas FOXE, Anne his wife and
John MACHELL.
Tenement in Ormset. *Faded.* (To William, bishop of Winchester. 1456-1460?)
                                                                    [WESTMORLAND.]

14   John ARUNDELL of Talvern and John TRETHERFF v. Roger TRELAWNY, late escheator.
Bond for defendant's account at the Exchequer. (After 1490.)   DEVON.

15   John ARTES v. William FYSKE.
Mortgage of a close in Laxfield. (1491-7 or 1514-1520.)   SUFFOLK.

16-17   William ARNOLDE, of Appleby, co. Leicester, v. John WRIGHTE, John DYET, judge of the court of Lichfield, and others.
Imprisonment by means of frivolous suits at Lichfield. (16th century.)   STAFFORD.

18   John, son and heir of John ASKEW, v. Clement PARKE.
Rent and fine of a messuage and land in Whitbeck. (16th century?)   CUMBERLAND.

19   Emote, late the wife of John AUNGER, v. John, son of Richard CHEDDER.
Rent of complainant's dower-lands in Angersleigh (Knyghtesly). (16th century.)   SOMERSET.

20   Agnes APRICE v. Richard [Bennet], abbot of BIDDLESDEN (Batelysden).
Debt awarded by arbitration and paid after the appointed date. (1504 or 1528.)   BUCKS.

21   John AYLWARD of London, haberdasher, and Alice his wife v. William OTLEY of Shrewsbury.
Defacement of a bond made to the said Alice. (1509 or later.)   LONDON, SALOP.

22-25   Simon AVERY v. Hugh PRUSTE (Pryst).
Mortgage of a messuage and land in Bomotysthorn. *Bill endorsed with divers orders.* (1511-2.)   DEVON.

26   Peter ALVERUS and Fulk LOPUS, merchants of Portugal, v. Richard POWELL of Wells.
Refused to give bond for price of 40 cwt. of ' woode ' (i.e. woad?) (1525.)   SOMERSET.

27-29   William ASHE of London, pewterer, v. Philip WHARTON of the same, broker.
Detention of deeds relating to tenements in St. Lawrence Lane and Birchin Lane. *Endorsed* with reference from the Council to Chancery. (Before 1540.)   LONDON.

30   Thomas ASTON and Bridget his wife v. Thomas GARRARDE and Edward LOGGE.
(*Copy of File* 1192, *No.* 40.) (1547-1551.)   STAFFORD.

31   More APOWELL, son and heir of Thomas Apowell, v. David DAVID (*sic*) ap Howell.
Detention of deeds relating to a messuage and garden in Monmouth. (1553-1558.)   MONMOUTH.

32-33   Thomas ALDERSAY and others, executors of Ralph Aldersay, citizen and merchant of Chester, v. Anne ALDERSAY, late the wife of the said Ralph.
Money and deeds belonging to the said Ralph and plate and household goods (*described*), late of Robert Byrkenhed, former husband of the said Anne. *See File* 1401, *No.* 2. (After 1554.)   CHESTER.

FILE 1491.

1-2   Robert ALLOTT and Roger Robynson v. William BRADFORTH and Anne his wife.
Messuages and lands in Ferriby and Fishlake, lease of the parsonage of Fishlake, and goods late of William Allott, deceased, former husband of the said Anne and father of the said Robert.   YORK.

3   Emma, executrix and late the wife of Thomas ANDREWS of Bury St. Edmunds v. Alice, late the wife of John GARRERD of the same, and administratrix of his goods.
Price of a flock of sheep.   SUFFOLK.

4-6   John, son of Thomas AVERYE, v. Richard AVEREY.
Manor of Down St. Mary, of the demise of John Gylle, late abbot of Buckfast.   DEVON.

7   John AWODE of the parish (' peryship ') of Barking, butcher, v. Stephen CLOSSE.
Messuage and land in Ripple Street and Ripple Marsh, Barking, of the feoffment of William Wyatt, gentleman.   ESSEX.

8   Jane ACTON v. Thomas ACTON.
Goods and jewels of the bequest of Edmund Acton, husband of complainant and kindsman of defendant. *See File* 277, *No.* 76. (*Cir.* 1504-1515.)   [SALOP.]

9-10   Robert ALMOND and Margaret his wife, aunt and heir of Thomas Lorkyn, v. Thomas, son and heir of John TABOUR of Slevys.
Lands in Margaretting already in dispute in this court. (Henry VIII or later.)   ESSEX.

11   John, son of Thomas ALYE, deceased, v. William ALLANSON, his step-father.
Land in Katerow (i.e. Catteral?) [? held] of the Earl of Derby. *Faded.* (Henry VIII or later.)   LANCASTER.

12-13   Philippa, late the wife of Humphrey ARUNDELL, and daughter and heir of John Beare, v. Nicholass HERLE, Elizabeth his wife, Hugh BOSCAWEN, and Philippa his wife.
Half a messuage and land in Probus claimed in right of Katherine Carmyno, deceased, mother of the female defendants. (Henry VIII or later.)   CORNWALL.

14-15   Thomas AWALEY v. John CROUCHE of Hexton, co. Herts, husbandman, son-in-law of Richard Parcell.
Detention of deeds relating to land in Southill. (Henry VIII or later.)   BEDFORD.

16-19   James ALDER(S)LEY, goldsmith and citizen of London, v. William HERMESTED, master of the Temple.
Non-payment for a lease of the parsonage of St. Mary Axe on the ground that defendant is ' proffessyde under the obediens of my lord of Seynt Johns.' (1532-3.)   LONDON.

20-22   Thomas ADAM v. John SCRASE.
Manor of Tarring, late of John Adam, deceased, father of complainant. (After 1533.)   SUSSEX.

23   Christopher ALEYN of London, gentleman, v. Francis SWANNE.
Lands in Old Romney and Lydd formerly of William Gybson of London, gentleman. *Faded.*
See File 940, No. 14. (After 1545.)   KENT.

24-25   David APPRYSE v. JOHN ap Robert and Griffin APPOWELL.
(Continuation of File 1191, No. 34) (1547-1551.)   DENBIGH.

26-27   William ATKYN and Cicely his wife, late the wife of William Jollye, v. Henry TYLNEY,
bailiff of the duchy of Lancaster, and others.
(Continuation of File 1190, No. 32.) (1547-1551.)   NORFOLK.

28-30   Hugh ASKEW, knight, late an officer of the cellar to King Henry VIII, v. Matthew
[STEWART], earl of Lennox.
Park of Whorlton and other lands. (*described*), whereof complainant is keeper. *Damaged.* (After
1547.)   YORK.

31-32   Vincent AMCOTTES v. Richard WYLLY.
Part price of a messuage in St. Michael's Lane. (1552-3.)   LONDON.

33-34   Thomas ASTRYE, gentleman, v. William MADISON (Mallysonne).
Detention of deeds relating to lands in Hitchin casually lost between Stoke Goldington and Harleston.
(After 1553.)   HERTS.

FILE 1492.

1   Ambrose BREDMAN and Ellen his wife v. Dame Margaret MAUNCELL.
Detention of deeds relating to the manor of Whipsnade, the manor called ' Clement is yn,' messuages,
land, rent, a ' baron,' etc., in Whipsnade, Eton (*i.e.* Eaton Bray), Studham, Dunstable, Houghton
[Regis], Sewell (in Dunstable), Kensworth (Kemworth), Caddington Billington, St. Clement's
parish without Temple Bar, and Milk Street, London, and a close adjoining the manor of
Tottenham Court. *See Files 464, No. 35; 606, No. 40; 643, No. 31.* (1529-1532.)
                                                       BEDFORD, MIDDLESEX, BUCKS, HERTS.

2   Ellen of the BOTRYE v. John CLOPTON her husband.
Suit for a divorce without her knowledge, and removal of her goods. (15th century or earlier.)

3   Adam BERESFORD v. Margaret, executrix and late the wife of William DETHYK, Thomas
his son, and others.
Arrears of a fifteenth, whereof the said William and the rest of the parties were collectors. (1416-7?)
See File 258, No. 35.   DERBY.

4   Margaret BEK v. John HESYLL *alias* Berker, gentleman.
Forcible entry and assault at Carlton, false imprisonment at Grantham, etc. *See File 9, No. 320.*
(1429 or later.)   LINCOLN.

5   John BACHE, grandson-in-law of William Hylle, v. John WHORWOD and Thomas HYLLE.
Detention of deeds relating to a messuage and land in Compton. *See File 466, No. 41.* (*Cir.* 1518-
1529).   STAFFORD.

6   Robert BROWNE, tanner, v. the twelve governors of BEVERLEY.
False imprisonment and refusal of bail. (Henry VII or later.)   YORK.

7-8   Margery, late the wife of William BURTON, v. Robert, grandson and heir of Nicholas
GEYNESFORD, feoffee to uses.
Lands late of John Mounshyll, in Cuddington and West Cheam (Westheyham). *Footnote to bill;*
Fiat ut petitur. (To the keepers; Early 16th century.)   SURREY.

9   Thomas BARKER, husbandman, v. John his brother.
Croft in Wimbish late of John their father, deceased. (16th century.)   ESSEX.

10   John BROKE v. George BROKE.
Detention of deeds relating to lands in Wednesbury. (16th century.)   STAFFORD.

11   William BROWNE of Shinfield, co. Berks, cooper, Edith his wife, late the wife of John
Helhouse, husbandman, and Richard HELHOUSE their son v. Thomas PYTTER of Shalden
and William GYLDEN.
Damage to lands in Heckfield in contempt of an order of this court. (16th century.)   HANTS.

12   Edward BYSSHOP of Leytonstone, gentleman, and Elizabeth his wife v. Robert BROWN.
Price of light grey cloth bought of Robert Bygbroke, former husband of the said Elizabeth.
(16th century.)   ESSEX.

13-14   Henry BYRDE and John PYERS v. Griffith JOHNS, Thomas LYCHEFFELDE, bailiff,
of Cardiff, John YEMAN and others, aldermen there, William JOHNS, John NORTHALL
(Northfolk) and others.
Destruction of a messuage in Cardiff late of James Tyrrell, knight, traitor. (1502-1547.)
                                                                                      GLAMORGAN.

15   Robert BEILBY v. Thomas POUNTFRET of Beverley.
Detention of deeds relating to messuages in York. (1504-1515?)   YORK.

16   Robert BARET of New Shoreham, co. Sussex, v. the bailiffs of DUNWICH and John
PALMER.
Action of debt to assist execution of a decree of this court concerning a messuage, garden and goods
in Yarmouth. *Corpus cum causa and subpoena.* (Henry VIII or later.)   SUFFOLK, NORFOLK.

17   Harry BEKWYTHE of Kirkby v. John JOHNSON, Annes his wife and others.
Bonds and goods of Cuthbert Bekwythe of Appleton, deceased, brother of complainant. (Henry VIII
or later.)   YORK, NORFOLK.

18-19   Henry BONE, husbandman, v. Thomas SMYTHE.
Weirs in the manor of Water Newton. *Mutilated.* (Henry VIII or later.)   HUNTINGDON.

20 John BORNE v. Alice COTHERS alias Pope, a woman 'eloptyd' from her husband.
Fish-shop at the High Cross of Ludlow of the demise of John Bussy and Thomas Box, bailiffs, of Ludlow. (Henry VIII or later.) SALOP.

21-22 Thomas BORYCHE alias Myle v. Peter STEWKELEY.
Refusal to complete a lease of messuages and land in Morebath. (Henry VIII or later.) DEVON.

23-24 Anthony BOURNE v. Thomas BYLE alias Rose of Chislett, Elizabeth his wife and Henry COURTE of St. Alphage's, Canterbury.
Detention of deed relating to a messuage and land in Smeeth late of Robert Fagge. (Henry VIII or later.) KENT.

25-26 Ralph BOWRYNG, vicar of Rugeley, v. Richard WESTON and others, inhabitants of Rugeley.
Croft belonging to complainant's church. (Henry VIII or later.) STAFFORD.

27 Anne BULKELEY v. John BULKELEY of Letcombe, co. Berks.
Tenements in Westwild. Damaged. (Henry VIII or later.)

28 William BALY of Week St. Lawrance, co. Somerset, v. Nicholas NEWELLES.
Messuage, land and wood called the chapel of Playsted (now Chapel Plaster) in Box, formerly of William Baly of Ford, great-grandfather of complainant. (After 1513.) WILTS.

29 Andrew BYLLYBBY, knight, v. John ORMESBY.
Detention of deeds relating to a messuage and land in Farlsthorp. See File 610, No. 1. (After 1513.) LINCOLN.

30-32 William BRYKYNDEN v. John SAVE and Elizabeth his wife.
Messuage, barn and land in Cranbrook, late of Roger Bate, deceased, father of the said Elizabeth.
See File 467, No. 46. (Cir. 1515-1529.) KENT.

33-35 Thomas BOWES, citizen and merchant tailor of London, v. John BIRON, knight and sheriff of Notts and William TOWNEROWE, his under-sheriff.
Evasion of a latitat against Henry Hall. (1523-1527, 1542 or 1551.) NOTTS.

36 John and Richard BERHAM v. William WALLER of Groombridge, esquire.
Action for price (already tendered) of coal taken from defendant's woods of Northuly and Southuly.
Mutilated. (After 1530.) KENT.

37 Henry Reynoldes, prior of BARHAM (Byrcham), v. Robert LOCKTON, gentleman.
Reviver of a suit by John Bybe, complainant's immediate predecessor, for a messuage, land and sheep-pasture at Barham in Linton (File 744, No. 7). (1533-1539.) CAMBRIDGE.

38-40 William BRABAN, vicar of Scarborough, v. Tristram TESHE (Tasshe).
(Continuation of File 950, No. 55.) (1540-1544.) YORK.

41-44 Thomas BOUND, Jane his wife and William BODY v. Robert LANGDON.
Messuage and land in Quethiock. Mutilated. (After 1544.) CORNWALL.

45-46 Christopher BYLBOROGH v. Robert IVEMAY, Peter BYLBOROGH and Agnes his wife.
(Continuation of File 1175, No. 69.) (1547.) YORK.

47-50 John BEAMUNT of Wivenhoe (Wevenhall), co. Essex, esquire, and George FORSTER, grandsons and heirs of William Tenderyng, esquire, v. Thomas BRAMPSTON and others.
Land in dispute between the manors of Harkstead and Chelmondiston. (Robert Forster is joined as complainant except in the bill.) (Before 1551.) SUFFOLK.

51 Robert BOTERELL and Elizabeth his wife, late the wife of Robert Morys, v. Edmund WARDE and Thomas COTON.
Detention of deeds relating to the manor of Aston Boterell and messuages and land in Yoxhall.
(Before 1553.) STAFFORD, SALOP.

52-53 Anthony BRAKYNBURY of Selaby (in Gainsford), co. Durham, esquire, v. Robert SYNGLETON, esquire, husband of Agnes, late the wife of Thomas Covell.
Rent charged on defendant's land in Fremington (in Grinton). (Before 1553.) YORK.

54 Ralph BULMER, esquire, v. Thomas HOMTON and Edward BROWNE.
Land in Rawston (i.e. Rostall, in Bentley?) in the manor (sic) of Sutton and Attewyke (i.e. Adwick-le-Street?) (Before 1553.) YORK.

55-57 John William BASSET and others v. Walter PYCKES.
Action for a debt paid to William Pyckes of Bristol, deceased, father of defendant. (1553 or later.)
Replication wanting. GLOUCESTER.

58-59 Richard BLACKWALLE v. James, brother of George PERGITOUR, deceased, and administrator of his goods.
Failure to complete a sale of lead. See File 1333, No. 32. (1553 or later.) DERBY.

60 William BLAKEWELL and Alyn SPYCER.
Petition to examine witnesses as to an entail of a messuage cottage and land in Edgware by Richard Rolf of Elstree, co. Herts, deceased. (1553-4.) MIDDLESEX.

61 Thomas BOLT of . . . any beer-brewer, v. William BALL, glover, sheriff of Chester.
Fee for teaching defendant the 'mistery of makyng and brewyng of beere.' (1553.) CHESTER.

62 John BRABAND, parson of St. Michael's, Crooked Lane, and Robert INGRAME and Nicholas LEVERETT, his churchwardens, v. John BROOKE.
Parsonage-house of the gift of William Walworth, knight. See File 1330, No. 65. (1553-1555.) LONDON.

63 Alice BROKEBANKE v. John SPALDYNG and William FOXE.
(Copy, with defects, of File 1331, No. 56.) (1553-1555.) LINCOLN.

64-66 George BROWNE, esquire, v. John THORGOOD, executor of Thomas Thorgood.
Ring belonging to Elizabeth, wife of complainant. Damaged. (1553 or later.) ESSEX.

67   Thomas BUSSHOPP of Shoreditch, co. Middlesex, v. Thomas DOWEMAN, his steward
of the manor of Pocklington.
Hamlet of Waplington belonging to the said manor. (1553 or later.)   YORK.

68   Robert BERWYCKE of Dedham, gentleman, v. Thomas RAMPSTON, gentleman, steward
of the hundred-court of Dedham.
Action by William Blosse of Lawford, husbandman, for a loan of 9 angel nobles in gold repayable
in 5l. worth of testers. Certiorari. (1554-8.)   ESSEX.

FILE 1493.

1-2   Joan, Mabel, Plesance, and Margaret, daughters and heirs of Thomas BOYS, v. John
BERNES.
Messuages and quit rents in St. Nicholas Acon, St. Martin Vintry, St. Thomas the Apostle,
St. Dennis, Lime Street, St. John Walbrook, St. Mary 'in Colbroke,' St. Lawrence Jewry,
St. Michael Cornhill, St. Mary Woolchurch-Haw, St. Mary Colechurch, St. Mildred Poultry,
St. Mildred Bread Street, and St. Peter Westcheap.   LONDON.

3   Thomas, son and heir of Thomas BYRSTYE, v. John WHELER.
Detention of deeds relating to land in Ardingly. (Henry VII or later.)   SUSSEX.

4-5   John BAKER and Alice his wife v. William CREKE (Crake).
Sale of corn and loan to Roger Colard, deceased, whose lands in Ash by Sandwich are now held by
defendant. (16th century.)   KENT.

6   Ralph BOSTOKE and Katharine his wife, late the wife of Thomas Whyttmore, deceased,
v. John WHYTTMORE, supervisor of the will of the said Thomas.
Goods of the said Thomas. (16th century.)   ————

7   Walter BAGTOR v. Richard MONE.
Cost of obtaining writs of certiorari and corpus cum causa for Elizabeth Mathew, daughter of
defendant, imprisoned at Exeter for felony. See File 281, No. 20. (Cir. 1504-1515.)   DEVON.

8   Isabel BAKER v. John BAKER and others, executors of William Baker her father.
Messuage in Church Eaton and share of goods. (Henry VIII or Edward VI).   STAFFORD.

9   John BANGE v. John CURTEYS.
Money promised in marriage with Joan, daughter of defendant, to whom complainant has given
a dower of lands in Netisherd. (Henry VIII or later.)   [NORFOLK.]

10-11   William BARKBY, citizen and scrivener of London, v. Peter de CASSA NOVA, serjeant
trumpeter.
Detention of deeds relating to messuages in Vintry Ward and the parish of St. James Garlickhithe.
See File 282, No. 23. (Henry VIII.)   LONDON.

12   Bartholomew BARRET v. [the bailiff of] the court of piepowder at WINCHESTER.
Action on a forged bond by John Grigge, servant to Scolas, mother of complainant, and false
imprisonment. Certiorari. (Henry VIII or later.)   HANTS, MIDDLESEX.

13   Robert BARWYKE, clerk of the King's stables, and Joan his wife v. Thomas DENTON.
Embezzlement of a lease of corn-tithes of Aspatria made by the late bishop and the dean and
chapter of Carlisle. (Henry VIII or Edw. VI.)   CUMBERLAND.

14   Hugh BOSTOCK of Huxley, drover, v. Richard LAYCIE.
Price of cattle. (1509-1553.)   CHESTER, SUFFOLK.

15   Ralph, son and heir of John BOSWELL of Breighton, co. Derby, esquire, v. John SAMPALL
and Robert WHITHACARS.
Messuages and land at Ladythorp in Campsall, Moss, Wragby and Pontefract acquired of Nicholas
Bollowe and Margaret his wife. (Henry VIII or Edward VI.)   YORK.

16-17   Robert BRYDD v. Ralph DOVE, esquire.
(Continuation of File 1202, No. 25.) (1547-1551.)   CHESTER.

18   Richard BURDEN, carrier, v. William KEYLWIKE.
Non-delivery of wheat. (Henry VIII or Edward VI.)   ————

19-20   Richard BUTT and Isabel his wife, daughter and heir of Robert Hayles, v. Thomas
DUKKETT, gentleman.
Messuage and land in . . . alyngton and Hoxne. (Henry VIII or Edward VI.)   SUFFOLK.

21-22   John BEALBURY of Liskeard v. Nicholas LOWER (Loure).
Woodland in St. Winnow and goods late of John Loure. (1519-1553.)   CORNWALL.

23-24   Edmund BRUDENELL v. Robert DOURY, gentleman, his son-in-law.
Part of a house in Chalfont St. Peter and rent reserved on a conveyance of complainant's property.
Mutilated. See File 289, No. 78. (1530-1547.)   BUCKS, ESSEX, ETC.

25   Richard BURY v. Thomas RYGBY, clerk.
Costs of a suit for half the manor of Walton, late of John Geylen. (1530-1547.)   NORTHAMPTON.

26-27   John BYTTERYNG, yeoman, v. Thomas GRYMWADE and Alice his wife, executrix, and
late the wife of Henry Turner of Lavenham, baker.
Over-driving of cattle from Lavenham and Cockfield to the pound of Bury St. Edmunds called
'the Court Yarde.' Commission. (1539-1547.)   SUFFOLK.

28-29   William BOLLAYNE, clerk, v. James BOLLAYNE, knight, his brother.
Share of the manor and park of Heveningham acquired of the King by defendant in exchange for
the manors of Hever, Seal, and Kemsing, and cost of building on the manor of Sall. (After 1539.)
                                                                          NORFOLK, KENT.

30   Anthony BROWNE, knight, and Robert BERWYKE, clerk of the King's stable, v. Ambrose
      LANCASTER, gentleman.
Loan by Thomas Clyfforde, knight, captain of Berwick, whose executors complainants are.
(Cir. 1544–1547.)   NORTHUMBERLAND.

31–34   Thomas BARBER of Faringdon and Richard WRIGHT of Wantage, butcher, v. Thobie
         PLEDALL, gentleman.
Refusal to accept a surrender of a close in defendant's manor of Faringdon. See File 1402, No. 8.
(1553–8.)   BERKS.

35–36   Gilbert BLACKELINGE v. Henry BLANDE and James ROBINSON, husbandmen.
Right of way to common of pasture and turbary at Crossdale in Sedbergh. (1553–8.)   YORK.

37–40   Arthur BLECHINGDON and Margery his wife, executrix of William Watt of Ivychurch,
         co. Kent, v. John GULDEFORDE (Gylleford), knight.
Tenement and half a barn in Guildford formerly of Thomas, earl of Sussex, attainted of treason.
Mutilated. (1553–1558.)   SURREY.

41–43   Ellen and John BROXHOLM v. Thomas BERRIE of Walesby.
Debt to William Broxholm, deceased, whose executors complainants are. (1553–1558.) LINCOLN.

44–48   William BRASBRYDGE v. Thomas BRACEBRIGE, esquire, his father, George GRYF-
         FYTH, knight, Anthony BOWLEY and John LUCAS, his servant, and . . .
Alienation of the manor of Kingsbury and other lands promised to complainant on his marriage
with Anne, daughter of Julyne Nethermyll. See Files 1291, No. 51; 1330, No. 66; 1406, No. 68.
(Cir. 1554.)   WARWICK.

49–51   Juliana, late the wife of John BOTHE of Thames Ditton, co. Surrey, gentleman, v. John
         GROMMEWALL (Grumwall), administrator of the goods of John Brereton, deceased.
Reviver of a suit for hospital lands called ' Holmefyeld.' Mutilated. (1554–8.)   CHESTER.

FILE 1494.

1   Henry, son and heir of John BAKER, gentleman, v. John BURY.
Messuage and land in Plympton-Earl.   DEVON.

2–4   George BARTON, parson of St. Helen's, . . . , v. Thomas OGLE and Thomas
       STAFFORD.
Rent. Mutilated.   ?

5   Nicholas BOSSE, labourer, v. John DREWE of Heston.
Imprisonment in the Marshalsea by covin with the ' bille berrer.'   [SURREY, MIDDLESEX.]

6   John BULPAN and Agnes his wife, daughter and heir of John Pylloke and of Agnes his
       wife, v. Maud PYLLOKE, executrix of the said John Pylloke.
Pasture in North Petherton formerly of John Sumpter. See Files 724, No. 33; 1410, No. 63.
(Cir. 1533–1555.)   SOMERSET.

7–8   John BULTE v. William STANBANKE.
Messuages and land in Sneynton late of Thomas Bulte. Bill illegible.   [NOTTS or YORK.]

9   John BUSHOP, clerk, executor of John Grendon, carrier, v. John HOLCOMBE and Joan
       his wife.
Yearly stipend promised by defendants to the said Grendon.   ———

10–12   John BYRKHEDE of York, merchant, v. Margaret, late the wife of Nicholas LANCASTRE.
Detention of deeds relating to messuages in York.   YORK.

13   John BENDYSSH, esquire, son and heir of Thomas Bendyssh and of Alice his wife, daughter
       of Walter Clopton, knight.
Commission to William Yerton, justice, to examine witnesses, as to a settlement of lands in Steeple
Bumpstead. (1417–1462.)   ESSEX.

14–18   John BUTLER v. Robert CRISTEMAS of London.
Arrest on his return from France with the body of King Henry V on parole to raise his ransom,
and dispute as to woad. Bill in 5 parts. (Henry VI.)   LONDON.

19–20   Margaret BUK v. the abbot of WALTHAM.
Money and jewels delivered to defendant in the presence of Roger, son of complainant, a canon
of Waltham, since apostate. (1444.)   ESSEX.

21   Thomas BARRETE of London, yeoman, v. Richard OODE (Wode) of the same, ironmonger.
Fraud in a payment to complainant's servant on behalf of Martin de Malewenda, Spaniard.
(Henry VII or later.)   LONDON.

22   Elizabeth BULKELEY, late the wife of Thomas Talbot, v. James TALBOT, knight.
Manors of . . . al, Hyde, Garoson, Southe Ashe, etc. Damaged. (1494.)   IRELAND.

23–25   Thomas, son and heir of Richard BARDESEY, v. Hugh STEPHENSON.
Detention of deeds relating to a house in Kingston-on-Thames. (16th century.)   SURREY.

26–28   John BRODERER v. the prior of LLANTHONY.
Messuages and land in Queddisly. Mutilated. (Before 1504.)   [GLOUCESTER.]

29   Elizabeth BAYN v. Thomas CRATHORN, esquire, and Guy CRATHORN.
Detention of deeds relating to messuages and lands in Castle Leavington, Crathorn, Ilton and
Kepwick (Kypyk). See Files 286; No. 7; 288, No. 14. (Cir. 1504–1515.)   YORK.

30   Peter BEVYLE v. Richard TREWEKE of Truro, and Otys LAURENS.
Promise to freight complainant's ship Peter of Falmouth for a voyage to ' Tanymount ' on condition
of respite of a payment for tin. (1504–1509?)   CORNWALL.

31   Richard, son and heir of Thomas BLANDE, v. Richard and John RAYNER.
Land. Damaged. (Henry VIII or Edward VI.)   LINCOLN.

32   William BROWNE, citizen and mercer of London and merchant of the staple of Calais,
          v. Edward TYRELL, late of Beech, gentleman, and Robert ARTHUR, yeoman of the guard.
Detention of deeds relating to reversion of a messuage, salt-cote and land in Stow after the death
of William Camper. (Henry VIII or Edward VI.)   ESSEX.

33-34   John BEKINGTON v. William HARRYSON.
Share of land and pasture in West Amesbury, formerly of Thomas Hobbes. *Pedigrees given. See
File 733, No. 28. (Cir. 1533–1538.)*   WILTS.

35   John BULMER, knight, v. James STRANWYSSH, knight.
Detention of deeds relating to a tenement at Wilton in Cleveland. *Mutilated.* (1533–1538.)
                                                                                 YORK.

36   William BUCKENHAM of Palgrave v. Roger MELL and others.
Warranty of land in Cratfield. *Mutilated..* (1553–8.)   SUFFOLK.

37   Edward BASSET v. James ORGAN, Nicholas POYNTZ, knight, and Stephen COLE his
          steward.
Tenement in the said Sir Nicholas's manor of Westerleigh. (1554–8.)   GLOUCESTER.

38-39   Nicholas BLABYE v. Elizabeth SAMON.
Original of File 1410, No. 31. (1554–8.)   WARWICK.

FILE 1495.

1   Laurence BAKER v. John BLAKFORD, husbandman.
Joint occupation of a tenement in the manor of Wiveliscombe promised on marriage with defendant's
daughter.   SOMERSET.

2   Richard BIXSTON v. William STARESMORE and Joan BIXSTON.
Detention of deeds relating to messuages in Great Bloxwich and Walsall.   STAFFORD.

3   Robert BLAKEMORE v. Roger BLAKEMORE.
Tenement in Maidenhead in the parish of Cookham, late of Robert Blakemore, deceased, father
of both parties.   BERKS.

4   William BOGGE and Margaret CHERY, executors of Thomas Chery, executor of John
          Chesse, v. Cecily . . .
Messuage in Great Munden formerly of Joan Chise, mother of the said John. *Mutilated.* HERTS.

5   . . . BOHAM(?), under-keeper of the bishop of Winchester's manor in Holborn, v. the
          mayor and sheriffs of LONDON.
Action of trespass by John Chapman concerning John Knolles, claimed by defendant as his
apprentice and by complainant as the bishop's servant. *Certiorari. Damaged.*   LONDON.

6   Lettice, late the wife of Richard BORDEN, v. John FREMAN, husband of Elizabeth, an
          executrix of the said Richard.
Money promised by the said Richard on his marriage.   ———

7   William BOUGHTON and George AGARD v. Joan MALORY.
Detention of deeds relating to the manor of Grene and messuages and lands in Alvechurch, Bylton,
Tansor and Barnwell, formerly of Henry Sutton. *Pedigree given.*
                                                 WORCESTER, WARWICK, NORTHAMPTON.

8   John BRANDON and Robert BOWYS v. John JERVYS.
Refusal to complete a sale of wheat.   ———

9   William BUSSHOP v. William JEYN *alias* Jenky.
Detention of deeds relating to a messuage in Dunster.   SOMERSET.

10   John BOTELER v. Cecil STYWARD.
Detention of deeds relating to tenements in Norwich. *Mutilated.* (15th century.) NORFOLK.

11-12   Adrian BAKER, William MEKLOW, and others, merchants of Southampton, v. Michael
          GODFRAY and John PERCHER.
Ship which proved to be ' not stanche nor seurly pechyd and dryssed.' (Henry VII or later.)
                                                                                 HANTS.

13   John BARLEY v. William SEWSTER of Steeple Morden, gentleman.
Seizure of corn at Ashwell. (Henry VII or later.)   HERTS.

14   John BROWN, clerk, executor of Ambrose Ede, clerk, v. William WALPOLE, gentleman.
Detention of deeds relating to messuages and lands in Houghton. (Henry VII or later.)
                                                                                 NORFOLK.

15   Thomas BROWN v. Joan, executrix and late the wife of John PORTER.
Imprisonment for price of sheep which died before Easter following their purchase. (Henry VII
or later.)   BEDFORD.

16   Katherine [?B]LAND v. the sheriffs of LONDON.
Imprisonment ' with manaclyng and feteryng ' by command of Henry Kebyll, alderman, for
refusal to accuse John West, priest, of incontinence. *Corpus cum causa.* (After 1502.)
                                                                                 LONDON.

17   John BENDISSH v. Walter CLERKE.
Promise to acquit complainant of a debt to Margaret Woode. (Henry VIII or later.) ———

18   John BOND of Coventry, draper, v. Margaret, late the wife of Thomas BANKES of York,
          draper, and Ralph PULLEYN of York, goldsmith.
Debt of the said Bankes, whose executors defendants are. (Henry VIII or later.)
                                                                        WARWICK, YORK.

19   John BRAYE v. Edward HERIOTTE and others.
Messuage and land in Wigmore, late of John Braye, deceased father of complainant.   (Henry VIII
or Edward VI.)   HEREFORD.

20   Christopher BYCKERDYKE v. William BALE, both of Cambridge.
' Dessyne of sylver spones ' lent by Richard Blaxton of the same.   (Henry VIII or Edward VI.)
                                                                                                              CAMBRIDGE.

21   William BAYLY, alderman of London, v. William LUFFKYN of Crayton (i.e. Creeting?),
clothman.
Action on a·bond for a debt already paid.   (1514 or later.)   LONDON, SUFFOLK.

22–23 . . . v. John KYNG and Katharine his wife.
Messuage and gardens in the parish of St. Michael Coslany [Norwich], late of Richard Braunche,
deceased, kinsman of complainant.   Bill mutilated.   (1529 or later.)   NORFOLK.

24   William BUTTON, gentleman, and William GARARD, scrivener, v. the sheriffs of LONDON.
Action by Michael Dormer, alderman, on a bond for price of land to be assured to William Hyde,
which has not been done.   Corpus cum causa.   (After 1531.)   LONDON.

25–31 ·Richard BAROWE (A Barough) v. Joan, executrix and late the wife of Vincent JUMPER,
and William their son.
Lease of the Bishop of Winchester's manor called Newcourt in Downton with live and dead stock.
(1538–1547.)   WILTS.

32   William, grandson and heir of John BLAK, v. John SHEPERREWE alias Harte and
Nicholas his son.
Tenements and cottage in Ogbourne St. Andrew held of the manor of Ogbourne St. George.
(Before 1547.)   WILTS.

33–35 Edward BUTLER, gentleman, v. John [MORDAUNT], lord Mordaunt.
Manor of Stotfold.   Damaged.   (1553–4.)   BEDFORD.

36   . . . BARKER, widow, v. the bailiffs of YARMOUTH.
Action by Robert Abs of Harley, co. Suffolk, clothier, for a debt of Robert Cornewell, partly paid.
Certiorari.   Mutilated.   (1554–8.)   NORFOLK.

37–38 John BRIDGEWATER, parson of Aldeburgh, v. John WYLLOWGHBYE (Willowe).
Tithes of Aldeburgh, defendant claiming to be vicar.   (1554–8.)   SUFFOLK.

FILE 1496.

1   John CLARYON v. Robert KYNG.
Detention of bonds already satisfied.   ———

2   Richard CLERK v. William STOKES, bailiff of Andover.
Seizure of money and false imprisonment.   Copy.   HANTS.

3–4   Edward CONWAYE and Alice his wife v. Richard DENYS and Marion his wife.
Land in Matford (in Heavitree), Exminster and elsewhere, late of Edward Hyllersdon, gentleman,
deceased, father of the said Alice and former husband of the said Marion.   Mutilated.   (Henry VII
or later.)   DEVON.

5   Edward CULPEPYR and Jane his wife v. John CLERK and Thomas CASTELL.
Land at the Stocks, late of John Hoddesdon, former husband of the said Jane.   Mutilated.
(Henry VII or later.)   LONDON.

6   The same v. Richard SHELDON and others.
Do., in the parish of St. Mary Woolchurch-Haw.   Faded.   (Henry VII or later.)   LONDON.

7   William COURTNEY, knight, v. John CROKKER, knight.
Bond given on defendant's behalf.   (After 1495.)   DEVON.

8–9   John COTTESMORE, knight, v. William HALS.
Promise to save complainant harmless on a bond made [for defendant's good conduct as escheator?].
Mutilated.   (1501 or later.)

10   Thomas CLERK, husbandman, v. Joan CLERK.
' Close or intack ' in Epworth, late of Edward Clerk, deceased, great-grandfather of complainant,
(Henry VIII or Edward VI.)   LINCOLN.

11–12 John COLROGER and John STEPHYN, husbandmen, v. Margaret TRENERTH and
Nicholas KYF.
Detention of deeds relating to a messuage and land in Merther, late of John Halvos, deceased.
Pedigree given.   (Henry VIII or Edward VI.)   CORNWALL.

13   John CONYNGESBYE and Elizabeth his wife v. Alice CROMER.
Lands in South Mimms, late of Reynold Frowike, deceased.   Mutilated Pedigree given.   (Henry VIII
or Edward VI.)   HERTS.

14   Christopher COO, esquire, v. the mayor and sheriffs of LONDON.
Action of Robert Constable, knight, for the full price of a ship and salt resold to complainant but
damaged while in the said Sir Robert's hands.   Certiorari.   (Henry VIII or later.)   LONDON.

15   Thomas CORNWALL and others v. David VAGHAN.
Detention of deeds relating to tenements in Bocking and Stebbing.   (Henry VIII or Edward VI.)
                                                                                                                        ESSEX.

16   Geoffrey, son and heir of Richard COVYLE, esquire, v. William MERTON and others.
Disturbance in the manor of Walsoken and marsh there, and wrongful assessment to the ' charges
of the cuntre.'   (Henry VIII or later.)   NORFOLK.

17-18 Arthur CRANE and Anne his wife *v.* Robert POSFORDE.
Goods of Robert Posforde, deceased, father of defendant and former husband of the said Anne, and residence in his house at Needham. (Henry VIII *or* Edward VI.) NORFOLK.

19-21 Crystyan, late the wife of Stephen CURDE of Ickleton, co. Cambridge, yeoman, *v.* Thomas HARRYSON and Elizabeth his wife.
Tenement (*described*) in Walden, late of Nicholas Adam, yeoman, deceased, father of complainant. (1511-1553.) ESSEX.

22-24 Ralph CALDWALL and Katherine his wife *v.* William SAUNDERS, John WARSOP, and Henry GUDIER.
Manors of Godyngton, Asthall, and Over Cornewall, and messuages, etc., in Synedoff Lane in London, Godyngton, St. Mary Cray, Paul's Cray, Orpington, Chelsfield, Strood, Frindsbury, Cobham, Higham, West Haddon and Staverton. *Damaged. Replication wanting.* (After 1515.)
LONDON, [OXFORD], KENT, NORTHAMPTON.

25-27 John CLAWCY, gentleman, *v.* John CHECHESTER, esquire, executor of Christopher Flemmyng, baron of Slane.
Rent in the manor of Croyde (Crydehoo), held by the said Lord Slane with the manors of Putsborough (in Georgeham) and Highbray. (After 1517). DEVON.

28 Nicholas CUTTER, bailiff of Sir William Say's manor of Pury-Fitchet (in Wembdon), *v.* John ELYS.
Tenement in the said manor. (After 1517.) SOMERSET.

29 John COTYNG *v.* Robert LAURENCE and others, feoffees to uses.
Tenements in St. Laurence, New Romney and in Newchurch, late of John Cotyng, deceased, father of complainant. (After 1531.) KENT.

30-31 Ralph COLLESON, labourer, and Agnes his wife, late the wife of Robert Varden, *v.* William, son of John BAXSTER, feoffee to uses, and Poll HUNNES (Honnes), labourers.
Messuage and land in Marham, late of the monasteries of Westacre and Marham. (1538-1553.)
NORFOLK.

32-33 John CANDISSHE, knight, and Margaret his wife *v.* Ralph KELYNG.
Tenement in Newcastle-under-Lyne (*described in answer*). (After 1542.) STAFFORD.

34-36 John, son of John CURLLE, deceased, *v.* John WESCOMBE, son of Elizabeth Rocwyll (Rokkell).
Tenement and cottage in the manor of Pixton (in Dulverton). *Previous decree cited.* (1545-7.)
SOMERSET.

37 Edmund CUSSHEN *v.* Richard BANYARD.
Detention of deeds relating to the manors of Stalworth's and Marham's and land and rent in Wymondham of the entail of John Cusshyn. *Mutilated. See File 965, No. 89.* (Before 1547.)
NORFOLK.

38-39 Richard CAGER and Agnes his wife *v.* Thomas CAGER and Robert his son.
Messuage and land in Hawkley, late held of Lord de la Warr's manor of Newton Valence by William Chistum, deceased, grandfather of the said Agnes. *See File 1293, No. 1.* (1547-1553.)
HANTS.

40-41 William CLAYETON of Breadsall Park, labourer, *v.* Thomas SACHEVERELL of Aston, gentleman.
Refusal to complete a lease of a messuage and land in Horsley. (1547-1553.) DERBY.

42-43 Philippa COWPER, daughter and heir of William Tylbroke, *v.* Thomas RUDDE.
Detention of deeds relating to a messuage and land in Carlton. (1553-4.) BEDFORD.

44-45 George CRESWELL *v.* John and Katharine HORNER.
(Continuation of *File 1339, Nos. 59-61.* (1553-5.) YORK.

46 Richard COLYNGBOURN and others *v.* John ANDREWE.
Land in Aylesbury demised for a year to Alice, mother of complainant. (1554-8.) BUCKS.

47-49 Thomas CULPEPER, gentleman, *v.* Robert BONHAM, esquire, and others.
Woods in the manor of Kelvedon Hall late of Thomas Blenerhaysett, knight, deceased, grandfather of Mary, wife of complainant. (1554-8.) ESSEX.

FILE 1497.

1 Elys CARMYNELL *v.* Simon de MARYN of London, grocer.
Petition for price of dinner and supper already paid for, which complainant ceased to attend, ' perceyvyng the great number of vacabundes and suspecte persones that contynually resorted unto the said house.' LONDON.

2 John CHOPE *v.* Thomas DUNNE and John SHEPPERD.
Detention of deeds relating to a messuage and land in Bradworthy. DEVON.

3 John CLERK of Basingstoke.
Petition on behalf of William Boubregge, accused of theft by John Saucer of Frome Selwood.
HANTS, SOMERSET.

4 Thomas CODLYNG, clerk, and others *v.* John DYKKES of East Dereham.
One-third of a messuage in Bawdeswell of the feoffment of John Millere. NORFOLK.

5-7 Thomas COK *v.* Thomas CROP and Margaret his wife.
Messuage in the borough of Liskeard bought of Margaret, late the wife of Richard Croppe (who answers). CORNWALL.

8 Thomas COLYN *v.* the mayor and bailiffs of EXETER and their clerk, and Agnes TOKER.
Refusal to permit complainant to see the record of a plea on which he had obtained a writ of certiorari. [*Certiorari and subpœna.*] DEVON.

9   John COLYNGBORN of Wooburn, husbandman, v. the sheriff of BUCKINGHAM.
False imprisonment by the under-sheriff.   BUCKS.

10   Nicholas COLYNS of Waltham in Middlesex, son and heir of William Colyns, v. Henry
HEWET, servant to John Russell, knight.
Detention of deeds relating to a messuage and land in Hitchin.   HERTS.

11   William COOKE of Over Burgate (in Fordingbridge) v. William TYRELL of Fordingbridge.
Detention of deeds relating to a messuage and land in the parish (sic) of Sandhill (i.e. Sandhill
manor in Fordingbridge).   HANTS.

12   . . . not COTERELL (a woman) v. John . . .
Messuage in St. Albans of the demise of Richard S[tode]ley, deceased. Mutilated.   HERTS.

13   John COBBETHORN and others, executors of Edmund [Stafford or Lacy?], bishop of Exeter,
v. Hugh WILLIAM, priest.
Fraudulently obtaining a release of a debt. (After 1419.)   ———

14   Henry, son and heir of Henry CACHEREL, v. Reynold DRYLAND of Selling.
Lands, rents and services in Sandwich conveyed by complainant to his own use on his departure
beyond seas with Lord Willoughby. (Cir. 1431–1452.)   KENT.

15   Nicholas CALTON, priest of the Chancellor's church of Wells, v. John REWE.
False charge of felony, detention of a bond and neglect of a suit against John Tipup (1435–1443).
SOMERSET.

16   Edmund, son and heir of Thomas COLT, and servant to ' the lord prynce,' v. John DYSON,
bailiff of Lichfield.
Seizure of goods in a dispute with Robert Coterell. Faded. (Henry VII ?)   STAFFORD.

17-18   Roger COTON, knight, and Margaret his wife, daughter and heir of Nicholas Norton, v.
William BOLTON and Margaret his wife.
Detention of deeds relating to a messuage and lands in Paddington, Westbourne, Kensington and
Knightsbridge. (After 1485.)   MIDDLESEX.

19   Margaret CHAFFER v. Nicholas WAREN of Shrewsbury, merchant.
Lease of a tenement in Watling Street, in the parish of All Hallows [Bread Street]. (16th century).
LONDON.

20-23   William CARSWILL and Jane HURST v. John UNDERHAY and William HANYS,
feoffees to user.
Messuage and land at Longford Lister (in Ugborough), late of Jane Hethfild, deceased. Pedigree
given. (1503 or 1527.)   DEVON.

24-26   Peter COWDREY v. Peter BOYLE, clerk.
(Continuation of File 300, No. 5.) See also Files 127, No. 63; 291, No. 7. (1504–1515.)
HANTS.

27   Edmund CHURCH v. William CAPELL, knight, alderman of London.
Non-payment of part price of the manor of South Wootton, and repudiation of release of a bond.
(Henry VIII.)   NORFOLK, LONDON.

28-29   John CLARE and Alice his wife, daughter and heir of Simon Taylor alias Nele, v. Stephen
GALLE, clerk.
Sheep of the bequest of the said Simon, claimed by defendant to buy vestments for the church of
Snitterton.   NORFOLK.

30-31   The same v. the same.
Detention and forgery of deeds relating to a messuage and land in Snitterton. (Henry VIII or
Edward VI.)   NORFOLK.

32-33   William CLUTTON and Margery his wife v. Martin, son and heir of Walter BOURE, feoffee
to user.
Messuage and land in Newent late of John Bukland, deceased, grandfather of the said Margery.
See File 296, No. 76. (Cir. 1510–1515.)   GLOUCESTER.

34-36   John CALWODLEY v. John CARLYON, parson of Stoodleigh.
Refusal to complete a lease of defendant's parsonage in expectation of which complainant had
surrendered a lien of two miles. See File 297, No. 93. (After 1513.)   DEVON.

37-39   Giles CAPELL, knight, v. Reynold HYGATE of Southminster.
Land in [Orsett ?] formerly of John [Hygate?]. Faded. [After 1513.]   ESSEX.

40-41   Richard COLLYN of Milton Abbot v. Ralph HARRYSON, vicar of Marystow.
Lease of part of land called the ' sentuarie,' in Marystow. (1530–1547.)   DEVON.

42-43   Audrey CLARK of South Elmham, daughter and heir of Richard Pedder, v. Rose DETHICK.
Wrongful occupation of a messuage and land at North Elmham, and procuring a session of the
manor court at a date unknown to complainant. (1549–1553 ?)   NORFOLK.

44-45   Peter COLSTONSOKE of Wood-Newton, in Northants, v. Robert COLSTONSOKE, John
CROSBYE, priest, and others.
(Continuation of File 1295, Nos. 36–38.) (1551–1553.)   CHESTER.

46   The inhabitants of COPPENHALL v. Thomas CHROMELEY and others, executors of
William Chomeley.
Bequest for making a cause way through Coppenhall and mending a lane called ' Annottes Laker.'
(1554-8.)   STAFFORD.

47-48   John CRAWNFEYLD of Cople, yeoman, v. Richard SAUNDERS of North Crawley, in
Bucks, late the husband of Agnes daughter of Thomas Pollyn.
Messuage and close in Cranfield late of William Crawnfeld of Cardington (Caryngton), husbandman
deceased, grandfather of complainant. (1554-8.)   BEDFORD.

49   Francis CROMWELL of London, gentleman, son and heir of Sir Richard Cromwell, *v.* Thomas
Llewelyn HYRE and others.
Trespasses and enclosures in the lordship of Cadoxton. (1554-8.)   GLAMORGAN.

FILE 1498.

1-2   John, son of Alexander CAREWE, esquire(?), *v.* John GLYN.
Money promised to complainant on his marriage with defendant's daughter.   ———

3   William CHAPMAN and Ellen his wife *v.* Ralph A THYKKYNGES.
Messuages and land in Great Drayton and Tunstall, late of Robert Bromeley, esquire, deceased,
grandfather of the said Ellen.   ———

4   John CHYLD, husbandman, *v.* Richard, son and executor of George SQUYER.
House called the ' Woode House ' in Witham, late of John Childe, deceased, whose executors were
Thomas, father of complainant, and Richard, father of the said George.   ESSEX.

5   Thomas COUPER *v.* John HOLLYER, executor of Joan, late the wife of William Nutbrown.
Detention of deeds relating to land in Bexhill (Bexle).   SUSSEX.

6   Thomas CARMYNOWE, gentleman of the King's chamber, *v.* Thomas SAYNTAWBYN
and others.
Tin obtained from complainant's lands in Kellyvregh and Nam Ysferne. *Mutilated.* (Henry VII
or later.)   CORNWALL.

7   William CODOURS *v.* the bailiffs of LUDLOW.
Action by Richard Whithall for price of cloth to be partly paid in malmsey and sugar. *Certiorari.*
(Henry VII or later.)   WALES (*now* SALOP).

8   Robert COKE and Elizabeth his wife *v.* Alice BRADWEY and others.
Detention of deeds relating to a messuage and land in Broad Campden. (Henry VII or later.)
        GLOUCESTER.

9   Piers COURTENEY, esquire, *v.* William COURTENEY, knight.
Detention of deeds relating to lands in Bere and Borowe of the gift of William Courteney, knight,
deceased, father of both parties. (1485-1535?)   SOMERSET.

10   Laurence CROMPTON *v.* the sheriffs of CHESTER, and Edward BEKK.
Action on a bond. *Certiorari and subpœna. Mutilated.* (Henry VIII or later.)   CHESTER.

11   John COROYE, merchant of Florence, factor to William Coroye and his company, *v.* [the
sheriffs of LONDON].
Attachment of·cloth of gold and silver, etc., at the suit of William Tyler, knight, and others.
Certiorari. Damaged. (After 1485.)   LONDON.

12-13   John CONGAN, yeoman, *v.* John PHILYP.
Messuage and land in South Raes, Treglonnen, and Treyew, late of John Congan, deceased, father
of complainant. *See Files 124, No. 78, and 396, No. 4.* (1486-1518.)   CORNWALL.

14-16   George COLUMBELL and Elizabeth his wife *v.* Thomas BRUMPTON.
Land, late of the said Elizabeth's father. *Faded.* (16th century.)

17-19   Richard CHARLES *v.* Robert BOREMAN.
Double sale of a ' berebruhouse ' and land in Appledore by Richard Newland. (1507.)   KENT.

20-21   Richard CADE *v.* Walter JAGO.
Messuages in [the parish of St. Martin?] Ludgate. *Mutilated.* (Henry VIII or later.)   LONDON.

22   Margaret CHAPMAN *v.* John CLARK.
Lands in Ugley. *Much damaged.* (Henry VIII or later.)   ESSEX.

23-26   James, Thomas and John COPPYN(G) *v.* Thomas ROBERTES and Margaret his wife.
Messuage and land in Boughton Monchelsea, late of John Coppyn, deceased, uncle of complainants.
(Henry VIII *or* Edward VI.)   KENT.

27   Laurence COUPER *v.* John ZELY.
Tenement in Briggewater and North Bowre (in Bridgwater?), late of John Baker. *Damaged.*
(Henry VIII or later.)   [SOMERSET.]

28   John COYNG, chaplain, *v.* the sheriffs of LONDON.
Action by Thomas Devynysh for false imprisonment. *Certiorari. Faded.* (After 1511.)
        LONDON.

29-30   Thomas CRAW of Boston, chaplain, *v.* Thomas PALMER.
(*Continuation of File 961, No. 55*). (1538-1544).   LINCOLN.

31   John COUNSTABLE, knight, *v.* Robert [HOLGATE], archbishop of York.
Promise of a lease for life of the rectory of Kinoulton. (1545-1553.)   NOTTS.

32-33   William COOKE, gentleman, *v.* Thomas ALLSOP.
Money sent to Trusley by Richard Coke. *Damaged.* (1554-8.)   DERBY.

34   Richard CORNEBY *v.* Jane CORNEBY.
Tenement called Corneby Hall late of complainant's father. *Faded.* (1554-8.)

35-36   John CRUSE (Cruys) *v.* James BRENDON.
Debt of —— Loure to John Bealbury, deceased, whose executors both parties are. *Faded.*
(1554-8.)   CORNWALL.

FILE 1499.

1 Thomas DOLPHYN of Birmingham, smith, and Alice his wife *v.* Roger BROMYCHE.
Mortgage of a tenement in Norton Heath by Roger (*sic*) Bromyche, brother of defendant, and
former husband of the said Alice.   WORCESTER.

2 Simon DONHAM, chaplain to [the Chancellor], and great-grandson and heir of Richard
Toppe, *v.* John SY . . . YE.
Detention of deeds relating to a messuage and land in Tunstall in Holderness. *Faded.* YORK.

3 Edward DREW *v.* John BASKERVYLL and others.
Assault on Henry Chylde, who obtained damages against complainant.   ———

4 Geoffrey DREWS, weaver of St. Mary-le-Strand, *v.* [the bailiff of the SAVOY].
Arrest by the procurement of Hugh Wever, condemned in the abbot of Westminster's court called
the pipepowders.' *Corpus cum causa.*   MIDDLESEX.

5-6 Simon DUNHAM, clerk, *v.* Peter DAVY.
Detention of deeds relating to land in Postwick said by defendant to be part of a ' senary ' held by
complainant by the right of parsonage. *Mutilated.*   NORFOLK.

7 William DURDAUNTE of London, grocer, *v.* the sheriffs of LONDON.
Action by Agnes, executrix, and late the wife of Nicholas Darley of London, grocer, on a com-
position for price of ' woode ' (*i.e.* woad ?) which proved to be of inferior quality. *Certiorari.*
   LONDON.

8 Elizabeth DYER *v.* the bailiffs of KINGSTON.
Action by defendants as bridge-wardens, pending an action for messuages and lands by complainant. *Certiorari. Mutilated.*   SURREY.

9 Joan DYER *v.* Robert MILLE of Maldon and John CAMPE.
Tenement in Hadleigh granted to complainant before her marriage by John Dyer, since her
husband, who died while she was on pilgrimage.   ESSEX.

10 Robert DYK of Beverley, labourer, *v.* the bailiffs of the provost of BEVERLEY.
Forged action of trespass by John Walasse following on other vexatious proceedings. *Corpus cum
causa.*   YORK.

11-12 Hoell (ap) Jevan DYOO of St. George *v.* (John) Jevan DYO.
Refusal to sign a bill for repayment of a debt.   GLAMORGAN.

13 John DOUNE *v.* Edmund WESTBY, bailiff of the franchise of the abbot of St. Albans.
Wrongful arrests and false return to a *corpus cum causa.* (*Cir.* 1394-1424 ?) [HERTS.]

14 Nicholas DYKER *v.* the mayor of [LONDON].
Cross suits for debt between complainant, John Hubank (Hughbank) of London, tailor, and
Christopher Plummer.. *Certiorari. Faded.* (1431 or later.)   [LONDON.]

15 William DEMOUNDE and May his wife *v.* Thomas GRYNFELD and others, executors of
Elizabeth Robessart, lady Bourchier.
Annuity granted for good service. *Footnote* discharging one of defendants. *Mutilated. See
File* 11, No. 114. (To the bishop of Bath, chancellor ; 1433-1443.) ———

16 Richard DIXSON of Muston, husbandman, *v.* Thomas AUNDERSON.
Money due to William, prior of Bridlington, and pasture for sheep promised on assignment of a
loan of land in [Muston ?]. *Damaged.* (After 1489.)   YORK.

17-19 Thomas DOWSYNG of London, poulterer, *v.* Henry BROTHERS of Shelswell.
Action concerning a bargain of rabbits forfeited as stale. (1497.) LONDON, OXFORD.

20 Patrick DURHAM, mariner, *v.* John NYCOLLES of London, skinner, attorney to John
Shyrwode, mariner.
Action on a bond extorted by force in an inn in Lombard Street. *Letters missive. See File* 495,
No. 37. (*Cir.* 1518-1529.)   LONDON.

21 William DAY of Wisbech, chandler, *v.* John ODAM of the same, butcher.
Contract for sale of all defendant's tallow during the joint lives of both parties. (1500-1532.)
   CAMBRIDGE.

22 Thomas DALBY, clerk, *v.* Thomas DOCKERAY, [prior of the Hospital of St. John of
Jerusalem in England].
Loan to the commanders of Ribston, Mount Grace, and Carbrook. *Mutilated.* (*Cir.* 1506-1515.)
   YORK, [NORFOLK.]

23-24 William DALYE and Isabel his wife *v.* William SMYTH of Stockerston.
Legacy of Richard, brother of defendant. *Paper bill.* (Henry VIII or later.) LEICESTER.

25 DAVID ap John ap Hugh *v.* JOHN ap Jenkyn and OWEN ap Griffith.
Detention of deeds relating to a messuage and land in Strate Marsell in the lordship of Powes.
(Henry VIII or Edw. VI.)   [MONTGOMERY.]

26 William DEANE, executor of Ralph Deane, *v.* John QUASHE of Norwich.
Price of fimble-hemp and ' sawthefyshes ' (*i.e.* saithe?) *Mutilated.* (Henry VIII or Edward VI.)
   NORFOLK.

27 Harry DRAKE, husbandman, *v.* Thomas RANDALL and others.
Land in Lamerton held in right of Cristian, wife of complainant, late the wife of Robert Hyll.
(Henry VIII *or* Edward VI.)   DEVON.

28 Thomas Croswell and Henry Derbye, churchwardens of DROITWICH, *v.* Thomas
BARRETT.
Waste on a tenement from which complainants provide the ornaments and vestments of the
church. *Mutilated.* (Henry VIII or Edward VI.)   WORCESTER.

29–30   John DANET and Anne his wife, daughter and heir of Thomas Elinebrugge, esquire, *v.*
Bartholomew [LINSTED], prior of St. Mary Overies.
Detention of deeds relating to lands, messuages, and a dovecote in Nutfield, Sutton, Merstham,
Gatton, Bletchingley, Chipstead, Croydon, Sanderstead, and Addington, and the manors of
Albury, Croham (in Croydon) and Chaldon.   (1513–1539.)   SURREY.

31–34   Katherine, late the wife of William DYKKES, *v.* Nicholas POTMAN.
Reviver of a suit concerning a messuage and land in Yarde *alias* Crayford   (*File* 404, *No.* 56.)
(After 1515.)   KENT.

35   William DYKON, priest, son and heir of Richard Dykon, *v.* Miles COLYNG, his brother-
in-law.
Detention of deeds relating to land in Haughton. (After 1518.)   DURHAM.

36   Laurence DUTTON, esquire, *v.* Richard EGERTON, clerk, feoffee to uses.
Entail of the manors of Dutton, Aston, Weston, Preston, Barterton, Legh, Ness in Wirrall, Little
Mouldsworth, Acton and Hapsford and messuages and lands there and in Clifton, Stony Dunham,
Great Barrow, Stoke, Picton, Arrow, Northwich, Halton, Thelwall, Ouston, Middlewich,
Stanthurle, and Over Runcorn. (After 1525.)   CHESTER.

37–38   John DREWE, Philippa his wife, Edmund YONGER, Edith his wife, John WYLLYSHAM,
and Rose his wife, *v.* Robert STYLLYARD and John BARKER, clerks.
Lands (*described*) in Bury St. Edmunds, late of Roger Cowper, deceased, grandfather of the female
complainants. *Faded.* (1530–1553.)   SUFFOLK.

39–42   John DANBURY of Walden, yeoman, *v.* Robert WRYGHT.
Pledge of a leasehold in Debden. (1533 or later.)   ESSEX.

43–44   William DEBNAM of Shorne, co. Kent, *v.* Robert BROWNE of Cranleigh and Robert
CHAUNDLER.
Houses and land in Haslemere, formerly of Thomas Pepham (Peperham), great-grandfather of
complainant. *See File* 775, *No.* 52. (*Cir.* 1533–1538.)   SURREY.

45–47   Robert DARWYN *v.* Thomas STANFELD, Richard FLYNTHAM, Nicholas FARMER,
and Oliver GIBSON.
Messuages and land in Torksey, Brampton, Upton and Kexby, late of Richard Darwyn and Alice
his second wife, deceased, parents of complainant. (1535–1553.) *See File* 1115, *No.* 7. LINCOLN.

48–51   Thomas, son of Gilbert DUTTON, *v.* John VENABLES of the Cross, near Northwich.
' Wichehouses or saltecotes ' in Northwich of the demise of John Buteler, late abbot of Vale Royal.
(1537–1547.)   CHESTER.

52–53   Elizabeth, wife of Philip DRACOT, knight, *v.* Maude, late the wife of Anthony FITZ-
HERBERT, knight.
Delivery to complainant's husband without her consent of a deed of feoffment of her jointure-
lands in Draycott[-in-the-Moor], Consall, Paynesley, Whistone (in Kingsley), Hasulles (*cf.* Hazel-
wall in Cheadle), Broadoak (in Kingsley), etc. (1538–1553.)   STAFFORD.

54–56   William DOLPHYN of London, draper, *v.* William SHUTFORD.
Arrest of complainant's ship when deserted by its mariners at Falmouth. *Mutilated.* (1540–1553.)
                                                                                CORNWALL.

57   John DAWNTESEY, gentleman, *v.* William WYLLYNGTON and Ambrose DAWNTESEY,
executors of William Dawntesey, alderman of London.
Mesne profits of the manor of Shipton Sollars, late of Anthony Twynnyho, esquire, deceased,
father-in-law of complainant. (1547–1553.)   GLOUCESTER.

58   Elizabeth DAUKES of Ambercote (*i.e.* Amblecote, co. Stafford?) *v.* John HARWARD and
Roger, son of Silvester Taylour.
Lands (*described*) in the manor of Chaddesley Corbett, late of John Dawkes, deceased, husband of
complainant. (1553–4.)   WORCESTER.

59   Robert DAVIES of Westminster and John DAVIES, executors of David ap Gruffydd ap
Llewellyn, *v.* REES ap John and ROBERT ap Elis, executors of John ap Rees ap David
Timo.
Bonds for a debt already paid. (1554–8.)   LONDON.

60   John DENHAM and Grace his wife *v.* Richard BRENT and John and Thomas, sons of
John HAM.
(Copy of *File* 1422, *No.* 25.) *Mutilated.* (1554–8.)   HANTS.

61–65   William DOWE (Dove) *v.* William TOMPSON and John his son.
Assignment of a lease from Christ's College, Cambridge, of the manor of North Hykeham.
(1556–8.)   LINCOLN.

66–67   John DUDLEY of [?Do]rkinge, co. Surrey, yeoman, *v.* Hugh ap Llewelyn LLOYD and
John SACKEVILE.
Joint lease from the Crown to complainant and William Sackevile, deceased, of messsuages, land
and rent in [Llan]luer, Ustate, Trevillan, and Lampeter [' Llanbether and Seynt Stephan '], late
of the monastery of Llanluer. *Mutilated.* (1554–8.)   CARDIGAN.

68–69   Thomas DYME(S), parson of Fetcham, *v.* John RYCKEMAN.
Seizure of tithe corn. *Answer wanting.* (1554–8.)   SURREY.

FILE 1500.

1　　Luke de ECCLESIA v. the judges of SOUTHAMPTON.
Action of covenant by Thomas Cook concerning goods of John de Bardes attached in complainant's
lands. *Certiorari.*　　　　　　　　　　　　　　　　　　　　　　　　　　　　HANTS.

2　　John ELYNGHAM, keeper of the King's pavilions, v. the sheriffs of LONDON.
Action by Alison, wife of Roger Benyngton, sometime of London, barber, complainant having
taken away from her his daughter, whom she had abducted and employed to tend her said
husband, a ' lazour:' *Corpus cum causa.*　.　　　　　　　　　　　　·LONDON.

3　　Thomas ELYS of Norwich, merchant, v. William WHEDERELL, bailiff of Ipswich.
Debt of Herman Rollesthorp, Dutchman, who was ' hosted ' with defendant.
　　　　　　　　　　　　　　　　　　　　　　　　　　　　　　　NORFOLK, SUFFOLK.

4　　Richard ESTCOTE and Agnes his wife v. Thomasyn, executrix, and late the wife of .John
WRANGWORTHY, and mother of the said Agnes.
Detention of deeds relating to messuages and land in Hartland.　　　　　　DEVON.

5　　Thomas,* prior of EARL'S COLNE, v. Elizabeth [DE VERE], countess of Oxford, and
others, executors of [John de Vere], late earl of Oxford.
Compensation for· land in Hedingham (Hynyngham) taken for the earl's park, defendants being
seized of the manor of Hinxton. *Mutilated.* (1461–1503.)　　　ESSEX, CAMBRIDGE.

6　　Roger ESTGATE v. Thomas LEMMAN, executor of Richard Bettys, vicar of Great
Witchingham.
Detention of a book called a ' portos ' and of evidences relating to lands in Bradfield. *See File*
199, *No.* 22. (After 1488.)　　　　　　　　　　　　　　　　　　　NORFOLK.

7–9　　James EMENS of Warwick, labourer, and Alice his wife v. John WYLSON and Hugh
CURSER (Corcer, Corveser).
Messuage and land, late of Roger Wylson of Great Worley (*i.e.* Wyrley?), baker, father of
complainant. (1496–1547.)　　　　　　　　　　　　　　　　　　　STAFFORD.

10–12　　The brethren of the gild of Corpus Christi in EATON v. Thomas KNYGHT.
Parcel of a messuage in Eaton, and rent charged on the adjoining one, which belongs to defendant.
(Henry VIII?)　　　　　　　　　　　　　　　　　　　　　　　　　BEDFORD.

13–15　　Robert (Ellis) EDMONDSON v. Geoffrey, Robert and Edward EDMONDSON.
Messuages and lands in Salley, late of Edward Edmondson, deceased, grandfather of complainant
and father of defendants. (Henry VIII *or* Edward VI.)　　　NOTTS (*rectius* DERBY).

16–17　　Henry ENGWYN .v. Alexander CARVANELL, yeoman, late the husband of Ellen,
executrix and formerly the wife of Martin Pendye (Pendry).
Balance of accounts. (Henry VIII or Edward VI.)　　　　　　　CORNWALL.

18　　·　Stephen ESTWICK of Lavendon (Landon) v. Ellen, late the wife of Richard KNIGHTE
of Holdenby, husbandman, and Robert KNIGHTE, administrators of the said Richard's
goods, and William KNIGHTE of Holdenby, husbandman.
Debt for sheep, the bond for which is lost. (1539–1547.)　　BUCKINGHAM, NORTHAMPTON.

19–20　　Robert ESTCHURCHE v. Nicholas WYCHEHALSE.
Refusal to complete a bond to save complainant harmless against John Webbe *alias* Toker after
giving an arbitral award against the latter in ' all matters and demaundes as well royall as
personell.' (After 1540.)　　　　　　　　　　　　　　　　　　　———

21–24　　ELIZABETH ap William *alias* Elizabeth verch Ellys v. WILLIAM ap John and JOHN
and KENRICK ap William.
Land in Ysceifiog, late of Howell ap William, deceased, husband of complainant, and son of the
defendant William. (1549–1553.)　　　　　　　　　　　　　　　FLINT.

25–26　　Anthony EDMUND and others v. Adlard WELBY.
(Continuation of *File* 1348, *No.* 10.) (1553–4.)　　　　　　　　　LINCOLN.

27–28　　Edmund ELLMES v. Elizabeth, late the wife of Thomas BRUDENELL, knight.
(Continuation of *File* 1348, *No.* 45.) (1553–4.)
　　　　　　　　　RUTLAND, LINCOLN, OXFORD, BUCKINGHAM, BERKS.

29–30　　George ESCROPE (Estrop, Estrope) v. John HALL and John, son and heir of Richard
VEALL, husbandman.
(Continuation of *File* 1348, *No.* 103.) (1553–4.)　　　　　　　YORK.

31–33　　Thomas EUSDON and Joan his wife v. Alice, late the wife of William COOKE, serjeant-
at-law.
Land in the said Cooke's manor of Milton. (1553–4.)　　　　　　　　　?

34–35　　Nicholas EVERAD, gentleman, v. John ATTMERE.
Debt partly recovered against complainant by John Bacon, esquire, a creditor of defendant.
(1556–8.)　　　　　　　　　　　　　　　　　　　　　　　　　　———

FILE 1501.

1　　John FAUKES, tenant of the Duchy of Lancaster, v. Henry INGLOUSE, knight.
Forcible entry and seizure of bedding, corn and cattle.　　　　　　　　NORFOLK.

2　　John FE .　.　.　:　v. Thomas RAWLYN.
Detention of deeds relating to a messuage and land in South　.　.　.　se. *Damaged.*　　?

* Not Thomas Cheltenham mentioned in V.C.H.

3   John FENLEY, shereman, and Margaret his wife, late the wife of John Brandon, citizen and shereman of London, *v.* the mayor and aldermen of LONDON.
Action by Margaret Porter for plate (*described*) and tablecloths given by her to the said Brandon and his wife for money and attendance in sickness. *Certiorari.*   LONDON.

4   Hercules de FERRARIIS, clerk, *v.* the sheriffs of LONDON.
Action by William Bayly, citizen and shereman of London, on a bond which he had promised to cancel, complainant having procured his release from arrest for offences concerning his allegiance and cured him of a disease. *Certiorari. See File* 310, *No.* 32. (*Cir.* 1504-1515).   LONDON.

5   Nicholas FISSHER of Strode *v.* William BROOKE of St. George's, Southwark.
Grant of all complainant's goods on a promise to 'make leve of' all his debts.   KENT, SURREY.

6   Richard FLAMOK and Margaret his wife *v.* John TRESODERYN.
Detention of deeds relating to messuages and land in Tresawle and Halveor (in St. Columb Major) and Carloggas (in St. Mawgan).   CORNWALL.

7-8   Miles, son and heir of Thomas FLEMMYNG, *v.* John TALBOT, executor of the said Thomas.
Detention of deeds relating to a messuage and land in Sampton.   [DEVON?]

9   Thomas FLETHAM, clerk, and Richard ELREDE, executors of Harry Newman, *v.* William HONOUR.
Messuage and land in Thurleby, bought of defendant who occupied them as testator's tenant-at-will.   [LINCOLN.]

10   Thomas FOLBERGH *v.* Henry INGLOUS, knight.
Forcible entry and vexatious suits.   NORFOLK.

11-15 James FOLJAMBE *v.* Vincent LOWE of Denby, esquire.
Manor of Denby and lands and rent in Woodhouse, Smalley, Codnor, and elsewhere. *Damaged.*
                                    DERBY.

16   Thomas FOXE *v.* John HUSBAND, feoffee to uses.
Messuages and land in Penkelek the More, late of William Foxe, deceased, father of complainant.   CORNWALL.

17-18 Elizabeth FRANKELEYN *v.* Avice, executrix, and late the wife of Thomas DYKSON, weaver.
Goods (*schedule annexed*) entrusted to the said Thomas by Cuthbert Colvile, deceased, father of complainant.   ————

19   Robert FREMAN, clerk, *v.* John CALY.
Detention of deeds relating to a messuage and land in Salhouse.   NORFOLK.

20-22 John FREND and Mary his wife *v.* John CHALKHILL and John CAVELEY, feoffees to uses, and Joan and Robert FREND.
Lands in Willesden and Harrow, late of Roger Frend, deceased, father of the said John Frend and husband of the said Joan. *Mutilated.*   MIDDLESEX.

23   John FREND of Maidstone, weaver, *v.* Nicholas HASELL, constable of Maidstone.
Arrest at defendant's own suit without writ or warrant. *Corpus cum causa.*   KENT.

24   Robert FREND, merchant tailor, *v.* the mayor and sheriffs of LONDON.
Action by William . . . on a bond for a debt already paid. *Certiorari. Faded.*   LONDON.

25   Henry FYSSHER, clerk, *v.* the sheriffs of LONDON.
Action of debt, account and trespass by Christopher Hall, gentleman, pending other suits. *Certiorari.*   LONDON.

26   James FENES, knight, *v.* Nicholas WYFFOLD, Katherine his wife, and John WALSHAWE.
Plate (including bottles called ' flaketis '), money and deed of gift of the same by John Brokle of London, alderman and draper, former husband of the said Katherine. (After 1442.)   LONDON.

27·   William FOXE *v.* the sheriffs of LONDON.
Divers suits by William Randys, girdler, ' a comen jurour . . . and so greatly favored amonges jurours,' who has assaulted complainant's wife. *Certiorari. Mutilated.* (To the keeper of the great seal; after 1460.)   LONDON.

28   Thomas FISSHERR and Alice his wife, of Aldbourne.
Imprisonment without indictment at Fisherton Anger, their case being removed by writ to Chancery. (Henry VII or later.)   WILTS.

29   John FLEMYNG of Exeter *v.* John LYMPENY, clerk.
Detention of deeds relating to messuages and land in St. Sidwell's and Petrockstow. (Henry VII or later.)   DEVON.

30-31 Richard FAGGER *v.* Richard COVERT, husband of Elizabeth, granddaughter of William Fagger.
Detention of deeds relating to tenements in Steyning. *See File* 93, *No.* 45. (*Cir.* 1486-1493.)
                                    SUSSEX.

32   Joan, late the wife of William FLYNT, and formerly of John HERT, *v.* John FYNEUX, knight, L.J.K.B., and others.
Reviver of a suit for lands in Wodechirch. (1495-1525.)   [KENT *or* CHESTER.]

33   . . . F . . GELL *v.* John TRENOWTHE.
Lands in Altarnun. *Mutilated.* (16th century.)   CORNWALL.

34-37 Lettice, a daughter of Sir John FOGGE, deceased, *v.* Jane FOGGE, late his wife, and John FOGGE, knight, her son.
Legacy partly payable out of lands of John Kyrrell (Kyryell) and partly out of goods of Bishop Goldwell. (After 1501.)   [KENT?]

38   John FISSHER, clerk, v. Harry BOWSELL, notary of London.
Refusal to give evidence concerning the prebend of Underton in the King's free chapel of Bridgnorth, or to produce deeds, including a copy of ' the pertygall.' (Henry VIII.)   SALOP.

39-41   Humphrey FITZWILLIAM v. William COPLEY.
Legacy of William Fitzwilliam, nephew of Dorothy, wife of defendant, payable out of the manors of Haddlesey and Darrington. (Henry VIII or later.)   YORK.

42   Robert FOX.
Petition to examine witnesses (*named*) as to a devise of a messuage and lands in Finchley and Totteridge by William Fox, deceased, father of complainant. (Henry VIII or Edward VI.)   MIDDLESEX, HERTS.

43   Christopher FYSSHER of London, mercer, v. the sheriffs of LONDON.
Action of trespass by John Neve of Colchester, clothier, arising out of a dispute as to a proposed marriage of Eleanor his daughter. *Certiorari.* (Henry VIII or Edward VI.)   LONDON, ESSEX.

44   William [FITZALAN], earl of Arundel, and Harry MATRAVERS (*sic*), lord Matravers, his son and heir apparent, v. George HEYDONE, esquire.
Rights of common belonging to the manors of Mileham and Beeston, etc. *Damaged.* (1512-1552.)   NORFOLK.

45-46   George FERANDOLFF, nephew and heir of John Ferandolff, v. James METCALFE and others, executors of the said John, and Richard HAWKESWELL, priest.
Detention of deeds relating to the manors and ' gresshinges ' of Spennithorne (Penythorn), Ferriby, etc. (*as in File 409, No. 4*). (*Cir.* 1515-1518.)   YORK.

47   Thomas FOWLER v. Roger RABON and the sheriffs of LONDON.
Action on a bond partly paid by Richard, father of complainant. *Subpœna and certiorari.* See File 408, No. 17. (*Cir.* 1515-1518.)

48-51   Robert FERMAN v. John DOCWRA.
Exchange of the manor of Walton for lands in Holoway and Hygate. *Damaged.* (After 1515.)   NORTHAMPTON, [MIDDLESEX].

52-53   Nicholas FRELOVE v. Ralph WATSON and William BROWNE, wardens of the fraternity of . . .
Tenements in No[rthampton] formerly of Joan, late the wife of John Glasebroke of Northampton, tailor, and afterwards wife of complainant. *Damaged.* (After 1517.)   NORTHAMPTON.

54-55   John FYNYMORE of Petersfield, husbandman, v. John, son of William REDYNG.
Detention of deeds relating to a tenement in Worldham (Wardelam), late of Thomas Grove and Alice his wife. (After 1523.)   HANTS.

56   Thomas [Chard *alias* Tybbes], abbot of FORD, v. Edward FETEPLACE, esquire.
Bond given by complainant for an annuity granted by John Chaffcombe out of the manor of Churchill intended to be out of that of Fyfield for services at his election as abbot of Bruern. (1527-1539.)   OXFORD.

57-58   William FREMAN and Agnes his wife, late the wife of William Smyth, v. Ralph SMYTH.
Messuage and land in Irthlingborough (Artylborough) of the gift of defendant. (Before 1530.)   NORTHAMPTON.

59   Godfrey FULLJAMBE, esquire, son and heir of Roger Fuljambe, v. Tristram REVELL of Barnyghwayt, gentleman.
Detention of deeds relating to a messuage, cottage and land in Brampton. *See Files 768, No. 26; 793, No. 41.* (*Cir.* 1533-1538.)   DERBY.

60-62   Humphrey FARLEY v. William WYNNE.
Messuages and land in the lordship of Upleadon in Bosbury, demised by William Weston, prior of the Hospitallers, on defendant's outlawry. *See File 983, No. 1.* (*Cir.* 1538-1544.)   HEREFORD.

63   Randall FOXHOLES, husbandman, v. John [Horwood?], abbot of VALE ROYAL.
Tenement in defendant's manor of Weaverham (Weverham, Werham). (Before 1545.)   CHESTER.

64-65   Alice FLEXNEY, executrix of Richard Flexney (Flaxney), both of Oxford, v. Laurence, son and executor of John BARRY of Ensham.
Money entrusted to the said John by Richard, son of the said Richard. *See File 1177, No. 48.* (*Cir.* 1547.)   OXFORD.

66-70   Robert FLECHER v. John GENES.
(*Continuation of File 1218, Nos. 14-15.*) (1547-1551.)   CHESTER.

71-72   William FULTHORN v. Thomas BRESE (Bryce) of Hockwold (Houghole), both husbandmen.
Refusal to complete a sale of a messuage and land in Feltwell in exchange for 5s. and a standing crop of barley. (1551-3.)   NORFOLK.

73-75   William FLEARE of Exeter and Elizabeth his wife, late the wife of John Brykenall of the same, merchant, v. John SOUTHCOTE of Shillingford, esquire.
Debt paid to divers persons by defendant's command. (1553-4.)   DEVON.

76   . . . ., younger sons of William FREMAN, deceased.
Petition to examine witnesses as to a devise by their said father of a tenement on Stotfold. *Damaged.* (1553-4.)   BEDFORD.

77   Christopher FRODINGHAM, gentleman, nephew of Thomas de la Ryver, deceased, and administrator of his goods, v. Richard CHOLMELEY, knight, Roger his son, and Jane, wife of the latter, and bastard daughter of the said Thomas.
Action in the Council of the North for goods of Elizabeth, mother of complainant, and for goods and messuages and land in Stearsby, late of the said Thomas: (1553-4.)   YORK.

78   Anthony FRANKYSHE of Ripon, gentleman, v. William ASHLEY, esquire, and others.
Bond given on defendant's behalf to Peter Thornton and others. (1554-8.)   YORK.

FILE 1502.

1   William GAVERGHAN v. John Harry NANSPIAN, son and executor of John Harry Wolkok.
Detention of deeds relating to messuages and land at Treluddro (in Newlyn). See Files 208, No. 58; 1509, No. 17. (Cir. 1493-1500.)   CORNWALL.

2   William GERVAS v. John PERYS.
Detention of deeds relating to messuages and gardens in the borough of Helston.   CORNWALL.

3   Arnold GILLAM, 'Gascoigne,' v. [the mayor of LONDON].
Action by John Skynner, weaver, for forcible seizure of cloths, wherein the said Skynner should have a jury of his neighbours. Certiorari.   LONDON.

4   William GLYN, gentleman, v. Thomas TREGARTHEN of Plymouth.
Land in Trevris. Damaged.   CORNWALL.

5   William GOODEMAN v. William DAWNE and Stephen RUGGEWAY, feoffees to uses.
Lands in Stodden (i.e. Staddon in Cheriton Bishop or Plymstock), late of John Goodeman, deceased, grandfather of complainant.   DEVON.

6   William GOUNDENHAM of Wellington v. William SPEKE, gentleman.
Frivolous ecclesiastical suits, unlawful distresses and assaults to compel complainant to sell a ' free place ' in Goundenham.   SOMERSET.

7   Robert GRENE of York, merchant, v. Edmund MATHEWE.
Action for price of wine which defendant had allowed himself in his account as complainant's attorney at Bordeaux.   YORK.

8   Ralph GWANYTER, clerk, v John TREWORGA, courtholder.
Detention of deeds relating to messuages and land in Gwanyter (i.e. Gwendra in Veryan ?).   CORNWALL.

9   John a GWILLIM and Margaret his wife v. Nicholas SAYMARD and others.
Messuage and land in Nibley, late of Nicholas Wodhouse and Katherine his wife, parents of the said Margaret.   GLOUCESTER.

10   John GYLES of London, skinner, v. William EDESON.
Detention of deeds relating to lands in Barlbrough.   DERBY.

11   William GOOLD, late servant to John Stopyngton, clerk, late master of the Rolls, v. Richard PRATTE, late mayor of Canterbury.
Condemnation of complainant without hearing his defence, and intimidation of his wife by arrest so that she ' durst never passe the dorres of the said Goold ne did the said Goolde one peny worth of goode.' See File 26, No. 194. (1456.)   KENT.

12-13   Thomas GURNELL, priest, v. William WORSLEY, canon of St. Paul's.
Vexatious suit to extort a resignation of complainant's vicarage in the collegiate church of Southwell. (1459-1479.)   NOTTS.

14-15   John, son and heir of William GAGE of Burstow (Bristowe), esquire, v. John MILLIS.
Action on a bond for payments in respect of defendant's marriage to complainant's sister, to whom he has refused to make a jointure. See Files 95, No. 51; 138, No. 43; 313, No. 4; 316, No. 54. (After 1485.)   SURREY.

16   Thomas GREY, marquis of Dorset, and Cecily his wife v. John BONVYLE, Katherine his wife, and William HODY, chief baron of the Exchequer, and Thomas BR . . . feoffees to uses.
Manors of Shute, Wishcombe (in South Leigh), and North Leigh, and messuages and lands in South Leigh, Chaldanger (in Membury), Waringston (in Buckerell); East Membury, Shute, Musbury, Membury, Whitford (in Shute), Petrous, Panteshays, Blakelegh, Lugshayne in Colyton (Leggeshays), More, Sidbury, and Axminster. (1486-1501.)   DEVON.

17-18   Walter GRYFFYGHT of Wichnor, knight, v. Robert TEMPLE and others.
Information of enclosures in Barton-under-Needwood ' whiche yf they were used in tyllage after tholde usage there wolde yerely have com thereof iij or iiij hundryth quarters of corne.' (After 1497.)   STAFFORD.

19-21   Thomas GAY v. William SWAN.
Obtaining a bill of debt of King Louis of France by means of a forged letter. (After 1498 ?)   WILTS.

22   Harry GOODWELL, an executor of Katherine Johnson of London, v. Sir John RYSLEY.
Land in the manor of Tottenham. Mutilated. (Henry VIII or later.)   MIDDLESEX.

23-24   Agnes GOODVFF v. John IPPYNG.
Land in Offley, late of John Shetfold, deceased, brother of complainant. Damaged. (Henry VIII or later.)   HERTS.

25   Eleanor, late the wife of Walter GRENOWE, v. John NEST, yeoman.
Site of the manor of Tredington of the demise of the abbot and convent of Tewkesbury. Mutilated. (Henry VIII.)   [WORCESTER.]

26   Thomas GASCOIGN, knight, v. Richard MASON, prior of the Black Friars (' the Toftes '),
York, and Guy URSWIK(?), esquire.
Detention of deeds relating to lands late of Edward Redman. *Damaged.* (1513-1538.)   YORK.

27   John GYLBERD of Greenway (in Churston Ferrers) v. William CAREWE, esquire, son
and heir of Edmund Carewe, knight, and Cecyll, executrix, and late the wife of William
COURTENEY, knight.
Manor of Galmpton and land in Brixham bought of the said Sir Edmund. *See File 412, No. 8.*
(*Cir.* 1515-1518.)   DEVON.

28   Robert GODDERD, shereman, dwelling in Sudbury, v. Thomas MYSTE.
Double sale of a messuage and land (*place not given*). (After 1529.)   SUFFOLK.

29   Richard GRENE of Chipping Norton v. John GOGISWELL.
Bond for a debt paid to Robert Busby. *Faded. See File 799, No. 4.* (1534-1547.)   OXFORD.

30-32   Alexander GARNET of Liverpool v. Edward GARNET.
Detention of deeds relating to messuages and gardens in Stockport. (1535-1553.)   CHESTER.

33   Thomas ap Llewelyn ap David GOZ *alias* Thomas ap Lewis v. Tudder ap David LLOID.
Land in the lordship of Denbigh formerly of Kenerek ap Eden[evet?] ap Cona, deceased, great-uncle
of complainant. *Endorsed* with a dismissal to the Prince's council. (1537-1547.)   DENBIGH.

34   The same, cousin and heir of Rice ap Madoc ap Rice, v. RICE ap Rice ap Madoc.
Detention of deeds relating to the same, described as in Llannefydd (Llanebith) and St. Asaph.
Like endorsement. (1537-1547.)   DENBIGH.

35   James GOLDSMYTH, citizen and fishmonger of London, v. William GOSTWIKE, esquire,
and Thomas LEE, gentleman.
Debt and legacy of John Gostwike, knight, whose executors defendants are. (After 1538.)
LONDON.

36   Elizabeth GREGORYE of Claydon, co. Oxford, daughter of Richard Grenewood, deceased,
v. Edmund . . ., Elizabeth his wife [late. the wife of Leonard Woodhull], and John
WOODHULL, son and heir of the said Leonard.
Messuage and land in Mollington of the demise of the late abbot and convent of Kenilworth.
Damaged. (1553-4.)   WARWICK.

37-39   John GAYRE (Gayer) v. Richard ERYSSY, Richard CAR(C)LEWE, and Alexander
PENHELLYK.
Messuages and land in St. Keverne. *Damaged.* (1554-8.)   CORNWALL.

40-42   Hugh, son and heir of John GREMES (Grymes), v. Henry JAMES *alias* Trehaverse.
Detention of deeds relating to a messuage and land in Tavistock. *Damaged.* (1554-8.)   DEVON.

43   Morgan GRIFFYTHE, yeoman, v. HOELL ap Meredith and others.
Bond for a debt of defendants of which complainant does not know the date. (1554-8.)   ———

FILE 1503.

1   John GODEREDE v. William DICONSON.
Detention of deeds relating to a messuage and land in Gisburne.   YORK.

2   Margaret, executrix and late the wife of John GROVE, v. William BERE.
Detention of deeds relating to lands in Northfleet and Southfleet. *Mutilated.* (Henry VII or later.)
KENT.

3   Robert GEFFOURNESON v. Joan, late the wife of John WERBURTON, knight, and
Peter WERBURTON, esquire.
Loan for wars in Scotland to the said Sir John, of whose goods defendants are administrators.
(After 1497.)   CHESTER.

4-6   Thomas GRAYSON and Joan his wife, late the wife of John Vynceynt, v. John SMYTH.
Grant of a messuage and land in Woodham Mortimer to the said John Vyncent and Joan for their
lives by John Smyth of Seven Wells, father of complainant. (16th century.)   ESSEX.

7   Thomas GRYFFYN, knight, and Edward his brother.
Petition to examine witnesses as to the meaning of the will of Ryce Gryffyn, esquire, eldest son of the
said Sir Thomas, whose executors complainants are, and of the ' sutes ' thereto. *Commission.*
(16th century.)   NORTHAMPTON.

8-9   John GOSTWYK v. Joan CARTER.
Cottage and land in Bletsoe, Risley, and Sharnbrook, late of Robert Carter, deceased, former
husband of defendant. (*Cir.* 1505-1529?)   BEDFORD.

10-11   Richard GODARD and Anne his wife v. the executors of Thomas ASHELEY and John
CRESSE(Y).
Part price of a messuage and curtilage in Ipswich late of Joan Mynter, mother of the said Anne
and John, and money received to release claims thereto. *Commission.* (Henry VIII or
Edward VI.)   SUFFOLK.

12-13   Edward GODE and Agnes his wife v. Thomas BENET and Joan his wife, late the wife of
Thomas Bucknell.
Money promised to the said Agnes on her marriage by the said Bucknell, her kinsman, who owned a
house in ' Pescodstrete,' Windsor. *Faded.* (Henry VIII *or* Edward VI.)   BERKS.

14-15   Robert GRENE of Coventry, grocer, and others, executors of Thomas Bonde of the same,
draper, v. Thomas PARKER and James BLADES of York, drapers, and Alice, wife of the
latter, late the wife of Alexander Jameson.
Debt for broadcloth bought by Robert Whityngham of York, draper, deceased, whose executors
are the said Alice, sometime his wife, and the said Thomas Parker. (The answer appears to have
been made to a former bill, of which this one is an amended version.) (Henry VIII *or* Edward VI.)
WARWICK, YORK.

16-18   John GYLBERT of London, barber, v. Thomas, grandson and heir of Robert BRYAN of
Barton-on-Humber, co. Lincoln.
Messuage called the Brewhouse, storehouse and land, formerly of John Byngham of Dover,
gentleman.   (Henry VIII or Edward VI.)   KENT.

19-20   Thomas [GREY], marquis of Dorset, v. John MAYNWARING, knight.
Land in Stoke-upon-Tern wrongfully acquired by George Maynwaring, late steward thereof.
(1513-1530.)   SALOP.

21   John GILBERT of Ashton, co. Wilts, gentleman, v. the mayor and aldermen of LONDON.
Imprisonment at the suit of John Stiles, citizen and merchant of London, on a bond mainly
satisfied by delivery of wool.   Certiorari.   (Cir. 1515-1518.)   LONDON.

22-24   William GAUNTE v. Anne, late the wife of George WALWYN.
Messuages and land in Standlake and More (i.e. Northmoor?), late of Simon Gaunte, deceased,
grandfather of complainant and father of defendant.   (After 1529.)   OXFORD.

25   William GOODOLPHYN, knight, and Henry NANSE v. William DAVIE and Peter
SANDRYE.
(Copy of File 1123, No. 30.)   (1544-1547.)   CORNWALL.

26-29   Henry GARDYNER v. John BOTHE and Elizabeth his wife.
(Continuation of File 1224, No. 1.)   (1547-1551.)   LINCOLN.

30   William GASCOIGN of Gawthorp, knight, v. Hugh DARELL and Eleanor his wife, late the
wife of Peter Middelton of Frindsbury, co. Kent, surveyor to Thomas [Cranmer], archbishop
of Canterbury.
Rent of the possession of the priory of Arthington paid to the said Middelton.   (Edward VI.)
                                                                                YORK.

31-33   Robert GRAY, gentleman, v. John and Raphael THROKMERTON, stewards of the manor
of Kenilworth, and John CLERKE (Taylor).
Close in the said manor acquired by Lawrence Grey, father of complainant.   (Edward VI.)
                                                                                WARWICK.

34-35   Edmund GRENE of Water Orton, co. Warwick, Alice his wife, John JENNYNS of
Lichfield, Maude his wife, William ROWLEY of Walsall, Elizabeth his wife, Richard
WALTON of Alrewas, Margery his wife, Henry CARTWRYGHT, and Agnes his wife, v.
Ellen, late the wife of Humphrey RYDDYNG.
Meadow in the lordship of Shenstone, late of John Ryddyng of Stone Hall, and Ellen his wife,
deceased, parents of the female complainants.   (Edward VI.)   STAFFORD.

36-40   Thomas GATELEY, yeoman, v. Edward BARDWELL, gentleman, Cicely his wife, formerly
Gateley, Edward BROKE, gentleman, and George CLEMENT.
Messuage and land in Grimston conveyed to Humphrey Jurdan, since deceased, to cut off an
entail.   (1553-4.)   NORFOLK.

41-42   Lawrence GRIFFITH of Westminster, yeoman, v. Jevan ap David, grandson of Hugh
BERTLEY (Barkeley), and Lewis WALTER.
Lands in Llandingat and Llanwrda acquired of Morgan ap David.   (1553-4.)   CARMARTHEN.

43-44   Thomas GALE, clerk, v. William COOKE.
Vicarage of Croydon.   (1554-8.)   SURREY.

45   William GEFFERY, master in Chancery and chancellor of Salisbury, v. Thomas ALRIDGES,
esquire.
Lands in Idbury and Fifield belonging to the church of Swinbrook.   (1554-8.)   OXFORD.

46-47   Martin GRYSSELYNGE of Plymouth, kinsman and heir of Peter Grysselinge, v. Elizabeth
late the wife of the said Peter.
Messuage and land in Saltash.   (1554-8.)   CORNWALL.

48-49   Inhabitants of GONERBY v. Thomas KNOTT.
(Continuation of File 1355, No. 45.)   (1554-8.)   LINCOLN.

FILE 1504.

1   .   .   ., late the wife of John HADDELEYE, v. Richard   .   .   .
Detention of deeds relating to the manor of Withycombe.   Mutilated.   DEVON.

2   Isabel HAGARSTON v. Alyne HYNDEMERSH, chaplain, and Richard FENDER, priest,
executors of Gawnen Hagarston.
Detention of deeds relating to a messuage in Scarborough.   See File 263, No. 1.   (1502-3.)   YORK.

3   John HAMOND of West Molesey, ' schowtman,' v. the mayor and sheriffs of LONDON.
Action laid in Surrey by John Calcrofte, who was hurt in an attack on complainant's ' schowte '
while moored off Paris Garden.   Corpus cum causa.   LONDON, SURREY.

4   William HAMPTON and Joan his wife, daughter and heir of John Crowche, v. John MAYE,
attorney at common law.
Detention of deeds relating to a sale of wood in Chatham made by John Nele, deceased.   KENT.

5   William HARDYNG, executor of Robert Newman [of] Salisbury, v. John, son of John
APPAT (Apport), and Edmund PENISTON, gentleman.
Account for linen and apprenticeship of the said John the elder.   Copy of pleadings, mutilated.
                                                                                WILTS.

6   Robert HILL v. the mayor and sheriffs of LONDON.
Imprisonment after an affray, complainant knowing no one to bail him.   Corpus cum causa.
                                                                                LONDON.

7 . . . HOBBES of South Molton v. Paul BALE, Agnes his wife, mother of complainant, and others.
Chamber and pasture in a tenement called ' Bremerydge ' (in South Molton). *Mutilated*. DEVON.

8 Nicholas HOPER v. William BRUGGE.
Detention of deeds relating to messuages and land in Dawlish. DEVON.

9 William HORNE v. William NEWENHAM, gentleman.
Assault with ' jakkys, salettes, glevys and longdebevys ' while collecting farm and dues in the Chancellor's market at Daventry. NORTHAMPTON.

10–12 Richard, son and heir of William HORTON, v. Henry, son and heir of George ZOUCH, and John BOTELER.
Reviver of a suit for a messuage and garden in Hertford and land. *Faded*. HERTS.

13 Hugh HORWODE v. Cristian MORE, widow, and Thomas . . .
Manor of Polhampton (in Overton), already in dispute in this court. *Faded*. HANTS.

14 Richard HUNTE v. Richard COLEPEPER and Thomas AT LEE, feoffees to uses.
Messuage, garden and land. *Mutilated*. (To the Archbishop.)

15 Robert HUNTE v. John TALTON and Harry BATEL, executors of Richard Baylly.
Refusal to complete a sale of messuages in Lynne. [NORFOLK.]

16 Robert HYNKELEY, bladesmith, v. William MONKE and John BONHAM, resident(?) in the franchise of the Savoy.
Attempt to get placed on an inquest into the franchise in the parish (*sic*) of Stepney, Whitechapel, and Shoreditch, to complainant's prejudice. MIDDLESEX.

17–18 Nicholas HONYMAN, cousin and heir of Robert Philpot, v. John (A)FRIGHT, feoffee to uses.
Messuage and land in Egerton formerly of Agnes Philpot. (Edward IV or later.) KENT.

19 John HEYSED v. Henry HEYSED and Nicholas (*sic*) his wife.
Detention of deeds relating to land in Hatherleigh and Waterhouse. *See File* 518, *No.* 30. (*Cir.* 1518–1529.) DEVON.

20 James HOBERT, attorney to the King, v. Robert DRURY, esquire.
Manor of Colling Brikling, bequeathed to the King by Edward Bensted, knight, in the event of his death without issue. (Henry VII.) CAMBRIDGE.

21 Robert HOLT and Elizabeth his wife, late the wife of Richard Spenser of Bury St. Edmunds, v. Elizabeth SPENSER.
Detention of deeds relating to a tenement near the butts at Nayland. (Henry VII or later.) SUFFOLK.

22 Amy HOO v. Thomas BRYAN and Thomas PLUMSTED.
Detention of deeds relating to tenements in St. Mary's the Less and St. Michael's, Norwich. (Henry VII or later.) NORFOLK.

23 John HALWILL and Walter COURTENEY, knights, and others v. Thomas STOILE.
Detention of deeds relating to a messuage and land in Nytherdurdon (in Northlew or Woolfardisworthy). (After 1485.) [DEVON.]

24 Henry HYNDE, Margery his wife, and Joan BRIGHT v. the sheriffs of LONDON.
Imprisonment in irons at the suit of Henry Cote, citizen and goldsmith and late alderman of London, for a trespass of David Paxton, against whom he has obtained execution. *Corpus cum causa*. (1498–1505.) LONDON.

25 Henry HANSHERT, clerk, v. William ASCOUGH, knight, and Elizabeth his wife.
Land in South Kelsey. *Mutilated*. (After 1501.) [LINCOLN.]

26 William HARRYS, servant to George Foster, knight, v. the sheriffs of LONDON.
Action by Roger Barnes, wounded in a street affray where complainant was present, and refusing to be treated by a surgeon till he had obtained a verdict. *Certiorari*. (After 1501.) LONDON.

27 John HOODE of London, tailor, v. John AXCE of the same, dyer.
Messuage in Watling Street, late of Bartholomew Fitzwillyams, and wool. *Damaged. See File* 321, *No.* 20. (*Cir.* 1504–1515.) LONDON.

28–29 Anne, late the wife of Edward HULME, v. William PERTYNGTON of Salford, co. Lancaster.
Tenement in Sunderland of the demise of the surveyors of Anne, countess of Derby. (1504–1547.) CHESTER.

30–31 Thomas HALLE of Bradford, tailor, v. Robert COXE of Belston, co. Somerset, William STYLEMAN of Hinton and Giles GORE of Sherley, co. Gloucester, gentlemen.
Messuages and land in Cliffe (Clifforde) Pypard and Christian-Malford, late of John Halle, deceased, kinsman of complainant and of the wives of the said Styleman and Gore. (Henry VIII or later.) WILTS.

32 John Hoyge and others, churchwardens of St. Nectan's, HARTLAND, v. John HUSBOND of Gawlish (in Hartland).
Destruction of a desk and organs in Hartland church to make himself a pew. (Henry VIII *or* Edward VI). DEVON.

33–35 Agnes, late the wife of Richard HODSHON, v. John HOWLYS of St. Helen's.
Detention of deeds relating to land in Arreton (Aderton) of the demise of Edward Coke, late of West Burton, co. Sussex, gentleman. (Henry VIII or later.) HANTS (I.W.)

36   Richard HORDER and Edith MAWDELEY *v.* Alice, executrix, and late the wife of Christopher PYKERELL, and Peter SYLVESTER.
Lease of a tenement called the Bush of Shaftesbury delivered to the said Christopher for examination.   (Henry VIII *or* Edward VI.)   DORSET.

37–38   Thomas HALSWYLL *v.* Humphrey BONVYLE.
Money secured on a tin-work.   *Damaged.*   (1530–1553.)   DEVON.

39   John HOLLOKE *v.* Thomas WYKE.
Messuage and lands called ' Coggars ' extended on a statute staple executed by Laurence Colway of Kenardington (Kennerton), co. Kent, labourer.   *Mutilated.*   (1530–1553.)   SUSSEX.

40–42   Robert HAMONDE *v.* Katherine, executrix and late the wife of Anthony BYRKES, clerk of the King's kitchen and of the Green Cloth.
Detention of deeds relating to the manor of Appledore, otherwise Abdall, in Oxney, Stone, and Wittersham.   (1531–1553.)   KENT.

43   Peter HALLOW of Sodburie (*i.e.* Sudbury ?) *v.* Thomas MYSTE, an executor of Thomas Sayer of Gestingthorp.
Legacy to Ellen, daughter of the said Sayer and wife of complainant.   *See File* 820, *No.* 29.
(*Cir.* 1533–1538.)   [SUFFOLK, ESSEX.]

44   Richard HASULS of Hanchurch, husbandman, for the infant son of John Hasuls, *v.* Robert HALYS.
Croft and pasture in the lordship of Newcastle-under-Lyme.   (*Cir.* 1533–1538.)   STAFFORD.

45–46   John HORSEPOLE of London, draper, *v.* Harry BRYNKLOWE and another.
Shop and land.   *Damaged.*   (*Cir.* 1533–1538.)

47   Nicholas HEYTH, archdeacon of Stafford, *v.* John JENENS and others, his tenants.
Lands in Penn.   (After 1535.)   STAFFORD.

48   James HOWELEYS *v.* John and Henry HOWLEYS his uncles.
Lands in Nettleston and Edington (both in St. Helen's), Brading, Trotton, Hertyshoyte, Angeston (*i.e.* Adgestone in Brading ?), Bembridge and North Sudham.   *Damaged.   See File* 824, *No.* 37.
(After 1536.)   HANTS (I.W.)

49   William HOBBERD *v.* James DANYELL.
Legacy of James Danyell, whose executor defendant is.   *Mutilated.*   (1537–1553.)   [NORFOLK.]

50–52   Ralph HOCKENHALL *v.* John DONNE, knight, son and heir of Richard Donne, esquire.
Messuage and land in Eaton of the demise of Giles Capell, knight.   (1540–1547.)   CHESTER.

53–54   Simon HORTON of Exeter, butcher, *v.* Henry GEYLL.
Price of sheep.   *Mutilated.*   (1545.)   DEVON.

55   William HEWYSTER, husbandman, tenant to John Hampden, knight, *v.* Robert BELSTON and John his brother.
Vexatious suits and forcible ejection from land in Bledlow.   *See File* 1179, *No.* 26.   (*Cir.* 1547.)
                                                                          BUCKINGHAM.

56–57   Roland HARRYSON, yeoman, *v.* . . . ., gentleman, William TOMSON and Robert CAVERLEY, his servants, and others.
Forcible ouster from a messuage in Denton.   (1549–1553 ?)   DURHAM.

58   Thomas HALL of South Mimms, yeoman, *v.* Agnes, late wife of Thomas NOWELL, and administratrix of his goods, and Robert BUCKETT of Hadley, labourer.
Money lent to complainant by the said Agnes when separated from her husband and repaid after their reconciliation.   *Damaged.*   (1553–4.)   MIDDLESEX.

59–62   Alice, late the wife of John HAYDON, and administratrix of his goods, *v.* John SEYNT-AUBYN and Michael ROSEWAREN.
Messuage and land called Traethen (*i.e.* Troon ?) in Camborne.   *Decayed.   See File* 1234, *No.* 24.
(1554–8.)   CORNWALL.

FILE 1505.

1   Robert HOXNE *v.* Robert FOWKELYNG.
Messuage and land.   *Mutilated.*   ?

2   Anne, late the wife of Walter, son and heir of Walter HAWKESWORTH, esquire, *v.* William GRYM, chaplain, feoffee to uses.
Deficiency in jointure lands in Mytton.   (After 1482.)   YORK.

3   Richard HALS and Joan his wife, daughter of Henry Smythe and of Isote his wife, both deceased, *v.* Thomas TAYLOUR.
Messuage and land in the parish of Rusheford (*i.e.* Brushford ?) of the demise of John Speke, knight.
(After 1483.)   DEVON.

4–5   Nicholas HYLLYNG *v.* William STEVYNS and John PAGE.
Balance of debt of Richard Predyux for cattle.   (Henry VII or later.)   DEVON.

6   William HAYNES of London, tallow chandler, *v.* the sheriff of LONDON.
Action of Edward Vaughan on a bond given on behalf of Thomas Martin, now departed into Wales.
Certiorari.   (*Cir.* 1486–1515.)   LONDON.

7   Robert HARYNGTON, esquire, *v.* John HARYNGTON.
Manor of Exton and mills there, late of Joan, formerly the wife of John Haryngton, deceased, and mother of complainant.   (16th century.)   RUTLAND.

8–10   John HUBBERT, citizen and mercer of London, v. Bartholomew de RUSE, merchant of Florence.
Bargains òf cloth of gold and other goods. *Damaged.* (After 1501.)   LONDON.

11   Thomas HACHOKE, capper of Stortford, v. Joan JAKYLTON and Elizabeth HACHOKE.
Houses in Flamborough. (Henry VIII or later.)   YORK.

12   John HALL of Henley-in-Arden, co. Warwick, son and heir of Thomas Hall, v. John VITTER.
Detention of deeds relating to the manor of Wytheworthe in the lordship of King's Norton, and rent, heriot and relief of a messuage and crofts there. (Henry VIII or Edward VI.) [WORCESTER.]

13   John HALLE, yeoman, v. Ralph PYKALL.
Detention of deeds relating to the manor-place of Stodley. *Mutilated.* (Henry VIII or Edward VI.) [LINCOLN ?]

14–15   Robert HALLEY v. Thomas CHEYNEY and John GARDYNER.
Detention of deeds relating to the manor of Champneys and land in Tring, late of John Cooper, deceased, great-uncle of complainant and father of Jane, late the wife of the said Thomas. (Henry VIII or Edward VI.)   HERTS.

16–17   Nicholas HALLYE v. Nicholas SMYTHE.
Legacy of William Bageshay, vicar of Hoope, of whose executors defendant is one. (Henry VIII or Edward VI.) [DERBY.]

18–19   Francis HARRYSON and Margaret his wife v. Elizabeth, wife of John CAWSTON of South Lambeth.
Spanish money and gold entrusted to defendant by William Tollyson of Southwark, clothworker, former husband of the said Margaret. *Paper copy, incomplete.* (Henry VIII or later.) SURREY.

20–21   Henry HARRYSON v. William WYBURGH, claiming to be a feoffee to uses, and Robert PAYNE.
Messuages in Bury St. Edmunds, late of James Harryson, deceased, father of complainant. (Henry VIII or Edward VI.)   SUFFOLK.

22   William HATHERLEY v. Roger MADGE of Bulkworthy (Bulcory).
Refusal to complete a conveyance of land in Hartland. (Henry VIII or Edward VI.)   DEVON.

23–25   John, nephew and heir of Robert HICHE, v. John COLLOPPE.
Detention of deeds relating to messuages and land in Melbourn. (Henry VIII or Edward VI.)   CAMBRIDGE.

26   Henry HILL v. William PEREN.
Surrender of a bond made to George Lambton of London, mercer, defendant promising repayment. (Henry VIII or Edward VI.)   LONDON.

27–29   Thomas HODGEIS v. Giles, son of Alice BRIDGE(S), and Edmund and John STOKES.
Messuage and pasture in Welland late of Robert Hodgeis *alias* Thomys, father of complainant. (Henry VIII or Edward VI.)   WORCESTER.

30–32   Thomas HOLDAR of Apperley, husbandman, v. William COX of Morton.
Detention of deeds relating to a messuage and lands in Chaddesley (Chatysley) and Tyrley. (Henry VIII or Edward VI.)   WORCESTER, GLOUCESTER.

33–34   John HOPKYNSON v. William COUTE and William WRIGHT.
Messuage and land in Maltby late of John Frances, deceased. (Henry VIII or Edward VI.)   LINCOLN.

35–36   William HYCKYS of Cromhall, clothier, v. Richard TYNDALE, yeoman.
Adultery with complainant's wife and conspiracy to murder him. (Henry VIII or·Edward VI.)   GLOUCESTER.

37   Joan HYNGHAM v. Nicholas EGHAM.
Detention of deeds relating to a tenement in Icklingham (Eclyngham). (Henry VIII or Edward VI.)   SUFFOLK.

38–39   John and Robert, sons of William HALL and of Elizabeth his wife, v. Edmund JOLYFF.
Lands in Tetney of the demise of the abbot and convent of Louth Park and Richard Wilkynson (After 1510.)   LINCOLN.

40   [William Dale], prior of St. Olave's, [HERRINGFLEET], and his convent v. Robert [BRONDE], prior of the Holy Trinity, NORWICH.
Rent(?) in Withingham (Wychlyngham). *Damaged.* (1515–1529.)   SUFFOLK.

41   Humphrey HUYSSHE, Jaket his wife, John PYTTE and Gonet his wife v. James CHECHESTRE, late of Hall (*i.e.* Hill in Frithelstock?).
Detention of deeds relating to lands in Swimbridge, Marwood, Bekynton (*i.e.* Abbots Bickington?) and Tawton, late of William Hall, deceased, great-grandfather of the female complainants. *See Files 520, No. 26; 416, No. 15.* (*Cir.* 1515–1529.)   DEVON.

42   John Bowes, Thomas Catcher and others, tenants of the manor of HACKNEY, v. John SHARPP, William SNAPPE, and others.
Common of pasture in Hackney marsh. (1532 or later.)   MIDDLESEX.

43   Thomas HALLE v. John ROGERS.
Messuages and lands in Calais, Marke and Oye, formerly of John Halle, deceased, grandfather of complainant, and of Margaret, wife of defendant. *See File 815, No. 24.* (*Cir.* 1533–1538.)   CALAIS.

44   Richard HEDDON v. [Agnes NORTHLEGH].
(Mutilated copy of *File 1012, No. 8.*) (1538–1544.)   DEVON.

45-46   Thomas, son and heir apparant of Philip HALL, and Alice his wife v. Thomas HALL, clerk, Thomas SEMAN, gentleman, and others, feoffees to uses.
Lands in Bristol and Redland (Thyrdland) promised to complainants on their marriage by John Hall of Langridge, co. Somerset, father of the said Alice. (Before 1539.)   GLOUCESTER.

47-48   HENRY ap David ap William ap Res v. JEVAN ap Kynryg ap Rice.
Crown lease of land at Carnychain in Gwaenysgor of the inheritance of Fulk, grandson of John Hope and late a minor in the King's ward. (1543-7.)   FLINT.

49-51   Thomas HOLLES of New . . ., servant to the Earl of Hertford, lord great chamberlain, v. John BANYSTER of London, esquire, and Edward KEPLE, clerk.
Bond given on behalf of the earl's chaplain. Mutilated. (1545-1551.)   LONDON.

52-54   William HARPAR v. John ZOUCH, Lord Zouch and St. Maur.
(Continuation of File 1232, No. 6.) (1547-1554.)   DEVON.

55-56   Richard HENNE v. John BARBOUR, great-grandson and heir of Thomas Browne alias Barbour.
Land in Rowley. Damaged. (Edward VI.)   STAFFORD.

57-60   Anthony HEVENYNGHAM, knight, and Mary his wife v. Dame Anne SHELTON.
Legacy of John Shelton, knight, deceased, husband of defendant and father of the said Mary. (A replication by Henry Fysher has been substituted for one by the said Sir Anthony and Mary.) (Edward VI.)   [NORFOLK.]

61   John HEXT v. John ROGER, husbandman.
Tenement in the manor of Staverton and goods promised to complainant on his marriage with defendant's daughter and on the death or marriage of complainant himself. (Edward VI.)
        DEVON.

62-63   Thomas HASYLFOOTE, Barbara his wife, and William FLECCHER v. George LASENBY.
Debt of John Fleccher, former husband of the said Barbara. Mutilated. (1553-5.)   ———

64-67   William HAWKYNS the younger of Plymouth v. Richard NYCOLLES.
Mansion house called Pepper's Green [or Tilney] adjudged in this court to Lancelot Middleton of Silksworth, co. Durham (File 1248, No. 59). (1553-4.)   NORFOLK.

68   James HEATHE and Elizabeth his wife, granddaughter and heir of John Page, v. Peter MORGAN of Bitton, co. Gloucester, gentleman.
Detention of deeds relating to tenements in Warminster, Devizes, and Tilshead. See File 1357, No. 47. (1553-4.)   WILTS.

69-72   HENRY ap Thomas v. WILLIAM ap John, JOHN ap William, and THOMAS ap Parry.
Messuage and mill with its watercourse in Nannerch of the bequest of Thomas ap Ellys, father of complainant. (1553.)   FLINT.

73-74   John HYDON v. Richard CORANT, John BOSSAVERN (Bussaveren), and others.
(Continuation of File 1356, Nos. 62-64.) (1553-5.)   CORNWALL.

FILE 1506.

1   John INGRAM, fishmonger of London, v. John BRAUNCHE, esquire, and others, feoffees to uses.
Manor of Briston (Bruston) devised by John (of) Bruston to Ellen, late his wife, now the wife of complainant.   NORFOLK.

2   Isabel, late the wife of Richard ISHAM, deceased, v. John ISHAM, esquire, and Alice his wife, parents of the said Richard.
Lands (not specified) promised to the said Richard and Isabel on their marriage. [NORTHAMPTON?]
Footnote.—Be this byll delivered to Trevylion of the Chancery.

3   John INGATE and Margaret his wife, executrix of John Davy, v. John HERYNG, feoffee to uses.
Messuage and land in Beccles. (Henry VIII or Edward VI.)   SUFFOLK.

4   Richard IRTON v. William MIDDILTON, knight, feoffee to uses.
Manors of Irton, Gosforth, Drigg, and Birker. See File 143, No. 45. (After 1513.) CUMBERLAND.

5   Harry JEFFERASON of Bolton Percy v. Thomas WYNDBYCH of Nocton, co. Lincoln, esquire.
Messuage [in or near] York. Mutilated. (Henry VII or later.)   YORK.

6-7   Henry JUSTICE, warden of the chantry of Winterbourne, v. Anthony BRADSTONE.
Detention of deeds relating to the lands of the chantry whereof defendant claims the patronage. (Henry VII or later.)   GLOUCESTER.

8   Thomas [Docwra], prior of the Hospital of ST. JOHN of Jerusalem in England.
Appeal from the report of a commission that he had let houses in Melchebourne, Greenham, Woolhampton and elsewhere with less than the customary quantity of land. Mutilated. (1502-1527.)   [BEDFORD], BERKS.

9   John JAMYS and Joan his wife v. Edmund NOKE and others.
Messuages and land in Hatfeld Brodhoke. See File 326, No. 38. (Cir. 1504-1515.) [ESSEX.]

10-11   Elizabeth JACKSON v. Thomas TURVYN (Turwyn), yeoman.
Close in Tickhill late of Sibill, late the wife of Thomas Ludlam and mother of complainant. (Henry VIII or Edward VI.)   YORK.

12   John JENKYN and Janet his wife, late the wife of Thomas Saundry, v. Peter MATHEW and others.
Messuage and land at Cosgarne in Gwennap of the demise of John Cosgarne. (Henry VIII or Edward VI.)   CORNWALL.

13   Hugh JOHNES(?) of the lordship of Wenlock v. the bailiffs of NEWPORT.
Action by Lettice Morgan for a debt of William Morgan, deceased, complainant being only his messenger. *Certiorari. Mutilated.* (Henry VIII or Edward VI.)   [SALOP.]

14-15   Richard JOHNSON *alias* Lewes v. Edmund FOXE.
Action before the bailiffs of Salisbury for a lease of tithes in Fordingbridge called ' the Marle.' *Mutilated.* (Henry VIII or Edward VI.)   WILTS, HANTS.

16-17   John JONES(?) v. John HUBARD of London, mercer.
Tenement of the demise of the master, brethren and sisters of St. Katherine's by the Tower. *Damaged,* (Henry VIII or Edward VI.)   LONDON.

18   William JONYS, a minor, v. John ap Evan ap Rice.
Tenement in Llandecwyn. *Mutilated.* (Henry VIII or Edward VI.)   MERIONETH.

19   David JOHNS v. Robert FYCHET.
Bond given on behalf of Roger Davyson, late of London, baker, for a lease of a bakehouse. (*Cir.* 1518-1529?)   LONDON.

20-22   John JILLOT (Jellott) of Woodbridge, son and heir of Edward Jillot, v. Edward BALDRY and Amy his wife.
Messuage and land in Yoxford, late of Henry Jillot, deceased, brother of the said Edward and former husband of the said Amy. *Answer directed to the said Edward ; replication wanting.* (After 1536.)   SUFFOLK.

23-25   John, son and heir of John JAMES v. Thomas JAMES and others.
Detention of deeds relating to lands in a ' went ' called Stronglond and elsewhere in Banham. *See File* 1014, *No.* 36. (*Cir.* 1538-1544.)   NORFOLK.

26-28   Constance JAMYS v. John TREVERE and others.
Lands at Bosoljack (Bosulsacke, Bosulsalke) in Madron, formerly of John Penpons, esquire. *See File* 1363, *No.* 18. (1554-8.)   CORNWALL.

29   William KEDWELLY of Ledbury, yeoman, John ASTON of the same, schoolmaster, and many others (*named*).
Petition concerning their indictment of the murder of John Milward and other felonies. *French. Much faded.*   HEREFORD.

30   The minister and brethren of St. Robert's by KNARESBOROUGH v. William GILBERT, priest, John LOKYNGTON, friar, *alias* Robert Middelton, and others.
Forgery of ' transumptes ' of bulls of indulgence and assumption of proctorship of complainant's order.   YORK.

31   Robert KNOLLES v. the mayor and [bailiffs] of COVENTRY.
Frivolous suits by John Hobley his master. *Damaged.*   WARWICK.

32   Edmund KYME of Bishop's Lynn, merchant, v. Alice WALPOLE.
Messuage in Mercer Rous Lynn, late of Edmund Spryngett, deceased, grandfather of complainants.   NORFOLK.

33   Maude, late the wife of Thomas KENDALE, v. Stephen KENDALE his brother, and Edmund KENDALE, priest, son of the latter.
Procuring from complainant a conveyance to religious uses of the manor of Trewenhelek (*i.e.* Trewen in Lanlivery?) contrary to the will of the said Thomas, who also held lands in Lostwithiel and Penlen (in Tywardreath?).   CORNWALL.

34   The same v. the same.
Do., threats that she was to be disposed of in marriage by William Bonevyll, knight, steward of the county, and forcible entry at Lostwithiel and seizure of deeds. (*Cir.* 1461?)   CORNWALL.

35   John KARR v. John LILBURN of Shawdon, nephew of the sheriff, Edmund his brother, and others.
Forcible entry on a messuage and land in West Lilburn, burning of a fold, and seizure of goods. (1475?)   NORTHUMBERLAND.

36   Emmot, late the wife of John KENDALE, v. Elizabeth, late the wife of Thomas MAL-HEVERER, knight, and administratrix of his goods.
Goods of the said John, and deeds relating to lands in Markington, Ingerthorpe, and Wallerthwaite obtained from William his son, an idiot. *See File* 329, *No.* 44. (1485-1515.)   YORK.

37   Richard KENCHE(?) of Preston, co. Northants, husbandman, v. William FYSSHEPOLE, tailor, and Henry TURNER, ' butterer,' both of Coventry, feoffees to uses.
Tenements in Brinklow. *Faded.* (Henry VII or later.)   WARWICK.

38   John KENDALL v. Richard STANNEBRYGGE, both of Felmersham, weavers.
Detention of deeds relating to a tenement in Felmersham. (Henry VII or later.)   BEDFORD.

39-40   Robert, son and heir of John KNYGHT, v. John STAPLE, gentleman, executor of the said John.
Detention of deeds relating to messuages and land in Rotherfield. *See File* 210, *No.* 7. (After 1493?)   SUSSEX

41   Roger KYTTOWE of St. Leonard's v. William . . . of Lansalloes and Joan his wife.
Detention of deeds relating to a messuage and land in Liskeard. (*Cir.* 1504-1515?)   CORNWALL.

42   John KYNG and Katherine his wife, daughter and heir of Robert Flagge of Needham Market, v. John BUGGE.
Detention of deeds relating to a messuage and land in Barking and Battisford (Basford). (Henry VIII or Edward VI.)   SUFFOLK.

43   John KYNG and Alice his wife v. Richard PYKERYNGE and Joan his wife.
Detention of deeds relating to messuages and land in Tanshelf, late of John Morpethe, deceased, father of the said Alice and former husband of the said Joan. (Henry VIII or Edward VI.)
                                                                                                                  YORK.

44-45   Nicholas KYTTOWE v. John MAYNARDE and others.
Blackmail. (Henry VIII or later.)   CORNWALL.

46   William KYNNERTON v. John NYGHTYNGALE, priest.
Detention of deeds relating to lands in Wolton (i.e. Walton?). (Cir. 1518-1529.)   STAFFORD.

47-48   John, grandson and heir of Jasper KYNASTON, v. Ralph KYNASTON his uncle.
Messuages and land in Ellesmere of the demise of Sir William Weston, prior of the Hospital of St. John of Jerusalem in England. Answer wanting. See File 837, No. 34. (After 1527.) SALOP.

49   Thomas KEYLE of London, stationer, v. John HAWKINS of London, grocer, and Margaret his wife, executrix of Richard Pynson of London, stationer.
Action for a debt released by the said Pynson pending a suit in this court (File 649, No. 32). (After 1530.)   LONDON.

50-51   Richard, grandson and heir of John KELYGRYU v. Richard TREGAYRE.
Detention of deeds relating to messuages and land in St. Hilary. See File 704, No. 20. (Cir. 1532-3.)   CORNWALL.

52   Thomas KEYE and Elizabeth his wife v. William RAMESDEN and Thomas SAYVYLL.
Manor of Leyghe Hall and other lands in Almondbury and Huddersfield (Ambreye and Hethersfeld), late of John a Wood, deceased, father of the said Elizabeth, and of Joan and Cicely, the wives of defendants. See Files 834, No. 1; 1019, No. 20. (Cir. 1533-1544.)   YORK.

53   William KYNG v. Betten and Henry KYNG.
Messuage in Crondall, late of William Kyng, deceased, grandfather of complainant and husband of the said Betten. (Cir. 1538-1544?)   HANTS.

FILE 1507.

1   Robert LANE v. the mayor and bailiffs of WINCHESTER.
Action by John Dregge for price of malt which was partly foul and worm-eaten. Certiorari.
                                                                                                                  HANTS.

2   Richard LITTILTON v. William BARKLEY, esquire.
Stewardship of the town and manor of Birmingham of the grant of Wilham Byrmyngham, esquire.
                                                                                                                  WARWICK.

3   John LOKSMYTH and Joan his wife, late the wife of Michael Ryx, v. John HENCLYFF, feoffee to uses.
Land in Teynham, late of the said Ryx, whose executors complainants are.   KENT.

4   Margaret ' that was the wyfe of Rauf of LONGEFORD, knyght,' v. Thomas of RADCLYF, knight, her brother.
Refusal to make a defeasance to a statute merchant made ' that the said Mergret shuld not be ravysshet.'   LANCASTER.

5   John LUCAS and John SHYRYNGTON, executors of John Loveney, all of Bristol, v. Nicholas HAWELEY of Dertemouth and Thomas GATER of Kyngesbrygge.
Forgery of a bond in the name of the said Loveney.   GLOUCESTER, [DEVON].

6   John LUTRELL v. John WYKES of Horbling.
Assault and procuring non-execution of writs.   LINCOLN.

7   . . .
Deposition as to the will of Ralph Lyngeyn, esquire, deceased, concerning lands in Sutton, Marden, Wisteston (in Marden), Fenne (cf. Venn's Green in Marden), Fromenton, and Church Withington. See File 15, No. 304. (Cir. 1442-1450.)   HEREFORD.

8   John LANE, tenant to the Earl of Stafford in Stanstead, v. William HODDESOLE of Ash, gentleman.
Joint purchase of wood in Stanstead. (Before 1444)   KENT.

9   John LEONARD, born in Brittany, v. [Richard BEST?].
Action for price of woollen cloth bought of Robert . . . of Taunton and Aunflise his wife, etc. Damaged. (1482.)   SOMERSET.

10   Thomas LEMAN, priest, kinsman and heir of John Leman the elder, v. John LEMAN the younger.
Detention of deeds relating to lands in Walpole. (Henry VII or later.)   NORFOLK.

11   Hugh LEWYS v. WILLIAM ap Evan and WILLIAM ap Howell.
3a. arable in La . . . an (i.e. Llanengan?) late of Lewis ap Howell, deceased, father of complainant. (Henry VII or later.)   CARNARVON.

12   John LOLLEHAM of Ramsey v. the bailiffs of HUNTINGDON.
Action by Lawrence Marten on a bargain for barley. Certiorari. (Henry VII.)   HUNTINGDON.

13   William LYNTER v. Thomas FRAMPTON.
Messuages and land. Mutilated. (Henry VII or later.)

14   Thomas LYON v. Thomas FYNCHE.
Detention of deeds relating to a messuage and land in Welburn. (Henry VII or later.)   YORK.

15-16   Otys LAURENS v. John DANYELL.
Detention of deeds relating to messuages and land in St. Clement's. See File 146, No. 38. (Cir. 1486-1515.)   CORNWALL.

17   John LOCHARD of Greet, gentleman, v. Edward BROUGHTON and Henry HALL and the sheriff of SALOP.
Action on a statute staple for a debt partly paid and wholly tendered. *Subpœna and certiorari.* (After 1494.)   SALOP.

18-19   Thomas LONKE and Agnes (Annes) his wife, daughter and heir of Roger Bartram, v. Richard, son and executor of William NORRES, knight, late guardian in socage to the said Agnes.
Messuages and lands in Whitchurch and Mapledurham. (After 1503.)   OXFORD.

20   Ralph LECHE, esquire, and Sampson LORDE, clerk, v. William KECHYN, nephew of Richard Kechyn, late parson of Broughton.
Part price of a lease of the parsonage of Broughton terminated by the death of the said Richard. (Henry VIII or Edward VI.)   LINCOLN.

21   Thomas LEE and Joan his wife, daughter and heir of David Staple(don), v. John CHAPMAN, Agnes his wife, and others.
Detention of deeds relating to lands in North Bu[ck]land (*i.e.* Buckland Brewer?) and Woolfardisworthy. *Mutilated.* (Henry VIII or Edward VI.)   DEVON.

22-23   Thomas LEE and William BOUNDE, executors of John Mounsteven the elder, v. Alice MONTSTEVYN and John MONTSTEVYN the younger.
Price of reversion of a messuage and land (*place not given*), sometime of William Boundefeld. (Henry VIII or Edward VI.)   ?

24   Robert LEGH, descendant and heir of John Legh, v. John SPURSTOWE, esquire.
Action on bonds extorted from complainant's father by imprisonment concerning messuages and land in High Leigh. *Pedigree given.* (Henry VIII or later.)   CHESTER.

25   Christopher LEVYNS v John NAYLER, alderman of Canterbury.
Goods and messuages in the parishes of St. Andrew, St. Mary Magdalen, and St. Paul, Canterbury, late of Joan Swan, deceased [grandmother of complainant?]. *Copy of proceedings, mutilated.* *See Files 332, No. 35; 425, No. 28.* (Henry VIII.)   KENT.

26-27   Griffith LEYSON v. Thomas GRESEMAN.
Pasture called the Horseshoe in Leominster adjoining the King's manor of Kingsland. (Henry VIII or Edward VI.)   HEREFORD.

28   Jevan LLOYD ap Rice v. Robert ap Rice ap Hoell GOZ.
Farm in Ruthin of the grant of Edward Byrte. (Henry VIII or later.)   DENBIGH

29   Reynold LOSSE v. William SUCKELYNGE and Elizabeth his wife.
Goods and account books of Ralph Owner of Dunwich, former husband of the said Elizabeth, whose executor complainant is. (Henry VIII or Edward VI.)   SUFFOLK.

30   John LYNGHAM v. Stephen POOLE and William EDWARD.
Money and cattle entrusted to defendants. (Henry VIII or Edward VI.)   SALOP.

31   Dame Elizabeth LASCARMA and Francis NORREIS, both of Greece, v. Robert MYLLER and Christopher BURTON, sheriffs of Lincoln.
Arrest while collecting alms for the redemption of the said Elizabeth's husband and children, prisoners with the Grand Turk. *Corpus cum causa.* (1511.)   LINCOLN.

31   Thomas LOVET.
Charge of destroying houses at Falcote in Wapenham. (After 1511.)   [NORTHAMPTON.]

33   Thomas LICHFELD v. Florence, wife of Richard BRETT, and late the wife of Edmund Grey, lord Grey of Wilton.
Agistment of the park of Bletchley. (1514-1529.)   BUCKINGHAM.

34-36   Henry LACY and Alice his wife, late the wife of Robert Oxenbrigge, v. Godard OXENBRIGGE, knight, and John OXENBRIGGE.
Half the said Robert's goods. *Damaged.* *See File 424, No. 35.* (*Cir.* 1515-1518.)   SUSSEX.

37   Thomas LOWE v. John BLORE.
Closes of pasture in the lordship of Ellaston of the demise of Ralph Longforth, knight. (After 1533?)   STAFFORD.

38   George LASSELLES, esquire, v. Richard RYCHARDSON of Clareborough, gentleman.
Manor of Sturton of the inheritance of Thomas Darcy, lord Darcy, attainted of treason. *Damaged.* (1537-1553.)   NOTTS.

39-40   William LANE v. Walter HADDON, Dorothy SAUNDERS, and others.
(Continuation of *File 1025, Nos. 7-8.*) (1538-1544.)   NORTHAMPTON.

41   Oliver LOWTHER v. William BROWNE and GRIFFITH ap Jevan.
Oaks bought by Florence Lowther, deceased, father of complainant, between the water of Dee and an old castle called Denys Brayne. (1544-1547.)   DENBIGH.

42-43   John LEE of Coleshill, co. Warwick, v. Rowland STANLEY and Margaret his wife.
Lands in Wimbolds Trafford, Egerton, Kinnerton, Broughton, Hawarden, Mancote (*i.e.* Mancoll?), Hersee by Pandeswood (*i.e.* Padeswood in Mold?), and Clotheley (Cotethlay super Aleyn), already in dispute in this court. *Pedigree given.* (Edward VI.)   CHESTER, [FLINT].

44-45   John LEKE v. Richard EDGE, Hugh HETHE, and others.
Suit to Horton and Grotton mills, belonging to the manor of Horton. (Defendants plead that possession of the manor does not prove the suit.) (Edward VI or Mary?)   STAFFORD.

46   William LYNELL v. Edward LYTELTON, esquire.
Messuage and land at Linehill in Penkridge (Lynell), late of Thomas Lynell and Alice his wife, parents of complainant. *See File 1307, No. 62.* (Edward VI.)   STAFFORD.

47   Robert LACY v. William FOTHERGILL.
Crown lease of land in Pickhill (Pickall) to John Norfolk. (1553-4.)   YORX.

48   Richard LEEKE of Osmondthorpe (in Edingley), co. Notts, yeoman, v. Thomas DADSLEY of Bottesford, miller, and Nicholas JULYAN, labourer.
Messuages and land in Bottesford and Normanton, formerly of Alexander Leeke, deceased, grand-father of complainant. (1553-4.)   LEICESTER.

49-50   Andrew LEWEN, husbandman, v. Ralph NORWOOD, esquire.
Contempt of two decrees of the Council of the Marches concerning messuages and lands in defendant's manor of Leckhampton. (1553-4.)   GLOUCESTER.

51   Thomas LLOYD alias Jevan of Llandefailog, husbandman, v. John THOMAS.
Land in Battle, late of Thomas Bede, deceased, great-uncle of complainant. (1553-4.)   BRECON.

52-53   John LONDON v. Agnes BAUGHE.
(Continuation of File 1365, No. 67.) (1553-4.)   WORCESTER.

54   Thomas LYNE and Richard TURNER, churchwardens of Bradley, v. Simon HARECOURTE, esquire, Thomas WATWOOD and William BUKBERD.
Cottages let to maintain a school in Bradley, and said by defendants to be chantry lands. (1553-4.)   STAFFORD.

55-57   Elizabeth (Joan) LYNTON (Lyntron) v. Ralph HOPTOUN, knight, and others.
(Continuation of File 1367, No. 99.) (1553-4.)   SOMERSET.

58-59   Nicholas and Henry LA v. William MARTEN.
(Continuation of File 1365, No. 1.) (1554-8.)   CORNWALL.

60   . . ., late bailiffs of LAUNCESTON, v. John AMADAS and William GAME, now bailiffs, and John ANDREW, a rebel.
Action concerning the escape of Richard Carlyan, late in complainants' custody. Mutilated. (1554-8.)   CORNWALL.

61   Rice LLOYD v. OWEN ap Griffith.
Price of sheep. (1554-8.)   ————

62   Rice LLOYD, servant to the Earl of Arundel, v. ROGER and JOHN ap David.
Refusal to complete a sale of a house, barn, and land in Llandrindod. (1554-8.)   RADNOR.

63   The same v. MALT verch Jevan, widow.
Wrongful occupation of the premises. (1554-8.)   RADNOR.

64-65   Edward LODGE v. Thomas RYDLEY and others.
Messuages, mill and land in Soulton, formerly of Edward Twyneo. Damaged. (1554-8.)   SALOP.

66-69   William LONGE and Alice his wife v. John RYPTON, William his son, and others.
Messuage and land at Tunstead in Tideswell (Tyddesworth) formerly of William Lytton. (1554-8.)   DERBY.

70   Katherine LUTTERELL, ward of the Crown, v. Richard EGCOMB, knight.
Land in the manor of Calstock, with the course of the Tamar, mills and a pigeon-cote formerly of Katherine, late the wife of Piers Egcombe, knight. (1554-5.)   CORNWALL.

FILE 1508.

1   . . . MAISTER of Canterbury v. [the bailiffs of CANTERBURY].
Action by Oliver . . . for price of camlet and linen paid by Edmund . . . Certiorari. Damaged.   KENT.

2   William MALTYN of Peopleton v. John WALSSHE of Whiteladies Aston, feoffee to uses.
Lands of complainant's wife (not described).   WORCESTER.

3   Richard MARYFF v. William CURWEN, vicar of Ugley.
Detention of deeds relating to land in Newport Pond.   ESSEX.

4   Edward MATHEWSON of London, wharfinger, v. the mayor and sheriffs of LONDON.
Action of trespass by William Ashbury, tallow-chandler and constable, dwelling in the parish of St. Botolph without Aldersgate, complainant having defended the constable of Tower Hill against an assault by him. Corpus cum causa. Mutilated.   LONDON.

5   Richard MAYDESTON.
Petition that John Arundell Trerys, knight, may be examined as to the truth of his replication in a former suit.   [CORNWALL.]

6   John MAYN and Joan his wife v. John BROMLEY.
Legacy of John Mayn of Salisbury, late the husband of the said Joan, whose executor defendant is.   WILTSHIRE.

7   Richard MEDE v. the mayor and bailiffs of BRISTOL.
False imprisonment and refusal of bail by John Langford, bailiff. Corpus cum causa.   GLOUCESTER.

8   John MERTON, chantry priest of St. Margaret in the church of St. Peter the Less, York, v. William WRIGHT of York, tailor.
Goods of Robert Wright, deceased, late priest of the same chantry.   YORK.

9   William MORE of Carthorpe v. Thomas ARDERN, esquire.
Seizure of a horse and cart and other goods from complainant's house.   YORK.

10   Robert MUSTE v. Thomas FOSTON, feoffee to uses.
Land in Stradsett, late of Thomas Muste, deceased, father of complainant. Mutilated.   NORFOLK.

11   John, son of Thomas MANFELD of Ardglass in Ulster, v. Richard SNELL.
Transfer of complainant's apprenticeship to defendant by order of the Chamberlain from Robert Pampe, citizen and paviour of London, who had paid him money weekly. Paper. (After 1459.)   LONDON.

12   William MARLYNG, gentleman, v. Richard his brother.
Detention of deeds relating to a messuage and land in Thaxted.   (Henry VII or later.)   ESSEX.

13   Henry MARMYON of Wollaton (Wolarton), gentleman, v. Thomas DIXSON, parson of Rippingale.
Loan.   (Henry VII or later.)   NOTTS., LINCOLN.

14   William MARSELEY of Tregenny, son and heir of Richard Maseley (sic), v. John GREBY.
Detention of deeds relating to the manor of Tregonyn in St. Tew (i.e. St. Ewe?).   Damaged.
(Henry VII or later.)   CORNWALL.

15   William MARSTON v. Henry HARTELEY and George RAWE of Ripon.
Obtaining delivery of wool by means of a false token.   (Henry VII or later.)   YORK.

16   William MAYNARD of Mayfield v. Richard SAXSPESSE.
Detention of deeds relating to land in Withyham.   (Henry VII or later.)   SUSSEX.

17   Michael MERDEN and Alice his wife, daughter of John Homersham, deceased, v. Simon HARRY and John HOMERSHAM.
Messuage and land in Smarden.   See Files 9, No. 87; 10, No. 60.   (Cir. 1431–1453.)   KENT.

18   Thomas MEGOR v. Roger .   .   .
Detention of deeds relating to land in Holme, late of Thomas Aylbourne, deceased, father of Joan, wife of defendant, and of Alice, mother of complainant.   Mutilated.   (Henry VII or later.)
BEDFORD.

19   Thomas METHAM, esquire, v. William CALISE and others.
Detention of deeds relating to a messuage and land in Kellington.   (Henry VII or later.)   YORK.

20   John MILLETON and Elizabeth his wife v. John Rychon KERVAR and Walter COK.
Detention of deeds relating to a messuage and land in Carg .   .   . ave of the gift of Alice Kelly.
(Henry VII or later.)   CORNWALL.

21   MORGAN and WILLIAM ap Res v. DAVID ap Hugh ap Grono ap Griffith.
Tenement in Krewedoge late of Morwyth, daughter of Evan Lloyd and grandmother of complainants.   (Henry VII or later.)   CARNARVON.

22   John MORYS v. John ARTHURE, yeoman.
Land in Bristol promised as indemnity for a bond given to Juliana Arthure.   (Henry VII or later.)
GLOUCESTER.

23   Adam MYLKE v. John CLARE.
Joint sale of fish in a fair at Ely, complainant being unable to work.   (Henry VII or later.)
CAMBRIDGE.

24   John MEYSAUNT, son and heir and executor of Alice Meysaunt alias Fleminge, v. Alice REYNOLD, daughter and heir of Thomas Chapman, feoffee to uses.
Messuage and land in Thaxted late of John Fleminge, deceased, husband of the said Alice Fleminge.
See File 148, No. 56.   (Cir. 1486–1515.)   ESSEX.

25–26   Edward, brother and heir of Thomas MYNSKIP, v. William and Thomas PRIOUR and John LAY (Lee).
Detention of deeds relating to a messuage in Castor.   See File 149, Nos. 24–25.   (Cir. 1486–1515.)
NORTHAMPTON.

27–28   Agnes MORTON v. Alice TAYLARD and others.
(Continuation of File 267, No. 35.)   (1502–3.)   LONDON.

29   Baldwin MALETT v. John HUYS of Honiton.
Debt due to Thomas Hacche of Woolley (in Bovey Tracy), gentleman, father-in-law of complainant.
(Cir. 1504–1515.)   DEVON.

30–31   Richard, son and heir of Philip MALLE v. John STYDOLD (Tedolf).
Detention of deeds relating to messuages and land in Fletching.   (Henry VIII or Edward VI.)
SUSSEX.

32   Elizabeth MALPAS v. the sheriffs of LONDON.
Action of debt and procurement of another suit by Gilbert Howell of London, tailor.   Certiorari.
(Henry VIII or Edward VI.)   LONDON.

33–34   Randell MANURYNG and Anne his wife, a daughter of Richard Cholmondeley,   Richard LEFTWYCHE, Edward MOLYNEUX, clerk, and others, feoffees to uses.
Legacy to the said Anne out of the manor of Cholmondeley.   (Henry VIII or later.)   CHESTER.

35–36   Ellen, late the wife of Robert MARKAM, gentleman, v. William MARKAM.
Manors of Lees Hall and Matleye in Scropton and Holme.   (Defendant pleads a conveyance to William Blount, lord Mountjoy, of the premises and of messuages and lands in Sapperton and Foston).   (Henry VIII.)   DERBY.

37–38   Alexander MARLER v. William SABRIGE.
Bond relating to the vicarage of Plymouth.   Mutilated   (Henry VIII.)   DEVON.

39–40   Thomas MASCALL v. Margaret MASCALL and others.
Messuage and land in Great Marlow late of John Mascall, deceased, father of complainant and husband of the said Margaret.   (Henry VIII or later.)   STAFFORD.

41   Stephen MATHEWE v. Robert TOBY of Kingsbridge.
Price of timber and wire.   (Henry VIII or Edward VI.)   DEVON.

42–43   MATTHEW ap Jevan v. Howell ap Guyllym HULLY and DAVID ap Jevan ap Rice.
Lands in the lordship of Clemyslond (Clonyslond).   Faded.   (Henry VIII or later.)   WALES.

44   John MAWDE and Elizabeth his wife, executrix and late the wife of John Thomson, v. Lettice THOMSON.
Action on a bond for a debt already paid.   (Henry VIII or Edward VI.)

45   John MAWDESLEY of Windsor, son of Gilbert Mawdesley of Clewer, gentleman, deceased,
        v. Richard WESTON, gentleman, feoffee to uses.
Refusal to make a release of tenements in Winkfield and elsewhere.   *Mutilated.*   (Henry VIII or
Edward VI.)   BERKS.

46   John, son and heir of John MAYNE of Biddenden, esquire, v. .   .   .   .
Action in the court of Lydd concerning a messuage and land in [?Romn]ey.   *Mutilated.*   (Henry
VIII or later.)   KENT.

47   Robert MAYSTERSON, prentice in London, v. Humphrey MANERING.
Messuage and land in Nantwich late of Alice Maisterson, deceased, mother of complainant and
husband of defendant.   (Henry VIII or Edward VI.)   CHESTER.

48   [Thomas?] MEYGOT and Alice his wife, late the wife of Nicholas Butler, v. Robert HEPSON
        (Hopson) and Walter FYSEWYKE.
Messuages and land in Louth.   (Henry VIII or Edward VI.)   LINCOLN.

49–50   John MORE *alias* Taylor of Thaxted, the younger, fishmonger, v. John MORE *alias* Taylor
        of Thaxted, the elder, and others, executors of William More *alias* Taylor of Thaxted, yeoman.
Detention of deeds relating to lands in Great and Little Sampford (Sandford).   (Henry VIII or
Edward VI.)   ESSEX.

51   William MORE of London.
Petition to be admitted *in forma pauperis* in a suit against John Haukes of Oulton for land in Beccles.
(Henry VIII or later.)   SUFFOLK.

52   Ursula MORECOKE *alias* Burgyes v. Morgan GEFFRE of Goudhurst.
Maintenance of defendant's child.   (Henry VIII or Edward VI.)   KENT.

53–54   George, grandson and heir of Thomas MULYS, v. Hugh YEO, William BRACHE and John
        NOTT.
Detention of deeds relating to messuages and land in Ernsborough in Swimbridge (Ernesdurgh) and
Collacot and Furze (both in Chittlehampton).   (Henry VIII.)   DEVON.

55   John MURDOK, groom of the Chamber, v. the mayor and sheriffs of LONDON.
Action by John Hoberd, merchant, on a bond to compel certain feoffees to convey to him the manor
of Bosom Hall.   *Corpus cum causa.*   (Henry VIII or Edward VI.)   LINCOLN, LONDON.

56   Elizabeth MYDDELTON v. William HANCOK of London, mercer.
Bond for a debt of Edward Clopton of London, mercer, for which jewels were pledged.   *Damaged.*
(Henry VIII or Edward VI.)   LONDON.

57   Henry MARTON, gentleman, v. Thomas NESFELD, gentleman, son and heir of William
        Nesfeld.
Refusal to complete a conveyance of lands in Flasby and Broughton-in-Craven.   (After 1512.)
                                                                                     YORK.

58–60   John MOYSY and Cristyan his wife, executrix and late the wife of John Woodman, v. John
        ADEWE of Stamford and Robert DAYE of Greatford, feoffee to uses.
Detention of the will of the said Woodman and of deeds relating to lands in Barholm and Stowe.
(1513–1553.)   LINCOLN.

61–63   Richard MASTERS v. William MASTERS.
Action pending a suit in this court (*File 856, No. 28?*) for messuages and lands in Burghill, Lyde
(Luyde Muchegros), Stretton, Wellington and Morton.   *Damaged.*   (After 1533?)   HEREFORD.

64   William MASTERS v. Richard MASTERS.
(Replication in the suit above mentioned?)   (After 1533?)   [HEREFORD?]

65   George West, master of the college of MANCHESTER, v. the abbot of .   .   .
Gown to be given to a member of the college.   *Much damaged.*   (1518–1539.)   LANCASTER.

66   Thomas MERYNGE v. Thomas WENTWORTHE.
(*Copy of File 543, No. 24.*)   (1518–1529.)   YORK.

67   Richard [Stoppes?], abbot of MEAUX, v. William WHYTYNG and John COLSON.
Detention of deeds relating to a messuage and land in Wawn.   (1523–1539?)   YORK.

68   Thomas MARCHAM v. Lewis TORFOTE and William ARGOLL.
Detention of deeds relating to a messuage called the *White Hart* and a garden in Water Lambith.
Mutilated.   (1524.)   [SURREY.]

69   Robert MALTON, yeoman, v. Thomas FOULESHURST, esquire.
' Oxon ' of land in Haslington.   (After 1525.)   CHESTER.

70   Alexander MERYNG v. the sheriffs of LONDON.
Action by John Whalley on a forged bond, pending a suit in this court (*File 658, No. 10*).
Certiorari.   (After 1529.)   LONDON.

71–72   Richard MORETON, great-nephew and heir of Nicholas Moreton, clerk, v. Thomas
        HERYNGMAN.
Messuages, shops and garden in Croydon bought of Matthew Barker. (Defendant pleads a decree of
the Star Chamber.)   (1530–1555.)   SURREY.

73–74   Robert MASTERSON v. Humphrey MAYNWARYNG.
(Continuation of File 856, No. 29.)   (1533–1538.)   CHESTER.

75   Richard MATHUE v. Andrew TOKER and Thomas John RICHARD.
Detention of deeds relating to messuages and land in the borough of Helston.   (1533–8.)   CORNWALL.

76   John MOORE v. the prior of LEEDS and Robert OXBRYGGE.
Tenement called the ' Kastell ' and lands in Ospringe.   (Before 1540.)   KENT.

77-78   Thomas MAWLE and others v. Richard VOYSY and others.
(Continuation of File 1143, No. 23.)   (1544-1547.)   ESSEX.

79   William MYCHYLL v. Thomas SEGAR.
(Copy of File 1146, No. 66.)   (1546.)   DORSET.

80-83   Edmund MARKAUNT v. Robert DANYELL, Agnes his wife and George his brother.
Goods and tenements in Westley and Great Horningsheath late of William Markaunt, gentleman,
father of complainant and former husband of the said Agnes, and tenements in Bury St. Edmunds
and Mildenhall.   Damaged.   (No. 85 is a replication in another suit.)   (Edward VI or later.)
SUFFOLK.

84-85   William MOGGERIGE v. Thomas STANTER.
Refusal to complete a sale of land in Hanging Langford of the demise of Edmund Mounepesson,
esquire.   See File 1184, No. 59.   (Edward VI.)   WILTS.

86-87   John MENYFEE of Honiton, co. Devon, yeoman, v. William FYSSHER and Juliana his
wife, late the wife of John Cooke, citizen and goldsmith of London.
Annuity granted out of defendant's manor of Stanton Barry by Thomas Pope, knight.   (1552-3.)
BUCKS.

88-89   John MAYSTER v. William HODGSON.
(Continuation of File 1308, No. 1.)   (1553-4.)   YORK.

90-91   John, son of John MEASURE and of Alice his wife, v. William GRESCROFT.
Land in Leake.   See File 1451, No. 32.   (1553-4.)   LINCOLN.

92-93   Robert MORIS v. Alban POUNDFELDE, yeoman.
Price of ewes.   (1553-4.)   SOMERSET.

94-95   William MURYELL (Maryell) v. Thomas NEWTON and others.
(Continuation of File 1368, Nos. 106-108.)   (1553-4.)   DERBY.

96   Elizabeth, late the wife of Thomas MONSON, v. Thomas MONSON her son.
Messuages and land in South Kelsey of the grant of John and William Monson.   (1554-8.)   LINCOLN.

97-98   Robert MYKELFYLD of London v. John HA(W)KES of the King's college of Windsor.
Debt due to John Aldersey, clerk, whose executor complainant is.   (1554-8.)   LONDON, BERKS.

99   Thomas M . . ., gentleman, v. John ODYNGSELLS, gentleman, son and heir of Richard
Odyngsells, and John LANGBROKE.
Refusal to complete a lease of the manor of Cabourn in Stamford-le-Hope and other lands.   Faded.
(1554-8.)   ESSEX.

100-101 William MARTEN v. Nicholas and Philippa LAA.
(Continuation of File 1368, No. 32.)   (1555-1558.)   CORNWALL.

FILE 1509.

1   'Robert N . . . TON v. John PARKER.
Detention of deeds relating to tenements in Exeter.   Faded.   DEVON.

2-4   John NYCHOLL, Margaret his wife, John STOKE, Alice his wife, Thomas POUGHLIP,
Margaret his wife, Richard GREYSTONE, and Emma his wife, v. Robert WOLFE, clerk,
descendant of Baldwin of Wythyfenne.
Land in Gorecote formerly of John Gorecote, ancestor of the female complainants.   Faded.
[CORNWALL ?]

5-6   . . . NYCOLLES and others, inhabitants of St. Tudy, v. John FYSSHER, John
FRYE, and others.
Making a rood-loft in the church of St. Tudy.   Mutilated.   [CORNWALL.]

7   George [NEVILL], lord Abergavenny, v. Katherine, executrix and late the wife of John
BOTELER.
Detention of documents relating to the said John's account as steward, feodary and surveyor of
the lordships of Allesley, Fillongley, and Dunkley.   (1476-1535.)   WARWICK.

8   Thomas NEVELL v. William DUE.
(Copy of File 78, No. 4.)   See also File 151, No. 20.   (1485-6.)   CORNWALL.

9   John, son and heir of Thomas NANSEGLOS v. Thomas ADAMS of Cambridge University.
Detention of deeds relating to a messuage and land in Exning.   (Henry VII or later.)   SUFFOLK.

10   Elizabeth, late the wife of Richard NAYLER, v. Robert CODE.
Messuage and lands in Hemswell and Eneterby (i.e. Snitterby?), late of Thomas Warde, deceased
father of complainant.   (Henry VII or later.)   LINCOLN.

11   Harry NORTHE, cook, v. [the sheriffs of LONDON, and Harry DENE, keeper of Ludgate
prison].
Bond given on behalf of William Laurence as the said Dene's deputy.   [Subpœna and certiorari.]
(Henry VII or later.)   LONDON.

12-13   Nicholas NYNE and Alice his wife v. Ralph and William WORSLEY and John FLECCHER,
chaplain.
Messuages and land in Wigan, Liverpool and [West] Derby, late of Richard Swynley, deceased,
father of the said Alice.   (Henry VII or later.)   LANCASTER.

14   William NOODE and others v. John NORRES of Chells (in Stevenage), gentleman, and
John GYN.
Closes of pasture in Stevenage conveyed by Richard Burwell for an obit in the church there.   See
File 216, No. 19.   (Cir. 1493-1500.)   HERTS.

15–16   Robert OLDEMEDOWE and Margaret his wife v. Edmund DAWKYN and Anne his wife.
Messuage and land in Upwell, late of Innocent, wife of Godfrey Gerico, and mother of the said
Margaret.   *See File* 244, *No.* 14.   (*Cir.* 1500–1501.)   CAMBRIDGE.

17   Harry NANSPIAN v. John HERRY.
Detention and forgery of deeds relating to lands in Chyaurme, Trenans, and Gwelecararthem (*i.e.*
Cararthen in Merther?).   (Henry VIII or Edward VI.)   *See Files* 208, *No.* 58 ; 1502, *No.* 1.   CORNWALL.

18   Thomas NELSON, clerk, v. the mayor and sheriffs of LONDON and James ABOROWGHE.
Actions for a robbery of plate confessed by Alice Taylor.   *Certiorari and subpœna.*   (Henry VIII
or later.)   LONDON.

19   Robert, grandson and heir of John NEWTON, v. Henry HOPKYNSON, Jane his wife, late
the wife of Henry Wyse, and others.
Detention of deeds relating to messuages and land in Newark and Kelham.   (Henry VIII or
Edward VI.)   NOTTS.

20   John NOLOTHE v. Joan and Nicholas NOLOTHE.
Legacy of Nicholas Nolothe, father of the said John, and Nicholas and former husband of the said
Joan.   *Mutilated.*   (Henry VIII or Edward VI.)   [SUFFOLK?]

21   Thomas NONNES of London, leather-seller, v. the sheriffs of LONDON.
Action 'attamyd' by Robynet Walker of London, beer-brewer, for a debt partly paid.   *Certiorari.*
(Henry VIII or Edward VI.)   ·   LONDON.

22–24   William NORMAN v. Henry BOSSE.
Refusal to complete a sale of a meadow in Outwell.   (Henry VIII or Edward VI.)   NORFOLK.

25   Thomas NORTON v. John COTYNGHAM and John ALVERICHE, feoffees to uses.
Messuage and land in South Malling of the settlement of William Norton.   (Henry VIII or later.)
KENT.

26   William NYGHTGALE v. William LOWE.
Arbitration as to land called a 'throughtgate' in North Leverton.   (Henry VIII or Edward VI.)
NOTTS.

27   John NEVYLL v. Robert and Andrew NEVYLE.
Lands in Carlton Kyme (near Dalton?) and Darlton, late of Robert Nevyll, deceased, father of all
parties.   *Copy.   Damaged.   See File* 548, *No.* 22.   (*Cir.* 1518–1529.)   LINCOLN, NOTTS.

28–29   John NEWBROUGH v. Thomas KYRTON, gentleman.
Manors of Berkley, Faroak (in Berkley), Standerwick, Oldford (in Frome and Berkley), and Skyd-
more (*i.e.* Upton Scudamore?), and messuages and lands there and in Shaftesbury,
Motcombe, Gillingham, Sturminster Newton Castle, Stalbridge, Wimborne Minster, Kingston
Lacy, Horton, Poole, Wareham, Stoborough, Corfe Castle, Galton (in Owermoigne), Blandford,
Shapwick and St. Clement Danes, formerly of John Newbrough of Lulworth, grandfather of com-
plainant.   *See File* 660, *No.* 47.   (*Cir.* 1529–1532.)   SOMERSET, DORSET, LONDON.

30   Thomas NORTON v. Joan SOMERFORD.
Detention of deeds relating to the manor of Naunton and lands there.   *See File* 660, *No.* 25.
(*Cir.* 1529–1532.)   WORCESTER.

31–32   Roger NORTHE v. Katherine RIDER and others.
Walkeringham Grange claimed under a lease from the abbot of Roche.   (Edward VI or later.)
NOTTS.

33   William NEWMAN v. Stephen CASTON, parson of Stratford.
Bond for defendant's first-fruits.   *Damaged.*   (Before 1553.)   SUFFOLK.

34–35   Ralph NORWOOD and others v. John [BRYDGES], lord Chandos.
(Continuation of *File* 1371, *No.* 58.)   (1553–4.)   GLOUCESTER.

36   John NEWPORTE v. John WHITE of Cardiff, executor of John White, receiver of pursage
and butlerage of Bridgwater.
Action by Thomas Pope for money due for two tuns of sack ('seckes').   *Mutilated.*   (1554–8.)
SOMERSET.

37   John NICOLLS v. William ELSON.
Tenement in Birmingham.   (1554–8.)   WARWICK.

38–39   William NORDEN of Stockland Gaunt, husbandman, v. Martin HUMFREY.
Bond partly paid and partly satisfied by another bond.   *Mutilated.*   (1554–8.)   SOMERSET.

40–42   William NORRES of Speke, co. Lancaster, knight, and Anne his wife, daughter of David
Myddelton, v. JOHN ap Howell and Elizabeth his wife.
Messuage and land in Wrexham.   (1554–8.)   DENBIGH.

43–45   Robert OSBERN v. the abbess and convent of BARKING.
Exclusion from the churchyard of Barking and from sacraments and dispute as to warden.
ESSEX.

46   Simon OUTELAWE v. Harry EVERARD.
Detention of deeds relating to land in Acle bought of defendant.   NORFOLK.

47   Reynold OUTHREDE and Edith his wife, great-granddaughter and heir of Thomas Tere
(Tyre), v. John FARROWE.
Detention of deeds relating to a messuage and land in Little Harrowden.   (Henry VII or later.)
NORTHAMPTON.

48   Richard OLYVER v. William WILBORE.
Receivership of the bishop of Rochester's lordship of Halling.   (Henry VIII or Edward VI.)
KENT.

49-50   Richard OXENFELD and John BALBERY v. Thomas, son and executor of Robert OXENFELD, and John ROBERT.
Debt of the said Robert Oxenfeld payable out of lands in Wakefield, Stanley and Allerthorpe. *Mutilated.* (Henry VIII or Edward VI.)   YORK.

51   William OLYFFE of Leicester and Agnes his wife v. Dame Elizabeth BARRYNGTON.
Balance of a legacy of William Boughton, father of the said Agnes, and sometime husband of defendant. (1540–1553.)   LEICESTER.

52   Rose, late the wife of John ORMESBY of Withern, v. Jane, late the wife of William WOODFORD, feoffee to uses.
Messuage and land in Woolthorpe (by Strubby), late of John Ormesby, father of the said John. (1544–1553.)   LINCOLN.

53   George ONYON v. Henry LONGE, knight.
Pasture in Calne (Calve), demised by the said Henry to Robert Ouyon and Alice his wife, both deceased. (1552.)   WILTS.

54-57   Thomas ONSLOWE, citizen and grocer of London, v. Francis WARDE and Joan his wife.
Contempt of former decrees (D. XI, 14, etc.) concerning lands in Baschurch. *Attachment.* (1554-8.)   SALOP.

FILE 1510.

1-2   John PARKER v. George PALMER.
Detention of deeds relating to a messuage in Braywell.   YORK.

3   John PERTESOYLL v. John FITZ GEFFREY, feoffee to uses.
Share of the manor of Pertesoyll in Risley, late of William Pertesoyll, deceased, father of complainant.   BEDFORD.

4   Harry PRICHARD v. David ap Guttyn LEWIS and Jevan ap Lewis KADLAN his brother-in-law.
Hunting and killing complainant's cattle on the common mountain of Aberdaron.   CARNARVON.

5   David PRESTON, esquire, v. John SKYFFELYN *alias* Brokestowe, esquire.
Forcible entry, destruction of corn, ejection of complainant's wife, etc., at Broxtow by the maintenance of Lord Grey of Codnor, dispute as to the marriage settlement of his wife, etc. *See File 9, No. 432.* (After 1431.)   NOTTS.

6   John PORTE and Lewis MARTYNUS, both of Lisbon, merchants, v. John BARON, merchant, and William ATTE WILLE (William WILLIAM), searcher, both of Exeter, and others.
Seizure of goods landed at ' Clyfton Dertemouth Hardenesse,' destruction of a sail of the ship *John* of Lisbon, arrest at Honiton by the jurisdiction of the staple, and contempt of a *corpus cum causa.* (Cir. 1438-9.)   DEVON.

7   William PARKER v. Richard MYLWARD.
Building promised on a burgage in Wotton-under-Edge demised to defendant. (Henry VII or later.)   GLOUCESTER.

8   Juliana and Margaret, daughters and heirs of Thomas PAUNFELD, v. Gilbert, son of John HORE of Childerley.
Lane in Chesterton, late of Margaret Paunfeld, deceased. (Henry VII or later.)   CAMBRIDGE.

9   John PEINTWYN v. Robert MAUNDEFELD.
Detention of deeds relating to a messuage and land in Great Wenden of the demise of William Richard. (Henry VII or later.)   ESSEX.

10-11   Richard POMELL (Panell) of Horseheath, husbandman, v. John NEWMAN.
Tenement in Linton, late of William Pomell, deceased, father of complainant. (Henry VII or later.)   CAMBRIDGE.

12   John POWER DE WILLMCOTE, yeoman, v. Richard POWER of Hall End in Polesworth, yeoman.
Detention of deeds relating to lands in Wilnecote (Wilmcote). (Henry VII or later.)   WARWICK.

13   Thomas PAYSSE of London, skinner, v. the mayor and aldermen of LONDON.
Action by Wynand Godfrey on a bet concerning the marriage of Thomas Cole and Jacomyne Walshe. *Certiorari.* (Cir. 1486-1493.)   LONDON.

14-15   John [de Eston], prior of PRITTLEWELL, and his convent v. Cicely WYTHER of London.
Action for rent of the manor of Shoebury, granted by John, late prior, in repayment of a debt. (1486-1525.)   ESSEX.

16   Reynold PEGGE v. Walter FROST and Anne his wife.
Detention of deeds relating to closes in Watford late of William Marion and others. *See File 244, No. 52.* (Cir. 1500-1501.)   HERTS.

17-19   John PAGE v. William COPLEY.
Mill in Emley, late held with lands in Haddlesey and Darrington by William Fitzwilliam, father-in-law of defendant. (Henry VIII or Edward VI.)   YORK.

20   William PALMER v. John HAVERD.
Lands and goods charged with legacies to the children of . . . Osbaldeston of Chadlington, gentleman, brother-in-law of complainant. *Mutilated.* (Henry VIII or later.)   OXFORD.

21   John PENROS v. John PENWARN of Mawnan and Joan JAKYS.
Land at Carlinick (in Mawnan). (Henry VIII or Edward VI.)   CORNWALL.

22   Thomas PERKYN of Guildford, baker, v. Hugh ASSHEBURY.
Imprisonment on an action of debt so as to hinder payment to Piers Clerk(?). *Damaged.*
(Henry VIII or later.)   SURREY..

23-25   John PERNELL v. Mary, late the wife of John SALMON, merchant and burgess of
Southampton.
Messuages and gardens in Southampton, late of John Parnell, deceased, father of complainant.
(Henry VIII or Edward VI.)   HANTS.

26   John POTTER v., John LAMBE the elder, John LAMBE the younger, and William GELOT.
Lands in Westerham late of John Lambe of Gylmyns, deceased, father of defendants John and
John (*sic*). (Henry VIII or Edward VI.)   KENT.

27-28   Randolph PRESTLAND v. Robert LEE, esquire, Anne his wife, John PRESTLAND of
Ridley, gentleman, and Thomas PALEN, husbandman.
Half a messuage and land at Prestland in Banbury late of William Prestland, deceased, grandfather
of complainant. (Henry VIII or Edward VI.)   CHESTER.

29   Geoffrey PROCTOUR v. Richard MALLOM, gentleman.
Refusal to complete a sale of lands in Malham. (Henry VIII or Edward VI.)   YORK.

30-32   John PENPONS v. Richard PENPONS his son.
Non-payment of an annuity and of complainant's debts (*specified*) in return for a grant of the
manors of Tregryll, Trewint, and Pengover (all in Menheniot), Trewent (in Duloe), Tregornowe
(*i.e.* Tregenna in St. Columb Minor?), Rosculyan (in Little Petherick) and Boscolleth, and seizure
of deeds from complainant's house at Tregose (*i.e.* Tregoss in Roche?). *Mutilated. See File* 1049,
No. 19. (*Cir.* 1515-1518.)   CORNWALL.

33-34   The same v. the same.
Seizure of deeds relating to the above (*reading* Tregorrowe *for* Tregornowe *and* Bescelleth *for* Boscolleth), and to manors and lands in Bosweman (*i.e.* Boswednan in Madron), Penhale, Bosulsek
(*i.e.* Bosolliack in Gulval), Trewren (*i.e.* Trewren in Madron?), Truruff (*i.e.* Trerieff in Madron?),
Bedrawthe (*i.e.* Bedruthan in St. Eval?), Penbygill (*i.e.* Penbugle north of Bodmin), Tretawne
(*cf.* Tawne in Cardinham), Penkylleke, Nanturna, Tregouth (*i.e.* Tregou in Lansalloes?), Ligana,
Treve(? n)ly, and Carrior. *See File* 436, *No.* 30.   CORNWALL.

35-36   Richard PENPONS v. John TOM and others, inhabitants of St. Columb.
Land in Tregoos (*i.e.* Tregoss in Roche or Tregoos in St. Columb Major?), late of John Penpons,
father of complainant. *Damaged. See File* 870, *No.* 16. (After 1515.)   CORNWALL.

37-38   Lewis POWES, gentleman, and others, administrators of the goods of Geoffrey Fyssher of
London, v. John GREVIS *alias* Coke of London, merchant tailor.
Debt for which defendant waged his law. (1516-7.)   LONDON.

39   John PENKEVELL, gentleman, v. John CARMYNOWE, esquire.
Rent reserved by John Penkevell, ancestor of complainant, on a grant of land in Penkevell to
John Trejagow, knight, and Harry Trejagu. *Pedigree given. See File* 555, *No.* 6. (*Cir.* 1518-
1529.)   CORNWALL.

40-41   Elizabeth, daughter and executrix of John PHILIPPE, v. Jane HUCHYN of Trecogow
(*i.e.* Trecugoe in St. Kew?), late the wife of John Huchyn, and William his son.
Messuage and land in Tremeteny and Frogham of the demise of Edmund Arundell, knight.
(After 1519.)   CORNWALL.

42   William PYNNOCK of Hanley, yeoman [and Elizabeth his wife, late the wife of Roger
Badger], v. John RUSSELL, knight.
Lands in the manor of Upton-on-Severn demised by the King to William Compton, knight,
deceased. *Mutilated.* (After 1528.)   WORCESTER.

43-47,   Richard PINSON of London, printer, v. Dame Isabel GREY and John WELLYS,
gentleman.
(Continuation of *File* 349, *No.* 40.) (1504-1530.)   LONDON.

48   Richard PLOMMER v. Dr. SMYTH, prebendary of St. Paul's.
(Deposition belonging to *File* 873, *No.* 34.) (1533-1538.)   ESSEX.

49   . . . executrix and late the wife of William PYPER, v. Thomas NOYSE and Jane his
wife, executrix, and late the wife of John Rymell.
Detention of a lease made to the said Pyper and Rymell by Roger Marciall, prior of St. Margaret's,
Marlborough. (*Cir.* 1534-5.),   WILTS.

50   John [Stonywell], abbot of PERSHORE, v. the bailiffs of WORCESTER, and Richard
HODYS, maniple of Gloucester College, Oxford.
Action of debt procured by John Teyle, clerk. *Certiorari and subpœna. Mutilated.* (1534-
1540.)   WORCESTER.

51-52   Thomas PAWSON v. John WOMMOCKE (Womoke) and John ROSSELL.
False imprisonment at Redford (*i.e.* Retford) and seizure of goods. (1540-1547.)   NOTTS.

53   Edward PLANKNEY v. Robert SALESBURY of Lleth (*i.e.* Llay?), gentleman.
Hindrance to courts held in the ' dominion ' of Dyffryn Clwyd on behalf of the bishop of Bangor.
(1540-1553.)   DENBIGH.

54-56   John PERTE, esquire, v. John GRAYE, gentleman.
Rent of a tenement in Salisbury Alley, St. Bride's, Fleet Street, fallen into arrear during complainant's absence as auditor in North Wales. (Edward VI.)   LONDON.

57-58   Hugh PHILLIPE and Eleanor his wife v. Alice FENDYK.
(Continuation of *File* 1252, *No.* 53.) (1547-1551.)   LINCOLN.

59–60　John PORT of Etwall [co. Derby.], knight, v. Richard TAYLYOR and others, inhabitants of Great and Little Leake.
Tithes of the demise of Julyan Crossebye, parson. (Edward VI.)　　　　　　　　NOTTS.
61–63　Dame Anne PAKINGTON v. John LITELTON and others.
(Continuation of File 1373, No. 1.)　(1553–4.)　　　　STAFFORD, MIDDLESEX, WORCESTER.
64　　George PONTESBURY v. George MERYKE.
Suit for messuage and land in Leatam dismissed from this court because under discussion in the Court of the Marches. (1553–4.)　　　　　　　　　　　　SALOP.

FILE 1511.

1　　John PEKE the elder v. Thomas DUFFELD, clerk, Thomas MOTEHAM, chaplain, feoffee to uses, and John HUNTYNGDON.
Messuage and meadow in Higham, wherein John Peke the younger, brother (sic) of complainant, had a life interest. Endorsed with note of answer.　　　　　　　　SUFFOLK.

2　　Harry [PERCY], earl of Northumberland, v. Katherine, late the wife of John PUTT.
Detention of deeds relating to the manors of Calceby, Mablethorpe and Burwell, and one-third of the manor and castle of Egremont. See File 434, No. 1. (Before 1537.)
　　　　　　　　　　　　　　　　　　LINCOLN, CUMBERLAND.

3　　Richard PLEYSTOWE v. the mayor of ROCHESTER.
Action by Thomas Lincoln, monk of Rochester, for sale of wine which was ' not able.' Corpus cum causa.　　　　　　　　　　　　　　　　KENT.

4　　George POLEYN v. Margery POLEYN.
Detention of deeds relating to messuages, lands and rent in King's-Weston, Laurence-Weston, Shirehampton, Charlton and Redland, late of Henry Poleyn, deceased, father of complainant and husband of defendant.　　　　　　　　　　　GLOUCESTER.

5　　William POLLARD, Jane his wife, . . . and . . . his wife, v. Richard .WATYSON(?) and John SE . TE.
Detention of deeds relating to tenements in Bodmyn, Truro and Egloshaile. Damaged. [CORNWALL.]

6　　Dorothy, wife of John POWER, gentleman, v. Thomas and Giles WELLYSBOURNE and Thomas POWER.
Abduction and concealment of the said John at Oxford.　　　　　　　OXFORD.

7　　John, son and heir of Thomas PRESTON and of Isabel his wife, v. William WATSON and others.
Detention of deeds relating to messuages and land in Garforth, formerly of William Westren. YORK.

8　　Hugh PROCTOUR v. John PROCTOUR, parson of half the church of Linton, William AYREY, and Alice YONGE.
Joint lease of the other half of the said church from Master Bakhous, parson thereof. See File 344, No. 58, (Cir. 1504–1515).　　　　　　　　　　　YORK.

9　　John PARKER v. the bailiffs of COLCHESTER.
Action by Thomas Thorpe, gentleman, for wine distrained as belonging to Roger Martyn, a defaulting tenant of complainant. Certiorari. (Henry VII or later.)　　　　ESSEX.

10–12　Richard PARRE v. John PAGE.
Land in Dyngley. Damaged. (Henry VII or later.)　　　　[NORTHAMPTON or BERKS.]

13　　John PATERSON of Lewtrenchard, cutler, v. John DOBELL and Joan his wife.
Detention of deeds relating to a house and garden in Tavistock. (Henry VII or later.)　DEVON.

14–15　Henry PAYN, tailor, v. Thomas Balle of LONDON, skinner.
Bond given on defendant's behalf to James Monkkaster of London, tailor. (Henry VII or later.)
　　　　　　　　　　　　　　　　　　　　LONDON.

16　　Henry [PERCY], earl of Northumberland, v. Thomas BULLYN, knight.
Detention of deeds relating to the manors of Northam, Slapton, ' Insula de Londay ', Torbryan, Dartmouth, Mapperton, Rampisham, Wraxall, Chilfroom, Woodsford (Wyrdesforde), ' Castrum Dors,' Haselbury, Sutton Poyntz, Puncknowle, Toller Porcorum, Swyre, Nether Kentcombe, Blundelshay in Whitchurch Canonicorum (Blondeshaye), Somerton Erleigh, Somerton Randolf, Batheaston, Shockerwick, Somerton, Kingsdon, Downhead, Frome Selwood and Oxenhall. See File 434, Nos. 3–6. (1483–1537).　　　DEVON, DORSET, SOMERSET, GLOUCESTER.

17　　[Walter] son and heir of William POURE.
Commission to examine witnesses as to land in Leysdown (Lysden), assigned to Thomas Seyguoir (Sygoure, Segour) till a debt should have been recovered therefrom. See File 559, No. 23. (Cir. 1518–1529).　　　　　　　　　　　　　　　KENT.

18–19　William PYGOTT and Maude his wife, daughter and heir of John Newe, v. Robert HATHEWOLF.
Detention of deeds relating to a messuage and land in Chobham. (Henry VII or later.) SURREY.

20–22　John P . . . YDE v. John SKYNNER.
Collection of debts assigned to complainant by . . . Turnour. Damaged. (Henry VII or (?)

23–25　John, son and heir of John POLPERE and of Maryell his wife, v. William TREWYNARD.
Detention of deeds relating to a messuage and land in Lelant (Lanant) and Carnsewe. (Cir. 1486–1493.)　　　　　　　　　　　　　　　CORNWALL.

26　　Thomas PYRYELL, yeoman, v. Robert APPYLTON and John RUTLAND.
Detention of deeds relating to lands in Whittlerford (Wyttysford). See File 348, No. 15. (Cir. 1504–1515).　　　　　　　　　　　　　　CAMBRIDGE.

27–28　Flower PEPERELL of Antony & Co. Cornwall v. John WARYNG.
Detention of deeds relating to a house in Plymouth. See Files 558, No. 55; 875, No. 20. (After 1518.)
　　　　　　　　　　　　　　　　　　　　DEVON.

29   Roger PORTER, citizen and 'upholder' of London, v. the mayor and sheriffs of LONDON.
Actions of debt by divers persons at the procurement of Percival Wylson, citizen and 'upholder'
of London. *Corpus cum causa.* (Henry VIII or Edward VI.)   LONDON.

30   Richard POWES of Glastonbury, gentleman, v. Agnes, late the wife of John LYDE, and
John WOODCROFT.
Heriot due from a cottage and land in the manor or parsonage of Street. (Henry VIII or Edward
VI.)   SOMERSET.

31   John POOET, priest, v. John PEGGYNNYS and Joan his wife.
Detention of deeds relating to messuages and lands in Launceston and Lifton. *Mutilated.* (1512.)
        CORNWALL. DEVON.

32   Alen PERCYE, clerk, v. Dame Margery BELYNGHAM and Oliver, prior of COMBE.
Detention of deeds relating to the manors of Ladbroke and Fenny Compton and messuages and lands
there and in Kingswood, Knightcote (in Burton Dassett) and Ryton (Reynton)-upon-Dunsmore.
See Files 552, *No.* 68; 873, *No.* 25; 1052, *No.* 8. (*Cir.* 1515–1544.)   WARWICK.

33   John PA[LMER?] v. the sheriffs of LONDON.
Action by . . . Baldewyn, [citizen] and haberdasher of London, on an account including
price of 'tenne celers of paynted bokeram.' *Certiorari. Mutilated.* (1529–1533.)   LONDON.

34   Philip PEN v. [Michael ORME and Thomas SKRYMSHER.]
Water-mill fishery and land in Forton of the demise of Dame Anne Seyntleger. *Index. Commission.*
(1529–1538.)   STAFFORD.

35   Hugh PRUST v. Jeffrey BURDON of Bideford, tanner.
Reversion of a tenement in Great Torrington sold as part of a contract for freight of complainant's
ships *Mary Bollen* and *Cateryn.* (After 1530.)   DEVON.

36   John PERLE v. John, prior of SHEEN.
Farm of Dewsall, formerly of Hyggyn ap Hyggyn. *Mutilated.* (Before 1534.)   HEREFORD.

37   Thomas PEERSON and Michael EDLIN, of East Woodhay, co. Hants, clerk, v. John RYALL.
Vicarage of Meere. *Damaged.* (1553–4.)   [SOMERSET or WILTS.]

38   John PEARLE v. John HYGGYNS.
Land in Dewsall. (1554–8.)   HEREFORD.

39–41   Nicholas POLGLAS [and others?] v. James and John TRELYVER and John SAMPSON.
Messuages and lands in Mawgan-in-Pyder, formerly of John Bercla. *Mutilated.* (1554–8.)
        CORNWALL.

42–43   Jane daughter of Edmund PURPETT v. John JERMY, knight.
Manor of Waldringfield and lands there and in Henley (Helmelee) and Newbarn. (1554–8.)
        SUFFOLK.

44   Robert PECOCKE, alderman of York, v. William KYDD and Thomas SOWDEN (Sowthen),
successively mayors of Boston.
Refusal to award execution for debt against William Johnson. (1557–8.)   LINCOLN.

45   John QUYLTER v. Walter GLOVER.
Price of kerseys. *Mutilated.* (Henry VIII or Edward VI.)   ———

46   Richard QUYNTRELL and Alice his wife, v. Robert BEARE.
Detention of deeds. *Mutilated.* (Henry VIII or Edward VI.)   [DEVON or CORNWALL?]

47–48   Edmund QUARR of Croscombe (Corscombe), clothier, v. Thomas, son of Edward POMEREY,
knight, deceased.
Reversion of a messuage, lands and fulling-mills in defendant's manor of Croscombe. (1530–1547.)
        SOMERSET.

49–50   Humphrey QUERNEBY and Elizabeth his wife, niece and heir of Thomas Mellores, v.
Henry FOSEBROKE.
Detention of deeds relating to houses and land in Nottingham. (*Cir.* 1547.) *Answer and replication
wanting.*   NOTTS.

FILE 1512.

1–2   John ROBERD and John MERCER v. Thomas BAKER.
Price of land in Hawkhurst late of Eleanor Bernys, whose executors complainants are.   KENT.

3   William ROGG[ER] v. John QUYNARTON.
Action in the court of Canterbury, 'wher the said John Quynarton hathe and maye have every
pannell served after his own entent,' for goods of Thomas Mayhew, stepson of defendant.   KENT.

4   Bryan ROUCLYFF, baron of the Exchequer, v. [John SLYNGESBY].
Armed riot and attempted assault at Colthorp. *Commission for arrest. Mutilated.* (1458–1494.)
        [YORK?]

5   John RATCLYFF v. Thomas NORTHEN and Agnes SEYNTNYCHOLAS.
Detention of deeds relating to a messuage and land in Sittingbourne. (Henry VII or later.) KENT.

6   William REVE and Rose his wife, late the wife of William Byschopp, gentleman, and daughter
of Thomas Armiger, v. Agnes WEST, mother of the said Byschopp.
Manor of Thistledown Hall in Burgh (Burffe), settled on the said Rose at her first marriage subject
to a rent payable to defendant. (Henry VII or later.)   SUFFOLK.

7   John RICHARDSON of Coningsby and Christian his wife v. Thomas ELLYS.
Deeds and goods late of George Redysdale, deceased, former husband of the said Christian.
(Henry VII or later.)   LINCOLN.

8 George ROBYNSON of London, barber, v. Ralph RELAND, bailiff, of Deptford, Thomas STANYS of London, broker, and Richard BAILI, a gentleman of the Earl of Lincoln.
Bond for price of goods to be bought by the said Baili. (Henry VII or later.) LONDON.

9 John ROWE v. Richard DAVY.
Detention of deeds relating to messuages and land in Abbotsham. (Henry VII or later.) DEVON.

10 John RUSSELL v. John RYDWARE.
Detention of deeds relating to lands in Stafford. (Henry VII or later.) STAFFORD.

11 Michael RUTHFOOS v. Robert POULE, clerk.
Detention of deeds relating to messuages and land in Crukmour (i.e. Crugmeer in Padstow?) and Trevethyn (i.e. Trewithen in St. Merryn?) bought of John Sperman. (Henry VII or later.)
CORNWALL.

12-14 Thomas REVE v. Robert WYGMORE.
Destruction of commissions in a suit in this court for lands in Tevetteshale. Mutilated. (After 1501.) [NORFOLK.]

15 John RAVENESBY, grandson and heir of John Malmyn, v. Thomas STOKESLEY.
Detention of deeds relating to a messuage, barn and land in North Mimms. See File 350, No. 13. (Cir. 1504–1515.) HERTS.

16 John [Lawrence], abbot of RAMSEY, v. . . . and John WYNDE.
Land [in Ramsey?] acquired by John Huntyngdon, late abbot. Mutilated. (1507–1538.)
HUNTINGDON.

17 Robert RAVENYNG v. William POTKYN, gentleman, feoffee to uses.
Messuage called the Bell on the Hoop in Bread Street and others in St. Mary Aldermary of the grant of Richard Chawre, alderman of London, grandfather of complainant. (Henry VIII.)
LONDON.

18 Margaret RAWLYNS v. [the sheriffs of LONDON].
Action of debt by Joan, executrix and late the wife of John Rawlyns, citizen and merchant tailor of London, against whom a verdict has already been given. Certiorari. (Henry VIII or later.)
LONDON.

19-21 Robert RICHARDSON, clerk, v. William TALBOTT, [clerk?].
Lease of the parsonage of Hargrave. Damaged. (Henry VIII or Edward VI.) NORTHAMPTON.

22-23 Jane, Denise, Alice and Constance, granddaughters and heirs of Walter ROBERTH, esquire, v. Thomas ROBERTH, gentleman.
Messuage and land in Goudhurst. (Henry VIII or Edward VI.) KENT.

24 Arnold ROGERS, Katherine his wife and Alice WESBYE v. John PYTTOWSE.
Tenement in Norwich late of John Polle, deceased, father of the female complainants. (Henry VIII or Edward VI.) NORFOLK.

25 John RONNELL v. Robert, son and heir of John MORTYMER.
Refusal to complete a lease of a messuage and land at East Gooseham in Moorwinstow. (Henry VIII or Edward VI.) CORNWALL.

26 . . . ter ROSE v. Harry TURNOUR.
Tenement in Kedington and Barnardiston late of William Barnardeston, esquire, whose executor complainant is. Faded. (Henry VIII or later.) SUFFOLK.

27-29 Jeffrey, son and heir of John RYCKARDES, by William·Hedgeman his guardian, v. Richard JENYNS and Agnes his wife.
Tenement in Horndon, formerly of John Ricardes, father of the said John and Agnes. (Henry VIII or Edward VI.) ESSEX.

30 William RYDER, executor of John Lytyll, v. Alice HINT, executrix of John Brown.
Price of wool. (Henry VIII or later.) ———

31 John RYPTON of Coventry, 'ferrer,' v. John TALLANES, mayor of Coventry, and Nicholas RIPTON, son of complainant.
Land in Coventry of the demise of a former mayor. (Henry VIII or Edward VI.) WARWICK.

32 John RASTELL v. the mayor and sheriffs of LONDON and Richard STAVERTON and others. (Duplicate of File 883, No. 8.) (1530–1536.) LONDON.

33 John ROSER of Parham v. Thomas BERTE and Joan his wife.
Tenements in Wetherden, Haughley and Bickton (i.e. Bacton?) late of John Roser, deceased, uncle of complainant. Mutilated. See File 880, No. 63. (Cir. 1533-8.) [SUFFOLK.]

34-36 John ROGERSON and others v. Thomas SMYTHE and John DUSTGATE (Busgate).
(Continuation of File 880, No. 57.) · (1534-1538.) SUFFOLK.

37-38 James ROGER of Chippenham, co. Cambridge, husbandman, and Joan his wife v. Reynold FYSTON and Margaret his wife.
Share of a messuage and land in Kentford (?) late of John Hadnam, deceased, father of the said Joan and Margaret. See File 1153, No. 45. (After 1536.) [SUFFOLK?]

39-41 William ROWDON of Hanging Langford v. William HUNTON of East Knoyle and Richard WHALE.
Price of cattle. (1536-1547.) WILTS.

42-44 John REYNER of Derby and Margaret REYNER, executors of Hugh Reyner of Derby, v. Godfrey (Geoffrey) WILDE, John FORMAN and others.
Loan to John Cha(u)lner of Crick, deceased, whose executors defendants are. (1538-1553.) DERBY.

45-46 Edmund ROKYS and Margaret his wife v. John KNYGHT.
Wages of the said Margaret before her marriage. (After 1539.) ———

47-48   William RAYNES *v.* John HASDEN, Joan his wife, William ORGAR, and Margaret his wife.
Messuage and gardens in Capel demised by complainant to the said Margaret with reservation of a
chamber. (1544-7.)   KENT.

49 52   John ROGER and Elizabeth his wife *v.* Harry ROCKADYN and Agnes GAY.
(Continuation of File 1154, Nos. 29-30, with an answer by Agnes Base in a suit on the same subject.)
(1545.)   GLOUCESTER.

53   Anne REEDE and William BACHELLER her tenant *v.* Henry BEDDYNGFYLDE, knight.
Action for lands in East Keale already in suit in this court. (1549-1553.)   LINCOLN.

54 55   Robert RABBETT *v.* Alice RABBETT and others.
(Continuation of File 1379, No. 1.) (1554-5.)   KENT.

56   Katharine, late the wife of John RADDON, and Nicholas their son *v.* James CRUSE and
John ROCHE.
Marsh in Norton of the grant of John Barnehouse, esquire, and Margaret his wife. *Damaged.*
(1554-8.)   ?

57   Thomas ROCHESTER and John BUT *v.* John HARRISON and William . . .
Lands in Billingford, Bawdeswell and elsewhere. *Faded.* (1554-8.)   NORFOLK.

58   Anthony ROLELESLEY *v.* William ROE and Jane his wife.
Messuage and land in Breadsall of the demise of John Dethicke. *Damaged.* (1554-8.)   DERBY.

59   Anthony ROSLEY *v.* Richard DETHICK, parson of Breadsall.
Contract for sale of tithe hay. (1554-8.)   DERBY.

FILE 1513.

1   John SAKKER and Margaret his wife *v.* John PYNGYLL of Exning.
Detention of deeds and profits of messuages and land in Willingham, late of John Rannow of
Exning, father of the said Margaret, whose executor defendant is.   CAMBRIDGE.

2   . . . son and heir of Christopher SALAGE and of Anne his wife *v.* Richard SALAGE.
Detention of deeds relating to the manor of Etchells (in Northenden and Stockport) and other
lands. *Damaged.*   CHESTER, WALES.

3   Robert SELOT *v.* John TYTYSHALE of Heveningham.
Bond given on defendant's behalf for price of a hired horse which died, and vexatious suit.
                                                                                                                      NORFOLK.

4   William SHEPARD of London, vintner, *v.* [. . .], alderman of LONDON.
Imprisonment under an alderman's command purchased by Richard Ryman, who has since re-
leased all suits. *Corpus cum causa.*   LONDON.

5-6   John son and heir of Raulyn SHORE *v.* John CHATERLEY of Derby, cordwainer.
Sale of land in All Hallows, Derby, and release of price extorted by threats and by forgery of a letter
from complainant's mother.   DERBY.

7   Joan SHORNE *v.* Edward YONG of London, haberdasher.
Murder of John, husband of complainant, attempt to throw the blame on Robert Colman, assault
in Cheap, and divers suits.   LONDON.

8-9   John SKELTON *v.* Roger LANE and William GRAY.
Goods of John Skelton, father of complainant, whose executors defendants are. *Schedule annexed.*

10   Rowland SMYTH *v.* John KNYSMYTH.
Detention of deeds relating to lands in Kelham.   NOTTS.

11   John SOUTH *v.* Robert CURTEYS, kinsman and heir of John Curteys of Cornwall, esquire.
Debt to Thomas Spark, citizen and grocer of London, whose widow took complainant to husband.
                                                                                                                      CORNWALL, LONDON.

12   John STOKKERE of London, merchant, *v.* Baty, late the wife of Robert MOREFF.
Loan to the purser of the ship *Marie* of 'Donewych in Pruys' (*i.e.* Danzig?), whereof the said
Robert was part owner.   LONDON.

13-14   Richard STRODE, esquire, *v.* [Richard MAYHOWE of Tavistock, merchant].
Sale of land in St. Budeaux, with the 'preheminence' of the sale of other lands. *Mutilated.*
                                                                                                                      DEVON.

15   Edward SYGAR *v.* Thomas LYGHE.
Shops and solars in Old Fish Street in the parish of St. Nicholas Cold Abbey of the entail of John
Sygar, grandfather of complainant.   LONDON.

16   William Wilflete, dean of the college of STOKE by Clare, *v.* John HOROLD.
Attempt to destroy the chancel of the parish church of Clare because complainant postponed its
renewal to other works in the college. (1461-9.)   SUFFOLK.

17   John STERNE of Bridport, co. Dorset, merchant, *v.* Richard REE, keeper of Exeter gaol.
Failure to produce John Fryston of Cambridge, clerk, and Walter Whyte of London, tailor,
arrested for sale of a chain of gilt copper as gold. [After 1462.]   DEVON.

18   Thomas SKOWE *v.* Robert POWER.
Detention of deeds relating to a tenement in Pudding Lane, St. Sepulchre's. (After 1472.) LONDON.

19-20   Margaret SANDYS *v.* William SANDYS, knight.
Marriage settlement with John, son of defendant, who died leaving complainant pregnant of a
child since born. (After 1478.)   ———

21   James SMYTH of London, draper, and Lettice his wife, late the wife of John Neve of
London, mercer, *v.* the mayor of LONDON.
Arrest at the suit of Richard Muston of London, draper, for expenses incurred on behalf of the
said Neve. (Richard III or later.)   LONDON.

22-23 Isabel and Elizabeth, daughters of John SCACEBY, deceased, v. Elizabeth SCACEBY, late his wife.
Detention of deeds relating to a messuage and land in Doncastre. (Henry VII or later.)   YORK.

24   Hugh, son and heir of James SCOLFELD, v. Ewan, son and heir of James RADCLIFF.
Detention of deeds relating to lands in Butterworth and Hundersfield (both in Rochdale). (Henry VII or later.)   LANCASTER.

25-28 Edward SERE, executor of John Turpyn of Barley End, v. William TATTENELL, feoffee to uses.
Lands in Pightlesthorn and Albury. (Annexed is an interpleader by Alice, late the wife of the said John.) (Henry VII.)   HANTS.

29   Richard SEYNTYLL v. John ATWILL of Exeter, late his guardian.
Continued occupation of lands in Morton (i.e. Moretonhampstead), Chagwourth (i.e. Chagford), South Tawton and Withycombe, and action on a bond for complainant's marriage. (Henry VII or later.)   DEVON.

30   Richard, son and heir of Robert SHENTON of Whittington, labourer, v. John BEELE of Williford (in Whittington).
Pasture (not specified) pledged by Nicholas Stanton, father of the said Robert, to Richard Beele, grandfather of defendant. (Henry VII or later.)   STAFFORD.

31   John SMYTH of Bristol, merchant, v. the mayor and bailiffs of BRIDGWATER.
Action by Richard Andrewes for price of Toulouse woad (' Tulles wood ') delivered by his wife in payment of a debt. Certiorari. (Henry VII or later.)   SOMERSET.

32   John SMYTH and Robert HORNECLYF v. the mayor and sheriffs of LONDON.
Action by William Dawncie of London, mercer, for a debt already satisfied. Certiorari. (Henry VII or later.)   LONDON.

33   Nicholas SMYTH and Mildred his wife v. Richard ACHAMBER ond others, feoffees to uses.
Messuage and land in Harrietsham, late of William Goolde, former husband of the said Elizabeth. (Henry VII or later.)   KENT.

34-37 Richard SMYTH and Joan his wife v. Edward LULHAM and Thomas PELHAM.
Detention of deeds relating to a messuage and land in Hoathly and Waldron. (Henry VII or later.)   SUSSEX.

38   William, son and heir of John SNELLYNG, v. Robert SNELLYNG, his uncle, and Simon STERTE of Rattery.
Detention of deeds relating to a messuage and land in Plympton. (Henry VII or later.) DEVON.

39   Anne SOMERFORD v. Walter LEVESON and John BAKER.
Detention of deeds relating to lands in Somerford. (Henry VII or later.)   STAFFORD.

40   Walter SQWYER and Anges his wife v. Roger PICAYS of Colchester and John PAGE or Ardleigh, feoffees to uses.
Tenement called the Vynehous in Colchester, late of Agnes Kyng, deceased, mother of the said Agnes. (Henry VII or later.)   ESSEX.

41-42 William STANE of Shelley, yeoman, grandson and heir of William Stane of Willingale, v. Robert, son and heir of Robert STANE.
Detention of deeds relating to messuages and land in Beauchamp Roding. (Henry VII or later.)   ESSEX.

43-44 William STURTON, husbandman, v. Thomas BOWER.
Messuage and land at Melton in Walton. (Henry VII or later.)   YORK.

45   John SUGGE v. William NODGE.
Detention of deeds relating to a messuage and land in Somerleton, late of John Nodge, deceased. Mutilated. [Henry VII or later.]   [NORFOLK.]

46   Thomas SYBNAM of St. Ives (Seynt Eve), co. Huntingdon, v. James LAURENCE of Wybuston, [co. Bedford], gentleman.
Bond for defendant's debt to John Hert, brewer of London. (Henry VII or later.)   ———

47   John STEVYNS, husbandman, v. Robert, prior of St. James's, BRISTOL.
Refusal to complete a lease of a close of pasture in Bitton. (1486-1539.)   GLOUCESTER.

48-49 William STYRTEVAUNT v. William ELMET.
Refusal to complete a lease of a messuage and land in Kelham (Kyllome). See File 164, No. 16. (1486-1515.)   NOTTS.

50   Edmund SYMKYS v. the bailiffs of BRIDGNORTH.
Action in the bailiffs' court by Hugh Preone, serjeant-at-mace, for impounding a horse which died. Certiorari. (1496 or 1520.)   SALOP.

51   Robert STOKES, late of Kegworth, gentleman, v. Hugh SHIRLEY, esquire.
Bond to indemnify Maude, late the wife of defendant. Endorsed Fiat ut petitur. Damaged. (After 1497.)   LEICESTER.

52-55 John SHARPE v. William HALLE, feoffee to uses.
Portion of a tenemnt in Reigate called the Checker, late of John Barett, deceased, uncle of com. plainant. (1503.)   SURREY.

56   Nicholas, son and heir of Thomas SYBYLL, esquire, v. John ROPER, esquire.
Detention of deeds relating to the manor of Chymbehams and lands in Farningham, Mappiscombe, Eynsford, Kingsdown, Rochester, and Gravesend, and the park of Grain. (After 1503.)   KENT.

57   Thomas, son and heir of Thomas STOTE, v. Stephen BENET.
Detention of deeds relating to a messuage and land in St. Neot's. (Cir. 1504-1515.)   CORNWALL.

X 2

58   Thomas SALWEY of Stanford *v.* Edmund BUTLER.
Verbal security given for a debt of Humphry Castyll, already paid. (Henry VIII or Edward VI.)
WORCESTER.

59   Margaret, granddaughter and heir of William SAMSON and of Ellen his wife, *v.* Richard SAM(P)SON.
Messuage and land in Biddenden promised by the said William in exchange for another in Clapham. (Henry VIII or Edward VI.)   BEDFORD.

60   William SEYMOUR and Joan his wife *v.* Robert and William SMYTH.
Messuages and lands in Thorpe and Calverley of the entail of Richard Smyth of Brouton, deceased. (Henry VIII *or* Edward VI.)   LINCOLN.

61-64   Laurence SIMON *v.* Richard HORDON, John CALLARD, and John SIMON.
Messuage and land at North Winsham in the manor of Braunton Dean, late of William Simon, deceased, father of the said Laurence and John. (Henry VIII or Edward VI.)   DEVON.

65   Thomas SKYPPWYTH of Utterby, esquire, *v.* William SKYPPWYTH, esquire.
Goods of Joan Bylysby, deceased, in the hands of John Aquarra, clerk, deceased, her co-executor with complainant, defendant claiming the said Aquarra as his bondman. (Henry VIII or Edward VI.)   LINCOLN

66-67   Roger and Edward, brothers of John SLEGGE, deceased, and administrators of his goods, *v.* Lewis PYDDER of London, tailor.
Loan and clothing left with defendant for repair. (Henry VIII or later.)   LONDON.

68   John SMYTHSON, clerk, *v.* the [bailiffs?] of YORK.
False charge by . . . Hall, clerk, of refusing to pray for the King. *Corpus cum causa. Mutilated.* (Henry VIII or Edward VI.)   YORK.

69-70   Nicholas SPENCER *v.* John BATEN.
Intimidation of a jury in an action of waste concerning land in Bramshall (*i.e.* Bramshaw or Bramshill?). (Henry VIII or Edward VI.)   HANTS.

71   Humphrey STEPHYNS, a grandson and heir of Richard Wulladon and of Elizabeth his wife, *v.* Richard UPCOTTE.
Detention and destruction of deeds relating to a moiety of a messuage, land and rent in Tamerton. (Henry VIII or Edward VI.)   CORNWALL.

72-73   John SUTTON, clerk, *v.* Margaret LYMFORD, Thomas GUDFEYLOWE, and Joan his wife.
Messuages and lands in Rushton Spencer and Cloudwall (*cf.* the Cloud, a hill partly in Rushton) held of the manor of Rushton by Richard Sutton, deceased, grandfather of complainant. (Henry VIII or Edward VI.)   STAFFORD.

74   John SWEYN *v.* Robert SAVAGE, husbandman.
Refusal to complete a sale of land in Reymerston. (Henry VIII or Edward VI.)   NORFOLK.

75-77   William SYGGAR, Agas his wife, Robert BRAYE and Joan his wife *v.* John A BROKE of Litlington.
Manor of Awke Hall and land and rent in Eastbourne late of John Soopar and Margaret his wife, deceased, grandparents of the female complainants. *Faded.* (Henry VIII or Edward VI.)   SUSSEX.

78   Alice SYMONDES *v.* Richard HALLESWYLL of Dartmouth, merchant.
Wine called bastard late of Robert Symondes of Barnstaple, merchant, deceased, husband of complainant. *See File* 442, *No.* 2. (*Cir.* 1515-1518).   DEVON.

79-80   Alson SYMONS, widow, *v.* John ADAM.
Detention of deeds relating to a messuage and land in Fremington. (Henry VIII or Edward VI.)   DEVON.

81   Richard SACHEVERELL, knight, *v.* William SEYGRAVE.
Detention of deeds relating to messuages and land in Frisby, Grimston and Wartnaby. (After 1513?)   LEICESTER.

82   Christopher SLYNGESBY, executor of Robert Knaresburghe, vicar of Floore, *v.* Richard MAYHOO of Tavistock, co. Devon, Margaret his wife, and Henry HAMLYN, citizen of Exeter.
Money due from Thomas Atkynson, citizen and barber-surgeon of London, deceased, for sheep taken from the said vicar for King Henry VII. (After 1515?)   NORTHAMPTON, DEVON.

83   Thomas SAUNDERS and others, feoffees to uses, *v.* Robert ANNABLE.
Messuage and land in Penn formerly bought of Cicely Sexton to find a priest with the profits to sing in the church of Amersham. (1523-1547.)   BUCKINGHAM.

84   Thomas SMYTH.
Petition to examine witnesses concerning the manor of Bradwell by Coggeshall, and messuages, land and rent in Bradwell, Pattiswick, Stisted, Rivenhall, Cressing (Kyrsyng) and Coggeshall whence complainant was commanded to avoid by Henry [Bourchier], earl of Essex. *Pedigree given.* (After 1528.)   ESSEX.

85   William STERKY and Maud his wife, granddaughter and heir of Richard Reve of Colnbrook, *v.* Joan REVE.
Detention of deeds relating to a messuage and land in Horton, Wraysbury, and Langley. *Mutilated. See File* 678, *No.* 30. (*Cir.* 1529-1532.)   BUCKINGHAM.

86-87   Edmund SADLER *v.* Hugh, prior of HUNTINGDON.
Sale of peas. *Mutilated.* (1532-1538.)   HUNTINGDON.

88 Henry SCROPE v. James STRANGWYS and others, feoffees to uses, etc.
Manors of Scruton and Kylvyngton, etc., of the bequest of John, lord Scrope. *Damaged.* (After 1533.) [YORK.]

89 Elizabeth SWYLLINGTON v. [Richard NEELE, esquire?].
Manor of Keythorp. *Mutilated. See File* 891, *No.* 61. (After 1533.) LEICESTER.

90 John SEYNTHILL, gentleman, v. the mayor of Exeter, and Humphrey BARNEHOWSE.
Action for time payable as price of a gelding and camlet which proved to be of bad quality. *Certiorari and subpœna.* (1536–1547.) DEVON.

91 The prior of St. Thomas's by STAFFORD v. James WYLSON and Margaret his wife, executrix, and late the wife of Thomas Robens.
Burgages and other lands in Stafford and goods of John Ashebye, deceased, whose executor was the said Robens. (Before 1539.) STAFFORD.

92–93 Richard STANLEY of Uttoxeter v. John JOHNSON of Bagot's Bromley (in Abbot's Bromley).
Messuage and land in Abbot's Bromley pledged to defendant. (1539–1547.) STAFFORD.

94 John STANLOWE of Coningsby, gentleman, v. Robert STANLOWE, his elder brother.
Lands in Hagworthingham of the grant of William Stanlowe of Stakeford, gentleman, deceased, father of both parties. (After 1539.) LINCOLN.

95–98 Richard SPYTTLE v. Hugh SPYTTLE.
Share of the manor of Lutley and land demised by Giles Strangways, knight, to Humphrey Spyttyll, deceased, father of both parties. (1540–1553.) [WORCESTER or STAFFORD.]

99 William STONE of Cirencester, tanner, v. Walter ROSE of Burford, shoemaker.
Debt for hides, the bond for which has been burnt. D.VI, 71. (1543?–1551.)
 GLOUCESTER, OXFORD.

100 Alice SAUNDERS v. Bertin HASELRYGE, esquire, her kinsman.
(Copy of *File* 1157, *No.* 1.) (1544–1547.) LEICESTER.

101 William SEWSTER v. Elizabeth, late the wife of John SEWSTER, gentleman, and John BYLL, gentleman.
Messuages and land in Ashwell acquired of Agnes Gascoyne. (Edward VI.) HERTS.

102–103 John STROBRYGGE v. John DRAKE of Musbury, esquire.
Refusal to complete a sale of a messuage called Hobertayn and other lands (*described.*) (Edward VI.)
 DEVON.

104–105 William SYNG and others v. John and William GELYS.
(Continuation of *File* 1269, *No.* 61.) (1547–1551.) DEVON.

106 Ralph SHERMAN, yeoman of the Ewry, v. James CANE.
Messuage and land at Tyseley in Tarporley, late belonging to ' Sturreis ' Chantry in St. Mary's, Shrewsbury. *See File* 1265, *No.* 29. (1549–1553.) CHESTER.

107–108 Ralph SHERMAN v. Maud HOUGHSLEY.
Do. (Tiresford). *Bill wanting.* (After 1535.) CHESTER.

109–110 William STANLEY, knight, v. Richard BARTIE (Bartue), esquire, and Katherine, duchess of SUFFOLK, his wife.
Plate, jewels, household stuff and horses, late of Charles [Brandon], duke of [Suffolk], deceased, grandfather of complainant and former husband of the said Katherine. (1550–1553.) ———

111–112 John SHERWELL v. Dorothy NO(W)ELL.
(Continuation of *File* 1315, *No.* 25.) (1551–3.) STAFFORD.

113–115 Robert SALYSBURYE, parson of Trotterscliffe, v. Thomas COWPER.
Award of a commission in a former suit for tithes. (1553–5.) KENT.

116–119 John, son of Stephen SAMPSON and of Joan his wife, and Benett and Ellen, children of John DELISTER and of Marian his wife, v. Nicholas TOLKYN (Tokkyn) and Juliana his wife, daughter and heir of William Brice.
Messuages and appurtenances in Rye, late of John Eston, deceased, brother of the said Joan and Marian. (Continuation of *File* 1315, *Nos.* 2–3.) (1553–4.) SUSSEX.

120–122 Edward SLEGGE of Comberton v. John HENNEGGE and others.
Price of corn, the bond for which is lost. (1553–4.) CAMBRIDGE.

123–126 Robert SMYTHE of Stepney, co. Essex (*sic.*), v. John RYVER and Margaret his wife.
Messuages and lands in Chattisham, Hintlesham, and Washbrook, late of John Bennet, deceased, grandfather of the said Robert and Margaret. (1553–4.) SUFFOLK.

127 John, son and heir of Richard SPENSER of Winchester, clothier, v. John GODFREY of the same, mercer.
Price of a tenement in the Pentice at Winchester sold by John Pedle of Hungerford, stepfather of complainant. (1553–4.) HANTS.

128–131 John SWAYNE of Blandford Forum, merchant, v. Anne and John CHETTELL.
Lands in Blandford St. Mary and Blandford Forum awarded to John Jobourne, late prior of Sheen, in a suit in this court against Henry Chettell. *Mutilated.* (1553–8.) DORSET.

132–133 John STORIE, LL.D., master in Chancery, v. John HAWLES (Hollis) of Wimborne, co. Dorset, Richard HYGGINS, and . . . his wife.
Farm of West Harnham and land there of the demise of John Bigges, late master of the college of St. Nicholas by the Valley in Salisbury, and the scholars thereof. *Mutilated.* (1554–8.) WILTS.

134 John STORYE, LL.D., and Thomas LEVYEN, clerk, v. John COXE (Cockes) of London, salter.
Debt to Richard Bowreman, clerk, deceased, of whose goods complainants are administrators. *Mutilated.* (1554–8.) LONDON.

135   Alexander SYMPSON of Skarthe (*i.e.* Scartho?), smith, *v.* Richard, William and Thomas COURTES, executors of Simon Marchant, late vicar of Skarthe.
Legacy in recompense for false charges in the Duchy court of Lancaster and elsewhere. (1554–8.)
LINCOLN·

136–138 Peter STRETCHE of Exeter, goldsmith, and William his son, *v.* John GREYNFYLDE of the same, esquire.
Farm of Cowley in Brampford Speke of the demise of Thomas [Grey], late marquis of Dorset. (1555–6.)
DEVON.

FILE 1514.

1   Thomas TATE, Alice his wife, John POERS and Margery his wife *v.* William BELGRAVE, Joan his wife, late the wife of John Ryvell, feoffee to uses, and others.
Messuages in Derby, late of William Fasemon, deceased, father of the female complainants. *See File* 9, *No.* 111. (*Cir.* 1431–1443.)
DERBY.

2   John TAYLOUR of London, girdler, *v.* the mayor and sheriffs of LONDON.
Action by William Martyn of London, girdler, and John Vanderbeson for price of goods compounded for. *Certiorari. Mutilated.*
LONDON.

3   Robert TENAUNT and Margaret his wife *v.* John PEKERYNG, gentleman, and William FITZWILLIAM of Lincoln, esquire, feoffees to uses.
Legacy of Thomas Pekeryng of London, esquire, father of the said Margaret.
YORK, LINCOLN.

4   John TETYSHALE *v.* Alice DAUTRE.
Lands in Herringfleet late of John Tetyshale, deceased, cousin of complainant and son of defendant.
SUFFOLK.

5   Ralph, son of Henry THORP, *v.* William ROUS.
Annuity promised out of the manor of Chaldefeld to Margaret, the repudiated wife of defendant and sister of complainant.
[WILTS.]

6   William TYLER and Margery his wife, dwelling in the borough of Southwark, *v.* the sheriffs of LONDON.
Action of trespass by Thomas Rowte, an officer in London, to prevent them from proceeding on an indictment for causing the death of their child. *Corpus cum causa.*
LONDON.

7   John TAILLOUR *alias* Clerke and Sibell his wife, executrix and late the wife of Thomas Cutler, *v.* John WOOD and Cristyne (Christean) his wife, executrix and late the wife of Thomas Bowne.
Money entrusted to the said Bowne to find a priest to sing for the soul of Joan Cutler, whose executor was the said Thomas Cutler. (Henry VII or VIII.)
——

8   Philip TAILLOUR *v.* the mayor and sheriffs of LONDON.
Action by John Hamond for price of sheep, which he claims before delivery. *Certiorari.* Henry VII or later.)
LONDON.

9   Richard TERRE of Steeple Claydon *v.* Richard TERRE of Westbury.
Cottage and land in Westbury late of Thomas Terre, deceased, father of complainant. *Mutilated.* (Henry VII or later.)
BUCKINGHAM.

10   Thomas TREVETHAN *v.* Stephen POLWHYLL.
Messuages, lands and rent in Padstow, Bodmin, St. Kew and Withiel, formerly of Walter Trevethan. *Commission. Cancelled.* (Henry VII or later.)
CORNWALL.

11   . . . er TREYANE *v.* Otone TREYANE and others, executors of George Treyane.
Detention of deeds. *Mutilated.* (Henry VII or later.)

12–14   Martin TROTT, yeoman, *v.* Richard and Robert CRAGGE.
Wrongful occupation of a messuage in Tiverton of the demise of Humphrey Predyox, esquire, and of furniture (*schedule given*). (Henry VII or later.)
DEVON.

15   John TURNOUR of Sandwich *v.* John WYNGATE.
Beans entrusted to complainant by Thomas Butler and falsely claimed by defendant as his purchase. (Henry VII or later.)
KENT.

16   Nicholas TYRRY *v.* Richard . . . and Thomas EVERARD of Glemsford, cloth-makers.
Price of 8,115 hoops. *Faded.* (Henry VII or later.)
SUFFOLK.

17   Henry TUDENHAM and John FYNCHAM *v.* John FYST of Bury.
Bond given on behalf of Richard, son of defendant, admitted to the fellowship of the Middle Temple at the request of William [Cadington], abbot of Bury. (After 1497.)
SUFFOLK.

18–20   Harry THORNEY and others, kinsmen and heirs of William Wynde, *v.* Richard BERETH.
Detention of deeds relating to land in Gamlingay. *Bill mutilated. See File* 246, *No.* 12. (1500–1501.)
[CAMBRIDGE.]

21   Christopher TRAVERS, administrator of the goods of Robert Norton, knight, deceased, *v.* William JONES.
Messuage and land called Pynbery. (1501–1515.)
GLOUCESTER.

22–24   William, prior of THOBY, and John REDE, canon thereof, *v.* William WHYTE of London, barber.
Plate pledged for a debt of Agnes, sister of the said John, since repaid. (The prior's name is omitted from the answer.) (1504–9.)
ESSEX.

25   John TIGO *v.* Richard CRYBBE.
Refusal to complete a sale of a messuage and land in King's Lynn (Lenn Bysshopp.) (*Cir.* 1504–1515?)
NORFOLK.

26   Robert TALINGE *v.* Henry STANNARD.
Crown debt of Thomas Sanderson, knight, deceased, of whose goods defendant is administrator.
Faded. (Henry VIII.)

27   William TOMPSON, baker, *v.* the mayor and sheriffs of LONDON.
Action of debt by John Grene of Navestock Hall, yeoman, and Ralph Dyer, husbandman. *Corpus cum causa.* (Henry VIII or later.)   LONDON, ESSEX.

28   Robert TRENER *v.* John . . .
Detention of deeds relating to tenements in Trereif, Bethkylae (both in Madron), Tremethek and Tregofora. *Mutilated.* (Henry VIII or Edward VI.)   CORNWALL.

29   Richard TUTTESHAM of Milton by Gravesend and Thomas AUSTEN of Milton by Sittingbourne, clerks, *v.* Katharine CHICHE.
Action on a bond but slightly infringed by Thomas Tutteshame, gentleman, whose executors complainants are. *Paper copy.* (Henry VIII.)   KENT.

30   John T . . . *v.* John COURTYS, [feoffee to uses].
Tenements in Lostwithiell and elsewhere. *Mutilated.* (Henry VIII or Edward VI.) [CORNWALL.]

31   John TWYTT of London, ironmonger, *v.* Roger BASING, late of London, merchant-tailor.
Money lent to defendant ' without any gaynes thereof only of love,' and partly repaid in woad and malmsey. *Endorsed* Whitehall. (*Cir.* 1518–1529?)   LONDON.

32   Thomas son of Elizabeth TATNELL *v.* William GRANGE.
Detention of deeds relating to a tenement acquired of defendant in Aston Clinton. *Faded.* (1533.)   BUCKINGHAM.

33   George TERRILL and Joan his wife, daughter and heir of Ralph Archlo of Buckingham, *v.* Thomas PACKINGTON, knight.
Detention of deeds relating to the manor of Croudwell. (*Cir.* 1553.)*   BUCKINGHAM.

34–36   Robert TOPP of Manston, husbandman, *v.* John BRIGHT and Elizabeth his wife, executrix and late the wife of Richard Horder of Shaftesbury, mercer.
Loan. *See File* 1271, *No.* 45. (1554–8.)   DORSET.

37–38   Edmund TRAFFORD of Trafford, co. Lancaster, esquire, *v.* Alice BYBBY, James MASEY (Massie) and others, tenants of lands in Sale and Godley.
Rents of the said lands pledged for a debt by Hamlet Massye, esquire, deceased. (1554–8.)   CHESTER.

39   The same *v.* Ralph CHADWYCKE and others.
Lands in Godley, Newton, Matley, Walton and Sale of the grant of the same Hamlet. (1554–8.)   CHESTER.

40–42   Richard TRAFFORD *v.* Robert HOLLYNGWORTHE and Agnes his wife.
(Continuation of File 1386, No. 49.) (1554–5.)   LEICESTER.

43   Philip TOWNSEND *v.* Jerome BLYTH.
(Copy of File 1478, No. 38.) (1556–8.)   DERBY.

FILE 1515.

1–2   Paul TAVERNER *v.* Francis STRADLYNG and Maude, late the wife of Thomas JUBBES.
Garden, lodge and dovecote in Back Lane by Lawford Gate, Bristol, demised to the said Thomas at will as a fee by William Taverner, deceased, uncle of complainant. (Henry VII or later.)   GLOUCESTER.

3–4   Joan TOKER, executrix of Henry Franke, ' cytyzen and of London grocer,' *v.* Margaret, late the wife of William USSHER of London, haberdasher, and William DALTON.
Debt of the said William Ussher, whose executors defendants are. (Henry VII or later.) LONDON.

5   William TYFFE of Walton-on-Thames *v.* the bailiffs of KINGSTON.
Action by John Lee for purchase of a ' hole pece of hopys ' sold by Robert Muswell in mistake for his own. *Certiorari.* (Henry VII or later.)   SURREY.

6   John TAILLOUR of Gloucester, mercer, *v.* the mayor and sheriffs of LONDON.
Action by Humphrey Lewes, citizen and mercer of London, for a debt partly paid and wholly tendered. *Certiorari.* (Henry VIII or Edward VI.)   LONDON.

7   John TAYLOUR, executor of Geoffrey Taylour, *v.* John SALMON.
Detention of deeds relating to a messuage, a house (*sic*) and horse-mil in Beccles. (Henry VIII or Edward VI.)   SUFFOLK.

8–9   George, son and heir of Richard TOMSON, *v.* William MAGELYN of Hole (*cf.* Bell Hole in Kirton-in-Holland?), gentleman.
Detention of deeds relating to a messuage in Kirton [-in-Holland?] (Henry VIII or Edward VI.)   LINCOLN.

10–11   Peter, son and heir of William TOPPE, *v.* Richard (William) BAUNFELD, John MOLLE, and others.
Tenement in the said Baunfeld's manor of North Molton. (Henry VIII or Edward VI.)   DEVON.

12–13   Thomas TREHANOK *v.* John TREFFRY ' de Seynt Madron,' son and heir of John Treffry.
Detention and forgery of deeds relating to a messuage and land at Tregwelan (*i.e.* Tregallan?) in Lanivet. (Henry VIII or Edward VI.)   CORNWALL.

14–15   Richard, son and heir of Thomas TREVOYN (Trevoan) *v.* Paul, son and heir of Thomas TRENOWITH.
Detention of deeds relating to land in Padstow and St. . . . . (Henry VIII or Edward VI.)   CORNWALL.

---

* The king's court is asked for, but Sir Thomas Packington was knighted by Queen Mary.

16–17   Hugh TUBBE *v.* John MEKELEY and Peter KNYGHT.
Rent, late of John **Tubbe**, deceased, father of complainant, issuing from land in Clifton.   (Henry VHI or Edward VI.)   NOTTS.

18   Thomas TYLMAN *v.* Alice DEVOREUX, executrix of John Devoreux of London.
.Detention of deeds relating to lands in Maidstone and Pluckley of the bequest of William Tylman, brother of complainant.   (Henry VIII of Edward VI.)   KENT.

19–21   John TOOKE, gentleman, *v.* Thomas BERYE and Denise his wife, executrix and late the wife of Thomas a Dele of Wye.
Detention of deeds relating to land in Boughton Aluph, Wye and Godmersham, formerly of Thomas a Dele of Godmersham.   (1530.)   KENT.

22   Elizabeth late the wife of William TEY *v.* John TEY his brother, and Henry [BOURCHIER], earl of Essex.
Action on a bond for conveyance of the keepership of Croydon park, executed when William was of unsound mind.   (Before 1540.)   SURREY.

23–24   Robert TYDERLEIGH of Upton Knoyle *v.* Elizabeth FITZJAMES.
Rent charged on defendant's half of the manor of Syles in Henstridge (Selyshemershe) by William More, esquire.   (After 1539.)   SOMERSET, DORSET.

25   John THOMSON, Austin friar of London, *v.* William WETHERALL, provincial of his order.
Exclusion of complainant from his chamber for failure to pay for a sermon which he had been excused in consideration of making a pulpit.   (Before 1541.)   LONDON.

26   Richard TUCK, gentleman, *v.* John LAURENS.
Failure to complete a lease of the manor of Solton in West Cliffe.   (After 1544.)   KENT.

27–29   Lionel TALMAGE *v.* Richard, son of Edmund BOKKYNGE, esquire.
Sale of messuages and land in Helmingham.   *Faded.*   (*Cir.* 1547–1551?)   SUFFOLK.

30–31.   Robert TEMŸS, esquire, *v.* William POYNTER, Thomas Bon, and Philip CLERK.
The Priest House and St. George's Hall in Weymouth, claimed by the said Clerk on behalf of the town.   (Edward VI.)   DORSET.

32–33   Robert TOKER of the parish (*sic*) of Dalwood *v.* Richard WARRE, esquire, and Richard WHYTMORE.
Tenement in the manor of Dalwood of the demise of Richard Warre, knight, deceased, grandfather of the said Richard.   (Edward VI.)   DORSET.

34–35   John TOWNELL, husbandman, and Joan his wife *v.* Oliver PERCYVALL.
Land in Holbrooke late of John Ingram, deceased, father of the said Joan.   (Edward VI.)   SUFFOLK.

36–37   Ermynell, late the wife of Robert THURSTON, and John THURSTON, executors of the said Robert, *v.* Richard TWYCHILL.
Reviver of a suit for the grange of Nether Broughton and Broughton Wood of the demise of the late abbot and convent of Croxton.   (1547–1558.)   LEICESTER.

FILE 1516.

1   Henry VERN . . . *v.* Richard LUDLOWE, knight.
Settlement of all defendant's lands, except some in Islington and elsewhere on Anne and Alice, his kinswomen and heirs apparent at their marriage with Thomas and Humphrey, sons of complainant.   *Mutilated.*   MIDDLESEX. SALOP.

2   . . . and . . . de VIVALDIS, merchants of Genoa, *v.* the sheriffs of LONDON.
Action by Sir Robert . . . on a bond for delivery of a Papal bull.   *Corpus cum causa.   Damaged.*   LONDON.

3–4   Thomas VYALL and Margaret his wife, *v.* John PARKER and Jane his wife.
Detention of deeds relating to lands in Poplar.   *See File* 230, *No.* 28.   (1502.)   MIDDLESEX.

5–6   Humphrey VYSE *v.* Thomas SKRYMSHER, son-in-law of Michael Swynnerton, and others.
Messuages and lands, late of John Vyse, deceased, grandfather of complainant.   *Mutilated.*   (Henry VIII or Edward VI.)   STAFFORD.

7   Anne, late the wife of John [de VERE], earl of Oxford, *v.* Robert VERNE, of Oxford University.
Deer-stealing in the parish of Lavenham (Laneham)   (1528.)   SUFFOLK.

8   George VEER, knight, and Margaret his wife, *v.* Thomas CHEYNEY, knight.
Detention of deeds relating to lands in Irthlingborough, Wellingborough, Irchester and Great and Little Addington, late of Elizabeth Cheyney, deceased, wife of defendant, whose heir the said Margaret is.   *Pedigree given.   See File* 587, *No.* 39.   (Before 1529.)   NORTHAMPTON.

9–11   Thomas VILLERS of Eaton, gentleman, *v.* Randall WOOD.
Messuage called the *Bell* in the Swine Market, Leicester, late of Alexander Vyllers, deceased, father of complainant.   (After 1533.)   LEICESTER.

12   John WACE, gentleman.
Commission to examine witnesses as to lands in Great Wycombe, Bishopston, Hartwell, Beaconsfield, Agmondesham, Chigwell and Finsbury Fields.   (Henry VII or later.)
BUCKS. HERTS. ESSEX. MIDDLESEX.

13   Henry, grandson and heir of Robert WARDE, *v.* Miles HOBARD.
Manor of Saham's in Kirby Bedon (Sames) and two thirds of the advowson of the church of Kirby Bedon pledged to James Hobard, knight, deceased, and held with other manors and lands in Kirby Bedon, Bramerton, Rockland, Framingham, Surlingham and Witchingham.   (Henry VII or later.)   NORFOLK.

14   Joan WEBSTER and John her son, *v.* Andrew BUG and others, feoffees to uses.
Lands and weirs in Barraway and Soham, late of Isabel Hede, deceased. (Henry VII or later.)
         CAMBRIDGE.

15   John WHITTON *v.* the mayor and sheriffs of CANTERBURY.
Action by . . . Cornewell for fraud in the sale of orchell. *Certiorari.* (Henry VII or later.)
         KENT.

16–19   Anthony WYNGFYLD, knight, and Elizabeth his wife, *v.* John FITZSOURS.
Manor of Haymund Froome and lands in Byshoppes Froome, late of Dame Margaret Vere. (Henry VII or later.)   HERTFORD (*i.e.* HEREFORD.)

20   Anthony WAKEMAN *v.* Richard WAKEMAN, of Sandhurst, co. Berks, yeoman.
Land in Worplesdon, late of Rose Heth, deceased, grandmother of complainant. (Henry VIII or Edward VI.)   SURREY.

21   John WALKER of Castern, gentleman, *v.* Agnes WALKER.
Detention of deeds relating to lands of John Walker, deceased, brother of complainant and husband of defendant. (Henry VIII or later.)   STAFFORD.

22   William WARMENTON and Margaret his wife, *v.* Humphrey FORTESCU and Mynson (*sic*) his wife.
Loan to John Wolff, deceased, brother of the said Margaret and former husband of the said Mynson. *Mutilated.* (Henry VIII or later.)   CORNWALL.

23–24   Henry WATTES and Joan his wife, executrix of Thomas Palmer, *v.* John BOSTON, servant of the said Thomas.
Goods of the said Thomas in the Inner Temple. (Henry VIII or Edward VI.)   LONDON.

25   John, son and heir of Richard WEBBE, *v.* Richard THOMAS.
Detention of deeds relating to land in Ticehurst. (Henry VIII or Edward VI.)   SUSSEX.

26–28   Martin WILCOCKES of Elmyngton (*i.e.* Edmonton?), co. Middlesex, yeoman, *v.* Maude STANFELD and others.
Messuages, cottages and land in Snydale, Normanton, Wrangbrook (near Hemsworth) and Kirkby, formerly of Christopher Wilcokes and Margaret his wife, grandparents of complainant. (Henry VIII or Edward VI.)   YORK.

29–30   Henry WILLIAMSON of London, clothworker, *v.* Henry TYLER of Sutton, son and heir of Richard Tyler.
House and garden in Southchurch, late of Thomas Williamson, clerk, deceased, uncle of complainant. (Henry VIII or Edward VI.)   ESSEX.

31–34   Alice, late the wife of Richard WOLLESTON, and formerly of Robert Meyde, *v.* Thomas CHECCHELEY, esquire, and Lawrence PYERS.
Rent reserved on a loan of complainant's dower lands in Wendy, Arrington and Croydon. *Replication wanting.* (Henry VIII or Edward VI.)   CAMBRIDGE.

35   Thomas WOMBWELL *v.* Margery JAMYS, executrix of Thomas Fane.
Profits of lands in Bidborough, Tonbridge, Speldhurst and Penshurst, granted on condition of an exchange which was not carried out. (Henry VIII or Edward VI.)   KENT.

36   Katharine and Elizabeth WYLBEY, William SYGO, and Dorothy his wife, *v.* Harry FERMOUR of East Barsham, gentleman.
Detention of deeds relating to the manor of Wilbeys and Pernow (Pernel) Hall in Hindringham, Avenell in Gunthorp and Wilbeys in Field Dalling, and lands there and in Bale, Sharrington, Barningham, Thursford and Great Snoring, late of Thomas Wilbey, deceased father of the female complainants. (Henry VIII or Edward VI.)   NORFOLK.

37–38   Henry WELBYE *v.* John HALL and Thomas WELBY.
Manor of Halstead (in Stixwould), late of Thomas Welbye, esquire, deceased, father-in-law of the said Hall. *Bill mutilated.* (1535–1547.)   LINCOLN.

39–40   Thomas, grandson and heir of Edward WARCOPP and of Agnes his wife, *v.* Lancelot, son and heir of Thomas LATON of Sexhow, esquire.
Seizure of deeds relating to land in Orton. *See File* 1276, *No.* 12. (After 1535.)   WESTMORLAND.

41   Ambrose WOLLEY of London, grocer, *v.* Oswald WYLLESTROPE, knight.
Attempts by defendant to invalidate his own title to the manor of Wilstrop sold to complainant. *See File* 1084, *No.* 44. (After 1538.)   YORK.

42–46   The dean and chapter of WELLS *v.* Richard NETHERWAYE (Nethewey, Wethwaye), parson of Wraxall.
Reviver of a suit for an annuity against Edmund Kenne, late parson (*File* 1092, *No.* 25.) (1541–1553.)   SOMERSET.

47–48   William WYNE of Bromsgrove in Worcester, husbandman, *v.* Edward BURTON, gentleman.
Messuage and ' noke ' of land in Withington of the demise of Thomas Blakeway, priest. (1541–1547.)   SALOP.

49   Leonard WHYTE of Pendennis, yeoman, *v.* Oliver HYDE of Abingdon, co. Berks, esquire, and Thomasyn his wife, late the wife of John Kykwyche, esquire.
Lease of a messuage and land at Catchfrench and Trevreng in St. Germans. (1546–7)   CORNWALL.

50–52   Ralph WALLER and Mary his wife, executrix of Geoffrey Cobbe of Gayton, *v.* John, son and heir of Christopher JENNEY, knight.
Bond for price of a capital messuage in Lynn, bought of John Stede. *Answer wanting.* (Edward VI.)   NORFOLK.

53–57   Ralph WARYNE, *v.* Thomas TRAFORD and others.
(Continuation of File 1282, No. 23.) (1547–1551.)   CHESTER.

58   John WOLCOTE of the county of the city of Exeter *v.* Richard MEYGER and Alice his wife, executrix and late the wife of John Hyll.
Detention of goods and deeds relating to pasture in Moretonhampstead. (After 1547.)   DEVON.

59–62   Robert WALTER and Richard, his son, *v.* Gabriel PLEDALL, esquire, surveyor of the manor of Wexcombe in Great Bedwyn (Westcombe), and Griffith CURTEYS, (Courties), steward.
Processing a false presentment of bondage (1554–8)   WILTSHIRE.

63   William WITTMELL *v.* Thomas BROTHURST of Heath Charnock, yeoman.
Detention of deeds. (1554–8.)   LANCASTER

FILE 1517.

1   Parnell WADLEY and others *v.* John [?BRA]MPTON and others.
(Duplicate of File 1481, No. 6?). *Much damaged.* (Shortly before 1558?)   [SALOP.]

2   Thomas WODYNGTON *v.* Thomas GROTT, priest (' preest '), and William PERSON, feoffees to uses.
Messuages and land in Ludlow bought of William Colwall.   SALOP.

3   Bartholomew WALE, haberdasher of London, *v.* the mayor and sheriffs of LONDON.
Action by Thomas Sonnyf for plate pledged by Reynold W[est?]. *Certiorari. Damaged.* (Henry VII or later.)   LONDON.

4   John WATSON *v.* Anne MERYNG and Robert SMYTH.
Tenement in Swanwick of the demise of Joan Ormond. *Mutilated.* (Henry VII or later.)   DERBY.

5   John WATTES *v.* Margaret BOORN.
Detention of deeds relating to land in Worstead. (Henry VII or later.)   NORFOLK.

6–7   John WYKES and Jane his wife *v.* Thomas OLYVER.
Detention of deeds relating to land in Kingston Seymour late of Robert Holbrooke, deceased, father-in-law of the said John and Thomas. (Henry VII or later.)   SOMERSET.

8   John WACE *v.* Nicholas BAXSTER.
Detention of deeds relating to a messuage in Bodney. *See File* 181, *No.* 59. (1486–1515.)   NORFOLK.

9–12   William WOODY and Elizabeth his wife, aunt and heir of Richard Clerk, *v.* John AWOODE and Henry DUFFELD of Estgre[nstede?], feoffee to his uses.
Messuage, land and rent in Croydon late of Alice, mother of the said Elizabeth. *Mutilated. See Files* 369, *No.* 30; 375, *No.* 40. (1504–1515.)   SURREY.

13–14   William WEVER of Shrewsbury, shoemaker, *v.* Edward MYNTON.
Refusal to complete a sale of a tenement in Collam Street, Shrewsbury, and waste. (Henry VIII or Edward VI.)   SALOP.

15–16   William WILLYES (Wellyes) *v.* William FRANKLEYN, son-in-law of Thomas Lewyn and of Maud his wife.
Detention of deeds relating to land in East Mallow. (Henry VIII or Edward VI.)   BERKS.

17–18   John WRENNE *v.* Thomas TOWE.
Detention of deeds relating to lands in Ryarsh. (Defendant pleads that he was not to give them up till the settlement of a dispute with Thomas Lyndale.) (Henry VIII or Edward VI.)   KENT.

19–21   Thomas WILLYS *v.* Robert OSBOURN, feoffee to uses.
Messuage in Norwich late of William Willys, deceased, father of complainant. (1515?) NORFOLK.

22   Edmund, son of Harry WEKES, deceased, *v.* Walter HARRY and Chrystyan his wife.
Refusal to complete a sale of a messuage in Bradworthy. *Decayed.* (After 1529.)   DEVON.

23–25   Francis WYTHE, an infant, grandson and heir of Thomas Wythe, *v.* Thomas RYCK-THORNE of Bobbington, co. Stafford, his stepfather and guardian.
Detention of deeds and profits of a messuage, land, ' salt fates and wallynges,' etc. (*described*) in Hampton Lovett and Droitwich, and erasure of the entry of complainant's birth from the ' church booke ' of Woodall. *Mutilated. See File* 917, *No.* 60. (After 1532.)   WORCESTER.

26   George WYLLOUGHBY and Anne his wife, late the wife of Thomas Lytylton, *v.* Walter WELSHE.
Messuages called ' Kynges' House ' and ' Clerkes House,' land, a water mill, fisheries in the lord's water of Avon, etc., in Elmley Castle and elsewhere. *Faded.* (1535–1547.)   WORCESTER.

27–28   Richard WETHECOMB of Northill, husbandman, *v.* William LUCAS of Northill, husbandman, son of Roger Lucas and of Margaret his wife, and William LUCAS the younger, husbandman, a minor.
Lands in Lewannick bought of Thomas Spore, esquire. (1545–8?)   CORNWALL.

29   Richard . . . RA . . . and Edward WHITCHYRCHE of London, haberdasher, *v.* the mayor and sheriffs of LONDON, and Thomas DONNE.
Action on a bond for a debt already paid to John Mayller. *Certiorari. Mutilated.* (Edward VI?)   LONDON.

30   The warden, fellows and scholars of WINCHESTER College *v.* Thomas CULPEPER.
Exchange of the manor and parsonage of Enford for the manors of Harmondsworth, Isleworth, Colthorpe (in Thatcham) and Shaw, and the parsonages of Heston, Isleworth and Hampton, with the advowsons of the vicarages (Defendant also held the manors of Hazleton, Enworthe and Naunton). *Mutilated.* (Edward VI.)   BERKS, MIDDLESEX, GLOUCESTER.

31-32   John WALES and Beatrice his wife v. Isabel KIGS, guardian of Thomas Kigs the younger.
Pasture in Wainfleet, All Hallows, late of Thomas Dalby, deceased, grandfather of the said Beatrice.
(1553-4.)   LINCOLN.

33   Edward, son and heir of John WARCOPP, v. William PRESTCOSSYNGE.
Rent of Rutter Close. (1553-4.)   WESTMORLAND.

34-35   Matthew WARCOPP v. Richard CLEBOURNE and others.
Tithes of Cleburn of the demise of Anthony Smetheson, parson. (1553-4.)   WESTMORLAND.

36-39   John WESTE of London, draper, and Elizabeth his wife v. George FLOWER and Thomas
PENNE.
Land in Stony Stratford late of William Vaughan and Alice his wife, deceased, parents of
complainant. *Mutilated.* D.XIV, 65. (1553-4.)   BUCKINGHAM.

40   William WATSON, citizen and draper of London, v. Cuthbert ELLYSON, mayor of
Newcastle-on-Tyne.
Price of flax. (1554-6.)   NORTHAMPTON.

41   William Feltham and Nicholas Lees, churchwardens of WESTHALL, v. Thomas, son and
heir of Richard DAVYE.
Reviver of a suit for the ' gyldland of Saynct Trynite ' in Westhall (*File* 1395, *No.* 33). (1554-
1558.)   SUFFOLK.

42-44   Robert WEBBE v. William EVERELL, Edmund ABELL and Eleanor his·wife.
(Continuation of File 1483, No. 30.) (1557-8.)   NORTHAMPTON.

FILE 1518.

1   Robert of WALCOTE v. the sheriff of LINCOLN.
Withholding a writ in a matter between complainant and Richard de la Launde.   LINCOLN.

2   Thomas WODYNGTON v. Richard HOCHESON, feoffee to uses.
Messuage, kitchen and garden in Lewisham bought of Robert Stevynson and Agnes his wife, late the
wife of William Marshall of London, tailor.   KENT.

3   Robert WYLLESON, Ellen his wife, William SADELER, Elizabeth his wife, John HAN-
WOOD, and Margaret his wife v. . . . PYKENHAM, clerk, Thomas TYRELL, knight, and
others.
Detention of deeds relating to messuages and land in Rayleigh, late of William Cuttyng, deceased,
father of the female complainants.   ESSEX.

4   Henry WYLLESTHORP, parson of Brafferton and Helperby, v. Thomas DE LE RIVERE,
' swyer.'
Spoil of wood ' growyng in defence ' of complainant's glebe in revenge for swearing the peace against
a felon who took ' zerly clothyng ' of defendant.   YORK.

5   John W . . . of Hambleden, husbandman, v. John WAGG of Turville.
Money entrusted to defendant, and price of barley. *Mutilated.* (After 1447.)   BUCKS.

6-7   John WALKEDEN, clerk, v. John BARFOTE and another.
Action in the name of John Dynham to hinder a suit for lands called Cricket Malherbie. (Henry
VII or later.)   SOMERSET.

8-9   John, son and heir of Richard WALKESTEDE, v. Edward LUSTEDE.
Land at West Betchworth in Dorking pledged to defendant. (Henry VII or later.)   SURREY.

10-11   William WALSHE v. William HUNTELEY.
Messuage, land and fishing in Quaddisley (?) formerly of James Walshe. *Faded.* (Henry VII or
later.)   [GLOUCESTER?]

12-17   Richard WAREN and Joan his wife, late the wife of Thomas Andrewes, and formerly of ——
Lovett, and John HAWES, v. William BERKBY of London, scrivener, and William
ANDREWES.
Messuage and land in Gateley of the bequest of the said Thomas. *Mutilated.* (Henry VII or later.)
                                                                                                                       NORFOLK.

18   John, son and heir of John WHYTE, v. Richard CARLYAN, clerk, and John CARLYAN.
Land in St . . . *Faded.* (Henry VII or later.)   CORNWALL.

19   Nicholas WODEWARD v. Eleanor SAYWARD and John her son.
Detention of deeds relating to land in Bagbere (in Thornbury *or* Little Torrington). (Henry VII
or later.)   DEVON.

20   Robert WORTHYNGTON of Abbot's Bromley, yeoman, v. Robert COKE, feoffee to uses,
and others.
Pasture in the lordship of (Marchington?) late of Robert Worthyngton of Marchington, deceased,
kinsman, and godfather of complainant. (Henry VII or later.)   STAFFORD.

21   Humphrey WALKER, citizen and bell-founder of London, v. the mayor and sheriffs of
LONDON.
Action by John Dalows and Joan his wife on a bond for price of copper used in making a pan for the
lady of [Sion], which was broken. *Corpus cum causa.* *Vacated.* *See File* 376, *No.* 32. (*Cir.* 1504-
1515.)   LONDON.

22   Robert WYE v. GWYLLYM (no surname).
Detention of deeds relating to land at Tregate in Llanrothel (Tregett) bought of John Drayton of
London, grocer. *See File* 375, *No.* 26. (*Cir.* 1504-1515.)   HEREFORD.

23   John Alestre, dean of the college of WARWICK, v. Richard FYSSHER and Richard
HURLEBOT.
Distress on lands in Cotton End, St. Nicholas, Warwick. *See File* 369, *No.* 12. (1505-1515.)
                                                                                                                       WARWICK.

24   Thomas WREWKE v. James, son and heir of Thomas SMERFELD.
Refusal to complete a sale of a messuage and land called Lathewoode in Elham (*i.e.* Ladwood,
now in Acrise?)   (1505 *or* 1529.)   KENT.

25   John WROTH and Isabel his wife v. Robert KYLLYGR[EW] of Wolleston in St. Ives,
gentleman.
Messuages and land at Boyland in St. Ives of the grant of Richard Boyland, deceased, father of the
said Isabel.   *Mutilated.*   (After 1507.)   CORNWALL.

26-27   William WODMANCY v. Robert GREY and Agnes his wife.
Detention of deeds relating to a messuage and land in Brantingham held of the bishop of Durham's
manor of Howden.   (Henry VIII or Edward VI.)   YORK.

28   Henry WRYGHT and Margery his wife v. Hugh KERCHEVER.
Lands in Flawborough and Dalyngton in Orston late of Joan Drury, deceased, mother of the said
Margery.   *Copy.* (Henry VIII or Edward VI.)   NOTTS.

29   Henry WATTES v. Thomas KNYGHT.
Account for cloth (*described*) and land held of the manor of Lambeth.   *Faded.*   (After 1535.)
                                                                                            SURREY.

30-32   Gilbert WILKYNSON of White Roding, co. Essex, son and heir of Jane late the wife of,
John Glyn, v. John SKUDDER, feoffee to uses, Robert KETELWELL of Sutton-at-Hone,
and others.
Tenement (*not described*) acquired of the said Ketelwell. (After 1536.)   KENT.

33   Thomas WOLLFF of St. Mary Cray, co. Kent, v. Richard WOLLFF, his younger brother.
Obtaining from Richard Wollff their father a grant of the reversion of a tenement in Marton on a
surprise of complainant's death. (1543-7.)   CHESTER.

34-36   Guy WADE v. Simon ANDREWES, John, son and heir of John ANDREWES, and
Clement (*sic*) his wife.
Detention of deeds relating to a messuage and land in Great and Little Munden.   (1554-8.)
                                                                                          HERTFORD.

37-40   Thomas, son and heir of John [WEST]BROKE of Langrish (in East Meon) v. Margaret
WESTBROKE,' late the wife of the said John, and formerly of Edward Langrishe.
Claim of dower in Petersfield, Steep, Liss and Prior's Dean in lieu of which the said John made a
bequest of rents.   (1555.)   HANTS.

41   John YELDHAM and Joan his wife, daughter of Thomas Dufhous, late citizen and fishmonger
of London, and of Alice his wife, v. William HANFORD, priest, and others, executors of the
said Alice.
40*l.* in gold bequeathed for an obit in the church of St. Magnus.   LONDON.

42   Richard Harry YONG of Hoxton, ' queuer ' (*i.e.* weaver?), v. William Henry YONG his
brother.
Detention of deeds relating to a messuage and land in Nycoll Fyld in the parish (*sic*) of Hoxton.
                                                                                         MIDDLESEX.

43-46   Edmund YATE v. John Recolver, prior of St. Mary Overies, SOUTHWARK.
Manor and parsonage of Mitcham.   *Decayed.*   (1496-9.)   SURREY.

47-48   John YEATE v. Richard SMYTH.
Detention of deeds relating to messuages and lands in Lympstone and Woodbury.   *See File* 377,
No. 27. (Cir. 1504-1515?)   DEVON.

49   Henry YE[RHAM, vicar of Hempstead?] v. John GALLANT, yeoman, and others.
Vicarage of Hempstead.   *Faded.*   (Cir. 1533-1538?)   NORFOLK.

50-51   John YONGE v. Agnes, late the wife of John MYLLER, and others.
Manor and parsonage of Thornham with the ' shepes coursse and lybertye of the foulde course
and fouldynge ' claimed under a lease of Richard Nixe, late bishop of Norwich.   (1536-1553.)
                                                                                           NORFOLK.

52-53   John YERDE v. John KYLLYGREWE.
Manor of Penroutte.   *Faded.*   (1554-8.)   [CORNWALL?]

FILE 1519.

The Archbishop of Canterbury.
[John Stafford, 1443-1450]

1   [Nicholas] GRENE, vicar of Stanes, v. John PUNCHON.
Bond given to avoid a (suborned) charge of incontinence with defendant's tenant, Christian Rideman.
Mutilated.   [MIDDLESEX.

The Archbishop of York.
[John Kempe, 1426-1432.]

2   John CROSBY of Habrough v. John TOMSON of Killingholme.
Arrest under forged warrants.   (Complainant offers testimony ' under xix seeles of gentelmenes
fraunkleynes and zomen ')   LINCOLN.

3   John GRENE *alias* of Chambre, dwelling with . . . CORNWAILL, knight, v. Stephen
COK and John COLYN of Berkhampstead.
Goods entrusted to defendants on complainant's departure over sea with King Henry V.   HERTS.

[The same, 1450–52.]

4   John PARFYT, servant to [Anne of Gloucester, styled] countess of Hereford, v. William CATTON and John BOTILLER *alias* Ronneham.
Lands of Johanne daughter and heir of William Grigges in East Tilbury, granted to complainant with her wardship by the said countess.   ESSEX.

The cardinal archbishop of York.
[The same.]

5   Roger BRIGGE,. gentleman, prisoner, v. Florence CRASSAGE.
Plate laid in pledge to raise archers for the [late duke] of Somerset ' when the siege was at Averaunce.' (Avranches).   —————
Note.—Either the heading is incorrect, or there was a false report of the duke's death.

6   Stephen CHAPMAN, mayor of Plymouth, v. John PAGE, burgess of Plymouth.
Hindrance in the execution of his duty as mayor by defendant, causing riots daily in the said town.
—*Paper.*   [DEVON.]

The cardinal archbishop of Canterbury.
[The same, 1452–4.]

7   William [de NOTTINGHAM, attorney-general ?] v. Thomas KNOYLE, Robert SAWCER, and John WHIPSTON.
Abduction of John, son and heir of John Leye, a ward of the King, and occupation of his manor of Stanton Fitzherbert and the advowson of its church.   WILTS.

The archbishop of York.
[George Neville, 1465–7.]

8–9   William CHATTOK and Willian BAYBROKE of London, fishmongers, v. Nicholas SCOT of Cley, John HADDELSEY of Hull, merchant, the abbot of RIEVAULX, [Ralph], Lord GREYSTOKE, John SNAYLES, and others.
Purchase of figs and raisins and other goods stolen from the ship *Mary* of Rouen at Sandwich by the crew of the *Carvel of Touke*, a ship of Thomas, Lord Ros, contrary to the statute 32 (*rectius* 31), Henry VI, c. 4.   NORFOLK, KENT.

The bishop of Lincoln.
[Thomas Rotherham ? *or* John Russell ? 1475–1483.]

10   Robert MARHAM v. Thomas SKETE.
Detention of deeds entrusted to defendant relating to complainants' inheritance.   —————

The archbishop of York.
[Thomas Rotherham.]

11–15   William GRYNDALL, clerk, v. William PURCHASE.   —————
Action by defendant on a bond for a debt partly paid.

16   Thomas LAMBROK, citizen and dyer of London, v. John SNORYNG, executor of Margery Wolfe.
Debt of the said Margery for dyeing wool and cloth.   LONDON.

17   Thomas NORYS and Johan his wife, executrix and late the wife of John Fyllo, *alias* Jaket, v. John BAMPTON, nephew and heir of Roger Jones, priest, feoffee to uses.
Messuages and land in the suburbs of Hereford, bought by the said Jaket of Walter, son of James Orchard.   HEREFORD.

18   William son and heir of Nicholas MOLYNEUX v. Thomas [BOURCHIER], cardinal archbishop of Canterbury, William [of WAYNFLETE], bishop of Winchester, William YELVERTON, knight, and Thomas LITTELTON, judge, and William PASTON, feoffees to uses.
A messuage called the ' Boar's Head ' in Southwark, acquired by the said Nicholas to himself and John Winter, deceased, and conveyed to defendants by John Fastolf, knight. *See File* 39, *No.* 233.   SURREY.

19   Thomas PENDE, citizen and draper of London, v. John ERETH, Alice BRICE and others.
Messuages in St. Christopher's represented by the said John to be security for a debt. [*Cf. No.* 23.]   LONDON.

[The same ?]

20   William HERBERD and Margery his wife, daughter and heir of William Medowe, v. Gilbert PALFREMAN and Robert COKKE, feoffees to uses.
Land in Whaplode. *Partly illegible.*   [LINCOLN.]

21   Robert BURTON, gentleman, v. Philip COURTENAY, esquire.
Assaults at Bigbury, A.D. 1459. Threats, embracery of juries, abduction of Robert son of Thomas Towson and William son of William Henston, sergeants-at-law, and illegal distress in Hoton and Noddon.   DEVON.

John [Morton], *archbishop of Canterbury* [1486–93.]

22   Francis CATESBY, and Philippa, his wife, late the wife of Jakes, son and heir of John Edy, v. Robert PYGOTT and John HANCOK, clerk, feoffees to uses, John PYGOTT, and others.
Manors, messuages, and land in Adstock, Oving, Yardley Gobion, Moor-End and elsewhere. *Mutilated. See File* 196, *No.* 84.   BUCKS, NORTHANTS.

23   Thomas PENDE, citizen and draper of London, v. Laurence NORMANTON, and Mary his wife, late the wife of John Erith, and others.
Occupation of messuages in St. Christopher's in contempt of a decree given in No. 19.   LONDON.

The cardinal archbishop of Canterbury.
[John Morton, 1493–1500.]

24   William CARNSUYOWE the elder and Thomas TRESCULERD, cousins and heirs of Humphrey Courteys, v. John RESKYMMER, esquire.
Detention of deeds relating to messuages and land in Treruf, Trewen and Newelyn.   CORNWALL.

25   John COLYNS and Agnes his wife v. Margaret MAYNARD.
Detention of deeds. *Faded.*   _____

26   John HENRY, dean of Hereford, and Thomas LAURENS, vicar of Allensmore, v. Richard DALABERE, knight.
Actions brought by defendant in defiance of a bond for arbitration.   HEREFORD.

27   The prior and friars Carmelites of NOTTINGHAM v. Edmund HOLME, priest.
Detention of a deed of composition between complainants and the parson of St. Nicholas, Nottingham, and occupation of land late of Alice Palmer.   NOTTINGHAM.

28–29   John WHITHER (Wether) and Alice (Alson) his wife v. Edward MORE, and Amy his wife.
A messuage called ' a bruhous ' devised to the said Alice by the will of Peter Pymbarde. (Decree endorsed.) *Partly illegible. Answer wanting.*   [MIDDLESEX ?]

30–31   Robert ONLEY, son of Robert Onley, knight, deceased, v. Richard COKES, clerk, and Thomas CHURCHEMAN, feoffees to uses, and John ONLEY, elder brother of complainant.
Land in Little Park Street, Coventry, bought of Giles Southam by the said Sir Robert.   WARWICK.

32   William BEELL of Lincoln, merchant, v. John WATSON.
Money expended on behalf of the city of Lincoln. *Mutilated.*   LINCOLN.

33–34   John HARRYS of Westerham, husbandman, v. John QUYDDYNGTON of Westerham.
Mortgage of land called ' Shynfield,' and forgery in lieu thereof of a deed granting the fee simple with the inscription therein of a parcel called ' Cadlocks.' *See File 318, No. 57.*   KENT.

The archbishop of Canterbury.
[Morton or Warham; 1486–1493; 1503–1515.]

35   Thomas, abbot of BUCKLAND, v. . . . DUNRYGGE, widow, and Richard DUNRYGGE.
A tenement called Hacche in the manor of Buckland, leased to John Dunrygge, to be surrendered on payment of 40 marks in grains of pure silver of the mines of Beer Ferris and other money, which the said John prevented by obtaining a lease of the said mines. *Partly illegible.*   DEVON.

36–37   Gregory Norwich, prior of BUSHMEAD, v. Peter EFFARD of Lincoln, executor of William Miller of Huntingdon.
Loan to the said William.   _____

38   Thomas Morice, prior of CARMARTHEN, v. the mayor and sheriffs of LONDON.
Action by Thomas Docwra, prior of the Hospital of St. John of Jerusalem in England, on a bond for rent of the commandery of Slebech and its appurtenances (*fully described*) leased to complainant by Robert Evers, prior in Ireland and Thomas Newporte, Turcopolier. *Certiorari.*
PEMBROKE, CARMARTHEN, ETC.

39   [James HUBBERD] attorney-general, v. . . . . .
The manor of Bennington, devised to the Crown by William, son and heir of John Bensted. *Mutilated.*   HERTS.

40   . . . v. Aubert LYVERMERE, feoffee to the use of Thomas . . .
Annuity. *Mutilated.*   LONDON.

41–43   James [. . .] master of St. James' Hospital, ELY, v. Thos. GRAY, knight, and John ROUCLYFF   CAMBRIDGE.

William [Warham], archbishop of Canterbury, 1503–1515.

44   George AGARDE and William BOUGHTON, heirs of Eleanor, sister and heir of Margaret Cecyll, v. Joan MALORY, widow.
Detention of deeds relating to the manor of Grove, messuages and land in Barnwell, etc. *Mutilated.*
WORCESTER, NORTHAMPTON.

45   Edward ARNOLD, Jane his wife, and Michael STRAYLE, v. Rose, executrix and late the wife of Thomas BURDON, father of the said Jane.
Action against the said Thomas by Adam . . ., whose executors the said Jane and Michael are. *Mutilated.*   _____

46–48   John ARUNDELL, knight, receiver of the [Duchy of Cornwall], v. Leonard FRYSKOBALD.
Debt to Ude Gough, late deputy to complainant, and himself indebted to the Crown. *Mutilated, answer wanting.*   CORNWALL.

49   [Maurice, Lord BERKELEY, nephew] and heir of [William], marquis Berkeley, v. ROBERT, prior of [. . .].
Detention of deeds relating to the manors of Epworth, Belton, Ouston, Kirkby Malzeard, Hovingham, Burton-in-Lonsdale, Melton Mowbray, Dalby, Chacombe, Bretby, Linton, Coton, Rosliston, Repton (Rappyngton), Melton, Heydon, Chatteris, and Morrow, late of Elizabeth, duchess of Norfolk, the manors of Goscote, Tatbury, Upton, Charleton, etc. *Mutilated.*
[LINCOLN], YORK, LEICESTER, DERBY, SUSSEX, CAMBRIDGE, GLOUCESTER.

50   John BENTLEY *v.* William THOMLYNSON of York, tanner.
Non-payment of money awarded by an arbitrator. *Mutilated.*   YORK.

51–52   Thomas Yarynton and others, churchwardens of BISHOP'S CLEEVE, *v.* William STILE
and Joan his wife, late the wife of Thomas Pendok.
Profits of a messuage and land in Gotherington under the will of the said Pendok.   GLOUCESTER.

53   Thomas Skewyngton, abbot of BEAULIEU, *v.* Jane, executrix and late the wife of Thomas
LANE.
Money received on behalf of the said abbey from the parsonage of St. Keveran.   [CORNWALL.]

54   Roger BESFORD, merchant of the Staple of Calais, *v.* the mayor, lieutenant, constables,
and fellowship of the said Staple.
Release of Henry Stokes, arrested on an action of account by complainant.   CALAIS.

55   Robert BOTHBY of Hougham, son and heir of Robert Bothby of Treswell, *v.* William
PORTER.
Detention of deeds relating to a messuage and land in Treswell. *See File* 288, *No.* 25.
                                                                                    NOTTINGHAM.

56   Lawrence B . . FFOLD *v.* William GRENEGATE.
Detention of deeds relating to a messuage and land in Newark.   NOTTINGHAM.

57   John COWLERD and Robert CLERKSUN *v.* John and Harry KYNG.
Detention of deeds relating to lands, rents, and services in Beckenham and Lewisham.   *Mutilated.*
See File 295, *No.* 1.   KENT.

58   Thomas Thomson, clerk, master of CHRIST'S COLLEGE, CAMBRIDGE and the fellows
and scholars of the same, *v.* Richard [FOX], bishop of Winchester, William [SMITH], bishop
of Lincoln, John [FISHER], bishop of Rochester, Hugh [OLDHAM], bishop of Exeter,
William KNYVET, Charles SOMERSET and others, knights, Lord HERBERT and others,
feoffees to uses.
The manors of Martock, Kingsbury Regis, Queen Camel, Sampford Peverel, Aller Peverel, Maxey,
Torpel and Bassingbournes in Fordham, the hundreds of Bulstone, Abdick, Horethorne and Halberton, the borough of Sampford Peverel, lands in Fordham and Iseleham, etc., wherewith the said
college was endowed by Margaret, countess of Richmond. *Mutilated.*
                                        SOMERSET, DEVON, NORTHAMPTON, CAMBRIDGE.

59–63   John Mors and John Joce, wardens of the gild of St. Anne, CROSCOMBE, *v.* John CARTER
the elder, Johanne his wife, and John CARTER the younger.
Money promised by William Champion, late warden of the said gild, whose executors the two last-
named defendants are.   SOMERSET.

64   Thomas CASSE *v.* William MALTBY.
Detention of deeds relating to messuages in Boston.   LINCOLN.

65   Robert Wittilbury, alderman of the gild of St. John, CROWLAND, and the brethren of
the same, *v.* John CHEVELEN.
Money lent from the stock of the gild to Robert Elderton, deceased, for which defendant became
surety. (Complainants, not being a corporation, cannot sue at common law.)   LINCOLN.

66   William Palden, clerk, master of the hospital of St. John, COVENTRY, *v.* Aden BERYSFORD
of Fenny Bentley.
Maintenance of Elyn daughter of defendant in the said hospital during 2½ years' probation,
after which she went out into the world. *See File* 286, *No.* 11.   WARWICKSHIRE.

67   Martin DOCWRA, William SYMPULL, and Alice his wife, daughter and co-heir of William
Betley, *v.* Walter SHERWOD.
Detention of deeds relating to messuages a mill and land in Coventry. *Mutilated.* WARWICKSHIRE.

68   John DALLY, clerk, and John LAURENCE, executors of John Baker, *v.* William GOSTEL-
LOWE.
Detention of deeds relating to messuages and land in Ramsey.   HUNTINGDON.

69–72   Richard [FOX], bishop of Winchester, and Humphrey CONYNGESBY, serjeant-at-law,
v. Thomas [FITZALAN], earl of Arundel, George BAYNBRIG, and Vincent FYNCHE.
Wardship of Jane, daughter of Roger Leukenoure, knight, son of Thomas Leukenoure, knight, and
custody of her manors of Trayton, Elsted, Didling and Dempford, etc. *Mutilated.*   SUSSEX.

73   William, abbot of St. Peter's, GLOUCESTER, *v.* Hugh GRENE, clerk, and William CLERK:
Detention of deeds relating to the priory of St. Guthlac, Hereford.   HEREFORD.

74   John Mohon and Thomas Walsh, wardens of the goods, ornaments, and 'catall' belonging
to the parish and parish house of LANTEGLOS, *v.* Thomas LAMELYN and Henry LETHIBY.
Rent due from the parsonage of Lanteglos, leased to defendants by the prior of St. John's, Bridgwater.   CORNWALL.

75–76   Thomas [STANLEY], earl of Derby, *v.* Richard SUTTON, John MORETON, and Thomas
STANLEY, servant of Jane Lady Strange, deceased.
Detention of deeds relating to the manors of Colham, Holborn, Wymington, Bicester, Millington,
Goring, Whichford, Compton, Knockyn, Hampton, Kinton in Great Ness (Nestraunge), Melton,
Overton Madoke and Mayllors, Sturminster Marshall, Bradworthy and Greywell, and Rotherwick,
late of the said Lady Strange.
        MIDDLESEX, BEDFORD, OXON, WARWICK, SALOP, CAMBRIDGE, HUNTS, DORSET, HANTS.

The archbishop of Canterbury.
[William Warham, 1503–1515.]

77   Robert CRESWELL *v.* John and Roger FENWYK.
Detention of deeds relating to lands, rents and services called Bellyngehams in Herst, Neubery
and Framlington.   NORTHUMBERLAND.

78   Robert, prior of ELSHAM v. John CHALENOR, recorder of London.
Rent of the parsonage of Blyton, whereon defendant promised a rebate.   LINCOLN.

[The same?]

79–81   Roger BELINGEHAM, knight, and Gilbert WHARTON of Kirkburn, v. John HIRTON.
Bond given on defendant's behalf. *Mutilated.*   WESTMORLAND.

After A.D. 1518.

82   Agnes HOLDYN, granddaughter and heir of Joan Acton, v. William LENCH, master of the
gild of St. Martin, Birmingham.
Detention of deeds relating to a burgage in Birmingham. (1518–1529.)   WARWICK.

83   Thomas SLATER of York, miller, v. Thomas MAGNUS, master of [St. Leonard's?] hospital,
[York], and Guy NELSON.
Lease of the castle mills, [York]. *Faded.* (1531.)   [YORK.]

84   Robert APRYCE and Cassandra his wife, late the wife of William Staunton and formerly of
Adlard Clemente, gentleman, v. Ralph RICHARDSON *alias* Evyngton of Frampton.
Land of the demise of Ellen Clony(?). *Mutilated.* (1533–8.)   LINCOLN.

85   .   .   .   *v.* [Roger Watson, abbot of LILLESHALL, and Thomas HOSIER.]
Grange, land and rent in Atyngham (*i.e.* Atcham), and tithes of the hamlet of Okynton (*i.e.*
Uckington in Wroxeter), of the demise of James, late abbot. *Mutilated.* (1533–8.)   [SALOP.]

86–87   John HAWKYNS v. Agnes HADERSYCHE, executrix and late the wife of Nicholas
Westbrooke.
(Continuation of File 811, No. 13.) (1538.)   STAFFORD.

88   George BROUGHTON v. William SMYTH.
(Continuation of File 949, No. 36. (1538–1544.)   [CORNWALL.]

89   John HUTTON v. Thomas POPE.
(Continuation of File 999, No. 53.) (1538–1544.)   ————

90–92   William JOHNSON of Alkborough v. John COUPER and John CRESSIE.
Messuage etc. held of the manor of Halton. *Mutilated.* (1538–1544.)   LINCOLN.

93   Thomas SENDE and Isabel his wife v. Stephen SHARPE.
Indecent assault at Wilton. *Damaged.* (1538-1544.)   WILTS.

94–96   Edward WOTTON, knight, and others, v. John BRYGES and Alice his wife.
(Continuation of File 1087, No. 51?) (1542.)   [WARWICK.]

97–98   The wardens and scholars of ALL SOULS' COLLEGE, Oxford, v. John BROWNE and
THOMAS [ap] Jenkyn.
Parsonage (sic) of Langenyth and Pennarth. *Bill wanting.* (After 1542.)   [GLAMORGAN.]

99   John BOYDELL and Joan his wife v. John STAPLE and Margaret his wife.
Legacy stated to have been partly paid to the late prioress of Amesbury at the said Joan's request in
order that she might become a nun there. *Replication only.* (1544–7.)

100   Gilbert COWPER v. the bailiffs of CAMBRIDGE.
Continued imprisonment and detention of goods after acquittal on a charge of illegal purchase of
corn. *Subpoena.* (1544–7.)   CAMBRIDGE.

101   William HYTCHCOK v. John GODARD.
Land in Tring, late of John Hitchcok, deceased, grandfather of complainant. *Mutilated.* (1544–7.)
        HERTS.

102   Richard PAYN v, James and John LECHERF, executors of John Lecherf, priest.
Tithes of St. Odwyn (*i.e.*, St. Owen's, Hereford?) *Faded.* (1544–7.)   HER[EF.]

103   .   .   .   *v.* William JUDE, prebendary of Peterborough, and others.
· Fishery, etc. in the manor of Peterborough of the demise of the late abbot and convent. *Mutilated.*
(1544–7.)   NORTHAMPTON.

104   Robert CLARKE v. John CADY.
(Continuation of File 1206, No. 24.) *Answer wanting.* (1547–1551.)   [NORF.]

105–106   [William LOWE?] v. William SPARRY.
Messuage and land in Northfield(?) (*Cir* 1551–3.) *Faded.*   WORCESTER.

107   Charles VAUGHAN and Jane his wife v. Robert PULVERTOFTE.
(Continuation of File 1479, Nos. 20–22.) (1556–8.)   [DORSET.]

EARLY CHANCERY PROCEEDINGS

BUNDLE 1520

1.　　Thomas ADYNGRAVE and Anne his [wife], daughter of
　　　Thomas PAGETT, *v.*_____
　Will of Thomas Pagett.　*Bill, fragment.*　(Henry VIII;
　Audley.)　·　　　　　　　　.　　　　　　　　　　　MIDDLESEX.

2.　　James APOTT of London, grocer, *v.* William NEVELL.
　?Debt.　*Bill, fragment.*　(Henry VIII *or* Edward VI;
　Wriothesley.)　　　　　　　　　　　　　　　　　　　?LONDON.

3.　　Nicholas AWDELEY, Thomas COOKE and Robert_____*v.*
　　　Walter WADLOND.
　Bond.　*Bill, fragment.*　(Henry VIII;　Audley.)　　　_____

4.　　Richard AWDELEY esquire *v.*_____
　Debt from lands in Sturminster Marshall and Newton
　Peveril.　*Bill, faded.*　(Henry VIII *or* Edward VI;
　Wriothesley.)　　　　　　　　　　　　　　　　　　　DORSET.

5.　　John BADLAND *v.* Nicholas TALBOT.
　Lands held by John Palmer.　*Answer and replication,
　mutilated.*　　　　　　　　　　　　　　　　　　　　_____

6.　　Thomasin BALLED and George BRYTTEN *v.* Margery
　　　BRYTTEN.
　Debt.　*Bill, mutilated.*　(Edward VI;　Paulet.)　　　_____

7.　　Humphrey BARNEHOUSE esquire *v.* Sir Hugh STUKELEY.
　Lands in ?Parnacott.　*Bill, faded.*　(Edward VI;
　Rich.)　　　　　　　　　　　　　　　　　　　　　　DEVON.

8.　　Joan BLAND, widow of William BLAND of London,
　　　haberdasher, *v.*_____
　Debt.　*Bill, fragment.*　(Henry VIII;　Audley.)　　LONDON.

9.　　William BRAFFYN *v.*_____
　Lands in Bradwell.　*Bill, fragment.*　(Edward VI;
　Rich.)　　　　　　　　　　　　　　　　　　　　　　_____

10.　　Thomas BROOKE and ?Anne his wife *v.* Richard
　　　DEVENYSHE.
　Bill, fragment.　(Edward VI;　Paulet.)　　　　　　_____

11.　　John BROUN *v.*_____
　Bill, fragment.　(Henry VIII;　Audley.)　　　　　_____

12.　　John BROWNE *v.* Nicholas ROOKWOOD.
　Answer.　　　　　　　　　　　　　　　　　　　　_____

13.　　William BROWNE *v.* Humphrey STILE esquire.
　House formerly of Dame Mawdelyn Tate of London.
　Bill, faded.　(Henry VIII;　Audley.)　　　　　　　LONDON.

EARLY CHANCERY PROCEEDINGS - BUNDLE 1520

14.   William BURNELL *v.* Thomas ATKINSON and Edward
PETINGER.
Indentures and leases.   *Answer and replication.*   ?LONDON.

15.   _____BURTON of London *v.* the Mayor and Sheriffs
of London.
Lease of a house from Dr. Brewrton, master of
St. Bartholomew's hospital.   *Bill, faded.*   (Henry VIII;
Audley.)   LONDON.

16.   Alice BYSET *v.* _____
Land in 'Kinggrowe' manor.   *Bill, mutilated.*
(Henry VIII *or* Edward VI; Wriothesley.)   ————

17.   Dame Elizabeth CONSTABLE, widow of Sir Marmeduke
CONSTABLE, *v.* _____
Debt.   *Bill, fragment.*   (Henry VIII; Audley.)   LONDON etc.

18.   Dr. ? DAKONS *v.* Richard bishop of Coventry and
Lichfield.
Return to writ of dedimus potestatem, *mutilated.*
(Edward VI; Rich.)   ————

19.   Hugh DANY_____*v.* David ap LAWRENS.
Abduction of wife and goods.   *Bill, fragment.*
(Edward VI; Rich.)   ————

20.   James ap DAVID of Bishopston *v.* _____
Lands late of Jevan ap Guillum.   *Bill, fragment.*
(Mary; bishop of Winchester.)   ?GLAMORGAN.

21.   Thomas DERBYE *v.* William_____
Lands formerly of William Derbye. • *Bill, mutilated.*
(Henry VIII *or* Edward VI; Wriothesley.)   ————

22.   Bernard DOBELL *v.* Henry HARRYS.
Debt.   *Answer, mutilated.*   ————

23.   _____of Surrey and Agnes his wife and Elizabeth
ELYOT of Guildford *v.* John AUNSELL.
Lands called 'Lawrences'.   *Bill, fragment.*
(Henry VIII; Audley.)   SURREY.

24.   John EYR, John BLENARHASS_____and Robert
GOSNOLDE the younger, executors of John
GOSNOLDE of Barham, Suffolk, *v.* _____
Leybourne and 'Coupe' woods.   *Bill, fragment.*
(Edward VI; Paulet.)   KENT.

25.   _____ and_____daughter of Thomas FELLIPPES *v.*
_____
Debt.   *Bill, fragment.*   (Edward VI; Rich.)   ————

26.   John FYSCH_____v. Arthur_____
?Debt. *Bill, mutilated.* (Edward VI; bishop of Ely.) _____

27.   Richard ?GRALLE *v.* Thomas ?BELCH_____
Bill, faded. (Henry VIII; Audley.)   _____

28.   John GROVE *v.* ? William GROVE.
Debt. *Bill, mutilated.*
(Mary; bishop of Winchester.)   WORCESTER.

29.   William HANCOK of Bromsgrove, tanner, *v.* John
            BRAYNE.
Debt. *Bill, mutilated.* (Henry VIII *or* Edward VI;
Wriothesley.)   _____

30.   John HAWARDE *v.*_____
Bill, fragment. (Mary; bishop of Winchester.)   _____

31.   Walter HENDLE and Margery his wife *v.* Alice
            COTTON widow.
Writ of dedimus potestatem. (26 Henry VIII.)   _____

32.   Elizabeth HETHE *v.* Richard PARKYNS and John
            PARKER.
Lease of houses. *Replication.*   _____

33.   Nicholas HUDSON and ? Dorothy his wife *v.* John
            BARTON, Thomas ADAM, John FORNE, and Roger
            NEWTON.
Lands in Wirksworth. *Bill, faded.* (Henry VIII;
Audley.)   DERBY.

34.   William HUXLEY *v.*_____
Lands in Denbigh. *Bill, fragment.* (Henry VIII;
Audley.)   DENBIGH.

35.   Henry HYOTT *v.* Edward BONSTALL, vicar of
            Nether Swell.
Vicarage of Nether Swell. *Bill, faded.* (Henry VIII
or Edward VI; Wriothesley.)   GLOUCESTER.

36.   John INGAT of Carlton *v.*_____
Sale of land at Winston. *Bill, fragment.*
(Henry VIII; Audley.)   SUFFOLK.

37.   John KE_____ *v.* _____
Bill, mutilated. (Henry VIII; Audley.)   SURREY.

38.   Bernard KNYGHT, a Venetian, *v.*_____
Bill, fragment. (Mary; bishop of Winchester.)   _____

39.   Edward KYNGDON *v.* William ?ACHORN and others.
Lands etc. of Thomas Beare. *Bill, fragment.*
(Henry VIII *or* Edward VI; Wriothesley.)   _____

EARLY CHANCERY PROCEEDINGS - BUNDLE 1520

40.   Jevan LECHE *v*. John ap DAVID.
   Debt.   *Bill*.   (Edward VI; Rich.)   ————

41.   _____ of London, son of Robert LEGGE, *v*._____
   Lands.   *Bill and answer, fragments*.   (Henry VIII;
   Audley.)   SALOP.

42.   Henry LEYE and Denise his wife and Matthew LEYE
           v. Sir John BONHAM.
   Lands formerly of Henry lord Brock.   *Writ of* dedimus
   potestatem *and answer*.   (1 & 2 Philip and Mary.)   ————

43.   John LIEVESO_____of Wolverhampton, merchant of
           the staple of Calais, *v*. Thomas MARTEN.
   ?Debt.   *Bill, fragment*.   (Edward VI;   Paulet.)   STAFFORD.

44.   David LLOYD *v*. William ap MORYS.
   Bill and answer, fragments.   (Edward VI;   Rich.)   ————

45.   _____son of John LOWE *v*. William LEE.
   Debt.   *Bill, fragment*.   (Edward VI;   bishop of Ely.)   ————

46.   John MALL_____N of London, bricklayer, and
           Margaret his wife *v*. Dame Elizabeth CONSTABLE,
           wife of Sir Marmaduke CONSTABLE.
   Debt.   *Bill, faded*.   (Henry VIII;   Audley.)   LONDON.

47.   Henry MANNOKKES of Streatham *v*._____
   Bill, fragment.   (Henry VIII;   Audley.)   ?SURREY.

48.   Alexander MARLER of London *v*._____
   ?Debt.   *Bill, fragment*.   (Henry VIII *or* Edward VI;
   Wriothesley.)   ————

49.   William MARTEN, William HOLMAN and Richard MARTEN *v*.
           Robert GYLLETT and Eleanor his wife.
   Will of William Rate, late husband of Eleanor Gyllett.
   Writ of dedimus potestatem *and answer*.   (34 Henry VIII.)   DORSET.

50.   William ?MARTEY of Butterwick *v*. Francis_____
   Lands in Freiston, Butterwick, Skirbeck, Toft, Boston
   and Friskney.   *Bill, mutilated*.   (Henry VIII *or*
   Edward VI;   Wriothesley.)   LINCOLN.

51.   John MASTERS *v*. Harry FRY.
   Lands etc. formerly of Margaret WYTCOMBE.   *Answer*.
   (Henry VIII.)   ————

52.   Geoffrey MATHEWE and Edith his wife *v*.
           Thomas_____
   Writ of dedimus potestatem, *mutilated*.   ————

53.   Richard MERCER of Newport, Essex, fletcher, *v*._____
   Bill, fragment.   (Henry VIII;   Audley.)   ————

54.   Peter_____ and Margery his wife, one of the
             daughters of Robert FOKEYS of_____, Norfolk,
             and Walter MOORE and Isabel his wife, another of
             Robert's daughters, *v*. William PAGE.
Messuages. *Bill, fragment.* (Henry VIII; Audley.)   ———————

55.   Thomas ap MORGAN *v*. Matthew ap Richard VAGHAN
             and Margaret_____
Return to writ of dedimus potestatum, *mutilated.*
(Mary; Archbishop of York.)   ———————

56.   Geoffrey M_____VE gentleman and Edith his wife
             v._____
Manor of Easton Bassett. *Bill, fragment.*
(Mary; Bishop of Winchester.)   WILTS.

57.   William MYLLEFURTHE *v*._____
Will. *Bill, fragment.* (Edward VI; Bishop of Ely.)   ———————

58.   William NALL *v*. Henry BYROM.
Debt. *Answer.*   ———————

59.   John ?NAYLOR *v*. Thomas GODDARD of Compton,
             Wilts.
Debt. *Bill, faded.* (Edward VI; Rich.)   ———————

60.   John PARSON *v*._____
?Debt. *Bill, fragment.* (Henry VIII; Audley.)   ———————

61.   Ralph PILKYNGTON_____ *v*. John GEE of____chester,
             Lancs., clothier.
Depositions before commissioners, fragment.
(Edward VI; bishop of Ely.)   LANCASHIRE.

62.   Anthony PORTER, son and heir of Richard PORTER,
             v. John GRYVELL.
Grant by Sir William Compton to Sir Edward Gryvell.
Bill, mutilated. (Henry VIII *or* Edward VI;
Wriothesley.)   ———————

63.   John PRUST, clerk, late abbot of Hartland, *v*.
             Edward_____
Arrest and imprisonment after the Dissolution for an
annuity granted before. *Bill, mutilated.*
(Henry VIII *or* Edward VI; Wriothesley.)   ?DEVON.

64.   Nicholas RO_____ *v*. John COLLES of Langton.
Lease. *Bill, fragment.* (Edward VI; Paulet.)   ———————

65.   Richard ap John ap ROGER and Roger JONES *v*.
             John ap GRYFFITH.
Lands of Gyttyn ap Jevan ap Eugyon; whether held by
gavelkind or borough English. *Answer.*   ———————

EARLY CHANCERY PROCEEDINGS - BUNDLE 1520

66.   Thomas ROLSTON and William WHYTINGTON *v.*_____
    Debt. *Bill, fragment.* (Henry VIII; Audley.)   —————

67.   _____RUDER of Walkeringham, Notts. *v.*_____
    Bill, fragment.   —————

68.   Ella SEMSON *v.*_____
    Marriage of Robert Semson, son of Ella, to Janet
    daughter of Thomas Banke of Johnby, Cumberland,
    husbandman. *Bill, fragment.* (Mary;
    bishop of Winchester.)   —————

69.   Humphrey SKYRES *v.*_____
    Will. *Bill, fragment.* (Henry VIII *or* Edward VI;
    Wriothesley.)   —————

70.   George SMYTH *v.* Agnes_____
    Writ of dedimus potestatem, *mutilated.*
    (37 [Henry VIII.])   —————

71.   _____?SNYDFYTH knight *v.*_____
    ?Debt. *Bill, faded.* (Henry VIII; Audley.)   —————

72.   Humphrey SOMERFORD *v.*_____
    Bill, fragment. (Henry VIII; Audley.)   ?SALOP.

73.   Ellis STEWARD *v.*_____and Agnes_____
    Return to writ of dedimus potestatem, *fragment.*
    (31 Henry VIII.)   STAFFORD.

74.   Richard David VAUGHAN *v.* Philip John David
        VAUGHAN, Robert MORGAN and Meredith GRUFFYTHE.
    Lands. *Bill, fragment.* (Henry VIII *or* Edward VI;
    Wriothesley.)   RADNOR.

75.   John WALSGROVE of Bristol *v.* William SANDYE of
        Great Malvern, husbandman.
    ?Debt and imprisonment. *Bill, faded and mutilated.*
    (Henry VIII; Audley.)   —————

76.   John WARBERLEY goldsmith *v.* John HICMAN
        goldsmith.
    Plate of William Rundell. *Rejoinder.*   —————

77.   John ZOUCHE knight, lord Zouche, *v.*_____
    Bill, fragment. (Henry VIII *or* Edward VI;
    Wriothesley.)   —————

78.   Richard_____*v.* John BARNARDE and Thomas
        MARSHALL.
    Lands. *Bill, faded.* (Henry VIII; Audley.)   —————

EARLY CHANCERY PROCEEDINGS - BUNDLE 1520

79.   Thomas_____v._____BATEMAN.
Judgment requested in a previous Chancery suit of 26
Henry VIII concerning land. *Bill, fragment.*
(Henry VIII *or* Edward VI; Wriothesley.)   PEMBROKE.

80.   Th[omas]_____v. Thomas BLAKBORN.
Failure to clean dykes on lands leased to defendant by
Robert Pulvertof. *Bill, fragment.* (Henry VIII;
Audley.)   ————

81.   Thomas_____v._____BLUMFILD.
Lands. *Bill, fragment.* (Henry VIII *or* Edward VI;
Wriothesley.)   SUFFOLK.

82.   William_____v. William BOCHER.
Debt. *Bill, mutilated.* (Henry VIII *or* Edward VI;
Wriothesley.)   ————

83.   _____v. Robert BROWNE of Crawley and Robert
CHAUNDELER.
Lands formerly of John Arnolde, Henry Chamsome, John
Whitenaye and Thomas Peperham. *Bill, fragment.*
(Edward VI; Rich.)   SURREY.

84.   _____v. Elizabeth wife and executrix of John
CLOSE.
Debt. *Bill, mutilated.* (Henry VIII; Audley.)   ————

85.   _____v. David COLE.
Lands and goods. *Bill and answer, fragments.*
(Henry VIII; Audley.)   DEVON.

86.   _____v. Robert CRAYNE and Elizabeth his wife.
Writ of dedimus potestatem, *mutilated.*
(38 [Henry VIII].)   ————

87.   _____v. Marion DENNYS.
Writ of dedimus potestatum, *fragment.*
(36 [Henry VIII].)   ————

88.   John_____v. Elizabeth ERDYSWYKE.
Debt at Stafford. *Bill, mutilated.* (Henry VIII;
Audley.)   STAFFORD.

89.   _____v. William FARRE, John WATSON and John
HODYNOT.
Surrender of land in manorial court. *Bill, mutilated.*
(Edward VI; Paulet.)   ————

90.   _____v. Humphrey FORTESCU and Mynson his wife.
Writ of dedimus potestatem, *mutilated.*
(36 [Henry VIII].)   ————

91.　　　　_____v. John GOODCHYLD, William DRAPER and
　　　　　Peter SMYTHEMAN.
　　Lands.　*Bill, fragment.*　(Henry VIII or Edward VI;
　　Wriothesley.)　　　　　　　　　　　　　　　　　　　　ESSEX.

92.　　　　_____v. Richard HANNEY, late abbot of B_____
　　Debt.　*Bill, fragment.*　(Henry VIII; Audley.)　　　——————

93.　　　　_____v._____HARPER.
　　Debt:　defendant imprisoned at Chester but released
　　on payment of bribe.　*Bill, fragment: writ to Mayor
　　and Recorder of Chester to inquire.*　(33 Henry VIII.)　　CHESTER.

94.　　　　_____v. Joan and Robert HARRYSON.
　　Lands.　*Bill, fragment.*　(Henry VIII; Audley.)　　　——————

95.　　　　_____v. John JENKYNS gentleman and Elizabeth
　　　　　his wife.
　　Lands in Watton.　*Answer, fragment.*　　　　　　　——————

96.　　　　Alice_____v. ?William MARTEN of Freiston,
　　　　　yeoman.
　　Debt.　*Bill, fragment.*　(Henry VIII; Audley.)　　　LINCOLN.

97.　　　　_____of Southampton, gentleman, v. Richard
　　　　　MATHEW.
　　Lease of lands of Francis Palmers of Linslade.　*Bill,
　　mutilated.*　(Henry VIII or Edward VI;　Wriothesley.)　BUCKINGHAM.

98.　　　　Bernard_____v. Gryffyn MEREDYTH.
　　Debt for provisions for soldiers going to France;　case
　　previously held in Exeter city court.　*Bill, mutilated
　　and faded.*　(Henry VIII or Edward VI;　Wriothesley.)　DEVON.

99.　　　　_____v. Peter MYDDELTON of co. York, gentleman.
　　Debt.　*Bill, mutilated.*　(Henry VIII; Audley.)　　YORK.

100.　　　　_____of Pucklechurch v. John OSBORNE of
　　　　　Marshfield.
　　Debt.　*Bill, fragment.*　(Henry VIII; Audley.)　　GLOUCESTER.

101.　　　　_____, ?vicar of Appledore, v. John PLANE.
　　　　　Thefts from Appledore church.　*Bill, faded and
　　mutilated.*　(Henry VIII; Audley.)　　　　　　　　KENT.

102.　　　　_____MELL, citizen and haberdasher of London, v.
　　　　　Walter POTTER, citizen and merchant of London.
　　Imprisonment for debt.　*Bill, fragment.*　(Henry VIII;
　　Audley.)　　　　　　　　　　　　　　　　　　　LONDON.

103.　　　　_____v. Hugh PYBETT.
　　Debt.　*Bill, fragment.*　(Henry VIII; Audley.)　　——————

104. _____v. Francis ROLLISTONE esquire.
Detention of household goods. *Bill, mutilated.*
(Edward VI; Rich.)

105. _____v. Robert SAKEFELLD gentleman.
Lease of 'Harvys Felld'. *Bill, fragment.* (Henry VIII
or Edward VI; Wriothesley.)   BEDFORD.

106. _____v. Richard STOKEY.
Lands of Robert Gaydon. *Bill, mutilated.*
(Henry VIII; Audley.)

107. _____of Devon, esquire, v. Richard STRODE of
Newnham.
Debt. *Bill, mutilated.* (Henry VIII or Edward VI;
Wriothesley.)   DEVON.

108. _____of Surrey v. William TAYLOUR and Richard
STOKTON.
Debt. *Bill, fragment.* (Henry VIII; Audley.)

109. _____v. Robert TEVEREY.
Lands in Little Thrompton and Long Eaton. *Bill, faded.*
(Henry VIII or Edward VI; Wriothesley.)   DERBY.

110. _____v. Thomas TURGES of Alton, Hants.
Debt. *Bill, mutilated.* (Henry VIII or Edward VI;
Wriothesley.)   LONDON.

111. _____v. Roger VALENTYNE yeoman.
Sale. *Bill, mutilated.* (Henry VIII; Audley.)   SUFFOLK.

112. _____v. John WALKER.
Deeds. *Bill, mutilated.* (Henry VIII; Audley.)

113. John_____v. William WALLYS.
Lease obtained by fraud. *Bill, mutilated.*
(Edward VI; Rich.)

114. _____v. John WAREN.
Debt. *Bill and answer, fragments.* (Henry VIII;
Audley.)

115. _____v. James WARREYNE.
Debt. *Bill, fragment.* (Henry VIII; Audley.)   BRISTOL.

116. _____v. Richard WESTRAM.
Lands. *Bill, fragment.* (Edward VI; bishop of Ely.)

117. _____v. William WYLLIAMS.
Bond concerning soap. *Bill, fragment.* (Henry VIII;
Audley.)   SOUTHAMPTON.

118. _____v. ?Thomas WYLSON.
Debt. *Bill, fragment.* (Edward VI; Rich.)

119.   _____v. Robert WYOTT.
Debt for board and lodgings: and trespass. *Bill,*
faded. (Henry VIII; Audley.)   _____

120.   _____v. Richard YVE gentleman.
Debt from the parsonage of West_____ *Bill, fragment.*
(Henry VIII; Audley.)   _____

121.   Alice_____v. William_____
Answer, fragment.   _____

122.   ·   Sir George_____v._____
Debt. *Bill, fragment.* (Edward VI; Rich.)   LONDON.

123.   _____and Joan_____v._____
Debt. *Bill, fragment.*   (Henry VIII; Audley.)   _____

124.   Richard_____v._____
Vicarage of Bilsby. *Bill, fragment.*   (Henry VIII or
Edward VI; Wriothesley.)   LINCOLN.

125.   William_____v._____
Lands called 'Ingeston' in Bishop's Frome.
Bill, fragment. (Henry VIII; Audley.)   HEREFORD.

126.   _____of co. Carmarthen, gentleman, v._____
?Shipwreck during trade with Portugal. *Bill, fragment.*
(Henry VIII; Audley.)   _____

127.   _____ of Essex, draper, v._____, his creditors.
Debt. *Bill, mutilated.*   (Edward VI; bishop of Ely.)   _____

128.   _____of London v._____
Sale of a messuage according to the custom of the manor
of Stepney. *Bill, fragment.* (Edward VI; Rich.)   MIDDLESEX.

129.   _____of Somerset, widow, v. Thomas_____and
            Christian_____
Land. *Bill, fragment.*   (Henry VIII; Audley.)   SOMERSET.

130.   _____v. Beatrice_____
Lands in Humberston. *Bill, fragment.*   (Edward VI;
Rich.)   LINCOLN.

131.   _____v. Sir Harry_____and_____
Debt. *Bill, fragment.*   _____

132.   _____v. Richard_____, John_____and Robert_____

Writ of dedimus potestatem, *fragment.*   _____

133.   _____ v. Robert_____
Lands formerly of Gikestas Francheham. *Bill,*
fragment.   (Henry VIII or Edward VI; Wriothesley.)   KENT.

EARLY CHANCERY PROCEEDINGS - BUNDLE 1520

134.   _____v. Stephen_____
House at Horsham etc.   *Bill, fragment.*   (Edward VI;
Bishop of Ely.)   SUSSEX.

135.   _____v. Steven_____
?Debt.   *Bill, fragment.*   (Henry VIII; Audley.)   DEVON.

136.   _____v. William_____and William_____
Debt.   *Bill, fragment.*   (Henry VIII; Audley.)   ESSEX.

137.   _____v._____
Lands of John Alen and others in Droitwich and Falsam.
Bill and answer, fragments.   (Henry VIII; Audley.)   WORCESTER.

138.   _____v._____
Rectory of Etr_____   *Bill, fragment.*
(Henry VIII; Audley.)   NORFOLK.

139.   _____v._____
Land.   *Bill, fragment.*   (Edward VI; Rich.)   ?BUCKINGHAM.

140.   _____v._____
Lands in Stoke by Clare.   *Bill, fragment.*
(Henry VIII; Audley.)   SUFFOLK.

141.   _____v._____
Debt in Warwick.   *Bill, mutilated.*   (Henry VIII;
Audley.)   WARWICK.

142.   _____v._____
Debt.   *Bill, fragment.*   (Edward VI; Bishop of Ely.)   _____

143.   _____v._____
Debt of Scotsman for lodgings.   *Bill, fragment.*
(Edward VI; Bishop of Ely.)   LONDON.

144.   _____v._____
. Debt resulting from former plea of plaintiff *v.* John
Mores of Farnham, esquire, and John Benet, late
citizen and grocer of London.   *Bill, mutilated.*
(Henry VIII; Audley.)   _____

145.   _____v._____
Land in Kinver.   *Bill, fragment.*   STAFFORD.

146.   _____v._____
Debt re coal from [Newcastle upon] Tyne for Calais and
elsewhere.   *Bill, fragment.*   _____

147.   _____v._____
Debt.   *Bill, fragment.*   (Henry VIII; Audley.)   NORFOLK.

148.   _____v._____
Rectory and church of Preston on Stour.   *Bill,*
fragment.   (Edward VI; Rich.)   GLOUCESTER.

EARLY CHANCERY PROCEEDINGS - BUNDLE 1520

149. _____v._____
Seizure of wood at Ipswich. *Bill, fragment.*
(Henry VIII; Audley.)   SUFFOLK.

150. _____v._____
Lands descending to John Osborne. *Bill, fragment.*
(Henry VIII; Audley.)   _____

151. _____v.._____
Lands in Fawley of William lord Seynt John. *Bill,*   SOUTHAMPTON,
fragment. (Henry VIII;*or* Edward VI; Wriothesley.)   DORSET.

152. _____v._____
?Debt. *Bill, fragment.* (Edward VI; Bishop of Ely.)   LONDON.

153. _____v._____
Debt. *Bill, fragment.* (Henry VIII *or* Edward VI;
Wriothesley.)   NORFOLK.

154. _____v._____
Manors of .Silverton and Rew and lands therein and in
Newland, Edge Barton, Lustleigh, Wadham and Newcott.
Bill, fragment. (Henry VIII *or* Edward VI;
Wriothesley.)   DEVON.

155. _____v._____
Lease of a messuage. *Bill, fragment.*   _____

156. _____v._____
?Debt. *Bill, fragment.* (Edward VI; Rich.)   _____

157. _____v._____
Land. *Bill, fragment.* (Edward VI; bishop of Ely.)   ESSEX.

158. _____v._____
Bill, fragment. (Edward VI; Rich.)   ?SUFFOLK.

159. _____v.._____
Bill, fragment. (Edward VI; Bishop of Ely.)   CORNWALL.

160. _____v._____
Fragment.   NORFOLK.

161. _____v._____
Bill, fragment. (Henry VIII; Audley.)   _____

162-164. *Fragments of bills.* (Henry VIII *or* Edward VI;
Wriothesley.)   _____

165-166. *Fragments of bills.* (Edward VI; Rich.)   _____

167-169. *Fragments of bills.*   _____

170. *Fragment of answer.*   _____

171-191. *Fragments.*   _____

EARLY CHANCERY PROCEEDINGS

BUNDLE 1521

1.   Richard A. BOROWE *v.* William RANDALL.
Plymouth. *Bill.*   DEVON.

2.   Richard ANDELEBY *v.* John FYLION *alias* KNEBWORTH. BEDFORD and
Estate of Eleanor Andeleby in Dunstable and Caddington. HERTFORD,
Bill only.   now BEDFORD.

3.   William ARKYLL *v.* Thomas POOLES and Alan ELAND.
Title deeds of property in Kirton in Holland.   LINCOLN.

4.   Thomas ARUNDELL *v.* Jane and Richard CHAMMOND.
Money matter. *Bill, mutilated.*   ——————

5.   William A___STED *v.* Wilmot HILLING and
Christopher BURY.
Money matter. *Bill, mutilated.*
(Philip and Mary; Heath.)   ——————

6.   Walter BABINGTON, Agnes his wife and Mary TRAVERS
v. Robert DILLON and George MOLES.
Profits of an enfeoffment to users of lands in Pyll in
Tawton Bishop, Landkey, South Radworthy, Rockley,
Whitefield [in Manwood], Barnstaple, Newton Bishop,
Fremington, Great and Little Torrington. *Bill.*
(Edward VI.)   DEVON.

7.   John BARNARDESTON *v.* John BATTE.
Grafton; manor. *Bill.* (Philip and Mary.)   WILTS.

8.   Thomas BATTERELL (?) *v.* Thomas WALL and Joan his
wife.
Estate of Thomas Russell. *Bill, mutilated.*   STAFFORD.

9.   Francis BAYKER *v.* Thomas BAWNE.
Parcel of the manor of Skerne. *Rejoinder.*
(Philip and Mary.)   [YORK].

10.   John BAWDYN, John COLYN, John GEDY, John PAWLYN
the younger and William BLYGHE *v.* John and Thomas
BLACKMOWRE, Robert WHALE and John HOIGGE.
Deeds of lands etc. in South Petherwin.   CORNWALL.

11.   Thomas BAWNE and Bridget his wife *v.* John SPENCER.
Title deeds of an oxgang of land in Gotham. *Mutilated.*
(Philip and Mary.)   NOTTINGHAM.

12.   John BELLOWE *v.* Francis BUNTING.
East Wykeham. *Bill.*   LINCOLN.

13.   Hugh BOSTOCKE and John DAVID *v.* Jevan DIO.
Unlawful arrest. *Bill.*   DENBIGH.

14.   John BOWRE, priest *v*. Sheriffs of LONDON.
Unlawful imprisonment in the Counter and Newgate.
Bill, mutilated.   (Henry VIII; Warham.)   MIDDLESEX.

15.   John BRAMEFELD *v*. Richard BOYDEN.
Debt.   *Bill, mutilated.*   CAMBRIDGE.

16.   Thomas BRANFORDE *v*. Mayor and Sheriffs of LONDON.
Petition for writ of *certiorari* concerning actions for
debt in courts of City of London.   *Faded.*
(Henry VIII; Wolsey.)

17.   John BROUN *v*. Randolph BILLINGTON.
Lease of a manor.   *Replication, mutilated.*

18.   John BRYMESGROVE, citizen and woolpacker of
London *v*. Thomas MARSHE and Agnes widow of Robert
Byron.
Petition for *certiorari.*   (Henry VIII.)

19.   Thomas BURTON and another *v._____*
Parsonage of Clipston.   *Bill, mutilated.*
(Philip and Mary; Gardiner.)   NORTHAMPTON.

20.   Owen BUTLER *v*. Walter VAUZGHAN.   CARMARTHEN
Title deeds of property with lordship of Ogmore.   and
                                              GLAMORGAN.

21.   William BYSSELL and Christian his wife, Ralph
LEY and Alice his wife, Mary HYLL, William
BYRDE and others *v*. Edward BROOKE and Agnes   WARWICK,
his wife.   WORCESTER,
Title deeds of Solihull, Dudley, Langley, Rowley,   STAFFORD,
Tillington and Hyll.   *Mutilated.*   (Edward VI.)   and SALOP.

22.   Thomas BYXFORD and Agnes his wife, daughter and
heir of William Markaund *v*. John WYLDON, clerk,
Thomas COUPERE and Cecilia his wife, executors
of William Wyldon.
Title deeds of a messuage and oxgang in Helmesley.
(Henry VIII.)   YORK.

23.   Henry CAPELL, knight *v*. Thomas GRIFFYN, knight.
Manor of Walton in Gordano.   (Philip and Mary.)   SOMERSET.

24.   Peter CHAMPENEYS *v*. William SCOTE, clerk and
Margaret his wife.
Marriage settlement of lands in Honiton and Aroliscombe.
Bill.   DEVON.

25-26.   Edward CHURCHELEY *v*. Thomas MOGGE and Thomas
POWTER.
Property of Thomas Mogge deceased.   *Mutilated.*
(Henry VIII.)

EARLY CHANCERY PROCEEDINGS - BUNDLE 1521

27.   William COKE, Robert KEYS *v.* Thomas KEYS, Margery
and Robert COWPER *alias* BYNGHAM.
Title deeds of property in Kilbourne, Horsley and
Horsley Woodhouse.   *Mutilated.*   (Mary.)   DERBY.

28.   _____COLBYN *v.* Henry and Alice CORDEN.
Pyworthy.   *Bill, mutilated.*   (Philip and Mary.)   DEVON.

29.   William COLE and Joan his wife, John RUNDELL and
Thomasyn his wife *v.* Thomas SPRYE and Joan his
wife, Hockeday and Thomas TREMLETT.
Title deeds of lands at East Liddaton in Brentor,
Dringwell in Thrusherton, and Thorne in Broadwoodwidger.
Bill.   DEVON.

30.   Elizabeth COLLYER, widow of Henry *v.* John STOCKER
and Joan his wife.
Estate of Henry Collyer.   *Bill.*   (Philip and Mary.)   DORSET.

31.   George COLLYNS *v.* John CLARKE, draper.
Debt.   *Bill.*   LONDON.

32.   Robert DANNE *v.* Owyn HOPTON.
Property of Priory of Blythburgh.   *Bill, mutilated.*
(Philip and Mary;   Heath.)   SUFFOLK.

33.   John DANYS, parson of Gunthorpe *v.* Gregory DANYS,
a Counsel.
Money matters, negligence in acting in plaintiff's case.
Bill.   NORFOLK.

34.   Sir Maurice DENYS *v.* Sir Nicholas POYNTZ.
Manors of Pucklechurch and Westerleigh parcel of Bishop
and Chapter of Bath and Wells.   *Mutilated.*
(Philip and Mary.)   GLOUCESTER.

35.   [John DONK(?)] *v.* [John INGE and Alice his
wife (?)].
A messuage, unspecified.   *Answer, mutilated.*
(Henry VIII.)   ———

36.   Thomas, Marquis of DORSET, *v.* William COTTON.
Custody of documents of bailiwick of Stoke upon Tern.
(Henry VIII.)   SALOP.

37.   Sir Roger DOR_____ER *v.* John A MORE.
Refusal to carry out agreement.   *Bill, faded.*   ———

38.   Walter EBELL *v.* Richard STAPYLTON, Edward CLERK.
Estate of James Clerk, deceased, parson of Borough
Green.   CAMBRIDGE.

39.   Hugh EDWARDS *v.* Jennet WARDE, wife of John.
Deeds of property within the franchise of Oswestry.
(Edward VI;   Wriothesley.)   SALOP.

EARLY CHANCERY PROCEEDINGS - BUNDLE 1521

40. William ELOND v. Richard SMART.
A silver pot. *Faded.*   _____

41. William ESTEBROKE the younger v. John BROCK.
Title deeds of messuage in [Drewnteignton]. *Mutilated.*
(Philip and Mary.)   DEVON.

42. John FERRER *alias* BAKER and Alice his wife v.
Sir John SYDENHAM.
Sandhill near Dunster. *Bill, mutilated.*
(Philip and Mary.)   SOMERSET.

43-47. Thomas FITZ and others v. Elizabeth FITZ, widow
of William, and Thomas and Ralph MILWARD. _____
Estate of William Fitz. *Mutilated.*   _____

48. Thomas FLOTMAN v. Henry and Agnes FLOTMAN.
Title deeds of premises in Starston and Needham, late
John Flotman. *Bill.*   NORFOLK.

49. John FOLKERD and Jane his wife v. Thomas POOLE
alias POLLE.
Kirton.   LINCOLN.

50. Thomas FORSTER v. Thomas MANFIELD.
Title deeds of premises in Northallerton. *Bill.*   YORK.

51. Robert FORTH v. William FORTH.
Hadleigh, Layham, Kersey and Monks Eleigh. *Bill.*   SUFFOLK.

52. Edmond FRYER v. Edward GREEN.
Money matter. *Bill, mutilated.*   _____

53. John FULLBROKE and Alice his wife v. Humfrey
COLE.
Deeds of lands. *Bill, mutilated.* (Philip and Mary.)   DEVON.

54. Thomas FULLWELL v. John GOODMAN.
Lease of lands of the Sub-Chartership of Wells
Cathedral. (Philip and Mary.).   SOMERSET.

55. William FYNCHAM v. Robert DRAKE.
Hockwold.   NORFOLK.

56. Mark GLENE v. Robert and William SPEDE.
Title deeds of a copyhold in Aylesbury. *Bill.*
(Henry VIII.)   BUCKINGHAM.

57. Thomas GODDARDE v. Guthlake OVERTON.
Manor of Rockley (Temple Rockley). *Bill, faded.*
(Henry VIII.)   WILTSHIRE.

58. Thomas GRANGER and Alice his wife v. Dunstan
BRAY.
Copyhold of Wargrave Manor.   BERKSHIRE.

59.   _____ap GRUFFYTHES, apprentice *v.* Thomas ap
GRUFFYTHES, Roger ap JOHN.
Estate of William ap Gruffythes in Dymeirchion. *Bill.*   FLINT.

60.   William GYE and Jane his wife *v.* Henry GYE.
Marriage settlement of lands etc. at Uphill in Gratton.
in Newton Ferrers. *Bill, mutilated.* (Edward VI;
Ely.)   DEVON.

61.   Thomas HARTE *v.* Ellen HARTE.
Custom of the manor of Uplyme. *Mutilated.*
(Edward VI.)   DEVON.

62.   John HASELWOD and Katherine his wife *v.* Edward
MARMYON, clerk, and Edith MARMYON, widow.
Title deeds of manors of Newton and Galby, lands in   LEICESTER
Lessingham, Rippingale and Dunsby, etc. *Bill.*   and
·(Henry VIII.)   LINCOLN.

63.   Arthur HEDOAR and Elizabeth his wife *v.*
AKRENE, John.
Title deeds of messuage in Partney. *Bill.*   LINCOLN.

64.   William HEYWARDE and his wife *v.* Anthony
HUDDELSTON.
Debt. *Bill, mutilated.*   GLOUCESTER.

65.   Hugh HILL *v.* Humphrey HILL.
Money matters.   _____

66.   Robert HILL and Margaret his wife *v.* William
ROBIN and Humphrey ARUNDELL.
Trehudreth in Blisland; · manor late of Thomas Luccomb. CORNWALL.

67.   _____[HILL] *v.* Sir Richard HILL.
St. Merryn. *Bill, mutilated.*   CORNWALL.

68.   Richard HOGGE *v.* William PONTE.
Dallington. *Bill.*   SUSSEX.

69.   Morgan HOLLAND *v.* Ryce DAY.
Money matter. *Bill.*   _____

70.   Morgan HOLLAND *v.* Robert ap OWEN.
Money matters. *Bill.*   _____

71.   Morgan HOLLAND *v.* Gryffyth WEYTH.
Money matters. *Bill.*   _____

72.   William HUDSON *v.* John JENKYNSON, John SKUTT,
Robert ROO and Richard SOUTHWARK, Master and
Wardens of the Merchant Tailors Company.
Mews called 'Saresson hedde' in Friday Street. *Bill.*
(Henry VIII.)   LONDON.

73.   William HUXLEY *v.* Fulke SALISBURY.
A great brass pot. *Bill, mutilated.*   _____

74.   Robert HYLL, clerk *v.* Geoffrey BLYTHE, Nicholas
DARYNGTON and William HYLL.
Advowson of the vicarage of St. Michael upon Wyse
(Wyre?) by(?)___nes in co. Lancaster, formerly college.
of St. Mary Magdalene, Shrewsbury.   _____

75.   William JENNYNS and, Joan his wife *v.* Hugh
SENKELEY and_____STAUNTON.
Copyholding of manor of Orsett. *Bill.*   ESSEX.

76.   Hugh JONES *v.* Alice and Richard GOBY.
Estate of Marmaduke Jones. *Bill, mutilated.*
(Henry VIII.)   _____

77.   John KAYLWEY *v.* Thomas GAWEN, esquire.
Lands in Gussage, Knowlton in Horton, late monastery of
Tarrant.   DORSET.

78.   James LAWTON *v.* John DODDE.
Land in High Hatton (Hatton Hyneheth). *Bill.*   SALOP.

79.   Thomas LEGET *v.* Richard TURNER and Elinor his
wife.
Deeds. *Bill.*   HERTFORD.

80.   Roger a LEGH and Agnes his wife *v.* John SCOTT.
Wood called 'Therste' in Woodmansterne and Arbright.
Mutilated. (Henry VII-VIII; Warham.)   SURREY.

81.   John LOCKSMITH *v.* John PERCIVAL.
Mudgedown (Moche Dene) and Avonhall. *Bill, mutilated.*   GLOUCESTER.

82.   John LUTTRELL, esquire *v.* David BROCKWAYE.
Advowson of Cheselbourne, late abbess and convent of
Cerne.   DORSET.

BUNDLE 1522

_..   William MARKEHAM and Frances his wife *v.* Chadd   WARWICK,
COKYN.   BEDFORD,
Estate of Humfrey Cokyn. *Bill.* (Henry VIII.)   NORTHAMPTON,
                                                            and LEICESTER.

2.   Robert MARTEN *v.* Thomas HOLTON, Margaret PECOKE.
Title deeds of land at Kirton. (Philip and Mary.)   SUFFOLK.

3.   William and Richard MARTEN and William HOLME(?)
v. Robert GYLLETT and Elianor his wife.
Money matter. *Bill.*   _____

EARLY CHANCERY PROCEEDINGS - BUNDLE 1522

4. Clemens MASON and Elizabeth his wife *v.* William
    DORRYNGTON the younger, William ARTHUR and
    another.
    Estate of William Dorryngton in Theydongamon.
    (Henry VIII.)   ESSEX.

5. John MAYNARD *v.* Henry HAMLYN, Robert HOKER,
    William HOSY.
    Administration of the Guildhall Court at Exeter. *Bill,*
    mutilated. (Henry VIII.)   DEVON.

6. John MERIK *v.* David HOELL.
    Tollhegod. *Bill.*   GLAMORGAN.

7. Joan MONYNG, widow of Robert *v.* John ARUNDELL.
    Debt. *Bill only.* (James I - Charles I.)   NORTHAMPTON.

8. Nicholas MOSTYN, Robert LOVELL, Hugh CLYFE,
    Hugh DART and others *v.* Katherine SNYDALL,
    Thomas DOWRYSH.
    Manor of Stockleigh English. *Bill, mutilated.*
    (Henry VIII.)   DEVON.

9. _____MOULTON and Margaret his wife *v.* William
    POUNDE.
    Lands on Hayling Island, late prior of Sheen
    Charterhouse, part of estate of John Moulton, deceased.
    Bill, mutilated.   SOUTHAMPTON.

10. Christopher MYGHELL *v.* John BANYARD.
    North Walsham. *Bill.*   NORFOLK.

11. William MYLFORTHE *alias* MYLFORDE *v.* Thomas
    COWPER.
    Estate of Laurence_____ *Bill.* (Henry VIII.)   _____

12. Alice and Joan MYLWARD *v.*_____Newerne in Lydney.
    Bill, mutilated. (Philip and Mary; Heath.)   GLOUCESTER.

13. Hugh NORRYS *v.* John GEORGE, John BLAKE, late
    abbot of Cirencester.
    Estate of Hugh Norrys the elder. *Bill.*   GLOUCESTER.

14. William NOTE and Joan his wife *v.* William SOPER.
    Annuity on property in New Sarum. *Bill.*   WILTS.

15. Francis PALMER *v.* Thomas WHUSON and Isabel his
    wife.
    Whitton. *Bill, faded.* (Henry VIII; Audley.)   LINCOLN.

16. John Palmer *v.* Masters and Wardens of the
    fellowship of COOPERS.
    Tenement called 'The Swane' and others adjoining.
    Replication.   _____

EARLY CHANCERY PROCEEDINGS - BUNDLE 1522

17.   Chedeoke PAULETT son of Marquess of Winchester *v.*
      Sir William FAYREFAX.
Manors of Bylborough and Sandworth in City. of York.
(Philip and Mary.)   YORK.

18.   John PECOCKE *v.* ---------
Petition for writ of *certiorari* .to Mayor and Sheriffs of
London concerning action brought by Thomas Lane against
plaintiff.   *Faded.*   (Henry VIII.)   ————————

19.   William PEGYN *v.* John and Richard PALMER.
The deeds of land in Moreton in the Marsh.
(Henry VIII.)   GLOUCESTER.

20.   Edmond PENFOUNDE and Elizabeth his wife .*v.*
      Margaret BERY.
Annuity from manor of Aveton Gifford.   *Bill.*   DEVON.

21.   John PENYFORD *v.* Thomas CLARKE, Thomas BURNEHAM.
Title deeds of premises in Barton under Needwood.
Bill, mutilated.   STAFFORD.

22.   Robert PERKYN *v.* William LEGH.
Title deeds of premises in Lichfield.   *Bill, mutilated.*   STAFFORD.

23.   David PHELIPPS *v.* John David LLOID, R. ap HOWELL.
Title deeds of 'Elwyn Vichan' in Llanwynia.   *Bill.*   CARMARTHEN.

24.   William PIGOTT and Isabel his wife *v.* John
      FOWKES the younger.
Title deeds of lands at Deanshanger.   *Bill, mutilated.*
(Edward VI; Ely.)   NORTHAMPTON..

25.   John PRISTES *v.* Humfre CROGYNTON and others.
Newton in Worfield.   *Bill.*   SALOP.

26.   John REYNER *v.* George PARKER.
Parsonage of Pattesley.   *Bill.*   (Philip and Mary.)   NORFOLK.

27.   Henry ROBINSON *v.* John BERE, clerk.
Church of Camborne.   *Bill.*   (Edward VI.)   CORNWALL.

28.   Roweland RYSCHOLD *v.* Thomas NIGHTINGALE and
      Alice his wife, Walter PATSALL and Thomas
      RYSCHOLD.
Panfield.   *Bill.*   ESSEX.

29.   Robert SAMWELL and Ellen his wife *v.* Robert
      CRAVENSHANK, John BADYLL, John REDE·
Deeds of a messuage in Great Stamseys in White Notley.   ESSEX.

30.   Robert SCAPULL and Tomasyn his wife *v.* John
      WESTOVER.
Property called 'Baclesford' in Chardstock.   *Bill.*   DORSET.
(Henry VIII.)   (now DEVON).

31.   Thomas SHARMAN *v.* Margaret Wrenne, widow.
Title deeds of property at Yaxley and Cranston.
Mutilated.   (Henry VIII.)   SUFFOLK.

32.   [_____SHERMAN (?)] *v.* Edward REDE and
        another.
Money matters, supply of bad goods.   *Bill, mutilated.*
Also petition for *certiorari* to the Mayor and Sheriffs
of Norwich.   NORFOLK.

33.   Robert SMYTHE *v.* William KOCKE, James WATMORE,
        clerk and Robert ALYCOCKE.
Title deeds of property in Normanton.   *Bill.*   NOTTINGHAM.

34.   Edward SOLE v. Francis PAYRONE (?).
Money matter.   *Bill, mutilated.*   _____

35.   Humphrey SOMERFORD *v.* Thomas, Richard and
        Elizabeth HICHECOCKES and Richard MARSHALL.
Edymond;   lands late of William Glover.   *Bill.*   SALOP.

36.   Matthew STAUNTON *v.* George TIRRELL.
Manor of Stoke Hammond.   (Philip and Mary.)   BUCKINGHAM.

37.   Thomas STEPHYNS the elder and Thomas the younger
        v. Sir John ABRYGGE.
Site of the parsonage of Chisledon, with appurtenances
in Chisledon, Hodson and Badbury, late monastery of
Hyde.   *Bill, mutilated.*   (Henry VIII.)   WILTS.

38.   _____STEYNTON, son of John *v.*_____
Title deeds of premises in Stretton by Sugwas.   *Bill.* HEREFORD.

39.   John STOKER *v.* William H_____
Crofton.   *Answer.*   DORSET.

40-41. Sir Nicholas STRELLEY *v.* Isabel SANDFORTH.
Grange of Thorpe Salvin [Thorpe Rygnall] late priory of
Worksop.   *Draft of Bill and Copy of Answer.*
(Philip and Mary.)   YORK.

42.   Alice SYMONS *v.* Paul SMYTH.
Title deeds to premises in Barnstable.   *Bill.*   DEVON.

43.   John TATHEWELL *v.* William TRAFURTH.
Deeds of manor of Trathwell.   (Henry VIII; Audley.)   LINCOLN.

44.   John THRIFT *v.* Robert HULCOPPE and William
        CURTIS.
Sutton.   *Bill.*   BERKS.

45.   Robert THROKEMORTON *v.* Robert HILL.
Park Manor.   *Bill.*   CORNWALL.

46.   William TOMSON and Agnes his wife *v.* William
         BALDWIN and Joan his wife.
Bequest under Will of Gilbert Wacy.   (Edward VI.)   ——————

47.   John TRESAMBALLE, Pasco CARPENTER,
         Churchwardens of St. Michael and St. Kebbe of
         Penkevill *v.* John CARMYNOWE, Thomas COCKE, clerk.
Bequest of John Paule, clerk.   *Bill.*   CORNWALL.

48.   Christofer TRYMNELL *v.* William TRYMNELL.
Property at Erlestoke.   *Mutilated.*   (Henry VIII;
Wolsey.)   WILTS.

49-50.   Robert TURBRIDGE *v.* John ap ITHELL, Harry ap John
         ap JENAN, Margaret SAYER.
Deeds of a tenement in Ruthin.   (Edward VI.)   DENBIGH.

51.   Richard TUXKYSWELL, Elizabeth his wife and Alice
         their daughter *v.* William HODY.
Deeds of a tenement called 'Wytwell' in Fiddington.
(Henry VIII.)   SOMERSET.

52.   Thomas TYRRELL *v.* John HOWYS and John WAGE.
'Collumbyn Hall'.   *Mutilated.*   (Philip and Mary.)   ——————

53.   Thomas VENABLES *v.* Sir John SABORGE and his wife,
         Thomas COTTON.
Petition for *procedends*, in suit on lands in Kinderton,
Middlewich, Sproston, Eccleston, Marston, Barteton,
Tetten and Newton in Wirrel (Newton beside Little Med).   CHESTER.

54.   Richard VYCARY *v.* John TOWNSEND, John FLEMING,
         Edmond WORTH and John WHITE.
Thorveton.   *Bill.*   DEVON.

55.   John WADE *v.* Elizabeth HOOD, widow.
Debt.   WARWICK.

56.   Alice WALKELATE, John HAYLEY and Elizabeth his
         wife, John MASSYE *v.* Henry MORETON and Margery
         his wife.
Title deeds of lands in Bentley in Stoke.
(Philip and Mary.)   STAFFORD.

57.   John WALROND *v.* John and Richard HAWKINS.
Copyholding of manor of Barrington.   *Bill.*   SOMERSET.

58.   Matthew WARCOPP *v.* Sir Barnard KIRKEBRIDE.
Advowson of Ormside.   *Bill.*   (Mary.)   WESTMORLAND.

59-60.   William WARING *v.* William HYGGYNS and Humphret
         OGLE.
Penance imposed by commissary's court at Hereford.
*Bill and notes prepared by the commission with
memorandum of decree, mutilated.*   (Henry VIII.)   ——————

EARLY CHANCERY PROCEEDINGS - BUNDLE 1522

61.   George WEBBE of Canterbury *v.* John VERGER.
Little Betteshanger, land in Elmstone and Preston.   KENT.

62.   Richard WHALLEY *v.* William BOWLES and Bonaventure
        BOWLES.
Failure to fulfil award on manor of Toton.   *Bill.*
(Philip and Mary.)   NOTTINGHAM.

63.   Richard WHALLEY, esquire *v.* Francis HEWETT.
Wardship of Edward Rye.   *Bill.*   (Mary.)   YORK.

64.   John WHITE *v.* John LAMBERT the elder and John the
        younger, Thomas CROCKE, John HUSBAND, John HILL,
        Thomas HYNDE, James FAVELL, John SMYTH, Thomas
        BYRTWYSSELL, William NELSON, Henry SARGYSON.
Lordship of Bordley in Craven.   YORK.

65.   John WHITE *v.* Thomas TOKER and Joan his wife.
Title deeds of 'The Close' in--------ell.
Bill, mutilated.   DEVON.

66.   John WHYTE *v.* Richard and John CARLYAN.
St. Stephen by Launceston.   CORNWALL.

67.   William WHYTTYNGHAM *v.* John WRYGHT.
Estate of Richard Whyttyngham.   (Henry VIII.)   LINCOLN.

68.   George WILLOUGHBY and Maude his wife *v.* Henry
        SHEMOND, John AMORE, Robert GEFFREY.
Rent from parcel of the manor of Great Amington.
(Philip and Mary;   Winchester.)   WARWICK.

69.   Geoffrey WOTTON and Margery his wife, John
        STEVEN and Isabel his wife *v.* Joan HAWE,
        William TOMBLYNSON *alias* DOBBEN.
Lease of a messuage.   *Mutilated.*   STAFFORD.

70.   John WRIGHT *v.* Thomas FULBARNE and Christopher
        BOWIS.
Money matter.   *Bill.*   (Philip and Mary.)   ————————

71.   William WYTHYNS *v.* Thomas CLERK, Abbot of the
        monastery of St. Werburgh in Chester.
Money matter.   *Bill.*   ————————

72.   Bartholomew YONGHUSBAND *v.* Edward and Robert
        BARTRAM.
Quittance from debt.   *Bill.*   NORTHUMBERLAND.

73-74.   ------*v.* James BRATBROOKE, Richard SPICER
         and another.
Parcel of manor (?) of Warborough.
(Philip and Mary.)   OXFORD.

75. _____v. Roger GRENE and John ALDERCHURCHE and
Margaret his wife.
Money matter. *Bill, mutilated.*
_____

76. Okker-NYGESON v. Thomas HAYSE.
Debt. *Bill, mutilated.*
SUSSEX.

77. _____citizen and haberdasher v. Roger HOLT and
John LYON.
Money matters, writ of error. *Bill, mutilated.*
(Mary; Gardiner.)
MIDDLESEX.

78. _____, Abbot of monastery of v. John NONNYE.
Money matter. *Bill, mutilated.*
_____

79. Henry_____and Joan his wife v. John OTWEY.
Potter Heigham. *Bill.*
NORFOLK.

80. _____v. Thomas REDE.
Title deeds of property in Idmiston. *Bill, mutilated.*
WILTS.

81. _____v._____
Money matter, Nicholas Sprynge, Henry Stapleton, and
John and Robert Gordon mentioned. *Bill, mutilated.*
(Philip and Mary.)
_____

82. _____v. Winifred_____
Money matters. *Answer, fragment.*
_____

83. John TAILLOUR, girdler, v. William MARTYN
alias MORTON.
Return to Commission
_____

.